PERSPECTIVES BUSINESS ETHICS

Third Edition

Laura P. Hartman
DePaul University

McGraw-Hill Irwin

Boston   Burr Ridge, IL   Dubuque, IA   Madison, WI   New York   San Francisco   St. Louis
Bangkok   Bogotá   Caracas   Kuala Lumpur   Lisbon   London   Madrid   Mexico City
Milan   Montreal   New Delhi   Santiago   Seoul   Singapore   Sydney   Taipei   Toronto

McGraw-Hill
Irwin

Published by McGraw-Hill/Irwin, a business unit of The McGraw-Hill Companies, Inc., 1221 Avenue of the Americas, New York, NY, 10020. Copyright © 2005, 2002, 1998 by The McGraw-Hill Companies, Inc. All rights reserved. No part of this publication may be reproduced or distributed in any form or by any means, or stored in a database or retrieval system, without the prior written consent of The McGraw-Hill Companies, Inc., including, but not limited to, in any network or other electronic storage or transmission, or broadcast for distance learning.

Some ancillaries, including electronic and print components, may not be available to customers outside the United States.

This book is printed on acid-free paper.

2 3 4 5 6 7 8 9 0 DOC/DOC 0 9 8 7 6 5 4

ISBN 0-07-288146-1

Vice president and editor-in-chief: *Robin J. Zwettler*
Editorial director: *John E. Biernat*
Senior sponsoring editor: *Andy Winston*
Marketing manager: *Lisa Nicks*
Lead project manager: *Pat Frederickson*
Freelance project manager: *Rich Wright, Omega Publishing Services*
Production supervisor: *Gina Hangos*
Design: *Mary Kazak*
Supplement producer: *Lynn M. Bluhm*
Senior digital content specialist: *Brian Nacik*
Cover design: *Sarah Studnicki*
Cover art: *© 2004 Andy Warhol Foundation for the Visual Arts/ARS, New York*
Typeface: *10/12 Times Roman*
Compositor: *Carlisle Communications, Ltd.*
Printer: *R. R. Donnelley*

Library of Congress Cataloging-in-Publication Data

Hartman, Laura Pincus
   Perspectives in business ethics / Laura P. Hartman—3rd ed.
      p. cm.
   Includes bibliographical references and index.
   ISBN 0-07-288146-1
   1. Business ethics. I. Title.
   HF5387.H3744 2005
   174'.4—dc22   2003070618

www.mhhe.com

For Emma and Rachel, to thine own selves be true.

Note to the Reader

This is a textbook that came to exist because I needed it. It's as simple as that. This approach may seem selfish (see Chapter 1 for discussion on ethical egoism); but I have found in my experience that, when professors write texts because they themselves have a strong need, the most effective text is usually produced.

The study of ethics includes an analysis of the interests of all of the individuals who hold a stake in the outcome of any dilemma or decision ("stakeholder analysis"). In teaching business ethics at both a graduate and undergraduate level, I found myself walking into the classroom with armloads of articles, cases, and other handouts that I used to present the perspectives of each stakeholder involved in a decision. This text seeks to provide perspectives on ethical issues in a variety of different formats—similar to my efforts involving handouts for class. It is expected that a professor may choose certain readings from a variety of chapters in order to best illustrate whatever issue she or he seeks to explore.

The text explores traditional ethics issues by providing multiple perspectives on the same issue. For instance, in providing an introduction to critical analysis, the text provides a reading on recent problems at Dow Corning and "where the ethicists went wrong" in their original glowing assessment of Dow Corning.

The materials in this book include:

1. Traditional textual explanations/definitions/discussion of new topics or ideas from a historical and foundational perspective.
2. Reprints of articles, whether seminal (older, traditional), or from present day analysis.
3. Short cases for brief explanatory questions and discussion in class.
4. Full-length cases for analysis with sufficient background information and guiding questions. These cases would also be supplemented either in the text or teachers' manual with projects and exercises.
5. Additional nontraditional materials such as song lyrics, excerpts from classical literature, short stories, and so on.

The varying formats not only present different perspectives, but also provide information and opinions in a manner most accessible by the students. As we all know, many of the more academic-focused articles are difficult to read, even for seasoned ethicists. The material presented in this text is sophisticated, yet relevant and accessible.

The focus of this approach is to encourage readers to open their minds to the variety of opinions on any given issue. The result of this approach is not to persuade readers that there is no right answer to these issues, but instead to ensure that all stakeholders' perspectives are considered before the decision maker reaches a conclusion. The readings for each section have been chosen with this representative interest in mind.

As you read, please also consider what opinions or perspectives are not represented in this text. I appreciate any and all suggestions/additions/modifications.

ACKNOWLEDGMENTS

This text is, in truth, the work of a host of scholars and business practitioners who offered their opinions as reviewers early on in the project, on previous editions, or who have allowed me to compile their work in order to present a more realistic and multiperspectival approach to the study of ethics in business decision making. I am deeply indebted to these individuals, for without their work and consideration, this text would not have come to pass. These include authors of chapter 6 (Zafar Iqbal) and chapter 7 (Ron Duska). In addition, I would like to thank my research assistants, David Thies (on the first edition), Amy McCann (on the second edition) and Brian Marks (on the third edition) for their tireless energy and exceptional research abilities in locating some of the more exceptional materials in the text, with a special thank you for their work on the thankless task of acquiring all of the permissions for the book. Finally, I thank Andy Winston and Emily Yim at McGraw-Hill/Irwin for their tireless support of this innovative project.

Laura P. Hartman
LHartman@depaul.edu
DePaul University, Executive Offices
1 E. Jackson Blvd.
Chicago, IL 60604
312/362-6569

Contents

Contents

ETHICAL THEORIES AND APPROACHES

The purpose of this text is not to teach ethics, but instead to offer a foundation in ethical thought, followed by a variety of perspectives on difficult ethical dilemmas. The reader is encouraged to critically evaluate each perspective using her or his personal ethical theory base. Using ethics to analyze business issues is merely one form of decision making, similar to profit maximization, legal compliance or religious beliefs. The difference, however, between ethics and these other bases for decisions is that ethics can serve as the foundation for each of the other methods. In reaching decisions, an individual may use ethics as a guide in legal or religious compliance, and even in maximizing profits.

We already use ethics as a basis for decision making. Assume your grandmother is on her deathbed. She looks at you and asks, as her last dying wish, that you follow her and your religion in a devout manner after she passes on. Assume, as well, that you do not plan to do this. Do you tell her that you will abide by her wishes, so that she might die a more peaceful death? Or are you honest with her and admit that you will not follow her wishes? Whichever your answer, consider *why* you feel the way you do. There is no law that requires one answer or another, not even a rule. You might believe that you should act one way or another because it is the "right" thing to do. This is your personal ethic.

Consider the response of the grandfather of Sir Adrian Cadbury, the owner of the second-largest chocolate company in Britain, when the Queen sought to purchase tins of chocolates to send to each soldier serving in the Anglo-Boer War in South Africa. Cadbury was opposed to the war and was uncomfortable reaping a profit from such a transaction. On the other hand, he was striving to move forward with the company and this would mean additional work for the firm. He decided to accept the order, but to do so only at cost with no additional amount for profit. The firm benefited from the work, but he did not reap a financial gain at the expense of the war.[1] Was this ethical? Would it have been unethical to deny the Queen's contract simply because he didn't approve of the purpose for which she intended to use the chocolate?

On the other hand, consider the $68 million Bausch & Lomb (B&L) agreed to pay to settle a consumer class action lawsuit. The plaintiffs complained that B&L had been selling three identical contact lenses under three different brand names for significantly different prices. B&L had attempted to market the lenses in different ways to different consumer groups at varying prices. Is this "wrong," "unethical"?

Volumes of literature are devoted in general terms to the question of defining ethics. Ethics involves judgments as to good and bad, right and wrong, and what ought to be. As defined by the philosopher Epicurus, ethics "deals with things to be sought and things to be avoided, with ways of life and with the *telos.*"[2] (*Telos* is the chief aim or end in life.) Ethics can be distinguished from "morals," which are rules or duties that govern our behavior as persons to persons (such as "do not tell lies" or "do not hurt another person") and from "values," which are ends or goals sought by individuals (such as health or happiness).[3]

An ethical dilemma exists when two or more values are in conflict, and we seek from ethics a resolution to this conflict. Business ethics refers to the measurement of business behavior based on standards of right and wrong, rather than relying entirely on principles of accounting and management. For purposes of this discussion, morals are one's personal guiding principles; ethics is the way those morals are applied to decisions.

Finding and following the moral course is not always easy for any of us, but the difficulty may be particularly acute for the businessperson. The bottom line is necessarily unforgiving. Hence, the pressure to produce is intense and the temptation to cheat may be great. Although the law provides useful guideposts for minimum behavior, no clear moral guidelines have emerged. Therefore, when a businessperson is faced with a difficult decision, a common tactic is simply to do what he or she takes to be correct at any given moment. Indeed, in one survey of ethical views in business, 50% of the respondents indicated that the word *ethical* meant "what my feelings tell me is right."

Philosophers have provided powerful intellectual support for that approach. *Existentialists,* led by the famed Jean-Paul Sartre, believe standards of conduct cannot be rationally justified and no actions are inherently right or wrong. Thus, each person may reach her or his own choice about ethical principles. This view finds its roots in the notion that humans are only what we will ourselves to be. If God does not exist, there can be no human nature, because there is no one to conceive that nature.

In Sartre's famous interpretation, existence precedes essence. First humans exist, then we individually define what we are—our essence. Therefore, each of us is free, with no rules to turn to for guidance. Just as we all choose our own natures, so must we choose our own ethical precepts. Moral responsibility belongs to each of us individually, and in our own ways.

---

[1]Sir Adrian Cadbury, "Ethical Managers Make Their Own Rules," *Harvard Business Review,* September/October 1987.

[2]Diogenes Laertius, *Lives of Eminent Philosophers* (Cambridge: Harvard University Press, 1925), book 10, chap. 30.

[3]This discussion of definitions is based on Lisa Newton's Vocabulary of Ethics in "Doing Good and Avoiding Evil, Part I.2," *http://www.rit.edu/~692awww/manuals/newton/dgae1p2.html.*

But, as we have seen countless times through history, what one woman or man believes is "right" or just, many others may believe is "wrong" or evil. Consider, for instance, Germany under Nazi rule. Adolf Hitler believed he was right in his brutal acts and decisions *as strongly as* the rest of the world believed he was wrong. Existentialists would say, perhaps, that there is no right answer in this situation, while others would argue for some universal principles of right and wrong. *Relativists* contend that the ethical answer depends on the situation (that ethics is relative). They may argue that those who followed Hitler were not necessarily unethical because of the circumstances of the situation. What is right in one situation may be wrong in another. The theories introduced in Chapter 1 and discussed throughout the text offer guidance in this area, though they are by no means the only routes to decisions. ■

Chapter 1

TRADITIONAL THEORIES

Until philosophers are kings, or the kings and princes of this world have the spirit and power of philosophy, and political greatness and wisdom meet in one, and those commoner natures who pursue either to the exclusion of the other are compelled to stand aside, cities will never have rest from their evils—no, nor the human race.

—PLATO, *Republic*

No regulatory system, however stringent, can provide against the consequences of human greed, folly or corruption.

—TIM YEO, *shadow secretary for the United Kingdom Department of Trade and Industry*

In answering the question in the Part 1 opening text about your grandmother's request at her deathbed, you resorted to **some form** of decision making. Perhaps you might call it "gut instinct." However, how certain are we or should we be of our gut instincts? How often have you awakened in the morning saying, "Oh, why did I make that decision yesterday? What was I thinking?" Our guts are not always trained to make complicated ethical judgments. We need to therefore exercise our guts by exploring ethical dilemmas at times when we are not actually faced with them. In that way, we are then better able to apply that reasoning when the challenge does present itself. We practice ethical decision making using moral reasoning. Moral reasoning is a more intentional form of decision making where we consider the basis for and implications of the decision before acting. We consider evidence and reach conclusions, or judgments, about the right and wrong way to act.

Theories of ethics allow us to explore these dilemmas with new eyes—to better understand the implications of our decisions and perhaps to allow us to adopt a normative perspective on the decisions of others. In other words, by considering the various options moral theory presents for resolving our dilemmas, we may become advocates of one particular option. In addition, ethical theories may offer support for our positions when the usual justification is "it just feels right." Instead, we are given a vocabulary with which to explain the basis of our conclusions or actions. However, moral reasoning can suffer from being too absolute (where one believes that the same rule applies, no matter the circumstance) or from being too relativistic (where the answer always seems to depend entirely on the circumstance); it is critical to explore the various ways in which the theories apply and determine which feels most appropriate for you.

In this chapter, we will review some ethical theories that might help you to explore dilemmas. The readings that follow include either the writing of the original theorist, an interpretation of the theory or an example of the theory applied.

TELEOLOGICAL ETHICAL SYSTEMS

Ethical theories may be divided into two categories: teleological and deontological. The distinction between the two is that teleological theories determine the ethics of an act by looking to the probable outcome or consequences of the decision (the ends), while deontological theories determine the ethics of an act by looking to the process of the decision (the means). The theory most representative of this approach is *utilitarianism,* which directs us to make decisions based on the greatest "good" (or "utility") for the greatest number as the end result. Jeremy Bentham (1748–1832) and John Stuart Mill (1806–1873) were the chief intellectual forces in the development of utilitarianism. The most basic form of utilitarian analysis is cost–benefit analysis where you tally the costs and benefits of a given decision and follow the decision that provides for the greatest overall gain.

While this approach is superficially easy to apply (majority rule, profit/loss statements), complexities remain. For instance, does one consider the impact on animals as well as humans in adding up the benefits and costs? Or, how does one weigh the "good"? If an action would render one person exquisitely happy and three people moderately unhappy, does the happiness of that one outweigh the unhappiness of the three? How do we measure happiness?

Utilitarianism is viewed as a strong and powerful theory because it is liberal; it appeals to no authority in resolving differences of opinion; and in fact, differences of opinion are irrelevant except as they create a majority or minority. It is also able to describe much of the process of human decision making, and its process seems "natural" and well suited to many decisions. It is an egalitarian process—no one person's "good" is valued more than another's. On the other hand, a weakness is that there is a possibility of "injustice" regarding the distribution of goods. Because the rights of any one person are not taken into account, no rights have any greater weight than others. Consequently, certain individuals may suffer great harm, while others receive only modest benefits. In addition, when the majority rules, who protects the minority? Who ensures that a minority voice is heard (if it even should be heard) and who ensures that new opinions are expressed so that intellectual growth is possible? Le Guin's parable of the Omelas that follows offers an extreme version of this particular challenge of utilitarianism.

Distributive justice is another teleological approach to ethical decision making and is based on a concept of fairness. Conceived by contemporary Harvard philosopher John Rawls, distributive justice holds that ethical acts or decisions are those that lead to an equitable distribution of goods and services. Therefore, it is critical to determine a fair method for distributing goods and services. Rawls suggests that we should consider how we would distribute goods and services if we were under a *"veil of ignorance"* that prevented us from knowing our status in society (i.e., our intelligence, wealth, appearance). He asks that we consider what rules we would impose on this society if we had no idea whether we would be princes or paupers. Would we devise a system of high taxes and expensive welfare projects that, presumably, would benefit the impoverished but prove costly to the wealthy? Or would we advocate a pure market-based system that demanded each of us to be responsible for our own needs and desires?

Rawls argues that under a veil of ignorance we would build a cooperative system in which benefits (e.g., income) would be distributed unequally only where doing so would be to the benefit of all, particularly the least advantaged. All those behind the veil would agree to that unequal standard because they could not know whether they would be among the advantaged or the disadvantaged. From this system of distributive economic justice, it follows that ethical justice is measured by the capacity of the act in question to enhance cooperation among members of society. That which is determined from behind the veil of ignorance is deemed ethical through the fairness of the end result. Note that this does not necessarily mandate an equal distribution; sometimes the fairest result is one that is unequal.

One way to understand the implications of distributive justice is to consider a difficult ethical dilemma. Imagine that you do not know what position you hold in connection with the outcome—you don't know whether you are going to be affected in a beneficial way or a detrimental way by the decision. Now, without that knowledge (under the veil of ignorance), what decision would you make? Rawls argues that you will make the most just and fair decision under this framework.

DEONTOLOGICAL ETHICAL SYSTEMS

A deontological system is based on rules or principles that govern decisions. The German philosopher Immanuel Kant (1724–1804) developed perhaps the most persuasive and fully articulated vision of ethics as measured by the rightness of rules, rather than by consequences. In this formalistic view of ethics, the rightness of an act depends little (or, in Kant's view, not at all) on the results of the act. Kant believed in the key moral concept of goodwill. The moral person is one of goodwill, and that person makes ethical decisions based on what is right, regardless of the consequences of the decision. Thus, the student who refuses to cheat on exams is morally worthy if her or his decision springs from a universal duty, but morally unworthy if the decision is merely born of self-interest, such as fear of being caught.

But, how does the person of goodwill know what is right? To respond, Kant propounded the *categorical imperative,* the notion that every person should act on only those principles that she or he, as a rational person, would prescribe as *universal laws* to be applied to the whole of mankind. (This approach has also been called *universalism.*) Universalism suggests that, in reaching a decision, we should consider whether it would be acceptable if everyone in every situation made this same decision—"Act only according to that maxim whereby you can at the same time will that it should become a universal law." This concept is similar to a parent asking a child, "How would you feel if everyone stole candy from their friends?" Or to the Golden Rule, directing you to act upon others only as you would have others act upon you. The weakness under these circumstances is that it could be circular—this rule would define as ethical a certain behavior we might consider to be unethical, as long as you believed it would be all right for everyone to act that way.

Kant believed that every rational creature can act according to his or her categorical imperative, because all such persons have "autonomous, self-legislating wills" that permit them to formulate and act on their own systems of rules. To Kant, what is right for one is right for all, and each of us can discover that "right" by exercising our rational faculties. Of course, Kant was not the only one to prescribe a moral system based on rules and rights. The Chinese scholar Confucius, born in 551 BCE, maintained an enormous set of rules by which he suggested one should live. These rules, or maxims, do not appear to us today to be complicated; instead, they seem now to be commonplace and pedestrian. They include the following:

What you do not wish done to yourself, do not do to others.

Do not wish for quick results, nor look for small advantages. If you see quick results, you will not attain the ultimate goal. If you are led astray by small advantages, you will never accomplish great things.

When you see someone of worth, think of how you may emulate. When you see someone unworthy, examine your own character.

Wealth and rank are what people desire, but unless they be obtained in the right way they may not be possessed.

Feel kindly toward everyone, but be intimate only with the virtuous.[1]

Universalism offers guidance with regard to the rules by which someone should make decisions. Kant recognized universal rights such as freedom of speech, freedom of consent, the right to privacy or freedom of conscience. A problem arises, however, when an individual does not know which rules to follow. For instance, you might be faced with a dilemma that pits freedom of speech against the right to privacy. Which rule wins? In addition, who is to determine these universal rights? As the world becomes increasingly enmeshed and as firms increasingly globalize, cultural conflicts regarding the exact nature of universal values occur. These issues and challenges of universalism are considered below.

In sum, applying universalism entails two queries: (1) Would it be all right for everyone to make the decision you are about to make? and (2) Would this decision infringe on any universal rights?

Another deontological approach is represented by the perspective of *religion.* No "theory" or approach to the evaluation of actions is more rule-based than religion. After all, the Ten Commandments are viewed by some as the most basic principles of behavior. Additional rules, such as "do unto others as you would have them do unto you," also spring directly from religious thought or writings, rather than reason or logic. The religious point of view is not so different from Kant's perspective, except that the universal principles come directly from religious beliefs rather than elsewhere. Whether one is Christian, Jewish, Muslim, Buddhist, or another faith, the deity's laws are viewed as absolutes that must shape the whole of one's life, including work. Faith, rather than reason, intuition or secular knowledge, provides the foundation for a moral life built on religion.

Finally, one might make decisions on the basis of *virtue ethics,* claiming that the key to good ethics lies not in rules, rights and responsibilities, but in the classic notion of character. As Plato and Aristotle contended, our attention should be given to strategies for encouraging desirable character traits such as honesty, fairness, compassion and generosity. The primary question in virtue ethics is not "What actions are universally right?" but "What is the best sort of life for human beings to live?" Virtue ethics applauds the person who is motivated to do the right thing and who cultivates that motivation in daily conduct. One would know the right thing by exercising judgment, rather than by applying a universal set of rules. One should make the decisions that a virtuous person would make. One way to exercise this theory is to consider someone whom you believe to be completely virtuous, a role model of ethical behavior, and then to act as you believe this person would act under these same circumstances. Aristotle believed that a person of good character enjoys being good, doing the right thing. In being good, you fulfill your nature and that of others.

---

[1]Confucius, *The Analects, passim,* cited in Huston Smith, *The World's Religions* (San Francisco: HarperSanFrancisco, 1991), p. 159.

ARISTOTELIAN MORAL VIRTUES

Courage
Self-control
Generosity
Magnificence
High-mindedness
Gentleness
Friendliness
Truthfulness
Wittiness
Modesty[2]

St. Thomas Aquinas, too, believed in the quest for the "right" thing or the "good" life. Aquinas, however, took the study of virtue one step beyond Aristotle when he divided virtue into the religious or theological virtues of faith, hope and charity and the intellectual virtues of prudence (wisdom), justice, temperance and fortitude.[3] Both Aristotle and Aquinas believed that any individual had the potential for virtue, as virtue was learned or acquired, rather than innate. Could a modern corporation realistically aspire to be "virtuous" according to Aquinas or Aristotle?

Virtue ethics might seem to be closely linked with universalism, where a set of principles is in the place of virtue ethics' set of traits. However, a part of the virtue ethics argument is that such persons are more morally reliable than those who simply follow the rules but fail to inspect, strengthen and preserve their own personal virtues.

HYBRID THEORIES

A king had some empty glasses. He said, "If I pour hot water into them they will crack. If I pour ice-cold water into them they will also crack." What did the king do? He mixed the hot and the cold water together and poured it into them and they did not crack. Even so did the Holy One, blessed be He, say, "If I create the world on the basis of the attribute of mercy alone, the world's sins will greatly multiply. If I create the world on the basis of the attribute of justice alone, how could the world endure? I will therefore create it with both the attributes of mercy and justice, and may it endure!"[4]

---

[2]Steven Mintz, "Aristotelian Virtue and Business Ethics Education," *Journal of Business Ethics* 15, no. 8 (August 1996), pp. 827–38, 830.

[3]Caryn Beck-Dudley, "No More Quandaries: A Look at Virtue through the Eyes of Robert Solomon," *American Business Law Journal* 34, no. 1 (Fall 1996), p. 119.

[4]Aba Hillel Silver, *Where Judaism Differed* (Northvale, NJ: Jason Aronson, 1987), cited in Huston Smith, *The World's Religions* (San Francisco: HarperSanFrancisco, 1991), p. 292.

Certain theories do not fit cleanly into one approach or another. For example, *personal libertarianism,* conceived by contemporary philosopher Robert Nozick, holds that morality springs from maximizing personal freedom and that individuals should be free from the interference of others in so doing. Justice and fairness, right and wrong, are measured not by equality of results (e.g., wealth) for all, but from ensuring equal opportunity for all to engage in informed choices about their own welfare. Hence, Nozick takes essentially a free market stance toward ethics. At first, this may seem to be a deontological theory because the primary concern is protecting the right to individual freedom, whatever the consequences. But the theory also looks to the results of an act in determining whether freedom has been restricted because of the decision. The primary value is liberty, and the ultimate gain is gain for one's self. However, Nozick does not contend that individuals seek only enjoyable experiences; he believes that individuals also seek to be the kind of people who are loved, who have friends, respect and so on.

Closely related to libertarianism is the concept of *ethical egoism.* The primary concern under ethical egoism is the maximization of the individual's self-interest, according to that individual. What is right is that which is right for the individual, while minimizing the impact of her or his choices on the rights of others. Ethical egoism identifies a means toward decision making (do what you want), while also identifying the greatest good as that which is the greatest good for the decision maker, hence a hybrid. Self-interest may be wealth, but it can also be fame, a happy family, a great job or anything else considered important to the decision maker.

Enlightened ethical egoism (also known as *enlightened self-interest*) considers the long-range perspective of others, or of humanity as a whole. It is important to the individual under this theory that the world is a "good" world; therefore, the individual may have a *self*-interest in curbing pollution or in community projects, even though she or he may not individually and personally benefit from the decision. Ian Maitland argues that the principle force that checks self-interest is, in fact, long-term self-interest, reinforcing morality and promoting civility and consideration for others.[5]

CONFLICTING UNIVERSAL VALUES— A CONTRADICTION IN TERMS?

To apply the above theories, it is critical to answer the question of whether there are any objective or universal "rights" and "wrongs." Is there anything that we would all agree is ethically wrong or ethically right? Western and Eastern concepts of right and wrong may not be that far off. For example, in a *Harvard Business Review* article, Wharton professor Thomas Donaldson demonstrates how Western and non-Western values may have a great deal in common. For instance, Donaldson links the Western values of individual liberty and human rights to the Japanese value of *kyosei* (living and working together for the common good) and the Muslim value of *Zakat* (the duty to give alms to the poor).[6]

---

[5]Ian Maitland, "The Human Face of Self-Interest," *Journal of Business Ethics* 38 (2002), pp. 3–17.
[6]Thomas Donaldson, "Values in Tension: Ethics Away from Home," *Harvard Business Review,* September/October 1996, pp. 48–62, 53.

But we have all heard the phrase, "When in Rome, do as the Romans." The essence of the rule is that one's action will be judged according to the norms of the environment in which it occurs. But this is not always the case; in many circumstances, we believe that our way is the right way and that alternatives are not acceptable. Consider the decision of Levi Strauss management to temporarily remove its manufacturing business from China to protest China's history of human rights abuses. While these actions might have been acceptable in the Chinese culture, or at least tolerated, Levi Strauss did not want to be a part of it.

Similarly, there was an uproar in mid-1996 when it was discovered that a clothing line sponsored by Kathie Lee Gifford was manufactured under conditions in other countries that appalled many Americans. Basketball player Michael Jordan was forced to defend his role as spokesperson for Nike shoes when similar conditions were found in foreign Nike plants. (See also the discussion of The Gap's operations in El Salvador in Chapter 5.)

On the other hand, the "when in Rome" justification has been used to ethically exculpate American firms that do business in other countries and that have offered [what we would consider to be] bribes in order to get certain jobs done. Consider what you would do if the only way to obtain a certain permit or contract is to offer a bribe and that "everyone does it." Consider Transparency International's annual Bribe Payers and Corruption Perceptions Indexes.[7] In 1999, TI found that Sweden scored 8.3 on a scale of 0–10 and South Korea scored a 3.4 (where 10 represented a perceived negligible level of bribery and 0 represented a perceived very high level of bribery). When businesspeople, risk analysts and the general public were asked about their perceptions of the degree of corruption with 10 representing highly clean and 0 representing highly corrupt, Denmark scored the highest with a 10 and Cameroon scored 1.5.

A firm may contend that, if it does not act in ways similar to firms native to a country, it may lose business or be unable to do business there. Does that make it acceptable? Americans generally believe that bribes are wrong or unethical because they allow certain parties to obtain a privilege not afforded to others. On the other hand, most Americans don't believe it is wrong or unethical to eat meat; while individuals in other countries believe that eating meat is wrong and unethical. In the United States, men are limited to one wife. In other countries, that is considered unthinkable and humiliating. Who is "right" in each of these conflicts? Who should answer that question?

Donaldson and colleague Thomas Dunfee suggest in their "integrative social contracts theory" (ISCT) that one can differentiate between those values which are fundamental across culture and theory ("hypernorms"[8]) and those values which are determined within moral "free space" and which are not hypernorms. Donaldson and Dunfee propose that one look to the convergence of religious, cultural and philosophical beliefs around certain core principles as a clue to the identification of hypernorms. Donaldson and Dunfee include as

---

[7]*http://www.transparency.de/documents/cpi/index.htm.*

[8]Thomas Donaldson and Thomas Dunfee, "Toward a Unified Conception of Business Ethics: Integrative Social Contracts Theory," *Academy of Management Review* 19 (1994), pp. 252, 264 (defining hypernorms as those principles that would limit moral free space, analogizing hypernorms to "hypergoods," "goods sufficiently fundamental as to serve as a source of evaluation and criticism of community-generated norms [within moral free space]." *Ibid.*).

examples of hypernorms freedom of speech, the right to personal freedom, the right to physical movement and informed consent. As you consider these far-reaching rights, do you believe that all reasonable thinkers would agree as to their predominance and worthiness of protection? And should the majority truly rule here, as ISCT dictates through its reliance on a "convergence" of opinions?

In line with Donaldson and Dunfee's effort to propose a means by which to apply ethical standards across borders, several proposed codes of conduct are presented in this section, including the U.S. Model Business Principles and the Caux Round Table Principles. Consider the similarities and differences between the proposed models of business behavior. If there are differences, do these differences in themselves evidence the fact that there is no general agreement regarding business conduct? If you were to create a model code of conduct for a global firm, would it resemble any of these codes? Consider the rights protected by the codes, agreements and guidelines represented in Table 1.1. How many x's are needed to raise an issue such as community involvement to the equivalent of a hypernorm? (Community involvement has three x's out of nine possibilities.)

Firms often complain that adhering to these codes of conduct is costly, imposing higher costs on them than those imposed on firms in other countries. Therefore, adherence to the codes places them at a competitive disadvantage in comparison to firms in other, less regulated countries. Some economists claim that international labor standards constitute "institutional intervention in competitive markets that impairs the workings of the invisible hand."[9] Free market economists believe that standards reduce efficiency, thereby increasing the cost of labor, lowering the employment of those affected and benefiting higher-cost competitors.[10] These economists suggest that people work in sweatshop conditions because it is the most rational means available to them for furthering their own ends. Moreover, these choices prove optimal for a developing country's economy, as they represent agreements among many producers and consumers of labor regarding desirable exchanges of labor (from the labor producers) and wages or other benefits (from the consumers of labor, in this case, multinational enterprises and the purchasers of their goods and services). In short, however much we may not like some of what we see in the labor conditions of developing nations, this is the market at work, and the market works to generate overall improvements in economic welfare for a society.

On the other hand, standards may be the only way to address a market failure—that is, the market fails to consider the nonfinancial conditions of employment and the nonfinancial impact of these conditions. Overall, some may argue, the global market may not be an effective arbiter of the trade-offs between improved working conditions and levels of economic development, production cost and product price. A nonindustrialized, developing country may tolerate various substandard practices if the result is a growing economy. Producers may tolerate some degree of labor practice constraint if the result does not raise the

---

[9]Richard B. Freeman, "A Hard-Headed Look at Labor Standards," *International Labor Standards and Global Economic Integration: Proceedings of a Symposium,* July 1994, p. 26.
[10]*Ibid.*

TABLE 1.1

Types of Standard and Issues Covered

	AA1000 Framework	GRI Guidelines	SA8000	GoodCorporation
Type of Standard				
Auditable standard or framework	×	×	×	×
Membership based, signatory standards				
International conventions				
Features				
Applicable to all organizations	×	×		SME's
Covers all business functions	×	×	Labor	×
Internationally recognized	×	×	×	
Compliance based	×	×	×	×
Requirement for reporting/disclosure	×	×		
Requirement for stakeholder engagement	×	×		Part
Requirement for performance measurement	×	×		
Requirement for governance/management	×	×	×	×
Requirement for embedded values	×			
Specific Issues Covered				
Stakeholder dialogue/engagement	×			
Environmental reference	×	×		×
Bribery and corruption				×
Political donations		×		
Workplace/employment	×	×	×	×
Health & safety	×	×	×	×
Supply chain	×	×	×	×
Employee involvement	×	×		×
Training and people development	×	×	×	×
Human rights		×	×	
Grievance/whistle-blowing			×	
Marketing/advertising practices				×
Trading/business practices		×		×
Community involvement	×	×		×
Restructuring				
Security		×		
Sustainable development	×	×		×

SOURCE: Copyright © 2002. Institute of Business Ethics. Reprinted with permission.

UN Global Compact	Ethical Trading Initiative Base Code	ILO Conventions	UN Declaration of Human Rights	OECD Guidelines for Multinationals
	×			
×	×			
		×	×	×
		Where ratified	×	×
	Supply	Labor	×	×
×		×	×	OECD Countries
	×	×	×	×
Partial				
				×
				×
×	×			×
×				×
				×
				×
×	×	×	×	×
×	×	×	×	×
	×			Limited Ref
		×		
		×		×
×	×	×	×	×
	×			×
				×
	×			×
				×
			×	×
				×

cost of production significantly. Consumers will tolerate modest price increases if they are assured that the worst labor practices have been eliminated. But markets are a poor mechanism for establishing appropriate boundaries. Many economists claim that, over time, markets will correct even the most substandard practices; but other economists and many noneconomists remain unconvinced.

Moreover, critics argue that regardless of what kinds of benefits do or do not accrue from substandard labor conditions, it simply is not right to subject individuals to extended periods of back-breaking and/or mind-numbing labor in conditions that put their health and welfare at risk. In short, any person deserves better conditions than these. Thus, in addition to the various pro and con arguments as to the real or illusory benefits and costs of poor working conditions for multinationals and developing countries, there remain fundamental objections to certain labor practices, the cogency of which does not depend on cost and benefit calculations. Basic concerns of human dignity and morality simply rule some practices out of bounds.

Harvard economist Richard Freeman asks whether there is any difference in the actual T-shirt produced by individuals under differing conditions. In other words, is there any difference between a T-shirt manufactured by political prisoners in a labor camp or sexually harassed women in a free trade zone in Central America and a T-shirt manufactured by workers under normal, acceptable conditions? If the price is the same, perhaps you will prefer the one made under "ethical" conditions. Perhaps you might even pay a slight premium for that shirt. However, the market shows fewer and fewer people are willing to pay a premium as the difference in price becomes greater. Freeman argues, therefore, that the market demand will sufficiently, efficiently and satisfactorily determine labor conditions for manufactured goods.[11]

Beyond compliance to a central code of business behavior, firms must be sensitive to cultural differences in those countries in which they do business. Campbell, the multinational soup purveyor, has learned that paying attention to cultural differences may mean the difference between reaping a profit and bearing a loss. Campbell discovered that other brands of dry soups were highly preferred to Campbell's canned, condensed soups in many countries. But Campbell's duck-gizzard soup had high sales in Hong Kong, and its Godiva Chocolate line sold well in Japan.[12] While meeting the soup flavor needs of a country may seem to be trivial in light of other ethical–cultural conflicts, Campbell was originally viewed as insincere and unresponsive by its foreign consumers. Not too trivial to Campbell.

Challenges to cultural sensitivity are strong, however; and similar criticism can be leveled against Donaldson and Dunfee's formulation. How many cultures have to agree on a norm for it to rise to the level of a hypernorm? If one culture's standards seriously violate a norm that is generally accepted by many other cultures, are you comfortable saying that the minority is wrong and the majority is right? Moreover, ethicist Richard Nielsen questions whether ISCT is a realistic conception when there is a lack of freedom of voice in

---

[11]*Ibid.,* p. 27.
[12]Joseph Weber, "What's Not Cookin' at Campbell's," *Business Week,* September 23, 1996, p. 40.

some communities.[13] Freedom of voice typically does not exist when there are significant power differences among segments of the relevant community, as would be the case with dictatorial governments and communities without effective labor unions and with high unemployment. Though most societies have due processes in form, the substance of due process is often lacking. Other ethicists contend that the basic requirements of norm establishment do not exist in so many cultures that ISCT proves to be unreliable.

So how is one to determine right from wrong in the global arena? Perhaps that is the most significant question in this text. As discussed above, right and wrong depend on the standards by which you are judging the act or decision. As national boundaries within our world market become increasing blurred, so too do the cultural differences. One may question whether this, in itself, is a beneficial result. In the end, one may be merely left with the differences between each human on the earth and the variances in their personal value structures. Perhaps as we all become more familiar with varying value perspectives, we might be more likely to better understand and, hopefully, to accept these differences as valuable rather than threatening.

In the readings that follow, consider the authors' contentions about what is "right" and "wrong." Do you agree with one of these approaches more strongly than another? In some readings, the approaches may seem more clearly in line with the theories discussed above than in others. Can you align the others with the traditional theories, or are they more likely hybrids of those discussed? Finally, how would you construct a global code of conduct that would be or should be applied worldwide?

---

[13]Richard P. Nielsen, "Do Internal Due Process Systems Permit Adequate Political and Moral Space for Ethics Voice, Praxis, and Community?" *Journal of Business Ethics* 24, no. 1 (March 2000), p. 1.

GROUNDING FOR THE METAPHYSICS OF MORALS

—IMMANUEL KANT

Immanuel Kant (1724–1804) was intrigued by the bases of human knowledge and understanding. In considering the origin of morals and morality, he concluded that reason is the final authority for morality. Only those actions that are undertaken from a sense of duty dictated by reason are moral; those acts that are dictated only by law or custom cannot be moral. In the following excerpt, Kant explains the categorical imperative, his basis for morality. Consider its close link to what we know as the Golden Rule.

[handwritten margin notes: "ordinary people w/ common sense", "2 Appeal to common Sense", "Rational moral Laws universal?", "posteriori", "begs"]

[It is clear from the foregoing that all moral concepts have their seat and origin completely a priori in reason, and indeed in the most ordinary human reason just as much as in the most highly speculative. They cannot be abstracted from any (empirical,) and hence merely contingent, cognition.] In this purity of their origin lies their very worthiness to serve us as supreme practical principles; and to the extent that something empirical is added to them, just so much is taken away from their genuine influence and from the absolute worth of the corresponding actions.] Moreover, it is not only a requirement of the greatest necessity from a theoretical point of view, when it is a question of speculation, but also of the greatest practical importance, to draw these concepts and laws from pure reason, to present them pure and unmixed and indeed to determine the extent of this entire practical and pure rational cognition, i.e., to determine the whole faculty of pure practical reason. [The principles should not be made to depend on the particular nature of human reason, as speculative philosophy may permit and even sometimes finds necessary; but, rather, the principles should be derived from the universal concept of a rational being in general, since moral laws should hold for every rational being as such.] In this way all morals, which require anthropology in order to be applied to humans, must be entirely expounded at first independently of anthropology as pure philosophy, i.e., as metaphysics (which can easily be done in such distinct kinds of knowledge). One knows quite well that unless one is in possession of such a metaphysics, then the attempt is futile, I shall not say to determine exactly for speculative judgment the moral element of duty in all that accords with duty, but that the attempt is impossible, even in ordinary and practical usage, especially in that of moral instruction, to ground morals on their genuine principles and thereby to produce pure moral dispositions and engraft them on men's minds for the promotion of the highest good in the world.

***

Everything in nature works according to laws. Only a rational being has the power to act according to his conception of laws, i.e., according to principles, and thereby has he a will. Since the derivation of actions from laws requires reason, the will is nothing but practical reason. If reason infallibly determines the will, then in the case of such a being actions which are recognized to be objectively necessary are also subjectively necessary, i.e., the will is a faculty of choosing only that which reason, independently of inclination, recognizes as being practically necessary, i.e., as good. But if reason of itself does not sufficiently determine the will, and if the will submits also to subjective conditions (certain incentives) which do not always agree with objective conditions; in a word, if the will does not in itself completely accord with reason (as is actually the case with men), then actions which are recognized as objectively necessary are subjectively contingent, and the determination of such a will according to objective laws is necessitation. That is to say that the relation of objective laws to a will not thoroughly good is represented as the determination of the will of a rational being by principles of reason which the will does not necessarily follow because of its own nature. . . .

[I]n the case of this categorical imperative, or law of morality, the reason for the difficulty (of discerning its possibility) is quite serious. The categorical imperative is an a priori synthetic practical proposition, and since discerning the possibility of propositions of this sort involves so much difficulty in theoretic knowledge, there may readily be gathered that there will be no less difficulty in practical knowledge.

In solving this problem, we want first to inquire whether perhaps the mere concept of a categorical imperative may not also supply us with the formula containing the proposition that can alone be a categorical imperative. For even when we know the purport of such an absolute command, the question as to how it is possible will still require a special and difficult effort, which we postpone to the last section.

If I think of a hypothetical imperative in general, I do not know beforehand what it will contain until its condition is given. But if I think of a categorical imperative, I know immediately what it contains. For since, besides the law, the imperative contains only the necessity that the maxim should accord with this law, while the law contains no condition to restrict it, there remains nothing but the universality of a law as such with which the maxim of the action should conform. This conformity alone is properly what is represented as necessary by the imperative.

Hence there is only one categorical imperative and it is this: Act only according to that maxim whereby you can at the same time will that it should become a universal law.

Now if all imperatives of duty can be derived from this one imperative as their principle, then there can at least be shown what is understood by the concept of duty and what it means, even though there is left undecided whether what is called duty may not be an empty concept.

The universality of law according to which effects are produced constitutes what is properly called nature in the most general sense (as to form), i.e., the existence of things as far as determined by universal laws. Accordingly, the universal imperative of duty may be expressed thus: Act as if the maxim of your action were to become through your will a universal law of nature.

We shall now enumerate some duties, following the usual division of them into duties to ourselves and to others and into perfect and imperfect duties.

1.   A man reduced to despair by a series of misfortunes feels sick of life but is still so far in possession of his reason that he can ask himself whether taking his own life would not be contrary to his duty to himself. Now he asks whether the maxim of his action could become a universal law of nature. But his maxim is this: from self-love I make as my principle to shorten my life when its continued duration threatens more evil than it promises satisfaction. There only remains the question as to whether this principle of self-love become a universal law of nature. One sees at once a contradiction in a system of nature whose law would destroy life by means of the very same feeling that acts so as to stimulate the furtherance of life, and hence there could be no existence as a system of nature. Therefore, such a maxim cannot possibly hold as a universal law of nature and is, consequently, wholly opposed to the supreme principle of all duty.

2.   Another man in need finds himself forced to borrow money. He knows well that he won't be able to repay it, but he sees also that he will not get any loan unless he firmly promises to repay it within a fixed time. He wants to make such a promise, but he still has conscience enough to ask himself whether it is not permissible and is contrary to duty to get out of difficulty in this way. Suppose, however, that he decides to do so. The maxim of his action would then be expressed as follows: when I believe myself to be in need of money, I will borrow money and promise to pay it back, although I know that I can never do so. Now this principle of self-love or personal advantage may perhaps be quite compatible with one's entire future welfare, but the question is now whether it is right. I then transform the requirement of self-love into a universal law and put the question thus: how would things stand if my maxim were to become a universal law? He then sees at once that such a maxim could never hold as a universal law of nature and be consistent with itself, but must necessarily be self-contradictory. For the universality of law which says that anyone believing himself to be in difficulty could promise whatever he pleases with the intention of not keeping it would make promising itself and the end to be attained thereby quite impossible, inasmuch as no one would believe what was promised him but would merely laugh at all such utterances as being vain pretenses.

3.   A third finds in himself a talent whose cultivation could make him a man useful in many respects. But he finds himself in comfortable circumstances and prefers to indulge in pleasure rather than to bother himself about broadening and improving his fortunate natural aptitudes. But he asks himself further whether his maxim of neglecting his natural gifts, besides agreeing of itself with his propensity to indulgence, might agree also with what is called duty. He then sees that a system of nature could indeed always subsist according to such a universal law, even though every man (like South Sea Islanders) should let his talents rust and resolve to devote his life entirely to idleness, indulgence, propagation and, in a word, to enjoyment. But he cannot possibly will that this should become a universal law of nature or be implanted in us as such a law by a natural instinct. For as a rational being he

necessarily wills that all his faculties should be developed, inasmuch as they are given him for all sorts of possible purposes.

4.   A fourth man finds things going well for himself but sees others (whom he could help) struggling with great hardships; and he thinks: what does it matter to me? Let everybody be as happy as Heaven will or as he can make himself; I shall take nothing from him nor even envy him; but I have no desire to contribute anything to his well-being or to his assistance when in need. If such a way of thinking were to become a universal law of nature, the human race admittedly could very well subsist and doubtless could subsist even better than when everyone prates about sympathy and benevolence and even on occasion exerts himself to practice them but, on the other hand, also cheats when he can, betrays the rights of man, or otherwise violates them. But even though it is possible that a universal law of nature could subsist in accordance with that maxim, still it is impossible to will that such a principle should hold everywhere as a law of nature. For a will which resolved in this way would contradict itself, inasmuch as cases might often arise in which one would have need of the love and sympathy of others and in which he would deprive himself, by such a law of nature springing from his own will, of all hope of the aid he wants for himself.

These are some of the many actual duties, or at least what are taken to be such, whose derivation from the single principle cited above is clear. We must be able to will that a maxim of our action become a universal law; this is the canon for morally estimating any of our actions. Some actions are so constituted that their maxims cannot without contradiction even be thought as a universal law of nature, much less be willed as what should become one. In the case of others this internal impossibility is indeed not found, but there is still no possibility of willing that their maxim should be raised to the universality of a law of nature, because such a will would contradict itself. There is no difficulty in seeing that the former kind of action conflicts with strict or narrow [perfect] (irremissible) duty, while the second kind conflicts only with broad [imperfect] (meritorious) duty. By means of these examples there has thus been fully set forth how all duties depend as regards the kind of obligation (not the object of their action) upon the one principle.

If we now attend to ourselves in any transgression of a duty, we find that we actually do not will that our maxim should become a universal law—because this is impossible for us—but rather that the opposite of this maxim should remain a law universally. We only take the liberty of making an exception to the law for ourselves (or just for this one time) to the advantage of our inclination. Consequently, if we weighed up everything from one and the same standpoint, namely, that of reason, we would find a contradiction in our own will, viz., that a certain principle be objectively necessary as a universal law and yet subjectively not hold universally but should admit of exceptions. But since we at one moment regard our action from the standpoint of a will wholly in accord with reason and then at another moment regard the very same action from the standpoint of a will affected by inclination, there is really no contradiction here. Rather, there is an opposition (*antagonismus*) of inclination to the precept of reason, whereby the universality (*universalitas*) of the principle is changed into a mere generality (*generalitas*) so that the practical principal of reason may meet the maxim halfway. Although this procedure cannot be justified in our own impartial judgment, yet it does show that we actually acknowledge the validity of the categorical imperative and (with all respect for it) merely allow ourselves a few exceptions which, as they seem to us, are unimportant and forced upon us.

We have thus at least shown that if duty is a concept which is to have significance and real legislative authority for our actions, then such duty can be expressed only in categorical imperatives but not at all in hypothetical ones. We have also—and this is already a great deal—exhibited clearly and definitely for every application what is the content of the categorical imperative, which must contain the principle of all duty (if there is such a thing at all). But we have not yet advanced far enough to prove a priori that there actually is an imperative of this kind, that there is a practical law which of itself commands absolutely and without any incentives, and that following this law is duty. . . .

If then there is to be a supreme practical principle and, as far as the human will is concerned, a categorical imperative, then it must be such that from the conception of what is necessarily an end for everyone because this end is an end in itself it constitutes an objective principle of the will and can hence serve as a practical law. The ground of such a principle is this: rational nature exists as an end in itself. In this way man necessarily thinks of his own existence; thus far is it a subjective principle of human actions. But in this way also does every other rational being think of his existence on the same rational ground that holds also for me; hence it is at the same time an objective principle, from which, as a supreme practical ground, all laws of the will must be able to be derived. The practical imperative will therefore be the following: Act in such a way that you treat humanity, whether in your own person or in the person of another, always at the same time as an end and never simply as a means. We now want to see whether this can be carried out in practice.

Let us keep to our previous examples.

First, as regards the concept of necessary duty to oneself, the man who contemplates suicide will ask himself whether his action can be consistent with the idea of humanity as an end in itself. If he destroys himself in order to escape from a difficult situation, then he is making use of his person merely as a means so as to maintain a tolerable condition till the end of his life. Man, however, is not a thing and hence is not something to be used merely as a means; he must in all his actions always be regarded as an end in himself. Therefore, I cannot dispose of man in my own person by mutilating, damaging or killing him. (A more exact determination of this principle so as to avoid all misunderstanding, e.g., regarding the amputation of limbs in order to save oneself, or the exposure of one's life to danger in order to save it and so on, must here be omitted; such questions belong to morals proper.)

Second, as concerns necessary or strict duty to others, the man who intends to make a false promise will immediately see that he intends to make use of another man merely as a means to an end which the latter does not likewise hold. For the man whom I want to use for my own purposes by such a promise cannot possibly concur with my way of acting toward him and hence cannot himself hold the end of this action. This conflict with the principle of duty to others becomes even clearer when instances of attacks on the freedom and property of others are considered. For then it becomes clear that a transgressor of the rights of men intends to make use of the persons of others merely as a means, without taking into consideration that, as rational beings, they should always be esteemed at the same time as ends, i.e., be esteemed only as beings who must themselves be able to hold the very same action as an end.

Third, with regard to contingent (meritorious) duty to oneself, it is not enough that the action does not conflict with humanity in our own person as an end in itself; the action must also harmonize with this end. Now there are in humanity capacities for greater perfection which belong to the end that nature has in view as regards humanity in our own person. To neglect these capacities might perhaps be consistent with the maintenance of humanity as an end in itself, but would not be consistent with the advancement of this end.

Fourth, concerning meritorious duty to others, the natural end that all men have is their own happiness. Now humanity might indeed subsist if nobody contributed anything to the happiness of others, provided he did not intentionally impair their happiness. But this, after all, would harmonize only negatively and not positively with humanity as an end in itself, if everyone does not also strive, as much as he can, to further the ends of others. For the ends of any subject who is an end in himself must as far as possible be my ends also, if that conception of an end in itself is to have its full effect in me.

Summary + 48:

Ten commandments   52

• Rape
• using others
• Suicide
• Lying promise
3 •
4 •
• Prostitution   47:45

THE TEN COMMANDMENTS

As discussed earlier, one of the earliest recorded codes of conduct is found in the Bible: the Ten Commandments. If you were given the opportunity to write 10, and only 10, commandments today, do you think that these would be the ones that you would choose? Are these sufficient? Are they realistic? In your opinion, is a good person one who follows these commandments?

1 Then God delivered all these commandments:

2 "I, the LORD, am your God, who brought you out of the land of Egypt, that place of slavery. 3 You shall not have other gods besides me. 4 You shall not carve idols for yourselves in the shape of anything in the sky above or on the earth below or in the waters beneath the earth; 5 you shall not bow down before them or worship them. For I, the LORD, your God, am a jealous God, inflicting punishment for their fathers' wickedness on the children of those who hate me, down to the third and fourth generation; 6 but bestowing mercy down to the thousandth generation, on the children of those who love me and keep my commandments.

7 "You shall not take the name of the LORD, your God, in vain. For the LORD will not leave unpunished him who takes his name in vain.

8 "Remember to keep holy the sabbath day. 9 Six days you may labor and do all your work, 10 but the seventh day is the sabbath of the LORD, your God. No work may be done then either by you, or your son or daughter, or your male or female slave, or your beast, or by the alien who lives with you. 11 In six days the LORD made the heavens and the earth, the sea and all that is in them; but on the seventh day he rested. That is why the LORD has blessed the sabbath day and made it holy.

12 "Honor your father and your mother, that you may have a long life in the land which the LORD, your God, is giving you.

13 "You shall not kill.

14 "You shall not commit adultery.

15 "You shall not steal.

16 "You shall not bear false witness against your neighbor.

17 "You shall not covet your neighbor's house. You shall not covet your neighbor's wife, nor his male or female slave, nor his ox or ass, nor anything else that belongs to him."

The Ten Commandments, Exodus 20: 1–17. The Bible.

THE JUSTIFICATION OF HUMAN RIGHTS

—DENIS G. ARNOLD

In order to think about human rights in a meaningful way, it is necessary to answer certain philosophical questions about their nature. Three of the most basic questions are the following: How can human rights be justified? What specific human rights exist? How do human rights differ from other rights, such as legal rights? Arnold considers each question in turn.

Human rights are rights enjoyed by humans not because we are members of the species *Homo sapiens,* but because fully functional members of our species are persons. Personhood is a metaphysical category that may or may not be unique to *Homo sapiens.* To be a person one must be capable of reflecting on one's desires at a second-order level, and one must be capable of acting in a manner consistent with one's considered preferences (Dworkin, 1988; Frankfurt, 1988). First-order desires are the assortment of desires that occupy one's conscious mind and compete for one's attention. Second-order desires are desires about those first-order desires. When one embraces a particular first-order desire at a second-order level, it becomes a preference. A mundane example will help to illustrate this concept. Each of us is likely to have found ourselves staring at a bedside clock after having turned off an early-morning alarm. Lying comfortably in bed, one might reflect on one's immediate desires: to get up and go for a run; to get up and prepare for an early morning meeting; or to roll over and return to sleep. The process of reflecting on these competing desires takes place at a second-order level of consciousness. It is the capacity to reflect on one's competing desires and to act in a manner consistent with our second-order preferences that distinguishes persons from mere animals. This is not to say that one cannot sometimes fail to act in a manner consistent with one's better judgment and still be regarded as a person. Indeed, most of us are intimately familiar with such weakness of the will. The point is that we enjoy this capacity, and we are capable of acting in a manner consistent with this capacity. Furthermore, if a human were constitutionally incapable of acting in a manner consistent with his or her second-order preferences, he or she would not be properly described as a person. It is in this sense that the idea of personhood is properly understood as metaphysical rather than biological (Melden, 1977).

Reprinted from Denis G. Arnold, "Human Rights and Business: An Ethical Analysis," in Rory Sullivan ed., *Business and Human Rights: Dilemmas and Solutions* (Sheffield, UK: Greenleaf Publishing, 2003). Reprinted with permission of the author and Greenleaf Publishing Co.

The derivation of human rights from the concept of personhood is one of the most important accomplishments of 20th century philosophy. Much of the most important foundational research on this subject has been produced by the philosopher Alan Gewirth. In his book *Reason and Morality* (1978), Gewirth provides a rigorous and detailed justification of human rights. As with any major philosophical theory, Gewirth's defense of human rights has been criticized on various grounds. However, Deryck Beyleveld has provided a masterful and persuasive defense of Gewirth's arguments concerning the justification of human rights in his own important work on the subject (Beyleveld, 1991). It is sometimes argued that human rights cannot be justified without appealing to specific religious or legal traditions. To see that this is not the case, it will be helpful to provide a summary of Gewirth's philosophical defense of human rights.

Gewirth begins with the idea that every person regards his or her purposes as good according to his or her own criteria. By rising each morning and pursuing their own individual goals, individuals demonstrate in a practical way those things that they value.[1] Such actions are possible only insofar as the necessary conditions of one's acting to achieve one's purposes are satisfied. In other words, via the act of pursuing their individual aims, individuals demonstrate that they value the necessary conditions of action. The necessary conditions of action are freedom and well-being. Without freedom and well-being, one cannot pursue those things which one values. Freedom is here understood as controlling one's behavior by one's unforced choice while having knowledge of relevant circumstances. Possessing well-being entails having the general abilities and conditions required for a person to be able to act in a manner consistent with his or her considered, or second-order, preferences. Anyone who pursues a particular good must, on pain of contradiction, claim that they have a right to freedom and well-being. As such, all persons must accept that others have rights to freedom and well-being. Gewirth puts the matter this way (Gewirth, 1978: 63):

> Since the agent [or person] regards as necessary goods the freedom and well-being that constitute the generic features of his successful action, he logically must hold that he has rights to these generic features, and he implicitly makes a corresponding rights claim.

Gewirth is not arguing, as some might think, that because persons require freedom and well-being in order to function, they are thereby entitled to freedom and well-being (MacIntyre, 1984). Such an argument, one grounded in *empirical necessity,* would not be convincing because it does not follow from the fact that one requires something, that one has a right to that thing. While Gewirth's argument does have an empirical component, it is properly understood as a transcendental argument in the Kantian tradition. A transcendental argument is one that establishes the truth of a proposition by appealing to necessary conditions of human experience. Gewirth's argument is that, as a matter of *rational consistency,* a person must acknowledge that she is a purposive being, and that the pursuit of her ends requires

---

[1]One might object to this view on the grounds that some people pursue ends that they themselves do not regard as valuable. Such an objection fails to undermine Gewirth's point since, on his account, one demonstrates that one regards some ends as valuable insofar as one pursues that end. Here Gewirth's position may be regarded as consistent with those social scientists who are interested in studying not what people say they value, but what they demonstrate they value through their actions.

freedom and well-being. Hence she must claim a right to freedom and well-being. To do otherwise would be irrational. Because all other persons share these qualities, she must— again, as a matter of rational consistency—ascribe these rights to all other beings. To deny that persons have the right to freedom and well-being is to deny that one is a purposive being. Since the denial is a purposive act, it contradicts the proposition being asserted. In this way, Gewirth provides a deep and satisfying justification for human rights. Because the justification is grounded in rational reflection on the human condition, it can be embraced by individuals of diverse religious faiths and different cultural identities.

At this point in our discussion, it is worthwhile to consider an objection to the foregoing argument concerning human rights. This criticism stems from the observation that the idea of human rights emerged from the Western philosophical tradition, but is taken to be universal in its applicability. The claim is then made that human rights are of less importance in the value systems of other cultures. For example, it is argued that "Asian values" emphasize order, discipline and social harmony, as opposed to individual rights. In this view, the freedom and well-being of individuals should not be allowed to interfere with the harmony of the community, as might be the case, for example, when workers engage in disruptive collective action in an effort to secure their rights. This view might also be used to defend the claim that the moral norms that govern Asian factory operations should emphasize order and discipline, not freedom and well-being.

Several points may be made in reply to this objection. First, Asia is a large region with a vast and heterogeneous population. As Amartya Sen and others have argued, to claim that all, or even most, Asians share a uniform set of values is to impose a level of uniformity that does not exist at present and has not existed in the past (Donnely, 1999; Sen, 1999, 2000; Tatsuo, 1999). Second, in secular, democratic Asian societies such as India, respect for individual rights has a long tradition. Indeed, there are significant antecedents in the history of the civilizations of the Indian subcontinent that emphasize individual freedom and well-being. For example, in the third century BC, the Emperor Ashoka granted his citizens the freedom to embrace whatever religious or philosophical system they might choose, while at the same time he emphasized the importance of tolerance and respect for philosophical and religious beliefs different than one's own (Sen, 1999). Third, even if it was the case that Asian cultures shared a uniform set of values that de-emphasized human rights, this would not by itself provide good reasons for denying or disrespecting the rights to freedom and well-being. This is because the justification of human rights provided above is grounded in rational arguments that are valid across cultures. Jack Donnely makes a similar point in his recent defense of universal human rights (Donnely, 1999: 87):

> *One of the things that makes us human is our capacity to create and change our culture. Cultural diversity has in recent years increasingly come to be valued in itself. Westerners have in recent centuries been especially insensitive in their approach to such differences. Nonetheless, the essential insight of human rights is that the worlds we make for ourselves, intentionally and unintentionally, must conform to relatively universal requirements that rest on our common humanity and seek to guarantee equal concern and respect from the state for every person.*

The critic is likely to retort that such a view reflects Western prejudices grounded in Enlightenment ideals. This response is unpersuasive. Diverse intellectual traditions have emphasized the importance of values derived from reason, rather than mythology, traditionalism, mere sentiment, or some other source. For example, in the 16th century the Moghul Emperor Akbar wrote (Sen, 2000: 37):

> *The pursuit of reason and rejection of traditionalism are so brilliantly patent as to be above the need for argument. If traditionalism were proper, the prophets would merely have followed their own elders (and not come with new messages).*

Akbar arranged to have philosophers representing diverse religious and philosophical beliefs engage in rational discussions regarding the merits of their competing views, and sought to identify the most persuasive features of each view. In so doing, Akbar was able to emphasize the power and force of rational analysis. Given that a similar emphasis on rational analysis concerning values may be found in the histories of other non-Western cultures, the claim that such analysis is uniquely Western is unpersuasive.

Human rights are moral rights that apply to all persons in all nations, regardless of whether the nation in which a person resides acknowledges and protects those rights. It is in this sense that human rights are said to be *inalienable.* Human rights differ from legal rights in that, unlike legal rights, the existence of human rights is not contingent upon any institution. Many nations grant their citizens certain constitutional or legal rights via foundational documents or legal precedent. However, the rights that are protected vary among nations. Some nations ensure that the rights of citizens are protected by effective policing and an independent judiciary. Frequently, however, poor citizens and disfavored groups are not provided with the same level of protection for their legal rights as the economic and political elite. Persons who are deprived of their rights do not thereby cease to have those rights. As A. I. Melden has argued (Melden, 1977: 167–68):

> *The complaint that persons are deprived of their human rights when, for example, they are subjected to forced indenture by their employers, is a complaint that their rights have been violated and implies, clearly, that they have rights they are unjustly prevented from exercising. If one were deprived of one's rights in the sense in which one would be deprived of things in one's physical possession by having them taken away, one would no longer have the rights, and there would be no grounds for the complaint. So it is with the denial of a person's right—this does not consist in denying that he has the right but, rather, in denying him, by withholding from him, that to which he has the right or the means or opportunity for its exercise.*

Employers may deny employees their inalienable right to freedom and well-being, whether or not local governments are complicit, but in doing so they in no way diminish the legitimacy of the claims of their employees to those rights. However, by virtue of their failure to operate from the moral point of view, such employers succeed in diminishing their own standing in the community of rights holders. . . .

REFERENCES

Beyleveld, D. (1991). *The Dialectical Necessity of Morality* (Chicago: University of Chicago Press).

Donnely, J. (1999). "Human Rights and Asian Values: A Defense of 'Western' Universalism." In J. Bauer and D. Bell (eds.), *The East Asian Challenge for Human Rights* (Cambridge, UK: Cambridge University Press): 60–87.

Dworkin, G. (1988). *The Theory and Practice of Autonomy* (Cambridge, UK: Cambridge University Press).

Frankfurt, H. (1988). *The Importance of What We Care About* (Cambridge, UK: Cambridge University Press).

Gewirth, A. (1978). *Reason and Morality* (Chicago: University of Chicago Press).

Gewirth, A. (1982). *Human Rights: Essays on Justification and Applications* (Chicago: University of Chicago Press).

MacIntyre, A. (1984). *After Virtue* (Notre Dame, IN: University of Notre Dame Press, 2nd ed.).

Melden, A. (1977). *Rights and Persons* (Berkeley, CA: University of California Press).

Sen, A. (1999). "Human Rights and Asian Values." In T. Machan (ed.), *Business Ethics in the Global Marketplace* (Stanford, CA: Hoover Institution Press): 37–62.

Sen, A. (2000). "East and West: The Reach of Reason," *The New York Review of Books,* July 20: 33–38.

Tatsuo, I. (1999). "Liberal Democracy and Asian Orientalism." In J. Bauer and D. Bell (eds.), *The East Asian Challenge for Human Rights* (Cambridge, UK: Cambridge University Press): 27–59.

UTILITARIANISM

—JOHN STUART MILL

John Stuart Mill (1806–1873) is most often linked with philosophical empiricism and utilitarianism. As a member of Parliament, he was a staunch defender of individual liberties and argued against state interference. In fact, he was one of the first advocates of women's equality. Mill's concept of utilitarianism was a modification of Jeremy Bentham's version in that Mill enriched the concept of pleasure. While Bentham believed that all pleasures, physical and intellectual, were of equal value, Mill considered the "higher" pleasures of the mind as superior. What are the implications of this belief on decision making?

WHAT UTILITARIANISM IS

The creed which accepts as the foundation of morals "utility" or the "greatest happiness principle" holds that actions are right in proportion as they tend to promote happiness; wrong as they tend to produce the reverse of happiness. By happiness is intended pleasure and the absence of pain: by unhappiness, pain and the privation of pleasure. To give a clear view of the moral standard set up by the theory, much more requires to be said; in particular, what things it includes in the ideas of pain and pleasure, and to what extent this is left an open question. But these supplementary explanations do not affect the theory of life on which this theory of morality is grounded—namely, that pleasure and freedom from pain are the only things desirable as ends; and that all desirable things (which are as numerous in the utilitarian as in any other scheme) are desirable either for pleasure inherent in themselves or as means to the promotion of pleasure and the prevention of pain.

Now such a theory of life excites in many minds, and among them in some of the most estimable in feeling and purpose, inveterate dislike. To suppose that life has (as they express it) no higher end than pleasure—no better and nobler object of desire and pursuit—they designate as utterly mean and groveling, as a doctrine worthy only of swine, to whom the followers of Epicurus were, at a very early period, contemptuously likened; and modern holders of the doctrine are occasionally made the subject of equally polite comparisons by its German, French and English assailants.

When thus attacked, the Epicureans have always answered that it is not they, but their accusers, who represent human nature in a degrading light, since the accusation supposes

---

John Stuart Mill, *Utilitarianism,* chaps. II and V.

human beings to be capable of no pleasures except those of which swine are capable. If this supposition were true, the charge could not be gainsaid, but would then be no longer an imputation; for if the sources of pleasure were precisely the same to human beings and to swine, the rule of life which is good enough for the one would be good enough for the other. The comparison of the Epicurean life to that of beasts is felt as degrading, precisely because a beast's pleasures do not satisfy a human being's conceptions of happiness. Human beings have faculties more elevated than the animal appetites and, when once made conscious of them, do not regard anything as happiness which does not include their gratification. I do not, indeed, consider the Epicureans to have been by any means faultless in drawing out their scheme of consequences from the utilitarian principle. To do this in any sufficient manner, many Stoic, as well as Christian, elements require to be included. But there is no known Epicurean theory of life which does not assign to the pleasures of the intellect, of the feelings and imagination, and of the moral sentiments a much higher value as pleasures than to those of mere sensation. It must be admitted, however, that utilitarian writers in general have placed the superiority of mental over bodily pleasures chiefly in the greater permanency, safety, uncostliness, etc., of the former—that is, in their circumstantial advantages rather than in their intrinsic nature. And on all these points utilitarians have fully proved their case; but they might have taken the other and, as it may be called, higher ground with entire consistency. It is quite compatible with the principle of utility to recognize the fact that some kinds of pleasure are more desirable and more valuable than others. It would be absurd that, while in estimating all other things quality is considered as well as quantity, the estimation of pleasure should be supposed to depend on quantity alone.

If I am asked what I mean by difference of quality in pleasures, or what makes one pleasure more valuable than another, merely as a pleasure, except its being greater in amount, there is but one possible answer. Of two pleasures, if there be one to which all or almost all who have experience of both give a decided preference, irrespective of any feeling of moral obligation to prefer it, that is the more desirable pleasure. If one of the two is, by those who are competently acquainted with both, placed so far above the other that they prefer it, even though knowing it to be attended with a greater amount of discontent, and would not resign it for any quantity of the other pleasure which their nature is capable of, we are justified in ascribing to the preferred enjoyment a superiority in quality so far outweighing quantity as to render it, in comparison, of small account.

Now it is an unquestionable fact that those who are equally acquainted with and equally capable of appreciating and enjoying both do give a most marked preference to the manner of existence which employs their higher faculties. Few human creatures would consent to be changed into any of the lower animals for a promise of the fullest allowance of a beast's pleasures; no intelligent human being would consent to be a fool, no instructed person would be an ignoramus, no person of feeling and conscience would be selfish and base, even though they should be persuaded that the fool, the dunce or the rascal is better satisfied with his lot than they are with theirs. They would not resign what they possess more than he for the most complete satisfaction of all the desires which they have in common with him. If they ever fancy they would, it is only in cases of unhappiness so extreme that to escape from it they would exchange their lot for almost any other, however undesirable in their own eyes. A being of higher faculties requires more to make him happy, is capable probably of more acute suffering and certainly accessible to it at more points than one of the inferior type; but in spite of these liabilities, he can never really wish to sink into what he feels to be a lower grade of existence. We may give what explanation we please of this unwillingness; we may attribute it to pride, a name which is given indiscriminately to some of the most and to some of the least estimable feelings of which mankind are capable; we may refer it to the love of liberty and personal independence, an appeal to which was with the Stoics one of the most effective means for the inculcation of it; to the love of power or to the love of excitement, both of which do really enter into and contribute to it; but its most appropriate appellation is a sense of dignity, which all human beings possess in one form or other, and in some, though by no means in exact, proportion to their higher faculties, and which is so essential a part of the happiness of those in whom it is strong that nothing which conflicts with it could be otherwise than momentarily an object of desire to them. Whoever supposes that this preference takes place at a sacrifice of happiness—that the superior being, in anything like equal circumstances, is not happier than the inferior—confounds the two very different ideas of happiness and content. It is indisputable that the being whose capacities of enjoyment are low has the greatest chance of having them fully satisfied; and a highly endowed being will always feel that any happiness which he can look for, as the world is constituted, is imperfect. But he can learn to bear its imperfections, if they are at all bearable; and they will not make him envy the being who is indeed unconscious of the imperfections, but only because he feels not at all the good which those imperfections qualify. It is better to be a human being dissatisfied than a pig satisfied; better to be Socrates dissatisfied than a fool satisfied. And if the fool, or the pig, are of a different opinion, it is because they only know their own side of the question. The other party to the comparison knows both sides.

It may be objected that many who are capable of the higher pleasures occasionally, under the influence of temptation, postpone them to the lower. But this is quite compatible with a full appreciation of the intrinsic superiority of the higher. Men often, from infirmity of character, make their election for the nearer good, though they know it to be the less valuable; and this no less when the choice is between two bodily pleasures than when it is between bodily and mental. They pursue sensual indulgences to the injury of health, though perfectly aware that health is the greater good. It may be further objected that many who begin with youthful enthusiasm for everything noble, as they advance in years, sink into indolence and selfishness. But I do not believe that those who undergo this very common change voluntarily choose the lower description of pleasures in preference to the higher. I believe that, before they devote themselves exclusively to the one, they have already become incapable of the other. Capacity for the nobler feelings is in most natures a very tender plant, easily killed, not only by hostile influences, but by mere want of sustenance; and in the majority of young persons it speedily dies away if the occupations to which their position in life has devoted them, and the society into which it has thrown them, are not favorable to keeping that higher capacity in exercise. Men lose their high aspirations as they lose their intellectual tastes, because they have not time or opportunity for indulging them; and they addict themselves to inferior pleasures, not because they deliberately prefer them, but because they are either the only ones to which they have access or the only ones which they are any longer capable of enjoying. It may be questioned whether anyone who has remained equally susceptible to both classes of pleasures ever knowingly and calmly preferred the lower, though many, in all ages, have broken down in an ineffectual attempt to combine both.

From this verdict of the only competent judges, I apprehend there can be no appeal. On a question which is the best worth having of two pleasures, or which of two modes of existence is the most grateful to the feelings, apart from its moral attributes and from its consequences, the judgment of these who are qualified by knowledge of both, or, if they differ, that of the majority among them, must be admitted as final. And there needs be the less hesitation to accept this judgment respecting the quality of pleasures, since there is no other tribunal to be referred to even on the question of quantity. What means are there of determining which is the acutest of two pains, or the intensest of two pleasurable sensations, except the general suffrage of those who are familiar with both? Neither pains nor pleasures are homogeneous, and pain is always heterogeneous with pleasure. What is there to decide whether a particular pleasure is worth purchasing at the cost of a particular pain, except the feelings and judgment of the experienced? When, therefore, those feelings and judgment declare the pleasures derived from the higher faculties to be preferable *in kind,* apart from the question of intensity, to those of which the animal nature, disjoined from the higher faculties, is susceptible, they are entitled on this subject to the same regard.

I have dwelt on this point as being part of a perfectly just conception of utility or happiness considered as the directive rule of human conduct. But it is by no means an indispensable condition to the acceptance of the utilitarian standard; for that standard is not the agent's own greatest happiness, but the greatest amount of happiness altogether; and if it may possibly be doubted whether a noble character is always the happier for its nobleness, there can be no doubt that it makes other people happier, and that the world in general is immensely a gainer by it. Utilitarianism, therefore, could only attain its end by the general cultivation of nobleness of character, even if each individual were only benefited by the nobleness of others, and his own, so far as happiness is concerned, were a sheer deduction from the benefit. But the bare enunciation of such an absurdity as this last renders refutation superfluous.

According to the greatest happiness principle, as above explained, the ultimate end, with reference to and for the sake of which all other things are desirable—whether we are considering our own good or that of other people—is an existence exempt as far as possible from pain, and as rich as possible in enjoyments, both in point of quantity and quality; the test of quality and the rule for measuring it against quantity being the preference felt by those who, in their opportunities to experience, to which must be added their habits of self-consciousness and self-observation, are best furnished with the means of comparison. This, being according to the utilitarian opinion the end of human action, is necessarily also the standard of morality, which may accordingly be defined "the rules and precepts for human conduct" by the observance of which an existence such as has been described might be, to the greatest extent possible, secured to all mankind; and not to them only, but, so far as the nature of things admits, to the whole sentient creation.

***

ON THE CONNECTION BETWEEN JUSTICE AND UTILITY

In all ages of speculation one of the strongest obstacles to the reception of the doctrine that utility or happiness is the criterion of right and wrong has been drawn from the idea of justice. The powerful sentiment and apparently clear perception which that word recalls with a rapidity and certainty resembling an instinct have seemed to the majority of thinkers to point to an inherent quality in things; to show that the just must have an existence in nature as something absolute, generically distinct from every variety of the expedient and, in idea, opposed to it, though (as is commonly acknowledged) never, in the long run, disjoined from it in fact.

***

. . . The idea of justice supposes two things—a rule of conduct and a sentiment which sanctions the rule. The first must be supposed common to all mankind and intended for their good. The other (the sentiment) is a desire that punishment may be suffered by those who infringe the rule. There is involved, in addition, the conception of some definite person who suffers by the infringement, whose rights (to use the expression appropriated to the case) are violated by it. And the sentiment of justice appears to me to be the animal desire to repel or retaliate a hurt or damage to oneself or to those with whom one sympathizes, widened so as to include all persons, by the human capacity of enlarged sympathy and the human conception of intelligent self-interest. From the latter elements the feeling derives its morality; from the former, its peculiar impressiveness and energy of self-assertion.

I have, throughout, treated the idea of a *right* residing in the injured person and violated by the injury, not as a separate element in the composition of the idea and sentiment, but as one of the forms in which the other two elements clothe themselves. These elements are a hurt to some assignable person or persons, on the one hand, and a demand for punishment, on the other. An examination of our own minds, I think, will show that these two things include all that we mean when we speak of violation of a right. When we call anything a person's right, we mean that he has a valid claim on society to protect him in the possession of it, either by the force of law or by that of education and opinion. If he has what we consider a sufficient claim, on whatever account, to have something guaranteed to him by society, we say that he has a right to it. If we desire to prove that anything does not belong to him by right, we think this done as soon as it is admitted that society ought not to take measures for securing it to him, but should leave him to chance or to his own exertions. Thus a person is said to have a right to what he can earn in fair professional competition, because society ought not to allow any other person to hinder him from endeavoring to earn in that manner as much as he can. But he has not a right to 300 a year, though he may happen to be earning it; because society is not called on to provide that he shall earn that sum. On the contrary, if he owns 10 thousand pounds 3% stock, he *has* a right to 300 a year because society has come under an obligation to provide him with an income of that amount.

To have a right, then, is, I conceive, to have something which society ought to defend me in the possession of. If the objective goes on to ask why it ought, I can give him no other reason than general utility. If that expression does not seem to convey a sufficient feeling of the strength of the obligation, nor to account for the peculiar energy of the feeling, it is because there goes to the composition of the sentiment, not a rational only but also an animal element—the thirst for retaliation; and this thirst derives its intensity, as well as its moral justification, from the extraordinarily important and impressive kind of utility which is concerned. The interest involved is that of security, to everyone's feelings the most vital of all interests. All other earthly benefits are needed by one person, not needed by another; and many of them can, if necessary, be cheerfully forgone or replaced by something else; but security no human being can possibly do without; on it we depend for all our immunity from evil and for the whole value of all and every good, beyond the passing moment, since nothing but the gratification of the instant could be of any worth to us if we could be deprived of everything the next instant by whoever was momentarily stronger than ourselves. Now this most indispensable of all necessaries, after physical nutriment, cannot be had unless the machinery for providing it is kept unintermittedly in active play. Our notion, therefore, of the claim we have on our fellow creatures to join in making safe for us the very groundwork of our existence gathers feelings around it so much more intense than those concerned in any of the more common cases of utility that the difference in degree (as is often the case in psychology) becomes a real difference in kind. The claim assumes that character of absoluteness, that apparent infinity and incommensurability with all other considerations which constitute the distinction between the feeling of right and wrong and that of ordinary expediency and inexpediency. The feelings concerned are so powerful, and we count so positively on finding a responsive feeling in others (all being alike interested) that *ought* and *should* grow into *must,* and recognized indispensability becomes a moral necessity, analogous to physical, and often not inferior to it in binding force.

If the preceding analysis, or something resembling it, be not the correct account of the notion of justice—if justice be totally independent of utility, and be a standard *per se,* which the mind can recognize by simple introspection of itself—it is hard to understand why that internal oracle is so ambiguous, and why so many things appear either just or unjust, according to the light in which they are regarded.

***

It appears from what has been said that justice is a name for certain moral requirements which, regarded collectively, stand higher in the scale of social utility, and are therefore of more paramount obligation, than any others, though particular cases may occur in which some other social duty is so important as to overrule any one of the general maxims of justice. Thus, to save a life, it may not only be allowable, but a duty, to steal or take by force the necessary food or medicine, or to kidnap and compel to officiate the only qualified medical practitioner. In such cases, as we do not call anything justice which is not a virtue, we usually say, not that justice must give way to some other moral principle, but that what is just in ordinary cases is, by reason of that other principle, not just in the particular case. By this useful accommodation of language, the character of indefeasibility attributed to justice is kept up, and we are saved from the necessity of maintaining that there can be laudable injustice.

The considerations which have now been adduced resolve, I conceive, the only real difficulty in the utilitarian theory of morals. It has always been evident that all cases of justice are also cases of expediency; the difference is in the peculiar sentiment which attaches to the former, as contradistinguished from the latter. If this characteristic sentiment has been sufficiently accounted for; if there is no necessity to assume for it any peculiarity of origin; if it is simply the natural feeling of resentment, moralized by being made coextensive with the demands of social good; and if this feeling not only does but ought to exist in all the classes of cases to which the idea of justice corresponds—that idea no longer presents itself as a stumbling block to the utilitarian ethics. Justice remains the appropriate name for certain social utilities which are vastly more important, and therefore more absolute and imperative, than any others are as a class (though not more so than others may be in particular cases); and which, therefore, ought to be, as well as naturally are, guarded by a sentiment, not only different in degree, but also in kind; distinguished from the milder feeling which attaches to the mere idea of promoting human pleasure or convenience at once by the more definite nature of its commands and by the sterner character of its sanctions.

SOME PROBLEMS
OF UTILITARIANISM

—Richard A. Posner

Utilitarianism is not without its detractors. Seventh Circuit Judge Richard Posner, who is well known for his staunch support of cost–benefit analysis in resolving legal disputes, explores several of these in this excerpt from The Economics of Justice.

Two features of utilitarian theory require clarification at the outset.[1] First, it is a theory of both personal morality and social justice. A good man is one who strives to maximize the sum total of happiness (his own plus others'), and the good society is one that seeks to maximize that sum total. Second, the maximand, as most utilitarians view it, is not a particular psychological state—ecstasy or euphoria or whatever—but is the broadest possible concept of satisfaction. Happiness, or utility, is maximized when people (or creatures) are able to satisfy their preferences, whatever those preferences may be, to the greatest possible extent. But this formulation does not exclude the possibility that A may know B's true preferences better than B does—the possibility, that is, of paternalism.

One of the principal criticisms of utilitarianism is that its domain is uncertain. Whose happiness is to count in designing policies to maximize the greatest happiness? Does the happiness of animals count? This issue has been addressed by J. J. C. Smart:

> *Perhaps strictly in itself and at a particular moment, a contented sheep is as good as a contented philosopher. However it is hard to agree to this. If we did we should have to agree that the human population ought ideally to be reduced by contraceptive methods and the sheep population more than correspondingly increased. Perhaps just so many humans should be left as could keep innumerable millions of placid sheep in contented idleness and immunity from depredations by ferocious animals. Indeed if a contented idiot is as good as a contented philosopher, and if a contented sheep is as good as a contented idiot, then a contented fish is as good as a contented sheep, and a contented beetle is as good as a contented fish. Where shall we stop?*[2]

Reprinted from *The Economics of Justice,* with permission of the author.

[1] For some recent expositions of utilitarianism see John Plamenatz, *The English Utilitarians* (1958); J. J. C. Smart, "An Outline of a System of Utilitarian Ethics," in Smart & Williams, *supra* note 2, at 3; Rolf E. Sartorius, *Individual Conduct and Social Norms: A Utilitarian Account of Social Union and the Rule of Law* (1975). Among the classical expositions see in particular Jeremy Bentham, *Introduction to the Principles of Morals and Legislation* (1789); Leslie Stephen, *The English Utilitarians* (1900). As noted earlier, I decline to empty the term utilitarianism of much of its distinctive meaning by defining it as the class of ethical doctrines in which the morality of a course of action is judged by its social consequences.

[2] Smart, *supra* note 1, at 16.

Smart does not answer his last question. Although he finds it "hard to agree" to equating the contented sheep with the contented philosopher, he can find no basis in utilitarian theory for distinguishing them and is left in the end to remark rather lamely that "the question of whether the general happiness would be increased by replacing most of the human population by a bigger population of contented sheep and pigs is not one which by any stretch of the imagination could become a live issue."[3]

Since utility in its broad sense is something possessed by many animals, the theory seems to require including sheep and pigs in the population whose happiness is to be maximized. Smart suggests as much. But there is something amiss in a philosophical system that cannot distinguish between people and sheep. In utilitarian morality, a driver who swerved to avoid two sheep and deliberately killed a child could not be considered a bad man, because his action may have increased the amount of happiness in the world.

We could say, with Frank Knight, that people don't *want* happiness or any other version of satisfaction that might embrace what animals want: "The chief thing which the common-sense individual actually wants is not satisfactions for the wants which he has, but more, and *better* wants."[4] But this is just a version of the old utilitarian game, which leads nowhere, of dividing preferences into "higher" and "lower" on inevitably shifting and subjective grounds.

Another boundary problem of utilitarianism concerns foreigners. Should American policy be to maximize the happiness of Americans, with foreigners' happiness given a zero weight? Or is a more ecumenical perspective required? And how about the unborn? To include them in the population whose happiness is to be maximized may yield policies on abortions, adoptions, homosexuality, savings and other issues different from those indicated if only the currently living are counted in the happiness census. Whether to include foreigners or the unborn is not an issue that utilitarianism can resolve directly, yet again it seems that if maximizing utility is to be taken seriously, the broadest possible conception of the relevant population must be used.

The problem of foreigners and the unborn is related to the old dispute over whether the utilitarian goal should be to maximize average or total happiness. If the poorer half of the population of Bangladesh were killed, the standard of living—and, for all one knows, the subjective happiness as well—of the remaining half would rise because of the higher ratio of people to land and other natural resources. However, the *total* happiness might be less. Similarly, a high birth rate may cause a reduction in the standard of living of a crowded country and, along with it, in the average happiness of the country, but this loss may be more than offset by the satisfactions, even if somewhat meager, of the added population. There is no clear basis in utilitarian theory for choosing between average and total happiness, but the latter is more consistent with a simple insistence on utility as the maximand.

In summary, the logic of utilitarianism seems to favor setting as the ethical goal the maximization of the total amount of happiness in the universe. Since this goal seems attainable only by making lots of people miserable (those of us who would have to make room

---

[3]*Id.* at 24–25.
[4]Frank Hyneman Knight, *The Ethics of Competition, and Other Essays* 22 (1935); see also *id.* at 32.

for all the foreigners, sheep or whatever), utilitarians are constantly seeking ways to contract the boundary. But to do so they must go outside of utilitarianism.

Another problem is the lack of a method for calculating the effect of a decision or policy on the total happiness of the relevant population.[5] Even within just the human population, there is no reliable technique for measuring a change in the level of satisfaction of one individual relative to a change in the level of satisfaction of another.

The Pareto approach may seem to offer a solution to the problem of measuring satisfaction. A change is said to be Pareto superior if it makes at least one person better off and no one worse off. Such a change by definition increases the total amount of (human) happiness in the world. The advantage of the Pareto approach is that it requires information only about marginal and not about total utilities. And there seems ready at hand an operational device for achieving Pareto superiority, the voluntary transaction, which by definition makes both parties better off than they were before. However, the condition that no one else be affected by a "voluntary" transaction can only rarely be fulfilled. Moreover, the voluntary-transaction or free-market solution to the problem of measuring utility begs two critical questions: whether the goods exchanged were initially distributed so as to maximize happiness (were the people with money those who derive the most happiness from the things money can buy?) and whether a system of free markets creates more happiness than alternative systems of resource allocation would.

Difficulty in deriving specific policies from ethical premises is not, however, unique to utilitarianism; it seems characteristic of ethical discussion generally. Among contemporary Kantian legal rights theorists,[6] one has only to compare Charles Fried and Richard Epstein, who, starting from seemingly identical premises regarding human respect and autonomy, derive sharply different policy implications.[7]

However, the fact that utilitarianism is no more indefinite than competing theories of moral obligation may not reconcile one to utilitarianism, especially if one favors limited government. Suppose, for example, that Bentham was correct in his belief that, lacking any real knowledge of the responsiveness to income of different individuals' happiness, we should assume that every one is pretty much alike in that respect. Then we need make only one additional, and as it happens plausible, assumption—that of the diminishing marginal utility of money income—to obtain a utilitarian basis for a goal of equalizing incomes. For on these assumptions it is easily shown that an equal distribution of income and wealth will produce more happiness than any other distribution[8] unless the costs of

---

[5]As Hayek puts it, the practice of utilitarianism presupposes omniscience. 2. F. A. Hayek, *Law, Legislation and Liberty* 17–23 (1976).

[6]I follow Bruce A. Ackerman, *Private Property and the Constitution* 71–72 (1977), in using the term "Kantian" to refer to a family of related ethical theories that subordinate social welfare to notions of human autonomy and self-respect as criteria of ethical conduct. Such theories need not, and usually do not, resemble closely the thought of Immanuel Kant, on which see Bruce Aune, *Kant's Theory of Morals* (1979).

[7]Among many other differences, Fried rejects Epstein's position that, *prima facie,* tort liability should be strict liability. *See* Charles Fried, *Right and Wrong* 107 (1978); and his *An Anatomy of Values: Problems of Personal and Social Choice* 187–189 (1970).

[8]*See* Jeremy Bentham, "The Philosophy of Economic Science," in 1 *Jeremy Bentham's Economic Writings* 81, 115–116 (W. Stark ed. 1952); Abba P. Lerner, *The Economics of Control: Principles of Welfare Economics* 35–36 (1944); Sartorius, *supra* note 16, at 131.

achieving and maintaining such a distribution equal or exceed the benefits. The qualification is critical, but it places the burden of proof on the opponent of income equalization in an area where proof is notoriously difficult to come by. This example illustrates a point made in the preceding chapter: if the impracticality of the felicific calculus is taken to justify the utilitarian's use of guesswork, the possibilities for plausible public intervention in private activities are unlimited.

The problem of indefiniteness blends into a related objection to utilitarian thought: what one might term the perils of instrumentalism. If happiness is maximized by allowing people to own property, marry as they choose, change jobs and so on, then the utilitarian will grant them the rights to these things, but if happiness can be increased by treating people more like sheep, then rights are out the window. People do not seem to be happier in totalitarian than in democratic states, but if they were, the consistent utilitarian would have to support totalitarianism. Utilitarianism thus seems to base rights of great importance on no firmer ground than an empirical hunch that they promote "happiness." That hunch cannot be verified by any tools we have or are likely to acquire—though some people will find one bit of evidence or another (for example, the Berlin wall) persuasive. Even within the framework of the liberal state, utilitarians who are not shy about making bold empirical guesses concerning the distribution of happiness can produce rather monstrous policy recommendations.[9]

"Moral monstrousness" is indeed a major problem of utilitarianism. Two types of monstrousness should be distinguished. One stems from the utilitarian's refusal to make moral distinctions among types of pleasure. Suppose that A spends his leisure time pulling wings off flies, while B spends his feeding pigeons, and because A has a greater capacity for pleasure than B, he derives more happiness from his leisure time. Putting aside the unhappiness of the fly, and the happiness of the pigeons, the consistent utilitarian would have to judge A a better man than B, because A's activity adds more to the sum of happiness than B's.

The other type of moral monstrousness arises from the utilitarian's readiness to sacrifice the innocent individual on the altar of social need. Alan Donagan gives the following example:

> *It might well be the case that more good and less evil would result from your painlessly and undetectedly murdering your malicious, old and unhappy grandfather than from your forebearing to do so: he would be freed from his wretched existence; his children would be rejoiced by their inheritances and would no longer suffer from his mischief; and you might anticipate the reward promised to those who do good in secret. Nobody seriously doubts that a position with such a consequence is monstrous.[10]*

Donagan seems correct in arguing that a consistent utilitarian would have to judge the murderer a good man. The utilitarian could, of course, point out that a *practice* of murdering obnoxious grandfathers would probably reduce happiness. Knowledge of the practice

---

[9]It should be mentioned, in fairness to the utilitarians, that Bentham is the principal, and inexhaustible, source of bizarre policy deductions from utilitarian premises. Nonetheless, utilitarians are frequently interventionist. *See, e.g.,* 3 Stephen, *supra* note 1, at 228–229, on J. S. Mill's interventionist proposals.

[10]Alan Donagan, "Is There a Credible Form of Utilitarianism?" In *Contemporary Utilitarianism* 187, 188 (Michael D. Bayles ed. 1968).

would make grandfathers very unhappy and in the long run would probably not benefit the heirs, because the practice would deter people from accumulating estates. But any utilitarian objections to creating an exception to the murder laws for killers of obnoxious grandfathers have no force at the level of personal morality once it is stipulated that the murder will go undetected. Yet to call the murderer in Donagan's example a "good man" does unacceptable violence to conventional moral notions.

Monstrousness is a less serious problem of utilitarianism at the level of social than of personal choice. It is one thing to pick an innocent person at random and kill him to achieve some social end and another to establish an institutional structure—criminal punishment, for example—which makes it inevitable that some innocent people will suffer. No punishment system could be devised that reduced the probability of erroneous conviction to zero. Yet even at the level of social choice, utilitarianism can lead to monstrous results. Were there a group of people at once so few relative to the rest of the society, so miserable, and so hated that their extermination would increase the total happiness of the society, the consistent utilitarian would find it hard to denounce their extermination, although he would be entitled to note the anxiety costs that might be imposed on people who feared they might be exterminated next.

If monstrousness is a peril of utilitarianism, moral squeamishness, or fanaticism, is a peril of Kantian theorists. Bernard Williams poses the case of Jim, the guest of an officer in a backward country who is about to have a group of political prisoners shot.[11] The officer tells Jim that if Jim will shoot one of the prisoners, he will release the others. Williams argues that Jim has no obligation to shoot a prisoner because there is a difference between doing evil and failing to prevent evil. But the difference is hard to see in the example. If Jim declines the officer's invitation, all the prisoners will die; if he accepts it, all but one will be saved. There is no trade-off. No one will be better off if Jim declines the invitation; all but one will be worse off.

Most Kantians try to avoid fanaticism by carving exceptions to the categorical duties they impose.[12] They will say that torture is wrong even if it could be shown (as Bentham believed) to maximize happiness on balance, but will then admit that if torturing one person were necessary to save the human race it would not be wrong to torture him. Once this much is conceded, however, there is no logical stopping point. What if two innocents must be killed to save 200 million Americans—10 to save 3 million Chicagoans—20 to save 60,000 residents of one Chicago neighborhood?

The tendency of Kantianism to merge into utilitarianism is illustrated by the moral philosophy of John Rawls. Although his premises are Kantian and he rejects utilitarianism because it does not take seriously the distinction between persons,[13] he defines justice as the outcome of collective choice by individuals in the "original position," that is, stripped of all their individual characteristics. He assumes that these shades choose principles of justice that will maximize their own utility, and because they are also assumed to be highly risk averse, they choose a principle that trades away much individual economic liberty for

---

[11]*See* Bernard Williams, "A Critique of Utilitarianism," in Smart & Williams, 77, 98–99.

[12]For an example of this approach *see* Fried, *supra* note 7, at 10.

[13]John Rawls, *A Theory of Justice* 27 (1971).

social insurance. Rawls's principle of social justice resembles Bentham's principle of maximizing income equality subject to the constraint of preserving the individual's incentive to engage in productive activity. In both cases, the optimal degree of equality depends on empirical hunches regarding the size and shape of individuals' marginal-utility schedules and the disincentive effects of egalitarian policies. The necessity of making such hunches imparts to Rawls's theory the same indefiniteness that plagues Bentham's. Rawls's concept of the "veil of ignorance" resembles the method by which the economist Abba Lerner deduced a norm of income equality from the greatest-happiness principle.[14] Lerner said that given our ignorance of the height of people's marginal-utility functions, the best assumption was that they are uncorrelated with income.[15] It is not surprising that another welfare economist, John Harsanyi, anticipated the core of Rawls's principle of justice (rational choice by people in the original position) by many years.[16]

To summarize, utilitarianism has serious shortcomings whether viewed as a system of personal morality or as a guide to social decision making; but Kantianism, the usual alternative, has its own serious defects; one of these is its resemblance to utilitarianism. . . .

---

[14]I am indebted to Gary Becker for this point.

[15]*See* Lerner, *supra* note 8.

[16]*See* John C. Harsanyi, "Cardinal Utility in Welfare Economics and in the Theory of Risk-Taking," 61 *J. Pol. Econ.* 434 (1953). Rawls acknowledges Harsanyi's contribution. *See* Rawls, *supra* note 13, at 137 n.11, 162 n.21. Harsanyi remains a sophisticated exponent of utilitarianism. *See* his "Morality and the Theory of Rational Behavior," 44 *Soc. Res.* 623 (1977).

THE ONES WHO WALK AWAY FROM OMELAS

—Ursula K. Le Guin

One of the concerns with utilitarian theory is that numbers do not always tell the full story. Le Guin illustrates this problem in the following story where one person's intense suffering is insufficient to outweigh the happiness of many. The story begins with a description of Omelas, one of the happiest cities you can imagine, full of festivals, music and joy for its inhabitants. This excerpt begins following Le Guin's description of that happiness. Consider how you would modify utilitarian theory to account for problems such as those described in this story.

. . . In a basement under one of the beautiful public buildings of Omelas, or perhaps in the cellar of one of its spacious private homes, there is a room. It has one locked door, and no window. A little light seeps in dustily between cracks in the boards, secondhand from a cobwebbed window somewhere across the cellar. In one corner of the little room a couple of mops, with stiff, clotted, foul-smelling heads, stand near a rusty bucket. The floor is dirt, a little damp to the touch, as cellar dust usually is. The room is about three paces long and two wide: a mere broom closet or disused tool room. In the room a child is sitting. It could be a boy or a girl. It looks about six, but actually is nearly ten. It is feeble-minded. Perhaps it was born defective, or perhaps it has become imbecile through fear, malnutrition and neglect. It picks its nose and occasionally fumbles vaguely with its toes or genitals, as it sits hunched in the corner farthest from the bucket and the two mops. It is afraid of the mops. It finds them horrible. It shuts its eyes, but it knows the mops are still standing there; and the door is locked; and nobody will come. The door is always locked; and nobody ever comes, except that sometimes—the child has no understanding of time or interval—sometimes the door rattles terribly and opens, and a person, or several people, are there. One of them may come in and kick the child to make it stand up. The others never come close, but peer in at it with frightened, disgusted eyes. The food bowl and the water jug are hastily filled, the door is locked, the eyes disappear. The people at the door never say anything, but the child, who has not always lived in the tool room, and can remember sunlight and its mother's voice, sometimes speaks. "I will be good," it says. "Please let me out. I will be good!" They never answer. The child used to scream for help at night, and cry a good deal, but now it only makes a kind of whining, "eh-haa, eh-haa," and it speaks less and less often. It is so thin there are no calves to its legs; its belly protrudes; it lives on a half-bowl of corn meal and grease a day. It is naked. Its buttocks and thighs are a mass of festered sores, as it sits in its own excrement continually.

They all know it is there, all the people of Omelas. Some of them have come to see it, others are content merely to know it is there. They all know that it has to be there. Some of them understand why, and some do not, but they all understand that their happiness, the beauty of their city, the tenderness of their friendships, the health of their children, the wisdom of their scholars, the skill of their makers, even the abundance of their harvest and the kindly weathers of their skies, depend wholly on this child's abominable misery.

This is usually explained to children when they are between eight and twelve, whenever they seem capable of understanding; and most of those who come to see the child are young people, though often enough an adult comes, or comes back, to see the child. No matter how well the matter has been explained to them, these young spectators are always shocked and sickened at the sight. They feel disgust, which they had thought themselves superior to. They feel anger, outrage, impotence, despite all the explanations. They would like to do something for the child. But there is nothing they can do. If the child were brought up into the sunlight out of the vile place, if it were cleaned and fed and comforted, that would be a good thing, indeed; but if it were done, in that day and hour all the prosperity and beauty and delight of Omelas would wither and be destroyed. Those are the terms. To exchange all the goodness and grace of every life in Omelas for that single, small improvement: to throw away the happiness of thousands for the chance of the happiness of one: that would be to let guilt within the walls indeed.

The terms are strict and absolute; there may not even be a kind word spoken to the child.

Often the young people go home in tears, or in a tearless rage, when they have seen the child and faced this terrible paradox. They may brood over it for weeks or years. But as time goes on they begin to realize that even if the child could be released, it would not get much good of its freedom: a little vague pleasure of warmth and food, no doubt, but little more. It is too degraded and imbecile to know any real joy. It has been afraid too long ever to be free of fear. Its habits are too uncouth for it to respond to humane treatment. Indeed, after so long it would probably be wretched without walls about it to protect it, and darkness for its eyes, and its own excrement to sit in. Their tears at the bitter injustice dry when they begin to perceive the terrible justice of reality, and to accept it. Yet it is their tears and anger, the trying of their generosity and the acceptance of their helplessness, which are perhaps the true source of the splendor of their lives. Theirs is no vapid, irresponsible happiness. They know that they, like the child, are not free. They know compassion. It is the existence of the child, and their knowledge of its existence, that makes possible the nobility of their architecture, the poignancy of their music, the profundity of their science. It is because of the child that they are so gentle with children. They know that if the wretched one were not there snivelling in the dark, the other one, the flute-player, could make no joyful music as the young riders line up in their beauty for the race in the sunlight of the first morning of summer.

Now do you believe in them? Are they not more credible? But there is one more thing to tell, and this is quite incredible.

At times one of the adolescent girls or boys who go to see the child does not go home to weep or rage, does not, in fact, go home at all. Sometimes also a man or woman much older falls silent for a day or two, and then leaves home. These people go out into the street, and walk down the street alone. They keep walking, and walk straight out of the city of Omelas, through the beautiful gates. They keep walking across the farmlands of Omelas. Each one goes alone, youth or girl, man or woman. Night falls; the traveler must pass down village streets, between the houses with yellow-lit windows, and on out into the darkness of the fields. Each alone, they go west or north, towards the mountains. They go on. They leave Omelas, they walk ahead into the darkness, and they do not come back. The place they go towards is a place even less imaginable to most of us than the city of happiness. I cannot describe it at all. It is possible that it does not exist. But they seem to know where they are going, the ones who walk away from Omelas.

ARISTOTELIAN ETHICS

—Camille Atkinson and Candice Fredrick

In the following excerpt, philosophers Atkinson and Fredrick challenge many of Aristotle's key definitions and processes. Such critical analysis is essential when applying theories from centuries ago to modern day issues. For instance, when Aristotle claims that one must receive a "proper upbringing in moral conduct," Atkinson and Fredrick appropriately question the implications of this statement. Consider the nature of a proper upbringing in Aristotle's time as compared with today's version of "moral conduct."

Before turning to this concept, Aristotle makes some important preliminary points about the study of ethics. First, ethical inquiry is not the kind of investigation in which the primary objective is abstract knowledge of the good (as it was for Plato before him); rather, the aim is to become a good person or develop a moral character (an objective similar to Kant's). Knowledge, therefore, has practical consequences, and it is only this kind of knowledge that ethics should be concerned with. "Will not the knowledge of this good, consequently, be very important to our lives? Would it not better equip us, like archers who have a target to aim at, to hit the proper mark? If so, we must try to comprehend in outline at least what this good is.

Aristotle is something of a pragmatist or realist in two respects: he does not regard knowledge as separate from action (i.e., theory is intimately connected to practice); and "the good" is something that can only be roughly or provisionally given (i.e., comprehended "in outline"). Ethics is not an exact science, nor is it conducive to mathematical formulation and/or demonstration. And, to expect it to be so would be a gross misunderstanding of what it entails. "For precision cannot be expected in the treatment of all subjects alike [and] a well-schooled man is one who searches for that degree of precision in each kind of study which the nature of the subject at hand admits."

A second claim Aristotle makes early on lends a degree of irony or paradox to the study of ethics. He asserts that before one can even begin to inquire into the nature of the good "one must first have received a proper upbringing in moral conduct." What does this mean? Is it an indication of Aristotle's elitism, as some would assert? It would appear that in order to become good, it is necessary to be good already. Or, that in order to learn what goodness consists of, one must have already been taught what it is. Doesn't this render any study of ethics superfluous at best, pointless at worst? For if one already possesses knowledge of the good, then there is no need for inquiring further. Or is there?

First, we must remember that an account of the good can only be given "in outline," so any investigation into it can never be complete or exhaustive. We will always need to fill in the blanks, so to speak; thus, our understanding of it will forever be merely provisional. Moreover, Aristotle is really making a much deeper point here: specifically, that the kind of practical wisdom necessary for moral action is not ultimately teachable. It is not simply a matter of learning some basic principles or formulas (like the axioms of geometry) and then applying them consistently in particular cases. If that were true, then why do we not have child prodigies, or geniuses of any age for that matter, in the field of ethics as we do in mathematics, music or chess? Far from being the mechanical application of universal principles (as Kant, or even Mill, would have us believe), ethical inquiry requires a certain disposition—a desire, tendency or willingness to do good—as well as a sufficient amount of life "experience" to draw from. This disposition is something that can only be nurtured over time, preferably from childhood on up.

In this sense, Aristotle seems to be validating one of our contemporary assumptions about human psychology; namely, that individuals are affected by their environment and are especially impressionable when they are young. What constitutes a "good upbringing" is certainly a matter of heated debate, and we do not assume that there is only one paradigm for such. But, the idea that it is necessary to instill some moral sensibility and sensitivity in children at an early age and to reinforce this throughout adolescence is rarely a matter of contention. Further, it should be equally clear that if someone has no basic desire to act rightly or avoid wrongdoing, if one does not care to discover what constitutes ethical or unethical action, then no amount of education will ever be sufficient to ensure moral behavior or check immoral behavior. So, what we find in this study of ethics is a blurring of the distinction between feeling and reasoning. Specifically, without the assumption that one cares about morality, we cannot even begin to inquire as to get to what might constitute moral action. Thus, Aristotle's ethics is written for those who at least *want* to know what goodness entails, and this is not something that can be taught in the strict sense.

What about Aristotle's second requirement, [that] of "experience"? What does this mean? Aristotle claims that practical wisdom itself is a form of "perception"—that is, the ability to "see" what kind of action is called for under particular circumstances or to discern what the good would consist of when faced with an actual situation in which a choice must be made. "Practical wisdom is concerned with particulars, as well [as with universals], and knowledge of particulars comes from experience. But a young man has no experience, for experience is the product of a long time." And, once more, this kind of experience cannot be gotten secondhandedly: in other words, it cannot be taught or learned in a formal or academic manner. However, it appears again as if we are stuck in a circle—to be wise requires experience, yet one first needs to be wise in order to reflect upon and understand one's various experiences, making sense of them in such a way that these experiences can provide material for moral deliberation.

Is this an instance of circular reasoning, which one must seek to avoid? Or, is it simply a fundamental and inescapable paradox of human existence? Aristotle suggests the latter, and we would concur. It is one of the essential tragedies of life and, at the same time, one of its cosmic jokes that when we need wisdom the most (when we are young), we are the least likely to have it, although we may think otherwise. When we do seem to have wisdom, we no longer need it as desperately, and can also recognize how elusive it really is. This seems to be life's ultimate paradox—the more we know, the more we know that we know so very little; and the less we know of life, the more certain we are. (Perhaps this is why those who are "experienced" so often try to give their wisdom away by dispensing it to others—again, ironically, to those who need it most but are also the least likely to want or appreciate it!) In sum, practical wisdom is concerned both with "universals" (general principles regarding the good that can only be given roughly or in outline) as well as with "particulars" (those unique and irreducible features of a concrete situation). . . . Martha Nussbaum makes some brilliant observations on this point in the *The Fragility of Goodness.*

NUSSBAUM ON ARISTOTLE

In Chapter 10 of her book, Nussbaum says that we need to ask "what Aristotelian general rules and accounts are and are not, and how the person of practical wisdom uses them." In the very next paragraph, she states that "[o]ne possibility is that the rules and universal principles are guidelines or rules of thumb: summaries of particular decisions, useful for purposes of economy and aids in identifying the salient features of the particular case." Of course, this is an interpretation that remains faithful to Aristotle's admonition that any general account of the good can only be given in outline and that practical wisdom must ultimately take its cue from, and respond to, the particulars of the case at hand. Aristotle criticizes general rules "both for lack of concreteness and for lack of flexibility." Is this not the heart of the criticism of Kant and Mill?—that their theories left both too much room for interpretation and too little room for responding to specific needs or demands. Thus, good deliberation can accommodate the intricacies and messiness of the concrete while simultaneously seeking the universal in the particular—that is, it does not assume that a rule "rules" the particulars; but rather, it allows them "to govern themselves and to be normative for correctness of rule." As Nussbaum states: "[g]ood deliberation accommodates itself to what it finds, responsively and with respect for complexity."

Another way of putting this is that means (the *how* of moral action) and ends (the objective or aim of morality) are codetermined, that "the end itself is only concretely specified in deliberating about the means appropriate to a particular situation." What this entails is that a general rule for action can only be deemed correct retrospectively, as we cannot know beforehand what will follow from the choices that we make. This does leave us vulnerable to some extent to what Nussbaum calls "moral luck," and we really can't expect much more given the complexities of human actions and relations. For instance, let us say that one is faced with a difficult choice between two jobs. While one may involve a substantial salary increase, it will also require moving her family to another state or city and taking on greater responsibility. The other job by contrast may provide greater security, more pleasant work and working relationships. How can she say ahead of time with any degree of assurance which will be the right choice? What she cannot do is not choose, for even that is ultimately a passive sort of choice. It may turn out that, after taking one of the positions, new information is revealed that confirms or validates the correctness of the choice made. But, how much of this is merely due to "good" luck? And, if the reverse were to occur—she regrets her decision after having acted upon it—could one really claim that the source of error was simply bad deliberation? How can we make sense of this element of moral luck?

Nussbaum distinguishes three features of choice that show why we will always remain vulnerable to these contingencies to some extent, or why it is the case that practical wisdom or moral deliberation can never be systematic. "First, there is the *mutability* or lack of fixity of the practical." As much as we may desire and seek the kind of security and stability provided by universal laws, we live in a world of change that is inherently insecure. Thus, practical wisdom must remain responsive, perhaps even creative, in order to meet the demands of a world that is always in process. Second, there is the *indeterminacy* of the practical. To illustrate this point, Nussbaum calls on an example taken from Aristotle himself where he shows that there can be no comprehensive definition of good joke telling. Just as it is clear that there is no science of humor, as it is closer to an art or creative skill, and that what constitutes a good sense of humor is both culturally and personally variable, so too should we regard ethical deliberation in this light. A good comedian, for example, must be responsive to his or her audience in the same manner in which the practically wise person must be capable of responding to the different demands of a particular situation. In a recent *Time* magazine article this point was made with regard to the debate surrounding artificial intelligence: specifically, that "the hardest thing for computers is the 'simple' stuff. Sure they can play great chess, a game of mechanical rules and finite options. But making small talk is another matter. So, too, with recognizing a face or recognizing a joke." In other words, the article claims, "the biggest challenge is giving machines common sense." This "common sense," whether it means the capacity to make or respond to a joke, perceive the tone in which something is said, or recognize which words or actions would be appropriate in a particular situation, is not something mechanical or scientifically objective. Lastly for Nussbaum, there is the feature of *non-repeatability*—namely, that we must recognize the existence of *ultimate* particulars. "This is in part a function of the complexity and variety already mentioned: the occurrence of properties that are, taken singly, repeatable in an endless variety of combinations makes the complex whole situation a non-repeatable particular."

There may be many salient or relevant circumstances that must be taken into consideration in any good deliberation. Again, her health and that of the child, her employment history, as well as the original agreement and interests of the company are all relevant features which, taken as a whole, are non-repeatable. Thus, her employer cannot apply general rules in a mechanical fashion—imposing them upon concrete cases without first "seeing" what the relevant issues are or determining whether or not they fit.

In sum, we cannot expect the kind of comfort afforded by the universal application of basic principles when confronted with ethical choices. Rules have only a limited usefulness: They must be regarded as guiding rather than as binding. They point the way, perhaps with a wave of the hand towards some general direction, but cannot function as definitive markers that point directly at something. Nussbaum refers to them as "tentative guides" or "summaries" that enable us "to be flexible, ready for surprise, prepared to see, resourceful at improvisation." For example, one may say that corporate downsizing is generally wrong, but this does not mean that it is so in all cases. As with lying, there may be good reasons for generally refraining from doing so. However, in some particular instances, there may be even more compelling reasons for not telling the truth or taking steps to reduce a company's overhead costs by eliminating jobs. This should then make clear why Aristotle insists that the person of practical wisdom must have a wealth of experience to draw from. People cannot be good at moral deliberation unless they have been able to cultivate their responsiveness, and maintain their composure under the stress of such decision making. It is this life and work history that allows the wise person to "see" what the universal is which is disclosed or revealed in a particular case. Though it is true that, in one sense, the case is nonrepeatable, in another sense, such would be "unintelligible without the guiding and sorting power of the universal."

We now need to turn to the role of this "universal," as thus far the "particular" has taken precedence. For ultimately, Nussbaum asserts that the relationship goes both ways with each illuminating the other. What then is this universal, and how does it act as a guide? And, how do particulars and universals codetermine each other?

It is the experienced person of practical wisdom who acts as the standard of good deliberation and judgment, according to Aristotle. This is the "thoroughly human being" who "does not attempt to take up a stand outside of the conditions of human life, but bases his or her judgment on long and broad experience of these conditions." Moreover, this is not an individual who seeks to escape from or suppress desires and passions (as Kant would have it), but one who has cultivated, and continues to cultivate, these important sources of motivation. However, what the practically wise person desires most of all is to act ethically, and this person will cultivate what is conducive to that. "He or she will be concerned about friendship, justice, courage, moderation, generosity; his desires will be formed in accordance with these concerns; and he will derive from this internalized conception of value many ongoing guidelines for action, pointers as to what to look for in a particular situation." For Aristotle, desires and inclinations are not merely animal impulses indicative of our bestial and amoral nature, as Kant would have us believe. Instead, they are "responsive intentional elements, capable of flexible ethical development." As choice is defined by Aristotle as "deliberate desire," thus placing it in between appetite and reason, it is only through moral choices that values can be made manifest in the world of human relations. And, just as our intellectual faculties can be developed or cultivated, so too can the affective side of our characters be molded along ethical lines or distorted in various ways. This underscores again Aristotle's concern with bringing up children in such a way that they are sensitized to moral issues as soon as possible, since "it is no small matter whether one habit or another is inculcated in us from early childhood; on the contrary, it makes a considerable difference, or, rather, all the difference."

But, who is this person of practical wisdom that brings the universal element to, or makes it manifest in, the particular situation? Is he or she merely an empty ideal or a real possibility? If the latter, then what can we do to encourage such character development?

Nussbaum speaks of this individual as one who is rooted in a community and is committed to a conception of the good life, which is expressed in and includes the values mentioned above. But, most specifically, this is a character who seeks moderation in everything. We could say that this is Aristotle's universal principle. However, it is one that is malleable, and its goodness is dependent upon who is interpreting or applying it. "Proper virtuous choice requires, if it is to be virtue, the combination of correct selection with correct passional response." And, presumably, it is the practically wise person who will have developed this harmonious relation between her passions and reason, which will allow her to make appropriate choices, or to "see" what the appropriate response would be, in any situation. Is this an unrealistic ideal? Perhaps, if we expect such a person to always and forever respond correctly and leave no room for human frailty, fallibility or luck. However, what is also problematic in Aristotle is the reliance upon the traditional values of the community. For this is a reliance that seems to preclude the possibility of criticism, which would allow one to determine whether these values had become outmoded, stagnant or even destructive. And, even if we accept some loose conception of friendship and justice, for example, as moral ideals, isn't it possible that the hardest ethical choice a person might be faced with would be one in which these two values conflict? In other words, to what principle do we appeal when the choice is between benefiting a friend or acting justly? Or, put more generally, what do we do when we must choose between two universal goods? Is Aristotle's concept of moderation at all helpful, or even relevant, here?

DISTRIBUTIVE JUSTICE

—JOHN RAWLS

Contemporary Harvard philosopher John Rawls is known as the fa-
ther of an ethical theory called distributive justice, which holds that
ethical acts or decisions are those that lead to an equitable distribu-
tion of goods and services. His description of this approach follows
below.

We may think of a human society as a more or less self-sufficient association regulated by a common conception of justice and aimed at advancing the good of its members.[1] As a co-operative venture for mutual advantage, it is characterized by a conflict as well as an identity of interests. There is an identity of interests since social cooperation makes possible a better life for all than any would have if everyone were to try to live by his own efforts; yet at the same time men are not indifferent as to how the greater benefits produced by their joint labors are distributed, for in order to further their own aims each prefers a larger to a lesser share. A conception of justice is a set of principles for choosing between the social arrangements which determine this division and for underwriting a consensus as to the proper distributive shares.

Now at first sight the most rational conception of justice would seem to be utilitarian. For consider: Each man in realizing his own good can certainly balance his own losses against his own gains.[2] We can impose a sacrifice on ourselves now for the sake of a greater advantage later. A[3] man quite properly acts, as long as others are not affected, to achieve his own greatest good, to advance his ends as far as possible. Now, why should not a society act on precisely the same principle? Why is not that which is rational in the case of one man right in the case of a group of men? Surely the simplest and most direct conception of the right, and so of justice, is that of maximizing the good. This assumes a prior understanding of what is good, but we can think of the good as already given by the interests of rational individuals. Thus just as the principle of individual choice is to achieve one's greatest good, to advance so far as possible one's own system of rational desires, so the principle of social choice is to realize the greatest good (similarly defined) summed over all the members of society. We arrive at the principle of utility in a natural way: by this principle a society is rightly ordered, and hence just, when its institutions are arranged so as to realize the greatest sum of satisfactions.

The striking feature of the principle of utility is that it does not matter, except indirectly, how this sum of satisfactions is distributed among individuals, any more than it matters, except indirectly, how one man distributes his satisfactions over time. Since certain ways of

John Rawls, "Distributive Justice." Reprinted by permission of the author.

distributing things affect the total sum of satisfactions, this fact must be taken into account in arranging social institutions; but according to this principle the explanation of common-sense precepts of justice and their seemingly stringent character is that they are those rules which experience shows must be strictly respected and departed from only under exceptional circumstances if the sum of advantages is to be maximized. The precepts of justice are derivative from the one end of attaining the greatest net balance of satisfactions. There is no reason in principle why the greater gains of some should not compensate for the lesser losses of others; or why the violation of the liberty of a few might not be made right by a greater good shared by many. It simply happens, at least under most conditions, that the greatest sum of advantages is not generally achieved in this way. From the standpoint of utility the strictness of commonsense notions of justice has a certain usefulness, but as a philosophical doctrine it is irrational.

If, then, we believe that as a matter of principle each member of society has an inviolability founded on justice which even the welfare of everyone else cannot override, and that a loss of freedom for some is not made right by a greater sum of satisfaction enjoyed by many, we shall have to look for another account of the principles of justice. The principle of utility is incapable of explaining the fact that in a just society the liberties of equal citizenship are taken for granted, and the rights secured by justice are not subject to political bargaining nor to the calculus of social interests. Now, the most natural alternative to the principle of utility is its traditional rival, the theory of the social contract. The aim of the contract doctrine is precisely to account for the strictness of justice by supposing that its principles arise from an agreement among free and independent persons in an original position of equality and hence reflect the integrity and equal sovereignty of the rational persons who are the contractees. Instead of supposing that a conception of right, and so a conception of justice, is simply an extension of the principle of choice for one man to society as a whole, the contract doctrine assumes that the rational individuals who belong to society must choose together, in one joint act, what is to count among them as just and unjust. They are to decide among themselves once and for all what is to be their conception of justice. This decision is thought of as being made in a suitably defined initial situation one of the significant features of which is that no one knows his position in society, nor even his place in the distribution of natural talents and abilities. The principles of justice to which all are forever bound are chosen in the absence of this sort of specific information. A veil of ignorance prevents anyone from being advantaged or disadvantaged by the contingencies of social class and fortune; and hence the bargaining problems which arise in everyday life from the possession of this knowledge do not affect the choice of principles. On the contract doctrine, then, the theory of justice, and indeed ethics itself, is part of the general theory of rational choice, a fact perfectly clear in its Kantian formulation.

Once justice is thought of as arising from an original agreement of this kind, it is evident that the principle of utility is problematic. For why should rational individuals who have a system of ends they wish to advance agree to a violation of their liberty for the sake of a greater balance of satisfactions enjoyed by others? It seems more plausible to suppose that, when situated in an original position of equal right, they would insist upon institutions which returned compensating advantages for any sacrifices required. A rational man would not accept an institution merely because it maximized the sum of advantages irrespective of its effect on his own interests. It appears, then, that the principle of utility would be rejected as a principle of justice, although we shall not try to argue this important question here. Rather, our aim is to give a brief sketch of the conception of distributive shares implicit in the principles of justice which, it seems would be chosen in the original position. The philosophical appeal of utilitarianism is that it seems to offer a single principle on the basis of which a consistent and complete conception of right can be developed. The problem is to work out a contractarian alternative in such a way that it has comparable if not all the same virtues.

In our discussion we shall make no attempt to derive the two principles of justice which we shall examine; that is, we shall not try to show that they would be chosen in the original position.[2] It must suffice that it is plausible that they would be, at least in preference to the standard forms of traditional theories. Instead we shall be mainly concerned with three questions: first, how to interpret these principles so that they define a consistent and complete conception of justice; second, whether it is possible to arrange the institutions of a constitutional democracy so that these principles are satisfied, at least approximately; and third, whether the conception of distributive shares which they define is compatible with commonsense notions of justice. The significance of these principles is that they allow for the strictness of the claims of justice; and if they can be understood so as to yield a consistent and complete conception, the contractarian alternative would seem all the more attractive.

The two principles of justice which we shall discuss may be formulated as follows: first, each person engaged in an institution or affected by it has an equal right to the most extensive liberty compatible with a like liberty for all; and second, inequalities as defined by the institutional structure or fostered by it are arbitrary unless it is reasonable to expect that they will work out to everyone's advantage and provided that the positions and offices to which they attach or from which they may be gained are open to all. These principles regulate the distributive aspects of institutions by controlling the assignment of rights and duties throughout the whole social structure, beginning with the adoption of a political constitution in accordance with which they are then to be applied to legislation. It is upon a correct choice of a basic structure of society, its fundamental system of rights and duties, that the justice of distributive shares depends.

The two principles of justice apply in the first instance to this basic structure, that is, to the main institutions of the social system and their arrangement, how they are combined together. Thus, this structure includes the political constitution and the principal economic and social institutions which together define a person's liberties and rights and affect his life-prospects, what he may expect to be and how well he may expect to fare. The intuitive idea here is that those born into the social system at different positions, say, in different social classes, have varying life-prospects determined, in part, by the system of political liberties and personal rights, and by the economic and social opportunities which are made available to these positions. In this way the basic structure of society favors certain men over others, and these are the basic inequalities, the ones which affect their whole life-prospects. It is inequalities of this kind, presumably inevitable in any society, with which the two principles of justice are primarily designed to deal.

Now the second principle holds that an inequality is allowed only if there is reason to believe that the institution with the inequality, or permitting it, will work out for the advantage of every person engaged in it. In the case of the basic structure this means that all inequalities which affect life-prospects, say, the inequalities of income and wealth which exist between social classes, must be to the advantage of everyone. Since the principle applies to institutions, we interpret this to mean that inequalities must be to the advantage of the representative man for each relevant social position; they should improve each such man's expectation. Here we assume that it is possible to attach to each position an expectation, and that this expectation is a function of the whole institutional structure: it can be raised and lowered by reassigning rights and duties throughout the system. Thus the expectation of any position depends upon the expectations of the others, and these in turn depend upon the pattern of rights and duties established by the basic structure. But it is not clear what is meant by saying that inequalities must be to the advantage of every representative man. . . . [One] . . . interpretation [of what is meant by saying that inequalities must be to the advantage of every representative man] . . . is to choose some social position by reference to which the pattern of expectations as a whole is to be judged, and then to maximize with respect to the expectations of this representative man consistent with the demands of equal liberty and equality of opportunity. Now, the one obvious candidate is the representative man of those who are least favored by the system of institutional inequalities. Thus we arrive at the following idea: the basic structure of the social system affects the life-prospects of typical individuals according to their initial places in society, say, the various income classes into which they are born, or depending upon certain natural attributes, as when institutions make discriminations between men and women or allow certain advantages to be gained by those with greater natural abilities. The fundamental problem of distributive justice concerns the differences in life-prospects which come about in this way. We interpret the second principle to hold that these differences are just if and only if the greater expectations of the more advantaged, when playing a part in the working of the whole social system, improve the expectations of the least advantaged. The basic structure is just throughout when the advantages of the more fortunate promote the well-being of the least fortunate, that is, when a decrease in their advantages would make the least fortunate even worse off than they are. The basic structure is perfectly just when the prospects of the least fortunate are as great as they can be.

In interpreting the second principle (or rather the first part of it which we may, for obvious reasons, refer to as the difference principle), we assume that the first principle requires a basic equal liberty for all, and that the resulting political system, when circumstances permit, is that of a constitutional democracy in some form. There must be liberty of the person and political equality as well as liberty of conscience and freedom of thought. There is one class of equal citizens which defines a common status for all. We also assume that there is equality of opportunity and a fair competition for the available positions on the basis of reasonable qualifications. Now, given this background, the differences to be justified are the various economic and social inequalities in the basic structure which must inevitably arise in such a scheme. These are the inequalities in the distribution of income and wealth and the distinctions in social prestige and status which attach to the various positions and classes. The difference principle says that these inequalities are just if and only if they are part of a larger system in which they work out to the advantage of the most unfortunate representative man. The just distributive shares determined by the basic structure are those specified by this constrained maximum principle.

Thus, consider the chief problem of distributive justice, that concerning the distribution of wealth as it affects the life-prospects of those starting out in the various income groups. These income classes define the relevant representative men from which the social system is to be judged. Now, a son of a member of the entrepreneurial class (in a capitalist society) has a better prospect than that of the son of an unskilled laborer. This will be true, it seems, even when the social injustices which presently exist are removed and the two men are of equal talent and ability; the inequality cannot be done away with as long as something like the family is maintained. What, then, can justify this inequality in life-prospects? According to the second principle it is justified only if it is to the advantage of the representative man who is worse off, in this case the representative unskilled laborer. The inequality is permissible because lowering it would, let's suppose, make the working man even worse off than he is. Presumably, given the principle of open offices (the second part of the second principle), the greater expectations allowed to entrepreneurs has the effect in the longer run of raising the life-prospects of the laboring class. The inequality in expectation provides an incentive so that the economy is more efficient, industrial advance proceeds at a quicker pace, and so on, the end result of which is that greater material and other benefits are distributed throughout the system. Of course, all of this is familiar, and whether true or not in particular cases, it is the sort of thing which must be argued if the inequality in income and wealth is to be acceptable by the difference principle.

We should now verify that this interpretation of the second principle gives a natural sense in which everyone may be said to be made better off. Let us suppose that inequalities are chain-connected: that is, if an inequality raises the expectations of the lowest position, it raises the expectations of all positions in between. For example, if the greater expectations of the representative entrepreneur raises that of the unskilled laborer, it also raises that of the semi-skilled. Let us further assume that inequalities are close-knit: that is, it is impossible to raise (or lower) the expectation of any representative man without raising (or lowering) the expectations of every other representative man, and in particular, without affecting one way or the other that of the least fortunate. There is no loose-jointedness, so to speak, in the way in which expectations depend upon one another. Now with these assumptions, everyone does benefit from an inequality which satisfies the difference principle, and the second principle as we have formulated it reads correctly. For the representative man who is better off in any pair-wise comparison gains by being allowed to have his advantage, and the man who is worse off benefits from the contribution which all inequalities make to each position below. Of course, chain-connection and close-knitness may not obtain; but in this case those who are better off should not have a veto over the advantages available for the least advantaged. The stricter interpretation of the difference principle should be followed, and all inequalities should be arranged for the advantage of the most unfortunate even if some inequalities are not to the advantage of those in middle positions. Should these conditions fail, then, the second principle would have to be stated in another way.

It may be observed that the difference principle represents, in effect, an original agreement to share in the benefits of the distribution of natural talents and abilities, whatever this distribution turns out to be, in order to alleviate as far as possible the arbitrary handicaps resulting from our initial starting places in society. Those who have been favored by nature, whoever they are, may gain from their good fortune only on terms that improve the well-being of those who have lost out. The naturally advantaged are not to gain simply because they are more gifted, but only to cover the costs of training and cultivating their endowments and for putting them to use in a way which improved the position of the less fortunate. We are led to the difference principle if we wish to arrange the basic social structure so that no one gains (or loses) from his luck in the natural lottery of talent and ability, or from his initial place in society, without giving (or receiving) compensating advantages in return. (The parties in the original position are not said to be attracted by this idea and so agree to it; rather, given the symmetries of their situation, and particularly their lack of knowledge, and so on, they will find it to their interest to agree to a principle which can be understood in this way.) And we should note also that when the difference principle is perfectly satisfied, the basic structure is optimal by the efficiency principle. There is no way to make anyone better off without making someone worse off, namely, the least fortunate representative man. Thus the two principles of justice define distributive shares in a way compatible with efficiency, at least as long as we move on this highly abstract level. If we want to say (as we do, although it cannot be argued here) that the demands of justice have an absolute weight with respect to efficiency, this claim may seem less paradoxical when it is kept in mind that perfectly just institutions are also efficient.

Our second question is whether it is possible to arrange the institutions of a constitutional democracy so that the two principles of justice are satisfied, at least approximately. We shall try to show that this can be done provided the government regulates a free economy in a certain way. More fully, if law and government act effectively to keep markets competitive, resources fully employed, property and wealth widely distributed over time, and to maintain the appropriate social minimum, then if there is equality of opportunity underwritten by education for all, the resulting distribution will be just. Of course, all of these arrangements and policies are familiar. The only novelty in the following remarks, if there is any novelty at all, is that this framework of institutions can be made to satisfy the difference principle. To argue this, we must sketch the relations of these institutions and how they work together.

First of all, we assume that the basic social structure is controlled by a just constitution which secures the various liberties of equal citizenship. Thus the legal order is administered in accordance with the principle of legality, and liberty of conscience and freedom of thought are taken for granted. The political process is conducted, so far as possible, as a just procedure for choosing between governments and for enacting just legislation. From the standpoint of distributive justice, it is also essential that there be equality of opportunity in several senses. Thus, we suppose that, in addition to maintaining the usual social overhead capital, government provides for equal educational opportunities for all either by subsidizing private schools or by operating a public school system. It also enforces and underwrites equality of opportunity in commercial ventures and in the free choice of occupation. This result is achieved by policing business behavior and by preventing the establishment of barriers and restriction to the desirable positions and markets. Lastly, there is a guarantee of a social minimum which the government meets by family allowances and special payments in times of unemployment, or by a negative income tax.

In maintaining this system of institutions the government may be thought of as divided into four branches. Each branch is represented by various agencies (or activities thereof) charged with preserving certain social and economic conditions. These branches do not necessarily overlap with the usual organization of government, but should be understood as purely conceptual. Thus the allocation branch is to keep the economy feasibly competitive, that is, to prevent the formation of unreasonable market power. Markets are competitive in this sense when they cannot be made more so consistent with the requirements of efficiency and the acceptance of the facts of consumer preferences and geography. The allocation branch is also charged with identifying and correcting, say, by suitable taxes and subsidies wherever possible, the more obvious departures from efficiency caused by the failure of prices to measure accurately social benefits and costs. The stabilization branch strives to maintain reasonably full employment so that there is no waste through failure to use resources and the free choice of occupation and the deployment of finance is supported by strong effective demand. These two branches together are to preserve the efficiency of the market economy generally.

The social minimum is established through the operations of the transfer branch. Later on we shall consider at what level this minimum should be set, since this is a crucial matter; but for the moment, a few general remarks will suffice. The main idea is that the workings of the transfer branch take into account the precept of need and assign it an appropriate weight with respect to the other commonsense precepts of justice. A market economy ignores the claims of need altogether. Hence there is a division of labor between the parts of the social system as different institutions answer to different commonsense precepts. Competitive markets (properly supplemented by government operations) handle the problem of the efficient allocation of labor and resources and set a weight to the conventional precepts associated with wages and earnings (the precepts of each according to his work and experience, or responsibility and the hazards of the job, and so on), whereas the transfer branch guarantees a certain level of well-being and meets the claims of need. Thus it is obvious that the justice of distributive shares depends upon the whole social system and how it distributes total income, wages plus transfers. There is with reason strong objection to the competitive determination of total income, since this would leave out of account the claims of need and of a decent standard of life. From the standpoint of the original position it is clearly rational to insure oneself against these contingencies. But now, if the appropriate minimum is provided by transfers, it may be perfectly fair that the other part of total income is competitively determined. Moreover, this way of dealing with the claims of need is doubtless more efficient, at least from a theoretical point of view, than trying to regulate prices by minimum wage standards and so on. It is preferable to handle these claims by a separate branch which supports a social minimum. Henceforth, in considering whether the second principle of justice is satisfied, the answer turns on whether the total income of the least advantaged, that is, wages plus transfers, is such as to maximize their long-term expectations consistent with the demands of liberty.

Finally, the distribution branch is to preserve an approximately just distribution of income and wealth over time by affecting the background conditions of the market from period to period. Two aspects of this branch may be distinguished. First of all, it operates a system of inheritance and gift taxes. The aim of these levies is not to raise revenue, but gradually and continually to correct the distribution of wealth and to prevent the concentrations of power to the detriment of liberty and equality of opportunity. It is perfectly true,

as some have said,[3] that unequal inheritance of wealth is no more inherently unjust than unequal inheritance of intelligence; as far as possible the inequalities founded on either should
satisfy the difference principle. Thus, the inheritance of greater wealth is just as long as it
is to the advantage of the worst off and consistent with liberty, including equality of opportunity. Now by the latter we do not mean, of course, the equality of expectations between
classes, since differences in life-prospects arising from the basic structure are inevitable,
and it is precisely the aim of the second principle to say when these differences are just. Indeed, equality of opportunity is a certain set of institutions which assures equally good education and chances of culture for all and which keeps open the competition for positions
on the basis of qualities reasonably related to performance, and so on. It is these institutions
which are put in jeopardy when inequalities and concentrations of wealth reach a certain
limit; and the taxes imposed by the distribution branch are to prevent this limit from being
exceeded. Naturally enough where this limit lies is a matter for political judgment guided
by theory, practical experience and plain hunch; on this question the theory of justice has
nothing to say.

The second part of the distribution branch is a scheme of taxation for raising revenue
to cover the costs of public goods, to make transfer payments, and the like. This scheme belongs to the distribution branch since the burden of taxation must be justly shared. Although
we cannot examine the legal and economic complications involved, there are several points
in favor of proportional expenditure taxes as part of an ideally just arrangement. For one
thing, they are preferable to income taxes at the level of commonsense precepts of justice,
since they impose a levy according to how much a man takes out of the common store of
goods and not according to how much he contributes (assuming that income is fairly earned
in return for productive efforts). On the other hand, proportional taxes that treat everyone
in a clearly defined uniform way (again assuming that income is fairly earned) and hence it
is preferable to use progressive rates only when they are necessary to preserve the justice
of the system as a whole, that is, to prevent large fortunes hazardous to liberty and equality
of opportunity, and the like. If proportional expenditure taxes should also prove more efficient, say, because they interfere less with incentives, or whatever, this would make the case
for them decisive provided a feasible scheme could be worked out.[4] Yet these are questions
of political judgment which are not our concern; and, in any case, a proportional expenditure tax is part of an idealized scheme which we are describing. It does not follow that even
steeply progressive income taxes, given the injustice of existing systems, do not improve
justice and efficiency all things considered. In practice we must usually choose between unjust arrangements and then it is a matter of finding the lesser injustice.

Whatever form the distribution branch assumes, the argument for it is to be based on
justice: we must hold that, once it is accepted, the social system as a whole—the competitive economy surrounded by a just constitutional legal framework—can be made to satisfy
the principles of justice with the smallest loss in efficiency. The long-term expectations of
the least advantaged are raised to the highest level consistent with the demands of equal liberty. In discussing the choice of a distribution scheme we have made no reference to the traditional criteria of taxation according to ability to pay or benefits received; nor have we
mentioned any of the variants of the sacrifice principle. These standards are subordinate to
the two principles of justice; once the problem is seen as that of designing a whole social

system, they assume the status of secondary precepts with no more independent force than the precepts of common sense in regards to wages. To suppose otherwise is not to take a sufficiently comprehensive point of view. In setting up a just distribution branch these precepts may or may not have a place depending upon the demands of the two principles of justice when applied to the entire system.

***

The sketch of the system of institutions satisfying the two principles of justice is now complete.

In order . . . to establish just distributive shares a just total system of institutions must be set up and impartially administered. Given a just constitution and the smooth working of the four branches of government, and so on, there exists a procedure such that the actual distribution of wealth, whatever it turns out to be, is just. It will have come about as a consequence of a just system of institutions satisfying the principles to which everyone would agree and against which no one can complain. The situation is one of pure procedural justice, since there is no independent criterion by which the outcome can be judged. Nor can we say that a particular distribution of wealth is just because it is one which could have resulted from just institutions although it has not, as this would be to allow too much. Clearly there are many distributions which may be reached by just institutions, and this is true whether we count patterns of distributions among social classes or whether we count distributions of particular goods and services among particular individuals. There are definitely many outcomes and what makes one of these just is that it has been achieved by actually carrying out a just scheme of cooperation as it is publicly understood. It is the result which has arisen when everyone receives that to which he is entitled given his and others' actions guided by their legitimate expectations and their obligations to one another. We can no more arrive at a just distribution of wealth except by working together within the framework of a just system of institutions than we can win or lose fairly without actually betting.

This account of distributive shares is simply an elaboration of the familiar idea that economic rewards will be just once a perfectly competitive price system is organized as a fair game. But in order to do this we have to begin with the choice of a social system as a whole, for the basic structure of the entire arrangement must be just. The economy must be surrounded with the appropriate framework of institutions, since even a perfectly efficient price system has no tendency to determine just distributive shares when left to itself. Not only must economic activity be regulated by a just constitution and controlled by the four branches of government, but a just saving-function must be adopted to estimate the provision to be made for future generations. . . .

NOTES

1. In this essay I try to work out some of the implications of the two principles of justice discussed in "Justice as Fairness," which first appeared in the *Philosophical Review,* 1958, and which is reprinted in *Philosophy, Politics and Society,* Series II, pp. 132–57.

2. This question is discussed very briefly in "Justice as Fairness," *see* pp. 138–41. The intuitive idea is as follows. Given the circumstances of the original position, it is rational for a man to choose as if he were

designing a society in which his enemy is to assign him his place. Thus, in particular, given the complete lack of knowledge (which makes the choice one of uncertainty), the fact that the decision involves one's life-prospects as a whole and is constrained by obligations to third parties (e.g., one's descendants) and duties to certain values (e.g., to religious truth), it is rational to be conservative and so to choose in accordance with an analogue of the maximum principle. Viewing the situation in this way, the interpretation given to the principles of justice earlier is perhaps natural enough. Moreover, it seems clear how the principle of utility can be interpreted; it is the analogue of the Laplacean principle for choice uncertainty. (For a discussion of these choice criteria, *see* R. D. Luce and H. Raiffa, *Games and Decisions* [1957], pp. 275–98.)

3. Example F. von Hayek, *The Constitution of Liberty* (1960), p. 90.
4. *See* N. Kaldor, *An Expenditure Tax* (1955).

THE ENTITLEMENT
THEORY

—Robert Nozick

*Nozick's theory is basically ethics according to contract rights. His
primary thesis is that liberty upsets patterns. You may have a basic
distribution of resources, but given free exchanges, that pattern of
distribution will be upset. As long as exchanges are freely entered
into, they must (by the definition of free) be ethical. Can you conceive of situations where this might not be so or where it might cause
a conflict?*

*Robert Nozick (b. 1938) believes that everyone is entitled to con-
tractual freedom, and that interfering with that freedom would be unethical. Freedom grants individuals the right to self-development and
self-fulfillment. Liberty is a greater societal value than justice. Contrast Nozick's concept of freedom and free exchange with Rawls's
patterned distribution.*

The minimal state is the most extensive state that can be justified. Any state more extensive
violates people's rights. Yet many persons have put forth reasons purporting to justify a
more extensive state. It is impossible within the compass of this book to examine all the reasons that have been put forth. Therefore, I shall focus upon those generally acknowledged
to be most weighty and influential, to see precisely wherein they fail. In this chapter we consider the claim that a more extensive state is justified, because it is necessary (or it is the
best instrument) to achieve distributive justice.

The term "distributive justice" is not a neutral one. Hearing the term "distribution," most
people presume that some thing or mechanism uses some principle or criterion to give out a
supply of things. Into this process of distributing shares some error may have crept. So it is
an open question, at least, whether *re*distribution should take place; whether we should do
again what has already been done once, though poorly. However, we are not in the position
of children who have been given portions of pie by someone who now makes last-minute adjustments to rectify careless cutting. There is no *central* distribution, no person or group entitled to control all the resources, jointly deciding how they are to be doled out. What each
person gets, he gets from others who give to him in exchange for something, or as a gift. In
a free society, diverse persons control different resources, and new holdings arise out of the

voluntary exchanges and actions of persons. There is no more a distributing or distribution of shares than there is a distributing of mates in a society in which persons choose whom they shall marry. The total result is the product of many individual decisions which the different individuals involved are entitled to make. Some uses of the term "distribution," it is true, do not imply a previous distributing appropriately judged by some criterion (for example, "probability distribution"); nevertheless, despite the title of this chapter, it would be best to use a terminology that clearly is neutral. We shall speak of people's holdings; a principle of justice in holdings describes (part of) what justice tells us (requires) about holdings. I shall state first what I take to be the correct view about justice in holdings, and then turn to the distribution of alternate views.

THE ENTITLEMENT THEORY

The subject of justice in holdings consists of three major topics. The first is the *original acquisition of holdings,* the appropriation of unheld things. This includes the issues of how unheld things may come to be held, the process, or processes, by which unheld things may come to be held, the things that may come to be held by these processes, the extent of what comes to be held by a particular process, and so on. We shall refer to the complicated truth about this topic, which we shall not formulate here, as the principle of justice in acquisition. The second topic concerns the *transfer of holdings* from one person to another. By what processes may a person transfer holdings to another? How may a person acquire a holding from another who holds it? Under this topic come general descriptions of voluntary exchange, and gift and (on the other hand) fraud, as well as reference to particular conventional details fixed upon in a given society. The complicated truth about this subject (with placeholders for conventional details) we shall call the principle of justice in transfer. (And we shall suppose it also includes principles governing how a person may divest himself of a holding, passing it into an unheld state.)

If the world were wholly just, the following inductive definition would exhaustively cover the subject of justice in holdings.

1. A person who acquires a holding in accordance with the principle of justice acquisition is entitled to that holding.
2. A person who acquires a holding in accordance with the principle of justice in transfer, from someone else entitled to the holding, is entitled to the holding.
3. No one is entitled to a holding except by (repeated) applications of 1 and 2.

The complete principle of distributive justice would say simply that a distribution is just if everyone is entitled to the holdings they possess under the distribution.

A distribution is just if it arises from another just distribution by legitimate means. The legitimate means of moving from one distribution to another are specified by the principle of justice in transfer. The legitimate first "moves" are specified by the principle of justice in acquisition.[1] Whatever arises from a just situation by just steps is itself just. The means of change specified by the principle of justice in transfer preserve justice. As correct rules of inference are truth-preserving, and any conclusion deduced via repeated application of such rules from only true premises is itself true, so the means of transition from one situation to another specified by the principle of justice in transfer are justice-preserving, and any situation actually arising from repeated transitions in accordance with the principle from a just situation is itself just. The parallel between justice-preserving transformations and truth-preserving transformations illuminates where it fails as well as where it holds. That a conclusion could have been deduced by truth-preserving means from premises that are true suffices to show its truth. That from a just situation a situation *could* have arisen via justice-preserving means does *not* suffice to show its justice. The fact that a thief's victims voluntarily *could* have presented him with gifts does not entitle the thief to his ill-gotten gains. Justice in holdings is historical; it depends upon what actually has happened. We shall return to this point later.

Not all actual situations are generated in accordance with the two principles of justice in holdings: the principle of justice in acquisition and the principle of justice in transfer. Some people steal from others, or defraud them, or enslave them, seizing their product and preventing them from living as they choose, or forcibly exclude others from competing in exchanges. None of these are permissible modes of transition from one situation to another. And some persons acquire holdings by means not sanctioned by the principle of justice in acquisition. The existence of past injustice (previous violations of the first two principles of justice in holdings) raises the third major topic under justice in holdings: the rectification of injustice in holdings. If past injustice has shaped present holdings in various ways, some identifiable and some not, what now, if anything, ought to be done to rectify these injustices? What obligations do the performers of injustice have toward those whose position is worse than it would have been had the injustice not been done? Or, than it would have been had compensation been paid promptly? How, if at all, do things change if the beneficiaries and those made worse off are not the direct parties in the act of injustice, but, for example, their descendants? Is an injustice done to someone whose holding was itself based upon an unrectified injustice? How far back must one go in wiping clean the historical slate of injustices? What may victims of injustice permissibly do in order to rectify the injustices being done to them, including the many injustices done by persons acting through their government? I do not know of a thorough or theoretically sophisticated treatment of such issues. Idealizing greatly, let us suppose theoretical investigation will produce a principle of rectification. This principle uses historical information about previous situations and injustices done in them (as defined by the first two principles of justice and rights against interference), and information about the actual course of events that flowed from these injustices, until the present, and it yields a description (or descriptions) of holdings in the society. The principle of rectification presumably will make use of its best estimate of subjunctive information about what would have occurred (or a probability distribution over what might have occurred, using the expected value) if the injustice had not taken place. If the actual description of holdings turns out not to be one of the descriptions yielded by the principle, then one of the descriptions yielded must be realized.

The general outlines of the theory of justice in holdings are that the holdings of a person are just if he is entitled to them by the principles of justice in acquisition and transfer, or by the principle of rectification of injustice (as specified by the first two principles). If each person's holdings are just, then the total set (distribution) of holdings is just. To turn these general outlines into a specific theory we would have to specify the details of each of the three principles of justice in holdings: the principle of acquisition of holdings, the principle of transfer of holdings and the principle of rectification of violations of the first two principles. I shall not attempt that task here. (Locke's principle of justice in acquisition is discussed below.) . . .

HOW LIBERTY UPSETS PATTERNS

It is not clear how those holding alternative conceptions of distributive justice can reject the entitlement conception of justice in holdings. For suppose a distribution favored by one of these nonentitlement conceptions is realized. Let us suppose it is your favorite one and let us call this distribution D_1; perhaps everyone has an equal share, perhaps shares vary in accordance with some dimension you treasure. Now suppose that Wilt Chamberlain is greatly in demand by basketball teams, being a great gate attraction. (Also suppose contracts run only for a year, with players being free agents.) He signs the following sort of contract with a team: In each home game, 25 cents from the price of each ticket of admission goes to him. (We ignore the question of whether he is "gouging" the owners, letting them look out for themselves.) The season starts, and people cheerfully attend his team's games; they buy their tickets, each time dropping a separate 25 cents of their admission price into a special box with Chamberlain's name on it. They are excited about seeing him play; it is worth the total admission price to them. Let us suppose that in one season one million persons attend his home games, and Wilt Chamberlain winds up with $250,000, a much larger sum than the average income and larger even than anyone else has. Is he entitled to this income? Is this new distribution, D_2, unjust? If so, why? There is *no* question about whether each of the people was entitled to the control over the resources they held in D_1; because that was the distribution (your favorite) that (for the purposes of argument) we assumed was acceptable. Each of these persons *chose* to give 25 cents of their money to Chamberlain. They could have spent it on going to the movies, or on candy bars, or on copies of *Dissent* magazine, or of *Monthly Review*. But they all, at least one million of them, converged on giving it to Wilt Chamberlain in exchange for watching him play basketball. If D_1 was a just distribution, and people voluntarily moved from it to D_2, transferring parts of their shares they were given under D_1 (what was it for if not to do something with?), isn't D_2 also just? If the people were entitled to dispose of the resources to which they were entitled (under D_1), didn't this include their being entitled to give it to, or exchange with, Wilt Chamberlain? Can anyone else complain on grounds of justice? Each other person already has his legitimate share under D_1. Under D_1, there is nothing that anyone has that anyone else has a claim of justice against. After someone transfers something to Wilt Chamberlain, third parties *still* have their legitimate shares; *their* shares are not changed. By what process could such a transfer among two persons give rise to a legitimate claim of distributive justice on a portion of what was transferred, by a third party who had no claim of justice on any holding of the others *before* the transfer? To cut off objections irrelevant here, we might imagine the exchanges occurring in a socialist society, after hours. After playing whatever basketball he does in his daily work, or doing whatever other daily work he does, Wilt Chamberlain decides to put in *overtime* to earn additional money. (First his work quota is set; he works time over that.) Or imagine it is a skilled juggler people like to see, who puts on shows after hours.

Why might someone work overtime in a society in which it is assumed their needs are satisfied? Perhaps because they care about things other than needs. I like to write in books that I read, and to have easy access to books for browsing at odd hours. It would be very pleasant and convenient to have the resources of Widener Library in my back yard. No society, I assume, will provide such resources close to each person who would like them as part of his regular allotment (under D_1). Thus, persons either must do without some extra things that they want, or be allowed to do something extra to get some of these things. On what basis could the inequalities that would eventuate be forbidden? Notice also that small factories would spring up in a socialist society, unless forbidden. I melt down some of my personal possessions (under D_1) and build a machine out of the material. I offer you, and others, a philosophy lecture once a week in exchange for your cranking the handle on my machine, whose products I exchange for yet other things, and so on. (The raw materials used by the machine are given to me by others who possess them under D_1, in exchange for hearing lectures.) Each person might participate to gain things over and above their allotment under D_1. Some persons even might want to leave their job in socialist industry and work full time in this private sector. . . . Here I wish merely to note how private property even in means of production would occur in a socialist society that did not forbid people to use as they wished some of the resources they are given under the socialist distribution D_1. The socialist society would have to forbid capitalist acts between consenting adults.

The general point illustrated by the Wilt Chamberlain example and the example of the entrepreneur in a socialist society is that no end-state principle or distributional patterned principle of justice can be continuously realized without continuous interference with people's lives. Any favored pattern would be transformed into one unfavored by the principle, by people choosing to act in various ways; for example, by people exchanging goods and services with other people, or giving things to other people, things the transferrers are entitled to under the favored distributional pattern. To maintain a pattern one must either continually interfere to stop people from transferring resources as they wish to, or continually (or periodically) interfere to take from some persons resources that others for some reason chose to transfer to them. (But if some time limit is to be set on how long people may keep resources others voluntarily transfer to them, why let them keep these resources for *any* period of time? Why not have immediate confiscation?) It might be objected that all persons voluntarily will choose to refrain from actions which would upset the pattern. This presupposes unrealistically (1) that all will most want to maintain the pattern (are those who don't, to be "reeducated" or forced to undergo "self-criticism"?), (2) that each can gather enough information about his own actions and the ongoing activities of others to discover which of his actions will upset the pattern, and (3) that diverse and far-flung persons can coordinate their actions to dove-tail into the pattern. Compare the manner in which the market is neutral among persons' desires, as it reflects and transmits widely scattered information via prices, and coordinates persons' activities.

It puts things perhaps a bit too strongly to say that every patterned (or end-state) principle is liable to be thwarted by the voluntary actions of the individual parties transferring some of their shares they receive under the principle. For perhaps some *very* weak patterns are not so thwarted. Any distributional pattern with any egalitarian component is overturnable by the voluntary actions of individual persons over time; as is every patterned condition with sufficient content so as actually to have been proposed as presenting the central core of distributive justice. Still, given the possibility that some weak conditions or patterns may not be unstable in this way, it would be better to formulate an explicit description of the kind of interesting and contentful patterns under discussion, and to prove a theorem about their instability. Since the weaker the patterning, the more likely it is that the entitlement system itself satisfies it, a plausible conjecture is that any patterning either is unstable or is satisfied by the entitlement system.

NOTE

1. Applications of the principle of justice in acquisition may also occur as part of the move from one distribution to another. You may find an unheld thing now and appropriate it. Acquisitions also are to be understood as included when, to simplify, I speak only of transitions by transfers.

FUNDAMENTAL INTERNATIONAL RIGHTS

—THOMAS DONALDSON

Thomas Donaldson identifies some of the items that should appear on a list of fundamental international rights. Donaldson defines a fundamental international right as satisfying three conditions: the right must protect something of great importance, the right must be subject to substantial and recurrent threats and the duties associated with the right must be limited in light of fairness and affordability.

. . . Though probably not complete, the following list contains items that appear to satisfy the three conditions and hence to qualify as fundamental international rights:

1. The right to freedom of physical movement.
2. The right to ownership of property.
3. The right to freedom from torture.
4. The right to a fair trial.
5. The right to nondiscriminatory treatment (freedom from discrimination on the basis of such characteristics as race or sex).
6. The right to physical security.
7. The right to freedom of speech and association.
8. The right to minimal education.
9. The right to political participation.
10. The right to subsistence.

This is a minimal list. Some will wish to add entries such as the right to employment, to social security or to a certain standard of living (say, as might be prescribed by Rawls' well-known "difference" principle). Disputes also may arise about the wording or overlapping features of some rights: for example, is not the right to freedom from torture included in the right to physical security, at least when the latter is properly interpreted? We shall not attempt to resolve such controversies here. Rather, the list as presented aims to suggest, albeit incompletely, a description of a *minimal* set of rights and to serve as a beginning consensus for evaluating international conduct. If I am correct, many would wish to add entries, but few would wish to subtract them.

Thomas Donaldson, *Fundamental International Rights.* Reprinted by permission of Oxford University Press, Inc.

The list has been generated by application of the three conditions and the compatibility proviso. Each reader may decide whether the 10 entries fulfill these conditions; in doing so, however, remember that in constructing the list one looks for *only* those rights that can be honored in some form by *all* international moral agents, including nation-states, corporations, and individuals. Hence, to consider only the issue of affordability, each candidate for a right must be tested for "affordability" by way of the lowest common denominator—by way, for example, of the poorest nation-state. If, even after receiving its fair share of charitable aid from wealthier nations, that state cannot "afford" kidney dialysis for all citizens who need it, then the right to receive dialysis from one's nation-state will not be a fundamental international right, although dialysis may constitute a bona fide right for those living within a specific nation-state, such as Japan.

Even though the hope for a definitive interpretation of the list of rights is an illusion, we can add specificity by clarifying the correlative duties entailed for different kinds of international actors. Because by definition the list contains items that all three major classes of international actors must respect, the next task is to spell out the correlative duties that fall upon our targeted group of international actors, namely, multinational corporations.

This task requires putting the "fairness-affordability" condition to a second, and different, use. This condition was first used as one of the three criteria generating the original list of fundamental rights. There it demanded satisfaction of a fairness-affordability threshold for each potential respecter of a right. For example, if the burdens imposed by a given right are not fair (in relation to other bona fide obligations and burdens) or affordable for nation-states, individuals and corporations, then presumably the prospective right would not qualify as a fundamental international right.*

In its second use, the "fairness-affordability" condition goes beyond the judgment *that* a certain fairness-affordability threshold has been crossed to the determination of *what* the proper duties are for multinational corporations in relation to a given right. In its second use, in other words, the condition's notions of fairness and affordability are invoked to help determine *which* obligations properly fall upon corporations, in contrast to individuals and nation-states. The condition can help determine the correlative duties that attach to multinational corporations in their honoring of fundamental international rights.

SAMPLE APPLICATIONS
Discrimination

The obligation to protect a person from deprivation of the right to freedom from discrimination properly falls upon corporations as well as governments insofar as everyday corporate activities directly affect compliance with that right. Because employees and

---

*It is worth noting that fundamental international rights are not the only type of rights. In addition there are legal rights and nation-specific moral rights. For example, the right to sue for damages under the doctrine of strict liability (where compensation can be demanded even without demonstrating negligence) is a legal right in the United States, although it would not qualify as a fundamental international right and is not a legal right in some other nation-states. Similarly, the right to certain forms of technologically advanced medical care such as CAT scanning for cancerous tumors may be a nation-specific moral right in highly industrialized countries (even when it is not guaranteed as a legal right) but could not qualify at this point in history as a fundamental international right.

prospective employees possess the moral right not to be discriminated against on the basis of race, sex, caste, class or family affiliation, it follows that multinational corporations have an obligation not only to refrain from discrimination, but in some instances to protect the right to nondiscriminatory treatment by establishing appropriate procedures. This may require, for example, offering notice to prospective employees about the company's policy of nondiscriminatory hiring, or educating lower-level managers about the need to reward or penalize on the basis of performance rather than irrelevant criteria.

Physical Security

The right to physical security similarly entails duties of protection. If a Japanese multinational corporation operating in Nigeria hires shop workers to run metal lathes in an assembly factory, but fails to provide them with protective goggles, then the corporation has failed to honor the workers' moral right to physical security (no matter what the local law might decree). Injuries from such a failure would be the moral responsibility of the Japanese multinational despite the fact that the company could not be said to have inflicted the injuries directly.

Free Speech and Association

In the same vein, the duty to protect from deprivation the right of free speech and association finds application in the ongoing corporate obligation not to bar the creation of labor unions. Corporations are not obliged on the basis of human rights to encourage or welcome labor unions; indeed they may oppose them using all morally acceptable means at their disposal. But neither are they morally permitted to destroy them or prevent their emergence through coercive tactics; for to do so would violate their workers' international right to association. The corporation's duty to protect from deprivation the right to association, in turn, includes refraining from lobbying host governments for restrictions that would violate the right in question, and perhaps even to protesting host government measures in countering the well-documented tendency of multinationals to mask immoral practices in the rhetoric of "tolerance" and "cultural relativity." According to this algorithm, no multinational manager can naively suggest that asbestos standards in Chile are permissible because they are accepted there. Nor can a manager infer that the standards are acceptable on the grounds that the Chilean economy is, relative to the multinational's home country, underdeveloped. A surprising amount of moral blindness occurs not because people's fundamental moral views are confused, but because their cognitive application of those views to novel situations is misguided.

What guarantees that multinationals possess the knowledge or objectivity to apply the algorithm fairly? As Richard Barnet quips, "On the 56th floor of a Manhattan skyscraper, the level of self-protective ignorance about what the company may be doing in Colombia or Mexico is high." Can Exxon or Johns Manville be trusted to have a sufficiently sophisticated sense of "fundamental rights," or to weigh dispassionately the hypothetical attitudes of their fellow citizens under conditions of "relevantly similar economic development"? My answer to this is "perhaps not," at least given the present character of the decision-making procedures in most global corporations. But this only serves to underscore the need for more sophisticated, and more ethically sensitive, decision-making techniques in multinationals. And I would add that from a theoretical perspective the problem is a contingent and practical one. It is no more a theoretical flaw of the proposed algorithm that it may be misunderstood or misapplied by a given multinational, than it is of Rawls's theory of justice that it may be conveniently misunderstood by a trickle-down Libertarian.

What would need to change in order for multinationals to make use of the algorithm? Most of all, multinationals would need to enhance the sophistication of their decision making. They would need to alter established patterns of information flow and collection to accommodate moral information. They would need to introduce alongside analyses of the bottom line, analyses of historical tendencies, health, rights and demography. And they might even find it necessary to introduce a new class of employee to provide expertise in these areas. However unlikely such changes are, I believe they are within the realm of possibility. Multinationals, the organizations capable of colonizing our international future, are no doubt also capable of applying—at a minimum—the same moral principles abroad that they accept at home.

MODEL BUSINESS PRINCIPLES

—U.S. DEPARTMENT OF COMMERCE

In an effort to codify the expectations of the American market, the U.S. Department of Commerce issued its Model Business Principles in 1995 as guidelines for business conduct in the United States and abroad. While the principles comprise a voluntary code of conduct, the Department hopes that they will encourage appropriate behavior.

Recognizing the positive role of U.S. business in upholding and promoting adherence to universal standards of human rights, the Administration encourages all businesses to adopt and implement voluntary codes of conduct for doing business around the world that cover at least the following areas:

1. Provision of a safe and healthy workplace.
2. Fair employment practices, including avoidance of child and forced labor and avoidance of discrimination based on race, gender, national origin or religious beliefs; and respect for the right of association and the right to organize and bargain collectively.
3. Responsible environmental protection and environmental practices.
4. Compliance with U.S. and local laws promoting good business practices, including laws prohibiting illicit payments and ensuring fair competition.
5. Maintenance, through leadership at all levels, of a corporate culture that respects free expression consistent with legitimate business concerns, and does not condone political coercion in the workplace; that encourages good corporate citizenship and makes a positive contribution to the communities in which the company operates; and where ethical conduct is recognized, valued and exemplified by all employees.

In adopting voluntary codes of conduct that reflect these principles, U.S. companies should serve as models, encouraging similar behavior by their partners, suppliers and subcontractors.

Adoption of codes of conduct reflecting these principles is voluntary. Companies are encouraged to develop their own codes of conduct appropriate to their particular circumstances. Many companies already apply statements or codes that incorporate these principles. Companies should find appropriate means to inform their shareholders and the public of actions undertaken in connection with these principles. Nothing in the principles is intended to require a company to act in violation of host country or U.S. law. This statement of principles is not intended for legislation.

U.S. Department of Commerce, U.S. Model Business Principles (1995).

MODEL BUSINESS PRINCIPLES: PROCEDURES

When President Clinton announced his decision to renew China's MFN status last year, he also announced a commitment to work with the business community to develop a voluntary statement of business principles relating to corporate conduct abroad. The President made clear that U.S. business can and does play a positive and important role promoting the openness of societies, respect for individual rights, the promotion of free markets and prosperity, environmental protection and the setting of high standards for business practices generally.

The Administration today is offering an update on our efforts to follow-through on the President's commitment to promote the Model Business Principles and best practices among U.S. companies. The Principles already have gained the support of some U.S. companies. A process is ongoing to elicit additional support for these Principles and to continue to examine issues related to them.

The elements of this process are as follows:

1. Voluntary Statement of Business Principles. The Administration, in extensive consultations with business and labor leaders and members of the Non-Governmental Organization (NGO) community, developed these model principles, which were reported widely in the press earlier this spring. This model statement is to be used by companies as a reference point in framing their own codes of conduct. It is based on a wide variety of similar sets of principles U.S. companies and business organizations already have put into global practice. The Administration encourages all businesses everywhere to support the model principles. (Copies of the model statement are available by calling the U.S. Department of Commerce Trade Information Center, 1–800-USA-TRADE.)
2. Efforts by U.S. Business. As part of the ongoing effort, U.S. businesses will engage in the following activities:
    (a) Conferences on Best Practices Issues. In conjunction with Business for Social Responsibility, a non-profit business organization dedicated to promoting laudable corporate practices, and/or other appropriate organizations, the Administration will work to encourage conferences concerning issues relating to the practices contained in the Model Business Principles. Such conferences can provide a forum for information-sharing on new approaches for the evolving global context in which best practices are implemented. (For further information on Business for Social Responsibility, contact Bob Dunn, President, (415) 865–2500.)
    (b) Best Practices Information Clearinghouse and Support Services. One or more non-profits will work with the U.S. business community to develop a clearinghouse of information regarding business practices globally. The clearinghouse will establish a library of codes of conduct adopted by U.S. and international companies and organizations, to be catalogued and made available to companies seeking to develop their own codes. The clearinghouse would be available to provide advice to companies seeking to develop or improve their codes, advice based on the accumulated experience of other companies. Business for Social Responsibility (described above) is highly respected and is one resource that businesses and NGO's alike can turn to for information on best business practices.

3. Efforts by the U.S. Government. The U.S. Government also will undertake a number of activities to generate support for the Model Business Principles:

    (a) Promote Multilateral Adoption of Best Practices. The Administration has begun and will continue its effort to seek multilateral support for the Model Business Principles. Senior U.S. Government officials already have met with U.S. company officials and U.S. organizations operating abroad as well as with foreign corporate officials to seek support for the Principles. For example, the American Chambers of Commerce in the Asia Pacific recently adopted a resolution by which their members agreed to work with their local counterparts in the countries in which they operate to seek development of similar best practices among their members. The United States also will present the Model Business Principles at the Organization for Economic Cooperation and Development (OECD) and the International Labor Organization (ILO) as part of these organizations' ongoing behavior. Therefore, on an annual basis, the Administration will offer a series of awards to companies for specific activities that reflect best practices in the areas covered by the Model Business Principles. The awards will be granted pursuant to applications by interested companies. NGOs and private citizens will be encouraged to call attention to activities they believe are worthy of consideration. (For further information on the Best Practices Awards Program, contact Melinda Yee, U.S. Department of Commerce, (202) 482–1051.)

    (b) Presidential-Business Discussions. The President's Export Council (PEC), a high-level advisory group of chief executive officers, provides a forum for the President to meet regularly with U.S. business leaders to discuss issues relating to U.S. industries' exports and operations abroad.

For further general information about the Model Business Principles, please contact Jill Schuker, U.S. Commerce Department, (202) 482–5151, or David Ruth, U.S. Department of State, (202) 647–1625.

THE CAUX PRINCIPLES

—THE CAUX ROUND TABLE

The Caux Round Table consisted of a group of international executives based in Caux, Switzerland. The group shared a belief that business organizations can be a powerful force for positive change in the quality of life for the world. The executives developed their principles based on the Minnesota principles created by the Minnesota Center for Corporate Responsibility in 1992. The Caux Principles are based in the conviction that we can all live together and act for the common good.

The Caux Principles are rooted in two basic ethical ideals: kyosei *and human dignity. The Japanese concept of kyosei means living and working together for the common good—enabling cooperation and mutual prosperity to coexist with healthy and fair competition. Human dignity relates to the sacredness or value of each person as an end, not simply as the means to the fulfillment of other's purposes or even majority prescription. The general principles in section 2 clarify the spirit of kyosei and human dignity while the specific stakeholder principles in section 3 are concerned with their practical application. After reading the principles, can you think of any issues that are not addressed?*

SECTION 1. PREAMBLE

The mobility of employment, capital, produce and technology is making business increasingly global in its transactions and its effects.

Laws and market forces are necessary but insufficient guides for conduct.

Responsibility for the politics and actions of business and respect for the dignity and interests of its stakeholders are fundamental.

Shared values, including a commitment to shared prosperity, are as important for a global community as for communities of smaller scale.

For these reasons, and because business can be a powerful agent of positive social change we offer the following principles as a foundation for dialogue and action by business leaders in search of business responsibility. In so doing we affirm the necessity for moral values in business decision making; without them, stable business relationships and a sustainable world community are impossible.

The Caux Round Table, *Caux Principles.* Reprinted with permission from *Business Ethics,* 52 S. 10th St., Suite 110, Minneapolis, MN 55403.

SECTION 2. GENERAL PRINCIPLES

Principle 1. The Responsibilities of Businesses:
Beyond Shareholders Toward Stakeholders

The value of a business to society is the wealth and employment it creates and the marketable products and practices it provides to consumers at a reasonable price commensurate with quality. To create such a value, a business must maintain its own economic health and viability, but survival is not a sufficient goal.

Businesses have a role to play in improving the lives of all their customers, employees and shareholders by sharing with them the wealth they have created. Suppliers and competitors as well should expect businesses to honor their obligations in a spirit of honesty and fairness. As responsible citizens of the local, national, regional and global communities in which they operate, businesses share a part in shaping the future of those communities.

Principle 2. The Economic and Social Impact of Businesses:
Toward Innovation, Justice and World Community

Businesses established in foreign countries to develop, produce or sell should also contribute to the social advancement of those countries by creating productive employment and helping to raise the purchasing power of their citizens. Businesses also should contribute to human rights, education, welfare and vitalization of the countries in which they operate. Businesses should contribute to economic and social development not only in the countries in which they operate, but also in the world community at large, through effective and prudent use of resources, free and fair competition and emphasis upon innovation in technology, production methods, marketing and communications.

Principle 3. Business Behavior: Beyond the Letter
of the Law Toward a Spirit of Trust

While accepting the legitimacy of trade secrets, businesses should recognize that sincerity, keeping of promises and transparency contribute not only to their own credibility and stability but also to the smoothness and efficiency of business transactions, particularly on the international level.

Principle 4. Respect for the Rules

To avoid trade frictions and to promote freer trade, equal conditions for competition and fair and equitable treatment for all participants, businesses should respect international and domestic rules. In addition, they should recognize that some behavior although legal, may still have adverse consequences.

Principle 5. Support for Multilateral Trade

Businesses should support the multilateral trade systems of the GATT/World Trade Organization and similar international agreements. They should cooperate in efforts to promote the progressive and judicious liberalization of trade, and to relax those domestic measures that unreasonably hinder global commerce, while giving due respect to national policy objectives.

Principle 6. Respect for the Environment

A business should protect and, where possible, improve the environment and promote sustainable development.

Principle 7. Avoidance of Illicit Operations

A business should not participate in or condone bribery, money laundering or other corrupt practices: indeed, it should seek cooperation with others to eliminate them. It should not trade in arms or other materials used for terrorist activities, drug traffic or other organized crime.

SECTION 3. STAKEHOLDER PRINCIPLES

Customers

We believe in treating all customers with dignity irrespective of whether they purchase our products and services directly from us or otherwise acquire them in the market. We therefore have a responsibility to: provide our customers with the highest quality products and services consistent with their requirements; treat our customers fairly in all aspects of our business transactions including a high level of service and remedies for their dissatisfaction; make every effort to ensure that the health and safety of our customers, as well as the quality of their environment, will be sustained or enhanced by our products and services; assure respect for human dignity in products offered, marketing and advertising; and respect the integrity of the culture of our customers.

Employees

We believe in the dignity of every employee and in taking employee interests seriously. We therefore have a responsibility to: provide jobs and compensation that improve workers' living conditions; provide working conditions that respect each employee's health and dignity; be honest in communications with employees and open in sharing information, limited only by legal and competitive restraints; listen to and, where possible, act on employee suggestions, ideas, requests and complaints; engage in good faith negotiations when conflict arises; avoid discriminatory practices and guarantee equal treatment and opportunity in areas such as gender, age, race and religion; promote in the business itself the employment of differently abled people in places of work where they can be genuinely useful; protect employees from avoidable injury and illness in the workplace; encourage and assist employees in developing relevant and transferable skills and knowledge; and be sensitive to serious unemployment problems frequently associated with business decisions and work with governments, employee groups, other agencies and each other in addressing these dislocations.

Owners/Investors

We believe in honoring the trust our investors place in us. We therefore have a responsibility to: apply professional and diligent management in order to secure a fair and competitive return on our owners' investment; disclose relevant information to owners/investors subject only to legal requirements and competitive constraints; conserve, protect and increase the owners/investors' assets; and respect owners/investors' requests, suggestions, complaints and formal resolutions.

Suppliers

Our relationship with suppliers and subcontractors must be based on mutual respect. We therefore have a responsibility to: seek fairness and truthfulness in all of our activities, including pricing, licensing and rights to sell; ensure that our business activities are free from coercion and unnecessary litigation; foster long-term stability in the supplier relationship in return for value, quality competitiveness and reliability; share information with suppliers and integrate them into our planning processes; pay suppliers on time and in accordance with agreed terms of trade; seek, encourage and prefer suppliers and subcontractors whose employment practices respect human dignity.

Competitors

We believe that fair economic competition is one of the basic requirements for increasing the wealth of nations and, ultimately for making possible the just distribution of goods and services. We therefore have a responsibility to: foster open markets for trade and investment; promote competitive behavior that is socially and environmentally beneficial and demonstrates mutual respect among competitors; refrain from either seeking or participating in questionable payments or favors to secure competitive advantages; respect both tangible and intellectual property rights; and refuse to acquire commercial information by dishonest or unethical means, such as industrial espionage.

Communities

We believe that as global corporate citizens, we can contribute to such forces of reform and human rights as are at work in the communities which we are open to. We therefore have a responsibility in those communities to: respect human rights and democratic institutions, and promote them wherever practicable; recognize government's legitimate obligation to the society at large and support public policies and practices that promote human development through harmonious relations between business and other segments of society; collaborate with those forces in the community dedicated to raising standards of health, education, workplace safety and economic well-being; promote and stimulate sustainable development and play a leading role in preserving and enhancing the physical environment and conserving the earth's resources; support peace, security, diversity and social integration; respect the integrity of local cultures; and be a good corporate citizen through charitable donations, educational and cultural contributions and employee participation in community and civic affairs.

INTERNATIONAL ETHICS STANDARDS FOR BUSINESS

NAFTA, Caux Principles and U.S. Corporate Codes of Ethics

—Patricia Carlson and Mark Blodgett

The authors compare the content of 31 corporate codes of ethics with the Caux Principles. Each of the codes is examined for representative words and phrases taken from the international code. The authors find that there remain areas of inadequate coverage in the corporate codes. The authors then discuss the three major ethical issues of NAFTA, comparing them to the Caux Principle.

NAFTA

This multilateral agreement was executed on January 1, 1994. Some of the main provisions of this unparalleled agreement deal with the elimination of tariff and non-tariff barriers and the facilitation of multinational corporate business operations. Also central to the agreement is a strong position on environmental protection (*San Diego Law Review*, 1994) and intellectual property. The agreement states that each party is to implement the provisions of the agreement so that "there will be a progressive elimination of all tariffs on goods qualifying as North American." It also calls for protection of the environment and intellectual property rights (Litka and Blodgett, 1995, p. 242). NAFTA's ample employment protections are of particular importance since Mexico does not enforce the liberal labor guarantees of its constitution that otherwise bear many similarities to U.S. and Canadian labor laws (Benton, 1993).

NAFTA's provisions deal with some of the most timely issues within the global environment. Do these issues reflect the concerns of businesses as players in a global ethical context? One indication of multinational concern is found in the Caux Round Table Principles of Business Ethics.

CAUX PRINCIPLES

Simultaneous with the implementation of the multilateral agreement (NAFTA) among the U.S., Canada and Mexico to promote free trade by eliminating tariff and non-tariff barriers

was the creation of the Caux Principles. Considered to be the first international code of ethics for business, the Caux Round Table Principles originated from a meeting of international business leaders in Caux, Switzerland. These business leaders represented the U.S., Europe and Japan. The Principles are based on an original set of principles known as the Minnesota Principles, developed by the Minnesota Center for Corporate Responsibility (MCCR) affiliated with the University of St. Thomas in the Twin Cities, Minnesota.

The Japanese influence is particularly notable since their concept of *kyosei,* "living and working together for the common good" (*Nation's Business,* 1996, p. 12), is one of two ethical concepts permeating the Caux Principles. The other concept is "human dignity," defined by the code as the "sacredness or value of each person as an end, not simply as a means to the fulfillment of other's purposes or even majority prescription." (*SBE Newsletter,* 1995, p. 14).

The Caux Principles promote action to further these two main concepts of fairness and respect for others by promoting free trade, environmental and cultural integrity and the prevention of actions that fall in the category of foreign corrupt practices as defined by U.S. law (bribery, money laundering, etc.). Among the principles that expand upon the concepts of fairness and respect for others are the following General Principles in Section 2 of the Caux Round Table Principles for Business:[1]

Principle 2. The economic and social impact of business

Principle 4. Respect for the rules

Principle 5. Support for multilateral trade

Principle 6. Respect for the environment

Principle 7. Avoidance of illicit operations

These principles are further explained as Stakeholder Principles of the Caux Round Table Principles for Business under the following topics: Customers, Employees, Owners/ Investors, Suppliers, Competitors and Communities. The purpose of this project was to examine codes of ethics from major corporations to determine whether they include the provisions of the Caux Principles. The following sections show the analysis of the data from the corporate codes of ethics and discuss the implications of the findings for responsible corporations acting in the international arena.

METHODOLOGY

The project was carried out in a large northeastern city during the months of February and March, 1994. Codes of ethics were solicited from businesses represented in the area, as evidenced by their presence in the Yellow Pages. The businesses were chosen based on two criteria: size and industry. Since larger businesses were considered most likely to have formal codes of ethics, the sample was limited to businesses with national prominence (national chains) or those easily recognizable as locally prominent. The industries selected

---

[1]The authors did not test the more general Caux Principles 1 or 3 in this project, since more extensive resources would be required. The authors investigated Caux Principle 3 in a previous project.

were: retail (fast food, grocery stores, department stores), financial services, utilities and health services.

Each business was contacted to determine the name of the person to whom a follow-up letter should be addressed. Once the name of the person was known, a letter soliciting the company code of ethics was sent by the researchers. A follow-up phone call to those businesses who had not responded within a two-month time period resulted in a response rate of 84%; 37 letters were sent, 31 codes were received.

Each corporate code of ethics was read by one of the researchers, and references to important concepts were noted. The researchers each read a subset of the other researcher's codes so that the coding would be uniform.

Salient concepts were decided upon before the coding process by combining principles mentioned in NAFTA with those from the Caux Principles. NAFTA is essentially an international trade agreement, which addresses the main issues of multinational trade, environmental protection, intellectual property and employment, among others. The Caux Principles contain a broad statement of ethical principles encompassing and enlarging upon these NAFTA provisions. The final coding scheme consisted of five all-encompassing concepts from the Caux Principles (see Table 1).

DATA

The typical composition of the codes of ethics includes three parts: (1) a cover letter, (2) a general statement at the beginning of the code, (3) a list of compliance situations in which ethical dilemmas may arise. A cover letter was included with 62% of the codes of ethics. The cover letter is always from the chairman of the board and/or the chief executive officer (CEO). The letter contains broad general statements about the importance of the code of ethics, and, in many cases, it is this document that instructs the employee about correct behavior when a situation is not specifically mentioned in the code of ethics. It is interesting

TABLE 1

Data Collection Coding Table

Caux Principle	Name of Principle	Evidence in Corporate Code of Ethics
Principle 2	The economic and social impact of business	Importance of ethnicity, employee culture, equal opportunity, equal conditions
Principle 4	Respect for the rules	Intellectual property, copyright, trade marks
Principle 5	Support for multilateral trade	Trade, relationship with suppliers, free trade
Principle 6	Respect for the environment	Improve or promote sustainable development, prevent waste, environmental protection
Principle 7	Avoidance of illicit operations	Corrupt practices, bribes, arms, other corrupt practices

to note that fully 38% of the companies attached so little importance to the code of ethics that no cover letter from upper management was included.

The general statement that prefaces the formal code of ethics usually consists of from two to six short paragraphs that include information about the importance of the code, who is held to obey the code, and it often contains information about the person who should be contacted when situations not covered in the code of ethics arise.

The final and longest part of the code of ethics (consisting of from 5 to 10 pages) is a list of compliance situations which could present an ethical dilemma to employees. The lists that are most helpful to employees are those that, in addition to listing the situations in formal terms, also give examples of actual situations (the examples are adapted to the particular industry). Some companies have only the lists without explanation or examples of situations. All of these sections were searched for references to the international ethics principles from the Caux Principles.

Each of the codes of ethics was examined for evidence of the five coding categories from Table 1. The data collected is shown in Table 2.

ANALYSIS

The primary objective of the study consisted in determining whether corporate codes of ethics contain any references that show an awareness of international ethical issues. This type of concern would be manifested by statements alluding to any of the General Principles of the Caux Round Table Principles for Business as shown in Table 1 above. The data collection resulted in the [Table 2] data set.

From the frequencies reported in the data set . . . the areas of major concern in corporate codes of ethics are evident. All of the codes of ethics contained references to illicit operations such as bribery and corrupt practices. Fully half of the codes of ethics contained references to the economic and social impact of business such as equal opportunity for all employees, the importance of ethnicity and equal conditions of work. Nearly one third of the companies were concerned about multilateral trade and relationships with suppliers. However, a majority of the companies did not mention intellectual property, copyright and trademarks; only four companies included statements about respect for the environment.

TABLE 2

Data Set

	The Economic and Social Impact of Business	Respect for the Rules	Support for Multilateral Trade	Respect for the Environment	Avoidance of Illicit Operations
Number of Codes of Ethics	15	8	11	4	31

When the information from Table 2 is considered, several concerns of business become apparent:

1. Businesses are very aware of the importance of instructing employees about one of the concepts—avoiding corrupt practices.
2. Businesses seem fairly aware of the importance of instructing employees about proper actions concerning two other concepts. The economic and social impact of business and support for multilateral trade are mentioned by at least one third of the codes of ethics.
3. Businesses are, however, for the most part, not instructing employees about actions regarding two important concepts—respect for the rules (illustrated by respect for intellectual property, copyrights, etc.) and respect for the environment—which are mentioned in only a few of the codes.

Organizations are apparently doing a good job of informing employees about only one out of the five principles, and they are doing an "OK" job for two more principles. What impact could the resulting lack of information have on employee actions in a domestic or an international setting? The importance of this question is discussed in the following section.

CONCLUSIONS AND RECOMMENDATIONS

The data show that employees are not informed about corporate preferences for action at least 50% of the time for four of the principles tested. In this scenario, corporations run the risk that employees will not know how to respond when faced with certain situations. This might lead to two undesirable results:

1. Employees might not act when action should be undertaken.
2. Employees might act in an inappropriate manner.

How important is correct action? From a societal point of view, the Caux Principles tell us that correct action is important and NAFTA tells us that correct action is important. Making incorrect choices concerning employment, trade, intellectual property or environmental protection will lead us to undesirable consequences such as child labor, unfair trade practices, pirating of copyrights, and environmental pollution. These actions have undesirable consequences at a societal level.

How important is correct action at an organizational level? In today's society organizations are expected to be responsible citizens at home. In our global economy organizations must also be responsible citizens abroad. This responsibility is enforced by laws and sanctions which organizations must respect or suffer the consequences in legal action.

Universal adoption of ethical standards such as the Caux Principles will enhance corporate codes of ethics as well as international treaties. From a practical point of view, when these ethical standards are translated into behavior, our global environment will be more desirable and organizations will be required to spend less time preparing for and carrying out litigation.

As members of the "local, national and global communities in which they operate, businesses share a part in shaping the future" (*Society for Business Ethics Newsletter*, 1995).

When corporations are actively promoting kyosei (living and working together for the common good) and human dignity (sacredness or value of each person) the result is a world society where employees, intellectual property and the environment are respected, trade is enhanced and business profits.

BIBLIOGRAPHY

1. Benton, Janine, "Extraterritorial Application of the ADA," *George Mason Independent Law Review,* vol. 2, no. 1, 1993, pp. 218–19.
2. Litka, M., and M. Blodgett, *International Dimensions of the Legal Environment of Business,* 3rd ed., South-Western College Publishing, Cincinnati, Ohio, 1995.
3. *Nation's Business,* vol. 84, no. 4, April, 1996.
4. *San Diego Law Review,* vol. 31, no. 4, Fall, 1994, pp. 1025–1055.
5. *Society for Business Ethics (SBE) Newsletter,* "Caux Roundtable Principles for Business," vol. 6, no. 1, May, 1995.

BUSINESS ETHICS
TIMELINE

—ETHICS RESOURCE CENTER

*The following timeline was developed by Jerry O'Brien at the Ethics
Resource Center and is included to provide some perspective on the
ethics implications of major business developments.*

Decade	Ethical Climate	Major Ethical Dilemmas	Business Ethics Developments
1960s	Social unrest. Anti-war sentiment. Employees have an adversarial relationship with management. Values shift away from loyalty to an employer to loyalty to ideals. Old values are cast aside.	• Environmental issues • Increased employee-employer tension • Civil rights issues dominate • Honesty • The work ethic changes • Drug use escalates	• Companies begin establishing codes of conduct and values statements • Birth of social responsibility movement • Corporations address ethics issues through legal or personnel departments
1970s	Defense contractors and other major industries riddled by scandal. The economy suffers through recession. Unemployment escalates. There are heightened environmental concerns. The public pushes to make businesses accountable for ethical shortcomings.	• Employee militancy (employee versus management mentality) • Human rights issues surface (forced labor, sub-standard wages, unsafe practices) • Some firms choose to cover rather than correct dilemmas	• ERC founded (1977) • Compliance with laws highlighted • Federal Corrupt Practices Act passed in 1977 • Values movement begins to move ethics from compliance orientation to being "values centered"

Decade	Ethical Climate	Major Ethical Dilemmas	Business Ethics Developments
1980s	The social contract between employers and employees is redefined. Defense contractors are required to conform to stringent rules. Corporations downsize and employees' attitudes about loyalty to the employer are eroded. Health care ethics emphasized.	• Bribes and illegal contracting practices • Influence peddling • Deceptive advertising • Financial fraud (savings and loan scandal) • Transparency issues arise	• ERC develops the U.S. Code of Ethics for Government Service (1980) • ERC forms first business ethics office at General Dynamics (1985) • Defense Industry Initiative established (1986) • Some companies create ombudsman positions in addition to ethics officer roles • False Claims Act (government contracting)
1990s	Global expansion brings new ethical challenges. There are major concerns about child labor, facilitation payments (bribes) and environmental issues. The emergence of the Internet challenges cultural borders. What was forbidden becomes common.	• Unsafe work practices in Third World countries • Increased corporate liability for personal damage (cigarette companies, Dow Chemical, etc.) • Financial mismanagement and fraud	• Federal Sentencing Guidelines (1991) • Class action lawsuits • Global Sullivan Principles (1999) • In re Caremark (Delaware Chancery Court ruling re Board responsibility for ethics) • IGs requiring voluntary disclosure • ERC establishes international business ethics centers • Royal Dutch/Shell International begins issuing annual reports on its ethical performance
2000s	Unprecedented economic growth is followed by financial failures. Ethics issues destroy some high-profile firms. Personal data is collected and sold openly. Hackers and data thieves plague businesses and government agencies. Acts of terror and aggression occur internationally.	• Cyber crime • Privacy issues (data mining) • Financial mismanagement • International corruption • Loss of privacy— employee's versus employer's • Intellectual property theft	• Business regulations mandate stronger ethical safeguards (Federal Sentencing Guidelines for Organizations; Sarbanes-Oxley Act of 2002) • Anticorruption efforts grow • Shift to emphasis on Corporate Social Responsibility and Integrity Management • Formation of international ethics centers to serve the needs of global businesses • OECD Convention on Bribery (1997–2000)

NOTE: The ethical climate and response to ethical dilemmas in the 1960s and 1970s blurs and loses some distinction across the decade boundaries due to the war in Vietnam, social upheaval and resulting stress on businesses.

Chapter 2

ETHICAL ANALYSIS AND APPLICATION
Corporate and Personal Decision Making

This above all: to thine own self be true, and it must follow, as the night the day, Thou canst not then be false to any man.

—SHAKESPEARE

To be nothing but yourself, in a world which is doing its best to make you everybody else, means to fight the hardest battle which any human being can fight, and never stop fighting.

—E.E. CUMMINGS

From here that looks like a bucket of water, but from an ant's point of view, it's a vast ocean; from an elephant's point of view, it's just a cool drink; and to a fish, of course, it's home.

—NORTON JUSTER

I am not afraid of storms, for I am learning to build my ship.

—LOUISA MAY ALCOTT

No professor teaches or takes a course in business ethics without hearing the all-too-familiar refrain, "Hey, isn't business ethics an oxymoron?" On the other hand, some argue that ethics is a natural market consequence of business—customers, clients, employees all want their firms to be ethical so it is in the firm's best interests to be so. Scholars George and John Steiner have identified six primary sources of ethics in the American business arena.

1.   *Genetic inheritance.* Although the view remains theoretical, sociobiologists have in recent years amassed persuasive evidence and arguments suggesting that the evolutionary forces of natural selection influence the development of traits such as cooperation and altruism that lie at the core of our ethical systems. Those qualities of goodness often associated with ethical conduct may, in some measure, be a product of genetic traits strengthened over time by the evolutionary process.

2.   *Religion.* Via a rule exemplified by the Golden Rule (or its variations in many religions) and the Ten Commandments, religious morality is clearly a primary force in shaping our societal ethics. The question here concerns the applicability of religious ethics to the business community. The question is all the more relevant because the Golden Rule is not limited to Western thought. Consider these words of Confucius:

> *There are four things in the Way of the profound person, none of which I have been able to do. To serve my father as I would expect my son to serve me. To serve my ruler as I would expect my ministers to serve me. To serve my elder brother as I would expect my younger brothers to serve me. To be the first to treat friends as I would expect them to treat me. These I have not been able to do.[1]*

Could the Golden Rule serve as a universal, practical, helpful standard for the businessperson's conduct?

---

[1]Confucius, *The Doctrine of The Mean,* chap. 13; *The Analects,* XIV, p. 28.

3. *Philosophical systems.* To the Epicureans, the quality of pleasure to be derived from an act was the essential measure of its goodness. The Stoics, like the Puritans and many contemporary Americans, advocated a disciplined, hardworking, thrifty lifestyle. These philosophies and others, like those cited earlier, have been instrumental in our society's moral development.

4. *Cultural experience.* Here, the Steiners refer to the rules, customs and standards transmitted from generation to generation as guidelines for appropriate conduct. Individual values are shaped in large measure by the norms of the society.

5. *Legal systems.* Laws represent rough approximations of society's ethical standards. Thus, the law serves to educate us about the ethical course in life. The law does not and, most would agree, should not be treated as a vehicle for expressing all of society's ethical preferences. Rather, the law is an ever-changing approximation of current perceptions of right and wrong.

6. *Codes of Conduct.* Steiner and Steiner identify three primary categories of such codes. Company codes, ordinarily brief and highly generalized, express broad expectations about fit conduct. Second, company operating policies often contain an ethical dimension. Policies as to gifts, customer complaints, hiring and other decisions serve as a guide to conduct and as a shield by which the employee can protect against unethical advances from those outside the firm. Third, many professional and industry associations have developed codes of ethics, such as the Affirmative Ethical Principles of the American Institute of Certified Public Accountants. (Codes of conduct are further discussed in Chapter 7.) In sum, codes of conduct seem to be a growing expression of the business community's sincere concern about ethics. However, the utility of such codes remains unsettled.

What forces determine which companies or businesspersons end up ethical and which do not? Why do people we consider to be "good" do "bad" things? Psychologist Lawrence Kohlberg believes that some individuals are simply better prepared to make ethical judgments than are others. He built a comprehensive theory of moral development in which he claimed that moral judgment evolves and improves primarily as a function of age and education.

Kohlberg, via interviews with children as they aged, was able to identify moral development as movement through distinct stages, with the later stages being viewed as more advanced than the earlier ones. Kohlberg identified six universal stages grouped into three levels.

At the postconventional level, the individual is able to reach independent moral judgments that may or may not conform with conventional societal wisdom. Thus, the Level 2 manager might refrain from sexual harassment because it constitutes a violation of company policy and the law. A manager at Level 3 might reach the same conclusion, but the decision would have been based on independently defined, universal principles of justice.

Kohlberg found that many adults never pass beyond Level 2. Consequently, if Kohlberg was correct, many managers may behave unethically simply because they have not reached the upper stages of moral maturity.

Kohlberg's model is based on very extensive longitudinal and cross-cultural studies over more than three decades. For example, one set of Chicago-area boys was interviewed at 3-year intervals for 20 years. Thus, the stages of moral growth exhibit "definite empirical

KOHLBERG'S SIX UNIVERSAL STAGES

Preconventional level (Level 1)

Stage 1:   Obey rules to avoid punishment.
Stage 2:   Follow rules only if it is in own interest, but let others do the same. Conform to secure rewards.

Conventional level (Level 2)

Stage 3:   Conform to meet the expectations of others. Please others. Adhere to stereotypical images.
Stage 4:   Doing right is one's duty. Obey the law. Uphold the social contract and order.

Postconventional or principled level (Level 3)

Stage 5:   Current laws and values are relative. Laws and duty are obeyed on rational calculations to serve the greatest number.
Stage 6:   Follow self-chosen universal ethical principles. In the event of conflicts, principles override laws.

characteristics" such that Kohlberg was able to claim that his model had been scientifically validated. While many critics remain, the evidence, in sum, is supportive of Kohlberg's general proposition.

Carol Gilligan offers a conception of moral development that runs contrary to Kohlberg's analysis. Instead of finding that individuals grow toward more autonomous, global decision making, Gilligan finds that individuals grow toward more complex webs of "caring" relationships. Gilligan's ethics of care was based on her findings that there exists a way of thinking about moral issues at variance with Kohlberg's sixth stage, and that this alternative was more common among women based on their different life experiences.

Gilligan found the following:

> *In a series of studies designed to investigate the relationship between conceptions of self and morality, and to test their association with gender and age, two moral voices could reliably be distinguished in the way people framed and resolved moral problems and in their evaluations of choices they made. One voice speaks of connection, not hurting, care and response; and one speaks of equality, reciprocity, justice and rights. . . . The pattern of predominance, although not gender specific, was gender related.[2]*

---

[2]Carol Gilligan, "Remapping the Moral Domain: New Images of Self in Relationship," in *Mapping the Moral Domain,* ed. C. Gilligan, J. Ward and J. McClean Taylor (Cambridge, MA: Center for the Study of Gender, Education and Human Development, Harvard University Press, 1988).

Gilligan, therefore had a different conception of moral development.

GILLIGAN'S CONCEPTION
OF MORAL DEVLOPMENT

First focus: Caring for self and ensuring survival.
   Transition stage: Self-focus as unacceptably selfish.
Second focus: Responsibility and material care for dependent others, self-sacrifice.
   Transition stage: Questions illogic of inequality between needs of others and self.
Third focus: Dynamic relationship between self and others.

Source: Carol Gilligan, *In a Different Voice* (Cambridge, MA: Harvard University Press, 1982).

Consider the similarities and differences between Gilligan and Kohlberg's analyses. In evaluating the actions of others, is it more helpful to consider their position along Kohlberg's scale or Gilligan's? Which seems more realistic as you apply it to others? Gilligan is often criticized for her "general" conclusion that women and men (as a result of life experiences) reason differently. Do you agree or disagree with that proposition?

MORAL DECISION MAKING IN BUSINESS: CORPORATE PROCESSES

A corporation, through its individual decision makers, might be viewed as having reached one of Kohlberg's levels. But is a corporation the same as a "moral person"? Of course, the corporation has long been treated as a person of sorts in the eyes of the law. We can legitimately hold the corporation legally blameworthy for employee wrongs. But can we attribute moral responsibility to the corporation? Ordinarily, we consider an individual morally responsible for act or event X only (1) if the person did X or caused X to occur and (2) if the person's conduct was intentional. Does a corporation ever do or cause any event? And even if a corporation could act, could it do so with intent? In a sense, can a corporation even think?

Philosopher Peter French posits that a corporation can be considered an "actor" since it has an organizational system of decision making (the organizational chart) and a set of policies and procedures for actions. Thus, the judgments and actions of individuals within the corporation are actually governed by the corporation itself (i.e., the will of the corporation). Critics of this approach argue that, while a corporation may be similar to an individual in some ways, it is distinct in others. For instance, the corporation does not have the same rights as individuals, such as the right to life.

Even if we are persuaded that the corporation could be treated as a moral actor, do we want to do so? We might answer yes because, in the event of wrongdoing, we could avoid the nearly impossible task of finding the guilty party within the corporate maze. Why not simply place the blame (or at least part of it) on the organization? But if we were to do so, would we somehow depreciate perhaps the central moral precept in our society—the notion that each of us must accept responsibility for our actions?

STAKEHOLDER ANALYSIS

Stakeholder analysis is one process by which a firm or an individual can apply the theories discussed in the previous chapter to reach an ethical decision. "Stakeholders" includes all of the groups and/or individuals affected by a decision, policy, or operation of a firm or individual. Stakeholder theory suggests that, to reach ethical decisions, we need to subscribe to the following decision-making process:

A. *Identification:* What is the moral dimension? What is the ethical issue? Often we don't even notice the ethical dilemma.
B. *Facts:* Gather all of the relevant facts. It is critical at this stage that we do not unintentionally bias our later decision by gathering only those facts in support of one particular outcome.
C. *Alternatives:* Identify the alternatives for your decision. Once you have gathered the facts, you will now be equipped to determine the variety of decision possibilities at your disposal. Explore not only the obvious choices, but also those that are less obvious and require some creative thinking or moral imagination to create.
D. *Stakeholders:* Now you are at a stage to identify the interested parties (i.e., stakeholders) based on the compiled facts and alternatives. Who is affected by our decision or any of the alternatives? What are their relationships, their priorities to me, and what is their power over my decision? Who has a stake in the outcome? Do not limit your inquiry only to those stakeholders to whom you believe you owe a duty; sometimes a duty arises as a result of the impact. For instance, you might not necessarily first consider your competitors as stakeholders; however, once you understand the impact of your decision on those competitors, an ethical duty may arise.
E. *Impact:* What is the impact of each alternative on each stakeholder?
F. *Guidance:* Can you discuss the case with relevant others, gather additional opinions or perspectives? Now is the time to consider the theories—What values are involved?
G. *Constraints:* Is the decision in line with legal and organizational rules?
H. *Comfort:* Are you comfortable with the decision? Can you live with it?
I. *Assessment:* Have you built in mechanisms for assessment of your decision and possible modifications, if necessary?

Each stakeholder or group of stakeholders, for instance, has interests that would be represented and considered throughout this analysis. Consider one group—customers. Their interests might include product safety, value for price, satisfaction, responsible communications, performance, compliance with regulations and so on. Shareholders are interested in stock returns, but also in timely and complete disclosures, corporate governance and compensation, compliance, the management of risk and reputation as it affects both the stock price and the firm itself.

Other questions that incorporate stakeholder analysis may prove just as useful. Philosophers/ethicists often ask the decision maker to consider whether she or he would feel all right if the *New York Times* (or a relevant daily newspaper) printed this decision as a front-page article, or whether it could be explained to a 10-year-old child so that the child thinks it is the right decision, or whether it will stand the test of time through generations in the firm.

Philosopher Laura Nash suggests asking 12 questions before reaching a decision in an ethical dilemma:

1. Have you defined the problem accurately?
2. How would you define the problem if you stood on the other side of the fence?
3. How did the situation occur in the first place?
4. Who was involved in the situation in the first place?
5. What is your intention in making this decision?
6. How does this intention compare with likely results?
7. Who could your decision or action injure?
8. Can you engage the affected parties in a discussion of the problem before you make your decision?
9. Are you confident that your decision will be as valid over a long period as it seems now?
10. Could you disclose without qualms your decision or action to your boss, your CEO, the board of directors, your family, or society as a whole?
11. What is the symbolic potential of your action if understood?
12. Under what conditions would you allow exceptions to your stand?[3]

Stakeholder analysis can be applied no matter what theory you're considering in terms of an ethical dilemma. For instance, if you were to apply a utilitarian analysis, you would need to consider the interests of all affected before being able to determine the greater good for the greatest number. If you are applying universalism to a particular decision, you would need to identify the individuals whose rights or needs might be affected by your decision and your duties with regard to those individuals. In applying a justice perspective, you would need to identify stakeholders and then consider how costs and benefits would be distributed among those stakeholders on the basis of your decision.

The Freeman reading that follows is one of the most influential and definitive discussions of stakeholder theory as it relates to business decision making. Recently, Patricia Werhane challenged whether this approach is sufficient and suggests that management decision making often is missing a more systems-based approach.[4] Instead, she contends, it is critical to understand not only the relationships between the corporation and the individual stakeholders but also those between and among the stakeholders themselves as a network of relationships and patterns. In so doing, you can better understand the interconnectedness of the entire system and therefore the potentially far-reaching implications of your decisions.

---

[3]Laura Nash, "Ethics Without the Sermon," *Harvard Business Review* 56, no. 6 (1981), pp. 80–81.
[4]Patricia Werhane, "Moral Imagination and Systems Thinking," *Journal of Business Ethics* 38 (2002), pp. 33–42.

APPLYING ETHICAL DECISION MAKING
TO PERSONAL DECISION MAKING

In "No Exit" by Sartre, Inez, a lesbian woman who drove her lover's husband to his death, says:

> *One always dies too soon—or too late. And yet one's whole life is complete at that moment, with a line drawn neatly under it, ready for the summing up. You are—your life, and nothing else.*

Consider Inez's statement. "You are—your life, and nothing else." Consider how you feel about your accomplishments, your challenges, your actions and decisions, and the manner in which you have treated your personal stakeholders. If we were to look at this life from the outside, would we find it to be "worthwhile," "good," "right," or any other positive judgment? You might believe that a part of our soul is left with each decision we make; and our lasting impact on this earth is evidenced by the "indentations" we make on the lives of others and our environment (i.e., stakeholders). If so, then you might also believe that we will all be judged on the basis of these indentations that we leave behind.

Do you consider that you act only in your own self-interest at all times, or would you contend that you ignore your personal interests in order to act in the interests of others at times? When you make a choice that is for your own good but against someone else's, are you accountable to that other individual for the impact of your decision. Some theorists argue that we act *only* in our own self-interest, that even something like an anonymous donation satisfies your personal need to do that act. Controversial author and philosopher Ayn Rand goes one step further and contends that those who do concern themselves with the interests of others do so to their own detriment or for purely selfish reasons. In discussing this "selflessness," the protagonist of Rand's novel, *The Fountainhead,* Howard Roark, states as follows:

> *And isn't that the root of every despicable action? Not selfishness, but precisely the absence of a self. Look at them. The man who cheats and lies but preserves a respectable front. He knows himself to be dishonest, but others think he's honest and he derives his self respect from that, second-hand. . . . The frustrated wretch who professes love for the inferior and clings to those less endowed, in order to establish his own superiority by comparison. The man whose sole aim is to make money. Now I don't see anything evil in a desire to make money. But money is only a means to an end. If a man wants it for a personal purpose—to invest in his industry, to create, to study, to travel, to enjoy luxury—he's completely moral. But the men who place money first go much beyond that. Personal luxury is a limited endeavor. What they want is ostentation: to show, to stun, to entertain, to impress others. They're second-handers.[5]*

Would you consider yourself someone Rand derides, a "second-hander"? Do you agree with her judgment, her derision of these types of individuals or would you instead stand up for the "second-hander"? How would Rand respond to the biblical case of Solomon and the

---

[5]Ayn Rand, *The Fountainhead* (New York: Signet Books, 1971), pp. 606–07.

two mothers. Two women came to King Solomon, both claiming to be the mother of a young child. The king said that he would cut the child in half and give each purported mother her half of the child. As he prepared to do this, one woman told him to stop and agreed to give the (entire) child to the other woman. King Solomon then determined that this must be the true mother of the child since she was prepared to give up her child in order to save him. Did the true mother act in her own best interests or the interests of another and how would Rand explain this decision?

The key issue in many of these questions is your personal accountability to all stakeholders. A 2000 National Business Ethics Survey conducted by the Ethics Resource Center found that, in comparison with a similar survey conducted in 1994, employees are more likely to report observed misconduct and they are more satisfied with their firms' handling of that report and the misconduct itself. If you were to observe misconduct, would you report it? What factors might influence your decision?

BUSINESS ETHICS AND DECISION MAKING IN PRACTICE

When questioned regarding the forces that contribute to unethical decision making in working life, managers point to the behavior of their superiors and the nature of company policy regarding wrongdoing. Hence, we assume that an organization committed to ethical quality can institute some structures and procedures to encourage decency. Codes of conduct are a common corporate ethics tool (discussed in further detail in Chapter 3). But the question remains: Can we somehow encourage ethical behavior and the consideration of stakeholders on the part of managerial decision makers?

As mentioned earlier, ethics is but one mode of decision making in the corporate environment. Is it possible to persuade corporate managers that ethics *should* be the basis of their decisions? Of course, if ethical behavior *always* led to higher profits as well as higher-quality products or services, the market would take care of everything. The ethical businessperson would be more likely to succeed than the unethical businessperson. However, while higher ethics may lead to higher profits (see Chapter 3), it does not *always* do so. We have all heard tales of those who successfully avoided responsibility for their unethical acts, while reaping millions in the meantime; or of those that actually go to jail for wrongful conduct, only to have their millions restored to them upon their release. As long as there is some perceived benefit to unethical behavior, some decision makers may be persuaded to leave their ethics at the door.

The Institute for Business, Technology and Ethics suggests the following "Nine Good Reasons" to run a business ethically:

1. Litigation/indictment avoidance
2. Regulatory freedom
3. Public acceptance
4. Investor confidence
5. Supplier/partner trust
6. Customer loyalty
7. Employee performance

8. Personal pride
9. It's right[6]

Modern theories of economics and ethics may also prove useful in understanding and encouraging ethical behavior in business. Consider the implications of a lawless system, where we relied solely on market forces to encourage behavior. Would companies be unleashed to act in unethical ways, or would there be any reason to believe that companies would refrain from wrongful conduct (or conduct we considered wrongful, since no law would be broken)? Does the market ensure fairness? Justice? Some scholars believe that the marketplace does foster ethical and honest behavior. It is argued that there is some market value to honesty and ethics—that consumers reward firms that are straight with them, firms in which they can place their trust. Consider drugstore giant Walgreen's adage, "The Pharmacy America Trusts," or Johnson & Johnson's, "Trust in Tampax." Truth might be the best policy, as the Roman philosopher Seneca noted that "time discovers truth."[7]

Economists Dwight Lee and Richard McKenzie support this contention. They explain that a businessperson may act honestly because of the high costs of dishonesty.[8] This is not to say that a businessperson cannot profit through dishonesty, simply that the risks/potential costs of dishonesty are higher than those of honesty.

> . . . [I]n addition to being a virtue from a strictly moral perspective, honesty is also important for quite instrumental reasons. An economy in which people deal with each other honestly produces more wealth than one in which people are chronically dishonest because more exchanges occur directing resources into their most productive employments.[9]

An earlier perspective is offered by St. Augustine in his treatise, "On Lying," where he explains "when regard for truth has been broken down or even slightly weakened, all things will remain doubtful."[10]

On the other hand, should *all* behavior be regulated, in every situation? Should fairness and justice be completely legislated? Recently, states have enacted laws prohibiting driver's licenses to individuals who failed to pay their family support. This was considered to be a crossover of law and behavioral justice. Paying family support really has nothing to do with whether one should be able to drive in that state; however, the state is using its muscle to persuade behavior it considers "right." In addition, in an effort to prevent even the appearance of impropriety, states have enacted conflict of interest statutes in connection with public workers. These statutes prohibit activities that might *lead* to or give the appearance of wrongful conduct, even where none exists.

Ethics demands the integrity to act according to our personal values as well as accountability for each decision that we make in our lives according to those values. ("Great

---

[6]Institute for Business, Technology and Ethics, *Ethix,* no. 22 (March/April 2002), p. 11.

[7]F. Richard Ciccone, "Truth and the American Way," *Chicago Tribune,* May 12, 1996, sec. 2, p. 8.

[8]Dwight Lee and Richard McKenzie, "How the Marketplace Fosters Business Honesty," *Business & Society Review,* Winter 1995, pp. 5–9.

[9]*Ibid.*, p. 5.

[10]St. Augustine, "On Lying," cited in Sissela Bok, *Lying: Moral Choice in Public and Private Life* (New York: Vintage Books, 1999).

minds don't think alike; they think for themselves!") If someone were asked to choose between allowing a loved one to die by following the law, or breaking the law in order to allow him or her to live, many may be willing to break the law. Their justification might be
"I had no choice—I had to do it to save my mother/brother/father/sister, etc." The truth is
that we all have choices. If you are asked to choose between terminating a subordinate or
losing your job, you might fire the worker, claiming, "I have no choice but to do this. Sorry."
In fact, you would have a choice—terminate the subordinate or lose your job. You may not
like the alternatives offered, but it is a choice nonetheless.

As a student or as an employee or employer, you face a variety of alternatives. It will
be up to you to determine the course of your actions. In a well-publicized case involving
the Electrical Manufacturers firm, recent college graduates were found guilty of conspiring
to fix prices and otherwise violate the antitrust statutes. In response to questions about their
guilt, the young employees claimed, "I got out of school and this was how it was done."
Does that explain the behavior to you? Consider how you would feel if you were (or had
been) asked to do something with which you were uncomfortable during your first year of
work. Do you think you would refuse? Would you quit? Of course, your response probably
depends on the nature of the request, but questioning accepted business practice is difficult,
no matter the cost.

Similarly, in her rather infamous short story, "The Lottery," author Shirley Jackson describes a small town where every citizen draws lots to see who will be subject to a stoning.
Why do these individuals participate in such an arcane annual ritual? Perhaps particularly
because it is a ritual, an accepted manner of practice in that town's culture and those who
do not participate may suffer greater woes. Of course, we would all like to believe that we
would never participate in such an event; but consider all of the rituals in which you do participate that perhaps you would not if you considered them more deeply.

In a 1991 study, researchers determined that business undergraduate students are the
most likely to have cheated on a test, when compared to pre-law students and the general
population.[11] In response to a statement claiming that *not* cheating is the best way to get
ahead in the long run, business students claimed, "This is the 90s. You snooze, you lose."[12]
Does this mean that, perhaps, there is a failure in ethics in the business arena because the
people who go into business already cheat? Or is it that business students are aware that the
business arena demands this type of unethical conduct so they prepare themselves for it
from the start? Competitiveness might blur the border between ethical and unethical. Either
way, as our parents once told us, simply because an environment is replete with a certain
type of behavior does not mean that we must follow suit, nor does it relieve us of our responsibility for actions in that environment ("If Janie jumps off a bridge, are you going to
follow," they would say).

---

[11]Rick Tetzeli, "Business Students Cheat Most," *Fortune,* July 1, 1991, p. 14. See also research of James Stearns and Shaheen Borna
that found that MBA students were more likely to cheat than convicted felons. "A Comparison of the Ethics of Convicted Felons and
Graduate Business Students: Implications for Business Practice and Business Ethics Education," *Teaching Business Ethics* 2 (1998),
pp. 175–95.
[12]Tetzeli, "Business Students Cheat Most," p. 18.

It may be telling regarding your future decision-making choices whether you believe that you will be held accountable for your actions, whether you believe that you will be caught, or more esoterically, whether you believe that "the world is out to get you," "you should do whatever you can to get ahead," "everyone cheats," "honest people lose in the end," or other cynical doctrines. Are these the type of people with whom you work, or for whom you work? Are these types of individuals more or less likely to act unethically? To be accountable for their actions? In the readings that follow, a variety of perspectives are offered in connection with this concept of free choice and accountability.

UNDERSTANDING PERCEPTUAL DIFFERENCES AND VARYING PERSPECTIVES: A DECISION-MAKING MODEL

Throughout this text, one are asked to reach your own conclusions and judgments in connection with ethical issues and dilemmas. In earlier sections, we have discussed a variety of models for decision making that may prove fruitful in this effort. In this section, several readings more specifically explain and/or highlight the multiperspectival approach that will be taken throughout the text.

The text presents you with a variety of perspectives in connection with each topic area or business ethics. The basis for this approach is the theory, first propounded by philosopher Ed Freeman, called "stakeholder analysis." Stakeholder theory asks a decision maker to consider, in reaching a decision, the interests of each individual or entity that holds a stake in that decision or who will be affected by the decision. The model of this approach was discussed earlier in the section on moral reasoning.

To consider the stakeholders of a decision, it is critical to be able to understand the interests of each party, to be able to empathetically evaluate what the potential impact on that stakeholder will be and what the stakeholders' perspective on the decision is likely to be. This is not as easy as it may first appear. For instance, one might not necessarily understand all of the parties who might be impacted, or one might not completely understand the nature of each party's interest, or even the effect the decision will have in the end.

> *It is often difficult for those who look on the tradition of the Red Man from the outside or through the "educated" mind to understand that no object is what it appears to be, but it is simply the pale shadow of a Reality. It is for this reason that every created object is* wakan, *holy and has a power according to the loftiness of the spiritual reality it reflects. The Indian humbles himself before the whole of creation because all visible things were created before him and, being older than he, deserve respect.*[13]

Several readings included in this section offer a practical application of stakeholder theory. For instance, the seminal business ethics case "The Parable of the Sadhu" offers a specific analysis of the interests and motivations of each decision maker in the parable.

---

[13]From a letter written by Joseph Epes Brown, quoted in Schuon, *The Feathered Sun,* 47, cited in Huston Smith, *The World's Religions* (San Francisco: HarperSanFrancisco, 1991), p. 379.

Werhane's "The Rashomon Effect" offers a similar demonstration in connection with the Ford Pinto case, a classic business ethics dilemma. Finally, an interpretation of Dow Corning's experience with silicone implants is included in an effort to illustrate how ethicists have viewed potentially unethical behavior. In reading later segments of this text, try to contemplate the variety of perspectives that may be offered on the same topic and consider your response only after evaluating the anticipated perspectives of each stakeholder in connection with the issue.

JUST BECAUSE IT'S LEGAL, IS IT ETHICAL?

—JEFFREY SEGLIN

Often business decision makers seek answers to ethical dilemmas from the law. However, as scholar and journalist Jeffrey Seglin discusses in the following article, the law is not always the appropriate oracle.

It's very possible for an owner or manager of a company to make a perfectly legal decision without ever exploring the ethical aspects of the decision. That's not to suggest that making a decision that is legal is inherently unethical. It's just that sometimes the law gives us an excuse to ignore whether the action we are taking is right or wrong.

The bankruptcy laws in the United States are a perfect example. In theory, they're a wonderful tool that give troubled business owners the opportunity to turn their businesses around rather than go under. When a company files for protection under chapter 11 of the bankruptcy code, it can keep its creditors at bay while it tries to work out a plan to reorganize itself so it can overcome its financial troubles. In theory, this is a good thing, because if the business emerges from chapter 11 protection rather than liquidating its assets in a chapter 7 bankruptcy filing, the chances are that creditors will ultimately be paid and the company itself will continue to contribute to the economy by creating jobs, paying taxes and engaging in commerce.

There "are many reasons why a business gets sick, but they don't necessarily mean it should be destroyed," observes Judge James A. Goodman, the chief bankruptcy judge for the district of Maine. Hundreds of thousands of businesses that at one time or another had financial difficulties survive today as the result of chapter 11 proceedings. They continue to contribute to employment, tax revenues and overall growth. It's counterproductive to destroy the business value of an asset by liquidating it and paying it out in a chapter 7 if that company shows signs of being able to recover in a reorganization. As for creditors, one of the provisions of the bankruptcy code is that in order for a reorganization to be confirmed, the creditor must get not less than he or she would have gotten in a chapter 7 liquidation. So why not go through with the reorganization?[1]

Judge Goodman argues that in spite of the fact that 80% of businesses that file chapter 11 protection never make it out of bankruptcy, the fact that 20% do makes the bankruptcy laws all the more worthwhile.

"If a doctor had a 20% success rate with terminal cancer cases, you'd say, 'That's incredible!' Well, that's what we've got—companies that are terminal. We take the nearly dead and show them how to operate better, and one-fifth survive. What's wrong with that?" the judge asks.

The fact that there are roughly 1.4 million bankruptcy filings a year hasn't helped calm the perception that bankruptcy is being used as a shield to keep those who owe from paying back those who are owed. But the reality is that, of those 1.4 million filings, the vast majority are personal filings rather than business filings.

According to the American Bankruptcy Institute, while the number of bankruptcies filed from October 1, 1997, to September 30, 1998, was up 5.1% over the previous year and hit a record number of 1,436,964, the vast majority of those—96.7%—were personal filings. Business bankruptcy filings actually decreased by 15.1% from the previous year to 47,125.[2]

Regardless of the numbers, the perception remains that the number of businesses hiding behind bankruptcy laws rather than repaying their debts is epidemic. Those who are involved closely in such cases, like Judge Goodman, argue that this perception is not accurate.

"Of course there are abuses," says Judge Goodman, "but in my opinion having been on the bench as a judge for 17 years and having practiced bankruptcy law for 20 years before that, the percentage of abuses is minimal. It's almost nil."[3]

But when a company fails, does the owner of that business have an ethical responsibility beyond the laws to make good on all of his debts, even if it means paying back creditors after the business has ceased operations? After all, after a company owner liquidates the assets of his business under chapter 7 bankruptcy protection and uses whatever proceeds are raised to pay off debtors, he can turn around and start a new company without ever paying off the people or businesses he owed money to when the prior company went bust.

Or are the bankruptcy laws, which forgive the business owner from the responsibility of paying back all that is owed, enough punishment? While it's perfectly legal to go out and start a new business without regard for past debts owed, some owners have made the decision that that's not enough, that they have a responsibility to make good on their past debts. And sometimes, the whole question gets mucked up in what side of the owing fence you're on.

ARE LAWS ABSOLUTION FROM HAVING TO THINK?

Forget whether or not you should have the responsibility to pay back your debts for a moment. The whole area of bankruptcy protection raises a far more interesting issue. And that's that it's a prime example of how laws and regulations, however well-intentioned, have resulted in a nation of business owners who are forgiven from having to think through the implications of their actions. If the law allows such and such behavior, the argument goes, then that's what I'm obligated to do—no more, no less.

Well, fine. But somewhere along the line, were business owners absolved from having to do some hard thinking on what their actions might mean? What they might say to the business community? What they might say about us and how we want to be perceived? Remember, this business community is likely one in which, post-dead company, you're going to be operating for a long, long time.

Now, don't get me wrong. I'm not suggesting that the laws are wrong or that after thinking through the meaning of your actions you might not decide to do precisely the same thing as you would have done had you just blindly followed the letter of the law.

When did we become a nation of people like Ilsa in the movie *Casablanca,* who looks longingly into Rick's eyes and sighs, "You'll have to do the thinking for both of us." Please. Just because the law makes it so doesn't mean we shouldn't have to think long and hard about our actions, just as we'd do in any other aspect of our business.

Be real, I can hear you saying it. (Or thinking it silently to yourself as you roll your eyes.) Who wants to sit around and participate in self-flagellation sessions where you go over in painful detail everything you owe to everybody you've disappointed—your customers, your vendors, your employees, your creditors and not least, yourself? Especially when you're in the midst of something as painful as losing your business and everything you built? I can think of few takers for the role. It's only when you're on the other side of the fence—when you're one of the ones being stiffed—that you spend time wondering loudly why the bankrupt business owner doesn't think about doing the right thing.

That's pretty much what happened to Daniel J. Driscoll, the owner of Darlyn Development Corp., a $4 million general contracting company in Marlboro, Massachusetts, when he found himself looking at the cover of the November 1995 issue of *Inc.* magazine. There, staring out from the cover with a plate of roasted chicken with all the fixings was George Naddaff, the entrepreneur who discovered Boston Chicken, at the time a fast-growing restaurant franchise success story that in 1993 had become one of the hottest public offerings on record.[4]

Mr. Driscoll was incensed. So he took pen to paper and wrote the magazine a letter. In part, he wrote: "While I find it wonderfully motivating that one business can flourish because of the ideas and actions of Mr. George Naddaff, I also find it infuriating that the same man could flaunt to the business world that he had $14 million to invest in a new venture, when he has not paid small businessmen like myself for his business ventures that failed." When asked about that failed venture in that November 1995 article, Naddaff told *Inc.* senior editor Joshua Hyatt: "I'd like to forget about it."[5]

"Why should a man who has all the money he did be able to walk away from a million-dollar debt?" Driscoll asked. "They should make it illegal. If you have the funds to pay your debt, then you shouldn't be able to walk away. . . . When he realized that his concept wasn't going to be the next Boston Chicken, he pulled the plug on it and fucked everybody."[6]

Naddaff and his partners at Olde World Bakeries, the corporation which owned Coffee by George, had invested roughly $5 million in the drive-through coffee kiosk concept before they realized it wasn't going to work. They decided to liquidate the business and arrived at an agreement to pay their creditors roughly 30 cents of every dollar that was owed. Driscoll was one of the creditors who had agreed to the payout.

Driscoll may have agreed to the payout, but he was none too pleased that it ever came to having to make this choice. What bothered Driscoll had nothing to do with whether Naddaff followed the law. Driscoll doesn't doubt that he did. But in spite of the fact that what Naddaff did was legal, Driscoll thinks he shouldn't have gotten off as easily as he did. Since Naddaff had the resources from his personal wealth or his other business dealings to make good on his debts, Driscoll believes that he should have been made to pay back his creditors in whole.

GOING BEYOND WHAT THE LAW REQUIRES

Regardless of the fact that the laws about how much of your personal assets are protected when a company goes out of business vary from state to state, some business owners who have been in the same position as Naddaff say that they believe the right thing to do in such circumstances is to go beyond what's required by the law to make good on your debts.

In 1985, Hawkeye Pipe Services Inc., a manufacturer of pipes for oil rigs, went out of business. Its founder, Bill Bartmann, owed more than $1 million to creditors. But Bartmann says he decided not to reach a liquidation agreement as Naddaff had with creditors. Nor did he file for bankruptcy. Instead, he decided that he would pay back all the money he owed, no matter how long it took him to do so.

"I was born and raised in Iowa, and back in the Calvinistic Puritan Protestant work ethic kind of environment, you were supposed to pay your bills," says Bartmann, who went on to found Commercial Financial Services Inc. (CFS), which in 1998, was a roughly $1 billion debt-collection company based in Tulsa, Oklahoma. "It just seemed inherently wrong to try to escape by using a law—granted, it was a valid law and I am a lawyer—as an escape hatch or excuse. It just didn't seem the proper thing to do."

After he closed the doors on Hawkeye Pipe Services, Bartmann says it took him two and a half years to pay everyone back in full. But he says he did.

"You know the American capitalistic system is the neatest on the globe," says Bartmann. "It's a wonderful environment to allow people to go out and assume the risks and rewards of life. Now, people understand the reward side very easily. I don't think they understand the reciprocal side is that they should be obligated to pay the piper if indeed there are any assets with which to do that. The question is do they have a responsibility beyond the legal requirements?"

In October 1998, an anonymous letter was written to CFS's bond ratings agencies which questioned CFS's collection rates. Bond ratings were pulled and CFS was cut off from that source of revenues. Bartmann resigned as CEO in late October 1998 and on December 11, the company filed for bankruptcy protection. Bartmann continued going into the office every day as a consultant for the company for the fee of $1 per year. But by late January, according to local press reports, he sent an e-mail to CFS employees saying that his daily presence at the company "had the potential of creating a conflict in how the company is run." In late June, it was reported that employees were notified by e-mail that the company was closing its doors. It remains to be seen if Bartmann has any intention to make sure that all of the debtors owed money by CFS are paid back in full should the company not reemerge from bankruptcy protection.[7]

Chris Graff is another company founder who thinks company owners have a responsibility that goes beyond what the law requires. Or, at least he believed he did. Graff is the President of Marque Inc., a successful ambulance manufacturer based in Goshen, Ind. But in a previous business, Graff didn't have such good fortune.

His furniture-making business, Geste Corp., went out of business in 1989. Graff auctioned off the company's assets, but, he says, "After the auction, I didn't have everybody paid off. I was about 10 grand short. So I went to work and paid it back out of my income." Graff says it took him roughly four months to pay back the money that was still owed.

"I guess it's just a moral or ethical issue for me," he says. "When we make a decision to do something, we should be able to explain that decision in the same way to anybody who asks, be it our spouse, our business partner, an employee, a creditor, or a customer. I have to sleep at night."

Beyond their take on whether it was moral or not, Bartmann and Graff were oblivious to the fact that their efforts to pay back their creditors all the money owed could have very practical aspects to it. "I understand how people view bankruptcy," said Bartmann. "I guess I rationalized it pretty quickly that although I was eligible to take the easy cure, to do so would forever taint me with that stigma."

As a result of going through the difficult chore of paying back all the money he owed his creditors, when Bartmann was trying to secure working capital for CFS, he used his earlier act as reassurance that "lending me money now again is the safest risk you're ever going to take."

REFERENCES

1. Robert A. Mamis, "Why Bankruptcy Works," *Inc.,* October 1996: 39.
2. "Bankruptcies Break Another Record During 12-Month Period Ending Sept.," November 23, 1998. Posted on American Bankruptcy website at www.abiworld.org.
3. Interview by the author with Judge James A. Goodman, January 1998.
4. In what seems to be a classic example of what goes around comes around, Boston Chicken filed for chapter 11 bankruptcy protection in October 1998. By the time of the filing, George Naddaff was not with the management team running the company. *See* Mike Hofman, "Boston Chicken Files Ch. 11 as Troubles Come Home to Roost," *Inc.* Online, October 7, 1998.
5. Joshua Hyatt, "The Next Big Thing," *Inc.,* November 1995: 62.
6. Jeffrey L. Seglin, "Brother, Can You Spare 30 Cents on the Dollar?" *Inc.,* April 1998. The case study told here was originally told in a different form in this article in *Inc.* magazine. Unless noted otherwise, while the telling of the story is new, the quotes from the subjects in this case are drawn from this article.
7. Shaun Schafer, "CFS Still Looks for Buyers," *Tulsa World,* January 27, 1999; and Julie Bryant, "Founder of CFS Won't Be in Office," January 22, 1999. Also: Clytie Bunyan and Andy Parsons, "You've Got No Job, E-Mail Says," *The Daily Oklahoman,* June 24, 1999.

IT SEEMS RIGHT IN THEORY BUT DOES IT WORK IN PRACTICE?

—NORM BOWIE

Can these theories work? Can theories guide business decision makers toward more ethical decisions? Often students and others who explore concepts of business ethics in connection with their application to the "real world" contend that these values work only in theory and not at all in practice. Consider Norm Bowie's defense of the discipline.

I have frequently used these arguments with executives who may find them theoretically persuasive, but who, nonetheless, think their practical implication is limited. They point out that in the real world in which business actually operates not everyone breaks contracts and not everyone freeloads. Some do but not all. Knowing that, isn't it to the strategic advantage of the firm to be the one who does break contracts or otherwise freeloads? After all, in terms of pure self-interest, the best world for a person or firm is one where everyone else plays by the rules except one, isn't it?

In asking that question I point out that one is no longer asking a question of ethics (the executives are already convinced that theoretically such activity is wrong), but rather a prudential question of strategy. Although Kant would feel no need to answer it, Kantian-type arguments can be brought to bear on the prudential question. The common approach of these arguments is to show that the self-defeating nature of actions based on maxims that cannot be universalized cut in long before complete universalization would take place. That was the point with my Georgetown student example. The fact that Georgetown students bounced more checks than the rest of the population did not bring about the collapse of payment by check. But it did for Georgetown students who did business in the proximity of Georgetown University.

What is significant but often overlooked by philosophers is that Kant's universalizability formulation of the categorical imperative is subject to empirical support. In some ways that should not be surprising. If someone tries to create a round square we can predict that no one will succeed. Similarly, if stealing or cheating when universalized is conceptually incoherent, then we would expect the collapse of certain institutions and practices if stealing or cheating became universal in our society, or at the very least those institutions would not be available for a subset of society. Now we do not have a case of universalized cheating any more than we have a case of absolute zero or a perfect vacuum. But we do have close approximations. We can empirically observe that Kantian-type effects take place when actions whose maxims cannot be universalized reach a certain threshold. We began the chapter by providing examples of what happens to credit when people do not pay their bills. A Kantian could predict that if enough checks of seafood customers bounce, the seafood store will stop taking checks. She could also predict that if people do not repay loans, the banks will fail.

There are positive stories that illustrate Kant's point as well. That is, there are stories showing that when a threshold of morality is reached, certain institutions become possible and, when economically feasible, will develop. Russia is in the process of starting a stock exchange. The difficulties in doing so, however, have been great, in part because company spokespersons would not provide accurate financial information about their companies. As a Kantian would expect, investors will not be forthcoming if they believe that the members of the exchange lie about their companies. Gradually, a few companies including Irkutsk Energo, Bratsky LPK and Rostelecom were able to establish a reputation as truthtellers. These companies were then able to attract investors and have done well. *The Wall Street Journal* put it this way:

> When the chief engineer of Irkutsk Energo addressed a gathering of 250 Western fund managers last March, he gave a straightforward presentation of the Russian utility's assets, liabilities and investment policy. This was anything but typical in Russia where enterprises usually withhold even basic information from investors. . . . This winter (1995) a few mavericks proved the value of corporate glasnost. As these companies drew foreign interest, others followed. Of the 50 most actively traded Russian companies, 10 are ardently wooing foreign investors. Last year there were two. . . . "There is a clear differentiation in the market between those companies that get it and those that don't," says Nancy Curtin, head of the Emerging Europe funds for Baring Asset Management.

In trying to establish a stock market, the Russians faced the problem that lying about the finances of the firm was perceived to be nearly universal. As a Kantian would expect, so long as the perception was held, Russian society could not have a stock market that reflected the rational values of the firms. Since investors knew that the information about the firms was false, there was no alternative way for them to get a reasonable figure about a firm's value. (Thus, the Securities and Exchange Commission provides a genuine contribution in the USA because it forces firms to be more truthful.) However, once a sufficient number of firms were perceived as being truthful about their finances, the stock prices of those firms rose rapidly to reflect rational expectations of the firms' worth.

And the success of these honest firms has led other firms to be more honest, to the point where the Russian stock market is thriving. The March 24, 1997, *Business Week* carried a story entitled "The Rush to Russia." In 1996 the Russian stock market was up 127% and it had already gained 65% in 1997. Of course, more honesty on the part of Russian companies is not the explanation for the rise in the stock market. Rather, sufficient honesty is a necessary condition for there to be a stock market at all.

As an aside, business ethicists are often asked how a business that wishes to be ethical should behave when other businesses are clearly behaving unethically. These executives would like to be ethical but believe they would be at a competitive disadvantage if they were ethical. And sometimes they would be. But, as our example of the Russian stock market shows, sometimes a firm has a clear competitive advantage if it is ethical when most other firms are not. Nearly all of us have horror stories to tell about auto-repair shops. Suffice it to say that the industry does not have a good reputation. Think of how successful an auto-repair shop would be if it had a reputation for honesty. This point is not merely theoretical. In Bloomington, Minnesota, I dealt with a devout Christian who left the repair facility of a major dealer to open his own repair facility. I was one of his first customers. I could call in the morning and get my car fixed that day. Within a year, I might have to wait nearly a week because he was so busy. In relating these positive examples, I am not arguing that one ought to be honest because it pays. I am pointing out that sometimes as a matter of fact it does. More remarkably in some cases it pays the most when most other competitors are not honest. Sometimes, contrary to popular opinion, the best competitive position for one is when all (or a large number of) your competitors are perceived to be (or are) dishonest and you are and are perceived to be honest. My car repairman in Minnesota occupies just that world.

The force of failure to follow the categorical imperative can be found in business practices themselves. Both the strategy literature and the popular business press extol the virtues of strategic alliances. In an era where companies are urged to focus on their core competencies (those things which they do most effectively), strategic alliances have become a crucial part of doing business. The Kantian moral philosopher would urge her firm to avoid alliances with firms that are not moral in Kant's sense, i.e., they constantly practice business according to maxims that are not universalizable, e.g., they lie or cheat. Why would a firm want to partner with another firm that lies and cheats, especially when all members of a partnership are jointly and severally liable for the product they jointly produce?

Supplier problems are not unique to the economies emerging from communism. Failure to heed Kant's dictum that a self-contradictory maxim cannot be universalized has created tremendous problems for General Motors and Volkswagen. General Motors promoted Jose Ignacio Lopez de Arroirtua (Lopez) on the basis of his success in lowering the cost of supplier products. His success in this area arose primarily through his practice of continually reopening negotiations with suppliers and providing the proprietary information of one supplier to other suppliers so that these suppliers could provide the product more cheaply. A morally sensitive person would characterize these activities as lying and stealing respectively. As we have shown, the maxims that permit lying and stealing cannot be universalized. Thus, what Lopez did was wrong.

And General Motors made an imprudent decision in promoting him. Is it any surprise that Lopez left GM for the German company Volkswagen, allegedly taking with him several associates and many cartons of GM's proprietary purchasing data? Furthermore, is it any surprise that, in a recent survey, the suppliers of auto parts rated GM worst of all the automakers? How will GM fare as it enters what *Fortune* calls the new economy where cars cost less because the auto industry relies more on cheaper high-quality suppliers? The strategic advice is that manufacturers should partner with their suppliers. But why would a supplier want to partner with a manufacturer that has promoted someone who lied and stole from them?

To strengthen this point, the November 25, 1996, issue of *Business Week* indicates that Lopez's former dealings with suppliers of GM have brought similar problems to Volkswagen.

Lopez is expected to be charged by German prosecutors with the theft of trade secrets. Meanwhile in the USA, GM began legal action against Volkswagen CEO Ferdinand Piech and other company executives for up to $4 billion in damages. On November 29, 1996, the Volkswagen Board accepted Lopez's "resignation." Shortly thereafter GM and Volkswagen reached a settlement, but Lopez's problems in both the USA and Germany remain.

In arguing that sound ethical business practices can support a positive bottom line, I am not arguing that this is always the case. Sometimes ethics does not pay but costs. In those cases Kantian morality requires that a business firm do what is ethically required even if it does not pay. However, I hope I have shown that doing what is morally required is not always unprofitable. Sometimes being moral enhances the bottom line rather than reduces it.

In summary, I have tried to show how Kant's universalizability formulation of the categorical imperative can be used to test the moral legitimacy of contemplated actions in business. In using that test we have an argument as to why certain actions like the breaking of contracts, stealing and competing unfairly are morally wrong. We have also seen that if immoral actions such as those cited cross a critical threshold, the business institutions that presuppose norms of truthfulness and fairness will become unstable and in extreme circumstances even cease to exist. Furthermore, through the use of numerous examples I have tried to show that Kant's arguments are of more than theoretical interest. They have predictable real-world applications.

THE ONE-MINUTE MORALIST

—ROBERT SOLOMON

Solomon posits a question that will be asked again and again by authors throughout this text: Does ethics in business lead to profits? Is good ethics good for business?

Once there was a bright young businessman who was looking for an ethical manager.

He wanted to work for one. He wanted to become one.

His search had taken him over many years to the far corners of the business world.

He visited small businesses and large corporations.

He spoke with used-car dealers, chief executive officers of Fortune 500 companies, management-science professors, vice presidents for strategic planning and one-minute managers.

He visited every kind of office, big and small, carpeted and tiled, some with breathtaking views, some without any view at all.

He heard a full spectrum of ethical views.

But he wasn't pleased with what he heard.

On the one hand, virtually everyone he met seemed frank, friendly and courteous, adamant about honesty even to the point of moral indignation. People were respectful of one another, concerned about their employees and loyal to their own superiors. They paid their debts and resented the lawsuits in which they considered themselves the innocent party, victims of misunderstanding and antibusiness sentiment. They complained about regulation and the implied distrust of their integrity. They proudly asserted that they were producing quality products or services that truly did satisfy consumer demand, making the world a better—even if only a very slightly better—place in which to live.

Their superiors were proud of their trustworthiness.

Their subordinates were confident of their fairness.

But, on the other hand, when they were asked for their views about ethics and business, what all of these people had to say was startling, to say the least.

The answers varied only slightly.

"You have to understand that it's a jungle out there!"

"Listen, I'm a survivor."

"If I don't do it, the other guy will."

"You've got to be realistic in this business."

"Profits—that's what it's all about. You do whatever you have to."

"The One-Minute Moralist," from *The New World of Business.* Reprinted by permission of Rowman & Littlefield Publishers.

And when our bright young businessman brought up the topic of business ethics, he invariably heard:

"There aren't any ethics in business"; or . . .

"*Business Ethics*—the shortest book in the world."

The latter usually with a grin.

At the same time, however, many executives shook their heads sadly and expressed the private wish that it were otherwise.

He met a few unscrupulous businessmen who admitted cutting corners, who had made a profit and were proud of it.

He met others who had cut corners and were caught. "This is a cutthroat world," they insisted, often contradicting this immediately by complaining about the injustice of being singled out themselves.

He met several self-proclaimed "ethical managers" who insisted that everyone who worked for them—and of course they themselves—had to be Perfectly Virtuous, to the letter of the Moral Law.

These managers' subordinates generally despised them, and their departments were rife with resentment. More than one employee complained about autocratic management and dogmatic ineffectiveness; a philosophical assistant manager pointed out the difference between morality and moralizing. Almost everyone pointed out that the principles that were so precisely printed out in both memos and plaques above their desks were usually impossible to apply to any real ethical issues. Their primary effect was rather to cast a gray shadow of suspected hypocrisy over everyday business life.

Our bright young businessman was discouraged. He could not understand why the conscientious, sociable, civilized, thoroughly ethical flesh-and-blood managers he met in the office talked in their off moments like the most cynical prophets of corporate Darwinism.

The flesh-and-blood managers complained that the public did not appreciate them.

The cynical prophets joked, "There are no ethics in business," and then wondered why people didn't trust them.

Our bright young businessman was perplexed: Could there be ethics in the real business world? he wondered. Were compromises and cut corners inevitable? he asked. Did the untrammeled pursuit of virtue have to be either hypocrisy or damaging to the bottom line, as he now feared?

And then he met the One-Minute Moralist.

The bright young businessman presented the One-Minute Moralist with his dilemma. The One-Minute Moralist answered him without hesitation.

"You don't understand ethics," he said. "And you don't understand business either.

"You set up an absurd dichotomy between ethical absolutism and the so-called real world, and then you wonder how ethics can possibly be at home in business, and whether business can function without cutting corners and making uneasy compromises. But cutting corners presumes that there are sharply delineated corners. And talking so uneasily of compromise (that is, compromising one's moral principles rather than compromising with other people) seems to assume that ethics consists of engraved principles rather than relations between people who (more or less) share values and interests.

"But ethics isn't a set of absolute principles, divorced from and imposed on everyday life. Ethics is a way of life, a seemingly delicate but in fact very strong tissue of endless adjustments and compromises. It is the awareness that one is an intrinsic part of a social order, in which the interests of others and one's own interests are inevitably intertwined. And what is business, you should ask, if not precisely that awareness of what other people want and need, and how you yourself can prosper by providing it? Businesses great and small prosper because they respond to people, and fail when they do not respond. To talk about being 'totally ethical' and about 'uneasy compromises' is to misunderstand ethics. Ethics is the art of mutually agreeable tentative compromise. Insisting on absolute principles is, if I may be ironic, unethical.

"Business, on the other hand, has nothing to do with jungles, survivalism and Darwin, whatever the mechanisms of the market may be. The 'profit motive' is an offensive fabrication by people who were out to attack business, which has curiously—and self-destructively—been adopted by business people themselves. Business isn't a single-minded pursuit of profits; it is an *ethos,* a way of life. It is a way of life that is at its very foundation ethical. What is more central to business—any kind of business—than taking contracts seriously, paying one's debts, and coming to mutual agreements about what is a fair exchange? Ethics isn't superimposed on business. Business is itself an ethics, defined by ethics, made possible by ethics. Two hundred years ago, Benjamin Franklin insisted that business is the pursuit of virtue. If you find yourself wondering or doubting whether virtue is possible in business, I suggest you reexamine your ideas about business.

"If you want to talk about hypocrisy, by the way, it is not just to be found in such bloated phrases as 'the untrammeled pursuit of virtue.' There is just as much hypocrisy in the macho, mock-heroic insistence that business is a tough-minded, amoral struggle for survival and profits rather than a staid and established ethical enterprise.

"Now you've had your Minute. When you think about business and ethics, don't worry about whether one is possible along with the other. In America, at least, nothing is more ethical than good business."

A STAKEHOLDER THEORY OF THE MODERN CORPORATION

—R. Edward Freeman

Freeman delineates the basics of stakeholder theory and challenges the primacy of the shareholder in corporate decisions.

INTRODUCTION

Corporations have ceased to be merely legal devices through which the private business transactions of individuals may be carried on. Though still much used for this purpose, the corporate form has acquired a larger significance. The corporation has, in fact, become both a method of property tenure and a means of organizing economic life. Grown to tremendous proportions, there may be said to have evolved a "corporate system"—which has attracted to itself a combination of attributes and powers, and has attained a degree of prominence entitling it to be dealt with as a major social institution.[1]

Despite these prophetic words of Berle and Means (1932), scholars and managers alike continue to hold sacred the view that managers bear a special relationship to the stockholders in the firm. Since stockholders own shares in the firm, they have certain rights and privileges, which must be granted to them by management, as well as by others. Sanctions, in the form of "the law of corporations," and other protective mechanisms in the form of social custom, accepted management practice, myth and ritual, are thought to reinforce the assumption of the primacy of the stockholder.

The purpose of this paper is to pose several challenges to this assumption, from within the framework of managerial capitalism, and to suggest the bare bones of an alternative theory, *a stakeholder theory of the modern corporation.* I do not seek the demise of the modern corporation, either intellectually or in fact. Rather, I seek its transformation. In the words of Neurath, we shall attempt to "rebuild the ship, plank by plank, while it remains afloat."[2]

My thesis is that I can revitalize the concept of managerial capitalism by replacing the notion that managers have a duty to stockholders with the concept that managers bear a fiduciary relationship to stakeholders. Stakeholders are those groups who have a stake in or claim on the firm. Specifically I include suppliers, customers, employees, stockholders and

---

R. Edward Freeman, "A Stakeholder Theory of The Modern Corporation." Reprinted with permission of the author.

the local community, as well as management in its role as agent for these groups. I argue that the legal, economic, political and moral challenges to the currently received theory of the firm, as a nexus of contracts among the owners of the factors of production and customers, require us to revise this concept. That is, each of these stakeholder groups has a right not to be treated as a means to some end, and therefore must participate in determining the future direction of the firm in which they have a stake.

The crux of my argument is that we must reconceptualize the firm around the following question: For whose benefit and at whose expense should the firm be managed? I shall set forth such a reconceptualization in the form of a *stakeholder theory of the firm*. I shall then critically examine the stakeholder view and its implications for the future of the capitalist system.

THE ATTACK ON MANAGERIAL CAPITALISM
The Legal Argument

The basic idea of managerial capitalism is that in return for controlling the firm, management vigorously pursues the interests of stockholders. Central to the managerial view of the firm is the idea that management can pursue market transactions with suppliers and customers in an unconstrained manner.

The law of corporations gives a less clearcut answer to the question: In whose interest and for whose benefit should the modern corporation be governed? While it says that the corporations should be run primarily in the interests of the stockholders in the firm, it says further that the corporation exists "in contemplation of the law" and has personality as a "legal person," limited liability for its actions, and immortality, since its existence transcends that of its members. Therefore, directors and other officers of the firm have a fiduciary obligation to stockholders in the sense that the "affairs of the corporation" must be conducted in the interest of the stockholders. And stockholders can theoretically bring suit against those directors and managers for doing otherwise. But since the corporation is a legal person, existing in contemplation of the law, managers of the corporation are constrained by law.

Until recently, this was no constraint at all. In this century, however, the law has evolved to effectively constrain the pursuit of stockholder interests at the expense of other claimants on the firm. It has, in effect, required that the claims of customers, suppliers, local communities and employees be taken into consideration, though in general they are subordinated to the claims of stockholders.

For instance, the doctrine of "privity of contract," as articulated in *Winterbottom v. Wright* in 1842, has been eroded by recent developments in products liability law. Indeed, *Greenman v. Yuba Power* gives the manufacturer strict liability for damage caused by its products, even though the seller has exercised all possible care in the preparation and sale of the product and the consumer has not bought the product from nor entered into any contractual arrangement with the manufacturer. Caveat emptor has been replaced, in large part, with caveat venditor.[3] The Consumer Product Safety Commission has the power to enact product recalls, and in 1980 one U.S. automobile company recalled more cars than it built. Some industries are required to provide information to customers about a product's ingredients, whether or not the customers want and are willing to pay for this information.[4]

The same argument is applicable to management's dealings with employees. The National Labor Relations Act gave employees the right to unionize and to bargain in good faith. It set up the National Labor Relations Board to enforce these rights with management. The Equal Pay Act of 1963 and Title VII of the Civil Rights Act of 1964 constrain management from discrimination in hiring practices; these have been followed with the Age Discrimination in Employment Act of 1967.[5] The emergence of a body of administrative case law arising from labor-management disputes and the historic settling of discrimination claims with large employers such as AT&T have caused the emergence of a body of practice in the corporation that is consistent with the legal guarantee of the rights of the employees. The law has protected the due process rights of those employees who enter into collective bargaining agreements with management. As of the present, however, only 30% of the labor force are participating in such agreements; this has prompted one labor law scholar to propose a statutory law prohibiting dismissals of the 70% of the workforce not protected.[6]

The law has also protected the interests of local communities. The Clean Air Act and Clean Water Act have constrained management from "spoiling the commons." In an historic case, *Marsh v. Alabama,* the Supreme Court ruled that a company-owned town was subject to the provisions of the U.S. Constitution, thereby guaranteeing the rights of local citizens and negating the "property rights" of the firm. Some states and municipalities have gone further and passed laws preventing firms from moving plants or limiting when and how plants can be closed. In sum, there is much current legal activity in this area to constrain management's pursuit of stockholders' interests at the expense of the local communities in which the firm operates.

I have argued that the result of such changes in the legal system can be viewed as giving some rights to those groups that have a claim on the firm, for example, customers, suppliers, employees, local communities, stockholders and management. It raises the question, at the core of a theory of the firm: In whose interest and for whose benefit should the firm be managed? The answer proposed by managerial capitalism is clearly "the stockholders," but I have argued that the law has been progressively circumscribing this answer.

The Economic Argument

In its pure ideological form managerial capitalism seeks to maximize the interests of stockholders. In its perennial criticism of government regulation, management espouses the "invisible hand" doctrine. It contends that it creates the greatest good for the greatest number, and therefore government need not intervene. However, we know that externalities, moral hazards and monopoly power exist in fact, whether or not they exist in theory. Further, some of the legal apparatus mentioned above has evolved to deal with just these issues.

The problem of the "tragedy of the commons" or the free-rider problem pervades the concept of public goods such as water and air. No one has an incentive to incur the cost of cleanup or the cost of nonpollution, since the marginal gain of one firm's action is small.

Every firm reasons this way, and the result is pollution of water and air. Since the industrial revolution, firms have sought to internalize the benefits and externalize the costs of their actions. The cost must be borne by all, through taxation and regulation; hence we have the emergence of the environmental regulations of the 1970s.

Similarly, moral hazards arise when the purchaser of a good or service can pass along the cost of that good. There is no incentive to economize, on the part of either the producer or the consumer, and there is excessive use of the resources involved. The institutionalized practice of third-party payment in health care is a prime example.

Finally, we see the avoidance of competitive behavior on the part of firms, each seeking to monopolize a small portion of the market and not compete with one another. In a number of industries, oligopolies have emerged, and while there is questionable evidence that oligopolies are not the most efficient corporate form in some industries, suffice it to say that the potential for abuse of market power has again led to regulation of managerial activity. In the classic case, AT&T, arguably one of the great technological and managerial achievements of the century, was broken up into eight separate companies to prevent its abuse of monopoly power.

Externalities, moral hazards and monopoly power have led to more external control on managerial capitalism. There are de facto constraints, due to these economic facts of life, on the ability of management to act in the interests of stockholders.

A STAKEHOLDER THEORY OF THE FIRM
The Stakeholder Concept

Corporations have stakeholders, that is, groups and individuals who benefit from or are harmed by, and whose rights are violated or respected by, corporate actions. The concept of stakeholders is a generalization of the notion of stockholders, who themselves have some special claim on the firm. Just as stockholders have a right to demand certain actions by management, so do other stakeholders have a right to make claims. The exact nature of these claims is a difficult question that I shall address, but the logic is identical to that of the stockholder theory. Stakes require action of a certain sort, and conflicting stakes require methods of resolution.

Freeman and Reed (1983)[7] distinguish two senses of *stakeholder.* The "narrow definition" includes those groups who are vital to the survival and success of the corporation. The "wide definition" includes any group or individual who can affect or is affected by the corporation. I shall begin with a modest aim, to articulate a stakeholder theory using the narrow definition.

Stakeholders in the Modern Corporation

Figure 1 depicts the stakeholders in a typical large corporation. The stakes of each are reciprocal, since each can affect the other in terms of harms and benefits as well as rights and duties. The stakes of each are not univocal and would vary by particular corporation. I merely set forth some general notions that seem to be common to many large firms.

FIGURE 1

A Stakeholder Model of the Corporation

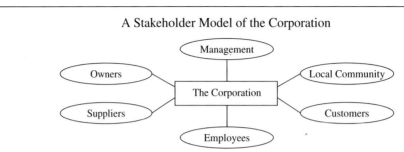

Owners have financial stake in the corporation in the form of stocks, bonds and so on, and they expect some kind of financial return from them. Either they have given money directly to the firm, or they have some historical claim made through a series of morally justified exchanges. The firm affects their livelihood or, if a substantial portion of their retirement income is in stocks or bonds, their ability to care for themselves when they can no longer work. Of course, the stakes of owners will differ by type of owner, preferences for money, moral preferences and so on, as well as by type of firm. The owners of AT&T are quite different from the owners of Ford Motor Company, with stock of the former company being widely dispersed among 3 million stockholders and that of the latter being held by a small family group as well as by a large group of public stockholders.

Employees have their jobs and usually their livelihood at stake; they often have specialized skills for which there is usually no perfectly elastic market. In return for their labor, they expect security, wages, benefits and meaningful work. In return for their loyalty, the corporation is expected to provide for them and carry them through difficult times. Employees are expected to follow the instructions of management most of the time, to speak favorably about the company, and to be responsible citizens in the local communities in which the company operates. Where they are used as means to an end, they must participate in decisions affecting such use. The evidence that such policies and values as described here lead to productive company-employee relationships is compelling. It is equally compelling to realize that the opportunities for "bad faith" on the part of both management and employees are enormous. "Mock participation" in quality circles, singing the company song, and wearing the company uniform solely to please management all lead to distrust and unproductive work.

Suppliers, interpreted in a stakeholder sense, are vital to the success of the firm, for raw materials will determine the final product's quality and price. In turn the firm is a customer of the supplier and is therefore vital to the success and survival of the supplier. When the firm treats the supplier as a valued member of the stakeholder network, rather than simply as a source of materials, the supplier will respond when the firm is in need. Chrysler traditionally had very close ties to its suppliers, even to the extent that led some to suspect the transfer of illegal payments. And when Chrysler was on the brink of disaster, the suppliers responded with price cuts, accepting late payments, financing and so on. Supplier and company can rise and fall together. Of course, again, the particular supplier relationships will depend on a number of variables such as the number of suppliers and whether the supplies are finished goods or raw materials.

Customers exchange resources for the products of the firm and in return receive the benefits of the products. Customers provide the lifeblood of the firm in the form of revenue. Given the level of reinvestment of earnings in large corporations, customers indirectly pay for the development of new products and services. Peters and Waterman (1982)[8] have argued that being close to the customer leads to success with other stakeholders and that a distinguishing characteristic of some companies that have performed well is their emphasis on the customer. By paying attention to customers' needs, management automatically addresses the needs of suppliers and owners. Moreover, it seems that the ethic of customer service carries over to the community. Almost without fail the "excellent companies" in Peters and Waterman's study have good reputations in the community. I would argue that Peters and Waterman have found multiple applications of Kant's dictum, "Treat persons as ends unto themselves," and it should come as no surprise that persons respond to such respectful treatment, be they customers, suppliers, owners, employees or members of the local community. The real surprise is the novelty of the application of Kant's rule in a theory of good management practice.

The local community grants the firm the right to build facilities and, in turn, it benefits from the tax base and economic and social contributions of the firm. In return for the provision of local services, the firm is expected to be a good citizen, as is any person, either "natural or artificial." The firm cannot expose the community to unreasonable hazards in the form of pollution, toxic waste and so on. If for some reason the firm must leave a community, it is expected to work with local leaders to make the transition as smoothly as possible. Of course, the firm does not have perfect knowledge, but when it discovers some danger or runs afoul of new competition, it is expected to inform the local community and to work with the community to overcome any problem. When the firm mismanages its relationship with the local community, it is in the same position as a citizen who commits a crime. It has violated the implicit social contract with the community and should expect to be distrusted and ostracized. It should not be surprised when punitive measures are invoked.

I have not included "competitors" as stakeholders in the narrow sense, since strictly speaking they are not necessary for the survival and success of the firm; the stakeholder theory works equally well in monopoly contexts. However, competitors and government would be the first to be included in an extension of this basic theory. It is simply not true that the interests of competitors in an industry are always in conflict. There is no reason why trade associations and other multiorganizational groups cannot band together to solve common problems that have little to do with how to restrain trade. Implementation of stakeholder management principles, in the long run, mitigates the need for industrial policy and an increasing role for government intervention and regulation.

The Role of Management

Management plays a special role, for it too has a stake in the modern corporation. On the one hand, management's stake is like that of employees, with some kind of explicit or implicit employment contract. But, on the other hand, management has a duty of safeguarding the welfare of the abstract entity that is the corporation. In short, management, especially top management, must look after the health of the corporation, and this involves balancing the multiple claims of conflicting stakeholders. Owners want higher financial returns, while customers want more money spent on research and development. Employees want higher wages and better benefits, while the local community wants better parks and day-care facilities.

The task of management in today's corporation is akin to that of King Solomon. The stakeholder theory does not give primacy to one stakeholder group over another, though there will surely be times when one group will benefit at the expense of others. In general, however, management must keep the relationships among stakeholders in balance. When these relationships become imbalanced, the survival of the firm is in jeopardy.

When wages are too high and product quality is too low, customers leave, suppliers suffer and owners sell their stocks and bonds, depressing the stock price and making it difficult to raise new capital at favorable rates. Note, however, that the reason for paying returns to owners is not that they "own" the firms, but that their support is necessary for the survival of the firm, and that they have a legitimate claim on the firm. Similar reasoning applies in turn to each stakeholder group.

A stakeholder theory of the firm must redefine the purpose of the firm. The stockholder theory claims that the purpose of the firm is to maximize the welfare of the stockholders, perhaps subject to some moral or social constraints, either because such maximization leads to the greatest good or because of property rights. The purpose of the firm is quite different in my view.

"The stakeholder theory" can be unpacked into a number of stakeholder theories, each of which has a "normative core," inextricably linked to the way that corporations should be governed and the way that managers should act. So, attempts to more fully define, or more carefully define, a stakeholder theory are misguided. Following Donaldson and Preston, I want to insist that the normative, descriptive, instrumental and metaphorical (my addition to their framework) uses of "stakeholder" are tied together in particular political constructions to yield a number of possible "stakeholder theories." "Stakeholder theory" is thus a genre of stories about how we could live. Let me be more specific.

A "normative core" of a theory is a set of sentences that includes among others, sentences like:

1. Corporations ought to be governed . . .
2. Managers ought to act to . . .

where we need arguments or further narratives which include business and moral terms to fill in the blanks. This normative core is not always reducible to a fundamental ground like the theory of property, but certain normative cores are consistent with modern understandings of property. Certain elaborations of the theory of private property plus the other institutions of political liberalism give rise to particular normative cores. But there are other institutions, other political conceptions of how society ought to be structured, so that there are different possible normative cores.

So, one normative core of a stakeholder theory might be a feminist standpoint, one rethinking how we would restructure "value-creating activity" along principles of caring and

EXHIBIT 1

A Reasonable Pluralism

	A. Corporations ought to be governed . . .	B. Managers ought to act . . .	C. The background disciplines of "value creation" are . . .
Doctrine of Fair Contracts	. . . in accordance with the six principles.	. . . in the interests of stakeholders.	—business theories —theories that explain stakeholder behavior
Feminist Standpoint Theory	. . . in accordance with the principles of caring/connection and relationships.	. . . to maintain and care for relationships and networks of stakeholders.	—business theories —feminist theory —social science understanding of networks
Ecological Principles	. . . in accordance with the principle of caring for the earth.	. . . to care for the earth.	—business theories —ecology —other

connection.[9] Another would be an ecological (or several ecological) normative cores. Mark Starik has argued that the very idea of a stakeholder theory of the *firm* ignores certain ecological necessities.[10] Exhibit 1 is suggestive of how these theories could be developed.

In the next section I shall sketch the normative core based on pragmatic liberalism. But, any normative core must address the questions in columns A or B, or explain why these questions may be irrelevant, as in the ecological view. In addition, each "theory," and I use the word hesitantly, must place the normative core within a more full-fledged account of how we could understand value-creating activity differently (column C). The only way to get on with this task is to see the stakeholder idea as a metaphor. The attempt to prescribe one and only one "normative core" and construct "a stakeholder theory" is at best a disguised attempt to smuggle a normative core past the unsophisticated noses of other unsuspecting academics who are just happy to see the end of the stockholder orthodoxy.

If we begin with the view that we can understand value-creation activity as a contractual process among those parties affected, and if for simplicity's sake we initially designate those parties as financiers, customers, suppliers, employees and communities, then we can construct a normative core that reflects the liberal notions of autonomy, solidarity and fairness as articulated by John Rawls, Richard Rorty and others.[11] Notice that building these moral notions into the foundations of how we understand value creation and contracting requires that we eschew separating the "business" part of the process from the "ethical" part, and that we start with the presumption of equality among the contractors, rather than the presumption in favor of financier rights.

The normative core for this redesigned contractual theory will capture the liberal idea of fairness if it ensures a basic equality among stakeholders in terms of their moral rights as these are realized in the firm, and if it recognizes that inequalities among stakeholders are justified if they raise the level of the least well-off stakeholder. The liberal ideal of autonomy is captured by the realization that each stakeholder must be free to enter agreements that create value for themselves, and solidarity is realized by the recognition of the mutuality of stakeholder interests.

One way to understand fairness in this context is to claim *a la* Rawls that a contract is fair if parties to the contract would agree to it in ignorance of their actual stakes. Thus, a contract is like a fair bet, if each party is willing to turn the tables and accept the other side. What would a fair contract among corporate stakeholders look like? If we can articulate this ideal, a sort of corporate constitution, we could then ask whether actual corporations measure up to this standard, and we also begin to design corporate structures which are consistent with this Doctrine of Fair Contracts.

Imagine if you will, representative stakeholders trying to decide on "the rules of the game." Each is rational in a straightforward sense, looking out for its own self-interest. At least *ex ante,* stakeholders are the relevant parties since they will be materially affected. Stakeholders know how economic activity is organized and could be organized. They know general facts about the way the corporate world works. They know that in the real world there are or could be transaction costs, externalities and positive costs of contracting. Suppose they are uncertain about what other social institutions exist, but they know the range of those institutions. They do not know if government exists to pick up the tab for any externalities, or if they will exist in the nightwatchman state of libertarian theory. They know success and failure stories of businesses around the world. In short, they are behind a Rawls-like veil of ignorance, and they do not know what stake each will have when the veil is lifted. What ground rules would they choose to guide them?

The first ground rule is "The Principle of Entry and Exit." In any contract that is negotiated, the corporation must have clearly defined entry, exit and renegotiation conditions, or at least it must have methods or processes for so defining these conditions. The logic is straightforward: each stakeholder must be able to determine when an agreement exists and has a chance of fulfillment. This is not to imply that contracts cannot contain contingent claims or other methods for resolving uncertainty, but rather that it must contain methods for determining whether or not it is valid.

The second ground rule I shall call "The Principle of Governance," and it says that the procedure for changing the rules of the game must be agreed upon by unanimous consent. Think about the consequences of a majority of stakeholders systematically "selling out" a minority. Each stakeholder, in ignorance of its actual role, would seek to avoid such a situation. In reality this principle translates into each stakeholder never giving up its right to participate in the governance of the corporation, or perhaps into the existence of stakeholder governing boards.

The third ground rule I shall call "The Principle of Externalities," and it says that if a contract between A and B imposes a cost on C, then C has the option to become a party to the contract, and the terms are renegotiated. Once again the rationality of this condition is clear. Each stakeholder will want insurance that it does not become C.

The fourth ground rule is "The Principle of Contracting Costs," and it says that all parties to the contract must share in the cost of contracting. Once again the logic is straightforward. Any one stakeholder can get stuck.

A fifth ground rule is "The Agency Principle" that says that any agent must serve the interests of all stakeholders. It must adjudicate conflicts within the bounds of the other principals. Once again the logic is clear. Agents for any one group would have a privileged place.

A sixth and final ground rule we might call "The Principle of Limited Immortality." The corporation shall be managed as if it can continue to serve the interests of stakeholders through time. Stakeholders are uncertain about the future but, subject to exit conditions, they realize that the continued existence of the corporation is in their interest. Therefore, it would be rational to hire managers who are fiduciaries to their interest and the interest of the collective. If it turns out the "collective interest" is the empty set, then this principle simply collapses into the Agency Principle.

Thus, the Doctrine of Fair Contracts consists of these six ground rules, or principles:

1. The Principle of Entry and Exit
2. The Principle of Governance
3. The Principle of Externalities
4. The Principle of Contracting Costs
5. The Agency Principle
6. The Principle of Limited Immortality

Think of these ground rules as a doctrine which would guide actual stakeholders in devising a corporate constitution or charter. Think of management as having the duty to act in accordance with some specific constitution or charter.

Obviously, if the Doctrine of Fair Contracts and its accompanying background narratives are to effect real change, there must be requisite changes in the enabling laws of the land. I propose the following three principles to serve as constitutive elements of attempts to reform the law of corporations.

The Stakeholder Enabling Principle

Corporations shall be managed in the interests of its stakeholders, defined as employees, financiers, customers, employees [*sic*] and communities.

The Principle of Director Responsibility

Directors of the corporation shall have a duty of care to use reasonable judgment to define and direct the affairs of the corporation in accordance with the Stakeholder Enabling Principle.

The Principle of Stakeholder Recourse

Stakeholders may bring an action against the directors for failure to perform the required duty of care.

Obviously, there is more work to be done to spell out these principles in terms of model legislation. As they stand, they try to capture the intuitions that drive the liberal ideals. It is equally plain that corporate constitutions which meet a test like the doctrine of fair contracts are meant to enable directors and executives to manage the corporation in conjunction with these same liberal ideals.

NOTES

1. Cf. A. Berle and G. Means, *The Modern Corporation and Private Property* (New York: Commerce Clearing House, 1932), 1. For a reassessment of Berle and Means' argument after 50 years, see *Journal of Law and Economics* 26 (June 1983), especially G. Stigler and C. Friedland, "The Literature of Economics: The Case of Berle and Means," 237–68; D. North, "Comment on Stigler and Friedland," 269–72; and G. Means, "Corporate Power in the Marketplace," 467–85.

2. The metaphor of rebuilding the ship while afloat is attributed to Neurath by W. Quine, *Word and Object* (Cambridge: Harvard University Press, 1960), and W. Quine and J. Ullian, *The Web of Belief* (New York: Random House, 1978). The point is that to keep the ship afloat during repairs we must replace a plank with one that will do a better job. Our argument is that stakeholder capitalism can so replace the current version of managerial capitalism.

3. *See* R. Charan and F. Freeman, "Planning for the Business Environment of the 1980s," *The Journal of Business Strategy* 1 (1980): 9–19, especially p. 15 for a brief account of the major developments in products liability law.

4. *See* S. Breyer, *Regulation and Its Reform* (Cambridge: Harvard University Press, 1983), 133, for an analysis of food additives.

5. *See* I. Millstein and S. Katsh, *The Limits of Corporate Power* (New York: Macmillan, 1981), Chapter 4.

6. Cf. C. Summers, "Protecting All Employees Against Unjust Dismissal," *Harvard Business Review* 58 (1980): 136, for a careful statement of the argument.

7. *See* E. Freeman and D. Reed, "Stockholders and Stakeholders: A New Perspective on Corporate Governance," in C. Huizinga, ed., *Corporate Governance: A Definitive Exploration of the Issues* (Los Angeles: UCLA Extension Press, 1983).

8. *See* T. Peters and R. Waterman, *In Search of Excellence* (New York: Harper and Row, 1982).

9. *See*, for instance, A. Wicks, D. Gilbert and E. Freeman, "A Feminist Reinterpretation of the Stakeholder Concept," *Business Ethics Quarterly*, Vol. 4, No. 4, October 1994; and E. Freeman and J. Liedtka, "Corporate Social Responsibility: A Critical Approach," *Business Horizons*, Vol. 34, No. 4, July–August 1991, pp. 92–98.

10. At the Toronto workshop Mark Starik sketched how a theory would look if we took the environment to be a stakeholder. This fruitful line of work is one example of my main point about pluralism.

11. J. Rawls, *Political Liberalism* (New York: Columbia University Press, 1993); and R. Rorty, "The Priority of Democracy to Philosophy" in *Reading Rorty: Critical Responses to Philosophy and the Mirror of Nature (and Beyond)*, ed. Alan R. Malachowski (Cambridge, MA: Blackwell, 1990).

IDENTIFYING STAKEHOLDER GROUPS

—ADIDAS-SALOMON

The report on the pages that follow provides an example of the application of stakeholder theory to corporate decision making. In its annual report, adidas-Salomon identifies those whom it perceives to be its stakeholders and describes the process by which it ensures stakeholder accountability.

By actively and systematically engaging with stakeholders, and involving them in the key decisions that shape day-to-day operations, we believe we can balance interests, build consensus and enhance the transparency of our business. We pursue a policy of open dialogue with stakeholders—debating issues and approaches and, where appropriate, forming partnerships to develop long-term solutions.

IDENTIFYING STAKEHOLDER GROUPS

The 2001 report defined stakeholders as those whom we affect and who affect us. This is a very diverse range of organizations, groups and people, and includes concerned consumers, employees, workers in our suppliers' factories and NGOs.

Not all of our stakeholders have a voice. We are still looking for ways to improve how we communicate with, and receive feedback from, all of our stakeholders. Our global social and environmental reporting initiative, launched in early 2001, was the first step in this process. This year, we have also begun to hold formal consultation meetings—we call them "stakeholder dialogues"—to engage key stakeholders and canvas their views on our SOE program. These dialogue meetings supplement the many individual points of contact, meetings and inquiries from stakeholders during the course of the year.

If we are to gauge the effectiveness of our current efforts and choose the right path for future actions, regular stakeholder dialogue and feedback is [*sic*] essential. From 2003 onward, stakeholder meetings will take place annually in each of the three key sourcing regions: Asia, the Americas and Europe.

TYPES OF ENGAGEMENT

In addition to the stakeholder dialogue sessions described above, we use a variety of techniques to engage with our stakeholders. The Works Council and one German union is [*sic*] represented on the Supervisory Board of the Group, so there is constant collaboration between management and staff. We conduct surveys with our staff to determine their views on social responsibility. We have convened roundtable discussions with external stakeholders in Asia, Europe and the Americas. We also work with other companies through memberships in trade associations and collaborative programs to improve the way we work with suppliers and communicate with stakeholders.

Staff and Management Surveys

In the first half of 2002 we conducted two internal surveys: one of staff, the other a cross-section of senior management. The primary purpose of the surveys was to gauge internal understanding of and support for the SOE program and to measure the effectiveness of internal communication and training on social and environmental issues.

The results show that employees feel it is important to work for a company that tackles social issues and that they believe adidas-Salomon to be an environmentally and socially responsible company. Employees also strongly supported the need to report on social and environmental issues internally, as we do externally. Overall, 72% of respondents confirmed they had heard of the SOE, with fewer knowing this term in Asia (63%) than in the Americas (67%) or Europe (94%). To close this gap in knowledge and understanding we are planning to make the 2002 social and environmental report available to every employee.

The senior management survey showed strong support for the SOE program. Of senior managers, 94% believe that SOE monitoring activities add value to the Group's performance and that formal reporting mechanisms support internal communications, but increased SOE training should be given. All managers believed that the SOE had brought about a positive improvement in factory conditions, with the same percentage acknowledging that the long-term future of SOE relies on factories developing their own internal systems and capabilities.

Respondents were also asked to rank the purpose of social and environmental compliance, based on six optional statements. The ranking reveals the importance given to SOE in bringing about factory improvement, in promoting the core values of the Group and in safe-

Our Stakeholders

Authorizers	Business Partners	Opinion Formers	Customers
Government	Employees	Journalists	Professional Sports
Trade Associations	Unions	Community Members	People
Shareholders	Suppliers	Special Interest Groups	Distributors
Board of Directors	Workers		Retailers
	Distributors		Individuals
	Service Providers		

guarding against risks to the Group's reputation. Interestingly, managers gave the lowest ranking to SOE as a means of competitive advantage, and of safeguarding against media or NGO criticism.

STAKEHOLDER MEETINGS

The first formal stakeholder meeting with NGOs took place in Hong Kong in December 2001. Since then we have built on this by coordinating two additional stakeholder meetings in Europe and in North America in 2002. Participants included representatives from other major brands, a trade association, a trade union, a social investment and tracking fund, a sustainability institute, a certification organization, and a number of human and labor rights NGOs.

Each meeting was managed and recorded by an independent advisor. Business for Social Responsibility [BSR] helped us with the selection of stakeholders in the United States and ran the Washington, DC, meeting. Adrian Henriques, a corporate social responsibility [CSR] consultant, oversaw the European stakeholder meeting in London, England.

RESPONDING TO SPECIFIC FEEDBACK

The SEA team engages continuously with local organizations such as NGOs, religious groups, trade unions and other special interest groups. Over the course of the year we have received many inquiries from the media, NGOs, worker rights groups, campaigners, academics, investment funds, students, shareholders and others about suppliers, the SOE program and our current practice. Where concerns or issues have been raised these have been fully investigated, assessed and a response given. In some cases, we have gone beyond a simple exchange of views, or information, and have worked collaboratively. Issues raised throughout the year include:

- Poor working conditions for football manufacturers in mainland China.

- Underage stitching of footballs in India and Pakistan.

- Working conditions in the footwear industry in Indonesia.

- Factory conditions at an accessories factory in Indonesia.

- Working conditions in an apparel factory in El Salvador.

- The use of kangaroo leather in the manufacture of soccer boots.

- Apparel factory closure in Thailand.

Details of how we respond to stakeholder feedback can be found at www.adidas-Salomon. com/en/sustainability/archive/.

Collaborative Efforts Following Feedback, PT Dada, Indonesia

The Workers Rights Consortium (WRC) is a non-profit organization that helps to enforce manufacturing Codes of Conduct adopted by US colleges and universities. In 2002, the

WRC published two reports covering its investigations of PT Dada, an Indonesian factory supplying caps to adidas-Salomon. Since mid-2001, adidas-Salomon had been aware of problems at PT Dada related to working conditions, workers' freedom of association and associated cases of harassment.

From the outset it was agreed that there was a need for constructive dialogue between the WRC, factory management and adidas-Salomon. adidas-Salomon led with the development and monitoring of action plans, setting timelines and supporting PT Dada with its remediation efforts. These action plans were shared with other buyers and with the WRC, who engaged three local monitors to get independent feedback from workers.

A Remediation Progress Report, published by the WRC in September 2002, detailed changes to their original recommendations and explained additional areas of remediation agreed with adidas-Salomon and PT Dada. The report acknowledges the very significant changes that have taken place at PT Dada and adidas-Salomon's "heavy efforts on issue-by-issue remediation work." Not all of the issues at PT Dada have been resolved and the collaborative efforts of the WRC and adidas-Salomon are continuing.

MEMBERSHIP AND COLLABORATION

We are actively involved with the World Business Council for Sustainable Development, Business for Social Responsibility, the World Federation of Sporting Goods Industry, the International Labour Organization and the Fair Labor Association. Typically our involvement means that we:

- Adhere to and promote codes of conduct.

- Support independent monitoring and capacity building.

- Develop and comment on guidelines and industry best practice.

- Are transparent.

SHARING KNOWLEDGE WITH OTHER BRANDS

adidas-Salomon is committed to sharing its knowledge and experience of social and environmental compliance. During 2002 we shared our current guidance materials and other information from the SOE program with a number of global brands. We used seven shared Fair Labor Association [FLA] audits as an opportunity to collaborate with Reebok and Nike during remediation of audit findings in the Americas, Asia and Europe.

The SEA team is in regular contact with counterparts in Nike, Reebok, Pentland, Puma and other major brands. They also share information with other CSR practitioners at mutually shared factory sites, and at business forums such as conferences and working groups. Every two to three months SEA team members in Hong Kong participate in a Buyers Compliance Group meeting. This meeting offers an informal forum for compliance officers to meet and exchange views on labour rights, legislative changes and other issues.

BENEFITS OF STAKEHOLDER DIALOGUE

- To bring about an improvement to factory conditions.
- To safeguard the Group against risks to reputation.
- To promote the values of the people (and of sport) who work for the Group and make them feel it is worth working for.
- To reduce our legal liabilities as a Group.
- To minimize criticism from the media and NGOs.
- To remain competitive with other brands.

MEASURING THE BUSINESS VALUE OF STAKEHOLDER RELATIONSHIPS

—Ann C. Svendsen, Robert G. Boutilier, Robert M. Abbott,
and David Wheeler

The following is a segment of a research project that sought to measure in quantitative terms the value of stakeholder relationships. This particular section focuses on evidence of the link between the quality of these relationships and business success, finding that there is a strong correlation between good stakeholder relationships and success. Though the question of a linkage between ethics, stakeholder relationships and the bottom line still persists, evidence of a positive correlation is persuasive.

EVIDENCE OF LINK BETWEEN QUALITY OF STAKEHOLDER RELATIONSHIPS AND BUSINESS SUCCESS

Stakeholder-Focus and Performance

The past 30 years have seen a rapid evolution in understanding about whether and how stakeholder relationships contribute to business success. While research which looks at the link between corporate social responsibility and financial performance have shown mixed results, there are a few significant studies which show there seems to be a strong correlation between good stakeholder relationships and business success.

Harvard researchers John Kotter and James Heskett, in their book *Corporate Culture and Performance* (1992), for example, showed that over an 11-year period, sales and employment growth at stakeholder-oriented companies were significantly higher than at shareholder-focused companies. Specifically, stakeholder-oriented companies reported four times the growth in sales and eight times the growth in employment. The authors argued that successful, visionary companies, although very diverse in other ways, put a lower priority on maximizing shareholder wealth and greater emphasis on serving the interests of a broad mix of stakeholders.

Arie de Geus reinforced this finding in his book, *The Living Company* (1997). Here, the author found that stakeholder-oriented companies remained in harmony with their environment by keeping "feelers" out and by developing strong relationships. He also noted that companies which survived for 25 years or longer tended to be cohesive, conservative in their financial dealings and more likely to have decentralized decision making.

In a Canadian context, a path-breaking study by Max Clarkson, former director of the Clarkson Centre for Business Ethics at the University of Toronto, found that firms that place a premium on ethics and social performance make the most money. Clarkson's research suggests that companies that concentrate exclusively on the bottom line often make poorer decisions. He suggested this may be because they lack information from stakeholders and the environment that would allow them to anticipate opportunities and solve problems when they are small and less costly to remedy (Clarkson, 1991).

Corporate Social Responsibility (CSR) and Financial Performance

A number of studies have used CSR databases to correlate measures of stakeholder relationship quality with financial performance (Collins and Porras, 1995; Waddock & Graves, 1997; Berman et al., 1999; Roman et al., 1999). Waddock and Graves and Berman et al. used measures for the quality of relationships with employees, customers, communities, minorities and women and the natural environment that were based on CSR ratings derived from the Kinder, Lydenberg, Domini (KLD) Socrates database. Waddock and Graves (1997) correlated companies' previous year CSR ratings with financial performance on measures such as return on assets (ROA), return on equity (ROE) and return on sales (ROS). They found quantitative support for the assertion that there is a connection between how a company treats its stakeholders and financial performance.

More recently, Berman et al. (1999) tried to determine which kinds of CSR behaviors were most strongly tied to ROA. They found that CSR behaviors that dealt with the company's relationships with employees and with customers had significant direct effects on ROA. The authors also examined the possible mediating role of company strategy, which was deduced from financial reports as selling intensity, capital expenditure efficiency or capital intensity. Behaviors related to communities, minorities and women and the natural environment proved to have a mediating effect, depending on the company's strategy.

Berman et al. speculated that mediating factors (e.g., impacts on the natural environment, and thus relationships with environmental groups) might not be of equal importance across industries. Similarly, relationships with minorities, as indexed by board and senior executive diversity, might be more important to financial performance in more racially and ethnically homogeneous geographic regions than in more diverse regions.

Rather more indirectly, correlations between social and environmental performance and stock price performance have been examined in the context of indices such as the Dow Jones Sustainability Index, the Innovest EcoValue Index and the Jantzi Social Index. Where these indices include the social dimension, their measurement is not based on the quality of stakeholder relationships. Rather, they equate social performance with observers' subjective ratings of actual corporate behaviors. In that respect, they focus on the outcomes or consequences of corporate stakeholder relationship quality. Moreover, the correlations are claimed to be the simultaneous manifestation in three dimensions of performance of a common factor, namely, management competence.

We propose to investigate the hypothesis that the ability to create and sustain high-quality stakeholder relationships is a necessary management competence, without which financial success becomes unlikely. In any case, the fact that such correlations exist does provide some empirical evidence for the existence of links between social and financial performance.

HOW DO STAKEHOLDER RELATIONSHIPS CREATE COMPETITIVE ADVANTAGE?

Increased attention to the link between positive stakeholder relationships and competitive advantage has been manifested in at least four areas:

  i. The failure to establish and nurture stakeholder relationships creates *shareholder risk.*
 ii. Strong relationships with and between employees, and with supply chain and business alliance partners are a prerequisite for *innovation.*
iii. A dense network of relationships provides resources and information necessary for the development of *new markets and opportunities.*
 iv. Relationships are the source of a good *reputation* and enhanced *brand value,* both of which create a myriad of business benefits.

Risk Reduction

Companies like McDonald's, Mitsubishi, Monsanto, Nestlé, Nike, Shell, and Texaco have suffered damage to their reputations and sales as a result of public awareness campaigns by advocacy stakeholder groups (Schwartz and Gibb, 1999; Wheeler et al., 2001a, b). At its most obvious, the Internet has made it possible for activists around the world to coordinate boycotts against corporations with direct impacts on sales, albeit usually by a rather small percentage of their potential markets. For example, activist sites such as http://www.corporations.org/corplist.html (updated to Oct. 31, 2000) list dozens of companies currently being boycotted.

In addition to sales impacts, there are probably more damaging long-term implications for shareholder value of controversies such as those suffered by the aforementioned companies. Although uncomfortable for companies to discuss and record, and difficult for them to quantify, they may include:

- Diminution of license to operate in certain markets (e.g., Monsanto and its genetically modified products in Europe).

- Diminution of "supplier" or "employer of choice" status (e.g., Shell's experience after the twin shocks of *Brent Spar* and Nigeria).

- Diminution of brand equity.

These impacts also result in direct costs as companies re-invest in reputation by, for example:

  a. Employing extra staff to monitor internal practices which are under question (e.g. Nike's experience with human rights controversies in its supply chain).

b. Tying up of senior management time during conflicts (e.g., McDonald's experience in its libel case against London Greenpeace).

c. Advertising spending (e.g., Shell's investments in corporate public relations post-Brent Spar and Nigeria).

d. Excessive compensation claims (e.g., Texaco's experience in dealing with charges of systematic racism in its U.S. business practices).

e. Costs of physical damage to property (e.g., McDonald's experience during anti-globalization protests).

Innovation

In today's highly competitive economy, innovation is of fundamental importance to business survival and success. Research shows that creating highly innovative work teams is largely dependent on establishing positive relationships both between management and employees and between employees themselves (Cooke and Wills, 1999; Leanna and van Burren, 1999).

Conversely, employees who are motivated by a common vision and set of goals, trust their colleagues and are linked into diverse and stimulating information networks will tend to be more innovative. In other words, positive relationships are necessary to transform an intangible asset (knowledge) into a tangible one (new processes, products and services).

Similarly, positive, trust-based relationships with suppliers and business partners are fundamental to spurring innovation, as well as enhancing effectiveness and efficiency. In the past, supply chain relationships were governed by arm's-length, explicit contracts. Considerable management effort was spent monitoring and controlling the behavior of suppliers and when contract terms are not met, attempting to remedy the problem and resolve conflicts. Today, supply chain relationships are more likely to be based on implicit, trust-based contracts that are negotiated and renegotiated as demands and opportunities change. This kind of relationship requires more flexibility and hence depends on shared knowledge, interaction and trust (Matthews et al., 1998).

Reputation

Research shows that a company's reputation is an important determinant of business success. A 1997 national study of consumer attitudes by Cone/Roper (1997) found that 76% of consumers would be likely to switch to a brand associated with a good cause. This represents an increase from 63% in 1993. Other studies show a downturn in the value of a company's stock when a company is accused of ethical wrongdoing.

Technology and the increased power of the media to influence public opinion have contributed to a rise in the importance of reputation. Companies recognize that their reputation depends on developing credible relationships with their employees, customers, nearby residents and suppliers. This is especially true in a networked world where everything about a company can be known globally and almost instantaneously.

The influence of reputation is perhaps best illustrated with reference to the well known cases of Shell in the UK and Merck in the U.S. On June 10, 1995 Shell UK began towing a used oil rig, the *Brent Spar,* into the North Atlantic to sink it. The disposal was the culmination of four years of study and was approved and supported by the regulators and, indeed, by British Prime Minister John Major when he was challenged on the point in Parliament. Greenpeace galvanized community opposition to the project, and compelled Shell to halt the project on June 20.

The costs to the company were considerable. Shell estimated that the direct cost to change the disposal decision was $200 million (U.S.). Additionally, boycotts and threats against Shell service stations led to lost sales. Fifty Shell service stations were vandalized, two firebombed and one raked with gunfire. Moreover, employee morale plummeted.

Within one month of the Shell episode, phosphorous trichloride leaked from Merck & Co. Inc.'s Flint River plant in Albany, New York. The leak produced a clearly visible toxic cloud above the plant. Forty-five people were taken to hospital, 400 workers were evacuated, and a TV crew broadcast the event. The community response ranged from indifference to laudatory support of Merck.

The reasons why Merck was given the benefit of the doubt are twofold. Firstly, the company's vision, forged in the 1920s, was built upon the core values of integrity, contribution to society, responsibility to customers and employees and the unequivocal pursuit of quality and excellence. As early as 1993, CEO George Merck articulated the operating philosophy of the company:

> *We pledge our every aid that this enterprise shall merit the faith we have in it . . . that those who hold aloft that torch of Science and Knowledge through these social and economic dark ages, shall take new courage and feel their hands supported.*

Merck believed that the company operated with the consent of the community and the company has, over the years, worked very hard to earn that consent. The company benefits from what Fombrun (1996) has called reputational capital.

Expanded Markets and Opportunities

The capability to engage essential stakeholders in positive relationships can give a firm a competitive advantage (Grant, 1998, 177). The advantage might be manifested in any number of ways in different industries and with different stakeholders. This phenomenon has been well demonstrated by Suncor in its development of oil sands in Alberta and BP in its securing of a community license to operate in Alaska (Wheeler et al., 2001a).

In the case of BP, a positive reputation for community involvement was key to its successful bid for oil rights in Alaska.

Brand Value

Spurred on by the rapid rise of the service sector, the quality of a company's relationships with its customers began to receive a great deal of attention in the 1980s. Customer satisfaction measurement merged with one-to-one (Peppers and Rogers, 1993) database marketing to become customer relationship value.

In a similar vein, brand loyalty has been recognized as a valuable intangible asset. Our growing understanding of the links among intangibles like customer satisfaction, customer loyalty and brand loyalty has facilitated estimates of the financial value of brands, the annual brand "rankings" by Interbrand for the *Financial Times* being a conspicuous example. The 2000 rankings estimated brand values for Coca-Cola and Microsoft at U.S. $72.5 and $70.2 billion respectively (*Financial Times,* 2000).

REFERENCES

Berman, Shawn L., Wicks, Andrew C., Kotha, Suresh, & Jones, Thomas M. (1999) "Does Stakeholder Orientation Matter? The Relationship Between Stakeholder Management Models and Firm Financial Performance." *Academy of Management Journal,* 42(5):488–506.

Clarkson, Max. (1991) "Good Business and the Bottom Line." *Canadian Business Magazine,* May, p. 28.

Collins, J. C. and Porras, J. I. (1995) *Built to Last: Successful Habits of Visionary Companies.* London: Century, Random House.

Cone/Roper. (1997) Cause Related Marketing Trends Report.

Cooke, Philip, and Wills, David. (1999) "Small Firms, Social Capital and the Enhancement of Business Performance Through Innovation Programmes." *Small Business Economics,* 13(3): 219–234.

deGeus, Arie. (1997) *The Living Company.* Boston: Harvard Business School Press. *Financial Times* 2000. "Coca-Cola Loses Its Fizz." Richard Tomkins, July 18, 2000.

Fombrun, Charles J. (1996) *Reputation: Realizing Value from the Corporate Image.* Boston: Harvard Business School Press.

Grant, R. M. (1991) "The Resource-Based Theory of Competitive Advantage: Implications for Strategy Formulation." *California Management Review,* 33(3): 114–135.

Kotter, John, and Heskett, James. (1992) *Corporate Culture and Performance.* New York: Free Press.

Leanna, Carrie R., and Van Buren III, Harry J. (1999) "Organizational Social Capital and Employment Practices." *Academy of Management Review,* 24(3): 538–555.

Mathews, R, Samouel, P., and Wheeler, D. (1998) "Supply Chain Alliances." In *A New Vision for Business.* Report of the Committee of Inquiry to the Prime Minister. Available via www.business-impact.org.uk/bi2/cofi.

Peppers, Don, and Rogers, Martha. (1993) *The One to One Future: Building Relationships One Customer at a Time.* New York: Currency/Doubleday.

Roman, R., Hayibor, S., and B. Agle, B. (1999) "The Relationship Between Social and Financial Performance." *Business and Society,* 38(1): 109–125.

Schwartz,. P., and Gibb,. B (1999) *When Good Companies Do Bad Things: Responsibility and Risk in an Age of Globalization.* Bloomington, IN: Indiana University Press.

Waddock, Sandra A., and Graves, S. (1997) "The Corporate Social Performance-Financial Performance Link." *Strategic Management Journal,* 19: 303–317.

Wheeler, D., Boele, R., and Fabig, H. (2001a) "Paradoxes and Dilemmas for Stakeholder Responsive Firms in the Extractive Sector—Lessons from the Case of Shell and the Ogoni." Manuscript submitted to the *Journal of Business Ethics.*

Wheeler, D., Capobianco, A., Perkin, M., and Stanford, S. (2001b) "Bridging the Digital Divide: Opportunities for Sustainability in the New Economy. A Canadian Perspective." *Paper presented to the CRUISE (Carleton University) Conference on Building Canadian Capacity. Sustainable Production and the Knowledge Economy.* Ottawa, April 2001.

DEMONSTRATING CORPORATE VALUES
What Are Society's Expectations of Business?

—DEBORAH SMITH

The growing demand from various sectors of society for companies to demonstrate their commitment to good corporate citizenship is finding a response among businesses. The perceived danger—that public statements of adherence to external standards will offer critics a larger target at which to shoot when things do go wrong—is being slowly eroded. In the following excerpt, Deborah Smith evaluates the stakeholders who comprise the term society *and their differing expectations of business.*

WHAT ARE SOCIETY'S EXPECTATIONS OF BUSINESS?
What Do We Mean by Society?

Companies face a bewildering array of choices for demonstrating that they are ethically and socially responsible. Into the fray of strategic options such as social reporting and accounting, regular stakeholder engagement and establishing subsequent commitments and programs, comes External Standards. Before looking at what these standards are and what they require it is worth a brief look at why they exist and from where the need for them has come.

One of the most common and possibly annoying questions companies continually face directly or indirectly through media speculation is—"What is expected of companies today by society?" This question will be to some extent sent in the opposite direction in the final chapter, but in dealing with this one first, the nebulous concept of "society" needs clarification. The dictionary definition is:

> *The persons, collectively considered, who live in any region or at any period; any community of individuals who are united together by a common bond of nearness; those who recognize each other as associates, friends and acquaintances.*

If complete credence were given to current media coverage in 2002, anybody would be forgiven for thinking that the developed world has an anti-corporate, anti-globalization revolution on its hands.

However, opinions not only vary wildly between individuals and groups according to their interests, but they can also change daily, or they certainly seem to! Opinion polls do not always deliver accurate results, as politicians and businesses alike can testify. For the purposes of this report, opinion and expectations have been grouped into the following categories: Consumers/General Public, Government, Investors, NGOs and Business.

Consumers/General Public

Some recent surveys and opinion polls provide a flavor of apparent consumer and opinion-former attitudes to corporate behavior.

- A Mori poll[1] found that 71% of the British public "agree that industry and commerce do not pay enough attention to their responsibilities."

- Research by the Future Foundation for a Co-Op Report "Who are the ethical consumers?"[2] found that almost 60% of consumers in the UK feel that companies cannot be trusted to make safe, durable products without the government setting industry standards. This compares with only 40% 20 years earlier.

- A survey by *Business Week*/Harris[3] in the United States found that 66% of the American public think that large profits are more important to big companies than developing safe, reliable, quality products for consumers.

- A Co-Op report on ethical consumerism[4] found that: "One in six of the population say they frequently buy or boycott products because of the manufacturer's reputation. Just over half of the population have bought a product and recommended a supplier because of its responsible reputation at some time in the last year.
  A quarter of consumers have investigated a company's social responsibility at least once."

On the face of it, consumers and the public seem to expect high standards of corporate behavior beyond making money. Generally, however, they do not trust companies. These sorts of results should be tempered with an awareness of various syndromes of polling and surveying. The "leading question" is one of them; asking questions on issues never really previously considered by respondents is another. A more interesting phenomenon has been identified by the authors of a Co-op report who talk about the 30:3 syndrome—this refers to the fact that a third of consumers profess to care about companies' policies and records on social responsibility, but ethical products rarely achieve more than a 3% market share.

What is often glossed over by commentators is that despite the seemingly unpopular reputation of business in general and certain ones in particular, the corporation is an institution whose existence, structure and activities are consistently sanctioned by society. One obvious manifestation of this, beyond our huge dependence on their share-price success for our pensions and investments, is consumers' endless responsiveness to cut-price competition.

---

[1]*MORI,* May 2000.
[2]*Who Are The Ethical Consumers?* Roger Cowe and Simon Williams, October 2000.
[3]*Business Week,* September 11, 2000.
[4]*Who Are The Ethical Consumers?,* Roger Cowe and Simon Williams, October 2000.

Investors

If there is one group in which real power and influence over companies is combined with a financial incentive, it is shareholders or investors. Leaving aside the "professional protestor shareholder" who often buys just a single share to enable their voting and presence at AGMs, there has been a significant growth in the impact that this group of society has had on corporate behavior.

A survey of 65 fund managers' attitudes to Social Responsible Investment included the following findings:[5]

- Over the last 12 months, more than 50% of fund managers taking part in the survey perceived an increase in interest in SRI from their pension scheme and other institutional clients.

- The key driver cited for this increased interest in SRI was client demand. Other important factors included government pressure, the implications of the publication of the Myners Report,[6] and the actions of competitors. Interestingly, the actions of pressure groups were seen as being largely irrelevant.

- Over 90% of respondents felt that corporate social responsibility was a key element of corporate reputation and brand.

- The majority (over 60%) of respondents felt that companies exhibiting strong environmental and social performance would outperform their peers.

Institutional investors are beginning to take an active interest in CSR issues. For example, Morley Fund Management has a policy of voting against resolutions to adopt the report and accounts of FTSE 100 companies that do not produce an environmental report. For FTSE 250 companies in high-risk sectors they will abstain if the company does not produce an environmental report. This applies to companies across their funds not just in their ethical ones. Morley believes that this policy is already leading to change in the companies in which they invest. The Co-Operative Insurance Society, an institutional shareholder of easyJet, raised concerns in early 2002 that contributed to the resignation of Stelios Haji-Ioannou, easyJet's founder and chairman. Criticisms voiced were that the controlling shareholder was allowed to appoint the chairman, that there were no independent directors on the board, that the share option scheme was "substantially flawed" and that the company had no environmental impact policy. easyJet subsequently agreed to establish an environmental policy.

Government

There is no doubt that government has notions of "legitimacy" of all kinds enshrined in its own license to operate. However, it is not clear how these are applied with clarity to the business world. In October 2000, in a keynote address to the Confederation of British Industry, Prime Minister Tony Blair told business leaders:

---

[5]*Socially Responsible Investment Survey 2002, Environment and Sustainability Services,* Deloitte & Touche, April 2002.
[6]*Myners Review of Institutional Investment in the UK,* Final Report March 2001.

I would also like to see more reporting on environmental and social performance. . . I am issuing a challenge, today, to all of the top 350 companies to be publishing annual environment reports by the end of 2001.

In 1999, a special U.K. position of Minister for Corporate Social Responsibility was created within the Department for Trade and Industry (DTI). This political appointment has, however, appeared to be lacking in any real measurability of impact. Amnesty International Business Group, for instance, stated that: "There's not a great deal of evidence that government is doing much to take the agenda forward. At times it looks as if it's playing catch-up."[7]

This reserve is reinforced in the latest DTI report on CSR.[8] It is refreshingly honest in stating that "the Government does not have all the answers and recognizes the need for the public sector to get its own house in order." However, it does not offer firm guidance on what it expects of companies or of itself, particularly in terms of transparency and accountability.

Contrast this with the French whose Parliament, in February 2002, published the requirements of a new law that mandates all French corporations to report on the sustainability of their social and environmental performance. Companies are required to disclose information on social and environmental issues, including human rights, local impacts and dialogue with stakeholders and it is compulsory for companies to clarify their policies and positioning on these matters, and then to build a structured and consolidated reporting system. This "new economic regulations" law has completely overhauled France's corporate law structure.

One of the key dynamics to affect the voluntary versus regulation debate on CSR is the pace and direction that the European Union is likely to pursue following the publication of its Green Paper on CSR. The subsequent consultation process has culminated in the establishment of a European Multi-Stakeholder Forum on CSR. The Forum is focusing on a variety of issues, including promoting the business case for corporate social responsibility in particular to SMEs; and benchmarking their social and environmental performance. It is made up of a mix of European-wide representative organizations of employers, trade unions, investors, consumers, civil society and business networks. In May 2002 there was some speculation that the EU may advance particular standards such as SA8000, create a new amalgamated business code from many existing ones or create some form of CSR Ombudsman. In addition, the European Parliament has drafted a parliamentary resolution which is expected to urge the Commission towards a commitment to mandatory social and environmental reporting for businesses with over 250 employees or a turnover greater than 4 million euros.

In the United States and Japan the messages from government to business in this area are much weaker—the USA's rebuttal of the Kyoto Treaty being the classic example.

---

[7] *Ethical Performance, Vol. 3, issue 10, page 1—"Flak for Alexander over CSR 'inaction.'"*
[8] *Business and Society—Corporate Social Responsibility Report 2002, Department of Trade and Industry.*

In summary, though further attention is being given by bodies like the Securities and Exchange Commission since the Enron affair in early 2002, governments are certainly expecting high standards of conduct by business, whether for the right reasons or not, and albeit with a distinct lack of joined-up international thinking so far.

NGOs

Despite the UK Government's call for companies to report on their environmental and social performance, there were indications in the first half of 2002 that few companies were doing so, or were devoting little space to the topic.

In response to this, a coalition of leading NGOs, including Friends of the Earth (FOE) and Oxfam, has called on the UK Government to insist that companies report because they believe that the voluntary approach has failed—they are promoting a Corporate Reform Bill (CORE) in Parliament. FOE Director Designate Tony Juniper commented: "The voluntary approach has failed. Now we need a new law to make sure that companies make these reports and take the results seriously."

This very explicit call for regulation differs from other tactics that have been and continue to be used by NGOs and pressure groups to persuade companies to be much more than profit-making entities. There is no doubt that NGOs have been very successful in bringing companies to the table on social and environmental agendas—the latter not always willingly and the former not always using the best tactics! NGO tactics include "naming and shaming" such as the production of league tables comparing different company performances on key issues such as supply chain labor exploitation,[9] or protests at AGMs or business summits, media campaigns, etc. The use of the Internet by pressure groups can be largely credited with generating the numbers of people who rallied behind anti-globalization demonstrations. This though, reinforces the view of some that it is the affluent countries and the middle classes amongst them, who can use this tool to be heard—and that therefore "social expectations" as recited are ones from their limited and privileged "first world" perspectives and values. Anti-corporate websites have their part to play in questioning the direction of global business development, but the readers themselves are usually let off the hook of taking any personal responsibility for changing anything.

Business Thoughts on What Is Expected from Them

On General Societal Expectations   The general sense amongst the business community is that they face ever mounting and ever changing pressures to consider the way they behave.

A survey of what business executives feel about CSR, carried out in September 2001[10] found that the majority of respondents (57%), felt that "companies need to become more accountable to shareholders." Almost two-thirds disagreed with the statement that "com-

---

[9]E.g., Christian Aid "Change at the Checkout" targeting supermarkets.

[10]The Changing Role of Business in Society—New Perspectives from Leaders in Business, Government and the Not-for-Profit Sector, Ashridge Centre for Business and Society, September 2001.

panies disclose all relevant information to all shareholders." A clear majority also felt that large institutional investors need to do more to hold management to account. When asked to speculate on the future, almost two-thirds of respondents reported that "shareholder activism will increase to encourage more responsible corporate behavior. Indeed, most think that investors will use social and environmental criteria more in their investment decisions."

But companies are increasingly aware that they need to impress more than their customers and investors. Initial company responses to the CSR agenda have ranged from "the headless chicken" response (running around in blind panic responding in the short term to the latest media headline on an issue) to those obsessed with proving perfect performance in every social and environmental issue possible. Some of those companies with greater experience of approaching and implementing CSR, are more balanced and less pressurized in their perspective. BASF, which has developed a comprehensive, multilayered sustainable development strategy, which includes observance of the Global Reporting Initiative and UN Global Compact standards states:

> *An increasing number of stakeholders do not only want to know how much we care—they want to know why we care and what's in it for us. They also counter-balance this view with "some stakeholders do not care at all—as long as we stand for low product prices and increasing share prices."[11]*

Other companies feel aggrieved that they are getting the blame for everything from host government incompetence and corruption to global warming. Those that have the resources to respond are reframing their entire business approach (arguably companies such as Shell and BP are doing this). Others need much clearer, more specific guidance, such as that offered by standards.

On Standards . . . and Societal Expectations

A review by AccountAbility,[12] "Mapping Standards for Corporate Social Responsibility," contained a number of comments from companies about whether current CSR standards are adequate in meeting society's expectations of them:

- "There are too many standards and companies don't know which one does what and whose they should follow. Opinion formers can't decide amongst themselves which is the 'best' one and everyone is peddling their own as superior. Even people in the industry can't really tell what distinguishes one from the next except the 'brand' of organization which developed it."

- "There are too many standards for companies to be able to know where to concentrate. There are also not enough standards in the sense that there are many substantive areas which would benefit from standards, but for which no standards exist, there needs to be just a few process standards, with sector specific protocols. And more substantive standards."

---

[11]*Taken from BASF conference presentation handout—issued at Ethical Corporation Conference,* April 24, 2002.
[12]*Mapping Standards for Corporate Social Responsibility,* AccountAbility, May 2002.

- "The issue of supply chain code proliferation is a real and difficult one. In our view codes should be based on common international reference points—the Universal Declaration of Human Rights and the ILO Conventions. As human rights are universal, the proper reference points for supply chain codes of conduct are global, rather than European."

So when BASF raise the valid question "do we really need an ISO norm for human rights?"[13] they are far from alone in expressing concern about too much red tape and bureaucracy that can be created by standards. The difficulty of course for any official body trying to establish a standard is balancing whose views are relevant and how to reflect them fairly and proportionately, with what are core, timeless issues.

NGOs and other social commentators also frequently express ambivalence about standards. The extract below, from an article about SA8000, although specifically addressing SA8000, applies to all social standards particularly compliance-based rather than process standards.

- ". . . The challenge that does hit a sharper note is that relating to the prescriptive nature of solutions. When it is so difficult to get to the heart of what workers in, for instance, Asian cultures really expect—and what really serves their interests—how likely is it that a standard which can be prescriptive as to outcomes or processes may end up having a negative outcome? SA8000 works against the criticism by basing itself only on internationally accepted norms—but there is a strong onus on the standard-setters to get this right. Otherwise managers are pushed onto managing the things that get counted—which may not be the things which count."[14]

To Sum Up

So it will be seen that those outside the world of business and commerce are concerned that companies of all sizes behave in ways that are consistent and verifiable. As well as external pressures, there are pressures from stakeholders (shareholders, employees, customers, suppliers and government) not only to state what their values and standards are, but also to have their performance verified.

---

[13]*Taken from BASF conference presentation handout—issued at Ethical Corporation Conference,* April 24, 2002.
[14]*Business Respect,* CSR Dispatches 26, Mallen Baker, March 2002.

THE PARABLE OF THE SADHU

—Bowen H. McCoy

This parable is based on the true experience of the author, Bowen McCoy, a senior executive from Morgan Stanley, who decided that he needed a sabbatical from the hectic life he had created. His answer was an extended trek through the Himalayas. The goal of this trek was to reach Muklinath, an ancient holy village on the other side of an 18,000-foot ice-covered pass. The parable offers McCoy's reflections upon his return from the experience.

Last year, as the first participant in the new six-month sabbatical program that Morgan Stanley has adopted, I enjoyed a rare opportunity to collect my thoughts as well as do some traveling. I spent the first three months in Nepal, walking 600 miles through 200 villages in the Himalayas and climbing some 120,000 vertical feet. On the trip my sole Western companion was an anthropologist who shed light on the cultural patterns of the villages we passed through.

During the Nepal hike, something occurred that has had a powerful impact on my thinking about corporate ethics. Although some might argue that the experience has no relevance to business, it was a situation in which a basic ethical dilemma suddenly intruded into the lives of a group of individuals. How the group responded I think holds a lesson for all organizations no matter how defined.

THE SADHU

The Nepal experience was more rugged and adventuresome than I had anticipated. Most commercial treks last two or three weeks and cover a quarter of the distance we traveled.

My friend Stephen, the anthropologist, and I were halfway through the 60-day Himalayan part of the trip when we reached the high point, an 18,000-foot pass over a crest that we'd have to traverse to reach the village of Muklinath, an ancient holy place for pilgrims.

Six years earlier I had suffered pulmonary edema, an acute form of altitude sickness, at 16,500 feet in the vicinity of Everest base camp, so we were understandably concerned about what would happen at 18,000 feet. Moreover, the Himalayas were having their wettest spring in 20 years; hip-deep powder and ice had already driven us off one ridge. If we failed to cross the pass, I feared that the last half of our "once in a lifetime" trip would be ruined.

The night before we would try the pass, we camped at a hut at 14,500 feet. In the photos taken at that camp, my face appears wan. The last village we'd passed through was a sturdy two-day walk below us, and I was tired.

During the late afternoon, four backpackers from New Zealand joined us, and we spent most of the night awake, anticipating the climb. Below we could see the fires of two other parties, which turned out to be two Swiss couples and a Japanese hiking club.

To get over the steep part of the climb before the sun melted the steps cut in the ice, we departed at 3:30 A.M. The New Zealanders left first, followed by Stephen and myself, our porters and Sherpas and then the Swiss. The Japanese lingered in their camp. The sky was clear, and we were confident that no spring storm would erupt that day to close the pass.

At 15,500 feet, it looked to me as if Stephen were shuffling and staggering a bit, which are symptoms of altitude sickness. (The initial stage of altitude sickness brings a headache and nausea. As the condition worsens, a climber may encounter difficult breathing, disorientation, aphasia and paralysis.) I felt strong, my adrenaline was flowing, but I was very concerned about my ultimate ability to get across. A couple of our porters were also suffering from the height, and Pasang, our Sherpa sirdar (leader), was worried.

Just after daybreak, while we rested at 15,500 feet, one of the New Zealanders, who had gone ahead, came staggering down toward us with a body slung across his shoulders. He dumped the almost naked, barefoot body of an Indian holy man—a sadhu—at my feet. He had found the pilgrim lying on the ice, shivering and suffering from hypothermia. I cradled the sadhu's head and laid him out on the rocks. The New Zealander was angry. He wanted to get across the pass before the bright sun melted the snow. He said, "Look, I've done what I can. You have porters and Sherpa guides. You care for him. We're going on!" He turned and went back up the mountain to join his friends.

I took a carotid pulse and found that the sadhu was still alive. We figured he had probably visited the holy shrines at Muklinath and was on his way home. It was fruitless to question why he had chosen this desperately high route instead of the safe, heavily traveled caravan route through the Kali Gandaki gorge. Or why he was almost naked and with no shoes, or how long he had been lying in the pass. The answers weren't going to solve our problem.

Stephen and the four Swiss began stripping off outer clothing and opening their packs. The sadhu was soon clothed from head to foot. He was not able to walk, but he was very much alive. I looked down the mountain and spotted below the Japanese climbers marching up with a horse.

Without a great deal of thought, I told Stephen and Pasang that I was concerned about withstanding the heights to come and wanted to get over the pass. I took off after several of our porters who had gone ahead.

On the steep part of the ascent where, if the ice steps had given way, I would have slid down about 3,000 feet, I felt vertigo. I stopped for a breather, allowing the Swiss to catch up with me. I inquired about the sadhu and Stephen. They said that the sadhu was fine and that Stephen was just behind. I set off again for the summit.

Stephen arrived at the summit an hour after I did. Still exhilarated by victory, I ran down the snow slope to congratulate him. He was suffering from altitude sickness, walking 15 steps, then stopping, walking 15 steps, then stopping. Pasang accompanied him all the way up. When I reached them, Stephen glared at me and said: "How do you feel about contributing to the death of a fellow man?"

I did not fully comprehend what he meant.

"Is the sadhu dead?" I inquired.

"No," replied Stephen, "but he surely will be!"

After I had gone, and the Swiss had departed not long after, Stephen had remained with the sadhu. When the Japanese had arrived, Stephen had asked to use their horse to transport the sadhu down to the hut. They had refused. He had then asked Pasang to have a group of our porters carry the sadhu. Pasang had resisted the idea, saying that the porters would have to exert all their energy to get themselves over the pass. He had thought they could not carry a man down 1,000 feet to the hut, reclimb the slope, and get across safely before the snow melted. Pasang had pressed Stephen not to delay any longer.

The Sherpas had carried the sadhu down to a rock in the sun at about 15,000 feet and had pointed out the hut another 500 feet below. The Japanese had given him food and drink. When they had last seen him he was listlessly throwing rocks at the Japanese party's dog, which had frightened him.

We do not know if the sadhu lived or died.

For many of the following days and evenings Stephen and I discussed and debated our behavior toward the sadhu. Stephen is a committed Quaker with deep moral vision. He said, "I feel that what happened with the sadhu is a good example of the breakdown between the individual ethic and the corporate ethic. No one person was willing to assume ultimate responsibility for the sadhu. Each was willing to do his bit just so long as it was not too inconvenient. When it got to be a bother, everyone just passed the buck to someone else and took off. Jesus was relevant to a more individualistic stage of society, but how do we interpret his teaching today in a world filled with large, impersonal organizations and groups?"

I defended the larger group, saying, "Look, we all cared. We all stopped and gave aid and comfort. Everyone did his bit. The New Zealander carried him down below the snow line. I took his pulse and suggested we treat him for hypothermia. You and the Swiss gave him clothing and got him warmed up. The Japanese gave him food and water. The Sherpas carried him down to the sun and pointed out the easy trail toward the hut. He was well enough to throw rocks at a dog. What more could we do?"

"You have just described the typical affluent Westerner's response to a problem. Throwing money—in this case food and sweaters—at it, but not solving the fundamentals!" Stephen retorted.

"What would satisfy you?" I said. "Here we are, a group of New Zealanders, Swiss, Americans and Japanese who have never met before and who are at the apex of one of the most powerful experiences of our lives. Some years the pass is so bad no one gets over it. What right does an almost naked pilgrim who chooses the wrong trail have to disrupt our lives? Even the Sherpas had no interest in risking the trip to help him beyond a certain point."

Stephen calmly rebutted, "I wonder what the Sherpas would have done if the sadhu had been a well-dressed Nepali, or what the Japanese would have done if the sadhu had been a well-dressed Asian, or what you would have done, Buzz, if the sadhu had been a well-dressed Western woman?"

"Where, in your opinion," I asked instead, "is the limit of our responsibility in a situation like this? We had our own well-being to worry about. Our Sherpa guides were unwilling to jeopardize us or the porters for the sadhu. No one else on the mountain was willing to commit himself beyond certain self-imposed limits."

Stephen said, "As individual Christians or people with a Western ethical tradition, we can fulfill our obligations in such a situation only if (1) the sadhu dies in our care, (2) the sadhu demonstrates to us that he could undertake the two-day walk down to the village, or (3) we carry the sadhu for two days down to the village and convince someone there to care for him."

"Leaving the sadhu in the sun with food and clothing, while he demonstrated hand-eye coordination by throwing a rock at a dog, comes close to fulfilling items one and two," I answered. "And it wouldn't have made sense to take him to the village where the people appeared to be far less caring than the Sherpas, so the third condition is impractical. Are you really saying that, no matter what the implications, we should, at the drop of a hat, have changed our entire plan?"

THE INDIVIDUAL VS. THE GROUP ETHIC

Despite my arguments, I felt and continue to feel guilt about the sadhu. I had literally walked through a classic moral dilemma without fully thinking through the consequences. My excuses for my actions include a high adrenaline flow, a superordinate goal and a once-in-a-lifetime opportunity—factors in the usual corporate situation, especially when one is under stress.

Real moral dilemmas are ambiguous, and many of us hike right through them, unaware that they exist. When, usually after the fact, someone makes an issue of them, we tend to resent his or her bringing it up. Often, when the full import of what we have done (or not done) falls on us, we dig into a defensive position from which it is very difficult to emerge. In rare circumstances we may contemplate what we have done from inside a prison.

Had we mountaineers been free of physical and mental stress caused by the effort and the high altitude, we might have treated the sadhu differently. Yet isn't stress the real test of personal and corporate values? The instant decisions executives make under pressure reveal the most about personal and corporate character.

Among the many questions that occur to me when pondering my experience are: What are the practical limits of moral imagination and vision? Is there a collective or institutional ethic beyond the ethics of the individual? At what level of effort or commitment can one discharge one's ethical responsibilities?

Not every ethical dilemma has a right solution. Reasonable people often disagree; otherwise there would be no dilemma. In a business context, however, it is essential that managers agree on a process for dealing with dilemmas.

The sadhu experience offers an interesting parallel to business situations. An immediate response was mandatory. Failure to act was a decision in itself. Up on the mountain we could not resign and submit our résumés to a headhunter. In contrast to philosophy, business involves action and implementation—getting things done. Managers must come up with answers to problems based on what they see and what they allow to influence their decision-making processes. On the mountain, none of us but Stephen realized the true dimensions of the situation we were facing.

One of our problems was that as a group we had no process for developing a consensus. We had no sense of purpose or plan. The difficulties of dealing with the sadhu were so complex that no one person could handle it. Because it did not have a set of preconditions that could guide its action to an acceptable resolution, the group reacted instinctively as individuals. The cross-cultural nature of the group added a further layer of complexity. We had no leader with whom we could all identify and in whose purpose we believed. Only Stephen was willing to take charge, but he could not gain adequate support to care for the sadhu.

Some organizations do have a value system that transcends the personal values of the managers. Such values, which go beyond profitability, are usually revealed when the organization is under stress. People throughout the organization generally accept its values, which, because they are not presented as a rigid list of commandments, may be somewhat ambiguous. The stories people tell, rather than printed materials, transmit these conceptions of what is proper behavior.

For 20 years I have been exposed at senior levels to a variety of corporations and organizations. It is amazing how quickly an outsider can sense the tone and style of an organization and the degree of tolerated openness and freedom to challenge management.

Organizations that do not have a heritage of mutually accepted, shared values tend to become unhinged during stress, with each individual bailing out for himself. In the great takeover battles we have witnessed during past years, companies that had strong cultures drew the wagons around them and fought it out, while other companies saw executives, supported by their golden parachutes, bail out of the struggles.

Because corporations and their members are interdependent, for the corporation to be strong the members need to share a preconceived notion of what is correct behavior, a "business ethic," and think of it as a positive force, not a constraint.

As an investment banker I am continually warned by well-meaning lawyers, clients and associates to be wary of conflicts of interest. Yet if I were to run away from every difficult situation, I wouldn't be an effective investment banker. I have to feel my way through conflicts. An effective manager can't run from risk either; he or she has to confront and deal with risk. To feel "safe" in doing this, managers need the guidelines of an agreed-on process and set of values within the organization.

After my three months in Nepal, I spent three months as an executive-in-residence at both Stanford Business School and the Center for Ethics and Social Policy at the Graduate Theological Union at Berkeley. These six months away from my job gave me time to assimilate 20 years of business experience. My thoughts turned often to the meaning of the leadership role in any large organization. Students at the seminary thought of themselves as antibusiness. But when I questioned them they agreed that they distrusted all large organizations, including the church. They perceived all large organizations as impersonal and opposed to individual values and needs. Yet we all know of organizations where peoples' values and beliefs are respected and their expressions encouraged. What makes the difference? Can we identify the difference and, as a result, manage more effectively?

The word "ethics" turns off many and confuses more. Yet the notions of shared values and an agreed-on process for dealing with adversity and change—what many people mean when they talk about corporate culture—seem to be at the heart of the ethical issue. People who are in touch with their own core beliefs and the beliefs of others and are sustained by them can be more comfortable living on the cutting edge. At times, taking a tough line or decisive stand in a muddle of ambiguity is the only ethical thing to do. If a manager is indecisive and spends time trying to figure out the "good" thing to do, the enterprise may be lost.

Business ethics, then, has to do with the authenticity and integrity of the enterprise. To be ethical is to follow the business as well as the cultural goals of the corporation, its owners, its employees and its customers. Those who cannot serve the corporate vision are not authentic business people and, therefore, are not ethical in the business sense.

At this stage of my own business experience I have a strong interest in organizational behavior. Sociologists are keenly studying what they call corporate stories, legends and heroes as a way organizations have of transmitting the value system. Corporations such as Arco have even hired consultants to perform an audit of their corporate culture. In a company, the leader is the person who understands, interprets and manages the corporate value system. Effective managers are then action-oriented people who resolve conflict, are tolerant of ambiguity, stress and change and have a strong sense of purpose for themselves and their organizations.

If all this is true, I wonder about the role of the professional manager who moves from company to company. How can he or she quickly absorb the values and culture of different organizations? Or is there, indeed, an art of management that is totally transportable? Assuming such fungible managers do exist, is it proper for them to manipulate the values of others?

What would have happened had Stephen and I carried the sadhu for two days back to the village and become involved with the villagers in his care? In four trips to Nepal my most interesting experiences occurred in 1975 when I lived in a Sherpa home in the Khumbu for five days recovering from altitude sickness. The high point of Stephen's trip was an invitation to participate in a family funeral ceremony in Manang. Neither experience had to do with climbing the high passes of the Himalayas. Why were we so reluctant to try the lower path, the ambiguous trail? Perhaps because we did not have a leader who could reveal the greater purpose of the trip to us.

Why didn't Stephen with his moral vision opt to take the sadhu under his personal care? The answer is because, in part, Stephen was hard-stressed physically himself, and because, in part, without some support system that involved our involuntary and episodic community on the mountain, it was beyond his individual capacity to do so.

I see the current interest in corporate culture and corporate value systems as a positive response to Stephen's pessimism about the decline of the role in the individual in large organizations. Individuals who operate from a thoughtful set of personal values provide the foundation for a corporate culture. A corporate tradition that encourages freedom of inquiry, supports personal values and reinforces a focused sense of direction can fulfill the need for individuality along with the prosperity and success of the group. Without such corporate support, the individual is lost.

That is the lesson of the sadhu. In a complex corporate situation, the individual requires and deserves the support of the group. If people cannot find such support from their organization, they don't know how to act. If such support is forthcoming, a person has a stake in the success of the group, and can add much to the process of establishing and maintaining a corporate culture. It is management's challenge to be sensitive to individual needs, to shape them and to direct and focus them for the benefit of the group as a whole.

For each of us the sadhu lives. Should we stop what we are doing and comfort him; or should we keep trudging up toward the high pass? Should I pause to help the derelict I pass on the street each night as I walk to the Yale Club en route to Grand Central Station? Am I his brother? What is the nature of our responsibility if we consider ourselves to be ethical persons? Perhaps it is to change the values of the group so that it can, with all its resources, take the other road.

THE RASHOMON EFFECT

—Patricia Werhane

The abstract of this article offers background to the piece. Consider how perspective alters judgment. Can you think of times when your perspective may have altered your judgment? What does this say of our justice system? What does it say of our information system as a whole? Do you obtain most of your news from (and therefore base your judgments on) television news shows? the newspaper? How might you ensure that your judgment is based on the most broad and unbiased perspectives?

The Academy Award winning 1960s Japanese movie Rashomon *depicts an incident involving an outlaw, a rape or seduction of a woman and a murder or suicide of her husband told from four different perspectives: that of the outlaw, the woman, the husband and a passer-by. The four narratives agree that the outlaw came upon the woman and her husband, the outlaw tied up the husband, sex took place between the woman and the outlaw in front of the bound husband, and the husband was found dead. How these events occurred and who killed the husband (or whether he killed himself) differs with each narrative.*

Applied ethics uses case stories to illustrate ethical issues, and it evaluates the stories or cases through moral theories and moral reasoning. The way we present cases or stories or describe the "facts," that is, the narratives we employ and the mental models that frame these narratives, affect the content of the story, the moral analysis and subsequent evaluation of events. Indeed, we cannot present a case or tell a story except through the frame of a particular narrative or mental model. When one narrative becomes dominant, we appeal to that story for the "facts," taking it as representing what actually happened. Yet we seldom look at the narrative we use nor are we often aware of the "frame" or mental model at work. If my thesis is not mistaken, then, it is just as important, morally important, to examine different narratives about the cases we use as it is to carry out the ethical analysis.

To demonstrate what I am talking about, I am going to recount narratives of a well-worn case, the Ford Pinto. I shall illustrate how different commentators present what one of them has called "independently supportable facts" (Schmitt and May, 1979, p. 1022). In each instance I cite, the commentator claims that he is presenting facts, not assumptions, commentary, or conjecture. Yet, for some reason, these "facts" seem to differ from each other. The accounts of the case I shall use are Mark Dowie's "Pinto Madness" from September/October 1977 *Mother Jones,* later revised and printed in *Business and Society;*

"Beyond Products Liability" by Michael Schmitt and William W. May from the *University of Detroit Journal of Urban Law,* Summer 1979; Manuel Velasquez's treatment of Pinto in his book *Business Ethics* (second ed.); Dekkers L. Davidson and Kenneth Goodpaster's Harvard Business School case, "Managing Product Safety: The Ford Pinto"; Ford Motor Company's statements from their law suit, *State of Indiana* v. *Ford Motor Company;* and Michael Hoffman's case/essay "The Ford Pinto," printed in *Taking Sides.* It will become evident that one narrative, Mark Dowie's, one of the earliest accounts of the case, becomes the dominant one.

> There is one indisputable set of data upon which all commentators agree. On May 28, 1972, Mrs. Lily Gray was driving a six-month-old Pinto on Interstate 15 near San Bernardino, California. In the car with her was Richard Grimshaw, a 13-year-old boy. . . . Mrs. Gray stopped in San Bernardino for gasoline, got back onto the freeway (Interstate 15) and proceeded toward her destination at 60 to 65 miles per hour. As she approached Route 30 off-ramp, . . . the Pinto suddenly stalled and coasted to a halt in the middle lane . . . the driver of a 1962 Ford Galaxie was unable to avoid colliding with the Pinto. Before impact the Galaxie had been braked to a speed of from 28 to 37 miles per hour.
>
> At the moment of impact, the Pinto caught fire and its interior burst into flames. The crash had driven the Pinto's gas tank forward and punctured it against the flange on the differential housing. . . . Mrs. Gray died a few days later. . . . Grimshaw managed to survive with severe burns over 90% of his body. (Velasquez, 199, p. 122; Grimshaw v. Ford Motor Co., p. 359).

In 1978 a jury awarded Grimshaw at least $125 million in punitive damages. *Auto News* printed a headline "Ford Fights Pinto Case: Jury Gives 128 Million" on February 13, 1978. The number $125 million is commonly cited and is in the court records as the sum of the initial punitive award. This award was later reduced on appeal to $3.5 million, a fact that is seldom cited.

What is the background for the development of the Pinto? According to public statements made by Lee Iacocca, then CEO of Ford, to meet Japanese competition Ford decided to design a subcompact car that would not weigh over 2,000 pounds nor cost over $2,000 (Davidson/Goodpaster, 1983). According to Davidson/Goodpaster, Ford began planning the Pinto in June 1967, ending with production beginning in September 1970, a 38-month turnaround time as opposed to the industry average of 43 months for engineering and developing a new automobile (Davidson/Goodpaster, 1983, p. 4). Mark Dowie claims that the development was "rushed" into 25 months (Dowie, p. 20); Velasquez says it occurred in "under two years" (Velasquez, p. 120); Hoffman claims that Ford "rushed the Pinto into production in much less than the usual time" (Hoffman, p. 133). While the actual time of development may seem unimportant, critics of the Pinto design argue that *because* it was "rushed into production" Pinto was not as carefully designed nor checked for safety as a model created over a 43-month time span (Dowie, Velasquez).

The Pinto was designed so that the gas tank was placed behind the rear axle. According to Davidson/Goodpaster, "At that time almost every American-made car had the fuel tank located in the same place" (p. 4). Dowie wonders why Ford did not place the gas tank over the rear axle, Ford's patented design for their Capri models. This placement is confirmed by

Dowie, Velasquez and some Ford engineers to be the "safest place." Yet, according to Davidson/Goodpaster other studies at Ford showed that the Capri placement actually increased the likelihood of ignition inside the automobile (p. 4). Moreover, such placement reduces storage space and precludes a hatchback design. Velasquez argues that "[b]ecause the Pinto was a rush project, styling preceded engineering" (p. 120), thus accounting for the gas tank placement. This fact may have been derived from Dowie's quote, allegedly from a "Ford engineer who doesn't want his name used," that "this company is run by salesmen, not engineers; so the priority is styling, not safety" (p. 23).

Dowie argues that in addition to rushing the Pinto into production, "Ford engineers discovered in pre-production crash tests that rear-end collisions would rupture the Pinto's fuel system extremely easily" (p. 18). According to Dowie, Ford crash-tested the Pinto in a secret location and in every test made at over 25 mph the fuel tank ruptured. But according to Ford, while Pinto's gas tank did explode during many of its tests, this was because, following government guidelines, Ford had to test the car using a fixed barrier standard wherein the vehicle is towed backwards into a fixed barrier at the speed specified in the test. Ford argued that Pinto behaved well under a less stringent moving-barrier standard, which, Ford contended, is a more realistic test (Davidson/Goodpaster; *State of Indiana* v. *Ford*).

Ford and the commentators on this case agree that in 1971, before launching the automobile, an internal study was conducted that showed that a rubber bladder inner tank would improve the reliability of Pinto during tests. The bladder would cost $5.08 (Dowie, p. 29; Schmitt and May, 1979, p. 1023), $5.80 (Davidson/Goodpaster), or $11 (Velasquez, p. 120). The $11 figure probably refers to a design adjustment that Ford would have had to make to meet a later new government rollover standard (see below). However, the idea of this installation was discarded, according to Ford because of the unreliability of the rubber at cold temperatures, a conjecture no one else mentions. Dowie also contends that Ford could have reduced the dangers from rear-end collisions by installing a $1 plastic baffle between the gas tank and the differential housing to reduce the likelihood of gas tank perforation. I can find no other verification of this fact.

All commentators claim that Ford did a cost/benefit analysis to determine whether it would be more costly to change the Pinto design or assume the damages for burn victims, and memos to that effect were evidence at the Grimshaw trial (*Grimshaw* v. *Ford Motor Co.,* 570). However, according to Davidson/Goodpaster and Schmitt/May, this estimate was done in 1973, the year *after* the Grimshaw accident, in response to evaluating a proposed new government rollover standard. To meet that requirement would cost $11 per auto, Ford calculated. Ford used government data for the cost of a life ($200,000 per person), and projected an estimate of 180 burn deaths from rollovers. The study was not applicable to rear-end collisions as commentators, following Dowie's story, claimed.

There are also innuendoes in many write-ups of this case that the $200,000 figure was Ford's price of a human life. Dowie says, for example, "Ever wonder what your life is worth in dollars? Perhaps $10 million? Ford has a better idea: $200,000." In fact, it was the U.S. government's 1973 figure.

How many people have died as a result of a rear-end collision in a Pinto? "By conservative estimates Pinto crashes have caused 500 burn deaths to people who would not have been seriously injured if the car had not burst into flames. The figure could be as high as

900," Dowie claimed in 1977 (p. 18). Hoffman, in 1984, repeats those figures word for word (p. 133). Velasquez, more cautious, claims that by 1978 at least 53 people had died and "many more had been severely burnt" (p. 122), and Schmitt and May, quoting a 1977 article in *Business and Society Review,* estimate the number at "at least 32" (p. 1024; May, p. 102 at 16). Davidson/Goodpaster claim that by 1978 NHTSA estimated there were 38 cases which involved 27 fatalities.

There was a second famous Pinto accident that led the State of Indiana to charge Ford with criminal liability. The facts in that case upon which all agree are reported by Hoffman as follows:

> *On August 10, 1978, a tragic automobile accident occurred on U.S. Highway 33 near Goshen, Indiana. Sisters Judy and Lynn Ulrich (ages 18 and 16, respectively) and their cousin Donna Ulrich (age 18) were struck from the rear in their 1973 Ford Pinto by a van. The gas tank of the Pinto ruptured, the car burst into flames and the three teenagers were burned to death. (p. 132)*

There are two points of interest in this case, points that helped to exonerate Ford in the eyes of the jury in the Indiana trial. First, in June of 1978 Ford recalled 1.5 million of its Pintos to modify the fuel tank. There is some evidence that the Ulrich auto had not participated in the recall (*State of Indiana* v. *Ford Motor Company*). Secondly, Ulrich's Pinto was hit from behind at 50 miles an hour by a van driven by a Mr. Duggar. Mr. Duggar, who was not killed, later testified that he looked down for a "smoke" when he then hit the car, although the Ulrichs had their safety blinkers on. Found in Duggar's van were at least two empty beer bottles and an undisclosed amount of marijuana. Yet this evidence, cited in the *State of Indiana* v. *Ford Motor Co.* case, are seldom mentioned in the context of the Ulrich tragedy, nor was Duggar ever indicted.

The point of all this is not to exonerate Ford nor to argue for bringing back the Pinto. Rather, it is to point out a simple phenomenon—that a narrative—a story—can be taken as fact even when other alleged equally verifiable facts contradict that story. Moreover, one narrative can become dominating such that what it says is taken as fact. Dowie's interesting tale of the Pinto became the prototype for Pinto cases without many of the authors going back to see if Dowie's data was correct or to question why some of his data contradicts Ford's and government claims. Moreover, Dowie's reporting of Grimshaw becomes a prototype for the narrative of Ulrich case as well, so that questions concerning the recall of the Ulrich auto and Mr. Duggar's performance were virtually ignored. Such omissions not only make Ford look better. They also bring into question these reports and cases.

Let me mention another set of stories, those revolving around the more recent Dow Corning silicone breast implant controversy. From the volumes of reports there are a few facts upon which everyone agrees. Dow Corning has developed and manufactured silicone breast implants since 1962. It is one of a number of manufacturers that include Bristol Myers Squibb, Baxter and 3M. In 1975 it changed the design of the implant to a thinner shell that, according to the company, was more "natural," thus less likely to harden over time. Out of the almost 2 million women who have had implants, at least 440,000 have joined class action suits or brought individual law suits claiming to have experienced a variety of illnesses, including autoimmune diseases such as lupus and rheumatoid arthritis, connective tissues diseases, scleroderma, cancer and various other malaises such as pain, fatigue, insomnia, memory loss and/or headaches (*New York Times,* 1995, p. C6; Angell, p. 18).

Since this is an evolving case not all the positions and narratives have sufficiently solidified to make exhaustive comparisons. But let me focus on three points. First, there is a very simple question, Do silicone breast implants cause cancer and other diseases, in particular, connective tissue or autoimmune diseases? Second, did the industry, and Dow Corning in particular, cover up or not inform physicians or women patients of the risks of implantation? Third, did Dow Corning fail "to acknowledge and promptly investigate signs of trouble?" (See bibliography for citations.)

The first question is the most simple and the most puzzling. A seldom cited fact in the case is that pacemakers and a number of other implants are made from silicone, because silicone is thought to be the most inert of all possible implant substances. Yet pacemaker wearers have not sued for illnesses that allegedly result from that implant. According to pathologist Nir Kossovsky, however, silicone breast implants can affect the immune system and cause a variety of harms to the system. This is particularly acute when an implant ruptures (Taubes, 1995). Yet in numerous independent epidemiological studies investigators have been unable to establish any but the weakest correlation between breast implants and cancer, connective tissue disease or autoimmune diseases (Sánchez-Guerrero et al., 1995; Giltay et al., 1994; McLaughlin and Fraumeni, 1994). The most extensive of these is a longitudinal study by Brigham and Women's Hospital of 87,318 women nurses from the ages of 30 to 55 covering their medical records over a 14-year span. This study, partly funded by the NIH, is the basis for what will be a larger study of 450,000 women. (It should also be noted that silicone breast implants were withdrawn from the market by the FDA, not because they were proven to be harmful but because the FDA concluded that the evidence was not strong enough to show they were not harmful.) Despite what an overwhelming number of scientists consider to be overwhelming evidence, a number of lawsuits have been won by claimants who argue they became ill because of implants.

The second question—Did Dow Corning cover up evidence?—is also equally puzzling. Dow Corning claims, of course, that they did not. This is partly because they instigated their own studies that found no conclusive link between implants and disease, and partly because from the very beginning they did in fact inform *physicians* about risks of implants, including possibility of rupture or hardening in some patients. It is only recently, since 1985, that Dow Corning has developed brochures to be distributed to candidates for implantation.

The third question seems to become moot if implants do not cause disease. Yet more is at stake here. Dow Corning and other silicone breast implant manufacturers depended on the narratives of science. They imagined that scientific evidence and only scientific evidence would count as evidence in the courts, that the media would not print a story to the contrary when such scientific evidence was conclusive, and that the emotional fact that women with implants became ill would become a dominant factor in what appeared to be a matter of science. We have here a number of narratives: the scientific evidence reports, Dow Corning's defense of their consent procedures, and lawsuits that focus on the illnesses. There is also a set of media narratives that focus on the emotional reactions of ill women (not all media narratives do this), the dominating examples of which are the *Business Week* article "Informed Consent" (Byrne, 1995) and John Byrne's book, which was produced from this reporting. This article focuses on the emotional trauma of Colleen Swanson, the wife of a Dow Corning manager, John Swanson, who recently resigned from Dow Corning after 27 years of employment. Colleen Swanson had had implants 17 years ago and has been suffering from a variety of illnesses almost since the end of the operation. While Byrne focuses on Colleen's emotional suffering he cites the epidemiological evidence but puts that evidence in doubt by stating:

> *Recent studies from Harvard Medical School and the Mayo Clinic, among others, have cast doubt on the link between implants and disease. But critics have attacked these studies on numerous grounds—among them that they look only for recognized diseases such as lupus, rather than the complex of ailments many recipients complain of. (Byrne, 1996, p. 116)*

Again I am not trying to whitewash this case. But it is interesting how the fact of illnesses in women with implants has been conflated with the causal claim of "illnesses caused by silicone breast implants." Perhaps it is the notion of causality that should be brought into question. The dominating emotional narratives have simply overshadowed the scientific ones. It is no wonder that Dow Corning cannot figure out what happened since they focused primarily on the scientific narratives. Moreover they seemed to assume that physicians performing implant surgery were all reasonable professionals who would inform their patients uniformly and thoroughly about the risks of implantation. (One cannot even with good conscience construct a narrative that claims that scientists are male-dominated and thus biased in their data analysis, because these studies have been conducted by men and women of a variety of scientific and medical backgrounds and nationalities.)

What can we say about the role of narratives? As I have argued elsewhere (Werhane, 1991, 1992) human beings do not simply perceive the data of their experiences unedited, so to speak. Each of us orders, selects, structures and even censors our experiences. These shaping mechanisms are mental models or schema through which we experience the world. The selection processes or schema are culturally and socially learned and changed, and almost no perspective or model is permanent or unalterable. But we never see the world except through a point of view, a model, or framing mechanism. Indeed, narratives that shape our experiences and influence how we think about the world are essential to the facts of our experience. At the same time, these mental models or schema and these narratives are not merely subjective. They represent points of view that others share or can share, and they are, or can be, what Amartya Sen calls "positionally objective." Sen writes:

> *What we can observe depends on our position vis-a-vis the objects of observation. . . . Positionally dependent observations, beliefs and actions are central to our knowledge and practical reason. The nature of objectivity in epistemology, decision theory and ethics has to take adequate note of the parametric dependence of observation and inference on the position of the observer.*

Position-dependency defines the way in which the object appears "from a delineated somewhere." This "delineated somewhere," however, is positionally objective. That is, any person in that position will make similar observations, according to Sen. I would add that the parameters of positionality are not merely spatial but could involve a shared schema. For example, managers at Ford had access to a lot of the same data about the Pinto. Ford's decision not to recall the Pinto despite a number of terrible accidents could be defended as a positionally objective belief based on the ways in which managers at Ford processed information on automobile crashes. (Gioia, 1991) Similarly, Dow Corning's reluctance to stop manufacturing silicone implants could be construed as positionally objective from their focus on scientific evidence and reliance on responsible surgeons. Colleen Swanson and other ill recipients of implants also adopt a positionally objective view, from their perspective as very ill people with implants.

However, a positionally objective point of view could be mistaken in case it did not take into account all available information. Thus, as Sen points out, in most cases one need not unconditionally accept a positionally objective view. Because of the variety of schema with which one can shape a position, almost any position has alternatives, almost every position has its critics. I would qualify that further. Even allegedly positionally objective phenomena are still phenomena that have been filtered through the social sieve of a shared mental model or schema.

As I have just demonstrated, some narratives are more closely based on actual experiences; others are taken from the narratives of others which we have accepted "as true"; still others are in the form of stories. For example, the movie *Wall Street* tells a story about Wall Street that reshapes our perception of investment banking. These perspectives are necessarily incomplete, they can be biased or they can be constituted by someone else's framing of experience. So, for example, as E. H. Gombrich the art historian relates, following Albrecht Durer's famous etching of a rhinoceros, for a very long time naturalists as well as artists portrayed rhinos with "armored" layers of skin, when in fact, a simple look at a rhino belies that conclusion (Gombrich). Similarly, Dowie's portrayal of the Pinto case became the prototype for other case descriptions. Byrne's *Business Week* article and his subsequent book on the Dow-Corning breast implant controversy appear to be becoming the prototype factual bases for analyzing that case. What happens in these instances is that "life imitates art," or the "grammar," the alleged data of the narrative creates the essence of the story.

Does this mean that one can never arrive at facts or truths? The short answer is "yes" or "no." The longer answer is more complicated. The thesis that experience is always framed by a perspective or point of view is closely related to another thesis, Wittgenstein's claim that "*[e]ssence* is expressed by grammar" (Wittgenstein, 1953, § 371), that is, in short, that all our experiences are framed, organized and made meaningful only through the language we employ to conceive, frame, think, describe and evaluate our experiences. Whether or not all experiences are linguistically constituted is a topic for another essay. What is important is what Wittgenstein does not say, that "essence is *created* by grammar" (Anscombe, 1976, p. 188). Nor did he hold that view, as I have argued in detail elsewhere (Werhane, 1992). To put the point in more Kantian terms, there is data or "stuff" of our experience that is not created or made up (although sometimes we can and do make up the content of our experiences when we envelop ourselves in fantasy) and, indeed, the distinction between "reality" and "fantasy" may be just that—that we do not make up the content of our experience. Nevertheless, that data or content or "stuff" is never pure—it is always constituted and contaminated by our perspective, point of view, or mental model.

At the same time, we are able to engage in "trans-positional" assessments or what Sen has called a "constructed 'view from nowhere.' " A trans-positional view from nowhere is a constructed critique of a particular conceptual scheme, and no positionally objective view is merely relative nor immune from challenge. This sort of assessment involves comparing various positionally objective points of view to see whether one can make coherent sense of them and develop some general theories about what is being observed. These trans-positional assessments are *constructed* views, because they too depend on the conceptual scheme of the assessors. From a trans-positional point of view conceptual schemes themselves can be questioned on the basis of their coherence and/or their explanatory scope. Although that challenge could only be conducted from another conceptual scheme, that assessment could take into account a variety of points of view. Still, revisions of the scheme in question might produce another conceptual scheme that more adequately or more comprehensively explained or took into account a range of phenomena or incidents. Together, studying sets of perspectives can get at how certain events are experienced and reported, and even, what mental models, schemes or narratives are at work in shaping the narratives about these experiences. While one can never get at those from a pure *tabula rasa,* nevertheless one can achieve a limited, dispassionate view from somewhere.

Near the end of *Rashomon* the narrator of the tale, who is also the bystander, decries the lack of trust in society engendered from the impossibility of ascertaining the truth. The cases we develop must be done with care. In using others' cases and narratives one should study not just the facts as presented in the case narratives. Rather, we need to examine the ways in which the facts are constituted to make a story or a case, and one should become aware of how some of those cases can become prototypical narratives that we imitate. The so-called "classics" like Pinto need to be revisited or they will become cliched prototypes. And we need to be wary of assumptions generated by these prototypes such as the assumption that Dow Corning caused egregious harms, perhaps even deliberately, to the over 2 million women who have their breast implants. While we cannot arrive at The Truth we can at least approximate it more fully. Only then will we who teach and write in applied ethics become, in the words of Henry James, "finely aware and richly responsible" (Nussbaum, 1990).

BIBLIOGRAPHY

Angell, Marcia. 1995. "Are Breast Implants Actually OK?" *The New Republic,* September 11, 17–21.
_____. 1996. *Science on Trial.* New York: W. W. Norton & Co.
Anscombe, G. E M. 1976. "The Question of Linguistic Idealism." *Essays on Wittgenstein in Honour of G. H. Von Wright.* Acta Philosophica Fennica, Vol. 28. ed. Jaakko Hintikka. Amsterdam: North Holland Publishing Co., 181–215.
Byrne, John A. 1995. "Informed Consent." *Business Week,* October 2, 104–116.
_____. 1996. *Informed Consent: A Story of Personal Tragedy and Corporate Betrayal.* New York, McGraw-Hill Companies.
Davidson, Dekkers, and Kenneth E. Goodpaster. 1983. "Managing Product Safety: The Ford Pinto." Harvard University Graduate School of Business Administration Case #9-383-129. Boston: Harvard Business School Press.
Dowie, Mark. 1977a. "Pinto Madness." *Mother Jones,* September/October, 18–32.
_____. 1977b. "How Ford Put Two Million Firetraps on Wheels." *Business and Society Review,* 23: 46–55.

"Ford Fights Pinto Case: Jury Gives 128 Million." 1978. *Auto News,* February 13, 1.

Gabriel, S. E., et al. 1994. "Risk of Connective-Tissue Diseases and Other Disorders after Breast Implantation." *New England Journal of Medicine,* 330: 1697–1702.

Giltay, Erik J., et al. 1994. "Silicone Breast Protheses and Rheumatic Symptoms: A Retrospective Follow Up Study." *Annals of Rheumatic Diseases,* 53: 194–196.

Gioia, Dennis. 1991. "Pinto Fires and Personal Ethics: A Script Analysis of Missed Opportunities." *Journal of Business Ethics,* 11: 379–389.

Gombrich, E. H. 1961. *Art and Illusion.* Princeton: Princeton University Press.

Grimshaw v. *Ford Motor Co.* 1978. No. 197761. Super CT. Orange County, CA, February 6.

Hoffman, Michael. 1984. "The Ford Pinto." Rpt. in *Taking Sides.* Ed. Lisa H. Newton and Maureen M. Ford. Dushkin Publishing Group, 132–137.

Kolata, Gina. 1995. "Proof of a Breast Implant Peril Is Lacking, Rheumatologists Say." *New York Times,* October 25.

McLaughlin, Joseph K., and Joseph F. Fraumeni Jr. 1994. "Correspondence Re: Breast Implants, Cancer and Systemic Sclerosis." *Journal of the National Cancer Institute,* 86: 1424.

Nussbaum, Martha. 1990. *Love's Knowledge.* New York: Oxford University Press.

Sanchez-Guerrero, Jorge, et al. 1995. "Silicone Breast Implants and the Risk of Connective-Tissue Diseases and Symptoms." *New England Journal of Medicine,* 332: 1666–1670.

Schmitt, Michael A., and William W. May, 1979. "Beyond Products Liability: The Legal, Social and Ethical Problems Facing the Automobile Industry in Producing Safe Products." *University of Detroit Journal of Urban Law,* 56: 1021–1050.

Sen, Amartya. 1993. "Positional Objectivity." *Philosophy and Public Affairs.*

State of Indiana v. *Ford Motor Co.* (1979), No. 11-431, Cir. Ct. Pulaski, IN.

Taubes, Gary. 1995. "Silicone in the System." *Discover,* December, 65–75.

Velasquez, Manuel. 1988. *Business Ethics,* 2nd ed. Englewood Cliffs: Prentice-Hall, Inc.

Werhane, Patricia H. 1991. "Engineers and Management: The Challenge of the *Challenger* Incident." *Journal of Business Ethics,* 10: 605–616.

_____. 1992. *Skepticism, Rules, and Private Languages.* Atlantic Highlands, NJ: Humanities Press.

_____. 1998. "Moral Imagination and Management Decision-Making." *New Avenues of Research in Business Ethics.* Edited by R. Edward Freeman. New York: Oxford University Press.

Wittgenstein, Ludwig. 1953. *Philosophical Investigations.* Trans. G. E. M. Anscombe. New York: Macmillan and Co.

IS BUSINESS BLUFFING ETHICAL?

—Albert Z. Carr

One of the most often discussed articles in many introductory business ethics courses, Albert Carr's article deftly asserts that bluffing in business may be ethical. Carr explains how bluffing (deceiving) in certain situations may be more acceptable than in others. On the other hand, there is a true benefit from a reputation for honesty in business, as well. Do you believe the distinctions Carr makes in his discussion are clear or arbitrary?

A respected businessman with whom I discussed the theme of this article remarked with some heat, "You mean to say you're going to encourage men to bluff? Why, bluffing is nothing more than a form of lying! You're advising them to lie!"

I agreed that the basis of private morality is a respect for truth and that the closer a businessman comes to the truth, the more he deserves respect. At the same time, I suggested that most bluffing in business might be regarded simply as game strategy—much like bluffing in poker, which does not reflect on the morality of the bluffer.

I quoted Henry Taylor, the British statesman who pointed out that "falsehood ceases to be falsehood when it is understood on all sides that the truth is not expected to be spoken"—an exact description of bluffing in poker, diplomacy and business. I cited the analogy of the criminal court, where the criminal is not expected to tell the truth when he pleads "not guilty." Everyone from the judge down takes it for granted that the job of the defendant's attorney is to get his client off, not to reveal the truth; and this is considered ethical practice. I mentioned Representative Omar Burleson, the Democrat from Texas, who was quoted as saying, in regard to the ethics of Congress, "Ethics is a barrel of worms."[1]—a pungent summing up of the problem of deciding who is ethical in politics.

I reminded my friend that millions of businessmen feel constrained every day to say *yes* to their bosses when they secretly believe *no* and that this is generally accepted as permissible strategy when the alternative might be the loss of a job. The essential point, I said, is that the ethics of business are game ethics, different from the ethics of religion.

He remained unconvinced. Referring to the company of which he is President, he declared: "Maybe that's good enough for some businessmen, but I can tell you that we pride ourselves on our ethics. In 30 years not one customer has ever questioned my word or asked to check our figures. We're loyal to our customers and fair to our suppliers. I regard my handshake on a deal as a contract. I've never entered into price fixing schemes with my

---

competitors. I've never allowed my salesmen to spread injurious rumors about other companies. Our union contract is the best in our industry. And, if I do say so myself, our ethical standards are of the highest!"

He really was saying, without realizing it, that he was living up to the ethical standards of the business game—which are a far cry from those of private life. Like a gentlemanly poker player, he did not play in cahoots with others at the table, try to smear their reputations or hold back chips he owed them.

But this same fine man, at that very time, was allowing one of his products to be advertised in a way that made it sound a great deal better than it actually was. Another item in his product line was notorious among dealers for its "built-in obsolescence." He was holding back from the market a much-improved product because he did not want it to interfere with sales of the inferior item it would have replaced. He had joined with certain of his competitors in hiring a lobbyist to push a state legislature, by methods that he preferred not to know too much about, into amending a bill then being enacted.

In his view these things had nothing to do with ethics; they were merely normal business practice. He himself undoubtedly avoided outright falsehoods—never lied in so many words. But the entire organization that he ruled was deeply involved in numerous strategies of deception.

***

THE POKER ANALOGY

We can learn a good deal about the nature of business by comparing it with poker. While both have a large element of chance, in the long run the winner is the man who plays with steady skill. In both games ultimate victory requires intimate knowledge of the rules, insight into the psychology of the other players, a bold front, a considerable amount of self-discipline and the ability to respond swiftly and effectively to opportunities provided by chance.

No one expects poker to be played on the ethical principles preached in churches. In poker it is right and proper to bluff a friend out of the rewards of being dealt a good hand. A player feels no more than a slight twinge of sympathy, if that, when—with nothing better than a single ace in his hand—he strips a heavy loser, who holds a pair, of the rest of his chips. It was up to the other fellow to protect himself. In the words of an excellent poker player, former President Harry Truman, "If one can't stand the heat, stay out of the kitchen." If one shows mercy to a loser in poker, it is a personal gesture, divorced from the rules of the game.

Poker has its special ethics, and here I am not referring to rules against cheating. The man who keeps an ace up his sleeve or who marks the cards is more than unethical; he is a crook, and can be punished as such—kicked out of the game or, in the Old West, shot.

In contrast to the cheat, the unethical poker player is one who, while abiding by the letter of the rules, finds ways to put the other players at an unfair disadvantage. Perhaps he unnerves them with loud talk. Or he tries to get them drunk. Or he plays in cahoots with someone else at the table. Ethical poker players frown on such tactics.

Poker's own brand of ethics is different from the ethical ideals of civilized human relationships. The game calls for distrust of the other fellow. It ignores the claim of friendship. Cunning deception and concealment of one's strength and intentions, not kindness and openheartedness, are vital in poker. No one thinks any the worse of poker on that account. And no one should think any the worse of the game of business because its standards of right and wrong differ from the prevailing traditions of morality in our society.

DISCARD THE GOLDEN RULE

This view of business is especially worrisome to people without much business experience. A minister of my acquaintance once protested that business cannot possibly function in our society unless it is based on the Judeo-Christian system of ethics. He told me:

> *I know some businessmen have supplied call girls to customers, but there are always a few rotten apples in every barrel. That doesn't mean the rest of the fruit isn't sound. Surely the vast majority of businessmen are ethical. I myself am acquainted with many who adhere to strict codes of ethics based fundamentally on religious teachings. They contribute to good causes. They participate in community activities. They cooperate with other companies to improve working conditions in their industries. Certainly they are not indifferent to ethics.*

That most businessmen are not indifferent to ethics in their private lives, everyone will agree. My point is that in their office lives they cease to be private citizens; they become game players who must be guided by a somewhat different set of ethical standards.

The point was forcefully made to me by a Midwestern executive who has given a good deal of thought to the question:

> *So long as a businessman complies with the laws of the land and avoids telling malicious lies, he's ethical. If the law as written gives a man a wide-open chance to make a killing, he'd be a fool not to take advantage of it. If he doesn't, somebody else will. There's no obligation on him to stop and consider who is going to get hurt. If the law says he can do it, that's all the justification he needs. There's nothing unethical about that. It's just plain business sense.*

This executive (call him Robbins) took the stand that even industrial espionage, which is frowned on by some businessmen, ought not to be considered unethical. He recalled a recent meeting of the National Industrial Conference Board where an authority on marketing made a speech in which he deplored the employment of spies by business organizations. More and more companies, he pointed out, find it cheaper to penetrate the secrets of competitors with concealed cameras and microphones or by bribing employees than to set up costly research and design departments of their own. A whole branch of the electronics industry has grown up with this trend, he continued, providing equipment to make industrial espionage easier.

Disturbing? The marketing expert found it so. But when it came to a remedy, he could only appeal to "respect for the golden rule." Robbins thought this a confession of defeat, believing that the golden rule, for all its value as an ideal for society, is simply not feasible as a guide for business. A good part of the time the businessman is trying to do unto others as he hopes others will not do unto him.[2] Robbins continued:

> *Espionage of one kind or another has become so common in business that it's like taking a drink during Prohibition—it's not considered sinful. And we don't even have*

Prohibition where espionage is concerned; the law is very tolerant in this area. There's no more shame for a business that uses secret agents than there is for a nation. Bear in mind that there already is at least one large corporation—one can buy its stock over the counter—that makes millions by providing counterespionage service to industrial firms. Espionage in business is not an ethical problem; it's an established technique of business competition.

"We Don't Make the Laws"

Wherever we turn in business, we can perceive the sharp distinction between its ethical standards and those of the churches. Newspapers abound with sensational stories growing out of this distinction:

> We read one day that Senator Philip A. Hart of Michigan has attacked food processors for deceptive packaging of numerous products.[3]

> The next day there is a congressional to-do over Ralph Nader's book, *Unsafe At Any Speed,* which demonstrates that automobile companies for years have neglected the safety of car-owning families.[4]

> Then another Senator, Lee Metcalf of Montana, and journalist Vic Reinemer show in their book, *Overcharge,* the methods by which utility companies elude regulating government bodies to extract unduly large payments from users of electricity.[5]

These are merely dramatic instances of a prevailing condition; there is hardly a major industry at which a similar attack could not be aimed. Critics of business regard such behavior as unethical, but the companies concerned know that they are merely playing the business game.

Among the most respected of our business institutions are the insurance companies. A group of insurance executives meeting recently in New England was startled when their guest speaker, social critic Daniel Patrick Moynihan, roundly berated them for "unethical" practices. They had been guilty, Moynihan alleged, of using outdated actuarial tables to obtain unfairly high premiums. They habitually delayed the hearings of lawsuits against them in order to tire out the plaintiffs and win cheap settlements. In their employment policies they used ingenious devices to discriminate against certain minority groups.[6]

It was difficult for the audience to deny the validity of these charges. But these men were business game players. Their reaction to Moynihan's attack was much the same as that of the automobile manufacturers to Nader, of the utilities to Senator Metcalf and of the food processors to Senator Hart. If the laws governing their businesses change, or if public opinion becomes clamorous, they will make the necessary adjustments. But morally they have in their view done nothing wrong. As long as they comply with the letter of the law, they are within their rights to operate their businesses as they see fit.

The small business is in the same position as the great corporation in this respect. For example:

> *In 1967 a key manufacturer was accused of providing master keys for automobiles to mail-order customers, although it was obvious that some of the purchasers might be automobile thieves. His defense was plain and straightforward. If there was nothing in the law to prevent him from selling his keys to anyone who ordered them, it was not up to him to inquire who or-*

dered them, it was not up to him to inquire as to his customers' motives. Why was it any worse, he insisted, for him to sell car keys by mail, than for mail-order houses to sell guns that might be used for murder? Until the law was changed, the key manufacturer could regard himself as being just as ethical as any other businessman by the rules of the business game.[7]

Violations of the ethical ideals of society are common in business, but they are not necessarily violations of business principles. Each year the Federal Trade Commission orders hundreds of companies, many of them of the first magnitude, to "cease and desist" from practices which, judged by ordinary standards, are of questionable morality but which are stoutly defended by the companies concerned.

In one case, a firm manufacturing a well-known mouthwash was accused of using a cheap form of alcohol possibly deleterious to health. The company's chief executive, after testifying in Washington, made this comment privately:

We broke no law. We're in a highly competitive industry. If we're going to stay in business, we have to look for profit wherever the law permits. We don't make the laws. We obey them. Then why do we have to put up with this "holier than thou" talk about ethics? It's sheer hypocrisy. We're not in business to promote ethics. Look at the cigarette companies, for God's sake! If the ethics aren't embodied in the laws by the men who made them, you can't expect businessmen to fill the lack. Why, a sudden submission to Christian ethics by businessmen would bring about the greatest economic upheaval in history!

It may be noted that the government failed to prove its case against him.

***

THE INDIVIDUAL & THE GAME

An individual within a company often finds it difficult to adjust to the requirements of the business game. He tries to preserve his private ethical standards in situations that call for game strategy. When he is obliged to carry out company policies that challenge his conception of himself as an ethical man, he suffers.

It disturbs him when he is ordered, for instance, to deny a raise to a man who deserves it, to fire an employee of long standing, to prepare advertising that he believes to be misleading, to conceal facts that he feels customers are entitled to know, to cheapen the quality of materials used in the manufacture of an established product, to sell as new a product that he knows to be rebuilt, to exaggerate the curative powers of a medicinal preparation or to coerce dealers.

There are some fortunate executives who, by the nature of their work and circumstances, never have to face problems of this kind. But in one form or another the ethical dilemma is felt sooner or later by most businessmen. Possibly the dilemma is most painful not when the company forces the action on the executive but when he originates it himself—that is, when he has taken or is contemplating a step which is in his own interest but which runs counter to his early moral conditioning. To illustrate:

The manager of an export department, eager to show rising sales, is pressed by a big customer to provide invoices which, while containing no overt falsehood that would violate a U.S. law, are so worded that the customer may be able to evade certain taxes in his homeland.

A company president finds that an aging executive, within a few years of retirement and his pension, is not as productive as formerly. Should he be kept on?

The produce manager of a supermarket debates with himself whether to get rid of a lot of half-rotten tomatoes by including one, with its good side exposed, in every tomato six-pack.

An accountant discovers that he has taken an improper deduction on his company's tax return and fears the consequences if he calls the matter to the president's attention, though he himself has done nothing illegal. Perhaps if he says nothing, no one will notice the error.

A chief executive officer is asked by his directors to comment on a rumor that he owns stock in another company with which he has placed large orders. He could deny it, for the stock is in the name of his son-in-law and he has earlier formally instructed his son-in-law to sell the holding.

Temptations of this kind constantly arise in business. If an executive allows himself to be torn between a decision based on business considerations and one based on his private ethical code, he exposes himself to a grave psychological strain.

This is not to say that sound business strategy necessarily runs counter to ethical ideals. They may frequently coincide; and when they do, everyone is gratified. But the major tests of every move in business, as in all games of strategy, are legality and profit. A man who intends to be a winner in the business game must have a game player's attitude.

The business strategist's decisions must be as impersonal as those of a surgeon performing an operation—concentrating on objective and technique, and subordinating personal feelings. If the chief executive admits that his son-in-law owns the stock, it is because he stands to lose more if the fact comes out later than if he states it boldly and at once. If the supermarket manager orders the rotten tomatoes to be discarded, he does so to avoid an increase in consumer complaints and a loss of goodwill. The company president decides not to fire the elderly executive in the belief that the negative reaction of other employees would in the long run cost the company more than it would lose in keeping him and paying his pension.

All sensible businessmen prefer to be truthful, but they seldom feel inclined to tell the *whole* truth. In the business game truth-telling usually has to be kept within narrow limits if trouble is to be avoided. The point was neatly made a long time ago (in 1888) by one of John D. Rockefeller's associates, Paul Babcock, to Standard Oil Company executives who were about to testify before a government investigating committee: "Parry every question with answers which, while perfectly truthful, are evasive of *bottom* facts."[8] This was, is, and probably always will be regarded as wise and permissible business strategy.

For Office Use Only

An executive's family life can easily be dislocated if he fails to make a sharp distinction between the ethical systems of the home and the office—or if his wife does not grasp that distinction. Many a businessman who has remarked to his wife, "I had to let Jones go today" or "I had to admit to the boss that Jim has been goofing off lately," has been met with an indignant protest. "How could you do a thing like that? You know Jones is over 50 and will have a lot of trouble getting another job." Or, "You did that to Jim? With his wife ill and all the worry she's been having with the kids?"

If the executive insists that he had no choice because the profits of the company and his own security were involved, he may see a certain cool and ominous reappraisal in his wife's eyes. Many wives are not prepared to accept the fact that business operates with a special code of ethics. An illuminating illustration of this comes from a Southern sales executive who related a conversation he had had with his wife at a time when a hotly contested political campaign was being waged in their state:

> *I made the mistake of telling her that I had had lunch with Colby, who gives me about half my business. Colby mentioned that his company had a stake in the election. Then he said, "By the way, I'm treasurer of the citizens' committee for Lang. I'm collecting contributions. Can I count on you for a hundred dollars?"*
>
> *Well, there I was. I was opposed to Lang, but I knew Colby. If he withdrew his business I could be in a bad spot. So I just smiled and wrote out a check then and there. He thanked me, and we started to talk about his next order. Maybe he thought I shared his political views. If so, I wasn't going to lose any sleep over it.*
>
> *I should have had sense enough not to tell Mary about it. She hit the ceiling. She said she was disappointed in me. She said I hadn't acted like a man, that I should have stood up to Colby.*
>
> *I said, "Look, it was an either-or situation. I had to do it or risk losing the business."*
>
> *She came back at me with, "I don't believe it. You could have been honest with him. You could have said that you didn't feel you ought to contribute to a campaign for a man you weren't going to vote for. I'm sure he would have understood."*
>
> *I said, "Mary, you're a wonderful woman, but you're way off the track. Do one know what would have happened if I had said that? Colby would have smiled and said, 'Oh, I didn't realize. Forget it.' But in his eyes from that moment I would be an oddball, maybe a bit of a radical. He would have listened to me talk about his order and would have promised to give it consideration. After that I wouldn't hear from him for a week. Then I would telephone and learn from his secretary that he wasn't yet ready to place the order. And in about a month I would hear through the grapevine that he was giving his business to another company. A month after that I'd be out of a job."*
>
> *She was silent for a while. Then she said, "Tom, something is wrong with business when a man is forced to choose between his family's security and his moral obligation to himself. It's easy for me to say you should have stood up to him—but if you had, you might have felt you were betraying me and the kids. I'm sorry that you did it, Tom, but I can't blame you. Something is wrong with business!"*

This wife saw the problem in terms of moral obligation as conceived in private life; her husband saw it as a matter of game strategy. As a player in a weak position, he felt that he could not afford to indulge an ethical sentiment that might have cost him his seat at the table.

Playing to Win

Some men might challenge the Colbys of business—might accept serious setbacks to their business careers rather than risk a feeling of moral cowardice. They merit our respect—but as private individuals, not businessmen. When the skillful player of the business game is compelled to submit to unfair pressure, he does not castigate himself for moral weakness. Instead, he strives to put himself into a strong position where he can defend himself against such pressures in the future without loss.

If a man plans to take a seat in the business game, he owes it to himself to master the principles by which the game is played, including its special ethical outlook. He can then hardly fail to recognize that an occasional bluff may well be justified in terms of the game's ethics and warranted in terms of economic necessity. Once he clears his mind on this point, he is in a good position to match his strategy against that of the other players. He can then determine objectively whether a bluff in a given situation has a good chance of succeeding and can decide when and how to bluff, without a feeling of ethical transgression.

To be a winner, a man must play to win. This does not mean that he must be ruthless, cruel, harsh or treacherous. On the contrary, the better his reputation for integrity, honesty and decency, the better his chances of victory will be in the long run. But from time to time every businessman, like every poker player, is offered a choice between certain loss or bluffing within the legal rules of the game. If he is not resigned to losing, if he wants to rise in his company and industry, then in such a crisis he will bluff—and bluff hard.

Every now and then one meets a successful businessman who has conveniently forgotten the small or large deceptions that he practiced on his way to fortune. "God gave me my money," old John D. Rockefeller once piously told a Sunday school class. It would be a rare tycoon in our time who would risk the horse laugh with which such a remark would be greeted.

In the last third of the 20th century even children are aware that if a man has become prosperous in business, he has sometimes departed from the strict truth in order to overcome obstacles or has practiced the more subtle deceptions of the half-truth or the misleading omission. Whatever the form of the bluff, it is an integral part of the game, and the executive who does not master its techniques is not likely to accumulate much money or power.

NOTES

1. *The New York Times,* March 9, 1967.
2. *See* Bruce D. Henderson, "Brinkmanship in Business," *Harvard Business Review,* March–April 1967, p. 49.
3. *The New York Times,* November 21, 1966.
4. New York, Grossman Publishers, Inc., 1965.
5. New York, David McKay Company, Inc., 1967.
6. *The New York Times,* January 17, 1967.
7. Cited by Ralph Nader in "Business Crime," *The New Republic,* July 1, 1967, p. 7.
8. Babcock in a memorandum to Rockefeller (Rockefeller Archives).

QUIZ YOURSELF ON BUSINESS ETHICS

—Dawn-Marie Driscoll, W. Michael Hoffman
and Edward Petry

*The following quiz was developed to help you to identify your own
ethical awareness and to give you a greater understanding of your
personal perspective.*

For questions 1 and 2, circle the answers you think are correct. More than one may qualify.

1. **Ethics is** _____
   a. A branch of philosophy that deals with values as they relate to human conduct.
   b. The study of what is good and right for people. It asks the question: How should I act, especially when my actions directly or indirectly affect others?
   c. A fad, a topic that is kept alive by the media on days when there is no hard news to report.

2. **Business ethics is** _____
   a. The application of ethical principles and methods of analysis to business.
   b. A topic of study that is now required at all business schools accredited by the American Assembly of Collegiate Schools of Business.
   c. An oxymoron.

In recent years there have been many tales of moral crises faced by organizations. How many of the following do you recognize? Again, more than one answer may be correct.

3. **Fraud and abuse was so common at NORTEL, Ltd., a giant Canadian telecommunications corporation, that:**
   a. It was estimated that one indictable offense occurred each and every working day.
   b. One manager defrauded the company for more than $6 million and then used the company's facilities to engage in widespread wiretapping, all the while amassing a private stockpile of arms.
   c. The company has since established a remarkably effective fraud prevention program and is emerging as a leader in the Canadian business ethics movement.

4. **For 15 minutes, executives at the Maine shipbuilder Bath Iron Works gave in to the temptation to cheat. Their ethical lapse:**
   a. Nearly destroyed the company's 100-year-old reputation for integrity.
   b. Put 8,000 jobs in peril.
   c. Ended the gubernatorial aspirations of the company's widely admired leader.
   d. Pushed the company to establish safeguards at the board and officer levels to increase ethical oversight at the top.

5. **A former president of the United Way was:**
   a. An entrepreneur and business genius who created the "greatest health and human services delivery system in history."
   b. A flawed leader who misused United Way funds to support a long-distance romance with a young woman just out of high school.
   c. Both of the above; in fact his successes helped shape an organization that all but made his failures inevitable.

What do business leaders think about the ethics of business? Deloitte & Touche surveyed more than a thousand officers and directors of corporations together with other business leaders. Are your views on the topic in sync with theirs? Circle the answers to questions 6 through 8 that you think are correct.

6. **Is the American business community troubled by ethical problems?**
   a. Yes
   b. No

7. **Has the issue of business ethics become overblown?**
   a. Yes
   b. No

8. **How do high ethical standards affect a company's competitive position?**
   a. Strengthen
   b. Weaken
   c. No effect

Has the increased acceptance of the concept of business ethics translated into actual changes in the workplace? In the years 1985, 1990 and 1992, the Center for Business Ethics surveyed the Fortune 1000 to find out what changes—if any—were being made to build ethics into corporate policies and programs. Circle the answers you think are correct for questions 9 through 13.

9. **What percentage of the Fortune 1000 are planning to expand efforts to incorporate ethics into their daily operations?**
   a. More than 90%
   b. About 50%
   c. Less than 25%

10. **The most common motive(s) given for implementing ethics initiatives is (are) to:**
    a. Improve profits
    b. Provide guidelines for conduct

c. Improve public image

d. Be socially responsible

11. **What percentage of the Fortune 1000 have written ethics policies?**
    a. More than 90%
    b. About 50%
    c. Less than 25%

12. **What percentage of the Fortune 1000 have employee ethics training?**
    a. More than 90%
    b. About 50%
    c. Less than 25%

13. **Since 1987, the number of large corporations with ethics officers (whose primary function is to create or maintain the company's ethics program) has:**
    a. Stayed about the same
    b. Increased slightly
    c. More than doubled

While there has been a decade of steady growth in the number of corporations implementing corporate ethics policies and programs, the new Federal Sentencing Guidelines for Organizations has certainly piqued the business community's interest and led to a sharp increase in its efforts. Circle the answers you think are correct for questions 14 through 16. More than one answer may be correct.

14. **The Guidelines apply only to large corporations.**
    a. True
    b. False

15. **Under the Guidelines organizations may be required to pay restitution and may be placed on probation for up to five years. The Guidelines also cite specific aggravating factors that can increase the organization's fine up to:**
    a. 400%
    b. 100%
    c. 50%

16. **The Guidelines call on organizations to create "effective programs to prevent and detect violations of law." These programs must include:**
    a. Established compliance standards.
    b. Specific individual(s) assigned to oversee compliance.
    c. Due care in delegating discretionary authority.
    d. Steps to communicate standards and procedures, e.g., training programs and publications.
    e. Steps to achieve compliance, e.g., monitoring, auditing and reporting systems.
    f. A record of consistent enforcement of standards.
    g. Procedures to review and modify the program after an offense.

Hopefully your company is one of those making a serious effort to build ethics into its daily operations. When an ethics dilemma arises, it's unfortunately often the case that, at least initially, you're still facing it alone. What should you do? Circle the answers you think are correct for questions 17 through 19. More than one may be correct.

17. **Possible scenarios: (1) You are an employee at a public utility and discover that rate payers' money is being used illegally to finance political campaigns. (2)You are an employee at a phone company that holds "pervert conventions" every year to "entertain" suppliers. (3) You have a choice of blowing the whistle to your company's officers and possibly facing retaliation or of going outside the company and blowing the whistle to the government and collecting a multi-million-dollar bonus.**

    When faced with such ethical dilemmas, which of the following questions should you ask yourself?
    a. Have I looked at the problem from the perspective of all the affected parties? Whose interests have priority?
    b. Who will be harmed and who will be helped? Is there an alternative course of action that will minimize harm?
    c. If I act unethically, can I get away with it?
    d. Am I confident that my decision will seem as reasonable over a long period of time as it does now?
    e. Would I be willing to disclose my decision to my boss, the board, the general public, my family?

18. **If the dilemma is still unresolved, one should:**
    a. Consult your company's written ethics policies.
    b. Use your company's hotline or helpline.
    c. Talk to your company's ethics officer or ombudsman.
    d. Call your mother.

19. **What companies have faced moral crises, learned their lessons and now serve as models for how to integrate ethics into their organizations?**

THE BUSINESS ETHICS QUIZ—ANSWERS
Question 1

The study of ethics is at least 5,000 years old, and ethics was first explicitly applied to business in the Code of Hammurabi around 2100 BC. If it's a fad, it's the longest one ever. . . . A and B are correct.

Question 2

A and B are correct. If one answered C, you're out of date. Businesses that ignore ethics are businesses at risk.

Questions 3–5

For each, all of the answers are correct.

Questions 6–8

According to the Deloitte & Touche Survey, 94% of the business leaders thought the American business community was troubled by ethical problems, only 32% thought the issue was overblown, and 63% thought high ethical standards strengthened competitiveness.

Questions 9–13

According to the Center for Business Ethics 1990 survey, more than 90% of the Fortune 1000 are planning to increase their business ethics efforts. Their principal motives were to provide guidelines for employee conduct and to be socially responsible (about 95% each). Only 43% said they were doing so to improve public image, and only 30% said they were motivated by profit. More than 90% of the Fortune 1000 have written ethics policies, and about 50% offer ethics training to employees. According to the Center for Business Ethics' Ethics Officer Survey of the Fortune 1000, the number of large corporations with ethics officers has more than doubled since 1987.

Questions 14–16

The Guidelines apply to business organizations of all sizes including those as small as 10 employees. They also apply to unions, governments and political subdivisions and non-profit organizations. If there is high-level complicity, a prior record of the same offense and obstruction of the investigation, the organization's fine could increase 400% above the stipulated base fine. The Guidelines call for an "effective program" that includes all of the listed components. Having such a program can reduce an organization's fine by up to 60%.

Question 17

If you answered C, go to jail, go directly to jail, do not pass Go and take this book with you!

Question 18

All four answers are correct. Answers A through C are the standard steps under any "effective program." Answer D is not required under the Guidelines, but it wouldn't hurt to call your mother more often, would it?

Question 19

A hint: They include one of the "baby bells" [and] a giant in the defense industry.

MORALITY
The Basic Rules
—ROBERT SOLOMON

Robert Solomon discusses the importance of moral rules and whether there may be a list of rules to govern behavior and proposes a definition of morality—three of the more difficult tasks in ethical theory!

I don't like violence. I'm a businessman. Blood is a big expense.
                    MARIO PUZO, *THE GODFATHER*

Ethics is a matter of *ethos,* participation in a community, a practice, a way of life. Business ethics is a function of the business ethos. Within itself, the mentality of business may be a game mentality, but not all of business ethics is defined by this gamelike business *ethos* or by the business community. The nature of business is circumscribed by society, which tends to encourage or discourage particular aspects of business on the basis of its own ideals and well-being. But there is also a more general set of basic rules that are not part of or partial to any particular society, community, or practice. These rules apply everywhere and determine the legitimacy of every practice. These are the rules of *morality.*

Morality is not the same as moralizing, and being moral does not mean being righteous. It means only *doing right.* Most of the time being moral is no big deal. One doesn't praise an accountant for not cheating on the corporation's tax return, and one doesn't praise an employee for not stealing from the company. Morality is most noticeable in its absence, except, perhaps, when a person succeeds in remaining moral under enormous pressure to be otherwise. But morality in general is not heroism; it is simply not doing what no one should think of doing in the first place. In practical business contexts, morality is rarely an issue, not because the possibility of immoral but lucrative behavior does not exist at every turn but because it is assumed—it *must* be assumed—that no amount of gain will justify a breach of morality. Morality and business are mentioned together when a business venture is *immoral,* and there is never a question of which—business or morality—will win that competition. Moral rules are the trump cards of every business transaction.

Given the importance of moral rules, one might like a list of them, but such an exercise is probably a waste of time. Anyone who doesn't know them already isn't going to learn anything. (It's not like learning a new computer language.) But, for starters, how about

Thou shalt not kill.

Thou shalt not steal.

Robert Solomon, "Morality: The Basic Rules," from *The New World of Business.* Reprinted by permission of Rowman & Littlefield, Publishers.

Thou shalt not commit adultery.

Thou shalt not bear false witness.

Thou shalt not cheat on thy taxes.

Thou shalt not knowingly do harm.

Don't be cruel.

Etc.

We could go on. There are moral rules that are in dispute, such as the morality of pre-marital sex and the morality of children's advertising. There are moral rules that conflict—especially in times of extreme stress, in wartime or the corporate equivalent thereof. But of morality itself there is surprisingly little to say (until we get to a highly theoretical level, which is not appropriate here). Moral laws are unambiguous and not open to debate. They simply say,

DON'T DO IT!

Against breaches of morality there are no good arguments, whatever a person's status, however powerful the company, however great the profits. In fact, considerable damage may be done by a company spokesman trying to argue against a moral rule, perhaps more damage than the original transgression itself. In this context, we should recall once again the Lockheed spokesman's heedless complaint, defending himself against a morally ambiguous charge: "When a company wants its products to be bought at all costs, [can it] realistically decline the request [for payoffs] on the grounds that it is not a good thing from the ethical point of view?"

The answer to that question is, simply, "Yes."

The practical problem with moral rules is never whether or not to accept them; it is rather how to apply them. Granted that one must accept the principle "Thou shalt not kill," does that include the lives of animals? Does it prohibit any risky industrial activity like mining coal, in which some employees will lose their lives? Does it prohibit the manufacture of any product, like guns or knives, that *might,* if abused, cause fatal injuries? Granted that one accepts the principle that one should not steal—that is, take someone else's property without paying a fair and agreed-upon price for it—does that mean that one should not take advantage of a company in trouble by buying up inventory or perhaps the company itself? Should a business person take advantage of the stupidity or negligence of a supplier or a customer—for example, if the first forgets to send a bill or the second overpays one? Granted that one should tell the truth and ought not to cheat on taxes, does that preclude such common business practices as tax deferrals and shelters?

What is morality, given that it occupies such an unchallengeable place in our (and every) society? Simply stated, morality consists of those rules that circumscribe legitimate activity for every citizen (or visitor). Such rules are the boundaries of a tolerable social life and guarantee the security of those things a society values most—individual life and well-being, obviously, but, in our society at least, extraordinary freedom, private property, personal and social relationships, freedom from terror and the "pursuit of happiness." But beyond this essential function, the nature of morality is a matter of violent dispute. There are those who insist that morality is inextricably tied to religion—or to a particular religion—and impossible without. There are those who insist on a strict interpretation of an exact set of moral rules, with no room for other interpretations and no exceptions based on current social facts and needs. And there are those who believe that morality is nothing but a set of local social restrictions that (with some risk) can be flouted or bypassed at will. (One sometimes finds people in business who defend the ultrastrict view of morality in their personal lives but are virtually amoral in professional life, thus provoking the most vehement critics of business.) But whatever else it may be, morality is at least the following:

1. *Morality is a living phenomenon,* no matter how ancient its codes and principles. Our primary moral precept is the autonomy of each individual and every generation to rethink and decide for themselves what is right and what is wrong.
2. *Morality is what one does,* not what one says or how loudly and publicly one regrets doing wrong afterward—a recent fashion. Apologizing on the national news after being convicted of a crime is not necessarily a mark of morality.
3. *Morality is a shared sense of values.* It is possible that only one person in the company is right and everyone else is wrong, but how do we recognize when that lone voice is indeed correct? Only because that lone voice finds a much larger audience outside the company, and agreement on the moral principles with which the company itself will be condemned.
4. *Morality isn't accidental.* It is not what one does that counts but what one does *knowingly.* Promoting the right person by mistake isn't being moral. Giving money to a charity by mistake isn't charity.
5. *Morality requires compassion.* Cold-blooded obedience of the rules isn't enough.
6. *Morality is a way of life,* a state of character. It's not a matter of forcing oneself to comply. The self-satisfaction of being a "good person" is motive enough.
7. *Morality is not a substitute for life.* We are a "cryptomoral" society that delights in clever criminals and charming con men, and not only in the movies. We are a law-abiding society, but we are also attracted to people who break the rules. No one who knows our society should ever expect a morally perfect business world. But such characters and their stories provide the spice of business life, not its substance. To be moral is an unquestioned good. To be a moralizing bore, a dogmatic stick-in-the-mud in the name of morality, is not good. In the words of Tom Peters, "The line between ethical purity and arrogant egocentrism is a fine one."

WHERE AND WHY DID BUSINESS ETHICISTS GO WRONG? THE CASE OF DOW CORNING CORPORATION

—DARYL KOEHN

Dow Corning is a contradiction in itself: It was one of the first firms to institute a senior-level code of conduct committee and received accolades from ethicists for forging ahead in this area, while it also declared bankruptcy after some claimed it ignored numerous complaints of serious medical problems in connection with its products: silicone breast implants. Later, it was alleged that Dow even destroyed a survey that disclosed the medical issues customers had with the implants. John Byrne was an engineer who expressed concern early on for the lack of safety testing.

Update to Dow Corning: In 1993, Dow Corning unveiled a $4.25 billion plan—the largest mass injury settlement ever—to settle all silicone breast implant claims (Thomas Burton, "Adding Insult to Injury," Progressive, July 1994, p. 8). Individual women would receive between $200,000 and $2 million each. Many criticized the plan as being extravagantly generous to certain claimants and "stingy" to others. By 1995, 440,000 women had joined in the settlement. However, 15,000 women decided to try their luck filing individual suits against Dow and opted out of the settlement (Michael Hoffman et al., The Ethical Edge, p. 134). Dow filed for bankruptcy in 1995, effectively freezing all claims and delaying payment to claimants for years. Four months after Dow's filing, a federal judge declared the original settlement dead.

In the following analysis, Daryl Koehn describes the history of the Dow Corning case and discusses why ethicists may originally have been misled regarding the ethical culture at Dow.

In the early 1980s, it seemed Dow Corning Corporation (DCC) could do no wrong. It hit the billion dollar sales mark in 1986. What is more, it maintained its competitiveness while

Daryl Koehn, "Where and Why Did Business Ethicists Go Wrong? The Case of Dow Corning Corporation," Reprinted by permission of the author.

acting in a fashion many judged ethically exemplary. In fact, a highly complimentary case study was done in 1984 by a Harvard business ethicist lauding various of the company's ethical initiatives. Yet by 1989, the company was in the midst of a public relations fiasco over its manufacture and marketing of silicone breast implants or "mammaries." The company had been found guilty of fraud for suppressing internal memos suggesting that these implants were less safe than the company's marketing literature represented them to be. Juries had awarded several multimillion dollar awards to women who claimed to have been seriously harmed by their implants. A criminal investigation had been launched into DCC's business practices. Although this investigation was subsequently dropped for lack of evidence, 15 members of Congress urged (in July 1995) Janet Reno, the U.S. Attorney General, to examine whether a senior manager of DCC had perjured himself when testifying before Congress several years earlier. In 1995, DCC filed for bankruptcy, claiming it did not have the funds necessary to fund the $4.23 billion settlement that had been reached for paying women who had been part of class action lawsuits against the company.

Whether or not silicone implants are safe is a highly contested matter. Some of DCC's own studies suggest they may not be safe. In particular, leaked silicone may harm the immune system. Later DCC studies seem to indicate that silicone is inert within the human body. Studies by researchers at University of Michigan and Mayo Clinic have been interpreted as showing that there is no link between silicone breast implants and autoimmune disease. However, critics have charged that these studies are suspect because the samples used were too small to be statistically significant and because the research was funded in part by DCC and the plastic surgeons who have a financial interest in showing that these implants are safe. While many women with implants firmly believe these implants to be the cause of their problems, their symptoms are diverse. Removal of the implants has not always improved their condition. Although the United States declared a moratorium on cosmetic surgeons implanting this product, the British government chose to leave them on the market after deciding women with implants were at no greater risk of contracting autoimmune disease than those without the implants.

This paper does not aim at resolving the scientific controversy regarding the safety of the implants. Nor does it try to build a case that DCC's production and manufacture of these implants were unethical. While I would question the goodness of many of DCC's reported actions, I am less interested in passing judgment on this company than in discovering what we can learn from its difficulties. To this end, I want to consider, first, why DCC won praise for its ethics initiatives; and second, what factors and forces, if any, business ethicists failed to consider when assessing the ethical goodness of DCC. I am interested in what mistakes business ethicists made in thinking about DCC's ethics and in learning what we can from these errors.

PART 1: THE ETHICS PROGRAM AT DCC

DCC sponsored many ethics initiatives. The company wrote and published a corporate code of ethics as early as 1977. While many codes emphasize matters of etiquette or remaining within the law, DCC's code was noteworthy for stressing integrity and respect. The 1977 code read: "The watchword of Dow Corning worldwide activities is integrity . . . We believe that business is best conducted and society best served within each country when business practice is based on the universal principles of honesty and integrity." The code goes on to say that "We recognize that our social responsibilities must be maintained at the high standards which lead to respect and trust by society. A clear definition of our social responsibilities should be an integral part of our corporate objectives and be clearly communicated to every employee."

Furthermore, the code was widely disseminated and was hung in the corridors of the corporation. The then CEO of the company, Jack Ludington, sent a letter to every employee urging him or her to read the code and to contact Ludington if they had any questions. Ludington and other managers of DCC consistently referred to the code of ethics in their speeches. Since various areas faced different ethical challenges, the areas were allowed to devise their own separate codes, although these codes still needed to be consistent with DCC's corporate code. Efforts were made to solicit employee feedback concerning the code and to keep the code current by revising it every two years. As John Swanson, the manager–business communications specialist who was the only permanent member of the Business Conduct Committee, put it, "The code of conduct is a 'living' statement, one that can change as accepted business practices change."

In addition, DCC instituted annual audits beginning in 1977 both to communicate the code and to solicit feedback as well as to monitor compliance. The audits were conducted by a newly created committee at DCC—the Business Conduct Committee. Up to 40 audits per year were conducted at the area level (e.g., in Mexico City, Toronto, Brussels, Hong Kong). Since different areas had different concerns (e.g., requests for bribes were more prevalent in Asia than in some other areas), the audits were tailored to the area being evaluated. Every effort was made to include regional personnel who were actually dealing with problems in the day-to-day business operation of the company. The results of the audit were documented and kept on file at headquarters, but the intent was not punitive. Rather the audits were an attempt to educate employees concerning the code and to highlight potential problems or ambiguities with the code itself. Some of the audit sessions were videotaped. These tapes were then shared with area personnel to educate them concerning the audit process.

Finally, the BCC developed corporate training modules on the code and a semi-annual opinion survey. The survey attempted to measure whether employees knew about the code and whether DCC's ethics initiatives were making a real difference in the life of the corporation.

Business ethicists praised DCC for its meaningful code and for its serious commitment to making ethics a regular part of business practice. It certainly looked as though management was serious about these various initiatives. Rising executives were regularly assigned to do a stint on the rotating Business Conduct Committee and were expected to spend up to 15% of their time per week on ethical issues. However, initiatives by themselves do not make a company ethical. In the next section, I explore several important dimensions of corporate life that were completely ignored by the *Harvard Business Review* study, dimensions that played a pivotal role in how DCC handled the growing public concern regarding the safety of silicone breast implants manufactured by the company.

PART 2: WHAT BUSINESS ETHICISTS FORGOT TO CONSIDER

Factor 1: Managerial Hubris

Although the CEO of DCC supported the ethics initiative, he met with some resistance from senior area personnel who believed that DCC was already a thoroughly ethical company. For example, Phil Brooks, a senior employee in Hong Kong, wrote a memo to Ludington arguing that DCC had no problem "and that our house doesn't need putting in order. Therefore we need to agree on the purpose of any Code and that purpose must arise from some need. What is the need if we already believe (as I do) that we are morally, legally and ethically correct in all aspects of our business conduct?"

The certainty implicit in this claim is remarkable. Given that DCC had just begun ethics audits to uncover what various managers' actual practices were, it seems odd to claim that one already knows that DCC is behaving completely correctly—legally, ethically and morally. The certainty that DCC was an entirely ethical company is doubly striking because it seems to have been widely held. As the controversy surrounding silicone breast implants deepened, another senior manager, Silas Braney, would proclaim, "I can say, without any qualification, that never in my 30 years at Dow Corning did I ever know of anyone doing anything illegal, unethical, or immoral." His sentiments echo those of CEO Ludington who, in the late 1970s, claimed that his corporate managers "would not intentionally do anything questionable and would even blow the whistle if they learned of any actual wrongdoing within the company." Again, the certainty seems rather misplaced, given that the company experienced a good deal of resistance to some parts of the code from some of its managers who believed that the code was making DCC uncompetitive. It is doubtful whether Ludington was warranted in asserting that DCC's employees would definitely blow the whistle on unethical practices by corporate employees if these employees in many cases (see Brooks quote above) did not accept that some of their past practices were in fact unethical.

More generally, such certainty on the part of management evinces an attitude that is antithetical to ethical reasoning. As Aristotle puts it, the "stuff" of ethical discourse is controversy because practical matters do not admit of the same degree of certainty as mathematical or scientific subjects. To reason ethically, therefore, consists at least in part in being willing to submit one's beliefs to the scrutiny and challenges of others. If agents begin with the position that they and their company have done no wrong, this very process of discussion is short-circuited. This shutting off of the possibility of discussion may itself be an ethical wrong, yet this possibility cannot get raised in this atmosphere of certainty.

All of the processes in the world will make little difference if people are fundamentally committed to the proposition that neither they nor their colleagues have done any wrong. One sees the consequences of this certainty quite clearly in the book on the breast implant controversy to which DCC insider John Swanson contributed. Key players at DCC are certain that the breast implants they helped to design and manufacture are absolutely safe. Indeed, they are so certain of their moral rectitude that they dismiss as "crazy" all of the women who think they have been harmed by their implants. Even after the Federal Drug Administration ordered companies manufacturing breast implants to prove that they were safe, some senior managers at DCC insisted that there was no ethical issue connected with the marketing of silicone breast implants. While the implants may turn out not to be the cause of these women's health problems, such demonizing of these women hardly seems consistent with DCC's professed commitment to respect the dignity of employees and of customers and to treat them fairly. It is, however, consistent with a certain hubris that appeared as early as 1977 in DCC's managers' view of the company's ethics initiatives. To the extent business ethicists quoted these hubristic claims but ignored the arrogance implicit in them, they were misled in their judgment of the company.

Factor 2: Corporate History

Another striking feature of HBR's analysis of DCC's ethics was the total disregard of the company's history. The case study looked at DCC at just one point in time—the late 1970s. While the case study was updated in the 1980s it still made no mention of the company's history. This oversight is striking because Dow Corning is a subsidiary of Dow Chemical. Managers moved between the two companies. Indeed, Keith McKennon, the manager brought in as the new CEO to provide decisive leadership at DCC as the lawsuits and bad publicity began to mount, was formerly an executive vice-president at Dow Chemical. Dow Chemical, in turn, had invented and marketed napalm, Agent Orange and, along with Merill-Dow, Benedictin, a morning sickness pill suspected of causing birth defects. These products all proved tremendously controversial in the late 1960s and 1970s. I do not here want to argue the morality of Dow Chemical's decision to produce these products nor the way in which the company responded to criticism of these products. It may be that any company in the chemical and pharmaceuticals business runs certain risks by producing powerful compounds whose long-term effects may not be immediately obvious. However, I do want to insist that this history and the behavior of the players in these earlier controversies is relevant to judging the ethics of Dow Corning because some of these same people were responsible for deciding how to respond to the press, whether to voluntarily pull the implants, how aggressively to respond to lawsuits, etc. In fact, CEO McKennon was apparently appointed to head DCC because he was internally regarded as the consummate "fireman" who successfully put out the Agent Orange controversy when it threatened to flame out of control.

A corporation is like a living organism. It has a history, and how it behaves in the present is a function of its past experiences, acquired habits and attitudes and the stories it tells itself concerning the past. To ignore such matters and to merely focus on the present behavior of corporate employees can and likely will lead both the business ethicist and the company astray. For if a company's management behaved questionably in the past, and if the company showed no willingness to engage in any soul-searching regarding these past actions, what reason is there to think that management will suddenly mend its ways and its habits just because a company institutes a code of conduct and sets up some ethics training sessions?

This tendency to ignore corporate history is endemic in the business ethics literature. We philosophers report some event or action. We raise a number of questions about behavior in this event, yet we rarely situate this event in the company's history or relate it to the company's past deeds. While this isolation of an action may give the illusion of analytic clarity, it seriously falsifies the actual process of choice. Choices are always made by human beings who have acquired certain habits of choice by dint of dealing with past crises and problems. To describe ethics processes such as DCC's "ethics audits" in isolation from the people doing and undergoing the audit will tell us little about the real value of these processes.

Factor 3: Corporate Culture

A third factor is the company's internal culture. By "culture," I mean both the totality of factors (history, environment, sanctions, etc.) that lead employees to embrace certain characteristic ways of viewing the world and this worldview itself, since, as it develops, it, too, becomes a controlling factor. The HBR case study attempts to characterize this culture. We read that "DCC's culture was open, informal and relaxed; little emphasis was placed on official status or a traditional organizational chart with clear-cut reporting relationships." As far as it goes, this judgment appears sound. DCC was known for being a highly matrixed company with many dotted line reporting relations. Employees routinely met in the halls to informally share information and to make decisions. The problem with this assessment of culture is not so much that it was wrong but that it was very incomplete. The HBR article assessed culture entirely in light of the company's reporting structure. However, we can also get a feel for culture by examining where people spend most of their time and energy, what behaviors are rewarded and who the heroes of the company are. When these are considered, we get a rather different view of DCC's culture.

At the time the HBR article was written, one out of every 10 employees of DCC was involved in new product development. This number is relatively high and suggests that there was a great deal of interest in not merely developing but also probably a good bit of pressure to successfully market new products to the consumer. Such pressure can result in a company rushing products to market before the product's safety has been adequately established. Swanson tells the story of how he had been sent to publicly announce a new silicon handwash; however, at the last minute he received a panicked call cancelling the product rollout because the product adversely affected monkeys. The rollout of breast implants may also have been premature. It appears, for example, that DCC provided implants to surgeons who placed them in women while the company was still doing initial safety testing on animals.

DCC was also distinguished by a tendency to lionize its scientists. The company's "hall of fame" featured pictures of the chemists who had made new discoveries concerning silicone or who had invented silicone-based products. There was a widespread perception among employees that to advance one had to be a scientist. The non-scientists within the company seemed to take the scientists' word as gospel. John Swanson relates how psychologically difficult it was for him to even consider the possibility that silicone might not be inert because he and his colleagues had been told for years by scientists that the material did not react with the body in any way. In short, the culture at DCC was one that prided itself on being scientifically expert.

On the one hand, a culture of people who pride themselves on their expertise may be driven by professional self-esteem to produce products that can be trusted not to harm the end-users. On the other hand, expertise may feed arrogance and lead employees to feel contempt for those who are not experts like them. At one point, DCC refused to take any questions from reporters on the ground that such people lacked scientific credentials. There is also a danger that expertise will lead those who view themselves as professionals to over-look the client's needs entirely. Thus we have doctors speaking of curing AIDs or the virus rather than the patient. A similar displacement seems to have occurred at DCC where both the surgeons and apparently the company itself restrictively defined a "failed implant" as one damaged in manufacture. The patient might experience pain or discomfort or require surgery to implant a new device, but these cases were not counted as failed implants. It was not until several years into the controversy over the implants that a CEO at DCC finally would say that the company's overriding responsibility was to women who had the im-plants. Although DCC's own code of corporate ethics gives priority to treating the customer fairly and with respect, the code proved no match for the corporate culture of expertise.

It might be objected that it is unfair to criticize business ethicists for failing to fully comprehend a corporation's culture. Persons who write case studies and consultants rarely have access to the corporate memos and jokes that often prove so revealing of a company's culture. Nor are they around long enough to get much of a feel for how the company oper-ates. There is some truth in this objection but it does not completely exonerate business ethi-cists. These facts suggest that we business ethicists need to be extremely circumspect when praising a company as ethically good. We need to be aware of our limitations and do the most we can to widen our focus to include other features of the culture, features of the sort described above.

Factor 4: The Wider Culture

The culture of a particular corporation is not freestanding. It is always embedded in the larger national culture (and global one, too, to the extent that it makes sense to speak of a global culture). Whether a corporation will act ethically depends at least in part on what pressures and expectations the wider culture brings to bear on the corporation and the way in which the corporation responds to them. In some cases, refusing to meet these expecta-tions may be the most ethical response, especially if these expectations are ill-formed, un-realistic or the product of suspect motivations. Business ethicists need to consider, therefore, whether the company in question has shown itself willing to sometimes say "no" to people.

In the case of DCC, the company faced pressure from plastic surgeons to develop a host of products they could use. In some cases, the silicone products were clearly of use in pro-moting people's health (e.g., a shunt used to drain fluid from the brain). However, breast implants did not unambiguously fall into this category. Although they could be, and were, used to rebuild the breasts of women who had mastectomies, most implants were used for purely cosmetic reasons. The plastic surgeons knew there was a huge market for these mam-maries and that there was big money to be made because a surgeon could do up to six im-plants per day at a charge of $1,000/implant (1970s dollar value). Furthermore, the plastic surgeons had the money and connections to increase this market. They lobbied hard to have small breasts defined as a disease so that insurance companies would pay for the breast en-largements the plastic surgeons were promoting.

From almost the moment DCC entered the implant market, it was involved with a prod-uct that was of questionable value and that was being promoted by doctors who had a vested interest in having women come to see themselves as defective. Although some women with small breasts may very well have low self-esteem, this condition hardly qualifies as a "disease" in the normal sense of the term. Many women with small breasts do not lack self-esteem so the symptomology is questionable. Furthermore, the condition generally is not debilitating in the way cancer or polio is. Even if some small-breasted women were to have difficulty functioning because of a lack of self-confidence, the "cure" arguably lies not in encouraging them to have surgery (with its attendant possible complications) but in fighting the propaganda that would have such women view themselves as inferior. It could be argued that this "disease" was manufactured to play on the fears of vulnerable parties who perhaps are already short on self-esteem. If this logic is sound, then DCC was in the business of not just manufacturing breast implants but of manipulating vulnerable people as well. DCC failed to ask itself early on: Why are we in this business anyway? The business ethicists who evaluated the ethics program at DCC also failed because they did not examine whether DCC product rollout process was thoughtful. Instead, they focused largely on the existence of a code of conduct and audits, neither of which directly speaks to the question of how DCC was dealing with external pressures and expectations.

Factor 5: Good Time Ethics

As I noted earlier, the HBR case study focused on processes of ethical review at DCC but did not consider in any detail exactly what cases were coming up for review. From the code, it was clear that DCC thought that it was most exposed in the area of bribery, kickbacks, or political contributions in its foreign operations. Swanson characterized the cases he dealt with as ranging from instances of alleged sexual harassment to cases where an employee was arrested for brawling in a barroom. What is most striking about this list is that many of the charges were one-time violations by a single employee. The cases did not involve systemic wrongdoing nor did they threaten any of the company's core business lines. After he left the company, Swanson himself characterized the company as having a "good time" ethics program—i.e., a program that functioned well only as long as the sums of money involved were not very large.

Philosophers surely need to be sensitive to the likelihood that acting well may be appealing to a company and its employees only as long as doing the right thing is not an expensive proposition. Before praising a corporation as ethical, business ethicists need to examine whether the company has faced any hard tests. Johnson & Johnson showed it was truly concerned about the customer when it recalled all of its Tylenol products after a customer had died from ingesting some of this product. One could argue that DCC's decision not to stop selling the silicone implants was of a different order. Both Johnson & Johnson and the police knew that the death was the result of some Tylenol having been tampered with, while the evidence linking the implants to many of the reported conditions was ambiguous. Given that there were risks as well in having the implants removed, DCC might have caused more harm by unduly alarming women and frightening them into "ex-plants." Still, the basic point remains: When evaluating a company's behavior, it is necessary to consider the extent to which the company has faced significant temptations not to do the right thing.

Factor 6: Character and Commitment

This last comment brings me to the sixth and final factor that business ethicists have tended to overlook in their case study—the issue of character and commitment. Paper codes and conduct committees are virtually worthless if people within the firm are not committed to avoiding wrongdoing. In fact, without such a commitment, a structure such as a business conduct committee may wind up being pernicious. Members may use the committee to avoid having to assume personal responsibility for their acts. Some literature suggests that people are less likely to do the right thing when they are a member of a group and take their cues from the collective than when they are confronting a crisis alone. This is not to say that, for people who are genuinely committed to acting well, the committee may provide a valuable sounding board for thinking through choices. But much will depend on the character and motivations of those on the board.

The problem thus becomes one of assessing the commitment of employees and management to acting well. All of the factors mentioned above need to be considered in arriving at a thoughtful judgment of this commitment. The DCC case suggests several other considerations especially relevant to the question of commitment. It is interesting that DCC was originally driven to adopt its ethical initiative only after Congress passed the Foreign Corrupt Practices Act in 1977. This act imposed fines on corporations and up to $10,000 in fines or five years in prison on individuals convicted of violating the act. The prospect of prison time no doubt proved sobering to many CEOs who were criminally liable if they "knew or had reason to know that their agents used the payments received from the U.S. concern to pay a foreign official for a prohibited purpose." The original impulse behind a move to develop an ethics initiative does not necessarily taint the entire resulting ethics initiative. Swanson, for example, apparently initially thought of the Business Conduct Committee as so much window dressing but over the years the committee and the rest of DCC's ethics program came to symbolize for him a genuine commitment to do the right thing. Nevertheless, if senior management understands its ethics program merely or largely as a strategy for avoiding getting into legal trouble, the company is not likely to do the right thing in those cases where it thinks it either will not be caught or can use the legal system to its advantage.

The corporate compensation system should be considered as well. At DCC, people were told, on the one hand, that they should avoid paying bribes to officials in order to get business; but, on the other hand, they believed they would be evaluated entirely on their contribution to the bottom line. The employees received a dual signal. Under such circumstances, employees may justifiably wonder about the sincerity of the company's commitment to doing the right thing.

Third, business ethicists should look to the possible effects of ownership structure (public vs. private) on a company's ethics. No doubt there are decent family-owned businesses. Clearly public ownership is neither a necessary nor a sufficient condition for encouraging ethically good behavior. Nevertheless, it may be that a company like DCC, which was accountable only to Dow Chemical and Corning Inc., will be less responsive to concerns about its actions than it would be if it were forced to confront and report to shareholders directly. Corporate structure does have ethical implications and should not be ignored.

Finally, it may prove insightful to ask employees who is responsible for ethics within their company. The right answer surely is: "I am." Every person who performs a deed places himself or herself within the ethical realm and becomes accountable for the actions he or she voluntarily initiates. Yet, at DCC, one man—Swanson—was viewed as "Mr. Ethics" and the "guardian of the company's ethics." The fact that Swanson apparently accepted these titles and the fact that they were given to him in the first place should have been a sign that something was seriously awry. No single person can know what others are doing around the world. Nor can he justly be held responsible for actions beyond his control that others initiate. Business ethicists seem to have been so impressed by Swanson's integrity that they forgot that one person does not a corporation make.

CONCLUSION

Although I have been critical of business ethicists' praise of Dow Corning, I am aware that I, too, might have spoken of the company's code and ethics program in glowing terms had I been the one writing a case study of the company back in 1977. However, the issue is not whether business ethicists sometimes err in their judgments but whether they show themselves willing to learn from their past errors. Like companies, we are judged by our histories and by our character and commitments. While it is the human condition to err, it is also part of our condition to be able to identify our mistakes as such and to learn from them. The above analysis represents one answer to the question of where and why we philosophers erred in our judgment of one company. The errors are generic in the sense that they are the sort we might make when evaluating any company and its actions. The good news is that, since these errors are generic, we can take the lesson learned from DCC to heart and do better the next time.

Chapter 3

CORPORATE ETHICAL LEADERSHIP
Corporate Culture and Reputation Management

The trouble with the rat race is that, even if you win, you're still a rat. —LILY TOMLIN

When we speak, we are afraid our words will not be heard, nor wel-
comed; but when we are silent, we are still afraid.
So it is better to speak,
Remembering that we were never meant to survive all.   —ANDRE LORDE

Take care to guard against all greed, for though one may be rich,
one's life does not consist of possessions.   —LUKE 12: 15

IMPLICATIONS AND ACCOUNTABILITY:
DOES ETHICS = VALUE?

Good ethics is good business. Have you heard that before? Did you believe it? Theorists argue about whether ethical decisions lead to more significant profits than unethical decisions. While we are all familiar with examples of unethical decisions leading to high profits,
there is general agreement that, in the long run, ethics pays. Lao Tzu in the *Tao Te Ching*
contends there is no crime greater than having too many desires and no misfortune greater
than being covetous.[1] How would Taoism view the acts and intentions of a profit-
maximizing firm in today's market?

Consider from a stakeholder perspective the demise of small bookstores all over the
country. In the past several years, large, multipurpose bookstores such as Borders Books
and Barnes and Noble have seemed to take over the literary consumption landscape.
Chicago alone has seen the collapse of a number of old standbys, bookstores that had been
in the city for years serving a specific, sometimes idiosyncratic, population rather than the
entire book-purchasing community. These stores (Krochs and Brentanos, Stuart Brent,
Guild Books and others) could not survive next to chain superstores that provide a greater
selection of low-priced alternatives.

Stuart Brent, a longtime bookseller on prestigious Michigan Avenue in Chicago, in 1996
was forced out of business by competition from Borders and other chain bookstores opening
down the street. Brent's store was one where the salespeople could remember your name,
where there were large comfy chairs in which to peruse the books, where there were experts
available on literary issues and where they knew just the right book for your Uncle Gordy.
Brent's sales went down 30% with the opening of a Borders bookstore three blocks away. "Supermarkets," he snorts. "Philistines. My father used to speak of 'men you'd have to stand on
tiptoes to talk to.' Where are those men today?" Even Mayor Richard Daley mourned the loss
in a telegram sent to Brent on closing day, "Michigan Avenue will miss you, as much as it was
enhanced by your fine store and elegant presence."[2] A traditional tale of David and Goliath?

---

[1]Lao Tzu, *Tao Te Ching,* Book 2, XLVI: 105.
[2]Jeff Lyon, "For Starters," *Chicago Tribune Sunday Magazine,* January 14, 1996, p. 6.

The chain superstores argue that it is not. Instead, these stores contend that they are merely serving the needs of their customers in a more effective, efficient manner and therefore deserve a larger share of the market. "It's no longer simply the big, stupid best-seller stores and the small, elegant, literary bookstores," says shopper and Northwestern University professor Joseph Epstien. "Places like Barnes and Noble and Borders stock the good books, too. I doubt that Stuart Brent had anything these stores don't, except in his specialty of psychoanalytic books."[3] Perhaps these larger bookstores aren't so much predators as they are simply players—answering the needs of the public.

Is there any responsibility of a large chain store entering a small community market? Consider as well the tales of Walgreen stores entering small towns where there is one established pharmacy equipped with a pharmacist who has been serving that public for many years. The pharmacist cannot compete with the economies of scale available to a large firm like Walgreen, so she closes her doors. Is Walgreen to blame? Perhaps. But is it at *fault*? It is using its size to a competitive advantage to reap greater profits for its owners.

Consider what ethical and unethical steps might be taken in the name of profits. Is offering a larger selection, lower prices and a different ambience unethical? Is an act ethical because it results in higher profit or in spite of it? Consider the examples suggested by Jason Lunday and opinion expressed in Al Gini's article. Accountability is directly addressed in the discussion of the Federal Sentencing Guidelines—some ask what better way to encourage ethical behavior than to financially reward those who engage in it and financially punish those who do not? On the issue of accountability, one might also want to check out the perspectives of various consumer and advocacy groups in connection with well-known businesses at any of the following websites:

- www.bankofamericafraud.org

- www.boycottameritech.com

- www.cokespotlight.org

- www.ihatestarbucks.com

- www.noamazon.com

- www.starbucked.com

- www.walmartsurvivor.com

Moreover, though there are many justifications for ethics in business, often the discussion returns to, well, returns—the business case for the return on investment. There is evidence that good ethics is good business; yet the dominant thinking is that, if one can't measure it, it is not important. Consequently, efforts have been made to measure the bottom-line impact of ethical decision making. Persuasive evidence of impact comes from a recent study titled, "Developing Value: The Business Case for Sustainability in Emerging Markets," based on a study produced jointly by SustainAbility, the Ethos Institute and the International Finance Corporation. The research found that, in emerging markets, cost

---

[3]John Blades, "Staying Alive," *Chicago Tribune,* March 20, 1996, sec. 5, pp. 1, 4.

savings, productivity improvement, revenue growth and access to markets were the most important business benefits of sustainability activities. Environmental process improvements and human resource management were the most significant areas of sustainability action. The report concludes that it does pay for businesses in emerging markets to pursue a wider role on environmental and social issues, citing cost reductions, productivity, revenue growth and market access as areas of greatest return for multinational enterprises (MNEs).

In addition, studies have found that there are a number of expected—and measurable—outcomes to ethics programs in organizations. Some look to the end results of firms that have placed ethics and social responsibility at the forefront of their activities, while others look to those firms who have been successful and determine the role that ethics might have played. With regard to the former, consider Johnson & Johnson, known for its quick and effective handling of its experience with tainted Tylenol. J&J had sales in 2001 of $33 billion, almost triple those of the previous decade and representing its 69th year of consecutive sales increases. It has had 17 consecutive years of double-digit earnings increases and 39 consecutive years of dividend increases. Its market value ended in 2001 at more than $180 billion, up from $38 billion in 1991—evidence that a firm that lives according to its strong values and a culture that supports those values not only can survive but can also sustain profit over the long term. CEO Ralph Larsen credits these successes directly to the J&J Credo. "It's the glue that holds our decentralized company together. . . . For us, the credo is our expression of managing the multiple bottom lines of products, people, planet and profits. It's the way we conceptualize our total impact on society."[4]

> *There is clear evidence that a good reputation gains a company more customers, better employees, more investors, improved access to credit and greater credibility with government. . . . The difference between a company with ethical capital and one with an ethical deficit—perceived or real—can even determine their "license to operate" in some emerging markets.[5]*

> *Whether at the World Trade Organization, or at the OECD, or at the United Nations, an irrefutable case can be made that a universal acceptance of the rule of law, the outlawing of corrupt practices, respect for workers' rights, high health and safety standards, sensitivity to the environment, support for education and the protection and nurturing of children are not only justifiable against the criteria of morality and justice. The simple truth is that these are good for business and most business people recognize this.[6]*

> *We all pay for poverty and unemployment and illiteracy. If a large percentage of society falls into a disadvantaged class, investors will find it hard to source skilled and alert workers; manufacturers will have a limited market for their products; criminality will scare away foreign investments and internal migrants to limited areas of op-*

[4]Ralph Larsen, "Leadership in a Values-Based Organization," Sears Lectureship in Business Ethics, Bentley College, February 7, 2002.

[5]J. Nelson/The Prince of Wales Business Leaders Forum, *Business as Partners in Development: Creating Wealth for Countries, Companies and Communities* (London: The Prince of Wales Business Leaders Forum, 1996), pp. 47, 52.

[6]Thomas d'Aquino, CEO of Canada's Business Council on National Issues, quoted in C. Forcese, "Profiting from Misfortune? The Role of Business Corporations in Promoting and Protecting International Human Rights," MA Thesis, Norman Paterson School of International Affairs, Carleton University, Ottawa (1997), referred to in C. Forcese, *Putting Conscience into Commerce: Strategies for Making Human Rights Business as Usual* (Montreal: International Centre for Human Rights and Democratic Development, 1997).

portunities will strain basic services and lead to urban blight. Under these conditions, no country can move forward economically and sustain development. . . . It therefore makes business sense for corporations to complement the efforts of government in contributing to social development.[7]

Our findings, both cross-sectional and longitudinal, indicate that there are indeed systematic linkages among community involvement, employee morale and business performance in business enterprises. To the best of our knowledge, this is the first time that such linkages have been demonstrated empirically. Moreover, the weight of the evidence produced here indicates that community involvement is positively associated with business performance, employee morale is positively associated with business performance and the interaction of community involvement—external involvement— with employee morale—internal involvement—is even more strongly associated with business performance than is either "involvement" measure alone.[8]

Through the readings that follow, this chapter seeks to delineate the nature of an ethical corporation and how one might lead that organization. What is ethical leadership and what are its implications? What is the impact of a corporation's culture; how does one build and sustain an ethical corporate culture and what are the costs of its failure?

ETHICAL LEADERSHIP

The results of a poll conducted by the World Economic Forum released in 2003 suggests that trust is not only declining in institutions worldwide, but also leaders are suffering from an even greater decline in public trust than the companies they lead. Given the scandals of 2000 forward, this finding may not be surprising since the general public blames corporate leadership—correctly in many cases—for the corruption and misdeeds in corporate America. Of the eight leadership categories tested, only the leaders of nongovernment organizations enjoy the trust of a clear majority of their public. In fact, of the eight categories, executives of multinational companies ranked seventh, beating out only leaders of the United States.[9] How does one counteract these perceptions and create instead a perception of ethical leadership?

Another survey may offer insight into these numbers. The results of a survey of 20,000 articles in the U.K press evidence that CEOs of large companies mention ethics or social responsibility issues in only 5% of their communications, compared to 40% that discuss financial matters. (This research was conducted before the collapse of Enron and, in a strange twist of research, the study found that CEOs in the oil and gas sector were the most likely to raise ethical issues!)

Overall, a perception of ethical leadership is most often based on the leaders' communication abilities and opportunities. When employees are satisfied with the way in which

---

[7]J. Ayala II, "Philanthropy Makes Business Sense," *Business Day* (Bangkok), September 25, 1995, and J. Ayala II, "Philanthropy Makes Business Sense," *Ayala Foundation Inc.* 4, no. 2 (July–September, October–November 1995), p. 3.

[8]D. Lewin and J. M. Sabater, "Corporate Philanthropy and Business Performance," *Philanthropy at the Crossroads* (Bloomington, IN: Indiana University, 1996), pp. 105–26.

[9]World Economic Forum, "Declining Public Trust Foremost a Leadership Problem," press release, January 14, 2003.

their leaders communicate, the results can be significant. These employees are more satisfied with their jobs; they feel that everyone is on the same team and working toward the same goal; they feel confident of their longevity with the firm; and they feel that their companies' products or services are better than their competitors'.[10] To create that perception, corporate leaders must do more than simply putting their values into action. They must learn to disseminate that ethical decision-making process.

The results of a qualitative study of the nature of ethical leadership emphasize the importance of being perceived as a leader with a people orientation, as well as the importance of leaders engaging in visible ethical action. Traits are also important and include receptivity, listening and openness, in addition to the more traditionally considered traits of integrity, honesty and trustworthiness. Finally, being perceived as having a broad ethical awareness and concern for multiple stakeholders, and using ethical decision processes are also important.[11] Those perceived as ethical leaders do many of the things "traditional leaders" do (e.g., reinforce the conduct they are looking for, create standards for behavior, etc.), but within the context of an ethics agenda. People perceive that the ethical leader's goal is not simply job performance, but performance that is consistent with a set of ethical values and principles. And, ethical leaders demonstrate caring for people (employees and external stakeholders) in the process.

However, as mentioned above, all of these traits and behaviors must be visible. If an executive is "quietly ethical" within the confines of the top management team, but more distant employees don't know about it, she or he is not likely to be perceived as an ethical leader. Traits and behaviors must be socially visible and understood in order to be noticed and influence perceptions.[12] People notice when an executive walks the talk and acts on concerns for the common good, society as a whole and the long term because executives are expected to be focused on the financial bottom line and the short-term demands of stock analysts. When they focus on these broader and longer-term concerns, people notice. Finally, making courageous decisions in tough situations represents another way ethical leaders get noticed. Ethical leaders are "courageous enough to say 'no' to conduct that would be inconsistent with [their] values."[13] This type of courageous decision making is certain to garner attention in the organization and to stand out from a neutral or unethical landscape, conveying information about the importance of standing up for what's right.

CORPORATE CULTURE

Every organization has a culture, represented by a shared pattern of beliefs, expectations and meanings that influence and guide the thinking and behaviors of the members of an organization or group. Though somewhat ethereal, it is important to consider the cultures of firms because it is the culture that encourages and influences decision making. Consider a

---

[10]Institute for Global Ethics, *Ethics Newsline* 5, no. 13 (April 1, 2002), citing Maritz Research Poll (January 14–17, 2002).
[11]L. Trevino, M. Brown and L. Hartman, "A Qualitative Investigation of Perceived Executive Ethical Leadership: Perceptions from Inside and Outside the Executive Suite," *Human Relations* 56, no. 1 (January 2003), pp. 5–37.
[12]*Ibid.*
[13]*Ibid.*

firm with a culture to play throughout the day—with Ping-Pong tables in the offices and a cafeteria replete with board games and other distractions, but everyone is also expected to remain in the office until all work is complete for that day, no matter how late that becomes. If you enter that firm with a 9 to 5 attitude, where you intend to give your all to work throughout the day but then to leave as the clock strikes 5, you might not have a "fit." The same might hold true for a firm's values. If you join a firm with a culture that supports other values than those with which you are comfortable, there will be values conflicts—for better or worse.

Some common elements of corporate culture include:

- There are no generically effective or ineffective cultures.

- Culture is self-reinforcing and socially learned.

- Strong, cohesive cultures are double-edged swords.

- Cultures are rooted in successful problem solving and actions.

- Culture's influence operates outside of our awareness.

- Culture is linked to organization performance.

- Cultural change takes time and requires multiple strategies.

A firm's culture can be its sustaining value—that which offers it direction during challenging times. It can, however, also constrain an organization to the common ways of managing issues—"that's how things have always been done here," "that's our prevailing climate." Consider a firm that has lingered for decades under weak management, a lack of any internal corporate controls, little oversight, a sales performance-based significant bonus plan and a product that has been successful because it has suited a need. Now that need has changed slightly and the firm is under pressure to survive. With "the way that we've always done it," employees may have the opportunity—even the imperative—to cut corners and make decisions that would never be tolerated in another culture. "When you've got the incentives [in the form of higher pay cause of bigger profits] to take risks, the system ought to at least throw up some red flags. People are going to overcompete and take risks and sometimes break laws."[14] Given recent downturns in the economy, this is precisely the environment at many organizations—"There is enormous pressure on corporations, never been greater earnings pressure. That will lead people at the top to press down [to workers]—'you will make money for the corporation.'"[15]

CORPORATE CULTURE AUDITS

How do you detect a potentially damaging or ethically challenged corporate culture—sometimes referred to as a "toxic" culture? The first clear sign would be a lack of any generally accepted base values for the organizations. In the absence of other values, the only

---

[14]Kenneth Bredemeier, "A Rogue within the Ranks," *Washington Post,* March 25, 2002, p. E1.
[15]*Ibid.*

value is profit—at any cost. Therefore, without additional guidance from the top, a firm is sending a clear message that a worker should do whatever it takes to reap profits. In addition, there are warning signs in the various component areas of the organization. How does the firm treat its customers, suppliers, clients, workers? The management of its internal and external relationships are critical evidence of its values. How does the firm manage its finances? Of course, a firm can be in a state of financial disaster without engaging in even one unethical act (and vice versa), but the manner in which it manages and communicates its financial environment is telling. PricewaterhouseCoopers offers guidance as to early warning signs of an ethically troubled organization that might indicate areas of concern regarding fraud, conflicts of interest, ineffective controls, imbalance of power, inappropriate pressure or other areas, including (but not limited to):

1. Inability to generate positive cash flows despite positive earnings and growth.
2. Unusual pressure to achieve accounting-based financial objectives.
3. Compensation tied closely or only to financial results.
4. Debt covenants violated (or close to being so).
5. Increased liabilities with no apparent source of funding.
6. Off-balance sheet transactions.
7. Complex or creative structures.
8. Ratios/trends that buck expectations or industry trends.
9. Large returns or revenue credits after the close of the period.
10. Large number of nonstandard adjusting entries.
11. History of unreliable accounting estimates.
12. Numerous related-party transactions.
13. Transactions with no/questionable business purposes.

In addition, PwC suggests the following organizational signals:

1. Unusually complex organizational structure; numerous entities with unclear purpose.
2. Insufficient management depth in key positions, especially positions that manage risks.
3. Rapid growth or downsizing placing stress on organizational resources.
4. Resignations of management or board members for reasons other than retirement, health or conflict of interest.
5. Member of board or senior management possibly involved in or aware of financial manipulation (resulting in restatement) still connected with the organization.
6. Finance/accounting staff understaffed.
7. Internal audit department undersized/understaffed.
8. No audit committee or ineffective committee.
9. Management conveys a lifestyle beyond financial means.
10. Scope of internal audit seems too narrow.
11. Failure to address weaknesses in controls or process.

The Institute for Business, Technology and Ethics cites the following eight traits of a healthy organizational culture:

1. Openness and humility from top to bottom of organization.
2. An environment of accountability and personal responsibility.

3. Freedom from risk-taking within appropriate limits.
4. A fierce commitment to "doing it right."
5. A willingness to tolerate and learn from mistakes.
6. Unquestioned integrity and consistency.
7. A pursuit of collaboration, integration and holistic thinking.
8. Courage and persistence in the face of difficulty.

Finally, the Institute of Business Ethics (U.K.) has created a self-assessment checklist for organizations that allows a company to determine where it stands with regard to core issues common to many social or business ethics standards (see Table 3.1).

Consider the messages sent to each and all stakeholders by these behaviors or activities. These are all responsible for creating a culture that permeates the entire organization.

TABLE 3.1

Self-Assessment Checklist for Businesses

Human Rights and Labor Practices

Business ethics	Do you have a code of business conduct, ethics or business principles in the company? Is it circulated to all employees and translated as appropriate? Is it available to all stakeholders?
Child labor	Do you comply with ILO conventions prohibiting employment of children under 15 years of age and preventing exposure of staff under 18 years of age to any hazardous conditions?
Suppliers	Do you encourage and/or monitor key suppliers for their compliance with basic workplace standards and human rights? Do you build such information into the selection and review process?
Discrimination, diversity	Do you have an equal opportunities policy? If so, how have you ensured that all staff are aware of your policy? Are salaries, appointments and promotions considered on merit? Is there an objective system of appraisal to enable this?
Freedom of association	Is your workforce freely able to form/join trade unions (or alternative collective units) and to bargain collectively?
Discipline/grievance	Is there a recognized and fair means of discipline in place? Similarly is there a formal and fair grievance process?
Human rights	Are the fundamental principles outlined in the UN Declaration of Human Rights captured in policies of employment and other relevant business practices? Do you have strict codes of conduct for any security personnel employed or contracted?
Health and safety	Do you have a senior manager responsible for ensuring that your product and operations do not pose an unacceptable risk to staff, contractors or visitors? Are all injuries recorded and causes investigated and remedied?
Working hours	Do any of your staff work more than a 48-hour week? If so, do you have systems in place to ensure compliance with the European Working Time Directive?

TABLE 3.1 (Concluded)

Remuneration/reward	Do you meet the minimum wage requirements in all of the countries in which you operate? Are all wages sufficient as to ensure staff can meet at least their basic human needs?

Community Involvement

Consultation	Do you consult communities on business decisions that may have significant impacts upon them before as well as after the event?
Responsibility	Where decisions have an adverse effect on a community, e.g., redundancies, do you take all reasonable steps to work with local communities to minimize these impacts?

Transparency and Accountability

Stakeholder engagement	Do you engage with external stakeholders? On what basis have you chosen your stakeholders? Do you build stakeholder views into decision making? Do you provide feedback to these stakeholders on your performance or impacts?
Performance measurement	Do you measure and monitor social performance using qualitative or quantitative indicators? Do you set improvement targets? Are such targets built into management objectives?
Disclosure/reporting	Do you publish or disclose your social performance or social impacts, e.g., via a social report, as part of your annual report or on your website? Is this done regularly? Do you invite feedback from readers?
External verification	Is your CSR management system or your social performance externally audited? Are the results of the audit published?
Sustainable development	Do you have an environmental management system in place? Do you regularly evaluate and seek to minimize your environmental impacts?

SOURCE: Copyright © 2002 Institute of Business Ethics. Reprinted with permission.

CORPORATE MISSIONS AND CODES

Before articulating the culture through a code of conduct or statement of values, a firm must first determine its mission. A code of conduct then may delineate this foundation both for internal stakeholders such as employees as well as external stakeholders such as customers. The code therefore both enhances corporate reputation and also provides concrete guidance for internal decision making, thus creating a built-in risk management system. When David Packard passed away, his business partner in creating HP, Bill Hewlett, commented, "As far as the company is concerned, the greatest thing he left behind him was a code of ethics known as the HP Way."[16] The vision can be inspiring—should be inspiring. Jim Collins, author of *Built to Last* and *Good to Great,* explains, "Contrary to business school doctrine, we did not find 'maximizing shareholder wealth' or 'profit maximization' as the dominant driving force or primary objective through the history of most of the visionary companies. They have tended to produce a cluster of objectives, of which money is only one—and not nec-

---

[16]James Collins and Jerry Porras, "Building Your Company's Vision," *Harvard Business Review,* September/October 1996.

essarily the primary one."[17] By establishing (especially through a participatory process) the core tenets on which a company is built, corporate leadership is effectively laying down the law with regard to the basis and objectives for all future decisions. As is evidenced by the Trevino article in this chapter, however, this is only the first step.

The 1990s brought a proliferation of corporate codes of conduct and mission statements as part of the corporate response to the Federal Sentencing Guidelines (see below)—a 2002 survey found that 75% of these mention the word *ethics*.[18] How successful these codes are depends in large part on the process by which they are conceived and written, as well as their implementation. As with the construction of a personal code or mission, it is critical to first ask yourself what you stand for or what the company stands for. Why does the firm exist, what are its purposes and how will it implement these objectives? Once you make these determinations, how will you share them and encourage a commitment to them among your colleagues and subordinates?

Implementation of a code often requires change—or at least the management of the current environment. Libby Hartman, Senior Director for Organizational Change Management at Cap Gemini Ernst & Young, cautions that one rarely sees change without the prior presence of pain. We don't abandon a current direction unless it is intolerable to continue. So, the first step is to evidence that pain—the basis for the intolerance. Why can't you continue as you are currently? Often the answer is easier if one considers the following image:

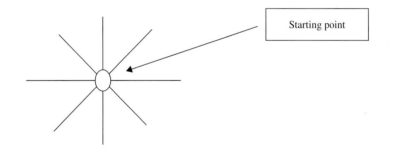

You may be very close in ideology if you're near the center but, if you happen to be on a different line than someone else, as time progresses, you'll grow further apart. It may not appear to be problematic in the beginning; but consider how far apart the two lines will become as the company matures.

The second step in support of this change is the articulation of a clear vision regarding the firm's direction. The Ethics Resource Center provides the following guidelines for writing an ethics code:

1. Be clear about the objectives that the code is intended to accomplish.
2. Get support and ideas for the code from all levels of the organization.

---

[17]Mark Satin, "We Need to Alter the Culture at Places Like Enron—Not Just Pass More Laws," *Radical Middle Newsletter,* March/April 2002, http://www.radicalmiddle/com.

[18]American Management Association Report, *2002 Corporate Values Survey.*

3. Be aware of the latest developments in the laws and regulations that affect your industry.
4. Write as simply and clearly as possible. Avoid legal jargon and empty generalities.
5. Respond to real-life questions and situations.
6. Provide resources for further information and guidance.
7. In all its forms, make it user-friendly because ultimately a code fails if it is not used.

The third step in this process is to identify clear steps as to how this cultural shift will occur. You have a code, but you can't simply "print, post and pray," as Ethics Resource Center president Stuart Gilman has referred to Enron's experience. Do you just post a sign on the wall that says, "Let's make more profits!" Of course not; you need to have processes and procedures in place that support and then sustain that vision. The same holds true for a vision of ethical conduct and the maintenance of an ethical culture.

Finally, to have an effective code that will successfully impact culture, there must be a belief throughout the organization that this culture is actually possible, achievable. If conflicts remain that will prevent certain components from being realized, or if key leadership is not on board, no one will have faith in the changes articulated.

In evaluating the establishment of codes of conduct according to a set of universal moral standards, Wharton professor Mark Schwartz developed a "code of ethics for corporate codes of ethics." Consider how the principles of trustworthiness, respect, responsibility, fairness, caring and citizenship can be embodied in the code creation process and the code, itself.

1. The above six standards should be included in the code, respected by other code content and given priority over bottom line concerns.
2. Code content should be understandable, achievable and justified.
3. All employees should be brought into the code creation process by offering each employee an opportunity to comment on the code.
4. Codes should be widely distributed and made fully accessible to the public.
5. Sufficient training, support and reinforcement should be provided in relation to the code.
6. The board of directors, CEO, president and all senior managers are obligated to demonstrate their support for the code, particularly by acting as role models through their own behavior.
7. Companies should enforce their codes and do so in a consistent and fair manner.
8. Sufficient protections should be provided to employees who report violations of the code.
9. Companies should ensure that a mechanism is in place to monitor and obtain feedback on their codes.[19]

Schwartz explains that the process by which one can change a culture is fluid. Such a transformation "occurs only after you have successfully altered some people's attitudes, which produces a modification in action, which may produce some group benefit for a period of time. People then need to see a connection between the modified behavior and the benefit, which then encourages them to adopt the new attitude, which then modifies their own behavior."[20]

---

[19]Mark Schwartz, "A Code of Ethics for Corporate Codes of Ethics," *Journal of Business Ethics,* no. 41 (2002), pp. 27–43.
[20]*Ibid.*

REPUTATION MANAGEMENT

Several readings in this chapter consider the corporate response to public demands for ethical behavior and the concern for the "appearance of propriety," the corporate reputation. As you review the readings in this section, ponder the following (facetious and sarcastic) recommendations for leadership offered by Gen. Colin Powell as a result of the frustration he experienced during the mishandling of the U.S. hostage crisis in Iran from 1979–81:

1. Release facts slowly, behind the pace at which they are already leaking to the public.
2. Don't tell the whole story until forced to do so.
3. Emphasize what went well and euphemize what went wrong.
4. Become indignant at any suggestion of poor judgment or mistakes.
5. Disparage any facts other than your own.
6. Accuse critics of Monday-morning generalship.
7. Accept general responsibility at the top, thus clearing everybody at fault below.[21]

Why do firms engage in ethical behavior? Earlier chapters have suggested profit motives but, as also discussed, an ethical decision does not always lead to the highest profits possible. Perhaps the firm engages in ethical decision making because "it's the right thing to do," as Sears Roebuck and Co. says in its ethics materials. Perhaps, however, as some of the readings in this section suggest, engaging in ethical behavior, implementing ethics programs, or instituting codes of conduct all contribute both to the internal culture of the firm as well as to the external stakeholders' perceptions of the firm. Is there anything wrong with paying attention to these external perceptions?

ENFORCING CULTURE: THE U.S. SENTENCING COMMISSION GUIDELINES

The United States Sentencing Commission, an independent agency in the United States Judiciary, was created in 1984 to regulate sentencing policy in the federal court system. Before that, disparity in sentencing, arbitrary punishments and crime control had been significant congressional issues. In mandating sentencing procedures, Congress through the USSC has been able to incorporate the original purposes of sentencing, bringing some of these challenges under control.

In 1987, the USSC prescribed mandatory sentencing guidelines that apply to individual and organizational defendants in the federal system, bringing some uniformity and fairness to the system. These prescriptions, based on the severity of the offense, assign most federal crimes to one of 43 "offense levels." Each offender also is placed into a criminal history category based upon the extent and recency of past misconduct. The court is then to input this information into a sentencing grid and determine the offender's guideline range (ranges are either in 6-month intervals or 25%, whichever is greater), subject to adjustments.

---

[21]Colin Powell and Joseph Persico, *My American Journey* (New York: Random House, 1995) p. 250.

The relevance of these guidelines to our exploration of ethics and, in particular, to our discussion of the corporate proactive efforts to create an ethical workplace, is that the USSC strived in its guidelines to create both a legal and an ethical corporate environment through these adjustments. The guidelines seek to reward corporations that create an effective compliance system so that they are not penalized (or the penalty is reduced) if they have an effective program but they find themselves in court as a result of a bad apple or two. On the other hand, firms that did not have effective compliance systems would be sentenced additionally to a term of probation and ordered to develop a program during that time.

The relevant language is found in section 8 of the guidelines, which identifies those specific acts of an organization that can serve as "due diligence" in preventing crime. These include:

1. Established effective compliance standards and procedures ("reasonably designed, implemented and enforced so that it will generally be effective in preventing and detecting criminal conduct").[22]
2. Assigned specific high-level person(s) to oversee compliance.
3. Used due care not to delegate important responsibilities to known high-risk persons.
4. Communicated its program effectively to all employees and agents.
5. Monitored and audited program operation and established a retribution-free means for employees to report possible violations to management.
6. Consistently disciplined employee violations.
7. Responded promptly and appropriately to any offenses and remedied any program deficiencies.[23]

Though these steps are likely to lead to an effective program, "[such a program] is more than checking off the seven items on a list. This concept of 'due diligence' is a restless standard, as flexible as changing events reflected in the day's headlines and as creative as the minds of potential wrongdoers."[24] For instance, the Guidelines require an investigation in response to a report of wrongdoing, but they also seem to require more than that. A firm must learn from its mistakes and take steps to prevent recurrences such as follow-up investigation and program enhancements. The USSC also mandates consideration of the size of the organization, the number and nature of its business risks, and the prior history of the organization, mitigating factors such as self-reporting of violations, cooperation with authorities, acceptance of responsibility, as well as aggravating factors such as its involvement in or tolerance of criminal activity, a violation of a prior order or its obstruction of justice. These standards are to be judged against applicable industry standards; however, this requires that each firm benchmark against comparable companies.

In a 1997 survey of members of the Ethics Officers Association, 47% of ethics officers reported that the guidelines were an influential determinant of their firm's commitment to

[22]USSC, *Guidelines Manual,* sec. 8A1.2, comment (n. 3(k)) (2000).
[23]*Ibid.*
[24]Joseph Murphy, "Lost Words of the Sentencing Guidelines," *Ethikos,* November/December 2002, p. 5.

ethics,[25] and another commission study showed that the guidelines influenced 44.5% of these officers to enhance their existing compliance programs.[26]

To provide some context to this exploration, consider which offenses are most likely to reap a fine for an organization. In 2001, the commission received information on 238 organizations sentenced under Chapter 8 (a 21.7% decrease from the previous year). The sentenced organizations had pled guilty in 92.4% of the cases—30% of fines and restitution were issued for cases of fraud, with the next most common crimes to be antitrust and import/export violations (6.7% each). Of those violations that are not included in the fine list, violations of environmental laws with regard to water topped the list at 13%. The mean restitution imposed was $4 million and the mean fine was $2 million.

As you read the following materials, put yourself in the position of someone who is establishing an organization from the ground up. What type of leader would you want to be? How would you create that image or perception? Do you create a mission statement for the firm, a code of conduct? What process would you use to do so? Would you create an ethics and/or compliance program and how would you then integrate the mission statement and program throughout your organization? What do you anticipate might be your successes and challenges?

APPLICATION TO THE GLOBAL BUSINESS ENVIRONMENT

As discussed with regard to the ethical principles governing global business in Chapter 1, there are a number of externally imposed, voluntary codes of conduct. The items in Chapter 1 refer to global business, while others might be promulgated by professional organizations or accrediting bodies, depending on the organization's industry or the practice involved (i.e., accounting, marketing and so on). Though valuable in many circumstances, the challenges with regard to these voluntary codes are myriad. For instance, based on what values should a global code be developed? Some firms have been accused of imposing American values worldwide, without any sensitivity to the cultural conflicts that might exist in some locations, nor to the sense of colonialism and paternalism that such an imposition creates. In addition, once a firm agrees to either its own codes or that of an outside body, how will the code be enforced? Who will ensure that a firm lives up to the prescribed standards?

With regard to labor codes, and in connection with apparel and footwear manufacturers and brands in particular, an entire industry of monitors has been established. These include internal monitors (firm employees), external monitors (outsiders hired by the firm to monitor its factories or contractors' factories), and external independent monitors (others hired by a third party to monitor according to prior agreement with the manufacturer or brand). The Fair Labor Association, for example, is an industry-supported organization that established a code of conduct and then monitors its signatories to ensure compliance. The

---

[25]Ethics Officers Association, "1997 Member Survey," 2000, p. 9.
[26]USSC, "Corporate Crime in America: Strengthening the 'Good Citizen' Corporation," 123–91 (1995).

signatory might have an entire internal monitoring structure but also will allow FLA monitors to visit their factories or contractor factories.

Critics of these voluntary codes and monitoring regimes claim that they replace effective governmental monitoring or regulation of labor environments. Others see voluntary codes simply as marketing tools, designed to enhance the firm's public relations image. They worry that codes can become mere window dressing and not address the key issues facing workers today, such as the right to organize.

MORAL LEADERSHIP AND BUSINESS ETHICS

—AL GINI

How do you judge the ethics of a leader? What makes one leader ethical and another unethical? Does it depend on the impact of that leader on her or his followers? Gini identifies the parameters within which we might appropriately judge a leader and the structural restraints imposed upon corporate leadership. Consider the impact of these restraints on the decisions and actions of leaders. Do they justify any (or all) leadership decisions?

How do we judge the ethics of a leader? Clearly, no leader can be expected to be perfect in every decision and action made. As John Gardner has pointed out, particular consequences are never a reliable assessment of leadership.[1] The quality and worth of leadership can only be measured in terms of what a leader intends, values, believes in or stands for—in other words, character. In *Character: America's Search for Leadership,* Gail Sheehy argued, as did Aristotle before her, that character is the most crucial and most elusive element of leadership. The root of the word "character" comes from the Greek word for engraving. As applied to human beings, it refers to the enduring marks or etched-in factors in our personality, which include our in-born talents as well as the learned and acquired traits imposed upon us by life and experience. These engravings define us, set us apart and motivate behavior.

In regard to leadership, said Sheehy, character is fundamental and prophetic. The "issues (of leadership) are those of today and will change in time. Character is what was yesterday and will be tomorrow."[2] For Sheehy, character establishes both our day-to-day demeanor and our destiny. Therefore, it is not only useful but essential to examine the character of those who desire to lead us. As a journalist and longtime observer of the political scene, Sheehy contends that the Watergate affair of the early 1970s serves as a perfect example of the links between character and leadership. As Richard Nixon demonstrated so well, said Sheehy: "The Presidency is not the place to work out one's personal pathology."[3] Leaders rule us, run things, wield power. Therefore, said Sheehy, we must be careful whom we choose as leaders. Because whom we choose, is what we shall be. If, as Heraclitus wrote, "character is fate," the fate our leaders reap will also be our own.

Putting aside the particular players and the politics of the episode, Watergate has come to symbolize the failings and failures of people in high places. Watergate now serves as a

Al Gini, "Moral Leadership and Business Ethics." Reprinted by permission. Al Gini is an associate professor of philosophy at Loyola University of Chicago and managing editor of *Business Ethics Quarterly.*

[1]John W. Gardner, *On Leadership* (New York: The Free Press, 1990), p. 8.

[2]Gail Sheehy, *Character: America's Search for Leadership* (New York: Bantam Books, 1990), p. 311.

[3]*Ibid.,* p. 66.

watershed, a turning point, in our nation's concern for integrity, honesty and fair play from all kinds of leaders. It is not a mere coincidence that the birth of business ethics as an independent, academic discipline can be dated from the Watergate affair and the trials that came out of it. No matter what our failings as individuals, Watergate sensitized us to the importance of ethical standards and conduct from those who direct the course of our political and public lives. What society is now demanding, and what business ethics is advocating, is that our business leaders and public servants should be held accountable to an even higher standard of behavior than we might demand and expect of ourselves.

Mutual Purposes and Goals

The character, goals and aspirations of a leader are not developed in a vacuum. Leadership, even in the hands of a strong, confident, charismatic leader remains, at bottom, relational. Leaders, good or bad, great or small, arise out of the needs and opportunities of a specific time and place. Leaders require causes, issues and, most importantly, a hungry and willing constituency. Leaders may devise plans, establish an agenda, bring new and often radical ideas to the table, but all of them are a response to the milieu and membership of which they are a part. If leadership is an active and ongoing relationship between leaders and followers, then a central requirement of the leadership process is for leaders to evoke and elicit consensus in their constituencies, and conversely for followers to inform and influence their leaders. This is done in at least two ways, through the use of power and education.

The term "power" comes from the Latin *posse:* to do, to be able, to change, to influence or effect. To have power is to possess the capacity to control or direct change. All forms of leadership must make use of power. The central issue of power in leadership is not, "Will it be used?" but, rather, "Will it be used wisely and well?" According to James MacGregor Burns, leadership is not just about directed results; it is also about offering followers a choice among real alternatives. Hence, leadership assumes competition, conflict and debate whereas brute power denies it.[4] "Leadership mobilizes," said Burns, "naked power coerces."[5] But power need not be dictatorial or punitive to be effective. Power can also be used in a noncoercive manner to orchestrate, direct and guide members of an organization in the pursuit of a goal or series of objectives. Leaders must engage followers, not merely direct them. Leaders must serve as models and mentors, not martinets. "Power without morality," said novelist James Baldwin, "is no longer power."

For Peter Senge teaching is one of the primary jobs of leadership.[6] The "task of leader as teacher" is to empower people with information, offer insights, new knowledge, alternative perspectives on reality. The "leader as teacher," said Senge, is not just about "teaching" people how "to achieve their vision" but, rather, is about fostering learning, offering choices and building consensus.[7] Effective leadership recognizes that in order to build and achieve community, followers must become reciprocally coresponsible in the pursuit of a common

---

[4]James MacGregor Burns, *Leadership* (New York Harper Torchbooks, 1979), p. 36.

[5]*Ibid.,* p. 439.

[6]For Senge the three primary tasks of leadership include: leader as designer; leader as steward; leader as teacher.

[7]Peter M. Senge, *The Fifth Discipline* (New York: Double/Currency Books, 1990), p. 353.

enterprise. Through their conduct and teaching, leaders must try to make their fellow constituents aware that they are all stakeholders in a conjoint activity that cannot succeed without their involvement and commitment. Successful leadership believes in and communicates some version of the now famous Hewlett-Packard motto: "The achievements of an organization are the results of the combined efforts of each individual."

In the end, says Abraham Zaleznick, "leadership is based on a compact that binds those who lead with those who follow into the same moral, intellectual and emotional commitment."[8] However, as both Burns and Rost warned us, the nature of this "compact" is inherently unequal because the influence patterns existing between leaders and followers are not equal. Responsive and responsible leadership requires, as a minimum, that democratic mechanisms be put in place which recognize the right of followers to have adequate knowledge of alternative options, goals and programs, as well as the capacity to choose between them. "In leadership writ large, mutually agreed upon purposes help people achieve consensus, assume responsibility, work for the common good and build community."[9]

STRUCTURAL RESTRAINTS

There is, unfortunately, a dark side to the theory of the "witness of others." Howard S. Schwartz in his radical, but underappreciated, managerial text *Narcissistic Process and Corporate Decay,*[10] argued that corporations are not bastions of benign, other-directed ethical reasoning. Nor can corporations, because of the demands and requirements of business, be models and exemplars of moral behavior. The rule of business, said Schwartz, remains the "law of the jungle," "the survival of the fittest," and the goal of survival engenders a combative "us against them mentality" which condones the moral imperative of getting ahead by any means necessary. Schwartz calls this phenomenon "organizational totalitarianism": Organizations and the people who manage them create for themselves a self-contained, self-serving world view, which rationalizes anything done on their behalf and which does not require justification on any grounds outside of themselves.[11] The psychodynamics of this narcissistic perspective, said Schwartz, impose Draconian requirements on all participants in organizational life: do your work; achieve organizational goals; obey and exhibit loyalty to your superiors; disregard personal values and beliefs; obey the law when necessary, obfuscate it whenever possible; and, deny internal or external discrepant information at odds with the stated organizational worldview. Within such a "totalitarian logic," neither leaders nor followers, rank nor file, operate as independent agents. To "maintain their place," to "get ahead," all must conform. The agenda of "organizational totalitarianism," said Schwartz, is always the preservation of the *status quo.* Within such a logic, like begets like, and change is rarely possible. Except for extreme situations in which "systemic ineffectiveness" begins to breed "organization decay," transformation is never an option.

---

[8]Abraham Zaleznik, "The Leadership Gap," *Academy of Management Executive* (1990), V.4, N.1, p. 12.

[9]Joseph C. Rost, *Leadership for the Twenty-First Century,* p. 124.

[10]Howard S. Schwartz, *Narcissistic Process and Corporate Decay* (New York: New York University Press, 1990).

[11]Howard S. Schwartz, "Narcissism Project and Corporate Decay: The Case of General Motors," *Business Ethics Quarterly,* V.1, N.3, p. 250.

In *Moral Mazes* Robert Jackall, from a sociological rather than a psychological perspective, parallels much of Schwartz's analysis of organizational behavior. According to critic and commentator Thomas W. Norton, both Jackall and Schwartz seek to understand why and how organizational ethics and behavior are so often reduced to either dumb loyalty or the simple adulation and mimicry of one's superiors. While Schwartz argued that individuals are captives of the impersonal structural logic of "organizational totalitarianism," Jackall contends that "organizational actors become personally loyal to their superiors, always seeking their approval, and are committed to them as persons rather than as representatives of the abstractions of organizational authority." But in either case, both authors maintain that organizational operatives are prisoners of the systems they serve.[12]

According to Jackall, all organizations (to be exact, he is specially referring to American business organizations) are examples of "patrimonial bureaucracies" wherein "fealty relations of personal loyalty" are the rule and the glue of organizational life. Jackall argued that all corporations are like fiefdoms of the middle ages, wherein the Lord of the Manor (CEO, President) offers protection, prestige and status to his vassals (managers) and serfs (workers) in return for homage (commitment) and service (work). In such a system, said Jackall, advancement and promotion are predicated on loyalty, trust, politics and personality as much as, if not more than, on experience, education, ability and actual accomplishments. The central concern of the worker/minion is to be known as a "can-do-guy," a "team player," being at the right place at the right time and master of all the social rules. That's why in the corporate world, says Jackall, 1,000 "atta-boys" are wiped away with one "oh, shit!"

As in the model of a feudal system, Jackall maintains that employees of a corporation are expected to become functionaries of the system and supporters of the *status quo.* Their loyalty is to the powers that be; their duty is to perpetuate performance and profit; and their values can be none other than those sanctioned by the organization. Jackall contends that the logic of every organization (place of business) and the collective personality of the workplace conspire to override the wants, desires and aspirations of the individual worker. No matter what a person believes off the job, said Jackall, on the job all of us to a greater or lesser extent are required to suspend, bracket or only selectively manifest our personal convictions.

> *What is right in the corporation is not what is right in a man's home or his church. What is right in the corporation is what the guy above you wants from you.*[13]

For Jackall the primary imperative of every organization is to succeed. This logic of performance, what he refers to as "institutional logic," leads to the creation of a private moral universe. A moral universe that, by definition, is totalitarian (self-sustained), solipsistic (self-defined) and narcissistic (self-centered). Within such a milieu truth is socially defined and moral behavior is determined solely by organizational needs. The key virtues,

---

[12]Thomas W. Norton, "The Narcissism and Moral Mazes of Corporate Life: A Commentary on the Writings of H. Schwartz and R. Jackall," *Business Ethics Quarterly,* V.2, N.1, p. 76.

[13]Robert Jackall, *Moral Mazes* (New York: Oxford University Press, 1988), p. 6.

for all alike, become the virtues of the organization: goal-preoccupation, problem solving, survival/success and, most importantly, playing by the "house rules." In time, said Jackall, those initiated and invested in the system come to believe that they live in a self-contained worldview which is above and independent of outside critique and evaluation.

For both Schwartz and Jackall, the logic of organizational life is rigid and unchanging. Corporations perpetuate themselves, both in their strengths and weakness, because corporate cultures clone their own. Even given the scenario of a benign organizational structure which produces positive behavior and beneficial results, the etiology of the problem, and the opportunity for abuse that it offers, represents the negative possibilities and inherent dangers of the "witness of others" as applied to leadership theory. Within the scope of Schwartz's and Jackall's allied analysis, "normative" moral leadership may not be possible. The model offered is both absolute and inflexible, and only "regular company guys" make it to the top. The maverick, the radical, the reformer are not long tolerated. The "institutional logic" of the system does not permit disruption, deviance or default. . . .

The term moral leadership often conjures up images of sternly robed priests, waspishly severe nuns, carelessly bearded philosophers, forbiddingly strict parents and something ambiguously labeled the "moral majority." These people are seen as confining and dictatorial. They make us do what we should do, not what we want to do. They encourage following the "superego" and not the "id." A moral leader is someone who supposedly tells people the difference between right and wrong from on high. But there is much more to moral leadership than merely telling others what to do.

The vision and values of leadership must have their origins and resolutions in the community of followers, of whom they are a part, and whom they wish to serve. Leaders can drive, lead, orchestrate and cajole, but they cannot force, dictate or demand. Leaders can be the catalyst for morally sound behavior, but they are not, by themselves, a sufficient condition. Leaders by means of their demeanor and message must be able to convince, not just tell others, that collaboration serves the conjoint interest and well-being of all involved. Leaders may offer a vision, but followers must buy into it. Leaders may organize a plan, but followers must decide to take it on. Leaders may demonstrate conviction and willpower, but followers, in the new paradigm of leadership, should not allow the leader's will to replace their own.[14] To reiterate the words of Abraham Zaleznick: "Leadership is based on a compact that binds those that lead with those who follow into the same moral, intellectual and emotional commitment."

Joseph C. Rost has argued, both publicly and privately, that the ethical aspects of leadership remain thorny. How, exactly, do leaders and collaborators in an influence relationship make a collective decision about the ethics of a change that they want to implement in an organization or society? Some will say, "Option A is ethical," while others will say, "Option B is ethical." How are leaders and followers to decide? As I have suggested, ethics is what "ought to be done" as the preferred mode of action in a "right-vs.-right," "values-vs.-values" confrontation. Ethics is an evaluative enterprise. Judgments must be made in regard to competing points of view. Even in the absence of a belief in the existence of a single universal, absolute set of ethical rules, basic questions can still be asked: How does it impact

---

[14]Garry Wills, *Certain Trumpets,* p. 13.

on self and others? What are the consequences involved? Is it harmful? Is it fair? Is it equitable? Perhaps the best, but by no means definitive, method suited to the general needs of the ethical enterprise is a modified version of the scientific method: (A) *Observation,* the recognition of a problem or conflict; (B) *Inquiry,* a critical consideration of facts and issues involved; (C) *Hypothesis,* the formulation of a decision or plan of action consistent with the known facts; (D) *Experimentation and Evaluation,* the implementation of the decision or plan in order to see if it leads to the resolution of the problem. There are, of course, no perfect answers in ethics or life. The quality of our ethical choices cannot be measured solely in terms of achievements. Ultimately and ethically, intention, commitment and concerted effort are as important as outcome: What/why did leader/followers try to do? How did they try to do it?

Leadership is hard to define, and moral leadership is even harder. Perhaps, like pornography, we only recognize moral leadership when we see it. The problem is, we so rarely see it. Nevertheless, I am convinced that without the "witness" of moral leadership, standards of ethics in business and organizational life will not occur or be sustained. Leadership, even when defined as a collaborative experience, is still about the influence of individual character and the impact of personal mentoring. Behavior does not always beget like behavior on a one-to-one ratio, but it does establish tone, set the stage and offer options. Although it is mandatory that an organization as a whole—from top to bottom—make a commitment to ethical behavior to actually achieve it, the model for that commitment has to originate from the top.[15] Labor Secretary Robert Reich recently stated: "The most eloquent moral appeal (argument) will be no match for the dispassionate edict of the market."[16] Perhaps, the "witness" of moral leadership can prove to be more effective.

---

[15]Dolecheck, "*Ethics: Take It From the Top,*" p. 14.
[16]William Pfaff, "It's Time for a Change in Corporate Values," *Chicago Tribune,* January 16, 1996, p. 17.

LEADERSHIP IN A VALUES-BASED ORGANIZATION

—Ralph Larsen

Ralph Larsen was the outgoing Chairman and CEO of Johnson & Johnson at the time that Bentley College invited him to speak at the Sears Lectureship in Business Ethics in February 2002. In his address, Larsen refers not only to ethical leadership embodied by J&J's now-famous response to the Tylenol disaster in Chicago but also to ethical leadership as it is exhibited every day at J&J and in the decisions of its people. Consider the value of the Credo to J&J and ask yourself whether the Credo would work at all firms. What needs to be present in order for a statement like the Credo to be effective?

I am very pleased to be here representing the more than 100,000 people of Johnson & Johnson, people who work so hard each day, not only building our business, but doing it in the right way.

I'm honored to be a part of this lecture series, and so, the first reason I'm here is because you asked. The second reason is that the older I get, the more I like hanging around with people younger than I am, people on the threshold of their careers. You keep us young and nimble. You have a way of distilling and challenging our thought processes. You remind us of what it's all about.

Last year I spoke with a young lady who was serving as a fellow in our corporate communications department. This is a program we have with the Rutgers School of Communications. These master's students work for us as interns for one or two years as they complete their program. I was struck by her story, and I wanted to share it with you today.

Well, somehow our company made an impression on this young girl in India, thousands and thousands of miles away from the headquarters where she ultimately worked. When she came to us she brought with her the expectation that we would be as community-oriented, thoughtful, values-oriented and as upstanding as she had seen on the outside. She also came with the full expectation that she would find an environment where she could express her values and feel encouraged to do the right thing.

Now, I share Sandhya's story with you because I think it's just terrific that a young person can be touched and motivated by our company's values. And I think it's even more encouraging that this motivation meant that she sought out a job with us. You too might have

---

This monograph was presented as a lecture in the Sears Business Ethics Lectureship at the Center for Business Ethics at Bentley College on February 7, 2002. Reprinted with permission from the Center for Business Ethics at Bentley College.

some preconceptions about the kinds of organizations you want to join, and if you do end up someplace with a strong set of core values, I can give you a glimpse of what to expect once you get there.

Obviously, I can speak only from my personal experience which is almost exclusively in Johnson & Johnson. As Chairman and CEO for the past 13 years, I have had the best job in corporate America—of that I am sure. The reason is that leading a company like Johnson & Johnson, with a strong foundation built on values and a heritage based on ethical principles, is very special. There are certain boundaries in place: things you simply don't do, well-accepted management practices that just won't work, changes that just won't stick, parts of our history that simply won't give way to certain new ideas.

Leading a company like this isn't for everybody. It's not a job that goes away at the end of the day. It's a responsibility that sinks into you, because often we wrestle with issues and problems that have no easy answers—no clear right or wrong. For all those challenges . . . challenges I'll go into in more detail in a minute . . . for all those leadership challenges, our core values also make leadership a whole lot easier. You see, values are our greatest point of leverage to get things done . . . achieve all we can achieve. Values are the foundation of our business success.

In his renowned book, *The Fifth Discipline,* Peter Senge uses something called a "trim tab" to explain certain theories of leverage within a system. In this case, how do you get something really big, like an oil tanker ship, to change course? Well, you move the rudder, of course. But the rudder itself is so big that there's water pressure keeping it where it is. So, there is this very small piece (a rudder for the rudder if you will) called a trim tab that compresses the water around the rudder. That action makes it easier for the rudder to move through the water. Easier, therefore, for the rudder to change the direction of the ship. You don't see the trim tab. You probably never even knew it was there, but it makes an incredible difference to the navigation of the ship.

Being bound together around the values . . . around our credo . . . being bound together around values is like the trim tab for leadership at Johnson & Johnson. What I mean is that because it is a deep point of leverage, it makes a huge difference. It's the point of leverage that makes leadership not only possible but also meaningful and enjoyable.

Johnson & Johnson's strong values have been instrumental in our charting a course that has proved successful, and for that I am very thankful.

- Sales last year were $33 billion, almost triple what they were a decade ago, representing our 69th consecutive year of sales increases.

- We've had 17 consecutive years of double-digit earnings increases.

- And we've had 39 consecutive years of dividend increases.

- And our shareowners have done very well. The market value of Johnson & Johnson ended last year at more than $180 billion, up from approximately $38 billion ten years ago.

The point is that our business is healthy and the future looks bright. The challenge is to keep it going and growing. I had the incredibly good fortune to be given the opportunity to lead not only a well-run business, but one that had a very strong guidepost about what we believe in.

At Johnson & Johnson, it's the glue that holds our decentralized company together. It's called our credo, and it is a 60-year-old deceptively simple one-page document. Our credo grew out of General Robert Wood Johnson's (the patriarch of our company) very simple, yet very profound management philosophy. In essence, it says that our first responsibility is to our customers, to give them high-quality products at fair prices. Our second responsibility is to our employees, to treat them with dignity and respect and pay them fairly. Our third responsibility is to the communities in which we operate, to be good corporate citizens and protect the environment. And then, it says that our final responsibility is to our shareholders, to give them a fair return.

In the final analysis, the Credo is built on the notion that if you do a good job in fulfilling the first three responsibilities, then the shareholder will come out all right. That is exactly what has happened over all these years, and that is what we continue to strive for today.

For us, the Credo is our expression of managing the multiple bottom lines of products, people, planet and profits. It's the way we conceptualize our total impact on society. It implicitly tells us what's important: honesty and integrity, respect for others, fairness and straight-dealing. Those are the ethical values on which we operate all over the world.

Johnson & Johnson is a very decentralized company with almost 200 operating companies in 51 countries around the world, selling products in more than 175 countries. These operating companies have their own management boards and are relatively independent. We use this structure because it helps us focus on the markets and people we serve. It's the only way Johnson & Johnson can be such a broadly based health care company.

We are probably best known as a company that is a leader in health care consumer brands you know so well—from Johnson & Johnson Baby Products and Band-Aids to over-the-counter medications such as Tylenol and Motrin.

***

Clearly, as the chief executive officer, I am ultimately accountable for everything that happens, both good and bad. But more than anything else, I am responsible for the tone at the top. To run a good and decent company with good and decent people. I work hard at setting the right tone. I spend a tremendous amount of time developing and selecting credo-based leaders and ensuring that we have the proper systems and controls in place.

But with more than 100,000 people throughout our family of companies, I must rely on all of our company leaders and their teams to do the right thing and work with me to instill credo values throughout their organizations. They share with me the challenge of being responsible for making sure we operate in accordance with our credo values in all that we do.

Coming into my job I had the advantage of knowing that our credo had been translated into dozens of languages. I knew that we had programs in place to help ensure that each new employee had read it and was told of its significance, and I knew that copies of it were prominently displayed in offices and plants all over the world. As a new chief executive officer, I viewed the credo as an important framework for management and a key point of leverage, of differentiation, in today's global marketplace. It gives us the incredible advantage of having a foundation of timeless principles that serve as the "glue" that holds our decentralized organization together through good times and challenging ones.

Now, it has occurred to me that I am making all this sound kind of simple. It is not. In a highly competitive, financially driven world with the tyranny of quarterly earnings and with multiple constituencies, actually living the credo in a meaningful way is a constant challenge. At the end of the day, our credo is all about personal responsibility.

As one read through it, each of the four responsibilities outlined starts with the preposition "to" and that is very important. Said another way, our credo isn't about us being responsible for something. A school child is responsible for her backpack. An assembly line worker is responsible for placing a product in a package. But when you are responsible to, you are responsible "to a person" or "to a group of people." And that's what our credo says . . . we are responsible to our customers, mothers and fathers, doctors and nurses; responsible to employees; responsible to people in communities. This is an intrinsically subjective area precisely because it's personal. It's about owing part of yourself to others. It's a serious responsibility.

I'm no linguist, and so I don't know where the root of the two uses of a particular word in French come together, but I am struck that the word to be physically burdened with lots of luggage, *chargé,* is the same word used to describe a person who has taken on a responsibility. It's part of a title to indicate you're in charge. The idea is simple; when you're in charge, you are responsible. And this responsibility weighs heavily, particularly when you have to balance the interests of different people, all people you are responsible to.

***

Several years ago, we made the decision to close approximately 50 small plants around the world. It involved laying off several thousand people, many in communities and countries in which I knew the people would have a very tough time finding comparable employment. We had never done anything like that before.

I worried about my responsibility to the men, women and their families who would lose their jobs. But our operating costs at these small plants were way out of line, and we were becoming less and less competitive. So yes, I was responsible to our employees in those plants, but I was also responsible to the patients who needed our products to keep them affordable. And I was responsible to all of our other employees around the world to keep the company healthy and growing. The harsh reality was that a great many more would be hurt down the road if I failed to act and we became less and less competitive.

In addition to our employees, I was also responsible to the tens of thousands of stockholders (individuals, retired folks, pension plans and mutual funds) who owned our stock. The facts were clear . . . I knew what had to be done, and we did it as thoughtfully and sensitively as possible. But the decision was hard, because it was personal.

At a deeper level, what became crystal clear was that competing on a global basis with Olympic-class companies had changed the ground rules forever. This new world meant that we could no longer guarantee that if you came to work every day and did your job well, you could count on being employed with us for life. That's the way it used to be, but that was a responsibility that we could no longer fulfill. Rather, we had to focus on making people employable for life. And that's where we put our resources, at life-long development of skill sets that could be used in many different companies and industries.

The bright side to all of this is that being responsible to people has a tendency to become mutual. If I am responsible to you, you are more likely to be responsible to me, and that means I have colleagues I can trust. People are committed to people, not just to paychecks. There's a sense that we are all in it together. In our case, we're all working to get life-saving and life-enhancing products to people who need them. Improving the quality of life and healing and curing disease is our heritage and mission. Being bound together in one purpose makes us able to achieve incredible heights, not only as a group but as individuals.

***

Once inside, new leaders, I think, can grasp what we're all about quite readily because we tend to wear our values on our sleeves and talk openly about them. The credo is part of our daily conversation as we wrestle with decisions of all kinds. This means that for the newcomer there is less confusion, less jockeying and less reticence to make decisions. In our company, it's clear where the lines are, and there's a lot of room to act until you get close to those lines. Our experience is that if we have an executive who tends to bump up against the ethical boundaries time and time again, sooner or later they get themselves, and often the company, in serious trouble and that's the end of their career.

The credo is not a rulebook. It is not a list of do's and don'ts. It outlines fundamental principles that apply to not only our corporate but also our personal behavior as we carry out our business responsibilities. It has proven, over time, to be a guiding force that appeals to the ethical aspirations of all kinds of people, from all kinds of places, from all spiritual and religious backgrounds. That is its magic.

At the highest levels of leadership, the greatest risks are often risks associated with moving into new businesses particularly by acquisition. Mergers and acquisitions are, by their very nature, highly risky endeavors. They can change the fundamental make-up of our business, and they can bring thousands of new people into our company overnight.

I'm often asked if our strong set of values propels or inhibits this process . . . does it scare people off, or make us unapproachable, or make it hard for people from acquired companies to fit in. Not a bit. I think our reputation for being a values-based company is a tremendous asset. It serves as a magnet for smaller companies who do not have the resources to fulfill their potential and want to become a part of the Johnson & Johnson family of companies.

The best evidence of this is that over the last 10 years, we have added more than 50 companies, products or technologies to our company. We've successfully transitioned from a company based heavily on our heritage consumer products to a science-based company on the leading edge of medical technology.

***

Leaders can make values a priority that gets measured and rewarded. We can work hard at making sure that the company's values are well-expressed, well-understood, explicit and visible in all that we do, in all of our programs, policies, products. But the most important thing is to set the proper personal example, the tone at the top.

Our values need to be visible to people like Sandhya, young people who will become the next generation of leaders. The leaders who will wrestle with increasingly complex problems in a complicated world. A world in which often there is no clear answer and where you are not sure of what the "right" thing to do is. Leaders with good judgment who know how to preserve important values and hold fast to them, while at the same time knowing when and how fast to change to meet the challenges of a new world.

If this all sounds interesting to you as you pursue your career, I would urge you to join a company rich in values. There are no perfect people, and there are no perfect companies. We all have our weaknesses and warts. But make sure the company you join has a set of core values that you are comfortable with, that you are proud of, and which will bring out the very best in you.

VENTURING BEYOND COMPLIANCE

—LYNN SHARP PAINE

Lynn Sharp Paine identifies two strategems to encourage and support an ethical corporate culture: legal compliance and organizational integrity. Consider which might be more effective from a long-term perspective? Which would be easier to implement? Which do you think is more prevalent in the business environment?

How can managers insure that individuals in their companies conduct business in a way that is responsible and ethically sound? This challenge involves organizational design and a number of specific managerial tasks.

WHY THE ETHICS FOCUS?

In the past decade, a number of factors have brought ethical matters into sharper focus.

Globalization Global expansion has brought about greater involvement with different cultures and socioeconomic systems. With this development, ethical considerations—such as the different assumptions about the responsibilities of business, about acceptable business practices, and about the values needed to build a cohesive, successful organization—become more important.

Technology The added capabilities of technology have created a new level of transparency and immediacy to business communication. Now the conduct of businesses around the globe is more exposed than it ever was before.

Competition Rising competition brings with it added pressure to cut corners. Simultaneously, leaders are looking for new ways to differentiate their companies and move them to a new level of excellence. Some believe that a proactive ethical stance can have a positive impact on the bottom line.

Public Perception and the Law There is a perceived decline in social ethics that yields uncertainty. Managers are no longer comfortable assuming that employees joining their companies possess the desired ethical values. And public expectations, too, have changed: That which was once deemed acceptable is now more readily scrutinized. New laws and stepped-up enforcement efforts have increased the risk of personal and organizational liability.

Lynn Sharp Paine, "Venturing beyond Compliance," *The Evolving Role of Ethics in Business,* report no. 1141-96-ch, pp. 13–16 (New York: The Conference Board, Inc., 1996). Email: *info@conference-board.org.*

TWO STRATEGIES EMERGE

Most managers are choosing either a *legal compliance* strategy or an *organizational integrity* strategy to support ethics in their companies. These strategies differ markedly in their conception of ethics, human behavior and management responsibility. While the organizational integrity strategy fully acknowledges the importance of compliance with the law, its aim is to achieve right conduct in general. Thus, it is more comprehensive and broader than the legal compliance strategy. Companies that adopt an organizational integrity strategy are concerned with their identity—who they are and what they stand for—and with how they conduct internal and external affairs. These matters are less clear-cut (and hence, more demanding) than those handled by a legal compliance approach.

These strategies differ in several fundamental ways:

Ethos The legal compliance strategy regards ethics as a set of limits, boundaries over which we must not cross. The compliance approach is externally driven. Here, ethics is viewed as something that *has* to be done.

The organizational integrity strategy defines ethics as a set of principles to guide the choices we make. Companies that adopt this approach choose their own standards for conducting business on an individual and company-wide basis.

Objectives The compliance approach is geared toward preventing unlawful conduct and criminal misconduct in particular. The integrity approach, by comparison, has a more lofty goal: to achieve responsible conduct across-the-board, even if not required by law.

Leadership While companies with a compliance approach place lawyers at the helm, the integrity approach is captained by company managers. To insure that their efforts are thorough and effective, these managers are assisted by lawyers, human resources specialists and other experts.

Methods The compliance focus emphasizes the rules people must not violate. It uses increased oversight and stepped-up penalties to enforce these rules. An integrity approach acknowledges the need for a brake on people's behavior from time to time, but treats ethics as a steering mechanism rather than the brake itself. Here, ethics infuses the organization's leadership, its core systems, and its decision-making processes.

Behavioral Assumptions Finally, the two approaches rest on very different philosophies of human nature. The compliance strategy's ideas are rooted in deterrence theory—how to prevent people from doing bad things by manipulating the costs of misconduct. The integrity strategy views people as having a fuller, richer set of needs and motivations. While it acknowledges that people are guided by material self-interest and the threat of penalties, it also identifies the other drivers of human nature—individual values, ideals and the influence of peers.

LIMITATIONS OF A COMPLIANCE-BASED APPROACH

Why go beyond compliance? While legal compliance is a must, a legal compliance approach to company ethics has several specific limitations:

- Compliance is not terribly responsive to many of the day-to-day concerns that managers and employees face. It follows the law, which is generally backward looking. For a company on the cutting edge of technology, of new financing mechanisms, of new practices, the law is not very helpful as a guide.

- The majority of hot-line calls are not about unlawful or criminal misconduct. They deal with gray areas and with issues of supervisory practice and fair treatment. A legal compliance approach does not provide answers to these types of questions. Therefore, it does not adequately address employees' real concerns and needs.

- The typical legal compliance program runs directly counter to the philosophy of empowerment. Empowerment gives employees discretion, resources and authority, and then trusts them to make good decisions. Compliance programs, though, reduce discretion, increase oversight and tighten controls. If a company tries to put forth an empowerment effort and a compliance-driven ethics program at the same time, the two will cancel each other out. This will result in a lot of employee cynicism.

- A legal compliance program is just not very exciting. Compliance is important, but the law was not designed to inspire human excellence so much as to set a floor for acceptable behavior. Since the law has to apply to everyone, its standards are not as demanding as we might choose for ourselves and for our companies.

CHALLENGES TO AN INTEGRITY-BASED APPROACH

If one are really interested in organizational effectiveness and organizational development rather than just avoiding liability, an integrity-driven approach is far more promising. But four challenges must be met before an organizational integrity approach can work:

1. *Developing an ethical framework.* Organizational integrity requires a much more robust concept of organizational identity and responsibility than does compliance.
2. *Aligning practice with principles.* This can be very problematic, especially in organizations whose structure, systems and decision processes run counter to the values and principles espoused by senior management.
3. *Overcoming cynicism.* In *The Cynical Americans,* Donald L. Kanter and Phillip H. Mervis' study of cynicism in the United States (San Francisco, Jossey-Bass Publishers, 1989, p. 1), it was revealed that almost 43% of Americans fit the profile of the cynic; that is, one who regards selfishness, dishonesty and fakery as at the core of human behavior. People often adopt cynicism as a self-defense mechanism. This frame of reference often prevents people from seeing reality, and can act as a barrier to instilling ethical values.
4. *Resolving ethical conflicts.* We all have conflicting responsibilities from time to time. If we are very creative, we may be able to solve potential conflicts before they unfold. Sometimes, though, hard trade-offs—between right and right, between two "goods"—must be made.

NAVIGATING WITH THE ETHICAL COMPASS

How do you begin to create an ethical compass or a framework for integrity? A useful starting point is to begin by answering some questions related to the four fundamental sources of responsibility.

- Purpose—What is the organization's fundamental reason for being—its ultimate aims?

- People—Who are the constituencies to whom the company is accountable and on whom it depends for success? What are their legitimate claims and interests?

- Power—What is the organization's authority and ability to act?

- Principles—What are the organization's obligations or duties, as well as its guiding aspirations and ideals?

If used as a set of reference points, these questions can help develop a framework against which to benchmark progress on ethical matters (see Exhibit 1).

EXHIBIT 1

The Four Points of an Ethical Compass

How can managers develop a framework for integrity?

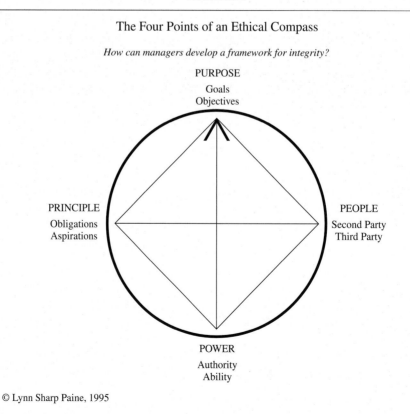

© Lynn Sharp Paine, 1995

The framework of ideas is only a start. Putting it into practice is the difficult part. People often wonder why a gap exists between the espoused values and everyday behavior, when in fact, a gap *should* exist to some degree. If you are fully satisfying your ideals and aspirations, most likely your standards are not high enough. If the gap between principle and practice becomes a chasm, though, it becomes hypocrisy, which is even worse.

MANAGEMENT: PUTTING IT TOGETHER

Integrity-based ethics management efforts have contributed to organizational effectiveness in several fundamental ways. Companies that have adopted such programs report fewer and less serious problems of misconduct. Often this is because problems are caught earlier and are dealt with at the onset. In some cases, an integrity approach can yield strengthened competitiveness: it facilitates the delivery of quality products in an honest, reliable way. This approach can enhance work life by making the workplace more fun and challenging. It can improve relationships with constituencies and can instill a more positive mindset that fosters creativity and innovation. And while an organizational integrity approach cannot guarantee bottom-line performance improvements, it is important to understand that ethics is a very practical matter. The purpose of ethics is to enhance our lives and our relationships both inside and outside of the organization.

Clearly, achieving and maintaining integrity requires intense commitment and involvement from managers company-wide. This goes beyond the so-called "tone" set by senior management. It involves specific leadership tasks and behaviors, starting with the development of the integrity framework. Managers must insure that company systems support responsible behavior. Then they must personally model responsible decision making. These leadership tasks are all essential to building the high-integrity organization.

ETHICAL BUSINESS: SURVEY RESULTS

—INSTITUTE OF BUSINESS ETHICS

Every three years, the Institute of Business Ethics (U.K.) surveys larger companies known to have codes of ethics/conduct/business principles about the use they make of them and their views about current business ethics issues. The principal findings follow.

WHO IS RESPONSIBLE FOR BUSINESS ETHICS?

CEOs turn to a wide spectrum of corporate functions to handle the ethical aspects of company behavior. Comparatively few (16%) retain it in their own department. This is further borne out by the response to a question asking *which department, function or person is responsible for the code.* Table 2 sets out the percentage responses in each of three years for which there is data.

TABLE 2

Departments Responsible for Codes of Ethics*

	2001	1998	1995
Corporate/External Affairs	**10%**	11%	1%
Human Resources	**20%**	12%	7%
Company Secretary and/or Legal Department	**46%**	44%	14%
Board/Board Committee/CEO	**16%**	12%	44%
Internal Audit/Finance	**14%**	7%	—
Other	**16%**	14%	34%

*Some multiple answers in 2001.

Nearly half of respondents look to the legal or compliance function to be responsible for ethical conduct of the organization. The human resources departments seem to be regaining their influence probably because of the rise of human rights issues at the workplace and with particular reference to the conduct of their suppliers. It is, however, the corporate governance functions that still predominate in business ethics. This reflects the attention that was paid in the 1990s to changes of practice following inclusion in the Stock Exchange listing requirements of the provisions of the Hampel Committee's Combined Code.[1]

---

[1]*The Hampel Report, Committee on Corporate Governance:* Final Report, 1998.

There is little sign yet that corporate affairs executives are being given increased responsibility for ethical policies following the publication of the Turnbull Report.[2] This requires among other things, that boards of companies assess and report on non-financial risks (i.e., threats to reputation, etc.) as well as the financial ones. It is certainly not too wild to suggest that many corporations will turn to their public affairs staff to advise on, and assume responsibility for, reputation management. It is therefore predicted that by 2004 (when the next survey is due), that function will appear further up the list of those that are responsible for business ethics. The rise in importance of the internal audit department should also be noted.

PURPOSE OF A CODE

Having an ethics policy now seems to be a well-established feature of the corporate strategy of larger organizations. IBE survey data indicates that in August 2001, 73 of the companies listed in the FTSE100 index either had a code of business ethics or had one in preparation. Others are known to be considering the matter seriously. Previous surveys have shown about the same proportion but the constituents of the index have changed significantly since the last count in 1999. Over half the respondents to the survey have had codes for more than three years, while only 7% have introduced them in the past year. See Table 3.

TABLE 3

For How Long Has Your Company Had a Code?	
Less than 1 year	7%
1–3 years	23%
3–5 years	18%
5–10 years	18%
More than 10 years	18%
No answer	16%

It is now seen as part of "good governance" to have and operate such a code.

A question was asked in the survey which sought to find out the motivation or purpose of companies in having an ethics policy. The answers indicate the main benefits that companies expect from the resources they spend on this aspect of their business. See Table 4.

TABLE 4

Importance of Codes to Companies (ranked by those giving each first priority)*	
Guidance to staff	31
Reduces risk	11
Helps to secure long term shareholder value	10
Helps to guard reputation	7
Shows we are a responsible company	5

*Some multiple answers.

[2]*Internal Control, Guidance for Directors on the Combine Code (aka the Tumbull guidance)* ICAEW, September 1999.

The prime motivation is that of giving guidance to staff on how to respond to ethical dilemmas. This is in sharp contrast to the 1998 survey when "guarding of reputation" was seen as the primary purpose by 75% of respondents whereas in 2001, it was down to 18%. Even if risk reduction is added to reputation protection, employee guidance still predominates as a motive today.

USE OF THE CODE

Having a code is a start, but how is [*sic*] it and its contents made known and what uses are made of it?

Table 5a indicates that practically all employees are provided with a copy of the code and increasingly, those outside the company are being informed about the organization's ethical stance.

TABLE 5a

Use of the Code

Circulated	2001	1998
Internally	93%	93%
Externally	46%	33%

The text of the code in the form of a booklet, memorandum or chapter in a staff handbook, or access via the intranet are still the preferred ways to publicize the code (see Table 5b). The intranet method was mentioned by a third of respondents compared with just 7% in 1998. Inclusion in new staff induction packs seems to be on the decline which is surprising. There is little evidence of the use of face-to-face briefing as a means of communication. Among methods of promulgating codes of business ethics internally which received only a few mentions were: noticeboards, CD-roms, calendars and videos.

TABLE 5b

Methods of Internal Publicity of the Code (multiple answers)

	2001	1998
Booklet/circular/staff manual	38	64
Included in induction pack	16	23
Face to face briefing	2	13
Intranet	33	7
Through line management	7	—
Compliance reviews	5	7
Others	13	

As pointed out above, there is less reluctance in 2001 to make companies' codes of ethics available to outsiders. 46% of respondents, compared with 33% in 1998, say they publicize their codes externally (see Table 5a). However, Table 5c shows that only 13% say they mention it in their annual reports which is a sharp decline compared with 1998. On the other hand, 25% of respondents post their code on their corporate website, which leads to the assumption that they are widely available. Because of this, companies are to some extent making themselves more vulnerable to comparisons of theory and practice as far as behavior is concerned.

TABLE 5c

External Publicity of the Code

	2001	1998
Annual Report	13%	47%
Given to stakeholders	—	32%
Dedicated report	5%	16%
Posted on website	26%	5%
Briefing to analyst/journalist	0	5%
Other	15%	—

Questions are often asked about the use of codes in overseas locations. Generally a code issued by the Board with the endorsements of the Chairman and for the Chief Executive Officer is applicable throughout the company irrespective of where the business operates. A question was asked for the first time about the translation of codes for use outside the English-speaking world. Table 6 sets out the answers.

TABLE 6

If You Have Locations Overseas, Do You Translate Your Code for Local Use?	
Yes	43%
No	37%
Not applicable	20%

Assuming that the "no" response implies that no translation of the code is undertaken by 37% of companies with non-English speaking staff in the UK or elsewhere, the response indicates that embedding of the code as part of the ethos or culture of the company is not taken very seriously by a significant number of larger businesses.

BUSINESS ETHICS TRAINING

The number of companies with codes who offer training on business ethics has fallen slightly compared with 1998 and remains stubbornly below 50% (Table 7).

TABLE 7

Do You Offer Training to Members of Staff on the Meaning and Use of Your Code?

	2001	1998
Yes	41%	46%
No	59%	54%

Table 7a sets out the principal methods of training provided by companies. They divide into three: 60% refer to staff seminars and 64% to inclusion in house manuals and guides (though how these are used is not clear). Thirdly, the use of the intranet for this type of training is mentioned by more than half of the respondents; in 1998 it was classified within the 20% of "other" methods used.

TABLE 7a

What Form Does the Training Take? (multiple answers)

	2001	1998
In-house training seminars	60%	50%
Intranet	56%	*
External training	0%	2%
Videos/games etc.	16%	30%
Staff manuals or guides	64%	30%
Other (*included Intranet in 1998)	20%	20%

IMPLEMENTATION OF THE CODE

Apart from the promulgation of the code to all businesses and individuals and the provision of training in relation to it, the main ways to make the code "live" involve reactions of staff to its contents and the use of it made by them.

Table 8 sets out responses in the last three surveys on the ways (if any) that are available to employees to raise questions concerning their own or others' conformity to, and interpretation of, their company code.

TABLE 8

Is There a Procedure to Raise Questions About the Code?

	2001	1998	1995
Yes	74%	70%	66%
No	26%	30%	34%

Provision of means for issues to be raised has now become a necessary part of any corporate ethics program. It is particularly important in the prevention of what has become known as whistleblowing. Staff are usually driven to make public any behavior which they consider to be harmful, illegal or unethical when there are no adequate procedures in an organization for raising such matters and having them addressed. The law now protects those who do go public on a matter but only if they have failed to get the issue taken seriously within the organization in which they work. The strongest deterrent to "speaking out" is the fear of reprisal. It is therefore interesting to note that in 2001, 91% of respondent companies say they protect the identity of the person raising concerns. This compares with 80% in 1998.

Another indication of how seriously a company takes its ethics program is whether conformity to the code is included in the employees' contracts of employment. Table 9 sets out results of a question on this matter.

TABLE 9

Is Conformity to Your Code Included in the Contract of Employment
Used by Your Corporation?

	2001	1998	1995
Yes	**53%**	42%	46%
No	**47%**	58%	54%

A majority of companies now include conformity to the code in contracts but there is still doubt about this among many respondents. This is partly because it implies that non-conformity would be grounds for dismissal. Clearly this would be the case for any deliberate and clear breaches. But ethical decisions based on conformity to a clause in a code—say, accepting a substantial gift from a supplier—are necessarily a matter of judgment and the reluctance of lawyers to agree to its inclusion in a contract of employment can be understood. Nevertheless, if a board of directors is serious about paying more than lip service to business ethics, a sure way of signalling this is to include it in a contract of employment and making it part of all induction training.

The extent to which codes are taken seriously can also be gauged from their use in corporate disciplinary procedures. It will be seen from Table 10 that it is becoming more common.

TABLE 10

Has Your Code Been Used in Disciplinary Procedures in Your Company?

	2001	1998	1995
Yes	**38%**	33%	32%
No	**62%**	67%	68%

38% compared with 33% in 1998 say that the code has been used to enforce the need to conform to standards of business conduct. As reputation risk is seen to be of growing importance, especially among companies with retail brands, anything which is seen to endanger the brand reputation will not be tolerated. This includes unethical conduct. It is likely then, that in future there will be a growth in the inclusion of conformity to a code in contracts of employment.

Some boards of directors have felt that there is not enough information about the way their organizations are seen to behave by those with whom they do business (their stakeholders). Others feel they may be vulnerable to accusations of unethical behavior and need to have assessments of where the weaknesses lie and what can be done to strengthen them. A question was asked about the use of ethical/social audits. The results are set out in Table 11.

TABLE 11

Have You Had, or Considered Having, an Ethical/Social Audit
of Your Company Carried Out?

	2001	1998
Have had an ethical/social audit carried out	15%	5%
Have considered an audit	35%	21%
Not interested in such an audit (or no answer)	50%	74%

The answers indicate a growing interest in this type of survey. Its value is that it provides a firm starting base on which to make a policy effective. As long as it includes questions to staff at different levels about their perceptions of the organization's behavior to their customers and other stakeholders as well as themselves, it will provide the ingredients for an ethics policy, including the provision and implementation of a code of business ethics.

As audits of this kind frequently form the basis for an external report for stakeholders, the growth in auditing also reflects a greater interest in using the company's commitment to ethics and social responsibility as part of overall communications.

CODE REVISION

One of the most important ways of keeping a company code of ethics effective is to have a process for its regular review and revision. A question asking if a process was in place to undertake this produced a somewhat surprising result as shown in Table 12.

TABLE 12

Have You a Process for Revision of Your Code?

	2001	1998	1995
Yes	77%	86%	76%
No	23%	14%	24%

It is not clear why there has been a drop in the number of companies having such a process. It could be because 30% of respondents have had a code for less than three years (see Table 3).

For those companies which do have a process, a question was asked about how it was done. Table 13 sets out the responses.

TABLE 13

How Was the Code Review Process Mainly Undertaken?

	2001	**1998**
Annual review by board	**17%**	40%
Decision of chairman/chief executive	**30%**	25%
Survey of staff	**11%**	11%
Consultation with stakeholders	**15%**	9%
Other	**27%**	15%

While it seems that an annual review by the board is less popular, CEOs are taking more initiative and stakeholders are being included by more companies in the review process, which is likely to be at a less frequent interval than yearly.

CURRENT BUSINESS ETHICS ISSUES

Respondents were asked about what ethical issues have been of recent concern to their companies. Most responded with more than one issue (see Table 14).

TABLE 14

Which Ethical Issues Have Recently Been of Concern to Your Organization? (multiple answers)

	Cited by
Supply chain issues/sourcing	38%
Bribery and corruption	32%
Remuneration of senior staff or board	30%
Work/life balance issues	28%
Product safety	25%
Other	18%
No answer	18%

Media attention in recent years on issues such as use of child labor, health and safety issues and other human rights matters in the organizations overseas where goods are sourced has raised important issues for importing companies. Some reputations have been severely tarnished when it was reported that companies had not taken into account these matters in their purchase and supply policies. It is not surprising, therefore, that this heads the list of current concerns. Bribery and board remuneration issues have continued to cause concern but work/life balance (better: work/home balance!) is a recent issue to appear in a list of corporate concerns.

MANAGING ETHICS AND LEGAL COMPLIANCE

What Works and What Hurts

—Linda Klebe Trevino, Gary R. Weaver, David G. Gibson
and Barbara Ley Toffler

Some ethics programs work and others do not. What are the differences between the two groups?

A survey of employees at six large American companies asked the question: "What works and what hurts in corporate ethics/compliance management?" The study found that a values-based cultural approach to ethics/compliance management works best. Critical ingredients of this approach include leaders' commitment to ethics, fair treatment of employees, rewards for ethical conduct, concern for external stakeholders and consistency between policies and actions. What hurts effectiveness most are an ethics/compliance program that employees believe exists only to protect top management from blame and an ethical culture that focuses on unquestioning obedience to authority and employee self-interest. The results of effective ethics/compliance management are impressive. They include reduced unethical/ illegal behavior in the organization, increased awareness of ethical issues, more ethical advice seeking within the firms, greater willingness to deliver bad news or report ethical/legal violations to management, better decision making because of the ethics/compliance program and increased employee commitment.

Ten years ago, a Business Roundtable report titled *Corporate Ethics: A Prime Business Asset* suggested that "there are no precise ways to measure the end results of the widespread and intensive efforts to develop effective corporate ethics programs. Despite this difficulty in measuring their accomplishments, corporate ethics and legal compliance programs have become even more widespread over the last decade. Companies are investing millions of dollars on ethics and compliance management. A recent survey of Fortune 1000 firms found that 98% of responding firms address ethics or conduct issues in formal documents. Of those firms, 78% have a separate code of ethics, and most distribute these policies widely

"Managing Ethics and Legal Compliance: What Works and What Hurts," by Linda Klebe Trevino, Gary R. Weaver, David G. Gibson, and Barbara Ley Toffler. Reprinted from *California Management Review* (Winter 1999), with permission of the University of California, Walter A. Haas School of Business.

within the organization. Many employees also receive ethics training and have access to a telephone line for reporting problems or seeking advice. Much of this activity has been attributed to the 1991 U.S. Sentencing Commission's Guidelines for organizational defendants. The Guidelines prescribe more lenient sentences and fines to companies that have taken measures to prevent employee misconduct.

What do these ethics and legal compliance programs actually accomplish? A firm's approach to ethics and legal compliance management has an enormous impact on employees' attitudes and behaviors. In this study, we found that specific characteristics of the formal ethics or compliance program matter less than broader perceptions of the program's orientation toward values and ethical aspirations. What helps the most are consistency between policies and actions as well as dimensions of the organization's ethical culture such as ethical leadership, fair treatment of employees and open discussion of ethics in the organization. On the other hand, what hurts the most is an ethical culture that emphasizes self-interest and unquestioning obedience to authority, and the perception that the ethics or compliance program exists only to protect top management from blame.

In order to investigate what works and what hurts in ethics and compliance management, we administered a survey to over 10,000 randomly selected employees at all levels in six large American companies from a variety of industries. The companies varied in their ethics/compliance program approaches. Because we were relying on employees' perceptions, we had to be concerned about socially desirable responses—having employees tell us what they thought we wanted to hear rather than the truth. We took a number of steps to guard against such biased responding. Surveys were completely anonymous, they were sent to employees' homes and they were returned directly to the researchers for analysis.

***

WHAT INFLUENCES ETHICS/COMPLIANCE PROGRAM EFFECTIVENESS?

There are several key organizational and program design factors that are associated with ethics/compliance management effectiveness. . . .

1. Program Orientation

Ethics/compliance programs can be designed with very different goals and orientations. Previous research has referred to two types of approaches, a compliance-based approach and an integrity or values-based approach. According to [L. S.] Paine ["Managing for Organizational Integrity," *Harvard Business Review,* March/April 1994, pp. 106–17], a compliance approach focuses primarily on preventing, detecting and punishing violations of the law, while a values-based approach aims to define organizational values and encourage employee commitment to ethical aspirations. She asserts that the values-based approach should be more effective than a compliance-based approach because a values-based approach is rooted in personal self-governance and is more likely to motivate employees to behave in accordance with shared values. She argues that compliance approaches can be counterproductive because they emphasize avoiding punishment instead of self-governance.

They define ethics in terms of legal compliance rather than ethical aspirations, and they implicitly endorse a "code of moral mediocrity."

A recent study of Fortune 1000 firms was conducted in part to determine the orientations of their ethics/compliance management efforts. The survey found that the compliance and values-based approaches are not mutually exclusive. Rather, most firms' approaches to ethics/compliance management combine these orientations in some way. Nevertheless, the compliance approach predominated over the values-based approach in over half of the firms. The U.S. Sentencing Guidelines (implemented in late 1991) contribute to the development of compliance approaches because fines and sanctions for companies convicted of crimes vary dramatically depending upon management's cooperation and whether the firm has a legal compliance program in place.

Given that a compliance-based approach predominates in most firms, our study needed to test the contention that a values-based approach is "better" (achieves more positive outcomes) than a compliance-based approach. Also, many companies hope to maintain or improve their public image and relationships with external stakeholders by adopting an ethics/compliance program. Therefore, we identified an orientation toward satisfying external stakeholders (customers, the community, suppliers) as a third approach in our study. Alternatively, employees sometimes suspect that an ethics/compliance program is introduced in part to protect top management from blame for ethical failures or legal problems. In fact, Paine associated this suspicion with a compliance-based program, suggesting that skeptical employees may see a compliance-oriented program as "nothing more than liability insurance for senior management." Another of Badaracco and Webb's interviewees put it this way: "I'm cynical. To me, corporate codes of conduct exist to cover the potential problems companies may have. It provides deniability. It gives the employers an excuse. . . . The top officers can say, 'These employees messed up. They violated our way of doing business' " [L. Badaracco and A. P. Webb, "Business Ethics: A View from the Trenches," Winter 1995, pp. 8–28]. Therefore, we also assessed the impact of a "protect top management from blame" orientation.

2. A Values Orientation Is the Most Effective Single Orientation

Across the six firms in this study, employees perceived the presence of each of the four orientations (compliance-based, values-based, external stakeholder and protect top management) to varying degrees, and all of them were important in influencing outcomes. However, it is clearly most important to have a program that employees perceive to be values-based. In these six companies, if employees perceived a values-based program, each of the seven outcomes studied was significantly more positive and the relationships were quite strong. Unethical/illegal behavior was lower, awareness of ethical/legal issues was higher, and employees were more likely to look for advice within the firm, to be willing to deliver bad news to management, and to report ethical violations. They also were more committed to the organization and more likely to believe that decision making was better because of the ethics/compliance program.

3. Compliance and External Orientations Are Also Helpful

Outcomes were also more positive if employees perceived a compliance or an external stakeholder orientation. Contrary to Paine's argument, if employees perceived a compliance-based program, all of the outcomes were significantly more positive. However, the relationships were not as strong as with the values orientation. If employees perceived an external stakeholder orientation, once again the same outcomes were significantly more positive. However, the relationships were even weaker than those for compliance orientation.

4. Combining These Orientations May Be Effective

The data also supported the idea that these orientations are not mutually exclusive. For example, values orientation is highly correlated with compliance orientation (correlation = .60) and with external stakeholder orientation (correlation = .53). So, it is clearly possible to design a program that combines these different orientations, while also emphasizing a values-based approach. A values orientation can be backed up with accountability systems and discipline for violators. Values can include a concern for customers, suppliers and the community as well as shareholders and internal stakeholders such as employees. The ideal mix of orientations likely depends on specific organizational circumstances, such as the organization's culture, product and industry.

5. "Protect Top Management" Is Clearly a Harmful Approach

Not surprisingly, where employees perceived that the ethics/compliance program was oriented toward protecting top management from blame, all of the important outcomes were significantly more negative. These relationships were particularly strong and negative for commitment to the organization, for the perception that it's okay to deliver bad news to management and that employees would report ethical/legal violations to management. In addition, unethical/illegal behavior was higher, employees were less aware of ethical issues and they were less likely to seek advice about ethical concerns. Furthermore, they did not believe that decision making was better because of the ethics/compliance program.

SUMMARY OF PROGRAM ORIENTATION FINDINGS

A key finding of this study is the importance of designing an ethics program that is perceived by employees to be first and foremost about shared organizational values and about guiding employees to act on their ethical aspirations. Such programs motivate employees to be aware of ethical or legal issues, report bad news to management, report ethical or legal violations and refrain from engaging in unethical or illegal conduct. In addition, unethical/illegal behavior is reduced, employee commitment is higher and employees believe that decision making in the organization is better because of the ethics program.

This values-based approach can be supplemented with an orientation toward legal compliance and satisfying external stakeholders. Valuing external stakeholders such as customers and the community has a positive impact on all outcomes, as does holding employees accountable for their behavior through monitoring and disciplinary systems. Discipline for rule violators serves an important symbolic role in organizations—it reinforces standards, upholds the value of conformity to shared norms, and maintains the perception that the organization is a just place where wrongdoers are held accountable for their actions.

Finally, a program must avoid conveying the message to employees that it exists to protect top management from blame. Having a program that is perceived in this way by employees may be worse than having no program at all. Recall Paine's proposal that employees were likely to associate a compliance approach with this "protect top management from blame" orientation. Our data did not support this contention. There was little association between employees' perceptions of the program as compliance-oriented and their perceptions of the program as being oriented toward protecting top management from blame. However, this protect-top-management orientation was even less likely to be associated with a program that employees perceived to be values-based. Perhaps the most important message to executives is that this protect-top-management perception is real. Employees judge top management's motives in implementing an ethics/compliance program. Also, it is important that they perceive it to be a sincere attempt to have all employees do what's right rather than just an attempt to create legal "cover" for executives in case of a legal mishap.

FORMAL AND INFORMAL ETHICS/COMPLIANCE PROGRAM CHARACTERISTICS

With regard to specific ethics/compliance program and organizational characteristics, we asked employees about formal characteristics including the official policies, procedures, offices and supporting structures (e.g., telephone hotline). We also asked for employees' perceptions of the more informal ways ethics and compliance concerns are handled every day (e.g., how well the company "follows through" on its policies).

FORMAL PROGRAM CHARACTERISTICS ARE RELATIVELY UNIMPORTANT

All six companies in the study had the "basics" of a comprehensive ethics/compliance program: an ethics/compliance office and officer, a formal code of conduct and a telephone hotline. Despite the existence of these formal program characteristics, employees may be more or less aware of them and more or less likely to use them. Therefore, we asked employees how familiar they were with the code's contents and how frequently they referred to the code for guidance. Interestingly, these factors had little impact on the outcomes, especially unethical conduct. It simply did not matter much whether employees were familiar with or referred frequently to the company's code of conduct. We also asked employees whether their company has a formal mechanism for raising ethical and legal compliance issues and concerns and whether ethics is a formal part of performance evaluation in the company. Both of these program characteristics are dynamic, requiring some kind of ongoing attention from the organization; whereas a code can be drafted, distributed and forgotten. To the extent that employees perceived the company to have a formal mechanism for raising concerns and to make ethics a formal part of performance appraisal, all of the outcomes were significantly more positive.

PROGRAM FOLLOW-THROUGH IS ESSENTIAL

With regard to program follow-through, we asked employees whether the company works hard to detect violators, whether the company follows up on ethical concerns raised by employees and whether there is consistency between ethics/compliance policies and actual organizational practices. Follow-through tells employees that a focus on ethics and legal compliance represents a sincere commitment on the part of management.

The more that employees in our study perceived the organization to be following through, the more positive were all of the outcomes. Further, employees' perceptions of follow-through were much more important than their perceptions of the formal characteristics. Employees' perception that the company's actions are consistent with its policies were particularly important. Employees need to perceive that policies are not just "window dressing" and that the company follows words with actions. Therefore, an approach that goes beyond the mere establishment of formal programs is necessary if employees are to be convinced that the organization really means what it says.

ETHICAL CULTURE IN THE ORGANIZATION

Managing ethics in organizations is not just about managing formal ethics/compliance programs. Researchers have suggested that the broader ethical context in an organization—referred to as the ethical climate or culture—is particularly important, perhaps more important than specific ethics/compliance program goals or characteristics. The elements of ethical culture that guide employee thought and action include leadership, reward systems, perceived fairness, ethics as a topic of conversation in the organization, employee authority structures and an organizational focus that communicates care for employees and the community.

EXECUTIVE AND SUPERVISORY LEADERSHIP

A decade ago, the Business Roundtable report *Corporate Ethics: A Prime Business Asset* referred to the crucial role of top management. "To achieve results, the Chief Executive Officer and those around the CEO need to be openly and strongly committed to ethical conduct, and give constant leadership in tending and renewing the values of the organization."

We were interested in the role of executive leadership because executives play a crucial role in creating, maintaining and changing ethical culture. We also wanted to investigate the role of supervisory leadership. Leaders at every level serve as role models, and employees have more daily contact with their supervisors than they do with executive leaders. Supervisors are responsible for rewards and punishments and they carry the message of how things are really done in the organization. Therefore, in separate sets of questions we asked employees for their perceptions of executive and supervisory ethical leadership.

Perceptions of these two groups were highly related (correlation = .78), suggesting that employees don't think differently about supervisors and executive leaders with regard to their attention to ethics and legal compliance. Essentially, if executive leaders value and pay attention to ethics, so do supervisory leaders.

Leadership was a key ethical culture factor—one of the most important factors in the study. Where employees perceived that supervisors and executives regularly pay attention to ethics, take ethics seriously and care about ethics and values as much as the bottom line, all of the outcomes were significantly more positive. Employees paint all leaders with the same broad ethical brush. When it comes to ethics, leaders are leaders, and the level (supervisory or executive) doesn't seem to matter much to employees.

FAIR TREATMENT OF EMPLOYEES

We also explored a less obvious aspect of ethical culture—employees' perceptions of general fair treatment in the organization. Why should general fair treatment of employees be related to ethics-related outcomes? First, the word *ethics* can mean different things to different people or groups. Kent Druyvesteyn, former ethics officer at General Dynamics, said that when managers say "ethics," employees hear "fairness." To most employees, ethics means how the organization treats them and their coworkers. This helps to explain why so many calls to ethics hotlines concern human resources issues of fair treatment in hiring, layoffs, performance appraisals and promotions. Also, recent research has highlighted the importance of fair treatment for ethics-related outcomes such as employee theft. When employees feel that they are treated unfairly, they may try to "balance the scales of justice" by engaging in unethical behaviors such as stealing from the organization. Some companies have acknowledged this connection between fair treatment and ethics management. For example, we know of a company that sees the elimination of executive dining rooms and other perks as important to making their ethics programs work. Employees see that rules apply to everyone because every employee, up to the CEO, has to have expense reports signed. "That sends a good message [to employees]. . . . Nobody is above the rules and code of conduct. . . . A high level person could get dismissed if they violated [a rule] as much as another person." Another company pegged executive pay to employee pay because of similar concerns about the implications of fair and consistent employee treatment for ethics management.

It is important to note that the survey questions concerning fair treatment had nothing to do with the ethics/compliance program. Rather, they were general questions that asked whether employees think of the company as fair in terms of rewards and punishments (do employees get the rewards and punishments they deserve), whether employees are treated fairly in general and whether supervisors treat employees with courtesy, dignity and respect. Employees' perception of fair treatment was strongly related to all outcomes and was one of the most important factors in the study. It had the strongest correlation with employee commitment and with the perception that it's acceptable to deliver bad news to management.

Companies demonstrate their good ethics to employees primarily through fair treatment. If a company passes the "fair treatment test," employees are more likely to be open to ethics and legal compliance initiatives and to cooperate in making them successful.

ETHICS IN DISCUSSIONS AND DECISIONS

We also asked employees whether people in the company talk openly about ethics and values and whether ethics and values are integrated into decisions. One of the ways ethics and values get "baked into" the corporate culture is to make these sorts of discussions the norm. Our previous experience with one company provides an example of how this should not be done. An oil company employee asked if he could bring an ethical problem to a meeting of divisional presidents. Their immediate response was, "If he wants to talk ethics, let him talk to a priest or a psychiatrist. The office is no place for it." Imagine what employees would think of a formal ethics/compliance program in such an environment.

In our study, perceptions that ethics is talked about and integrated into decision making were important for all outcomes. Open discussion of ethics and values in the company was particularly important for employee commitment, the perception that it's acceptable to deliver bad news, the belief that employees would report an ethics violation and that decision making is better because of the ethics/compliance program.

REWARD SYSTEMS THAT SUPPORT ETHICAL CONDUCT

Good managers know that people do what's rewarded and avoid doing what's punished. Therefore, an ethical culture should include a reward system that supports ethical conduct. We asked employees whether ethical behavior is rewarded and unethical behavior is punished in their organizations. Perceptions of both of these dimensions were important for all outcomes. However, employee perceptions that ethical behavior is rewarded were more important than were perceptions that unethical behavior is punished. The belief that ethical behavior is rewarded was particularly important for employees' commitment and their perceptions that it's okay to deliver bad news to management and that employees would be likely to report ethical violations.

UNQUESTIONING OBEDIENCE TO AUTHORITY

An ethical organizational culture must emphasize each individual's accountability and responsibility for his or her own actions and an obligation to question authority when something seems wrong. An unethical culture is more likely to require unquestioning obedience to authority—"Just do as I say and don't ask any questions." In this study, we found that where employees perceived a structure that expects unquestioning obedience to authority, all outcomes were significantly more negative. Most affected were employee commitment to the organization, willingness to report an ethical or legal violation and willingness to deliver bad news to management.

ORGANIZATIONAL FOCUS

Research on ethical climate has found that employees' perceptions of the organization's focus are associated with both unethical behavior and employee commitment. In this study, we considered three types of focus: employee focus (where employees perceive an organizational focus on what's best for them and their coworkers); community focus (where employees perceive an organizational focus on what's best for customers and the public); and self-interest focus (where employees perceive that everyone in the organization is simply out for himself or herself).

Where employees perceived the organization to be focused on what's best for employees (employee focus) or for customers and the public (community focus), all of the outcomes were significantly more positive. However, where employees perceived that people in the organization were mostly out for themselves (self-interest focus), all outcomes were significantly more negative.

SUMMARY OF ETHICAL CULTURE FINDINGS

As a set, the ethical culture factors emerged as the most important influential factors. Of these factors, leadership, fairness perceptions, the perception that ethics is discussed in the organization and the perception that ethical behavior is rewarded were the most significant factors in the study. As to "what hurts" in ethics/compliance management, two culture factors were quite harmful. Outcomes were more negative where employees perceived an expectation of unquestioning obedience to authority, and where they perceived a focus on self-interest rather than concern for employees and/or the community.

WHAT WORKS AND WHAT HURTS IN ETHICS/COMPLIANCE MANAGEMENT: PRESCRIPTIONS FOR ACTION

What should firms be doing if they want to achieve the most positive outcomes from their ethics/compliance management efforts? What should they avoid doing?

1. Tap the Trenches—Employee Perceptions Matter

Badaracco and Webb recently presented "a view from the trenches" in a report that summarized the results of in-depth interviews with recent graduates of the Harvard MBA program. These young managers reported pressures to be unethical, insufficient help from formal ethics programs and executives who were "out-of-touch" on ethical issues. The authors recommended in-depth interviews with lower-level employees to learn more about employee perceptions. While few companies have the resources to conduct in-depth interviews with a large number of employees, they can conduct surveys and focus groups to learn what their employees are thinking. Employees can tell a company a great deal about what's going on in its trenches. Our survey suggests that they are willing to report both the positive and the negative, such as the extent to which they perceive strong ethical leadership, employee fair treatment and consistency between words and actions, or the extent to which they perceive a focus on self-interest and unquestioning obedience to authority. Obviously, asking these questions may make ethical issues more salient to employees. Therefore, asking the questions assumes that you want to know the answers and that you are willing to take corrective action.

2. Build a Solid Ethical Culture

The ethics officer in a Fortune 500 company once stated, "I have a hard time when people [ask] me, 'Tell me about your company's ethics plan.' I want to tell them about everything we do. Because in my mind, everything we do is part of it." This quote demonstrates that ethics/compliance management is first and foremost a cultural phenomenon. As noted, ethical culture factors were among the most powerful factors in this study. It is not enough to have formal policies and programs. To achieve desired outcomes, concerns for ethics and legal compliance must be baked into the culture of the organization. Therefore, attention to the ethical culture should come first in any corporate ethics/compliance effort. Executive leaders and supervisors must regularly show they care about ethics and shared values (including demonstrating that values are as important as the bottom line), and they must show that they care through words and consistent actions. Consider employees' reactions when the CEO of a major bank who preached responsible use of corporate resources sent a corporate plane to California to pick up a pair of shoes for his wife. This CEO didn't understand that his actions spoke louder than his words.

3. Create a Values-Based Program That Incorporates Accountability and Care for Stakeholders

When it comes to creating a formal ethics/compliance program, managers need not choose between values-based and compliance-based approaches. Rather, these approaches are complementary. They are further complemented by an approach that is concerned about external stakeholders. However, to be most effective, formal efforts to manage ethics and legal compliance should be oriented primarily toward values. A values approach can include valuing customers and the community, as well as employee accountability for ethical conduct.

4. Focus on Formal Program Follow-Through

Some companies approach ethics/compliance management with the idea that all they need to do is check off the U.S. Sentencing Commission's seven requirements for due diligence by appointing an ethics officer, writing and distributing a formal code of conduct, communicating standards via codes and training programs and setting up hotlines and investigative procedures. The results of this study suggest that simply putting formal staff, structures and procedures into place does little to influence important outcomes. More important were employees' perceptions that the company follows through on its formal codes, policies and procedures by working hard to detect violators and by following up on ethical concerns raised by employees. Most important was the perception that actual practice is consistent with formal policies. Again, actions speak louder than words.

***

CONCLUSION

Contrary to the Business Roundtable's decade old statement, our study found that there are ways to measure the end results of corporate ethics and compliance programs. There are a number of important outcomes that can be measured reliably via employee surveys and that can be linked to key program and organizational influences.

A values-based cultural approach to ethics/compliance management works best. This approach requires the sincere commitment of leadership at all levels, including ongoing attention to key issues such as fair treatment of employees, rewards for ethical conduct, concern for external stakeholders and consistency between words and actions. The ethics/compliance program itself should be values-based, motivating employees to aspire to ethical conduct, encouraging them to question authority when ethics are at stake and holding them accountable for rule violations. The results of such an approach are impressive. They produce highly committed employees who are aware of ethics and compliance issues, who seek advice within the organization and who are willing to deliver bad news to their managers or report ethical/legal violations. Results also include less unethical/illegal behavior in the organization and better decision making because of the organization's ethics/compliance efforts.

CORPORATE CODES OF CONDUCT

—International Labour Organization, Bureau for Workers' Activities

Corporate codes of conduct have no globally accepted definition. The concept usually refers to companies' policy statements that define ethical standards for their conduct; however, there is great variance in the ways these statements are drafted. The following document prepared by the International Labour Organization offers an in-depth discussion of the origins of corporate codes of conduct, their various formats, transparency, monitoring and enforcement.

BACKGROUND
Defense Industry Scandals

Worldwide interest in corporate conduct was initially awakened in the 1980s by scandals in the defense industry and on Wall Street. Companies viewed business ethics as a way of promoting self-regulation and deterring government intervention and regulatory action. Corporate interest quickly led to the "institutionalization" of business ethics programs, consisting largely of codes of conduct, ethics officers and ethics training. (See, KPMG, *The Age of Ethics.* KPMG is the abbreviation for the names of the founding members: Klynveld, Peat, Marwick, Goerdeler. KPMG is a business services firm operating in 155 countries.)

Among the first companies to establish codes of conduct were General Electric, General Dynamics, Martin Marietta (now Lockheed Martin), and other defense contractors. These companies had all experienced procurement scandals (although General Dynamics and Martin Marietta were not formally charged with wrongdoing). Now, the defense sector actively polices itself. In 1986, 17 contractors signed the Defense Industry Initiative on Business Ethics and Conduct, which declares that each of the companies will review its ethical practices annually.

Naturally, corporate codes of conduct existed prior to the movement of the 1980s. For example, Johnson & Johnson's *Credo* was published in 1943. As early as 1935, General Robert Wood Johnson urged his fellow industrialists to embrace what he termed "a new industrial philosophy." Johnson defined this as the corporation's responsibility to customers, employees, the community and stockholders. According to Johnson & Johnson, the corporation has drawn heavily on the strength of the *Credo* for guidance through the years—at no time was this more evident than during the Tylenol® crises of 1982 and 1986, when the company's product was adulterated with cyanide and used as a murder weapon. (Johnson & Johnson's home page: http://www.j&j.com.)

Following the pricing scandals that rocked the defense industry in the 1980s, General Electric became a prime example of an American corporation in need of an image overhaul. In response, the company created a corporate ombudsman's office, originally for the purpose of examining its government defense contracts. The company also drew up a summary of in-house rules on ethical concerns, called "Integrity: The Spirit & the Letter of Our Commitment," which is 80 pages long and is available in most languages that are spoken in the General Electric worldwide network, including Arabic and Urdu. In early 1993, the office started a network of toll-free help lines for each business unit in the United States. Employees can call the hot lines anonymously to ask questions about the guidelines and to report suspected violations.

***

Consumer Power

While the long arm of the law is a factor in business decision making, sometimes the arm of ethics is longer still. Consumer power is increasingly being wielded to affect company behavior. The boycott mechanism has long been a means for political protest; for many years, a significant number of consumers avoided buying South African products. Recently, however, boycotts have been called to protest against the actions of specific companies. Nestlé's sales suffered from the boycott protesting about its policy on selling baby formula in the third world, and Shell was forced to change its plans for disposal of the Brent Spar oil platform when German consumers stopped buying Shell petrol. A 1995 poll of 30,000 consumers in the UK showed that one in three had boycotted stores or products in the past because of concerns about ethical standards, and 6 in 10 were prepared to boycott in the future. Almost two in three of those surveyed were more concerned about ethical issues now than five years ago. (See, International Society for Business, Economics and Ethics, *How Ethical Auditing Can Help Companies Compete More Effectively at an International Level?*)

Pressure groups are growing more professional and more vociferous. While in the past, unethical behavior by a company might have been kept quiet through skilled public relations, there is now a greater likelihood that employees from within a company will alert relevant pressure groups, as loyalty to employers has lessened while concern for the public good has grown. It is also more likely now than in the past that the pressure group will be successful in generating significant publicity about the incident. (International Society for Business, Economics and Ethics, *How Ethical Auditing Can Help Companies Compete More Effectively at an International Level?*)

In response to consumer pressure, a whole sector of ethical corporations has arisen in recent years. Some companies have made principled withdrawals from countries where they could otherwise manufacture profitably—this was the course taken by Levi Strauss in China. Levi Strauss has adopted a strong "good guy" image, because of its refusal to use subcontractors that exploit workers in developing countries. Protest from outraged consumers may force companies manufacturing in India or Thailand to sack the underage children they were previously employing. Codes prohibiting child labor have been introduced, especially among apparel manufacturers, merchandisers and retailers. (See the apparel company codes in the list of company codes.)

Globalization

Consciousness of the growing interdependence of all people on the earth—globalization—calls for more uniform treatment of people and their environment in every corner of the world. Globalization is one factor that has pushed multinationals to initiate uniform standards of conduct in all countries in which they operate. It may have seemed acceptable decades ago for Shell to apply lower environmental standards to its drilling in Ogoniland than those applied in Europe or North America, but in an era of acute consciousness of the interdependence of the world ecosystem, the same standards are rightly expected on every continent.

In 1986, Frederik Philips (former President of Philips Electronics) and Olivier Giscard d'Estaing (Vice-Chairman of INSEAD) founded the Caux Round Table of business leaders from Europe, Japan and the United States. Caux is committed to energizing the role of business and industry as a vital force for innovative global change. At the urging of Ryuzaburo Kaku, Chairman of Canon Inc., the Round Table has focused attention on the importance of global corporate responsibility in reducing social and economic threats to world peace and stability. Caux Round Table Principles for Business were drafted by a committee composed of Japanese, European and U.S. business representatives, and include a relatively long section on workers' rights.

NUMBER OF CODES

Although, a number of surveys have been carried out on corporate codes of conduct, it is difficult to estimate how common they actually are. Certainly, codes are very common among those companies that respond to surveys, but the rate of response tends to be low. For example, only 264 companies out of 1,900 responded to the Conference Board survey in 1991.

However, this survey is important, because it is the only international survey that follows up on the results of a previous survey, conducted in 1987. By and large, the participants were the same companies that had participated in the earlier survey, from the United States (186 companies), Canada (34 companies) and Europe (40 companies). Most of the companies surveyed were large, with median annual sales of the participants at $1 billion.

In 1991, 82% of the responding companies had codes of conduct. As was the case in 1987, companies in the financial sector were less likely to have codes (57%). Nearly half of the codes discussed or submitted by survey respondents had been enacted since the last study was published (45%). Codes were much more typical of U.S. companies than of European companies. (The Conference Board, *Corporate Ethics Practices,* 1992.)

KPMG surveyed 1,000 Canadian companies in 1996, but only 251 responded. Of these, 83% indicated that they have a published mission statement, and 66% reported having a code of conduct. (See KPMG, *1997 Business Ethics Survey Report.*)

In an International Center for Human Rights and Democratic Development (ICHRDD) survey in 1996, the proportion of Canadian companies that had codes of conduct was much smaller. Only one in five of the 43 Canadian companies that responded reported having adopted a code of conduct for international operations. A total of 98 companies were surveyed. (See, ICHRDD, *Canada's Largest Corporations Lack Codes of Conduct on Treatment of Workers Overseas.*)

FORMATS OF CODES

In the Conference Board survey, the *compliance code* was the most common code type in all regions. Over 90% responded that their company's statement requires particular types of employee or company behavior. Three-fourths of the responding organizations with codes said their statement is a credo that explains the company's accountability to its key constituencies (e.g., employees, customers and suppliers). *Management philosophy declarations* are the least common format—still, more than half of the companies with codes use this type of statement. Canadian firms are more likely to use philosophy declarations than are U.S. or European firms. (The Conference Board, *Corporate Ethics Practices,* 1992.)

Survey responses indicated that most codes are hybrids of more than one type. Of the three types, the compliance code is likely to have been in existence the longest. The median date of adoption for compliance statements is 1985.

The reports of 1987 and 1991 indicate that code drafting is a dynamic process. Nearly two-thirds of the compliance codes were revised between the two surveys.

In the KPMG survey (251 Canadian companies in 1996), 79% of companies with a published code of conduct said that the code is appropriately described as a set of "Guiding Principles," while 32% felt that "Rules and Regulations" was a fitting label.

In a U.S. Department of Labor survey, which focused on child labor in the apparel industry, 33 of 42 companies that provided reportable responses had corporate codes of conduct, statements of principles, or compliance certificates specifically addressing child labor in overseas production. Twelve further respondents did the same through contract requirements contained in purchase orders, letters of credit, or buying agent agreements. Nine respondents used a combination of both types of policy, while six had no policy on overseas child labor. (See United States Labor Department, The Apparel Industry and Codes of Conduct, Chapter E: Development of Apparel Industry Codes of Conduct.)

A comparison of the codes of conduct . . . provides an idea of how differently codes can be formulated. An example of a specific and clear format is Halliburton's code, in which concepts and scope are well defined. Administration of the code is clear and unambiguous, including such issues as allocations of responsibility, delegation of substantial discretionary authority, communication of policies, monitoring and auditing, the reporting system, investigation of violations and disciplinary measures. Under each issue regulated by the code, there are sections regarding the purpose, policy and procedures related to the issue. However, this code seems to be an exception. Most codes are rather brief and general statements, which leave a good deal of room for interpretation and contain no administrative details.

***

CONTENT OF CODES
All Issues

The Conference Board questionnaire identified 13 issue areas dealt with in corporate codes. Most codes include some formal statement of the company's fundamental principles. Nine specific issues in codes were named by more than 66 companies. Among these, six relate in some degree to the employee's contract with the company.

Purchasing guidelines and security of proprietary information—issues focused on employee honesty—were the only specific areas of concern cited by over half the code companies. Of the remaining human resource-oriented issues, three acknowledge company commitments to the employee (workplace safety, confidentiality of employee records and employee privacy), and one focuses on employee obligations (intellectual property safeguards). The three remaining major subject areas relate to corporate social accountability—for example in environmental, marketing and product safety responsibility.

There were few regional variations in subject matter. Codes in the United States are more likely to include sections on the security of proprietary information. Workplace safety is a more frequent subject of European ethics statements.

Over the period between the 1987 and 1991 surveys, 20% of the European companies had added environmental responsibility to their codes. Among U.S. companies, the most common addition was fundamental guiding principles of company. Among Canadian companies, the most common additions related to intellectual property and marketing.

Besides fundamental guiding principles, environmental responsibility was the only issue added in over 10% of the codes. (For examples of environmental accountability statements, see the codes of Nestlé and Waste Management.)

The interest in environmental problems has grown in the last ten years especially among chemical companies. Member companies of the Chemical Manufacturers' Association have adopted six codes of management practices under the Responsible Care initiative, which was launched in 1988: Community Awareness and Emergency Response, Pollution Prevention, Process Safety, Distribution, Employee Health and Safety and Product Stewardship.

In the KPMG survey of 251 Canadian companies in 1996, participants were first asked to score for importance seven issue areas in their codes of conduct. The scoring was on a scale of 1 to 4, and the criteria for scoring was [sic] the potential risk to their business posed by the issue area in question. The most important categories identified by the respondents were employee and workplace issues and the handling of company assets.

Next, the companies were asked to rank individual issues as to their associated risk factor. Worker health and safety was the second most important issue in rank.

***

TRANSPARENCY OF CODES
Dissemination

According to the Conference Board report, companies were more willing to discuss their codes openly in 1991 than in 1987, when only a handful of respondents returned a copy of their code with a completed questionnaire. In 1991, more than one-third of companies with ethics statements supplied them with the questionnaire.

According to the KPMG survey of 251 Canadian companies in 1996, external distribution of the code was reported by less than 30% of respondents that had codes of conduct.

The ICHRDD survey of 43 Canadian companies in 1996 indicated that Canadian companies are reluctant to speak about their relations with workers abroad. Even companies that report having codes of conduct are reluctant to share them with the public. The study suggests that "Canadian business places a very low priority on communicating its response to issues it confronts in its overseas operations to the non-governmental sector. A large number of firms expressed no . . . interest in the subject."

According to the U.S. Department of Labor survey of 42 U.S. apparel companies in 1996, a few companies made an effort to communicate information on their codes of conduct and monitoring programs to the general public, including their shareholders: Levi Strauss and The Gap have sections on their codes of conduct in their annual reports to shareholders.

Distribution

Within the Company   According to the Conference Board report, there is a clear trend in favor of distributing the company's code to all employees. In 1987, nearly two-thirds of the responding code companies gave it to all their employees. Among 1991 survey participants, 77% followed this practice. The figure for Canada (83%) was slightly higher than that in the United States or Europe. Of companies that have codes, 22% limited distribution to top and middle management (down from over one-third in 1987), and just three companies gave the code only to top managers.

Distribution to employees in overseas divisions is common, but not universal—72% of survey participants engaged in this practice. Canadian companies were somewhat less likely to distribute codes in this manner than were U.S. or European companies.

European companies were more likely to modify their documents for use outside the home country (25%) than were U.S. (14%) or Canadian companies (13%). In fact, nearly half of all European companies had branches, subsidiaries or divisions with their own codes (45%). This practice is much less common in U.S. and Canadian firms.

The KPMG survey (251 Canadian companies in 1996) revealed that just over 80% of companies with a published mission statement believed that "the average employee is likely to be aware of it." A lower proportion of those with mission statements (73%) indicated that the mission statement was often referred to in policies and other statements. A published code of ethics, practice or conduct was somewhat less common. Of those who had a published code of conduct, all but 4% indicated that the codes were widely distributed internally.

To Contractor Companies   According to the U.S. Department of Labor survey (42 U.S. apparel companies in 1996), only a very few respondents indicated that they have tried to ensure that production workers in overseas facilities know about their code or policy by specifically requiring that copies of such statements be posted. Only three companies stated that they unconditionally require contractors to post their code. The Gap requires that its code, which has been translated into 39 languages, be posted in each contractor facility. Liz Claiborne, which has translated its Standards of Engagement into more than 10 different languages, requires all contractors to post the Standards in the local language in common areas, such as cafeterias or locker rooms, of every facility where Liz Claiborne products are made. Phillips-Van Heusen stated that it insists that every facility post its "PVH Shared Commitment" poster, which contains guidelines and standards on worker's rights. The poster is printed in English and Spanish, and is sent to Asia with instructions for it to be translated into local languages. Nike and Sara Lee stated that their codes are posted at some facilities. Nike indicated that its code is posted in all its footwear contractors' factories in two or three languages, but this is not necessarily the case for its apparel contractors. Nike stated that its footwear contractors produce exclusively for Nike, while its apparel contractors often produce for many other companies. Nike often uses individual apparel contractors for only a short period of time. Sara Lee indicated that it posts notices of employees' rights at its wholly owned facilities in English and the host language.

Managers of two-thirds (47 out of 70) of surveyed plants that currently export to U.S. apparel companies indicated that they were aware of codes of conduct issued by their U.S. customers. Based on company visits, awareness among managers about codes of conduct was highest in El Salvador (all eight companies visited knew about the codes) and Guatemala (six out of nine companies knew). In three other countries visited—the Dominican Republic, Honduras and the Philippines—managers interviewed were more evenly divided between those who were aware and those who were not. In India, only two out of seven producers visited were aware of the codes of conduct of their U.S. customers. However, only 34 of the 47 companies that indicated they were aware of codes of conduct had available a copy of the code (or contractual provision) that they could show and discuss with the visiting Department of Labor official. Thus, managers at less than half of the plants visited were able to produce a code of conduct upon request.

The plant visits by Department of Labor officials suggest that while posting of a U.S. garment importer's codes of conduct seems to be common practice in El Salvador, it is not the norm in the garment industries of the other countries visited. In all, 21 of the 70 plants visited by the officials had posted a code of conduct of a U.S. customer, and seven of these were in El Salvador (out of eight total plants visited in that country). Elsewhere, two plants visited in the Dominican Republic had codes of conduct posted, one plant in Honduras, two in Guatemala, two in India and seven in the Philippines.

Although a significant number of suppliers knew about the U.S. corporate codes of conduct, meetings with workers and their representatives in the six countries visited suggested that relatively few workers were aware of the existence of codes of conduct, and even fewer understood their implications.

The lack of awareness on the part of workers about codes of conduct may be attributable in part to the relatively low level of effort on the part of producers to inform their workers about the codes. Management regards codes of conduct—and compliance with labor law—as a management problem, and approaches the monitoring and supervision of these matters as management responsibilities. Workers are not seen by management as having a role in these activities.

Managers in 22 of the companies visited told the Department of Labor officials that they informed workers about codes of conduct—13 companies indicating they do so orally, and only 9 stating that they do so both orally and in writing. Of all the plants that were visited in the six countries, there was only one example of a producer that had an explicit policy of informing workers about the code of conduct of its U.S. customer. (For more detailed, company specific, information, see United States Department of Labor, The Apparel Industry and Codes of Conduct, section Transparency.)

***

MONITORING OF THE CODES

Just over 40% of the participants in the KPMG survey (251 Canadian companies in 1996) indicated that there was a senior-level manager whose role specifically includes the implementation, monitoring or assurance of the ethics program. Of the 102 companies with such a senior manager, 16 reported that this manager had the title "Compliance Officer," while three indicated that the title of this manager was "Ethics Officer." Most often (in 22 cases), the "Human Resources Manager" was indicated as having this responsibility.

Of the 251 responses, 76 indicated there was a position within the firm that had responsibility for enabling "upstream communication" and equitable resolution of ethics or compliance problems. Of these, 14 reported that this role is a full-time assignment. In companies that reported this type of "ombudsperson" role, almost two-thirds had established the position three or more years prior to the survey.

In 78% of the responding companies, there was no formal policy to protect employees that report ethics violations or non-compliance with the law or with company policies. Of the 54 companies that indicated they did have such a policy, over half said that the policy was supported by a confidential hot-line or similar procedure.

A specific policy on conflicts of interest and specific guidelines in this regard were reported by 58% of all respondents. Of these, three-quarters require a compliance sign-off, and almost half have reviewed or updated the policy within the last year.

Over 60% of the respondents reported that they had never undertaken a comprehensive review of their ethics-related policies and performance. Over half of the companies that have undertaken such a review indicated that it was completed within the year prior to the survey.

According to the U.S. Department of Labor survey (42 United States apparel companies in 1996), eight companies had no monitoring system to implement their codes of conduct. A further 28 companies had developed internal monitoring systems, using local or regional company personnel or employees from United States corporate offices to monitor labor practices. Internal monitoring may be used by companies that are reluctant to grant access to their facilities, procedures and business practices to outside monitors. It is most common among large, vertically integrated companies (i.e., those in which the corporation owns or directly controls all stages of the production process). Internal monitoring is less common for companies, particularly retailers, that do not own or control the factories that make the products they sell. Some retailers internally monitor only those plants producing private-label merchandise, which they import directly. United States retailers and manufacturers who use hundreds or thousands of foreign contractors may find it a logistical or financial hardship to monitor all of the facilities from which they source.

Buying agents were relied on to monitor compliance with corporate codes by 12 companies in the survey. This procedure avoids the financial and logistical burden of monitoring, but also removes the U.S. corporation from the direct line of control in implementing its policy. Only four companies used an outside auditor, and only two an NGO for the monitoring of their codes. (For more detailed, company specific, information, see United States Department of Labor, The Apparel Industry and Codes of Conduct, Implementation of Apparel Industry Codes of Conduct.)

All 70 of the plants exporting garments to the United States that were visited by Department of Labor officials confirmed that they are subject to regular visits by their U.S. customers or their agents to verify product quality and to coordinate production and delivery schedules. About 90% of the companies visited stated that monitors or inspectors verifying product quality generally also examined working conditions in the plant, with emphasis on safety and health issues (climate control, ventilation systems, fire escapes, etc.).

Whether monitoring visits are announced or unannounced differs widely from company to company. In 41 of the companies interviewed (58%), monitoring visits by the U.S. importer, its agent or its representatives were announced in advance. In 13 companies (18%) they were unannounced, while there were both announced and unannounced visits in 16 companies (23%).

While monitoring for product quality and even for health and safety conditions is customary in the garment industry, the field visits by Department of Labor officials suggest that monitoring for compliance with labor-related provisions of the U.S. garment importer's codes of conduct is not. This applies particularly to child labor. Where such monitoring does occur, the degree to which it extends to all labor standards addressed by the codes—as opposed to exclusively safety and health issues—seems to vary widely across suppliers. Foreign suppliers that are wholly owned by a U.S. corporation, or contract directly with a U.S. corporation with a presence abroad, seem to be subject to the most frequent and most thorough monitoring of codes of conduct, including those related to child labor and other labor standards.

Monitoring the implementation of child labor provisions of codes of conduct is very challenging. Generally, the closer the relationship between a U.S. garment importer and the actual producer of the items, the greater the ability of the U.S. company to influence labor practices in the production process, including prohibitions on child labor. Conversely, it is more complex and challenging to implement labor policies in longer chains of procurement and production—in one example drawn from the Philippines, there were five steps between producer and final buyer. With more levels of buying agents, contractors and subcontractors, the U.S. importer has less ability to influence labor practices.

The field visits also revealed numerous instances of contractual monitoring of codes of conduct. Contractual monitoring is most prevalent in the case of U.S. retailers, which do not have a significant presence abroad.

In these situations, the burden of monitoring compliance with the U.S. importer's child labor policies rests with the foreign agent, contractor or subcontractor, typically through a self-certification process. In these instances, the role of the U.S. importer in monitoring compliance of its code of conduct is minimal. In Honduras, Fabena Fashions is required by Macy's and Wal-Mart to sign a contract including a no-child-labor clause. In Tirupur, India, the producer Chenduran Textiles exports about one-half of its output to the United States. Its main U.S. customer is Tropic Textiles of New York City, a supplier to Wal-Mart. Tropic requires Chenduran to certify that no slave or child labor is used in the production of goods through a paragraph in the contract or bill of lading. Tropic accepts Chenduran's self-certification of the clause and does not have any in-country monitoring, education, implementation or enforcement programs. Also in India, Pankaj Enterprises is an exporter of mid-grade apparel items based in New Delhi that exports to the United States. Pankaj's U.S. buyers require that no child labor be used in the manufacture of garments. Pankaj buys its fabric, and guarantees that no child labor is used in the production of garments through a self-certification process. There is no monitoring by the importer or its agents.

In some instances, U.S. importers use a combination of contractual and active monitoring, using auditors from the importer itself or its agents to verify compliance. In the Philippines, Liz Claiborne has a policy of monitoring and supervising its contractors, which must certify that they are in compliance with the code of conduct. In addition, contractors are subject to frequent visits from Liz Claiborne's Philippines office, which monitors implementation of the code of conduct as well as quality control. Warnaco requires that contractors certify that child labor has not been used, and also audits suppliers in Honduras for full compliance with its child labor policies, including age verification. Macy's, Wal-Mart and The Limited have checked personnel records at Fabena Fashions to verify the age of workers. In India, Zoro Garments supplies 75% of its production to the U.S. market. Zoro's major U.S. customers are Rustic River, Quick Silver, Blue Print and JCPenney, while Phillips-Van Heusen is a former customer. According to Zoro's management, representatives of U.S. customers have visited Zoro's factory occasionally for quality control inspections. Most of these visits were walk-throughs with some general questions raised about the use of child labor, but no checklist of requirements was administered. Phillips-Van Heusen had previously raised the subject of codes of conduct with Zoro's management and asked the company to fill out a questionnaire. When Zoro was producing for Phillips-Van Heusen, there was a clause in its contract related to child labor. Primo Industries in El Salvador, a contractor for Liz Claiborne, Lands' End, Polo and JCPenney, met with Liz Claiborne several years ago to discuss and sign the Liz Claiborne code of conduct. The plant manager told Department of Labor officials that Liz Claiborne is "the toughest on child labor." He also said that American inspectors visit the plant approximately twice a month to check on quality control and see whether their rules and regulations are being implemented.

Based on field visits, it appears that most monitoring conducted by U.S. corporations primarily covers quality control issues. As such, there seems to be relatively little interaction between monitors on the one hand, and workers and the local community on the other. It also appears that monitors have a technical background in production and quality control and are relatively untrained with regard to the implementation of labor standards. (For more detailed, company-specific information, see United States Department of Labor, The Apparel Industry and Codes of Conduct, chapter E: Monitoring.)

ENFORCEMENT OF THE CODES

None of the surveys discussed above dealt with the issue of enforcement of codes internally within the companies themselves, in cases where management or employees of the company may violate the code. A quick overview indicates that most codes do not include any enforcement provisions or are not specific regarding enforcement measures. For example, the Boeing code states simply that "violations of the company standards of conduct are cause for appropriate corrective action including discipline."

However, there are also codes that are specific regarding disciplinary measures. A good example is Halliburton's code, which states that:

1. The Company shall consistently enforce its Code of Business Conduct through appropriate means of discipline. Pursuant to procedures adopted by it, the Executive Committee shall determine whether violations of the Code of Business Conduct have occurred and, if so, shall determine the disciplinary measures to be taken against any employee or agent of the Company who has so violated the Code of Business Conduct.

    The disciplinary measures, which may be invoked at the discretion of the Executive Committee, include, but are not limited to, counseling, oral or written reprimands, warnings, probation or suspension without pay, demotions, reductions in salary, termination of employment and restitution.

    Persons subject to disciplinary measures shall include, in addition to the violator, others involved in the wrongdoing such as (i) persons who fail to use reasonable care to detect a violation, (ii) persons who if requested to divulge information withhold material information regarding a violation and (iii) supervisors who approve or condone the violations or attempt to retaliate against employees or agents for reporting violations or violators.

2. Documentation. Subject to the applicable document retention program, the Company shall document its compliance efforts and results to evidence its commitment to comply with the standards and procedures set forth above.

According to the U.S. Department of Labor survey (42 U.S. apparel companies in 1996), companies that pass the screening process and become contractors of U.S. corporations may face a range of corrective measures should they fall short in complying with the code of conduct.

In Guatemala, although garment contractors and subcontractors were unable to articulate the U.S. companies' policies to address violations of their codes of conduct, they expressed great concern about the possibility of losing their contracts if they were found to have child labor problems. A representative of Phillips-Van Heusen stated that in May 1996, his company had identified three young workers (under 15 years of age) in a plant operated by a subcontractor in San Pedro de Sacatepequez. Upon learning of their presence, Phillips-Van Heusen required the company to dismiss the three young workers immediately.

In the Dominican Republic, many companies stated that U.S. clients had requested changes in the physical conditions of the factories during their visits to the companies. These changes often included requirements for eating facilities, restrooms and more lighting or ventilation. In most cases, changes affecting working conditions were related to safety and health issues. Most of the companies that had contracts with Levi Strauss in the Santiago Zona Franca said that all companies were requested to reinforce, move or rebuild wooden mezzanines—where sewing machines were stationed—as a fire safety precaution.

Undergarment Fashions mentioned that JCPenney, in addition to performing periodic visits to the plant, also had a rating system to evaluate the contractor's performance. Under this rating system, a company must receive at least 50 points in order to maintain its current contract. If the company does not obtain a satisfactory rating, it is put on probation and given a reasonable period of time to make the requested changes.

High Quality Products, located in Zona Franca Los Alcarrizos, a contractor for the Jones Apparel Group, said that Jones Apparel terminated a contract with Bonahan Apparel (in Zona Franca Bonao) because of Bonahan's refusal to recognize the establishment of a union in its plant.

In Honduras, Rothschilds made a number of recommendations regarding clean toilets, lighting, ventilation, drinking water and hours of work for 14- and 15-year-old workers at Global Fashions.

In part because of the priority to improve quality, but also because of a concern about violations of labor standards (and child labor provisions in particular), U.S. garment importers have cut back sharply on subcontracting and also reduced the number of their foreign suppliers. From the point of view of foreign garment producers, the streamlining of suppliers in the U.S. garment industry has resulted in clear winners and losers.

On the one hand, suppliers to the United States market that can meet the considerations of quality and timeliness of product while complying with codes of conduct have been rewarded with continued orders. They have also received additional orders which have been diverted to them from producers that rely on subcontracting schemes.

On the other hand, marginal suppliers—in terms of quality and timeliness of output, physical plant or ability to comply with labor standards—have lost their contracts with United States importers. They have had to resort to sales to other, less profitable markets, including their own domestic market.

Continued access to the U.S. market is a very large incentive for overseas garment producers to meet quality and timeliness requirements and to comply with codes of conduct. Thus, the prospect of continued ability to ship to the United States reinforces compliance with appropriate standards. Foreign countries also have a great deal at stake, as unused import quota allocations translate into the loss of export revenue in the short term and loss of the import quota in the longer term. (For more detailed, company specific, information, see United States Department of Labor, The Apparel Industry and Codes of Conduct, chapter F: Enforcement.)

PROFITABLE ETHICAL
PROGRAMS

—Jason Lunday

*In response to a previous e-mail to a listserver on teaching business
ethics, Jason Lunday identifies some apparently successful ethical
business practices from the annals of business history.*

. . . Some apparently successful ethical business practices:

(In some cases, the companies claim a very direct bottom-line effect to certain ethical
practices. Others claim that their ethical practices contribute to an overall corporate climate
which cuts waste, encourages efficiency, promotes community/marketplace goodwill, allowing the company a healthy bottom line.)

1. 3M—through its Pollution Prevention Program (3P), initiated in the mid-1970s,
the corporation claims to have decreased its production and emission of air, solid and water pollutants by billions of pounds AND saved the company over $500 million during its
first 15 years. It did so by using its expertise in innovation to find new ways of manufacturing which led to fewer pollutants. To qualify for the 3P program, ideas had to meet three
of four measures, only one of which was cost savings. [See Alfred Marcus, *Business and
Society: Strategy, Ethics and the Global Economy,* Irwin, Chicago, 1996.]

While 3M was considered the first, I understand that a large number of companies have
successfully accomplished similar environmental initiatives, reducing pollutants and saving money. Contact the Management Institute for Environment and Business, Washington,
DC, for examples.

2. Levi Strauss—with a strong history of employee goodwill, LSCO has worked for
numerous years to insure that its employee policies demonstrate respect for workers and their
lives. It has consistently paid workers at the top of the industry and granted benefits uncom-
mon among its competitors (like year-round employment). Further, it has encouraged strong
employee communication and idea-sharing. It has expected that such treatment would create mutual respect. This apparently came true when a South American operation effectively
communicated one of its new product launches to headquarters during a time of overall lagging sales. The idea, Dockers, became the biggest product introduction in U.S. history and
reinvigorated the company. [See Jeffrey Edwards and Jason Lunday, *Levi Strauss & Co.: The
South Zarzamora Street Plant,* Darden Graduate Business School Case Bibliography.]

There are other stories of how factory employees have taken pay cuts, done without
raises, and accepted other risks at certain times because of the company's fair treatment and
with an expectation that such a well-managed company will overcome periodic difficulties.

3. South Shore Bank—the company came up with the great idea to help its local community, a depressed area of Chicago, where few could get bank loans. In finding ways to

---

grant credit where other banks would not, South Shore not only helped a community pick itself back up, it increased bank earnings.

[Sorry, don't have a reference handy. South Shore has won Business Ethics Magazine's annual award in recent years, so a past edition of the magazine will overview the company's story.]

4.   Johnson & Johnson—need we say more on this one? For a treatment of this, see *Managing Corporate Ethics,* Francis Aguilar, Oxford University Press, New York, 1994.

5.   Delta Air Lines—Delta also has a strong history of employee relations, to the extent that, for years, it was the only non-unionized airline. This allowed the carrier flexibility during recessions to move workers around in order to maximize manpower in key areas. It also traditionally allows the airline to have employees perform multiple tasks so that it does not have to hire additional workers. The airline had, for many years, consistently been at the top of the Department of Transportation's lowest complaint list. It generally is still there, occasionally being beat out by Southwest. Employee goodwill because of the company's treatment also helps the company keep a very low employee/seat miles ratio. Some years back, because of exceptional treatment, the employees chipped in and bought the company a passenger jet. Delta has also ended up as one of the country's most admired companies for many years. [Personal unpublished research—if you want article references, just ask. I've got a lot.]

6.   Lincoln Electric—arc welding. Company claims that strong employee orientation has allowed it to earn exceptional profits. [See *Managing Corporate Ethics,* Francis Aguilar, Oxford University Press, New York, 1994.]

7.   Honda—attention to customer quality allowed it strong entrance into U.S. market. [*Business and Society,* Alfred Marcus, Irwin, Chicago, 1996.]

8.   BFI—effort to help New York rid itself of corruption in the trash hauling business gave the company early entry into a lucrative market. [See recent *Fortune* cover story.]

9.   Socially responsible companies Body Shop, Ben & Jerry's, Tom's of Maine, etc.: each claims that their orientation to meeting stakeholder needs—in a variety of forms—allowed them to become large players in their respective markets. [See *Body and Soul,* Anita Roddick, *The Soul of a Business,* Tom Chappell, don't know Ben & Jerry's book.]

10.   Merck—another company at the very top of Fortune's Most Admired Companies. The company ended up paying millions of dollars to formulate, manufacture and distribute a drug which cures river blindness, which is generally found in poor regions of lesser developed countries. The goodwill alone from this has apparently, like J&J and Tylenol, given it many consumers' trust. Granted, it would be difficult to quantify how much that is worth, but I doubt that Vagelos or the current chairman would deny it has been worth a lot.

11.   Sears, Roebuck—when questions arose about possible inappropriate sales practices of product warranties, which, by the way, were making BIG money for the retailer, they retrained their associates to ensure that the warranties were not being pushed on customers or otherwise sold unethically. Expecting a drop in warranty sales, they instead were hit with a sizeable increase. [See *Ethikos* back issue, can't remember the date. Also, personal consulting experience with them.]

Business ethics books are generally filled with cases of companies which have gotten into trouble. We don't see enough of the good stories since, I suppose, we simply expect this. However, the positive examples can go a long way in encouraging prosocial behavior, which, like deterrence theory, is another aspect of business ethics.

CORPORATE CODES
AND ETHICS
PROGRAMS

—MICHAEL C. DECK

In the following selection, Michael Deck explains research conducted to gather and to analyze 200 codes of conduct. The researcher found that while many firms have codes, they are not always communicated to stakeholders, nor are they always adhered to. Consider whether any firm you have worked for has had a code and whether you felt it was completely integrated into the decision-making functions of the firm.

STAKEHOLDER THEORY

Our research program has examined more than 70 Canadian corporations over the last 10 years. As we studied the data, it became clear that the managers of successful companies no longer regard shareholders as the sole and necessarily most important stakeholders in the corporation. The concept of shareholders endowed with a right to the maximization of profits is being replaced by the concept of stakeholders, of which shareholders comprise only one group. The shareholder is no longer the preeminent stakeholder, to be rewarded at the expense of other stakeholders. . . .

What this research shows is that when management or the board of a company favor one group of stakeholders at the expense of other primary stakeholder groups, difficulties always develop. When shareholders are favored unfairly, when maximizing the bottom line takes full priority, customers or employees or suppliers invariably will be shortchanged. . . .

MANAGING ETHICS IN THE WORKPLACE

If we agree that values, ethics and moral principles are essential to sound decision making, how does a manager go about managing that aspect of the organization?

In looking for an answer to that question, we thought it would make sense to begin looking for the values, ethics and moral principles of an organization in its Code of Ethics. Beginning three years ago, our Centre undertook to gather and to analyze 200 corporate codes. We learned that while corporations do indeed have values, ethics and moral principles, these are not always communicated in a code of ethics and may in fact be quite different from what the code might lead one to believe.

Michael C. Deck, "Corporate Codes and Ethics Programs," www.kpmg.ca/ethics/eth_clks.htm First presented at "Business Practices under NAFTA: Developing Common Standards for Global Business," University of Colorado–Denver, December 8–10, 1994. Reprinted by permission of the author.

While it would be ingenuous to think that ethical behavior within an organization can be changed simply by posting a list of high sounding principles, it is equally naive to imagine that the ethics of an organization "just happens and there's nothing to be done about it."

Every organization, as Steven Brenner points out, has an ethics program, whether it knows it or not.[1] The ethics program is that set of factors both explicit and implicit which communicate corporate values, define parameters of decision making and establish the ground rules for behavior. This is similar to what Robert Jackall has described as "institutional logic." An effective ethics program encourages behavior consistent with corporate principles.

Explicit elements of a corporate ethics program include the things which an organization says it believes in, and the efforts made to communicate those principles directly. The centerpiece of the explicit components is the corporate code. In order to evaluate the effectiveness of a corporate code, the purpose of the code must be considered. Corporate codes can serve a variety of purposes: from "image enhancing" to "due diligence defense," from guidance for employees who want to "do the right thing" to helping an employee resist pressure from a superior. The corporate code and its implementation can raise issues of ethics to a conscious level and legitimate discussion.[2]

Our research on about 200 corporate codes revealed some interesting details about their nature and purpose.[3] Using the Stakeholder Model, we sorted out the statements made in these codes according to which stakeholder's interests were being addressed. One observation is that most of the text in these codes is concerned with the duty and responsibility of the employee to the company. Put more strongly, it seems that the most common purpose of a corporate code is to protect the firm from its employees. This is borne out by the observation that the most frequently cited "reason why" for ethical behavior is that violations will hurt the company. The problem with this approach is that if the possibility of getting caught (and incurring the penalty) is apparently small, then the reason for ethical behavior evaporates. . . .

The analysis of these codes also looked at the "approach" used for each statement, categorizing each as Guiding Principle, Act & Disclose, Seek Advice or Rule. These categories lie along a scale which we describe as "Source of Control."

. . . This analysis [made it] clear that there were really three basic types of codes, differentiated by the source of control.

The terms *"Code of Ethics," "Code of Conduct"* and *"Code of Practice"* are often used interchangeably. It is useful, however, to distinguish among these terms in order to establish a basic typology. Each basic code type has a different intent and purpose.

Codes of Ethics are statements of values and principles which define the purpose of the company. These codes seek to clarify the ethics of the corporation and to define its responsibilities to different groups of stakeholders as well as defining the responsibilities of its employees. These codes are expressed in terms of credos or guiding principles. Such a code says: "This is who we are and this is what we stand for," with the word "we" including the company and all its employees, whose behavior and actions are expected to conform to the ethics and principles stated in the code.

Codes of Practice are interpretations and illustrations of corporate values and principles, and they are addressed to the employee as individual decision maker. In effect they say: "This is how we do things around here." Such a code seeks to shape the expression of the corporation's stated values through the practices of its employees. Codes of practice tend to rely on guidelines for decision making, using such rules of thumb as "act and disclose" or "seek advice." This approach takes a view of ethics as "what we do because it is our character."

Codes of Conduct are statements of rules: "This is what one must (or must not) do," as distinct from the code of ethics, which is stating: "This is how we expect one to behave." Codes of Conduct typically are comprised of a list of rules, stated either affirmatively or as prohibitions. Penalties for transgressions may be identified and systems of compliance and appeal defined. Potential conflicts of interest are often described, with appropriate rules for guidance. This approach takes a view of ethics as what is not to be done (or seen not to be done) in view of the consequences.

In practice, corporate codes tend to include elements of all three types, but for analytical purposes it is helpful to consider these three basic types as benchmarks. Each of the three types is useful and each can be appropriate or necessary in particular business and organizational settings. For example, in a divisionalized corporation, it would be appropriate to draft a Code of Ethics in order to enunciate the company's overall purpose and the guiding principles and ethics that govern its actions and behavior. At the divisional and functional area levels, different and divisionalized Codes of Conduct and Practice are appropriate, so long as the rules, examples and guidelines are not in conflict with the statement of the corporation's guiding principles and ethics. . . .

HAVE ETHICS PROGRAMS FAILED?

It is interesting to note at this point that recent research has found no significant correlation between corporations having a code of ethics and a reduction in ethical violations.[4] Is the problem that the code was badly written? Probably not. Is there a problem with implementation? A more likely suspect, since, of the 90% of companies that have codes, only 28% do any training. There is, however, another factor which, I would suggest, accounts for these findings. I referred earlier to the implicit components of an ethics program. It may well be that the failure of the explicit components to produce results is the result of their having to fight an uphill battle against the implicit components.

If the goal is to produce behavior which is in line with the explicit values, principles and ethics of the organization, then congruency between the explicit and implicit components of the ethics program is essential.

To evaluate the potential effectiveness of an ethics program we propose several criteria which can be applied to the explicit components, beginning with the published code of ethics/practice/conduct. Assuming that the corporate code is satisfactory, the next step is to evaluate implementation efforts. Ultimately, the success and effectiveness of the program will depend on the next step, which is an honest and objective audit of the "implicit" components.

One danger of using a phrase such as "ethics program" is that it might suggest a requirement for a large scale, disruptive and expensive process. Just the opposite is true. As I said at the beginning of this section, every corporation already has an ethics program. What is proposed here is a framework for looking at the effectiveness of what is already in place and for identifying what, if any, aspects need strengthening or modification. The ethical ground rules, values and practices of an organization develop incrementally over time and will require time to change.

NOTES

1.   Brenner, S. N., "Ethics Programs and Their Dimensions," *Journal of Business Ethics,* Vol. 11: 391, 399, 1992.
2.   Metzger, M., D. R. Dalton, and J. W. Hill, "The Organization of Ethics and the Ethics of Organizations: The Case for Expanded Organizational Ethics Audits," *Business Ethics Quarterly,* Vol. 3, Issue 1, 1993, pp. 27–43.
3.   The details of this research are expanded in M. B. E. Clarkson and M. C. Deck, "Applying the Stakeholder Management Model to the Analysis and Evaluation of Corporate Codes," in *Business and Society in a Changing World Order,* pp. 55–76 (Best Papers volume of the 1992 Conference of the International Association for Business and Society), Dean C. Ludwig, Editor. Edwin Mellen Press, New York. 1993.
4.   Rich, A. J., C. S. Smith, and P. H. Mihalek: 1990, "Are Corporate Codes of Conduct Effective?" *Management Accounting* (September), pp. 34–35.

DO CODES OF CONDUCT DELIVER THE GOODS?

—MAUREEN QUIGLEY

Mission statements are constantly and consistently developed by firms, though there is only some conclusive evidence of their impact. Maureen Quigley asks the questions that many corporations therefore would like answered!

Companies adopt a range of ways and means to tackle ethical problems found within their supply chains, such as abuse of safety standards in factories in developing countries. Each approach has inherent strengths and pitfalls, yet each represents a step in a process of improving conditions. Companies most commonly start by adopting codes of conduct and internal monitoring systems. But are such steps enough? Experiences of the Pentland Group suggest that companies facing the difficult and complex demands of ethical trading will need more than formulaic codes or monitoring.

A code can be an essential first step. It defines key principles and aspirations, and companies can often use their purchasing power to urge suppliers' compliance with it. Yet such leverage is limited in scope because:

- It hinges on a buyer committed to taking a large percentage of a supplier's production.

- It offers no advantage to smaller companies that lack significant purchasing power.

- It could be used unfairly to discriminate against small to medium-sized enterprises.

- It is piecemeal, tackling issues on factory-by-factory basis rather than addressing larger root causes.

- It may be used cosmetically to guard corporate reputations rather than improve conditions.

A second, more progressive phase is where a company implements a code of conduct, either by imposing it on suppliers or by more collaborative means, then works to integrate the principals of the code into its own supply chain management and other management systems. The blending together of principals and actions is essential to sustainable ethical trading.

Nonetheless, the roots of the problems and dilemmas found in manufacturing are too complex to be sorted out on a factory-by-factory basis. Tackling problems found in worker health and safety involves looking at external forces and conditions, such as the capacity of civic institutions to regulate, enforce and provide essential services to businesses and workers. The route to lasting improvement is to overcome contextual barriers, inefficiencies and inequalities commonly associated with underdevelopment, that impede sustainable change. Companies that seek to be a positive force for change need to take a developmental approach that is characterized by (although not limited to):

- Local ownership of issues.

- Collaborative relationships with suppliers.

- Multi-sectoral partnerships.

- Capacity building of institutions.

These values define a long-term strategy that fuses integrated management systems with partnership development. Traces of this method have been found traditionally within extractive industries. However, it is an option and an opportunity for companies of varying size and in all sectors. Strategic partnerships enable small companies to overcome vast resource requirements of a developmental approach by complementing partners' expertise and material contributions. Partnerships cannot be limited to suppliers and workers, but must include competitors, local and foreign governmental institutions and NGOs if they are to build a comprehensive strategy for change.

Debate within ethical trading circles remains steeped in issues of how best to monitor and to evaluate company codes. As more companies develop codes, it is clear that codes represent only part of a process. Given the vast effort expended on monitoring, one must question whether resources might be better applied to treating the root causes of problems rather than to monitoring symptoms. Advocates for ethical trading must be aware of the risk of failing to see the forest for the trees. The challenge for corporations, nongovernmental organizations, unions and governments is to develop viable, collaborative programs to root out the causes of human rights abuses and unsatisfactory working conditions.

HOFFMAN-LAROCHE CASE
A Sentencing Guidelines Milestone

—Jeffrey M. Kaplan

When the corporate sentencing guidelines went into effect in November 1991, prosecutors, compliance officers and others noted that fines under the new law could reach as high as $290 million or even greater. After the Daiwa Bank *prosecution in 1996—which resulted in a $340 million criminal fine—punishment beyond the $290 million figure was no longer just a theoretical possibility. Later that year, a Delaware court, in the* Caremark *decision, raised the prospect of individual liability for a fine under the corporate sentencing guidelines, by permitting shareholders to sue directors personally for losses arising from failure to ensure that their company had put in place "an effective program to prevent and detect violations of law," which is the guidelines' articulation of a meaningful compliance program.*

Now, another sentencing guidelines milestone has been reached. In May 1999, F. Hoffman-LaRoche, Ltd.—a large Swiss pharmaceutical company—was convicted of an antitrust conspiracy and fined $500 million. This is the largest criminal fine in the history of American law.

According to documents filed in court and other accounts, Hoffman-LaRoche, BASF AG (a German firm) and Rhone Poulenc SA (of France), engaged in a conspiracy from 1990 to 1999 to control the price and sales volume of a wide range of vitamins used as nutritional supplements or to enrich human food and animal feeds (including vitamins A, B2, B5, C, E and beta carotene). The conspiracy involved annual meetings to plan production, divide the market and fix prices, with follow-up sessions to enforce compliance. One member of the cartel referred to it as "Vitamins, Inc."

U.S. Assistant Attorney General for Antitrust, Joel Klein, said that "[t]his conspiracy has affected more than $5 billion of commerce in products found in every American household." According to some estimates, prices of vitamins were pushed up by 15–40%.

In addition to the record fine against Hoffman-LaRoche, BASF AG will pay a fine of $225 million, which is also one of the largest financial penalties ever imposed in a criminal case. Rhone Poulenc, on the other hand, was not prosecuted at all. Because it brought evidence of the conspiracy to the government's attention, it was a beneficiary of the Antitrust

Jeffrey M. Kaplan, "Hoffman-LaRoche Case: A Sentencing Guidelines Milestone," *Ethikos and Corporate Conduct Quarterly* 13, no. 1 (July/August 1999), pp. 1–11. Reprinted with permission of *Ethikos and Corporate Conduct Quarterly*.

Division's amnesty program. According to Gary Spratling, Deputy Assistant Attorney General, Rhone Poulenc's cooperation "led directly to the charges and the decision of the defendants" to plead guilty.

The fines will likely not be the only costs to the companies for their offenses. They also face class action lawsuits from businesses that bought vitamins. Hoffman-LaRoche and BASF have announced that they will attempt to settle the cases, but doing so may be costly in light of the admission of liability. Additionally, Karel Van Miert, the EU Competition Commissioner, declared after the U.S. prosecutions were announced, "This kind of cartel needs to be fined very heavily. It needs to be punished." Indeed, authorities in Canada, Europe and Australia have begun their own investigations into the matter.

In addition, the former head of Roche's global marketing division, Dr. Kumo Sommer, was charged with participating in the conspiracy and with lying to government investigators. He agreed to plead guilty, serve four months in prison, and pay a $100,000 fine. (The extent of *individual* financial liability under the sentencing guidelines is often underappreciated. In one recent antitrust case, an executive was fined $10 million.)

Hoffman-LaRoche is clearly an important prosecution. But looking beyond the headlines, what are the implications of this case for those engaged in business ethics and compliance work?

LESSON 1: THE NEED FOR STRONG ANTITRUST COMPLIANCE

Many of the largest fines under the corporate sentencing guidelines have involved antitrust violations. In addition to the penalties against Hoffman-LaRoche and BASF, at least three other companies have been fined $100 million or more in the past few years. Indeed, there are apparently about 35 federal grand juries investigating price-fixing in a variety of industries. The number of *state* investigations is harder to ascertain but could also be large, given the increasing emphasis on antitrust enforcement at the state level (as evidenced, among other ways, by the participation of many state attorneys general in the *Microsoft* case).

Despite this, many companies—particularly those that are moving from purely regulated into more entrepreneurial endeavors—have not adopted meaningful antitrust compliance measures. The risk of such inaction is great, given that the Antitrust Division has been on record for several years in setting forth the types of steps it expects to see in compliance programs. These include, according to Deputy Assistant Attorney General Spratling, "both regular and unannounced audits of price changes, discount practices and bid sheets, conducted by those familiar with the firm's past and present business practices and trained in recognizing questionable divergence, [and] [b]oth regular (scheduled) and unannounced audits of front-line pricing and bidding personnel to test their level of understanding of the antitrust laws and their degree of compliance with a program's requirements and standards relating to prevention and detection, backed up by disciplinary mechanisms and potential penalties for failures."

Spratling has also emphasized that "the elements of a compliance program, particularly the audit elements, should be 'customized'—that is, designed and targeted to the firm's specific organization, operation, personnel and business practices."

In the face of this clear guidance and the dramatically escalating penalties for non-compliance, any company's failure to take meaningful antitrust compliance measures will likely be inexplicable to the government, shareholders and others.

LESSON 2: THE VALUE OF SELF-REPORTING

The importance of *timely* self-reporting could not be more starkly apparent than from the results of the vitamin price-fixing conspiracy. Two firms—Hoffman-LaRoche and BASF—will pay fines totaling $725 million. Yet the third conspirator—Rhone Poulenc—avoided prosecution altogether, because it was the first to report the crime to the government.

While the value of such cooperation may be most dramatically evident in the antitrust area (given the amnesty program), the same general principle applies to virtually every other risk area as well. Indeed, the *Daiwa Bank* case, involving a $340 million fine under the corporate sentencing guidelines, was premised largely on the defendant's *late* reporting of a crime by one of its employees.

Yet self-reporting requires more than good intentions (or, in the case of some companies, a formal self-reporting policy). Unless companies have the means to *uncover* internal wrongdoing it is unlikely that they will receive the type of early warning that is often the key to prompt self-reporting. For this and other reasons, compliance auditing—emphasized in Spratling's recommendations—should not be limited to the antitrust area.

***

LESSON 5: THE WORST IS LIKELY YET TO COME

Assistant Attorney General Klein announced that with the Hoffman-LaRoche and BASF pleas, the Antitrust Division had "already secured more than $900 million in criminal fines in this fiscal year," which, he said, is "more than three times our previous annual record; in fact, more than the total amount of fines in the entire history of U.S. antitrust enforcement."

But records are clearly made to be broken, and it is likely that some prosecutors are already looking for a way to top the $500 million mark. Indeed, as great as the penalties were against Hoffman-LaRoche, they actually could have been worse. Spratling noted that the sentencing guidelines would have permitted a fine of as high as $1.3 billion.

Which company will make history with the first *billion* dollar fine? It will likely be one whose executives fail to heed the lessons of *Hoffman-LaRoche.*

SO THEN WHY DID
YOU DO IT?

—John Dunkelberg and Debra Ragin Jessup

What causes unethical behavior and what can we learn from those individuals who have had spectacular ethical lapses? The profiles of several prominent individuals, including Dennis Levine and Charles Keating, are examined in the following article to try to provide some insight into what might lead them down the slippery slope to criminal and unethical behavior. What was found was that all those examined certainly knew they were breaking the law and that most went to extraordinary lengths to cover up what they were doing. Additionally, the authors found that each individual had attained a position of authority that enabled them to break the law without being seriously challenged by others who knew, or suspected, what was being done. Each person was highly compensated for their efforts; yet they chose to engage in unethical and illegal activities in the pursuit of lust, a little more money or power.

A recent study examined the background and environment of 129 individuals who either pled guilty or were found guilty of a crime that generated an article in *The Wall Street Journal* between January 1, 1990, and December 31, 1997. No general pattern emerged from that paper of the variables studied that could explain their criminal activity. The current paper, however, will delve into a deeper examination of some of these individuals in an attempt to see what lessons can be learned from their stories. They range from a man with very little education who became the CEO of a large defense contractor to a couple of attorneys with a privileged upbringing who worked for the most prestigious law firms in Chicago. What led these people down the slippery slope to criminal activity and what penalties did they pay? More importantly, what can we learn from their mistakes?

The individuals presented in this paper include: Dennis Levine who pled guilty to four felony charges of insider trading, Charles Keating who was found guilty of 73 counts of racketeering and fraud involving Lincoln Savings and Loan, Robert Fomon who was the CEO of E. F. Hutton during its rise as a lending brokerage firm and subsequent demise caused by unethical leadership . . . and Robert Citron who pled guilty to six felony counts of securities fraud involving the loss of $1.64 billion in Orange County funds. . . .

DENNIS LEVINE—INSIDER TRADING

Dennis Levine was born and raised as the youngest of three brothers, in a Jewish middle class area of Queens. His father sold aluminum and vinyl siding to support his family and Dennis admired his work ethic. Dennis, however, aspired to a higher standard of living. From an early age, he wanted to be a Wall Street player and he seemed dazzled by expensive clothes, cars and large estates. He was not, however, willing to work hard to achieve his goals and did not excel as a student or as an athlete in high school. He went on to graduate from Baruch College with an undistinguished record. He obtained a job with Citicorp and, after not getting a promotion, moved to Smith Barney. Within a year, he was sent to Paris and soon set up a Swiss bank account. To Dennis the Swiss bank account meant that he was "playing like the big boys now." On his return to the New York office he talked his way into the mergers and acquisition department. Within his team he was noted for his dismal math skills and an inflated view of his skills and contributions, but he was part of a group that worked on the details of mergers before they were known to the public.

Dennis saw the price of stocks moving up before mergers were announced and was convinced that everybody was getting rich on insider information but him. During his Citicorp days, Dennis had met and become friends with Robert Wilkis. Wilkis had an excellent education, Harvard, then Stanford Business school, and who spoke five languages fluently. Within a week of his move to Smith Barney, Dennis had called Wilkis with a stock tip and Wilkis purchased a couple of hundred shares. The stock rose dramatically and the beginning of a partnership that would end in jail sentences, large fines and public humiliation was formed. Dennis and Wilkis agreed to trade only on the other's information, never share tips with anyone else, and to use code names when calling the other partner. The knowledge and monetary benefits gained from one "friend" proved insufficient to satisfy Dennis Levine's dreams and he soon recruited a ring of associates. As a group they worked for almost all of the major firms engaged in the merger and acquisition practice during a time when this business was very lucrative. They traded information gathered as part of their confidential work with these firms. Using this information, Dennis Levine's trading profits grew to over $11.6 million in less than five years. He even had an arrangement with Ivan Boesky in which Levine would be paid a percentage of any "profits" Boesky made with the "tips" he received from Levine. The revelation of this insider trading ring would make national headlines and shake the faith of the financial system as it had been rarely shaken before.

After his arrest, Dennis agreed to cooperate with the government, implicating all the people with whom he had traded information, even placing calls that were recorded by the government investigators to those with whom he had conspired. In pleading guilty, he agreed to pay restitution to the Securities Exchange Commission of the $11.6 million in alleged trading profits. He was allowed to keep his Park Avenue co-op, his personal effects, including a BMW and personal savings, but lost all of his real estate investments, retirement account, Drexel shares and his beloved Ferrari Testarossa (with only 3,847 miles on it). He was sentenced to two years in prison. The night before going to prison, he tried to explain to his five-year old son why he would be away for the next couple of years. He said that there are rules for big people just like there are rules for children and that he had broken those rules and now must pay. His son listened and then said, "Daddy, did one know what one were doing was wrong?" Dennis answered, "Yes." His son then replied: "So then, why did you do it?"

Dennis had indeed known the rules. He had used cash to fly to Geneva, and later to a bank in the Bahamas, where he set up secret bank accounts under coded names. He used code names in dealing with his co-conspirators, photocopied secret documents and agreed to a formula providing cash payments for his tips to Ivan Boesky. On one occasion, he even stole his father's passport and photocopied it for a trip to Nassau. He knew he was to blame for his own actions but he had a huge desire for fast, easy money. "Money became the way you gauged your level of success, compared to those about you," and the more money the better. "When I was an associate, I wanted to be a Vice-President, when I was a VP, I wanted to be a Senior VP, and when I was a Senior VP, I wanted to be a managing director." On another occasion Dennis noted that when "I was earning $20,000, I wanted $100,000; when I was making $100,000, I wanted $200,000; when I was making $200,000, I wanted $1 million, and then $3 million." There was never any satisfaction.

Insider trading reached its peak in the late 1980s. The scandal brought national attention to such infamous names as Mike Milken, who paid a fine of over $1 billion and spent time in jail, and Martin Revson, of Revlon fortune fame, who traded tips with a group of his well-known socialite friends known as the Southhampton Seven. Why were these men, and dozens of others, willing to trade their good reputations for the small additional marginal utility of a little more money? Maybe because they did not think that if they broke the rules sooner or later they would have to answer the question, "So then why did you do it?"

CHARLES KEATING—SAVINGS AND LOAN SCANDAL

Charlie Keating was raised in very modest conditions. His father, who had managed a local dairy, became disabled when Charlie was seven by Parkinson's disease. He received a Jesuit school education and was known as an excellent student. However, he flunked out of the University of Cincinnati and then enlisted in the Navy as a fighter pilot but he never saw combat. After World War II, he went back to college, received a liberal arts degree, and won gold medals in the NCAA and Pan American Games in the breaststroke. After college he earned a law degree and later started working for Carl Lindner, Jr., a well-known multimillionaire in Cincinnati. During this time, he built a national reputation for his hatred of pornography and in one year flew over 200,000 miles around the country giving talks on the subject. He kept lots of pornography around just to show people how bad it was. Interestingly, at least twelve of his secretaries had breast enlargements, allegedly because Charlie loved to walk around and look down their blouses.

In 1976, Charlie Keating and Carl Lindner parted company. Charlie moved to Phoenix, Arizona, and took over American Continental Corporation (ACC), a home building business with assets of half a million and liabilities of over $110 million. By 1983 the firm was in the black and building over eight homes a day. During this turn-around, Charlie hired all employees and almost all the men were white, tall and blue-eyed. The women were blond, good-looking and buxom. He fired people easily and often but paid those that he kept excellent wages. The offices of ACC were all white, the carpeting, walls and even the desks, and the desktops were always utterly clear of any material.

In September of 1983, Keating bought Lincoln Savings and Loan for $54 million, although its net worth was $34 million. Lincoln had $1.2 billion in assets of which $250 million were judged to be "risky ventures." By 1984, assets had grown to $2.5 billion and the risky ventures had grown to $1.6 billion. Much of the growth in assets had come from brokered loans. (Brokered loans are those sold by brokers who obtain the highest yield possible from the competing financial institutions for these FDIC-insured deposits. Thus the U.S. Government became the insurer of these very risky loans.) Ultimately these brokered loans would total about $5 billion of Lincoln's assets.

With this money, Charlie went on a spending spree. He built or refurbished hotels in Detroit and Phoenix, spending hundreds of millions of dollars on the finest décor. A residential real estate scheme in the desert outside of Phoenix included plans for thousands of homes, a PGA-caliber golf course and a huge clubhouse. Over $100 million of these federally insured deposits went in Ivan Boesky's investment schemes and hundreds of millions into Mike Milken's junk bonds. There were over 52 large real estate deals that never had a credit check and the real estate appraisals were grossly inflated. Files on these loans would be brought "up-to-date" months after the loan was made and corrected to existing regulations.

Charlie Keating gave generously, of money from ACC, to charitable groups. He was proud of his Catholic faith and gave millions to Mother Teresa, in India, and Father Bruce Ritter, in New York. To live in style, Keating had a $2 million home in Phoenix, a $5 million home in Florida, and a fabled retreat in the Bahamas. The care and feeding of his pilots and aircraft was over $35 million. Parties for his staff were first class with one Christmas party costing over $460,000. Since he saw himself as a business tycoon, he spent like one with one meal for four at Le Cirque in Manhattan costing over $2,495 and a single stop to buy a few sports jackets and slacks at Giorgio's on Rodeo Drive totaling $7,694. He and his family flew often and all over the world. In addition, he kept the regulators at bay by giving large sums to political campaigns including five senators (John Glenn, John McCain, Dan Riegle, Dennis DeConcini and Alan Cranston) all later known as the Keating Five. With all the money flowing to others, Charlie also paid himself and his top staff extremely well. He and his family were paid $34 million over five years. In 1987, he had over $5 million in income, but no personal donations to charity.

With spending like this the end was, of course, in sight. ACC used very creative accounting to show a profit and thus kept Charlie Keating going. With over 54 subsidiaries, ACC would buy properties from one subsidiary and sell to another and book the profit. Upstreaming is another example of the schemes used to keep this giant cash machine going. In this scheme, Lincoln would loan money to an individual who would use the money to purchase an asset. The asset would be sold at a higher price and the profits were booked. Since these two transactions were linked, the buyer is a straw buyer, not a real buyer, and this makes the deal a felony. However, with the spending out of control, even schemes of this type could not keep ACC viable.

In September of 1989, ACC declared bankruptcy. The corporation showed $6 billion in assets, but a couple billion was missing. The next day the U.S. Government took over Lincoln Savings and Loan. The case was the largest bank fraud case ever. Lincoln was charged with using straw buyers, sham land sales, inside stock deals, upstreaming of money and fraudulent loans. Charlie Keating was charged with 73 counts of fraud but he claimed he was innocent. Instead he became the poster boy for all that went wrong with the S&L failures in the late 1980s. He was tried, found guilty and sentenced to 10 years in prison and required to pay a fine of $250,000. The judge in this case described Charlie Keating's treatment of Lincoln as "an adult taking candy from a helpless child." Judge Sorkin also wondered how the accountants and the law firms involved with ACC and Lincoln could not have seen the problems. At the time of sentencing Keating was sixty-six years old.

Why did a man who publicly made so much of love of his family and his Catholic religion, his hatred of pornography and drugs, use fraudulent techniques to enrich himself, his family and his friends? His motivation seemed not to be the money but the power and acceptance that money brings. He was earning his way into a club that he coveted, the Boesky, Milken, Lindner club. As a swimmer he had been driven to win because he liked the applause. As the CEO of a company it was the power and seduction and control of people and events.

ROBERT FOMON—CHAIRMAN OF THE BOARD OF E. F. HUTTON

Wall Street probably has never occupied so prominent a place in the public's consciousness as it did during the 1980s. A great bull market was in progress and many individuals were amassing fortunes buying and selling, both stocks and corporations. The news media made several of these individuals virtual heroes and extolled their financial and business acumen. Unfortunately too many of these heroes later turned out to be frauds who made money through unlawful manipulations. Others skirted just inside the law but employed dubious ethical tactics to accumulate wealth during this time. When money comes so easily to so many, few are willing to stop and critically examine how the money is being made. As a result, several corporations became spectacular failures during this time but all these failures were preventable. E. F. Hutton was but one of these firms and its demise is worth examining (Stevens, 1989 and Sterngold, 1990).

E. F. Hutton started in 1904, on April Fool's Day, and grew into a brokerage powerhouse using such famous marketing lines as: "I'm J. Paul Getty and E. F. Hutton is my broker," and "When E. F. Hutton talks, people listen." In the 1970s and the first six years of the 1980s, Hutton was led by Robert Fomon a short, paunchy man who was adept at manipulating images and people. Bob Fomon's early life was one of little joy and less love. His mother died of cancer when he was four. His father, a physician, had very little desire to have the responsibility of raising children, so he sent his three sons to be raised by his wife's spinster sister. He visited his sons no more than twice a year, at Christmas and during his summer vacation. Bob Fomon was a prankster throughout his school years and was thrown out of a Catholic high school and then a public high school just before graduation. He went to the University of Southern California and graduated, with a very undistinguished record, in 1947 with a fine arts degree. After a brief fling in law school he dropped out and tried to determine what he should do with his life.

Through his fathers' connections, Fomon had met many people from the moneyed side of society and he liked the life they led. He saw the stock brokerage business as one that could be quite lucrative. After being rejected by Merrill Lynch and Dean Witter, a friend of his father helped him get a job with E. F. Hutton. Although he demonstrated little in the way of investment acumen, he had a remarkable knack of selling himself to the country club set and they eagerly handed him their business. After building a power base in California, he rose to be the CEO of Hutton through a mixture of charm and double-cross. The charm included a mixture of hard drinking with other brokers in his office and tales of his prowess as a seducer of women.

During his tenure as CEO, E. F. Hutton grew through the raiding of top brokers from other firms and the purchase of other brokerage firms to become one of the nation's most well regarded brokerage houses. Although in an industry that preferred to maintain a rather staid image, Bob Fomon retained his notorious personal behavior of hard drinking and womanizing. When he was in his fifties, he was dating young women in their late teens and early twenties. He also contributed to this rakish behavior with scandalous public statements. For example, he once was quoted describing women as objects of decoration, better seen than heard. Interestingly, his second marriage was to Sharon Kay Ritchie, a former Miss America. Although Hutton did little business in Paris, Fomon had Hutton open an office there, which was overseen by girlfriends from California. Another girlfriend, a young lady in her twenties, was given the job as head of advertising although she had no training of any kind in this field. He also had Hutton pick up the hotel tab for guests at his daughter's wedding and his son charged over $100,000 in expenses in just one year.

Encouraged by E. F. Hutton's culture and to maintain the profit growth, the firm started several questionable practices that would later not only be embarrassing but lead to its ultimate demise. One of these practices was the selling of products, such as tax shelters, that were notable more for the high commissions generated for Hutton brokers than the tax benefits generated for their customers. To help secure public finance business (selling tax-exempt bonds) in various states, Hutton entertained some state officials at brothels. Several brokerage units found money laundering to be profitable business and, in one case, a customer regularly paid for his security purchases with a gym bag full of small bills. To obtain the lucrative commissions from selling bonds, Hutton underwrote some "junk" bonds with the par value guaranteed, thus if the bonds' ratings slipped, Hutton could, and did, lose millions of dollars. Hutton also entered into the risky second mortgage business charging up to eighteen percent interest, plus up-front fees that pushed the rates closer to forty percent. All of these practices paled before the grand scheme that gained Hutton much unneeded notoriety—check kiting.

By 1980, E. F. Hutton was looking for new ways to make profits; and many of its brokerage units across the United States wrote large checks against uncollected balances to create a float for Hutton and inflate its bank balances. Hutton engaged in an illegal practice known as "pinwheeling." A pinwheel occurred when multiple checks were passed from one Hutton account to another to earn interest on the float. This is a felonious action and Hutton's accountants, Arthur Andersen, had warned management about it. Playing the float was too lucrative a practice to be stopped and became Hutton's most profitable product, earning $95.9 million in one year. The end, however, was in sight.

In 1985 Hutton pled guilty to over 2,000 felony counts of defrauding its banks of several million dollars, and customers started fleeing the company in large numbers. Several of the tax shelters defaulted, the junk bonds were down-rated and Hutton had to buy them back at par value, costing the firm additional millions. The Providence, Rhode Island, office was charged with laundering money for organized-crime figures and entertaining customers in a notorious call-girl ring involving several Brown University coeds. With its capital almost gone, Hutton put itself up for sale. Shearson purchased the once proud firm, in what amounted to a fire sale, in December of 1987. In the aftermath, 8,000 of Hutton's 18,000 employees lost their jobs, but Bob Fomon and the directors of the firm were rewarded handsomely for their stewardship. For example, Bob Fomon sold his 230,000 shares of Hutton stock before the problems at the firm became public knowledge. His golden parachute gave him $4 million in cash, $500,000 a year for seven years, plus a pension of $612,450 for life. The directors also gave him an additional 76,000 shares of stock worth about $3 million.

Of all the individuals studied in this paper, only Bob Fomon was never charged with a crime, yet he presided over a firm that had an impeccable reputation before his arrival and was notorious for its sordid activities at the end. His unethical behavior led the firm to its demise and cost many of his employees their livelihood.

***

ROBERT CITRON

Robert Citron had been the Orange County Treasurer-Tax Collector for over 24 years when he was indicted for securities fraud. As treasurer, he was responsible for investing billions of dollars in county tax revenue. His investment record was amazing in that he had consistently matched or outperformed managers in other counties. Why did his investment empire crumble before his eyes, landing Orange County in the largest municipal bankruptcy in U.S. history?

Citron was born in Los Angeles and grew up in Burbank. He never finished college and had been married to the same woman for 39 years and lived in the same house for 22 years. As treasurer, Citron was responsible for the county's investment pool. His investment record showed an average return of 9.03% during the ten years just prior to the bankruptcy, which was double what comparable pools made. Citron was known as one of the best county finance officers in the nation and once received an award naming him one of the top five best government investors nationwide.

Citron's strategy was simple, he used the investment pool's U.S. treasury bill and bonds as collateral to borrow short-term loans at low interest rates. He then invested the borrowed funds in mid-term corporate bonds and securities that paid a higher rate of return. This type investment strategy can result in large returns if the interest rates stay low and stable. However, if interest rates rise, the entire investment strategy collapses.

The public was forewarned about the potential problems with Citron's investment strategy when he ran for reelection in 1994. John Moorlach, his political opponent, questioned his investment practices. Of course, this criticism fell on deaf ears because Citron had been singled out as one of the best county finance officers in the nation. He had also received an award for one of the five best government investors nationwide. Nevertheless, Moorlach persisted throughout the campaign, accusing Citron of "overly risky strategy that left the county's investment pool vulnerable to rising interest rates."

It appears that Moorlach had a crystal ball. When interests rates went up, Citron's world collapsed. On December 6, 1994, Citron resigned due to reports that the county's investment fund had lost $1.5 billion in value due to rising interest rates and risky investment transactions. In fact, the interest rate increases wiped out, on paper, almost one of every five dollars in the fund. Citron gave no reason for his resignation; however, his lawyer said that "no one shares the county's pain more than Mr. Citron."

After his resignation, someone who knew Citron said that his successful investments made him believe he was infallible, that he started to believe his own press. Others said that Citron loved to be praised and he spoke often of his own accomplishments.

Citron was charged with defrauding investors and misappropriating public money in connection with the county's investment pool. He pled guilty and the evidence showed that he diverted over $100 million in other agencies' money into the county's account. Prior to sentencing, Citron's attorney sought information that would implicate others involved, stating that they were "more sophisticated and knowledgeable about matters concerning securities and accounting." He also said that Citron "relied on financial and legal experts." Everyone was shocked to discover in court, that two of the "experts" were a mail-order astrologer and a psychic. The psychics were right about one thing: Citron was told that December of 1994 would be a bad month, but after that, his money worries would be over.

Citron was sought and was given leniency by the judge for his cooperation with the prosecutors. The judge sentenced Citron to one year in the county jail and a fine of $100,000. He was also placed on probation for five years, ordered to perform 1,000 hours of community service and undergo psychological counseling.

Citron reported to the county jail on January 10, 1997, and stayed 20 minutes, then went home. The sheriff agreed to let him serve his time by doing clerical work during the day and returning home at night. What do you know, the psychics were right again, they said he wouldn't go to jail.

***

CONCLUSION

The objective of this paper was to provide a detailed look at individuals whose level of illegal or unethical behavior brought them national attention in order to learn something about what caused them to fall into their destructive pattern of action. A possible common thread seems to be an addictive behavior that started with a simple, almost insignificant, act that grew into an uncontrollable habit of unethical and illegal behavior. The drive for this irrational behavior seems to be a feeling of power that comes from having more control over others, more money, or a higher status position.

All of these individuals share common characteristics even though they all took different paths to success. They all had attained a level of success in their field that was enviable by others yet they decided to break the rules, risking and then losing everything. So why did they do it? They were all driven by a desire to have more power, more money or more recognition. They were driven to the point of obsession and lacked the ability to rationally assess their conduct. Specifically, all of the individuals studied, acted as though they believed they were above the rules. Add the autonomy that came with their jobs and you have the perfect combination for disaster.

What can we learn from these ethical lapses? We offer these suggestions. First, create an ethical environment that encourages and rewards ethical behavior. This can be done in a variety of ways. Professor Robin discusses this issue in his book, *Questions & Answers about Business Ethics* (1999). He tells us to combat unethical behavior,

> the company must constantly support and develop the culture. The culture should make it clear that peers will find unethical behavior unacceptable and will report it, thus, the perceived probability of getting caught increases. When ethical misdeeds are detected, the company should punish the individual fairly but openly.

Thus, it is imperative that companies implement policies and procedures that make it clear that unethical conduct will be detected and the employee punished. The punishment should be direct, publicized and long-lasting. The company must send a message that unethical conduct will not be tolerated.

Additionally, Professor Robin tells us that "employees entering the workplace are looking for guidelines for acceptable behavior." New employees will look to role models and mentors to set the standard for ethical behavior. The "ethical tone" of the business must be set by top management and trickle down to the entry-level employees. If the ethics of top management is beyond reproach, this sends a clear message that ethical conduct and success go hand in hand.

Secondly, these individuals have taught us that there must be balance between power and autonomy. The desire to commit unethical acts is nothing without the autonomy to do so. Autonomy is the factor in the equation that sends intelligent successful people over the ethical edge. They believe they are invincible because no one is looking over their shoulder. We certainly cannot assume that all highly successful people would behave unethically; however, we can guard against the possibility by refraining from giving an individual complete autonomy over their duties.

In conclusion, ethical behavior within the business structure has to be a priority, right up with making a profit. Ethical business environments do not miraculously appear. The ethical business environment must be meticulously cultivated and failure to do so can result in great loss to the company, the profession, and society.

REFERENCES

Binstein, M., and C. Bowden: 1993, *Trust Me: Charles Keating and the Missing Billions* (Random House, New York).

Frantz, D.: 1987, *Levine & Company: Wall Street's Insider Trading Scandal* (Henry Holt and Company, New York).

Robin, D.: 1999, *Questions & Answers about Business Ethics: Running an Ethical and Successful Business* (Thomson Learning, Cincinnati, OH).

Sterngold, J.: 1990, *Burning Down the House: How Greed, Deceit, and Bitter Revenge Destroyed E. F. Hutton* (Summit Books, New York).

Stevens, M.: 1989, *Sudden Death: The Rise and Fall of E. F. Hutton* (NAL Books).

Stewart, J.: 1991, *Den of Thieves* (Simon & Schuster, New York).

Traub, J.: 1990, *Too Good to Be True, The Outlandish Story of Wedtech* (Doubleday, New York).

Chapter 4

CORPORATE SOCIAL RESPONSIBILITY AND SOCIAL REPORTING

Business has to take account of its responsibilities to society in coming to its decisions, but society has to accept its responsibilities for setting the standards against which those decisions are made.[1]

—SIR ADRIAN CADBURY

[1]Sir Adrian Cadbury, "Ethical Managers Make Their Own Rules," *Harvard Business Review,* September/October 1987.

By "social responsibility," we mean the intelligent and objective concern for the welfare of society that restrains individual and corporate behavior from ultimately destructive activities, no matter how immediately profitable, and leads in the direction of positive contributions to human betterment, variously as the latter may be defined.[2]

—Kenneth R. Andrews

Fill your bowl to the brim
and it will spill.
Keep sharpening your knife
and it will be blunt.
Chase after money and security
and your heart will never unclench.
Care about people's approval
and you will be their prisoner.
Do your work, then step back.
The only path to serenity.

—Tao Te Ching

You never expect justice from a company, do you? They neither have a soul to lose nor a body to kick.

—Sydney Smith,
1771–1845, English
writer, clergyman

This chapter addresses the central questions of (1) whether there exists a social responsibility of business and, if so (2) how firms can meet and evidence their fulfillment of this responsibility. This question of whether the responsibility exists has been asked numerous times in a variety of ways, with just as many answers. Central to this question is perhaps the underlying determination of what responsibility business has at all to anyone. Do you ask yourself whether your friends, colleagues, parents or others have a *social* responsibility? Probably, at some point. You might see your colleague drop some trash on the floor and walk on. You may feel that this person should stop and pick it up instead of continuing. Your belief about the responsibility of business may be no more than this—a firm should clean up after itself, so to speak. On the other hand, there are some theorists who believe that firms owe something back to the society that supports it, and that this debt is greater than the debt of the individual members of society.

IS THERE A SOCIAL RESPONSIBILITY OF BUSINESS?

The first article in this section by Milton Friedman is perhaps the best-known argument for a purely *profit-based* social responsibility of business (though Adam Smith was probably among the first to articulate this concept). Friedman is not ignoring ethical responsibility in

---

[2]Kenneth R. Andrews, *The Concept of Corporate Strategy* (Homewood, IL: Irwin, 1971), p. 120.

his analysis; he is merely suggesting that decision makers are acting ethically if they follow their firm's self-interest. Primeaux expands on Friedman's analysis in order to find a corporate social responsibility within a profit-maximizing framework. Consider the qualities of a successful firm—it meets the needs of its market. If the market demands socially responsible behavior, a firm may only be successful by demonstrating this behavior. On the other hand, if the market places no value at all on socially responsible behavior, it is unlikely that a firm would be encouraged by profit to exhibit this behavior. Professor James Wilson explains that, "While free markets will ruthlessly eliminate inefficient firms, the moral sentiments of man will only gradually and uncertainly penalize immoral ones. But, while the quick destruction of inefficient corporations threatens only individual firms, the slow anger at immoral ones threatens capitalism, and thus freedom itself."[3]

Though purporting on the surface to disagree with Friedman, Kenneth Dayton, former chairman of the Dayton-Hudson Corporation, actually seems to best articulate the balance between Primeaux and Friedman:

> *We are not in business to make maximum profit for our shareholders. We are in business . . . to serve society. Profit is our reward for doing it well. If business does not serve society, society will not long tolerate our profits or even our existence.[4]*

In fact, this is not an argument in favor of social responsibility for society's sake but instead an argument for the sustainability of an organization through meeting the needs of its supporting constituencies.

The general public, however, seems to disagree with Friedman's underlying presumption. A *BusinessWeek*/Harris poll of over 1,000 Americans found that 95% reject the notion that a corporation's role is limited to profit maximization.[5] Further, there may be other arguments for a socially responsible firm. Employees who are well-treated in their work environments may prove more loyal, and more effective and productive in their work. Liz Bankowski, director of social missions at Ben & Jerry's Homemade Ice Cream Company, claims that 80 to 90% of employees work at Ben & Jerry's because "they feel they are part of a greater good."[6] The impact on the bottom line, therefore, stems not only from customer preference but also from employee preference. The problem with a focus on preference, however, is that social responsibility becomes merely social marketing. That is, a firm may use the image of social responsibility to garner customer support or employee loyalty while the facts do not evidence a true commitment. Are motivations relevant? Paul Hawken, co-founder of Smith & Hawken gardening stores and an advocate of business social responsibility, reminds us that

> *You see tobacco companies subsidizing the arts, then later you find out that there are internal memos showing that they wanted to specifically target the minorities in the arts because they want to get minorities to smoke. That's not socially responsible. It's using social perception as a way to aggrandize or further one's own interests exclusively.[7]*

---

[3]James Wilson, quoted by Elmer W. Johnson at the Hansen-Wessner Memorial Lecture, "Corporate Soulcraft in the Age of Brutal Markets," Northwestern University, May 2, 1996.
[4]Kenneth Dayton, Dayton-Hudson Corporation, 1996.
[5]*Business Ethics,* November/December 1996, p. 6.
[6]Joel Makower, *Beyond the Bottom Line* (New York: Simon & Schuster, 1994), p. 68.
[7]*Ibid.,* p. 15.

What about the perspective of the *receiving* organization? Should an organization simply accept funding from any possible source? Consider the dilemma an organization faces, for instance, when a donor offers funds that would further the organization's objectives but the donor's image is completely contrary to those of the organization? Does the organization have the right or responsibility to question the motives of its benefactor? Since a major contribution often amounts to a type of partnership arrangement, should organizations be concerned about linking their images to that of their donors?[8] The answers to these questions may, in fact, lie more in the intention of the recipient than in that of the donor.

On the other hand, if the market does not encourage responsibility for social causes, should a firm engage in this behavior? And, indeed, is this responsibility only that of firms, or are we responsible for supporting firms that fail to exhibit socially responsible behavior? If we stand by and allow irresponsible actions to take place using profits garnered by our purchases, do we bear any responsibility?

There exist disagreements even among scholars who advocate a social responsibility. For instance, to whom does the firm owe this responsibility? To the employees? The community? The consumers? All stakeholders? As we have seen in previous sections, it may not be possible to satisfy the needs of each and every stakeholder in a situation. Therefore, what is the prioritization of this social responsibility? Consider the case of the spotted owl and the loggers in the Pacific Northwest. Logging poses a danger of extinction to the spotted owl, but discontinuing logging activities poses a hardship on the logging communities and those connected with them. Animal rights activists consider the interests of society in preserving the spotted owl to be predominant, while others consider the interests of the loggers and their communities to be predominant. Whether you are persuaded by the fact that this is a conflict between humans and animals or by the fact that a species might be endangered, the answer is found only in your personal prioritization scheme.

WHAT IS THE NATURE OF CORPORATE SOCIAL RESPONSIBILITY?

Is profit for the firm the only guiding principle of socially responsible activities, or should the impact of its decision on others be considered, even where the law allows the decision? Shell Oil's rehabilitative actions subsequent to NGO pressure in one circumstance seem not to have been motivated by a legal duty to act. However, interestingly enough, a recent appellate court decision held that a lawsuit against Shell for allegedly aiding and abetting in the torture and murder of Nigerian activists who opposed drilling on their lands was allowed to proceed (in a decision dated September 14, 2000).[9] In the time since the activities discussed in the case, Shell has strived to create an awareness regarding corporate social responsibility both for itself and in its industry. "Corporate citizenship is not a luxury, especially in these difficult times," said P. B. Watts, chairman, Royal Dutch/Shell Group of Companies, during a recent annual shareholder meeting. "It's a sensible part of doing business."[10]

---

[8]I appreciate the assistance of Jennifer Wiggins in regard to social responsibility and the arts. These questions derived from her work on this topic.
[9]*Wiwa v. Royal Dutch Petroleum Co.,* 99-7223 (2000).
[10]"Corporate Citizenship: A Luxury in Difficult Times?" World Economic Forum Knowledge Navigator, April 2, 2002.

Similarly, the Dodge brothers sued Henry Ford in a legendary case seeking to answer this very same type of question. Mr. Ford believed that there should be a Ford in every garage; in other words, that Ford cars should be made for and be affordable by everyone in America. At the time of the lawsuit, this meant a reduction in the price of a Ford from $440 to $360 and a refusal to pay stock dividends. John and Horace Dodge, both Ford shareholders, believed that Ford's primary objective should be to make profit for its shareholders.

"My ambition," said Ford, "is to employ still more men, to spread the benefits of this industrial system to the greatest possible number, to help them build up their lives and their homes. To do this, we are putting the greatest share of our profits back in the business."[11] Ford's counsel argued that "although a manufacturing corporation cannot engage in humanitarian works as its principal business, the fact that it is organized for profit does not prevent the existence of implied powers to carry on with humanitarian motives such charitable works as are incident to the main business of the corporation." The court was not persuaded that it should interfere with the reasonable business judgment of the Ford Motor Co. as it did not find that the alleged motives of the directors "menace the interests of the shareholders."

Ford seemingly convinced the court that it was a valid and perhaps laudable claim that "a Ford in every garage" might be an effective long-term business strategy. In fact, consider the long-term gains. If you bought your first car and it was a Ford, you might be more likely to stick with that particular manufacturer; and you might tell others how affordable the cars were, and so on. Investment in loyalty and shared beliefs between the manufacturer and its customers has been shown in countless industries to be a profitable profit-maximizing process. Note that, as their interests seemed to be more short-term than those evidenced by Mr. Ford, the Dodges eventually opened their own firm producing Dodge automobiles to compete directly with Ford.

Perhaps the answer to the quandary of the nature of social responsibility lies somewhere in the middle of all of these arguments. Philosopher Ayn Rand contends that our one and only social responsibility is to ourselves, but that this concern does not act as a barrier to helping others:

> *The moral purpose of one's life is the achievement of happiness. This does not mean that he is indifferent to all men, that human life is of no value to him and that he has no reason to help others in an emergency—but it does mean that he does not subordinate his life to the welfare of others, that he does not sacrifice himself to their needs, that the relief of his suffering is not his primary concern, that any help he gives is an act of generosity, not of moral duty.*[12]

IN THE END, DOES GOOD ETHICS MEAN GOOD BUSINESS?

As we considered at the beginning of Chapter 3, the question of whether good ethics—in this case, specifically corporate social responsibility—translates into fiscal responsibility is not yet completely settled. A landmark study by Professors Stephen Erfle and Michael

---

[11]*Dodge v. Ford Motor Co.,* 204 Mich. 459; 170 N.W. 668 (1919), excerpt.
[12]Ayn Rand, *The Virtue of Selfishness* (New York: New American Library, 1964), p. 49.

Frantantuono found that firms that were ranked highest in terms of their records on a variety of social issues (including charitable contributions, community outreach programs, environmental performance, advancement of women and promotion of minorities) had greater financial performance as well. Financial performance was better in terms of operating income growth, sales-to-assets ratio, sales growth, return on equity, earnings-to-asset growth, return on investment, return on assets and asset growth.[13]

Another recent study by Murphy and Verschoor reports that the overall financial performance of the 2001 *Business Ethics Magazine* Best Corporate Citizens was significantly better than that of the remaining companies in the S&P 500 index, based on the 2001 *Business Week* ranking of total financial performance.[14] In addition, the researchers found that these same firms had a significantly better reputation among corporate directors, security analysts and senior executives, as well, as measured by the 2001 *Fortune* survey of "Most Admired Companies." A follow-up study to validate these findings was conducted by the United Kingdom–based Institute of Business Ethics. The IBE found that, from the perspectives of economic value added, market value added and the price-earnings ratio, those companies who had a code of conduct outperformed those who did not over a five-year period.[15] The higher performance translated into significantly more economic value added, a less volatile p/e ratio (i.e., perhaps a more secure investment) and 18% higher profit/turnover ratios. The research concluded:

> This study gives credence to the assertion that "you do business ethically because it pays." However, the most effective driver for maintaining a high level of integrity throughout the business is because it is seen by the board, employees and other stakeholders to be a core value and therefore the right thing to do . . . [A] sustainable business is one which is well managed and which takes business ethics seriously. Leaders of this type of business do not need any assurance that their approach to the way they do business will also enhance their profitability, because they know it to be true.[16]

Previous studies had found both supporting and conflicting results (though supporting seems to outweigh conflicting). Professor Ullman summarizes the results of previous empirical studies on the relationship between social and financial performance as follows:

- Seven showed a positive relationship between social and financial performance.

- Three showed a negative relationship between social and financial performance.

- One showed a positive relationship between the promotion of women and financial performance and a negative relationship between charitable contributions and financial performance.

---

[13]Makower, *Beyond The Bottom Line,* pp. 70–71.
[14]Curtis Verschoor and Elizabeth Murphy, "The Financial Performance of Large U.S. Firms and Those with Global Prominence: How Do the Best Corporations Rate?" *Business & Society* Review 107, no. 3 (2002), pp. 371–80. See also Elizabeth Murphy and Curtis Verschoor, "Best Corporate Citizens Have Better Financial Performance," *Strategic Finance,* v. 83, no. 7 (January 2002), p. 20.
[15]Simon Webley and Elise More, *Does Business Ethics Pay?* (London: Institute of Business Ethics, 2003), p. 9.
[16]*Ibid.,* p. 33.

- One showed a U-shaped relationship, meaning that extreme social performance (good or bad) was negatively related to financial performance.

- Two found no effect.[17]

Take a look at the Reputation Quotient material and consider whether a better reputation should be the guiding motivation for these types of activities. Does Johnson & Johnson reap a financial benefit from being ranked as the most reputable company in America by ResponsibilityInc? Many people are skeptical of firms who engage in philanthropy, for instance, because they question the firms' motivation. They ask themselves what the company is getting out of a sponsorship, for example. When Philip Morris Co. spends $250 million on an advertisement campaign that communicates its charitable activities, some might question why the company engaged in the charitable activities in the first place. On the other hand, Procter & Gamble Co. was harshly criticized by respondents to a survey seeking to rank firms on the basis of their corporate philanthropy, saying that P&G did "absolutely nothing to help" after the September 11 tragedy.[18] However, in truth, the company provided more than $2.5 million in cash and products but simply did not publicize that contribution. The same held true for Honda Motor Co., which donated cash, all-terrain vehicles and generators for use at the World Trade Center site. Seemingly unaware of these efforts, respondents instead believed them to lack compassion for their failure to support America. The Grand Bank case included in this chapter poses this quandary with regard to publicizing corporate good deeds.

Note that a reputation is relevant to many stakeholders—not just purchasing consumers. A survey conducted in the United Kingdom found that 33% of workers in that country were "very likely" to seek new employment during the next year because of their current employer's poor record on corporate social responsibility.[19] Employers are also more likely to seek out new hires with a demonstrated awareness of social and environmental responsibility—in fact, a *Wall Street Journal* survey found that 77% of corporate recruiters said it is important to their hiring decisions.[20] Moreover, investors are sinking almost $1.3 billion into socially responsible mutual funds, effectively putting their money where their mouths are.[21] Arnold Hiatt, former CEO, Stride Rite Corp., explained,

> *Look at a well-run company and you will see the needs of its stockholders, its employees and the community at large being served simultaneously.[22]*

---

[17]A. Ullman, "Data in Search of a Theory: A Critical Examination of the Relationships Among Social Performance, Social Disclosure and Economic Performance of U.S. Firms," *Academy of Management Review,* July 1985, pp. 545–57.

[18]Ronald Alsop, "For a Company, Charitable Works Are Best Carried Out Discreetly," *The Wall Street Journal,* January 16, 2002, Marketplace Section, p. 1.

[19]The Work Foundation, "The Ethical Employee," http://www.theworkfoundation.com/research/publications/ethical.jsp (2002).

[20]Ronald Alsop, "Corporations Still Put Profits First, But Social Concerns Gain Ground," *The Wall Street Journal,* October 30, 2001, p. B12.

[21]A. J. Vogl, "Does It Pay to Be Good?" *Across the Board,* January 2003.

[22]Cited in Linda Ferrell, "Strategic Philanthropy," http://www.e-businessethics.com/lf/strategic.html.

IF THERE IS A CORPORATE SOCIAL RESPONSIBILITY, HOW DOES A FIRM EVIDENCE ITS SATISFACTION OF THAT RESPONSIBILITY?

Additional readings in this chapter discuss the options available to firms in connection with reporting related to social and environmental issues. This topic is all the more important these days as we move from a unique occurrence where a firm shares information with regard to social and environmental issues to a quasi-regulatory environment that arose in the mid-1990s where firms produce reports pursuant to generally accepted principles. In fact, the French Parliament enacted a new law in France in March 2002 that required all French corporations listed on the Paris Stock Exchange to report on the sustainability of their social and environmental performance. In fall 2002, PricewaterhouseCoopers reported the results of a survey evidencing that two-thirds of multinationals in Europe and 41% in the United States provide information on their "triple bottom line" performance—economic, social and environmental performance.

Even in focusing on social reporting, there is no one structure of group of topics for a corporate social report. Though some elements are mandatory pursuant to other regulations, such as corporate charitable contributions, pension fund adequacy, employee share ownership schemes and employment data, other information is not otherwise required to be disclosed in the United States. This additional information may include energy savings, consumer protection efforts, product safety, health and safety efforts beyond OSHA, employee training, vendor agreements or codes of conduct, mission statements and/or statements of social responsibility.

Firms are engaging in this voluntary reporting process for a variety of reasons. The benefits to a transparent organization include a positive impact on reputation, enhanced shareholder relations, clearer and more transparent corporate governance and greater trust within the investment community.

Formal efforts at standardized corporate responsibility reporting began in the early 1990s. In 1991, seven companies had published sustainability reports;[23] at that time, however, much of the reports' focus was on the environment. The reporting trend has since transformed itself, addressing not only environmental issues, but also economic and social performance.[24] Since that time, the number of corporations documenting their social behavior has exploded into a global legion (as of 2001, the number of companies that published sustainability reports reached 531).[25] And, just as the number of companies adopting corporate social reports has grown, so too has the number of initiatives aimed at standardization dealing with the topic of international corporate behavior. Business leaders, even after acknowledging the importance of corporate social reporting, are being pinned into a situation where simply having a governance committee and a corporate social report is no

---

[23]Patricia Panchak, "Editor's Page—Time for a Triple Bottom Line," IndustryWeek.com (June 1, 2002), http://www.industryweek.com/Columns/Asp/columns.asp?ColumnId=871 (accessed February 27, 2003).

[24]SustainAbility, "Engaging Stakeholders Reports," http://www.sustainability.com/publications/engaging/social-report-morel.asp (accessed January 24, 2003).

[25]Panchak, "Editor's Page."

longer good enough[26]—after all, Enron received accolades in corporate governance and corporate citizenship.[27] Accountability, credibility and transparency are now all a necessity in the company's social reporting procedure.

A broad compendium of global initiatives, principles and standards designed to stimulate change and to promote good corporate citizenship and encourage innovative solutions and partnerships, has emerged. Several organizations have created processes or standardized reporting structures to assist organizations in quantifying their social reporting as well as in creating benchmark data against which they can gauge their activities and decisions. Though many of these are industry specific (such as the Clean Clothes Campaign), others apply cross-industry. The organizations include:

Global Reporting Initiative

Global Sullivan Principles

Social Accountability 8000

UN Global Compact

OECD Guidelines for Multinational Enterprises

ILO Conventions

AA1000

ISO 14000

These voluntary initiatives are considered credible and authentic because of their association with reputable international organizations and agencies,[28] despite the absence of formal regulatory schemes.[29] Each of the following initiatives shares a common mission: to promote an economic environment where smart, sustainable development and good corporate citizenship coexist.[30]

Global Reporting Initiative

Established in 1997, the Global Reporting Initiative (GRI) is a foundation-funded program that established a generally accepted sustainability-reporting framework to which corporations adhere. The reporting criterion covers all aspects of a company's performance—economic, environmental and social. The GRI recognizes the limits of an international, "one-size-fits-all" approach toward corporate reporting and therefore developed sector-

---

[26]"Special Reports: Responsible Business 2001—Corporate Responsibility," FinancialTimes.com, http://specials.ft.com/responsiblebusiness2001/FT34TVZJ4TC.html (accessed February 27, 2003).

[27]Vogl, "Does It Pay to Be Good?" pp. 16–23.

[28]Malcolm McIntosh, Ruth Thomas, et al., "International Standards for Corporate Responsibility," *Ethical Corporation Magazine,* January 2003, pp. 22–29.

[29]*Ibid., infra* n.26, p. 22.

[30]*Ibid.*

specific guidelines or "sector supplements" for companies to follow.[31] The GRI distinguishes itself from the list of voluntary initiatives due to its performance indicator system: The GRI encourages companies to establish watermarks for performance and then to report on their successes and failures in reaching those targets.[32] The GRI is a means for companies to communicate with their multiple stakeholders across regions and nations as well as a way for companies to monitor their progress in sustainable development. Other attributes include strong governance, accessibility and transparency, as well as the ability to create strong partnerships throughout the globe. To date, 55 companies in Europe and America have adopted the GRI.[33]

Global Sullivan Principles

As opposed to the auditable framework of the GRI, the Global Sullivan Principles comprise a set of internal ethical business operating principles.[34] Conceived in 1977, the Sullivan Principles were the brainchild of the late Reverend Leon Sullivan. The Global Sullivan Principles have a tripartite structure that includes corporations, higher education and civic involvement. This tripartite initiative exemplifies Rev. Sullivan's commitment to ethical conduct, which, he believed, is not limited to businesses alone—instead it is the responsibility of the entire community. However, because the Global Sullivan Principles omit the right to freedom of association as a core labor standard, they lack support from the labor organization community.[35] Currently, more than 170 companies, including public sector and religious organizations, subscribe to the Global Sullivan Principles; the vast majority of signatories are within the United States.[36]

Social Accountability 8000

Created in 1997 by the Social Accountability Institute (SAI), a not-for-profit, nongovernmental organization, and the Council on Economic Priorities (CEP), Social Accountability 8000 (SA8000) is a standard based on a commitment to establishing a cross-industry standard for workplace conditions and independent verification.[37] Unique to SA8000 is this independent verification, which allows the standard to be implanted in any nation and within any industry of any size and its monitoring arm, the Council on Economic Priorities Accreditation Agency (CEPAA). The SA8000 focuses on the core labor rights of the ILO Conventions, the International Declaration of Human Rights and the UN Convention on the Rights of the Child, addressing key issues such as child labor, compulsory labor, health and

---

[31]Global Reporting Initiative, "Dialogue on Current and Future Directions: Some Key Issues and Perspectives for and from Our Stakeholders," http://www.globalreporting.org/Feedback/Dialogue/index.htm (accessed January 20, 2003).

[32]McIntosh, Thomas, et al., "International Standards for Corporate Responsibility," *infra* n.26, p. 25.

[33]*Ibid., infra* n.26, p. 27.

[34]Global Reporting Initiative, "Global Reporting Initiative & Global Sullivan Principles," http://www.globalreporting.org/AboutGRI/SullivanPrinciples.pdf.

[35]McIntosh, Thomas, et al., "International Standards for Corporate Responsibility," *infra* n.26, p. 25.

[36]*Ibid., infra* n.26, p. 27.

[37]Global Reporting Initiative, "Global Reporting Initiative & SA8000," http://www.globalreporting.org/AboutGRI/SA8000.pdf.

safety, freedom of association, increased educational attainment for employees, discrimination and working hours and wages.[38] It applies to manufacturers and suppliers, but retailers can also adhere to it. The auditing process is required every three years and includes minimum performance requirements, employee interviews, as well as an open complaints and appeals system. Presently, there are more than 190 companies in 31 countries that have SA8000 certifications.[39]

United Nations Global Compact

On January 31, 1999, United Nations Secretary General Kofi Annan presented to the World Economic Forum at Davos his proposal for a Global Compact.[40] On July 26, 2000, Kofi Annan's vision was set into action.[41] The Secretary General's Global Compact made the issue of corporate social responsibility paramount, challenging business leaders around the world to take part in the global initiative. The Global Compact is comprised of nine principles, surrounding the issues of human rights, labor standards and environment.[42] Participating companies must publish annual reports and display on their websites specific examples of how they put the Global Compact principles into practice. Like the other initiatives, the Global Compact is voluntary and has no enforcement arm. The initiative's openness is designed "to stimulate and to promote good corporate citizenship and encourage innovative solutions and partnerships."[43] Its openness was also designed to carry out the Global Compact's two objectives: (1) incorporate the Global Compact and its nine principles into a business's strategy and operations; (2) facilitate a partnership among key stakeholders and promote partnerships in support of U.N. goals.[44] The United Nations' reputation and moral authority is one reason more than 649 companies and cities have adopted the Global Compact.[45]

OECD Guidelines for Multinational Enterprises

The Organization for Economic Cooperation and Development is a forum of 30 member countries whose mission is to encourage sustainable business practices and "to improve the fit between business and society by clarifying the rights and responsibilities of governments and enterprises in the area of international business."[46] First established in 1976 and then revised in 2000, the OECD Guidelines for Multinational Enterprises "is the only comprehensive code of conduct agreed to by multiple nations," addressing issues like disclosure of material information, employment relations, consumer interests, competition, science and

[38]Global Reporting Initiative, "Global Reporting Initiative & Global Sullivan Principles."

[39]McIntosh, Thomas, et al., "International Standards for Corporate Responsibility," *infra* n.26, p. 26.

[40]United Nations Global Compact, "The Global Compact: About the GC," http://www.unglobalcompact.org/Portal/.

[41]*Ibid.*

[42]United Nations Global Compact, "The Global Compact: Nine Principles," http://www.unglobalcompact.org/Portal/.

[43]UN Global Compact, "The Global Compact: FAQ," http://www.unglobalcompact.org/Portal/.

[44]UN Global Compact, "The Global Compact: Overview," http://www.unglobalcompact.org/Portal/.

[45]McIntosh, Thomas, et al., "International Standards for Corporate Responsibility," *infra* n.26, p. 27.

[46]Global Reporting Initiative, "Global Reporting Initiative & OECD Guidelines for MNEs," http://www.globalreporting.org/AboutGRI/OECDGuidelines.pdf.

technology diffusion and environmental management.[47] The Guidelines are unique in that they adopt local practices instead of international-agreed standards and that each OECD country has a contact point, serving as a form of customer service. Similar to the ILO conventions, the OECD Guidelines for MNEs are intended for governmental commitment, making it all the more difficult to hold companies directly accountable. Thirty-four governments have signed on to these operating principles.[48]

International Labor Organization Conventions

The International Labor Organization (ILO) is the oldest of the UN agencies. Like the Global Sullivan Principles, the ILO is a tripartite structure, composed of government, labor and employers' organizations. The ILO's tripartite structure, coupled with its early establishment, enhances the credibility of the organization as well as its conventions. The three-tiered system does, however, create a quite lengthy and arduous decision-making process. And, like the other global initiatives, the ILO conventions have a weakness when it comes to enforcement and implementation. The International Labor Organization has enacted more than 180 conventions throughout its history, addressing a wide range of labor issues, including the freedom of association, prohibition of compulsory labor, prohibition of child labor, employment of disabled persons, equal remuneration/equal work and health and safety.[49] The conventions' positive elements—international reach, history and tripartite structure—give it credibility in addressing the topic of social reporting.[50]

AA1000 and AA1000 Series

The AccountAbility 1000 Series, developed in 1999, concentrates on improving the accountability and overall performance of organizations by way of increasing the quality of social and ethical accounting, auditing and reporting.[51] This global initiative is overseen by the Institute of Social and Ethical AccountAbility, an international, not-for-profit, professional institute dedicated to the promotion of social, ethical and overall organizational accountability, as well as members from business (profit and nonprofit), academic and consultant groups.[52] Developed by its International Council, the AA1000 is the first systematic stakeholder-based approach to address institutional accountability and performance enhancement.[53] The AA1000 has evolved into the AA1000 Series (AA1000s), which is an extension to the AA1000 Framework, a standard engineered to improve accountability and performance by "learning through stakeholder engagement."[54] The AA1000s provides comprehensive outlines and guidelines

[47]*Ibid.*

[48]McIntosh, Thomas, et al., "International Standards for Corporate Responsibility," *infra* n.26, p. 27.

[49]International Labor Organization (ILO), "What Are International Labour Standards?" http://www.ilo.org/public/english/standards/norm/whatare/index.htm.

[50]McIntosh, Thomas, et al., "International Standards for Corporate Responsibility," *infra* n.26, p. 23.

[51]Global Reporting Initiative, "Global Reporting Initiative & AA1000 and AA1000 Series," http://www.globalreporting.org/about/iniaa1000.asp (accessed March 27, 2003).

[52]*Ibid., infra* n.49.

[53]*Ibid.*

[54]AccountAbility, "AA1000 Series: Introducing AA1000," http://www.accountability.org.uk/aa1000/default.asp (accessed March 28, 2003).

for stakeholder engagement, supporting social, ethical and environmental accountability systems. Unveiled in 2002, the Assurance Standard (which has as its focus strengthening the credibility of social and sustainability reporting) was the first addition to the AA1000 Framework. The AA1000 Assurance Standard complements the GRI in that it provides an outline for independent third parties to assure and audit sustainability reporting. At press time, AccountAbility was developing two other modules: one with an emphasis on risk and the other with a focus on measuring and communicating the quality of stakeholder engagement.[55]

While the scope of the GRI includes economic, environmental and social performance and public reporting, the scope of the AA1000 is social and ethical accounting, auditing and reporting, stakeholder dialogue and accountability and quality assurance. Though both emphasize satisfying the information and decision-making needs of a full range of stakeholder groups, the AA1000 is based on accountability principles and the process of social accounting and stakeholder engagement, while GRI is a disclosure framework based on reporting principles, characteristics and indicators.

ISO 14000

Developed in 1996 by the International Organization for Standardization in Geneva, Switzerland, the ISO 14000 series is a voluntary initiative that places an emphasis on environmental management standards and operations (i.e., management systems, auditing, labeling, performance evaluation, life cycle assessment).[56] Its core mission is to provide voluntary environmental management standards to enhance companies' ability to manage environmental impacts and risks, and to improve environmental performance. The series' commitment to the improvement of the corporate environmental atmosphere—management systems, auditing, performance evaluation, life cycle, etc.—is what distinguishes this initiative from others mentioned above. The standards promote continual improvement without specifying actual standards of performance. Unlike the SA8000, the 14000 series was first developed at a national level before expanding internationally. The key stakeholders for the ISO 14000 series are the standard-creating organizations within the ISO member community, but also include environmental NGOs, professional, research, governmental and other nonprofit institutions. The ISO series includes a number of standards; those that deal directly with external reporting include the ISO 14001 (which is the model adopted by organizations for their environmental management system), the ISO 14004 (which extends the definition of environmental management systems to include a general framework for external auditing) and the ISO 14031 (a process by which companies can assess and report on their environmental behavior).[57] The ISO's greatest attribute is its development of management systems, which is why several hundred thousand facilities subscribe to the standards;[58] however, due to the series' substantial implementation cost ($25,000 to $128,000), it is difficult for small and mid-size companies to adopt and implement.[59]

---

[55]*Ibid., infra* n.52.

[56]Global Reporting Initiatives, "GRI and Other Initiatives, ISO 14000," http://www.globalreporting.org/about/iniiso14000.asp (accessed March 27, 2003).

[57]*Ibid., infra* n.54.

[58]McIntosh, Thomas, et al., "International Standards for Corporate Responsibility," *infra* n.26, pp. 26–27.

[59]*Ibid.*

Collectively, these global initiatives are at the forefront in addressing corporate responsibility, and developing practices and codes of conduct that will promote sustainable development and corporate citizenship. However, a number of issues do exist or have yet to be addressed. Among them: conflict resolution between initiatives; level of enforcement, if any—local, national, or international; discrimination against smaller firms, because of the high costs associated with initiatives. Beyond those problems associated with the actual initiatives, skepticism exists among the general public with respect to social reports themselves. Among the questions critics pose: Are the social reports credible, relevant and effective, especially now when every corporation seems to have one? Are social reports a fad trying to lure shareholders back into the market? Are the organizations, themselves, even credible? In a time where corporations are held suspect, corporate social reporting is leading the charge in freeing businesses' tainted image. The recent vim in corporate responsibility has emerged in part to sustain those market economies and regain corporate value, but ultimately the goal is to help companies across the map change their behavior, so as to realize that everyone is a stakeholder in their company.

THE SOCIAL RESPONSIBILITY OF BUSINESS IS TO INCREASE ITS PROFITS

—MILTON FRIEDMAN

In perhaps the seminal article in the challenge to corporate social responsibility, Nobel Prize–winning economist Milton Friedman articulates his objections to the presumption that business owes something extra to our social environment. Consider the recent influx of "socially conscious" firms (or at least those that appear socially conscious) in the marketplace: Ben & Jerry's, The Body Shop, Working Assets Long Distance and others. Is this the direction of the future? Should this be the direction of the future?

When I hear businessmen speak eloquently about the "social responsibilities of business in a free-enterprise system," I am reminded of the wonderful line about the Frenchman who discovered at the age of 70 that he had been speaking prose all his life. The businessmen believe that they are defending free enterprise when they declaim that business is not concerned "merely" with profit but also with promoting desirable "social" ends; that business has a "social conscience" and takes seriously its responsibilities for providing employment, eliminating discrimination, avoiding pollution and whatever else may be the catchwords of the contemporary crop of reformers. In fact they are—or would be if they or anyone else took them seriously—preaching pure and unadulterated socialism. Businessmen who talk this way are unwitting puppets of the intellectual forces that have been undermining the basis of a free society these past decades.

The discussions of the "social responsibilities of business" are notable for their analytical looseness and lack of rigor. What does it mean to say that "business" has responsibilities? Only people can have responsibilities. A corporation is an artificial person and in this sense may have artificial responsibilities, but "business" as a whole cannot be said to have responsibilities, even in this vague sense. The first step toward clarity in examining the doctrine of the social responsibility of business is to ask precisely what it implies for whom.

Presumably, the individuals who are to be responsible are businessmen, which means individual proprietors or corporate executives. Most of the discussion of social responsibility is directed at corporations, so in what follows I shall mostly neglect the individual proprietors and speak of corporate executives.

Milton Friedman, "The Social Responsibility of Business Is to Increase Its Profits." Reprinted by permission of *The New York Times*.

In a free-enterprise, private-property system, a corporate executive is an employee of the owners of the business. He has direct responsibility to his employers. That responsibility is to conduct the business in accordance with their desires, which generally will be to make as much money as possible while conforming to the basic rules of the society, both those embodied in law and those embodied in ethical custom. Of course, in some cases his employers may have a different objective. A group of persons might establish a corporation for an eleemosynary purpose—for example, a hospital or a school. The manager of such a corporation will not have money profit as his objectives but the rendering of certain services.

In either case, the key point is that, in his capacity as a corporate executive, the manager is the agent of the individuals who own the corporation or establish the eleemosynary institution and his primary responsibility is to them.

Needless to say, this does not mean that it is easy to judge how well he is performing his task. But at least the criterion of performance is straightforward and the persons among whom a voluntary contractual arrangement exists are clearly defined.

Of course, the corporate executive is also a person in his own right. As a person, he may have many other responsibilities that he recognizes or assumes voluntarily—to his family, his conscience, his feelings of charity, his church, his clubs, his city, his country. He may feel impelled by these responsibilities to devote part of his income to causes he regards as worthy, to refuse to work for particular corporations, even to leave his job, for example, to join his country's armed forces. If we wish, we may refer to some of these responsibilities as "social responsibilities." But in these respects he is acting as a principal, not as an agent; he is spending his own money or time or energy, not the money of his employers or the time or energy he has contracted to devote to their purposes. If these are "social responsibilities," they are the social responsibilities of individuals, not of business.

What does it mean to say that the corporate executive has a "social responsibility" in his capacity as businessman? If this statement is not pure rhetoric, it must mean that he is to act in some way that is not in the interest of his employers. For example, that he is to refrain from increasing the price of the product in order to contribute to the social objective of preventing inflation, even though a price increase would be in the best interests of the corporation. Or that he is to make expenditures on reducing pollution beyond the amount that is in the best interests of the corporation or that is required by law in order to contribute to the social objective of improving the environment. Or that, at the expense of corporate profits, he is to hire "hard-core" unemployed instead of better qualified available workmen to contribute to the social objective of reducing poverty.

In each of these cases, the corporate executive would be spending someone else's money for a general social interest. Insofar as his actions in accord with his "social responsibility" reduce returns to stockholders, he is spending their money. Insofar as his actions raise the price to customers, he is spending the customers' money. Insofar as his actions lower the wages of some employees, he is spending their money.

The stockholders or the customers or the employees could separately spend their own money on the particular action if they wished to do so. The executive is exercising a distinct "social responsibility," rather than serving as an agent of the stockholders or the customers or the employees, only if he spends the money in a different way than they would have spent it.

But if he does this, he is in effect imposing taxes, on the one hand, and deciding how the tax proceeds shall be spent, on the other.

This process raises political questions on two levels: principle and consequences. On the level of political principle, the imposition of taxes and the expenditure of tax proceeds are governmental functions. We have established elaborate constitutional, parliamentary and judicial provisions to control these functions, to assure that taxes are imposed so far as possible in accordance with the preferences and desires of the public—after all, "taxation without representation" was one of the battle cries of the American Revolution. We have a system of checks and balances to separate the legislative function of imposing taxes and enacting expenditures from the executive function of collecting taxes and administering expenditure programs and from the judicial function of mediating disputes and interpreting the law.

Here the businessman—self-selected or appointed directly or indirectly by stockholders—is to be simultaneously legislator, executive and jurist. He is to decide whom to tax by how much and for what purpose, and he is to spend the proceeds—all this guided only by general exhortations from on high to restrain inflation, improve the environment, fight poverty and so on and on.

The whole justification for permitting the corporate executive to be selected by the stockholders is that the executive is an agent serving the interests of his principal. This justification disappears when the corporate executive imposes taxes and spends the proceeds for "social" purposes. He becomes in effect a public employee, a civil servant, even though he remains in name an employee of a private enterprise. On grounds of political principle, it is intolerable that such civil servants—insofar as their actions in the name of social responsibility are real and not just window-dressing—should be selected as they are now. If they are to be civil servants, then they must be elected through a political process. If they are to impose taxes and make expenditures to foster "social" objectives, then political machinery must be set up to make the assessment of taxes and to determine through a political process the objectives to be served.

This is the basic reason why the doctrine of "social responsibility" involves the acceptance of the socialist view that political mechanisms, not market mechanisms, are the appropriate way to determine the allocation of scarce resources to alternative uses.

On the grounds of consequences, can the corporate executive in fact discharge his alleged "social responsibilities"? On the other hand, suppose he could get away with spending the stockholders' or customers' or employees' money. How is he to know how to spend it? He is told that he must contribute to fighting inflation. How is he to know what action of his will contribute to that end? He is presumably an expert in running his company—in producing a product or selling it or financing it. But nothing about his selection makes him an expert on inflation. Will his holding down the price of his product reduce inflationary pressure? Or, by leaving more spending power in the hands of his customers, simply divert it elsewhere? Or, by forcing him to produce less because of the lower price, will it simply contribute to shortages? Even if he could answer these questions, how much cost is he justified in imposing on his stockholders, customers and employees for this social purpose? What is his appropriate share and what is the appropriate share of others?

And, whether he wants to or not, can he get away with spending his stockholders', customers', or employees' money? Will not the stockholders fire him? (Either the present ones or those who take over when his actions in the name of social responsibility have reduced the corporation's profits and the price of its stock.) His customers and his employees can desert him for other producers and employers less scrupulous in exercising their social responsibilities.

This facet of "social responsibility" doctrine is brought into sharp relief when the doctrine is used to justify wage restraint by trade unions. The conflict of interest is naked and clear when union officials are asked to subordinate the interest of their members to some more general purpose. If the union officials try to enforce wage restraint, the consequence is likely to be wildcat strikes, rank-and-file revolts and the emergence of strong competitors for their jobs. We thus have the ironic phenomenon that union leaders—at least in the U.S.—have objected to Government interference with the market far more consistently and courageously than have business leaders.

The difficulty of exercising "social responsibility" illustrates, of course, the great virtue of private competitive enterprise—it forces people to be responsible for their own actions and makes it difficult for them to "exploit" other people for either selfish or unselfish purposes. They can do good—but only at their own expense.

Many a reader who has followed the argument this far may be tempted to remonstrate that it is all well and good to speak of Government's having the responsibility to impose taxes and determine expenditures for such "social" purposes as controlling pollution or training the hard-core unemployed, but that the problems are too urgent to wait on the slow course of political processes, that the exercise of social responsibility by businessmen is a quicker and surer way to solve pressing current problems.

Aside from the question of fact—I share Adam Smith's skepticism about the benefits that can be expected from "those who affected to trade for the public good"—this argument must be rejected on grounds of principle. What it amounts to is an assertion that those who favor the taxes and expenditures in question have failed to persuade a majority of their fellow citizens to be of like mind and that they are seeking to attain by undemocratic procedures what they cannot attain by democratic procedures. In a free society, it is hard for "good" people to do "good," but that is a small price to pay for making it hard for "evil" people to do "evil," especially since one man's good is another's evil.

I have, for simplicity, concentrated on the special case of the corporate executive, except only for the brief digression on trade unions. But precisely the same argument applies to the newer phenomenon of calling upon stockholders to require corporations to exercise social responsibility (the recent G.M. crusade for example). In most of these cases, what is in effect involved is some stockholders trying to get other stockholders (or customers or employees) to contribute against their will to "social" causes favored by the activists. Insofar as they succeed, they are again imposing taxes and spending the proceeds.

The situation of the individual proprietor is somewhat different. If he acts to reduce the returns of his enterprise in order to exercise his "social responsibility," he is spending his own money, not someone else's. If he wishes to spend his money on such purposes, that is his right and I cannot see that there is any objection to his doing so. In the process, he, too, may impose costs on employees and customers. However, because he is far less likely than a large corporation or union to have monopolistic power, any such side effects will tend to be minor.

Of course, in practice the doctrine of social responsibility is frequently a cloak for actions that are justified on other grounds rather than a reason for those actions.

To illustrate, it may well be in the long-run interest of a corporation that is a major employer in a small community to devote resources to providing amenities to that community or to improving its government. That may make it easier to attract desirable employees, it may reduce the wage bill or lessen losses from pilferage and sabotage or have other worthwhile effects. Or it may be that, given the laws about the deductibility of corporate charitable contributions, the stockholders can contribute more to charities they favor by having the corporation make the gift than by doing it themselves, since they can in that way contribute an amount that would otherwise have been paid as corporate taxes.

In each of these—and many similar—cases, there is a strong temptation to rationalize these actions as an exercise of "social responsibility." In the present climate of opinion, with its widespread aversion to "capitalism," "profits," the "soulless corporation," and so on, this is one way for a corporation to generate goodwill as a by-product of expenditures that are entirely justified in its own self-interest.

It would be inconsistent of me to call on corporate executives to refrain from this hypocritical window-dressing because it harms the foundations of a free society. That would be to call on them to exercise a "social responsibility"! If our institutions, and the attitudes of the public make it in their self-interest to cloak their actions in this way, I cannot summon much indignation to denounce them. At the same time, I can express admiration for those individual proprietors or owners of closely held corporations or stockholders of more broadly held corporations who disdain such tactics as approaching fraud.

Whether blameworthy or not, the use of the cloak of social responsibility, and the nonsense spoken in its name by influential and prestigious businessmen, does clearly harm the foundations of a free society. I have been impressed time and again by the schizophrenic character of many businessmen. They are capable of being extremely farsighted and clear-headed in matters that are internal to their businesses. They are incredibly short-sighted and muddle-headed in matters that are outside their businesses but affect the possible survival of business in general. This short-sightedness is strikingly exemplified in the calls from many businessmen for wage and price guidelines or controls or income policies. There is nothing that could do more in a brief period to destroy a market system and replace it by a centrally controlled system than effective governmental control of prices and wages.

The short-sightedness is also exemplified in speeches by businessmen for social responsibility. This may gain them kudos in the short run. But it helps to strengthen the already too prevalent view that the pursuit of profits is wicked and immoral and must be curbed and controlled by external forces. Once this view is adopted, the external forces that curb the market will not be the social consciences, however highly developed, of the pontificating executives; it will be the iron fist of government bureaucrats. Here, as with price and wage controls, businessmen seem to me to reveal a suicidal impulse.

The political principle that underlies the market mechanism is unanimity. In an ideal free market resting on private property, no individual can coerce any other, all cooperation is voluntary, all parties to such cooperation benefit or they need not participate. There are no values, no "social" responsibilities in any sense other than the shared values and responsibilities of individuals. Society is a collection of individuals and of the various groups they voluntarily form.

The political principle that underlies the political mechanism is conformity. The individual must serve a more general social interest—whether that be determined by a church or a dictator or a majority. The individual may have a vote and say in what is to be done, but if he is overruled, he must conform. It is appropriate for some to require others to contribute to a general social purpose whether they wish to or not.

Unfortunately, unanimity is not always feasible. There are some respects in which conformity appears unavoidable, so I do not see how one can avoid the use of the political mechanism altogether.

But the doctrine of "social responsibility" taken seriously would extend the scope of the political mechanism to every human activity. It does not differ in philosophy from the most explicitly collectivist doctrine. It differs only by professing to believe that collectivist ends can be attained without collectivist means. That is why, in my book *Capitalism and Freedom,* I have called it a "fundamentally subversive doctrine" in a free society, and have said that in such a society, "there is one and only one social responsibility of business—to use its resources and engage in activities designed to increase its profits so long as it stays within the rules of the game, which is to say, engages in open and free competition without deception or fraud."

MAXIMIZING ETHICS AND PROFITS

—Patrick Primeaux, S.M.

Patrick Primeaux offers a practical rejoinder to critics of Friedman, arguing for the possibility of a balance between money and ethics that is based on a theory of profit maximization.

Business is the highest level of human activity and the highest level of social good. Some of the greatest pieces of art the world has ever known are a good meal, a Boeing 747, a BMW, a PC, a CAT scanner, a refrigerator. By any measure, the kind of behavior needed to produce these works of art constitutes the highest level of human activity and the highest level of social good. After all, it is people engaged in business who deliver all the goods and services the community wants—better health care, schools for our children, food for our tables and shelter for our families.

Business demands excellence and creativity. Men and women in business are artists and scientists. The activities in which they engage are like those required to produce a great symphony, a well-written play, a fine painting, a vintage wine, or a new scientific discovery. These activities demand excellence and require an abundance of creativity.

These words appear in the opening chapter of a book John Stieber and I wrote about business ethics.[1] Stieber and I want to reflect a positive and optimistic evaluation of business and of the men and women in business. However, when we read newspapers, watch television, or listen to business people conversing, we know that this positive evaluation of business is not universally accepted. Everyone knows that men and women in business are interested in one thing: money. And, as everyone also knows, men and women in business will do anything that has to be done to make money. That's the name of the game. That's what business is really all about.

If that's the case, why bother talking about ethics? When Milton Friedman claims that the ethical mandate of business is to increase shareholder profit, he's talking about money and he's talking about ethics. Connecting the two, he probably did more than any other theorist to advance business ethics. Now we hear executives of major corporations giving commencement speeches about ethics. "What will it look like on the front page of the *New York Times?*" and "Think of yourself as running for mayor" they propose as guiding principles for ethics in business. What they are advising is business as usual. Do what you have to do to maximize profits, but make it look good to the public and to the Securities and Exchange Commission. We might commend them for their practicality, but why not ask them to be-

---

Patrick Primeaux, S.M., "Maximizing Ethics and Profits." Reprinted by permission of the author.

[1]For a fuller examination of the theory and implications of the argument reflected in this essay, see Patrick Primeaux and John Stieber, *Profit Maximization: The Ethical Mandate of Business* (San Francisco: Austin & Winfield, 1995) and an article of the same title in the *Journal of Business Ethics* 13, no. 4 (1994), pp. 287–94.

come even more practical? Why don't they recommend, as Charles E. Quinn does, that everyone simply invest in a personal paper shredder?

The problem for business and for business ethics is the equation of business with money, specifically bottom-line accounting profits, and the pressure to increase those profits quarterly or annually. That motivating objective is itself reflective of an ethical code. It consists of an ethical principle, and demands a certain kind of behavior consistent with that principle. The organization is structured, people are hired, jobs are described, managers are held accountable, raw materials are acquired and technology engaged to increase that bottom line. Everything and everybody within the company is directed by that profit-maximizing principle and expected to conform to its demands.

Stieber and I want to create another ethical code for business, one which still takes money seriously. We also want to provide a framework or blueprint for business and for people in business to be able to appreciate the ethics of business, and to regulate themselves rather than waiting for political, legal and religious demands to be imposed on them from the outside. In other words, we want to tie business ethics to profit maximization, but to a broader understanding of profit maximization than that usually ascribed to rational, numerical bottom-line accounting profits.

When numbers become more important than anything else, everything and everyone in the company becomes valued in those same mathematical and numerical terms. When people or things are valued for their contribution to increased profit margins, they are identified numerically and treated as such. They are themselves valued simply with respect to their contribution to profits. The philosopher would say that they are objectified for utility. They are treated as objects and valued simply for their contribution to production. It is when this happens that business and men and women in business leave themselves wide open to criticism and to regulation from the law, from philosophy or from religion.

That's the problem with Friedman's ethical imperative. It is too myopic, too focused on bottom-line accounting profits alone and, because of that, values the factors of production only insofar as they are useful for production and for rationally-and-numerically determined profits. It also reflects Friedman's values, what is important to him, how he views people and the world, especially the world of nature which provides the raw resources which go into productivity. It is evident that the values he wants to encourage are focused exclusively on utility, on usefulness to production. Is there not another value system which appreciates people and things for their own positive existence, their own presence in the world, rather than how they can be useful to us? Asking that question raises questions about ourselves.

What are our values? What do we value? Who do we value? How do we value ourselves? The subject and objects of each of these questions, as well as the contexts of the questions themselves, suggest that we are presuming different meanings of the word *value*. In the first case, we're asking about morals or ethics, about behavior. In the second question, we're inquiring about objects. In the third, the focus is on people other than ourselves. The fourth question is about ourselves, about self-identity. However, although used in different ways to ask different questions, the contextual nuances suggest a commonality and continuity of behavior, possessions, others and ourselves. How can all of these be connected?

They are connected by value, and value suggests relationship. To ask questions about value is to ask questions about relationship, about how we perceive ourselves, others—perhaps God—and the objects we possess. Value not only suggests relationships, but similarity and continuity within our perceptions and considerations of the things we have, the people we meet and the persons we are becoming. Today, in our world, that bonding is primarily economic.

The first meaning of the word *value* in *Webster's* is "a fair return or equivalent in goods, services, or money for something exchanged," and the second is "the monetary worth of something: marketable price."[2] The third meaning is "relative worth, utility, or importance," and the fourth is "a numerical quantity assigned or computed." These definitions not only provide answers to our questions, but lead us to conclude that who and what we value, as well as our values, are defined primarily in economic terms: money, utility, numerical quantity. Not only is money an object, it is an object that can be quantified numerically. Its utility, its usefulness, is also quantified numerically.

But, let's not focus on money alone. Surely what we value, as well as our values, cannot be determined by money alone. They can also be determined by what money can buy and what money can provide. Even then, that focus on money is too myopic, as would be any appreciation for economics that would concentrate on money alone, or even on what money can buy. It is that understanding of economics which is misleading, for it subjects economics to numbers and accounting principles.

Profit maximization is not, however, only an accounting notion. There is also an economic definition of profit maximization which is much broader in scope and reference than any accounting formulation. Actually, the two are almost identical, defining profits as total revenues minus total costs (TR − TC). The real difference surfaces within total costs. The accountant would define total costs with respect to fixed costs and variable costs (TC = FC + VC). The economist would widen that definition to include opportunity costs so that total costs involves fixed costs, variable costs and opportunity costs (TC = FC + VC + OC).

So what? The inclusion of opportunity costs within decision making opens the doors to a broader perspective. That broader perspective goes beyond money and numbers. It moves beyond the bottom line to question a whole list of concerns which go into, and contribute to, that bottom-line maximization of profits. In other words, economic profit maximization is not content to focus on the numbers. Economic profit maximization wants to know how those profits are realized.

What are opportunity costs? Opportunity costs are usually defined as the forgone goods and services that could have been produced from a given set of scarce resources that was used to produce some other goods and services. There are two key phrases in this definition of opportunity costs that should help us understand their role in business decision making. The two phrases are "the forgone goods and services" and "from a given set of resources."

Assume that a business has a fixed amount of money from the earnings it has retained to invest for its owners. Further, suppose it decides to start a used car lot in an Amish town. Once these resources ("a given set of resources") are committed to the project, they can

---

[2]Henry Bosley Woolf, ed., *Webster's New Collegiate Dictionary* (Springfield, MA: G. & C. Merriam Company, 1981).

never be used to produce any other goods and services for the community such as health care, education, or housing ("forgone goods and services").

Besides the usual kinds of business considerations associated with this decision (location, lease, hiring, taxes, etc.), there is a serious ethical consideration to be addressed. The Amish do not drive cars. Were the decision makers insensitive to this ethical behavior, the project would fail and the resources would be lost.

If the project were to fail because the management of this company was insensitive to the ethics of the situation, the opportunity costs for the community would be that of a whole set of scarce resources used to produce something consumers did not want, i.e., did not value. These wasted resources can never be used to produce anything else. The opportunity cost for the firm is the loss of money from a set of scarce resources that could have been used for another project.

From a more philosophical perspective there are some implications of opportunity costs we can apply to ourselves as men and women in business as well as to the business itself. First, opportunity costs imply that in every decision, in every choice, there is a negation, a rejection. This means that statements like "it's OK as long as no one gets hurt" become downright silly. Someone or something is always hurt, negated, or rejected in any choice to pursue one opportunity rather than another. Second, opportunity costs remind us that we can't have or do everything because resources are scarce. In other words, opportunity cost decision making serves to make the obvious even more so. Anything and everything is a scarce resource. Third, opportunity costs suggest that every decision about anything is an ethical decision. To choose one thing over another, or one course of action in preference to another, implies values. It also implies good and bad, right and wrong. This is especially the case when decisions are made about scarce resources. The very appreciation of scarcity suggests that any abuse or misuse of any resource is wrong. Fourth, opportunity-cost decision making opens wide the horizons of consideration. It moves beyond any immediate and short-term concerns to refer to implications and considerations for the widest possible scope of reference. It moves beyond numbers to encompass the whole of human experience, the whole of the world's ecology. That is, it encourages us to consider anything and everything that could possibly affect profits—both within and without the company. The establishment of a used-car lot in an Amish community fails precisely because the religious traditions of the people of that community were ignored. In opportunity-cost decision making, nothing can be ignored. To do so would incur opportunity costs, waste scarce resources and would, for that reason, provide the grounding for unethical behavior.

How do we know whether a company is being ethical or not? To do so we would have to investigate its use of scarce resources. Within economics, we have a framework of reference within which to pursue that investigation. We can isolate the factors of production, and examine the costs associated with those factors. The factors of production are, of course, the scarce resources that enter into production.

The factors of production are usually described as four: land, labor-time, creativity/entrepreneurship and capital. The costs associated with land are paid as rent, to labor-time as wages, to creativity-entrepreneurship as profit, to capital as interest. Tying the costs of production to the factors of production implies an ethical imperative based in efficiency. To use these resources inefficiently leads to waste, abuse and misuse. That inefficiency translates into unnecessary costs, and reflects not only inefficiency, but waste of scarce resources.

Since the time of Adam's and Eve's eviction from the Garden of Eden, everything and anything has become a scarce resource. While in the Garden, they had everything they wanted. Why? They had an infinite number of resources available to them. Outside the Garden, they found that resources were limited. Moreover, they quickly discovered that to acquire the things they wanted, these scarce resources had to be used efficiently.

They also quickly discovered that once an animal was slaughtered for food and clothing, that animal would never be able to provide additional food and clothing. There would be other animals, though, and for a time it might have seemed that these existed in limitless, infinite numbers. As time progressed, and as the earth became more and more populated, the number of animals available for food and clothing became more and more scarce. In today's world, we can easily argue from casual observation and ordinary experience, that anything and everything is a scarce resource; that once used for one purpose, the resource no longer exists for any other purpose.

In economics, that realization of the scarcity of resources is translated into the principle of opportunity costs. Actually, the monetary value we attach to human labor and time, as well as to personal creativity, land and even money, is itself an indication of scarcity. Once any of these resources is brought into production, any opportunity for an alternative use is forgone. Measuring its actual use with respect to its potential use, provides an indication of the value of a given resource, i.e., a measure of whether or not the person or thing is employed towards its maximum value or potential. To do otherwise would prove inefficient, for it would involve waste, abuse, or misuse of a valuable and scarce resource. It would also be inefficient, for it would result in unwarranted costs.

The principle of opportunity costs can be assessed personally as well as corporately. Given the many choices we have in life, the college student can choose between preparing for an exam the following day or socializing with friends. As opportunity-cost decision making implies both choice and negation, to choose to spend time and expend energy poring over class notes and text books necessitates the rejection of the company of one's friends. The costs of studying are weighed with the costs of socializing for the scarce resources of time and energy require a choice. To choose one requires the negation of the other. The question to ask is, which will be more efficient? Another question to ask is, which will cost more in the long run?

We need to ask the same question when choosing between two desirable alternatives in business. A really intelligent, responsible and productive secretary who is paid a salary commensurate with market standards, even though contributing more than required or expected of that standard, provides a practical and common example. The decision hinges on capital and the most efficient use of that capital. Should he receive a higher salary, or should that same money—a scarce resource—be used to increase bottom-line accounting profits? Choosing to direct the money towards profits could mean the secretary leaving the firm for higher-salaried employment by another firm. The costs of hiring and training a replacement, perhaps one contributing less than the former secretary, could exceed the costs of a salary raise. In that case, the scarce resource of the original secretary, as well as the scarce resource of capital, would be wasted and misused, especially in the long run. Directly pertaining to ethics, no one would consider the decision bearing on this case to be a good one. With respect to costs, no one would judge this use of the person as well as of capital to be good and efficient.

Perhaps the most abused of the factors of production is that of creativity/entrepreneurship. Although afforded a market-level salary, our exceptionally efficient secretary is not rewarded. Only senior managers and directors are considered worthy of pay for the creativity of their decisions, especially those of bringing creative people into the firm. A creative and entrepreneurial spirit can, however, be found at every level of the organizational structure and also rewarded in a manner proportionate to contribution to profit. Our exemplary secretary should be compensated for her creativity. So also should the janitor who saves the company money by using cleaning supplies sparingly while, at the same time, complying with the dictates of her job description.

Opportunity-cost decision making leads to profit-maximization insofar as it recognizes the scarcity of all of its resources, and uses those resources as efficiently as possible. To evaluate whether a company is profit-maximizing, then, one needs to look beyond bottom-line accounting profits to identify what those profits represent. To do that, one would have to study the costs incurred by each of the factors of production, to assess those costs in terms of opportunity costs, and to evaluate those opportunity costs from a long-term perspective. This kind of assessment would answer the most important question of practical and ethical concern: Are all of the factors of production being used as efficiently as possible?

This perspective commends itself for good business and good business ethics because it originates directly within business theory and practice. It also commends itself because it encourages business to move beyond bottom-line accounting profits to consider people and things not only as valuable for production, but also as valuable in themselves—as scarce resources having value and dignity. It also commends itself because we could then equate good business and good business ethics.

THE DIVINE RIGHT OF CAPITAL

Is Maximizing Returns to Shareholders a Legitimate Mandate?

—MARJORIE KELLY

In response to what she sees as the problems of capitalism—bloated CEO pay, sweatshops, speculative excess to stagnant wages, corporate welfare and environmental indifference—Marjorie Kelly explores the question of whether maximizing shareholder wealth is an appropriate mandate for business. This mandate, she contends, arises from the unconscious belief that property owners (wealth holders, shareholders) matter more than others resulting in an economic aristocracy.

Where does wealth come from? More precisely, where does the wealth of major public corporations come from? Who creates it?

To judge by the current arrangement in corporate America, one might suppose capital creates wealth—which is odd, because a pile of capital sitting there creates nothing. Yet capital-providers (stockholders) lay claim to most wealth that public corporations generate. They also claim the more fundamental right to have corporations managed on their behalf. Corporations are believed to exist for one purpose alone: to maximize returns to shareholders. This principle is reinforced by CEOs, *The Wall Street Journal,* business schools, and the courts. It is the law of the land—much as the divine right of kings was once the law of the land. Indeed, "maximizing returns to shareholders" is universally accepted as a kind of divine, unchallengeable mandate.

It is not in the least controversial. Though it should be.

What do shareholders contribute, to justify the extraordinary allegiance they receive? They take risk, we're told. They put their money on the line, so corporations might grow and prosper. Let's test the truth of this with a little quiz:

Stockholders fund major public corporations—True or False?

False. Or, actually, a tiny bit true—but for the most part, massively false. What's intriguing is that we speak as though it were entirely true: "I have invested in AT&T," we say—imagining AT&T as a steward of our money, with a fiduciary responsibility to take care of it. In fact, "investing" dollars don't go to AT&T but to other speculators. Equity "investments" reach a public corporation only when new common stock is sold—which for major corporations is a rare event. Among the Dow Jones Industrials, only a handful have sold any new common stock in 30 years. Many have sold none in 50 years.

The stock market works like a used car market, as accounting professor Ralph Estes observes in *Tyranny of the Bottom Line.* When you buy a 1989 Ford Escort, the money doesn't go to Ford. It goes to the previous owner. Ford gets the buyer's money only when it sells a new car. Similarly, companies get stockholders' money only when they sell new common stock—which mature companies rarely do. According to figures from the Federal Reserve and the Securities and Exchange Commission, about 99%of the stock out there is "used stock." That is, 99 out of 100 "invested" dollars are trading in the purely speculative market, and never reach corporations.

Public corporations do have the ability to sell new stock. And they do need capital (funds beyond revenue) to operate—for inventory, expansion and so forth. But they get very little of this capital from stockholders. In 1993, for example, corporations needed $555 billion in capital. According to the Federal Reserve, sales of common stock contributed 4% of that. I used this fact in a pull-quote for a magazine article once, and the designer changed it to 40%, assuming it was a typo. It's not. Of all capital public corporations needed in 1993, stockholders provided 4%.

Well, yes, critics will say—that's recently. But stockholders did fund corporations in the past.

Again, only a tiny bit true. Take the steel industry. An accounting study by Eldon Hendriksen examined capital expenditures in that industry from 1900 to 1953, and found that issues of common stock provided only 5% of capital. That was over the *entire first half of the 20th century,* when industry was growing by leaps and bounds.

So, what *do* stockholders contribute, to justify the extraordinary allegiance they receive? Very little. And that's my point.

Equity capital is provided by stockholders when a company goes public, and in occasional secondary offerings later. But in the life of most major companies today, issuance of common stock represents a distant, long-ago source of funds, and a minor one at that. What's odd is that it entitles holders to extract most of the corporation's wealth, forever. Equity investors essentially install a pipeline, and dictate that the corporation's sole purpose is to funnel wealth into it. The pipeline is never to be tampered with—and no one else is to be granted significant access (except executives, whose function is to keep it flowing).

The truth is, the commotion on Wall Street is not about funding corporations. It's about extracting from them.

The productive risk in building businesses is borne by entrepreneurs and their initial venture investors, who do contribute real investing dollars, to create real wealth. Those who buy stock at sixth or seventh hand, or 1,000th hand, also take a risk—but it is a risk speculators take among themselves, trying to outwit one another like gamblers. It has little to do with corporations, except this: Public companies are required to provide new chips for the gaming table, into infinity.

It's odd. And it's connected to a second oddity—that we believe stockholders *are* the corporation. When we say, "A corporation did well," we mean its shareholders did well. The company's local community might be devastated by plant closings, its groundwater contaminated with pollutants. Employees might be shouldering a crushing workload, doing without raises for years on end. Still we will say, "The corporation did well."

One does not see rising employee income as a measure of corporate success. Indeed, gains to employees are losses to the corporation. And this betrays an unconscious bias: that employees are not really part of the corporation. They have no claim on wealth they create, no say in governance and no vote for the board of directors. They're not citizens of corporate society, but subjects.

Investors, on the other hand, may never set foot inside "their" companies, may not know where they're located or what they produce. Yet corporations exist to enrich investors alone. In the corporate society, only those who own stock can vote—like America until the mid-1800s, when only those who owned land could vote. Employees are disenfranchised.

We think of this as the natural law of the free market. It's more accurately the result of the corporate governance structure, which violates free-market principles. In a free market, everyone scrambles to get what they can, and they keep what they earn. In the construct of the corporation, one group gets what another earns.

The oddity of it all is veiled by the incantation of a single, magical word: "ownership." Because we say stockholders "own" corporations, they are permitted to contribute very little, and take quite a lot.

What an extraordinary word. One is tempted to recall Lycophron's comment, during an early Athenian slave uprising against the aristocracy. "The splendour of noble birth is imaginary," he said, "and its prerogatives are based upon a mere word."

GLOBAL CORPORATE CITIZENSHIP

The Leadership Challenge for CEOs and Boards

—WORLD ECONOMIC FORUM

The following is a joint statement by a task force of the World Economic Forum CEOs. The task force recommends a Framework for Action that chief executives, chairmen, board directors and executive management teams can use to develop a strategy for managing their company's impact on society and its relationships with stakeholders. The framework produces a template for a leadership process within the company and is intended to be complementary to the various voluntary corporate citizenship principles and guidelines that have been developed in specific issue areas. Although the statement uses the language of corporate citizenship, the reader should understand that definitions and approaches may vary, with terms such as corporate responsibility, sustainable development and triple bottom line also used by other sources in place of corporate citizenship. The aim of the following effort was not to focus on specific definitions but instead to emphasize the point that these issues are not add-ons but fundamental to core business operations and to identify some key leadership actions that can be adapted by most business leaders to their own circumstances.[1]

A FRAMEWORK FOR ACTION

1. *Provide leadership:* Set the strategic direction for corporate citizenship in your company and engage in the wider debate on globalization and the role of business in development.
    (i) Articulate purpose, principles and values internally and externally.
    (ii) Promote the 'business case' internally.
    (iii) Engage the financial sector.
    (iv) Enter the debate on globalization and the role of business in development.

---

[1]Adapted from introduction to "Global Corporate Citizenship."

2. *Define what it means for your company:* Define the key issues, stakeholders and spheres of influence which are relevant for corporate citizenship in your company and industry.
   (i) Define the issues.
   (ii) Agree on company's spheres of influence.
   (iii) Identify key stakeholders.

3. *Make it happen:* Establish and implement appropriate policies and procedures and engage in dialogue and partnership with key stakeholders to embed corporate citizenship into the company's strategy and operations.
   (i) Put corporate citizenship on the board agenda.
   (ii) Establish internal performance, communication, incentive and measurement systems.
   (iii) Engage in dialogue and partnership.
   (iv) Encourage innovation and creativity.
   (v) Build the next generation of business leaders.

4. *Be transparent about it:* Build confidence by communicating consistently with different stakeholders about the company's principles, policies and practices in a transparent manner, within the bounds of commercial confidentiality.
   (i) Agree what and how to measure.
   (ii) Develop a graduated program for external reporting.
   (iii) Be realistic.

1. Provide Leadership

Set the strategic direction for corporate citizenship in your company and engage in the wider debate on globalization and the role of business in development. Experience has shown that for corporate citizenship to flourish, CEO, board and senior management leadership are essential.

(i) Articulate Purpose, Principles and Values Internally and Externally Business leaders play a crucial role in serving as role models and champions by communicating and behaving in a manner that is consistent with the company's stated principles, values and purpose. Platforms for doing this include:

- Annual general meetings and other briefings with investors.

- Annual report and other corporate publications.

- Regular meetings and communications with employees.

- Interaction with trade, industry and business associations.

- Other focused stakeholder dialogues and communications.

- Non-executive roles on other company boards.

- Conference platforms and media interviews.

- Daily actions that "walk the talk."

(ii) Promote the "Business Case" Internally   Business leaders are uniquely placed in highlighting to their employees in a persuasive manner the costs of "getting it wrong" in terms of economic, social and environmental performance and the business and societal benefits of "getting it right."

(iii) Engage the Financial Sector   The shareholder-driven and short-term nature of the financial markets is often cited as an obstacle to social and environmental innovation both within companies and in the market more generally. Leaders in the financial sector play an important role in increasing awareness of these issues among their peers, but all business leaders can engage proactively with their major institutional investors, bankers and insurers on issues related to their companies' social and environmental risks, innovations and business opportunities.

(iv) Enter the Debate on Globalization and the Role of Business in Development   There is a growing need to ensure that the public debate on these subjects is an open and rational one, backed as much as possible by solid evidence, practical examples and experience of the business contribution to development. Business leaders can play a role by being forthright about the benefits and constructive about the shortcomings of trade, investment and globalization. They can actively engage in dialogues aimed at defining the different roles and responsibilities of governments, business and civil society in helping to make globalization work for more people and countries.

2. Define What It Means for Your Company

Define the key issues, stakeholders and spheres of influence which are relevant for corporate citizenship in your company and industry. Broad areas of action for corporate citizenship can be identified, although the specific issues, dilemmas and strategies will vary for different companies.

(i) Define the Issues   Corporate citizenship is often talked about in the abstract, but it is fundamentally concerned with real and compelling issues. They will vary in nature and importance from industry to industry and location to location. The environmental issues faced by an energy company, for example, will be of a different magnitude compared to those faced by a pharmaceutical company, and tackling HIV/AIDS in the workplace will take on added intensity for operating units in Southern Africa, compared to those in Europe. At the same time, expectations of a company or industry sector's responsibility for addressing a particular issue are likely to vary between different stakeholders. Setting the boundaries of a company's role and responsibility *vis à vis* government and other actors is therefore often a question of dialogue and negotiation. In most cases, however, global corporate citizenship will include elements of:

- *Good corporate governance and ethics*—including compliance with the law, existing regulations and international standards, efforts to prevent bribery and corruption and other issues addressed through ethical conduct policies or statements of business principles.

- *Responsibility for people*—for example, product and employee safety programs to ensure that consumers and people involved in the sourcing, production and distribution of products are not placed at risk; also human and labor rights which may include equal opportunities, non-discrimination, prevention of child labor, freedom of association and fair wages within the workforce and along supply chains and in some cases, issues such as indigenous peoples' rights and the use of security forces in zones of conflict.

• *Responsibility for environmental impacts*—for example, maintaining environmental quality, adopting clean and eco-efficient production processes, sharing environmental technologies and for some industries, engaging in global challenges such as climate change and bio-diversity protection.

• *Broader contribution to development*—efforts to contribute to broader social and economic benefits in host countries and communities, for example: building local business linkages; spreading international business standards; increasing access to essential products and services for poorer communities such as credit, water, energy, medicines, education and information technology; and so on. These contributions to development may be part of a company's core business operations or part of its social investment, philanthropic or community relations activities, depending on the industry sector and company concerned.

(ii) Agree on Company's Spheres of Influence   Companies and business leaders have different spheres of influence, where they have different levels of authority and ability to manage their impacts and to influence the actions of their own employees, stakeholders and others. These spheres of influence include:

• *Core business operations*—business leaders have their greatest authority and responsibility within their own business activities, in the manner in which they

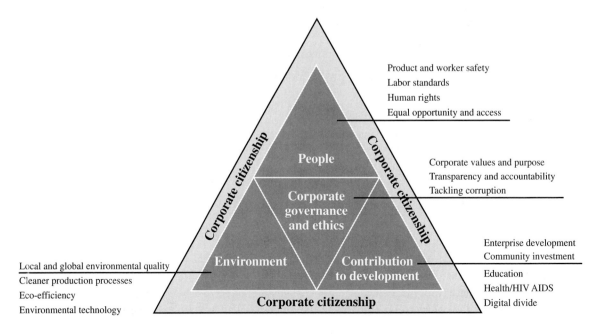

source, produce, market, distribute and in certain cases dispose of their products and services. Their primary focus should therefore be on their core activities in the workplace, the marketplace and along their supply chain. Companies can have an especially valuable influence and multiplier impact through their supply chain, although in many cases joint ventures and other ownership structures along the supply chain limit the level of direct influence that a head office can exert.

- *Host communities*—for companies with a major physical presence, the surrounding communities where they operate are another important sphere of influence where they need to consult with community leaders to address issues of common interest and concern. In some cases, "host communities" may cover a wide geographic area or region.

- *Industry associations*—many business leaders have relationships with trade, industry and business associations, ranging from chambers of commerce and organizations of employers, to sector bodies and issue-specific business leadership groups. This is another sphere of influence where they can support innovative thinking and new approaches to tackling wider economic, social and environmental issues.

- *Public policy realm*—many companies, especially major investors, are engaged in public policy dialogues either directly or through their trade and industry associations, at the local, national and international levels. Although not traditionally considered an aspect of corporate citizenship, this is an area where the private sector can have an important impact and where transparency and alignment with other corporate activities is increasingly important.

(iii) Identify Key Stakeholders (i.e., those who contribute to the success of the corporation and those who are affected by it). As with issues and spheres of influence, a company's stakeholders will fall into similar broad categories, with variations depending on industry sector and other circumstances:

- *Investors, customers and employees* are important stakeholders for almost all companies. Many have long-standing experience on defining and communicating with these groups on a wide range of issues including social, ethical and environmental issues.

- *Other stakeholders* may or may not be important depending on the company and industry sector. They may include business partners, industry associations, local communities, trade unions, non-governmental organizations, research and academic institutions, the media and government bodies—from local municipalities to regional, state and national governments and international bodies such as those in the United Nations system.

3. Make It Happen

Establish and implement appropriate policies and procedures and engage in dialogue and partnership with key stakeholders to embed corporate citizenship into the company's strategy and operations. All the right words and statements will achieve little without embedding the company's principles and values and its commitment to corporate citizenship in the way people carry out and are supported in their daily work.

(i) Put Corporate Citizenship on the Board Agenda   For example, by establishing appropriate board policies and structures that embed corporate citizenship in the strategic direction of the company and monitor social and environmental performance. These structures can include board committees, external advisory panels and selection of diverse non-executive directors. Recent research in the United States and Europe by the U.S.-based Conference Board, the International Business Leaders Forum and SustainAbility indicates that a growing number of companies are establishing board committees focused on ethics, environment, corporate responsibility and similar issues.

(ii) Establish Internal Performance, Communication, Incentive and Measurement Systems   These form the heart of embedding corporate citizenship into a company's "DNA" and senior executives play a vital role in ensuring that management systems are developed and implemented in a manner that is appropriate to the company's purpose, values and operational circumstances.

(iii) Engage in Dialogue and Partnership   Having identified the company's stakeholders, managers at all levels of the company are important intermediaries in building opportunities for productive dialogue and partnership, but senior management has an especially important outreach role particularly on sensitive and/or strategically important issues and especially with key stakeholders.

(iv) Encourage Innovation and Creativity   Innovative new technologies, products and services can help to address many environmental and social challenges. By creating incentives and support for social and eco-innovation inside the company and encouraging external partnerships with relevant innovators, researchers and customers, business leaders can help to provide a framework for new product development that meets business objectives, as well as other development needs. Examples include carbon emissions trading initiatives, energy efficient products and technologies, innovative medical and education pricing mechanisms, social and eco-labelling, sustainable product sourcing, fair trading networks and so on.

(v) Build the Next Generation of Business Leaders   Leadership development is an important element of "making it happen" and today's business leaders play a vital role in helping to develop tomorrow's. They can ensure that issues of corporate citizenship form an integral part of mentoring and coaching initiatives and executive development programs. They can also influence the teaching and research of corporate citizenship in business schools and act as role models for business students.

4. Be Transparent About It

Build confidence by communicating consistently with different stakeholders about the company's principles, policies and practices in a transparent manner, within the bounds of commercial confidentiality. One of the most consistent demands that companies are facing from different stakeholders, ranging from institutional investors to social and environmental activists, is to be more transparent about their wider economic, social and environmental performance.

(i) Agree What and How to Measure   In most companies communication efforts are initially focused internally to identify what to measure and how to measure it, in consultation with employees and key business partners, but in some companies also in consultation with external stakeholders. Business leaders play a role in agreeing on the most appropriate indicators or other methods for assessing the company's performance and directing and monitoring progress against these.

(ii) Develop a Graduated Program for External Reporting   Once the company has decided how best to evaluate its progress against the issues or stakeholders identified as being important, senior management has a role to play in communicating this externally and in ensuring that such communication is regular and consistent. If problems occur, CEO or senior management involvement, openness and timely discussion are important in order to build or sustain trust.

(iii) Be Realistic   There is a danger of trying to move too fast, or promising too much in terms of organizational change and other deliverables, which can result in the creation of unrealistic expectations and/or low trust amongst stakeholders, both inside and outside the company. Executive management teams play an important role in setting the pace and managing expectations by agreeing on clear strategies, timetables or roadmaps for implementing the company's evolving commitments to corporate citizenship.

THE CASE FOR ACTION

For most business leaders there is a compelling case for taking action on issues relating to global corporate citizenship:

- First, an individual business case, that in today's world good corporate citizenship makes sound business sense. It is increasingly in the shareholders' interests for a company to have a clear purpose and set of values, not just a matter of public relations and avoiding negative publicity.

- Second, a broader case, that business prospers in societies that are prosperous. As such, business leaders and the owners of businesses have a direct interest in the process of globalization continuing and extending its benefits to more people around the world.

A detailed analysis of the "Case for Action," including a list of recent research and surveys undertaken in this area, is available on the World Economic Forum website.

The "Business Case"

Producing safe goods and services that customers want to buy and doing so profitably and within the law, form the crucial basis for being a good corporate citizen, without which business can offer little else to society over the longer term. There is growing anecdotal and empirical evidence that companies are better able to achieve this by: having a clear sense of purpose and values; taking into account the interests of a broad set of stakeholders, including but not only shareholders; and actively managing their wider economic, social and environmental impacts. Over the past decade, largely as a result of changing societal expectations of business and the challenges of operating in new markets, these factors have become more important drivers that can either enhance or undermine a company's financial performance.

A growing number of research projects and surveys have highlighted the linkages between the quality of a company's stakeholder relationships and/or its wider economic, social and environmental performance, both real and perceived, and key value drivers such as:

- Risk profile and risk management.

- Ability to attract, motivate and retain talented employees.

- Reputation and brand equity.

- Effectiveness at learning and innovation, especially in complex and dynamic environments.

- Investor relations and access to capital, especially in terms of the growing socially responsible investment community.

- Competitiveness and market positioning, in terms of gaining entry to new markets and building or sustaining customer loyalty in existing markets.

- Operational efficiency, in terms of reducing input and transaction costs, increasing process efficiencies and improving quality of products and services.

- Licence to operate, in terms of responding to and influencing regulation, as well as public opinion and confidence.

This is not to say that doing what is right will always pay or that there will always be a "win-win" situation without any trade-offs. Sometimes costs will be incurred or opportunities forgone that outweigh financial gains, especially in the short term, due to the need to adhere to the company's business principles and values, its risk management criteria and/or its voluntary standards that go beyond legal compliance. Defining what these are and communicating to investors and other stakeholders how they are likely to influence the company's long-term and short-term performance is a key element of business leadership.

Building Prosperous Societies and Sharing the Benefits of Globalization

There is little doubt that legitimate and legal businesses prosper in societies where:

- The citizens are educated and healthy, with freedom of expression and movement and access to opportunity.

- There is democracy, with the government operating effectively in terms of collecting taxes, promulgating sensible regulation within a liberalized and competitive economic environment, facilitating required investments in physical and social infrastructure and services, providing a fair and effective framework for commercial law and ensuring an absence of corruption.

- There is a vibrant private sector, with a growing small and medium-sized enterprise sector and an efficient and effective financial services sector.

- There is physical safety and the absence of violent conflict.

Only 4% of Americans surveyed in 2000 by a *BusinessWeek*/Harris Poll agreed that U.S. corporations should have only one purpose— to make the most profit for their shareholders—and their pursuit of that goal would be the best for America in the long run. 95% agreed that U.S. corporations should have more than one purpose and that they also owe something to their workers and the communities in which they operate. Too much corporate power?

Source: *BusinessWeek,* September 2000.

During 2001, the U.S.-based Conference Board, working with the Asian Institute of Management, Instituto Ethos in Brazil and the International Business Leaders Forum, undertook one of the largest ever CEO surveys on the role of business in society. Over 700 leading CEOs responded from Europe, Asia, Africa, the Middle East, the United States and Brazil. Economic and political stability and the availability of an educated and skilled workforce were cited as the two most important factors for them to continue to succeed as a business in the future. The CEOs perceived their roles in addressing these factors as partnership first and leadership second. The two factors ranked as most important to their future success in addressing broader societal issues were more effective management within the company of the company's external involvements and clear leadership from government.

Source: "The New Role of Business in Society: A Global CEO Survey," The Conference Board, 2002.

In today's world there are more opportunities than ever before to build such societies, but enormous challenges. No sector has the capacity to address these challenges alone. Governments and inter-governmental institutions have a more critical role than ever, but they cannot do it alone. The power and creativity of the market needs to be mobilized more than ever before, but is insufficient on its own. An active and open civil society and civic engagement is crucial, but not enough. New modalities of interaction and joint problem solving, both formal and voluntary, need to be developed. While the public sector has primary responsibility for creating effective domestic and international institutions and investing in human development, the private sector has an important contribution to make.

Against this backdrop, business leaders have a direct interest in working with each other and with governments, inter-governmental institutions and civil society organizations to harness the opportunities and resolve the challenges posed by globalization. Failure to develop these new approaches and failure to gain and sustain public support for globalization may seriously undermine progress on trade and investment. This in turn may undermine not only business opportunities and economic growth, but also the potential to reduce poverty and to invest in environmental sustainability.

Companies from all sectors and of all sizes can make a contribution. Small, medium and micro-enterprises have an especially important role to play in job creation, in raising productivity levels and in helping to lift people out of poverty. But so do large-scale and multinational companies. For many citizens business in general and multinational companies in particular represent the "face" and key drivers of globalization and, rightly or wrongly, they are often seen as part of the problem rather than part of the solution. Business leaders need to demonstrate their ability and willingness, and their existing efforts and experiences, in being part of the solution to the challenges of globalization, either individually or in partnership with others.

The UN estimates that the number of transnational corporations has increased from some 37,000 in 1990 to over 60,000 in 2001, with around 800,000 foreign affiliates and millions of suppliers and distributors along their value chains. Private sector capital flows to developing countries, driven largely by these companies, now outstrip official development assistance (ODA). There are growing calls from politicians, academics and activists for an increase in ODA. Even if such an increase occurs, however, the role of trade and private investment cannot be ignored. According to the World Bank, developing countries stand to gain over three times the $43 billion they get annually in overseas aid from further trade liberalization—enough to lift an additional 300 million people out of poverty by 2015.

As stated at the outset, the primary duty of companies must be to meet market needs through the efficient and profitable use of resources, thereby preserving and expanding the invested capital of shareholders, while taking into account the interests of a broader set of stakeholders. Efficient allocation of resources is what drives economic growth, and economic growth is the *sine qua non* of improved living standards. As the primary agent of economic growth in market economies, the core responsibility of business to society is therefore to produce safe and cost-effective goods and services thereby generating profits, creating jobs and building wealth.

Having said this, business cannot afford to ignore the wider social, economic and environmental impacts of its activities, both positive and negative. Nor can it ignore the wider challenges faced by governments in terms of investing in human development, infrastructure and institutions, both national and international, that help to create a sound enabling environment and healthy societies. By supporting governments, inter-governmental organizations and civil society in creating such an enabling environment and building such societies, business will prosper over the longer term.

EXAMPLES

There are numerous examples of individual CEOs and their companies addressing some or all of the points outlined in the *Framework for Action.* The following examples focus on "collective leadership" at the national, global or industry sector level. Many of them involve not only the private sector, but also the public sector and civil society organizations. Examples of other partnerships and individual company profiles can be found on the websites of the companies and other organizations listed in the acknowledgements.

The Global Compact was proposed by UN Secretary General Kofi Annan at Davos in January 1999. He called on business leaders to embrace and enact within their own corporate activities nine core principles derived from universally accepted agreements on human rights, labor and the environment. Today the Global Compact brings together several hundred companies, with some of the world's leading trade union bodies, human rights and environmental organizations in a global learning forum, policy dialogues and variety of development projects. Companies engage in the initiative through the written support of their CEOs. (www.unglobalcompact.org).

Tackling Global Health Issues

CEO leadership has been central to the establishment of a number of international initiatives to address global health concerns. *The World Economic Forum Global Health Initiative (GHI)* is designed to foster greater private sector engagement in the global battle against HIV/AIDS, tuberculosis and malaria. In cooperation with the World Health Organization and UNAIDS, the GHI brings together businesses, NGOs, civil society and academic institutions in a partnership, focusing on corporate best practices, resource gaps, partnership opportunities, philanthropy and the role of business in advocacy. (www.weforum.org). *The Global Business Council on HIV/AIDS* (www.businessfightsaids.org) is an international group of business leaders dedicated to advocating for an increased business response to AIDS both in the workplace and in the community. *The Global Alliance for Vaccines and Immunization* (www.vaccinealliance.org) was officially launched in January 2000 at Davos, with a mission of combining public and private resources and competencies to support immunization activities. It is a coalition of governments, the WHO, UNICEF and the World Bank; philanthropic foundations; the International Federation of Pharmaceutical Manufacturers Associations (IFPMA); and technical and research institutes.

Overcoming the Digital Divide

CEOs in the ICT sector and beyond have engaged in a variety of policy dialogues and practical initiatives to bridge the "digital divide" both within and between nations. Examples include: the G8 *Digital Opportunity Task Force* (www.dotforce.org) which consisted of leaders from the public, private and not-for-profit sectors; the UN's multi-stakeholder *ICT Task Force* (www.unicttaskforce.org); and the *World Economic Forum's Global Digital Divide Initiative* (www.weforum.org/digitaldivide). Business leaders are also supporting practical projects such as the Digital Partnership (www.iblf.org/digitalpartnership) and NetAid (www.netaid.org); and others such as those listed on the World Economic Forum website.

Investing in Sustainable Development

This has been an area of increased CEO leadership. The International Chamber of Commerce (www.iccwbo.org) and World Business Council for Sustainable Development (www.wbcsd.org) have established *Business Action for Sustainable Development* (www.basd-action.net) as a network and platform to provide business input and partnership examples to the World Summit for Sustainable Development in 2002.

Promoting Good Corporate Governance

Business leaders are playing a role in several initiatives to promote good corporate governance. Examples include: *The International Corporate Governance Network,* pension funds and financial institutions with over $8 trillion in assets under management working towards global convergence on standards of governance (www.icgn.org); and business support for *Transparency International* to tackle corruption. (www.transparency.org). Another aspect of good governance is the efforts to promote sustainability reporting such as the *Global Reporting Initiative.* (www.globalreporting.org).

Corporate Citizenship at the Sector Level

The World Business Council for Sustainable Development and UNEP (www.uneptie.org) have played an important role in promoting sector-based initiatives for sustainable development in industries as diverse as mobility, cement, pulp and paper, information technology, banking and finance. Other examples include the *E7 network* of electricity companies (www.E7.org); the *International Hotels Environment Initiative* (www.ihei.org); and the *Global Mining Initiative.* (www.globalmining.com).

Supporting National Development

At the national level business leaders are supporting initiatives focused on goals such as education, local enterprise and job creation and rural development. Examples include: *Philippine Business for Social Progress* (www.pbsp.org.ph); the *National Business Initiative in South Africa* (www.nbi.org.za); *Instituto Ethos in Brazil* (www.ethos.org.br); *Business in the Community* in the UK (www.bitc.org.uk); and *Landcare* in Australia. (www.landcareaustralia.com.au).

Engaging Tomorrow's Leaders

Today's business leaders are supporting networks such as the *World Economic Forum's Global Leaders for Tomorrow,* which consists of young leaders from the public and private sectors and civil society, and *AIESEC,* the world's largest student-run organization (www.aiesec.org) to promote sustainable development and corporate citizenship. A small but growing number of business schools have started to invest in research and teaching in this area supported by some CEOs (see www.aspeninstitute.org/isib for some leading examples).

SURVEYS FIND MANY CONSUMERS HOLD COMPANIES RESPONSIBLE FOR THEIR ACTIONS

—PricewaterhouseCoopers,
Charles Fombrun and
The Reputation Institute

In the first global survey of its kind, 40% of 22,000 consumers around the world reported that during 1999 they have responded negatively to actions by a company perceived as not socially responsible. Half of this number, or one in five worldwide, reported avoiding a company's product or speaking out against it to others. These results are consistent with a U.S. survey sponsored by PricewaterhouseCoopers and The Reputation Institute, conducted online, which found that a surprising number of consumers said they act on their feelings about companies at the cash register. In fact, a quarter of the 10,830 Reputation Institute survey respondents said that during 1999 they had boycotted a company's products or urged others to do so when they didn't agree with its policies and actions. In looking at the final list, consider whether any of these firms might find themselves in different positions if the survey were conducted today!

WE KNOW YOUR RQ. DO YOU?

Want to know what stakeholders really think of your company? Wish you could find out how they rate you compared with the competition?

The Harris-Fombrun Reputation Quotient[SM] (RQ) is designed to help identify the relative placement of your company's reputation among competitors in the marketplace. It also reveals the areas that might be weakening your position. Developed jointly by Harris Interactive and Professor Charles Fombrun of New York University's Stern School of Business and Executive Director of the Reputation Institute (*www.reputations.org*), RQ is a syndicated study that draws on Harris Interactive's global database of more than 6.2 million cooperative respondents.

WHAT DOES RQ MEASURE?

We know what drives your company's reputation, and who you have to please. The Reputation Quotient study uncovers what key stakeholder groups—the General Public, Customers, Corporate Employees, General Investors and Consumer Boycotters—think about your company. It tells you how they feel about the six dimensions that are the key components of every company's reputation, as well as the *20 attributes* that make up those dimensions. The study can help you identify ways you can leverage this information to your reputation's advantage.

- Emotional Appeal: How much the company is liked, admired and respected.

- Products & Services: Perceptions of the quality, innovation, value and reliability of the company's products and services.

- Financial Performance: Perceptions of the company's competitiveness, profitability, growth prospects and risk.

- Vision & Leadership: How much the company demonstrates a clear vision, strong leadership, and an ability to recognize and capitalize on market opportunities.

- Workplace Environment: Perceptions of how well the company is managed, what it's like to work there and the quality of its employees.

- Social Responsibility: Perceptions of the company as having high standards in its dealings with people, good causes and the environment.

Data from the RQ study are carefully weighted to ensure that the sample is representative of the specified population. The RQ can also be administered by telephone, by mail or in person when online interviews are not possible.

THE 20 ATTRIBUTES OF REPUTATION

The Harris-Fombrun Reputation Quotient develops a company's rating among competitors based on 20 attributes comprising the six dimensions of reputation.

- *Emotional Appeal*
  Have a good feeling about the company.
  Admire and respect the company.
  Trust the company a great deal.

- *Products & Services*
  Stands behind its products and services.
  Develops innovative products and services.
  Offers high quality products and services.
  Offers products and services that are a good value for the money.

- *Financial Performance*
  Has a strong record of profitability.
  Looks like a low-risk investment.

Looks like a company with strong prospects for future growth.
Tends to outperform its competitors.

- *Vision & Leadership*
  Has excellent leadership.
  Has a clear vision for its future.
  Recognizes and takes advantage of market opportunities.

- *Workplace Environment*
  Is well-managed.
  Looks like a good company to work for.
  Looks like a company that would have good employees.

- *Social Responsibility*
  Supports good causes.
  Is an environmentally responsible company.
  Maintains high standards in the way it treats people.

PURPOSE OF THE STUDY

To identify the *companies* that a representative sample of Americans hold in highest regard, and to rate those companies based on the six dimensions of reputation using the Harris-Fombrun Reputation Quotient[SM] (RQ). *The Wall Street Journal* published these results on the front page of its Marketplace section on September 23, 1999.

HOW WAS THE STUDY CONDUCTED?

The study was carried out in two phases during July 1999 and August 1999. In Phase 1, Harris Interactive conducted online and telephone interviews with 4,500 respondents throughout the U.S. Respondents were asked to nominate the companies they believed to have the best and worst reputations. The nomination process utilized both open-ended questions (i.e., unprompted), as well as close-ended questions using a prompted list of 60 companies developed by an expert panel. In Phase 2, another 10,830 respondents provided detailed ratings of the 30 best-regarded companies and a control group of 10 other companies.

The 40 companies selected to be rated (i.e., the 30 RQ Gold companies and the Comparison 10) were based on the number of nominations received in Phase 1. It is important to note that a company did not have to have been included in the prompt list in Phase 1 (the Nomination Phase) in order to be included in Phase 2 (the RQ Rating Phase). In fact, 12 of the 30 companies that make up the RQ Gold had not appeared on the prompt list for the nomination phase.

Final results were weighted to be representative of the U.S. adult population. Weighting variables included both demographic and other, non-demographic variables.

RQ scores were then calculated for each company based on respondents' ratings (using 7-point scales) on the 20 individual attributes. Each company's RQ was calculated by summing the ratings on the 20 attributes as a percentage of the total possible score (i.e., 7×20). Each of the 40 rated companies was evaluated by an average of 445 respondents.

Each RQ rating has an "estimated sampling tolerance" of $+/-$ 1.5. In comparing any two RQ scores, a difference of 1.96 would be considered significantly different at the 90% confidence level.

THE 30 BEST-REGARDED COMPANIES IN AMERICA

1. Johnson & Johnson
2. Coca-Cola
3. Hewlett-Packard
4. Intel
5. Ben & Jerry's
6. Wal-Mart
7. Xerox
8. Home Depot
9. Gateway
10. Disney
11. Dell
12. General Electric
13. Lucent
14. Anheuser-Busch
15. Microsoft
16. Amazon.com
17. IBM
18. Sony
19. Yahoo!
20. AT&T
21. FedEx
22. Procter & Gamble
23. Nike
24. McDonald's
25. Southwest Airlines
26. AOL
27. Daimler-Chrysler
28. Toyota
29. Sears
30. Boeing

THE ETHICS OF MARKETING GOOD CORPORATE CONDUCT

—Mary Lyn Stoll

Companies that contribute to charitable organizations rightly hope that their philanthropic work will also be good for the bottom line. Marketers of good corporate conduct must be especially careful, however, to market such conduct in a morally acceptable fashion. Although marketers typically engage in mild deception or take artistic license when marketing goods and services, these sorts of practices are far more morally troublesome when used to market good corporate conduct. The author below argues that although mild deception is not substantially worrisome with respect to the marketing of most goods and services, it is a far greater moral blunder to use such methods in the marketing of good corporate character. These erode trust and demonstrate a lack of adequate respect for the moral good. In light of these concerns, the author suggests that such practices must be re-examined when applied to the marketing of good corporate conduct. Finally, she develops a revised set of ethical guidelines that are needed in order to address the problems peculiar to the marketing of morally praiseworthy behavior.

Companies that contribute to charitable organizations rightly hope that these contributions will not go unnoticed by consumers, investors and members of local communities. Whether it is a line of acknowledgement in a brochure for Earth Day or a national advertising campaign, companies want consumers to know about the good that they do in the hopes that their good deeds might also be good for the bottom line.

In one sense, this is utterly unproblematic. Good companies are rewarded for good deeds and this in turn encourages other companies to follow suit in giving back to the community. Companies that publicly proclaim their desire to be a positive force in the community will also be more likely to face continued public scrutiny, and this will in turn provide a further incentive to avoid wrongdoing. In another sense, however, advertising concerning corporate donations can be morally problematic. When a company spends far more on advertising their good deeds than it spends on the deeds themselves, it is questionable whether or not such actions are truly morally praiseworthy and whether or not this sort of advertising is unacceptably misleading. Although advertising campaigns are generally less than forthright concerning all of the relevant facts, mild deception in marketing corporate character is a much more serious offense. When advertising campaigns concerning corporate philanthropy are selectively advanced as a means of reacting to negative public perceptions resulting from prior misdeeds, this too raises serious ethical concerns. At the same time, however, the benefits of positive publicity for good deeds must not be undercut as an incentive for companies to engage in morally acceptable behavior. A set of guidelines for dealing with the marketing of good corporate conduct is needed in order to deal with these sorts of issues. Thus, standard views of marketing ethics must be adjusted to deal with the moral peculiarities of marketing good deeds. In this paper, I will begin with standard views of marketing ethics and then discuss how such accounts must be revised in order to deal with the peculiarities of marketing corporate good conduct. I will then use two case studies, one of unacceptable marketing of corporate conduct and one of very careful marketing of good corporate conduct, to suggest more adequate guidelines towards which business persons in marketing may turn when formulating advertising campaigns concerning good corporate conduct.

I. STANDARD VIEWS OF MARKETING ETHICS

Since the primary justification for the market is that it is effective in meeting consumers' desires for goods and services, it follows that marketing tactics ought not undermine the effective performance of this function. To be effective in meeting consumer needs, however, the market must be one in which exchange is truly voluntary so that consumers will be able to make informed decisions in procuring the goods and services they actually want. According to David Holley, marketing ethics includes at least three major tenets: (1) Both the buyer and seller must be adequately informed concerning what is purchased and what is paid for that purchase. (2) Neither buyer nor seller is compelled through coercion, severely restricted alternatives or other relevant constraints on the ability to choose. And (3) Both buyer and seller are capable of making a rational decision concerning the transaction (Holley, 1987). Without these sorts of constraints in place, buyers and sellers will not be able to trust one another. Without such trust the parties involved will find the business transaction much more cumbersome and time consuming than it would be if each party adhered to such minimal ethical guidelines. Apart from the expected utility for both consumers and businesses that results from such a system, one might also hope that both parties would adhere to these guidelines out of a respect for one of the most basic of moral obligations: a respect for others' ability to make informed autonomous decisions for themselves. Whether one ultimately favors a Utilitarian, Kantian, Contractarian, or virtue based ethic, there are certainly good moral reasons on any one of these accounts to be honest, non-coercive and non-deceptive in business transactions.

The extent to which market practices actually meet these criteria is still a matter of intense debate. John Kenneth Galbraith, for instance, has argued that business does not simply satisfy consumer desires and needs (Galbraith, 1985). Galbraith claims that advertisers coerce us by aiding in the creation of consumer desires that may be in conflict with the greater good. Advertisers may also induce desires that are contrary to a more full and satisfying life that individuals would be more likely to pursue if not for a constant barrage of advertisements inducing slavish devotion to procuring frivolous goods and services. This poses moral problems in creating a society in which individual virtue is fostered above base materialism.

Others, such as Theodore Levitt, would argue that the virtues of non-deception, non-coercion and honesty in advertising ought to be more circumscribed. These theorists would defend practices of puffery in which sellers make exaggerated or fanciful claims with respect to a product. Although such practices are clearly more a matter of persuasive tactics than of simply providing customers with the information necessary to making well reasoned decisions, one might argue that such mild deception is morally acceptable and may even serve a social good. In this regard, Levitt has argued that this sort of advertising can help to elevate the mundane aspects of everyday existence with imaginative promise serving a function more akin to art than huckstering (Levitt, 1970). Robert Arrington has further argued that so long as the pursuit of desires fostered or even created by business is consciously affirmed by the individual, autonomy and rationality are not compromised (Arrington, 1982).

Richard Lippke objects to this line of reasoning arguing that the net effect of mass-advertising does in fact induce beliefs, desires and attitudes that encourage the suppression of rational decision making and thereby the suppression of autonomous individuals who define themselves through these sorts of decisions. Lippke maintains that the frequency with which individuals are subjected to such ads and the repetitive nature of the ads are akin to oppression by a very loud and persistent bully who simply will not give one the time or space to think for oneself. Targeting the vulnerable, legitimizing emotional appeals, oversimplifying claims, relying upon superficiality and encouraging shoddy standards for proof of claims are all common practices in mass advertising that serve to subvert free, rational, and autonomous decision making. This barrage of advertising teaches individuals that highly selective representation of information relevant to decision making and the overstatement of possible benefits are legitimate means of affecting the decision-making practices of others. Again, these practices are antithetical to encouraging rational self-determination (Lippke, 1989). Lippke sums up his objections to standard marketing practices as follows:

> *(These messages) tell individuals . . . that they cannot believe or trust what others say, that anything (or nothing!) can be proved, that evidence contrary to one's claims may be ignored and that words can mean whatever anyone wants them to mean. They tell persons that success in communication is a matter of persuading others no matter how it is done. Such attitudes about thought and communication starkly oppose the habits and attitudes constitutive of critical competence: clarity, rigor, precision, patience, honesty, effort, etc. (Lippke, 1989, p. 45).*

Lippke further objects to standard mass marketing practices in so far as such practices allow advertisers to define the ideal of the good life by manipulating our desires and by exploiting our insecurities rather than allowing individuals the mental space to think critically for themselves about what is constitutive of the good life. According to Lippke, at best the mass onslaught of advertising to which we are subjected distracts us from the things that truly matter to us such as developing friendships or dealing with personal flaws and insecurities in a clearheaded way. At worst, mass advertising exploits our insecurities in order to increase sales and deprives us collectively of critical thinking tools needed to make free and well-reasoned decisions. Thus, Lippke argues for even greater restraint in marketing practices in order to assure that critical reasoning skills are fostered and that notions of what constitutes the good life are well reasoned rather than merely market manipulated (Lippke, 1989).[1]

II. MORAL PROBLEMS PECULIAR TO THE MARKETING OF CORPORATE GOOD CONDUCT

Clearly there is much debate concerning the degree to which standard advertising practices in either particular cases or *en masse* are morally problematic. One might reasonably argue that a certain amount of deception in advertising is relatively harmless so long as consumers bear in mind the extent to which our culture presupposes the principle of *caveat emptor* and the extent to which advertisers may take creative license in depicting a symbolic imagery with which they hope a product will be associated.[2] One might also reasonably argue that advertising, especially in mass quantities and constant doses, does in fact threaten rational autonomy and ought to be reformed so as to truly respect individuals by fostering practices of non-coercion, and non-deception as well as critical reasoning skills. But when it comes to marketing good corporate conduct as morally praiseworthy, the stakes are raised both for those who hope to protect consumers from morally unacceptable business practices and for businesses that hope good corporate conduct will also be good for the bottom line. Here, I will argue that the marketing of good corporate conduct represents a very special case of advertising in which it is especially important that such marketing is carried out in a responsible fashion.

In an increasingly global economy with a relatively weak system of international law, consumers need to know that they can depend upon the media to serve as a watchdog over companies that engage in unacceptable behavior. Even if government cannot punish the errant company, surely public moral outrage will often prove just as sure a punishment as any regulatory fine.[3] If companies can "manage" the dispersal of information relevant to moral judgments of corporate behavior through the marketing of isolated instances of good corporate conduct even in cases where immoral conduct is the rule rather than the exception, consumers lose a vital tool in making well reasoned decisions about the products and practices they choose to support. If, on the other hand, a company chooses to go above and beyond the call of duty with respect to meeting moral obligations to its stakeholders, even when this may be more costly, it needs to rely upon the marketing of good corporate conduct to make up for such losses and to explain the moral concerns that may be driving its prices slightly higher. In order to better discern what the standards for marketing good corporate conduct should be, I will first examine a case in which the marketing of good corporate conduct is done in a fashion that is morally problematic and then later discuss another case of appropriate advertising of good corporate character. These examples will serve as illustrations of broader points concerning the sorts of guidelines that marketers ought to consider when marketing good corporate conduct.

Philip Morris' troubles with unethical, and often illegal, behavior are well known. The company has been accused and convicted repeatedly of having knowingly deceived customers concerning the health risks of smoking and of having targeted children who lack adequate skills to make well-reasoned decisions concerning the purchase of the product. Philip Morris and others in the tobacco industry are all faced with a peculiar marketing problem in that their product is addictive. This is one clear case in which business can actually create and sustain a desire within the consumer to continue to purchase a product simply because the product itself has chemically addictive properties. Although tobacco companies must rely upon other factors to induce the initial purchase of tobacco products, once the consumer has begun to purchase the industry's products, he or she will be unlikely to stop. This is part of the reason why the public has generally found the marketing of cigarettes to children to be especially repugnant. Since use of the product inherently introduces elements of coercion after its initial use due to its chemically addictive properties, it is especially pernicious to target those who can not yet make well reasoned autonomous decisions with respect to this initial purchase.

To offset much of the negative publicity associated with Philip Morris' own involvement in these sorts of deceptive and manipulative practices, Philip Morris has launched a campaign know as "People." The campaign is meant to highlight many of the positive things that Philip Morris has achieved through its philanthropic donations to charitable organizations. These ads included print ads in prominent magazines publicizing money that Miller, a Philip Morris Company, has set aside for scholarships and job training for technical college students. Other ads highlight the money that Philip Morris has given to the Meals on Wheels program for homebound persons who need help in getting adequate nourishment and the company's Supplier Diversity Program meant to ensure increased partnerships with minority owned businesses. While all of these are noble and worthwhile philanthropic endeavors, *Adbusters* has recently criticized Philip Morris for spending $108 million on advertising these purported good deeds and only $60 million on corporate donations to these charitable organizations (*Adbusters,* 2001). When a company spends far more on advertising its good deeds, then on facilitating good deeds, it is questionable whether or not the actions are truly morally praiseworthy and whether or not this sort of advertising is unacceptably misleading. The issue is further complicated by the fact that this ad campaign focusing upon areas of corporate excellence in one area, charitable giving, has been developed partly as a response to public censure over corporate misdeeds in another area, namely misinforming consumers concerning health risks and marketing an addictive product to children.

One might respond by insisting that there is nothing wrong with letting consumers know all of the relevant information concerning their moral judgments of Philip Morris, including the good that Philip Morris has done. Furthermore, if one advocates a stockholder view of the corporation and its moral obligations, philanthropic donations are only justified insofar as they help the company to turn a profit for stockholders (Friedman, 1970; Hasnas, 1998). Thus spending more on advertising philanthropy than on the philanthropy itself is entirely justified on such a view.

Even though a stockholder view of corporate obligation is itself highly contentious amongst many business ethicists, even if managerial obligations are so drastically limited as this sort of theory suggests, I would maintain that there is still good reason to think that these practices are immoral. Even stockholder theorists maintain that pursuit of profit is only justified given certain basic constraints. Although it is true that the company has a right, and perhaps even an obligation, to let consumers know all of the relevant facts concerning its corporate character, it does not thereby follow that an advertising campaign is the most appropriate means by which to disseminate such information. For all of the reasons that Lippke gives for thinking that mass advertising is morally problematic in general, advertising to disseminate relevant information concerning corporate character is even more problematic. Ads are generally designed to appeal to the emotions and quick judgment rather than to reasoned discussion. Ads commonly rely upon a select subset of information rather than providing all of the relevant information needed to make a decision. While these practices may be common and perhaps even relatively harmless when used to advertise products, they are far more suspect when used to advertise the company's moral character. Especially with something so serious as one's considered moral judgment, attention to careful reasoned decision making and access to all of the relevant facts is necessary. This does not mean that advertising with respect to corporate good conduct is inherently wrong. It does follow, however, that many practices commonly used in marketing are thoroughly inappropriate to advertising corporate good conduct.

The Philip Morris campaign, "People," bears two fundamental morally unacceptable features. First, the campaign uses the value attached to right conduct as a mere means towards increased profit and positive brand associations. Right conduct is a far more valuable aspect of human existence than mere profit on any account. Using something of higher value, and perhaps even of the utmost value, to promote something of secondary value is unacceptable and indicates a lack of respect for what matters most, namely good character and right conduct. Take, for instance, the case of someone seeking to win an election for homecoming queen who makes several very visible appearances at the local soup kitchen or at a community service day just before the election. She rarely ever engages in community service activities otherwise and would not participate in these activities if not for the contest. There is clearly something wrong with her behavior. Part of the problem is the way in which this approach appeals to the values associated with the moral good to promote something of lesser value, namely this particular individual's winning a contest for beauty and popularity. Feigning high moral character or attempting to gain esteem merely to achieve some other lesser end indicates a lack of respect for moral values that are clearly of a higher value than the secondary ends these values are used to promote.

In the case of Philip Morris, this problem is exacerbated by the fact that Philip Morris has used the value that individuals associate with what is morally good and right in order to offset the damage that it has done to its own business through its past failures to act in a fashion that is respectful of what right conduct demands. Thus, the company has displayed an utter disregard for values attached to the moral good twice over: first by deceiving customers concerning health risks and preying upon children who are especially vulnerable, and second by profaning the moral law yet again by selectively appealing to it only to regain profits lost as punishment for its earlier indiscretions.

It might be objected that this sort of criticism of Philip Morris presupposes that good corporate conduct can never be marketed in an ethically acceptable fashion since businesses would always market good corporate conduct with an eye towards whether or not the action would result in increased profit. Thus, all marketing of good corporate conduct in effect merely uses the value of the moral good or right, something of the utmost value, for the pursuit of profit, something of secondary value. But just as individuals that engage in good conduct may reap the rewards of moral praise without thereby impugning the moral praiseworthiness of their actions, so too companies may reap the rewards of moral praise even when this entails greater profit without it thereby following that the action was done solely for the purpose of gaining profit by whatever means necessary. There is nothing intrinsically wrong with receiving deserved moral praise especially when this praise allows a company to offset potential financial costs of engaging in ethical conduct. On the other hand, there is something wrong with deliberately manipulating public sentiment so as to reap the rewards of moral praise even when the recipient does not ultimately deserve such praise. In the case of the Philip Morris "People" campaign, the fact that (1) far more was spent on advertising the good deeds than on the good deeds themselves and (2) the campaign was designed in part to help the company avoid deserved moral blame for prior misdeeds, indicates that moral praise may not be appropriate.

III. APPROPRIATE MARKETING OF GOOD CORPORATE CONDUCT

In order to market good corporate conduct in a morally acceptable fashion, one must constantly bear in mind that such marketing is premised upon the notion that the company should benefit from deserved moral praise but that companies ought not use the values associated with the moral good and with right conduct solely as a means towards increasing profit. When evaluating the moral character of either a person or an organization it is of the utmost importance that honesty, non-deception and non-coercion are maintained. If marketers engage in mild deception or slight manipulation when selling a new perfume or motor oil, the stakes are nowhere near as high as when such deception or manipulation occurs with respect to evaluations of moral character. In the first case, deceptive marketing may lessen somewhat the value that a consumer attaches to a particular brand of perfume or of oil and may decrease slightly one's sense of trust in others. In the second case, deceptive marketing practices may result in a lesser value attached to morality itself and may greatly decrease one's trust of others. After all, if an organization is willing to lie about even its own moral character, something of the utmost value, then it is likely that this same organization will lie about anything whatsoever.

The importance of honesty with respect to evaluations of moral character entails that marketers of good corporate conduct must not only avoid even mild deception or subtle manipulation but that the company itself must be open to further critical evaluation to ensure that honest presentation of relevant facts is available. Honest presentation of the facts concerning moral judgments of corporate conduct are especially important not only because they are judgments concerning something of the utmost importance, namely right conduct, but also because it is only with accurate estimations of the moral rightness of corporate character that companies will continue to be motivated to do what is right. Since companies may be quite powerful, and often extend their activities beyond the boundaries of any given country, it is especially important that companies be motivated by fear of deserved moral reprobation if their activities are to be constrained by moral considerations even when the law does not so constrain their actions. It is also especially important that companies which do not deserve the benefits of moral praise, including a possible willingness on the part of consumers to pay more for the product or service, do not as a rule reap those benefits. Otherwise their competitors, who may incur such costs, will be unable to compete with others in the industry that do not incur such costs but reap the same financial benefits nonetheless. To secure both of these ends, it is thus crucial that the marketing of good corporate conduct go hand in hand with an openness to external audits to ensure the accuracy of information provided. For this reason, the Body Shop provides a good example of appropriate marketing of good corporate conduct. Not only does the Body Shop market itself as a company sensitive to the needs of persons living in third world countries, opposed to unnecessary animal testing, and opposed to preying upon women's insecurities with respect to masculinist notions of beauty, it also opens itself up to outside audits on a regular basis.[4]

The Body Shop has carved out a niche for itself as a company with a reputation for social responsibility. Instead of simply using standard chemical ingredients, the Body Shop has sought out natural ingredients and products that can be produced in third world countries, especially by poor women, for which it then pays a decent price. The "Trade Not Aid" campaign is thus designed to address the company's obligations to social justice. Early on, the Body Shop also sought to produce products that were not tested on animals and which included ingredients that had not been tested on animals in the recent past. Finally, the Body Shop, rather than launching the standard cosmetics advertising campaigns with dangerously thin models promising sexual prowess and eternal youth, launched a campaign with a more realistic looking Barbie doll to highlight the ways in which the industry as a whole engages in marketing practices that prey upon women's insecurities in a patriarchal youth obsessed society. The company also makes a concerted effort to avoid marketing that creates needs for women that would not exist otherwise and lists all ingredients on its labels even when this is not required by law. The Body Shop's commitment to honesty in marketing even extended so far as to labeling one hair treatment product with the warning that it contained henna which is smelly and resembles manure (Hartman and Beck-Dudley, 1999).[5] In the judgment of many reflective consumers, these examples are paradigmatic of the nature of good corporate moral conduct. Rather than launching a barrage of repetitive television ads, the company avoided marketing good corporate conduct in this fashion. Instead it relied upon word of mouth, news stories, a book by the company's founder, pamphlets and posters in store windows to get the message across.

But perhaps even more importantly, the Body Shop is subject to regular social audits with outside input in order to ensure that the company is responsive to concerns voiced by workers, customers and citizens.[6] This is what helps to guarantee that whatever benefits it gains from the perceived moral praiseworthiness of its actions are in fact deserved. The company has run five independently verified environmental statements since 1992. The company has also done a number of more general social audits in order to give voice to various stakeholders and their concerns. When the company faced scrutiny over its decisions, for instance putting petroleum based ingredients in its products, it made an honest attempt to address such concerns. Although it first questioned the methods used by reporters breaking the story and wrote a letter to *Business Ethics,* under false pretenses, defending its position, the Body Shop later explained how it felt that the public had simply misunderstood its stated policy and after a social audit vowed to control its "grouchiness" when faced with critical scrutiny (Sillanpaa, 1998).[7] Since all ingredients are listed even when the law does not require it and since outside audits are routinely carried out, the Body Shop arguably deserves whatever benefits it gains from marketing its good corporate conduct.

While not all companies will find it feasible to engage in honesty in marketing to quite the extent that the Body Shop has done, all companies should aspire to being as honest and as careful not to manipulate or coerce judgments concerning the marketing of good corporate conduct. Since there is so much more at stake, it is especially important that the considered moral judgments of consumers rest upon accurate information rather than the occasionally manipulative and often opaque presentation of information in standard marketing campaigns. Because it is so important both with respect to motivating companies to respect the constraints upon action imposed by moral laws and with respect to promoting and protecting a general respect for the values associated with the moral good and right action, marketing of good corporate conduct must be undertaken with special care and honesty. This honesty must be guaranteed by an openness and willingness by companies to engage in outside social audits with respect to the good corporate conduct from which the company hopes to benefit.[8] Using Philip Morris' example of how companies may market good conduct in a way that is disrespectful of the moral good and of right action and the Body Shop's example of how good corporate conduct may be made public in a morally acceptable fashion, marketers can gain some idea of what appropriate marketing of good corporate conduct entails. Marketers must consistently bear in mind the importance of marketing good corporate conduct in a fashion that does not treat the value of right conduct as secondary in value to the procurement of profit. This may be achieved by making a special effort to be honest in advertising good corporate conduct.

IV. CONCLUSION

I have argued that a certain level of deception or less than forthright presentation of relevant facts by those marketing products may not be particularly harmful so long as individuals are aware of such practices and able to make well-reasoned decisions concerning the effects of such campaigns upon their purchasing decisions. But such practices are much more serious when used to promote purported good corporate conduct. While it is not wrong, *per se,* for a company to market and benefit from moral praise for good corporate conduct, it is wrong for companies to use the values associated with the moral good and with right action as a mere means to gaining greater profit. Deception with respect to corporate character is more problematic since: (a) It is a far greater omission and a far greater attack upon the institution of trust as such to lie about facts relevant to determining the moral praiseworthiness of an action or institution than to engage in deception with respect to marketing a good or service. (b) This practice undermines moral motivation for companies to actually engage in right action rather than merely appearing to merit moral praise. Further, (c) It is wrong to use something of the utmost value, such as the moral good or right action, as a mere means to something of lesser value such as profit. In order for companies to engage in the marketing of good corporate conduct in a morally acceptable fashion, companies must not produce a barrage of ads that encourage faulty reasoning and must stem practices of selective presentation of relevant facts more common in other areas of marketing; companies must also in general recognize a greater obligation to clarity, honesty and non-coercion in presenting facts relevant to the company's garnering the benefits of perceived morally praiseworthy action. To achieve this end, it is also important that companies which engage in the marketing of good corporate conduct make every effort to ensure that consumers are granted access to relevant information and that outside audits with respect to the good corporate conduct marketed are available. This is likely one of the only ways to ensure that the benefits of moral praise garnered by making moral praiseworthiness of corporate actions more widely known through marketing strategies are in fact justly deserved.

ACKNOWLEDGEMENTS

I would like to thank attendees of the Eighth Annual International Conference Promoting Business Ethics for their helpful advice and recommendations on an earlier version of this paper.

NOTES

1. For more on objections to the pervasiveness of mass advertising and its effect upon autonomy, see Sneddon, 2001.
2. On the extent to which the principle of *caveat emptor* is presupposed by and or limited by United States culture and law, see Carson, 2001.
3. For more on public censure as a means of affecting corporate behavior, see Maynard, 2001.
4. I do not mean to suggest that the Body Shop is a perfectly virtuous company, merely that they have done a particularly good job with marketing good corporate conduct. There may have never been a perfectly virtuous person, but this does not entail that the concept of the virtuous person cannot guide our actions as an ideal towards which we may strive. So too, even if there has never been a perfectly virtuous company, it need not follow that the ideal of the virtuous company cannot be a useful guide to action. A clearer conception of this ideal may be developed by examining various companies that embody one or more virtues or a specific virtue even if no one company embodies all possible virtues appropriate to businesses.
5. For more on the ethics of women's advertising, see Cohan, 2001.
6. For further information on the benefits of social audits in guaranteeing good corporate conduct, see Hess, 2001.
7. Although it would have been better had the Body Shop reacted in a less aggressively defensive manner when faced with initial public scrutiny, the company is still a good model. Even though its behavior in the past has not always been perfect, the company has the added virtue of recognizing past failures and making strides to improve upon them. Corporate character can not be thought of as static. A company with good character, like an individual with good character, is constantly evolving. This evolution and growth in the face of past failures is as much a part of good character as is any corporate virtue.
8. When a company decides to market its charitable donations to nonprofits using the logos of nonprofit organizations, it is again especially important that honesty is maintained. This kind of marketing is a particular sort of marketing good corporate conduct. It is especially important that such ads do not encourage consumers to infer that nonprofit organizations have endorsed the company or its product even when they have not. Failure to make this clear or failure to disclose whether or not nonprofits were paid for the use of their logo in such ads is yet another case of using the values associated with the moral good and with right conduct to advance something of secondary value, namely profit. For more on this particular sort of marketing good corporate conduct, see also Wulfson, 2001.

REFERENCES

Adbusters: Journal of the Mental Environment: 2001, 36, 1–6.

Arrington R.: 1982, "Advertising & Behavior Control," *Journal of Business Ethics* 1, 3–12.

Carson, T.: 2001, "Deception and Withholding Information in Sales," *Business Ethics Quarterly* 11(2), 275–306.

Cohan, J. A.: 2001, "Towards a New Paradigm in the Ethics of Women's Advertising," *Journal of Business Ethics* 33, 323–337.

Friedman, M.: 1970, "The Social Responsibility of Business Is to Increase Its Profits," *New York Times Magazine* (September 13), 33.

Gailbraith, J. K.: 1985, "Persuasion—and Power," in J. R. Desjardins and J. J. McCall (eds.), *Contemporary Issues in Business Ethics* (Wadsworth Publishing Company, Belmont, CA), pp. 142–147.

Hartman, C. and C. L. Beck-Dudley: 1999, "Marketing Strategies & the Search for Virtue: A Case Analysis of the Body Shop International," *Journal of Business Ethics* 20, 249–263.

Hasnas, J.: 1998, "The Normative Theories of Business Ethics: A Guide for the Perplexed," *Business Ethics Quaterly* 8(1), 19–42.

Hess, D.: 2001, "Regulating Corporate Social Performance: A New Look at Social Accounting, Auditing and Reporting," *Business Ethics Quarterly* 11(2), 307–330.

Holley, D. M.: 1987, "A Moral Evaluation of Sales Practices," *Business & Professional Ethics Journal* **5**, 3–21.

Levitt, T.: 1970, "The Morality of Advertising," *Harvard Business Review* 48, 84–92.

Lippke, R. L.: 1989, "Advertising & the Social Conditions of Autonomy," *Business & Professional Ethics Journal* 8, 35–58.

Maynard, M. L.: 2001, "Policing Transnational Commerce: Global Awareness in the Margins of Morality," *Journal of Business Ethics* 30, 17–27.

Sillanpaa, M.: 1998, "The Body Shop Values Report—Towards Integrated Stakeholder Auditing," *Journal of Business Ethics* 17, 1443–1456.

Sneddon, A.: 2001, "Advertising and Deep Autonomy," *Journal of Business Ethics* 33, 15–28.

Wulfson, M.: 2001, "The Ethics of Corporate Social Responsibility and Philanthropic Ventures," *Journal of Business Ethics* 29, 135–145.

CORPORATE TITHING AT GRAND BANK

—RAM SUBRAMANIAN

The following case describes a bank's quandary with whether to publicize the nature of its good deeds and the implications of its decision. Consider who exactly comprises Grand Bank's stakeholders and what is the nature of their specific claims. In addition, consider in general what an organization should do with its free cash flow (surplus after providing for all necessary investments). How should Charles Stoddard respond at the upcoming board meeting?

Charles Stoddard, the chairman and CEO of the Grand Rapids, Michigan-based Grand Bank, put down the telephone with a thoughtful look on his face. A major stockholder of his bank had just told him that the bank should advertise its unique practice of donating 10% of its annual pre-tax profits to charitable organizations within the community. The bank had hitherto not publicized this practice and had no intention of doing so. However, the stockholder had argued with Stoddard that publicizing this practice would benefit the bank and allow it to successfully differentiate itself in the competitive metropolitan Grand Rapids banking market. In addition, the publicity could spur other banks and businesses to follow suit.

Stoddard had promised to bring this issue up at next week's Board meeting. However, Stoddard realized that the Board would expect him to brief them on what he felt were the pros and cons of publicizing the corporate tithing program. He had a week to assess the stockholder's request and frame his opinion on the management's response.

HISTORY

Grand Bank Financial Corporation[1] (hereafter referred to as "Grand Bank") was a closely held banking company based in Grand Rapids, Michigan. It was founded in 1987 by Charles Stoddard, a Harvard MBA, with more than 30 years in banking, including a stint as the chairman of Michigan National Bank-Central. Stoddard pitched the idea of a small, community-based bank that offered personalized service as an antidote to the large, impersonalized bank that relied increasingly on automation to gain efficiencies.

Copyright 2003 Ram Subramanian, reprinted with permission of the author.

This case study was prepared as a basis for class discussion rather than to illustrate either effective or ineffective handling of an administrative situation. All individuals and events described are real. The author wishes to thank Charles Stoddard without whose help this case could not have been written. The author also wishes to thank his colleague, Barry Castro, for providing the motivation and support to write the case.

[1]www.grandbank.com.

EXHIBIT 1

Grand Bank's Mission Statement

Grand Bank, locally owned and managed, offers integrated financial services to executives, professionals, senior citizens, small businesses and others desiring more personal service. It is committed to providing a superior level of personal service and sharing its profits with the local community.

Source: Grand Bank.

Dan Vos, an erstwhile director of the bank, proposed the idea of making tithing an integral part of the bank's mission. The concept of tithing had its origin in the Bible and it referred to contributing 10% of one's income to charity. This concept was rare among banks: To the best of Stoddard's knowledge, Atlantic Stewardship Bank of New Jersey was the only bank that had a similar program.[2] The prospectus that was used to get investment from 125 stockholders clearly identified the role of the proposed bank in the community. It stated that 10% of the bank's annual pre-tax profit would be earmarked for charitable giving to the community. One half of the designated amount would be given to charitable organizations as decided by a committee of two insiders (the CEO and the President of the bank) and four outside directors. The other half would be donated to charities designated by the bank's stockholders. Each stockholder could specify donation of an amount equal to his/her proportion of shares held. Exhibit 1 contains the bank's mission statement.

On December 31, 2001, the bank had assets of $263 million (an 18% increase over the previous year) and net earnings of $2.8 million (a 26% increase over fiscal 2000). Its return on equity was 15%, the highest in the region amongst banks of comparable size. Corporate tithing amounted to $451,000 in 2001 and cumulatively amounted to more than $2.3 million since 1987.

COMPETITIVE POSITION

Grand Rapids was Michigan's second largest city after Detroit and was home to major office furniture companies such as Steelcase and Knoll, to Amway, the multi-level marketing organization, and to a large number of automotive suppliers. John Brown, the president of the Grand Rapids Area Chamber of Commerce, remarked that the key to the city's current economic success was the development of a diverse manufacturing sector, that included industrial machinery, metal, food, paper and printing products. Brown stated that "in the next decade, Grand Rapids will be called upon to provide economic leadership for the state of Michigan, and I think we're well prepared for that task."[3] Exhibit 2 profiles the demographics of the metropolitan Grand Rapids area.

---

[2]www.asbnow.com.
[3]Grand Rapids Area Chamber of Commerce, 2000 Business Directory, page 5.

EXHIBIT 2

Demographic Profile of Metropolitan Grand Rapids

- The metropolitan Grand Rapids area consists of the counties of Kent, Ottawa, Muskegon and Allegan.
- The 1999 population of this area was 1,052,092, which was an 11.97% increase in the 1990–1999 period. The population growth in Michigan during 1990–1999 was 6.12%, and for the U.S. it was 9.22%.
- The forecasted population for this area in 2010 was 1,188,211, an increase of 12.94% between 1999 and 2010.
- The average median household income in 1996 for the four counties in the metropolitan Grand Rapids area was $40,375. The average annual growth between 1990 and 1996 was 1.125%. This was in comparison to Michigan's median household income of $35,940 (average annual growth of −0.1%) and $35,172 (average annual growth of 0.3%) for the U.S. as a whole.

SOURCE: Demographic Profile for Grand Rapids and Lakeshore Areas, 2001, published by the Seidman School of Business, Grand Valley State University.

Banking in the metropolitan Grand Rapids area was dominated by large banks such as Old Kent Financial Corporation, Huntington, National City, Bank One and Comerica (Exhibit 3 profiles the top area banks). However, mergers and acquisitions (for example the acquisition of Old Kent by Fifth Third Bank, Comerica's takeover of Manufacturers' Bank and Chemical Bank's acquisition of Bank West) of the major banks led to opportunities for formation of new smaller banks. The Michigan Office of Financial and Insurance Services noted that in 2001, seven new banks were formed in the State, compared to nine in 2000, seven in 1999 and one in 1995, two in 1994 and zero in 1993.[4] Many of the smaller niche banks formed because of the merger and acquisition wave of the 1990s were started by displaced former bank executives. The community banks placed a premium on customer service and community involvement. This emphasis appealed to retail customers and small businesses who were dissatisfied by the impersonality of the big banks. The small, niche banks enjoyed robust increases in both loans and deposits. Spurred by a strong local economy and further consolidation among the major banks, this was expected to continue.

Grand Bank's Chairman Charles Stoddard talked about Grand Bank's future in the 2000 annual report:

> *The management of the bank is enthusiastic about its prospects for 2001. With declining interest rates, loan demand is expected to increase, especially for residential mortgages. Moreover, last fall's announcement of Fifth Third Bancorp's takeover of Old Kent Financial clearly provides opportunities for us. History demonstrates that there is always customer dislocation because of mergers. It is amazing how the local financial landscape has changed since we started in 1987. Then, there were 16 separate banks in the greater Grand Rapids area with 8 of those located downtown. Today, in 2001, there are 28 banks with 14 located downtown. Of the eight downtown banks in 1987, only Grand Bank and one other have the same name today.*

---

[4]Cited in Mark Sanchez, "Market Still Seems to Be Good for New Banks," *Grand Rapids Business Journal,* June 18, 2001: B11, B18.

EXHIBIT 3

Profile of Selected Area Banks

Bank	No. of W Michigan Locations	2001 Total Loans ($000s)	2001 Total Deposits ($000s)
Fifth Third Bank	155	5,700,000	6,600,000
Bank One	47	3,122,000	1,467,700
Comerica	48	2,048,000	2,155,391
Standard Federal	62	2,100,000	1,920,000
Huntington	90	1,874,000	2,283,574
National City Bank	28	800,000	NA
Macatawa	16	438,000	419,000
Mercantile	2	500,000	420,000
Grand Bank	1	180,850	193,587

BANK OPERATIONS

Grand Bank's internal operations were carried out in four areas: client services, lending services, trust services and operations. The bank had one place of business and no branch offices. Exhibit 4 contains the bank's financial statements.

THE TITHING PROGRAM

On a continuing basis, the bank received requests from community organizations for funding support. Stoddard and others at the bank designed a one-page application (Exhibit 5) that was mandatory for all applicants. The applicant had to be a non-religious, 501(C)(3) organization (i.e., tax-exempt) that had to indicate on the application how the funds would benefit the community.

Once the half-yearly financial statements were finalized (around mid-January and mid-July of each year), a committee consisting of Stoddard, Tom Wesholski, President and four outside directors, reviewed the applications. Five percent of each half's profits were then contributed to the community organizations that requested funding. After the annual accounts were finalized and the net income for the fiscal year determined, Stoddard sent out a letter to each of the stockholders of the bank that requested the stockholder to identify a community organization of the stockholder's choice that deserved funding. The amount of the funding available to a stockholder to contribute to the community organization was determined by the stockholder's investment in the bank. For example, a stockholder who owned 1% of the bank was allowed to designate 1% of the tithing pool to a community organization of his or her choice. The bank then made the payment to the community organization indicating that the organization was selected to receive funding by the specific stockholder. Thus, the charity received an unsolicited donation; the stockholder received recognition for designating the donation; and the bank received a tax-deduction, which Stoddard called a "triple win."

EXHIBIT 4

Grand Bank's Financial Highlights
As of and for the years ended December 31, 1998 through 2001
(In thousands, except for per share information)

Year ended December 31,	2001	2000	1999	1998
Net interest income	$8,139	$7836	$6470	$6022
Provision for loan losses	470	490	304	543
Other income	3,467	2482	2457	2327
Other expenses	7,668	6360	5865	5431
Net income	2,822	2251	1777	1564
Dividends declared	270	270	254	231

Per Share Information	2001	2000	1999	1998
Net income—basic	$ 18.01	$ 16.68	$13.16	$11.94
Net income—diluted	17.59	16.35	12.95	11.86
Dividends declared	2.00	2.00	1.88	1.76
Book value	126.23	110.14	94.30	83.88

December 31,	2001	2000	1999	1998
Investment securities	$ 13,648	$ 14,433	$ 11,834	$ 14,938
Gross portfolio loans	220,691	180,850	149,503	123,347
Deposits	222,116	193,587	152,066	124,419
Stockholders' equity	17,036	14,865	12,727	11,313
Total assets	263,422	223,930	178,665	149,022

Ratios	2001	2000	1999	1998
Return on average assets	1.02%	1.12%	1.06%	1.11%
Return on average equity	15.01	16.32	14.75	14.98
Allowance for loan losses as a percentage of total portfolio loans	1.30	1.30	1.31	1.34
Net interest income as a percentage of average earning assets	3.53	4.02	4.01	4.42
Dividends declared as a percentage of earnings	11.10	11.99	14.28	14.79
Stockholders' equity as a percentage of total assets	6.47	6.64	7.12	7.59

EXHIBIT 5

Grand Bank Charitable Contribution Request Application

(If you have not applied before, please include a copy of your budget, Board of directors and your 501 (c)(3) status certification)
Please print all requested information including organization address.
1. NAME AND ADDRESS OF ORGANIZATION
2. IS IT A LOCAL NON-RELIGIOUS "501 (c)(3)" ORGANIZATION?
3. IS THIS A REQUEST FOR A CAPITAL CAMPAIGN?
4. REQUESTED AMOUNT OF CONTRIBUTION:
5. TOTAL AMOUNT OF FUND DRIVE:
6. PERCENTAGE OF CAMPAIGN FUNDS TO BE USED FOR ACTUAL PROJECT (AS OPPOSED TO FUND-RAISING EXPENSES):
7. USE OF PROCEEDS:
8. BENEFIT TO THE COMMUNITY:
9. IF GRAND BANK DECIDES TO CONTRIBUTE, IS THERE ANY RECOGNITION FOR GRAND BANK?

NAME OF INDIVIDUAL SUBMITTING INFORMATION   PHONE #

SOURCE: Grand Bank.

THE DECISION

In an essay in the local newspaper, Stoddard had indicated his preference for not publicizing the bank's tithing program. He had remarked:

> *I am aware of several local businesses that practice corporate tithing in a quiet, non-public way. Their motive is not to seek public recognition or to use the charity as marketing gimmicks. They believe that it's simply the right thing to do.*[5]

However, Stoddard could also see the point of view of the stockholder who had asked that the program be publicized. In a high-growth, opportunity-filled, albeit highly competitive marketplace, this could be a way to differentiate Grand Bank from others. It could strengthen the bank's claim that it was a bank founded to serve the local community.

Stoddard realized that there were merits in the arguments for and against publicizing the bank's tithing program. He wondered what he should recommend to the board at the upcoming meeting?

---

[5]Charles C. Stoddard, "Tithing for Corporations," *Grand Rapids Press,* November 3, 1996: E1, E6.

CASE STUDY FOR COMPANIES DEALING WITH SECURITY FORCES

Shell Linking Security to Human Rights in Nigeria

—INTERNATIONAL BUSINESS LEADERS FORUM

Since 1958, Shell Oil has extracted about $30 billion in crude oil beneath a small area in Nigeria known as the Rivers State, or Ogoniland. It is claimed that the oil has served to greatly enrich the corporate coffers of Royal Dutch/Shell and to provide unimaginable wealth to the corrupt Nigerian dictator of the week, currently General Sani Abacha. Shell's detractors point to the impoverished people of Ogoniland, who received little in exchange for the resources from which they might have benefited. Nigeria depends on oil production for 80% of its revenues; Shell is the biggest player in this game. As such, the international media and other activist groups have held Shell responsible for "turning a blind eye to the monstrous human-rights abuses, murders, rapes and other forms of intimidation that have occurred in the quest to keep the oil flowing in Ogoniland."

What is the nature of social responsibility? In the discussion below, you are asked to consider a firm's responsibility to a community where it conducts operations. Is profit for the firm the only guiding principle, or should the impact of its decision on others be considered, even where the law allows the decision? Shell's rehabilitative actions subsequent to NGO pressure seem not to have been motivated by a legal duty to act. However, interestingly enough, an appellate court decision held that a lawsuit against Shell for allegedly aiding and abetting in the torture and murder of Nigerian activists who opposed drilling on their lands was allowed to proceed (in a decision dated September 14, 2000).[1]

[1] *Wiwa v. Royal Dutch Petroleum Co.*, 99-7223 (2000).

For many years, people living in the Niger Delta have endured violations of their civil and political rights by the Nigerian security forces. While inter-ethnic conflicts and demands by minority groups for autonomous recognition have been at the heart of some conflict in the Delta, the overlay of oil production and inequities in the distribution of the proceeds have exacerbated tensions. The widely held perception amongst communities within oil producing areas is that they have suffered adverse social and environmental consequences of oil production, while realizing none of the benefits.

The absence of a visible government presence within the Delta has led to oil companies—Shell in particular—becoming the focus of discontent and sometimes violent protest. The often heavy-handed responses of the state security forces have prompted concerns internationally, most notably following the execution of Ken Saro-Wiwa in November 1995. Securing the safety of employees and company assets while respecting human rights is one of the main challenges facing Shell in Nigeria, given the social and political context of its operations.

The Shell Petroleum Development Company (SPDC), a joint venture operated by Shell, is responsible for 40% of Nigeria's total output and 55% of onshore production.

In the 1990s, protests relating to oil production—linked to environmental damages and the failure of local people to realize economic benefits—have escalated in the Delta region. One of the most notorious incidents occurred at a Shell facility at Umuechem in October 1990, when 80 unarmed demonstrators were killed and hundreds of houses burned by the Mobile Police—a notorious paramilitary force linked to numerous abuses of human rights. A judicial commission of enquiry concluded that the mobile police had displayed "a reckless disregard for lives and property."

In the early 1990s, the Movement for the Survival of the Ogoni People (MOSOP) campaigned for a greater share of oil revenues, political autonomy and ownership of the oil beneath their land. It demanded $6 billion in rent and royalties from Shell and compensation of $4 billion for environmental degradation. MOSOP also accused Shell of colluding with the government in the genocide of the Ogonis. Faced with increasing intimidation, Shell withdrew from Ogoni land in early 1993. The murder of four Ogoni leaders and the subsequent execution in November 1995 of nine MOSOP leaders—due to their alleged involvement in the murders—attracted widespread international condemnation. It also led many advocacy NGOs to call for a boycott of Shell to hold it accountable for "environmental abuses and tolerance of injustice."

The international human rights organization, Human Rights Watch, has catalogued a depressing cycle of protest and repression in the Delta. These include alleged instances of harassment, unlawful detentions, beatings, torture and killings. These actions are often prompted by demands for compensation following oil spills, or protests. International concerns at human rights infringements in Nigeria have also been raised in various reports and resolutions of the UN's Human Rights Committee. The focus of protest and repression has recently shifted from Ogoni-land to the territory occupied by the Ijaw people, the fourth largest ethnic group in Nigeria. This follows the issue of the Kaiama Declaration by an Ijaw Youths Conference in December 1998, calling for the withdrawal of the Nigerian military and oil companies. Yet Shell and other oil companies have a legitimate interest in providing a secure environment for employees and in protecting oil infrastructure. Hostage-taking of oil workers and kidnappings increased in the area. For Shell, striking a balance between providing security to its employees and protecting human rights has proved to be difficult, particularly since security is primarily the responsibility of the State's security forces.

In early 1996, Shell embarked on a major consultative exercise known as "Societies changing expectations." Largely prompted by public reaction to the Brent Spar incident and allegations of complicit involvement in human rights abuses in Nigeria, human rights emerged as one of the key concerns of consultees. This led to a revision of the company's Business Principles, which now explicitly commit Shell to "respect the human rights of their employees" and "express support for fundamental human rights in line with the legitimate role of business." In 1998, the company produced a management primer on Business and Human Rights.

Shell also engaged with a range of stakeholders such as Amnesty International and Human Rights Watch regarding the security aspects of its Nigerian operations starting in 1996. This led to a revision of Shell's rules of engagement with the state security forces—the police and the military—to accommodate the UN Basic Principles on the Use of Force and Firearms and the UN Code of Conduct for Law Enforcement Officials. The experience in Nigeria has prompted a more broadly based review of security provision, and the development and adoption in 1998 of group-wide Use of Force Guidelines. These provide for *inter alia* seeking assurances from state forces that the use of force will respect human dignity and peoples rights, will be proportional to the threat, will minimize damage and injury and advising them that they will be held accountable for any excessive use of force.

All Shell security personnel are to receive adequate training in operating procedures that are consistent with relevant codes of conduct. The guidelines stipulate the "rules of engagement" for calling in or contracting with state security forces. They also provide advice on acceptable courses of action and responses against those who represent a threat to the security or safety of personnel or company assets.

Shell recognizes the need to improve stability within the Niger Delta if the current security situation is to improve. The ongoing programs for renovation of faulty infrastructure play a small but important part of this strategy. More importantly, the people in the Delta need to become beneficiaries from oil production—rather than its casualties.

There is an emerging consensus that for peace and stability to be restored to the Niger Delta, the communities must view themselves as net beneficiaries from oil production. Achieving that shift in perspective is no easy task, given the legacy of past failures by governments, persecution by security forces, inter-ethnic rivalries and the sense that oil companies have put profits before principles. Shell believes that it has a contribution to make towards helping change perceptions. This includes a responsibility to continue to demonstrate support for human rights. Whether or not communities finally come to see themselves as beneficiaries depends not only on Shell, but also crucially on the Nigerian government and on the ethnic groups living in the Delta.

The case of Shell in the Niger Delta illustrates the extent to which the social and economic development of local communities and the level of state repression are inextricably linked to the security of company personnel and installations.

CHIQUITA'S PATH FROM PARIAH TO PARADIGM

—JEM BENDELL

Jem Bendell examines the cultural change at what is now a leading food company in corporate responsibility—Chiquita Brands International. He explains that most decision makers do not decide to "do" CSR because of the business case we have discussed earlier in this chapter. Instead, he explains, most have done so because they wanted to, or because they felt pushed, and only then have they sought to make the numbers work. The recent history of Chiquita Brands International is illustrative.

Like me, I guess many of you have listened to presentations on the business case for corporate responsibility or the rationale for having good stakeholder relations, whether delivered by consultants, academics or managers themselves. Cue the picture of bubbles on sticks ("stakeholders"), radiating out from a big bubble ("corporation"), which is always in the center ("of course"). And for the next slide, why not some survey results on staff morale before and after a new social policy or report? And for the finale, perhaps a quote or two from a famous CEO saying that GOOD business makes good BUSINESS?

These are the tenets being preached at corporate responsibility conferences around the world. Yet such evangelizing can give a false impression of why companies have engaged in what we call corporate citizenship. Neat and tidy presentations of messy and emotional situations will not help us understand why changes have occurred, what could occur in future and the limits of such change. How so?

Well, in the-world-according-to-PowerPoint, managers are assumed to calculate the reasons for being nice to everyone, or at least more people than before, and then to do it (or try to). Companies that have faced reputational crises are offered up as examples of what happens to those who don't follow the gospel of PowerPoint. Yet if we think about the people we know, does this story seem true? I have not yet met any manager who decided to push their company in a more socially or environmentally friendly direction because of a bubbles-and-sticks stakeholder map or some statistics on the money to be made in doing so. I have met dozens who now choose to explain their actions to key audiences, such as investors and peers, by pointing to the business case. But I have not met a single manager who decided to "do" CSR because of the business case. Instead, most have done so because they wanted to, or because they felt pushed, and only then have they sought to make the numbers work.

DRIVEN TO CHANGE

Chiquita is a prime example of a company being driven by, on the one hand, the will of some of its managers to make a positive difference and, on the other, the power of civil society criticism to compel further change. With 26,000 workers and a 100-year history of carrying out the socially, environmentally and politically contentious activity of producing and trading bananas, the company's move to position itself as a responsible corporation is significant. In the past Chiquita was implicated in political corruption, repression of trade unions and environmental degradation, among other concerns. Moreover, when in 1997 I first began looking at the company's social and environmental record it was widely considered to be very closed and defensive towards criticism. Now there is "a new spirit of openness" and the company has been applauded for signing an agreement with the International Union of Food and Agricultural Workers (IUF) and for its activity within the Ethical Trading Initiative (ETI). "Even two years ago, union and NGO members of the ETI would likely have voted against Chiquita's membership. But we've earned their support by proving through our progress and our transparency that we are genuinely committed to Corporate Responsibility," says the European Director of Corporate Responsibility and Public Affairs, George Jaksch.

THE BEGINNING

This turnaround began in 1991, in Costa Rica. The small Central America republic was the scene of some bitter disputes between the industry and environmentalists over the expansion of banana plantations. Problems included deforestation, water pollution, worker health and safety, discrimination and trade union rights. Rows were played out in the media, with Chiquita's local management experiencing a rude awakening to its social and environmental responsibilities. This led to discussion with various stakeholders, and as a result the local management decided to work with the non-governmental organizations (NGOs) Fundacion Ambio and Rainforest Alliance to implement an environmental management and certification program, which came to be known as the Better Banana Project. In 1995 the Costa Rican management team publicized its efforts, and consequently head office summoned it to Cincinnati to find out what it was doing. The commitment and vision of Costa Rica managers Carlos Vega and David McClaughlin must have carried the day, as the senior management decided to extend the program across all its Latin American operations. Five years later all the plantations Chiquita owned on the continent had been certified.

During that time the European division of Chiquita had asked for more action on social issues, given the growing consumer concern about working practices in poorer countries. This complemented the Rainforest Alliance's own interests, as environmental challenges began to be understood in the context of sustainable development, which included social concerns. However, by 1996 the Better Banana Project was coming under criticism from local trade unions and organic farmers as being greenwash. Their argument was that the project ignored workers' rights, which were often abused on banana plantations, was not effectively monitored and helped Chiquita present a green image that could undermine the fledgling market for organic bananas. Some questioned the mandate and independence of the non-governmental inspectors. Director of the union SITRAP, Gilbert

Bermudez, told me at the time, "Chiquita pays, Chiquita commands." This experience meant that Chiquita managers began to realize the accountability of those they worked with was essential to the perception of their work.

Another rude awakening came in 1998 when the *Cincinnati Enquirer* published an ex-pose of the dirtier sides to Chiquita's operations. The accusations were wide, including po-litical corruption, owning secret companies, poisoning workers by crop-dusting while they worked in the fields and squashing trade union activity in some areas. The report was all the more colorful for including the transcripts of internal voicemail messages about the re-porters' investigations. The company defended itself and sued the paper for theft of the tapes. Nevertheless, behind the scenes there was some reflection about the story and the general theme that Chiquita was a huge company with no scruples. As Steve Warshaw noted, "In the wake of particularly damaging media coverage, we embarked on a disci-plined path toward corporate responsibility." This path was made all the more necessary as, the following year, European activists such as Banana Link began a media and consumer campaign targeting supermarkets including Asda and Tesco so that they would demand that Chiquita address problems with pesticide use and trade union rights.

FINANCIAL CONSIDERATIONS

All this stakeholder strife was occurring while the company was experiencing financial dif-ficulty. 1999 saw a massive collapse in banana prices and Chiquita was worse hit as it had banked on Europe's opening its markets to Latin American bananas as a result of a dispute at the World Trade Organization (WTO). Its financial difficulties led to bankruptcy pro-ceedings at the end of 2001. Despite this it continued its initial investment in social re-sponsibility. For example, in 2001 Chiquita published its first Corporate Responsibility Report, in which it admitted to past failings and announced a change of heart. It committed itself to working toward a workplace standard established by Social Accountability Inter-national (SAI), signed an agreement with the IUF and became a member of the ETI.

This story shows how Chiquita managers experienced for themselves the changing power relations in a global economy, with civil society being able to exert influence on its operations. As Steve Warshaw told CNN last year, "The question is 'where is the strong arm in the industry?' And the answer is that the strong arm is not in our hands today. The way the banana industry operates today is very similar to other industries. Whether you're deal-ing with environmental groups, government units or organized labor . . . if you can come up with a cooperative spirit that leads to mutual improvement, it works. I don't think that we can afford not to be responsible. We live in a very transparent time where everyone knows everyone's business."

We could say that those rude awakenings I mentioned earlier had changed Chiquita managers' perceptions of self. As their understanding of society changed, so they came to appreciate their impacts on society and the environment and their responsibility in ad-dressing these rather than passing the buck. Warshaw again: "Our understanding of our role in society, and what it means to be a responsible corporate citizen, is quite different from what it was not long ago."

That this is a shift in corporate consciousness is further illustrated by the company's emphasis on how its corporate responsibility work stems from core values. It grounds its work on four key values, which it developed after consultation with over 1,000 employees. Its code of social responsibility is intended as a mobilization of these values. The emphasis on values also means that one's intent is key. Hence the company has been open to admitting its failings, believing honesty is important. Throughout its corporate responsibility report "we make note of those places where we fall short of our expectations . . . we have come to realize that we are unlikely to resolve issues or problems unless and until we talk about them openly—among ourselves and in collaboration with others."

IS HONESTY THE BEST POLICY?

Perhaps not, if you are only doing CSR because of the business case. I say this because being honest is not a risk-averse strategy. In April Human Rights Watch (HRW) released a report on child labor and union rights in Ecuador. Stephen Coats, Executive Director of Labour Education in the Americas Project (US/LEAP), said that, "Chiquita's decision to respond to HRW's questionnaire in detail was the right decision, but opened it up to further criticism than, say, Del Monte's decision not to respond. Others, like the highly respected IUF, were able to use the report to differentiate between the major transnationals and give Chiquita proper credit for the steps it has been taking in contrast to its competitors." So it is difficult to say whether being proactive on CSR and honest about your performance creates or reduces risk.

Of course, trying to put a figure on risk is an imprecise task and is usually done to support decisions that are going to be made anyway, rather than inform them. In any case, by using factors such as defined hazards and known probabilities, risk calculations can ignore three key limitations. First, there is what we know we don't know, sometimes called uncertainty in scientific circles. Then there is what we don't know we don't know, often called indeterminacy. Finally there is what we can't know because of the fallibility of human cognition. By ignoring these limitations of our ability to know and therefore manage, risk assessments can actually create risk by giving management a false sense of certainty over their business environment.

Chiquita managers are not, to my knowledge, part-time theoretical physicists. So these ideas didn't shape their thinking, but their experience of a complex business environment gave them a similar understanding so that calculating the specific benefits, financially, of corporate responsibility work was not a pre-requisite to that work. For example, they made a US$20 million capital investment in the environmental program and more in operating costs but didn't assess the financial dividends of the work, instead seeing it as a prerequisite to doing business in some markets.

A NEW FOCUS MOVING FORWARD

Nevertheless, management must be able to explain itself to investors. In the last few years the financial return to Chiquita's investors has been poor to non-existent. The new Chairman and CEO, Cyrus F. Freidheim, was brought in to return the company to profitability. Therefore the new focus must be on the business case for corporate responsibility, and the company now has people tasked with putting figures on the tangible and intangible benefits of it. The greatest effect of this shift in emphasis may be in the story that Chiquita management tells the world.

The company is beginning to explain its actions using the business case for corporate responsibility and sustainability, and suggests its actions were a deliberate strategic decision, rather than something compelled by external forces or personal values. Therefore those areas where it is easier to demonstrate financial benefit will be championed. For example, in June, Cyrus F. Freidheim mentioned its "War on Waste" in the tropics as a key part of its efforts to reduce costs. Nevertheless, it seems there can be no turning back from its investments in the broader CSR agenda. Why? The company recently launched a TV advertising campaign aimed at families, inviting parents to "Give them something good"— referring to their children. The messages in this campaign are children, responsibility, caring, health and goodness. You don't have to be Einstein to see the potential damage from negative publicity on these themes. Consequently their corporate responsibility work has become an indispensable part of their new branding and marketing.

As we try to rationalize what managers do, could do, or should do and determine the business case for corporate responsibility, let us not create some myth about what is driving these changes. Business is about people, not numbers. And it's people both inside and outside business who have been putting social and environmental issues on the corporate agenda. Bubbles, sticks, surveys and stats may all look good, but they don't capture the complexity and emotional nature of contemporary business. Life ain't no PowerPoint presentation.

THE GLOBAL REPORTING INITIATIVE

The Global Reporting Initiative (GRI) was established in late 1997 with the mission of developing globally applicable guidelines for reporting on the economic, environmental and social performance, initially for corporations and eventually for any business, governmental or non-governmental organization. The GRI was convened by the Coalition for Environmentally Responsible Economics (CERES) in partnership with the United Nations Environment Programme (UNEP), along with active participation from corporations, NGOs, accountancy organizations, business associations and other stakeholders from around the world.

The GRI has developed a set of core metrics intended to be applicable to all business enterprises, sets of sector-specific metrics for specific types of enterprises and a uniform format for reporting information integral to a company's sustainability performance. The GRI's Sustainability Reporting Guidelines were released in exposure draft form in March 1999. The GRI Guidelines represent the first global framework for comprehensive sustainability reporting, encompassing the "triple bottom line" of economic, environmental and social issues.

The GRI's Sustainability Reporting Guidelines are designed to help organizations publish reports:
- *In a way that provides stakeholders with reliable and relevant information that fosters dialogue and inquiry.*
- *Through well-established reporting principles, applied consistently from one reporting period to the next.*
- *In a way that facilitates reader understanding and comparison with similar reports.*
- *In a form that provides management across different organizations with valuable information to enhance internal decision making.*

Kofi Annan, secretary general of the United Nations, has remarked that "the Global Reporting Initiative is an admirable response to one of the primary challenges of our times: making global markets more stable and inclusive." Companies as diverse as 3M, ABB, Alliant Energy, Anheuser-Busch Companies, AT&T, BASF, Ericsson, Ford Motor Co., International Finance Corporation, Johnson & Johnson, McDonald's, Nike, Poloroid, Toshiba, Volkswagen and many more (see http://www.globalreporting.org/GRIGuidelines/Reporters.htm) have all adopted the GRI in their reporting structures.

Below you will find excerpts from the introduction to the GRI as well as the guidelines themselves.

BENEFITS OF REPORTING

For the 2,000 or more companies worldwide that are already reporting, the business justification for economic, environmental and social reporting is fact, not hypothesis. While no reporting organization may ever see the full range of potential benefits, observers point to the following common views in the business community:

- Effective management in a global economy, where information (reliable or unreliable) travels at Internet speed, requires a proactive approach. Measuring and reporting both past and anticipated performance is a critical management tool in today's high-speed, interconnected, "24-hour news" world.

- Today's strategic and operational complexities require a continual dialogue with investors, customers, advocates, suppliers and employees. Reporting is a key ingredient to building, sustaining and continually refining stakeholder engagement. Reports can help communicate an organization's economic, environmental and social opportunities and challenges in a way far superior to simply responding to stakeholder information requests.

- Companies increasingly emphasize the importance of relationships with external parties, ranging from consumers to investors to community groups, as key to their business success. Transparency and open dialogue about performance, priorities and future sustainability plans help to strengthen these partnerships and to build trust.

- Sustainability reporting is a vehicle for linking typically discrete and insular functions of the corporation—finance, marketing, research and development—in a more strategic manner. Sustainability reporting opens internal conversations where they would not otherwise occur.

- The process of developing a sustainability report provides a warning of trouble spots—and unanticipated opportunities—in supply chains, in communities, among regulators and in reputation and brand management. Reporting helps management evaluate potentially damaging developments before they develop into unwelcome surprises.

- Sustainability reporting helps sharpen management's ability to assess the organization's contribution to natural, human and social capital. This assessment enlarges the perspective provided by conventional financial accounts to create a more complete picture of long-term prospects. Reporting helps highlight the societal and ecological contributions of the organization and the "sustainability value proposition" of its products and services. Such measurement is central to maintaining and strengthening the "license to operate."

- Sustainability reporting may reduce volatility and uncertainty in share price for publicly traded enterprises, as well as reducing the cost of capital. Fuller and more regular information disclosure, including much of what analysts seek from managers on an ad hoc basis, can add stability to a company's financial condition by avoiding major swings in investor behavior caused by untimely or unexpected disclosures.

***

"IN ACCORDANCE" CONDITIONS

Organizations that wish to identify their report as prepared in accordance with the 2002 GRI *Guidelines* must meet five conditions:

1. Report on the numbered elements in Sections 1 to 3 of Part C.
2. Include a GRI Content Index as specified in Section 4 of Part C.
3. Respond to each core indicator in Section 5 of Part C by either (a) reporting on the indicator or (b) explaining the reason for the omission of each indicator.
4. Ensure that the report is consistent with the principles in Part B of the *Guidelines*.
5. Include the following statement signed by the board or CEO: "This report has been prepared in accordance with the 2002 GRI *Guidelines*. It represents a balanced and reasonable presentation of our organization's economic, environmental and social performance."

***

GRI REPORT CONTENT

The following five sections contain the reporting elements and performance indicators for the 2002 GRI *Guidelines*. Reporting elements are numbered (e.g., 1.1, 2.10) and performance indicators are contained in tables in Section 5. The elements and indicators are listed in bold type. Some are supported by additional guidance or explanation in standard type.

1. Vision and Strategy

This section encompasses a statement of the reporting organization's sustainability vision and strategy, as well as a statement from the CEO.

1.1 Statement of the organization's vision and strategy regarding its contribution to sustainable development. Present overall vision of the reporting organization for its future, particularly with regard to managing the challenges associated with economic, environmental and social performance. This should answer, at a minimum, the following questions:

- What are the main issues for the organization related to the major themes of sustainable development?

- How are stakeholders included in identifying these issues?

- For each issue, which stakeholders are most affected by the organization?

- How are these issues reflected in the organization's values and integrated into its business strategies?

- What are the organization's objectives and actions on these issues?

Reporting organizations should use maximum flexibility and creativity in preparing this section. The reporting organization's major direct and indirect economic, environmental and social issues and impacts (both positive and negative) should inform the discussion. Reporting organizations are encouraged to draw directly from indicators and information presented elsewhere in the report. They should include in their discussion any major opportunities, challenges or obstacles to moving toward improved economic, environmental and social performance. International organizations are also encouraged to explicitly discuss how their economic, environmental and social concerns relate to and are impacted by their strategies for emerging markets.

1.2 Statement from the CEO (or equivalent senior manager) describing key elements of the report. A statement from the reporting organization's CEO (or equivalent senior manager if other title is used) sets the tone of the report and establishes credibility with internal and external users. GRI does not specify the content of the CEO statement; however, it believes such statements are most valuable when they explicitly refer to the organization's commitment to sustainability and to key elements of the report. Recommended elements of a CEO statement include: highlights of report content and commitment to targets; description of the commitment to economic, environmental and social goals by the organization's leadership; statement of successes and failures; performance against benchmarks such as the previous year's performance and targets and industry sector norms; the organization's approach to stakeholder engagement; and major challenges for the organization and its business sector in integrating responsibilities for financial performance with those for economic, environmental and social performance, including the implications for future business strategy. The CEO statement may be combined with the statement of vision and strategy.

2. Profile

This section provides an overview of the reporting organization and describes the scope of the report. Thus, it provides readers with a context for understanding and evaluating information in the rest of the report. The section also includes organizational contact information.

Organizational Profile   Reporting organizations should provide the information listed below. In addition, they are encouraged to include any additional information that is needed for a full picture of the organization's operations, products and services.

2.1 Name of reporting organization.

2.2 Major products and/or services, including brands if appropriate. The reporting organization should also indicate the nature of its role in providing these products and services, and the degree to which the organization relies on outsourcing.

2.3 Operational structure of the organization.

2.4 Description of major divisions, operating companies, subsidiaries and joint ventures.

2.5 Countries in which the organization's operations are located.

2.6 Nature of ownership; legal form.

2.7 Nature of markets served.

2.8 Scale of the reporting organization: number of employees; products produced/services offered (quantity or volume); net sales; and total capitalization broken down in terms of debt and equity.

In addition to the above, reporting organizations are encouraged to provide additional information, such as: value added; total assets; and breakdowns of any or all of the following:

- Sales/revenues by countries/regions that make up 5% or more of total revenues;

- Major products and/or identified services;

- Costs by country/region; and

- Employees by country/region.

In preparing the profile information, organizations should consider the need to provide information beyond that on direct employees and financial data. For example, some organizations with few direct employees will have many indirect employees. This could include the employees of subcontractors, franchisees, joint ventures and companies entirely dependent on or answerable to the reporting organization. The extent of these relationships may interest stakeholders as much or more than information on direct employees. The reporting organization should consider adding such information to its profile where relevant. Reporting organizations should choose the set of measures best suited to the nature of their operations and stakeholders' needs. Measures should include those that can be used specifically to create ratios using the absolute figures provided in other sections of the report. All information should cover that portion of the organization that is covered by the report.

2.9 List of stakeholders, key attributes of each and relationship to the reporting organization. Stakeholders typically include the following groups (examples of attributes are shown in parentheses): communities (locations, nature of interest); customers (retail, wholesale, businesses, governments); shareholders and providers of capital (stock exchange listings); suppliers (products/services provided, local/national/international operations); trade unions (relation to workforce and reporting organization); workforce, direct and indirect (size, diversity, relationship to the reporting organization); and other stakeholders (business partners, local authorities, NGOs).

Report Scope   2.10 Contact person(s) for the report, including e-mail and Web addresses.

2.11 Reporting period (e.g., fiscal/calendar year) for information provided.

2.12 Date of most recent previous report (if any).

2.13 Boundaries of report (countries/regions, products/services, divisions/facilities/joint ventures/subsidiaries) and any specific limitations on the scope. If reporting boundaries do not match the full range of economic, environmental and social impacts of the organization, state the strategy and projected timeline for providing complete coverage.

2.14 Significant changes in size, structure, ownership, or products/services that have occurred since the previous report.

2.15 Basis for reporting on joint ventures, partially owned subsidiaries, leased facilities, outsourced operations and other situations that can significantly affect comparability from period to period and/or between reporting organizations.

2.16 Explanation of the nature and effect of any re-statements of information provided in earlier reports, and the reasons for such re-statement (e.g., mergers/acquisitions, change of base years/periods, nature of business, measurement methods).

Report Profile   2.17 Decisions not to apply GRI principles or protocols in the preparation of the report.

2.18 Criteria/definitions used in any accounting for economic, environmental and social costs and benefits.

2.19 Significant changes from previous years in the measurement methods applied to key economic, environmental and social information.

2.20 Policies and internal practices to enhance and provide assurance about the accuracy, completeness and reliability that can be placed on the sustainability report. This includes internal management systems, processes and audits that management relies on to ensure that reported data are reliable and complete with regard to the scope of the report.

2.21 Policy and current practice with regard to providing independent assurance for the full report.

2.22 Means by which report users can obtain additional information and reports about economic, environmental and social aspects of the organization's activities, including facility-specific information (if available).

3. Governance Structure and Management Systems

This section provides an overview of the governance structure, overarching policies and management systems in place to implement the reporting organization's vision for sustainable development and to manage its performance. Discussion of stakeholder engagement forms a key part of any description of governance structures and management systems. Some of the information listed in this section may overlap with information in other publications from the organization. GRI is sensitive to the need to avoid unnecessary duplication of effort. However, for the sake of ensuring full and complete contextual information for users of sustainability reports, it is important to cover the items listed below in combination with other information on the organization's economic, environmental and social performance. Organizations may wish to cross-reference between different documents, but this should not be done at the expense of excluding necessary information in a sustainability report.

Structure and Governance   3.1 Governance structure of the organization, including major committees under the board of directors that are responsible for setting strategy and for oversight of the organization. Describe the scope of responsibility of any major committees and indicate any direct responsibility for economic, social and environmental performance.

3.2 Percentage of the board of directors that are independent, non-executive directors. State how the board determines "independence."

3.3 Process for determining the expertise board members need to guide the strategic direction of the organization, including issues related to environmental and social risks and opportunities.

3.4 Board-level processes for overseeing the organization's identification and management of economic, environmental and social risks and opportunities.

3.5 Linkage between executive compensation and achievement of the organization's financial and non-financial goals (e.g., environmental performance, labor practices).

3.6 Organizational structure and key individuals responsible for oversight, implementation and audit of economic, environmental, social and related policies. Include identification of the highest level of management below the board level directly responsible for setting and implementing environmental and social policies, as well as general organizational structure below the board level.

3.7 Mission and values statements, internally developed codes of conduct or principles and polices relevant to economic, environmental and social performance and the status of implementation. Describe the status of implementation in terms of degree to which the code is applied across the organization in different regions and departments/units. "Policies" refers to those that apply to the organization as a whole, but may not necessarily provide substantial detail on the specific aspects listed under the performance indicators in Part C, Section 5 of the *Guidelines.*

3.8 Mechanisms for shareholders to provide recommendations or direction to the board of directors. Include reference to any policies or processes regarding the use of shareholder resolutions or other mechanisms for enabling minority shareholders to express opinions to management.

Stakeholder Engagement   Stakeholder engagement activities should reflect the organization's stakeholders as identified in the Profile section.

3.9 Basis for identification and selection of major stakeholders. This includes the processes for defining an organization's stakeholders and for determining which groups to engage.

3.10 Approaches to stakeholder consultation reported in terms of frequency of consultations by type and by stakeholder group. This could include surveys, focus groups, community panels, corporate advisory panels, written communication, management/union structures and other vehicles.

3.11 Type of information generated by stakeholder consultations. Include a list of key issues and concerns raised by stakeholders and identify any indicators specifically developed as a result of stakeholder consultation.

3.12 Use of information resulting from stakeholder engagements. For example, this could include selecting performance benchmarks or influencing specific decisions on policy or operations.

Overarching Policies and Management Systems   GRI has included policy indicators in both Section 3 (Governance Structure and Management Systems) and Section 5 (Performance Indicators), using the general principle of grouping information items closest to the most relevant aspect. The broader, overarching policies are most directly related to the governance structure and management systems section of the report. The most detailed level of policy (e.g., policies on child labor) may be captured in the performance indicator section of the report. Where the reporting organization perceives an overlap in the GRI framework, it should choose the most appropriate location in its report for the information.

3.13 Explanation of whether and how the precautionary approach or principle is addressed by the organization. This could include an example that illustrates the organization's approach to risk management in the operational planning or the development and introduction of new products.

3.14 Externally developed, voluntary economic, environmental and social charters, sets of principles or other initiatives to which the organization subscribes or which it endorses. Include date of adoption and countries/operations where applied.

3.15 Principle memberships in industry and business associations, and/or national/international advocacy organizations.

3.16 Policies and/or systems for managing upstream and downstream impacts, including: supply chain management as it pertains to outsourcing and supplier environmental and social performance; and product and service stewardship initiatives. Stewardship initiatives include efforts to improve product design to minimize negative impacts associated with manufacturing, use and final disposal.

3.17 Reporting organization's approach to managing indirect economic, environmental and social impacts resulting from its activities.

3.18 Major decisions during the reporting period regarding the location of, or changes in, operations. Explain major decisions such as facility or plant openings, closings, expansions and contractions.

3.19 Programs and procedures pertaining to economic, environmental and social performance. Include discussion of: priority and target setting; major programs to improve performance; internal communication and training; performance monitoring; internal and external auditing; and senior management review.

3.20 Status of certification pertaining to economic, environmental and social management systems. Include adherence to environmental management standards, labor or social accountability management systems, or other management systems for which formal certification is available.

THE GRI—THE WILL TO SUCCEED IS NOT ENOUGH

—MALLEN BAKER

Not everyone is completely enthusiastic about the advent of the GRI—and for a variety of reasons. Deloitte Touche, for instance, issued a statement claiming that "we do believe that the core indicators required by the 2002 Exposure Draft are too voluminous and will discourage too many organizations from even attempting to report under the GRI Guidelines. Further, we believe that the required boundaries of a sustainability report should not exceed the reporting entity's circle of control because it is unlikely that the reporting entity would have the ability to obtain the requisite information or determine its accuracy. Management may present supplementary, or additional, information on such matters, where relevant. We are concerned that the GRI is proceeding down a path of attempting to make a sustainability report be everything to everyone rather than focusing on how the reporting entity's sustainability performance can be measured overall. While we recognize that the latter form of a sustainability report will not suit each and every stakeholder's perceived needs, we believe it will result in a far more meaningful presentation."

What follows is another perspective from Mallen Baker, who explained in a separate article, "The danger for the GRI is that businesses are impatient to move forward—and if they are to embrace reporting, which many of them are starting to do, they want to see the value. These multi-stakeholder coalitions are all very well, but when the evidence suggests that very few of these stakeholder groups then go on actually to read the reports, or to engage with the content within them, you have the recipe for a passing fad that will pass before the rule book has finished being written. Alternatively—and this is quite a likely option—businesses will realize that reports need to focus only on those audiences who are used to gaining their information from reports—mostly the financial sector. And the rules for such reports will more quickly be established through a dialogue between the companies and those audiences. Then they will have to work out just how they communicate with the other audiences—the local communities, the employees and the customers."

Mallen Baker, *Business Respect,* No. 27 (April 2002), http://www.mallenbaker.net/csr/CSRfiles/GRI.html. Reprinted with permission of the author.

As the old saying goes, one shouldn't make important the things that are easy to measure—rather measure the important however hard that may be. But from all of these counts, the current GRI crop fares poorly. Much of the information requested is of only passing relevance to the impact or health of the business—and for a list of 57 indicators there isn't room for dead weight. All of these measures will take considerable company resources to gather—if some of the indicators are ill-conceived it runs the risk of bringing the whole CSR reporting imperative into some disrepute.

Most of the economic indicators fall into this. What information do I get from knowing the percent of purchasing spent per supplier and main invoicing country? Even if I get a list of subsidies received broken down by geographical region, how am I meant to interpret that in the context of social responsibility?

Whilst I am wading through these, and a host of similar details relating to cash flows—what I am not getting so far is any kind of assessment of the impact on society of the company's core products or services—which is rather a grievous omission. I may personally believe that society must make space for the possibility of a socially responsible tobacco company, but I would expect such a one to report fully on the current impact of the product—something not required by the core indicators of the GRI as framed here.

But the biggest problem is that once you get past the economic and the environmental indicators, the GRI gives up the ghost on performance measurement altogether, and falls back on describing policies and practices. The existence of a policy to prevent this, the existence of a procedure to ensure that. But no performance measurement.

If the company has a policy to exclude child labor, personally I would like verification that neither it, nor its key suppliers, employs children. Call me picky. If it has policies to evaluate human rights performance in its supply chain, it must be relevant to look at how that is evaluated, and how performance is communicated.

Of the 57 core indicators, no less than 22 simply ask for policies or procedures. The ability to track over time how such policies play out in terms of performance is highly questionable.

It does seem that the GRI has been pulled in several directions at once, and will end up pleasing nobody unless the main intellectual content of what it has been set up to do is sorted out. Its indicators are not business-led enough—there is a huge demand on companies to collect information the value of which to them will be rather questionable. But then on the side of the other stakeholders—those with an interest in the activity of companies—the preponderance of measures relating to policies being in place rather than performance means that these will be unsatisfying from the point of view of disclosure.

The committees and the subcommittees have been formed. The rites of institutionalization have taken place. There is a huge will all round for the GRI to create a global consensus on what constitutes core data for social reporting. Now it needs to deliver the goods. If it doesn't do this—and doesn't do it quite soon, it will weaken the power and role of social reporting immeasurably.

Part Two

ETHICS IN THE BUSINESS DISCIPLINES

Chapter 5

ETHICS AND HUMAN RESOURCES MANAGEMENT
Values in the Employment Relationship

We can invest all the money on Wall Street in new technologies, but we can't realize the benefits of improved productivity until companies rediscover the value of human loyalty.

—FREDERICK REICHHELD,
DIRECTOR, BAIN & CO.

In 1960, about one-third of the American workforce was represented by unions. Today, that figure is about 11%. Collective bargaining, established to protect the interests of workers, has proven inadequate to the task. Not surprisingly, federal and state regulations governing work practices have exploded. The variety of protections is prodigious: anti-discrimination laws, wage and hour laws, worker safety laws, unemployment compensation, workers' compensation and social security, to name a few.

The purpose of this chapter is to present ethical dilemmas that face the worker, whether she or he is an employee on an assembly line, the manager of a restaurant or the CEO of a large corporation. While the perspectives change, similar conflicts (and stakeholders) present themselves. The predominant theme is that at some point in each person's life, she or he will be an employee or an employer, and it is critical to recognize the stakes each player may have in any given dilemma. The chapter will provide a textual background relating to the employment relationship, its origins and its regulation, as well as readings relevant to this topic.

We all have decisions about how we will treat others in the workplace and how we will ask to be treated. Ethics at work and in human resource management is about our relationships with others and with our organizations. Recent research supports a slew of earlier findings that "companies that place employees at the core of their strategies produce higher long-term returns to shareholders than do industry peers."[1] The same holds true for inter-

---

[1] Walker Information, "Committed Employees Make Your Business Work," *Employee Relationship Report,* http://www.walkerinfo. com/products/err/ee_study.cfm (1999).

personal relationships. Notwithstanding these truths, less than half of U.S. workers feel a strong personal attachment to their organization or believe that the organization deserves it. Only one in four workers is truly loyal to their place of work. When asked about the greatest influence on their commitment, workers responded that the most important factor is fairness at work, followed by care and concern for employees—all key components of an ethical working environment.

In developing a response to these concerns and influences, one might consider the role of emotion in the workplace. Though a relatively new area of research, studies evidence that management can have a significant impact on the emotions of their workers, and this impact can greatly affect productivity and loyalty, as well as perceptions of fairness, care and concern. Scholars Neal Ashkanasy and Catherine Daus suggest that managers pay attention to the emotional impact of various jobs within their workplace and model a positive emotional environment.[2] Rewards and compensation structures can clearly impact the emotions of workers, as can the composition of teams or the power relationships within a workplace. Finally, transformational leadership strategies can emphasize positive emotional health and a powerful vision for the organization.

Sears put this concept to the test when it asked its workers what is important to them. This is a sensitive question because, if a firm asks and then does not respond to those areas of importance, it is effectively ignoring the priorities of its workers. Sears did ask, though, and learned a great deal. The company found that the job factors that are most important to workers include:

- Whether they like their work.

- Whether their work gives them a sense of accomplishment.

- Whether they are proud to say they work at Sears.

- Workload.

- Working conditions.

- Treatment by supervisors.

- Optimism about the future of the company.

- Whether they feel that Sears is competing effectively.

- Whether they understand the company's business strategy.

- Whether they see a connection between their work and the company's objectives.[3]

Consider how you would respond to these factors with regard to your current or a previous job. How would you have prioritized the above concerns?

---

[2]Neal Ashkanasy and Catherine Daus, "Emotion in the Workplace," *Academy of Management Executive* 16, no. 1 (2002), p. 76.
[3]Workforce Online, "What's Most Important to Employees," http://workforceonline.com/sears/attitude.html (1999).

When employees see that a firm values their emotions, as well as exhibits values such as honesty, respect and trust, they feel less pressure, feel more valued as employees and are also more satisfied with their organizations.[4] Since reporting has become such a key issue in recent scandals, consider whether a more satisfied employee is more or less likely to report misconduct. (See later articles in this chapter on whistleblowing for a more in-depth discussion.)

DOWNSIZING

How do we act more ethically in downsizing? In a speech to the Ethics Officers Association, John Challenger suggested that we should consider planning, timing, notice, impact (on those who will go and those who will stay) and stakeholder perceptions.[5] We can make better choices, Challenger argues. The decision regarding downsizing should be made by a representative group so that all stakeholder interests can be considered and to earn the trust of those who will be impacted. Since employees should be kept aware of business conditions, the need for a downsizing effort should not come as a great surprise. However, the question of notice is debatable. Some might argue that a firm should give notice of the downsizing as soon as it determines the need, and then let those who will be impacted know of the choice as soon as that list is devised. On the other hand, the uncertainty and rumors that are sure to develop between the announcement of a downsizing effort and the decision about who will be terminated may outweigh the benefits gained in early notification. In addition, allowing a worker to remain in a position for a period of time once she or he has been notified of impending termination might not be the best option. A worker may interpret your early notice as an effort to get the most out of this worker before departure rather than an effort to allow them time to come to grips with the departure.

When a firm decides to downsize, as with any other termination, it is critical to lessen any unnecessary impact and to allow the individual to depart with dignity (i.e., unless there is some other reason, a security guard following the terminated employee until they leave the building might not be the best option). Above all, during a time when relationships might be strained, it is most critical to be honest and forthright and to have sensitivity to the experiences of those you plan to impact.

As inevitable as downsizing may seem during downturns in the economy, some firms have survived decade after decade without any layoffs. How do they do it? One firm, Nucor, has not laid off a worker in 20 years. However, the firm maintains a three-day workweek with an average wage of $8 per hour. When large contracts come in, it expands to a seven-day workweek and $22 per hour wage. Other firms have entered into agreements with their workers where the firm promises not to terminate workers for reasons of the economy as long as the workers agree to lower wages or decreased hours during tough periods. For instance, in December 1998, Volkswagen in Brazil was suffering under the collapse of that country's economy and the resulting 25% downturn in the Brazilian car market. However, it avoided terminations at its 20,000-worker plant by moving to a four-day workweek.

---

[4]Ethics Resource Center, *National Business Ethics Survey* (2000).
[5]John A. Challenger, "Downsizing: The Better Ways," *Ethikos,* January/February 2002, p. 7.

DISCRIMINATION

One might think that, after four decades of anti-discrimination laws on the books, one might be hard pressed today to find discrimination remaining in the workplace. Unfortunately, this is far from the case. In fact, though overt acts of discrimination might be decreasing, covert forms of discrimination are still at play. For instance, in recent research, University of Chicago scholars Marianne Bertrand and Sendhil Millainathan found that there remains discrimination simply on the basis of one's name.[6] In order to determine the extent of discrimination in the labor market on the basis of the racial sound of a name, these researchers answered help-wanted ads in Boston and Chicago newspapers by sending résumés. Though the résumés were all exactly the same in their substance, they were different in the names attached to them. This change produced a major difference in the number of callbacks received for each résumé. Names that were traditionally associated with Caucasians (such as Jill, Allison, Neil and Brad) drew 50% more callbacks than did those traditionally associated with African Americans (such as Aisha, Ebony, Tremayne and Leroy). Even when the researchers increased the quality of the résumés, higher-quality résumés from African American–sounding candidates received no more callbacks than the original résumé. The only bright spot in the research was the finding that Chicago employers in African-American neighborhoods discriminated less than those in other communities.

Additional studies reinforce these findings that bias on the job is also common. Rutgers Law School professors Alfred and Ruth Blumrosen conducted a study in 2002 that concluded that about 2 million workers were affected by intentional discrimination in 1999.[7] Within those numbers, about 22,000 employers were found to be "hard-core" discriminators, employing below-average numbers of women and minorities for 10 years. Their numbers were so low that the Blumrosens found that there was only a 1% chance that the discrimination occurred randomly.

Though these findings might seem disappointing, many employers bemoan greater and greater regulation of their workplaces. The law allows employers to make decisions on any basis, other than a few prohibited bases (age, religion, race, disability, gender, national origin, color).

Moreover, we don't often recognize areas of Western culture that contain or perpetuate covert discrimination. In her article, "White Privilege: Unpacking the Invisible Knapsack,"[8] Peggy McIntosh identifies a number of daily conditions on which a white person in Western society can basically count in connection with their daily living, explaining that

---

[6]Marianne Bertrand and Sendhil Millainathan, "Are Emily and Brendan More Employable Than Lakisha and Jamal?" University of Chicago, Graduate School of Business, unpublished paper, November 18, 2002.

[7]Alfred and Ruth Blumrosen, "The Reality of Intentional Job Discrimination in Metropolitan America—1999," http://www.eeol.com/1999_NR/1999_nr.htm. See also Reed Abelson, "Study Finds Bias on the Job Is Still Common," *New York Times,* July 24, 2002.

[8]Peggy McIntosh, "White Privilege: Unpacking the Invisible Knapsack," *Peace and Freedom,* July/August 1989, pp. 10–12.

this privilege is like "an invisible weightless knapsack of provisions, maps, passports, code-books, visas, clothes, tools and blank checks," such as:

- I can go shopping alone most of the time, pretty well assured that I will not be followed or harassed.

- I can open a newspaper or turn on the television and see people of my race represented positively.

- I can do well in a challenging situation without being called a credit to my race.

- I am never asked to speak for all of the people in my racial group.

On the other hand, if we change the above references to gender rather than race, women often face challenges that are distinct from those faced by men. For instance, women and men are both subject to gender stereotyping, but suffer from different expectations in that regard. A woman who is aggressive in the workplace is often considered to be a bully, while a man is deemed to be doing what he needs to do to get ahead. In fact, there even exists a corporate coaching program for women who are considered to be "bullies" called "Bully Broads." The program is designed to help women to understand how their conception of what it takes to get ahead (often learned through interactions with men, for that matter) might cause others with whom they work to consider them to be bullies. But can you imagine a similar program for men? Probably not. Aggressive men are viewed as going after what they want, not letting anything get in their way and so on.

In an article discussing the coaching program, not one mention was made regarding how this behavior might have been learned nor whether it should be all right for women to engage in behavior similar to male counterparts.[9] The goal of the program is to boost productivity because "it is difficult to produce if others do not want to work with you." How would this same story sound if it had to do with one race acting too much like another? How would you feel about the story if it suggested that a certain group of people should "know their place" or people won't want to work with them?

The fact is, when any employment decision is made, discrimination exists. Does that surprise you? Isn't it appropriate for an employer to discriminate based on actual qualifications such as education and experience (for some jobs)? In fact, employers can, should and do discriminate based on perfectly acceptable grounds. You wouldn't find it strange or wrong for a business to require a human resources degree for applicants to a position as vice president of human resources. American law merely forbids discrimination on a *few, specific, non-job-related* factors (such as religion and race).

Can the Market "Fix" Discrimination?

If the market were left to its own devices, wouldn't you expect firms that discriminate to fall by the wayside? That is, if a firm hires its employees based on prejudices and discriminatory views (such as women can't do a certain job), then it is limiting its pool of possible

[9]Good Morning America, "Powerfully Nice," abcnews.com, July 16, 2001.

employees. Another firm that does not discriminate can choose from the larger pool and is more likely to obtain the *most* qualified individual for the job. Judge Richard Posner explains the economic impact of this theory in terms of race discrimination as follows:

> *In a market of many sellers, the intensity of the prejudice against blacks will vary considerably. Some sellers will have only a mild prejudice against them. These sellers will not forgo as many advantageous transactions with blacks as their more prejudiced competitors (unless the law interferes). Their costs will therefore be lower, and this will enable them to increase their share of the market. The least prejudiced sellers will come to dominate the market in much the same way as people who are least afraid of heights come to dominate occupations that require working at heights: they demand a smaller premium.*[10]

Under what circumstances would Posner's argument fail? Consider the implications if the discriminating firm held a monopoly on its good or service. What is the effect of regulation such as Title VII on Posner's argument? Consider his approach above as you read the excerpt from his text later in this chapter.

DIVERSITY

Efforts toward the elimination of discrimination in employment over the past 30 years have, indeed, resulted in a more diverse workforce. Diversity refers to the presence of differing cultures, languages, ethnicities, races, affinity orientations, genders, religious sects, abilities, social classes, ages and national origins of the individuals in a firm. Ninety percent of employees in U.S. businesses believe they have a diverse workforce where they work.[11] This is not surprising since the pool of eligible and interested workers is becoming more and more diverse, as well. It is estimated that, by 2010, only 20% of the workforce will be white, able-bodied men under 45.[12] As one might expect, the management composition at firms with diversity programs is significantly more diverse than those at firms who do not have such programs and 79% of senior managers at those firms say that cultivating a more diverse workforce is part of the organization's overall business strategy.

This diversity has brought with it countless benefits to the workplace, but has also created conflicts that were not previously present. Where individuals from different backgrounds are brought together for the first time, *and* where negative stereotypes previously ruled interactions between these two groups, sensitivity to the potential for conflict is necessary. Efforts at multiculturalism, defined as the acknowledgment and promotion of diversity through celebration and appreciation of various cultures in the workplace, is one response.

Part of hiring for a diverse environment raises issues of potential cultural conflicts so a firm needs to be prepared to manage those areas of friction as it embarks on the creation

---

[10]Richard A. Posner, *Economic Analysis of Law,* p. 616.
[11]"Diversity Policies Have Positive Impact on Company Business Performance," New York Times Company Press Release, February 13, 2003.
[12]Business in the Community, "Workplace," http://www.bitc.org.uk/resources/research/statbank/workplace/index.html.

of a diverse workforce. On the other hand, there is nothing inappropriate about seeking to ensure that workers will be able to support the particular values of a firm. How can you ensure the latter while also encouraging diversity? Some scholars suggest that job applicants be screened with regard to their values—but how? Though not an area to be taken lightly, most firms go with a "gut" instinct. In the same way that one might apply the "can you sleep at night" test to an ethical dilemma after considering all of the implications, so too might you trust this factor to the same test. It is not discriminatory to refuse to hire someone about whom you simply have a "bad feeling," unless that bad feeling is based on a perception that their difference is the only challenge.

The cost of ignoring diversity is high, not only in terms of ensuring the greatest productivity, creativity and other performance-based measures, but also in terms of legal liability. Texaco experienced what Texaco insiders refer to simply as "the crisis" in 1996 when it was required by a settlement to sign a $175 million check to settle a racial discrimination lawsuit. The settlement was based on taped conversations of executives using racist language as well as documented compensation discrimination against minority employees, hundreds of whom were being paid below the minimum salary for their job level.

However, often a firm reaches its depths before it emerges anew—Texaco's current numbers tell a much different story. In 1998, minority hires accounted for 40% of all new employees, including some key senior executives, and more than 20% of promotions. Texaco pledged to spend at least $1 million with minority and women contractors within five years and, of course, diversity training is now mandated for all workers, with management compensation tied to the attainment of success in implementing new initiatives.

Often, an effort to encourage greater diversity may also be seen as a form of "reverse discrimination"—in other words, discrimination against those individuals who are traditionally considered to be in power or the majority, such as white men. The term, itself, however, doesn't make much sense since discrimination can go in any direction. Everyone has a gender, a race, a national origin. Discrimination on any of these bases, whether against a man or a woman, an Asian or a Native American—all of these are prohibited. Consequently, firms that seek to promote diversity must be careful in doing so in order to protect against liability. See the Hettinger article for a more expansive discussion of this issue.

Other problems exist that one might not necessarily consider. For example, reflect on a report by the U.S. Commission on Civil Rights that addresses the unique predicament of Asian Americans. The report documents widespread discrimination against Asian Americans, who have long been seen as having escaped the national origin barriers that face other cultures. The report contends that the typical Asian stereotype of being hardworking, intelligent and successful is actually a detriment to Asian Americans. This stereotype results in the problems of poor Asians being overlooked, in preventing successful Asian Americans from becoming more successful, in placing undue pressure on young Asian Americans to succeed in school and in discrediting other minorities by arguing that "if Asian Americans can succeed, so can other minorities."[13] In an article highlighting the report, *Fortune* mag-

---

[13]"Up from Inscrutable," *Fortune,* April 6, 1992, p. 20.

azine intuits that the problem is really that the commission is "being driven crazy by the fact that Asian Americans have been succeeding essentially *without the benefit of affirmative action.* The ultimate problem is not that they may make other minorities look bad—it is that they are making the civil rights bureaucracy look irrelevant."[14] Some theorists argue that formal affirmative action measures have often served to create a greater divide rather than to draw people closer.

Affirmative Action

The struggle for civil rights in the workplace sometimes cannot be achieved, in the short run, simply by avoiding discriminatory practices. Obviously, obeying the law is expected of all. However, as a matter of social policy, we have decided that mere compliance with the civil rights laws, guaranteeing equal opportunity in the workplace, is not always adequate to correct the wrongs of discrimination. Among other problems, a great deal of time ordinarily would need to pass before the lingering effects of past discrimination would no longer be felt if we were to do nothing more than not practice discrimination. Therefore, we have decided as a society to implement the policy that we label "affirmative action" as a means of remedying past wrongs and preventing the same in the future. In following an affirmative action plan, employers consciously take positive steps to seek out minorities and women for hiring and promotion opportunities, and they often employ goals and timetables to measure progress toward a workforce that is representative of the qualified labor pool.

Affirmative action efforts arise in two ways: (1) courts may order the implementation of affirmative action after a finding of wrongful discrimination, and (2) employers may voluntarily adopt affirmative action plans. Some may do so because they believe it is a wise management strategy or because they approve of affirmative action as a matter of social policy, or both. Others may adopt affirmative action because they wish to do business with the federal government. All government contractors must meet the affirmative action standards of the Office of Federal Contract Compliance Programs. As discussed above, those standards consist essentially of established goals and timetables for strengthening the representation of "underutilized" minorities and women.

Good Policy?

Affirmative action is one of the most hotly disputed social issues in contemporary life. Minorities and women have been the victims of discrimination. Should white males "pay" for those wrongs? Critics decry affirmative action as "reverse discrimination." They argue that affirmative action is paternalistic and encourages the view that minorities and women can progress only with the aid of white males. Studies confirm that affirmative action plans stigmatize minorities and women in the minds of co-workers. Minorities and women are often assumed to have achieved their positions via "quotas" and not as the result of their efforts and abilities.

---

[14]*Ibid.*

Now, many white males feel that they are surrounded and under siege by the forces of affirmative action and multiculturalism. Even if so, *Newsweek* argues that being a white man is still a very comfortable role in contemporary America:

> *But is the white male truly an endangered species, or is he just being a jerk? It's still a statistical piece of cake being a white man, at least in comparison with being anything else. White males make up just 39.2% of the population, yet they account for 82.5% of the Forbes 400 (folks worth at least $265 million), 77% of Congress, 92% of state governors, 70% of tenured college faculty, almost 90% of daily-newspaper editors, 77% of TV news directors. They dominate just about everything but NOW and the NAACP.*[15]

Affirmative Action in Practice

United Steelworkers of America v. Weber is perhaps the clearest Supreme Court statement to date about the permissible boundaries of affirmative action. Weber, a white male, challenged the legality of an affirmative action plan that set aside for black employees 50% of the openings in a training program until the percentage of black craft workers in the plant equaled the percentage of blacks in the local labor market. Weber was denied entry to the training program. The federal district court and the federal court of appeals held for Weber, but the U.S. Supreme Court reversed. Therefore, under *Weber,* race-conscious affirmative action remedies *can* be permissible. Several qualities of the Steelworkers' plan were instrumental in the Court's favorable ruling:

1. The affirmative action was part of a plan.
2. The plan was designed to "open employment opportunities for Negroes in occupations that have been traditionally closed to them."
3. The plan was temporary.
4. The plan did not unnecessarily harm the rights of white employees. That is—
   (a) The plan did not require the discharge of white employees.
   (b) The plan did not create an absolute bar to the advancement of white employees.

Therefore, affirmative action in situations like that in *Weber* does not constitute unlawful reverse discrimination. The Supreme Court clarified the law's affirmative action commands a bit further in the *Burdine* case, in which the Court asserted that Title VII does not require the employer to hire a minority or female applicant whenever that person's objective qualifications were equal to those of a white male applicant. Therefore, "the employer has discretion to choose among equally qualified candidates, provided the decision is not based upon unlawful criteria."

DRUG TESTING

Whether an employer tests its employees for drug usage requires a delicate balance between the right of the employer to protect its interests and the right of the employee to be free from wrongful intrusions into her or his personal affairs. Since the employer is often responsible

---

[15] M. A. Jaimes Guerrero, "Affirmative Action," *American Behavioral Scientist* 41, no. 2 (1997), p. 246.

for legal violations of its employees committed in the course of their job, the employer's interest in retaining control over every aspect of the work environment increases. On the other hand, employees may argue that their drug usage is only relevant if it impacts their job performance. Until it does, the employer should have no basis for testing.

Country singer Tom T. Hall would likely advocate drug testing as he croons, "If you hang all the people, you'll get all the guilty." Consider the possibilities of incorrect presumptions in connection with drug testing. For instance, in his book, *Drug Abuse in the Workplace: An Employer's Guide for Prevention,* Mark de Bernardo suggests that crudely wrapped cigarettes, razor blades or eye droppers, frequent trips to the bathroom, or dressing inappropriately for the season may be warning signs of drug use.[16] On the other hand, it does not take a great deal of imagination to come up with other, more innocuous alternative possibilities. Yet, an employer may decide to test based on these "signs."

In a study examining the attitudes of college students to drug testing programs, researchers found that "virtually all aspects of drug testing programs are strongly accepted by some individuals and strongly rejected by others."[17] The only variable that the researchers found indicative of a student's attitude was whether the student had ever used drugs in the past. Where a student had never used drugs, she or he was more likely to find drug testing programs acceptable.[18] In general, the following factors contribute to greater acceptance and approval by workers:

A. Programs that use a task force made up of employees and their supervisors.
B. A completely random program.
C. Effective communication of procedures.
D. Programs that offer treatment other than termination for first time offenders.
E. Programs with no distinction between supervisory and other workers.

COMPENSATION

One of the most heated issues in any discussion of human resource management is salary. Often workers believe that they are underpaid for their work, that employers might not always treat them fairly or that they are not appreciated. One of the most sensitive areas in connection with salary and fairness is gender discrimination. As we have discussed, Title VII of the 1964 Act places race, color and national origin among those "protected classes" against which discrimination is forbidden. In addition, the Equal Pay Act of 1963 specifically provides that men and women must be paid equal pay for equal work. Accordingly, failure to fairly compensate workers may constitute both a legal and ethical breach.

An employer seeking to avoid a violation of Title VII or the Equal Pay Act can adjust its wage structure by raising the pay of the disfavored sex. Lowering the pay of the favored

---

[16]Mark A. de Bernardo, *Drug Abuse in the Workplace: An Employer's Guide for Prevention,* available from the U.S. Chamber of Commerce, 1615 H Street, NW, Washington, DC 20062.
[17]Kevin Murphy, George Thornton and Douglas Reynolds, "College Students' Attitudes Toward Employee Drug Testing Programs," *Personnel Psychology* 43 (1990), p. 615.
[18]*Ibid.*

sex violates the act. Paying women and men the same amount for the same work is simple enough in principle, but the legal issues have proved slippery, indeed. For example:

1. Is travel reimbursement a "wage"? Maternity payments? [According to the federal government—No.]
2. Must the plaintiff establish a *pattern* of sex-based wage discrimination? [According to the federal government—No.]
3. Are jobs unequal in effort and thus "unequal work" when a part of one job includes tasks that females are physically unable to perform? [No, if those tasks do not constitute a substantial part of the job.]

In the leading case of *Corning Glass Works v. Brennan,* the Supreme Court was faced with the question of whether different shifts constituted differing "working conditions." Women had been engaged in glass inspection on the day shift. Corning added a night shift of inspectors, which, due to state "protective" laws, was composed entirely of males. The night shift demanded and received higher wages than the female day inspectors. The Supreme Court held that the time of day in and of itself is not a *working condition.* That term, the Court said, refers to "surroundings" and "hazards." However, shift differentials could lawfully constitute a "factor other than sex" if established by the employer.

Comparable Worth

Equal pay for equal work is hardly a radical notion, but equal pay for work of comparable value would, if fully realized, dramatically alter the nature of the American labor market. *Comparable worth* calls for determining the compensation to be paid for a position based on the job's intrinsic value in comparison to wages being paid for other jobs requiring comparable skills, effort and responsibility and having comparable worth to the organization.

The argument is that the dollar value assigned to jobs held predominantly by men is higher than the value assigned to jobs held predominantly by women. To proponents of comparable worth, such disparities cannot be explained by market forces. They argue that women are the continuing victims of sex discrimination in violation of Title VII of the Civil Rights Act of 1964.

A variety of studies have contrasted pay scales in traditionally female jobs with those in traditionally male jobs where the jobs are judged to be of comparable worth. For example, licensed practical nurses in Illinois in 1983 earned an average of $1,298 per month, while electricians earned an average of $2,826. A 1987 Child Welfare League study fixed the median salary of garbage collectors at $14,872 annually, as compared with $12,800 for child care workers. The same study found social workers with master's degrees earned about $21,800 per year, while auto salespeople averaged $22,048.

There may be market explanations for the inequality between wages in occupations that are traditionally male-dominated as opposed to those jobs that are traditionally female-dominated. Economist and jurist, Judge Richard Posner, explains:

> *[While] irrational or exploitive discrimination is one possibility[,] another is that male wages include a compensatory wage premium for the dirty, disagreeable and often strenuous jobs that men dominate presumably because their aversion to such work*

is less than women's. Another (these are not mutually exclusive of course) is differences in investments in market-related human capital (earning capacity). If a woman allocates a substantial part of her working life to household production, including child care, she will obtain a substantially lower return on her market human capital than a man planning to devote much less time to household production, and she will therefore invest less in that human capital. Since earnings are in part a return on one's human capital investments (including education), women's earnings will be lower than men's. In part this will show up in the choice of occupations: Women will be attracted to occupations that don't require much human capital. Of course the amount of time women are devoting to household production is declining, so we can expect the wage gap to shrink if the economic model is correct.[19]

Posner concludes by qualifying his comments, "if the economic model is correct." Why might you believe that this model would not be correct or that the wage gap may not shrink completely? If actual prejudice (i.e., pre-judging) exists, that is, women are *believed* to be less valuable as workers than men, regardless of their *actual* abilities, then employers may continue to hire men at higher wages. In other words, even though women are actually spending less time at home and the household and child care duties are more likely to be split, employers may still *believe* that women will get pregnant and quit. Given this prejudice, employers will not pay women commensurate with men, notwithstanding market influences. Do you agree?

A number of companies, state governments and several foreign countries practice some form of comparable worth, but most continue to rely on the market as the best measure of worth. The U.S. Supreme Court has yet to directly explore the substance of the comparable worth debate. In the *Gunther* case, the Court held, in effect, that Title VII does not forbid the comparable worth theory. However, the federal appeals court decisions to date have rejected the comparable worth theory in the context of Title VII sex discrimination.

SEXUAL HARASSMENT

One additional area of recent concern, especially in connection with the balance of power in the workplace, is sexual harassment. Sexual harassment evolved through a traditional application of Title VII: treating someone differently because of her or his gender is unlawful under Title VII. There are two types of sexual harassment that fit within this broad prohibition: quid pro quo and hostile environment. Quid pro quo exists where a supervisor offers an employment benefit in exchange for sexual activity or where a supervisor refuses to give an employee deserved benefits unless she or he engages in sexual activity. Hostile environment sexual harassment is not so easily defined. The Supreme Court, through a host of cases, explains that a hostile environment exists where a work environment is severely or pervasively altered such that a reasonable person would find it offensive or abusive.

The definition of a hostile environment is thus rather complicated and amorphous. The court has defined it in such a way as to make it a hybrid of a subjective and objective test. First, the plaintiff must show that the environment would be considered offensive to

---

[19]Richard Posner, *Economic Analysis of Law* (Boston: Little Brown & Co., 1986), pp. 313–14.

a reasonable person (objective analysis); then the plaintiff must *also* show that she or he, individually, was offended by the situation (subjective analysis). For this reason, it is difficult to state conclusively whether any given circumstance might be considered to be sexual harassment. On the other hand, we are given some parameters. The facts that give rise to the claim must be severe or pervasive. A onetime event would not constitute sexual harassment unless it is severe; and a relatively benign event might become sexual harassment where it is pervasive.

HUMAN RESOURCE VALUES IN CONFLICT?

One of the key issues facing business in today's globalized economy is the potential for cultural or legal conflicts in connection with worldwide labor management. Though the issues stir our consciences, their resolution is not so clear. Let's consider, for example, the case of child labor. As we begin to understand the circumstances facing children worldwide, we can see that a simple prohibition might not offer us the best possible solution. But what options exist?

In developing countries children begin work at ages as young as three years. Children may work in unhealthy conditions. However, they also live in unhealthy conditions. The labor opportunities that exist almost always preclude children from obtaining an education as children often work on a full-time basis.[20] However, if children are not working, their options are not as optimistic as those for children in developed economies. There are not always sophisticated education systems or public schools. Often children who do not work in the manufacturing industry are forced to work in less hospitable "underground" professions such as drug dealing or prostitution simply in order to provide for their own food each day.

Unfortunately, in extreme cases, children are forced into slavery as a result of this need for work, often in the guise of indentured servitude or apprenticeship training. When discussing the nature of children's work, ILO Bureau of Statistics reports that

> [m]ost children working as paid employees were paid much less than the prevailing rates in their localities, even when compared with the legal minimum wages—receiving only one-sixth of the minimum rate in one survey finding; also the younger the working

---

[20]See Lammy Betten, *International Labor Law* (1993), p. 316 (noting that child labor legislation may lead to a movement of child labor from the formal to the informal sectors of the economy). See also Ministry of Labor, Manpower and Overseas Pakistanis & SEBCON (Pvt) Ltd., *Qualitative Survey on Child Labor in Pakistan* (Islamabad: International Labor Organization/OPEC, 1996) [ILO study in Pakistan evidences that, among the child laborers interviewed, 72% had no access to education at all.]; Alan R. Myerson, "In Principle, a Case for More 'Sweatshops,'" *New York Times,* June 22, 1997 (online version: http://www.ncpa.org/pd/pdint152.html); and "Labor Secretary Herman Speaks out Against Child Labor," *Apparel Industry Magazine* 58, no.11 (November 1997), p. 12 [Mohammed Hafizul Islam Chowdhury, an apparel manufacturer from Bangladesh, asks, "Why are Americans against child labor? It's good in my country because it keeps children off the streets and out of prostitution."]; and Stephen Golub, "Are International Labor Standards Needed to Prevent Social Dumping?" *Finance & Development,* December 1997, pp. 20, 22, http://www.imf.org/external/pubs/ft/fandd/1997/12/pdf/golub.pdf.

child, the lower the wage payment. On average girls worked longer hours than boys but were paid less than their working brothers doing the same type of work. . . . Generally children were not paid for overtime work.[21]

Children make up a substantial portion of the labor force in undeveloped countries.[22] The International Labor Organization estimates that in developing countries there are 250 million child laborers between the ages of 5 and 14, with at least 120 million working full time.[23] Most children work in agriculture, service industries, or prostitution. Because work takes children out of school, more than half of the child labor force will never be literate.[24] And because of substandard working conditions, child employees will grow less than those who didn't work as children and the child workers' bodies will be smaller, even into adulthood.[25] By the time child laborers reach adulthood, most will irrevocably be sick or deformed; the children are unlikely to live to be 50 years old.[26]

Though few, if any, would argue for the continuation of these circumstances, economists are at odds regarding what to do about them. As you review the readings in this chapter, consider how you might respond if you were a sourcing manager who found youth workers in the factory of a new supplier.

[21]Kebebew Ashagrie, *Methodological Child Labor Surveys and Statistics: ILO's Recent Work in Brief* (Geneva: International Labor Organization, 1997), p. 10, http://www.ilo.org/public/english/120stat/actrep/childlab.

[22]The ILO reports that in the Philippines more than 60% of working children are exposed to hazardous working conditions and 40% of those exposed experience serious injuries or illnesses including those that result in amputations and loss of body parts. International Labor Organization, *Child Labor: Targeting the Intolerable* (Geneva: International Labor Organization, 1998), http://www.ilo.org/public/english/90ipec/publ/clrep96.htm.

[23]International Labor Organization, *Child Labor: Targeting the Intolerable, infra* note 21, at p. 7, http://www.ilo.org/public/english/90ipec/publ/clrep96.htm. See also International Labor Organization, *Child Labor Today,* ILO/CLK/1 (Geneva: International Labor Organization, June 10, 1996), p. 1. For additional statistical information in this area, see also International Labor Organization, *Facts and Figures on Child Labor* (1999), http://www.ilo.org/public/english/child/download/worstfrm/statistics.pdf.

[24]International Labor Organization, *World Employment Report 1998–1999* (Geneva: International Labor Organization, 1999).

[25]World Health Organization, *Children at Work: Special Health Risks, Technical Report Series No. 756* (Geneva: International Labor Organization, 1987); K. Satyanarayan et al., "Effect of Early Childhood Nutrition and Child Labor on Growth and Adult Nutritional Status of Rural Indian Boys Around Hyderabad," *Human Nutrition: Clinical Nutrition,* no. 40 C (1986).

[26]*Ibid.*

THE ETHICS OF DOWNSIZING

—Frank Navran

Frank Navran addresses some of the primary concerns about downsizing practices.

IS DOWNSIZING EVER ETHICAL?

Organizations in every segment of business, industry, government and education are downsizing. The very act of forcing people to leave their employment is rife with ethics-related questions. In this article, we will consider one of the most fundamental questions: *Is downsizing ever ethical?*

The truth is that unless an organization was designed expressly and overtly for the purpose, it is not in business to provide employment. Jobs are the by-product of successful organizational endeavors, not their intended output.

Furthermore, downsizing is not necessarily a desperate move on the part of failing organizations. It can be, and probably should be, a strategic choice designed to serve the best interests of an organization. We should not be constrained by the false belief that current organizational effectiveness or financial success is a de facto argument against doing what is necessary to ensure continuing success. A healthy profit picture and downsizing are not mutually exclusive.

But this is only a partial answer to the question. We have merely said that organizational downsizing is not intrinsically unethical. To answer more fully, we have to look at a number of issues. First, some definitions:

Values—this term refers to a set of beliefs. Values are how one defines what is right, fair and good. This definition applies whether we consider individual values, organizational values or societal values.

Ethics—here we mean choices and the observable, behavioral manifestation of values-based decisions.

Ethical dilemma—this is a situation where every viable option requires the decision maker to choose between conflicting values. Under these conditions, any decision under consideration will violate one or more values even as it honors others.

Ethical congruence—a situation where one's decision is consistent with, aligns with, the applicable set(s) of values. Under these circumstances, a choice to take some action will harmonize with the decision maker's values.

Bearing these definitions in mind, we find that determining whether the decision to downsize is ethical means determining whether that choice is congruent with the values of at least two different constituencies:

Those who must leave the organization against their will.

Those who remain after the downsizing.

To frame the ethical issues faced by these two constituencies, we must first agree on a set of values to use as a reference point. For this discussion, we will employ four values suggested by Kenneth W. Johnson, JD. He uses the acronym EPIC to define the values set:

E = Empathy: Caring about the consequences of one's choices as they affect others. Being concerned with the effect one's decisions have on those who have no say in the decision itself.

P = Patience: Taking time to consider and deliberate the long-term consequences of a choice before making that choice and acting upon it.

I = Integrity: Making choices that are consistent with each other and with the stated and operative values one espouses. Striving for ethical congruence in one's decisions.

C = Courage: Choosing to do what one believes is right even if the result will not be to everyone's liking or may lead to personal loss.

THOSE WHO MUST LEAVE

Being forced to leave a job, irrespective of separation allowances, pension enhancements or any of the other tools used by organizations to soften the blow, feels wrong. It feels like it must violate some values, and typically it does.

Empathy—the act of dismissal can be unempathetic, since it negatively affects those who are forced to give up their chosen path, no matter what future success may await them and since they typically feel as though they had no voice in the decision.

Patience—if the decision to downsize is perceived to be a faddish response to competitive pressures it will appear impatient or premature to those who must leave. If it is perceived as anything less than a well-developed, strategic response to demands on the organization, then it fails the patience criterion.

Integrity—where there was either an implied or spoken promise of continuing employment as the repayment for employee loyalty and/or the successful completion of assigned work, the decision—and hence the organization and its leaders—may be thought to lack integrity.

Courage—downsizing can sometimes be seen to be about creating victims and displacing blame rather than accepting responsibility and choosing the more difficult, moral high ground.

THOSE WHO REMAIN

Surviving a downsizing has its own ethical issues. Surviving employees will often share perceptions about the ethics of this decision with those who are being forced to leave. They also experience their own emotional reactions—anger, guilt, fear and depression—when asked to take up the slack by doing more work, learning new tasks, and all for the same or less money than before the downsizing occurred.

Empathy—asking people to do more with less and for less can seem unfair. Downsizing organizations put terrible pressures on their surviving employees, and that often affects their families as well. This can seem to show a lack of caring on the part of decision makers, an insensitivity to the reality that employees are people with full lives and responsibilities outside of work.

Patience—organizations which downsize often have a sense of urgency about realizing the promised benefits of doing more with less. If this rush to a new order is seen to be without a basis in fact, and if the decision makers are viewed as being unaware of what is needed to get the job done, then the decision can be seen to violate the patience ethic.

Integrity—in organizations where downsizing is imposed at the same time that executive and/or stockholders are receiving substantial bonuses, there can be the perception of a double standard. When the organization's stated values include an assertion that "we value our employees," downsizing can be seen to violate the integrity value.

Courage—if executives blame their superiors (CEOs, boards of directors, special interests or stockholders) for the necessity to downsize, and speak or act as though they had no choice, the message can be that they lacked the courage to do what is right, to stand up for those who have served them loyally, no matter the personal risk. This is viewed as cowardice.

CONCLUSION

As with most complex organizational issues, the question of whether downsizing is ethical has no easy answer. Perhaps the best that can be hoped for is that the decision makers apply the EPIC test to their choice:

> *That they demonstrate empathy for all of those affected by their decision: the employees who leave and those who remain behind. That they display patience, avoiding a premature knee-jerk reaction. That the decision be based on a critical understanding of its stimuli and its consequences. That they show integrity as they strive to live according to their word and match their actions to their professions of belief. And finally that they have the courage to do the right thing, even when the right thing may be the more difficult thing to do.*

PINNACLE BRANDS
A Strike Puts Employees Up to Bat
—GILLIAN FLYNN

When baseball struck out in 1994, Pinnacle Brands Inc., a trading card company, could have followed others' leads with layoffs. Instead, it tossed the ball to employees, challenging them to save their jobs with money-making ideas.

Downsizing in general and even single terminations present some of the greatest challenges to management in terms of emotional struggles. Companies, however, often mistakenly believe that these terminations are their only options for survival. Pinnacle thought otherwise and, in its creativity, salvaged positions and employees slated for termination. Would this work in other firms?

Are you American? Then you must love baseball. And you probably still wince a bit at the debacle of 1994, when those on-field heroes, the boys of summer, packed up their gear and headed home. The strike hit us hard. Most Americans were beyond bitter—we felt robbed, cheated out of our national pastime. There was no joy in Mudville, nor any other baseball-loving town.

If you think the average Joe was upset, consider the organizations linked to baseball because it's not just a national pastime, it's a national business. Take, for instance, trading card companies. When baseball shut down, so did a huge chunk of their sales. Smaller card companies literally went bankrupt. Larger ones survived, but only after huge headcount slashes.

Of the top five trading card manufacturers, only one got through the strike with no layoffs: Pinnacle Brands Inc. It did so by issuing an intriguing challenge to its employees: If they could devise new ways to replace the $40 million of lost trading card revenue, they would keep their jobs. Pinnacle's workforce emerged from the strike victorious with a sales jump of 80% in two years. In a season without heroes on the baseball field, these employees became heroes on the business field.

ONE STRIKE CAN MEAN YOU'RE OUT (OF BUSINESS)

It was a tense spring at Pinnacle Brands. Each day the murmurs of a 1994 strike grew stronger, so did employees' fears. At that time, baseball cards represented 65% of Pinnacle's business. "Here we were getting ready for what could be a no-baseball season," remembers Carlo Frappolli, vice president of HR. "When the stars aren't hitting home runs and aren't pitching no-hitters, people don't want to buy their cards. Everyone was nervous."

Frappolli and Chairman & CEO Jerry Meyer began discussing what-ifs. A strike would all but nullify the company's need for 190 full-time employees. However, both Meyer and Frappolli strongly believed workers should be viewed as revenue producers, not expense items. Unlike executives at many companies, their first reaction wasn't to lay people off. Pinnacle's regard for its workforce is reflected in the company's operating philosophies, four of which directly address the employer-employee relationship:

- Treat all employees with dignity and respect.

- Deliver good news with grace.

- Deliver bad news quickly and with brutal honesty.

- Reward for results, not efforts.

In the first week of July, the strike ceased to be a rumor. Soon, the season was canceled. There was no good news to deliver, but the remaining three operating principles were about to come into play. Upon the official declaration of the season as null and void, Meyer convoked employees for a meeting. He delivered two messages. First, he quickly and honestly explained to employees that the company had just hit a dangerously rough patch. It was sink-or-swim time. Second and most important, he delivered the game plan: "He told the folks, 'I'm not going to save your jobs. You're going to save your jobs. You know what you can change and what you can do differently,' " says Frappolli.

Carolyn Corbin, founder of the Center for the 21st Century in Dallas, a think tank on future socioeconomic issues, believes Pinnacle's approach should serve as a role model for companies going through similar crises. "Very few companies take that risk," she says. "But in a way, it's not a risk at all because it puts the responsibility on the people to 'pay for themselves.' There isn't cash flow anymore, it's people flow: People will have to be generating, directly or indirectly, revenue for their keep or they can't stay."

The majority of Pinnacle employees remained wary at first, particularly the production people, who'd been subjected to continual cyclical layoffs under the company's former owner. Carol Anderson, an executive assistant in the finance division, recalls the workforce jitters: "Everybody sort of said, 'Uh-oh, what does this mean to us?' I think everybody went home that night a little nervous. But I thought we should give it a shot. At least it was we'd all sink or swim together, not just lay off people."

Meyer and Frappolli provided encouragement by setting up opportunities for employees to gather in informal teams and discuss ideas. Teams were deliberately cross-departmental. For instance, if employees had a new-product idea, a team would include someone from the creative end, a person from photography, people from marketing and finance. This gave employees insight into each step of a process so they didn't get blindsided halfway into a plan because they lacked the necessary perspective. It wasn't long before some amazing ideas started floating past supervisors' desks.

PINNACLE HAS A WINNING SEASON

One of the very first bright ideas came not from the COO or CFO, but someone just as in tune with the company's operations: Pinnacle's custodian. She came to Frappolli with a simple observation: The company spent approximately $50,000 a year on refrigerated sodas and bottled waters for every conference room and most executive offices, as well as personalized cups to boot. "So we stopped that," says Frappolli. "If executives feel they need to have sodas, they should go out and buy them themselves. That idea came from someone who sweeps the floors."

As soon as an employee's suggestion proved useful, Pinnacle immediately recognized him or her by printing out a big colorful poster with the person's name on it and many thanks. Some employees were spotted for a dinner with a spouse or friend at any Dallas restaurant of their choice. Others got round-trip airfare to visit nearby cities. "We tried to personalize it," says Frappolli. "Maybe we'd get them a signed football if they were a player's big fan. We tried to give things that mean something to that person."

Another simple but effective idea came in response to a newly developing area. Pinnacle had begun making pogs for Frito-Lay's division in Mexico; a 3-D pog went into every bag of chips. To understate it, the item was popular. The introduction of pogs spurred sales from 40 million bags of chips a week to 80 million and there's only 50 million people in all of Mexico. Problem was, the orders were growing so exponentially, Pinnacle couldn't keep up. In danger of losing the contract, a manufacturing supervisor set his carpentry—yes, carpentry—skills to work. On his own time, he made a "shaker table." The homemade contraption literally shakes the pogs as they come onto a ramp so they shoot down different avenues, allowing more workers to pack them. It increased Pinnacle's production capacity by tenfold—the company shipped over a billion pogs that summer. "If you looked at this table, you'd think your 10-year-old could have made it," says Frappolli. "But it's a good idea and no one had thought of it. It let us hit the order."

Employees were encouraged not just to concentrate on their own areas, but also to think outside the box. A public relations manager, for instance, was looking at the 1996 Olympics with dollar bills in his eyes. He'd been to previous Olympics and had seen how well pins had sold. He contacted one of the few companies licensed to sell Olympic pins in Atlanta, a company that lacked the distribution channels Pinnacle had established. Now that company makes the pins and Pinnacle distributes them. The venture brought in almost $20 million in revenue.

Throughout the process, Pinnacle struggled against formalizing it too much. Employees would contact either Frappolli or their supervisors with ideas. "I found from my days at large companies that programs can bog you down," says Frappolli. "With us it's if you've got a good idea that will work, let's do it. Let's quantify savings so we know it works and then reward that employee." How did the company know if an idea would work? It grabbed all the stakeholders and asked them if it was worth trying. The company tried to emphasize the positive. Maybe the first idea wasn't a home run, but if employees remained encouraged, they might hit the next one out of the ballpark.

One of the employees who scored big was Anderson. As an employee in the finance department, she was privy to the exorbitant costs of trademark searches. Every time the company came up with a new name for a trading card, it had to pay a trademark attorney to do a search to make sure it hadn't been trademarked. Anderson decided to create a database for Pinnacle, to track what trademarks it owned and which ones it had searched in the past. Although she had no training in legal or intellectual-property issues, she wasn't afraid to ask a lot of questions. Anderson worked to set up the system—at home and on weekends, even on lunch breaks—for almost three months before it was up and running. It has saved more than $100,000.

Toward the close of '94, there still hadn't been even a peep about layoffs. Employees were revitalized. "Each day and each week and each month they saw we weren't laying people off and our competition was—some were laying off half their workforces, shutting entire plants down," says Frappolli. "They saw we weren't doing any of that and it really built some steam."

Pinnacle was lucky it had a tough and energized workforce, because it wasn't in the clear until fall 1995. Baseball sales are strong this spring, however, and the company is breathing a collective sigh of relief. But the message remains clear—just because we're bouncing back doesn't mean we should relax. Keep the ideas coming. Says Corbin: "What Pinnacle has done is to tell employees, 'Keep justifying your job. Earn your keep if you want to stay here.' Rather than the organization choosing who stays and who goes, the people themselves choose through their actions. What Pinnacle is doing is the most honest, empowering thing it can do."

Anderson says employees are still at it—she herself is exploring a new database. She gives much of the credit to the Pinnacle culture. "It's an atmosphere in which you can take on as much responsibility as you want," Anderson says. "If you were to leave Pinnacle— and I have no intention of doing so—you could honestly look your employer in the face and say, 'I can do anything you throw at me.' "

Truly mutual admirers, Frappolli says a lot of the credit goes to the Pinnacle workforce— a uniquely excellent group of people. "I think it would be dangerous to say that this is a template that could work across America," he says. "You need special kinds of people who believe in themselves and understand that they control their own destiny. These employees know that if they deliver results they're going to have a job and if they don't they might not. They prefer to bet on themselves rather than having a company take care of them."

Pinnacle's mission statement is "to provide unexpected delight in everything we do." In its rally against layoffs, the company certainly provided unexpected delight to a business community jaded by "unavoidable" downsizings. When the crowds cheer to the crack of the bat this week, we should reserve a portion of the adulation for the heroes off the field.

WHEN FEAR OF FIRING DETERS HIRING

—Jeffrey L. Seglin

If a firm believes that a termination is more likely to be challenged on discriminatory grounds by a woman or minority, is that firm less likely to hire those individuals in the first place? This is the concern expressed by some in this article. How can we prevent this counter-intuitive result?

Over the last few years, several people have spoken to me about their reluctance to hire people whose race, color, creed or national origin—or age, disability or sex—put them in protected classes under anti-discrimination law.

The reasoning goes this way: You have to be absolutely sure that someone in a protected class is the best possible candidate, because people in these categories can make your life miserable with litigation if you ever have to dismiss them.

"It's a dirty little secret" that people are thinking this way, said Tama Starr, president of Artkraft Strauss, a sign-making company in New York, and one of the few business people who has spoken out on the subject. Those who subscribe to these ideas "have to choose between different protected classes and weigh the risk of hiring them," she said, adding, "This is a very obnoxious way to think."

Managers tread on swampy ethical terrain when they allow fear of possible problems to deter them from hiring apparently capable minority applicants—or to hesitate so long over a decision that a candidate loses interest or gives up in frustration.

The fear of discrimination suits is not wholly groundless. A 1997 survey conducted by the Society for Human Resource Management found that of 616 personnel executives who responded, 53% said their organizations had been sued at least once by former employees in the last five years; nearly half the 611 suits they reported involved claims of discrimination.

But Martha R. A. Fields, chief executive of Fields Associates, a management consulting firm in Cambridge, Mass., says the risk of a suit is often an excuse that masks a deeper motive for not hiring people in protected classes. It is more likely, Ms. Fields said, that managers really just feel safer hiring people like themselves.

Some people, she said, find it easy to think to themselves: "If I know people who are like me, I know the good, bad and the ugly about them. If I don't know them and I see images of them in the media, I'm, like, 'Oh man, those black people, they might be welfare-dependent, or criminals, or crime victims. I don't know if I really want to bring that into my organization.'"

Increasingly, such bias is economically irrational as well as unethical. "The demographics of this country are shifting in major ways," Ms. Fields noted, as minority groups, especially Hispanic people, account for a rapidly growing share of the population and its purchasing power. "Consumers want to see people like themselves in organizations," Ms. Fields said.

Another underlying problem is managers who are poor at managing. Some who speak these fears are simply afraid to fire anyone—not just someone in a protected class—and shy away from situations they perceive as requiring them to take a chance.

To avoid hiring problem employees from any group, managers just "need to do a good job of checking résumés, identifying the time gaps and verifying simple facts," said Mary C. Dollarhide, an employment lawyer with Paul, Hastings, Janofsky & Walker in Stamford, Conn. For $200 to $300, a manager can also get a criminal background check on a candidate and a docket search to see if he or she often files lawsuits. "If you do your due diligence, you're going to stand a much better chance of not bringing in the gripers, complainers, bad actors and poor performers," Ms. Dollarhide said.

But a thorough screening does not absolve managers of having to manage. "If you get somebody in your midst whom you fail to discipline because you're afraid you're going to get slammed for having reprimanded someone in a protected class, well, guess what: The failure to do that is going to land you in exactly the same spot," Ms. Dollarhide said. "If the employee is terminated, he can sue and you're left with no records to support your case."

Much sound management translates into ethical behavior. Employees who are treated fairly, honestly and directly are both less likely to require dismissal and less likely to sue over it later.

That frees everyone to concentrate on the business they enjoy. "I still believe that people are good and honest and they want to do a nice job," said Ms. Starr of Artkraft. "Having to fight through more stupidity just hampers everybody's humanity."

SOME ISSUES IN EMPLOYMENT DISCRIMINATION ON GROUNDS OF RACE, SEX AND AGE

—RICHARD POSNER

Seventh Circuit Court Judge and lecturer at the University of Chicago Richard Posner offers his market theory as applied to discrimination. Posner addresses three issues: why unions have long refused to admit black workers, comparable worth and mandatory retirement. Posner is known for his logical, well-reasoned analyses, though they are not always in line with society's preferred result. Are you persuaded by the judge's arguments? If you were asked to debate him on these issues, what would be your arguments or criticisms of his reasoning?

. . . Racial discrimination in employment is a part of a larger issue—that of the causes and cures of racial discrimination. . . . Here we shall discuss one specialized topic in racial discrimination and also employment discrimination against women and the aged.

Many unions long refused to admit black workers. Why? Economics suggests an answer. As we have seen, unions seek to raise the wage rate above the competitive level; and to the extent they succeed, an excess demand for union jobs is created. There are various ways in which this excess demand could be eliminated. One would be by auctioning off union membership. The successful bidders would be those willing to pay an entrance fee equal to the present value of the difference between the union wage scale and the wages in their next best employment. This would be the method of rationing used if unions were simply firms enjoying monopoly power over labor—firms that bought labor at the competitive wage and resold it to employers at a monopoly wage. But unions are not firms; they are representatives (however imperfect) of the workers, and they will not adopt a rationing method that would deny the union membership any net wage gains from membership. The problem with nonmonetary rationing methods, however, is that they induce applicants to expend real resources. If admission to the union is based on work skills, for example, applicants will incur real costs to obtain the requisite skills, and the competition in obtaining skills may result in eliminating the expected monopoly profits of union membership . . . What makes criteria involving race or some other relatively immutable status (such as being the son of a union member) attractive is that they do not invite heavy expenditures on qualifying; the costs of changing one's race or parents are prohibitive.

The central economic question relating to employment discrimination against women is explaining the persistently higher average wage of men compared to women (women's wages per hour are on average about 60% of men's wages).[1] Irrational or exploitive discrimination is one possibility. Another is that male wages include a compensatory wage premium for the dirty, disagreeable and strenuous jobs that men dominate presumably because their aversion to such work is less than women's. Another (these are not mutually exclusive possibilities, of course) is differences in investments in market-related human capital (earning capacity). If a woman allocates a substantial part of her working life to household production, including child care, she will obtain a substantially lower return on her market human capital than a man planning to devote much less time to household production, and she will therefore invest less in that human capital. Since earnings are in part a return on one's human capital investments (including education), women's earnings will be lower than men's.[2] In part this will show up in the choice of occupations: Women will be attracted to occupations that don't require much human capital. Of course the amount of time women are devoting to household production is declining, so we can expect the wage gap to shrink if the economic model is correct.

Comparable worth refers to the movement, now being pressed in courts and legislatures, for raising the wage level of job classifications filled primarily by women (e.g., secretarial work) to that of predominantly male job classifications (e.g., truck driving).[3] The proposal is to determine the actual worth of the different jobs, and if the worth is the same equalize the wages (by raising the lower wage level) regardless of the market conditions. The effort to divorce worth from market value is troubling to an economist. If a truck driver is paid more than a secretary, even though the secretary works just as long hours and has as good an education, the economist's inclination will be to assume that the market is compensating a skill that is in shorter supply, or is offsetting a disamenity, rather than making arbitrary distinctions based on fast-vanishing stereotypes. The economist would therefore assume that if measurements of comparable worth failed to pick up the different worths of the two types of job, this was because of the crudeness of the measuring devices rather than the absence of real differences.

---

[1] With certain adjustments the real percentage is estimated for 1974 at 66%, in *Improvements in the Quality of Life: Estimates of Possibilities in the United States, 1974–1983,* at 194 (Nestor E. Terleckyj ed. 1975).

[2] See Jacob Mincer & Haim Ofek, "Interrupted Work Careers: Depreciation and Restoration of Human Capital," 17 *J. Human Resources* 3 (1982); Jacob Mincer & Solomon W. Polachek, "Family Investments in Human Capital: Earnings of Women," 82 *J. Pol. Econ.* S76 (1974); "Trends in Women's Work, Education and Family Building," 3 *J. Labor Econ.* 51 (1985).

[3] See June O'Neill, *Comparable Worth* (Urban Institute and U.S. Commn. on Civil Rights, unpublished, Jan. 29, 1985); June O'Neill & Hal Sider, *The Pay Gap and Occupational Segregation: Implications for Comparable Worth* (Urban Institute and U.S. Commn. on Civil Rights, unpublished, Dec. 29, 1984); *Comparable Worth: Issue for the 80's* (U.S. Commn. on Civil Rights, 1984); *Comparable Worth: An Analysis and Recommendations* (U.S. Commn. on Civil Rights, 1985).

In any event, consider what the consequences will be if comparable worth is implemented. If wages in jobs now dominated by women are raised, the number of jobs available will shrink, as employers seek to substitute other, and now cheaper, inputs (e.g., word processors for typists), and as customers substitute other products for those made by firms whose wage bills and hence prices have risen because of comparable worth. At the same time, men will start competing more for those jobs, lured by the higher wages. So female employment in a job classification that had been (for whatever reason) congenial to women may (why not will?) drop. Some displaced women will find new employment in the predominantly male occupations such as truck driving—perhaps replacing men who have become secretaries! But these women may not be happier in their new jobs; after all, there is nothing to stop a woman today from becoming a truck driver if that is what she wants to be. Finally, under comparable worth the incentives of women to invest in human capital usable in the traditional men's jobs will drop as the relative wages in those jobs drop, so that in the end occupational sex segregation may not be greatly affected.

Federal law forbids public or private employers to force their employees to retire before the age of 70, with the exception of a few job classifications such as airline pilot. The economist is naturally troubled by the government's intervening in the decision of a private employer to use age as a basis for terminating employment either on a retail or wholesale (mandatory retirement age) basis. The reply is that the use of age is arbitrary. Although this is true, it does not provide a good economic reason for government intervention in the employment market. The use of a single, readily determinable characteristic such as age as the basis for an employment decision economizes on the costs of information. True, there is diseconomy as well as economy: Sometimes a more competent older worker will be replaced by a less competent younger one. But that does not make the employer's use of age as a proxy for competence, crude as the proxy is, inefficient. The employer's objective is to minimize the sum of the costs of suboptimal retention decisions resulting from lack of individualized assessment of workers' abilities and the information costs of making such assessments.[4] If the sum is minimized by having a mandatory retirement age, the employer will have a mandatory retirement age; otherwise he will not. There is no externality calling for government intervention.

---

[4]This decisional problem is strikingly like that of deciding how much procedure to provide to litigants.

SUCH STUFF AS DREAMS ARE MADE ON

A Short Primer on Why We Should Not Be Ready to Throw Out Affirmative Action

—DAWN D. BENNETT-ALEXANDER

Bennett-Alexander contends that lost in a good deal of the legal and lay dialogue of whether the consideration of race violates the Equal Protection Clause in decisions involving the granting of benefits of any kind is the very simple recognition that the Court has always permitted the use of such distinctions among seemingly similarly situated persons when, upon closer inspection, there is a difference which supports doing so. Also lost in the fray is the fact that the arguments opposing the use of affirmative action are generally predicated on the presumption that one is dealing with two groups equally situated, so that giving one an advantage through affirmative action puts the other at a disadvantage and is therefore unfair.

In her treatise, Bennett-Alexander makes the compelling argument that the affirmative action discourse virtually ignores the impact of the 300+ years of institutionalized racism and discrimination against blacks, the effects of which still continue today, and the concomitant benefit to whites, which results in the two races being in significantly different positions in society. In her view, because of these significant differences, the use of the minimal (though admittedly imperfect) tool of affirmative action to continue to try to equalize the position of blacks makes sense, reflects the country's goal of equality, is legally supportable and appropriate, and is not a denial of equal protection.

Once again the Court is called upon to review school desegregation plans to determine whether the plans meet constitutional standards. The distinctive feature of these cases, consolidated on appeal, is that they also require us to reexamine school desegregation standards in the light of the Civil Rights Act of 1964. . . .

When the United States Supreme Court in 1954 decided Brown v. Board of Education,[1] *the members of the High School Class of 1966 had not entered the first grade.* Brown I *held that separate schools for Negro children were "inherently un-*

Excerpted from a paper originally presented at the Academy of Legal Studies in Business Annual Meeting, Nashville, TN (August 14, 2003). ©Dawn D. Bennett-Alexander, 2003. Reprinted with permission.
[1]*Brown v. Board of Education,* 347 U.S. 483 (1954) (*Brown I*). See *Brown v. Board of Education,* 349 U.S. 294 (1955) (*Brown II*).

equal." Negro children, said the court, have the "personal and present" right to equal educational opportunities with white children in a racially nondiscriminatory public school system. For all but a handful of Negro members of the High School Class of '66 this right has been "of such stuff as dreams are made on".[2,3]

INTRODUCTION

Much has been made of the U.S. Supreme Court's June 23, 2003, decisions in the University of Michigan companion cases of *Grutter v. Bollinger*[4] and *Gratz v. Bollinger.*[5] In those cases the Court once again upheld the concept of affirmative action[6] in college admissions, but struck down the use of points given for race as a way to implement the concept. *Grutter* involved a law school admissions policy in which the law school gave no specific points for being a minority, but instead tried to gear its program to admitting a "critical mass" of minorities for each incoming class based on the specifics of the class. *Gratz* involved review of an undergraduate admissions policy in which minority applicants were given a specific number of points toward the total needed for admission.[7] The Court upheld the law school's plan, but not the one for undergraduate admissions.

The Michigan case, as it is commonly referred to, was one of the most eagerly awaited decisions in recent history. The deeply divisive issue had not been given such serious review since the Court's 1978 decision in *Regents of the University of California v. Bakke,*[8] in which the Court first endorsed the use of the concept of affirmative action in college admissions. However, much had happened during the 26-year interim, both in society as well as in the Court, so the decision was sure to draw attention. There were more *amicus curiae* briefs filed in the case, both for and against the use of affirmative action in college admissions as well as employment, than had been seen in the Court in recent history.[9] The case drew a good deal of acrimony from conservatives who believed the time had come to abandon the use of affirmative action.

---

[2]Shakespeare, *The Tempest,* Act IV.

[3]*United States v. Jefferson County Board of Education,* 372 F. 2d 836 (5th Cir. 1966), *aff'd en banc,* 380 F.2d 385 (5th Cir. 1967). Judge John Minor Wisdom, a legendary southern jurist and scholar, was one of the small band of judges in the South in what scholars call "Southern jurisprudence." The term refers to the mostly Republicans handpicked by President Dwight Eisenhower's attorney general, Herbert Brownell, who had a quiet passion for civil rights. These jurists developed new constitutional doctrine in many cases during the civil rights era and the U.S. Supreme Court signaled its general support. A few months before his death in 1999, at age 93, Judge Wisdom said he was uncertain which was more important, how far blacks have come in overcoming discrimination, or "how far they still have to go." Jack Bass, "How the G.O.P. Created Affirmative Action," *New York Times,* May 31, 2003.

[4]4123 S. Ct. 2325, 2003 U.S. LEXIS 4800 (July 23, 2003).

[5]123 S. Ct. 2411, 2003 U.S. LEXIS 4801 (July 23, 2003).

[6]As used in this paper, affirmative action is any plan designed for a university or workplace to consciously include qualified blacks, women or others who have traditionally been excluded, who once included, must perform in order to stay.

[7]Points were also given for several other things such as socioeconomic disadvantage, attendance at a high school in a predominantly underrepresented minority population or underrepresentation in the unit to which the student was applying (for example, men who sought to pursue a career in nursing). *Gratz* at 4.

[8]438 U.S. 265 (1978).

[9]For a list and the full text of the *amicus* briefs, see the *Chronicle of Higher Education* website at: http://chronicle.com/indepth/michigan/documents/documents.htm.

The Court's decision to continue to hold that affirmative action in college admissions does not deny equal protection to the white students affected by such action has been alternately hailed as the basis for cruelly continuing the country's racial divide, by its opponents, or the Court's recognition of the continuing need for the use of race-conscious efforts in ridding the country of its vestiges of racial discrimination, by its supporters.

More than 40% of Americans believe affirmative action is no longer necessary to achieve diversity in the workplace, according to a July survey by the Employment Law Alliance.[10] Recent Pew polls found that Americans support affirmative action in theory, but have difficulty with it in practices (5/14/03), and blacks are more likely than whites to believe there is bias in college admissions (6/24/03).[11]

The position of this paper is that lost in the lofty legal rhetoric surrounding the discussion of affirmative action is the reality of the difference in the lives of blacks and whites in this country—a profound omission. A difference that affects us from the minute we are born until the minute we die. A difference that manifests itself from the gamut of the subtle to the profound. From something as simple as blacks not being able to see themselves accurately reflected in the mass media, to still having crimes committed against them like the heinous dragging death of James Byrd Jr. as recently as 1998 by three white men in Jasper, Texas, or, in what has been called the "worst miscarriage of justice in Texas history," a white police officer perjuring himself in Tulia, Texas, to obtain the conviction of 36 blacks on drug charges, and the district attorney knowing he was doing so.[12] A difference that more than justifies the constitutional position the Court has taken in refusing to agree that affirmative action, as a concept, denies equal protection of the law. The Constitution allows differently situated people to be treated differently, and that is what justifies affirmative action. What we conveniently forget in our national discourse is just how profound this difference in the lives of blacks and whites is, and therefore, why such a thing as affirmative action is still necessary.

It is my position that by neglecting to take a good hard look at this country's, often, very recent, racial history in any kind of detail, it becomes easy to argue that we are all equal and affirmative action gives an unfair advantage to blacks and other minorities.[13] Even the

---

[10]"Debate Revived on Workplace Diversity," *USA Today,* July 21, 2003, p. 4B.

[11]*USA Today,* August 1, 2003, p. 15A; Pew Research Center for the People and Press, http://people-press.org/reports/print.php3?PageID=709.

[12]"Court Cases Raise Conduct Concerns," *USA Today,* June 26, 2003, p. 2A. Twelve of the defendants were released this year, four years after their convictions, when their convictions were thrown out because of the false testimony. Tulia is a predominantly white town, and the arrests resulted in more than 10% of Tulia's black population being arrested. *Jet* Magazine, April 24, 2003, p. 54. The Texas Board of Pardons and Paroles has unanimously recommended pardons for 35 of the convicted defendants. "Pardons Urged for 35 in Texas Drug Cases," *USA Today,* July 31, 2003, p. 10A.

[13]In this paper I will confine myself to the issue of affirmative action and blacks since that is what the law initially set out to address and it is that history that I look at. By doing so, I do not in any way intend it to lessen the importance of affirmative action as it relates to other groups.

Court's choice to treat the parties as equals, and using the compelling state interest as a basis for supporting the difference in treatment, begs this issue. Using a compelling state interest assumes that the parties' positions are equal but one is being treated differently. This paper's position is that the parties' positions are not equal, therefore there is not even a need to use the test.

In reaching the conclusion that the country is not ready to discard affirmative action, I am only stating what is obvious when one looks at all the facts rather than only the ones that conveniently suit an argument. The refusal to address the issue head-on and be honest about the position of blacks in this country relative to whites and the consequences and vestiges of a system the country adhered to for well over 300 years should not continue. Reaching such a conclusion does not mean that blacks should be given a handout or that they should be considered inferior. Far from it, though this is a convenient argument used by opponents. On the contrary, blacks have made tremendous strides in the years since the 1964 Civil Rights Act, despite the obstacles in their way and the handicaps they operate under. But it is ludicrous to think they are in the same position in this country as whites when it comes to any significant factor one cares to use, whether it is education, employment, wages, health, housing, crime, purchasing power, influence, or anything else.

Blacks know this and deal with it every day. However, most whites do not. We still live in a fairly homogeneous society, with little racial intermixing on any real level. Ignorance of the true lives of blacks is part of what goes with being white in the U.S.[14] As a result, on the face of it, many whites are ignorant of the true plight of blacks, but on the other hand, tend to say they think things are pretty much the same for everyone. That could not be farther from the truth. One simple question asked by comedian Chris Rock gets to the heart of the matter and demonstrates how true this is: Would you want to be black? The reason most whites would answer "no" to this question lies at the heart of why blacks and whites in the U.S. are not equally situated, and why it makes sense to be able to constitutionally support affirmative action and continue its use.

Whites may not be able to articulate the specifics of why they would not want to be black, but they know in their deepest recesses that being black is not the same as being white in this country, and that being black has definite disadvantages.[15] Because those disadvantages manifest themselves in a myriad of ways in the lives of blacks, the two groups,

---

[14]See, for instance, Peggy McIntosh, "White Privilege: Unpacking the Invisible Knapsack," *Peace and Freedom,* July–August 1989, pp. 10–12; Jim Cole, *Prejudicial Behavior from Those Who Report They Are Not Prejudiced,* Alex Kotlowitz & Suzanne Alexander, "Tacit Code of Silence on Matters of Race Perpetuates Division: Blacks Tend to Be Reluctant to Share Experiences; Whites Often Shun Topic; 'A Very Difficult Tightrope,'" *The Wall Street Journal,* 1995; Thomas Ross, *The Just Stories: How the Law Embodies Racism,* Beacon Press, 1997; Ellis Cose, *Color-Blind: Seeing Beyond Race in a Race-Obsessed World,* Harper Collins, Pub., 1997; Ellis Cose, *The Rage of a Privileged Class,* Perennial Press, 1995.

[15]Peggy McIntosh, "White Privilege: Unpacking the Invisible Knapsack," *Peace and Freedom,* July–August 1989, pp. 10–12.

despite some surface appearances, are not the same and affirmative action should remain a weapon in the arsenal of alternatives used to try to have America live up to its promise of equality. It is not yet time to throw out affirmative action. We have only used it for a very short time (about 25 years) considering our country's 300+ year history, and clearly there is still much work to do. Whites, who tend to appreciate progress hard won, often overlook the system blacks operated under in this country since its birth and the devastating impact it has had, and continues to have on black families, jobs, education, crime, self-esteem, achievement, self-concept and believing in the possibilities white Americans hold so dear. There is *no way* to accurately look at the relative positions of blacks and whites in this country *without* considering this.

After looking at the differences in the relative positions of blacks and whites in our country, it becomes clear that affirmative action is an appropriate and necessary (though highly imperfect and even undesirable) means of addressing lingering inequality. It is not my intent to argue the mechanics of affirmative action, or really even the constitutionality of it. It is also not intended to exclude other groups, argue the relative merits of one kind of affirmative action over another, or to preclude consideration of other possible alternatives to affirmative action related to the workplace or education. Rather, my intent is to take a hard look to at least some of the reality of the lives of blacks, in particular, to see if there is still a need for affirmative action.

In the final analysis, given the history of our country and its present day vestiges of the system we lived under by law until just 40 or so years ago (and de facto until well into the 1970s), the conclusion is that affirmative action is constitutional, still necessary, and in the end, the very least we can do to try to, as President Bush recently said, reach our "destination" of "liberty and justice for all."[16]

Make no mistake about it: this is a paper with a view. It is not an attempt at an arm's-length discourse on the relative merits, or not, of affirmative action. I say right up front that I firmly believe it is not yet time for affirmative action to be discarded. Dealing with hundreds of white students every year in discussing these topics, and countless employees, managers and supervisors in consulting in this area, I have a substantial knowledge of what they say they believe and know about these issues. Most people want to do the right thing, but, as the Pew poll reflected, have a real problem in putting that into effect.

I have seen what happens when white students who believe in fairness are exposed to the reality of blacks' lives so often lost in the discussion of affirmative action. Once they realize how different life is for blacks than for whites and why, these students who came into class thinking affirmative action was absolutely unfair, end up angry that this is all their country, professing equality, has to offer blacks.

Like my students, I believe in the promise of the U.S. to live up to its constitution, to live up to its promise, and to continue to allow interim measures such as affirmative action until it does so. This is truly "such stuff upon which dreams are made on."

---

[16]Remarks of the president at Goree Island, Senegal (at the site where Africans were put onto ships for the Middle Passage, their journey across the Atlantic, during slavery), *USA Today,* July 9, 2003, p. 4A.

COLOR BLIND VS. COLOR CONSCIOUS

The Constitution is both color blind and color-conscious. To avoid conflict with the equal protection clause, a classification that denies a benefit, causes harm or imposes a burden must not be based on race. In that sense the Constitution is color blind.

But the Constitution is color-conscious to prevent discrimination being perpetuated and to undo the effects of past discrimination. The criterion is the relevancy of color to a legitimate government purpose.[17]

Opponents of affirmative action often speak of a wish for "color blindness." They do not distinguish between color blindness and color-consciousness. There is a significant difference. Color blindness presumes that everyone is the same. That is not so. With a racial history like ours, there are times when in order to reach the goal of color blindness, color-consciousness must first be used. Affirmative action does this. I do not believe that is necessarily a bad thing. If anything is "bad," it is the system that created the circumstances that made either necessary in the first place. While we cannot undo the past, we can certainly try to rectify its ill effects. We do not do this by ignoring them.

We would all love to be judged solely on the basis of merit, but that has never been the case. Color has always mattered in this country and has always worked to exclude blacks from the picture altogether. Now, when race is taken into consideration in an attempt to address the situation this created, people want to say we should be color blind. You can't just create a bad situation and walk away from it. There are consequences and circumstances created that must be addressed. You cannot just pretend it never happened. In order to fix the situation our racial past created, race must now be taken into consideration through affirmative action.

There is a difference between using race to hurt and using it to remedy. To not recognize that is like saying the medical doctor's creed of "first do no harm," means the doctor cannot set someone's broken leg because of the pain the patient may feel. The two kinds of pain/harm are not the same. The intent is to not further harm the patient, while the pain is necessary as part of the healing. So it is with the goal of color blindness. It is a lofty goal and worth pursuing, but to get there involves considering color, but for the right reasons. Considering it for purposes of trying to minimize the effects of 300+ years of discrimination against blacks is certainly a right reason. Thinking things will take care of themselves without help is ludicrous. We gave that a try in the 99 years between the end of the Civil War and the passage of the Civil Rights Act of 1964. It was, to say the least, a crashing failure.

ARE WE ALL THE SAME? THE MYTH OF RACIAL PARITY

A belief in fundamental fairness is, in fact, what fuels opposition to the concept of affirmative action. That makes perfect sense if you live, as most whites do, in a world in which you have every reason to think things are fair and merit reigns supreme; a world in which race has no value in decisions because virtually everyone is of your race. But blacks know another world.

---

[17]Judge John Minor Wisdom in *United States v. Jefferson County Board of Education,* 372 F.2d 836 (5th Cir. 1966), *aff'd en banc,* 380 F.2d 385 (5th Cir. 1967).

One of the problems with trying to discuss the issue of affirmative action is that whites generally believe that the same opportunities are open to all. This simply is not so. Economically challenged whites can change that by making money. However, blacks will always be black and in our country that carries negative baggage. When those two people are put in a workplace to apply for a job or visit a neighborhood to find a place to live, the white person still has the edge. Does this mean the person is better? No. Does it means blacks feel sorry for themselves and just sit out the game? Absolutely not. What it does mean is that there must be a recognition of this truth and the impact that this has on the opportunities available to all.

Further complicating the issue is the fact that our society has rarely had a truly beneficial dialogue about race. As Ellis Cose says, we either talk in "shouts or whispers."[18] When blacks mention discriminatory treatment to them, whites, unfamiliar with such things, often minimize blacks' concerns or say they must be being overly sensitive. Blacks, used to such treatment, as well as the history of race in this country, become angry and frustrated at whites' lack of understanding.[19]

The end product is an unwillingness of either side to put themselves forward in any significant way to try to help the situation. This, in turn, gives whites even less exposure to the reality of black lives and all they are left with is the news and other media exposure they are privy to. This, of course, gives them an unrealistic view of blacks that only further alienates the two groups (since society is geared toward whites, blacks are given much more exposure to them in ways that whites are not exposed to blacks).

In that context, whites are left with simply allowing things to stay on the surface so that feathers are not ruffled. They see blacks at their jobs, shopping, in school and perhaps even in their neighborhood, etc., and assume everyone is on the same level. This could not be farther from the truth.

Even if a black person has money, tons of it, or has position, like Colin Powell or Condoleeza Rice, they are still black, and in this country, that means they are treated differently. If you took away the position from either of them, they'd just be another black person, subject to the same discrimination as any other black. This has been shown often enough when such well-heeled blacks are put in a position where their status is not known and they are treated poorly based purely on their race. It happened to Oprah in her early days after coming to Chicago. A department store employee didn't realize who she was and mistreated her.[20] Male actors have had it happen when they do something as simple as go for a run in their posh neighborhoods, only to be stopped by the police and treated as if they are criminals for being there (before, of course, the cop finds out it is a celebrity).[21] This is

---

[18]Ellis Cose, *The Rage of a Privileged Class,* Harper Collins, Pub., 1984.

[19]Alex Kotlowitz & Suzanne Alexander, "Tacit Code of Silence on Matters of Race Perpetuates Division: Blacks Tend to Be Reluctant to Share Experiences; Whites Often Shun Topic; 'A Very Difficult Tightrope,' " *The Wall Street Journal,* 1995.

[20]She later "retaliated" by coming back and buying tons of stuff—much to the embarrassment of the store clerk and the store manager.

[21]A situation like this occurred with Eddie Murphy in Las Vegas. It would be funny if it wasn't such a sad reflection of race in our society. Different variations of the facts have floated around, but Murphy says the basic story is true. The essentials are that he got on an elevator with a black male friend just as the door was closing. Two white women were on the elevator. Murphy and his friend were nicely dressed (rather than looking like "thugs"). Murphy said to his friend, "Hit the floor." The two women screamed and got down on the floor. The men looked at them like they were crazy. Once they realized what the women thought, they started laughing. Of course, Murphy meant for his friend to push the elevator button for their room floor. However, the women thought they meant for the women to get on the elevator floor so that the men could commit some sort of crime against them. Murphy later surprised the women by paying their hotel bill. It is possible, but not likely, that the women would have reacted the same way if the men had been white.

the reality blacks know and live with every day, but it isn't even on the radar screen for whites,[22] so they assume blacks must be mistaken or overreacting when they disclose it.

In 1994, a white University of Maryland student decided that he would see for himself if there really was a difference in treatment between blacks and whites. He heard his black friends constantly talking about race and being treated poorly, and because he never saw it, he suspected it wasn't really true. He decided to take Psorlen pills to turn himself dark and live a semester as a black male. He lasted only two days. He said that he stopped because he "just couldn't stand the hate." It was far worse than he thought it would be, but not in the way he was expecting. There was little of the obvious, overt racism he had been expecting.[23] Rather, it was the constant daily grind of the subtle (and not so subtle) difference in treatment that he knew had never happened when he was white.[24] This difference in treatment manifests itself in the daily lives of blacks in ways that make our lives quite different than those of whites.

It is instructive to take a look at some recent items of interest to see how blacks shape up compared to whites, so we can see if they are, in fact, similarly situated. First we will look at a few statistics, then at some anecdotal information.

STATISTICS

We all know that statistics can be pretzeled into anything anyone wants to make of them. But I thought I would present a few statistics I have come across recently that form quite a picture when looked at in tandem. View them more as an overall snapshot rather than a microscope slide. The purpose is not a scientific scrutiny of any one particular statistic, but rather to provide an overview of how blacks and whites shape up in a number of areas.

Wages and Income

- According to the Census Bureau's recent report on its annual look at educational achievement in America culled from a March 2002 survey, on average, a white man with a college diploma earned about $65,000 in 2001, while black and Hispanic men with college degrees earned 30% less. Black men with high school diplomas earned about 25% less than similarly educated whites. Black men with master's degrees earned 20% less than their white counterparts.[25]

---

[22]I say it isn't on the radar screen, but see Glenn C. Loury, *The Anatomy of Racial Inequality,* Harvard University Press, 2002, p. 23, in which Loury discusses the concept of "self-confirming racial stereotypes." He theorizes that whites create certain stereotypes in blacks by treating them certain ways and it essentially becomes a self-fulfilling prophecy. For instance, if college admissions officers do not think blacks can do as well as whites and agree to admit them with lower scores than whites for purposes of diversity, blacks, who can, in fact, perform as well, have no incentive to achieve higher scores because they can get in with lower ones.

[23]Joshua Solomon, "Skin Deep; Reliving 'Black Like Me': My Own Journey into the Heart of Race-Conscious America," *The Washington Post,* October 30, 1994.

[24]In a later interview that was more in-depth than the news article, the student said that in truth, blacks would be even angrier if they knew how good whites *really* had it. www.thecode.net/interviews/solomons.html.

[25]Genaro C. Armas, "White Men with Degrees Are Still Wage Kings," *Salt Lake Tribune,* March 21, 2003; *Jet* Magazine, March 2003, p. 18.

- The median income for white households in 2001 was $44,517; for blacks it was $29,470.[26]

- Adjusting for inflation, the typical full-time black male worker made less in 2001 ($31,921) than the typical white male worker made in 1967 ($33,704).[27]

- The median 2001 income for white full-time male workers was $40,790; for a black male worker, $31,921.[28]

- The typical white family has more than 11 times as much net wealth—assets minus debt—as the typical black family. White families had median net wealth of $94,900 in 2001, according to the Panel Study of Income Dynamics. Black families had $8,500, including home equity.[29]

- The black poverty rate is almost triple that of whites. The official 2001 black poverty rate (issued in September 2002) was 22.7%, compared with 7.8% for whites.[30]

- In a 2002 speech, Franklin Raines, the first black CEO of a Fortune 500 company (Fannie Mae), said that if America had racial equality, blacks would have nearly $2,000 billion more in income, 2 million more college degrees, nearly 2 million more managerial and professional jobs and 3 million more homeowners. They would have $760 billion more in home equity value, $200 billion more in the stock market, $120 billion more in retirement funds, $80 billion more in the bank, for a total of over $1 trillion more in wealth.[31]

Employment

- Black male teenage unemployment rate is 22.4% as opposed to 10.7% for whites.[32]

- Black unemployment is twice that of whites. The unemployment rate as of April of this year was 10.6% for blacks and 5.2% for whites.[33]

- Unemployment among black is rising at a faster pace than in any similar period since the mid-1970s, and the jobs lost have been mostly in manufacturing, where the pay for blacks has historically been higher than in many other fields.[34]

---

[26]U.S. Census Bureau, DeNevas-Walt, Robert Cleveland, *Poverty in the United States, 2001, Current Population Reports, Current Income,* issued September 2002. http://www.census.gov/prod/2002pubs/p60-218.pdf.

[27]*Ibid.*

[28]*Ibid.*

[29]Panel Study of Income Dynamics, http://www.isr.umich.edu/src/psid/test2.gif.

[30]U.S. Census Bureau, DeNevas-Walt, Robert Cleveland, *Poverty in the United States, 2001, Current Population Reports, Current Income,* issued September 2002, http://www.census.gov/prod/2002pubs/p60-219.pdf.

[31]Speech delivered at 135th Charter Day Convocation at Howard University, March 8, 2002.

[32]Bureau of Labor Statistics, http://www.bls.gov/news.release/youth.t02.htm.

[33]Walt Byars, "Is There a Connection Between Discrimination and the Black Unemployment Rate?" Newsfilter.org, http://www.newsfilter.org/articles/black_unemployment.htm.

[34]Louis Uchitelle, "Black Unemployment Rises at Mid-70s Pace," *New York Times,* July 12, 2003.

- The 2003 Racial and Gender Report Card published by the Institute for Diversity and Ethics in Sport at the University of Central Florida, considered to be the definitive assessment of hiring practices in professional and amateur sports in the United States, found that minority hiring decreased in pro and college sports.[35]

- A study by professors at the University of Chicago Graduate School of Business and the Massachusetts Institute of Technology recently found that applicants with "ethnic" first names were 50% less likely to get a call for a job interview, compared to whites with the "non-ethnic" names.[36]

- Echoing the findings of others who have found "linguistic profiling" a growing concern, the executive director of the National Fair Housing Alliance says that their tests show that when blacks and whites leave messages on the answering machine, whites get the return calls and blacks do not.[37]

Education

- Students in six big cities (urban areas with predominantly black populations) are less proficient in reading and writing than their national peers, according to figures from the National Center for Educational Statistics' National Assessment of Educational Progress.[38]

- A new report from the Civil Rights Project at Harvard University found that charter schools provide black students with a more "intensely segregated school" experience than other public schools. Many of these schools are located in urban areas where racial segregation is most severe.[39]

- African Americans are far more likely than white children to be designated mentally retarded or emotionally disturbed and therefore in need of special education. Even when appropriately placed in special education classes, minority children often receive poorer services than disabled white children.[40]

- In Modesto, California, black students are two times as likely as their white peers to be expelled. During the 1998–99 school year, only one state (South Carolina) suspended 9% or more of its white students, but 35 states suspended that percentage of blacks, according to the Civil Rights Project at Harvard University. Black students

---

[35]*Jet* Magazine, 2003, pp. 46–47.

[36]The professors sent about 5,000 résumés in response to want ads in *The Boston Globe* and *Chicago Tribune.* They found that the "white" applicants they created received one response—a call, letter or e-mail—for every 10 résumés mailed, while "black" applicants with equal credentials received one response for every 15 résumés sent. The study authors said the results can solely be attributed to name manipulation. CNN.com, January 26, 2003.

[37]Steve Osunsami, "Voice Recognition: Can 'Hello' Cost You a Home If You're Black?" ABCNews.com, December 6, 2002.

[38]*USA Today,* July 23, 2003, p. 6D.

[39]"A Charter-Schools War," *Newsweek,* July 21, 2003, p. 8.

[40]*Racial Inequity in Special Education,* Daniel J. Losen and Gary Orfield, Eds., The Civil Rights Project at Harvard University and the Harvard Education Press, Pub., 2002.

made up 30% of the population of Miami-Dade County public schools in 2000–01, but accounted for half the school arrests, according to the Advancement Project. Indiana University charted the discipline patterns of 11,000 middle school students in a major urban district in Indiana and found that black students were more than twice as likely as their white peers to be sent to the principal's office or suspended and four times more likely to be expelled. While white students were reprimanded for behaviors like smoking and vandalism, black students were more often disciplined for things like excessive noise and disrespect.[41]

Health

- The life expectancy for blacks in 2001 increased to 72.2; it still lagged behind whites' 77.7 years.[42]

- Blacks are 40% more likely than whites to die of stroke, according to a Centers for Disease Control and Prevention report.[43]

- A recent CDC study found a 114% increase in suicide among black males age 10–19 from 1980 to 1995—larger than any other group. There was a 233% increase for blacks age 10–14, compared with a 120% increase for whites in their same age group. Among black males age 15–19, the suicide rate increased 146%, compared with 22% for white males.[44]

- The black infant mortality rate is more than double that of whites.[45]

Criminal Justice

- While blacks make up 12% of the population; of the 1.3 million prisoners in state and federal systems last year, 45% were black, 34% were white and 21% were Hispanic or another ethnicity. About 10% of all black men ages 25–29—or about 123,000 men—were in state or federal prisons last year.[46]

- According to a study by Amnesty International, blacks and whites are murdered in about equal numbers, but 80% of the 845 people executed since the United States resumed the death penalty in 1977 were put to death for killing whites. A disproportionate number of those executed were black and many were convicted by

---

[41]Jodie Morse & Wendy Cole, "Learning While Black," *Time Atlantic,* May 20, 2002.

[42]*Jet* Magazine, March 31, 2003, pp. 4–5.

[43]"Study Flags Racial Disparity in Stroke Deaths," *USA Today,* February 21, 2003, p. 3A.

[44]"What Drives Black Men to Suicide?" *USA Today,* November 25, 2002, p. 15A.

[45]BIBS, www.state.nj.us/health/bibs/education/1unsolved.html.

[46]*USA Today,* July 28, 2003, p. 3A, citing a U.S. Justice Department study released on July 27, 2003.

juries containing no blacks.[47] Blacks who murder whites are 15 times more likely to be executed than if they murdered other blacks.[48]

- Blacks comprise 12% of the U.S. population, but 41% of those on death row and 35% of those executed between 1977 and 2001.[49]

- An Illinois study found juries were three times more likely to sentence a defendant to death if the victim was white rather than black.[50]

- In Pennsylvania, racial and ethnic minorities account for 66% of the state prison population but only 12% of the Commonwealth's population.[51]

- A study commissioned by Gov. Glendening of Maryland that considered data from 6,000 homicide prosecutions over two decades found that blacks who kill whites are significantly more likely to face the death penalty in Maryland than are blacks who kill blacks or white killers. The study found that choices made by prosecutors about whom to charge with capital crime accounted for almost all of the racial disparity.[52]

Housing

- In one of the most exhaustive studies of residential segregation ever undertaken, a two-year analysis of census data by the U.S. Census Bureau determined that blacks remained the most highly segregated residents in the country.[53]

- Blacks have the lowest rates for home ownership and mortgage approval, but the highest foreclosure rate of all racial groups.[54]

- The total home ownership rate in the U.S. is 67.9%. The rate for whites is 71.8%; the rate for black home ownership is 47.3%.[55]

---

[47]*Death Penalty Discrimination,* CBSNews.com, http://www.cbsnews.com/stories/2003/04/24/national/main550986.shtml.

[48]"Blacks Much More Likely to Face Death Penalty, Study Says," *Jet* Magazine, April 2003, citing Amnesty International's report, "Death by Discrimination—The Continuing Role of Race in Capital Cases."

[49]Justice Department's Bureau of Justice Statistics, *Death Penalty Discrimination,* CBSNews.com, http://www.cbsnews.com/stories/2003/04/24/national/main550986.shtml.

[50]*Death Penalty Discrimination,* CBSNews.com, http://www.cbsnews.com/stories/2003/04/24/national/main550986.shtml. Illinois Gov. George Ryan cited these findings in January when he commuted 167 death sentences. *Jet* Magazine, February 24, 2003.

[51]Pennsylvania Department of Corrections and U.S. Bureau of Justice Statistics.

[52]Adam Liptak, "Death Penalty Found More Likely When Victim Is White," *New York Times,* January 8, 2003.

[53]*Jet* Magazine, December 16, 2002, p. 4.

[54]*Jet* Magazine, June 2003, p. 10.

[55]U.S. Census Bureau, Housing Vacancies and Homeownership Annual Statistics: 2002, http://www.census.gov/hhes/www/housing/hvs/annual02/ann02t20.html.

Family

- According to a recently released Census Bureau report, 43% of black families were headed by single women in 2002, compared to 13% of white families.[56]

Discrimination

- In 2001, 66% of blacks, but only 45% of whites told Gallup pollsters that race "will always be a problem" in the U.S. This was the widest gap recorded in the nine years Gallup has asked the question.[57]

- According to a seven-volume Harvard study issued in late 1999, race operates pervasively at many levels, manifesting itself in everything from highly segregated housing to labor markets that prefer hiring some racial groups over others. They found that stereotyping is often at play, particularly when it comes to where people want to live and whom they will hire. Blacks "continually end up at the bottom in terms of preferences for neighbors as well as when employers talk about hiring preferences." The study found that minorities make less money and work fewer hours than their white counterparts. It also found that they had a significantly harder time landing a job.[58]

CONCLUSION

It is ludicrous to think that America's long and tortured history with blacks would have no impact on how things stand today. The system put in place to control slaves, and the subsequent violence and intimidation used to control free blacks after the end of the Civil War was psychological as well as physical. You cannot for 300+ years deny education to people, deny all but the most menial employment to them, deny decent living conditions to them, deal unfairly with them in the criminal justice system, health care system, military system and other aspects of life and expect that it does not have an impact that will be felt for longer than the short period we have had non-discrimination laws. Having blacks be deprived of basic things like jobs and education and feeding them a constant diet of violence, subservience, being told they were less than and could not achieve was bound to have an impact.[59] In many ways, this continues today as blacks are still overrepresented in negative news stories and media representations. Their lives are rarely portrayed or understood in their full dimension. This sticks with whites who then deal with blacks in their daily inter-

---

[56]*Jet* Magazine, 2003, p. 5.

[57]DeWayne Wickham, "Bush Can Escape Grip of Right Wing's Bigotry," *USA Today,* December 24, 2002, p. 13A.

[58]*The Multi-City Study of Urban Inequality,* co-sponsored by the Russell Sage Foundation, the Ford Foundation and the Harvard University Multidisciplinary Program in Inequality and Social Policy. Initiated in the early 1990s, the project attempted to understand the patterns of racial inequality in modern, metropolitan areas and how race has been affected by economic changes.

[59]Na'im Akbar, *Chains and Images of Psychological Slavery,* New Mind Productions, 1984.

actions and fuels the actions that result in blacks having such different lives and opportunities than whites.

A basic American tenet is that we believe in equality. Our primary opposition to affirmative action is based on thinking blacks and whites are equally situated so giving a leg up to blacks is unfair.[60] In this paper, this perceived equality was shown to be fallacious. Blacks and whites in America are not similarly situated. Because of the peculiar history of race and race relations in this country, there are still deep differences between the reality of the lives and opportunities of blacks and whites. With the presumption that everyone is equal that undergirds opposition to affirmative action struck down, there is then no reason to continue to oppose it.

There is even less reason for the opposition to be based on the constitutional basis of affirmative action plans being a denial of equal protection. Since blacks, though gaining, significantly, lag behind whites in virtually every indicator used to determine the quality of life in this country, due in large part to their unique racial history and lingering vestiges, giving them consideration through affirmative action is an appropriate and justifiable thing to do. This is particularly so when statistical evidence significantly reflects the difference in their lives and studies indicate discrimination is based on negative stereotypes that have little or nothing to do with whether blacks should receive whatever is under consideration.

Even if a black student is given the benefit of an affirmative action plan, that student must still perform satisfactorily in school or be dismissed. Even if a black employee is given the benefit of an affirmative action plan, that employee must perform up to par or be terminated. The end product of affirmative action for blacks and society so far outweighs the insignificant burden it places on others with more and better opportunities, until it is still worth doing. That is to say, allowing affirmative action in college admissions gives the recipient a means to be able to become a productive, contributing member of society. Who would not want that? Given the statistics we have seen above, not being able to get into the school of their choice will not significantly adversely affect whites, who generally have significantly more opportunities open to them than blacks.

It is all well and good to want to look forward rather than backward, but when the past has such an inescapable impact on the present, it is difficult to do. Ignoring the past and the vestiges with which we are presently dealing will not make those vestiges go away. We have tried that route and it does not work. That is why we are still dealing with this issue 138 years after the end of the war that was supposed to put us all in the same position.

---

[60]Actually, there seems to be little opposition to plans that primarily benefit whites such as college admission programs that take into consideration whether an applicant's parent or grandparents attended the institution, whether the parents have contributed to the institution financially, or whether the applicant is being recommended by someone rich, famous or well-known, who, it is perceived, could help the school. Since blacks were not permitted to attend many schools until after the civil rights legislation, and jobs and education were denied to them until then, there is little chance they can benefit from such plans.

The most incredible aspect of all of this is that blacks have managed to come as far as they have despite the odds they have been working with. To have to beg for a few crumbs by way of an affirmative action plan is too ridiculous to be believed. An entire race was entirely excluded from anything even *close* to the mainstream of life in this country from this country's inception all the way up until nearly forty years ago, and for some bizarre reason, white society seems to think that we are all now in the same place. What sense does that make? None. We aren't, and affirmative action is the least we can do to address it.

> *It has been suggested that affirmative action harms minorities by causing whites to respect them less. This idea is laughable and cynical at best. If respect for minorities existed prior to affirmative action there would not have been a need for its implementation. I agree that it has harmed some minorities, but by different means. First, many minority applicants have been excluded from education or employment at institutions that would not consider further minority applicants once their "quota" was met. Second, affirmative action caused many white Americans to become jealous, resentful and scared because they saw their privileged position in society diminishing.[61]*

It is time to face the truth. This country's racial past still has strong vestiges very much with us today. Even though recent days have seen the passing of some of the staunchest pillars of our near past of segregation like Strom Thurmond and Lester Maddox, it only took this past January's fiasco with Trent Lott to see how much that past is still with us. The institution of slavery followed by Jim Crow was self-perpetuating, but we can and must stop it. Good and decent folks who never owned slaves, wore a hood, burned a cross or participated in a night ride to terrorize blacks, were just as responsible for the system that they silently allowed others to conduct and that they received the benefits of. There is no question that a 300+ year history of white supremacy benefited all whites. Doing nothing can sometimes be as damaging as doing the wrong thing.

Affirmative action is a very modest way to try to address the inequities built into our society by a system that had been in place since the inception of this country until very recently. Ignoring that fact will not make it go away. Affirmative action should be used, while alternatives are explored, to address this.

Despite the statistics provided in this paper, blacks have made *incredible* strides in the past forty years. However, we must consider where we started from. Now that we have some of the basics taken care of, we can get down to the real work of equality of opportunity and what it means for the quality of lives of blacks and their continued contribution to all of America.

That is truly such stuff as dreams are made of. . . .

---

[61]Larry Smith, Drogheda, Ireland, *USA Today,* July 1, 2003, p. 11A.

WHAT IS WRONG WITH REVERSE DISCRIMINATION?[1]

—NED HETTINGER

Many people think that it is obvious that "reverse discrimination" is unjust. Calling affirmative action policies "reverse discrimination" itself suggests this result. The following discussion evaluates numerous reasons given for this alleged injustice. Most of these accounts of what is wrong with reverse discrimination are found by the author to be deficient. The explanations for why reverse discrimination is morally troubling persuade him only that it is unjust in a relatively weak sense. This result has an important consequence for the wider issue of the moral justifiability of affirmative action. If social policies that involve minor injustice are permissible (and perhaps required) when they are needed in order to overcome much greater injustice, then he argues that the mild injustice of reverse discrimination is easily overridden by its contribution to the important social goal of dismantling our sexual and racial caste system.

By "reverse discrimination" or "affirmative action" I shall mean hiring or admitting a slightly less well qualified woman or black, rather than a slightly more qualified white male,[2] for the purpose of helping to eradicate sexual and/or racial inequality, or for the purpose of compensating women and blacks for the burdens and injustices they have suffered due to past and ongoing sexism and racism.[3] There are weaker forms of affirmative action, such as giving preference to minority candidates only when qualifications are equal, or providing special educational opportunities for youths in disadvantaged groups. This paper seeks to defend the more controversial sort of reverse discrimination defined above. I begin by considering several spurious objections to reverse discrimination. In the second part, I identify the ways in which this policy is morally troubling and then assess the significance of these negative features.

SPURIOUS OBJECTIONS

1. Reverse Discrimination as Equivalent to Racism and Sexism

In a discussion on national television, George Will, the conservative news analyst and political philosopher, articulated the most common objection to reverse discrimination. It is unjust, he said, because it is discrimination on the basis of race and/or sex. Reverse discrimination against white males is the same evil as traditional discrimination against blacks and women. The only difference is that in this case it is the white male who is being discriminated against. Thus if traditional racism and sexism are wrong and unjust, so is reverse discrimination, and for the very same reasons.

But reverse discrimination is not at all like traditional sexism and racism. For the motives and intentions behind it are completely different, as are its consequences. Consider some of the motives underlying traditional racial discrimination.[4] Blacks were not hired or allowed into schools because it was felt that contact with them was degrading, and sullied whites. These policies were based on contempt and loathing for blacks, on a feeling that blacks were suitable only for subservient positions and that they should never have positions of authority over whites.

Slightly better qualified white males are not being turned down under affirmative action for any of these reasons. No defenders or practitioners of affirmative action (and no significantly large segment of the general public) think contact with white males is degrading or sullying, that white males are contemptible and loathsome, or that white males—by their nature—should be subservient to blacks or women.

The consequences of these two policies differ radically as well. Affirmative action does not stigmatize white males; it does not perpetuate unfortunate stereotypes about white males; it is not part of a pattern of discrimination that makes being a white male incredibly burdensome.[5] Nor does it add to a particular group's "already overabundant supply" of power, authority, wealth and opportunity, as does traditional racial and sexual discrimination.[6] On the contrary, it results in a more egalitarian distribution of these social and economic benefits.

If the motives and consequences of reverse discrimination and of traditional racism and sexism are completely different, in what sense could they be morally equivalent acts? If acts are to be individuated (for moral purposes) by including the motives, intentions and consequences in the act's description, then clearly these two acts are not identical.

Someone might argue, however, that although the motives and consequences are different, the act itself is the same: reverse discrimination is discrimination on the basis of race and sex, and this is wrong in itself independently of its motives or consequences. But discriminating (i.e., making distinctions in how one treats people) on the basis of race or sex is not always wrong, nor is it necessarily unjust. It is not wrong, for example, to discriminate against one's own sex when choosing a spouse. Nor is racial or sexual discrimination in hiring necessarily wrong. This is shown by Peter Singer's example in which a director of a play about ghetto conditions in New York City refuses to consider any white applicants for the actors because she wants the play to be authentic.[7] If I am looking for a representative of the black community, or doing a study about blacks and disease, it is perfectly legitimate to discriminate against all whites. Their whiteness makes them unsuitable for my (legitimate) purposes. Similarly, if I am hiring a wet-nurse, or a person to patrol the women's change rooms in my department store, discriminating against males is perfectly legitimate.

These examples show that racial and sexual discrimination are not wrong in themselves. This is not to say that they are never wrong; most often they clearly are. Whether or not they are wrong, however, depends on the purposes, consequences and context of such discrimination.

2. Race and Sex as Morally Arbitrary and Irrelevant Characteristics

A typical reason given for the alleged injustice of all racial and sexual discrimination (including affirmative action) is that it is morally arbitrary to consider race or sex when hiring, since these characteristics are not relevant to the decision. But the above examples show that not all uses of race or sex as a criterion in hiring decisions are morally arbitrary or irrelevant. Similarly, when an affirmative action officer takes into account race and sex, use of these characteristics is not morally irrelevant or arbitrary. Since affirmative action aims to help end racial and sexual inequality by providing black and female role models for minorities (and non-minorities), the race and sex of the job candidates are clearly relevant to the decision. There is nothing arbitrary about the affirmative action officer focusing on race and sex. Hence, if reverse discrimination is wrong, it is not wrong for the reason that it uses morally irrelevant and arbitrary characteristics to distinguish between applicants.

3. Reverse Discrimination as Unjustified Stereotyping

It might be argued that reverse discrimination involves judging people by alleged average characteristics of a class to which they belong, instead of judging them on the basis of their individual characteristics, and that such judging on the basis of stereotypes is morally unjust.

But the defense of affirmative action suggested in this paper does not rely on stereotyping. When an employer hires a slightly less well qualified woman or black over a slightly more qualified white male for the purpose of helping to overcome sexual and racial inequality, she judges the applicants on the basis of their individual characteristics. She uses this person's sex or color as a mechanism to help achieve the goals of affirmative action. Individual characteristics of the white male (his color and sex) prevent him from serving one of the legitimate goals of employment policies, and he is turned down on this basis.

Notice that the objection does have some force against those who defend reverse discrimination on the grounds of compensatory justice. An affirmative action policy whose purpose is to compensate women and blacks for past and current injustices judges that women and blacks on the average are owed greater compensation than are white males. Although this is true, opponents of affirmative action argue that some white males have been more severely and unfairly disadvantaged than some women and blacks.[8] A poor white male from Appalachia may have suffered greater undeserved disadvantages than the upper-middle class woman or black with whom he competes. Although there is a high correlation between being female (or being black) and being especially owed compensation for unfair disadvantages suffered, the correlation is not universal.

Thus defending affirmative action on the grounds of compensatory justice may lead to unjust treatment of white males in individual cases. Despite the fact that certain white males are owed greater compensation than are some women or blacks, it is the latter that receive compensation. This is the result of judging candidates for jobs on the basis of the average characteristics of their class, rather than on the basis of their individual characteristics. Thus compensatory justice defenses of reverse discrimination may involve potentially problematic stereotyping.[9] But this is not the defense of affirmative action considered here.

4. Failing to Hire the Most Qualified Person Is Unjust

One of the major reasons people think reverse discrimination is unjust is because they think that the most qualified person should get the job. But why should the most qualified person be hired?

a. Efficiency   One obvious answer to this question is that one should hire the most qualified person because doing so promotes efficiency. If job qualifications are positively correlated with job performance, then the more qualified person will do a better job. Although it is not always true that there is such a correlation, in general there is, and hence this point is well taken. There are short term efficiency costs of reverse discrimination as defined here.[10]

Note that a weaker version of affirmative action has no such efficiency costs. If one hires a black or woman over a white male only in cases where qualifications are roughly equal, job performance will not be affected. Furthermore, efficiency costs will be a function of the qualifications gap between the black or woman hired, and the white male rejected: the larger the gap, the greater the efficiency costs.[11] The existence of efficiency costs is also a function of the type of work performed. Many of the jobs in our society are ones which any normal person can do (e.g., assembly line worker, janitor, truck driver, etc.). Affirmative action hiring for these positions is unlikely to have significant efficiency costs (assuming whoever is hired is willing to work hard). In general, higher prestige positions are the ones in which people's performance levels will vary significantly, and hence these are the jobs in which reverse discrimination could have significant efficiency costs.

While concern for efficiency gives us a reason for hiring the most qualified person, it in no way explains the alleged injustice suffered by the white male who is passed over due to reverse discrimination. If the affirmative action employer is treating the white male unjustly, it is not because the hiring policy is inefficient. Failing to maximize efficiency does not generally involve acting unjustly. For instance, a person who carries one bag of groceries at a time, rather than two, is acting inefficiently, though not unjustly.

It is arguable that the manager of a business who fails to hire the most qualified person (and thereby sacrifices some efficiency) treats the owners of the company unjustly, for their profits may suffer, and this violates one conception of the manager's fiduciary responsibility to the shareholders. Perhaps the administrator of a hospital who hires a slightly less well qualified black doctor (for the purposes of affirmative action) treats the future patients at that hospital unjustly, for doing so may reduce the level of health care they receive (and it is arguable that they have a legitimate expectation to receive the best health care possible for the money they spend). But neither of these examples of inefficiency leading to injustice concern the white male "victim" of affirmative action, and it is precisely this person who the opponents of reverse discrimination claim is being unfairly treated.

To many people, that a policy is inefficient is a sufficient reason for condemning it. This is especially true in the competitive and profit oriented world of business. However, profit maximization is not the only legitimate goal of business hiring policies (or other business decisions). Businesses have responsibilities to help heal society's ills, especially those (like racism and sexism) which they in large part helped to create and perpetuate. Unless one takes the implausible position that business' only legitimate goal is profit maximization, the efficiency costs of affirmative action are not an automatic reason for rejecting it. And as we have noted, affirmative action's efficiency costs are of no help in substantiating and explaining its alleged injustice to white males.

b. The Most Qualified Person Has a Right to the Job   One could argue that the most qualified person for the job has a right to be hired in virtue of superior qualifications. On this view, reverse discrimination violates the better qualified white male's right to be hired for the job.

But the most qualified applicant holds no such right. If you are the best painter in town, and a person hires her brother to paint her house, instead of you, your rights have not been violated. People do not have rights to be hired for particular jobs (though I think a plausible case can be made for the claim that there is a fundamental human right to employment). If anyone has a right in this matter, it is the employer. This is not to say, of course, that the employer cannot do wrong in her hiring decision; she obviously can. If she hires a white because she loathes blacks, she does wrong. The point is that her wrong does not consist in violating the right some candidate has to her job (though this would violate other rights of the candidate).

c. The Most Qualified Person Deserves the Job   It could be argued that the most qualified person should get the job because she deserves it in virtue of her superior qualifications. But the assumption that the person most qualified for a job is the one who most deserves it is problematic. Very often people do not deserve their qualifications, and hence they do not deserve anything on the basis of those qualifications.[12] A person's qualifications are a function of at least the following factors: (a) innate abilities, (b) home environment, (c) socio-economic class of parents, (d) quality of the schools attended, (e) luck and (f) effort or perseverance. A person is only responsible for the last factor on this list, and hence one only deserves one's qualifications to the extent that they are a function of effort.[13]

It is undoubtedly often the case that a person who is less well qualified for a job is more deserving of the job (because she worked harder to achieve those lower qualifications) than is someone with superior qualifications. This is frequently true of women and blacks in the job market: they worked harder to overcome disadvantages most (or all) white males never faced. Hence, affirmative action policies which permit the hiring of slightly less well qualified candidates may often be more in line with considerations of desert than are the standard meritocratic procedures.

The point is not that affirmative action is defensible because it helps insure that more deserving candidates get jobs. Nor is it that desert should be the only or even the most important consideration in hiring decisions. The claim is simply that hiring the most qualified person for a job need not (and quite often does not) involve hiring the most deserving candidate. Hence the intuition that morality requires one to hire the most qualified people cannot be justified on the grounds that these people deserve to be hired.[14]

d. The Most Qualified Person Is Entitled to the Job   One might think that although the most qualified person neither necessarily deserves the job nor has a right to the job, still this person is entitled to the job. By "entitlement" in this context, I mean a natural and legitimate expectation based on a type of social promise. Society has implicitly encouraged the belief that the most qualified candidate will get the job. Society has set up a competition and the prize is a job which is awarded to those applying with the best qualifications. Society thus reneges on an implicit promise it has made to its members when it allows reverse discrimination to occur. It is dashing legitimate expectations it has encouraged. It is violating the very rules of a game it created.

Furthermore, the argument goes, by allowing reverse discrimination, society is breaking an explicit promise (contained in the Civil Rights Act of 1964) that it will not allow race or sex to be used against one of its citizens. Title VII of that Act prohibits discrimination in employment on the basis of race or sex (as well as color, religion or national origin).

In response to this argument, it should first be noted that the above interpretation of the Civil Rights Act is misleading. In fact, the Supreme Court has interpreted the Act as allowing race and sex to be considered in hiring or admission decisions.[15] More importantly, since affirmative action has been an explicit national policy for the last 15–20 years (and has been supported in numerous court cases), it is implausible to argue that society has promised its members that it will not allow race or sex to outweigh superior qualifications in hiring decisions.

In addition, the objection takes a naive and utopian view of actual hiring decisions. It presents a picture of our society as a pure meritocracy in which hiring decisions are based solely on qualifications. The only exception it sees to these meritocratic procedures is the unfortunate policy of affirmative action. But this picture is dramatically distorted. Elected government officials, political appointees, business managers and many others clearly do not have their positions solely or even mostly because of their qualifications.[16] Given the widespread acceptance in our society of procedures which are far from meritocratic, claiming that the most qualified person has a socially endorsed entitlement to the job is not believable.

5. Undermining Equal Opportunity for White Males

It has been claimed that the right of white males to an equal chance of employment is violated by affirmative action.[17] Reverse discrimination, it is said, undermines equality of opportunity for white males.

If equality of opportunity requires a social environment in which everyone at birth has roughly the same chance of succeeding through the use of their natural talents, then it could well be argued that given the social, cultural and educational disadvantages placed on women and blacks, preferential treatment of these groups brings us closer to equality of opportunity. White males are full members of the community in a way in which women and blacks are not, and this advantage is diminished by affirmative action. Affirmative action takes away the greater than equal opportunity white males generally have, and thus it brings us closer to a situation in which all these groups have an equal chance of succeeding through the use of their talents.

It must be noted that the goal of affirmative action is to bring about a society in which there is equality of opportunity for women and blacks without preferential treatment of these groups. It is not the purpose of the sort of affirmative action defended here to disadvantage white males in order to take away the advantage a sexist and racist society gives to them. But noticing that this occurs is sufficient to dispel the illusion that affirmative action undermines the equality of opportunity for white males.[18]

LEGITIMATE OBJECTIONS

The following two considerations explain what is morally troubling about reverse discrimination.

1. Judging on the Basis of Involuntary Characteristics

In cases of reverse discrimination, white males are passed over on the basis of membership in a group they were born into. When an affirmative action employer hires a slightly less well qualified black (or woman), rather than a more highly qualified white male, skin color (or sex) is being used as one criterion for determining who gets a very important benefit. Making distinctions in how one treats people on the basis of characteristics they cannot help having (such as skin color or sex) is morally problematic because it reduces individual autonomy. Discriminating between people on the basis of features they can do something about is preferable, since it gives them some control over how others act towards them. They can develop the characteristics others use to give them favorable treatment and avoid those characteristics others use as grounds for unfavorable treatment.[19]

For example, if employers refuse to hire you because you are a member of the American Nazi Party, and if you do not like the fact that you are having a hard time finding a job, you can choose to leave the party. However, if a white male is having trouble finding employment because slightly less well qualified blacks and women are being given jobs to meet affirmative action requirements, there is nothing he can do about this disadvantage, and his autonomy is curtailed.[20]

Discriminating between people on the basis of their involuntary characteristics is morally undesirable, and thus reverse discrimination is also morally undesirable. Of course, that something is morally undesirable does not show that it is unjust, nor that it is morally unjustifiable.

Just how morally troubling is it to judge people on the basis of involuntary characteristics? Notice that our society frequently uses these sorts of features to distinguish between people. Height and good looks are characteristics one cannot do much about, and yet basketball players and models are ordinarily chosen and rejected on the basis of precisely these features. To a large extent our intelligence is also a feature beyond our control, and yet intelligence is clearly one of the major characteristics our society uses to determine what happens to people.

Of course there are good reasons why we distinguish between people on the basis of these sorts of involuntary characteristics. Given the goals of basketball teams, model agencies and employers in general, hiring the taller, better looking or more intelligent person (respectively) makes good sense. It promotes efficiency, since all these people are likely to do a better job. Hiring policies based on these involuntary characteristics serve the legitimate purposes of these businesses (e.g., profit and serving the public), and hence they may be morally justified despite their tendency to reduce the control people have over their own lives.

This type of argument can be applied to reverse discrimination as well. The purpose of affirmative action is to help eradicate racial and sexual injustice. If affirmative action policies help bring about this goal, then they can be morally justified despite their tendency to reduce the control white males have over their lives.

In one respect this sort of consequentialist argument is more forceful in the case of affirmative action. Rather than merely promoting the goal of efficiency (which is the justification for businesses hiring naturally brighter, taller or more attractive individuals), affirmative action promotes the non-utilitarian goal of an egalitarian society. In general, promoting a consideration of justice (such as equality) is more important than is promoting efficiency or utility.[21] Thus in terms of the importance of the objective, this consequentialist argument is stronger in the case of affirmative action. If one can justify reducing individual autonomy on the grounds that it promotes efficiency, one can certainly do so on the grounds that it reduces the injustice of racial and sexual inequality.

2. Burdening White Males Without Compensation

Perhaps the strongest moral intuition about the wrongness of reverse discrimination is that it is unfair to job-seeking white males. It is unfair because they have been given an undeserved disadvantage in the competition for employment; they have been handicapped because of something that is not their fault. Why should white males be made to pay for the sins of others?

It would be a mistake to argue for reverse discrimination on the grounds that white males deserve to be burdened, and that therefore we should hire women and blacks even when white males are better qualified.[22] Young white males who are now entering the job market are not more responsible for the evils of racial and sexual inequality than are other members of society. Thus, reverse discrimination is not properly viewed as punishment administered to white males.

The justification for affirmative action supported here claims that bringing about racial and sexual equality necessitates sacrifice on the part of white males who seek employment. An important step in bringing about the desired egalitarian society involves speeding up the process by which blacks and women get into positions of power and authority. This requires that white males find it harder to achieve these same positions. But this is not punishment for deeds done.

Thomas Nagel's helpful analogy is state condemnation of property under the right of eminent domain for the purpose of building a highway.[23] Forcing some in the community to move in order that the community as a whole may benefit is unfair. Why should these individuals suffer rather than others? The answer is: Because they happen to live in a place where it is important to build a road. A similar response should be given to the white male who objects to reverse discrimination with the same "Why me?" question. The answer is: Because job-seeking white males happen to be in the way of an important road leading to the desired egalitarian society. White males are being made to bear the brunt of the burden of affirmative action because of accidental considerations, just as are homeowners whose property is condemned in order to build a highway.

This analogy is extremely illuminating and helpful in explaining the nature of reverse discrimination. There is, however, an important dissimilarity that Nagel does not mention. In cases of property condemnation, compensation is paid to the owner. Affirmative action policies, however, do not compensate white males for shouldering this burden of moving toward the desired egalitarian society. So affirmative action is unfair to job-seeking white males because they are forced to bear an unduly large share of the burden of achieving racial and sexual equality without being compensated for this sacrifice. Since we have singled out job-seeking white males from the larger pool of white males who should also help achieve this goal, it seems that some compensation from the latter to the former is appropriate.[24]

This is a serious objection to affirmative action policies only if the uncompensated burden is substantial. Usually it is not. Most white male "victims" of affirmative action easily find employment. It is highly unlikely that the same white male will repeatedly fail to get hired because of affirmative action.[25] Furthermore, the burden job-seeking white males face—of finding it somewhat more difficult to get employment—is inconsequential when compared to the burdens ongoing discrimination places on women and blacks.[26] Forcing job-seeking white males to bear an extra burden is acceptable because this is a necessary step toward achieving a much greater reduction in the unfair burdens our society places on women and blacks. If affirmative action is a necessary mechanism for a timely dismantlement of our racial and sexual caste system, the extra burdens it places on job-seeking white males are justified.

Still the question remains: Why isn't compensation paid? When members of society who do not deserve extra burdens are singled out to sacrifice for an important community goal, society owes them compensation. This objection loses some of its force when one realizes that society continually places undeserved burdens on its members without compensating them. For instance, the burden of seeking efficiency is placed on the shoulders of the least naturally talented and intelligent. That one is born less intelligent (or otherwise less talented) does not mean that one deserves to have reduced employment opportunities, and yet our society's meritocratic hiring procedures make it much harder for less naturally talented members to find meaningful employment. These people are not compensated for their sacrifices either.

Of course, pointing out that there are other examples of an allegedly problematic social policy does not justify that policy. Nonetheless, if this analogy is sound, failing to compensate white males for the sacrifices placed on them by reverse discrimination is not without precedent. Furthermore , it is no more morally troublesome than is failing to compensate less talented members of society for their undeserved sacrifice of employment opportunities for the sake of efficiency.

CONCLUSION

This paper has shown the difficulties in pinpointing what is morally troubling about reverse discrimination. The most commonly heard objections to reverse discrimination fail to make their case. Reverse discrimination is not morally equivalent to traditional racism and sexism since its goals and consequences are entirely different, and the act of distinguishing between people on the basis of race or sex is not necessarily morally wrong. The race and sex of the candidates are not morally irrelevant in all hiring decisions, and affirmative action hiring is an example where discriminating on the basis of race or sex is not morally arbitrary. Furthermore, affirmative action can be defended on grounds that do not involve stereotyping. Though affirmative action hiring of less well qualified applicants can lead to short run inefficiency, failing to hire the most qualified applicant does not violate this person's rights, entitlements or deserts. Additionally, affirmative action hiring does not generally undermine equal opportunity for white males.

Reverse discrimination is morally troublesome in that it judges people on the basis of involuntary characteristics and thus reduces the control they have over their lives. It also places a larger than fair share of the burden of achieving an egalitarian society on the shoulders of job-seeking white males without compensating them for this sacrifice. But these problems are relatively minor when compared to the grave injustice of racial and sexual inequality, and they are easily outweighed if affirmative action helps alleviate this far greater injustice.[27]

NOTES

I thank Cheshire Calhoun, Beverly Diamond, John Dickerson, Jasper Hunt, Glenn Lesses, Richard Nunan, and Martin Perlmutter for help with earlier drafts of this essay.

1. With regard to the introduction, Thomas Nagel uses the phrase "racial caste system" in his illuminating testimony before the Subcommittee on the Constitution of the Senate Judiciary Committee, on June 18, 1981. This testimony is reprinted as "A Defense of Affirmative Action" in *Ethical Theory and Business,* 2nd edition, ed. Tom Beauchamp and Norman Bowie (Englewood Cliffs, NJ: Prentice-Hall, 1983), pp. 483–487.
2. What should count as qualifications is controversial. By "qualifications" I refer to such things as grades, test scores, prior experience and letters of recommendation. I will not include black skin or female sex in my use of "qualification," though there are strong arguments for counting these as legitimate qualifications (in the sense of characteristics which would help the candidate achieve the legitimate goals of the hiring or admitting institution). See Ronald Dworkin, "Why Bakke Has No Case," *The New York Review of Books,* November 10, 1977.
3. This paper assumes the controversial claim that we live in a racist and sexist society. Statistics provide immediate and powerful support for this claim. The fact that blacks comprise 12% of the U.S. population, while comprising a minuscule percentage of those in positions of power and authority is sufficient evidence that our society continues to be significantly racist in results, if not in intent. Unless one assumes that blacks are innately less able to attain, or less desirous of attaining, these positions to a degree that would account for this huge under-representation, one must conclude that our social organizations significantly disadvantage blacks. This is (in part) the injustice that I call racism. The argument for the charge of sexism is analogous (and perhaps even more persuasive given that women comprise over 50% of the population). For more supporting evidence, see Tom Beauchamp's article "The Justification of Reverse Discrimination in Hiring" in *Ethical Theory and Business,* pp. 495–506.
4. Although the examples in this paper focus more on racism than on sexism, it is not clear that the former is a worse problem than the latter. In many ways, sexism is a more subtle and pervasive form of discrimination. It is also less likely to be acknowledged.
5. This is Paul Woodruff's helpful definition of unjust discrimination. See Paul Woodruff, "What's Wrong with Discrimination," *Analysis,* vol. 36, no. 3, 1976, pp. 158–160.
6. This point is made by Richard Wasserstrom in his excellent article "A Defense of Programs of Preferential Treatment," *National Forum* (The Phi Kappa Phi Journal), vol. VIII, no. 1 (Winter 1978), pp. 15–18. The article is reprinted in *Social Ethics,* 2nd edition, ed. Thomas Mappes and Jane Zembaty (New York: McGraw-Hill, 1982), pp. 187–191. The quoted phrase is Wasserstrom's.
7. Peter Singer, "Is Racial Discrimination Arbitrary," *Philosophia,* vol. 8 (November 1978), pp. 185–203.

8. See, for example, Robert Simon, "Preferential Hiring: A Reply to Judith Jarvis Thomson," *Philosophy and Public Affairs,* vol. 3, no. 3 (Spring 1974).

9. If it is true (and it is certainly plausible) that every black or woman, no matter how fortunate, has suffered from racism and sexism in a way in which no white male has suffered, then compensation for this injustice would be owed to all and only blacks and women. Given this, arguing for affirmative action on the grounds of compensatory justice would not involve judging individuals by average features of classes they are members of. Still it might be argued that for certain blacks and women such injustices are not nearly as severe as the different type of injustice suffered by some white males. Thus one would have to provide a reason for why we should compensate (with affirmative action) any black or woman before any white male. Perhaps administrative convenience is such a reason. Being black or female (rather than white and male) correlates nicely with the property of being more greatly and unfairly disadvantaged, and thus race and sex are useful rough guides with which to determine who is most in need of compensation. This does, however, involve stereotyping.

10. In the long run, however, reverse discrimination may actually promote overall societal efficiency by opening the gates of a vast reservoir of untapped potential in women and blacks.

11. See Thomas Nagel, "A Defense of Affirmative Action," p. 484.

12. This is Wasserstrom's point. See "A Defense of Programs of Preferential Treatment," in *Social Ethics,* p. 190.

13. By "effort" I intend to include (1) how hard a person tries to achieve certain goals, (2) the amount of risk voluntarily incurred in seeking these goals and (3) the degree to which moral considerations played a role in choosing these goals. The harder one tries, the more one is willing to sacrifice and the worthier the goal, the greater are one's deserts. For support of the claim that voluntary past action is the only valid basis for desert, see James Rachels, "What People Deserve," in *Justice and Economic Distribution,* ed. John Arthur and William Shaw (Englewood Cliffs, NJ: Prentice-Hall, 1978), pp. 150–163.

14. It would be useful to know if there is a correlation between the candidate who is most deserving (because she worked the hardest), and the one with the best qualifications. In other words, are better qualified candidates in general those who worked harder to achieve their qualifications? Perhaps people who have the greatest natural abilities and the most fortunate social circumstances will be the ones who work the hardest to develop their talents. This raises the possibility, suggested by John Rawls, that the ability to put forward effort is itself a function of factors outside a person's control. See his *A Theory of Justice* (Cambridge, MA: Harvard University Press, 1971), pp. 103–104. But if anything is under a person's control, and hence is something a person is responsible for, it is how hard she tries. Thus if there is an appropriate criterion for desert, it will include how much effort a person exerts.

15. See Justice William Brennan's majority opinion in *United Steel Workers and Kaiser Aluminum v. Weber,* United States Supreme Court, 443 U.S. 193, (1979). See also Justice Lewis Powell's majority opinion in the *University of California v. Bakke,* United States Supreme Court, 438 U.S. 265 (1978).

16. This is Wasserstrom's point. See "A Defense of Programs of Preferential Treatment," p. 189.

17. This is Judith Thomson's way of characterizing the alleged injustice. See her "Preferential Hiring," *Philosophy and Public Affairs* vol. 2, no. 4 (Summer 1973).

18. If it is true that some white males are more severely disadvantaged in our society than are some women and blacks, affirmative action would increase the inequality of opportunity for these white males. But since these individuals are a small minority of white males, the overall result of affirmative action would be to move us closer toward equality of opportunity.

19. James Rachels makes this point in "What People Deserve," p. 159. Joel Feinberg has also discussed related points. See his *Social Philosophy* (Englewood Cliffs, NJ: Prentice-Hall, 1973), p. 108.

20. He could work harder to get better qualifications and hope that the qualifications gap between him and the best woman or black would become so great that the efficiency cost of pursuing affirmative action would be prohibitive. Still he can do nothing to get rid of the disadvantage (in affirmative action contexts) of being a white male.

21. For a discussion of how considerations of justice typically outweigh considerations of utility, see Manuel Velasquez, *Business Ethics* (Englewood Cliffs, NJ: Prentice-Hall, 1982), Chapter Two.

22. On the average, however, white males have been unfairly benefited by the holding back of blacks and women, and hence it is not altogether inappropriate that this unfair benefit be removed.

23. Nagel, "A Defense of Affirmative Action," p. 484.

24. It would be inappropriate to extract compensation from women or blacks since they are the ones who suffer the injustice affirmative action attempts to alleviate.

25. This is a potential worry, however, and so it is important to insure that the same white male does not repeatedly sacrifice for the goals of affirmative action. The burdens of affirmative action should be spread as evenly as possible among all the job-seeking white males.

26. I thank Cheshire Calhoun for reminding me of this point.

27. Of course one must argue that reverse discrimination is effective in bringing about an egalitarian society. There are complicated consequentialist arguments both for and against this claim, and I have not discussed them here. Some of the questions to be addressed are: (1) How damaging is reverse discrimination to the self-esteem of blacks and women? (2) Does reverse discrimination promote racial and sexual strife more than it helps to alleviate them? (3) Does it perpetuate unfortunate stereotypes about blacks and women? (4) How long are we justified in waiting to pull blacks and women into the mainstream of our social life? (5) What sorts of alternative mechanisms are possible and politically practical for achieving affirmative action goals (for instance, massive early educational funding for children from impoverished backgrounds)?

THE QUESTION
OF WAGES

—RUTH ROSENBAUM

*In discussing employee compensation, the question of wage levels of-
ten goes beyond the "going rate" to a concern for whether the "going rate" is where it should be. Is this the ethical wage to be paying
a worker? Ruth Rosenbaum provides some definitional context for the
discussion below.*

In the United States at this time many city governments are considering a requirement that
companies that do business with the government pay a "living wage." The federal government and some state governments have recently enacted legislation to raise the "minimum
wage." Union leaders call for "just wages." Persons who have moved from receiving federal or state assistance into low-paying jobs sometimes talk about "slave wages." Middle
and upper-level management personnel who have been laid off face big "reductions" in
their salaries, or wages. The media carries reports of scandalous conditions of sweatshops
worldwide. Truly, work and the financial remuneration for that work are central to people's
lives and are in the forefront of the difficulties of the world's globalized economy.

In addressing this issue, the Center for Reflection, Education and Action (CREA) uses
a set of working definitions of wage levels that describes the purchasing power that workers are able to earn. Awareness of these levels can assist in discussions and decisions about
wages. While many higher wage levels exist, CREA has found that the following terminology and definitions are the most helpful in discussions.

Level 1: Marginal Survival Wage. This wage level does not provide for adequate
nutritional needs. Starvation is prevented, but malnutrition, illnesses and early
deaths are the result.

Level 2: Basic Survival Wage. This wage level allows for meeting immediate survival
needs, including basic food, used clothing, minimal shelter and fuel for cooking.

Level 3: Short Range Planning Wage. This level meets basic survival needs, and
in addition provides the possibility of a small amount of discretionary income.
Such income allows for minimal planning beyond living from paycheck to paycheck. It allows for occasional purchase of needed item(s) as small amounts can
be set aside after meeting basic survival needs.

Level 4: Sustainable Living Wage. This wage level meets basic needs including food, clothing, housing, energy, transportation, healthcare and education. It provides sufficient money to enable participation in culturally required activities (including celebrations of births, weddings, funerals and related activities).

Level 5: Sustainable Community Wage. This level provides enough discretionary income to allow the workers to support the development of small businesses in a local community, including the support of cultural and civic needs of that community, and preservation of the environment for future generations.

CREA has used another construct set in systemic analysis study groups, and found them to be helpful in considering wages. This set involves looking at wages from the perspective of whether they are legal, ethical, moral and just.

1.   Legal: Legal minimum wage means no more than what companies can pay without violating the law of the country or state. Legal minimum wages are not predicated on nutritional needs, or any other needs workers have on an on-going basis. Often, they are predicated or based on a country's or a region's perceived need to attract businesses. When this happens, workers' wages become a competitive advantage or disadvantage, depending upon one's viewpoint. Corporations seek production sites where wages are kept as low as possible by the legal standards, so that the corporation itself may become more "profitable." We see this reflected in the numerous codes of conduct which individual corporations and industries are producing. These corporate standards assert that what the company is doing is legal, that the company adheres to the minimum wage laws of the countries in which it operates. These corporate standards, communicated to the public as both legal and acceptable, then become normative, despite their negative effects on workers.

2.   Ethical: Leaving aside philosophical discussion of the meaning of ethics, it is important to recognize that business ethics, medical ethics, etc., have become colloquially understood as behavior which is acceptable within a particular group. Therefore, business ethics or the ethics within a particular business segment can be understood as industry's self-defined and self-accepted standard of practice. In other words, what the industry says about itself as acceptable practice becomes the accepted public standard. Again, we see this reflected in industry codes of conduct. The ethical standard for workers' wages has become that which keeps the corporation competitive. At the opposite poles of corporate organization, we see CEO salaries increasing at incredible rates while workers at the bottom of the corporate structure are often forced by the system to compete in a race to the bottom. The expression that is used for this industry standard of wages is "the prevailing industry wage/salary."

3.   Moral: When we raise moral questions about wages, we are immediately forced to raise the question as to the purpose of wages. From a moral standard, the wages of the workers should reflect the contributions they make to the corporations in which they are employed. Likewise, workers should be able to meet their own needs and the needs of their

dependents. It is important in this context to define need not as "bare minimum" but as those needs which allow the worker and his/her family to be productive, contributing members of their communities.

From a religious perspective, the moral standards regarding wages proceed from the belief that each and all human beings are made in the image and likeness of a divine Creator. Human beings are not to be seen as machines, which need a minimum of fuel and maintenance in order to produce. To be a human being means to be both an individual person and a person in relationship, and therefore the wages earned for the work a person does should reflect the requirements of those relationships. These include significant time to spend with one's family, the need for a workday short enough for people to develop relationships and to serve their communities, wage levels sufficient to allow for the sustainable growth of their communities.

4.   Just: Justice deals with the distribution of the benefits from Earth's resources, or the benefits resulting from the production and sale of products and services by any corporation or business. Justice requires that we raise the issue of the ongoing concentration of wealth throughout the world in the hands of the few within each country, and in the hands of some countries more than others. The unequal concentration of wealth in the hands of a few deprives the vast majority of persons the benefit of those resources.

In both our private and our public conversations about wages, we need to be very careful to use terminology that accurately reflects what we are trying to say and to accomplish. Are we talking about wages that are legal, ethical, moral or just? How does it make a difference? Within faith communities, is not part of our role to raise questions/initiate conversation regarding corporate responsibility and wages that moves from standards of legality and corporate ethics to the standards of moral and just wages?

Considering these various levels and constructs helps us to identify our own experiences of money and wages, and to examine more critically the wage levels that exist in our own and in other parts of the world. We are led to ask: Who determines these wage levels? How? On what authority? Why? What is the source of the mind-set that it is acceptable for some groups of people to be given wages for their work that keeps them and their families at the lowest levels, even when their work is the groundwork for an enterprise? What cultural and societal values and standards are operative? Who sets and enforces these standards? On what authority? How? Why?

Examining questions such as these helps us to look deeper into the underlying systemic causes of the injustices in our economic system and opens us up to creative ways of acting for a more just world. Indeed, they force us to examine our own attitudes, values and standards, and to try to understand where they came from and to name them in honesty and humility. CREA has found that it is the persons on the bottom, those far from the sources of power, who can raise the most perceptive questions, and provoke the sharpest analysis. Listening to their experiences and their analysis may not be comfortable, but it will help fill in our own gaps of knowledge, bring us closer to truth and our world closer to justice.

IS PAY EQUITY EQUITABLE?

—LAURA B. PINCUS (HARTMAN) AND NICHOLAS J. MATHYS

In the following article, Nicholas Mathys and I argue that a simplistic evaluation of pay equity does not consider the intrinsic rewards offered by some positions. These rewards might include greater autonomy, flexibility, different work tasks or others. When these intrinsic rewards are coupled with the salary paid in those positions, perhaps the compensation is similar to a higher-paying job with fewer intrinsic rewards.

. . . Much has been written about the disparity in wages between men and women. The familiar phrase, "70 cents on the dollar" has been repeated as the basic comparison between the value of women in employment to that of men.[1] However, though allegedly slightly higher today than at the time of its first calculation, it is the contention of these authors that this figure overstates the compensation disparity which exists between male and female workers. Furthermore, the extent of that disparity has been greatly exaggerated by prior research and writing that has failed to recognize all of the variables that must be considered in the determination of "compensation." Instead, prior research has focused on the *specific* disparity between the dollar amount of the wages paid to women and the wages paid to men in similar positions. It has failed to adequately answer the question: "Why are people paid what they are paid?" As one researcher states: "whereas women may feel underpaid, they may not feel undercompensated."[2] For instance, as women are more likely to be the individuals who care for children, women may place a higher value on positions which offer flexible hours, work at home possibilities or day care centers at the workplace.

The Equal Pay Act as it was originally envisioned applied only to workers performing the *same* job. As the comparable worth movement developed, the Act took on a broader application; equal pay was now arguably warranted for "similar" jobs. The definition of "similar" was expanded to include not only equal positions but also jobs that had equal worth as defined by job evaluation analyses. The authors are in entire agreement with the original, narrow application of the Equal Pay Act, requiring that individuals in the same position should be paid equal compensation, regardless of their gender. It is the determination of what constitutes equal compensation that begs the question.

"Is Pay Equity Equitable?" by Laura Pincus (Hartman) and Nick Mathys. Reprinted by permission of the authors.
[1] C. Kleiman, "Women's Lower Pay Adds Up to Lower Pensions," *Chicago Tribune* (November 18, 1991). B. C. Norris, "Comparable Worth, Disparate Impact; and The Market Rate Salary Problem: A Legal Analysis and Statistical Application," *California Law Review,* 71, 730 (1983). G. Meng, "All the Parts of Comparable Worth," *Personnel Journal,* 99 (November 1990); J. Hollenbeck, D. Ilgen, C. Ostroff and J. Vancouver, "Sex Differences in Occupational Choice, Pay and Worth: A Supply-Side Approach to Understanding the Male-Female Wage Gap," *Personnel Psychology,* 40, 715 (1987).
[2] Hollenbeck et al., pp. 715, 717.

The issue which serves as the focal point in this paper is not whether the jobs are similar, but whether the areas in which the positions are dissimilar constitute, in themselves, a difference in compensation. In other words, the functional responsibilities of a male-dominated position and a female-dominated position may be similar (as determined by job evaluation techniques), but the female may receive greater intrinsic compensation (as explained below) and less remunerative compensation than the male. Therefore, the employer's defense under the Equal Pay Act is not that the male and female employee are performing different jobs, but instead that the compensation received is actually of equal value though not in equal ratios of monetary gain and other benefits. . . .

WHAT CONSTITUTES COMPENSATION?

Compensation, at least in theory, represents the reward to an individual for contributions made to the organization—first for job-related contributions and second (at least for some jobs) for performance contributions. *Equity theory* holds that there is a large number of potential contributions and benefits that are recognized and considered relevant to both parties in the employment exchange. It is the sum total of all these contributions made by the individual employee and rewards (financial and otherwise) offered by the organization that goes into the determination of equity (see Figure 1). It is our contention that the proponents of pay equity focus almost exclusively on pay to determine whether people are being "treated equitably," when it is obvious that pay (or compensation) is only one motivation (albeit a major one) why people accept a position or desire a particular career.

FIGURE 1

Equity Model for Employment Exchange

Contributions Being Brought to Organization by Individual	Rewards (Benefits) Being Offered to Individual by Organization

Balance Needed

Skills/Abilities	A. *Extrinsic*
Education	—Pay
Experience	—Fringe Benefits
"Potential"	—Job Security
Performance	—Promotion Opportunities
Personality Traits	—Social Relations
Energy Level	—Closeness to Home
Values	—Organization Culture
Flexibility	—Organization Working Relationships
	B. *Intrinsic*
	—Challenge
	—Variety
	—Autonomy
	—Significance of Task
	—Sense of Achievement

Let's expand on this. The variety of rewards offered in the employment exchange is large. However, they fall into two general categories: those that are *intrinsic* (provided by the job itself) and those that are *extrinsic* (provided by factors outside the job). Examples of extrinsic rewards include pay, fringe benefits, job security, social satisfaction and recognition by one's supervisor. Examples of intrinsic rewards include a sense of accomplishment attained from the job, its challenge, variety and degree of autonomy.

In determining the variants of pay equity, organizations and unions (along with economists) have tended to focus their attention on the economic basis of the employment exchange. On the other hand, psychologists and other behavioral scientists have taken a broader view by identifying a sizable number (over 100) of nonfinancial rewards in studies on job satisfaction.[3] Following are some examples of nonfinancial rewards desired by individuals.

To some employee groups, job security and safety issues may be important. The pleasant, sanitized working conditions in many office settings attract more job candidates than do more hazardous, less-skilled jobs resulting in lower pay being offered to those candidates. Also, many positions in governmental agencies are viewed as more secure against layoffs than "equivalent" private sector positions. Greater job security along with better fringe benefits usually offered by the public sector can explain much of the seeming disparity between the pay of jobs in the public and private sector.

Other people look for friendships and sociability from their job. For these people, jobs that allow for social interaction will be viewed more favorably than those that require individual work.

Some workers desire scheduling flexibility as an important nonfinancial reward and may trade this for (be satisfied with) less pay. Students, spouses with small children and individuals holding two or more jobs, among others, are often found in this group.

Another nonfinancial reward factor is job status. Many financial institutions have many layers of "vice-presidents" who are not paid at the levels suggested by the title. The title can be viewed as "psychic" pay.

Finally, to some the job may be seen as a "cause" or "calling." The sense of achievement and satisfaction of fulfilling a desired purpose in life or the emotional significance of the task may "compensate" for lower than normal financial rewards. Examples of some occupational groups affected are artists, many jobs dealing with social issues and causes and educators.

The conclusion drawn from the above is that comparable worth exponents ignore the differences in intrinsic and nonfinancial rewards offered by jobs of "comparable worth" even in the same organization. These differences need much further study rather than assuming away all things but pay, and calling it equity.

Worse yet, comparable worth proponents constantly use misleading comparisons such as "women are paid approximately 70¢ per $1 paid to men."[4] These differences are the re-

---

[3]E. E. Lawler, *Pay and Organizational Effectiveness: A Psychological View* (New York: McGraw-Hill, 1971); F. Herzberg, *Work and The Nature of Man* (Cleveland: World Books, 1966).

[4]U.S. Bureau of the Census, *Current Population Reports,* Series P-60, No. 174 (Washington, D.C.: U.S. Government Printing Office, 1992), pp. 112–118.

sult of so many factors (such as type/level of jobs, experience differences, industry differences, personal characteristics, etc.) that one cannot assume the "unexplained" difference is proof of discrimination.

FACTORS AFFECTING PAY DIFFERENCES

Even if only pay is looked at, we believe pay equity proponents drastically overstate the extent of pay differences between men and women. In order to determine the extent of pay differences in similar jobs, one needs to hold constant the effects of factors such as the following.

Type of industry and company: Studies suggest that employees in some jobs can receive as much as a 20% increase simply by switching industries in the same geographic area while performing basically similar jobs.[5] Also, firms and industries that have a greater ability to pay their employees should not be compared with those that are less profitable.[6] For example, in Chrysler's efforts to stave off bankruptcy, the company requested and obtained pay concessions from UAW workers.

Size of organization: Research indicates that small companies usually pay less than large organizations.[7] Other research suggests that women "like" smaller companies.[8] Pay differences between genders may result, but are women less satisfied?

Marital status: Macro economic data shows that the economic effects of marriage and parenthood are significant and often directly opposite in their effects on men and women. For instance, marriage increases a man's participation rate in the labor force compared to single men and reduces a woman's labor force participation rate compared to single women.[9] Also, a married man's hours worked annually increase with the number of children, while a married woman's hours tend to decrease with more children.[10] Thus married men with children work more and earn more than single men, while the reverse is true for women. In fact, women who remain single earn over 93% of the income of single men (18 years old and over).[11] In the end, the major difference is *not* between men and women but between married women and everyone else.

Age group: Research indicates that the gender wage gap is larger for older than younger workers. At age 20–24 the gap is 89% and widens to 65% for those 55–64 years

[5]E. Groshen, "Sources of Wage Dispersion: How Much Do Employers Matter?" Working paper, Harvard University Department of Economics (1985).

[6]G. Bahar, M. Jensen and K. Murphy, "Compensation and Incentives: Practice vs. Theory," *Journal of Finance,* 593–616; B. Gerhardt and G. Milkovich, "Organizational Differences in Managerial Compensation and Financial Performance," F. Foulkes, Ed., *Executive Compensation in 1990s* (Boston: Harvard Business School Press, 1990).

[7]W. Mellow, "Employer Size and Wages," *Review of Economics and Statistics,* 495–501 (1982); D. Evans and L. Leighton, "Why Do Smaller Firms Pay Less?" *Journal of Human Resources,* 26, 3, 562–580 (1989); A. Weiss and H. Landau, "Wages, Hiring Standards and Firm Size," *Journal of Labor Economics,* 2, 4, 477–479 (1984).

[8]W. Oi, "Neglected Women and Other Implications of Comparable Worth," *Contemporary Policy Issues,* 4, 2, 21–32 (1986).

[9]W. Bowen and T. Finegan, *The Economics of Labor Force Participation* (Princeton: Princeton University Press, 1969).

[10]S. Smith, "Estimating Annual Hours of Labor Force Activity," *Monthly Labor Review* (February 1983), p. 19.

[11]U.S. Bureau of the Census, pp. 124–127.

of age. Factors accounting for this gap could include a greater career orientation of the post-Civil Rights age group and the fact that women bear the brunt of child care responsibility, resulting in pay erosion over time because of being placed on the "mommy track."[12]

Experience: We have already noted that, on the average, men work more hours per week than women (roughly 6% more). Although the gap is narrowed over time, this results in the fact that after 16 years out of school, women still average half as much labor market experience as men.[13] Since women still lag behind men in the total workforce experience (especially in older age groups), it is important that age cohort studies take this into account. This can be done by comparing younger age groups (20–30 years old) to reduce the effect or by comparing men and women with the same years of experience. Research shows that the male/female pay differential is reduced by about half when years of experience rather than age cohorts are used.

Education: Currently men and women are graduating from college in nearly equal numbers. The careers women are entering are changing and so too are the college majors chosen by women. This is significant, since a college major is the strongest factor affecting income of college graduates. A major in engineering or accounting brings the highest income for both men and women while a major in education brings the lowest.[14] In 1964, nearly half (42.5%) of all bachelors degrees earned by women were in education. By 1981 it declined to 18%. Today the fields attracting women are those that were traditionally male-dominated, especially in the professional areas. In 1964, women earned fewer than 5% of medical, law and MBA degrees. In 1984, one-fourth of medical degrees, one-third of law degrees and one-fourth of MBAs were earned by women.

These facts are significant, since research shows clearly that it is *type* of education not *years* of education that matters. Common sense suggests that a degree in the humanities is not equivalent to a degree in electrical engineering. Research studies that use years of education as proxies for all the differences in an individual's skills, abilities and quality of education received are doomed to reach erroneous conclusions. . . .

DIRECTION FOR FURTHER RESEARCH

The failure of researchers to properly identify the extent of disparity and to recognize the degree of equality actually evidenced in the area of gender compensation results in negative consequences. Through increased awareness, continued education and greater opportunities for women, the magnitude of gender-based employment discrimination is being reduced.

First, the continued use of statistics such as "women are paid 70 cents on the dollar compared to men" fosters an atmosphere of distrust in the workplace. When added to the normal secrecy of most organizational compensation systems, the chance for heightened barriers between men and women is increased. It is time for responsible people to discuss the gender-based pay issue on grounds that take into account all relevant reward factors and

---

[12]E. Erlich, "The Mommy Track," *Business Week* (March 20, 1989), 123–128.

[13]V. Fuchs, "Women's Quest for Economic Equality," *Journal of Human Resources,* 26, 3562–80 (1991).

[14]J. Estelle, N. Abraham, J. Conaty and D. To, "College Quality and Future Earnings," Working Paper, SUNY-Stonybrook Department of Economics (1989).

sound statistical bases. Lacking an understanding of statistics, many women are led to believe that they are underpaid compared to men doing the same job.

Second, researchers need to undertake studies that hold constant factors known to affect compensation besides gender. These factors were discussed above and include types of industries and companies, size of organization and a variety of personal work-related characteristics such as age, years of work experience, type and extent of education and marital status. In addition, the effect that intrinsic reward factors have on market forces that may affect pay should be considered and evaluated.

Third, requiring employers to increase the amounts they pay to women will critically reduce the opportunities available to women who are marginal performers.[15] If an employer is compelled to raise the wages of any of its employees, that employer may not be able to afford the same number of employees. The added cost is likely to force the employer to reduce the number of people employed. In determining which employees to discharge, the employer likely will retain the best performers and terminate those whose performance is marginally adequate. Unfortunately, among this group will be women who are most in need of protection against discrimination. In addition, this solution reduces the flexibility of other benefit options. These options include flexible hours and day care programs, which may be valued as compensatory benefits, but employers will lose the incentive to provide women and others benefits which they actually value greatly.

REDUCING GENDER-BASED WAGE DIFFERENCES

In lieu of a pay equity analysis, there are a number of solutions that would help to reduce any actual disparities which remain between the compensation of men and women. First, the education of women in the United States must begin to emphasize career opportunities for women in non-traditional occupations at an early age.[16] Our conventional pigeonholing of women in certain career paths and men in others must be removed in favor of a more balanced approach based on skill and potential rather than preconceived, traditional expectations. Women should receive similar educational preparation and counseling for any occupation and be equally equipped to obtain similar positions as men, allowing them to more effectively exert their market power. Ironically, many of the counselors giving advice in our primary and secondary schools are themselves women.

Second, there is a need to emphasize the societal need as well as the economic benefit to the employer to provide day care, parental leave, flexible hours/shifts and other non-monetary compensation which allow women to remain in employment positions instead of following the "mommy track" and retreating from their positions at the onset of children. If one accepts the reality that women are equally qualified for almost every position as men, then the inability to retain women upon the birth of their children must be seen as the loss to the workforce of valuable resources. As women (and their spouses) advance to higher decision-making levels in organizations, these benefits are more often being implemented.

---

[15]L. Fischel, "Comparable Worth and Discrimination in Labor Markets," *U. Chi. L. Rev.,* 53, 891.
[16]Hollenbeck et al., 1987, pp. 715, 718.

If employers were to provide support for working mothers, these individuals would not suffer the economic and social pressure felt by many to leave the workforce, and employers would benefit from the increased pool of potential employees. In addition, research has shown that firms which provide this support report strengthened employee loyalty, decreased absenteeism and increased productivity.[17]

Third, women must be increasingly aware of the value of their market power. In the long run, pay equity and comparable worth will not assist the greatest population of female workers, individuals who have merely adequate abilities. Firms may be less willing to take a chance with a potential employee if employers believe that they will have difficulty terminating them because of potential liability. For instance, suppose an employer has the option of hiring a female applicant or a male applicant, both of whose applications evidence adequate abilities. The employer may hesitate in hiring the female applicant because, if she does not work out and is terminated, there is a greater risk of a discrimination action. In addition, the employer could hire the male applicant at a lower wage than his other employees until such time as that individual proves himself, even though he would generally hire all workers at the same wage. On the other hand, the employer does not have this flexibility in hiring the female applicant because the law requires the employer to pay to her the same wage as a male in the position for which he is hiring her.

Wages are determined by the market, not by any ex ante determination of relative merit. As stated earlier, if women act rationally as a group, they would be able to create a supply and demand ratio that would force the wages for women up to meet that lack of supply. Women are forced to make decisions with which, perhaps, men have not traditionally been faced. What must be understood is that, in the past, women were willing to accept low paying positions because, as a general rule, they had husbands who would support them. The ones that did not were forced to take positions solely based on the salaries offered, and may have forgone portions that they truly would have preferred. Now, more women do not have that marital support and may be forced into certain positions due to the salaries offered.

The answer to this market imperfection, therefore, is not only to require employers to provide women wages equal to those men receive (as this would lead to a supply and demand curve that is superficially supported), but also to encourage women to identify and exercise their market power, as do other underrepresented classes.

---

[17]W. List, "Employers Find Rewards in Employment Equity," *Canadian Business Review,* 35 (Spring 1989).

A FREE MARKET APPROACH TO COMPARABLE WORTH

—Laura B. Pincus (Hartman)

The following article supports Posner's criticisms of comparable worth theory. I argue that the market should be able to correct any discrepancy between male and female wages and that, if it does not correct this difference, there are other means by which women (using market power) may be able to argue for increased wages.

The issue of comparable worth exemplifies the imperfection of market effects. The argument made by proponents of comparable worth is that women earn between 59% and 65% of men's earnings because they are systematically segregated into jobs that are traditionally held by women and traditionally underpaid. Champions of comparable worth argue that each job has an inherent value irrespective of the market, that the market thus is imperfect in its valuation of females in these positions, and that the law should create a hierarchy of job positions that are comparable in worth and set wages accordingly. They refuse to accept that an employee's economic worth is determined by his or her salary. Due to this flawed approach, they fail to recognize that incomparable wages derive not from faulty wage-value scales but from the supply and demand curves that are formed.

Proponents argue instead that the supply curve for female employees is skewed in certain positions due to discrimination in the marketplace. Assume that nursing and auto maintenance require approximately the same skill level (I am making no realistic comment, this is only an example). Next assume that female nurses comprise 90% of the nurses in this country and that male auto mechanics comprise 90% of the mechanics in this country. Proponents of a comparable worth system would contend that these percentages (or similar ones) exist due to two related reasons: Women are forced into nursing because this is accepted as a job which "should" be staffed by women, and they are forced out of other positions that are predominantly male because of similar discriminatory employment barriers. As the employers know that the women have no bargaining power because they have no other jobs to go to that will pay more, they do not have to pay women as much as they would have to pay men to lure them to the same positions.

The purpose of this paper is to address the arguments proposed by proponents of a comparable worth system using the analytical approach defined as "objectivism" and to explain why regulation of employment decisions is best left to market forces. Objectivism is a political and social philosophy first developed and cultivated by author and philosopher Ayn Rand. The essence of objectivism is the recognition that Woman or Man is an end in herself or himself. One applies this concept through the utilization of an "objective absolute," which regards reality as set by the Reason of Nature. Facts are recognized as independent of one's emotions or influences [i.e., wishing it will happen does not make is so]. No one person decides what is right or wrong, nature does not decide; Man and Woman merely observe and attempt to act in furtherance of what is right. While some may identify this conclusion as moral realism, this is incorrect as morality is subjective while "right" and "wrong," according to Rand, are objective.

As there is one set of absolutes by which all are governed, the distinctions among individuals exist by virtue of characteristics unique to each individual. Objectivism thus encourages every individual to realize his or her own independence, a right derived from his or her nature as a rational being. This does not mean, as most critics believe, that one naturally has the right to do as he or she pleases, no matter the cost to others or to society. What it does mean is that individuals have the right to exist for their own sakes, neither sacrificing their selves to others nor requiring the sacrifice of others to themselves. The individual recognizes all others' right to the same freedom and may not restrict that right.

The most volatile topic of objectivism, and of Rand's writings, is her concept of "egoism" or "rational selfishness." Rand explains that an "egoist" is one who does not sacrifice others but instead stands above the need of using others in any manner.[1] She contends that this is the only form of close association and mutual respect possible between individuals.[2] "Rational selfishness" is a concept that does not embrace a moral evaluation of good or evil but merely acknowledges that selfishness, by definition, is a concern with one's own interests. As long as one is a rational being, he or she will act at all times in his or her own best interest, within the confines of his or her power. This concept is best defined by examining the difference between one's interest in creation and one's interest, instead, in theft. The distinction between the two lies in the object of the pursuit, the object each actor values and each actor's conception of his or her own self-interest. Rand argues that, as there is a set of absolute rules, a rational person motivated by self-interest will view creation of the object as a proper goal, as opposed to theft of the object.

Critics view such support of selfishness as detrimental to our fundamental social structure as there will be no charity, no giving of one's self for the benefit of others. However, the critics incorrectly assume that one cannot gain from the activities mentioned, that pure altruism exists and that such altruism is good (in its meaning as "opposed to evil"). These assumptions are not logical conclusions. First, one gives to charity or helps one in need because he or she has a desire to do so. Failure to act upon the desire precludes self-satisfaction. The impetus behind charitable acts is therefore satisfaction of the actor through satisfaction of the desires of the recipient. There is personal gain to the actor. Second, due to the fact that one's motivation for all that he or she does during his or her lifetime is self-interest, altruism, in its most strict sense of selflessness, cannot possibly exist. Third, altruism in this traditional sense

---

[1]Ayn Rand, *For The New Intellectual* (New York: Random House, 1961), p. 94.
[2]*Ibid.*

is insulting to rational minds as it permits no concept of humans except as "sacrificed animals and profiteers-on-sacrifice, as victims and parasites" as opposed to a more genuine and realistic portrayal of men and women as self-supporting and self-respecting individuals.[3]

The moral obligation owed by one human being to another is only the obligation of rationality one owes to himself or herself. This rationality comes only through thought. The egoist is the creator, and the selfless man is the one who does not think but instead learns from the thoughts of others. Man and Woman have the power to be independent thinkers, individuals and free, self-interested actors in their lives. Any denial of these freedoms will also deny our society of the whole of its parts.

Society, accordingly, can benefit from the exercise of self-interest on the part of all of its members. The American governmental system encourages self-interested behavior through its political-economic system: laissez-faire capitalism. The American system is one which prescribes that individuals do not act as victims and slayers but instead as equal traders, by free, voluntary exchanges for their mutual benefit.[4] The role of the capitalist government is merely to protect individual rights, requiring a complete separation of the government and the country's economics. This has not, and potentially may not, be accomplished in the United States. Yet, this is the ideal system in which to protect one's rights.

As can be inferred from objectivist theory, it is not the duty of the government to exercise an individual's rights, it is the duty of each individual to assert those rights, and the government only will intervene in situations where one's rights infringe upon another's. In a perfect capitalist society, the market controls all that is produced, the price at which it is produced and the manner in which it is produced. There should be no outside influences that dictate some conclusion other than that reached by clear market demands. Critics argue that the market may lead to unfair consequences; yet, it is the concept of "unfair" that is the issue, not the market. An actor will act in such a way that he or she will influence the market to some extent; yet, due to the fact that he or she is behaving rationally, these influences must be fair by definition. That which is rational and logical must be fair. Without this certainty, there could be no objective determination of "equity." Therefore, the imperfections of market effects occur solely due to irrational decisions made by players in that market.

In connection with the concept of comparable worth, and applying the fundamental theories of objectivism, the argument that all women are trapped in "female occupational ghettos" appears insupportable. First, there are positions open to women in areas which may be dominated by men. If women cannot obtain those positions, there is already a legal remedy against that type of discrimination through enforcement of Title VII of the Civil Rights Act.

Second, it is not a valid argument that women have been in certain positions for many years and thus should not have to change their jobs merely to obtain a higher paying job. This is the nature of the market. If women act rationally as a group, they might be able to create a supply and demand ratio that would force the wages for nurses up to meet that lack of supply. What these women are contending, however, is that they would like to stay in their present positions and also make the amount of money they feel that they deserve. The employers obviously do not feel threatened that these women will leave if they pay them a

---

[3]Ayn Rand, *The Virtue of Selfishness* (New York: New American Library, 1964), p. xii.
[4]"Introducing Objectivism," *The Objectivist Newsletter* (August 1962), p. 35.

low salary, NOT because they know that the women have nowhere else to go, but because this has been their experience.

What must be realized under such a scenario is that, in the past, women were willing to accept low paying positions because, as a general rule, they had husbands who would support them. The ones that did not were forced to take positions solely based on the salaries offered, and may have forgone positions that they truly would have preferred. Now, more women do not have that marital support and may be forced into certain positions due to the salaries offered. Men must do this also; it is naive to believe that this is not the case.

The answer to this market imperfection, therefore, is not to provide women with higher wages in certain positions which they claim are undervalued. This would lead to a supply and demand curve that is superficially supported, forcing resources into areas where the demand is slight and leaving other areas which are objectively valued by participants in the market without sustenance. Without voluntary exchange by independent judgment there could be no trade, save for that which was dictated. An actor acts in her or his own self-interest and is therefore attracted by the full scope of rewards of a particular activity or job. If there is an intrinsic value to each position in employment, given to it my market definition of priority of resource allocation, is there not also an intrinsic value to other things? And therefore, prices, too, must be set. Why are women's shoes more expensive than men's? Women's clothes? Women's soap? If we intend to retain a free market economy, the question of value of services or of goods must be left for the market.

Objectivism does not oppose the reality that women are as valuable as are men in the perfect employment market. While there are irrational actors who play in this market, they will not prevail. The rational profit seekers, acting in their self-interest, will realize the potential of women. Females continue to be viewed by some remnants of the historical discriminators as less able to participate. To force a specific treatment of these new entrants without allowing the market to respond on its own will do nothing more than prove to these traditionalists that the problem of discrimination cannot be handled on a rational level of reason. "To deal with men [women] by force is as impractical as to deal with nature by persuasion."[5] All that is necessary is some demonstration of the value of the female worker, of which there has been much, in order to force a market response. I refuse to demean women to the extent that I feel do these critics. Women are capable of asserting their independence and in doing so, they will vie for positions that are traditionally male-dominated, and if refused they will use the law to prevent their discrimination. Their sense of self must be exalted, not the value that they feel our male-dominated society should place on them. There are examples of this everywhere one looks, yet many simply claim that this is not enough and that more should be done to pave their way to independence. Until they begin to act in their own self-interest, and use the market that exists to further their position in this society, they will continue to be treated as if they are not independent, and as if they have no selves.

---

[5]Ayn Rand, *Philosophy: Who Needs It?* (New York: New American Library), p. 32.

WHISTLEBLOWING AND TRUST

Some Lessons from the ADM Scandal

—DARYL KOEHN

"Whistleblowing" occurs when an employee informs the public of inappropriate activities going on inside the organization. More limited definitions of the term include the requirement that the whistleblowing relate to an activity requested of the whistleblower, such as when an individual is asked to lie on federal reporting documents to protect the firm. Philosopher Norman Bowie contends that whistleblowing is not justified unless the following characteristics are present:

1. It is done based on an appropriate moral motive.

2. The individual has exhausted all internal channels for dissent.

3. The individual's belief regarding the inappropriate conduct is based on evidence that would persuade a reasonable person.

4. The individual has carefully analyzed the situation to determine the serious nature of the violation, the immediacy of the violation and the specificity of the violation.

5. The individual's action is commensurate with responsibility for avoiding and/or exposing moral violations.

6. The individual's action has some chance of success, exposing and/or avoiding the moral violation (Norman Bowie, Business Ethics *[Englewood Cliffs, NJ: Prentice Hall, 1982], pp. 142–43).*

"No servant can serve two masters. He will either hate one and love the other, or be devoted to one and despise the other (Luke 16:13). Koehn evaluates the concept of trust as it applies to the Archer Daniels Midland whistleblowing case. In doing so, she highlights the responsibilities of both the whistleblower and the firm. Interestingly enough, she concludes that there are times when whistleblowing is not ethically correct. Do you agree with her conclusion? Is she persuasive?

The 1980's witnessed a flurry of articles regarding the ethics of whistleblowing. These articles tended to focus on three issues: (1) the definition of whistleblowing; (2) whether and when it was permissible to violate one's obligations of loyalty to colleagues or one's profession/corporation; and (3) whether a threat to the public interest actually obligates someone with knowledge of this threat to make this knowledge public.[1] These same issues have surfaced in recent discussions of the act of whistleblowing by Mark Whitacre at Archer Daniels Midland. While I do not think these three issues are morally irrelevant to a discussion of whistleblowing, I am troubled by the fact that the entire discussion to date has focused on the issue of duty. In this commentary, I want to focus less on the question of duty and more on the question of personal, corporate and public trust: Does whistleblowing foster or destroy moral trust? What makes whistleblowers and the companies for whom they work worthy of employee and public trust?

I shall use the alleged events at ADM to explore these questions. The reader should keep in mind that I am not writing a case history of whistleblowing at ADM. At the time of this writing, we have yet to hear much of the company's side of the story nor do we know exactly what evidence Whitacre has to support his allegation that the company engaged in price-fixing with their competitors. What matters for my purposes here is not that these events did occur but that they could have occurred and they raise serious and interesting questions for corporate, individual and public behavior.

PART ONE: WHISTLEBLOWING
AND ITS EFFECTS ON TRUST

It will be helpful to begin with a working definition of a whistleblower. Following Sissela Bok, I shall define whistleblowers as persons who "sound an alarm from within the very organization in which they work, aiming to spotlight neglect or abuses that threaten the public interest."[2] Several features of this definition are relevant to thinking about trust. First, the whistle-blower claims to be acting in the public interest. He or she tries to occupy the moral high ground by calling attention to some matter the whistleblower thinks the public will be, or should be, concerned about. I say "concerned about" rather than simply "interested in" because the whistleblower claims to be more than a mere tattler. If I were to disclose the religious preferences of my boss, we would not think such disclosure constituted whistleblowing because it is hard to see what public interest is involved. Given the very real risks of being fired, demoted, ostracized, or attacked by those the whistleblower is accusing of negligence or abuse, the whistleblowers generally must think of themselves as on something akin to a mission. They try to portray themselves as acting on behalf of an interest higher than their own—the public interest.

I dwell on this point to emphasize that the whistleblower has made some assumptions as to what constitutes the public interest. He may have erred in his assessment of the nature of the public interest. Or he may have misevaluated his "facts." The facts may be unsound, or they may be sound yet irrelevant to the public interest. If we take trust as the trustor's belief that he or she is the recipient of the good will of the trusted party, the whistleblower can be thought of as portraying himself as a trustworthy person who has acted in good will toward the public and who merits the public's trust. Mark Whitacre, for example, portrayed himself as the white knight of the consumer, a consumer whom ADM had allegedly declared to be the enemy.[3] However, if Whitacre's accusations result in the demise of ADM and the loss of a major supplier of consumer goods, we may well wonder whether Whitacre has acted in fact in the public's interest. Moreover, Whitacre himself arguably has something of a skewed view of public interest since he seems perfectly willing to engage in predatory, monopolistic pricing.[4] According to his own account, he balked at his company's pricing policy only when his colleagues tried to engage in price-fixing.[5] Given that the customer is hurt by monopolistic pricing as well as price-fixing, his whistleblowing at this late date may be less an attempt to aid the customer and the public than to save his own skin. More generally, if and when a whistleblower's motives are mixed, we have some reason to wonder, on the one hand, whether he is trustworthy and, on the other hand, to perhaps be more sympathetic to a company who charges that the whistleblower has betrayed it and the public as well.

Second, the whistleblower believes that there is a substantial audience who will attend to her disclosures. If an employee calls up the press and discloses that the CEO wears blue shirts to work every day, his announcement is likely to be greeted by the reporter with a stifled yawn, if not a burst of profanity. To say that the whistleblower's disclosure is in the public interest just is to say that it has the makings of a good story. The tale, therefore, will likely attract the press and maybe the regulatory authorities as well. It can quickly become sensationalized as people begin to speculate on the extent and magnitude of the alleged corporate misconduct. Furthermore, the regulatory authorities may begin an elaborate investigation on the theory that any abuse known by one individual may just be the tip of the iceberg. The Federal authorities, for example, are not merely subpoenaing many of ADM's records; they have also asked for the records of many of ADM's competitors.[6] There is a very real danger of a witchhunt, for as Bok reminds us, secret police almost always rely on informers and have a history of widening the charges against those accused.[7] Such reflections suggest that it is incumbent upon a whistleblower who truly wants to merit the public's trust to try to explore issues internally before going public with her accusations.

There are, of course, difficulties associated with going public internally. I shall say more about these shortly. My point here is that whistleblowing may harm public trust in our institutions, rather than restore it, if whistleblowing creates a whirlwind of suspicion and the impression that corruption is everywhere. Fellow employees of whistleblowers may be justifiably irritated at a colleague who makes accusations to the press without ever running these same charges by them or without seeking their interpretation of actions and events within the corporation. It may be unfair for the corporation to try to dismiss a whistleblower as a troublemaker with few social skills. On the other hand, the whistleblower may very well be someone who is overly suspicious or inclined to make wild accusations without verifying her facts. Moreover, if the whistleblower does not try to work internally first to try to resolve what she perceives as a problem, it is difficult to see how she can claim to be trying to right the problem. It is striking that Whitacre, by his own account, had heard allegations of price-fixing for many years and had simply ignored them,[8] treating them as though they were someone else's problem. But if he really cared for the company and for the public interest, why did he not investigate these charges when he first heard them? Given that he was in line to be president of ADM, he surely should have worried about this problem and taken steps to address a problem that he was bound to inherit. Conversely, one wonders why he would have wanted to be president of a company that was in his judgment engaged in dastardly deeds. At a minimum, it seems as though he should have interested himself many years ago in the question of whether and why ADM had a history of tolerating price-fixing.

Another way of putting the point is as follows: Whistleblowers are part and parcel of the corporate culture on which they blow the whistle. They are often rather senior because it is those issuing orders who usually have the most control over and the most knowledge about what is occurring within the corporation. At the point of public disclosure, the whistleblower assigns responsibility for the abuse to someone else and thereby distances himself from any responsibility. But matters are rarely so clean. If one has worked many years for a company, taken a salary from them, followed their policies, then one is arguably complicitous in the practices of that corporation. The traditional discussion of whistleblowing pits the individual's loyalty to the company against his loyalty to himself. But this formulation presupposes that that self is a private self, totally independent of the company. I am saying that the self is a company self as well. And while it may be convenient for the whistleblower to talk as though it is him against the big bad company, such talk is suspect to the extent that the whistleblower has supported that company. Blowing the whistle may not increase public trust to the extent the public is rightly suspicious of the whistleblower's own history within the corporation.

Third, the whistleblower is levelling an accusation of neglect or abuse at particular persons within the corporation. These accusations are not pleasant for the accused whose lives may be permanently disrupted by what may turn out to be false charges. At a minimum, the lives of the accused will be unsettled for a substantial amount of time as the press picks up the story and as investigations run their course. While no one should be above the law, we also should not be insensitive to the need for due process. We should also remember that passions almost always run high around whistleblowers' accusations because the whistleblower's charge applies to present activities of a corporation or profession.[9] No one blows the whistle or shows much interest in past abuses with few present effects or in remote, unlikely future events. The alleged danger is present and the person's emotions are engaged, which is all the more reason for exercising extreme caution in making charges and in evaluating them.

The above observations suggest that corporate employees and leaders rightly are concerned about the effect of whistleblowing not merely on corporate morale but on the ability of employees to work together in relative harmony. This harmony becomes close to impossible when the atmosphere is a highly charged one of mutual suspicion. Note that I am not saying that an employee has an overriding loyalty of duty to the group for which he works. It may well be, as Ronald Duska has argued, that the corporation is not the kind of group to which one can be loyal.[10] In any case, there is no prima facie duty to be loyal to any group. A profession such as medicine is worth serving not because it is a group but because its end—the health of individuals—is a genuine good. The end, not the group per se, commands group members' loyalty. We do not, for example, say that agents have a prima facie duty to the Ku Klux Klan or the mafia. The person who leaves such a group does not override a prima facie duty. Rather, there never was a duty to be a part of a group engaged in unethical behavior.

My point then is not that the employee acts wrongly because whistleblowing is disloyal. The wrongness in the whistleblowing consists instead in acting to destroy the workplace atmosphere if and when this destruction could have been avoided by adopting a less accusatory stance or by working within the corporation. Whistleblowing may destroy trust. And trust within a corporation is good when the trust is a reasoned trust, born of open and probing discussions with one's peers regarding matters of joint concern. Whistleblowing should be evaluated in light of its consequences for this reasoned trust, not in light of its effects on irrational loyalty or its relation to a non-existent prima facie duty of group loyalty.

PART TWO: RESPONSIBILITIES OF BOTH WHISTLEBLOWER AND CORPORATION

This last comment raises what I take to be the central moral issue connected with whistleblowing: What can both whistleblower and corporation do to foster reasoned trust and to avoid a situation in which employees feel they have to go outside the company to get their concerns addressed?

Given the very real dangers associated with whistleblowing and the all-too-human propensities toward self-righteousness and misinterpretation, it is clear that the would-be whistleblower and corporation alike should make every effort to discuss perceived abuses and negligence before it gets to the point where the whistleblower thinks a public accusation must be made. The corporation thus has a responsibility to provide a regular forum for free and open discussion of possible abuses. Participants should have equal and reciprocal rights to question one another, to bring evidence, etc. They should not be penalized in any way for participation in this forum. It is striking that ADM had no such forum. In fact, communication was so bad within the company that the CEO's own son apparently did not know until after the fact that the father had called in the FBI to help investigate whether production at ADM was being sabotaged.[11]

Conversely, the whistleblower must be willing to come forward and be identified. It is close to impossible for the accused to mount a defense or even seek clarification when the accuser is anonymous. This requirement to publicly participate increases the odds that the would-be whistleblower will doublecheck her facts before going public. Discussion will also tend to dispel employees' perception that corruption is everywhere. In fact, regular discussion should deflate a good deal of the anger and anxiety regarding corporate problems. Employees will come to see that, yes, their corporation has problems and oversights but, yes, their corporation is routinely and professionally addressing these difficulties. Participation in such a forum will require a good deal of courage on the part of employees and a good bit of restraint on the part of a corporate hierarchy tempted to retaliate against any and all perceived threats.

Second, it is incumbent on corporate leadership to examine the tasks they impose on their employees. An employee can only be morally required to do that which is possible. If the employee is placed in an untenable position, then he will feel anxious, trapped and may be driven to try to escape from this position by taking his predicament public in an effort to gain public sympathy and support. Whitacre, for example, apparently was expected to do cut-rate pricing with a view to grabbing a large market share while at the same time showing either minimal losses or a profit.[12] Price-fixing becomes a temptation in a corporate environment with these unreasonable expectations, and reasoned trust is not given much of a chance to flourish. For their part, the employees must critically examine the position they are being asked to assume. It is curious that Whitacre professed unease about recruiting competitors for their expertise when he himself seems to have been recruited from a German competitor precisely for his expertise![13] Uncritical naivete on the part of employees becomes morally culpable to the extent that they fail to raise objections that would promote in-house discussion of possible unethical practices.

Third, a company that desires the reasoned trust of its employees must grant the employees access to information about the company's practices. When a whistleblower accuses a company of malpractice, all employees of the corporation feel slightly tainted and anxious. They may feel betrayed not just by the whistleblower but also by the company whom they perceive as having hid relevant information from them. Secrecy encourages corporate paranoia. One of the best ways to combat it is to run as open a corporation as possible. The more access employees have, the more the corporation can legitimately hold them accountable for their actions and the more responsibility the employees will feel for actions they have known about and have had a chance to discuss. If there is genuine access to information about corporate practices, employees have a responsibility to seek out and to consider the implications of this information. It becomes less legitimate for them to bury their heads in the sand and then at some late date cry "Foul!" And this is how it should be in corporations where all parties are genuinely committed to acting well.

Fourth, and finally, all members of the corporation have a responsibility to critically examine their actions, even if they have been taught to perform these acts and been rewarded for doing so. A recent study comparing Japanese and American managers' attitudes towards ethics showed that the American managers were far more focussed on marketing than their foreign competitors and tended to think of immorality as occurring largely within marketing. This focus is problematic in several ways. It encourages managers to overlook ways in which they are treating their employees badly (e.g., by imposing unreasonable job requirements upon them). Furthermore, to the extent that American managers see only particular marketing practices as immoral, they fail to consider whether marketing itself may not be in some ways immoral. For example, does the idea of "targeting" specific groups of people for specific products wind up instrumentalizing the customer? If this customer is little more than a means to selling this product, it is not much of a leap to begin to think (as ADM allegedly did) of the customer as an enemy whose demand for low prices is keeping the company from attaining maximal profit.[14] More thought needs to be given to the nature of the core practices of business and less attention devoted to the bribery, price-fixing, etc., which may merely be symptoms of a sick practice. Unless and until these practices are well-scrutinized by the people who are engaged in them and who have the most knowledge about them, we should expect to continue to have a series of nasty abuses springing up and surprising us.

The corporate atmosphere also should be scrutinized. ADM's anti-bureaucratic rhetoric is a case in point. Whitacre mentions it several times and indicates that ADM has historically prided itself on its ability to get things done.[15] However, what gets dismissed as bureaucracy is often the system of checks and balances within the firm. Anti-bureaucratic rhetoric may encourage, at worst, an attitude of lawlessness and at best, a "can-do" approach which may, as in the case of Whitacre, breed enthusiasm but not do much for thoughtfulness.

CONCLUSION

While whistleblowing sometimes may be the only way to call attention to serious abuses by professions or corporations, whistleblowing is not unambiguously ethically good. It is perhaps best seen as an option of last recourse. Rather than concentrating on when whistleblowing is moral, our time would be better spent thinking about how to improve corporate and professional environments so that employees and clients will not be driven to adopt this strategy.

NOTES

1. Ronald Duska, "Whistleblowing and Employee Loyalty," in Tom L. Beauchamp and Norman E. Bowie, *Ethical Theory and Business* (Englewood Cliffs, NJ: Prentice Hall, 1993), pp. 312–316.
2. Sissela Bok, "Whistleblowing and Professional Responsibility," in Beauchamp, *op.cit.*
3. Mark Whitacre as told to Ronald Henkoff, "My Life as a Corporate Mole for the FBI," in *Fortune,* Sept. 4, 1995, pp. 56–62.
4. *Ibid.*
5. *Ibid.* Ronald Henkoff comments that Whitacre's preferred approach to pricing "sounds a lot like predatory pricing," in Henkoff, "So Who Is This Mark Whitacre, and Why Is He Saying These Bad Things about ADM," in *Fortune,* Sept. 4, 1995, pp. 64–67.
6. See "Suicide Hurts Government's ADM Case," Monday, August 14, 1995, at clari.news.crime.murders on the Worldwide Web.
7. Bok, *op.cit.*
8. Whitacre, *op.cit.*
9. Bok also discusses the fact that the charges apply to present wrongdoing. Bok, *op.cit.*
10. Duska, *op.cit.*
11. Whitacre, *op.cit.*
12. *Ibid.*
13. *Ibid.*
14. *Ibid.*
15. *Ibid.*

THREE WOMEN'S MORAL COURAGE

Why We Care

—Rushworth Kidder

When Time *magazine announced its "Person of the Year" choice in December 2002, it handed a triple crown to three women. Were they dashing female CEOs? High-maintenance entertainers? Athletic stars? No, the 2002 award focused on three whistleblowers: Enron's Sherron Watkins, WorldCom's Cynthia Cooper and the FBI's Coleen Rowley. The dominant theme, in other words, was practical, applied ethics. Rushworth Kidder discusses why this choice is a critical message about moral courage.*

Time magazine's writers duly noted similarities among the three ["People of the Year" for 2002]: Each worked from within to expose wrongdoing—financial mismanagement at Enron and WorldCom, a culture of nonresponse at the Bureau. Each worked in high-profile organizations—Enron known for its devastating corporate collapse, WorldCom for its record bankruptcy filing of $3.8 billion and the FBI for charges that it failed to investigate leads that might have helped prevent the 9/11 attacks.

What's more, each woman worked in relative obscurity, neither at the top nor in the limelight. Each, by filing a complaint, was seeking to reform an organization she dearly loved, not setting out to destroy something she despised. Each depended on her job for a livelihood. And each was a woman.

For their part, these three told *Time* they don't think gender has much to do with their actions. They can't abide the term "whistleblower." They remain emotionally attached to their organizations: Of the three, only Watkins has since left her employer—and has taken serious flak, initially for failing to go public with her accusations, and now for capitalizing on her experiences through her share of a half-million-dollar book advance. Still, she and her co-awardees are acutely aware of the stresses that whistleblowing involves.

At bottom, however, there's another overriding commonality: moral courage, a term strangely muted in the *Time* account. In varying degrees, each of these women understood the danger they faced, found the will to endure the risk and based her action on clear moral principle. These three characteristics—awareness, endurance and principle—are the defining features of moral courage.

And that helps us answer the big question surrounding *Time*'s choice: Why, this year, give an award for moral courage? What is it in our culture, the ethos of our time, our zeitgeist that makes it so important to honor the courage to be moral?

In part, of course, it's our want of heroes, our longing for bold leadership in an age of insecurity. The tragedy of 9/11 supplied us with a few heroes in the form of firefighters. Now the pendulum has swung to a different sort of courage, where what's endangered is not life and limb but reputation, ethical standards and the need for principle.

And in part, it's just the reverse: our desire for something to moderate the glut of executive swashbuckling. Weary of the excesses of corporate rapacity, we reach out for the modesty and humility of a moral leadership that carefully tracks the right numbers, establishes a culture of trust, subordinates style to substance and tells the truth.

But there's something else, I think, driving this thirst for moral courage. Call it the Age of Disjunction. These days there's an unusual disconnect between words and action, theory and practice, assertion and demonstration. Increasingly, it seems, there's an inertia that keeps goodness in a state of suspended animation while badness rolls on of its own momentum. It's an age fixed on show and surface, a two-dimensional televisual culture that militates against depth and penetration. Result: an almost hypnotic inability to bring things to conclusion. Perhaps that's what T. S. Eliot had in mind when, in "The Hollow Men," he noted that "Between the motion/And the action/Falls the Shadow."

In a fascinating moment in their *Time* interview, these women glimpsed that shadow. "In this country," said Watkins, "we have a vacuum in leadership. . . . We value splashy leaders."

"People who move to the top," added Cooper, "are typically racehorses, not workhorses. And they're very charismatic."

"And the dark side of charisma," replied Watkins, "is narcissism."

That's not your usual whistleblower talk. But it speaks to a key point about moral courage. Because it seeks truth, moral courage probes for depth. In the end, what unites these three women is their discomfort with the superficial. For them, neither the glitz of WorldCom, the bland denials of Enron, nor the veneer of old traditions at the FBI was compelling. They wanted something more profound.

So, ultimately, do we. Sobered by 9/11, rocked by corporate scandals, clouded by rumors of war, we long to unite motion and action, dissolve the shadow and connect our ideas and our lives. That can be hard, discomforting work. That three women did it—and that some editors thought what they did was supremely important—is a sign of hope for the new year.

WHISTLEBLOWING: A GLOBAL PERSPECTIVE

—LORI TANSEY MARTENS AND AMBER CROWELL

The events surrounding the demise of Enron and Arthur Andersen have focused renewed attention on whistleblowing. Companies have long known the advantages of encouraging employees to report bad news through internal, corporate channels. U.S. companies, in particular, have adopted a sophisticated array of options to facilitate whistleblowing, including 24-hour hotlines and corporate ethics offices. However, multinational companies face significant challenges when they try to encourage whistleblowing across a wide variety of cultures, many of which have deeply ingrained biases against whistleblowing. The following article examines those cultural differences and their impacts on reporting.

Ronald Berenbeim, Principal Researcher at the Conference Board, notes that companies regard the reporting of questionable practices to be critical to the success of their ethics and compliance initiatives. Yet whistleblowing is one of the least well developed elements of global business practices programs. Even with corporate hotlines in place, low international employee usage continues to be a problem for many organizations.[1]

CULTURAL IMPEDIMENTS

There are a number of cultural and other factors that discourage international employees from reporting misconduct. These include:

Divided Loyalties: Divided loyalties represent a significant challenge in Asia. Dr. Terence Tsai, Assistant Professor of Management at the Chinese University of Hong Kong, notes, "In parts of East Asia, members of the corporation are a family; if you view them as family members, it's wrong to report them."

In Japan, lifetime employment and a strict seniority system can discourage workers from questioning management decisions, dictating, instead, that employees show unbounded loyalty to their co-workers. In Korea, a subordinate's loyalty to a superior is even greater than his or her loyalty to the company. These cultural norms may make it difficult for organizations to establish an environment that accepts whistleblowing.

History: For some countries, recent history exacerbates a bias against whistleblowing. In China, for example, attempts to introduce corporate hotlines can remind employees of the horrors of the Cultural Revolution when citizens were encouraged to report "illegal activities" to authorities, which included children reporting against parents, students against teachers and neighbors against neighbors. In Germany, encouraging anonymous or confidential reporting can bring to mind Gestapo tactics from WWII. Here, the aversion to whistleblowing has been heightened by recent revelations of the far-reaching informant networks of the Stasi in the former East Germany.

Logistics: Numerous time zones and languages are only two of the many logistical factors that prevent international employees from using corporate whistleblowing resources. International 800-numbers and international collect calls either do not work or are unknown in many countries. In some locations, even gaining access to a telephone can be problematic. Guy Dehn, Director of the UK-based Public Concern at Work, confirmed in a recent interview, "If you're in a village in Northern Indonesia, where are you going to get the telephone to call the Alert Line? At a public telephone with others listening?"

Fear of Retribution: Despite assurances from corporate headquarters that retribution will not be tolerated, many international employees fear otherwise. International operations may be far-removed from the watchful eyes of a corporate ethics office, making it difficult to monitor retaliatory actions against whistleblowers.

Professor Tsai remains skeptical about the reality of whistleblower protection in Asia, stating, "Information tends to leak out though 'informal networks' in Hong Kong, Taiwan and China, and the whistleblower's future becomes difficult." In addition to the real threat of losing a job, whistleblowers can also be subject to legal sanctions and loss of personal reputation. As Dr. Ruben Apressyan, Head of the Department of Ethics at the Russian Academy of Sciences, noted, "A whistleblower in Russia subjects him/herself to a lot of trouble because of possible persecution (legal or criminal) from company managers or owners. In some cases, the whistleblower will also be met with public suspicion that questions the sincerity of his/her intentions."

Finally, in certain parts of the world, the risk to whistleblowers can be life-threatening. Roy Jones, Senior Policy Advisor for the Trade Union Advisory Committee (TUAC) to the Organization for Economic Cooperation and Development (OECD), noted that over the years the TUAC has received reports about trade unionists and employees who have been murdered in countries from Russia to Guatemala for exposing corruption.[2]

PROTECTING WHISTLEBLOWERS

Despite these challenges, there is growing international interest in promoting whistleblowing as an important tool to combat global corruption and corporate misconduct. This interest has led to the formation of an international network of whistleblower protection organizations. The objective of the network is to promote and protect whistleblowing in the public interest.[3]

Tom Devine, Legal Director for the Government Accountability Project (GAP) and author of the Model International Whistleblower Protection Statute, reports that GAP has received requests for legislative assistance from all over the world, including Argentina, Australia, Canada, Great Britain, Korea, Russia and Slovakia. A brief summary of some of the legislative developments in whistleblower protection is listed below:

United Kingdom—The U.K. Public Interest Disclosure Act protects most workers from retaliation by their employer, including dismissal, disciplinary action or a transfer that otherwise would not have happened. Unless the employer can show a valid reason for the dismissal or detriment, an employment tribunal may order the company to compensate the employee for the losses suffered, and in rare cases, mandate reemployment.[4]

European Union—After a procurement scandal at the European Commission, the EU published a charter for whistleblower protection in 2000. The charter identifies the terms under which commission staff may "blow the whistle," imposes a duty upon officials to report suspected wrongdoing and outlines the channels for reporting malpractice.[5] GAP has characterized the legislation as a "Trojan Horse," however, because it limits whistleblower protection to internal disclosures of wrongdoing.

South Africa—The Protected Disclosures Act 26 of 2000 prohibits an employer from subjecting an employee to an "occupational detriment" (e.g., disciplinary action, suspension, dismissal, demotion, harassment, etc.) for raising concerns about unlawful or irregular conduct. Whistleblower protection is limited, however, to individuals who disclose their concerns according to specifically defined procedures.[6]

Israel—Following the lead of legislation passed in South Africa and the United Kingdom, Israel adopted whistleblower legislation that protects corporate and government workers.

Ghana—A Whistleblower Protection Act, similar to that of South Africa, has been proposed in Ghana to offer rewards and protection to people who volunteer information leading to the prosecution of white collar criminals. The success of the proposed legislation hinges, in part, upon the repeal of existing laws that make it impossible for public officers to make disclosures.[7]

South Korea—The Anti-Corruption Act of 2001 established the Korea Independent Commission Against Corruption, whose mission includes the encouragement, protection and compensation of whistleblowers. In spite of early signs of success (i.e., over 800 reports of corruption were alleged in the first two months of operation), the Commission is struggling through growing pains and regulatory limitations. The Commission is prohibited from questioning the accused, and in its first action against corruption, it failed to keep the identities of the accused strictly confidential.[8]

Devine notes that while enacting whistleblower legislation is difficult, translating laws into reality is an even more elusive task. Many organizations face similar challenges to implementation within their global business practices programs. In the face of so many obstacles, how can multinational corporations increase the willingness of employees around the world to report questionable conduct?

Several corporations have found successful ways to work within cultural norms, and their achievements can present a model for other organizations. Their approaches and strategies will be highlighted in Part II of this article, due to appear in the July/August issue of *ethikos.*

FOOTNOTES

1. Berenbeim, Ronald E. *Company Programs for Resisting Corrupt Practices: A Global Study.* (New York: The Conference Board, 2000.)
2. Jones, Roy. *Fighting Corruption: The Role of Trade Unions.* 9th Annual International Anti-Corruption Conference (IACC), October 9–15, 1999.
3. Further information on the International Network of Whistleblower Protection Organisations can be found at http://www.whistleblower.org/international.
4. http://www.pcaw.org.uk/.
5. "More Power to Tell All for Whistleblowers," *Sunday Business,* December 3, 2000.
6. http://www.iss.co.za/Pubs/Papers/47/Paper47.html.
7. "Combating Corruption Give Whistleblowers Cover," *Ghanaian Chronicle,* February 20, 2001.
8. "Fight Against Corruption," *The Korea Herald,* April 4, 2002.

HUMAN RIGHTS AND GLOBAL LABOR PRACTICES

—Denis G. Arnold

Denis Arnold considers the nature of fundamental human rights as it might be applied to global labor practices. After evaluating what should be considered to be fundamental human rights of workers, he contends that a more comprehensive understanding of basic human rights can encourage business decision makers to make morally better decisions about labor challenges.

Ethical concerns are at the core of the dispute concerning global labor practices. Critics charge multinational enterprises (MNEs) with the inhumane and unjust treatment of workers in developing nations. Economists retort that satisfying the demands of these critics will result in fewer jobs in developing nations, thereby reducing social welfare. In order to properly evaluate these claims, and others like them, it is first necessary to provide an analysis of the ethical obligations of MNEs regarding global labor practices.

One set of ethical norms that is a prominent feature of contemporary public discourse, especially as it pertains to international affairs, is that of human rights. The promulgation of the United Nations Universal Declaration of Human Rights, together with the advocacy of organizations such as Amnesty International and Human Rights Watch, has led to the widespread acceptance of human rights as a basic tool of moral evaluation by individuals of widely divergent political and religious beliefs. Increasingly, the language of human rights is a prominent feature of debates regarding globalization and global labor practices. This essay explains how an understanding of basic human rights can help MNE managers to produce morally innovative solutions to global labor challenges.

GLOBAL LABOR PRACTICES

Suppose that an MNE sourcing manager must choose between two offshore factories that wish to serve as suppliers. Both suppliers operate factories in a developing nation with an emerging democracy that has completed two rounds of free and fair elections. Workers in this nation have recently become entitled to freedom of association, collective bargaining and a national health care program funded by social security payroll deductions. However, the ability of government officials to enforce these laws is minimal, as the enforcement agencies are underfunded and understaffed, while residual corruption undermines the enforcement of labor

"Human Rights and Global Labor Practices" by Denis G. Arnold, reprinted from Denis G. Arnold, "Human Rights and Business: An Ethical Analysis," in Rory Sullivan, ed., *Business and Human Rights: Dilemmas and Solutions* (Sheffield, UK: Greenleaf Publishing, 2003). Reprinted with permission from the author and Greenleaf Publishing.

429

laws. Furthermore, there is a well grounded concern on the part of government officials that the enforcement of existing labor laws will result in higher costs for MNEs, and that because of this MNEs will place fewer orders in its domestic manufacturing sector.

The two suppliers submit bids, together with product samples. Both sets of samples meet minimum quality standards. However, the bid of Supplier A is 20% more than the bid of Supplier B. The bid differential is attributable to the fact that Supplier A has substantially higher employee costs than Supplier B. Supplier A provides workers legally required overtime pay; deducts and pays to the government social security payroll taxes; provides bonuses for meeting specified quality standards; provides annual pay raises; provides opportunities to workers for promotion; and has invested in health and safety measures in order to prevent basic risks to the lives and health of employees while at work. Employees of Supplier A who work 50–60 hours per week are able to avoid conditions of overall poverty as defined by the United Nations (UNDP 2000).

Supplier B, on the other hand, does not pay workers as required for overtime; deducts but does not turn over social security payroll taxes to the government; provides no bonuses or regular pay raises; provides no opportunities for promotion (instead making exclusive use of foreign nationals as supervisors); and has taken no measures to prevent basic risks to the lives and health of employees. Employees of Supplier B who work 50–60 hours per week typically live in conditions of extreme poverty.

It is platitudinous, but necessary, to observe that different individuals may agree that the correct choice is obvious, yet disagree about *which* choice is correct. Various interested parties—factory workers, economists, MNE shareholders, customers and so on—will each have their own distinct perspectives. For example, some labor or human rights activists might reason as follows: "The very existence of Supplier A is unusual, as most factories in developing countries better fit the description of Supplier B. The opportunity to work with Supplier A should be embraced by the MNE, since doing so will promote human and labor rights. The additional costs are minimal for an MNE." Some MNE sourcing managers, or individuals sympathetic to the arguments put forth by such managers, might reason as follows: "Supplier B is the norm in nearly all developing countries. It is the responsibility of national governments to enforce existing labor laws uniformly. When governments do not enforce such laws uniformly, an MNE cannot be expected to bear the costs of adhering to local labor laws, let alone the costs of providing the comfortable working conditions and high wages present in Supplier A. To do so would place the MNE at a competitive disadvantage."

What more can be said in defense of the view that the MNE manager should choose Supplier A? In order to properly answer this question, it is necessary to provide a justification and explanation of basic human rights. . . .

HUMAN RIGHTS AND LABOR PRACTICES

We have seen in the essay included in Chapter 1 of this text how a right to freedom and a right to well-being can be justified. If persons have a right to freedom and well-being, then at a minimum other persons have an obligation to refrain from interfering with those rights. It is in this sense that rights entail corresponding duties on the part of other persons. What are the specific obligations or duties of MNE managers with respect to the freedom and well-being of employees and how are these obligations to be balanced against the obligations of managers to their employers?

Because freedom and well-being are basic rights, the obligation to respect those rights is equally basic. As such, no labor practices may be undertaken that will violate a worker's right to freedom and well-being. MNEs are in a unique position to ensure that basic rights is respected in the workplace by virtue of their power and the vast resources under their command. In the words of the United Nations: "Society no longer accepts the view that the conduct of global corporations is bound only by the laws of the country they operate in. By virtue of their global influence and power, they must accept responsibility and be accountable for upholding high human rights standards" (UNDP 2000: 80). MNEs typically have well defined internal decision structures that provide an internal mechanism for enforcing human rights standards. The internal decision structure of an organization is comprised of its offices and levels of responsibility, together with the rules that allow managers to differentiate between enterprise-level decisions, and the decisions of individual employees (French, 1979; 1995). For this reason, morally innovative managers are well positioned to play a constructive role in ensuring that the rights of workers in developing nations are respected.

MNE managers should regard respect for their employees' rights to freedom and well-being as constraints on the activities they undertake on behalf of their employers. However, the rights to freedom and well-being are very general. Greater specificity regarding the content of these rights must be provided. Let us begin with freedom. Previously we characterized freedom as controlling one's behavior via one's unforced choice, while having knowledge of relevant circumstances. Gewirth provides a helpful summary of the content of the right to freedom (Gewirth 1982: 56–57):

> *This consists in a person's controlling his actions and his participation in transactions by his own unforced choice or consent and with knowledge of relevant circumstances, so that his behavior is neither compelled nor prevented by the actions of other persons. Hence, a person's right to freedom is violated if he is subjected to violence, coercion, deception or any other procedures that attack or remove his informed control of his behavior by his own unforced choice. This right includes having a sphere of personal autonomy and privacy whereby one is let alone by others unless and until he unforcedly consents to undergo their action.*

Possessing freedom entails having the general abilities and conditions required for a person to be able to act in a manner consistent with his or her second-order preferences. A right to freedom, then, involves the right to pursue one's own goals and preferences without interference from others. Specifically, it includes control over one's own physical integrity, freedom of belief and expression and freedom of association. Traditionally, the right to freedom is thought to be as extensive as is compatible with a like right to freedom for all. Such freedom is not, however, unlimited. It may be rightfully curtailed if a person's actions illegitimately infringe upon the freedom or well-being of others.

The rights one enjoys as a human being are not unlimited in the sense that one is free to exercise all of them under any circumstances. Legitimate restrictions may be placed on the exercise of one's rights by both the state and private enterprise. It is, for example, not an illegitimate infringement of one's right to freedom of belief and expression if an employer prohibits proselytizing on behalf of one's religious convictions while at work. Such activity is typically disruptive and as such incompatible with the purposes for which employees are hired. Furthermore, employees are free to engage in such activity when they are not working. Restricting employee activity in this manner does not infringe on an employee's dignity as a person. There are, however, certain restrictions on employee freedom that always violate human dignity because they treat the employee as a tool rather than as a person. Control over one's physical integrity is one such example. This freedom could, for example, be violated by a rule that permitted only one bathroom break each day.

Several international covenants and conventions are available to MNEs interested in specific guidance with respect to their global labor practices. For example, the Articles of the United Nations Universal Declaration of Human Rights (UDHR) (1948) provide specific examples of what it means to respect an employee's right to freedom at work (see Figure 1). Articles 3, 4 and 5 provide a basis for the prohibition of all forced labor, indentured servitude, corporeal punishment of employees by supervisors and seriously unsafe working conditions. Article 23, Section 4 provides a basis for the prohibition of the termination of employees for organizing or joining a trade union.

FIGURE 1

Articles of the UDHR Concerning the Right to Freedom with Special
Relevance to the Obligations of MNEs to Workers

Article 3: Everyone has the right to life, liberty and security of person.

Article 4: No one shall be held in slavery or servitude; slavery and the slave trade shall be prohibited in all their forms.

Article 5: No one shall be subjected to torture or to cruel, inhuman or degrading treatment or punishment.

Article 23, Section 4: Everyone has the right to form and to join trade unions for the protection of his interests.

Now let us turn to well-being. As we have seen, well-being entails having the general abilities and conditions required for a person to be able to act autonomously. The most important component of well-being, and the one that we shall focus upon here, is basic goods. Basic goods are the general physical and psychological capabilities necessary for human functioning. In recent years, the relationship between well-being and human functioning has received a great deal of attention from economists and philosophers. Some of the most important work on this topic has been produced by Amartya Sen (1985, 1987, 1999b) and Martha Nussbaum (2001). Their distinctive variety of quality of life assessment, known as the capabilities approach, had become increasingly influential. This is partly due to the fact that it has been adapted by the UNDP and has been incorporated into the UNDP Human Development Reports since 1993. The relationship between human functioning and well-being is usefully articulated by Sen (1985: 197–198):

> *The primary feature of well-being can be seen in terms of how a person can "function," taking that term in a very broad sense. I shall refer to various doings and beings that come into this assessment as functionings. These could be activities (like eating or reading or seeing),*

or states of existence or being, e.g., being well nourished, being free from malaria, not being ashamed by the poverty of one's clothing or shoes (to go back to a question that Adam Smith discussed in his Wealth of Nations*).*

It is important to note that not all persons will have the same capacity to function well with the same goods. Variations in the transformation of goods into constituent elements of well-being will vary significantly among persons. For example, as noted by Sen (1985: 198–199):

Take, for example, the consumption of food, on the one hand, and the functioning of being well nourished, on the other. The relationship between them varies with (1) metabolic rates, (2) body size, (3) age, (4) sex (and if a woman, whether pregnant or lactating), (5) activity levels, (6) medical services, (7) nutritional knowledge and other influences.

Access to the basic goods necessary for human functioning does not mean that a person who enjoys the basic goods necessary to function well will do so. Two individuals may have access to the same goods necessary for each of them to achieve the same level of well-being, yet fail to do so because one of them made choices that reduced his or her ability to function well. For this reason it is necessary to emphasize an individual's *capability* to function. What are these capabilities? Nussbaum (2001) identifies ten capabilities as necessary for humans to enjoy well-being (see Figure 2). The list is itself the product of years of cross-cultural study and discussion and represents a sort of overlapping consensus on the part of individuals with widely disparate views of human life. Nussbaum is careful to point out both that the list is open-ended, and that items on the list may be interpreted somewhat differently in different societies. However, each item on the list is of central importance and as such it must be regarded as a significant loss when a person falls below any one of the central areas.

The Articles of the UDHR provide a valuable resource for determining what it means for an employer to respect an employee's right to well-being (see Figure 3). Article 23, Section 2

FIGURE 2

Central Human Functional Capabilities (Nussbaum 2001: 78–80)

1. **Life.**   Being able to live to the end of a human life of normal length; not dying prematurely, or before one's life is so reduced as to not be worth living.
2. **Bodily Health.**   Being able to have good health, including reproductive health; to be adequately nourished; to have adequate shelter.
3. **Bodily Integrity.**   Being able to move freely from place to place; having one's bodily boundaries treated as sovereign, i.e., being able to be secure against assault, including sexual assault, child sexual abuse and domestic violence; having opportunities for sexual satisfaction and for choice in matters of reproduction.
4. **Senses, Imagination and Thought.**   Being able to use the senses, to imagine, think and reason—and to do these things in a "truly human" way, a way informed and cultivated by an adequate education, including, but by no means limited to, literacy and basic mathematical and scientific training . . . .
5. **Emotion.**   Being able to have attachments to things and people outside of ourselves; to love those who love and care for us, to grieve at their absence; in general, to love, to grieve, to experience longing gratitude and justified anger. Not having one's emotional development blighted by overwhelming fear and anxiety, or by traumatic events of abuse or neglect.

(continued)

FIGURE 2 (Concluded)

(Supporting this capability means supporting forms of human association that can be shown to be crucial in their development.)

6. Practical Reason.   Being able to form a conception of the good and to engage in critical reflection about the planning of one's life. (This entails protection for the liberty of conscience.)

7. Affiliation.

   A.   Being able to live with and towards others, to recognize and show concern for other human beings, to engage in various forms of social interaction; to be able to imagine the situation of another and have compassion for that situation; to have the capability for both justice and friendship. (Protecting this capability means protecting institutions that constitute and nourish such forms of affiliation, and also protecting the freedom of assembly and political speech.)

   B.   Having the social bases of self-respect and non-humiliation; being able to be treated as a dignified being whose worth is equal to that of others. This entails, at a minimum, protections against discrimination on the basis of race, sex, sexual orientation, religion, caste, ethnicity, or national origin. In work, being able to work as a human being, exercising practical reason and entering into meaningful relationships of mutual recognition with other workers.

8. Other Species.   Being able to live with concern for and in relation to animals, plants and the world of nature.

9. Play.   Being able to laugh, play, to enjoy recreational activities.

10. Control over One's Environment.

   A. Political.   Being able to participate effectively in political choices that govern one's life; having the right of political participation, protections of free speech and free association.

   B. Material.   Being able to hold property (both land and movable goods), not just formally but in terms of real opportunity; and having property rights on an equal basis with others; having the right to seek employment on an equal basis with others; having the freedom from unwarranted search and seizure.

provides a basis for the prohibition of discrimination based on arbitrary characteristics such as race or sex. Article 23, Section 2 and Article 25, Section 1 provide a basis for paying employees wages that are consistent with living with dignity. They also provide a basis for thinking that it is the responsibility of MNEs to ensure that social security and other taxes are paid to appropriate governmental authorities. Article 24 provides a basis for the view that employees are entitled to wages adequate for a dignified standard of living without working extensive overtime hours.

Some individuals who are concerned with the welfare of workers in developing nations will disagree with the conclusion that MNE labor practices must not violate a

FIGURE 3

Articles of the UDHR Concerning the Right to Well-being with Special
Relevance to the Obligations of MNEs to Workers

Article 23

(2) Everyone, without any discrimination, has the right to equal pay for equal work.

(3) Everyone who works has the right to just and favorable remuneration ensuring for himself and his family an existence worthy of human dignity, and supplemented, if necessary, by other means of social protection.

FIGURE 3 (Concluded)

Article 24

Everyone has the right to rest and leisure, including reasonable limitation of working hours and periodic holidays with pay.

Article 25

(1) Everyone has the right to a standard of living adequate for health and well-being of himself and of his family, including food, clothing, housing and medical care and necessary social services, and the right to security in the event of unemployment, sickness, disability, widowhood, old age or other lack of livelihood in circumstances beyond his control.

worker's right to freedom and well-being. The claim is frequently made, with varying degrees of sophistication, that respecting employee rights will result in greater harm than good. For example, in a recent book David Henderson argues that the expenditure by MNEs of corporate resources in the interest of human rights will result in workers being made worse off (Henderson 2001). Henderson's conclusion is shared by Ian Maitland who claims that "attempts to improve on market outcomes may have unforeseen tragic consequences" for workers in developing nations (Maitland 2001: 603). The core argument of both Henderson and Maitland, as it pertains to formal sector workers in developing nations, is that the imposition of wages or labor standards greater than those demanded by the market will increase costs, and that this will inevitably lead to layoffs and higher unemployment. How persuasive is this argument?

To see that voluntarily improving employee wages and working conditions will not inevitably lead to the "tragic consequences" that Henderson and Maitland predict, consider the following points.[1] First, with regard to the lowest paid formal sector wage earners in developing countries, the assumption that productivity is independent of wage levels is mistaken. Put simply, workers whose minimum daily dietary requirements are met, and who have basic non-food needs met, will have more energy and better attitudes at work; will be less likely to come to work ill; and will be absent with less frequency. Workers are thus likely to be more productive and loyal. Increased productivity resulting from better nutrition and increased employee loyalty alone may offset the cost of higher wages. The wage which, if reduced, would make the firm worse off because of a decrease in worker productivity is known as the efficiency wage. Firms that pay employees at rates higher than the efficiency wage may enjoy other economic advantages such as reduced training costs as a result of greater employee loyalty. Second, it is economically feasible for MNEs to raise wages and improve working conditions in factories in developing economies without causing increases in unemployment. MNEs may *choose* to improve wages and working conditions while maintaining existing employment levels. Profit margins vary among products. For the manufacturers of brand name retail goods, a significant increase in labor costs may be readily absorbed as an operating expense. Indeed, the expense may be offset by the value added to the good insofar as consumers demonstrate a preference for products produced under conditions in which the rights of workers are respected. Third, there may be cases where

---

[1]For a more thorough reply to this objection see Arnold and Bowie (2003).

increased labor costs are not offset by greater productivity, and where the increase in costs cannot be readily absorbed as an operating expense. For example, manufacturers of generic goods with low profit margins *may* find it difficult to simply absorb the cost of increased labor expenses. In such cases, the added cost of labor may instead be balanced by internal cost-cutting measures;[2] or it may be passed on to consumers via higher prices;[3] or it may be passed on to the owners of the business enterprise via lower return on equity.[4] In such cases, the costs of respecting human rights must be regarded as a necessary condition of doing business. This point should not be problematic for anyone who recognizes the existence of basic human rights. For insofar as we recognize the rights of other persons, we have an obligation to respect those rights. It is by acting in a manner that respects basic human rights that we raise ourselves above other species.

CONCLUSION

The vast majority of workers in most developing nations operate outside or at the periphery of formal employment relations. As formal sector employment increases in these nations, MNEs that demonstrate respect for the rights of workers can be expected to have an influence on the local norms governing labor practices which is disproportionate to the number of workers that they actually employ. This is because they, together with morally innovative indigenous employers, will be setting the standard against which other employers must be measured. The result will be a substantially improved quality of life for the growing ranks of workers in the formal sector. Correspondingly, morally innovative MNEs and their suppliers can be expected to enjoy the most productive and loyal indigenous workers since they will be ranked among the most desirable employers. Furthermore, as increasing numbers of workers leave the informal sector in pursuit of better opportunities in the formal sector, less pressure will be exerted on the scarce productive resources of the informal sector. This should permit an enhanced standard of living for those remaining in the informal sector. Far from causing a decrease in overall social welfare by spurring unemployment, MNEs that demonstrate respect for worker rights are well positioned to enhance the welfare of citizens in developing nations.

---

[2] One set of obvious targets for expense reduction is the cost of supporting significant numbers of home country managers in the country of the supplier. While some presence may be necessary, it will often be more cost effective to employ host country nationals in this capacity. Another attractive set of targets is executive perks. While such perks vary significantly among firms, it does appear morally inconsistent to argue that improving the welfare of the factory workers is cost prohibitive while executive perks remain substantial.

[3] Given the frequently fierce competition among the manufacturers of generic products targeted at cost conscious consumers, it may be difficult for one retailer to remain competitive while raising prices to cover increased labor costs, while others do not. For this reason, industrywide standards concerning labor practices may prove valuable as a way of distributing costs equitably.

[4] To keep investors informed regarding such policies it will be important to report on efforts to protect worker rights in annual reports and other appropriate communications.

REFERENCES

French, P. (1979) "The Corporation as a Moral Person," *American Philosophical Quarterly* 16: 207–217.

French, P. (1995) *Corporate Ethics* (Fort Worth, TX: Harcourt Brace).

Gewirth, A. (1978) *Reason and Morality* (Chicago: University of Chicago Press).

Gewirth, A. (1982) *Human Rights: Essays on Justification and Applications* (Chicago: University of Chicago Press).

Henderson, D. (2001) *Misguided Virtue: False Notions of Corporate Social Responsibility* (London: Institute for Economic Affairs).

Maitland, I. (2001) "The Great Non-Debate over International Sweatshops," in T. Beauchamp and N. Bowie (eds.), *Ethical Theory and Business* (Englewood Cliffs, NJ: Prentice Hall, 6th ed.).

Nussbaum, M. (2001) *Women and Human Development* (New York: Cambridge University Press).

Sen, A. (1985) "Well-being, Agency and Freedom: The Dewey Lectures 1984," *Journal of Philosophy* 82: 169–203.

Sen, A. (1987) *On Ethics and Economics* (Oxford: Blackwell Publishers).

Sen, A. (1999a) "Human Rights and Asian Values," in T. Machan (ed.), *Business Ethics in the Global Marketplace* (Stanford, CA: Hoover Institution Press): 37–62.

Sen, A. (1999b) *Development as Freedom.* (New York: Alfred A. Knopf, Inc.).

Sen, A. (2000) "East and West: The Reach of Reason," *The New York Review of Books,* July 20: 33–38.

UNDP. (2000) *Human Development Report 2000* (New York: Oxford University Press).

TEE-SHIRTS AND TEARS
Third World Suppliers to First World Markets
—Laura B. Pincus (Hartman)

It is important to note that these conditions do not exist only in foreign markets. U.S. Secretary of Labor Robert Reich made the following remarks in a keynote address at a conference on international labor standards:

> *I have had occasion over the past year to study a country in which many workers who have tried to organize themselves have been fired for their activities. It is a country in which there are sweat shops of the worst Third World variety. In fact, there are sweat shops in which young children are working.*
>
> *It is a country in which many workers are still exposed to hazards that kill and maim them. In this country just a week ago today, I had occasion to visit a plant to serve papers on a plant manager and a company—a very, very large company—where one worker was killed recently. Other workers had been maimed, suffering lost fingers and mangled arms, and yet the company still, still, refused to change its ways and come into compliance.*
>
> *The country I'm talking about is, obviously, the United States. I issue a warning to all of us—a warning to all Americans dealing with the issue of international labor standards. We must guard against too much self-righteous indignation. (Robert B. Reich, "Keynote Address,"* International Labor Standards and Global Economic Integration: Proceedings of a Symposium, *July 1994, p. 1.)*

The hottest places in hell are reserved for those who, in a period of moral crisis, maintain their neutrality.

—Dante

Recent media attention has heightened our awareness of labor conditions in third world countries. While Americans otherwise may have been able to write off substandard labor conditions as another case of cultural variations, these recent cases garnered domestic interest as a result of the parties involved. Their names are about as American as Apple Pie.

The Gap. Kathie Lee Gifford. Even Michael Jordan. These are the contractors, the investors, the spokespeople who represent "sweatshops" where, allegedly, young girls are allowed only two restroom visits per day and, allegedly, the days sometimes consist of 21 straight hours of work.

LABOR CONDITIONS IN THE UNITED STATES

America's garment industry today grosses $45 billion per year and employs more than one million workers.[1] Uproar began in the Fall of 1995 when Secretary of Labor Robert Reich announced the names of several large retailers who may have been involved in an El Monte, California, sweatshop operation. Notwithstanding the fact that the retailers are not liable for the conditions if they have no knowledge of them, the companies involved in this situation agreed to adopt a statement of principles which would require their suppliers to adhere to U.S. federal labor laws.[2]

Reich followed this announcement with an appearance on the *Phil Donahue Show* where he discussed a situation at another plant that employed Thai workers at less than $1.00 per hour and kept its workers behind a barbed wire fence. Retailers respond that it is difficult, if not impossible, to police their suppliers and subcontractors, who may total more than 20,000 in some cases. And the pressures of the situation are only becoming worse. The apparel industry, which has borne the brunt of Reich's focus, is highly competitive, and extremely labor-intensive. Competition from companies in other countries that do not impose similar labor condition requirements is fierce. Consequently, one is not surprised to learn that a 1994 Labor Department spot check of garment operations in California found that 93% had health and safety violations.[3]

Manufacturers may have a bit more to be concerned about than retailers. Reich has recently involved a little-used provision in the Fair Labor Standards Act that holds manufacturers liable for the wrongful acts of their suppliers and that allows for the confiscation of goods produced by sweatshop operations.

Reich has now appealed to the retailers and manufacturers alike to conduct their own random spot checks. "We need to enlist retailers as adjunct policemen. At a time when business says to government, 'Get off our back. We can do it ourselves,' we're giving them the opportunity," Reich notes.[4] In June 1995, Reich established a consortium to police working conditions made up of manufacturers. The group, called Compliance Alliance, will police contractors conducting regular audits and will identify firms that pay less than minimum wage or otherwise violate the provisions of the Fair Labor Standards Act.[5] . . .

The Clinton Administration's voluntary Model Business Principles, published in May 1995, are relevant to this discussion. The principles encourage all businesses to adopt and implement voluntary codes of conduct for doing business around the world and suggest appropriate code coverage. . . .

AMERICAN ATTENTION DRIFTS
TOWARD OTHER COUNTRIES

Neil Kearney, general secretary of the International Textile, Garment and Leather Worker's Federation, describes the garment workplace as follows:

> *The reality today is that most of the 30 million jobs in the fashion industry around the world are low paid, often based in export processing zones where worker rights are usually suppressed. Wages are frequently below the subsistence level and falling in real terms. . . .*
>
> *Management by terror is the norm in many countries. Workers are routinely shoved, beaten, kicked, even when pregnant. Attempts to unionize are met with the utmost brutality, sometimes with murder.*[6]

Once the American public considered its own conditions, it looked to other countries to see how labor was treated there. Following Reich's slap on the hand to American manufacturers, media attention turned toward the conditions in Third World countries and toward American responsibility for or involvement in those conditions. In 1970, there were 7,000 multinational companies in the world. Today, there are more than 35,000.[7] The topic of conditions in those multinationals was destined for afternoon talk shows once it was announced that television personality Kathie Lee Gifford endorsed a line of clothing that had been made for Wal-Mart in Honduran sweatshops. These operations employed underage and pregnant women for more than 20-hour days at $.31 per hour. The conditions were extremely hot and no worker was allowed to speak during the entire day.

The situation was brought to the attention of the press by Charles Kernaghan, director of the National Labor Committee, based in New York City. Kernaghan informed Gifford, and the press, of the conditions in the plant and asked her to respond. Gifford's immediate response was to immediately break off her relationship with the company.[8] Unfortunately, this is not what is always best for the exploited workers. Instead, Kernaghan impressed upon her the need to remain involved and to use her position and reputation to encourage a change in the conditions at the plants.

These arguments may remind the reader of those waged several years ago regarding divestment from South Africa. Proponents of investment argued that the only way to effect change would be to remain actively involved in the operations of the South African business community. Others argued that no ethical company should pour money into a country where apartheid conditions were allowed to exist. The same arguments can and have been made about conducting business in Third World countries, and Gifford found herself right in the middle of them.

THE EL SALVADORAN LABOR ENVIRONMENT

El Salvador is a country that has been ravaged by internal conflicts culminating in a civil war that lasted for many years. In 1992, with the advent of peace, the country sought to rebuild what it had lost during wartime and is now considered one of the fastest growing economies in Latin America.[9] The objective of the El Salvadorans involved in the rebuilding process was to help the poor to overcome the conditions of poverty, dependence and oppression that they had experienced during the conflict. While the objectives of private investors may be different, all seem to share a common interest in social stability and development. Economist Louis Emmerij notes that the leading cause of social unrest is "the lack of sufficient and renumerative employment opportunities, bad living conditions and the lack of perspective and hope."[10]

In developing countries like El Salvador, long-term strategies for improving a poor household's ability to generate disposable income on a sustained basis must consider if households have the skills, education and know-how to allow them to operate in the market. These strategies include support for training and education, access to markets and access to technology and credit. A large part of the labor problem in the *maquiladores* is the lack of agreement between the workers and management as to the minimum level of productivity expected per day, the level of compensation for a worker who achieves that level and who should assume the burden of training in order to increase productivity.

Yet, low wages are the prime magnet for multinational firms coming to El Salvador. In 1990, a glossy full-colored advertisement appeared in a major American apparel trade magazine showing a woman at a sewing machine and proclaiming, "Rosa Martinez produces apparel for U.S. markets on her sewing machine in El Salvador. *You* can hire her for 57 cents an hour." One year later, the same ad announced that Rosa's salary had gone down—"*You* can hire her for 33 cents an hour."[11] It appears that the publicists felt that Rosa's salary originally looked too high in the eyes of the market players.

Critical to understanding these conflicts is an understanding of the Salvadoran culture itself. Salvadoran workers are not exempt from the consequences of their history. When they enter the workplace, they expect to be exploited and do not trust management. In addition, as a result of the repressive conditions in El Salvador during the war, the society suffers from a general lack of candor and a tendency on the part of individuals to protect themselves by not telling the truth.[12] But this quality is different from the deception that occurs in American business dealings. In this situation, it serves as a means of self-protection in a culture that offers little else. Moreover, the government does not protect individual and business interests, thereby allowing cartels to develop, flourish and continue.

The author of this case had the opportunity to travel to El Salvador in 1996 in order to observe a class in financial administration at an El Salvadoran university. During the course of a quiz in the class, the professor had reason to leave the classroom for a moment. Upon his return, he found that the students were now collaborating on the answers to the quiz. During the discussion that later ensued regarding the students' actions, the students articulated a need to help each other to succeed. They felt that they should bind together in order to help them all to move forward. If this meant helping a colleague who did not have time to study because he had to work to support his family, in addition to attending school, that seemed acceptable, if not necessary and ethical.[13]

During that same course, the graduate students (most, if not all, of whom worked full-time in professional positions) were asked to identify the principal barriers to trust in Salvadoran business relationships, and the means by which those barriers could be broken down. Students responded as follows (translated from Spanish):

> One barrier is that the big businesses are formed at the level of families and friends that form a close nucleus, prohibiting others from entering.

> The government does not enact laws to guarantee business interests and growth without the intervention of stronger, "bully" businesses.

There is a failure of information—only certain people have access to the most important, business-related information. There is no requirement that business share information, even at a level that would mimic the American SEC requirements.

Create legal mechanisms that sanction companies violating the rules. These sanctions *do not* exist. Companies use illicit means to take advantage of their competitors and employing the same means is the only way to compete.

The period since the war has seen an increase in vandalism at an individual and corporate level, making it difficult to carry on a business.[14]

Consider the expectation of conflict in this scenario recounted by Fr. David Blanchard, Pastor of the Our Lady of Lourdes Church in Calle Real Epiphany Cooperative Association:

> In February of 1994, the cooperative had a serious labor conflict. The women became quite adept at sewing lab coats. But in February 1994, when the only contract available was for sewing hospital bathrobes, a serious labor conflict arose. Unfortunately, the women who were elected by their peers to negotiate with the contractor made some serious errors in judgment when they calculated the time required to sew this item.
>
> At the time, some women were earning 80 colones daily (twice the minimum wage). Most were making 50 colones. Only a few apprentices were making less than the minimum wage.
>
> With the transition to sewing bathrobes, production and therefore income, was cut in half. Six of the highest wage earners subsequently staged a sit-down strike at their machines, claiming that they were being oppressed.
>
> Father Blanchard asked, "Who negotiated your contract?"
>
> "Our representatives," they said.
>
> "Who elected your representatives?"
>
> "We did."
>
> "Who will suffer if this work is not completed?"
>
> "We will."
>
> These women had entered this project with no prior skills. They had received high-quality and expensive technical, legal and social training. They were all self-employed, but when their wages plunged, they felt oppressed, frustrated and angry, and ended up leaving the cooperative. . . . Some of these women will continue to suffer in poverty. It is certain that they are victims. But they are the victims of hundreds of years of oppression and not of the immediate circumstances sewing hospital bathrobes. They responded to the problems created by the lack of education and their lack of abilities by generating conflict.[15]

Blanchard remarks that Salvadoran industrialists and managers are even more strident in generating conflict in the workplace. For instance, consider the case of the Mandarin factory and many other similar plants throughout El Salvador.

THE MANDARIN PLANT AND ITS LABOR CONDITIONS

The San Salvador Mandarin International plant was established in order to assemble goods to be shipped to the United States under contract with major U.S. retailers such as The Gap and Eddie Bauer. The plant was built in the San Marcos Free Trade Zone, a zone owned by the former Salvadoran Army Colonel Mario Guerrero and created with money from the Bush Administration's U.S. Agency for International Development (USAID). David Wang, the Taiwanese owner of the plant, subsequently hired Guerrero as its personnel manager. In addition, the company also hired ex-military, plain-clothed armed guards as security for the plant.[16] Factories in El Salvador, as in the United States, need protection for workers, for personal property and for real property.

While personnel managers are not security guards, such appointments have become commonplace with Salvadoran industrialists precisely because they expect conflict in the workplace. However, in many situations, their personnel managers generate the conditions of conflict and attempt to control the conflict through the same methods employed during wartime.[17] For example, Colonel Guerrero himself told the workers at one point, "I have no problem, but perhaps you do; either the union will behave, leave, or people will die."[18]

While The Gap was one of the first companies to have a code of conduct for overseas suppliers (along with Reebok), this strategy might not be effective in the El Salvadoran business environment. Charles Kernaghan, director of the National Labor Committee in Support of Democracy and Human Rights in El Salvador (NLC), believed that a preexisting code of conduct was practically useless and stated the following in an interview with *Business Ethics* magazine in June 1996:

> *Consider the history of El Salvador's military, which specialized in the killing of nuns and priests and trade unionists. It is laughable to think that these same people will carry out a company's code of conduct. And there were no legal avenues to challenge any violation because the ministry of labor there is so ill-funded and ill-trained. So you can't depend on the laws. And the women were afraid to speak out.[19]*

After a bitter union-management struggle regarding working conditions and the termination of 100 union workers, the union and management reached an agreement. Unfortunately, the Mandarin did not abide by this agreement.

As North Americans became more and more aware of the working conditions in El Salvador, they began to take action against the retailers. On August 16, 1995, more than one hundred workers from UNITE (Union of Needles Trades and Industrial & Textile Employees) demonstrated in front of a Gap outlet store in downtown Toronto in protest of the working conditions at Gap suppliers. At the same time, thousands of miles south of Toronto, Guerrero claimed that "the working conditions here are good for us and good for the Salvadoran workers, but bad for those seeking to keep jobs in the United States. . . . [Without the jobs in the maquilas,] young women would have few other work options apart from prostitution or crime."[20] The story becomes further blurred, however, when Guerrero's comments are compared with an earlier statement by Mandarin owner David Wang in connection with the wages paid to Mandarin workers: "If you really ask me, this is not fair."[21]

Workers' wages make up less than 1% of the retail cost of GAP shirts. Is it any wonder that the company made $310 million in 1994, and paid its CEO Donald Fisher $2 million plus stock options?[22]

From Gap Sourcing Principles & Guidelines: "Workers are free to join associations of their own choosing. Factories must not interfere with workers who wish to lawfully and peacefully associate, organize or bargain collectively. The decision whether or not to do so should be made solely by the workers."[23]

Based on claims of a violation of its sourcing principles and in an effort to ameliorate the situation, The Gap decided to discontinue its relationship with the Mandarin (following in the footsteps of other previous Mandarin contractors such as Eddie Bauer, Liz Claiborne, J. Crew and Casual Corner); however, this action prompted strong cries of concern from labor activists. Contrary to the intentions of The Gap, this resolution was viewed as irresponsible and lacking in accountability.[24] Those concerned with the rights of workers in El Salvador contested The Gap's decision, claiming that this would be the worst possible solution to the problems in a country where 60% of the labor force is unemployed.[25] As a result of other pullouts, the Mandarin has had to cut its work force from 1,300 to 300, and 32 other maquilas have already shut down.[26] "Instead of acting responsibly and seeing that conditions are improved at Mandarin, the Gap is trying to wash its hands and to shift production to other maquilas in other countries with equally bad conditions."[27]

The Gap's original perspective is not without its supporters. Joan Spero, business executive and Secretary of State for Economic Affairs, explains: "A world community that respects democracy and human rights will provide a more hospitable climate for American trade and commerce. . . . Repression fosters instability in the long run and puts investment at greater risk of expropriation and loss."[28] Consider as well the following comments of John Duerden, former president of Reebok:

> As a public company, we have an ethical responsibility to build value for Reebok's shareholders—but not at all possible costs. What we seek is harmony between the profit-maximizing demands of our free-market system and the legitimate needs of our shareholders, and the needs and aspirations of the larger world community in which we are all citizens.[29]

"A VICTORY FOR ALL OF US WHO ARE DETERMINED TO ELIMINATE SWEATSHOPS AT HOME AND ABROAD"[30]

The situation took a drastic turn in December 1995 when Reverend Paul Smith called a meeting between The Gap's senior vice president for sourcing, Stan Raggio, Gap Sourcing Guidelines Director Dottie Hatcher, Gap consultant James Lukaszewski, Reverend David Dyson of the Interfaith Center for Social Responsibility and Charles Kernaghan (NLC). The Gap was feeling pressure from all sides. On the one hand, labor, religious, consumer, solidarity, children's and women's groups were arguing for dramatic changes in working conditions. On the other hand, the National Retailers' Federation contested the complaints and encouraged The Gap to ignore the demonstrations.

The Gap responded to the consumers, issuing a letter stating that it is "committed to ensuring fair and honest treatment of the people who make [its] garments in over 40 countries worldwide,"[31] and, in the words of the NLC, "took a major step forward in accepting direct responsibility for how and under what conditions the products it sells are made."[32] As a result of the meeting, The Gap agreed to implement an independent monitoring system in El Salvador, using the Human Rights Ombudsperson in El Salvador to monitor factories' compliance with its labor guidelines, as long as the Mandarin agreed to rehire the fired union activists.

The NLC and others saw this decision by The Gap as a benchmark against which all other multinational retailers will be measured. Says Kernaghan, "The message is clear: if you make it, you are responsible."[33] Not everyone agrees with Kernaghan's assessment. Larry Martin of the American Apparel Manufacturer's Association believes otherwise: "They've [labor] given us a black eye that most of us don't deserve. Most of us monitor contractors we use here and offshore."[34] One might understand Martin's concerns for the rest of American retailers when one considers the comments of U.S. Labor Secretary Robert Reich: "This raises the question for other big retailers who haven't moved in this direction—why not?"[35]

Most recently, the Salvadoran minister of labor established a government commission to review conditions in the free trade zone and indicated that foreigners would no longer be permitted to monitor the implementation of work codes in El Salvador.[36] This begs the question of why The Gap doesn't simply allow the El Salvadoran government to monitor the work conditions of the plant? Father Blanchard offers the following response:

> *We must consider what are the global consequences for disbanding this effort after less than one month in existence.*
>
> *For example, recently we have learned that the Commerce Department of the United States has informed the international fishing industry that it will not allow the importation of shrimp that are caught with nets that also snare turtles. All fishermen who use nets, and who wish to sell their produce in the United States, must use turtle-free nets. What is more, the industry must allow independent monitoring by outside agencies.*
>
> *Salvadoran law permits the use of turtle-snaring nets. The United States has no authority to control the Salvadoran shrimp industry (one of the largest sources of external revenue for the Government of El Salvador). It has complete authority to determine the conditions under which shrimp may be imported into the United States.*
>
> *The question remains: why not simply rely on the government of El Salvador to supervise compliance, especially given the importance of the shrimping industry in this country.*
>
> *The answer lies in norms for the modernization of government and general guidelines for development being promulgated by the World Bank, the InterAmerican Development Bank and other loaning agencies. Governments that contribute to international loaning agencies insist on down-scaling government and allowing compliance to be monitored by the private sector in alliance with independent monitoring groups. In this scheme, Congress passes the law defining the kinds of nets that are required in the shrimp industry; people concerned about the welfare of turtles contribute to organizations like the International Wildlife Fund to guarantee that these laws are enforced; organizations like the International Wildlife Fund in turn collaborate with the fishing industry to guarantee that the norms are followed. When all is said and done, if nobody cares about the welfare of turtles, the laws are not passed and compliance never takes place.*
>
> *What is good for turtles is also good for human beings.*[37]

ENDNOTES

1. Department of Labor, "No Sweat Initiative: Fact Sheet," http://www.dol.gov/dol/esa/public/forum/ fact.htm.
2. Susan Chandler, "Look Who's Sweating Now," *Business Week,* October 16, 1995, pp. 96, 98. (In March, 1996, 72 Thai workers at the El Monte sweatshop were awarded more than $1 million in back wages in connection with the scandal. George White, "Sweatshop Workers to Receive $1 Million," *L.A. Times,* March 8, 1996, p. B1.)
3. *Ibid.,* p. 98. The study also found that 73% of the garment makers had improper payroll records, 68% did not pay appropriate overtime wages, and 51% paid less than the minimum wage.

4.   *Ibid.,* pp. 96, 98. Self-inspection may also be necessitated by the drop in the number of inspectors assigned by the Labor Department to investigate wage and hour law violations. Since 1989, that number has fallen from almost 1,000 to less than 800. Also see Andrea Adelson, "Look Who's Minding the Shop," *New York Times,* May 4, 1996, p. 17.

5.   Stuart Silverstein, "Self-Regulatory Group to Police Clothes Makers' Work Conditions," *L.A. Times,* June 20, 1995, p. D1.

6.   http://www.dol.gov/dol.opa/public.forum/kearnery.txt.

7.   Douglass Cassel, "Human Rights Violations: What's a Poor Multinational to Do?" Remarks before the Chicago Council on Foreign Relations, February 7, 1996, p. 10.

8.   "Gifford Counters Sweatshop Charges," May 2, 1996, p. 40 (Reuters).

9.   Michael McGuire, "Lost in the Junkyard of Abandoned U.S. Policy," *Chicago Tribune,* April 7, 1996, sec. 2, pp. 1, 4.

10. Louis Emmerij, *Social Tensions and Social Reform: Toward Balanced Economic, Financial and Social Policies in Latin America* (Washington, DC: Social Agenda Policy Group, Inter-American Development Bank, 1995), p. 7, *cited in* letter from Fr. David Blanchard, pastor, O. L. Lourdes in Calle Real Epiphany Cooperative Association, to Aaron Cramer, Director, Business and Human Rights Program, Business for Social Responsibility, February 6, 1996, p. 2.

11. Bob Herbert, "Sweatshop Beneficiaries," *New York Times,* July 24, 1995, p. A13.

12. Blanchard letter, p. 8, citing research by Fr. Ignacio Martin-Baro, a social psychologist and one of the six Jesuit priests slain in November 1989 at the University of Central America in El Salvador. The war has additional effects on the people of El Salvador, even if they were not alive at the time of the recent conflicts. For example, one American student recorded in his journal, "9/3/95: One of the little children handed me an old bullet that he must have found. I imagine there must be many bullets out there in the field. I just wanted the day to be over, for me and for this little boy." Student manuscript in possession of the author.

13. First-hand experience of the author, February 1996.

14. Student manuscripts in possession of the author (June 1996).

15. Blanchard letter, p. 5.

16. Terry Kelly, "The GAP: Brutality Behind the Facade," part of *World History Archives,* located at http://neal.ctstateu.edu/history/world.history/archives/canada/canada002.html, p. 1 (1995).

17. Blanchard letter, p. 6.

18. Kelly, "The GAP," p. 2.

19. Mary Scott, "Going After The Gap," *Business Ethics,* May/June 1996, p. 20.

20. Letta Taylor, "Salvadoran Clothing Factory Accused of Worker Abuse," *Roanoke Times and World News* (December 31, 1995), p. D4.

21. Bob Herbert, "Not a Living Wage," *New York Times,* October 9, 1995, p. A17.

22. Kelly, "The GAP," p. 2.

23. Gap, Inc., *Code of Vendor Conduct,* sec. VIII, 1996. See also Christian Task Force on Central America, "Urgent Action El Salvador," http://www.grannyg.bc.ca/CTFCA/act1295a.html (November 29, 1995), p. 1.

24. Letta Taylor, "Salvadoran Clothing Factory Accused of Worker Abuse," *Roanoke Times and World News,* December 31, 1995, p. D4; Joanna Ramey, "Worker Rights Groups Slam Gap for Ending El Salvador Contract," *Women's Wear Daily,* November 30, 1995.

25. Letta Taylor, "Salvadoran Clothing Factory," p. D4.

26. *Ibid.*

27. Christian Task Force on Central America (CTFCA), "Urgent Action El Salvador," http://www.grannyg.bc.ca/CTFCA/act1295a.html, November 29, 1995, p. 2.

28. Quoted by Douglass Cassel, "Human Rights Violations: What's a Poor Multinational to Do?" remarks before the Chicago Council on Foreign Relations, February 7, 1996, p. 9.

29. Quoted by Cassel, "Human Rights Violations," p. 9.

30. Words of Jay Mazur, UNITE President, in National Labor Committee, "Gap Victory," http://www.alfea.it/coordns/work/industria/gap-victory.html, February 1996.

31. CTFCA, "Urgent Action El Salvador."

32. National Labor Committee, "Gap Agrees to Independent Monitoring Setting New Standard for the Entire Industry," http://www.alfea.it/coordns/work/industria/gap.agrees.html.

33. Quoted in Industrial Workers of the World, "Unions Win Victory in Gap Battle," *The Industrial Worker,* http://fletcher.iww.org/~iw/feb/stories/gap.html, February 1995. See also Mary Scott, "Going After The Gap," *Business Ethics,* May/June 1996, pp. 18–20 ("What the Gap has done is historic. It will be a good pilot project to see if third party monitoring works," said Conrad McKerron, social research director of Progressive Asset Management).

34. Quoted in Paula Green, "The Gap Signs Accord on Conduct Code with U.S. Labor Group," *The News-Times,* http://www.newstimes.com/archives/dec2295/bzf.htm, December 22, 1995, p. 2.

35. Quoted in United Auto Workers, "The Gap Agrees to Improve Conditions in Overseas Plants," *Frontlines,* http://www.uaw.org/solidarity/9601/frontlinesjan96.html, January 1996, p. 1.

36. Memo from Fr. David Blanchard to Mark Annerm, Coordinator, Independent Monitoring Team, April 19, 1996, p. 4.

37. *Ibid.,* pp. 5–6.

BUSINESS AND CHILD LABOR

A Management Primer

—SHELL OIL CO.

As discussed earlier in this chapter, child labor is a complex problem affecting all regions of the world. Though closely linked to poverty, its roots often lie in a complicated interaction of social, economic, cultural and political factors. Although opinions differ as to how best to eliminate child labor, there is a strong consensus that the worst forms of child labor should be tackled as a matter of urgency. At first glance, child labor may seem a strange concern for Shell Oil, one of the world's largest energy multinationals. However, the commitment to support fundamental human rights included in the Shell General Business Principles means that Shell strives not to exploit children in any of its activities, either directly or indirectly. This requires a sound understanding of where the problem is most likely to be encountered, how it can be recognized and how it is best tackled. This primer—one of a series from Shell that addresses human rights related issues— does not offer easy answers to the problem of child labor. It does, however, provide the information and references necessary to gain a practical understanding of the issue.

SECTION 1. THE NATURE AND CAUSES OF CHILD LABOR
1.1 What is child labor?

The first problem facing anyone with an interest in child labor is the difficulty in defining what it means. When is a child sufficiently old to start work? At what point does acceptable "work" become exploitative "labor"? To some extent the answers to these questions will vary from culture to culture and country to country.

Undertaking a few hours of work per week on a voluntary basis can be beneficial to children. Such work is not detrimental to health or education and may indeed help the child to increase its social skills, benefit from informal education, learn a useful trade, and, of course, earn money. Yet millions of children worldwide are obliged to undertake work of a very different nature. "Child labor" is used to refer to a type and intensity of work that hampers children's access to education, damages their health, their development within their families and deprives them of their childhood or their self-respect. However, where the line between "work" and "labor" falls, remains a matter of considerable debate.

The most widely recognized, though not universally accepted, definition is provided by the International Labor Organization (ILO) Minimum Age Convention (138). This defines the minimum ages for employment as follows: at 13 years, children may undertake light work, ie work which will not prejudice a child's attendance at school. At 15 years, regular work is permissible, whilst at 18 years, or the age of majority if earlier, the child becomes an adult and so able to undertake any form of work.

In countries "whose economy and educational facilities are insufficiently developed," lower age limits apply on a transitional basis. Children of 12 years are eligible for light work, and children of 14 years are able to undertake regular work. Under certain circumstances, the age limit for hazardous work may also be reduced to 16 years.

(Note: the youngest Shell company employee is 15 years old and works part-time in Europe.)

1.2 How big is the problem today?

Child labor is known to be a worldwide problem today. It is however, difficult to determine the exact magnitude of the problem due to the lack of accurate, detailed statistics. The ILO estimates that over 250 million children between the ages of 5 and 14 years are currently engaged in some form of paid work, of whom around 120 million are thought to be working full time.[1] In addition, UNICEF suggests that there are a further 150 million children who undertake regular, but

FIGURE 1

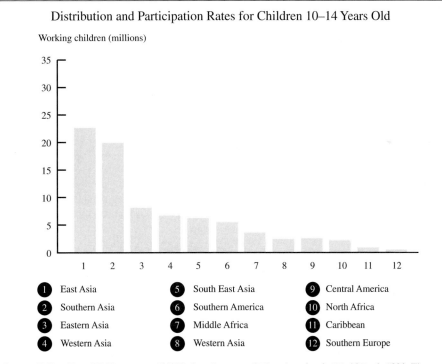

Distribution and Participation Rates for Children 10–14 Years Old

Working children (millions)

1 East Asia	5 South East Asia	9 Central America
2 Southern Asia	6 Southern America	10 North Africa
3 Eastern Asia	7 Middle Africa	11 Caribbean
4 Western Asia	8 Western Asia	12 Southern Europe

Source: Fallon, P. and Z. Tzannatos, *Child Labor: Issues and Directions for the World Bank,* 1998, The International Bank for Reconstruction and Development/World Bank: Washington, DC.

---

[1]McIntosh, M., *et al., Corporate Citizenship; successful strategies for responsible companies.* 1st ed. 1998, London: Financial Times; Pitman Publishing.

unpaid work such as helping with domestic activities. This suggests that worldwide, as many as 400 million children may be involved in some form of regular work or labor.

The largest number of child workers is found in Asia, which accounts for over 60% of the world's total child workforce. However, it is believed that this number has largely stabilized, and may be reducing. Increased income, the spread of education and decreasing family size are credited with this change.[2]

In Africa however, the converse situation is found. Around 40% of all African children, between the ages of 5 to 14 years are thought to be engaged in some form of work.[3] Economic crises, combined with political instability, have led to the breakdown of essential social services, rapid population growth, reduced standards of living, widespread displacement and the break up of families. The impact of the HIV/AIDS pandemic has exacerbated the problem. Together, these factors have encouraged a growth in child labor.

Although Africa and Asia together account for a very substantial proportion of all child labor, the problem is not confined to certain continents, nor is it confined to countries with a low level of industrialization. It is estimated, for example, that in Europe some 89,000 children in the 10 to 14 age range[4] are engaged in work. Eastern Europe has been particularly badly affected in recent years as an upsurge in child labor has occurred in the wake of the transition to a market economy.[5] There may also be large differences between countries in the same region.

So, it can be seen that although the challenge of child labor is at its greatest within less industrialized countries, the issue is truly global and affects substantial numbers of individuals.

1.3 Are all forms of child labor the same?

Child labor occurs in many different guises and is more prevalent in some sectors than in others. Children are most commonly found working on farms, in households and in the informal manufacturing sector, comprising small factories, workshops, foundries etc.[6] These economic sectors are relatively inaccessible to protective legislation and so the children working within them are at risk of exploitation.

DEBT BONDAGE

In this modern form of slavery a child's labor is provided as security against a loan made to the parents, often to finance an event required by social or religious tradition. The child must work for the lender until the debt is paid off. The lender may add to the debt an inflated charge for feeding the child, thereby ensuring that the debt cannot be repaid. The burden of the debt can be passed from one generation to the next, whilst ownership of the debt may also be traded.

---

[2]International Labor Office and U.N.C. Fund. *Strategies for Eliminating Child Labor: prevention, removal and rehabilitation, in International Conference on Child Labor.* 1997 Oslo.

[3]International Labor Organization, *Facts and Figures on Child Labor,* 1999, ILO: Geneva.

[4]Fallon, P. and Z. Tzannatos, *Child Labor: Issues and Directions for the World Bank,* 1998, The International Bank for Reconstruction and Development/World Bank: Washington DC.

[5]International Labor Organization, *Facts and Figures on Child Labor,* 1999, ILO: Geneva.

[6]International Labor Office and U.N.C. Fund, *Strategies for Eliminating Child Labor: prevention, removal and rehabilitation, in International Conference on Child Labor.* 1997 Oslo.

However, some forms of child labor are even more hazardous. The ILO has recently defined the "worst forms" of child labor as being: slavery, prostitution, involvement with illegal activities such as drug trafficking and other work likely to jeopardize the health, safety or morals of children.[7] Again the problem is global. Child prostitution, for example, is a problem in many parts of the world, including Europe and North America, where at least 100,000 children are thought to be involved.[8] Children have been forced into work in areas as diverse as South American sugar cane plantations and South East Asian railways,[9] whilst others face the potential of a life of slavery arising from debt bondage.

Not all children labor in physically or mentally detrimental conditions, however. Some children work on a voluntary basis, possibly in their home environment, under the protection of one or both parents. The hours that the children work may interfere with their education, but their physical well being is not at great risk. However, if the working hours are too long, the child too young or the type of work undertaken is harmful, the benefits gained are likely to be outweighed by the long term damage caused to the child's physical and mental development. The key lies in an appropriate balance between work and education.

1.4 Why include children in the workforce?

Children are sought after as workers for a variety of reasons. Lower cost is certainly a key element; one survey found that children received just one sixth of the minimum national wage.[10] However, children are also in demand because they are easily controlled, quick to learn basic skills, often willing to work long hours, non-unionized, uneducated and unable to complain to the authorities.

The inclusion of children in the workforce has often been justified on the grounds that their "nimble fingers" are able to undertake tasks that adults are unable to complete. This has been a popular and ostensibly logical argument for tasks such as rug-making and bead-threading. However, it has now been largely discredited; the finest rugs with the smallest knots are made by skilled adult workers, and not by inexperienced children.

1.5 What are the causes of child labor?

The causes of, and attitudes towards, child labor are complex and are usually rooted in cultural, social and economic structures and traditions. A number of particularly important factors can be identified, as follows:

Poverty   The World Bank has shown that there is a close correlation between Gross Domestic Product (GDP) per capita and the incidence of child labor. In countries with a GDP per capita of $200, children make up over 10% of the total workforce. At $500 per capita the proportion falls to 5%. At $5,000 per capita the figure falls to around 2.5%. This relationship is confirmed by the ILO which has shown that the more elementary the nature of the economic activity undertaken within the country, the larger the relative size of the child

---

[7]International Labor Organization, *Proposed Convention on the prohibition and immediate elimination of the worst forms of child labor,—ILO 87th Session Report IV(1),* 1999, ILO.

[8]UNICEF, *The State of the World's Children,* 1997, Oxford University Press: Oxford.

[9]Brazier, C., *Respite—and respect, in New Internationalist. 1997.* pp. 7–10.

[10]Ashagrie, K., *Statistics on Working Children and Hazardous Child Labor,* 1998, Editor. International Labor Office: Geneva.

labor force. Less industrialized countries tend to have a higher demand for agricultural and less skilled workers than do industrialized countries, and this demand may be readily met by the use of child laborers.

The relationship between poverty and child labor is not, however, a simple one. Issues such as income distribution, fertility, education, malnutrition, the status of women, together with the structure and framework of the economy can all affect the likely incidence of child labor. However, whilst the economic status of a country may create a climate that encourages child labor, basic human need may provide the catalyst that causes families to send their children to work. According to the World Bank, more than 1.3 billion people currently live on less than $1 per day—the internationally defined poverty line.[11] It is estimated that children contribute 20 to 25% of the income of the families within this group.[12] Given that in these families most of the family income is spent on basics such as food and shelter, it can be seen that here the child's contribution is a necessity, not a luxury.

Absence of Primary Schooling   The absence of universal, free, compulsory and non-discriminatory primary schooling deprives children of their best opportunity to avoid the risks and deprivation associated with child labor. Primary education ensures that children are physically removed from the work place for at least a few hours a day and provides an opportunity for the child to gain the skills and knowledge needed to break away from the cycle of poverty.

Education can help overcome the tendency for poor regions to be centers of child labor. The State of Kerala in India, for example, combines a very low level of income with a low level of child labor. This is widely attributed to its provision of almost universal primary education. However, provision of primary education alone does not guarantee a reduction in child labor. The local social climate must also encourage families to take advantage of education where it is available.

Social Structures and Attitudes   Social attitudes can be a significant factor influencing the prevalence and nature of child labor. In almost all societies, certain groups suffer discrimination with some children being treated more favorably than others. In some cases this can lead to the favored child receiving an education, whilst the less favored child enters the workforce. In many societies, it is believed that time spent on the education of girls and children from poor or low status/low caste families is wasted. A working life, whether paid or unpaid, is seen as the appropriate future for such children from a very early age. The attitude of some employers, who stand to benefit from such low cost labor, helps to reinforce this cycle of deprivation. Where such attitudes are deeply ingrained, they may present a significant obstacle to those seeking to eradicate child labor.

It can be seen therefore that there exists a range of factors that combine to provide both the motivation and the opportunity for child labor.

---

[11]International Labor Office and U.N.C. Fund. *Strategies for Eliminating Child Labor: prevention, removal and rehabilitation, in International Conference on Child Labor.* 1997, Oslo.
[12]International Labor Organization, *IPEC: finding out about child labor,* 1998, ILO.

1.6 What are the consequences?

Excessive levels of work undertaken by children can have detrimental consequences for the children themselves, for their parents and for the communities in which they live.

For children the consequences may be broken down into three categories: educational, physical and psychological. The developmental problems and want of future opportunity that accompany the lack of a basic education have already been highlighted.

WORKING WITH THE FAMILY

Save the Children Fund is active in a number of programs in Sialkot, Pakistan, an area best known as a world center for football stitching. Following investigative work that revealed a high incidence of child labor, SCF is now working with UNICEF and two local NGOs, Bunyard and Bait u Mal, to establish Village Education & Action Centers. These provide non-formal education and literacy training. SCF is also working, in the face of some cultural resistance, to help women continue in paid employment, thereby securing the family's earnings and reducing reliance upon child wages.

Source: International Organization of Employers.

Physical problems can arise from working in often cramped and unsafe or unsanitary conditions. Whilst impaired growth is suffered by many child laborers, additional, more specific problems may also be faced depending on the work carried out. Respiratory diseases, for example, are common where the work place is filled with particles, as in the rug making or metal polishing trades. Severe cuts, even loss of a limb, may be suffered from using knives, machetes or unguarded cutting equipment. Sight can be irreparably damaged by spending years working in poorly lit conditions.

Extended periods spent working in such poor conditions can in themselves cause long-term emotional and psychological problems. However, it is those children at risk of sexual or deliberate psychological abuse that may experience the greatest psychological damage. Children in domestic service, children working away from home and children in the sex trade, are most likely to suffer the long-term trauma of such abuse.

Child labor has consequences for adults too. There is an emotional cost when children work far from home, as the bond between child and parent can become strained or irreparably broken. There is also a potential financial cost. The availability of a very cheap labor force may suppress local wages and may ultimately contribute significantly to adult unemployment. Ironically, this can lead to an ever greater reliance upon child income, possibly even causing children to be removed from school, thereby creating a vicious circle.

1.7 Do the governments of countries with a high level of child labor care about what is happening?

Many such governments are indeed concerned about the issue, recognizing the long-term detrimental impact of child labor on the country as a whole. However, the countries where the problem is most prevalent are often the poorest, and thus limited in what they can do by the resources available to them.

However, it is not simply a question of funding. Authorities working to overcome child labor may also face resistance from affected communities, where children are traditionally seen as an acceptable component of the workforce, and from those with a vested interest, such as the owners of the factories and farms where the children work. Corruption within local law enforcement agencies can also hinder the effective application of any policy that might be introduced.

Furthermore, in the short term, the economic case against child labor may not be completely clear cut. As countries compete for global investment on the basis of labor costs, the inclusion of low-waged children within the workforce may seem to represent an efficient means by which to find a place on the international economic stage. This issue is discussed further in section 2.2.

SECTION 2. INTERNATIONAL ISSUES IN CHILD LABOR
2.1 The legal framework

The first point of regulation for child labor is the national legislation of each country. Although specific requirements may vary significantly, almost all countries have laws that define the minimum age at which children may enter the workforce, together with schooling regulations, work place regulations and more.

However, child labor is also the subject of a variety of international conventions and recommendations, foremost amongst which are the instruments of the International Labor Organization (ILO).

OLD ENOUGH TO WORK?

The age at which it is deemed acceptable for children to undertake certain tasks varies from country to country. In 1991, age limits included the following:

12 years: Egypt—seasonal work, Benin—light agriculture, Senegal—seasonal work

13 years: Denmark—shop assistant, Tunisia & Switzerland—light non-industrial

14 years: Cyprus—construction, India—explosives, Sri Lanka—street trades

15 years: Thailand—bars, Italy—machinery in motion, Dominican Republic—mining

Source: *Conditions of Work Digest* Vol 10, No1, 1991, Part II, Annex; quoted UNICEF, *The State of the World's Children* 1997.

International Labor Organization   The ILO was founded in 1919 and in its first year of operation set itself the goal of abolishing child labor, adopting the "Minimum Age (Industry) Convention" which prohibited work by children under 14 years. Since then, 20 Conventions and 10 Recommendations have been endorsed by ILO member states,[13] the most significant of which is the Minimum Age Convention, 1973 (138) and its associated Recommendation, 1973 (146). The key requirements of ILO 138 on member states are to:

- Pursue a national policy to abolish child labor.

- Set a minimum age for admission to work (including both work for another person or for himself/herself).

- Gradually increase the lower age limit on work to a level consistent with the fullest physical and mental development of young people.

At the time of writing, Convention 138 has been ratified by 84 countries. This includes four Asian countries.[14]

In June 1999, the ILO revisited the issue of child labor. At the 87th Session of the ILO, a new Convention concerning the prohibition and immediate elimination of the worst forms of child labor, together with an associated Recommendation, were unanimously adopted. Convention 182, "Worst Forms of Child Labor Convention 1999," addresses the extremes of child labor such as slavery, debt bondage and child prostitution and calls for "immediate and comprehensive action for the elimination of the worst forms of child labor."[15]

United Nations   Although the ILO Conventions offer the most direct and comprehensive commitment to the elimination of child labor, other pertinent documents include the United Nations Universal Declaration of Human Rights and its two underlying Covenants. The first, the International Covenant on Economic, Social and Cultural Rights, calls for compulsory free primary education, whilst the second, the International Covenant on Civil and Political Rights, prohibits slavery, servitude and forced labor and calls for the protection of minors. Further details about these instruments can be found in the Primer "Business and Human Rights."

The United Nations Convention on the Rights of the Child is of special relevance to child labor. This enshrines for children rights such as primary education, freedom of association, freedom of thought, rest and leisure, participation in cultural and artistic life. It seeks to protect children from any threat that might be hazardous to them or be harmful to their health, education, physical, mental, spiritual or social development. It expressly addresses child labor in Article 32, calling for countries to: define a minimum age for admission to employment; regulate the hours and conditions of employment and apply sanctions to ensure enforcement of

[13]Bureau of Statistics & International Program on the Elimination of Child Labor, *Methodological Child Labor Surveys and Statistics,* 1997, International Labor Organization: Bureau of Statistics: Geneva.
[14]International Organization of Employers, *Employers' Handbook on Child Labor: A guide for taking action.* 1998, Geneva: IOE with Bureau for Employers' Activities and International Programme on the Elimination of Child Labour.
[15]International Labor Organization, *Proposed Convention on the prohibition and immediate elimination of the worst forms of child labor.—ILO 87th Session Report IV(1),* 1999, ILO.

A CENTURY OF CHANGE

Key legislative landmarks in the international reappraisal of child labor include:

1919:   ILO Minimum Age (Industry) Convention No. 5: Establishes 14 years as the minimum age for industrial work

1930:   ILO Forced Labor Convention No. 29: Provides for the suppression of forced labor in all its forms

1966:   UN International Covenant on Civil and Political Rights: Article 8 confirms that slavery and forced labor are unacceptable

1966:   UN International Covenant on Economic, Social & Cultural Rights: Article 10 seeks protection for young people from economic or other exploitation and requires each State to set a minimum employment age

1973:   ILO Minimum Age Convention No. 138: Introduces an obligation to ensure that children are not employed at an age younger than that for completion of compulsory schooling. Associated Recommendation 146 calls for countries to raise minimum employment to 16 years.

1989:   UN Convention on the Rights of the Child: Affirms the child's right to the full range of civil, political, social, economic and cultural rights, including protection from work that is counter to the child's interests.

1999:   ILO Worst forms of child labor Convention No. 182: addresses the extremes of child labor calling for their immediate elimination

employment legislation. The Convention on the Rights of the Child has been ratified by all countries of the United Nations, except the United States of America and Somalia.[16]

International Programme on the Elimination of Child Labour   Whilst legal instruments help to define internationally acceptable standards of behavior with regard to working children, the complexity of the problem makes achieving these standards very difficult, particularly for resource limited countries. In 1992, the ILO launched the International Programme on the Elimination of Child Labour (IPEC). At an international level, IPEC seeks

---

[16]International Organization of Employers, *Employers' Handbook on Child Labor: A guide for taking action.* 1998, Geneva: IOE with Bureau for Employers' Activities and International Programme on the Elimination of Child Labour.

to contribute to a worldwide movement against child labor by providing information and support. At a national and a community level, IPEC helps to raise awareness and understanding of the issue, and to find appropriate ways of eliminating the worst forms of child labor, taking into account the social and economic circumstances of the country in question. Funded by 18 donor countries, IPEC now has projects in over 50 countries worldwide.[17]

WORKING CHILDREN SPEAK OUT

International meetings have been organized to enable working children to voice their concerns. For example, in 1998, representatives of the Movements of Working Children and youth of Africa, Latin America and Asia met in Dakar (Senegal). The Dakar Declaration presents the decisions taken by the International Movement of Working Children.

The Dakar Declaration

1. We will ask the ILO to give us a chance to speak during its upcoming conference in Geneva so we can express ourselves on the convention on the "intolerable forms of child labor."
2. We are against prostitution, slavery and drug trafficking by children. These are CRIMES and not WORK.
3. The decision makers should distinguish between work and crime.
4. We are fighting every day against hazardous work and against exploitation of child work.
5. We are also fighting for the improvement of life and working conditions of all children in the world.
6. We want all the children in the world to have, one day, the right to make a choice between working and not working.
7. Work should be in accordance with the capacity and development of each and every child and not depend on his/her age.

The nature of the projects varies from country to country according to specific needs.

2.2 Globalization and child labor

The increasing globalization of the world economy brings both benefits and drawbacks for working children. Foreign direct investment (FDI) by major companies can help create jobs, increase export earnings and ultimately alleviate the poverty that is so closely linked with child labor. However, countries trying to encourage FDI may seek to gain competitive advantage over rival investment locations by offering the lowest possible cost of production. This may involve providing a cheap and compliant workforce, an increasing proportion of which may be children.

---

[17]International Labor Office, *Operational aspects of the International Programme on the Elimination of Child Labour (IPEC), in Committee on Technical Cooperation,* ILO. 1998.

THE HARKIN BILL—A CASE OF
UNINTENDED CONSEQUENCES?

In 1992 Tom Harkin, a U.S. senator sponsored by a major trade
union, put forward the "Child Labor Deterrence Act" which sought
to prohibit the import of goods manufactured wholly or in part by
children under the age of 15.[18] During 1993, although the Act was
still only a discussion document, over 50,000 Bangladeshi children
were dismissed from their jobs,[19] by employers anxious not to lose
lucrative export contracts. UNICEF and Save the Children Fund
suggest that the majority of these children moved into less well paid
and more hazardous occupations,[20] although some sources suggest
that around 8,000 of them may subsequently have enlisted in
school.[21] The situation was particularly difficult for girls, who comprised around 80% of the sacked workforce. The Harkin Bill deprived them of the opportunity to earn money working with their
mothers within the comparative protection of the factory gates, and
the social mores prevalent in Bangladesh at that time denied them
the possibility of education.

The Harkin Bill concerned unilateral action by one rich country
and so is not truly analogous to the introduction of a social clause on
a multilateral basis. Yet it does provide some indication of the unforeseen consequences that could arise from blanket international
action that is insensitive to local needs. Whether the original intention of the Harkin Bill was humanitarian or protectionist, the consequence for children seems to have been predominantly negative.

Although only about 5% of the world's child labor force is thought to be engaged in
export sector industries,[22] it is nevertheless a significant and visible problem. This has
prompted discussion in the context of international trade negotiations, concerning the introduction of a "social clause" to international trade agreements. Such a clause would result in the imposition of penalties on countries or companies failing to observe core labor
standards, such as ILO Convention 138.

Proponents of a linkage between trade and labor standards include trade unions, some
NGOs and a range of governments, primarily from developed countries. Noting that "as the
global free trade agenda becomes a reality, sustainable and equitable development risks being undermined in the name of cut-throat competition," they see introduction of some form

[18]Durai, J., *Helping business to help stop child labor,* 1996, Anti-Slavery International: London.
[19]Alam, S., *Thank you, Mr Harkin, sir!* in *New Internationalist.* 1997.
[20]Save the Children Fund, *A labor of necessity,* in *www.oneworld.org/textver/scf/childlab/feature.htm.* 1998.
[21]Alam, S., *Thank you, Mr Harkin, Sir!* in *New Internationalist.* 1997.
[22]UNICEF, *The State of the World's Children,* 1997, Oxford University Press: Oxford.

of punitive measure, such as trade sanctions, as essential.[23] This would ensure that one country does not "undermine another by abusing basic {labor} standards." Those against such a linkage, including the International Organization of Employers and the governments of many developing countries, see it as potentially protectionist, and observe that enforcement could draw the World Trade Organization into matters of domestic governance. Furthermore, those in favor of self-regulation point towards the negative consequences that a blanket ban on child labor could have for developing countries in general and for the child workforce in particular.

The case for and against attempts to eradicate child labor through compulsory means remains unclear, as the example of the Harkin Bill illustrates (see box). However, despite the divergence of views concerning appropriate means, there exists a consensus that the international community must act swiftly and effectively to address the worst excesses of child labor wherever they are found.

SECTION 3. CHILD LABOR—THE ROLE OF BUSINESS

3.1 Is child labor really an issue for businesses?

Child labor is an ethical issue for the global community, including businesses. The primary responsibility for eliminating child labor may be seen as lying with national governments and international bodies such as the ILO and UN. However, as the discussion on globalization has shown, international businesses are one element in a complex set of factors that can result in, or conversely help reduce, child labor. As part of the global community therefore, businesses have an obligation to take responsibility for the influence that they wield.

A ROLE FOR TRADE ASSOCIATIONS

A number of regional and national trade associations and employer bodies have begun work to help member companies tackle the problem of child labor. The Employer's Confederation of the Philippines, for example, started an awareness raising program in April 1997. This seeks to provide member companies both with practical guidance on how to eliminate child labor and with a voice in the national debate on the issue. In addition it is undertaking research to examine the linkages between procurement and subcontracting policies and child labor.

However, businesses should be aware of child labor for commercial reasons too. Increasingly the public is voicing concerns regarding the issue and in today's information based societies, such concerns can be aired freely and spread rapidly. Any company found to be involved with child labor risks damage to its reputation. Whilst this may be of secondary concern to the needs of abused children, it is still an important consideration.

---

[23]ICFTU, *No time to play: child workers in the global economy,* 1996, 16th ICFTU World Congress.

3.2 So how do companies tackle the problem?

There are three main types of approach used by companies to address the issue of child labor.

- Labels which seek to ensure that a single product or product type is free from child labor.

- Codes of conduct and supplier guidelines, usually tailored to the specific issues faced by that company.

- A pan-industrial standard for social responsibility, including child labor, to which a company might seek to adhere.

Labelling   A number of products now carry a label indicating to consumers that the product was manufactured under fair and equitable conditions and without the use of child labor. The Brazilian Footwear Industry's Pro-Child Corporate Educational Institute, for example, has developed a corporate seal to endorse child labor free products, whilst the Rugmark Foundation's logo is now internationally trade-marked for use to indicate child labor free hand-knotted rugs and carpets.

Critics suggest that labelling is generally too simplistic an approach by which to combat such a complex problem. It is extremely hard to guarantee that a product has been manufactured without the use of child labor, and as has already been discussed, removing children from the workforce entirely may not be a suitable solution. However, such labels can bring benefits when they are supported by a rigorously applied audit process.

THE RUGMARK

Rugmark is a voluntary scheme that seeks to control the worst excesses of the rug and carpet industry by encouraging loom owners to register their looms and hence qualify to apply the rugmark to their product. Loom owners must:

- Commit to working without illegal child labor.
- Provide a comprehensive list of all looms in their company.
- Pay at least the minimum wage.
- Have at least one third of all looms inspected before acceptance within the scheme.
- Agree to unannounced inspections.
- Contribute 1% of export revenue into a central fund to rehabilitate and support exploited children.

Once accepted each carpet is labelled with a unique reference, enabling the ultimate buyer to contact the Rugmark Foundation and verify the exporter, the type of carpet and the loom on which it was made.

Codes of Conduct and Supplier Guidelines   These have proved to be a popular approach to the problem, with many companies having introduced their own guidelines. Some NGOs have developed, or provide advice on developing, such codes.

CODE OF CONDUCT IN ACTION

Clothing company C&A has developed a supplier code of conduct which expressly states that exploitation of child labor is "absolutely unacceptable." The code is a legally binding requirement for each merchandise order, and is enforced by SOCAM, an independent audit company originally established by C&A. SOCAM auditors are required to have a detailed understanding both of the garment industry and of the region or country in which they will operate; often they will be of the local nationality. Audits are unannounced; detected infringements of the code lead to varying types of sanction from a warning, through contract suspension, to removal from the company's suppliers list.

Source: C&A.

In the absence of external monitoring and verification, codes of conduct may be seen as, and indeed prove to be, little more than rhetoric and may even prove counterproductive if introduced without sufficient thought. However, codes of conduct can be useful when introduced by companies with a detailed understanding of the complexities of child labor.

Standards   The Council for Economic Priorities, a U.S. based organization, has developed a new standard called Social Accountability (SA) 8000. Produced in consultation with a variety of blue chip multinationals, primarily in the retail sector, the standard provides guidelines for company performance regarding a wide range of human rights issues, including child labor. SA8000 is significant as it provides the first serious move towards a pan-industrial standard. However, there remain significant concerns as to how useful a prescriptive standard can be in tackling the complexities of problems such as child labor.

Each of the three approaches offers a different mechanism by which to avoid the exploitation of children in the workforce. The common characteristic of the three is that to be fully effective, each approach also requires some form of audit activity. This in itself presents a problem, as the next section illustrates.

3.3 Can auditors really ensure that children are not involved in the supply chain?

No, not completely. Establishing whether child labor exists at a given site may be difficult. Verifying performance is a key part of the process, but is much more complicated than it sounds. Problems faced by auditors include:

- Physical violence against auditors, particularly where the audit has revealed problems.

- Use of false identity cards for underage workers.

- Complex "lay off" arrangements, in which the source of the product becomes almost untraceable.

- Inaccessibility of the site to be audited.

- Complex company structures, enabling a legitimate company to pass off a nonlegitimate supply source, such as a prison, as one of its departments.

- Gender issues; in many cultures, the auditor must be the same gender as the interviewee.

- Linguistic problems; arising through mistranslation or from the use of staff speaking regional dialects, or other languages.

3.4 What lessons can be learned from the experience of other companies?

Perhaps the most important lesson is the need to recognize the complexity of the problem, together with the potential ramifications of any action taken. Experience illustrates that different groups in society may perceive the problem of child labor in very different ways. Indeed, sometimes these views may be in conflict and this could present a company with a dilemma.

OVERCOMING THE AUDIT CHALLENGE

Some of the approaches used to overcome problems faced whilst auditing supplier codes of conduct include:

- Use of UNICEF growth charts to assess a child's age.
- Questioning children on their work at school, rather than asking their age.
- Use of illustrated booklets to explain health and safety issues to illiterate workers.
- Inclusion of local NGOs in the audit process.

Take for example a company that prioritizes the views of its customer stakeholders. Where customers demand that the company "stop using child labor," as has happened with some retailers, the company might concentrate on ensuring that children are not employed at its own or its suppliers' premises. The company might see such a move as necessary in order to avoid any association with child labor, thereby preserving its reputation with customers. The risk with such a response is that simply removing children from the workforce, and therefore taking away their income, may have predominantly negative consequences, possibly leading to the child becoming involved in more hazardous work than before.

A company which focuses on the needs of its supplier and local community stakeholders might well have a different response to the same problem. Rather than seeking to eliminate all work undertaken by children, it might choose instead to change the nature of the work, in line with ILO recommendations and ideally in consultation with a local community-based organization. The risk with this approach is that although the children may benefit from restructured working hours and conditions, the company may be exposed to allegations of exploitation from quarters where the complexity of the child labor issue is not understood.

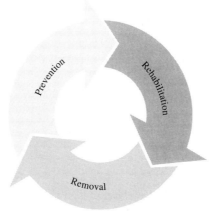

Eliminating child labor demands an integrated approach

. . . Any response to child labor must be clearly thought through, with the views of many different stakeholders being taken into account. Wherever the role of children is to be changed, whether it is to be eliminated, or reduced in scope, the benefit to both company and child will be greatest if the changes are introduced in a controlled fashion, possibly over a period of time. Whatever the response, good communication with all affected stakeholders will be essential.

STANDARDS OF ENGAGEMENT

Authenticity/Inspiration/Commitment/Honesty

—ADIDAS-SALOMON

As mentioned earlier in this text, many firms have created and published codes of conduct and other like statements subsequent to targeted attacks by activists. adidas-Salomon had been subject to similar attacks but also had discovered through its own internal mechanisms that some of its supplier operations were not operated at the same standards as its own operations. In 1998, adidas-Salomon published its Standards of Engagement (SoE) with the aim of ensuring that all of its suppliers' factories are safe, fair places to work. Updated in 2001, the SoE are patterned after the ILO conventions and the model code of conduct of the World Federation of Sporting Goods Industries and reflect attention to labor, safety, health and environmental issues.

These are the core values of the adidas-Salomon Group. We measure ourselves by these values and we measure our business partners in the same way.

Consistent with these values, we expect our business partners—contractors, subcontractors, suppliers and others—to conduct themselves with the utmost fairness, honesty and responsibility in all aspects of their businesses.

The Standards of Engagement are tools that assist us in selecting and retaining business partners who follow work place standards and business practices consistent with our policies and values. As guiding principles, they help identify potential problems so that we can work with business partners to address issues of concern as they arise. Business partners must develop and implement action plans for continuous improvement in factory working conditions. Progress against action plans will be monitored by business partners themselves, our internal monitoring team and external independent monitors.

Specifically, we expect our business partners to operate work places according to the following standards and practices.

GENERAL PRINCIPLE

Business partners must comply fully with all legal requirements relevant to the conduct of their businesses.

EMPLOYMENT STANDARDS

We will do business only with business partners who treat their employees fairly and legally with regard to wages, benefits and working conditions. In particular, the following standards apply:

Forced labor: Business partners must not use forced labor, whether in the form of prison labor, indentured labor, bonded labor or otherwise. No employee may be compelled to work through force or intimidation of any form.

Child labor: Business partners must not employ children who are less than 15 years old or less than the age for completing compulsory education in the country of manufacture, where such age is higher than 15.

Discrimination: Business partners must make recruitment and post-hiring decisions based on ability to do the job, rather than on the basis of personal characteristics or beliefs. Business partners must not discriminate in hiring and employment practices on the grounds of race, national origin, gender, religion, age, disability, marital status, parental status, association membership, sexual orientation or political opinion.

Wages and benefits: Wages are essential for meeting the basic needs of employees and reasonable savings and expenditure. In all cases, wages must equal or exceed the minimum wage required by law or the prevailing industry wage, whichever is higher, and legally mandated benefits must be provided. Wages must be paid directly to the employee in cash or check or the equivalent. Information relating to wages must be provided to employees in a form they understand. Advances of, and deductions from, wages must be carefully monitored and comply with law. In addition to compensation for regular working hours, employees must be compensated for overtime hours at the rate legally required in the country of manufacture or, in those countries where such laws do not exist, at a rate exceeding the regular hourly compensation rate.

Hours of work: Employees must not be required, except in extraordinary circumstances, to work more than 60 hours per week including overtime or the local legal requirement, whichever is less. Employees must be allowed at least 24 consecutive hours rest within every seven-day period, and must receive paid annual leave.

Freedom of association and collective bargaining: Business partners must recognize and respect the right of employees to join and organize associations of their own choosing and to bargain collectively. Where law specifically restricts the right to freedom of association and collective bargaining, business partners must not obstruct alternative and legal means for independent and free association or collective bargaining. Additionally, business partners must implement systems to ensure effective communication with employees.

Disciplinary practices: Employees must be treated with respect and dignity. No employee may be subjected to any physical, sexual, psychological or verbal harassment or abuse.

HEALTH AND SAFETY

A safe and hygienic working environment must be provided, and occupational health and safety practices which prevent work-related accidents and injury must be promoted. This includes protection from fire, accidents and toxic substances. Lighting, heating and ventilation systems must be adequate. Employees must have access at all times to sanitary facilities, which should be adequate and clean. Business partners must have health and safety policies that are clearly communicated to employees. Where residential facilities are provided to employees, the same standards apply.

ENVIRONMENTAL REQUIREMENTS

Business partners must make progressive improvement in environmental performance in their own operations and require the same of their partners, suppliers and subcontractors. This includes: integrating principles of sustainability into business decisions; responsible use of natural resources; adoption of cleaner production and pollution prevention measures; and designing and developing products, materials and technologies according to the principles of sustainability.

COMMUNITY INVOLVEMENT

We will favor business partners who make efforts to contribute to improving conditions in the countries and communities in which they operate.

EMPLOYMENT STANDARDS

In 2002 we continued to measure our suppliers' performance against the SOE employment standards and developed both training programs and rating tools and standardized our action plans. We also addressed many of our stakeholders' most pressing concerns—child labor, fair wages and labor rights.

Training Programs

Our training initiatives are designed to build capacity within factory management staff, so that their efforts to improve work conditions become integral to the factory's management style and sustainable over the long term.

After the launch of the Guidelines on Employment Standards in late 2001, the SEA team began training suppliers in use of the guidelines. The training sessions took place in the suppliers' own factories and in regional workshops. The guidelines set out the legal background to the standards, provide practical examples of non-compliance and suggest solutions, outline a number of case studies and provide sample documentation [such as a standard payroll template]. In the context of the training sessions, this content has been translated into simple and pragmatic training modules. Similarly, the suggested solutions in the guidelines are being used as the basis to develop factory action plans where remediation of poor labor conditions is required. The guidelines are being translated into Chinese and will be available by the end of the first quarter 2003.

Sharing Best Practice meetings complement the manual-based training. The meetings, held annually throughout Asia, give factories a chance to become more aware of the progress that has been made, and the good practices that are being developed within their business. At the meetings, factories with best practices in the areas of labor, H&S and the environment are invited to share their experiences and compliance models with other suppliers. In China the local SEA staff has established a Factory SOE Sharing Club so that factories can exchange ideas and practices more regularly. Some specific supervisor training projects have been undertaken—most notably the Grow Together training project in Indonesia. The main purpose is to raise awareness of compliance issues and the needs of workers among factory supervisors and middle management. This project will be promoted in other countries throughout the Asia region in 2003.

Labor Rating Tool

The original version of the labor audit report document, which is completed by SEA staff when they visit a factory to check on working conditions, has been reviewed and improved. Much of the original content is still valid and forms the basis of our approach to labor issues. However, as the SOE program has developed, it has become clear that some standards require more detailed investigation and deeper analysis. Consequently, the original labor audit report has been re-worked into a labor rating tool, and additional lines of investigation have been included. Specifically, the tool gives greater attention to freedom of association and collective bargaining, wages and benefits, the supplier's general corporate behavior and the extent of cooperation by its management. The tool will be field tested until October 2003.

Standardized Labor Action Plan

The SEA team is now working with a standardized labor action plan. The plan is linked directly to the labor rating tool, as each section mirrors those of the rating tool both in identification of problems and solutions suggested. Following an audit, the SEA team uses their expertise and experience to judge which parts of the plan need amending or fine-tuning for a specific factory or case. The purpose of the plan is to ensure that team members do not miss any possible issues or problems, thus making sure that the information we give factories in action plans is consistent from country to country and region to region.

Fair Wages

To define what we mean by a "fair wage" the SOE were updated in 2001 to include a re-worded clause on wages and benefits. These changes called for adidas-Salomon suppliers to gain a better understanding of the basic needs of factory workers, as well as their discretionary savings and spending patterns. While making these changes to the SOE we recognized that neither we nor our suppliers had any real data to work with, nor any standard method to determine a fair wage level. Our objective is to seek an answer to the question, raised by workers and our other stakeholders: what is a sufficient wage to cover basic needs and reasonable savings and expenditure? The second step will be to find pragmatic mechanisms to translate the answer into a workable model, to identify appropriate wage levels across all countries.

Fair Wage Study, Indonesia

In 2001 we commissioned a local NGO, Lembaga Penelitian, Pendidikan dan Penerangan Ekonomi dan Sosial [the Institute for Social and Economic Research, Education and Information or LP3ES] to carry out a pilot study into fair wages in Indonesia. adidas-Salomon has committed to publishing the results of the study in 2003 and will host a multi-stakeholder workshop to discuss and debate the findings. To capture the widest possible range of views, the workshop will be extended to labor rights organizations, local NGOs, academics, unions, government officials and adidas-Salomon suppliers.

Working Hours

Working alongside sourcing departments, the SOE team continued to collect information about working hours from a large number of factories throughout 2002. The footwear factories in Asia, together with many apparel and hardware suppliers, provided monthly working hours reports. These were randomly verified by adidas-Salomon staff through interviews with workers and cross-referencing the reports with factory payroll and time records. The data and interviews reveal a trend in footwear toward greatly reduced working hours, often to below the 60-hour work week limit outlined in the SOE.

However, it is clear that working hours continue to pose one of our biggest challenges. In 2003, we will continue to research ways that working hours can be reduced while not adversely affecting wage levels. The project aims to identify the many complex causes of excessive working hours, and set out the findings in a working report. Following that, a task force within the Group will consult with factories, material suppliers, retail groups and NGOs to map out possible solutions to the problem. Other major brands, who are working on the same issue within their own supplier base, have also provided valuable feedback on the causes of excessive working hours and possible solutions.

Child Labor

During the course of 2002, adidas-Salomon continued its work on child labor through two projects: the Sialkot monitoring project, and the follow-up and assessment of the child labor education project in Vietnam.

Local Monitoring of Child Labor, Pakistan   In 1997, the ILO, UNICEF and the Sialkot Chamber of Commerce and Industry signed a partner agreement to eliminate child labor in Pakistan's football manufacturing industry. As part of its commitment to that agreement, the ILO established an independent workplace monitoring system to check for underage workers in registered stitching centers. adidas-Salomon suppliers have three registered football stitching centers in Sialkot.

Since 1997, the ILO has progressively trained and transferred expertise to a team of local monitors. These monitors now form the nucleus of a new body, known as the Independent Monitoring Association for Child Labor (IMAC), which will take forward and sustain the monitoring efforts.

As part of the program, a local NGO assessed the education needs of Sialkot's children and devised and delivered education and training interventions, partly funded by adidas-Salomon.

International NGO Assessment of Education Project, Vietnam   An education program was established to provide young people who had been employed at a footwear factory with an education and vocational skills. An assessment of this program was carried out by Save the Children, Sweden, through local staff and researchers who conducted broad-scale interviews with interested parties, from management and workers, to teachers and the local community. The assessment provided constructive commentary on the management of the project and highlighted areas where adidas-Salomon failed to get at the root causes of the problem. It also highlighted where a more inclusive approach could have been taken with local government education officials, the trade unions, women's groups in the area and the local community. The assessment provides a critical framework for future projects and efforts by the Group in the area of child labor. It also advocates support to local families by the employment of juvenile workers, where allowed by law, under specially controlled conditions.

Migrant Workers

adidas-Salomon gave an increasing amount of attention to the plight of migrant workers throughout the industry in 2002. This issue has been highlighted through the worker interview process and our closer links with the NGO groups who monitor workplace conditions for migrant workers, a group particularly vulnerable to exploitation. We have identified a large number of migrant workers within our own supply chain, moving from Indonesia, Vietnam, the Philippines, Nepal, Bangladesh and China to relatively more developed countries such as Korea, Japan, Taiwan, Singapore and Malaysia.

While we have been developing a heightened awareness of the issue, the UN Convention on the Protection of the Rights of all Migrant Workers and Members of their Families has been the subject of serious focus and debate. On 11 December 2002. East Timor acceded to the Convention, meaning that the requisite number of ratifications was achieved and the Convention enters into force early 2003. Not only will member states be required to report on their efforts with regard to migrant workers in their countries, but suppliers and buyers who profit from the labor of migrant workers will be forced to address discrimination, under-payment of wages, excessive recruitment fees and forced labor conditions.

Monitoring Migrant Worker Conditions, Taiwan   Taiwanese manufacturers rely heavily on foreign contract workers, the majority of whom come from Thailand, the Philippines, Indonesia and Vietnam. Numbers of these workers have recently exceeded 300,000, making the rights of migrant workers a pressing issue in these countries.

In 2002 the SEA team reviewed common problems faced by migrant workers in Taiwan that might breach the SOE or local labor laws. The result is a set of clear guidelines for the employers of migrant workers that covers placement fees, wage and benefit deductions, overtime pay and working hours. Efforts to improve migrant worker conditions are also being developed at government level. In late 2002, the Thai and Taiwan governments signed a labor cooperation agreement aimed at improving conditions for Thai workers. adidas-Salomon's role will be to ensure workplace compliance with the agreement.

Worker Representation and Management—Worker Communications

Throughout our training workshops and factory visits in 2002 we focused on the issue of management-worker communication. Communication and bargaining mechanisms take a variety of forms in various countries. In China, the focus has been on establishing effective HSE committees, direct management-worker discussion groups suggestion boxes, worker magazines and counselling centers.

Towards the end of 2002, the SEA team began a process of consultation with the ILO, government manufacturing association representatives in Beijing, Chinese academics and other brands to identify ways in which worker representative groups in China might be developed within the current legal framework. We are currently exploring through discussion with NGOs and workers how the development of such organizations might be more "grass-roots" driven. In other countries, such as Indonesia, our focus has been on projects and actions that promote multi-union coexistence in factories and proper collective bargaining processes.

Labor Rights Awareness in Local Government and the Workplace, China   The development of labor intensive industries, particularly in Guangdong province, has seen a growth in labor disputes as well as an increased focus on labor safety standards in both private and state-owned enterprises. Workers often do not understand their rights and obligations within the employment relationship and are unable to find this information.

The Institute of Contemporary Observation [ICO], a local NGO, scoped a project to promote labor rights protection and assistance. Cooperation with several multi-national businesses has resulted in a user-friendly manual with information about basic labor conditions such as working hours and wage payments, industrial safety, how to report a work-related injury and claim compensation, what to do in a labor dispute and where to go for advice. adidas-Salomon helped to set up the project and has played an important role in the development of the manual. The team assigned to the project deals with labor disputes and workers' claims on a daily basis.

Worker-Management Communication, El Salvador   The case of an apparel factory in El Salvador demonstrates the benefit of improved worker-management communication. The factory received attention from the European media for poor health and safety practices and discriminatory employment practices. To improve the factory's treatment of workers, a solution was to develop better communication between workers and management and to involve workers in the compliance process.

The structure of the factory communication committee, including its meetings, and its elections of worker representatives, evolved substantially in 2002. There have been discernable changes in the process of creating and administering the worker management committee, with established procedures to conduct elections, institutional scheduling of meetings, recording meeting minutes and effective communication channels between workers, committee representatives and management.

The content of these meetings originally covered topics such as planning the company's social events and organizing factory sports teams. Recently the committee has identified and implemented changes that improved the quality and health standards in the factory canteen. The committee has also instituted a community donations program that identifies medical need in the local community and manages distribution of appropriate medical supplies.

Future committee activities will address continuing education and training of workers, improved feedback methods between the committee and its constituencies, and expanding the community donations program.

International and Local Supplier Factories

APPAREL

Labor Standards	Asia	Americas	Europe
*	12	0	4
**	80	7	45
***	132	88	144
****	26	13	17
*****	0	0	0
Total rated to date†	250	108	210
Total rated in 2002	153	94	113
Total factories in region	299	138	180

† Active factories only
‡ Accessories and gear

FOOTWEAR

Labor Standards	Asia	Americas	Europe
*	1	0	0
**	1	2	1
***	5	3	4
****	6	3	0
*****	2	0	1
Total rated to date†	15	8	6
Total rated in 2002	18	8	1
Total factories in region	21	8	6

HARDWARE‡

Labor Standards	Asia	Americas	Europe
*	2	0	0
**	32	0	2
***	35	8	10
****	14	6	2
*****	0	0	3
Total rated to date	83	14	17
Total rated in 2002	46	18	8
Total factories in region	100	36	40

Supplier Scoring System

Following an audit, each factory is rated and an action plan is written. The five grades of our supplier scoring system are:

*

There are numerous severe non-compliance issues. The factory has been given notice that business will be terminated unless there is immediate improvement.

**

There are some non-compliance issues and the factory is responding to the action plan slowly or with reluctance. The factory is monitored regularly.

***

There are minor non-compliance issues, and the factory is responding to the action plan positively.

****

Generally there are no non-compliance issues, and there are some best practices in place, confirmed in documentation.

*****

There are no non-compliance issues and all of the factory's management system and practices are in place, confirmed in documentation.

The table summarizes the performance of our suppliers against both our labor and HSE standards. The table uses the supplier scoring system described above to compare performance.

THE BASE CODE

—Ethical Trading Initiative

The Ethical Trading Initiative (ETI) has developed a code of labor practice—the "Base Code"—reflecting the most relevant international standards with respect to labor practices. The Base Code, which is founded on the ILO standards, is accompanied by a set of general principles concerning implementation. ETI member companies are expected to adopt this Base Code, or to adopt their own code so long as it incorporates the Base Code. Member companies must require that suppliers meet agreed standards within a reasonable time frame, and that performance in this regard is measured, transparent and, ultimately, a precondition to further business.

ETI understands that the observance of some provisions in the code may not be immediately realizable in all cases. Some suppliers may be unable to meet all the terms within a short time or, in some cases, they may be constrained by national law. Reasonable time frames and the existence of any constraints not controllable by the supplier may be taken into account. Failures to observe certain standards require rapid corrective action for member companies to continue any business relationship with the supplier concerned. These include the use of forced, bonded or involuntary prison labor as well as physical abuse or discipline, and extreme forms of intimidation.

At the time of joining ETI, member companies may stipulate the scope of application of their code provided that this is clearly indicated in the preamble of their code and that company publicity concerning the code also indicates its scope of application. The scope of application may be certain products made or marketed by the company or to the activities of any designated part of the company. In any event, the code shall always apply to all work performed within the scope of application.

1. Employment is freely chosen.
    1.1 There is no forced, bonded or involuntary prison labor.
    1.2 Workers are not required to lodge "deposits" or their identity papers with their employer and are free to leave their employer after reasonable notice.

2. Freedom of association and the right to collective bargaining are respected.

   2.1 Workers, without distinction, have the right to join or form trade unions of their own choosing and to bargain collectively.

   2.2 The employer adopts an open attitude towards the activities of trade unions and their organizational activities.

   2.3 Workers representatives are not discriminated against and have access to carry out their representative functions in the workplace.

   2.4 Where the right to freedom of association and collective bargaining is restricted under law, the employer facilitates, and does not hinder, the development of parallel means for independent and free association and bargaining.

3. Working conditions are safe and hygienic.

   3.1 A safe and hygienic working environment shall be provided, bearing in mind the prevailing knowledge of the industry and of any specific hazards. Adequate steps shall be taken to prevent accidents and injury to health arising out of, associated with or occurring in the course of work, by minimizing, so far as is reasonably practicable, the causes of hazards inherent in the working environment.

   3.2 Workers shall receive regular and recorded health and safety training, and such training shall be repeated for new or reassigned workers.

   3.3 Access to clean toilet facilities and to potable water, and, if appropriate, sanitary facilities for food storage shall be provided.

   3.4 Accommodation, where provided, shall be clean, safe and meet the basic needs of the workers.

   3.5 The company observing the code shall assign responsibility for health and safety to a senior management representative.

4. Child labor shall not be used.

   4.1 There shall be no new recruitment of child labor.

   4.2 Companies shall develop or participate in and contribute to policies and programs which provide for the transition of any child found to be performing child labor to enable her or him to attend and remain in quality education until no longer a child; "child" and "child labor" being defined in the appendices.

   4.3 Children and young persons under 18 shall not be employed at night or in hazardous conditions.

   4.4 These policies and procedures shall conform to the provisions of the relevant ILO standards.

5. Living wages are paid.

   5.1 Wages and benefits paid for a standard working week meet, at a minimum, national legal standards or industry benchmark standards, whichever is higher. In any event wages should always be enough to meet basic needs and to provide some discretionary income.

5.2 All workers shall be provided with written and understandable information about their employment conditions in respect to wages before they enter employment and about the particulars of their wages for the pay period concerned each time that they are paid.

5.3 Deductions from wages as a disciplinary measure shall not be permitted nor shall any deductions from wages not provided for by national law be permitted without the expressed permission of the worker concerned. All disciplinary measures should be recorded.

6. Working hours are not excessive.

6.1 Working hours comply with national laws and benchmark industry standards, whichever affords greater protection.

6.2 In any event, workers shall not on a regular basis be required to work in excess of 48 hours per week and shall be provided with at least one day off for every seven day period on average. Overtime shall be voluntary, shall not exceed 12 hours per week, shall not be demanded on a regular basis and shall always be compensated at a premium rate.

7. No discrimination is practiced.

7.1 There is no discrimination in hiring, compensation, access to training, promotion, termination or retirement based on race, caste, national origin, religion, age, disability, gender, marital status, sexual orientation, union membership or political affiliation.

8. Regular employment is provided.

8.1 To every extent possible work performed must be on the basis of recognized employment relationship established through national law and practice.

8.2 Obligations to employees under labor or social security laws and regulations arising from the regular employment relationship shall not be avoided through the use of labor-only contracting, subcontracting or home-working arrangements, or through apprenticeship schemes where there is no real intent to impart skills or provide regular employment, nor shall any such obligations be avoided through the excessive use of fixed-term contracts of employment.

9. No harsh or inhumane treatment is allowed.

9.1 Physical abuse or discipline, the threat of physical abuse, sexual or other harassment and verbal abuse or other forms of intimidation shall be prohibited.

The provisions of this code constitute minimum and not maximum standards, and this code should not be used to prevent companies from exceeding these standards. Companies applying this code are expected to comply with national and other applicable law and, where the provisions of law and this Base Code address the same subject, to apply that provision which affords the greater protection.

THE GREAT NON-DEBATE OVER INTERNATIONAL SWEATSHOPS

—Ian Maitland

Recent years have witnessed a dramatic growth in the contracting out of production by companies in the industrialized countries to suppliers in developing countries. The contracting arrangements have drawn intense fire from critics who have charged that the companies are (by proxy) exploiting workers in so-called international sweatshops. The paper addresses the issue of what are appropriate wages and labor standards in international sweatshops. It evaluates the specific charges made by critics from the standpoints of (a) their factual and (b) their ethical sufficiency. The paper also uses the investigation of sweatshops as a setting for adjudicating between competing views about what those standards should be. It pays particular attention to (but is not limited to) labor conditions at the plants of Nike's suppliers in Indonesia.

Recent years have seen a dramatic growth in the contracting out of production by companies in the industrialized countries to suppliers in developing countries. This globalization of production has led to an emerging international division of labor in footwear and apparel in which companies like Nike and Reebok concentrate on product design and marketing but rely on a network of contractors in Asia and Central America, etc., to build shoes or sew shirts according to exact specifications and deliver a high quality good according to precise delivery schedules. These contracting arrangements have drawn intense fire from labor and human rights activists who charge that the companies are (by proxy) exploiting foreign workers. The companies stand accused of chasing cheap labor around the globe, failing to pay their workers living wages, using child labor, turning a blind eye to abuses of human rights and being complicit with repressive regimes in denying workers the right to join unions and failing to enforce minimum labor standards in the workplace, and so on. Many companies have tried to address these concerns by developing codes of conduct for their overseas suppliers. This workshop will examine the desirability and pitfalls of such codes of conduct.

The campaign against international sweatshops has largely unfolded on television and, to a lesser extent, in the print media. What seems like no more than a handful of critics has mounted an aggressive, media-savvy campaign which has put the publicity-shy retail giants on the defensive. The critics have orchestrated a series of sensational "disclosures" on prime time television exposing the terrible pay and working conditions in factories making jeans for Levi's or sneakers for Nike or Pocahontas shirts for Disney. One of the principal scourges of the companies has been Charles Kernaghan who runs the National Labor Coalition (NLC), a labor human rights group involving 25 unions. It was Kernaghan who, in 1996, broke the news before a congressional committee that Kathie Lee Gifford's clothing line was being made by 13- and 14-year-olds working 20-hour days in factories in Honduras.[1] Kernaghan also arranged for teenage workers from sweatshops in Central America to testify before congressional committees about abusive labor practices. At one of these hearings, one of the workers held up a Liz Claiborne cotton sweater identical to ones she had sewn since she was a 13-year-old working 12-hour days. According to a news report, "[t]his image, accusations of oppressive conditions at the factory and the Claiborne logo played well on that evening's network news."[2] The result has been a circus-like atmosphere—as in Roman circus where Christians were thrown to lions.

Kernaghan has shrewdly targeted the companies' carefully cultivated public images. He has explained: "Their image is everything. They live and die by their image. That gives you a certain power over them." As a result, he says, "these companies are sitting ducks. They have no leg to stand on. That's why it's possible for a tiny group like us to take on a giant like Wal-Mart. You can't defend paying someone 31 cents an hour in Honduras . . . ."[3] Apparently most of the companies agree with Kernaghan. Not a single company has tried to mount a serious defense of its contracting practices. They have judged that they cannot win a war of sound bites with the critics. Instead of making a fight of it, the companies have sued for peace in order to protect their principal asset—their image.

Major U.S. retailers have responded by adopting codes of conduct on human and labor rights in their international operations. Levi Strauss, Nike, Sears, JCPenney, Wal-Mart, Home Depot, Phillips-Van Heusen now have such codes. As Lance Compa notes, such codes are the result of a blend of humanitarian and pragmatic impulses: "Often the altruistic motive coincides with 'bottom line' considerations related to brand name, company image and other intangibles that make for core value to the firm."[4] Peter Jacobi, president of global sourcing for Levi Strauss, has advised: "If your company owns a popular brand, protect this priceless asset at all costs. Highly visible companies have any number of reasons to conduct their business not just responsibly but also in ways that cannot be portrayed as unfair, illegal or unethical. This sets an extremely high standard since it must be applied to

---

[1]Stephanie Strom, "From Sweetheart to Scapegoat," *New York Times,* June 27, 1996. According to Strom, "Shortly after [Kernaghan] effectively charged Mrs. Gifford with exploiting children in the pursuit of profit, news broke of a factory in New York's garment district where workers making blouses for the Kathie Lee Gifford line had not been paid. Mrs. Gifford dissolved into tears on her talk show, while her husband, Frank, the football player and broadcaster, hurried to the factory, Seo Fashions, and doled out three $100 bills to each of the workers. . . .[Kernaghan] recently apologized saying he and his organization 'never intended to hurt anyone personally and are truly sorry for any pain caused to Kathie Lee Gifford. . .' "

[2]Joanna Ramey & Joyce Barrett, "Apparel's Ethical Dilemma," *Women's Wear Daily,* March 18, 1996.

[3]Steven Greenhouse, "A Crusader Makes Celebrities Tremble," *New York Times,* June 18, 1996, p. B4.

[4]Lance A. Compa & Tashia Hinchliffe Darricarrere, "Enforcement Through Corporate Codes of Conduct," in Compa and Stephen F. Diamond, *Human Rights, Labor Rights and International Trade* (Philadelphia: University of Pennsylvania Press, 1996), p. 193.

both company-owned businesses and contractors . . . ."[5] And according to another Levi Strauss spokesman, "In many respects, we're protecting our single largest asset: our brand image and corporate reputation."[6] Nike recently published the results of a generally favorable review of its international operations conducted by former American U.N. Ambassador Andrew Young.

Recently a truce of sorts between the critics and the companies was announced on the White House lawn with President Clinton and Kathie Lee Gifford in attendance. A presidential task force, including representatives of labor unions, human rights groups and apparel companies like L. L. Bean and Nike, has come up with a set of voluntary standards which, it hopes, will be embraced by the entire industry.[7] Companies that comply with the code will be entitled to use a "No Sweat" label.

OBJECTIVE OF THIS PAPER

In this confrontation between the companies and their critics, neither side seems to have judged it to be in its interest to seriously engage the issue at the heart of this controversy, namely: What are appropriate wages and labor standards in international sweatshops? As we have seen, the companies have treated the charges about sweatshops as a public relations problem to be managed so as to minimize harm to their public images. The critics have apparently judged that the best way to keep public indignation at boiling point is to oversimplify the issue and treat it as a morality play featuring heartless exploiters and victimized third world workers. The result has been a great non-debate over international sweatshops. Paradoxically, if peace breaks out between the two sides, the chances that the debate will be seriously joined may recede still further. Indeed, there exists a real risk (I will argue) that any such truce may be a collusive one that will come at the expense of the very third world workers it is supposed to help.

This paper takes up the issue of what are appropriate wages and labor standards in international sweatshops. Critics charge that the present arrangements are exploitative. I proceed by examining the specific charges of exploitation from the standpoints of both (*a*) their factual[8] and (*b*) their ethical sufficiency. However, in the absence of any well-established consensus among business ethicists (or other thoughtful observers), I simultaneously use the investigation of sweatshops as a setting for trying to adjudicate between competing views about what those standards should be. My examination will pay particular attention to (but will not be limited to) labor conditions at the plants of Nike's suppliers in Indone-

---

[5]Peter Jacobi in Martha Nichols, "Third-World Families at Work: Child Labor or Child Care," *Harvard Business Review,* January–February 1993.

[6]David Sampson in Robin G. Givhan, "A Stain on Fashion; The Garment Industry Profits from Cheap Labor," *Washington Post,* September 12, 1995, p. B1. According to *The Wall Street Journal*'s G. Pascal Zachary, "Ethics aside, Levi's was frankly concerned with its image among hip customers." Zachary quotes Robert Dunn, who helped design Levi's code of conduct, as saying, "Anyone seeking to protect their brand and company reputation will realize these policies make business sense. The alternative is to put ourselves at risk." "Exporting Rights: Levi Tries to Make Sure Contract Plants in Asia Treat Workers Well," *The Wall Street Journal,* July 28, 1994.

[7]Steven Greenhouse, "Voluntary Rules on Apparel Labor Proving Elusive," *New York Times,* February 1, 1997.

[8]As Thomas Donaldson rightly says, "In general, the solution to most difficult international problems requires a detailed understanding not only of moral precepts, but of particular facts." *The Ethics of International Business* (New York: Oxford University Press, 1989), p. 90. This case is especially fact-intensive.

sia. I have not personally visited any international sweatshops, and so my conclusions are based entirely on secondary analysis of the voluminous published record on the topic.

WHAT ARE ETHICALLY APPROPRIATE LABOR STANDARDS IN INTERNATIONAL SWEATSHOPS?

What are ethically acceptable or appropriate levels of wages and labor standards in international sweatshops? The following four possibilities just about run the gamut of standards or principles that have been seriously proposed to regulate such policies.

1. *Home-country standards:* It might be argued (and in rare cases has been[9]) that international corporations have an ethical duty to pay the same wages and provide the same labor standards regardless of where they operate.[10] However, the view that home-country standards should apply in host-countries is rejected by most business ethicists and (officially at least) by the critics of international sweatshops. Thus Thomas Donaldson argues that "[b]y arbitrarily establishing U.S. wage levels as the bench mark for fairness one eliminates the role of the international market in establishing salary levels, and this in turn eliminates the incentive U.S. corporations have to hire foreign workers."[11] Richard DeGeorge makes much the same argument: If there were a rule that said that "American MNCs [multinational corporations] that wish to be ethical must pay the same wages abroad as they do at home, . . . [then] MNCs would have little incentive to move their manufacturing abroad; and if they did move abroad they would disrupt the local labor market with artificially high wages that bore no relation to the local standard or cost of living."[12]

2. *"Living wage" standard:* It has been proposed that an international corporation should, at a minimum, pay a "living wage." Thus DeGeorge says that corporations should pay a living wage "even when this is not paid by local firms."[13] However, it is hard to pin down what this means operationally. According to DeGeorge, a living wage should "allow the worker to live in dignity as a human being." In order to respect the human rights of its workers, he says, a corporation must pay "at least subsistence wages and as much above that as workers and their dependents need to live with reasonable dignity, given the general state of development of the society."[14] As we shall see, the living wage standard has become a rallying cry of the critics of international sweatshops. Apparently, DeGeorge believes that it is preferable for a corporation to provide no job at all than to offer one that pays less than a living wage.

---

[9]Arnold Berleant has proposed that the principle of equal treatment endorsed by most Americans requires that U.S. corporations pay workers in developing countries exactly the same wages paid to U.S. workers in comparable jobs. See Donaldson, *Ethics of International Business,* pp. 97–98.

[10]Formally, of course, workers at Nike's suppliers are not Nike employees. But critics say this is a distinction without a difference, and I will not distinguish the two cases in this paper.

[11]Donaldson, p. 98.

[12]Richard DeGeorge, *Competing with Integrity in International Business* (New York: Oxford University Press, 1993), p. 79.

[13]DeGeorge, *Competing with Integrity,* pp. 356–57.

[14]*Ibid.,* p. 78.

3. *Donaldson's test:* Thomas Donaldson believes that "it is irrelevant whether the standards of the host country comply or fail to comply with home country standards; what is relevant is whether they meet a universal, objective minimum."[15] He tries to specify "a moral minimum for the behavior of all international economic agents."[16] However, he concedes that this "leaves obscure not only the issue of less extreme threats but of harms other than physical injury. The language of rights and harm is sufficiently vague so as to leave shrouded in uncertainty a formidable list of issues crucial to multinationals."[17] He accepts that "many rights . . . are dependent for their specification on the level of economic development of the country in question."[18] Accordingly, he proposes a test to determine when deviations from home-country standards are unethical. That test provides as follows: "The practice is permissible if and only if the members of the home country would, under conditions of economic development relevantly similar to those of the host country, regard the practice as permissible."[19] Donaldson's test is vulnerable to Bernard Shaw's objection to the Golden Rule, namely that we should not do unto others as we would have them do unto us, because their tastes may be different. The test also complicates matters by introducing counterfactuals and hypotheticals (if I were in their place [which I'm not] what would I want?). This indeterminacy is a serious weakness in an ethical code: It is likely to confuse managers who want to act ethically and to provide loopholes for those who don't.[20]

4. *Classical liberal standard:* Finally there is what I will call the classical liberal standard. According to this standard a practice (wage or labor practice) is ethically acceptable if it is freely chosen by informed workers. For example, in a recent report the World Bank invoked this standard in connection with workplace safety. It said: "The appropriate level is therefore that at which the costs are commensurate with the value that informed workers place on improved working conditions and reduced risk."[21] Most business ethicists reject this standard on the grounds that there is some sort of market failure or the "background conditions" are lacking for markets to work effectively. Thus for Donaldson full (or near-full) employment is a prerequisite if workers are to make sound choices regarding workplace safety: "The average level of unemployment in the developing countries today exceeds 40%, a figure that has frustrated the application of neoclassical economic principles to the international economy on a score of issues. With full employment, and all other things being equal, market forces will encourage workers to make trade-offs between job

---

[15]Thomas Donaldson, *The Ethics of International Business* (New York: Oxford University Press, 1989), p. 100.

[16]Donaldson, *Ethics of International Business,* p. 145.

[17]*Ibid.,* p. 100.

[18]*Ibid.,* p. 101.

[19]*Ibid.,* p. 103.

[20]Donaldson rather loftily dismisses the objection that his "algorithm" makes excessive demands on the sophistication and "ethical sensitivity" of managers. "[F]rom a theoretical perspective the problem is a contingent and practical one. It is no more a theoretical flaw of the proposed algorithm that it may be misunderstood or misapplied by a given multinational, than it is of Rawls's theory of justice that it may be conveniently misunderstood by a trickle-down Libertarian." *Ethics of International Business,* p. 108. That seems to be equivalent to saying that the operation was a success but the patient died. Surely ethical guidelines for multinational managers are practical or they are irrelevant.

[21]World Bank, *World Development Report 1995, "Workers in an Integrating World Economy"* (Oxford University Press, 1995), p. 77.

opportunities using safety as a variable. But with massive unemployment, market forces in developing countries drive the unemployed to the jobs they are lucky enough to land, regardless of the safety."[22] Apparently there are other forces, like Islamic fundamentalism and the global debt "bomb," that rule out reliance on market solutions, but Donaldson does not explain their relevance.[23] DeGeorge, too, believes that the necessary conditions are lacking for market forces to operate benignly. Without what he calls "background institutions" to protect the workers and the resources of the developing country (e.g., enforceable minimum wages) and/or greater equality of bargaining power, exploitation is the most likely result.[24] "If American MNCs pay workers very low wages . . . they clearly have the opportunity to make significant profits."[25] DeGeorge goes on to make the interesting observation that "competition has developed among multinationals themselves, so that the profit margin has been driven down" and developing countries "can play one company against another."[26] But apparently that is not enough to rehabilitate market forces in his eyes.

THE CASE AGAINST INTERNATIONAL SWEATSHOPS

To many of their critics, international sweatshops exemplify the way in which the greater openness of the world economy is hurting workers. According to one critic, "as it is now constituted, the world trading system discriminates against workers, especially those in the Third World."[27] Globalization means a transition from (more or less) regulated domestic economies to an unregulated world economy. The superior mobility of capital, and the essentially fixed, immobile nature of world labor, means a fundamental shift in bargaining power in favor of large international corporations. Their global reach permits them to shift production almost costlessly from one location to another. As a consequence, instead of being able to exercise some degree of control over companies operating within their borders, governments are now locked in a bidding war with one another to attract and retain the business of large multinational companies.

The critics allege that international companies are using the threat of withdrawal or withholding of investment to pressure governments and workers to grant concessions. "Today [multinational companies] choose between workers in developing countries that compete against each other to depress wages to attract foreign investment."[28] The result is a race for the bottom—a "destructive downward bidding spiral of the labor conditions and wages of workers throughout the world . . . ."[29] Kernaghan claims that "It is a race to the bottom over who will accept the lowest wages and the most miserable working conditions."[30] Thus,

---

[22]Donaldson, *Ethics of International Business,* p. 115.

[23]*Ibid.,* p. 150.

[24]DeGeorge, *Competing with Integrity,* p. 48.

[25]*Ibid.,* p. 358.

[26]*Ibid.*

[27]Kenneth P. Hutchinson, "Third World Growth," *Harvard Business Review,* November–December 1994. (In 1994, Hutchinson was executive director of the Asian-American Free Labor Institute in Washington, D.C., an affiliate of the AFL-CIO).

[28]Terry Collingsworth, J. William Goold & Pharis J. Harvey, "Time for a Global New Deal," *Foreign Affairs,* January–February 1994, p. 8.

[29]Collingsworth et al., p. 8.

[30]David Holmstrom, "One Man's Fight against Sweatshops," *Christian Science Monitor,* July 3, 1996.

critics charge that in Indonesia wages are deliberately held below the poverty level or subsistence in order to make the country a desirable location. The results of this competitive dismantling of worker protections, living standards and worker rights are predictable: deteriorating work conditions, declining real incomes for workers and a widening gap between rich and poor in developing countries. I turn next to the specific charges made by the critics of international sweatshops.

Unconscionable Wages

Critics charge that the companies, by their proxies, are paying "starvation wages"[31] and "slave wages."[32] They are far from clear about what wage level they consider to be appropriate. But they generally demand that companies pay a "living wage." Kernaghan has said that workers should be paid enough to support their families[33] and they should get a "living wage" and "be treated like human beings."[34] Jay Mazur of the textile employees union (UNITE) says, "On the question of wages, generally, of course workers should be paid enough to meet their basic needs—and then some."[35] According to Tim Smith, wage levels should be "fair, decent or a living wage for an employee and his or her family." He has said that wages in the maquiladoras of Mexico averaged $35 to $55 a week (in or near 1993) which he calls a "shockingly substandard wage," apparently on the grounds that it "clearly does not allow an employee to feed and care for a family adequately."[36] In 1992, Nike came in for harsh criticism when a magazine published the pay stub of a worker at one of its Indonesian suppliers. It showed that the worker was paid at the rate of $1.03 per day which was reportedly less than the Indonesian government's figure for "minimum physical need."[37]

Immiserization Thesis

Former Labor Secretary Robert Reich has proposed as a test of the fairness of development policies that "Low-wage workers should become better off, not worse off, as trade and investment boost national income." He has written that "[i]f a country pursues policies that . . . limit to a narrow elite the benefits of trade, the promise of open commerce is perverted and drained of its rationale."[38] A key claim of the activists is that companies actually impoverish or immiserize developing country workers. They experience an absolute decline in living standards. This thesis follows from the claim that the bidding war among developing countries is depressing wages.

---

[31]*Nightline* (ABC), June 13, 1996.

[32]Kernaghan cited in Larry Rohter, "To U.S. Critics, a Sweatshop; for Hondurans, a Better Life," *New York Times,* July 18, 1996.

[33]Greenhouse, "A Crusader Makes Celebrities Tremble."

[34]William B. Falk, "Dirty Little Secrets," *Newsday,* June 16, 1996.

[35]Greenhouse, "Voluntary Rules."

[36]Tim Smith, "The Power of Business for Human Rights," *Business & Society Review,* January 1994, p. 36.

[37]Jeffrey Ballinger, "The New Free Trade Heel," *Harper's Magazine,* August 1992, pp. 46–47. "As in many developing countries, Indonesia's minimum wage . . . . is less than poverty level." Nina Baker, "The Hidden Hands of Nike," *Oregonian,* August 9, 1992.

[38]Robert B. Reich, "Escape from the Global Sweatshop; Capitalism's Stake in Uniting the Workers of the World," *Washington Post,* May 22, 1994. Reich's test is intended to apply in developing countries "where democratic institutions are weak or absent."

Critics deride the claim that sweatshops are benefiting the poor by means of a global version of "trickle down" economics.[39] They reject as flawed "claims that U.S. [free trade] policies are leading to the growth of huge middle classes—in such countries as China, India and Indonesia—that will drive the world economy in the 21st century."[40] This picture, they say, is belied by the fact that "Most of the 'global South'—some 45% of humanity who reside mainly in the 140 poorest countries of the Third World—is locked in poverty and left behind as the richer strata grow. . . ."[41]

Widening Gap Between Rich and Poor

A related charge is that international sweatshops are contributing to the increasing gap between rich and poor. Not only are the poor being absolutely impoverished, but trade is generating greater inequality within developing countries. Another test that Reich has proposed to establish the fairness of international trade is that "the gap between rich and poor should tend to narrow with development, not widen."[42] Critics charge that international sweatshops flunk that test. They say that the increasing GNPs of some developing countries simply mask a widening gap between rich and poor. "Across the world, both local and foreign elites are getting richer from the exploitation of the most vulnerable."[43] And, "The major adverse consequence of quickening global economic integration has been widening income disparity within almost all nations . . . ."[44] There appears to be a tacit alliance between the elites of both first and third worlds to exploit the most vulnerable, to regiment and control and conscript them so that they can create the material conditions for the elites' extravagant lifestyles.

Collusion with Repressive Regimes

Critics charge that, in their zeal to make their countries safe for foreign investment, Third World regimes, notably China and Indonesia, have stepped up their repression. Not only have these countries failed to enforce even the minimal labor rules on the books, but they have also used their military and police to break strikes and repress independent unions. They have stifled political dissent, both to retain their hold on political power and to avoid any instability that might scare off foreign investors. Consequently, critics charge, companies like Nike are profiting from political repression. "As unions spread in [Korea and Taiwan], Nike shifted its suppliers primarily to Indonesia, China and Thailand, where they could depend on governments to suppress independent union-organizing efforts."[45]

---

[39]Collingsworth et al., p. 8.

[40]Robin Broad & John Cavanaugh, "Don't Neglect the Impoverished South," *Foreign Affairs,* December 22, 1995, p. 18. See also the typical muckraking piece by Merrill Goozner: "As the global economy pushes ever deeper into the poorest precincts of the developing world, its benefits aren't trickling down. . . . There is mounting evidence that the rising tide of rapid development is not lifting all boats, especially in China and Indonesia, the first and fourth most populous countries on earth." Goozner, "Asian Labor: Wages of Shame; Western Firms Help to Exploit Brutal Conditions," *Chicago Tribune,* November 6, 1994, p. 1.

[41]Broad & Cavanagh, "Don't Neglect the Impoverished South."

[42]Reich, "Escape from the Global Sweatshop."

[43]Hutchinson, "Third World Growth."

[44]Broad & Cavanagh, "Don't Neglect the Impoverished South." See also Goozner, "Wages of Shame."

[45]John Cavanaugh & Robin Broad, "Global Reach; Workers Fight the Multinationals," *The Nation,* March 18, 1996, p. 21. See also Bob Herbert, "Nike's Bad Neighborhood," *New York Times,* June 14, 1996.

484   *Chapter 5 Ethics and Human Resources Management*

EVALUATION OF THE CHARGES AGAINST INTERNATIONAL SWEATSHOPS

The critics' charges are undoubtedly accurate on a number of points: (1) There is no doubt that international companies are chasing cheap labor.[46] (2) The wages paid by the international sweatshops are—by American standards—shockingly low. (3) Some developing country governments have tightly controlled or repressed organized labor in order to prevent it from disturbing the flow of foreign investment. Thus, in Indonesia, independent unions have been suppressed.[47] (4) It is not unusual in developing countries for minimum wage levels to be lower than the official poverty level. (5) Developing country governments have winked at violations of minimum wage laws and labor rules. However, most jobs are in the informal sector and so largely outside the scope of government supervision.[48] (6) Some suppliers have employed children or have subcontracted work to other producers who have done so. (7) Some developing country governments deny their people basic political rights. China is the obvious example; Indonesia's record is pretty horrible but had shown steady improvement until the last two years. But on many of the other counts, the critics' charges appear to be seriously inaccurate. And, even where the charges are accurate, it is not self-evident that the practices in question are improper or unethical, as we see next.

Wages and Conditions

Even the critics of international sweatshops do not dispute that the wages they pay are generally higher than—or at least equal to—comparable wages in the labor markets where they operate. According to the International Labor Organization (ILO), multinational companies often apply standards relating to wages, benefits, conditions of work and occupational safety and health, which both exceed statutory requirements and those practiced by local firms.[49] The ILO also says that wages and working conditions in so-called Export Processing Zones (EPZs) are often equal to or higher than jobs outside.[50] The World Bank says that the poorest workers in developing countries work in the informal sector where they often earn less than half what a formal sector employee earns. Moreover, "informal and rural workers often must work under more hazardous and insecure conditions than their formal sector counterparts."[51]

The same appears to hold true for the international sweatshops. In 1996, young women working in the plant of a Nike supplier in Serang, Indonesia, were earning the Indonesian legal minimum wage of 5,200 rupiahs or about $2.28 each day. As a report in the *Washington Post* pointed out, just earning the minimum wage put these workers among higher-

[46]For example, see Gideon Rachman, "Wealth in Its Grasp, A Survey of Indonesia," *Economist,* April 17, 1993.
[47]Adam Schwartz, "Pressures of Work," *Far Eastern Economic Review,* June 20, 1991, p. 14.
[48]Schwartz, "Pressures."
[49]International Labor Organization, *World Employment 1995* (Geneva: ILO, 1995), p. 73.
[50]ILO, p. 73.
[51]World Bank, *Workers in an Integrating World Economy,* p. 5.

paid Indonesians: "In Indonesia, less than half the working population earns the minimum wage, since about half of all adults here are in farming, and the typical farmer would make only about 2,000 rupiahs each day."[52] The workers in the Serang plant reported that they save about three-quarters of their pay. A 17-year-old woman said: "I came here one year ago from central Java. I'm making more money than my father makes." This woman also said that she sent about 75% of her earnings back to her family on the farm.[53] Also in 1996, a Nike spokeswoman estimated that an entry-level factory worker in the plant of a Nike supplier made five times what a farmer makes.[54] Nike's chairman, Phil Knight, likes to teasingly remind critics that the average worker in one of Nike's Chinese factories is paid more than a professor at Beijing University.[55] There is also plentiful anecdotal evidence from non-Nike sources. A worker at the Taiwanese-owned King Star Garment Assembly plant in Honduras told a reporter that he was earning seven times what he earned in the countryside.[56] In Bangladesh, the country's fledgling garment industry was paying women who had never worked before between $40 and $55 a month in 1991. That compared with a national per capita income of about $200 and the approximately $1 a day earned by many of these women's husbands as day laborers or rickshaw drivers.[57]

The same news reports also shed some light on the working conditions in sweatshops. According to the *Washington Post,* in 1994 the Indonesian office of the international accounting firm Ernst & Young surveyed Nike workers concerning worker pay, safety conditions and attitudes toward the job. The auditors pulled workers off the assembly line at random and asked them questions that the workers answered anonymously. The survey of 25 workers at Nike's Serang plant found that 23 thought the hours and overtime worked were fair, and two thought the overtime hours too high. None of the workers reported that they had been discriminated against. Thirteen said the working environment was the key reason they worked at the Serang plant while eight cited salary and benefits.[58] The *Post* report also noted that the Serang plant closes for about 10 days each year for Muslim holidays. It quoted Nike officials and the plant's Taiwanese owners as saying that 94% of the workers had returned to the plant following the most recent break.

The *New York Times*'s Larry Rohter went to Honduras where he interviewed more than 75 apparel workers and union leaders and made visits to half a dozen plants, including the one that made clothes for the Gifford line. Workers and employers told Rohter that managers at some companies verbally abused their workers on a regular basis, but at other plants they treated their employees well. "What residents of a rich country see as exploitation,"

---

[52]Keith B. Richburg & Anne Swardson, "U.S. Industry Overseas: Sweatshop or Job Source?: Indonesians Praise Work at Nike Factory," *Washington Post,* July 28, 1996.

[53]Richburg & Swardson, "Sweatshop or Job Source?" The 17-year-old was interviewed in the presence of managers. For other reports that workers remit home large parts of their earnings see Seth Mydans, "Tangerang Journal; For Indonesian Workers at Nike Plant: Just Do It," *New York Times,* August 9, 1996, and Nina Baker, "The Hidden Hands of Nike."

[54]Donna Gibbs, Nike spokeswoman on ABC's *World News Tonight,* June 6, 1996.

[55]Mark Clifford, "Trading in Social Issues; Labor Policy and International Trade Regulation," *World Press Review,* June 1994, p. 36.

[56]Larry Rohter, "To U.S. Critics, a Sweatshop; for Hondurans, a Better Life," *New York Times,* July 18, 1996.

[57]Marcus Brauchli, "Garment Industry Booms in Bangladesh," *The Wall Street Journal,* August 6, 1991.

[58]Richburg & Swardson, "Sweatshop or Job Source?"

Rohter reported, "can seem a rare opportunity to residents of a poor country like Honduras, where the per capita income is $600 a year and unemployment is 40%."[59]

There is also the mute testimony of the lines of job applicants outside the sweatshops in Guatemala and Honduras. According to Lucy Martinez-Mont, in Guatemala the sweatshops are conspicuous for the long lines of young people waiting to be interviewed for a job.[60] Outside the gates of the industrial park in Honduras that Rohter visited "anxious onlookers are always waiting, hoping for a chance at least to fill out a job application [for employment at one of the apparel plants]."[61]

The critics of sweatshops acknowledge that workers have voluntarily taken their jobs, consider themselves lucky to have them and want to keep them. Thus Barnet and Cavanagh quote a worker as saying, "I am happy working here. I can make money and I can make friends."[62] But they go on to discount the workers' views as the product of confusion or ignorance, and/or they just argue that the workers' views are beside the point. Thus, while "it is undoubtedly true" that Nike has given jobs to thousands of people who wouldn't be working otherwise, they say that "neatly skirts the fundamental human-rights issue raised by these production arrangements that are now spreading all across the world."[63] Similarly the NLC's Kernaghan says that "[w]hether workers think they are better off in the assembly plants than elsewhere is not the real issue."[64] Kernaghan and Jeff Ballinger of the AFL-CIO concede that the workers desperately need these jobs. But "[t]hey say they're not asking that U.S. companies stop operating in these countries. They're asking that workers be paid a living wage and treated like human beings."[65] Apparently these workers are victims of what Marx called false consciousness, or else they would grasp that they are being exploited. According to Barnet and Cavanagh, "For many workers . . . exploitation is not a concept easily comprehended because the alternative prospects for earning a living are so bleak."[66]

Immiserization and Inequality

The critics' claim that the countries that host international sweatshops are marked by growing poverty and inequality is flatly contradicted by the record. In fact, many of those countries have experienced sharp increases in living standards—for all strata of society. In trying to attract investment in simple manufacturing, Malaysia and Indonesia and, now, Vietnam and China, are retracing the industrialization path already successfully taken by East Asian countries like Taiwan, Korea, Singapore and Hong Kong. These four countries got their

---

[59]See also Henry Tricks, "Salvador Textile Workers Face Bad Times," Reuters, March 8, 1996; Freddy Cuevas, "Sweatshop, or a Boon?" *St. Paul Pioneer Press,* July 17, 1996; and Seth Mydans, "Tangerang Journal."

[60]Lucy Martinez-Mont, "Sweatshops Are Better than No Shops," *The Wall Street Journal,* June 25, 1996.

[61]Rohter, "To U.S. Critics a Sweatshop."

[62]Barnet & Cavanagh, *Global Dreams* (New York: Simon & Schuster, 1994), p. 327. Similarly, Nina Baker reported that "Tri Mugiyanti and her coworkers [at the Hasi plant in Indonesia] think they are lucky to get jobs at factories such as Hasi." Baker, "The Hidden Hands of Nike."

[63]Barnet & Cavanagh, *Global Dreams,* p. 326.

[64]Rohter, "To U.S. Critics a Sweatshop."

[65]William B. Falk, "Dirty Little Secrets," *Newsday,* June 16, 1996.

[66]Barnet & Cavanagh, "Just Undo It: Nike's Exploited Workers," *New York Times,* February 13, 1994.

start by producing labor-intensive manufactured goods (often electrical and electronic components, shoes and garments) for export markets. Over time they graduated to the export of higher value-added items that are skill-intensive and require a relatively developed industrial base.[67]

As is well known, these East Asian countries have achieved growth rates exceeding 8% for a quarter century.[68] As Gary Fields says, the workers in these economies were not impoverished by growth. The benefits of growth were widely diffused: These economies achieved essentially full employment in the 1960s. Real wages rose by as much as a factor of four. Absolute poverty fell. And income inequality remained at low to moderate levels.[69] It is true that in the initial stages the rapid growth generated only moderate increases in wages. But once essentially full employment was reached, and what economists call the Fei-Ranis turning point was reached, the increased demand for labor resulted in the bidding up of wages as firms competed for a scarce labor supply.[70]

Interestingly, given its historic mission as a watchdog for international labor standards,[71] the ILO has embraced this development model. It recently noted that the most successful developing economies, in terms of output and employment growth, have been "those who best exploited emerging opportunities in the global economy."[72] An "export-oriented policy is vital in countries that are starting on the industrialization path and have large surpluses of cheap labor."[73] Countries which have succeeded in attracting foreign direct investment (FDI) have experienced rapid growth in manufacturing output and exports.[74] The successful attraction of foreign investment in plant and equipment "can be a powerful spur to rapid industrialization and employment creation."[75] "At low levels of industrialization, FDI in garments and shoes and some types of consumer electronics can be very useful for creating employment and opening the economy to international markets; there may be some entrepreneurial skills created in simple activities like garments (as has happened in Bangladesh). Moreover, in some cases, such as Malaysia, the investors may strike deeper roots and invest in more capital-intensive technologies as wages rise."[76]

According to the World Bank, the rapidly growing Asian economies (including Indonesia) "have also been unusually successful at sharing the fruits of their growth."[77] In fact, while inequality in the West has been growing, it has been shrinking in the Asian

---

[67]Sarosh Kuruvilla, "Linkages Between Industrialization Strategies and Industrial Relations/Human Resources Policies: Singapore, Malaysia, The Philippines and India," *Industrial & Labor Relations Review,* July 1996, p. 637.

[68]Gary S. Fields, "Labor Standards, Economic Development and International Trade," in Stephen Herzenberg & Jorge Perez-Lopez (eds.), *Labor Standards and the Development of the Global Economy* (Washington, D.C.: U.S. Department of Labor, Bureau of International Affairs, 1990), p. 23.

[69]Fields, p. 25.

[70]*Ibid.*

[71]The ILO's Constitution (of 1919) mentions that: ". . . the failure of any nation to adopt humane conditions of labor is an obstacle in the way of other nations which desire to improve the conditions in their own countries." ILO, *World Employment 1995,* p. 74.

[72]ILO, p. 75.

[73]*Ibid.,* p. 76.

[74]*Ibid.,* p. 77.

[75]*Ibid.,* p. 78.

[76]*Ibid.,* p. 79.

[77]World Bank, *The East Asian Miracle* (New York: Oxford University Press, 1993), p. 2.

economies. They are the only economies in the world to have experienced high growth *and* declining inequality, and they also show shrinking gender gaps in education.[78]

This development strategy is working for Indonesia. According to a recent survey in *The Economist,* "Indonesia is now well and truly launched on the path of export-led growth already trodden by countries such as Malaysia, Thailand and South Korea."[79] "In 1967, when the president, Suharto, first took that job, Indonesia's GNP of $70 per person meant that it was twice as poor as India and Bangladesh. Since then Indonesia's economy has grown at a rate of almost 7% a year in real terms. . . . By the early 1990's, average annual incomes had spurted to $650 a person—twice what they had been a decade earlier—as gross national product had expanded at an average clip of 6.8%."[80] Indonesia has spent significant sums on health, education and the advancement of women and the provision of credit to low income families and small-scale entrepreneurs.[81] It has also spread its wealth to the rural areas. Rural electrification and road construction have made rapid strides. By 1993, about half of the Indonesian countryside was expected to have electricity, up from 35% the previous year. Largely because of improvements in rural medical facilities and sanitation, the infant mortality rate has fallen by nearly 60% since the early 1970's.[82] These facts are reviewed here because they are so starkly different from the much darker picture painted by the critics of international sweatshops.

Profiting from Repression?

What about the charge that international sweatshops are profiting from repression. It is undeniable that there is repression in many of the countries where sweatshops are located. But economic development appears to be relaxing that repression rather than strengthening its grip.[83] The companies are supposed to benefit from government policies (e.g., repression of unions) that hold down labor costs. However, as we have seen, the wages paid by the international sweatshops already match or exceed the prevailing local wages. Not only that, but incomes in the East Asian economies, and in Indonesia, have risen rapidly. Moreover, even the sweatshops' critics admit that the main factor restraining wages in countries like Indonesia is the state of the labor market. "Why is Indonesia the bargain basement of world labor?" ask Richard Barnet and John Cavanagh of the Institute for Policy Studies. Their principal explanation is that "[t]he reserve army of the unemployed is vast; 2.5 million people enter the job market every year."[84] The high rate of unemployment and underemployment acts as a brake on wages: Only about 55% of the Indonesian labor force can find more than 35 hours of work each week, and about 2 million workers are unemployed.[85]

---

[78]World Bank, *East Asian Miracle,* pp. 2–4, 47.

[79]*Economist,* "Wealth in Its Grasp."

[80]Marcus W. Brauchli, "Indonesia Is Striving to Prosper in Freedom But Is Still Repressive," *The Wall Street Journal,* October 11, 1994.

[81]Barbara Crossette, "U.N. Survey Finds World Rich-Poor Gap Widening," *New York Times,* July 15, 1996, citing *U.N. Human Development Report 1996* (New York: Oxford University Press, 1996).

[82]Philip Shenon, "Hidden Giant—A Special Report; Indonesia Improves Life for Many But the Political Shadows Remain," *New York Times,* August 27, 1993, p. 1.

[83]See, for example, Brauchli, "Indonesia Is Striving to Prosper."

[84]Barnet & Cavanagh, "Just Undo It: Nike's Exploited Workers."

[85]Schwartz, "Pressures of Work."

The critics, however, are right in saying that the Indonesian government has opposed independent unions in the sweatshops out of fear they would lead to higher wages and labor unrest. But the government's fear clearly is that unions might drive wages in the modern industrial sector *above* market-clearing levels—or, more exactly, further above market. It is ironic that critics like Barnet and Cavanagh would use the Marxian term "reserve army of the unemployed." According to Marx, capitalists deliberately maintain high levels of unemployment in order to control the working class. But the Indonesian government's policies (e.g., suppression of unions, resistance to a higher minimum wage and lax enforcement of labor rules) have been directed at achieving exactly the opposite result. The government appears to have calculated that high unemployment is a greater threat to its hold on power. I think we can safely take at face value its claims that its policies are genuinely intended to help the economy create jobs to absorb the massive numbers of unemployed and underemployed.[86]

LABOR STANDARDS IN INTERNATIONAL SWEATSHOPS: PAINFUL TRADE-OFFS

Who but the grinch could grudge paying a few additional pennies to some of the world's poorest workers? There is no doubt that the rhetorical force of the critics' case against international sweatshops rests on this apparently self-evident proposition. However, higher wages and improved labor standards are not free. After all, the critics themselves attack companies for chasing cheap labor. It follows that, if labor in developing countries is made more expensive (say, as the result of pressure by the critics), then those countries will receive less foreign investment, and fewer jobs will be created there. Imposing higher wages may deprive these countries of the one comparative advantage they enjoy, namely low-cost labor.

We have seen that workers in most "international sweatshops" are already relatively well paid. Workers in the urban, formal sectors of developing countries commonly earn more than twice what informal and rural workers get.[87] Simply earning the minimum wage put the young women making Nike shoes in Serang in the top half of the income distribution in Indonesia. Accordingly, the critics are in effect calling for a *widening* of the economic disparity that already greatly favors sweatshop workers.

By itself that may or may not be ethically objectionable. But these higher wages come at the expense of the incomes and the job opportunities of much poorer workers. As economists explain, higher wages in the formal sector reduce employment there and (by increasing the supply of labor) depress incomes in the informal sector. The case against requiring above-market wages for international sweatshop workers is essentially the same as the case against other measures that artificially raise labor costs, like the minimum wage. In Jagdish Bhagwati's words: "Requiring a minimum wage in an overpopulated, developing country, as is done in a developed country, may actually be morally wicked. A minimum wage might help the unionized, industrial proletariat, while limiting the ability to save and invest rapidly which is necessary to draw more of the unemployed and nonunionized rural poor into gainful employment and income."[88] The World Bank

---

[86]*Economist,* "Wealth in Its Grasp," pp. 14–15.

[87]World Bank, *Workers in an Integrating World Economy,* p. 5.

[88]Jagdish Bhagwati & Robert E. Hudec, eds., *Fair Trade and Harmonization* (Cambridge, MA: MIT Press, 1996), vol. 1, p. 2.

makes the same point: "Minimum wages may help the most poverty-stricken workers in industrial countries, but they clearly do not in developing nations. . . . The workers whom minimum wage legislation tries to protect—urban formal workers—already earn much more than the less favored majority. . . . And inasmuch as minimum wage and other regulations discourage formal employment by increasing wage and nonwage costs, they hurt the poor who aspire to formal employment."[89]

The story is no different when it comes to labor standards other than wages. If standards are set too high they will hurt investment and employment. The World Bank report points out that "[r]educing hazards in the workplace is costly, and typically the greater the reduction the more it costs. Moreover, the costs of compliance often fall largely on employees through lower wages or reduced employment. As a result, setting standards too high can actually lower workers' welfare. . ."[90] Preversely, if the higher standards advocated by critics retard the growth of formal sector jobs, then that will trap more informal and rural workers in jobs which are far more hazardous and insecure than those of their formal sector counterparts.[91]

The critics consistently advocate policies that will benefit better-off workers at the expense of worse-off ones. If it were within their power, it appears that they would reinvent the labor markets of much of Latin America. Alejandro Portes' description seems to be on the mark: "In Mexico, Brazil, Peru and other Third World countries, [unlike East Asia], there are powerful independent unions representing the protected sector of the working class. Although their rhetoric is populist and even radical, the fact is that they tend to represent the better-paid and more stable fraction of the working class. Alongside, there toils a vast, unprotected proletariat, employed by informal enterprises and linked, in ways hidden from public view, with modern sector firms."[92]

Moreover the critics are embracing a development strategy—one that improves formal sector workers' wages and conditions by fiat—that has been tried and failed. It is in the process of being abandoned by Third World countries around the globe. Portes, who is no advocate of unfettered markets,[93] has warned against the overregulation of labor markets in developing countries. He says: "For those who advocate a full set of advanced regulations to be implemented in all countries, I offer the example of those less developed nations which attempted to do so and failed. More often than not, their sophisticated legal codes did

---

[89]World Bank, *Workers in an Integrating World Economy*, p. 75.

[90]*Ibid.*, p. 77. As I have noted, the report proposes that the "appropriate level is therefore that at which the costs are commensurate with the value that informed workers place on improved working conditions and reduced risk. . . ." (p. 77).

[91]World Bank, *Workers in an Integrating World Economy*, p. 5.

[92]Compare the World Bank's analysis: "But unions can also have negative economic effects. In some countries they behave like monopolists, protecting a minority group of relatively well-off unionized workers at the expense of the unemployed and those in rural and informal markets, whose formal sector employment opportunities are correspondingly reduced." World Bank, *Workers in an Integrating World Economy*, p. 80. For estimates of the size of the "union wage effect"—the difference in compensation between otherwise similar workers that is attributed to union membership—in different countries, see sources cited in *ibid.*, p. 81.

[93]Portes does not advocate "a removal of all state regulation in order to let popular entrepreneurial energies flourish" but believes that "[t]here is no alternative to state intervention in the labor market. . . .[B]asic rights which have become consensually accepted throughout the civilized world. . ." Alejandro Portes, "When More Can Be Less; Labor Standards, Development and the Informal Economy," in Herzenberg & Perez-Lopez, *Labor Standards and the Development of the Global Economy*, p. 234.

not so much reflect labor market realities as the influence and prestige of things foreign. The common end-result was an acute labor market dualism which protected a privileged segment of the labor force at the expense of the majority."[94] It is precisely to escape the web of overregulation of their own making that developing countries have established so-called "special production zones" (SPZs). The governments of "heavily regulated countries attempting to break into export markets have adopted the strategy of establishing [SPZs] in remote areas away from the centers of union strength. What is 'special' about these zones is precisely that provisions of the existing tax and labor codes do not apply to them and that they are generally 'union-free.' "[95]

Of course it might be objected that trading off workers' rights for more jobs is unethical. But, so far as I can determine, the critics have not made this argument. Although they sometimes implicitly accept the existence of the trade-off (we saw that they attack Nike for chasing cheap labor), their public statements are silent on the lost or forgone jobs from higher wages and better labor standards. At other times, they imply or claim that improvements in workers' wages and conditions are essentially free: According to Kernaghan, "Companies could easily double their employees' wages, and it would be nothing."[96]

In summary, the result of the ostensibly humanitarian changes urged by critics are likely to be (1) reduced employment in the formal or modern sector of the economy, (2) lower incomes in the informal sector, (3) less investment and so slower economic growth, (4) reduced exports, (5) greater inequality and poverty.[97] As Fields says, "The poor workers of the world cannot afford this."[98]

CONCLUSION: THE CASE FOR NOT EXCEEDING MARKET STANDARDS

It is part of the job description of business ethicists to exhort companies to treat their workers better (otherwise what purpose do they serve?). So it will have come as no surprise that both the business ethicists whose views I summarized at the beginning of this paper— Thomas Donaldson and Richard DeGeorge—objected to letting the market alone determine wages and labor standards in multinational companies. Both of them proposed criteria for setting wages that might occasionally "improve" on the outcomes of the market.

---

[94]Portes, "When More Can Be Less," p. 234.

[95]*Ibid.*, pp. 228–29.

[96]Rohter, "To U.S. Critics a Sweatshop." The focus on labor conditions in the export sectors of developing economies, when conditions are worse elsewhere, has attracted charges of "protectionism in the guise of humanitarian concern." Paul Krugman, "Does Third World Growth Hurt First World Prosperity?" *Harvard Business Review,* July–August 1994, p. 113. Critics are accused of advocating increased labor rights in third world export industries in order to reduce the competitive threat to first world jobs. Prime Minister Mahathir of Malaysia is outspoken on this point: Western pressure, he says, "is intended to stop multinationals from manufacturing in developing markets." "Striking a Balance; Pressured by Workers and the West, Asia Fights to Stay Competitive," *Asiaweek,* October 26, 1994. According to Krugman, "Developing countries are already warning, however, that such standards are simply an effort to deny them access to world markets by preventing them from making use of the only competitive advantage they have: abundant labor. The developing countries are right." Paul Krugman is right.

[97]Gary S. Fields, "Employment, Income Distribution and Economic Growth in Seven Small Open Economies," *The Economic Journal,* 94 (March 1984), p. 81.

[98]Fields, "Labor Standards," p. 21.

Their reasons for rejecting market determination of wages were similar. They both cited conditions that allegedly prevent international markets from generating ethically acceptable results. Donaldson argued that neoclassical economic principles are not applicable to international business because of high unemployment rates in developing countries. And DeGeorge argued that, in an unregulated international market, the gross inequality of bargaining power between workers and companies would lead to exploitation.

But this paper has shown that attempts to improve on market outcomes may have unforeseen tragic consequences. We saw how raising the wages of workers in international sweatshops might wind up penalizing the most vulnerable workers (those in the informal sectors of developing countries) by depressing their wages and reducing their job opportunities in the formal sector. Donaldson and DeGeorge cited high unemployment and unequal bargaining power as conditions that made it necessary to bypass or override the market determination of wages. However, in both cases, bypassing the market in order to prevent exploitation may aggravate these conditions. As we have seen, above-market wages paid to sweatshop workers may discourage further investment and so perpetuate high unemployment. In turn, the higher unemployment may weaken the bargaining power of workers vis-a-vis employers. Thus such market imperfections seem to call for more reliance on market forces rather than less. Likewise, the experience of the newly industrialized East Asian economies suggests that the best cure for the ills of sweatshops is more sweatshops. But most of the well-intentioned policies that improve on market outcomes are likely to have the opposite effect.

Where does this leave the international manager? If the preceding analysis is correct, then it follows that it is ethically acceptable to pay market wage rates in developing countries (and to provide employment conditions appropriate for the level of development). That holds true even if the wages pay less than so-called living wages or subsistence or even (conceivably) the local minimum wage. The appropriate test is not whether the wage reaches some predetermined standard but whether it is freely accepted by (reasonably) informed workers. The workers themselves are in the best position to judge whether the wages offered are superior to their next-best alternatives. (The same logic applies *mutatis mutandis* to workplace labor standards.)

Indeed, not only is it ethically acceptable for a company to pay market wages, but it may be ethically unacceptable for it to pay wages that exceed market levels. That will be the case if the company's above-market wages set precedents for other international companies which raise labor costs to the point of discouraging foreign investment. Furthermore, companies may have a social responsibility to transcend their own narrow preoccupation with protecting their brand image and to publicly defend a system which has greatly improved the lot of millions of workers in developing countries.

SWEATSHOPS AND RESPECT FOR PERSONS

—DENIS G. ARNOLD AND NORMAN E. BOWIE

The following essay explores how the theories of Immanuel Kant can be applied to the issue of global labor rights. By applying Kant's theory of universalism, the author find that fundamental rights exist for workers and that there is an ethical obligation on the part of employers to respect those rights.

In recent years labor and human rights activists have been successful at raising public awareness regarding labor practices in both American and off-shore manufacturing facilities. Organizations such as Human Rights Watch, United Students Against Sweatshops, the National Labor Coalition, Sweatshop Watch and the Interfaith Center on Corporate Responsibility have accused multinational enterprises (MNEs), such as Nike, Wal-Mart and Disney, of the pernicious exploitation of workers. Recent violations of American and European labor laws have received considerable attention.[1] However, it is the off-shore labor practices of North American and European based MNEs and their contractors that have been most controversial. This is partly due to the fact that many of the labor practices in question are legal outside North America and Europe, or are tolerated by corrupt or repressive political regimes. Unlike the recent immigrants who toil in the illegal sweatshops of North America and Europe, workers in developing nations typically have no recourse to the law or social service agencies. Activists have sought to enhance the welfare of these workers by pressuring MNEs to comply with labor laws, prohibit coercion, improve health and safety standards and pay a living wage in their global sourcing operations. Meanwhile, prominent economists wage a campaign of their own in the opinion pages of leading newspapers, arguing that because workers for MNEs are often paid better when compared with local wages, they are fortunate to have such work. Furthermore, they argue that higher wages and improved working conditions will raise unemployment levels.

One test of a robust ethical theory is its ability to shed light on ethical problems. One of the standard criticisms of Immanuel Kant's ethical theory is that it is too abstract and formal to be of any use in practical decision making. We contend that this criticism is mistaken and that Kantian theory has much to say about the ethics of sweatshops.[2] We argue that Kant's conception of human dignity provides a clear basis for grounding the obligations of employers to employees. In particular, we argue that respecting the dignity of workers requires that MNEs and their contractors adhere to local labor laws, refrain from coercion, meet minimum safety standards and provide a living wage for employees. We also respond to the objection that improving health and safety conditions and providing a living wage would cause greater harm than good.

I. RESPECT FOR PERSONS

Critics of sweatshops frequently ground their protests in appeals to human dignity and human rights. Arguably, Kantian ethics provides a philosophical basis for such moral pronouncements. The key principle here is Kant's second formulation of the categorical imperative: "Act so that you treat humanity, whether in your own person or in that of another, always as an end and never as a means only."[3] The popular expression of this principle is that morality requires that we respect people. One significant feature of the idea of respect for persons is that its derivation and application can be assessed independently of other elements of Kantian moral philosophy. Sympathetic readers need not embrace all aspects of Kant's system of ethics in order to grant the merit of Kant's arguments for the second formulation of the categorical imperative. This is because Kant's defense of respect for persons is grounded in the uncontroversial claim that humans are capable of rational, self-governing activity. We believe that individuals with a wide range of theoretical commitments can and should recognize the force of Kant's arguments concerning respect for persons.

Kant did not simply assert that persons are entitled to respect, he provided an elaborate argument for that conclusion. Persons ought to be respected because persons have dignity. For Kant, an object that has dignity is beyond price. Employees have a dignity that machines and capital do not have. They have dignity because they are capable of moral activity. As free beings capable of self-governance they are responsible beings, since freedom and self-governance are the conditions for responsibility. Autonomous responsible beings are capable of making and following their own laws; they are not simply subject to the causal laws of nature. Anyone who recognizes that he or she is free should recognize that he or she is responsible (that he or she is a moral being). As Kant argues, the fact that one is a moral being entails that one possesses dignity.

> *Morality is the condition under which alone a rational being can be an end in himself because only through it is it possible to be a lawgiving member in the realm of ends. Thus morality, and humanity insofar as it is capable of morality, alone have dignity.*[4]

As a matter of consistency, a person who recognizes that he or she is a moral being should ascribe dignity to anyone who, like him or herself, is a moral being.

Although it is the capacity to behave morally that gives persons their dignity, freedom is required if a person is to act morally. For Kant, being free is more than freedom from causal necessity. This is negative freedom. Freedom in its fullest realization is the ability to guide one's actions from laws that are of one's own making. Freedom is not simply a spontaneous event. Free actions are caused, but they are caused by persons acting from laws they themselves have made. This is positive freedom. Onora O'Neill puts the point this way.

> *Positive freedom is more than independence from alien causes. It would be absent in lawless or random changes, although these are negatively free, since they depend on no alien causes. Since will is a mode of causality it cannot, if free at all, be merely negatively free, so it must work by nonalien causality. . . it [free will] must be a capacity for self-determination or autonomy.*[5]

When we act autonomously we have the capacity to act with dignity. We do so when we act on principles that are grounded in morality rather than in mere inclination. Reason requires that any moral principle that is freely derived must be rational in the sense that it is universal. To be universal in this sense means that the principle can be willed to be universally binding on all subjects in relevantly similar circumstances without contradiction. The fact that persons have this capability means that they possess dignity. And it is as a consequence of this dignity that a person "exacts respect for himself from all other rational beings in the world."[6] As such, one can and should "measure himself with every other being of this kind and value himself on a footing of equality with them."[7]

Respecting people requires honoring their humanity; which is to say it requires treating them as ends in themselves. In Kant's words,

> *Humanity itself is a dignity; for a man cannot be used merely as a means by any man . . . but must always be used at the same time as an end. It is just in this that his dignity . . . consists, by which he raises himself above all other beings in the world that are not men and yet can be used, and so over all* things.[8]

Thomas Hill Jr. has discussed the implication of Kant's arguments concerning human dignity at length.[9] Hill argues that treating persons as ends in themselves requires supporting and developing certain human capacities, including the capacity to act on reason; the capacity to act on the basis of prudence or efficiency; the capacity to set goals; the capacity to accept categorical imperatives; and the capacity to understand the world and reason abstractly.[10] Based on Kant's writings in the *Metaphysics of Morals,* we would make several additions to the list. There Kant argues that respecting people means that we cannot be indifferent to them. Indifference is a denial of respect.[11] He also argues that we have an obligation to be concerned with the physical welfare of people and their moral well being. Adversity, pain and want are temptations to vice and inhibit the ability of individuals to develop their rational and moral capacities.[12] It is these rational and moral capacities that distinguish people from mere animals. People who are not free to develop these capacities may end up leading lives that are closer to animals than to moral beings. Freedom from externally imposed adversity, pain and want facilitate the cultivation of one's rational capacities and virtuous character. Thus, treating people as ends in themselves means ensuring their physical well being and supporting and developing their rational and moral capacities.

With respect to the task at hand, what does treating the humanity of persons as ends in themselves require in a business context—specifically in the context of global manufacturing facilities? In an earlier work Bowie has spelled out the implications of the Kantian view for businesses operating in developed countries.[13] Here we apply the same strategy in order to derive basic duties for MNEs operating in developing countries. Specifically, we derive duties that apply to MNEs that are utilizing the vast supplies of inexpensive labor currently available in developing economies. To fully respect a person one must actively treat his or her humanity as an end. This is an obligation that holds on every person *qua* person, whether in the personal realm or in the marketplace. As Kant writes, "Every man has a legitimate claim to respect from his fellow men and is *in turn* bound to respect every other."[14] There are, of course, limits to what managers of MNEs can accomplish. Nonetheless, we believe that the analysis we have provided entails that MNEs operating in developing nations have an obligation to respect the humanity of their employees. We discuss the implications of this conclusion below.

It is noteworthy that an application of the doctrine of respect for persons to the issue of the obligations of employers to employees in developing economies results in conclusions similar to the capabilities approach developed by Amartya Sen.[15] Over the last twenty years Sen has argued that development involves more than an increase in people's incomes and the GNP of the country. He argues that we should be concerned with certain basic human capabilities, the most important of which is freedom. Sen's perspective is similar in important respects to our own because both are concerned with providing work that enhances the positive freedom of the worker. The United Nations utilizes both the Kantian view and the capabilities view as a dual theoretical foundation for its defense of human rights. Among the rights identified by the UN are freedom from injustice and violations of the rule of law; freedom to decent work without exploitation; and the freedom to develop and realize one's human potential. It argues that all global actors, including MNEs, have a moral obligation to respect basic human rights.[16]

* * *

V. WORKING CONDITIONS

Critics of MNEs argue that many workers are vulnerable to workplace hazards such as repetitive motion injuries, exposure to toxic chemicals, exposure to airborne pollutants such as fabric particles and malfunctioning machinery. One of the most common workplace hazards concerns fire safety. In factories throughout the world workers are locked in to keep them from leaving the factory. When fires break out workers are trapped. This is what happened in 1993 when a fire broke out at the Kader Industrial Toy Company in Thailand. Over 200 workers were killed and 469 injured. The factory had been producing toys for U.S. companies such as Hasbro, Toys "R" Us, JC Penney and Fisher-Price.[17] In Bangladesh alone, there have been seventeen fires that have resulted in fatalities since 1995. A recent fire at Chowdhury Knitwears claimed 52 lives.[18]

Workers are also exposed to dangerous toxic chemicals and airborne pollutants. For example, a Nike-commissioned Ernst & Young Environmental and Labor Practices Audit of the Tae Kwang Vina factory outside Ho Chi Minh City, Vietnam, was leaked to the press. Among the many unsafe conditions reported by Ernst & Young at this 10,000-person facility was exposure to toluene (a toxic chemical used as a solvent in paints, coatings, adhesives and cleaning agents) at 6 to 177 times that allowed by Vietnamese law.[19] . . . In addition to toluene, workers at the Tae Kwang Vina factory were exposed to airborne fabric particles and chemical powders at dangerous levels. It is implausible to think that the (mainly) young women who work in the Tae Kwang Vina factory were informed about these health risks before they were hired. Ernst & Young reports that the employees received no training concerning the proper handling of chemicals after they were hired. Since that time Nike has overseen substantial health and safety improvements at the Tae Kwang Vina factory, and at the other Southeast Asian factories with which it contracts. Nonetheless, available evidence indicates that unsafe workplace conditions remain common among MNE factories.[20] Consider, for example, the report of Mexican maquila worker Omar Gil:

> *Back in 1993 I got my first job in a maquiladora, at Delphi Auto Parts. They paid 360 pesos a week (about $40). There was a lot of pressure from the foreman on the assembly lines to work hard and produce, and a lot of accidents because of the bad design of the lines. The com-*

pany didn't give us adequate protective equipment to deal with the chemicals—we didn't really have any idea of the dangers, or how we should protect ourselves. The Union did nothing to protect us.

From Delphi I went to another company, National Auto Parts. In that plant we made car radiators for Cadillacs and Camaros, and there was a lot of sickness and accidents there too. I worked in the area with the metal presses. There were not ventilators to take the fumes out of the plant, and they didn't give us any gloves. We had to handle the parts with our bare hands, and people got cut up a lot. I worked in an area with a lot of lead. If you worked with lead, you're supposed to have special clothing and your clothes should be washed separately. But the company didn't give us any of that. We had to work in our street clothes.

For all of that they paid 400 pesos a week (about $43). We had no union, and there was the same pressure for production from the foreman and the group leaders as I saw at Delphi.

Now I work at TRW, where I've been for about a month and a half. There's really no difference in the conditions in any of these plants—if anything, my situation now is even worse.[21]

If our analysis is correct, then those MNEs that tolerate such health and safety risks have a duty to improve those conditions. Lax health and safety standards violate the moral requirement that employers be concerned with the physical safety of their employees. A failure to implement appropriate safeguards means that employers are treating their employees as disposable tools rather than as beings with unique dignity.

We cannot provide industry-specific health and safety guidelines in the space of this essay. However, we believe that the International Labour Organization's carefully worked out Conventions and Recommendations on safety and health provide an excellent template for minimum safety standards.[22] For example, the ILO provides specific recommendations regarding airborne pollutants in "Occupational Exposure to Airborne Substances Harmful to Health" (1980) and exposure to chemicals in "Safety in the Use of Chemicals at Work" (1993). Ethicists, business people and labor leaders with widely divergent views on a number of issues can agree on a minimum set of health and safety standards that should be in place in factories in the developing world. We return to this issue in Section VII.

VI. WAGES

One of the most controversial issues concerning sweatshops is the demand that employers raise the wages of employees in order to provide a "living wage." Workers from all over the world complain about low wages. For example,

> *Employees of a maquiladora in Ciudad Acuna, Mexico, owned by the Aluminum Company of America (Alcoa), calculated that to buy the most basic food items needed by a factory worker—items such as beans, tortilla, rice, potatoes, onions and cooking oil, and excluding such "luxuries" as milk, meat, vegetables and cereal—cost U.S.$26.87 per week. At the time, weekly wages at the plant ranged only from $21.44 to $24.60.*[23]

While a living wage is difficult to define with precision, one useful approach is to use a method similar to that used by the U.S. government to define poverty. This method involves calculating the cost of a market basket of food needed to meet minimum dietary requirements and then adding the cost of other basic needs. The Council on Economic Priorities uses this approach to define a wage that meets basic needs in different countries. Their formula is as follows:

1. Establish the local cost of a basic food basket needed to provide 2,100 calories per person.
2. Determine the share of the local household income spent on food. Divide into 1 to get total budget multiplier.
3. Multiply that by food spending to get the total per person budget for living expenses.
4. Multiply by half the average number of household members in the area. (Use a higher share if there are many single-parent households.)
5. Add at least 10% for discretionary income.[24]

The United Nations Development Program employs a similar method to distinguish between three different levels of poverty (see Table 1).[25]

TABLE 1

Types of Poverty	Deficiencies	Measures
Extreme Poverty (also known as Absolute Poverty)	Lack of income necessary to satisfy basic food needs	Minimum caloric intake and a food basket that meets that requirement
Overall Poverty (also known as Relative Poverty)	Lack of income necessary to satisfy basic non-food needs	Ability to secure shelter, energy, transportation and basic health care
Human Poverty	Lack of basic human capabilities	Access to goods, services and infrastructure

It is our contention that, at a minimum, respect for employees entails that MNEs and their suppliers have a moral obligation to ensure that employees do not live under conditions of overall poverty by providing adequate wages for a 48-hour work week to satisfy both basic food needs and basic non-food needs. Doing so helps to ensure the physical well-being and independence of employees, contributes to the development of their rational capacities and provides them with opportunities for moral development. This in turn allows for the cultivation of self-esteem.[26] It is difficult to specify with precision the minimum number of hours per week that employees should work in order to receive a living wage. However, we believe that a 48-hour work week is a reasonable compromise that allows employees sufficient time for the cultivation of their rational capacities while providing employers with sufficient productivity. In addition, MNEs and their suppliers have an obligation to pay appropriate host nations taxes and meet appropriate codes and regulations to ensure that they contribute in appropriate ways to the creation and maintenance of the goods, services and infrastructure necessary for the fulfillment of human capabilities. Anything less than this means that MNEs, or their suppliers, are not respecting employees as ends in themselves.

VII. ECONOMIC CONSIDERATIONS

In a recent paper, Ian Maitland criticizes both the labor and human rights activists who have accused MNEs of unjust labor practices, as well as MNEs, such as Nike, that have responded by acquiescing to some of the activists demands.[27] . . . In addition to assessing the veracity of claims regarding worker exploitation, he sets out to determine "the ethically appropriate levels of wages and labor standards in international sweatshops."[28] He argues that philosophers . . . who object to letting market determinations alone set wage standards, are misguided on the grounds that "attempts to improve on market outcomes may have unforeseen tragic consequences."[29] Maitland's arguments regarding ethically appropriate levels of wages and labor standards may be summarized as follows:

1. Workers in the urban, formal sector of developing nations earn better wages than do workers in the rural, informal sector.
2. The imposition of wages or labor standards greater than that demanded by the market increases costs.
3. Increased costs result in layoffs and slow investment in the formal sector.
4. Formal sector layoffs result in a surplus supply of labor in the informal sector.
5. A surplus of informal sector workers depresses income in the informal sector.
   Conclusion: higher wages or labor standards increase poverty and limit economic growth in developing nations.

Appealing as it does to textbook economic theory, Maitland's conclusion retains an authoritative quality. Naive critics of MNEs fail to take into consideration rudimentary economic theory, and cynical corporate managers ignore these economic realities in order to preserve their brand images and corporate reputations. Maitland has done a valuable service by raising issues of central importance to the welfare of millions of powerless and impoverished people. However, is his conclusion correct? In the remaining portion of essay we argue that it is not.

First, despite his faith in the ability of international markets alone to generate ethically acceptable wage and labor standards for MNEs and their contractors . . . Maitland does not himself defend an unrestricted market approach. It is not clear, however, that Maitland recognizes this fact. The most obvious evidence in support of this conclusion is his criticism of corporate managers who, he believes, merely seek to appease their critics. "Not a single company has tried to mount a serious defense of its contracting practices. They have judged that they cannot win a war of soundbites with the critics. Instead of making a fight of it, the companies have sued for peace in order to protect their principal asset—their image."[30] Thus, according to Maitland, corporate managers have made the strategic decision to respond to market forces—in this case consumers' preferences and other marketing considerations—in the manner they deem most consistent with profitability. Given Maitland's faith in the free market, one might expect him to criticize this strategy because it is inefficient.[31] However, Maitland does not pursue this approach. Instead, he argues that managers should not appease their critics—even if managers regard this as the strategy most consistent with profitability—because doing so will have undesirable economic and moral outcomes, namely, higher unemployment and slower economic growth. There is, then, a contradiction at the heart of Maitland's analysis. He argues in favor of improvements to current market outcomes, while at the same time he argues against attempts to improve on market outcomes on the grounds that doing so will result in undesirable moral consequences.[32]

Second, some of the most compelling evidence in support of the proposition that MNEs can improve workplace health and safety conditions while avoiding "tragic outcomes" comes from MNEs themselves. Companies such as Levi Strauss, Motorola and Mattel have expended considerable resources to ensure that employees in their global sourcing operations work in healthy and safe environments. For example, Levi Strauss & Company stipulates that "We will only utilize business partners who provide workers with a safe and healthy environment."[33] Levi Strauss is known for acting in a manner consistent with this policy. Motorola explicitly endorses the idea of respect for persons in their Code of Business Conduct. The Code is built on two foundations:

> Uncompromising integrity *means staying true to what we believe. We adhere to honesty, fairness and "doing the right thing" without compromise, even when circumstances make it difficult.*
>
> Constant respect for people *means we treat others with dignity, as we would like to be treated ourselves. Constant respect applies to every individual we interact with around the world.*[34]

The physical instantiation of these principles can be seen in a Motorola factory in Tianjin, China:

> *In the company cafeteria, workers queue up politely for a variety of free and nutritious meals. One area is set aside for a pregnancy well-care program. A booth is open at which appointments can be made with the company medical staff. There is a bank branch dedicated to employee needs. It is a scene that one might expect in a Fortune 500 corporate campus in the United States. The overwhelming sense is of a pleasant, orderly place in which people are fulfilled in their work.*[35]

Recently Mattel announced the creation of a global code of conduct for its production facilities and contract manufacturers. It has spent millions of dollars to upgrade its manufacturing facilities in order to improve worker safety and comfort. Furthermore, it has invited a team of academics lead by S. Prakash Sethi to monitor its progress in complying with its self-imposed standards and to make their findings public.[36] This is believed to be the first time that a major MNE has voluntarily submitted to external monitoring. The examples set by Levis Strauss, Motorola and Mattel provide evidence that MNEs are capable of improving worker health and safety without causing further hardship in the communities in which they operate.

Finally, it is not clear that improving employee wages will inevitably lead to the "tragic consequences" that Maitland and others predict. The economic issues under consideration are complex and we cannot address them here in the detail they deserve. Nonetheless, several reasons may be provided for thinking that Maitland's conclusion is incorrect. With regard to the lowest paid formal sector wage earners in developing countries, the assumption that productivity is independent of wage levels is dubious.

> *As exceptionally low wages are raised, there may be increases in productivity either because of induced management improvements or because of greater labor efficiency due to a decrease in wasteful labor turnover and industrial disputes and to improvements in workers'*

morale and nutrition resulting, in turn, in an increase in the workers' willingness and capacity to work and a reduction in the incidence of debilitating diseases, time off due to illness and accidents caused by fatigue. If higher wages, at least over a certain range, are accompanied by certain improvements in labor productivity, it is conceivable that labor costs could decrease rather than increase and to such an extent that employment would not fall.[37]

Put simply, workers whose minimum daily caloric intakes are met, and who have basic non-food needs met, will have more energy and better attitudes at work; will be less likely to come to work ill; and will be absent with less frequency. Workers are thus likely to be more productive and loyal. Economists refer to a wage that if reduced would make the firm worse off because of a decrease in worker productivity as the efficiency wage. Empirical evidence supports the view that increased productivity resulting from better nutrition offsets the cost of higher wages.[38] Thus, if workers are being paid less than the efficiency wage in a particular market there are good economic reasons, in addition to moral reasons, for raising wages. Higher productivity per hour could also help alleviate the need for overtime work and facilitate a 48-hour work week.

One might object that our analysis implies that MNE managers are unaware of the correlation between wages and productivity, and that such ignorance on the part of MNE managers is implausible. Our reply is twofold. First, workers in developing nations *are* frequently paid less than the efficiency wage in those labor markets. Second, findings from an El Salvadoran Ministry of Labor study of maquiladora factories are instructive. Researchers found that "According to the production managers interviewed, some companies use North American and Asian efficiency and productivity levels as a parameter for establishing production goals, without considering the different nutritional conditions and technical capacity of our workers."[39] We believe that such erroneous assumptions have been widespread among MNE managers.

Part of Maitland's analysis rests on the assumption that increased labor costs will inevitably result in higher unemployment in competitive markets. Maitland is correct to identify this view as a common belief among many economists, especially as it relates to minimum wage legislation.[40] However, this view has been challenged in recent years. In their influential recent book-length study of the impact of minimum wage increases on employment, David Card and Alan Krueger argue that their reanalysis of the evidence from the United States, Canada, the United Kingdom and Puerto Rico indicates that the existing data does not provide compelling evidence for the textbook view.[41] In addition, Card and Krueger analyzed new data for recent increases in the minimum wage in the U.S. Their analysis is complex, but the results of their analysis are straightforward. "In every case . . . the estimated effect of the minimum wage was either zero or positive."[42] Increased labor costs appear to have been passed on to consumers in the form of higher prices without increasing unemployment. Again, this data undermines the textbook view regarding the impact of increases in the minimum wage. Economist Richard Freeman summarizes the impact of Card and Krueger's work as follows:

The Card-Krueger work is essentially correct: the minimum wage at levels observed in the United States has had little or no effect on employment. At the minimum, the book has changed the burden of proof in debates over the minimum, from those who stressed the potential distributional benefits of the minimum to those who stress the potential employment losses.[43]

After evaluating recent work on the impact of minimum wages, economists William Spriggs and John Schmitt reached a more determinate conclusion: "The overwhelming weight of recent evidence supports the view that low-wage workers will benefit overwhelmingly from a higher federal minimum."[44]

Two points concerning wages should be distinguished. First, conclusions concerning the impact of U.S. minimum wage legislation on unemployment cannot automatically be assumed to apply to developing nations. Careful study of the unique conditions of those labor markets is necessary before corollary claims can be assessed. Nonetheless, the textbook view rests significantly on studies concerning the U.S. labor market. As such, we believe that the burden of proof remains with those who maintain that increased labor costs must inevitably result in higher unemployment. Second, we wish to emphasize that we are not taking a position in this essay on increasing federally mandated minimum wages in developing nations. Rather, our contention is that it is economically feasible for MNEs to voluntarily raise wages in factories in developing economies without causing increases in unemployment. MNEs may choose to raise wages while maintaining existing employment levels. Increased labor costs that are not offset by greater productivity may be passed on to consumers, or, if necessary, absorbed through internal cost cutting measures such as reductions in executive compensation.

VIII. CONCLUSION

As Kant argues, it is by acting in a manner consistent with human dignity that persons raise themselves above all things. Insofar as we recognize the dignity of humanity, we have an obligation to respect both ourselves and others.[45] We have argued that MNE managers that encourage or tolerate violations of the rule of law; use coercion; allow unsafe working conditions; and provide below subsistence wages, disavow their own dignity and that of their workers. In so doing, they disrespect themselves and their workers. Further, we have argued that this moral analysis is not undermined by economic considerations. Significantly, MNEs are in many ways more readily able to honor the humanity of workers. This is because MNEs typically have well defined internal decision structures that, unlike individual moral agents, are not susceptible to weakness of the will.[46] For this reason, MNE managers who recognize a duty to respect their employees, and those of their subcontractors, are well positioned to play a constructive role in ensuring that the dignity of humanity is respected.

ENDNOTES

1. See, for example, Susan Chandler, "Look Who's Sweating Now," *BusinessWeek,* October 16, 1995; Steven Greenhouse, "Sweatshop Raids Cast Doubt on an Effort by Garment Makers to Police the Factories," *New York Times,* July 18, 1997; and Gail Edmondson, et al., "Workers in Bondage," *BusinessWeek,* November 27, 2000.
2. For the purposes of this paper we define the term as any workplace in which workers are typically subject to two or more of the following conditions: income for a 48-hour workweek less than the overall poverty rate for that country (see Table 1); systematic forced overtime; systematic health and safety risks that stem from negligence or the willful disregard of employee welfare; coercion; systematic deception that places workers at risk; and underpayment of earnings.
3. Immanuel Kant, *Foundations of the Metaphysics of Morals,* Lewis White Beck, trans. (New York: Macmillan, 1990), p. 46.

4. Kant, *Foundations of the Metaphysics of Morals,* p. 52.

5. Onora O'Neill, *Constructions of Reason* (Cambridge: Cambridge University Press, 1989), p. 53.

6. Immanuel Kant, *The Metaphysics of Morals,* Mary Gregor, trans. (Cambridge: Cambridge University Press, 1991), p. 230.

7. *Ibid.*

8. *Ibid.,* p. 255.

9. Thomas Hill Jr., *Dignity and Practical Reason in Kant's Moral Theory* (Ithaca: Cornell University Press, 1992).

10. *Ibid.,* pp. 40–41.

11. Kant, *Metaphysics of Morals,* p. 245.

12. *Ibid.,* pp. 192–193 and 196–197.

13. Norman E. Bowie, *Business Ethics: A Kantian Perspective* (Malden, MA: Blackwell, 1999). See pp. 41–81 for further discussion of the second categorical imperative.

14. Kant, *Metaphysics of Morals,* p. 255.

15. His latest book is *Development as Freedom* (New York: Anchor Books, 1999). Martha Nussbaum has developed her own version of the capabilities approach, one that pays particular attention to the unique circumstances of women's lives. *Women and Human Development: The Capabilities Approach* (Cambridge: Cambridge University Press, 2000).

16. United Nations Development Programme, *Human Development Report 2000* (New York: Oxford University Press, 2000).

17. Varley, ed., *The Sweatshop Quandary,* p. 67.

18. Bearak, "Lives Held Cheap in Bangladesh Sweatshops."

19. "Ernst & Young Environmental and Labor Practice Audit of the Tae Kwang Vina Industrial Ltd. Co., Vietnam." Available at http://www.corpwatch.org/trac/nike/ernst/audit.html.

20. See, for example, Varley, ed., *The Sweatshop Quandary,* esp. pp. 59–398.

21. Campaign for Labor Rights, "The Story of a Maquiladora Worker: Interview with Omar Gil by David Bacon" (September 6, 2000). Available at http://www.summersault.com/~agj/clr/alerts/thestoryofamaquiladoraeworker.html.

22. International Labour Organization, "SafeWork: ILO Standards on Safety and Health." Available at http://www.ilo.org/public/english/protection/safework/standard.htm.

23. After the complaint was raised in a shareholder meeting Alcoa raised the wages of the workers by 25%. Pamela Varley, ed., *The Sweatshop Quandary,* p. 63.

24. Aaron Bernstein, "Sweatshop Reform: How to Solve the Standoff," *BusinessWeek,* May 3, 1999.

25. *Poverty Report 2000: Overcoming Human Poverty* (New York: United Nations Development Programme, 2000).

26. Self-esteem is grounded in the conscious recognition of one's dignity as a rational being.

27. Ian Maitland, "The Great Non-Debate over International Sweatshops," reprinted in Tom L. Beauchamp and Norman E. Bowie, *Ethical Theory and Business,* 6th ed. (Englewood Cliffs, NJ: Prentice Hall, 2001), p. 595. First published in *British Academy of Management Conference Proceedings* (September 1997), pp. 240–265.

28. *Ibid.*

29. *Ibid.,* p. 603.

30. *Ibid.,* p. 594.

31. Such an argument would likely maintain that corporate managers fail to recognize that a public relations strategy that includes higher wages and improved workplace standards is more costly than an alternative strategy that does not. The details of such a strategy would then need to be worked out.

32. Maitland, "The Great Non-Debate over International Sweatshops," p. 602.

33. *Ibid.,* p. 539.

34. Motorola, "Code of Business Conduct." Available at http://www.motorola.com/code/code.html.

35. Santoro, *Profits and Principles,* p. 6.

36. S. Prakash Sethi, "Codes of Conduct for Multinational Corporations: An Idea Whose Time Has Come," *Business and Society Review* 104: 3 (1999): 225–241.

37. Gerald Starr, *Minimum Wage Fixing* (Geneva: International Labour Organization, 1981), p. 157.

38. C. J. Bliss and N. H. Stern, "Productivity, Wages, and Nutrition, 2: Some Observations," *Journal of Development Economics* 5 (1978): 363–398. For theoretical discussion see C. J. Bliss and N. H. Stern, "Productivity, Wages, and Nutrition, 1: The Theory," *Journal of Development Economics* 5 (1978): 331–362.

39. Republic of El Salvador, Ministry of Labor, Monitoring and Labor Relations Analysis Unit, "Monitoring Report on Maquilas and Bonded Areas." Available at http://www.nlcnet.org/elsalvador/0401/translation.htm.

40. See, for example, the essays collected in Simon Rottenberg, ed., *The Economics of Legal Minimum Wages* (Washington, DC: The American Enterprise Institute, 1981).

41. See David Card and Alan B. Krueger, *Myth and Measurement: The New Economics of the Minimum Wage* (Princeton: Princeton University Press, 1995). See also the special symposium on *Myth and Measurement* in *Industrial & Labor Relations Review* (July 1995) with contributions by Charles Brown, Richard Freeman, Daniel Hamermesh, Paul Osterman and Finis Welch; David Neumark and William Wascher, "Minimum Wages and Employment: A Case Study of the Fast-Food Industry in New Jersey and Pennsylvania: Comment," *The American Economic Review* (December 2000): 1362–1396; and David Card and Alan B. Krueger, "Minimum Wages and Employment: A Case Study of the Fast-Food Industry in New Jersey and Pennsylvania: Reply," *The American Economic Review* (December 2000): 1397–1420. For a discussion of the living wage issue in the context of the U.S. economy see Robert Pollin and Stephanie Luce, *The Living Wage: Building a Fair Economy* (New York: The New Press, 1998).

42. Card and Krueger, *Myth and Measurement,* p. 389.

43. Richard B. Freeman, "In Honor of David Card: Winner of the John Bates Clark Medal," *Journal of Economic Perspectives* (Spring 1997): 173.

44. William Spriggs and John Schmitt, "The Minimum Wage: Blocking the Low-Wage Path," in Todd Schafer and Jeff Faux, *Reclaiming Prosperity: A Blueprint for Progressive Economic Reform* (Armonk, NY: ME Sharpe, 1996), p. 170.

45. Kant, *Foundations of the Metaphysics of Morals,* p. 255.

46. For a fuller defense of this position see Peter A. French, *Corporate Ethics* (Fort Worth, TX: Hartcourt Brace, 1995), pp. 79–87.

CASE STUDIES OF INNOVATIVE RESPONSES TO CHALLENGING GLOBAL LABOR ISSUES

—Laura Hartman, Denis G. Arnold and Richard Wokutch

We are all parties to the conflicts incited by globalization; we don't have to leave our dens to see images of protest on television screens. Unfortunately, further investigation often only clouds the controversies for those not intimately involved. Frequently multinational enterprises are left with little direction or guidance regarding a recommended response to these disputes.

Attention usually focuses on multinationals' real or alleged "sweatshop" treatment of workers in developing economies. However, many firms either have been spurred on by this attention toward ameliorating workplace conditions; had begun the process at the time the media uproar began; or have always maintained superior standards for the workplace. Insufficient attention has been paid to firms who engage in truly good and beneficial activities with regard to their workforces, where the result is not a "sweatshop" environment but is instead a healthy workplace where laborers are respected and are treated with dignity.

The following two case studies present creative management approaches to resolving global labor challenges, approaches that are critical if workers' rights are to be respected within the constraints faced by developing countries and multinational enterprises.

ADIDAS-SALOMON

adidas-Salomon, formerly called adidas, was founded in 1949 and named after its founder Adolf (Adi for short) Dassler. It primarily produces athletic shoes, apparel lines and sports equipment.[1] The company was nearly bankrupt until it shifted production to Asia in the early 1980's and strengthened its budget for marketing.[2] In the year ending December 31,

Case Studies of Innovative Responses to Challenging Global Labor Issues. Excerpted from *Rising Above Sweatshops* by Laura Hartman, Denis G. Arnold and Richard Wokutch (Praeger Publishers, 2004). Reprinted with permission.

2001, adidas-Salomon had net income of 208 million euros (approximately $183 million) on net sales of 6.11 billion euros (approximately $5.35 billion).[3] Footwear accounted for approximately 44% of sales and apparel 36% during that year.[4]

Worldwide, adidas-Salomon contracts with approximately 950 factories.[5] For the adidas brand alone adidas-Salomon contracted with 570 factories in 2000 of which 267 were in Asia, 122 were in North and South America, and 181 were in Europe.[6] While adidas-Salomon comprises only a small percentage of many of the apparel factories' business, most of its footwear suppliers produce almost exclusively for adidas-Salomon. This allows them greater leverage in those circumstances to request modifications with regard to labor practices or issues surrounding safety, health and the environment. Given its leverage with suppliers, adidas-Salomon has conceded that "outsourcing supply does not mean outsourcing social responsibility."[7] The number of adidas-Salomon contractors is declining over time as adidas-Salomon consolidates its supplier base.

Case: Responding to the Challenge of Child Labor in Supplier Factories

One of the most challenging issues any MNE might face is what to do about child labor found at a supplier or vendor. First, let's be clear about terminology. For purposes of this case, "child labor" refers to paid workers who are under 16 years of age. "Juvenile labor" refers to paid workers between the ages of 16 and 18. "Youth workers" refers to any worker under 18, grouping together the two previous subgroups.[8] The ILO Convention No. 182, against the Worst Forms of Child Labor, came into force on November 19, 2000. That convention defines "child" to be anyone younger than 18 years of age. According to the new ILO estimates, there are some 250 million children 5–14 years old who are toiling in economic activity in developing countries, with almost half working on a full-time basis.[9] Even economically developed countries currently employ child and juvenile labor, albeit with restrictions, and so one should carefully review the social and economic structure within which the labor exists.

While the easy, black-white answer may be to rid all factories of all workers under 18 years of age, that is generally not the best answer for the children or the families involved. This is because alternative activities such as full-time education programs or childcare are not universally available, forcing these youths to perhaps engage in less desirable, though profitable, activities such as prostitution or drug dealing.[10] Moreover, notwithstanding the possible educational alternatives in some environments, this proposed solution completely ignores the financial impacts of terminating the employment of a youth worker. The income generated by the youth worker may, at the very least, assist in supporting that particular youth's fundamental needs (food, clothing and shelter); and, at the very most, it may be critical in supporting the entire family.

Children Found in Factory   adidas found itself facing this particularly challenging dilemma when it performed a first-time audit of a footwear supplier in Vietnam. On her audit of the factory, the auditor found documents that did not seem to make sense and confirmed these inconsistencies through worker interviews. She would ask some of the workers how old they were and would hear an appropriate (i.e., compliant) answer. However, as a follow-up, she would ask the worker what their "animal year" was (a fact known by all Vietnamese in accordance with the Vietnamese zodiac calendar), and they would not be able to respond immediately, without taking time to figure it out. Given this information, the auditor continued her investigation and later identified just under 200 of the factory's 2,000 workers as underage, according to adidas' SoE.

The auditor found both child workers as well as juveniles. Both groups were subject to the same responsibilities, pay, hours and overtime requirements as other workers, in violation of adidas' SoE. According to the SoE and its Guidelines on Employment Standards, child laborers are not permitted at all: business partners may not employ children who are less than 15 years old, or who are younger than the age for completing compulsory education in the country of manufacture where such age is higher than 15. adidas also requires that juvenile workers must be assigned to age-appropriate, safe duties, with a maximum of seven hours per day with no overtime.[11]

Next Steps   After reporting this information, Kitty Potter, adidas' Regional Labour Manager–Asia, realized that the solution was more complicated than simply letting all of these youths leave the workplace. In this *inspiration or vision setting* situation, however, while the SoE division was contemplating its response, several dozen child workers were immediately terminated, sometimes accompanied by threats should they return, without the knowledge of adidas at the time. adidas SoE staff now knew that something must be done—and quickly—to avoid losing contact with other youth workers, forcing these kids to consider alternatives far worse than the work environment they were forced to leave.

Potter and senior adidas production staff immediately told the factory manager that no more youths could be encouraged to leave, under any circumstances. adidas felt incredible pressure to act without delay in establishing some parameters for the situation, even though a more drawn-out process might have resulted in greater buy-in and participation from the factory, and a longer consultation period with the youths. adidas contacted an NGO called Verité (a non-government organization that focuses on human rights and standards in global outsourcing) for assistance. Verité recommended a Vietnamese education coordinator. At the same time, adidas drafted some basic notices to the children, on behalf of the factory. The notices explained that the factory would offer a program of educational classes and vocational training to the workers under 18. The students had to decide whether they would commit to the program. The notice required them to discuss the issue with family members and give their consent to enter into the program. It was clear to the adidas SoE team members that most of the students did not have a full understanding of what was going to happen and many of them were naturally suspicious.

Possible Solutions?   Working with Verité and an education coordinator, adidas was able to develop what later became adidas global policy for managing similar situations, that is, a global vision:

> *The supplier meets with the worker and tries to persuade them to go back to school. If the worker agrees to return to school, schooling fees and other costs are paid for by the factory until the worker completes compulsory education. Any continued employment is conditional on enrolling the worker in a work study program of continued education.*

The factory continues to pay the average monthly wage for the worker until the worker finishes school. This will make up for any lost income that the worker's family depends on in order to cover the basic needs of the family. The worker is required to provide the personnel manager proof of enrollment in school in order to continue receiving the monthly salary and school payments.

Finally, the factory agrees to provide a job for the worker once the worker has completed compulsory education.[12]

Motivation for Response   Part of the motivation behind this standard is that, if a supplier chooses to use children as laborers and that supplier is caught, they must pay the child plus send them to school; so it is a negative incentive. In implementing this standard, adidas was *integrating* its policies into operating practices with its suppliers. adidas monitors the payments to the youths in both programs in order to ensure that each receives payment equal to their average monthly wages over the year preceding the introduction of the program. In the case of the juvenile workers who will continue to work on a reduced shift, this has a significant impact since those individuals were originally paid on a piece-rate basis (i.e., based on productivity). The juvenile workers will accordingly produce less since they can only work seven hours a day; yet they will be paid based on their average wage from the previous year during which, of course, they were able to produce more in an eight-hour shift.

For children up to 16 years of age, in cooperation with teachers from the local government schools, the factory put into place a full-day education program with coverage similar to that covered in local schools. Topics included math, literature, chemistry, physics, biology and history. Children would arrive and depart from the factory at the same times they originally traveled, but would spend the workday in a large classroom in a space specifically designated for the program by the factory. Pre-program assessments were completed to accurately place each student in an education-appropriate program and teachers from a local province were hired to conduct the classes.

For juveniles of 16 and 17 years old, adidas felt that it was important to offer them continuing education programs in "lifestyle skills" subjects such as computer skills, the Vietnamese Labor Code, the environment, safety (both personal and in the workplace, with a focus on fire safety), AIDS/HIV, sexual education, hygiene. Not only would these programs assist the juveniles in areas of personal development, but adidas felt that it was necessary to occupy the workers in the afternoons so they wouldn't go find other work in alternate factories, thus subverting the current efforts.

Status   When the program began, they had 13 students enrolled in the younger program and 133 students in the juvenile program. As of June 2001, only 56 students remained involved in the program since many had already reached the age of 18. Eleven of these students are less than 16 years old (following an academic program equivalent to the 6th, 7th and 8th grade levels); 43 are juveniles participating in the lifestyle education programs and two are older workers who have chosen to participate in these latter courses.

It was determined that the education programs would take place at a location right at the factory itself. This would reduce any possible transportation problems in actually going to the program (since the youths could already get to the factory). In addition, by installing the program on-site, adidas was better equipped to monitor the program and the youths' compensation than if the youths attended programs in their communities.

While adidas was of tremendous assistance in the establishment of the programs themselves, they did not contribute to the programs on a financial level. "We wanted them to know that we believed this was their responsibility and not a 'rescue,' " says Potter. In order to facilitate payments, and because it was Verité's policy to enter into a contractual relationship with the multinational rather than the factory (to ensure payments and assure leverage between the MNE and the factory), adidas paid to Verité a quarterly advance for the work anticipated while the factory paid adidas retrospectively on a monthly basis for work performed. Under these arrangements, the risk was carried in full by adidas; but this arrangement also afforded adidas the leverage it needed in order to ensure compliance by the factory. In the final months of the program, an assessment by another NGO and local Vietnamese researchers will be conducted. The assessment will be fully funded by adidas, but the results of, and any recommendations in, the assessment will be available to all the parties involved in the program.

Assessment   This was adidas' first experience with child labor of this magnitude. Therefore, there was a great deal of *innovation, improvement* and *learning* that was accomplished in connection with this particular program regarding education programs, juvenile development programs and the employment of youths. In this situation, it was evidently vital to have a program in place as soon as possible in order to prevent greater harms. However, if adidas and Verité were to begin this process again, both would prefer to have a longer advance time to prepare the program. Under normal circumstances, the organizations would have been able to develop a comprehensive needs assessment, to test the participants for appropriate placements and to develop programming assured to meet the needs of the students. Unfortunately, often it is impossible to plan for these circumstances as they arise unexpectedly and demand immediate attention and crisis management.

The best method for advance preparation, therefore, is to determine exactly how the firm would respond under this scenario and to have in place as much of the preparation as possible so that it can be activated within a short time span. Under current circumstances, adidas and Verité had to "launch and learn" at the same time and only later make corrections based on some of the challenges that later arose (see below).

Moreover, one of the *indicators,* attendance, has been an issue in the programs. The factory experienced some attrition from the program after the students' annual leave time which one of the supplier's education coordinators explained might be due to the fact that "they're tired of school; they would rather just come back and make money."

Both Potter and Heather White of Verité suggest that, as discussed above, innovation and improvement are possible with more lead time. For example, a program could be designed based on subject demand rather than expert recommendations. In other words, perhaps the prospective students (especially in the juvenile lifestyles program) could be consulted regarding the precise topics of which they seek a greater understanding. In that way, the factory would be providing the educations that these youths want, rather than (or in addition to) that which is determined to be what they should have. For instance, a survey conducted after the program had begun revealed that the two most alluring topics for these older students were family life issues and family planning.

Potter also notes that a greater, more in-depth understanding of each individual youth's family and social situation might have allowed adidas and the factory to have engaged in a more effective, "holistic" approach to each person's particular circumstances. Perhaps by reviewing these circumstances, adidas and the factory could ameliorate some of the pressures that had led to the youth in the workplace in the first place.

Identified Areas of Challenge   Students have also noted the lack of interactivity in the classes, particularly the afternoon classes for the juvenile workers. These juveniles would have worked a seven-hour shift before coming to class. It is crucial, therefore, that these classes draw the students out through interaction and participatory teaching styles. "They just want to go home," explains Thuy Duong Le, the adidas labor auditor for this supplier. The objective is therefore to marry cultural values with modern, sophisticated teaching methods. In this way, the class becomes more attractive and the students are better able to learn in these circumstances. adidas engaged the services of an additional individual representing Verité named Minh Phuoc, in order to respond to these issues by creating a training program for the teachers involved.

Attendance, however, is a tricky balance. Those in developed countries generally consider the value of any education to be tremendous and, when compensated, the opportunity to go to school in lieu of work to be an easy choice. To the contrary, however, in this situation in Vietnam, many of these students would have preferred to work (or as in the case of the juvenile workers, to work longer hours) and to earn more money than to go to school at all. Unfortunately, there are woefully few examples of peer workers who have received their education and thereby excelled or succeeded in the workplace. Young factory workers in Vietnam do not look to their immediate supervisors or line managers above them and see educated Vietnamese colleagues. Instead, the leadership of these factories, from the president level down to the supervisors and line managers, is foreign-based expatriates. For example, in each of the factories this author visited, the ownership and management rested abroad, either in Taiwan or Korea. Therefore, without internal management programs or leadership training, the Vietnamese youth see no advantage at all in pursuing an education when they could otherwise be earning more money.[13]

Connecting this lack of role models to the attendance issue, the factories need to walk the fine line between requiring the young worker to attend school or lifestyle programs and asking too much of a worker, thereby encouraging that young person to quit and work for a different factory that would allow them to work more and not place these demands on them. Consider the impact of this struggle on the education program itself. Testing and grading is not necessarily part of the program because you would not want students to "drop out." The program must be sufficiently interesting to encourage students to remain, even if they foresee no economic benefit from doing so. And, as long as the labor law prohibiting workers under 16 and limiting the hours and types of work for 16 and 17 year olds is not strictly enforced, these youths *will* have alternative employment to which they can turn.

Finally, both Verité and adidas suggest that the program could be more successful if they would have had the time to involve the factory management in a more significant way from the start. As it was, adidas had no choice but to move quickly and hire outside consultants, who then created a program to implement immediately. Given a longer time frame, factory management would have been able to play a greater role and might thereby have "bought into" the program a bit more from its very inception, as well as been able to sell it a bit more strongly on the factory floor. In so doing, perhaps both adidas and the factory management would have been able to link this program into larger economic initiatives, thus planning for greater self-sustainability.

NIKE, INC.

Nike was founded in 1964 by Philip H. Knight as "BRS (Blue Ribbon Sports)," and later changed to "Nike" in 1972. Phil Knight remains Nike's Owner, Chairman and CEO today. Nike, based in Beaverton, Oregon, has more than 22,000 employees and over 800 contracted suppliers in about 52 countries throughout the world, employing more than 550,000 workers on any given day creating sports and fitness footwear, apparel, equipment and accessories for worldwide distribution (over 400 of these suppliers are located in Asia).[14] Approximately 175 million pairs of shoes are manufactured each year for Nike, contributing in part to Nike's annual revenue for 2001, which totaled almost $10 billion.[15] Nike's Code of Conduct, first sent out to manufacturers in 1992 and the second to be developed in the entire industry,[16] binds all Nike contract manufacturers and requires that all "manufacturing partners must post this Code in all major workspaces, translated into the language of the worker, and must endeavor to train workers on their rights and obligations as defined by this Code and applicable labor laws."[17] In its code, Nike sets a standard for its partnerships by seeking contractors who are committed to best practices and continuous improvement in the following areas:

- Management practices that respect the rights of all employees, including the right to free association and collective bargaining.

- Minimizing our impact on the environment.

- Providing a safe and healthy workplace.

- Promoting the health and well-being of all employees.

Specifically, Nike's code binds its partners to core standards of conduct, as set forth below:

1. Forced labor
2. Child labor
3. Compensation
4. Benefits
5. Hours of work/overtime
6. Environment, safety and health
7. Documentation and inspection[18]

Case: The Nike Jobs and Microenterprise Program

Conceived in 1997 and beginning in 1998, Nike established a microenterprise loan program to provide some support for women in the communities surrounding its suppliers. The purpose of the program is to allow women a chance to build small businesses that will ultimately boost their family's economic well-being, as well as contribute to the community's overall development. Though there is no direct financial gain for Nike, "the mircoloan program helps to create a more healthy community, which then provides other sources of income in the community, better workers and additional sources of support for the families of current workers, raising the whole village's standard of living," says Nike representative Chris Helzer.

Microloans respond to another difficult challenge in the Southeast Asian region. Nike has a global prohibition against any at-home work. However, this might have the impact of discriminating against women who, for social and cultural reasons, have either chosen not to work or are not allowed to work outside of the home. Therefore, by prohibiting any at-home outsourcing, these women may not have any financial means to protect their rights in other areas. The microloan program can provide this financial stability without outsourcing Nike manufacturing.

In each country in which the program is located, Nike has teamed with local NGOs in an effort to ensure that ongoing support is available for borrowers and that the programs are well *integrated*. The Vietnam programs were established as a joint effort between Nike, Colorado-based Friendship Bridge (an NGO devoted to creating loan programs for developing economies that was involved in the first three years of the program) and the local Vietnamese Women's Unions (who notify and solicit the borrowers). Currently, there have been approximately 3,200 loans in place with the average loan standing at approximately $65 [maximum loan = 1 million Vietnamese Dong ($\sim$ $75 US) and the minimum loan = 500,000 VND ($\sim$ $37 US)]. Total Nike investment to date has been approximately 3.5 billion VND ($244,755 US) which includes an administrative fee paid to Friendship Bridge. Usually women will borrow the minimum amount for their first loan and increase the amounts for subsequent loans.

The Vietnam program includes potential borrowers within a 30-mile radius of Nike suppliers. The loan program currently operates in 6 villages in the Dong Nai province and 12 villages in the Cu Chi province. The borrowers must submit a business plan and go through basic business training and health seminars before the plans and loans are approved. The business plan must include a provision for saving a part of the money earned and mini-classes are available to borrowers regarding good saving habits. An additional component of the program requires children of borrowers to remain in school.

Those receiving the loans included groups of women who team together to borrow funding to raise small livestock, to produce incense sticks and other basic manufactured items (garments) or to tend to rice fields in the production of rice paper for spring rolls. More than 2,300 rural women and former workers have received funds to help them in creating small businesses and, in Vietnam specifically, there have been *no defaults* on the loans.[19]

The loans are granted in a "trust bank" format to teams of individuals in order to build in a support structure to the program. The 5–20 team members of each trust bank guarantee each other's loans. The borrowers meet weekly or monthly to make loan repayments, share business tips, address community concerns and receive training in both business topics such as financial management as well as personal subjects such as nutrition, hygiene, child care and so on. After repaying loans, trust bank members can qualify for larger loans, and their payments are recycled to others in the form of new loans. Trust Bank clients have maintained an average repayment rate of 97% or better.

In Indonesia, the microenterprise loan program is offered in conjunction with Opportunity International, an NGO that has fighting global poverty as its primary goal. The basis of the program is the belief that a very small loan [such as less than US$100] may allow individuals to expand their inventory or to buy their raw materials in bulk, so that they can increase their profit margin, improve their business and perhaps begin to accumulate savings.

Through a partnership with an NGO called the Population and Community Development Association and Union Footwear, Nike also supports a microenterprise program in northeastern Thailand where it helped to establish a rural village stitching center and surrounding infrastructure such as a vegetable bank, a tree bank, a school and a women empowerment center. Nike invested in order to provide jobs and to support the rural development of the region, reversing migration to the city and to build cash crop projects. For Nike, this type of assistance represents a small loan that can put thousands of individuals to work. These efforts represent significant local community improvement and innovation efforts associated with the program.

The program was developed and structured with the intent of self-sufficiency within several years. Based on interest charged and reinvestment of capital, the program will soon be able to afford its loans with no additional infusion of capital from Nike.

ENDNOTES

1. http://www.adidas-salomon.com/en/overview/
2. Hoovers Online, "adidas-Salomon: (Capsule)," http://www.hoovers.com/co/capsule/2/0,2163,92632,00.html.
3. adidas-Salomon, "Overview, History," *infra* n. 1
4. *Ibid.*
5. adidas-Salomon, "Clearer: Social and Environmental Report 2001" (Herzogenaurach, Germany: adidas-Salomon, 2000), p. 20.
6. adidas-Salomon, "Our World: Social and Environmental Report 2000," *infra* n. 5, pp. 22–23. These figures are for export production only. Additional factories supply production for sale in local markets only.
7. *Ibid.,* p. 14.
8. The Global Reporting Initiative uses the term "young workers," and defines it as "a person who is above the applicable minimum working age and younger than 18 years of age." Global Reporting Initiative, *Child Labor Protocol, Draft for Public Comment* (May 17, 2002).
9. Kebebew Ashagrie, "Statistics on Working Children and Hazardous Child Labor in Brief" (Geneva: ILO, 1998), http://www.ilo.org/public/english/standards/ipec/simpoc/stats/child/stats.htm (accessed July 15, 2002).
10. However, some advocacy groups fail to consider all perspectives. For example, the Global Reporting Initiative's discussion on its Child Labor Indicators fails to take into account the impact of the termination of children beyond their removal from the workplace.
11. adidas-Salomon Guidelines on Employment Standards, (2001), part two, chapter 3, pp. 1–8.
12. *Ibid.,* p. 5.
13. These same circumstances also provide no incentive for the factory to provide additional education, or management or leadership training, since they do not expect the Vietnamese workers to manage the factory.
14. Nike, Inc., "Corporate Responsibility Report, 2001," p. 1; *see also* Amanda Tucker, Nike Director of Compliance for the Americas, during presentation transcribed in Richard Wokutch, "Nike and Its Critics," *Organization & Environment,* v. 14, n. 2 (June 2001), pp. 207–237, 212.
15. Nike Annual Report 2001, http://www.nike.com/nikebiz/invest/reports/ar_01/pdfs/financials.pdf (accessed July 15, 2002).
16. Nike's code was second behind Levi Strauss, which disseminated its code in December 1991.
17. Nike, "Code of Conduct," http://www.nike.com/nikebiz/nikebiz.
    jhtml?page=25&cat=compliance&subcat=code (accessed July 15, 2002).
18. *Ibid.*
19. Phil Knight, "New Labor Initiatives" (May 12, 1998), text at http://cbae.nmsu.edu/~dboje/NIKphilspeech.html (accessed July 15, 2002), also reported in "PBS Newshour," http://www.pbs.org/newshour/forum/may98/nike.html (accessed July 15, 2002) (confirmed in discussions with Dusty Kidd). For additional information on the loan program, see http://www.nike.com/nikebiz/nikebiz.jhtml?page=26&item=asia (accessed July 15, 2002) and http://www.nike.com/nikebiz/nikebiz.jhtml?page=25&cat=communityprograms&subcat=smbizloans (accessed July 15, 2002).

Chapter 6

ETHICS AND MARKETING

Zafar Iqbal, *DePaul University*

(continued)

According to common perception, it seems almost antithetical to include the terms *marketing* and *ethics* in the same sentence. Marketing is typically perceived as something that is "done" to customers; something that customers have to "watch out for." Marketing, generally equated with advertising and selling, is viewed as a set of tactics used by firms to induce unsuspecting customers to buy products and services that they do not need, at prices that are much too high. More generous critics understand that marketing is necessary in today's society and are willing to concede that marketing is at best a "necessary evil."

Marketers respond to the above criticisms by pointing to a more expansive definition of marketing as the "process of planning and executing the conception, pricing, promotion and distribution of ideas, goods, services to create exchanges that satisfy individual and organizational goals."[1] In other words, marketers are merely providing their customers with products and services at prices that satisfy the customers. Furthermore, because markets are competitive, firms have to advertise and promote in order to differentiate their offerings from those of the competitors. By including customer satisfaction as a critical outcome of the marketing process, marketers state that they are providing products that are needed and/or wanted by their customers—if customers are satisfied, then clearly the products are needed.

From the standpoint of ethical theory, the above response of marketers to criticisms of marketing employs teleological reasoning—the outcome of customer satisfaction, a good outcome, justifies the means used by marketers to achieve the outcome. The critics counter this reasoning by emphasizing that the criticisms of marketing are deontological, i.e., concerned with the means employed by marketers, irrespective of the outcome. In fact, most criticisms of marketing ethics pertain to the tactics used by marketers: "create demand for unnecessary products"; "fail to provide complete information"; "create misleading advertising"; "mark up prices when demand is high"; "charge different prices for different customers"; and so on. A teleological response to a deontological criticism seems to only exacerbate the battle.

This is not to say that marketers do not have a deontological response for their critics. Marketers have created and adopted a code of ethics that is mainly deontological, i.e., it deals with how marketers must conduct their activities, irrespective of outcomes (see Appendix A to this chapter text). In addition, studies in marketing ethics suggest that deontological issues pervade practicing managers' use of ethics. For example, sales managers' decisions to discipline or reward the behavior of salespeople are guided primarily by the inherent rightness or wrongness of the salespeople's behaviors (deontological considerations)

---

[1]*Dictionary of Marketing Terms,* 2nd ed., ed. Peter D. Bennett (Chicago: American Marketing Association, 1995).

and only secondarily by the consequences of the behaviors on the organization (teleological).[2] In a survey of 1,076 marketing professionals asking for the most difficult ethical issues they face in their work, respondents cited the following: bribery (gifts, questionable payments), fairness (conflicts of interest, manipulation), price issues (differential or predatory pricing), products (safety, infringement), personnel confidentiality, advertising (puffing versus misrepresentation), manipulation of data and purchasing (reciprocity in supplier selection).[3] As seen from Appendix A, most of the above issues have been addressed by the American Marketing Association code of ethics.

However, creating a code of ethics and subscribing to it in practice can be two entirely different matters. A comprehensive study of marketing professionals' responses to ethical issues in marketing research found that judgments of ethics were largely influenced by deontological considerations. These judgments, rather than teleological considerations, influenced marketing professionals' decisions to either reward or punish an ethical or unethical behavior.[4] In other words, inherent rightness or wrongness of an action determined a marketing professional's judgment of whether that action was ethical or not, rather than whether that action led to good or bad outcomes. A more comprehensive study of marketers' responses to a variety of ethical dilemmas demonstrated that most marketing professionals had some sense of ethics when making marketing decisions.[5]

The above facts indicate that most practicing marketers do take ethics into account when making decisions. Moreover, marketing as a discipline has responded by creating a code of ethical conduct that seems to take into account the most serious ethical concerns in the marketing discipline. So then, are we to assume that the issue of marketing ethics has been resolved successfully by marketing practitioners?

FAR FROM RESOLUTION

It is difficult to pick up a newspaper or a magazine without finding some issue in marketing being subjected to criticism for lack of ethical sensitivity. In the recent past, some typical issues have included, among others, truth in advertising (the old favorite), planned obsolescence product decisions (products intentionally failing after a predetermined amount of time), data privacy, selling practices, price gouging (natural gas in California, gasoline in Illinois) and marketing to minors (alcohol and tobacco). It is somewhat surprising that ethical issues keep arising despite both teleological (customer satisfaction) and deontological (code of ethics) methods adopted by marketing professionals to prevent unethical behavior. What might explain these recurring lapses in ethics on the part of marketers? There are five possible explanations for the above anomaly.

---

[2]Shelby Hunt and Arturo Vasquez-Parraga, "Organizational Consequences, Marketing Ethics, and Sales Force Supervision," *Journal of Marketing Research* 30 (1993), pp. 78–90.

[3]Lawrence Chonko and Shelby Hunt, "Ethics and Marketing Management: An Empirical Investigation," *Journal of Business Research* 13 (1985), pp. 339–59.

[4]Daulatram Lund, "Deontological and Teleological Influences on Marketing Research Ethics," *The Journal of Applied Business Research* 17, no. 2 (2001), pp. 65–82.

[5]Daulatram Lund, "An Empirical Examination of Marketing Professionals' Ethical Behavior in Differing Situations," *Journal of Business Ethics* 24 (2000), pp. 331–42.

1. *It's legal, isn't it?* The easiest response of most marketing professionals to accusations of ethical lapses is to resort to a legal shelter. It is not just that legal and ethical issues are often the same in the minds of marketing professionals. It is more than that. There is a perceptible trend to determine the wrongness and rightness of a decision by referring to the legality of an issue rather than using either an internal or external ethical reference point. Given the rise in the amount of total litigation that business today faces, it is not surprising that most business decisions are viewed through a legal filter. Increasingly, the defensive posture adopted during product launches, advertising campaigns, contests, pricing offers and distribution agreements involves an extensive legal analysis before implementation. This alone is a heavy and costly burden for most businesses to shoulder. Most firms, however, shoulder this burden because the cost of illegal behavior is very high. Ethics, on the other hand, does not have as widely accepted a corresponding framework with a commensurate downside. Given limited resources and intense time pressures, the tussle between the law and ethics results in the law substituting for ethics.

2. *Do customers really care about ethics?* If there is one (near) guarantee in the marketing behavior of firms, it is that firms will (eventually) stop offering what customers do not care about. So the question indeed bears consideration—do customers care about ethics when making purchasing decisions? Because, if the answer is negative, then firms have a reason to avoid thinking of ethics when making decisions. The answer to the above question is not unequivocal. Even though customers today are extremely sophisticated, this does not necessarily translate into their favoring ethical firms over unethical firms. This is not to say that customers are unethical, but that when purchasing products and services, customers seem to care about other aspects of the purchase before they consider whether a firm is ethical or not.[6] Customers consider ethics in a purchase decision when the ethical issue affects them directly. Given the increase in complexity in most products and services and the corresponding increase in the information associated with products, it is not surprising that customers seem too overwhelmed to consider ethics as an additional factor. If customers place ethics lower down in the hierarchy of needs when actually purchasing, marketers lose incentive to pursue ethical behavior.

3. *Where are the ethics police?* Typically ethical lapses by firms are made public by consumer advocacy groups, concerned citizens and members of the media. Given the number of firms engaging in marketing activities, it is difficult for just the above groups alone to police all marketing behavior for ethical violations. Legal enforcement has a budget, personnel and a clear mandate from easily communicated laws. Ethical enforcement (in whatever form it exists) has none or very little of the above and hence cannot control most ethical violations.

4. *Ethical environment: a moving target.* Like most other forms of firm environment, ethical environments change rapidly. Even the best-intentioned marketers are sometimes caught by surprise by an ethical issue. Even firms that allocate significant resources to

---

[6]Marylyn Carrigan and Ahmad Attalla, "The Myth of the Ethical Consumer—Do Ethics Matter in Purchase Behavior," *Journal of Consumer Marketing* 18, no. 7 (2001), pp. 560–77.

ensuring ethical behavior of their employees are taken unawares. For example, The Body Shop, a company at the forefront of ethical intentions and behavior, was caught unaware when the magazine *Business Ethics* published an exposé of its alleged false claims.[7] The allegations claimed that the company had misled its customers by falsely claiming the level of indigenous and natural materials used in its cosmetics. A subsequent social audit, sponsored by The Body Shop, revealed overall favorable results for The Body Shop, though the firm did not fare so well in other nonsponsored reports, leaving the issue somewhat unresolved. However, the fact that a company with an avowed ethical mission can sometimes fall behind the times does not bode well for firms with less stringent ethical missives.

5. *Following the money: changing incentives.* In addition to customer satisfaction, obviously another critical outcome that firms seek is profits. The nature of profits and the duration allowed by shareholders for firms to achieve desired levels of profits make firms act within an extremely short time frame. Quarterly earnings and profit reports have existed for a long time, but the intense scrutiny and the (almost) brutal punishment meted out to firms falling below expectations has caused many managers to manage for the short term. The short-term mentality is perhaps not conducive for encouraging ethical behavior. Results from ethical behavior are typically long term, often vague and sometimes even unclear. Given the pressures from short-term-oriented shareholders with very sharp teeth and comparing those to longer-term, sometimes weak pressures from ethical interest groups with unclear dental records, the choice of behavior is startlingly clear—ethics takes a back seat.

SO, NOW WHAT?

In the clamor of the battle, one conclusion stands clear—ethical behavior is critical. We have seen the implications of unethical behavior throughout this text and earlier chapters have outlined the positive implications of ethical conduct for any firm. Both marketers and ethicists agree that ethics are important. Ethicists agree that marketing activities are vital for the functioning of an economy and society and that pursuing profits benefits a large section of society, particularly when compared to the option of not pursuing profits. Marketers, for their part, agree that brand name matters and that corporate reputation is an integral part of the value of a brand. In turn, ethics are a large part of corporate reputation. What might allow the two sides to focus on these commonalities rather than the differences that separate them? We consider two possible solutions here:

1. *Self-regulation.* Marketers are very well trained in responding to environmental changes—after all, two key environmental stakeholders are completely the responsibility of marketing, namely customers and competitors. Marketers have always modified their marketplace behavior in response to changes that affect their interactions with the above two stakeholders. Marketers are quick to attack competitors when incidences of marketplace discrimination occur (e.g., Microsoft and its competitors), or

---

[7]John Bavaria, Eric Baker and Simon Billenness, "Body Shop Scrutinized," from *Insight,* published by Franklin Research and Development.

when competitors behave illegally. Marketers seek any source of competitive advantage over competition. It then behooves ethicists to continually raise issues of ethics because smart marketers will treat these issues as opportunities for gaining competitive advantage over competitors that fail to respond to the ethical environment. Other marketers will imitate these pioneers and we will have the beginnings of self-regulated ethical behavior on the part of marketers. An example of the above is the cosmetics industry. Firms like The Body Shop have raised the bar in ethics and other cosmetics companies are (slowly) responding. The number of firms that now claim that their cosmetics are "not tested on animals" is rising. Some degree of self-regulation within the cosmetics industry is occurring where competitors are quick to use lapses in ethics by others as a source of competitive advantage.

2. *Benefiting society and the bottom line.* The role of corporate social responsibility is gaining importance. Many private companies have moved to the forefront of promoting social causes.[8] For example Rockport Co.'s campaign to educate Americans on the benefits of walking has been credited with starting the fitness walking craze. It goes without saying that Rockport clearly benefited by more Americans walking (sales jumped 20-fold in 10 years) and that makes the purists among the ethicists question the motives behind Rockport's intentions. But from a teleological perspective, both society and Rockport achieved good outcomes. From a deontological perspective (somewhat tainted, because outcomes drove actions), Rockport behaved ethically. Most theorists agree that theories are approximations of reality—they make comprehension, explanation and prediction easier. In such a situation, it is perhaps sensible to allow marketers to achieve their goals (customer satisfaction and profits) by insisting on ethical behavior (the ethicists' goals) and not always questioning the motives behind the actions of marketers.

So, in conclusion, if society benefits, marketers benefit and marketers behave ethically, why not let that happen? Perhaps then the phrase "marketing ethics" will not be perceived to be an oxymoron.

ORGANIZATION OF THE CHAPTER

The articles selected for inclusion in this chapter are intended to raise ethical issues and conflicts in six areas of marketing.

1. *Advertising.* Two controversial issues in advertising involve the portrayal of women in advertising and racial insensitivity. Advertising is used by marketers as a means of communication with their target market. Interestingly, in a survey of advertising executives, the most common ethical problem cited was "treating clients fairly."[9] However, in treating clients fairly, advertisers also need to keep ethical concerns of their target markets in mind.

---

[8]Paul Bloom, Pattie Yu Hussein and Lisa Szykman, "Benefiting Society and the Bottom Line," *Marketing Management,* Winter 1995.
[9]Shelby Hunt and Lawrence Chonko, "Ethical Problems of Advertising Agency Executives," *Journal of Advertising* 16, no. 4 (1987), pp. 12–24.

2. *Product obsolescence.* Most of us have purchased a computer and subsequently found that, within a very short period of time, the computer is outdated compared to the current offerings in the market. While many of us attribute this circumstance to the rapid advance of technology, we forget that the choice of introducing the latest technologies lies with the marketers.

3. *Marketing research and data mining.* The rapid expansion of information technology has made the collection, storage and manipulation of customer data tremendously economical. Marketers, like Amazon.com, credit card companies, banks, health care organizations, among others, seeking competitive advantage have amassed vast data warehouses. This trend is compounded by the use of sophisticated analytic software that detects patterns in behavior—the resultant is a loss in customer privacy.

4. *Pharmaceutical marketing.* The ethical conflicts raised by direct advertisement of pharmaceuticals to customers coupled with increased budgets for marketing to physicians have raised costs of health care—or have they?

5. *Marketing to minors.* The ethics of marketing to children is an explosive issue, in general. While the issues of marketing alcohol and tobacco to minors have been subject to legislation, how should other products and brands be handled?

6. *Pricing issues.* Two issues are suggested by the readings—the first issue deals with "dynamic pricing," the act of instantaneously adjusting prices based on current demand (e.g., the price of a beverage in a vending machine rises or falls as a function of ambient temperature). The second related issue addressed in the readings concerns price gouging.

APPENDIX A: AMA CODE OF ETHICS[10]

Members of the American Marketing Association are committed to ethical professional conduct. They have joined together in subscribing to this Code of Ethics embracing the following topics:

Responsibilities of the Marketer

Marketers must accept responsibility for the consequences of their activities and make every effort to ensure that their decisions, recommendations and actions function to identify, serve and satisfy all relevant publics: customers, organizations and society.

Marketers' Professional Conduct must be guided by:

1. The basic rule of professional ethics: not knowingly to do harm;
2. The adherence to all applicable laws and regulations;
3. The accurate representation of their education, training and experience; and
4. The active support, practice and promotion of this Code of Ethics.

---

[10]*American Marketing Association's Code of Ethics,* www.marketingpower.com.

Honesty and Fairness

Marketers shall uphold and advance the integrity, honor and dignity of the marketing profession by:

1. Being honest in serving consumers, clients, employees, suppliers, distributors and the public;
2. Not knowingly participating in conflict of interest without prior notice to all parties involved; and
3. Establishing equitable fee schedules including the payment or receipt of usual, customary and/or legal compensation for marketing exchanges.

Rights and Duties of Parties in the Marketing Exchange Process

Participants in the marketing exchange process should be able to expect that

1. Products and services offered are safe and fit for their intended uses;
2. Communications about offered products and services are not deceptive;
3. All parties intend to discharge their obligations, financial and otherwise, in good faith; and
4. Appropriate internal methods exist for equitable adjustment and/or redress of grievances concerning purchases.

It is understood that the above would include, but is not limited to, the following responsibilities of the marketer:

In the area of product development and management:

*   disclosure of all substantial risks associated with product or service usage;

*   identification of any product component substitution that might materially change the product or impact on the buyer's purchase decision;

*   identification of extra cost-added features.

In the area of promotions:

*   avoidance of false and misleading advertising;

*   rejection of high-pressure manipulations, or misleading sales tactics;

*   avoidance of sales promotions that use deception or manipulation.

In the area of distribution:

*   not manipulating the availability of a product for the purpose of exploitation;

*   not using coercion in the marketing channel;

*   not exerting undue influence over the reseller's choice to handle a product.

In the area of pricing:

- not engaging in price fixing;

- not practicing predatory pricing;

- disclosing the full price associated with any purchase.

In the area of marketing research:

- prohibiting selling or fundraising under the guise of conducting research;

- maintaining research integrity by avoiding misrepresentation and omission of pertinent research data;

- treating outside clients and suppliers fairly.

Organizational Relationships

Marketers should be aware of how their behavior may influence or impact the behavior of others in organizational relationships. They should not demand, encourage or apply coercion to obtain unethical behavior in their relationships with others, such as employees, suppliers, or customers.

1. Apply confidentiality and anonymity in professional relationships with regard to privileged information;
2. Meet their obligations and responsibilities in contracts and mutual agreements in a timely manner;
3. Avoid taking the work of others, in whole, or in part and representing this work as their own or directly benefiting from it without compensation or consent of the originator or owner; and
4. Avoid manipulation to take advantage of situations to maximize personal welfare in a way that unfairly deprives or damages the organization of others.

Any AMA member found to be in violation of any provision of this Code of Ethics may have his or her Association membership suspended or revoked.

AMERICAN MARKETING ASSOCIATION CODE OF ETHICS FOR MARKETING ON THE INTERNET

Preamble

The Internet, including online computer communications, has become increasingly important to marketers' activities, as they provide exchanges and access to markets worldwide. The ability to interact with stakeholders has created new marketing opportunities and risks that are not currently specifically addressed in the American Marketing Association Code of Ethics. The American Marketing Association Code of Ethics for Internet marketing provides additional guidance and direction for ethical responsibility in this dynamic area of marketing. The American Marketing Association is committed to ethical professional conduct and has adopted these principles for using the Internet, including online marketing activities utilizing network computers.

General Responsibilities

Internet marketers must assess the risks and take responsibility for the consequences of their activities. Internet marketers' professional conduct must be guided by:

1. Support of professional ethics to avoid harm by protecting the rights of privacy, ownership and access.
2. Adherence to all applicable laws and regulations with no use of Internet marketing that would be illegal, if conducted by mail, telephone, fax or other media.
3. Awareness of changes in regulations related to Internet marketing.
4. Effective communication to organizational members on risks and policies related to Internet marketing, when appropriate.
5. Organizational commitment to ethical Internet practices communicated to employees, customers and relevant stakeholders.

Privacy

Information collected from customers should be confidential and used only for expressed purposes. All data, especially confidential customer data, should be safeguarded against unauthorized access. The expressed wishes of others should be respected with regard to the receipt of unsolicited e-mail messages.

Ownership

Information obtained from the Internet sources should be properly authorized and documented. Information ownership should be safeguarded and respected. Marketers should respect the integrity and ownership of computer and network systems.

Access

Marketers should treat access to accounts, passwords and other information as confidential and only examine or disclose content when authorized by a responsible party. The integrity of others' information systems should be respected with regard to placement of information, advertising or messages.

GOT . . . BEER?!

Better Than Milk, New Survey Shows!

—PEOPLE FOR THE ETHICAL TREATMENT OF ANIMALS

The following publicity item was created and disseminated by People for the Ethical Treatment of Animals (PETA) as part of its publicity campaign surrounding the treatment of dairy cows. The campaign was specifically directed at college campuses and, subsequent to its inception, was severely chastised by groups including Mothers Against Drunk Driving (MADD) as inappropriate and insensitive to the drinking problems and pressures often found on college campuses. In response to MADD's concerns, PETA pulled the "Got . . . Beer?" campaign materials from college settings, "notwithstanding the enormously positive response from college students," and redirected those interested to its "Dump Dairy" campaign, instead. Included below are materials from both campaigns. Do you believe the "Got . . . Beer?" campaign is inappropriate on college campuses? Is the "Dump Dairy" campaign as effective as "Got . . . Beer?"

"Got . . . Beer?! Better Than Milk, New Survey Shows!" Reprinted with permission of People for the Ethical Treatment of Animals (PETA).

People for the Ethical Treatment of Animals

is urging college students to wipe off those milk mustaches and replace them with ... foam? The largest animal rights group in the world is releasing the results of research showing that beer is actually better for you than milk. PETA is giving away bottle openers that say, "Drinking responsibly means not drinking milk–save a cow's life," to college students who visit www.MilkSucks.com.

The dairy industry spends more than $300 million every year to convince people to drink gallons of the white stuff, but PETA's sentiments are with savvy health officials who warn that dairy products have four major drawbacks. Milk and cheese: 1) are loaded with fat and cholesterol and devoid of complex carbohydrates; 2) are frequently contaminated with pesticides and drugs; 3) are linked to diabetes, heart disease, and certain cancers; and 4) may even cause osteoporosis, the very disease that the dairy industry loves to use as a selling point in its ads, because the excess protein in dairy products leaches calcium from the bones. (The Harvard Nurses' Study shows almost twice as many bone breaks among women who drink three glasses of milk a day as compared to women who drink little to no milk.)

Here's why beer is better

A nutritional comparison of beer and milk reveals that:

* Beer has zero fat; milk is loaded with it.

* Beer has zero cholesterol; milk contains 20 mg of cholesterol in every 8-oz. serving.

* Beer doesn't contain hormones or antibiotics, while milk contains an ever-increasing variety of the pesticides and antibiotics fed to cows, including rBGH, the notorious growth hormone that can give guys breasts.

* Beer has half a gram of fiber in every cup; milk has no fiber whatsoever.

* Beer has only 12 mg of sodium per 122 mg. Milk is sky-high in sodium.

* The high-animal protein content of milk actually leaches calcium from the bones. In the U.S., Norway, and Sweden–where people consume the most dairy products–women have the highest rates of osteoporosis in the world. Regions of the world where dairy products are not part of the culture, such as China and Japan, are virtually osteoporosis-free. A study published by the *Journal of Clinical Nutrition* found that by the time she is 65, the average female American dairy-drinker will have lost 35 percent of her original bone density. The average female American vegetarian will have lost only 18 percent.

- Unless you drink the stuff on your way up Mount Everest, beer won't give you a stroke. However, dairy products contribute to almost every disease except carpal tunnel syndrome, including stroke; iron-deficiency; allergies; cancers of the prostate, breast, colon, and ovaries; asthma; heart disease; and even the common cold (milk helps promote the production of mucus).

PETA's main "beef" is, of course, about the treatment of the mother cows and their calves on factory farms. Today's dairy cow is treated like nothing more than a milk machine–chained by her neck in a concrete stall for months, her udders genetically modified to produce so much extra milk that they sometimes drag on the feces and urine covered cement. She is kept pregnant by artificial insemination to keep milk production high; her male calves are traumatically taken away from her at 1 to 2 days old and chained inside cramped dark crates to be killed for veal. The milk that is meant for them ends up on our supermarket shelves. There are no retirement homes for dairy cows. When their usefulness to dairy farmers is over, they get shoved into a truck and sent off to slaughter.

PETA's College Action Campaign coordinator Morgan Leyh counsels, "Colleges have been busy banning kegs from campus. But we say, 'Ditch the dairy, not the beer!' "

United States Department of Agriculture Nutritional Data for Milk and Beer.		
	MILK (1 cup, 2% milk)	**BEER (1 cup)**
Fat (g)	5	0
Fiber (g)	0	.5
Sodium (mg)	122	12
Cholesterol (mg)	20	0
Calories	122	97

Of course, while all this is true, PETA recommends fresh juices, soy milk, and mineral water–even soda–over milk <u>or</u> beer.

March 16, 2000

Dean Wilkerson
National Executive Director
Mothers Against Drunk Driving
511 E. John Carpenter Fwy., Ste. 700
Irving, TX 75062-8187

1 page via fax:972-869-2206 (hard copy to follow)

Dear Mr. Wilkerson:

We have seriously considered MADD's concerns about PETA's "Got Beer?" parody materials, and we have decided to pull our materials that refer to drinking beer from college campuses. We will, of course, continue the anti-milk campaign, but from a different angle.

As I think you appreciate, PETA's aim was never to promote beer drinking. Our materials recommend fruit juices, soy milk, and mineral water over milk or beer. We included beer in our nutritional comparison to focus attention a bit irreverently, on the fact that milk is so awful for you that even a glass of beer—widely recognized as no health food—would be a better choice than a glass of milk.

We will now refocus our "Milk Sucks" Campaign on the terrible suffering of hyper-ovulated, artificially inseminated, worn-out mother cows and their calves who are torn from their mothers and made to suffer so that college students and others can drink the milk that nature intended for them. As a result of our campaign, over 1,500 college students have decided to get involved in the fight against dairy. They will be asked to help post up our new "Missing" ads, modeled after the "Missing" ads on milk cartons and featuring a veal calf raised for veal.

We're pleased that the spotlight on our anti-dairy campaign has been able to help MADD bring more attention to the issue of drunk driving, while also drawing attention to the cruelty and unhealthiness of dairy products. Because all of us here feel that your work is so valuable, I am enclosing $500 in individual contributions to MADD from PETA employees. We will also add a link from our "Got Beer?" Web site to MADD's Web site.

Good luck in your good work. Please wish us well in ours!

Very truly yours,

Ingrid Newkirk
President

Mothers Against Drunk Driving

511 E. John Carpenter Fwy. Suite 700 • Irving, Texas 75062-8187 • Telephone (214) 744-MADD • FAX (972) 864-2206/2207 • www.madd.org
NATIONAL OFFICE

March 21, 2000

Ms. Ingrid Newkirk
President
People for the Ethical Treatment of Animals
501 Front Street
Norfolk, VA 23510

VIA FAX: 757-562-0457 (hard copy to follow)

Dear Ms. Newkirk:

We received the hard copy of your faxed letter dated March 16, 2000, along with the $500.00 contribution. While we appreciate the acknowledgement of MADD's mission, we feel we must return the enclosed donations from your organization and staff members. If you truly wish to support MADD's efforts, please do the right thing and stop asking students to drink alcohol.

As our national president stated in a letter faxed March 16, we are extremely disappointed to see that the "Got Beer" campaign continues to appear on the PETA Web site. While pulling the irresponsible campaign from college campuses is an important step, you are continuing to encourage students – many under the legal drinking age of 21 – to drink beer instead of milk through your Web site. Again, we ask that you immediately remove all "Got Beer" campaign references and terminate your link to MADD's Web site. We are unable to accept your contributions or allow a link to the MADD site because of the implied association with PETA's animal rights issues – issues which are unrelated to our mission to stop drunk driving, support the victims of this violent crime and prevent underage drinking.

We received numerous phone calls and e-mails from the public and PETA supporters voicing their concerns about the "Got Beer" campaign. We hope to hear from you soon regarding our requests.

Sincerely,

Dean Wilkerson
Executive Director

cc: MADD Board of Directors

PEOPLE FOR THE ETHICAL
TREATMENT OF ANIMALS

501 FRONT STREET
NORFOLK, VA 23510
TEL 757-622-PETA
FAX 757-622-0457

www.peta-online.org
info@peta-online.org

March 24, 2000

Mr. Dean Wilkerson
Executive Director
MADD
511 E. John Carpenter Fwy., Ste. 700
Irving, TX 75062-8187

Dear Mr. Wilkerson:

Your recent letter would have been well received if, instead of attacking us and insulting our staff and their families, you had acknowledged any of the good that has come out of the PETA campaign — for your organization, which received a greater platform at a crucial time for your issue than in any previous year, i.e. just before Spring Break, and for the issues that concern not only MADD but all decent people, namely drunken driving (which PETA has never advocated), underage drinking (which PETA has never advocated), and binge drinking (which PETA has never advocated). As someone here said, MADD got more exposure in two days than it has had in two years.

We realize that MADD used PETA as an easy target and we do not resent that. Without your drawing the media to our campaign, PETA would not have been able to let as many people as we did know that modern milk production is abusive to cows, promotes the notoriously cruel veal industry, and produces a product that eventually kills more people than drunken driving, through coronary artery disease, stroke, cancers, and other milk- (and meat-) related diseases.

Not that I would presume to know your agenda, but surely, now that the media fuss has abated, MADD should be rechanneling its energies into more productive avenues, say, for example, the fact that every sporting event of widespread interest to high school and college students is sponsored by beer and alcohol companies? That would seem more useful than niggling about our Web site. When college students or older people ask what the fuss was all about, we are not about to tell them that they're not intelligent enough to read the facts and make up their own minds. Let me also make it clear, PETA is not against beer-drinking, it is against milk-drinking, for ethical reasons. Beer-drinking is legal in this country and PETA has never suggested that any individual under the legal drinking age start drinking the stuff. When visitors to www.MilkSucks.com read our materials, they realize that.

Finally, by returning contributions from people who work at PETA, whereas you do not presumably return contributions from people who work at Budweiser or Coors, or even at the National Rifle Association or Ku Klux Klan headquarters, you have allowed your prejudices regarding our humane agenda to let you refuse money that MADD could have used to help stop problem drinking. Instead of seizing the opportunity to welcome new individual members, you have, instead, left a bad taste in their mouths. That is a shame and a missed opportunity to keep up MADD's good work.

Very truly yours,

Ingrid E. Newkirk
President

AN INTERNATIONAL
ORGANIZATION DEDICATED
TO PROTECTING
THE RIGHTS OF ALL ANIMALS

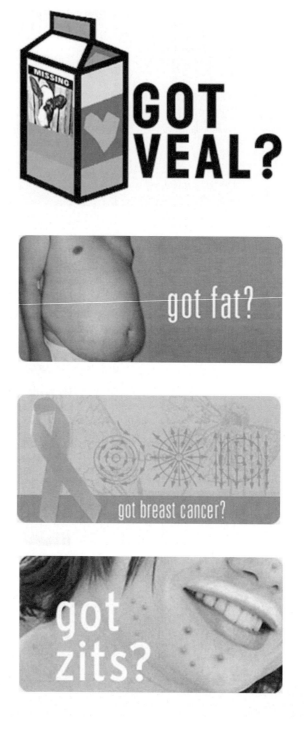

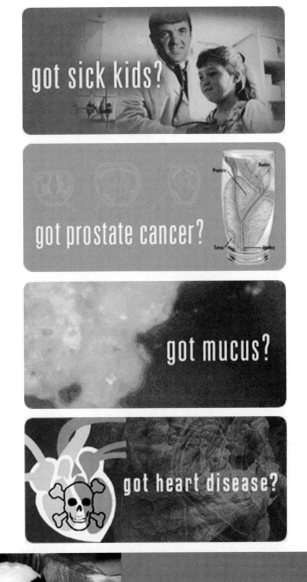

PORTRAYAL OF WOMEN IN ADVERTISING

—Camille Atkinson and Candice Fredrick

The authors explain that women and in particular young girls, experience advertising differently than men. Are you persuaded by their discussion? If so, what can be done to combat the potential for negative impact on women's self-esteem?

While all factions share similar concerns and worries regarding children's exposure to an unbridled media, young girls are a particularly vulnerable group, especially when speaking of the effects of advertising. In a sexist society where any trait labeled "feminine" tends to be devalued or exploited, young girls learn through the media how to behave and look if they want to obtain the beauty and character of the "ideal" woman.[1] Early in their lives, women have a sense that something about them isn't quite right and appearance takes on monumental importance as the girl matures. Open a magazine, any magazine, or pass a string of billboards along a highway and you will see the image of the beautiful woman: extremely thin, large breasted, sexually available, with flawless skin. This prototypical "beauty" is seen everywhere; clothes and products are designed for her and those who aspire to be like her. This is quite a feat when we consider that 33% of American women wear a size 16 or larger![2] What should one do when besieged with this paradigm if she does not measure up (speaking both literally and figuratively)? This archetypal figure represents a body type that only 5% of women actually possess. However, the beauty industry has come to the rescue: make-up; products to eliminate wrinkles, blemishes, cellulite or any other physical flaw; plastic surgery, exercise videos and dieting tips.

Because such products are aggressively advertised, eating disorders are all too common among young women who accept the myth of the "perfect" body. These disorders, which involve both physical and mental health issues, are on the rise in the United States; whereas 30 years ago, they were almost entirely unheard of. Today, they are being called "the socio-cultural epidemic of our time."[3] This is underscored when we consider that the revenues of the diet industry are $33 billion. Furthermore, 72% of women report that they will be on a diet in any given year[4]—despite the fact that 95% of people who look to the diet industry to lose weight gain it all (and then some) back again.[5]

Can we even imagine men following a similar path to meet such a narrowly defined ideal? Of course some men diet, but we cannot find examples of men looking like hunger posters or behaving childlike in order to be attractive to women. Nor does the average man pick at a salad or raw vegetables at dinner, instead of ordering a meal. Men are afforded the dignity of being able to age gracefully and still be considered attractive. Showing a few wrinkles and gray hair is even deemed sexy for men. Many actors are cast as a desirable

---

leading man despite graying or the loss of hair and weathered skin. Newscasters can show evidence of their age if they are male; but we are hard-pressed to find women who can successfully look or act their age and remain employable on television or the big screen.

In her book *The Beauty Myth,* Naomi Wolf talks about how this obsession with perfection came into being.[6] In the 1950s, advertising revenues soared as manufacturers targeted the American housewife, who was often bored with the repetitive tasks of housekeeping. Household products were marketed to make her life easier and more efficient. However, with the advent of a 1960s style feminism and economic instability, many women entered the workforce. Shrewd business people recognized that they needed a new "hook" that did not pertain only to the closed environment of the home. Advertisers sought an obsession that women could take with them to work and this is how cosmetic/toiletries promotional campaigns began. By 1989 this strategy was well entrenched with beauty products offering $650 million in advertising revenues to magazines; while soaps, cleansers and polishes yielded only one tenth that amount.[7]

Even certain gains coming out of the women's movement of the 1960s and 1970s have been given an ironic spin by advertisers. For example, the idea that a woman could be naturally beautiful without props has been co-opted and entire lines of products have been developed to promote the "natural look." A look, however, that could only be obtained with the help of the beauty industry. Now women can wear make-up without it being apparent that they are doing so and seem instead to be blessed with "natural beauty." Even eye color can be changed with tinted contact lenses—the general preference being blue. Moreover, this obsession has created new categories of what counts as attractive, such as the over-forty-but-forever-young look.[8] Scientific approaches to skin care, cosmetic surgery and fitness programs promise to stave off the inevitable changes of maturing and magazine articles relating to diet increased 70% from 1968 to 1972. Articles on diet continued to rise steadily from 60% in the year 1979 to 66% in the month of January 1980 alone.[9] One of the models of the "fit for life," eternally attractive yet over-forty woman, is the actress and fitness guru Jane Fonda. She is also a woman with a long, sad history of eating disorders—over twenty years of eating and purging. Openly speaking of her disorder she said: "Society says we have to be thin and while most of us don't have much control over our lives, we can control our weight, either by starving to death or by eating all we want and not showing the effect.[10] In order to "not show the effect" yet still eat heartily a pattern of binge-and-purge must be routinely followed. Fonda speaks of her bulimia as the secret device she used to maintain the physical perfection that was expected of her. Now the publicly stated approach to controlling her weight is physical fitness and "sensible eating."

It is ironic that the goal in each case is the same: control over one's body. Of course, physical fitness does not carry the health dangers of an eating disorder, but the message is no different: find a way to maintain this image of self-control and ideal beauty, regardless of whether or not this reflects a deeper truth and no matter what the cost. The unfortunate message remains that women need to find ways to reach these ideals of eternal youth and physical perfection, though perhaps through "healthier" channels. Something is amiss here, for in either case the burden falls upon women alone. That is, few people question these ideal images or ask how they originated. Perhaps men, too, should wonder why they hold onto such a narrow definition of what is beautiful and look at the damage it may be doing to their wives, lovers, daughters, mothers and sisters.

One criticism is that women themselves have helped to create or, at least, perpetuate this false conception of beauty that is portrayed in the media and advertising. After all, it is they who buy the magazines that typecast them into an ideal that is so hopeless and debilitating (as Andy Rooney argued in a *60 Minutes* episode). It is women who submit their bodies and themselves to diets, surgery and whatever else it takes to remain young, attractive and competitive. But what are they actually competing for? Is male attention the main goal or obtaining a husband? Are these reasons sufficient for explaining why a woman would risk her health and happiness? If so, how can this account for the "lipstick lesbians" who also buy into the advertising ideal? Why *do* so many women buy into a view of themselves that is virtually impossible and ultimately self-defeating? These kinds of questions are rarely asked, except by self-proclaimed feminists, and answers can only be speculative at best. However, maybe the "why" queries—or search for causes—are ultimately less important than asking, what should we do now? Or, where does one go from here if she wants to overcome these fears of being less than "perfect"? Perhaps one can begin simply by becoming more aware.

Could it be that a commitment to understanding how the professional (advertisers) affects the personal (women's lives) merely reflects a prejudice of a small group of highly educated, professional women influenced by the feminist movement? And, that most are not even interested in how deeply advertising has affected them? This is a criticism leveled by Camille Paglia, the antifeminist writer and lecturer, who basically feels the women's movement is run by East Coast, elitist intellectuals who are making "much ado about nothing." This view supposes that there is something wrong with being educated or an intellectual and that there is something wrong with this type of woman reflecting upon the position of women in general. It takes a combination of strength, financial resources and independence to face and overcome the traditionally prevailing model of women's worth or lack thereof. If we accept this, then it is only the educated, financially independent woman who can afford to critically examine this media image and attempt to bring this awareness to others. Women already caught up in the cycle of emotional as well as financial dependency on men lack the resources which would enable them to think, let alone act, in ways that might put their already modest standard of living in jeopardy. Many women have to channel their energies on just surviving and caring for children; they have little time left for contemplating or challenging the pros and cons of constricting gender roles but they are nonetheless hurt by them. It takes time, confidence and security to confront the status quo.

Regardless, what is wrong with one group of women fighting the battles for those who cannot? Wouldn't seeing yourself as "your sister's keeper" be consistent with a care ethics that values relationships? If financially independent women are in a better position to raise others' consciousness and effect change, doing so should be a virtue not a fault. Moreover, there is a long respected tradition in our country in which those who are privileged speak out and help those who are less fortunate. The Kennedy family has been such an example of this *noblesse oblige*—that is, the moral obligation that goes along with power, wealth and social standing.

The image of women in advertising and other media is so ingrained in society that people don't even recognize it as damaging. Even in college classes, it is only after researching advertising in depth that students start to look critically at advertisements that have long been viewed as benign or neutral. Educating the public facilitates heightened sensitivity to the fact that advertisers work extremely hard, with the help of experts, to have anything but a "neutral" effect on the consumer.

For advertisements to be effective they have to play on fears that are based, at least partly, in reality. And, in fact, many women are afraid of losing love and domestic stability as they age and become less youthful in appearance. Moreover, almost half of all marriages end in divorce and the old story of a man leaving his middle-aged wife for a younger woman is not a myth. Advertisers find easy prey in the very real anxiety many women feel. Men do not have this same kind or degree of concern. As stated before, men can have gray hair and wrinkles and still be considered sexy. And in movies when mature men are teamed with a love interest, the woman is usually much younger and this seems quite "normal." But, more importantly, men are not financially dependent on women the way women are on men, despite social and political advancements. As Wollstonecraft indicated so many years ago: women are prized for their physical beauty and this is one of the few sources of "power" granted them. This may also explain why even some lesbians, who do not look to men for emotional or financial support, continue to aspire to the same standards of beauty. Specifically, beautiful women tend to be valued in ways that the "average" woman is not. They are seen as more powerful, competent or, simply, as overall better human beings. Women in Hollywood complain that there are fewer and fewer scripts for them as they mature, regardless of their talent or abilities. Even with all that plastic surgery can do for those who are wealthy enough to afford it, one cannot stay young eternally and fighting the inevitable process of aging is depressing and time-consuming. It saps women's energy to such a degree that sometimes they have little left over for more productive activities. And perhaps this is the objective: keeping women on the defensive about how they look allows them to be taken less seriously making them less threatening to men.[11] Whether or not one agrees with this, it is still clear that women have to be convinced to enter into this futile chase for eternal youth and this impossible ideal of beauty for many businesses to realize profit.

It would not be fair to blame advertising alone for how women are portrayed in media images, but there can be no doubt that business and profit play a significant role and, at the very least, exacerbate sexist assumptions regarding what is feminine and attractive. It is hoped that the next generation of women will not be blindly led by the beauty industry. For transcending cultural conditions is no easy task when a society has been so saturated. Women and men working in the field of ethics can teach students to critically examine advertisements and consider their effects on themselves. Most importantly they need to be empowered to avoid the trap of thinking that media images are innocuous or that the beauty industry, in particular, is only giving the public what they want.

NOTES

1. Jean Kilbourne, *Still Killing Us Softly* [videocassette] (Cambridge, Mass.: Cambridge Documentary Films, 1987).
2. *People Magazine,* June 3, 1996.
3. Eva Szekely, *Never Too Thin* (Toronto: The Women's Press, 1988), p. 12.
4. Jean Kilbourne, *Slim Hopes* [videocassette] (Northhampton, Mass.: Media Education Foundation, 1995).
5. *Ibid.*
6. Naomi Wolf in her book *The Beauty Myth* offers a good historical explanation of how the beauty myth came into being and the ensuing beauty culture that has been built around this myth. She is an excellent source for further research on the relationship between feminism and this change of advertising focus.
7. Naomi Wolf, *The Beauty Myth* (New York: Anchor Books, 1991), p. 66.
8. For a good discussion of "over 40" beauty, see "Changing Landscapes," by Wendy Chapkis, *Women Images and Reality* (Mountain View, Calif.: Mayfield Publishing Co., 1995), pp. 94–95.
9. Naomi Wolf, *The Beauty Myth,* p. 67.
10. Leo Janus, "Jane Fonda, Finding Her Golden Pond," *Cosmopolitan,* January 1985, p. 170.
11. See Susan Faludi, *Backlash* (New York: Doubleday Publishing, 1992).

ASIAN-AMERICAN AFFAIRS

—Taro O'Sullivan

*The article refers to a series of T-shirts created by Abercrombie &
Fitch (A&F) that showed cartoon caricatures of Asian Americans
complete with slogans. When questioned about the shirts, an A&F
spokesperson said the company thought the Asian-American community would find the T-shirts funny and would buy them. Instead the
T-shirts were derided as "racist" and "promoting old stereotypes"
and were the subject of nationwide protests organized by Asian-
American organizations. What would prompt a marketer, in today's
society, to create and advertise products such as these?*

THE TWO WONGS OF ABERCROMBIE & FITCH

"Wong Brothers Laundry Service: Two Wongs Can Make It White." That is what the latest
Abercrombie & Fitch T-shirts said, complete with Asian cartoon caricatures we used to see
during World War II.

"It is not and never has been our intention to offend anyone," Abercrombie spokesman
Hampton Carney said. He actually said the company thought the Asian-American community would find the shirts funny and buy them. To quote him, he said: "We thought they were
cheeky, irreverent and funny and everyone would love them. But that has not been the case."
Indeed it has not.

Abercrombie & Fitch is a large corporation that markets its clothing line all over the
world. Just what were they thinking when they thought up this idea? "Cheeky, irreverent
and funny." It blows my mind. If they were to produce T-shirts with caricatures of African
Americans along the lines of the old Sambo restaurants and made fun of a community using other racist props like fried chicken and watermelon, wouldn't that go over like a lead
balloon? Every African-American advocacy organization would be demanding resignations
and apologies. And they would get it too. I have not seen an apology from the folks at Abercrombie & Fitch in any of the publications I researched for this piece, just that they were
pulling the T-shirts from the shelves. Meanwhile, e-Bay is selling the shirts on its site for
over $230 each.

What would Abercrombie & Fitch marketing people do if I came into their boardroom
and tried to sell them a T-shirt that said "White Trash Debutante" and included a white female in curlers with a trailer park in the background. Would they let me proceed? I think
not! So why do they come out with this kind of nonsense? Are we left out of the decision-

making process so much that it simply doesn't matter anymore? I'd like to see how many people of color they employ in their Ohio headquarters.

As soon as I found out about the shirts, I wrote to give them my humble opinion, as did many Asian-American individuals and organizations across the country. Abercrombie & Fitch pulled the shirts from the stores immediately. A victory? Not even close!

The fact that a national company like this one would do such a thing illustrates how we are perceived as a group. We are not taken seriously if their marketing people thought we would actually like this garbage. They thought we would think it was funny! How fundamentally moronic and out of sync with reality.

The danger with this kind of racism is that it trivializes the issue and makes those of us who complain look like we are too sensitive. The reality, however, is that we cannot tolerate this, or any other kind of discrimination. The line has to be drawn. Gender discrimination, particularly against women, is very difficult to address because of this type of trivialization. We as men make fun of women, thinking it is just humor. We don't consider it might be wrong and offensive and we keep offending.

The offenders should never decide the appropriateness of such jokes. If a joke offends someone, the offenders need to stop. No if's, and's or but's! If we are to eliminate hurtful behaviors, then we must not make exceptions just because some people don't want to stop. Abercrombie & Fitch did the correct thing by recalling the T-shirts from its stores. For that, I must commend them. Still, what were they thinking?

If these T-shirts were sold, young people would be wearing them across the United States. The message it would have sent makes me very nervous. Every time we see others make fun of Asian Americans in this way, it desensitizes us to the point where it becomes okay to think of people in these terms. Subtly to be sure, but it still re-enforces stereotypes of Asians. It becomes the small crack in a large dam that eventually leads to a major breach. If it is okay to make fun of Asians, that same person will eventually make fun of others.

Power and privilege is something that is difficult to manage. Those who have it most often fail to realize they possess it. They don't understand how they could be doing so much damage. Often, those who have power and privilege don't really need to care.

I am glad Abercrombie & Fitch took this offensive piece of cotton wear off the market, but we have to be vigilant. They aren't the only ones we have to watch. My daughter is flooded with Madison Avenue images of what a woman ought to look and act like. She has to deal with the peer pressure of little girls learning about objectification as though it was a good thing. Children are continuously bombarded with the message that they are sexual beings without the re-enforcement that they are that and a whole lot more. The other attributes of being a woman are sadly not noticed. There is no healthy balance. We have a very long way to go before I can sleep well at night, but at least tonight, I'll be able to sleep a few minutes more than last night.

WHY ABERCROMBIE & FITCH STILL DOESN'T GET IT

—Andrew Chin

This article refers to the same set of T-shirts created by Abercrombie & Fitch discussed previously. The argument made here goes further in stating that the company should be made to pay for the damage that it has caused. The article highlights some measure of that payment. Considering that the company got free publicity (although mostly negative), was the apology sufficient?

After thousands of Asian-American university students and the Organization of Chinese Americans raised their voices last week, forcing Abercrombie & Fitch to recall a new line of T-shirts featuring Asian cartoon characters, this is what Thomas Lennox, the company's senior public relations official, had to say: "It's not and never has been, our intention to offend anyone. These graphic T-shirts were designed with the sole purpose of adding humor and levity to our fashion line."

As "damage control" press conferences go in the corporate world, you will not find a more artful example of evasion and misdirection. The media accepted Lennox's statement without further questioning, even though:

- No one ever accused Abercrombie & Fitch of *intending* to offend Asian Americans. The purpose of the protests was to call the company's attention to the fact that the T-shirts were offensive, because it was obvious that nobody in authority at the company knew that they were.

- No one ever suggested that the T-shirts were designed in a spirit other than of humor and levity. But the caricatures were deliberately chosen with historical antecedents in mind. If most Asian Americans cannot look back on those early stereotypical images and laugh, it is because we recognize the discriminatory effects of racial stereotyping as a persisting problem and not as an amusingly quaint fashion of a bygone era.

When viewed in light of Lennox's statement, Abercrombie's recall of the T-shirts does not constitute an apology. Abercrombie's only regret is that Asian Americans have mobilized, with the effect that the company would now find it unprofitable to continue marketing the T-shirts.

Some activists are continuing to seek a pledge from Abercrombie that such designs won't be repeated. But this proposal only calls for the company to make what has already been shown to be a sound business decision.

Instead, Abercrombie should be held responsible for the false and misleading message it has sent the public: that it's harmless fun to portray Asian Americans as coolies, laundrymen and rickshaw drivers, because everyone knows better and there no longer exist any problems of racial discrimination, harassment and violence based on the misconception that Asian Americans are exotic foreigners.

Federal Trade Commission rules require a business who engages in misleading advertising to spend 25% of its advertising budget on corrective advertising. By analogy, activists should demand that Abercrombie dedicate one-fourth of the costs it incurred in designing, manufacturing, distributing and marketing the T-shirts to educate its own employees and the general public regarding historical and continuing racial discrimination against Asian Americans.

Even without a genuine apology and corrective measures from Abercrombie, the company's decision to recall the T-shirts may be viewed as a small victory for Asian-American activism. Activists should extend on this gain, keeping in mind that the Abercrombie T-shirt fiasco was not an isolated incident, but is simply a visible manifestation of our community's general experience of marginalization by the dominant culture.

ORIENTALIST KITSCH

Abercrombie & Fitch's T-shirts Resurrect

Caricatures and Complications

—MIMI NGUYEN

The author, in reference to the Abercrombie & Fitch T-shirts, suggests she was "hardly shocked" because they represented a "tidal wave of kitsch merchandising." She increases the frame of reference to the past century and states that marketers have always engaged in this kind of behavior. Do you agree?

Desperate never looks good on a preppie. After a series of blows to the clothiers' significance on the landscape of cool, the Gap, J. Crew and Abercrombie & Fitch are facing a crisis of cultural and financial capital. Over the last few years, stocks and sales slumped in an embarrassing snub of the brands and the boom of store openings yielded less profit than the retailers had hoped.

But when Ohio-based Abercrombie & Fitch released a line of T-shirts in April depicting Chinese laundry workers and smiling Buddhas, captioned by groan-worthy puns, the brand found itself launched into the newspapers and television news with the aid of media-savvy Asian-American college students protesting the reproduction of century-old caricatures. Activists criticized the T-shirts for denigrating Asian men, trivializing "an entire religion and philosophy," and offending Asian Americans.

And even as company spokespersons claimed innocence and regret, protests were staged outside the retailers' stores, boycotts were organized across e-mail lists and demands for "respect" for Asian Americans as a lucrative market were sounded.

I have to confess, I would rather wear plastic garbage bags and orange legwarmers (which I would do now if I could find some) than sport the sartorial remnants of Reagan-era preppie. And I was hardly shocked by the "Get Your Buddha on the Floor" or "Wok-n-Bowl, Let the Good Times Roll—Chinese Food and Bowling" T-shirts, only the latest splashes in the tidal wave of kitsch merchandising and "orientalia" that's been stocking store shelves for years now.

But what this particular instance *does* reveal is that the demand for mimetic realism and "positive" images of racial and ethnic populations in popular culture is often inadequate—and fails to address the other, often more complicated messages embedded in these caricatures.

I am not arguing that Abercrombie & Fitch is funny, daring or even interesting. (Again, have you *seen* the clothes? Strictly dullsville.) This line of T-shirts is dumb and boring, on top of the printing of these caricatures. On the other hand, Abercrombie & Fitch's now in-famous "Wong Brothers Laundry Service—Two Wongs Can Make It White" T-shirt is not meant to function as an "accurate" representation of Chinese masculinity. (Although the correlation between "white" and "right" in the pun is both banal and striking.)

The clothiers acknowledge these are not realistic images. To accuse the company of "misrepresenting" Chinese or Asian men, culture, whatever, with negative stereotypes, is to forgo the messier aspects of contemporary cultural politics. The standard criticism—articulated during the controversy as a matter of "misleading [consumers] as to what Asian people are"—does not suffice.

While these images are surely reproductions of racist caricatures—that is not up for debate—to criticize them as "misrepresentations" assumed that the meaning of visual im-ages is obvious and the only way to think about representation is through its relation to realism. These analyses argue that Abercrombie views Asian Americans as laundry workers or (as one angry editorial writer put it) a "mass of con-sumers [so] full of self-hate and self-loathing that they will latch onto any negative stereotype of themselves and parade it around town like a yellow minstrel."

Unfortunately, the implications of this ap-proach limit images to two categories: stereotyp-ical (negative) and realistic (positive); and Asian Americans to two categories: authentic (protest-ing) or assimilated (buying). The criticism that these T-shirts "sell Asian self-hate and shame," or that Asian Americans who might buy these T-shirts are "whitewashed," ignores the possibil-ities for other kinds of consumers, images or in-terpretations of commodities.

We know by now that no mass cultural production is shaped outside of corporate management and market influence. We know capitalist culture is able to assimilate even the most revolutionary, or in this case reviled, sorts of images or themes and in the process often reproduces and repackages uneven social relations. But it may be that because we already know these things, we can begin to ask other questions about *how* this happens. This does not mean we abandon the analysis of popular culture for its reproduction of racist stereotypes, gender norms or social restrictions; on the contrary, by thinking about things like form and aesthetics, it might mean that we are able to take the politics of popular culture more seriously.

The corporatization of thrift store chic by retailers like The Gap and Abercrombie & Fitch and other chain stores like Urban Outfitters, has produced "Rub My Belly Buddha" and "Art's Auto Body" tees in a simulation of a secondhand sensibility and follows the rise of kitsch (so often typed as "trashy" or "low class") as the cultural capital of "cool." In this instance, we need to examine the emergence of what could be termed "orientalist kitsch," in which the caricature is resurrected and marketed. The first thing we have to account for is that the reproduction of an image of a historical stereotype *right now* is *not* the reproduction of the meaning of the stereotype in its original social creation. If we understand these commodity images as kitsch, we can engage this particular image of Chinese laundry workers as a function of marketing strategies such as parody and irony.

The public relations arm of Abercrombie suggested that these T-shirts were meant to be funny. Ironic, right? But in this instance, irony is conservative in its operation. It implies that if a long enough view is taken, all histories, current events and individual dramas are insignificant in the "immensity of life." The production of these caricatures is not a gesture to reinstate turn-of-the-century Chinese exclusion, legal discrimination or even the emasculation of Chinese men, *as much as it is a dismissal of these histories as meaningful in the present.*

The same effect is at work in the recycling of revolutionary iconography or heavy metal tour T-shirts. This leveling effect depoliticizes the social powers and conditions that produced these individuals, populations or movements. South American guerillas, heavy metal progenitors and Chinese laundry workers are made to occupy the same horizon as commodity images or arrested moments divorced from their specific historical significance.

Of course, what distinguishes the "Two Wongs" T-shirt from one featuring Che Guevara or Judas Priest is that it is an image of a racist stereotype. Nevertheless, this transformation process (turning caricature into kitsch) is a different order of naughty than the argument that these images faithfully reproduce stereotypes can explain.

These images reproduce stereotypes only to turn them into *kitsch,* signifying instead a deliberate "eh" to historical significance or meaning. That it is a racist stereotype makes this an admittedly anxious operation, as it skittles between declaring a "postracist" state and resurrecting old ghosts and bad memories.

Accordingly, the T-shirts cannot be understood outside of their status as kitsch commodities and whose cultural capital circulates *precisely because of their "bad taste"*—witness their resale for as much as $250 on eBay as collectors' items. In the language of kitsch, "bad taste" is a valuable quality and "bad taste" sells to the hip, urban consumer of tiki bars, wobbly-headed dashboard dogs, mullet paraphernalia and Buddha T-shirts. And because these items are typed as "trashy" or "low class"—the (sometimes faux) detritus of thrift stores and garage sales—their purchase as kitsch is accompanied by the necessary wink, which distinguishes the wearers of the T-shirts from those who might really work at Art's Auto Body. This is a wink with no memory or history, or in the case of Abercrombie, a wink with no *concern* for memory or history.

But while "bad taste" may function to reiterate class distinctions and depoliticize the commodity, it can also serve as a complicit critique of "good taste" and the hope for a "positive" image, by forcing us to consider *what these are*. What makes for "good taste"? (Martha Stewart? High culture?) What does a "positive" image look like? (Middle-class? The good girl who doesn't kiss on the first date?) Clearly both are mediated values, which (usually) reproduce class distinctions and a hygienic version of aesthetics and populations.

Abercrombies' reinvention of the elite classics—polo shirts, chinos, whatever—has for years balanced the brand image on the sensibility of a privileged whiteness steeped in hedonism. The thick quarterly catalogs feature luscious models, many recruited from college campuses and most of the Anglo-Saxon type, frolicking nude or lounging in stately dorm rooms and lush football fields in suggestive (and often homoerotic) poses. This provocative approach garnered the censure of cultural conservatives; the right-wing fundamentalist Bob Jones University banned the Abercrombie logo from its South Carolina campus two years ago, while Michigan's attorney general pushed Abercrombie to shrink-wrap and slap "adults only" labels on the catalogs.

I cite this history of censure not to cheer Abercrombie & Fitch for daring to frighten the cultural conservatives (which frankly isn't hard), but to highlight the complaints about its complicated brand image, dependent upon the coupling of class and race privilege with a "natural" sensuality.

Rather than examine the complex and often contradictory modes of representation and social powers mobilized by this brand image, the recent criticisms of Abercrombie for retailing controversies like the "Wong" T-shirts too easily and quickly articulate a conservative leaning toward "good taste" and realism. An article in a left-leaning Asian-American student newspaper accuses the retailer of "skirting the rules," and that the "Abercrombie & Fitch catalog stunts encourage behavior [like underage sex] that flaunts social conventions."

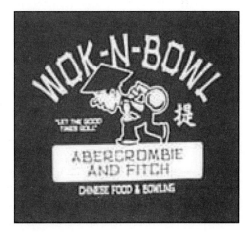

Since I'm generally for the "skirting" and questioning of social norms, the pairing of an Asian-American critique of racism with a social conservatism of sexual propriety and obeisance to "rules" seems to be a disturbing and dangerous strategy. Here, the critique of a racist stereotype is hinged upon the reproduction of class distinctions of "good taste" and social norms of "positive" behavior models. Wow, problematic much?

This complaint about "skirting the rules," like the suggestion that Abercrombie & Fitch "respect" Asian Americans as a target market (which itself skirts dangerously close to a "model minority" hurrah), forces us to re-imagine the stakes and strategies in Asian-American cultural politics. I am *not* arguing to invalidate the critique of the caricature, only that we complicate that critique.

In any case, Abercrombie & Fitch has so far profited from the controversy. And, for the record, I don't think they ever believed their own publicity, that "we thought Asians would love this T-shirt." Shares in Abercrombie sold at $33.30, a 52-week high, on April 18, the day the T-shirts were pulled from store shelves and the company offered its apologies. (And what has gone for the most part unremarked during the protests is the sweatshop labor that no doubt produces the casual clothing in factories and free trade zones in Asia and Central America.)

But to demand purity in pop culture makes no sense. Instead of dismissing popular culture (and its audience) for the fact of its messy manufacture, we need to probe further to examine the character and range of any given commodity form's power and possibility, what moment of crisis or contradiction it might represent, what meanings it might afford. (One colleague of mine adopts the tactic of repossessing and rehistoricizing the "bad taste" of racist kitsch as a desanitization of Benetton-style liberal multiculturalism, though this is a contingent strategy.) At the very least, these controversies should remind us that *all* images and representations are staged—stereotypical or realistic, negative or positive—and, as such, we're only as authentic as "our" kitsch, which is to say, not at all.

THE CASE OF PLANNED OBSOLESCENCE

—JAMES HEELY AND ROY NERSESIAN

The following is a hypothetical case that deals with planned product obsolescence—a deliberate product strategy adopted by companies to make current generations of product obsolete within a set period of time in order to induce customers to enter the market again for the next generation of products. Remember, this is a deliberate strategy with the timing of introduction firmly within the control of the marketers. Consider dimensions of the problem, i.e., pros and cons. Is there an ethical dilemma, and if so, how do you resolve it?

A fictitious case of a company president who is considering deliberate product obsolescence to boost the firm's sales and profits is presented. The company makes consumer products that use a steel alloy that does not wear out with usage. The firm enjoys an excellent reputation for quality, but it cannot increase sales because the product does not have a substantial replacement market. The president is proposing that the firm invest in R&D to find a metal alloy that will last for at least seven years, but not over eight years, so that the product will have to be replaced by then. The production manager has reservations about the plan. He is concerned about the ethics of diverting shareholder profits to finance the project and of using R&D funds to degrade the longevity of the product.

The president of a major consumer products company with an excellent reputation for quality was concerned about increasing the company's sales and profits. The company makes a consumer product that requires very close manufacturing tolerances for it to work. Any relaxation of these tolerances results in almost immediate product failure and negative "word-of-mouth" advertising. Consequently, actions taken to ensure that the product works when it is sold also mean that the product can last for generations. Passing down of the product from mother to daughter was a familiar phenomenon.

John, the president of the company, decided to hold a private meeting with Phil, the production manager and Henry, the chief financial officer, to discuss a scheme to improve the company's financial future.

He began the meeting with the following comment: "Once we make a sale, we make a sale forever. In a sense, our current model competes head on with a model made half a century ago. Where would Ford be today if everyone still drove around in Tin Lizzies?"

As John distributed a sales graph, he noted, "Our new models look more modern, have one or two enhancements, but they don't make our old models obsolete. That's our essential marketing problem. Our sales depend on formation of new families and population

"The Case of Planned Obsolescence," by James Heely and Roy Nersesian. Reprinted with permission from the Institute of Management Accountants, Montvale, NJ, USA, www.imanet.org.

growth and very little on replacement. But if we had a seven- or eight-year life to our product line, our sales would look like this." Phil and Henry stared at the graph that depicted actual sales over the last 10 years and predicted sales if the product had a finite eight-year life.

"And while you're so spellbound by what you see, here's another view of the situation in terms of profits," said John as he handed out another graph. Phil and Henry were amazed at the difference between these two lines.

Henry quipped, "These are not my projections."

"No, they're not," said John. "I'm as capable of projecting revenues and earnings as you are Henry. But these are not projections. Here is what sales and profits would have been if our customers had turned in an eight-year-old model for a new one. We have plenty of spare capacity in our plants to accommodate the increase in sales if we had a seven- or eight-year life expectancy. Our fixed costs are not only fixed, but high because of past overinvestment in plant capacity that occurred before we came on the scene. These fixed costs are weighing heavily on our bottom line. We can cut plant capacity, but that means heavy writedowns. We cannot increase sales because they are tied to the formation of new families. But we do have a tremendous replacement market if only the product needed replacement."

Phil spoke up. "John, we're not going to have another repeat of your fiasco of loosening up the tolerances and having the first product recall this company has ever had in its history?"

"No. I want to find a metal alloy that will maintain its technical specifications for at least seven, but not over eight years. After that, normal wear and tear will have reached a point where the manufacturing tolerances are no longer satisfied. Then the product must be replaced."

Phil became agitated. "Our R&D division was initially responsible for helping the steel industry to develop an alloy that could be used to manufacture parts easily with extremely close tolerances. In so doing, we also ended up with a steel alloy that essentially does not wear out with usage."

"That's right, Phil—that's exactly what your R&D people did. Now they are going to develop an alloy that meets the specifications for seven or so years and then fails to do so."

"That is not exactly what our R&D people consider R&D."

"I know. That's why I want a new division set up by people who are emotionally and intellectually in tune with what I want done."

"John, let me acquaint you with a few technical facts I think you are overlooking in the planned degradation of our product."

"Call it market enhancement."

"Market enhancement by product obsolescence and market enhancement by making a superior quality product—there is a difference."

"A big one, Phil. And what happens when we bring out a new model, which is basically the old model in a new exterior plus an enhancement or two? Nothing. Our sales do not change because the consumers are still satisfied with the old model. Our profit margins are mired in the same old rut. If we can introduce product obsolescence in a manner that our customers will never notice—and I maintain that no one will be disappointed in a product that gracefully dies after seven full years of superior service—we can improve profits dramatically. Or we can continue business as usual."

"There is more to corporate life than profits, John. There is such a thing as consumer satisfaction. Besides, there are technical considerations. Metal wears uniformly with time. For our products to work for seven years and then start to fail, we need to find an alloy that wears very little for seven years and erodes like crazy thereafter. It'll cost a fortune to find such a metal because the various parts are exposed to different wear factors. It would be extremely difficult to have them all timed to fall out of specification on the seventh anniversary of the product."

"I know that; only one part will be made of this alloy. The rest will be made as now. As you say, we need an alloy that wears very little for seven years, then turns to putty the day after our warranty expires."

"We have no parts that are integral with the housing. To do that, we will have to redesign the product totally."

"Then we'll have to do it."

"We have no experience or expertise in metallurgy. We solved the metallurgical problem decades ago. We will have to obtain this expertise to identify such an alloy. That will take time and a lot of money."

"That's why I propose setting up a separate organization for this project."

"The casing for our product, as you well know, is made of standard metal as it's not exposed to the operation of the product. We would now be making casing of two metals—one to form the exterior and some portion of which to be part of the operation. Bimetallic casings will be expensive to design and to manufacture."

"Then we'll just have to expend the funds in product and process development to find a way to do it at current costs."

"John, slow down." Henry rose from his chair. "We need to think this matter through."

"What is there to think through, Henry? Can't you see the difference between two lines where we quadruple our profits?"

"Okay, let me give you something to think about. What about the millions we're going to spend on R&D to cheapen our product? Do you think that will affect earnings adversely?"

"Capitalize them, Henry, like you capitalize everything else. Then we'll write off these expenses against earnings a decade away in time."

"I can only capitalize what I am permitted to capitalize and R&D is not on the list. It will have to be expensed as funds are expended. This will hurt our current earnings. If this effort is of a magnitude of expenditure that I think it is, we may even have to cut our dividend."

"Henry, think long term."

"John, what about the impact on the short-term price of the stock as earnings tumble and dividends are cut?"

"Well, I don't plan to own any of the stock myself and I don't think our pension plan ought to own any. I'm going to be exercising my options and clearing out. What are you going to be doing, Henry?"

"I think you've got a problem with insider trading, John. That's what I think."

"Okay, I'm going to do nothing. What do you think the future value of the stock of this company is going to be when you and I retire? Profits will be four times what they would have been if we do nothing. Sure the shareholders will take a hit, but it's only for the development time to find the right alloy and redesign our product line. Do you think that the shareholders are going to vote against us if we feel that an increase in R&D spending is in their long-term interest?"

"John, you don't know if all these efforts will be successful and you haven't taken into account inventory writedowns from introducing a new product line, nor the seven- or eight-year hiatus before your planned obsolescence time bomb goes off."

"We've brought out new models in the past and have managed our inventory to minimize writedowns. Look, gentlemen, I am not looking for final agreement. I just want to take this a step further to start laying out costs and benefits."

"John, let me do a little advanced homework for you now. I don't think this will be a small expenditure of funds. Phil, do you have any idea what we are talking about in cost and time?"

"Certainly millions and certainly not less than three years, including bringing out the new model—my guess is somewhere around $10 million and five years of effort, assuming we want to guarantee success."

"But look at profits, look at the value of your pension benefits if we are successful."

"John, contain yourself—five years to bring the product out, another five or 10 years before the new product line reaches sufficient market share to make replacement meaningful and then another seven or so years for the timebomb to mature in the form of sales. This is truly one of the longest long-term plans I have ever seen in my professional life and for what? I am bothered by the concept and spending R&D funds to degrade the longevity of our product. R&D connotes product improvement and you are using R&D to introduce product obsolescence. Furthermore, is it ethical to divert shareholder profits for such an expenditure, even to the point of threatening the dividend? Is this the best we can do with the funds entrusted to us by the shareholders of the company?"

"Then, Henry, what do you suggest?"

ETHICAL "GRAY AREAS" IN COMPETITIVE INTELLIGENCE

—Jennifer Raisor

Suppose you've just arrived home from attending a cutting-edge conference in your industry. You open the packet of materials you collected to discover it's not yours; you've picked up someone else's files by mistake. Leafing through them, you realize that they belong to one of your competitors and that they are full of sensitive information that would be extremely valuable to your company. "I have to return them," you think. But before that . . . would it be all right to make a copy or two? Shall you skim through the files and take a few notes? After all, you didn't steal the material—it was left lying around in public. Upon return, perhaps the owner would assume you've looked through them anyway, so why not do so? Is it "permissible" to take a peek? The following article explores the issue of competitive intelligence and corporate espionage through several case studies, striving to arrive at a definition of "ethical corporate intelligence gathering."

WHAT IS COMPETITIVE INTELLIGENCE?

The ethical problem posed by this scenario may seem straightforward enough. In competitive industries, however, such as high-tech engineering and manufacturing, computers, financial services and industrial and commercial electronics, timely access to information like this could make the difference between success and obsolescence.[1] A company's survival may depend on how quickly and effectively it can gather information about its competitors' plans for products and services. Companies thus place a great deal of pressure on employees to locate and analyze sensitive information by whatever means possible.[2] In order to meet the company's expectations, employees often feel they must operate at the very limits of ethical behavior. How far should they go to gather information?

This sensitive information is called "competitive intelligence," and the employees responsible for collecting and processing it are known as competitive intelligence professionals

"Ethical 'Gray Areas' in Competitive Intelligence," by Jennifer Raisor, reprinted with permission of the author.

[1]Thomas Furtado, "Ethical Dilemmas Regarding Competitive Intelligence," Council for Ethics in Economics (Case 3, 1995), reprinted in L. Hartman, *Perspectives in Business Ethics,* 2nd ed. (Burr Ridge, IL: McGraw-Hill/Irwin, 2002), p. 307.

[2]Darren Charters, "The Challenge of Completely Ethical CI and the CHPI Model," *Competitive Intelligence Review* 12, no. 3 (Third Quarter 2001), p. 3.

or practitioners. Although people have no doubt collected information about their rivals throughout the ages, the term "competitive intelligence" (CI) and recognition of the profession are relatively recent. The Society of Competitive Intelligence Professionals (SCIP), an organization devoted to education and networking among people working in the industry, was founded in 1986.[3] SCIP actively promotes the profession of CI, claiming that it makes a crucial difference to a company's bottom line:[4] One statistic it presents is that within a given industry, companies with CI programs have greater earnings per share than those without CI programs.[5] Companies recognize this advantage and more and more are implementing CI systems. According to a 1997 survey of U.S. companies by The Futures Group, 60% of those surveyed had a system for collecting information on competitors; 82% of companies with annual revenues over $10 billion had such a system.[6]

SCIP describes competitive intelligence as the "legal collection and analysis of information regarding the capabilities, vulnerabilities and intentions of business competitors, conducted by using information databases and other 'open sources' and through ethical inquiry."[7] This definition takes care to articulate that the sensitive information sought by CI practitioners exists in the public domain and can be obtained both legally and ethically. One example of an open source is patents, copyrights and trademarks. While these are traditionally methods for ensuring legal protection for one's own intellectual property, the applications and related documents are in the public domain for outsiders to access. A company can study these to gain an understanding of status of their competitors' research.[8] Another example of an open source is secondary published literature, which is also available in the public domain.[9]

Perhaps the best source of competitive information is a competitor's own employees.[10] Some employees are disgruntled for various reasons and wish to betray the company by revealing its secrets; others hope to receive financial compensation in exchange for confidential information.[11] Such employee behavior is evidently on the rise: in a 2001 survey conducted by the magazine *Information Security,* 22% of the 2,545 companies surveyed reported electronic theft, sabotage or intentional destruction of proprietary information by insiders.[12]

A CI practitioner need not unearth a mole to ensure success, however. Many employees are simply negligent.[13] In what is surely one of the most famous examples in recent memory, a U.S. State Department laptop computer containing "highly classified" informa-

---

[3]http://www.scip.org/about/index.asp.

[4]http://www.scip.org/ci/faq.asp.

[5]*Ibid.*

[6]*Ibid.*

[7]http://www.scip.org/ci/.

[8]Furtado, p. 308.

[9]Alfonso Sapia-Bosch and Robert S. Tancer, "Navigating through the Legal/Ethical Gray Zone: What Would *YOU* Do?" *CI Magazine* 1, no. 1 (April–June 1998), p. 4.

[10]Furtado, p. 308.

[11]Scott Tyler Shafer, "Corporate Espionage: The Enemy Within," *Red Herring,* January 2002, p. 78.

[12]Shafer, p. 78.

[13]Furtado, p. 308.

tion disappeared from its office in 2000. A State Department spokesman said that department officials didn't know whether the computer had been stolen or merely lost.[14] Companies as well as government agencies constantly battle problems with employees leaving laptop computers or files lying around in public or speaking to colleagues or on the phone loudly in public places.[15]

Other sources of sensitive information include the suppliers and customers of a competitor. Like the competitor's employees, they may be negligent, or they may deliberately divulge information in an attempt to wrangle a competitive edge.[16] Trade shows and conferences and networking at interest and professional group events are also opportunities to seek sensitive information.[17]

Of the various techniques used to extract sensitive information, some of the most widely used include reverse engineering, which involves examining and analyzing a competitor's existing product available on the market, surveys, interviews, simulations, observation and benchmarking, which involves comparing your competitor's operations with your own company's.[18] Less orthodox methods include breaking into a competitor's facility, hacking into a competitor's computer system and wiretaps.[19]

II. COMPETITIVE INTELLIGENCE, CORPORATE ESPIONAGE AND THE LAW

Break-ins, wiretaps . . . all of this seems vaguely familiar, but in a different context. To those unfamiliar with the industry, such methods smack of the more exciting passages of Ian Fleming or John LeCarre. Is the term "competitive intelligence" just a euphemism—a kind of Orwellian Newspeak, even—for what's really going on: corporate espionage?

There is no doubt that corporate espionage is alive and well and on the increase. In a recent study conducted by the American Society for Industrial Security and PricewaterhouseCoopers, in 1999 companies in the Fortune 1000 suffered losses of more than $45 billion due to stolen sensitive information.[20] The average Fortune 1000 company reported 2.45 incidents; the loss per incident was estimated at over $500,000.[21] In the especially competitive field of high technology, companies sustained nearly $120 million in losses.[22] The average company reported 67 incidents and the loss per incident was, on average, around $15 million.[23]

---

[14]http://www.cnn.com/2000/US/04/17/state.computer.02/.

[15]Furtado, p. 308.

[16]*Ibid.*

[17]*Ibid.*

[18]http://strategis.ic.gc.ca/sc_mangb/cip/engdoc/ci_intro.html.

[19]Furtado, p. 308.

[20]Thomas A. Hemphill, "Oracle vs. Microsoft: Corporate Espionage or Competitive Intelligence?" *Business and Society Review* 107, no. 4, pp. 506–07.

[21]*Ibid.*, p. 507.

[22]*Ibid.*

[23]*Ibid.*

The U.S. law with the greatest impact on the way competitive intelligence gathering is conducted is the Economic Espionage Act of 1996 (EEA). The act makes it a federal offense to steal or obtain trade secrets by "fraud, artifice, or deception" or to conspire to do so, which means that buying information so obtained is also a crime.[24] "Trade secret" is defined as

> *all forms and types of financial, business, scientific, technical, economic or engineering information, including patterns, plans, compilations, program devices, formulas, designs, prototypes, methods, techniques, processes, procedures, programs or codes, whether tangible or intangible and whether or how stored, compiled or memorialized if the owner of the information has reasonably tried to keep it secret.*[25]

This law has helped to clearly delineate the differences between competitive intelligence and corporate espionage. After conducting a policy study, SCIP concluded that the profession of competitive intelligence is completely consistent with the EEA.[26] According to an undated press release issued by SCIP, entitled "Competitive Intelligence Is Not Corporate Espionage," corporate espionage is illegal; competitive intelligence is not.[27] Clearly illegal means of collecting information include break-ins, computer hacking and wiretaps. Other means not so obviously illegal, however, also qualify as corporate espionage. Practices such as interviewing a competitor's employee and identifying oneself as a graduate student conducting research for a thesis, for example, would constitute a case of obtaining information by fraud. This would also fall within the purview of the EEA and would, therefore, qualify as corporate espionage.

III. ETHICAL CONCERNS

As long as it is not illegal, is any method of gathering sensitive information acceptable? Sometimes information is gathered in a way that is not illegal—that is, it does not violate the EEA or any other law—but still poses an ethical dilemma.[28] CI practitioners often refer to these situations as "gray zones." Examples of gray zones include finding a lost document, overhearing competitors talking in a bar, or removing one's name tag at an industry gathering. None of these activities actually violate the explicit provisions of the EEA. They all, however, raise serious ethical questions.

For SCIP, CI practitioners must do more than stay within the four corners of the law. SCIP holds them to a much higher ethical standard. However, how well do practitioners in the field understand this standard and do they live up to it? To find out, SCIP conducted a law-and-ethics survey entitled "What Would *YOU* Do?" involving 728 CI practitioners.[29] SCIP began with this assumption: "If people know what is right, they are likely to do the

---

[24]Economic Espionage Act of 1996.

[25]*Ibid.*

[26]Hemphill, p. 507.

[27]*Ibid.*, p. 506.

[28]Furtado, p. 308.

[29]Sapia-Bosch, p. 1.

right thing."[30] Based on that assumption, SCIP developed five scenarios and asked CI practitioners to choose a response from those provided.[31]

After taking the survey, academics and a legal advisor discussed the legality and ethicality of the various responses. Those who conducted the study were surprised to find that respondents who had been members of SCIP for less than one year responded correctly to the case studies more often than those who had been members longer.[32] In addition, while CI practitioners with up to one year of experience performed "fairly well" and those with more than five years of experience responded with the most correct answers, those with two to three years of experience most often answered incorrectly.[33] It seems problematic that those in the middle group in terms of CI experience performed the most poorly. Furthermore, for each of the cases, significant percentages of respondents gave unethical responses, indicating that there is no industry-wide consensus on what is ethical behavior in the practice of competitive intelligence.

IV. CASE STUDIES: ORACLE AND LOPEZ[34]

Two recent, well-publicized incidents highlight the difference between corporate espionage and competitive intelligence. In 2002, software manufacturer Oracle Corporation hired an investigative agency to sniff around organizations that had openly supported Microsoft Corporation while it was being sued by the U.S. Department of Justice for having a monopoly in the operating system market.[35] Although evidence that Microsoft financially supported these organizations had already been published in the news, Oracle, after its investigation was exposed, claimed that it was necessary to expose further improprieties.[36] Oracle's chief executive officer, Larry Ellison, declared that Oracle was providing a "public service" and that he felt "very good" about Oracle's actions.[37]

The particulars of the investigation were revealed in the news. An alleged employee of the investigative agency entered the building of one of the organizations using a cardkey obtained under suspicious circumstances and lied about her identity to bargain with the cleaning staff to buy the organization's trash.[38] Although Oracle claims that it repeatedly instructed the agency to use only legal methods and received assurances that this was the case, these actions were clearly illegal.[39] Thus, although Oracle characterized its activities as "competitive intelligence," the activities, if true, clearly constitute corporate espionage.[40]

---

[30]*Ibid.*, p. 3.
[31]*Ibid.*
[32]*Ibid.*, p. 12.
[33]*Ibid.*
[34]Hemphill, pp. 501–511.
[35]*Ibid.*, pp. 501–503.
[36]*Ibid.*, pp. 501–502.
[37]*Ibid.*, pp. 501, 505.
[38]*Ibid.*, p. 504.
[39]*Ibid.*, pp. 505, 508.
[40]*Ibid.*

Even if these actions did not violate the EEA, a CI practitioner should have concerns about the ethical implications of these methods.

An earlier case involved a high-ranking executive's move to a different company in the same competitive industry. In 1993, Jose Ignacio Lopez de Arriortua resigned as the head of global purchasing at General Motors, where he had been so successful that he was voted Auto Industry Man of the Year.[41] He left to take a similar position at Volkswagen.[42] Although an employee's move always presents the threat of sensitive information leaking, in this case, GM accused Lopez of actually stealing confidential documents about GM's plans and products and taking them to Volkswagen and brought a suit.[43] Lopez resigned from Volkswagen, which eventually settled out of court to the tune of $100 million in damages.[44]

V. ETHICAL COMPETITIVE INTELLIGENCE

The fact that CI practitioners respond so variably on surveys and that high-ranking executives conduct themselves in ethically questionable ways with such self composure highlights the fact that there is little consensus on how far a company should go in collecting sensitive information, barring outright illegal methods. In fact, most CI practitioners believe that others in the industry are conducting activities in an unethical manner.[45] None argue, however, that unethical CI is appropriate. The problem lies in formulating the necessary principles, ensuring that CI practitioners receive the appropriate training in them and enforcing the principles. Certain factors have been identified as making a significant difference. For example, in the law-and-ethics survey discussed above, respondents whose companies had an ethics policy, a general code of business conduct or a specialized CI policy gave more correct responses than respondents whose companies lacked such guidelines.[46] This reveals the important role played by policies addressing ethics in general or competitive intelligence activities in particular.

SCIP has established a Code of Ethics that both encompasses and extends beyond legality:

SCIP CODE OF ETHICS FOR CI
PROFESSIONALS

- To continually strive to increase the recognition and respect of the profession.

- To comply with all applicable laws, domestic and international.

---

[41]Furtado, p. 310.
[42]*Ibid.*
[43]*Ibid.*, pp. 309–310.
[44]Sapia-Bosch, p. 2.
[45]Charters, p 1.
[46]Sapia-Bosch, p. 12.

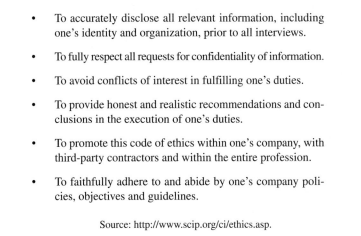

- To accurately disclose all relevant information, including one's identity and organization, prior to all interviews.

- To fully respect all requests for confidentiality of information.

- To avoid conflicts of interest in fulfilling one's duties.

- To provide honest and realistic recommendations and conclusions in the execution of one's duties.

- To promote this code of ethics within one's company, with third-party contractors and within the entire profession.

- To faithfully adhere to and abide by one's company policies, objectives and guidelines.

Source: http://www.scip.org/ci/ethics.asp.

Going a step further, academic Darren Charters has proposed a model for completely ethical CI called the "CHIP model."[47] He asserts that CI practitioners must rigorously evaluate contemplated CI activities against "established ethical frameworks."[48] The acronym "CHIP" stands for Community virtues (signifying virtue ethics in its community aspect), Harm (a descriptive term for utilitarian ethics), Individual as end (indicating Kantian ethics) and Personal virtues (again signifying virtue ethics, this time in its individual aspect).[49] The CHIP model weaves together these various ethical strands to provide a systematic way for CI practitioners to assess whether CI activities are ethical. The model provides a framework for practitioners whose companies either lack a defined policy or whose company policy does not cover all contingencies.[50]

There is a common thread running through SCIP's assertions about ethics and CI, Charters' model and other champions of the inherently ethical nature of SCIP. A common refrain is that ethical CI can be conducted with absolutely no impact on the quality of the results: there is "no need to steal, lie or cheat to accomplish goals."[51] Are organizations, academics and practitioners protesting too much? Is it not naïve to argue that CI can actually be conducted more effectively when it is conducted ethically? Or are they simply acknowledging that the risk of failing to collect sensitive information as effectively as possible is simply the price to pay for maintaining a high standard of ethics?

[47]Charters, pp. 13–16.
[48]*Ibid.*, p. 1.
[49]*Ibid.*, pp. 13–14.
[50]*Ibid.*, p. 1.
[51]Sapia-Bosch, p. 12.

ETHICAL ISSUES IN QUALITATIVE RESEARCH ON INTERNET COMMUNITIES

—GUNTHER EYSENBACH AND JAMES TILL

The authors raise the issue of "listening in on" and surveying communities of customers that form on the Internet to discuss certain product- and company-related issues. Increasingly, we find that customers are creating websites and discussion forums online either as support groups, help forums or complaint sites. Marketers are using the information generated on these sites to help them develop an understanding of their customer base. What are the ramifications of this approach for marketers? Do you see an ethical dilemma and future problems for marketers using this approach? How can you help them resolve the issues raised?

The Internet is the most comprehensive electronic archive of written material representing our world and people's opinions, concerns and desires. Physicians who surf the Internet for the first time are often stunned by what they learn on websites set up by lay people or patient self support communities. Material on these venues can be a rich source for researchers interested in understanding the experiences and views of people and patients. Qualitative analysis of material published and communicated on the Internet can serve to systematize and codify needs, values, concerns and preferences of consumers and professionals relevant to health and health care. While the Internet makes people's interactions uniquely accessible for researchers and erases boundaries of time and distance, such research raises new issues in research ethics, particularly concerning informed consent and privacy of research subjects, as the borders between public and private spaces are sometimes blurred.

INTERNET COMMUNITIES

Internet communities provide a way for a group of peers to communicate with each other. They include discussion boards on websites, mailing lists, chat rooms, or newsgroups. Examples of health related mailing lists can easily be found by inserting a key word such

---

as "cancer" in the search box at the Topica website (www.topica.com/). One example is the Breast Cancer Mailing List, based at Memorial University in Newfoundland (www.bclist.org), which provides a forum for those seeking peer support and information, with an emphasis on information on treatment and disease, practical information (such as relevant online resources), personal experiences and emotional support.

QUALITATIVE RESEARCH ON THE INTERNET

Qualitative research seeks "to acknowledge the existence of and study the interplay of multiple views and voices—including, importantly, lay voices."[1] Internet postings are accessible for qualitative research of these voices—for example, to determine information needs and preferences of consumers or to investigate how health related information can best be converted into knowledge and disseminated widely.[2]

Three different types of Internet based research methods can be distinguished.[3] One is passive analysis, such as studies of information patterns on websites or interactions on discussion groups without the researchers actually involving themselves. Examples include the study of helping mechanisms and content of online self help groups for colorectal cancer,[4] breast cancer,[5] Alzheimer's disease,[6] and eating disorders.[7] The second type of online research is through active analysis, in which researchers participate in communications—for example, to determine the accuracy of responses to healthcare questions on the Usenet.[8] In the third type researchers identify themselves as such and gather information in the form of online semistructured interviews, online focus groups, or Internet based surveys or use the Internet to recruit participants for "traditional" research.

SUMMARY POINTS

Internet communities (such as mailing lists, chat rooms, newsgroups or discussion boards on websites) are rich sources of qualitative data for health researchers.

Qualitative analysis of Internet postings may help to systematize and codify needs, values and preferences of consumers and professionals relevant to health and health care.

Internet based research raises several ethical questions, especially pertaining to privacy and informed consent.

Researchers and institutional review boards must primarily consider whether research is intrusive and has potential for harm, whether the venue is perceived as "private" or "public" space, how confidentiality can be protected and whether and how informed consent should be obtained.

INTERNET COMMUNITIES' MEMBERS DO NOT EXPECT TO BE RESEARCH SUBJECTS

There is increasing evidence that researchers posting or "lurking" on such communities may be perceived as intruders and may damage the communities. King quotes a group member who, realizing that the community had been monitored by a researcher, retreated from a mailing list with the remark: "When I joined this, I thought it would be a support group, not a fishbowl for a bunch of guinea pigs. I certainly don't feel at this point that it is a safe environment, as a support group is supposed to be, and I will not open myself up to be dissected by students or scientists."[9]

One subscriber to the Breast Cancer Mailing List responded to one of the frequent requests from researchers interested in obtaining insights into patients' personal experiences with breast cancer: "Why can't researchers do it the 'hard way' as they used to . . . and leave us alone on the Breast-Cancer list?"[10] Sharf reported that among 14 people from a mailing list contacted to obtain informed consent, one woman was "somewhat hostile, assuming that [the researcher] had behaved voyeuristically, taking advantages of people in distress" and that "the idea of using the conversations as data had not occurred to many members."[11]

We searched the Dejanews archive (http://groups.google.com/) to find comments of newsgroup participants responding to researchers' requests. Entering the search terms "research survey project health" identified 85 messages from researchers. By following the message threads, we could find newsgroup participants' reactions, which were often negative. Among the concerns expressed was that often "the researcher isn't familiar with newsgroup culture—problems akin to those occasionally experienced by anthropologists when they try to interpret the behavior of cultures they really don't understand. And on the rare occasions when I've seen someone who's part of that culture attempt to study the group he/she is part of, it resulted in a rippling sense of resentment and betrayal among those who find such things underhanded."

PUBLIC SPACES OR PRIVATE ROOMS?

Informed consent, privacy and confidentiality are basic ethical tenets of scientific research on people.[12–14] To determine whether informed consent is required, you first have to decide whether postings on an Internet community are "private" or "public" communications. This distinction is important because informed consent is required "when behavior of research participants occurs in a private context where an individual can reasonably expect that no observation or reporting is taking place."[15] On the other hand, researchers "may conduct research in public places or use publicly available information about individuals (such as naturalistic observations in public places and analysis of public records or archival research) without obtaining consent,"[15] and "research involving observation of participants in, for example, political rallies, demonstrations or public meetings should not require Research Ethics Board review since it can be expected that the participants are seeking public visibility."[16]

Although publication on the Internet may have parallels to publishing a letter in a newspaper or saying something in a public meeting, there are important psychological differences, and people participating in an online discussion group cannot always be assumed to be "seeking public visibility." On the Internet the dichotomy of private and public sometimes may not be appropriate and communities may lie in between.

Several measures can be used to estimate the perceived level of privacy. Firstly, if a subscription or some form of registration is required to gain access to a discussion group then most of the subscribers are likely to regard the group as a "private place" in cyberspace.[17]

Secondly, the number of (real or assumed) users of a community determines how "public" the space is perceived to be: a posting to a mailing list with 10 subscribers is different from a posting to a mailing list with 100 or 1,000 subscribers. However, as messages sent to mailing lists are sometimes also stored in Web accessible archives, the actual number of people accessing messages may be greater than assumed and may be impossible to determine.

Thirdly and perhaps most importantly, the perception of privacy depends on an individual group's norms and codes, target audience and aim, often laid down in the "frequently asked questions" or information files of an Internet community. For example, SickKids is a discussion list for children who are ill. The information file about the mailing list states that "adults will NOT be permitted to participate on this list as its purpose is to provide kids with their own personal place to share." It seems clear that children who send messages to this list are unlikely to be "seeking public visibility." Similarly, a virtual self support group of sexual abuse survivors was reported to have a group policy explicitly discouraging interested professionals who were not sexual abuse survivors from joining the group,[9] yet a decision was made to analyze postings without obtaining prior or retrospective consent from the group members.[18]

CAN INFORMED CONSENT BE WAIVED?

If it is thought that a community may be perceived to be private, the next question is whether informed consent for passively analyzing the postings is needed or whether this requirement can be waived. In clinical studies non-intrusive research such as retrospective use of existing medical records may be conducted ethically without the express consent of the individual subjects if the material is anonymized at the earliest possible stage, if there is no inconvenience or hazard to the subjects and if the institutional review board has reviewed and agreed to the research protocol.[19] Similar considerations may be applied to passive analysis of messages on mailing lists. When considering potential hazards to group participants or the community as a whole, privacy issues are especially important and it should be considered whether publication of the results (especially when mentioning the group name) may negatively affect group members or harm the community as a whole. Much will depend on what data will be collected and how they will be reported, how vulnerable the community or sensitive the topic is and the degree to which the researcher interacts with group members.

HOW CAN INFORMED CONSENT BE OBTAINED?

If a researcher and the institutional review board feel that obtaining informed consent is necessary, how should it be obtained? For mailing lists, there are basically two possibilities. The first is to send an email to the mailing list describing the research prospectively and giving participants the opportunity to withdraw from the list. The second is to ask retrospectively each person whose postings have been or will be used, giving them the possibility to withdraw themselves from the analysis.

The first approach is intrusive and can be done only for those mailing lists or chat rooms where the entry of new members can be monitored, so that they can be briefed on the ongoing research. There is also a considerable danger that announcing the research may influence future communication patterns or provoke many members to opt out (which may damage the community). The second approach is much less intrusive, can ensure that researchers correctly interpret statements of participants and may even avoid false stories of personal illness being analyzed.[20] However, this approach is cumbersome and time consuming,[11] especially as email addresses may be no longer valid and many participants may not respond.

Obtaining permission from the "list owner" (the individual responsible for maintaining the mailing list) or moderator (if any) is rarely an adequate way for a researcher to obtain "community consent," as neither can properly claim to speak for all of the participants in a mailing list. However, they may know the online community better than the researcher, so they can be a useful starting point to find out what the group norms are and what would be the best way of obtaining informed consent from group members.

PRIVACY AND CONFIDENTIALITY

The Internet holds various pitfalls for researchers, who can easily and unintentionally violate the privacy of individuals. For example, by quoting the exact words of a newsgroup participant, a researcher may breach the participant's confidentiality even if the researcher removes any personal information. This is because powerful search engines such as Google can index newsgroups (groups.google.com), so that the original message, including the email address of the sender, could be retrieved by anybody using the direct quote as a query. Participants should therefore always be approached to give their explicit consent to be quoted verbatim and should be made aware that their email address might be identifiable. Another reason why researchers should contact individuals before quoting them is that the author of the posting may not be seeking privacy but publicity, so that extensive quotes without attribution may be considered a misuse of another person's intellectual property.

CONCLUSIONS

The main problem with using Internet communities for research is that researchers may have difficulty separating spaces regarded as private from spaces regarded as public. We recommend that researchers and institutional review boards should carefully consider these points when developing and reviewing research protocols and should involve members of the group they want to study in these considerations (see box). Our examples show how complex such considerations may be, being further compounded by our lack of knowledge about the psychological aspects of cyberspace, the risks and benefits of Internet-based research and the technical complexities involved. Best practice guidelines for Internet research and compilations of case studies, from the perspective of both researchers and Internet communities, are needed.

PROPOSED CONSIDERATIONS FOR
RESEARCHERS AND INSTITUTIONAL
REVIEW BOARDS BEFORE STUDYING AN
INTERNET COMMUNITY*

Intrusiveness—Discuss to what degree the research conducted is intrusive ("passive" analysis of Internet postings versus active involvement in the community by participating in communications)

Perceived privacy—Discuss (preferably in consultation with members of the community) the level of perceived privacy of the community. (Is it a closed group requiring registration? What is the membership size? What are the group norms?)

Vulnerability—Discuss how vulnerable the community is: for example, a mailing list for victims of sexual abuse or AIDS patients will be a highly vulnerable community.

Potential harm—As a result of the above considerations, discuss whether the intrusion of the researcher or publication of results has the potential to harm individuals or the community as a whole.

Informed consent—Discuss whether informed consent is required or can be waived. (If it is required how will it be obtained?)

Confidentiality—How can the anonymity of participants be protected (if verbatim quotes are given originators can be identified easily using search engines, thus informed consent is always required)?

Intellectual property rights—In some cases, participants may not seek anonymity, but publicity, so that use of postings without attribution may not be appropriate.

*Researchers should explicitly address these issues
in their research protocol.

All authors of the quotes from newsgroups and mailing lists have given their consent to quote them.
  Contributors: Both authors contributed equally to this manuscript.
  Funding: JET's contributions were partially supported by an award from the National Cancer Institute of Canada.
  Competing interests: None declared.

1. Barbour RS. The role of qualitative research in broadening the 'evidence base' for clinical practice. *J Eval Clin Pract* 2000;6:155–63.
2. Eysenbach G. Consumer health informatics. *BMJ* 2000;320:1713–6.
3. Eysenbach G., Wyatt JC. Facilitating research via the internet. In: McKenzie B, ed. *Internet and medicine.* Oxford: Oxford University Press (in press).
4. Klemm P, Reppert K, Visich L. A nontraditional cancer support group. The internet. *Comput Nurs* 1998;16:31–6.

5. Sharf BF. Communicating breast cancer on-line: support and empowerment on the internet. *Women Health* 1997;26(1):65–84.

6. White MH, Dorman SM. Online support for caregivers. Analysis of an internet Alzheimer mailgroup. *Comput Nurs* 2000;18:168–76.

7. Winzelberg AJ. The analysis of an electronic support group for individuals with eating disorders. *Comput Human Behav* 1997;13:393–407.

8. Seaboldt JA, Kuiper R. Comparison of information obtained from a Usenet newsgroup and from drug information centers. *Am J Health Syst Pharm* 1997;54:1732–5.

9. King SA. Researching internet communities: proposed ethical guidelines for the reporting of results. *The Information Society* 1996;12(2):119–28.

10. Till JE. Research ethics: internet-based research. Part 1: On-line survey research. http://members.tripod.com/~ca916/index-3.html. (updated 18 Nov 1997, accessed 20 Jan 2001).

11. Sharf BF. Beyond netiquette. The ethics of doing naturalistic discourse research on the internet. In: Jones S, ed. *Doing internet research.* London: Sage; 1999:243–56.

12. World Medical Association. Declaration of Helsinki: ethical principles for medical research involving human subjects. www.wma.net/e/policy/b3.htm (update 7 Oct 2000, accessed 20 Jan 2001).

13. Jones RA. The ethics of research in cyberspace. *Internet Res* 1994;4(3):30–5.

14. Frankel MS, Siang S. *Ethical and legal issues of human subjects research on the internet—report of an AAAS workshop.* Washington, DC: American Association for the Advancement of Science, 1999.

15. American Sociological Association, American Sociological Association code of ethics. www.asanet.org/members/ecoderev.html (updated 1 Aug 1999, accessed 12 Jan 2001).

16. Social Sciences and Humanities Research Council of Canada. Tri-Council policy statement: ethical conduct for research involving humans. www.sshrc.ca/english/programinfo/policies/Index.htm (updated 14 Sep 2001).

17. Mayer M, Till JE. The internet: a modern Pandora's box? *Qual Life Res* 1996;5:568–71.

18. Finn J. An exploration of helping processes in an online self-help group focusing on issues of disability. *Health Soc Work* 1999;24:220–31.

19. Royal College of Physicians Committee on Ethical Issues in Medicine. Research based on archived information and samples. Recommendations from the Royal College of Physicians Committee on Ethical Issues in Medicine. *J R Coll Physicians Lond* 1999;33:264–6.

20. Feldman MD. Munchausen by internet: detecting factitious illness and crisis on the internet. *South Med J* 2000;93:669–72. (*Accepted 4 October 2001*)

THE ETHICS
OF DATA

—CLINTON WILDER AND JOHN SOAT

The data industry has come under harsh criticism for the amount and means of data about customers collected. Every customer touch-point is a potential source of information for marketers. Consider the ethics of collecting this information and the extent to which it has the potential of eroding customer privacy in unprecedented ways.

Steve Hoberman works for one of the largest process-manufacturing companies on the East Coast. Hoberman is a data architect in the company's IS division. He generates reports for the company's marketing and sales executives based on information in its data warehouse. He considers himself an expert in database design and has a master's degree in IT from Carnegie Mellon University.

You might think Hoberman would know all there is to know about his company's data policies, or at least he'd be generally aware of what the company does with its data. But ask him whether his company sells data to third parties. "No," he answers right off, but then, thinking about it, "I guess I don't know for sure." Does he care? "Not really," he says. "I'm an enabler. I solve people's problems." Hoberman says he translates management's need to interpret data into a tool executives can use to help the business. "Beyond that point," he says, "I don't care."

As an IT professional, Hoberman isn't unusual in his lack of awareness of his company's data policies, nor is he unusual in his insistence that he doesn't need to know those policies. As the debate over data privacy grows louder and more acrimonious, IT professionals increasingly find themselves in the middle of the controversy, whether they know it or not—and a disturbing number don't know it. IT is what makes the collection, manipulation and dissemination of data possible. And while data has been collected and sold since the invention of the abacus, the furious pace at which that industry has grown over the past 10 years can be laid directly at the feet of the technology industry.

What do professionals in the "data industry"—data marketers and vendors of database and data-mining technology—think of the ethical implications, if any, of what they do? What about IT professionals who specialize in data storage and management? Many data marketers equate their ethical obligations with following the letter of the law. As for data-technology vendors, by and large they feel removed from the issue. Many IT professionals, even some directly involved in creating marketing databases, profess an ignorance—willed or not—of any implications to what they do outside their immediate business obligations.

The data industry has come under harsh review. There is a raft of federal and local laws under consideration to control the collection, sale and use of data. American companies have yet to match the tougher privacy regulations already in place in Europe, while personal and class-action litigation against businesses over data-privacy issues is increasing. Privacy advocates, educators and industry observers say it's time for the data industry and the IT community in general, to embrace the issue and drop the duck-and-cover mentality that pervades the controversy. "This whole area is a minefield," says Brian Staff, marketing VP at database supplier Informix Corp., which was recently acquired by IBM.

Earlier this year, N2H2 Inc. learned about the politics of the privacy debate the hard way. The Seattle company, which provides 40% of the Internet filtering software used in U.S. schools, decided last year to enter a new business: the sale of aggregated data. In a partnership with marketing powerhouse Roper Starch Worldwide, N2H2 began marketing the data, called Class Clicks, that its filtering tools collected on the Web-site usage trends of elementary and high-school students. The data contained no names or personal information and complied with the new federal Children's Online Privacy Protection Act.

Yet N2H2's new line of business brought such loud howls of protest from online privacy advocates that the company scrapped the effort in February. "We went above and beyond the call to make sure there was no way to trace anything back to a school or an individual," says Ken Collins, N2H2's director of analytic services. "It was all aggregated data, but it still triggered a bunch of flags in public perception. It was a confusing and chaotic mess."

There's no doubt that data marketers feel under scrutiny. "If we don't get it right and we allow abuses to happen, the whole industry will pay the price for years," says Paul Gustafson, VP of business development and product management for IQCommerce Corp., which builds the IT behind online promotions for companies such as Unilever and Johnson & Johnson. "There's an awful lot at stake and we're a long way away from having all the answers."

Many companies in the consumer-information business describe ethical business practices primarily in terms of complying with existing laws, such as the 31-year-old Fair Credit Reporting Act or the recently ratified Gramm Leach Bliley Act that regulates consumer financial data. "We try to balance how we use information while complying with laws and regulations and doing things in an ethical manner," says Rich Crutchfield, executive VP at Equifax Corp. in Atlanta, the world's largest provider of credit data.

"There's a tremendous amount of federal, state and contract law out there dealing with privacy," says David Lee, an executive VP at ChoicePoint Inc., which compiles public-record information for insurance carriers, the FBI and the U.S. Marshals, among other customers. "We view ourselves almost as a regulated industry." At ChoicePoint, chief privacy officer Michael de Janes is also the company's general counsel.

Clearly, business and government leaders aren't satisfied with how data privacy has been handled so far. The growth of a management position known as the chief privacy officer is an attempt by companies—across many industries, not just those in the data business—to indemnify themselves against potential liability over data issues, both internal and external.

As well they should. Along with the privacy laws already on the books, there are 50 bills pending in Congress concerning privacy and more in state and local governments.

THE UPSHOT

IT pros can no longer abstain from the ethics and privacy debate:

- As online marketing grows, so do ethical implications of database management.

- New privacy laws thrust IT into the data-ethics fray.

- Ethics training is just beginning to appear in college IT curricula.

- More on the emergence of chief privacy officers at informationweek.com/837/ethics_cpo.htm.

- Find part one of our series on ethics and IT at informationweek.com/825/ethics.htm.

Data marketers are keenly aware of the growing momentum behind those legislative efforts and what it might mean for their industry. "We want to avoid heavy-handed regulation with unintended consequences," says John Ford, chief privacy officer at Equifax. "Why use a vise grip when a pair of tweezers will do?"

One of the most controversial of the new privacy laws is the Health Insurance Portability and Accountability Act. Former President Clinton signed the bill into law in 1996, but Congress never devised specific rules governing medical data, so that onerous task was deferred to the Department of Health and Human Services. The department released 1,500 pages of rules in December (available at www.hhs.gov/ocr/regtext.html), Congress ratified them last month and companies have two years to comply.

Patients are promised the ability to access their medical records; previously, that was allowed in only 28 states. Also, they can make changes to inaccuracies in their medical files. Health-care entities covered under HIPAA must receive written consent from patients to use their medical data. Health-care companies must also hire a privacy officer and train employees in how to handle the sensitive data. Those who misuse data face up to 10 years in prison and $250,000 in fines.

HIPAA won't affect some data-collection methods. Medical Marketing Service in Wood Dale, Ill., and A. Caldwell List Co. in Atlanta aren't using official records or under-the-table schemes to gather the information they sell to data marketers. They get it voluntarily from ailment sufferers who respond to direct-mail or online questionnaires that promise coupons, discounts and samples in exchange for a bevy of personal data. "We not only get ailment information, but also data on college degrees, income, age, hobbies, address and phone number, if they have an American Express or Visa card and whether they plan to travel or buy [specific] things in the next six months," says Tori Weathersby, senior sales executive at A. Caldwell. For the millions who respond, they're informed of the marketing possibilities on the questionnaires.

HIPAA also doesn't cover dot-coms, so when an individual fills out a health-care assessment on a medical Web site, that information is fair game for any marketing efforts. "There's a false sense of security that consumers and patients would have at an E-health dot-com," says Paul Tang, chief medical information officer at the Palo Alto Medical Foundation, a health-care provider and medical research group in northern California. Tang is also chairman of the public policy committee of the American Medical Informatics Association. "A critical point is that they're not doing anything that's currently illegal. So it's really a 'consumer beware' situation," he says.

Data marketers realize they have a public-perception problem. The Direct Marketing Association represents 5,000 consumer-marketing and data-collection companies. Pat Faley, VP of ethics and consumer affairs for the association and the former VP of public responsibility at American Express, heads a staff of 10 who focus on consumer-protection and privacy issues. The association has specific privacy guidelines that its members must follow or they can be kicked out of the group—and last year, it did just that to three members, including Columbia University's Graduate School of Business, that refused to certify their adherence to the guidelines. "They felt it was not the appropriate role for a trade associa-

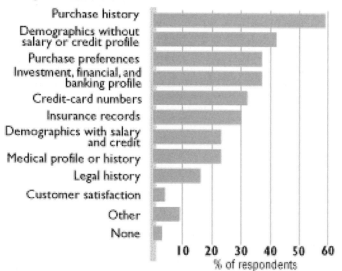

Selective Shopping

Which of the following types of data are collected from your customers?

Note: Multiple responses allowed.

DATA: INFORMATIONWEEK RESEARCH BUSINESS ETHICS STUDY 2001 OF 250 IT AND BUSINESS PROFESSIONALS

tion, but we obviously disagree," Faley says. "Any company that violates their customers' privacy gives the entire industry a black eye."

A common refrain among technology providers and the companies collecting and mining data is that ethical, privacy-respecting practices simply make good business sense. "Poor privacy practices harm relationships," says Rachael Shanahan, chief privacy officer at Unica Corp., a supplier of customer-relationship management software. "Any company that doesn't understand the value of the customer relationship won't be around for very long."

But most database-technology vendors don't believe it's their place to dictate how their customers can or can't use their products. "We're like the companies that make the metal that goes into guns—one step removed," says Informix's Staff. "It's hard to see how we could impose any controls on how [Informix technology] is used."

Oracle's head database developer, Ken Jacobs, admits he has conflicting feelings when his dinner is interrupted by a telemarketer—who has perhaps culled his name from an Oracle database. "I sometimes ask myself, 'Do I really want to help these people?' " he says with a laugh. But Jacobs, the database-industry leader's VP of product strategy for server technologies, says he doesn't know how Oracle could enforce any edicts on how its products are used, or not sell to a customer it considered unethical. "I don't think we'd be in a position to do that," he says. "Would the hardware people not sell them hardware? Or the electric company not sell them electricity?"

Far from apologizing for what they do, many in the data industry say they perform a valuable function for society. "One of the key things that fuels our economy is easy access to credit information," says Equifax's Crutchfield. "You can buy a car in an hour because the auto company can see [your credit data] instantly."

Business-intelligence software vendor Business Objects SA tries to convince companies that aren't in the information business that they're passing up a potentially large source of revenue by not analyzing and selling data they collect. "We ran a seminar session called 'You're Sitting on a Gold Mine and Don't Know It,' " says David Kellogg, senior VP of marketing at Business Objects.

Another vendor touts the capability of its products to go beyond the generally accepted norm of aggregation—categorizing data by demographic details without referencing specific names—as a competitive advantage. "Marketers can indeed target personally identifiable individuals, going beyond aggregation," says Paul Rodwick, VP of market development and strategy at E.piphany Inc. "Companies want a deep relationship with their customers and technologies like ours help prevent spam because marketers can do finer segmentation and market to people who are actually interested in what they're selling."

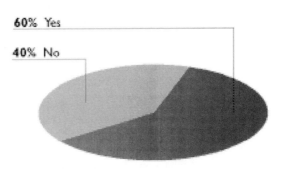

Privacy Proclamations
Does your company have a publicly displayed privacy policy?

60% Yes

40% No

DATA: INFORMATIONWEEK RESEARCH BUSINESS ETHICS STUDY 2001 OF 250 IT AND BUSINESS PROFESSIONALS

That all makes sense to at least one IT professional. "To me, there's nothing bad here," says database designer Hoberman. "I don't see anything wrong with collecting all this information about us. I live for information. The more information you have, the better. It's all good stuff."

Are there guidelines or an ethical code to help database experts sort out their responsibilities? Should there be? Some senior IT managers say database professionals don't bear much responsibility at all. "I never really thought about [usage of data] from the database administrator's position," says Lou Saviano, director of IT services and infrastructure development at Osram Sylvania, the Danvers, Mass., division of Osram GmbH. "A database administrator would never make the decision on how the data is used. That would be a sales and marketing call."

That also goes for outside consultants who create databases for clients, says Trey Johnson, a data-warehouse architect for Encore Development, an E-business consulting firm in Jacksonville, Fla. "We're just building tools," Johnson says. "The customers are ultimately responsible for how they're using these tools." Johnson admits it's possible that Encore would create a tool that would collect data at a fairly personal level, but the responsibility for how that technology is used "falls squarely on the shoulders of the companies that use these tools," he says. "That's where privacy starts and ends."

Tang, of the Palo Alto Medical Foundation, has a different view—that IT professionals should go beyond creating the tools and take an active role in building their companies' privacy policies. Not only has Palo Alto implemented strict policies for users of patient medical data, it's also adopted policies for how the IT department handles such information. "Every time you make a purchase or upgrade of a system, you should consider the security features built in and make sure they're sufficient to handle privacy regulations, governed either by professional ethics or law," he says. "I don't think that's been at the top of anyone's mind for any industry, including health care. We live in a new world and this should be a key component of any new system."

The ethical "duties" of a database administrator revolve around maintaining the integrity, security, reliability and availability of a company's data, says Bill Burke, director of information services, strategic operations, at supply-chain software vendor i2 Technologies Inc. That means preventing information about a consumer's credit history or an employee's human-resources records from becoming corrupted, that no "inadvertent or malicious damage" is done to the data, Burke says. Making such data secure, both from access by outside hackers and inappropriate use by internal employees, is also part of a database administrator's ethical responsibility. "You have the salary of everyone from the janitor to the CEO on file," Burke says.

A mitigating factor is that database professionals have limited control over the operation of other parts of the companies they work for, says Kimberly Floss, who recently left a job as a database administrator for the Leo Burnett advertising agency in Chicago. For example, responsibility for data integrity, while primarily the database administrator's, also lies with the organizations that operate the applications that supply data to the company's database and even with the third-party application providers that supply that software. But database administrators have to be knowledgeable about those systems as well as their own, Floss says. "The responsibility of the DBA, in my view, has increased."

When it comes to data privacy and the changes that IT is bringing, the industry hasn't done enough to raise ethical questions, says David Ozar, director of the Center for Ethics at Loyola University in Chicago. The speed at which things are changing is no excuse. Ozar compares it with human genome research, where technology may be outstripping the ethical debate, but there's at least an active discussion about it in the professional and academic community. "There was a self-conscious effort to say 'Let's talk about the fundamental questions here,' " Ozar says. "I don't think IT has anything comparable."

RULES OF INTERNET CONDUCT NEED TO EVOLVE

A group of IT professionals, business executives, scholars and *InformationWeek* editors gathered at Loyola University earlier this year for a roundtable discussion about IT and business ethics. Participants ranged from the CIO of a stock-trading network to a lawyer to a philosophy professor. Some excerpts follow; to read a longer version of the roundtable, visit informationweek.com/837/ethics_rt.htm.

- Henry Venta, Loyola University of Chicago, business school dean: "Are we going to give enough time for these rules of conduct to develop as they normally do? We might be making rash decisions; that's why there's not a lot of support among the technology community, for example, for widespread regulation."

- Stuart Townsend, CIO, Archipelago stock-trading network: "The real reason for regulation isn't to protect the individual, but to protect society so that society can benefit from these advances. If everyone stops giving information on the Internet about themselves, the whole thing grinds to a halt."

- David Ozar, Loyola philosophy professor and Center for Ethics director: "Most large corporations have at least some kind of ethics committee running a compliance program. But in a lot of corporations, this process is veneer, just in case some federal judge has to sentence us some day and we want him to think we look good."

- Mike Zdeb, attorney, Childers & Zdeb: "There's this notion that because you use '.com' or you use the word 'Internet' as an adjective that somehow the ordinary, everyday rules of common sense, ethics and legal rules don't apply."

- Mary Arnberg, HR director of law firm Sidley Austin Brown & Wood: "The pace of change in technology has far

> outpaced everyday living, so people are confronted with what's the right thing and the wrong thing to do with the technology that they have. There aren't guidelines in place that help people decide what it is they should do and there's just so much technological capability out there. It's really a free-for-all."
>
> - James Burke, president, JPB Group: "It starts with the individual, the personal ethics of the people running the firm. If they don't have those ethics or that yardstick to work on, it will cascade through the corporation very rapidly."

The problem is that many IT people don't know very much about the privacy debate. "You find that there's a general lack of understanding about privacy, about the laws and regulations," says Larry Ponemon, president of Guardent Inc., a Waltham, Mass., security service provider. Before Guardent, Ponemon was a partner with PricewaterhouseCoopers, where he established the consulting firm's ethics and corporate-compliance practice. He's considered one of the leading experts on privacy. "[IT professionals] will say things like 'We know our company has a privacy policy, but I don't know where it is.' They don't understand how it affects their business processes," Ponemon says.

That's dangerous, says Ira Rothken, principal of the Rothken Law Firm in San Francisco. Rothken is a lead counsel in a class-action lawsuit in California against online data marketer DoubleClick Inc. in a privacy-invasion dispute over the use of cookies, the Internet device many Web sites use to keep track of visitors. While Rothken says IT executives aren't likely to be cited in a data-privacy lawsuit unless they've done something criminal, they should understand the legal environment. "An IT person would be acting below the standard of care not to know the laws and regulations in their area," he says.

Where do IT professionals find training in ethics? Not in college—at least not yet. Database designer Hoberman says he never once discussed ethics during his time at Carnegie Mellon. "I don't really mention the word *ethics*. I talk about privacy and security," says Daniel Norris, a professor of management information systems at Iowa State University who specializes in teaching database management and computer security. The subject of ethics comes up only in relation to security, he says, and the students themselves never bring it up. "If it won't help them on the job, they don't want to talk about it," he says.

Norris says there's a push at Iowa State to integrate ethics into the curriculum and that the school has created an ethics center. As far as the computer-science department is concerned, "it's going to be a slow process," he says.

But not if Doris Lidke can help it. Lidke is a professor of computer and information sciences at Towson University in Towson, Md. She's also a member of the Accreditation Board of Engineering and Technology, which accredits computer-science departments across the country.

Lidke recently headed a task force to explore the possibility of creating a computer-science curriculum that specializes in very large systems, to prepare graduates to work with, say, air-traffic control systems. The task force was made up of equal parts academics and business executives, the latter from companies such as Boeing Co. and Citibank as well as a large phone company and a large computer manufacturer. In developing a list of potential subjects for such a curriculum, Lidke and her colleagues were surprised to see one nontechnology topic score as high in terms of priorities as user-interface and systems integration. "We were quite surprised that [ethics] was one of the things that absolutely had to be in the curriculum," she says. This summer, the Accreditation Board of Engineering and Technology will add a new subject to its list of mandatory courses: one credit hour of ethics study.

The teaching of business ethics has grown rapidly in recent years, but linking ethics to IT and to decisions about the way data is collected and used, is long overdue. Jody Giles, VP and CIO of shoemaker Vans Inc. in Santa Fe Springs, Calif., says he had

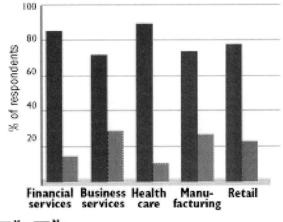

Customer Profiling by Industry
Does your company collect data from its customers?

Yes ▪ No ▪

Base: 50 financial-services sites; 50 business-services sites; 50 health-care sites; 50 manufacturing sites; 50 retail sites

DATA: INFORMATIONWEEK RESEARCH BUSINESS ETHICS STUDY 2001 OF 250 IT AND BUSINESS PROFESSIONALS

to rely on the expertise of @Once, the company's E-mail-distribution partner, when Vans began marketing to teenagers online. "Had they not made me aware of the Children's Online Privacy Protection Act, I wouldn't have known a thing about it," Giles says. "This is a new, emerging issue that comes with the technology. They didn't teach me about it when I was taking ethics classes in business school."

With Eileen Colkin, Robin Gareiss, Diane Rezendes Khirallah, Chris Murphy, and Rick Whiting.

THE PHARMS AND DOCTORS: CORRUPTING MEDICINE

—Wanda Hamilton

The author lays out a trenchant criticism of marketing practices used by pharmaceutical marketers to persuade physicians to adopt specific brands of pharmaceuticals. Also criticized is the relationship between top professional medical journals and pharmaceutical advertising budgets. Is this any different from any other marketing channel, wherein both "push" and "pull" marketing are standard practices?

It begins on the first day of medical school and lasts through to retirement and it is the only reliable "cradle to grave" benefit that doctors can truly count on any more. . . . It starts slowly and insidiously, like an addiction, and can end up influencing the very nature of medical decision-making and practice. It first appears harmless enough: a textbook here, a penlight there and progresses to stethoscopes and black bags, until eventually come nights "on the town" at academic conventions and all-expenses paid "educational symposia" in lovely locales. The Lancet editorial is talking about pharmaceutical industry perks to physicians and influence on medical education in the U.S. (*The Lancet,* 356:781, Sept. 2, 2000).

The corporate world owns many of our political representatives in Washington, DC. The medical situation is not very different: industry owns physicians and dictates the course of education, research and ultimately the practice of medicine in degrees previously unimaginable. Augusto Sarmiento, MD, Letter to the Editor, *JAMA,* 286(3), July 18, 2001.

The phrase, "First, do no harm" has been eliminated from the "modified" Hippocratic oath currently administered to graduating medical students in the U.S. The initial sentence in the Physicians' Oath now reads: "I do solemnly swear by whatever I hold most sacred, that I will be loyal to the profession of Medicine and generous to its members."

The relationship between physicians and the pharmaceutical industry is unavoidably intimate because physicians depend on pharmaceutical products to treat patients. Nevertheless, there is substantial evidence that pharmaceutical company influence on physicians, medical education and patient treatment is far more pervasive and insidious than even some physicians themselves realize and it involves far greater ethical problems than physicians' acceptance of gifts of penlights, free lunches and all-expense-paid trips to symposia. For example, documents released by the U.S. House of Representatives Commerce Committee indicate that some doctors make money billing Medicare and Medicaid for more than they actually pay for drugs, a practice made possible by the manufacturers of the drugs.

> *Drug companies artificially inflate wholesale prices, investigators say, because Medicare and state Medicaid programs base their reimbursement on those numbers. Their goal is to have the highest wholesale price—and the lowest actual selling price.*
>
> *That way, they can market their drugs to doctors based on how much money the doctors can make by billing government programs for the higher amount.*
>
> *"Profit maximization—it's in the bag," reads a 1997 marketing memo from Glaxo Wellcome touting one of its drug's wholesale price advantage over a competitor's similar product.*
>
> *The Glaxo marketing document shows that a busy oncology practice using its 32 milligram bag of anti-nausea treatment could net $13 million a year—$2 million more than if the practice used its competitor's product. All because the wholesale price, which no one except the government actually pays, is higher.* (Julie Appleby, "Drug Makers Accused of Price Scheme," *USA Today,* Sept. 27, 2000, p. 1B.)

Shocking as it might be, this wholesale price inflation by pharmaceutical companies to increase profits for themselves and physicians at the expense of the taxpayers is apparently quite legal.

It's also quite legal for big pharmaceutical companies to track individual physician's prescription patterns and then attempt to change those patterns, even if it means encouraging the physician to prescribe a more expensive drug when a less expensive drug is just as effective.

> *Over the past decade, with the advent of sophisticated new computer technology, pharmaceutical manufacturers have been quietly compiling résumés on the prescribing patterns of the nation's health care professionals, many of whom have no idea that their decisions are open to commercial scrutiny.*
>
> *These "prescriber profiles" are the centerpiece of an increasingly vigorous—and apparently successful—effort by drug makers to sway doctors' prescribing habits. To create them, pharmaceutical marketers are buying information from pharmacies, the federal government and the American Medical Association, which generates $20 million in annual income by selling biographies of every American doctor.* Sheryl Stolberg and Jeff Gerth, "High-Tech Stealth Being Used to Sway Doctor Prescriptions," *New York Times,* Nov. 16, 2000. In addition to increased calls from drug sales reps, physicians may be offered such perks as "consultation fees" in an effort to influence their drug prescribing practices.

And there are many other ways pharmaceutical companies influence physicians' choices of prescription drugs—billions of dollars worth of free samples, advertising in medical publications and direct-to-consumer advertising:

- *"The pharmaceutical industry gave $7.2 billion worth of samples to U.S. doctors in 1999"* (Gavin Yamey, "Pen 'Amnesty' for Doctors Who Shun Drug Companies," News, *BMJ,* 322:69, Jan. 13, 2001).

- *"Of the $13.9 billion that the drug companies spent promoting their products last year, 87%, or about $12 billion, was aimed at doctors and the small group of nurse practitioners and physicians' assistants who can prescribe some medications, about one million prescribers all told."* Stolberg and Gerth, "High-Tech Stealth Being Used to Sway Doctor Prescriptions," *New York Times,* Nov. 16, 2000. Many medical journals gain most of their revenue from pharmaceutical ads.

- *"Doctors wrote 34.2% more prescriptions in 1999 than in 1998 for the 25 drugs promoted direct to consumers that contributed most to overall drug spending. Doctors wrote only 5.1% more prescriptions for all other prescription drugs."* Fred Charatan, "US Prescription Drugs Sales Boosted by Advertising," News, *BMJ,* Sept. 30, 2000.

- *"We know that 66% of patients that ask the doctor for a particular product get it."* Thomas Ebeling, head of pharmaceuticals at Novartis. Quoted in David Pilling, "Direct Promotion of Brands Gives Power to the Patients," *Financial Times,* April 28, 2001.

These marketing practices in themselves do not necessarily compromise a physician's prescription patterns. What is more problematic is that even highly ethical physicians depend on experts in their fields, professional journals, symposia and reference books for their information on drugs and these sources are largely funded by the pharmaceutical industry. For example, prominent physicians may be paid by pharmaceutical companies to promote the companies' drugs to other physicians.

> *One pharmaceutical company employs several eminent British cardiologists to lecture to other doctors around the country to promote the company's drugs. The cardiologists, known to company employees as The Road Show, are each paid 3,000 to 5,000 [U.K. pounds] . . . plus traveling expenses for a 1 hour evening talk in the UK. . . . Some members of The Road Show have spoken fortnightly for the company. As a result they receive more money each year from the company than their annual salary from their hospital or university. . . . Some have admitted to me that they have kept silent about adverse effects of drugs to avoid loss of lucrative research contracts with a manufacturing pharmaceutical company. Some opinion leaders involved in pharmaceutical research now command speaker fees that are so high that their engagements are negotiated by an agent.* Wilmshurst P, "Academia and Industry," *The Lancet* 2000; 356:338–344, July 22, 2000.

Many of the top professional medical journals such as *The New England Journal of Medicine, JAMA* and the *British Journal of Medicine* receive the bulk of their funding from pharmaceutical advertising. In addition, many of the journals' editorial writers, peer reviewers and even many of the researchers whose studies appear in the journals have financial connections to the pharmaceutical industry. And many of the published drug studies themselves are funded by the very pharmaceutical companies manufacturing the drugs.

The New England Journal of Medicine published a study concluding that 30% of study subjects using bupropion (Glaxo Wellcome's Zyban) as a smoking-cessation aid stayed off cigarettes for at least a year. Not only was the study funded by Glaxo Wellcome, but "eight of the 12 doctors involved in the study declared a link to the pharmaceuticals giant" ("Antidepressants Beat the Craving," BBC News, March 4, 1999). Studies not funded by the manufacturer have found the drug's success rate is half that claimed in the Glaxo Wellcome funded study. Further, the *NEJM* article did not highlight the considerable health risks posed by the drug.

Even worse is the common practice of pharmaceutical companies buying editorials and paying physicians and researchers to affix their names to journal articles they did not write.

> *The practice of buying editorials reflects the growing influence of the pharmaceutical industry on medical care. Thompson defines a conflict of interest as a "set of conditions in which professional judgment concerning a primary interest (such as a patient's welfare or the validity of research) tends to be unduly influenced by a secondary interest (such as financial gain)." The boundaries between these interests are becoming more and more difficult to perceive, especially when information for physicians is carefully orchestrated by a public-relations firm. Indeed, the goal of public-relations firms that ghostwrite editorials and do other work for drug companies is to blur the distinction between primary and secondary interests.*
>
> *In the past, publications were written by a study's principal investigator. More recently, a practice that one might call the nonwriting author-nonauthor writer syndrome has developed. . . . The syndrome has two features: a professional medical writer ("ghostwriter") employed by a drug company, CRO [contract research organization], or medical communications company, who is paid to write an article but is not named as an author; and a clinical investigator ("guest author") who appears as an author but does not analyze the data or write the manuscript.*
>
> *In one study, 19% of the articles surveyed had named authors who did not contribute sufficiently to the articles to meet the criteria for authorship. . . .* The foregoing quotations are all from Brennan T, "Buying Editorials," *The New England Journal of Medicine,* 331:10, Sept. 8, 1994.

In addition to professional journals, physicians also rely on symposia and professional meetings to update themselves on information about drugs, but many of these are also funded by pharmaceutical companies.

> *Most of the CME [Continuing Medical Education], the plenary sessions and almost 75–80% of the general as well as specialty symposia are sponsored by one or the other pharmaceutical company.* Kagalwala T, M.D, "The Conferences Are a Charade," May 26, 2001, *BMJ* Electronic response Jackson T, "Are you being duped?" *BMJ* 2001; 322:1312, May 26, 2001. The Jackson article is a review of a 24-page guide published as a supplement in the May, 2001 edition of *Pharmaceutical Marketing.* Jackson writes:

"So what exactly does this guide say? It advises marketers, in identifying opinion leaders, not to 'risk wasting money' on doctors 'who you eventually hear have no credibility with their peers.' Instead, marketers should aim for those who are 'on the editorial boards of key publications for ultimate target audiences,' on scientific committees, members of key professional societies, representatives of national or international guideline committees and key players on formulary committees. 'The key aim,' says the guide, 'is to ensure that you are working with a mix of people who can ultimately be called upon to communicate on your behalf in different situations.' "

Other sources of drug information for physicians are reference works, such as the *Physicians' Desk Reference* [PDR] and national and international guidelines. But the PDR "was originally developed as a promotional device" and "there is no mechanism by which all clinically relevant dose-response data or important post release discoveries are regularly and rapidly incorporated into it" (Cohen J, "Dose Discrepancies Between the *Physicians' Desk Reference* and the Medical Literature, and Their Possible Role in the High Incidence of Dose-Related Adverse Drug Events," *Archives of Internal Medicine,* 161(7): 957–964, April 9, 2001). And the national and international guideline panels are loaded with researchers having strong financial ties to the pharmaceutical industry, as is the case with the U.S. Clinical Practice Guideline on Treating Tobacco Use and Dependence.

The lack of objective drug information available to physicians may account for at least some of the steep rise in fatal medication errors:

> *An examination of all U.S. death certificates over the 10-year period [between 1983 and 1993], the most recent data available to the researcher, found that fatal medication errors had increased 2.6-fold. But among outpatients, the jump in such deaths was 8.5-fold.* Richard Knox, "Researchers Report Surge in Deaths Due to Medication Errors," *The Boston Globe,* Feb. 27, 1998, p. A1. In addition to medication errors, it is estimated that more than 100,000 Americans die each year from adverse effects of prescription drugs and that 1,000,000 more are injured so severely they must be hospitalized.

It also may account for many physicians' misinformation on the health effects of smoking and environmental tobacco smoke.

GODDAMN THE PUSHER MAN

Why Does Everybody Seem to Hate the
Pharmaceutical Industry?

—RONALD BAILEY

A defense is offered for certain marketing practices adopted by pharmaceutical companies. Pharmaceutical companies have the right, argues the author, to recover the costs of creating new drugs. By curtailing the activities of pharmaceutical companies, the author states that society suffers in the long term. Once again we see the clash between deontological and teleological perspectives. Can you offer a mechanism of resolution?

Drug companies saved my marriage.

Get that smirk off your face, for this is not a tale of Viagra. Two years ago, I asked Pamela to marry me. She said yes, making me a happy man—arguably the happiest man on Earth. But that tender moment was only possible because of what I am more than willing to call a miracle drug. You see, Pamela owns two cats and she had made it clear that if I was going to live with her, I was going to have to live with her two cats as well. "I gave up my cats for my first husband and I'm not going to do it for a second one," she declared.

The problem is that I am allergic to cats. The solution is the new antihistamine Zyrtec, developed by Pfizer in 1995. I take one pill a day and the felines can rub their fluffy tails across my nose without provoking so much as a sniffle. (Zyrtec doesn't cause drowsiness, either.) So now we are living happily ever after in wedded bliss. A month's supply costs $66.25 at my local pharmacy, but what price love?

Yet the development of products such as Zyrtec—not to mention Viagra and birth-control pills—has not bought pharmaceutical companies a lot of love. Quite the opposite. When Al Gore listed "Big Drug Companies" along with "Big Oil, Big Tobacco and Big Polluters" as foes of the American people in his acceptance speech at last year's Democratic National Convention, he wasn't going out on a limb. He was tapping into widespread bad feelings toward pill makers. John Le Carré, the best-selling British writer famous for his Cold War spy novels, casts pharmaceutical companies as the new global villains in his 2000 novel *The Constant Gardener*. Communist dictators are out as bad guys and drug company CEOs are in.

The pill-pushing industry is now one of the top targets of politicians and much of the public for ire, wrath and (possibly) regulation. The most frequent complaint is that prescription drugs cost too much, that their costs are spiraling out of control. There's no question that Americans are spending more on prescription drugs than they used to. In 1997, our total spending on drugs increased by 14.2% from the previous year; in 1998, it went up 15.7%; and in 1999, it rose again by 18.8%. During that same time span, the overall inflation rate never rose above 3% per annum.

So the drug companies must be gouging patients and health care providers, right? No. Many critics have made the mistake of confusing more spending with higher prices. In other words, prices aren't going up—we're buying more. Spending on prescription drugs is rising rapidly because Americans like me are buying more pills; our medicine cabinets are bulging with new treatments for whatever ails us.

Between 1993 and 1999, overall inflation rose 19% while drug prices increased 18.1%. In some years inflation outstripped drug price increases, while in others drug prices rose faster than inflation. For example, in 1996 inflation was 3.3% and drug prices increased only 1.6%; in 1998, inflation rose 1.6% and drug prices went up 3.2%. The vast majority of the spending increase on drugs—some 78%—has occurred because doctors and patients are taking advantage of the more and better drugs that are now available.

During the 1990s, the pharmaceutical industry developed nearly 400 new drugs, many of which act as substitutes for older, more expensive medical treatments. When other industries develop new products that people want—personal computers, say, or cell phones—we typically laud them for their innovation and willingly plunk down our money.

So why are pharmaceutical companies in the doghouse, especially since they are making products that save and enrich our lives? The answer includes political opportunism, large doses of ignorance regarding the drug industry's economics and an entitlement mind-set among many consumers. Those are potent sentiments that, in today's policy climate, are particularly troubling. If enacted, the most common proposed solutions to the prescription drug "problem" would actually undermine an industry that has greatly enriched our quality of life.

COST ANALYSIS

Just how much are Americans spending on prescription medicines and what are they getting in return? According to the Bureau of Labor Statistics, the average consumer spends just over 1% of her annual income on pharmaceuticals, about the same amount that gets spent on tobacco and alcohol. The elderly, who are by far the largest consumers of medicine, spend roughly 3% of their annual income on drugs, about the same amount they spend on entertainment. Households with seniors 65 to 74 years old spend $1,587 on entertainment and $698 on drugs, while those over 74 years old spend $875 on entertainment and $719 on drugs. (The average income for 65-to-74-year-olds is $28,928; for those over 74 it is $23,937.)

As mentioned before, Americans are indeed spending more on prescription medicines in absolute terms. Average expenditures per household were $301 in 1993 and $370 in 1999. But spending totals aren't the end of the analysis. A more important question is whether we are getting value for our money. According to Columbia University economist

Frank Lichtenberg, the answer is absolutely yes. Between 1960 and 1997, life expectancy at birth for Americans rose from 69.7 years to 76.5 years. "Increased drug approvals and health expenditure per person jointly explain just about 100% of the observed long-run longevity increase," writes Lichtenberg in a working paper done last year for the National Bureau of Economic Research. Lichtenberg found that for an expenditure of $11,000 on general medical care, there is a gain of one life-year on average. (A life-year in this context is simply an extra year of life that a patient gains by being treated.) However, spending just $1,345 on pharmaceutical research and development gets the same result. Economists have calculated that, on average, people value an extra year of life at about $150,000. (That figure is based on people's willingness to engage in risky jobs.) Assuming an average value of $150,000 per life-year, the benefits from medical care expenditures outweigh the costs by a factor of more than 13; the benefits of drug R&D are more than 100 times greater than its costs. As important, drugs can also reduce health care costs. In "Do (More and Better) Drugs Keep People Out of the Hospital?"—a 1996 study published in the *American Economic Review*—Lichtenberg found that "a $1 increase in pharmaceutical expenditure is associated with a $3.65 reduction in hospital-care expenditure."

The story of stomach-acid-blocking drugs such as Tagamet and Zantac illustrates how drugs save money by keeping patients out of the hospital. In 1977, the year in which such drugs were introduced, surgeons performed some 97,000 operations for peptic ulcers. In 1993, despite population growth, that number had shrunk to 19,000. The shift from surgery to highly effective pills—a change that has made life better for tens of thousands of people with stomach problems—is the sort of quiet development that escapes much attention. The Boston Consulting Group's health care practice reported that it saves patients and insurers at least $224 million in annual medical costs.

Other examples abound. In 1991, for instance, the benefits that drugs offered became painfully apparent when New Hampshire, in a cost-saving measure, adopted spending caps on the number of reimbursable medications that Medicaid patients could receive. The result was that nursing home admissions doubled among chronically ill elderly patients and raised government costs for institutional care by $311,000, which was 20 times more than was "saved" by imposing spending caps on drugs. As John Calfee, a drug policy analyst at the market-oriented American Enterprise Institute, has noted, drugs that break apart blood clots cut hospitalization and rehabilitation costs for stroke victims by about four times the cost of the drug. In his recent monograph *Prices, Markets and the Pharmaceutical Revolution,* Calfee also reports that schizophrenia drugs costing $4,500 per year save more than $70,000 in annual institutional treatment costs.

A yearlong study of 1,100 patients done by Humana Hospitals found that using drugs to treat congestive heart failure increased pharmacy costs 60%, but cut hospital costs by 78%, for an overall savings of $9.3 million. Better still, the death rate dropped from an expected 25% to 10%. In Virginia, an asthma study found that new asthma drugs cut emergency room visits by 42%. And, relevant to my cat situation, a study by the consulting firm William M. Mercer concluded that every $1 spent on non-sedating antihistamines yielded a $3.07 return to employers, due to increased productivity and reduced accident costs.

"The ability of pharmaceuticals to reduce the total expenditures for health care, as well as business costs, is important but secondary," concludes Calfee. Modern drug therapy means "patients and consumers . . . are gaining . . . better health, longer life, reduced pain and discomfort and other blessings."

OBSCENE PROFITS

OK, grant some critics of the industry. Drugs dramatically cut some medical costs, they say, but the drug makers are reaping huge—obscene, really—profits. In fact, drug company profits as conventionally calculated do run to as much as 20%, while 5% profit margins are typical of many other American industries. That 20% figure, however, is deceptive, since the standard accounting procedures used to calculate drug company profits write off R&D costs as "current expenses." No other industry has nearly as high R&D expenses, so when other industries write off their R&D it doesn't have as much effect on their rate of return calculations. If pharmaceutical R&D were depreciated over time, then annual profits for the industry drop to around 9%.

That's still almost double the average rate of return. What explains it? Drug discovery and development is a notoriously risky business. "Some 5,000 to 10,000 molecules are screened and only one will make it to being a drug," explains Kees Been, vice president for business and marketing at Biogen Inc., a leading biotech pharmaceutical company based in Cambridge, Massachusetts. "From discovery to launch takes 12 to 16 years. Only 30% of all products ever invented returned more than what was invested in them," adds Been. That means that 70% of the drugs currently available for treating and curing people are in fact economic losers for the companies that developed them.

A 1999 study by Duke University economists Henry Grabowski and John Vernon for the Tufts University Center for the Study of Drug Development analyzed the sales of a cohort of drugs introduced between 1988 and 1992. The study found that the top 10% of new drugs accounted for more than half the total sales revenues of drugs. "The returns to R&D projects in pharmaceuticals have similar properties to that of venture capital investments," conclude Grabowski and Vernon. In other words, drug companies, like venture capital firms, throw money at a lot of different high-risk projects knowing that virtually none will pan out, but that a few may score real jackpots.

These jackpots cover the losses on the other projects and, perhaps more important, pay for future bets. In this way, revenues from such blockbuster drugs as Prozac for depression, Celebrex for arthritis pain, Viagra for erectile dysfunction and Lipitor for controlling cholesterol levels do more than cover the costs of the majority of drugs that do not make a profit; they also fuel further research.

Investment in R&D for any given drug is not trivial. Typically, it costs between $300 million and $500 million to bring a single drug from being a gleam in a lab jockey's eye to delivery to the marketplace. Yet one argument that critics often make is that drug companies sell their pills for dozens, if not hundreds, of times more than it costs to make them. The liberal policy magazine *American Prospect* made just this case in its September 11, 2000, issue, in an article titled, "The Price Isn't Right." The piece cites an analysis that claims Bristol-Myers Squibb can manufacture a patient's 18-month supply of the popular cancer drug Taxol for just $500, but charges over 20 times more than the manufacturing costs.

This kind of "analysis" is just willfully stupid. For many products whose value is essentially embodied in intellectual property—drug makers get a 20-year patent on new drugs—copies can be manufactured very cheaply once the product has been developed. Hence, it may cost hundreds of millions of dollars to create the first copy of a computer program, but the second copy is little more than the cost of the CD onto which it can be downloaded. The same holds true for most pharmaceuticals. Manufacturing that first pill takes millions in conducting research and clinical trials, in processing regulatory filings and building a factory, in establishing distribution channels and generating advertising. The second pill may indeed take only pennies to make physically, but virtually all the money to create it has already been spent by the time that second pill goes into a pharmacist's bin.

"A pill is very small, so people have the intuition that it shouldn't have a high price," says Alison Keith, who recently stepped down as head of economic and science policy analysis at pharmaceutical giant Pfizer. "But a better way to think about our medications is that they are small tablets wrapped in huge envelopes of information."

DOUBLE BILLING?

A related charge regarding pharmaceutical costs is the idea that patients are actually paying for drugs twice—the first time as taxpayers through government-funded scientific research and again as patients, when they go to their local drugstore to pick up their prescriptions. "Research funded by the public sector—not the private sector—is chiefly responsible for a majority of the medically significant advances that have led to new treatments of disease," argues *The American Prospect.*

Is that true? The annual budget of the National Institutes of Health, the major government grant-giving institution for medical research, was $17.8 billion in 2000 and is expected to rise to $20.5 billion this year. Meanwhile, the pharmaceutical companies' R&D budgets totaled $26.4 billion last year—almost 50% more than the 2000 NIH budget. (Industry R&D expenditures equal more than 20% of what pharmaceutical companies make in total sales, making the industry the most research-intensive business in the world.) What roles do government and private-sector research actually play in the drug discovery and development process?

"Government-supported research gets you to the 20-yard line," explains Duke's Grabowski. "Biotech companies get you to the 50-yard line and [the big pharmaceutical companies] take you the rest of the way to the goal line. By and large, government labs don't do any drug development. The real originator of 90% of prescription drugs is private industry. It has never been demonstrated that government labs can take the initiative all the way" to drugstore shelves.

George Whitesides, a distinguished professor of biochemistry at Harvard University, similarly appreciates the role of often-government-funded research labs at universities in the early stages of drug development. But he stresses that "pure" research rarely translates into usable products. "The U.S. is the only country in the world that has a system for transmitting science efficiently into new technologies," he argues. That system includes research universities that produce a lot of basic science and get a lot of government money. In turn, startup companies take that lab science and develop it further. "Startups take 50% of the risk out of a product by taking it up to clinical trials," explains Whitesides. "Industry has an acute sense of what the problems are that need addressing." Without private industry to mine the insights of university researchers, taxpayers would have paid for a lot of top-notch scientific papers, but few if any medicines.

Frank Lichtenberg, the Columbia economist, has a slightly different take on the question of whether patients are paying twice for drugs. He cites the example of Xalatan, a glaucoma drug developed by Pharmacia & Upjohn. Last April, *The New York Times* ran a news story suggesting that although some of the original research on Xalatan was backed by a $4 million NIH grant in 1982, the "taxpayers have reaped no financial reward on their investment." Not so fast, says Lichtenberg. In 1999, Xalatan represented 7% of sales for Pharmacia & Upjohn, so Lichtenberg reasonably assumes that 7% of the company's $344 million in corporate income tax payments that year can be attributed to Xalatan. Thus Pharmacia & Upjohn paid about $24 million in income taxes on its 1999 sales of Xalatan. Just counting that one year of increased taxes as if it were the only return ever for a 17-year-old investment, Lichtenberg calculates that this yields a very respectable 11% return on the taxpayers' money. In fact, future sales are very likely to be higher, "so the return on the taxpayers' investment is likely to be considerably greater."

PLACEBO EFFECT

"Big drug companies are putting more money into advertising and promotion than they are into research and development," said Al Gore on the campaign trail, neatly summarizing another popular complaint against the pharmaceutical industry. This widespread assertion, however, is just plain wrong. In 1999, for instance, the pharmaceutical industry spent $13.9 billion on advertising and promotion. (Half the promotion costs, incidentally, were for drug samples that doctors give to patients for free.) R&D expenditures for 1999 were more than $24 billion.

There are, to be sure, more drug ads around these days. In 1997, the Food and Drug Administration, concerned about a couple of First Amendment lawsuits against its regulations, relaxed its restrictions on advertising prescription drugs. Since then, there has been an explosion of direct-to-consumer television and print ads for prescription drugs. In 1999, pharmaceutical companies spent $1.8 billion appealing directly to consumers. Industry critics charge that advertising directly to consumers causes patients to demand drugs they don't need. As Gore put it, drug makers were nefariously "spending hundreds of millions of dollars on television and on magazine advertising to persuade people to buy newer and more expensive medications when less expensive versions work just as well."

Such charges raise several issues. First, do less-expensive medicines work just as well as those "newer and more expensive ones"? In a study of the benefits and costs of newer drugs, Lichtenberg shows that older drugs are, in general, not as good as newer drugs. Using data from the 1996 Medical Expenditure Panel Survey, an in-depth national survey of the health care expenditures of more than 22,000 people, Lichtenberg developed an econometric model to compare the costs and benefits of using older and newer drugs to treat similar medical conditions. He concluded that "the replacement of older by newer drugs results in reductions in mortality, morbidity and total medical expenditure." Lichtenberg also found that "*denying people access to branded drugs* [as opposed to cheaper generic drugs] *would increase total treatment costs, not reduce them and would lead to worse outcomes*" (emphasis in original). Newer is clearly better.

What about the claim that advertising simply tricks consumers into demanding more expensive drugs? Obviously, advertising can generate interest in a product—that, after all, is the whole point. But the idea that advertising can simply create a demand for a worthless product is no less convincing when it comes to medical care than it is for other goods and services. If anything, it is less so in this case, since the advertiser needs to convince two buyers—the patient and her doctor—to make a sale.

More to the point, such criticisms ignore basic realities of the health care market. "There are substantial societal benefits to health from consumer advertising," says Alison Keith from Pfizer. "Patients have a lot of information about themselves that otherwise would not go into the medical system." A survey in 1999 by *Prevention* magazine estimated that direct-to-consumer advertising encouraged nearly 25 million patients to talk with their doctors about illnesses or medical conditions that they had never discussed before. In my case, a television ad for Zyrtec showing people being pursued by herds of allergen-generating cats alerted me to its marriage-saving possibilities. As important, by providing information outside of the traditional doctor-patient relationship, direct-to-consumer advertising can also give patients some protection against incompetent or indifferent physicians who have failed to keep up with new developments.

"The industry . . . also downplays the fact that many 'new' drugs aren't medical breakthroughs," complains *The American Prospect,* jabbing away at the pharmaceutical industry, looking to win its argument on points if not by knockout. "About half of industry research is aimed at developing me-too drugs," that treat problems already addressed by existing medications, it adds. The implication is that companies are simply trying to take market share away from each other without providing any "real" benefits to patients.

Such a scenario ignores the simple fact that companies are likely to be researching similar drugs to begin with and that one firm has to be first to market. But so-called me-too drugs actually benefit patients, not simply by offering different treatments for similar conditions—Tagamet and Zantac, for instance, have different active ingredients—but by driving down prices in a given treatment category. "The period of one-brand dominance for an innovating drug within a breakthrough therapeutic category has unmistakably shortened," writes AEI's Calfee. This faster competition leads to price cuts among competing medicines. Hence, when new anti-depressant medications were introduced in the mid-1990s, they cost only 53% as much as Prozac did when it first hit shelves in 1988 and had the field more or less to itself. Similarly, new cholesterol-lowering drugs that came to market in the mid-1990s cost 60% less than pioneering effort Mevacor did when it first showed up in 1987.

FIRST, DO NO HARM

The Hippocratic Oath famously insists that doctors do nothing to worsen a patient's condition: First, do no harm. Unfortunately, when it comes to most policy recommendations regarding prescription drugs, the potential for harm, usually in the form of price controls and universal, mandatory coverage, lurks everywhere.

Central to virtually all "reform" agendas is reining in those drug company profits. Will that contain health care costs? "Suppose we seize all pharmaceutical profit," suggested Sidney Taurel, CEO of Eli Lilly & Co., in a speech last October. "Drugs are just 8% of total health care. To simplify the arithmetic, let's stretch and say [profits are] 20% of sales. Twenty percent of 8% equals just 1.6% of total health care costs. Does that sound like a solution to you?" Despite its political appeal, it's not much of one. In fact, that sort of thing would almost certainly retard the development of new drugs by destroying the incentive for research. (It's not called the profit *motive* for nothing.)

Given their relatively small cost as a percentage of health care dollars and overall household consumption, why have drugs raised the ire of politicians and populists so forcefully? The short answer is third-party payments. "Most of the drugs are not being paid for by users. Third parties are paying but not getting the benefits, so they are very concerned about costs," explains AEI's Calfee. As doctors prescribe more drugs to cure and ameliorate the ills that afflict their patients, this means that health insurance and managed-care providers are spending more on drugs. Insurers, in turn, pass along the additional spending to their customers, companies who provide job-based medical coverage, whose bottom lines are squeezed by the additional spending.

In many cases, spending on drugs does lower health care costs, but often enough the new drugs do cost more than earlier, less effective therapies, so third-party payers are shelling out more money while patients are getting greater benefits. From a strictly actuarial point of view, it's cheaper for patients to drop dead of heart attacks than for the government or insurers to pay for years of cholesterol-lowering life-extending drugs. Employers who don't want to pay the rising costs for employee health insurance and politically potent seniors who have been schooled by Medicare to think that all health care is a right, complain to legislators that drug costs are out of control. Such complaints focus on increased spending on drugs, while ignoring the costs saved through pharmaceutical treatments and the suffering and disability that afflicted patients before pharmaceutical companies developed the new drugs.

The policy initiatives that respond to such complaints are fraught with problems. Those that simply award consumers more money specifically earmarked for drugs amount to little more than corporate welfare, by giving pharmaceutical companies a new revenue stream. More typically, though, policies that address prescription drugs end in some sort of price control scheme that, by undercutting the possible return to investment in the pharmaceutical industry, will over time harm patients by reducing the supply of new drugs. Trying to devise some sort of drug benefit for seniors—a major goal of the Bush administration—is treacherous policy territory, since misguided or ham-handed regulation can have serious consequences, especially with respect to not-yet-invented drugs. During the debate over the Clinton health plan, notes AEI's Calfee, just the threat of price controls spooked pharmaceutical R&D. "Growth in research spending dropped off dramatically from 10% annually to about 2% per year," according to Calfee.

Yet the perception that drug prices—and drug company profits—are too high is likely to drive policy. Last year, Congress passed legislation allowing the reimportation of drugs manufactured in America from Canada, where drug prices are significantly lower due to price controls, which are in place in some form in virtually all developed nations outside the

U.S. The law drew part of its moral authority from the fact that American drug companies routinely sell their drugs abroad at lower prices than they do in the U.S. Why shouldn't Americans get as good a deal? asked lawmakers.

Essentially, companies are selling their products abroad at prices well below their long-run development costs, but above their current manufacturing costs. While the drug companies can make some money this way, it's not enough to generate the profits necessary to fund their enormous R&D costs. Indeed, it is because of our relatively unregulated market that the U.S. provides the rest of the world with new drugs. Over the past two decades, companies in the U.S. have produced nearly 50% of the world's leading pharmaceuticals. Today, U.S. drug companies make all 10 of the world's best-selling drugs. Due to other countries' price controls, pharmaceutical research and development has increasingly been centered in the United States.

With regard to Congress' reimportation scheme, former Secretary of Health and Human Services Donna Shalala refused to certify the program on the grounds that she "could not demonstrate that it is safe and cost effective." However, if Tommy Thompson, the new HHS secretary, approves the program, it will be Canadians and not Americans who will be in for a rude price shock. "The drug companies will not sell to Canada at the current rate," says Calfee. "They will raise their prices to Canada in order to not undercut their markets in the U.S." As evidence, he cites a 1999 General Accounting Office report which found that a "law requiring drug companies to grant Medicaid the best price offered to managed care firms effectively raised the managed care prices rather than lowered Medicaid prices." Instead of lowering prices, reimportation and matching-discount requirements eliminate any incentive to give discounts at all.

We are entering a golden age of pharmaceutical research. With the completion of the Human Genome Project, "all pharmaceutical targets until the end of time are now known," said Biogen's Kees Been, at a presentation in December at the Massachusetts Institute of Technology. At the same meeting, Sean Lance, CEO of Chiron, a biopharmaceutical company located near San Francisco, predicted, "We are going to win over HIV, malaria and tuberculosis because of biotech."

Such certitude—bordering on arrogance—would be irredeemably smug, if not for the pharmaceutical industry's track record in raising the quality of life. "In the 1950s and '60s, doctors performed millions of tonsillectomies and put grommets in the ears of children to prevent earaches. Now we know that they don't work," said Lance. "In 10 years' time, we're going to look back and laugh at what we're thinking are complicated issues and technologies today."

If we want the pharmaceutical and biotech companies to find and market new life-saving, life-enhancing drugs to cure and treat heart disease, cancer, dementia, diabetes, AIDS and other illnesses, then Congress and President Bush would be wise to let the sort of relatively unfettered market competition that has worked well in the past continue into the future. "There is no substitute for the profit motive for inducing and guiding research," says Calfee. In a recent article in *Science,* Jurgen Drews, chairman of International Biomedicine Management Partners and former head of global research at Hoffman-La Roche, concludes that "free markets will be capable of generating the technical and institutional instruments that are needed to apply scientific advances to the solution of societal problems." True enough. But only if we let them.

MARKETING TO
CHILDREN HARMFUL

Experts Urge Candidates to Lead Nation
in Setting Limits

—CENTER FOR MEDIA EDUCATION

The following press release contains a letter urging political candidates to set limits to marketing to children. Consider the role of children as consumers and the arguments that marketers make to justify their marketing spend to target minors.

Kathryn Montgomery, president of the Center for Media Education (CME), has joined a prestigious coalition of more than 50 scholars, educators, health care providers and child advocates that sent a letter to presidential candidates Al Gore, George W. Bush, Ralph Nader and Pat Buchanan, urging the next administration to take a leadership role to drastically reduce the amount of marketing aimed at children. The full text of the letter follows, below.

"Parents are increasingly alarmed by the level, types and pervasiveness of advertising in the lives of their children," said Montgomery. "They're saying 'enough!' "

Led by Harvard Medical School faculty, Susan Linn and Alvin F. Poussaint of the Media Center of Judge Baker Children's Center, the letter is signed by some of the nation's foremost scholars and leaders in pediatric health care, education and child advocacy, including Marian Wright Edelman, founder and president of the Children's Defense Fund; T. Berry Brazelton, author and pediatrician; Roald Hoffman, Nobel laureate; Howard Gardner, psychologist, education innovator and recipient of a MacArthur fellowship; and Peggy Charren, founder of Action for Children's Televison.

Coming on the heels of the FTC's report that media companies market violence to children and the General Accounting Office's report that marketing in schools is a growth industry, the letter cites mounting evidence of the harmful effects of intensive marketing, from childhood obesity to family stress. Stating that "Parents need help from policy makers to protect children from this unprecedented and unethical assault," the signers ask the next administration to take steps such as convening a White House conference on corporate marketing and its effects on children; allocating research funds from the National Institutes of Health to investigate the psychosocial and health consequences of intensive marketing to children and working with Congress and state governments to designate schools as ad free zones.

The Media Center
Judge Baker Children's Center
3 Blackfan Circle
Boston MA: 02115
617-232-8390 x2328

October 12, 2000

Dear [CANDIDATE]:

As health care professionals, educators, child advocates and parents, we are writing to express our alarm at the barrage of marketing targeting American children. Because marketing to children is so pervasive, affecting all aspects of their lives from health to safety and education, we believe it constitutes an escalating public health problem that must be addressed by the next administration.

As you know, marketing to children has received a great deal of media attention recently. The September 11th FTC report on marketing violence to children states unequivocally that media executives intentionally market products to children that their own rating system publicly deems inappropriate for them. Three days later, the General Accounting Office issued a report documenting the rapid growth of corporate marketing in schools. But the problem is far more pervasive.

Children have become big business in the United States. Corporations now spend over $12 billion a year marketing to children,[1] almost double the amount spent in 1992.[2] Companies employ increasingly sophisticated technology, extensive market research and the expertise of child psychologists in their efforts to manipulate children into buying things. And they have been very successful—today children influence purchases totaling over $500 billion a year.[3]

Children, especially young children, are more susceptible to marketing than adults. They tend to believe what they see, don't understand that ads are meant to sell them something[4] and have trouble differentiating between commercials and programming.[5] With the deregulation of children's television in 1984, it became possible to use programs to market toys. The distinctions between ads and shows became even more difficult to make. Preteens and teens are more savvy about ads, but research suggests that understanding advertising techniques does not diminish its strong influence on their choice of products.[6] This is not surprising since advertising often appeals more to emotion than intellect.

By the time they graduate from high school, American children view an estimated 360,000 commercials on television alone.[7] They are also inundated with indirect marketing—products linked to media characters, cross promotions through toy giveaways at fast food restaurants and product placements in movies and television. Children are bombarded with marketing from the moment they wake up until bedtime. And there's growing evidence that it's harmful to them.

Last month the American Academy of Pediatrics and a coalition of other professional organizations concluded, after reviewing 1000 studies conducted over 30 years, that violent media is linked to aggressive behavior.[8] Yet professional wrestling programs, which are rated TV-14 and violent movies such as X-Men (rated PG-13) market violent action figures to preschoolers.

And at a time when childhood obesity has become a major public health problem, purveyors of food high in fat, sugar and calories are the biggest television advertisers during children's peak viewing time.[9] Studies show that childhood obesity is linked to television viewing,[10] and that obese children appear to be more susceptible to the "feel good" messages embedded in food advertising.[11]

As advertisers sell children high fat foods, they also present them with models who are impossibly slim. Forty percent of 9- and 10-year-old girls report dieting.[12] And studies document that discontent with body image rises with increased exposure to fashion magazines, which are bursting with ads.[13]

Even the way children play is affected by advertising—and not for the better. The most heavily advertised and best selling toys are linked to media programs. Yet children often play less creatively with toys based on characters from television and film.[14]

The combination of ubiquitous media and virtually unrestricted marketing practices make obsolete the conventional wisdom—promoted by the industry—that parents can protect their children from commercial culture. Unless families retreat to the woods, it's inescapable. To some extent, parents can mitigate the effects of marketing, but even if advertising is limited at home, children are exposed at friends' houses, on the street, the playground, in supermarkets and even in school.

Other industrialized democracies have laws to protect children from the attempts of adults to influence them in this way. For example, Sweden and Norway prohibit television advertising directly targeting children below 12 years of age. In Greece, commercials for toys are banned until 10 PM, and in Belgium it is forbidden to broadcast commercials during children's programs as well as during the five minutes before and after them.[15]

Parents need help from policy makers to protect children from this unprecedented and unethical assault. We believe that the next president of the United States should assume a strong leadership role in establishing policies that protect children from marketing targeted at them, with the explicit goal of substantially reducing the amount of advertising to which our youth are exposed. We recommend that the next president work with Congress to take the following protective steps:

- *Convene a White House conference on corporate marketing and its effects on children. Such a conference will serve as a springboard for national dialogue and lay the groundwork for creating appropriate policy.*

- *Allocate research funds from the National Institutes of Health to investigate the psychosocial and health consequences of intensive marketing to children.*

- *When voluntary approaches fail, establish federal regulations on marketing to children, including all toy-based media programs.*

- *Ban advertising to children of products known to be harmful to them.*

- *Designate schools as advertising-free zones.*

- *Establish a rating systems for toys that conforms to the ratings for the media programs to which they are linked.*

- *Hold market research with children to the same ethical standards of human subject review as academic research.*

Children pay for marketing. They pay with their safety, their health, their well-being and their family relationships. They deserve a government committed to protecting them from exploitation. Please respond specifically to our concerns, our recommendations and tell us your plan to substantially reduce the amount of corporate advertising aimed at children.

REFERENCES

1. McNeal, James (Texas A&M University), quoted in: Campbell K, Davis-Package K. "How Ads Get Kids to Say, I Want It!" *The Christian Science Monitor.* September 18, 2000:1.
2. Corporations spent $6.9 billion on marketing to children in 1992. Lauro PW. "Coaxing the Smile That Sells: Baby Wranglers in Demand in Marketing for Children." *New York Times.* November 1, 1999:C1+.
3. Packaged Facts. "The Kids Market." New York: MarketResearch.com, March 2000.
4. Liebert RM, Sprafkin JN. *The Early Window: Effects of Television on Children and Youth.* 3rd ed. New York: Pergamon Press, 1988.
5. Atkin CK. "Television Advertising and Socialization to Consumer Roles." In: Pearl D, Bouthilet L, Lazar J. eds. *Television and Behavior: Ten Years of Scientific Progress and Implications for the Eighties.* Rockville, MD: National Institute of Mental Health, 1982:191–200.
6. Ross RP, et al. "When Celebrities Talk, Children Listen. An Experimental Analysis of Children's Responses to TV Ads with Celebrity Endorsement." *Journal of Applied Developmental Psychology.* 1984; 5:185–202.
7. Shelov S, et al. "Children, Adolescents and Advertising." Statement from the American Academy of Pediatrics Communications Committee. *Pediatrics.* 1995; 95:295–297.
8. "Joint Statement on the Impact of Entertainment Violence on Children." American Academy of Pediatrics, the American Academy of Child and Adolescent Psychiatry, the American Psychological Association and the American Medical Association. Report to a congressional public health summit. August 2000.

9.   Taras HL, Gage M. "Advertised Foods on Children's Television." *Archives of Pediatric Adolescent Medicine.* 1995; 149:649–652.

10. Dietz WH, Gortmaker ST. "Do We Fatten Our Children at the Television Set? Obesity and Television Viewing in Children and Adolescents." *Pediatrics.* 1985; 75:807–812.

11. Lewis MK, Hill J. "Food Advertising on British Children's Television: A Content Analysis and Experimental Study with Nine Year Olds." *International Journal of Obesity.* 1998; 22:206–214.

12. Schreiber GB, et al. "Weight Modification Efforts Reported by Black and White Preadolescent Girls: National Heart, Lung and Blood Institute Growth and Health Study." *Pediatrics.* 1996; 98:63–70.

13. Field AE, et al. "Exposure to the Mass Media and Weight Concerns Among Girls." *Pediatrics.* 1999; 103:E36.

14. Carlsson-Paige N, Levin D. *The War Play Dilemma.* New York: Teachers College Press, 1987.

15. Valkenburg P. "Media and Youth Consumerism." *Journal of Adolescent Health.* 2000; 27:54.

WEB OF DECEPTION
Threats to Children from Online Marketing

—Karyn Montgomery and Shelley Pasnik

This report lays out the facts of children's online behavior. It further reveals the techniques adopted by marketers to create branded communities online and create brand loyalty. This could be a simple case of target marketing, market research and customer satisfaction if it were not for the fact that these are minors. Consider the dimensions of the ethical dilemma and what possible recommendations one could make to encourage the marketers to be more ethical in targeting children.

Armed with sophisticated new research, advertisers and marketers have begun to target the rapidly growing numbers of children online. World Wide Web sites and other interactive online services are being designed to capture the loyalty and spending power of the "lucrative cybertot category." A variety of new interactive advertising and marketing techniques have been developed specifically for this new medium. Many of them threaten to manipulate children and rob them of their privacy. If allowed to develop without any intervention, these practices will become widespread and even more egregious.

The Center for Media Education (CME) has just completed a major investigation of online advertising and marketing practices directed at children. For the past six months, CME has monitored online developments, analyzed Web sites and areas of proprietary services directed at children, surveyed trade publications and special reports and interviewed experts within the media and advertising industries.

This investigation has uncovered a number of disturbing new practices. They pose two kinds of threats: (1) invasion of children's privacy through solicitation of personal information and tracking of online computer use; and (2) exploitation of vulnerable, young computer users through new unfair and deceptive forms of advertising. Many of the practices described in the following pages are already in place. Industry sources expect other, more problematic practices to be rolled out in the near future.

Invasion of Children's Privacy　　Marketers have devised a variety of techniques to collect detailed data and to compile individual profiles on children. For example, children are offered free gifts such as T-shirts or chances to win prizes like portable CD players if they will fill out online surveys about themselves. Tracking technologies make it possible to monitor every interaction between a child and an advertisement. The ultimate goal is to create personalized interactive ads designed to "microtarget" the individual child.

Unfair and Deceptive Advertising   Other online advertising practices have been developed which would violate long-standing safeguards protecting children in other media. But because neither the proprietary online services (e.g., America Online, CompuServe, Prodigy) nor the World Wide Web are subject to such regulations, marketers are able to pursue children with few or no restraints. As a consequence, advertising and content are often seamlessly interwoven in new online "infomercials" for children. Entire electronic advertising "environments" have been built to entice children to spend countless hours playing with such popular product "spokescharacters" as Tony the Tiger, Chester Cheetah and Snap! Crackle! & Pop! Interactive forms of product placement are being developed to encourage children to click on icons in their favorite games and play areas and immediately be transported to advertising sites.

This report is an early warning to parents, child advocates, health professionals and policy makers unaware of the new practices for targeting children online. There is now a window of opportunity to develop safeguards to protect children. The Center for Media Education is calling on the Federal Trade Commission to conduct a full investigation of online marketing and advertising directed at children. CME also recommends implementation of the following principles to guide development of online commercial children's services:

1. Personal information (including click stream data) should not be collected from children, nor should personal profiles of children be sold to third parties.
2. Advertising and promotions targeted at children should be clearly labeled and separated from content.
3. Children's content areas should not be directly linked to advertising sites.
4. There should be no direct interaction between children and product spokescharacters.
5. There should be no online microtargeting of children and no direct-response marketing.

* * *

MANIPULATING CHILDREN ONLINE

There is a long tradition of government and self-regulatory policies to protect children from unfair and deceptive television advertising. These safeguards are based on substantial research documenting the special vulnerabilities of children to the powerful appeals of marketers.[31] This research has shown that young children cannot distinguish between programs and the commercials that surround and interrupt them. Nor can they easily resist the persuasive product pitches by program hosts. Like the teachers and parents in children's lives, these authority figures—whether real-life or animated—wield special powers to influence youngsters. Because of children's vulnerabilities to advertising, there are rules at the Federal Communications Commission that (1) require "separators" between children's programs and commercials; (2) forbid the host of a children's show from pitching products at children; and (3) limit the amount of advertising time in children's programs.[32]

The rapidly evolving world of cyberspace has no such rules or traditions. Where advertising and marketing to children are concerned, it is an unregulated media environment.[33] Marketers are able to develop innovative forms of online advertising with virtually no restraints. In the absence of a regulatory framework for protecting children from marketing abuses online, many marketers are exploiting the particular susceptibilities of children of different ages.

The following online marketing and advertising practices are becoming increasingly prevalent in children's areas. Each practice violates safeguards that have been in place for decades.

Luring Children with Branded Environments

The goal of many advertisers online is to capture and hold the attention of children for as long as possible. Unlike television, in cyberspace, time does not restrain ad length—an ad's effectiveness is measured in part by the amount of time each child spends "in" the ad. "[I]f you create an ad that's as much fun as the content," such as "games that kids can play that involve the products. . . . then there'll be a reason for kids to click on the ads and interact with them and enjoy them," explained Joanne Roberts, head of Kids Site 3000 on America Online.[34]

Banners are one of the most common forms of advertising on the World Wide Web. Online banners function more as gateways than billboards along the side of a road. When children click on a banner, they are whisked away to an interactive advertising environment, with activities designed to keep children engaged for extended periods of time.

- Kidstuff, Pathfinder's children's area, is sprinkled with ad banners, inviting young computer users to visit Colgate's Web site. These banners must compete for children's attention with nearby icons for other Kidstuff offerings including *Sports Illustrated for Kids* and *Where's Waldo.* In order to compete, Colgate uses pictures of cartoon characters and phrases like "follow me" and "tour the world" to shift children's attention away from such information-based content to its product promotions. (http://pathfinder.com/@@LMptUtKjqQAAQOKo/pathfinder/kidstuff/kidstuff.html)[35]

- Once in the Colgate Kid's World, children are kept busy asking the Tooth Wizard questions, interacting with the Story-Coloring Book and making virtual journeys in the Tour the World section. All of these activities center around Colgate's toothpaste. (http://www.colgate.com/Kids-world/)[36]

- The Nabisco Neighborhood is a branded environment that beckons children to come and play. Although some of the information contained in this site appears to be geared toward adult consumers, the Nabisco Playground is clearly designed for children—a "place where you can play for hours on end and never worry about the sun going down or running out of quarters." The playground occupies children with games, (such as the search for "The Nabisco Thing") to build brand loyalty and increase product awareness. (http://www.nabisco.com/)[37]

- To maximize the time children spend there, the Oscar Mayer CyberCinema features: an online Sega contest and game; a narrated, interactive guided history of the Wienermobile; and a Super Bowl party and Cyber Halftime Show, with real-time audio. The Oscar Mayer® Wiener Jingle© and Bologna Song© can also be downloaded for sing-along purposes. (http://www.oscar-mayer.com/)[38]

- Disney recently launched its revamped Web site, sending Mickey and all of his cartoon friends into cyberspace. Chock full of information about the books, movies, toys, theme parks, software, music, cable channels and home videos that comprise the Magic Kingdom's empire, this site is very easy for kids to get lost in. In the *Toy Story* section alone, children can download movie clips, sound clips, computer icons, wallpaper patterns, coloring book pages and a "Toy Story" concentration game. The bottom of each page of the Web site includes a "Sign-in" button, which invites visitors to share personal information and to receive regular Disney online updates. The site also hypes its new online shopping area, The Disney Store, which is overflowing with children's merchandise. (http://www.disney.com/)[39]

Seamlessly Integrating Advertising and Content

As the online world becomes more and more commercialized, advertising is being seamlessly integrated with content. The boundaries that once separated ads from content are blurring and in many cases being eliminated altogether. Advertisements are either skillfully woven into programming or are presented as programs or "content" themselves. According to *Red Herring,* a trade publication for investors: "What is really happening [on the Web] is what will ultimately happen on interactive television: the infomercialization of all programming. Services will deliver some content, with lots of appeals (some soft, some hard) to purchase. Requesting literature and additional information (read: volunteering for a mailing list), and actual buying, will be easily enabled. . . . This is not advertising as you and I understand it, but a more viewer-engaged, browse-and-buy genre just beginning to emerge as a form of programming unto itself."[40]

Unlike television, where commercials interrupt a program, online advertisers are blending advertising and content. As Saatchi & Saatchi's Erica Gruen explains: "Anything that is perceived as an interruption of the flow state, whether it's artwork being downloaded or an ad that is obtrusively splattered on a screen is going to get a negative reaction." Consequently, the practice of disguising advertising as content may well become the norm for commercial children's sites. The safeguards in children's television programming implemented to separate program content from advertising are not only absent from the online media, but have also been replaced by a set of operating principles designed to achieve the opposite effect.

In addition to the branded environments already discussed, many other Web sites are melding advertising and content:

- Frito Lay's Web site offers a number of entertaining interactive areas for children, including a "Dreamsite" section where children are asked to design their dream date. Although children are first asked to describe the guy or gal of their dreams, eventually they are asked to choose which Frito Lay snack their virtual date prefers. Upon choosing, the dream date is pictured holding the snack. (http://www.fritolay.com/)[41]

- The Crayola Web site entertains children with interesting facts about the colorful crayons, provides them with the results of the Crayola Big Kid Classic contest and tells them to be on the look out for the 100 billionth crayon. In celebration of this crayon-making milestone, Crayola has added a new special color—blue ribbon—to its 96 Big Box. Children are subtly told that if they find a blue ribbon crayon wrapped in special foil in their 96 Big Box, they will win "more than a thousand great prizes."

The most important activity at this site is selling Crayola's products. (http://www.crayola.com/home.html)[42]

Interactive product placement is another online practice that blends program content and advertising. Children can click on various product icons woven into a story or game and be transported to Web sites for these products. Microsoft's Bill Gates describes how product placement is likely to work in the future: "If you are watching the movie *Top Gun* and think Tom Cruise's aviator sunglasses look really cool, you'll be able to pause the movie and learn about the glasses or even buy them on the spot—if the film has been tagged with commercial information."[43] Today's products are routinely woven into the new genre of on-line soap operas called "cybersoaps."

Product placement in children's areas online is in its first stage.

- Nickelodeon ingeniously integrates clickable products into its area on AOL. Silly pictures—like an electric plug, a set of teeth and a piggy bank—serve as icons for each section of Nickelodeon's area. Mixed with these are other icons that, when clicked, produce interactive advertisements. When children open one of these advertisements, they are encouraged to go directly to that advertiser's Web site.[44]

- One of the sites easily reached from Nickelodeon's area on AOL is MooTown's Web site UdderNet, where there are a variety of activities tied to MooTown Snackers (snack foods). Children are invited to play the Cow Chip Toss Game and MooTown Hide and Seek. The Global Lunch Box is used to gather personal information from visitors. (http://www.mootown.com)[45]

Eventually children will be able to click on various products woven into stories and be transported to Web sites for those products. The interactive nature of online media will foster the development of new forms of product placement. Unlike products placed at fixed points in movies, products could be placed more dynamically online. Children engaged in interactive narratives may be able to use the special powers of certain products over and over again.

Establishing Relationships through Spokescharacters

A few years ago, the Fox Children's Network tried to launch a children's cartoon program based on Chester Cheetah, the animated character that advertises Fritos corn chips. But when consumer and parent groups raised concerns in the press that such a series would violate the rules against program-length commercials, the network quickly backed off. Today such blatant forms of overcommercialization are the norm in cyberspace.

The prohibition against host-selling in children's TV programming was designed to protect children from the manipulative use of symbolic authority figures.[46] In the online world, the no-host principle is not only being violated, but hosts are also being used to interact with children in exploitative new ways. Saatchi & Saatchi's Gruen observes that: "Marketers here have an unparalleled opportunity to get kids actively involved with brands. Brand characters, brand logos, brand jingles, brand video, by cutting, pasting and coloring with these elements . . . it's very important that kids can change what they see and manipulate what they see and author new things based on elements that we give them to put together. Advertisers can then give kids public places to post these characters and also provide activities for kids to do together. And all, of course, within the brand environment and using brand spokescharacters or other brand icons."[47]

Children's online areas are quickly being populated by a growing number of animated characters and products. Their purpose is to develop relationships with children that will foster brand loyalty. They are hosting online sites and offering children endless opportunities to play with them.

- FRITOnet, the Web site for Frito Lay, Inc., invites children to enter "Chester's Closet." Here, the marketing mascot tries to win children over with computer-related gifts. Chester Cheetah says: "If your desktop is a little cluttered and crude, get some help from this cool cyber-dude. . . ." The downloadable pictures of this hip spokescharacter are meant to heighten brand awareness and build brand loyalty. (http://www.fritolay.com/)[48]

- The Web site for Kellogg's makes full use of Snap, Crackle & Pop, Tony the Tiger and Toucan Sam. The three elves are the hosts of the Clubhouse, welcoming children to explore the different rooms and encouraging them to participate in all the various activities. Youngsters can color pictures of the spokescharacters, download Rice Krispies Treats recipes and do word-find puzzles. The Kellogg General Store sells licensed merchandise; Tony the Tiger watches, Toucan Sam sweatshirts and Snap, Crackle & Pop T-shirts are just a few of the items that can be ordered online. (http://www.kelloggs.com/)[49]

In addition to spokescharacters who sell separate products, there are also spokescharacters who are products and sell themselves.

- Building on the enormous licensing success of the television show, the Mighty Morphin Power Rangers Web site is a promotion for the movie. This site brings children closer to the six Rangers with downloadable sound bites and film clips and information about the villains they battle. The site offers young fans the opportunity to have a personal letter delivered to one of the characters. "Click on any of the Power Rangers below to send them a quick note . . . I will get your letter delivered, no matter where in the universe the Power Rangers and Monsters are and I will forward their reply to you within 24 hours!" (http://www.delphi.com/power/powrhome.htm)[50]

- Warner Bros. populates its Web site with both new spokescharacters (Animaniacs, Pinky & The Brain, Freakazoid) and classic spokescharacters (Sylvester, Tweety, Bugs Bunny). Children can play Dr. Scratchansniff's Eye, Ear, Nose Identity Game online, or download the Connect-The-Dots and Jigsaw Puzzle games. The Studio Store sells clothes, mugs and art sets from the WB collection. Customers can make their purchase online or use the toll-free number. (http://www.warnerbros.com/)[51]

- The Mail Room in the Batman Web site invites children to send messages to Gotham. Beneath the colorful characters is the invitation to "Just click on any character above to E-mail them. (Their answers may surprise you.) And be sure to leave your comments on Gotham's Bulletin Boards." Not only does this site give children a forum to chat with other superhero fans, it gives them the opportunity to communicate with the caped crusader himself. (http://www.batmanforever.com)[52]

It is easy to imagine how engaging and persuasive these spokescharacters will become when brought to life with full-motion video and enhanced computer animation. Children under the age of five, cannot easily distinguish between fantasy and real-live characters.[53] Elementary school children strongly identify with fictional characters, attempting to re-create stories and imitate behavior that they have seen. When combined with microtargeting, the potential for manipulation by spokescharacters becomes even greater. Marketers will be able to develop ongoing relationships with children through their spokescharacters. Many children may eventually become "keypals"—the online equivalent to penpals—with advertisements.

* * *

CONCLUSION

The following principles should guide the development of regulations for online advertising and marketing to children:

1. *Personal information (including clickstream data) should not be collected from children, nor should children's personal information be sold.* Since most children neither understand the importance of privacy (their family's or their own), nor can resist the blandishments and bribes offered for personal information, the online collection of such information from them should be prohibited. Likewise, technological monitoring of interactions between children and online advertising should not be allowed. Children's personal information, however gathered (from organizations or mailing lists), should not be sold or distributed.

2. *Advertising and promotions targeted at children should be clearly labeled and separated from content.* The integration of advertising and content should be proscribed in children's content areas. Advertising should not be disguised as content and children should understand which is which. Product placement should not be allowed.

3. *Children's content areas should not be directly linked to advertising sites.* Children who go to a content area should be allowed to fully explore and use it without having to constantly resist the skillful efforts of advertisers to lure them away. Discrete underwriting should be allowed, but not hyperlinks designed to catapult children into captivating advertising environments.

4. *There should be no direct interaction between children and product spokescharacters.* Just as rules are in place to shield children from the influence of such spokescharacters on TV, it is crucial that similar protections be developed for online services. The interactive nature of the new medium gives spokescharacters the potential for even greater influence over children.

5. *There should be no online microtargeting of children and no direct-response marketing.* Advertising pitches specifically tailored to each individual child should also be prohibited. Online ads fully utilizing animation, video, sound, 3-D and interactivity, are likely to become the most persuasive advertising ever. To allow them to be individually crafted to each child based on his or her particular preferences would give online advertising unprecedented power over children. Children should also be protected from direct response marketing online which combines a hard sell with incentives to make immediate impulse purchases.

These principles do not prohibit all online advertising directed at kids, but do establish clear boundaries between content and advertising. By placing limits on egregious and exploitative practices, they require that children be treated fairly, truthfully and appropriately. Working together, policy makers, parents and industry leaders could ensure that children make the most of the exciting educational and cultural opportunities in cyberspace, while avoiding deceptive advertising, manipulative marketing and a wholesale loss of privacy.

NOTES

31. Sponsored by the American Psychological Association, *Big World, Small Screen* summarizes 30 years of research on television's effects on viewers. A Huston et al, *Big World, Small Screen: The Role of Television in American Society* (Lincoln: University of Nebraska Press, 1992). S. Kline also examines the effect of commercial television on children's development in *Out of the Garden: Toys, TV and Children's Culture in the Age of Marketing* (London and New York: Verso, 1993). D. Pearl, E. Bouthilet, J. Lazar, eds. *Television and Behavior,* Vol. 2 (Washington, DC: U.S. Government Printing Office, 1982). E. Palmer and A. Dorr, eds. *Children and the Faces of Television: Teaching, Violence, Selling* (New York: Academic Press, 1980). E. Wartella, "A Cognitive Development Study of Children's Attention to Television Commercials," *Communications Research,* Vol. 1, 1974.

32. D. Kunkel, "The Role of Research in the Regulation of U.S. Children's Television Advertising," *Knowledge: Creation, Diffusion, Utilization,* Vol. 12 No. 1, September 1990, Sage Publications, Inc.

33. The Federal Communications Commission has no regulations governing advertising on online communications. Recent telecommunications legislation outlaws so-called "indecent" content online, but no regulations govern advertising to children. The Federal Trade Commission has jurisdiction to protect consumers, including children, from deceptive or unfair advertising in all media. But the FTC has promulgated no rules or guidelines to govern children's advertising in cyberspace.

34. J. Roberts, "Defining the Digital Consumer IV Agenda: Digital Kids Pre-Conference Seminar," New York, NY, October 25, 1995.

35. March 21, 1996 contents of Web site.

36. March 21, 1996 contents of Web site.

37. March 19, 1996 contents of Web site.

38. March 21, 1996 contents of Web site.

39. March 24, 1996 contents of Web site.

40. K. Davis and R. O'Driscoll, "Roadmap for the Internet," *The Red Herring,* March 1995.

41. March 15, 1996 contents of Web site.

42. March 23, 1996 contents of Web site.

43. Bill Gates, *The Road Ahead* (NY: Viking Penguin, 1995).

44. March 21, 1996 contents of Web site.

45. March 21, 1996 contents of Web site.

46. D. Kunkel, "Children and Host-Selling Television Commercials," *Communication Research,* Vol. 15, 1988.

47. E. Gruen, "Defining the Digital Consumer IV Agenda: Digital Kids Pre-Conference Seminar," New York, NY, October 25, 1995.

48. March 22, 1996 contents of Web site.

49. March 22, 1996 contents of Web site.

50. March 21, 1996 contents of Web site.

51. March 23, 1996 contents of Web site.

52. March 24, 1996 contents of Web site.

53. In addition to the works already cited, the following may deal with advertising and children: A. Huston, B. Watkins and D. Kunkel, "Public Policy and Children's Television." *American Psychologist,* Vol 44, 1989. S. Ward, G. Reale and D. Levinson, "Children's Perceptions, Explanations and Judgments of Television Advertising: A Further Exploration," in E. Rubinstein, G. Comstock and J. Murray (Eds.), *Television and Social Behavior,* Vol. 4 (Washington, DC: U.S. Government Printing Office, 1972).

ONLINE DYNAMIC PRICING
Efficiency, Equity and the Future of E-commerce

—Robert M. Weiss and Ajay K. Mehrotra

This article lays out the legality of "dynamic pricing"—the practice of instantaneously adjusting prices to reflect demand. The authors argue against regulation and suggest reasons as to why it may make economic sense to allow dynamic pricing.

* * *

IV. THE ECONOMICS BEHIND DYNAMIC PRICING

Economic theory has demonstrated the social benefits and perhaps even the necessity, of price discrimination. Although most textbooks dealing with economics discuss price discrimination only in the context of monopoly power,[22] the notion of charging different individuals different prices for the same good or service may also appeal to those industries with inherently high fixed costs. In those cases where start-up costs are high, but operating expenses are relatively low, price discrimination may lead to a socially efficient use of resources. Consider the airline industry again. The start-up costs of creating a new airline are enormous. The expense of purchasing or even leasing a fleet of planes by itself requires a substantial amount of capital. But once an airline has covered its initial fixed costs, the marginal expense of flying an additional passenger is relatively small—in some cases literally "peanuts." For such high fixed cost/low marginal cost industries, price discrimination is not just a boon; it is a necessity.

Without a sufficient amount of demand for air travel, airlines would not be able to cover their high initial fixed costs, not to mention their marginal expenses. But because airlines are able to charge some customers more—namely less price-sensitive business travelers—they are able to cover their fixed costs, while offering less expensive fares to the more price-sensitive leisure travelers. If carriers were forced to sell all their seats at the same price, they would, in theory, likely not raise enough revenue to cover their fixed costs. Hence, they would possibly be forced out of business, or would price-out a significant portion of their customer base and not optimize their profits. By charging different prices, airlines are able to provide their services to both sets of travelers—at prices often

---

below their respective absolute willingness to pay. Such differential pricing has the added advantage of allowing the airline companies to optimize their profits.[23]

Airlines are not the only companies dependent upon price discrimination. Just about any industry that faces a high set of fixed costs and relatively low variable costs—such as book publishing or the movie industry—will resort to some form of price discrimination.[24] Indeed, today's digital economy is filled with numerous firms defined by a structure of high fixed costs and low marginal costs. The technology of digitalization itself has transformed the cost structure of many industries competing in cyberspace. Internet publishing, for example, has dramatically reduced the marginal cost of producing magazines and journals.[25] In theory, nearly anyone with a desktop publishing program can put together an online newsletter or periodical with little expense. But, as the continuous proliferation of Web sites suggests, just having a presence online is generally not enough. Contrary to conventional wisdom, entry into the world of digital publications is not as facile as it may first appear. Any serious online publisher must devote a significant amount of initial resources to developing a brand name and this development often entails a well-funded advertising and marketing budget. Thus, the high fixed costs of developing an online brand, together with the low marginal cost of reproducing digital products has come to define the cost structure of Internet publishing.[26]

Other online companies face similar concerns. Because much of cyberspace remains uncharted territory, e-commerce companies have been engaged in a race against time to be the first to claim key digital space as part of their branding and marketing efforts. While the operating expenses of providing their goods and services may have been decreased by the efficiencies of new technologies, the initial fixed cost of developing a reliable brand remains relatively high.[27] With these cost requirements, many e-commerce companies may feel compelled to charge different prices for the same goods and services.

The question remains, however, whether such price discrimination is fair. When two reasonably similar individuals are charged different prices for the same goods and services, there seems to be something patently wrong. Price discrimination appears to elicit a visceral negative reaction. Airline customers, in particular, are often astonished and irked when they learn what others seated next to them have paid for their tickets. On the other hand, many customers may be willing to tolerate a certain amount of price discrimination, if it is necessary to assure the provision of particular goods and services, such as air travel; or if it aids those individuals, such as students and seniors, who are living on a fixed income.

However, in those cases where price discrimination is not socially necessary or acceptable, the question becomes: is there any other economic justification for charging different prices for identical goods and services? One answer may be that customized offers add value to online transactions. In the euphemistic language of today's e-commerce, "personalized pricing" could be defended as a measure that provides the latest, up-to-date information to consumers. Customers who are willing to pay more for a broader choice of goods and services may simply view dynamic pricing as an "information fee" levied by retailers who are willing to tailor offers to the past buying habits of consumers—essentially giving them what they want, before they even know it. While such a group of price-insensitive buyers may exist, they are surely in the minority.

As an additional justification for dynamic pricing, information technology economists have argued that "personalized pricing" is simply an extension of traditional marketing practices.[28] When the operating costs of reproducing another unit are close to zero—as they are for many information-based industries—companies have an incentive to price their goods according to consumer value, not production costs. Proponents of personalized pricing contend that prices based on value and not cost, benefit not only companies, but also those consumers who are offered relatively lower priced goods and services, since these customers pay only as much as they value the good or service.

Setting aside economic explanations for dynamic pricing, the concern for equity remains: is it fair to charge different prices for the same items to different people according to their willingness to pay? From a legal perspective, is dynamic pricing a violation of current law? If not, is it because the old laws have not kept up with the new technological changes embodied in e-commerce? Indeed, should there even be a set of rules or regulations governing dynamic pricing?

VI. THE LEGALITY OF DYNAMIC PRICING

The multitude of issues posed by the advent of the Internet has fundamentally challenged many of the bedrock theories of contemporary law. Law reviews and legal journals, not to mention the popular press, are filled with articles about the present tension between law and technology. Jurisdiction, privacy, intellectual property, criminal law and free speech are just some of the areas of law that have come under increased strain in the digital age. Although the issue of price discrimination in e-commerce has received little attention, the burgeoning potential of this new pricing strategy has broad implications for the intersection of law and technology. Like other novel issues of cyberspace law, online dynamic pricing begs the question of whether existing legal rules can be used to address the possible unfairness of Internet price discrimination. If current legal rules are inadequate to deal with this new pricing system, perhaps a new legal regime, or some other form of monitored self-regulation, is necessary.

At first blush, it appears that existing legal rules could combat the inequity concerns raised by online price discrimination. United States antitrust law, for example, specifically deals with price discrimination. The Robinson-Patman Act of 1936, which amended Section 2 of the Clayton Act, makes it "unlawful for any person . . . to discriminate in price between different purchasers of commodities of like grade and quality . . . where the effect . . . may be substantially to lessen competition or tend to create a monopoly."[29] Simply put, the Robinson-Patman Act "requires that sellers treat all competing customers on the same basis, unless there is some recognized legal justification for different treatment."[30]

Despite the broad language of the statute, the Robinson-Patman Act has had limited applicability in the recent past and may even be irrelevant in the context of online dynamic pricing. The Department of Justice has not enforced the Act since 1977 and the Federal Trade Commission ("FTC") has only used it sparingly.[31] More importantly, Robinson-Patman, as a provision of U.S. antitrust laws, has focused primarily on attacking the anti-competitive dealings of intermediary vendors, rather than on protecting consumer welfare directly.[32] In fact, because the Act is concerned chiefly with preserving the structural integrity of competitive markets, business-to-consumer e-commerce is unlikely to be affected by the statute's provisions. With the large number of e-commerce companies currently competing in the business-to-consumer space, it is highly unlikely that those willing to engage in online price discrimination will have any anti-competitive effects on the market. It is more likely that the large number of competitors (as well as the increasing prevalence of price comparison Web sites and shopping bots) will act as a curb on possible price discrimination. Rational consumers, skeptical of an online company's pricing practices, will take their business to a competing company in whom they have greater trust and faith.

Beyond antitrust law, at least one set of consumers has creatively attempted to use existing criminal law to address price discrimination in mail-order catalogues.[33] In 1996, Denise Katzman filed a class action lawsuit against Victoria's Secret Catalogue alleging that the catalogue company violated the Racketeer Influenced and Corrupt Organizations Act ("RICO") by providing different discounts to different groups of customers.[34] Katzman claimed that she received a Victoria's Secret catalogue that offered a smaller discount than a nearly identical catalogue sent to a male co-worker. Moreover, Katzman asserted that in previous years Victoria's Secret also engaged in price discrimination by mailing multiple versions of the same catalogue, offering identical items at different prices to different classes of customers.[35] In her complaint, Katzman argued that the catalogue company's discriminatory pricing structure constituted "racketeering activity under the RICO stature [sic]."[36] To demonstrate the predicate acts of racketeering required by the statute, Katzman contended that sending multiple versions of a mail-order catalogue with different prices for the same goods constituted mail fraud.

The courts rejected Katzman's innovative legal arguments. Judge Robert W. Sweet of the U.S. District Court for the Southern District of New York dismissed Katzman's claims, ruling that "offering different discounts to different catalogue customers does not constitute mail fraud under any reading of the law."[37] In addition, Judge Sweet declared that Katzman's filings were "objectively unreasonable."[38] Because defendants were compelled to respond to "a patently meritless complaint" that caused "unwarranted adverse publicity,"[39] Judge Sweet imposed sanctions against Katzman's attorney for filing a frivolous suit, ordering him to pay defendants legal fees in the amount of $5,000.[40] The appeals court affirmed Judge Sweet's decision.[41]

The rulings in *Katzman* seem to suggest that retailers can, for legitimate business purposes, make distinctions between buyers. As long as the price differences are based on reasonable business practices such as rewarding loyal customers and do not discriminate against race, gender or other impermissible categories, dynamic pricing appears to be legal. Since current law seems to permit reasonable forms of price discrimination in the tangible world, the issue becomes whether there ought to be a new legal regime for governing online dynamic pricing practices. The normative question turns on whether there ought to be some other form of regulation addressing the evolving pricing practices of e-commerce companies.

Denizens of cyberspace—especially businesses occupying digital space—have been advocating self-regulation as the best suited form of governance for the Internet in general and e-commerce in particular. Some legal commentators have argued that the Internet has developed an indigenous cultural aversion to state intervention and that bottom-up private ordering and grass-roots social control have become important Internet norms.[42] Although the stability and prevalence of these Internet norms remains a contested issue,[43] the evolution of online privacy policies illustrates the populist penchant for online self-regulation. In the early years of the Internet, Web site privacy policies were quite rare. It was not until some sites began to violate the implied trust of their visitors by revealing personal information that online privacy policies emerged as a competitive, commercial advantage. Those sites with explicit privacy policies garnered more visitors and hence greater advertising revenue. Soon Internet users developed an expectation of privacy and confidentiality in the information that they provided and online privacy policies became a standard component of nearly every online presence.[44]

Online privacy policies did not, however, simply emerge *de novo* from consumer pressure. The formal institutional structure of state regulation also played an important part. In the summer of 1998, the need for online privacy policies was given the force of law when the FTC settled claims against the popular Web site, GeoCities. In response to an FTC complaint alleging that GeoCities had engaged in misleading data collection practices, GeoCities agreed to a consent order that required it to post a clear and prominent notice to members and visitors explaining how their personal information would be collected and used.[45] The consent order naturally captured the attention of many e-commerce companies.

The "self-regulation" advocated by the Internet faithful has not meant "no regulation." The Internet community has developed *ad hoc* institutions—such as newsgroups and chat sites—that circulate information and provide the leverage for public pressure against inappropriate cyberspace behavior. Similarly, several online ventures have emerged that attempt to foster the self-regulatory aspects of e-commerce. One such company, TRUSTe, operates much like the better business bureau, stamping its seal of approval on those digital enterprises that conform to established privacy principles and comply with TRUSTe's oversight and consumer resolution process.[46] Several online shopping comparison sites have recently been using these quality control organizations to check the stated business policies and customer relations practices of the e-retailers associated with their sites.[47] Though these quality measurement companies originated with the concern for online privacy, there is no reason why such organizations could not also monitor Internet pricing practices. After all, consumer confidence in the fair pricing procedures of online companies is a critical component in developing the trust necessary to facilitate the growth of e-commerce.

It is quite possible that if the Internet community deems dynamic pricing to be a violation of the implicit trust and loyalty of e-commerce, these quality control sites could intervene to prevent consumer exploitation. Even without these sites, Internet consumers appear to be appealing to the underlying competitive nature of e-commerce. Shopping comparison Web sites and shopping bots could be viewed as a market response to the consumer demand for increased information about prices and products. In other ways, the Internet community has already been able to admonish practitioners of price discrimination without the assistance of any formal, institutional intervention. Amazon's experiments with dynamic pricing were ultimately discovered at an online chat site dedicated to DVDs. It was online consumers themselves, connecting and communicating via the Internet and e-mail, who brought a halt to Amazon's "price tests."[48]

Yet, despite the success of self-regulation, the decentralized nature of the World Wide Web suggests that there is still a role for law and the formal institutions of the state to circumscribe what could potentially be a highly unfair business practice. Even self-regulation has limits in an environment where technology is constantly improving and the creation of Web sites is escalating at a dizzying pace. If e-commerce continues to grow at the astronomical rate that most experts anticipate, keeping track of the number of proliferating sites and monitoring their quality may require more formal types of collective action. In these instances, the FTC may be the ideal institution to oversee the evolving pricing strategies of e-commerce. The FTC's Bureau of Consumer Protection, for example, has as its self-proclaimed mandate the obligation "to protect consumers against *unfair,* deceptive, or fraudulent practices."[49] Just as it stepped into the fray regarding online privacy policies, the FTC could begin by simply monitoring the pricing practices of e-commerce companies and issuing reports about the status of online dynamic pricing.[50]

Presently, the FTC has remained reticent in the discussions concerning online dynamic pricing. But if industry analysts are correct and dynamic pricing becomes the wave of the future, the FTC will have no choice but to intervene to insure that dynamic pricing remains a reasonable business practice—one that does not exploit the potential of new technology to extract a consumer's entire willingness to pay. With its experience in dealing with price discrimination and its knowledge of e-commerce, the FTC has the authority and capacity to monitor and guide e-commerce pricing practices. That does not mean, however, that the FTC should rule with a heavy hand. Rather, it would be more appropriate for the agency to initially respect the cultural norms of the Internet community, to allow online forms of self-regulation to develop, permitting institutions such as TRUSTe to guide and protect consumer concerns. In monitoring the Internet's attempts at self-regulation, the FTC should intervene in those cases where the competitive forces of the market and the information flow of the Internet community may not be able to keep pace with the escalating dynamics of e-commerce. As a monitoring agency and an arbiter of last resort, the FTC can operate within the indigenously developing norms of the Internet community while insuring the principles of consumer protection.

NOTES

22. *See generally* Paul A. Samuelson & William D. Nordhaus, *Economics* 617–19 (Elisa Adams et al. eds., 13th ed. 1989).

23. A simple numerical example may highlight the social efficiency of price discrimination: Suppose that an airplane can be hired at a cost of $200. Suppose further that five business travelers are willing to pay $25 each to travel, while another 10 leisure travelers are only willing to pay as much as $10 each. If the price of travel is set at $10, all 15 potential customers will be willing to buy, but the total revenue of $150 is not sufficient to cover the airplane's costs. If the price is set higher than $10, the leisure travelers are priced out of the market and the airplane company can only make a maximum of $125 from the business travelers—still not enough to cover costs. If the company can distinguish between the two sets of travelers—business and leisure—and charge them different prices according to their willingness to pay, the company could cover its costs and at the same time satisfy both sets of passengers. Charging business travelers $24 and leisure travelers $9 would satisfy both sets of travelers (allowing them to pay less than their respective maximum willingness to pay) and yield the airplane company a profit of $10. For a similar example see, Scott Woolley, "I Got It Cheaper Than You," *Forbes,* Nov. 2, 1998, at 82.

24. Book publishers price discriminate by charging higher prices for the initial run of hardback books, as opposed to the paperback prices of subsequently released versions. Similarly, the movie industry price discriminates not only in charging different prices for different customers, such as adults versus students and senior citizens,

but also by releasing video and DVD versions of movies well after the initial run. Online companies also use this strategy of delay by charging customers more for more up-to-date information. For example, online brokers often charge more for real-time stock quotes. *See* Carl Shapiro & Hal R. Varian, *Information Rules: A Strategic Guide to the Network Economy* 4, 53–82 (Harvard Business School Press ed., 1999).

25. *See generally Internet Publishing and Beyond: The Economics of Digital Information and Intellectual Property* (Hal R. Varian & Brian Kahin eds., MIT Press 2000).

26. *Ibid.*

27. For those e-commerce companies that already have a sustained brand in the world of bricks-and-mortar, the establishment of an online presence may not be as costly. But the start-up costs of transforming a well-known brand into an online presence remain. *See* Erick Schonfeld, "Schwab Puts It All Online," *Fortune,* Dec. 7, 1998, at 94.

28. *See* Shapiro and Varian, *supra* note 24, at 19–52.

29. 15 U.S.C. § 13(a) (2001).

30. David A. Balto, Emerging Antitrust Issues in Electronic Commerce, Speech Before 1999 Antitrust Institute (Nov. 12, 1999), Distribution Practices: Antitrust Counseling in the New Millennium, *at* http://www.ftc.gov/speeches/other/ecommerce.htm.

31. Herbert Hovenkamp, *Federal Antitrust Policy: The Laws of Competition and Its Practice* 572 (2d ed. 1999).

32. A recent example of a Robinson-Patman case is *National Ass'n of Coll. Bookstores v. Cambridge Univ. Press,* 990 F. Supp. 245 (S.D.N.Y. 1997).

33. *Katzman v. Victoria's Secret Catalogue et al.,* 167 F.R.D. 649 (S.D.N.Y. 1996). Although it is unclear whether e-commerce issues could be governed by conventional mail-fraud provisions, the pricing practices of mail-order catalogue companies are analogous to online dynamic pricing. *See* Joseph P. Bailey, Intermediation and Electronic Markets: Aggregation and Pricing in Internet Commerce, 124–25 (1998) (unpublished Ph.D. dissertation, Massachusetts Institute of Technology) (*available at* http://www.rhsmith.umd.edu/lbpp/jbailey/pub/phdthesis.html).

34. 18 U.S.C. §§ 1961, 1962 (2001). Although RICO is essentially a criminal statute, it does provide for civil damages to private parties who have been injured "by reason of" a RICO violation. 19 U.S.C. § 1964(c).

35. *Katzman,* 167 F.R.D. at 654. Victoria's Secret's previous differential pricing practices were the subject of a WCBS-New York television news broadcast. Like Amazon, Victoria's Secret attributed the difference in prices for identical items as a temporary "pricing test." *See* Marilyn Much, "Catalogs Shrewd Pricing: The Newest Type of Bias?" *Investors Business Daily,* Jan. 18, 1996, at A4; CNN, "Suit Accuses Victoria's Secret of Price Gouging," Cnnfn.com, *at* http://cnnfn.cnn.com/archive/news/9601/03/briefs/.

36. *Katzman,* 167 F.R.D. at 654.

37. *Ibid.* at 660. Katzman also sued under the Lanham Act, claiming that Victoria's Secret's price discrimination was a form of misrepresentation amounting to trademark infringement. The court dismissed this claim for lack of standing. *Ibid.* at 658.

38. *Ibid.* at 660.

39. *Ibid.* at 661.

40. *Ibid.* For more on Katzman's legal counsel, see generally Amy Stevens, "Tempest in a C Cup: What's Underneath Victoria's Secret Suit; A Lawyer and His Friend Get Different Catalogs, Then Head to the Courthouse," *The Wall Street Journal,* May, 1 1996, at A1.

41. *Katzman v. Victoria's Secret Catalogue,* No. 96-7929, 1997 U.S. App. LEXIS 16440 (2d Cir. 1997).

42. The issue of Internet governance has been a popular topic among legal scholars. Some of the more thoughtful scholarship supporting online self-governance includes: David R. Johnson & David Post, "Law and Borders—The Rise of Law in Cyberspace," 48 *Stanford Law Review* 1367 (1996); Trotter Hardy, "The Proper Legal Regime for Cyberspace," 55 *University of Pittsburg Law Review* 993 (1994); Henry H. Perritt, Jr., "Cyberspace Self-Government: Town Hall Democracy or Rediscovered Royalism?" 12 *Berkeley Technology Law Journal.* 413 (1997).

43. Legal scholars have also questioned the effectiveness of self-regulation of cyberspace based on social norms. Among these critiques are: Neil Weinstock Netanel, "Cyberspace Self-Governance: A Skeptical View from Liberal Democratic Theory," 88 *California Law Review* 395 (2000); Mark A. Lemley, "The Law & Economics of Internet Norms," 73 *Chicago-Kent Law Review* 1257 (1998).

44. Seth Fineberg, "Candidness Is Key: New Study Looks at Evolution of Privacy Policies," ChannelSeven, Apr. 12, 2000, *at* http://www.channelseven.com/adinsight/surveys_research/2000features/surv_20000412.shtml.

45. "FTC and GeoCities Settle First Internet Privacy Lawsuit," *Computer Law Strategist,* Sept. 1998, Vol. 15, No. 5, p. 9.

46. *See generally The TRUSTe Story,* at http://www.etrust.com/about/about_truste.html.

47. The popular technology Web site CNET.com, for example, recently began using merchant review ratings provided by Gomez.com, in its MySimon price comparison Web pages. *See* "MySimon Recognized for Excellence by Industry Expert," *PR Newswire,* Sept. 13, 2000, *available in* LEXIS, News Library, PR Newswire file.

48. David Streitfeld, "On the Web, Price Tags Blur; What You Pay Could Depend on Who You Are," *Washington Post,* Sept. 27, 2000, at A1; Linda Rosencrance, "Outrage Prompts Amazon to Change Price-testing Policy," *Computerworld,* Sept. 18, 2000, at 14.

49. FTC, *Profile of the Bureau of Consumer Protection* (emphasis added), *at* http://www.ftc.gov/bcp/bcp.htm.

50. How the FTC chooses to act could well depend upon whom dynamic pricing affects the most. If online dynamic pricing is gouging affluent Internet consumers, one may wonder if such a privileged group may not have more effective means, namely its consumer power, to combat such pricing practices.

COKE: IT'S THE REAL (GREED) THING

—CHARLES MEMMINGER

An impassioned appeal made by a consumer against dynamic pricing, this article provides a consumer's point of view on dynamic pricing. Can one reconcile the consumer's argument with that of the marketer made in the previous article?

Coca-Cola made one of the biggest marketing blunders in history when it launched its "New Coke," and now it's preparing to make an even bigger boner.

According to recent news stories, Coke is testing new soda machines that can jack up the price of drinks depending on how hot the weather is.

If there ever was a plan nearly guaranteed to outrage customers, this is it. In fact, it is such a lunk-headed idea, I almost believe Pepsi agents infiltrated Coke's board of directors and launched this turkey.

Think about it. Every time you go up to a Coke machine, you'll have no idea how much you'll have to pay. It could be a buck or it could be 55 cents. Yesterday, you paid 70 cents for a Coke; today, they want you to pay $1.25. For the *same* product.

Coke officials defend the plan by saying it just capitalizes on the concept of supply and demand. Wrong. It is price gouging at its worst. It is insulting to customers. It is taking advantage of a bad situation.

And it discriminates against people who live in warm climates. If this harebrained idea goes through, Hawaii residents will once again have to pay a higher price for a product simply because we live on an island near the equator.

The technology of self-pricing soda machines is not all that complicated. All you do is stick a sensor in the machine that changes the price of the drinks depending on the temperature. But just because you *can* do something, doesn't mean you should.

I suppose they also could rig the machines so that when there are only a few remaining Cokes in the machine, the price would go up. That's supply and demand also.

But it's not right. In fact, supermarkets and hardware stores are hammered by the public when they try to raise the prices of food, water and building supplies before or after a hurricane. You could argue that it is just supply and demand but would you continue to shop at a store you knew took advantage of you when the going got tough?

Coke is crazy. It spends millions of dollars in advertising trying to present itself as a caring, sensitive company. Remember the commercial which had people around the globe singing, "I'd like to teach the world to sing in perfect harmony. I'd like to buy the world a Coke and keep it company . . ."?

I envision a new commercial with a hundred happy automated Coke machines singing, "We'd like to gouge the world with Coke and squeeze out every dime, when you're hot and nearly broke, it is Coke extortion time!"

I believe in a free market. Coke might have a legal right to jimmy its prices based on how hot and bothered its customers are. But customers are going to see this gambit for what it is, not free-market entrepreneurship but greedy profiteering. It reeks of taking advantage of people when they are suffering physically. Charging more for a certain product simply because hot weather is making people more thirsty is unscrupulous bordering on immoral. More importantly, from a marketing point of view, it's just plain stupid.

I'm no marketing whiz, but if I were on the board of Pepsi, I'd be loving this idea. I'd rig all Pepsi machines with the same sensors that the Coke machines have. Except, as the temperature went up, the cost of Pepsi would go down. Right along with Coca-Cola stock.

LET 'EM GOUGE

A Defense of Price Gouging

—JERRY TAYLOR AND PETER VANDOREN

The authors defend price gouging. Do you agree?

Gasoline prices have gone up from a national average of $1.22 a year ago to a startling $1.71 today. The industry says it's supply and demand. Consumer activists say it's gouging. Who's right? Well, both are.

The supply and demand explanation is straightforward. On top of the Venezuelan labor strike and war jitters in the Middle East, the winter in the Northeast—a region that relies heavily on heating oil—has been unusually cold. Refineries have accordingly been making heating oil rather than gasoline, so gasoline supplies are relatively scarce. Scarce gasoline = rising prices.

But what constitutes price gouging? To many, "gouging" is selling something at the highest level that the market will bear regardless of production costs. By that definition, we are indeed being gouged at the pump. Gasoline prices have risen faster than the price of crude oil.

But pricing goods and services at the highest level that the market will bear is what everyone in a capitalist economy does every day. Moreover, it happens regardless of whether prices are rising or falling. Oil companies were trying just as hard to charge what the market would bear in December 2001 when gasoline was $1.13 a gallon as they are now. Given present scarcities, however, the market can bear a higher price today than yesterday.

Why the constant government investigations only when prices are rising? Because to many, pricing significantly above cost is immoral and politicians and the press are in the business of finding immoral dragons to slay.

What has really set the moralizers off this time is the revelation that the gouging is often both tightly targeted and coldly calculated. The industry calls it "zone pricing." Essentially, oil companies examine small geographic areas, consider how much retail competition exists, estimate the willingness of motorists to look elsewhere for gasoline and price accordingly. Consumer activists are aghast that oil companies would go so far to extract every penny they can out of a gallon of gas.

Price discounting, however, clearly benefits the consumers who receive the discounts. But how about those consumers who pay prices higher than the discount? Economists of all stripes who've studied the effect of differential pricing based on the willingness of consumers to search for lower prices have concluded that consumers overall are likely to benefit if sales are higher with price discrimination than without it. That's because those consumers less sensitive to prices pay more of the fixed costs of doing business.

Regardless, most people view the practice of zone pricing in gasoline markets as unfairly taking advantage of consumers. Yet many of those same people—who will curse a blue streak if you put them in front of a camera and ask them about "Big Oil"—are as we speak putting their houses on the market and enthusiastically gouging the living daylights out of anyone looking for a new home. And what's more, they're zone pricing! Surprisingly, however, no one ever rages against real estate price gouging. In fact, the opposite is the case. Business reporters gush about returns and politicians pledge to do whatever it takes to keep the real estate bubble afloat.

So is price gouging okay if you're the gouger but not the gougee? It would appear so. But in reality, price gouging—like spinach—may be unappealing at first bite but it's good for everyone in the long run. Gougers are sending an important signal to market actors that something is scarce and that profits are available to those who produce or sell that something. Gouging thus sets off an economic chain reaction that ultimately remedies the shortages that led to the gouging in the first place. Without such signals, we'd never know how to efficiently invest our resources. Moreover, we'd have no idea what to conserve. It's no exaggeration to state that, without such price signals, our economy would look like Cuba's.

There's a catch, however. If the government artificially restricts supply, those price signals will fall on deaf ears. Local zoning ordinances, for instance, often prevent real estate developers from answering the call from desperate home-buyers. They also frequently prevent new service stations from popping up to challenge the local micro-monopoly.

Blame not the price gouger. Blame the government that won't let the price gouger do his job.

Chapter 7

ETHICS IN FINANCE AND ACCOUNTANCY

RONALD DUSKA, *American College*

Enron, WorldCom, Tyco, Adelphia, Cendant, Rite Aid, Sunbeam, Waste Management, HealthSouth, Andersen, Ernst & Young, KPMG, Deloitte & Touche, Pricewaterhouse-Coopers, J. P. Morgan, Merrill Lynch, Morgan Stanley, Bear Sterns SSB: These are the names of companies, accounting firms and investment firms that have all been implicated in some ethically questionable activity in the past few years, activities that have resulted in fines or criminal convictions. Most of the unethical behavior involved some aspect of finance from manipulating special purpose entities to show growth, to cooking books, to instituting questionable tax dodges, to allowing investment decisions to color the objectivity of investment research and advice. Ethics in the financial services area is perhaps the most visible area in business ethics in the first years of the new millennium. Accounting and investment firms that were looked upon as the guardians of integrity in financial dealings are exposed as violating the fiduciary responsibilities entrusted to them.

The vast array of ethical issues in the financial markets and services sector is too large to be addressed in one section of a business ethics text. We will concentrate on a few areas. We will begin with an overall appraisal of ethics in finance. This essay will analyze the ethical elements of the market system on both a macro and micro level. Beginning with a defense of capitalism as a system, the essay will move on to describe the financial markets system and explain the role of intermediaries in that system. Financial markets, by turning finance into a commodity, make it possible to grow economies by providing capital and credit that help in the exchange of goods characteristic of the wider market. The selling of money, or better the marketing of money, makes all sorts of exchanges possible. But exchanges involve marketing and selling, practices that always have an ethical component. The essay lays out a litany of those malpractices, followed by an analysis of the necessity to avoid deception and fraud in marketing. The essay next examines the various roles played in the financial markets and turns to ways of regulating behavior—the self-regulation of the professional and the regulation of the legal environment. The essay concludes with suggestions for ways to improve ethical behavior.

ENRON AND ANDERSEN

The watershed event that made the ethics of finance prominent was the collapse of Enron and its accounting firm, Arthur Andersen. William Thomas's essay, "The Rise and Fall of Enron," details the steps taken that led to the downfall of those companies, including the introduction of "mark to marketing" accounting and complex special purpose entities that were used to access capital or hedge risk. The Enron case "has wreaked more havoc on the accounting industry than any other case in U.S. history."[1] It brought into focus the necessity of the independence of auditors and the responsibilities of accountants like never before. But the ethical responsibility of accountants was not unknown.

THE ETHICS OF THE ACCOUNTING PROFESSION

Accounting is a unique profession in the financial world because the accountant is responsible for giving the financial pictures that are necessary for companies to stay in existence, and the auditors are responsible for verifying that the pictures are accurate and truthful. The difficulties facing accountants in being objective and independent were not unknown before the Enron debacle, though. The section provides an eerily prescient

---

[1]C. William Thomas, "The Rise and Fall of Enron," *Journal of Accountancy,* April 2002, p. 7.

piece on the responsibilities of accountants in the form of a major address by John Bogle, the founder of Vanguard, which he gave in October 2000 shortly before the unraveling of Enron and Andersen. Entitled "Public Accounting: Profession or Business?" it begins by asserting the necessity of the integrity of financial markets and details threats to that integrity. Those threats came to fruition with the collapse of Enron and Andersen and the subsequent disclosures and scandals involving the financial services profession. Bogel calls for the need for accountants to be independent, and then contrasts the difference between being a mere business marketing a product and being a profession. When companies move from being professions to mere business marketers, problems arise. Such a move creates a conflict of interest between the good of the client and the profit needs of the company. Bogel looks at issues that affect the accounting profession today: the question of basic accounting issues, earnings management, stock options, abusive tax shelters, and independence.

The *Business Week* article "Accounting in Crisis" spells out what reforms are necessary to get accounting back on an ethical track, many of which were addressed in the Sarbanes-Oxley legislation, which we will turn to in the next section. Most of those reforms are reiterated in an address Henry M. Paulson Jr., the chairman and CEO of Goldman Sachs, gave to the National Press Club in June 2002. It developed the by now popular theme of how to restore investor confidence. It looks briefly at the role accounting needs to play, the role of corporate governance, and the problems with conflicts of interest and investment research.

CONFLICTS OF INTEREST IN THE FINANCIAL MARKETS

But what are these conflicts of interest in the financial arena? Marianne Jennings in "Conflicts of Interest: They're Not as Difficult as They Seem" sets forth a succinct account of them. Perhaps the leading example of the unethical effects of conflicts of interest is manifested in the shocking fact that ten of the top investment firms in the country had to pay fines for actions that involved conflicts of interest between research and investment banking. Companies that engaged in investment banking would pressure their research analysts to give high ratings to companies whose stocks they were issuing, whether those ratings were deserved or not. The problem is spelled out by William H. Donaldson, the chairman of the SEC, on the occasion of a global settlement of approximately $1.5 billion for such breaches between those companies and the SEC, NASAA, NASD and NYSE.

THE SARBANES-OXLEY ACT OF 2002

Since the beginning of the millennium scandals in the financial services sector have taken a toll on investor confidence. Kant's point of asking what would happen if everybody did something is well taken. The more it is clear that there is deceit and chicanery and evasiveness and cutting corners going on, the less trustworthy those engaged in financial services become. Relying on professions to police themselves did not seem to work, so the U.S. Congress passed the Sarbanes-Oxley Act of 2002.

A summary of what that legislation requires done by PricewaterhouseCoopers is included. The reaction to Sarbanes-Oxley has been mixed. Dawn-Marie Driscoll weighs in with "Sarbanes-Oxley: Pardon Me If I'm Underwhelmed," which is countered by Rebecca Walker's "Weighing Sarbanes-Oxley: Changes Appear to Be Profound." The difference between the two appraisals seems to rest on the question of whether we can legislate morality. The answer will depend on the extent to which regulations with sanctions are effective.

Whatever the case, James Clarke spells out what ethical requirements Sarbanes-Oxley will have on members of boards of trustees with "Board Governance Post Enron." Clarke insists the ethical responsibility of the board members is to care for the institution and be loyal to it.

ABUSIVE TAX SHELTERS

Accounting firms, firms dealing with derivatives, makers of commodity markets and large brokerage and investment firms are not the end of the problem in financial services today. In the interlocking world of financial markets one of the most egregious unethical practices, which has until now gone largely unremarked, is the practice of abusive tax shelters. Taxes are not part of the financial services market, but the avoidance of taxes is an impetus behind all sorts of financial instruments created and sold by financial planners, tax lawyers, tax accountants and financial services firms. Given the voluntary nature of our tax system, it is imperative for the general welfare that all constituents pay their fair share of taxes. Yet a large portion of the financial markets is intent on finding loopholes or "dodges" to help clients pay less than their fair share and thus free ride on the backs of the ordinary taxpayer. For a voluntary system to be healthy, entities with power and privilege need to participate in what is always a necessary inconvenience, paying taxes, for the good of the whole. In April 2001 the IRS named 25 companies who evaded $4 billion in taxes in improper shelters. It is a practice reported on by Cassell Bryan-Law in a *Wall Street Journal* article, "Accounting Firms Face Backlash over the Tax Shelters They Sold." The article points out how accounting firms help their corporate clients exploit the loopholes in the modern-day tax codes.

The large accounting firms form teams dedicated to gaming the tax codes for the benefits of their clients, as long as the clients promise not to divulge the schemes. Hence these major accounting firms are under attack for tax advice that violates the spirit of the tax law by exploiting the letter of the tax laws.

Tax accountants' code of ethics requires they take their responsibility to the general public seriously. Section 5.06 of the AICPA's Statement of the Responsibility of Tax Preparers states, "CPAs have a duty to the tax system as well as to their clients." Section 5.05 states, "Our self-assessment tax system can only function effectively if taxpayers report their income on a tax return that is true, correct and complete." The abuse of tax shelters does not meet those requirements.

Finally, David A. Lifson, who chaired the Tax Executive Committee of the AICPA, said: "We (the AICPA) strongly oppose the undermining of our tax system by convoluted and confusing tax sophistry. Clearly there are abuses . . . However . . . taxpayers should be entitled to structure transactions to take advantage of *intended* incentives." (A statement to the House of Representatives Committee of Ways and Means in hearings on corporate tax shelters, November 10, 1999.) But this clearly proscribes abusing the system by taking advantage of *unintended* incentives, the loopholes that conform to the letter but violate the spirit of the law.

INSIDER TRADING

No discussion of the ethics of finance would be complete without consideration of the practice of insider trading. Ivan Boesky, in the 1980s, was sent to prison for the crime of insider trading. Ken Lay and his colleagues at Enron have been accused of insider trading. They allegedly dumped their stock, knowing of the inevitable downturn in the stock's worth, while encouraging others to hold on to it. This is patently unfair.

The Securities and Exchange Commission defines insider information in the following way.

> *"Insider trading" refers generally to buying or selling a security, in breach of a fiduciary duty or other relationship of trust and confidence, while in possession of material, nonpublic information about the security. Insider trading violations may also include "tipping" such information, securities trading by the person "tipped" and securities trading by those who misappropriate such information. Examples of insider trading cases that have been brought by the Commission are cases against: corporate officers, directors and employees who traded the corporation's securities after learning of significant, confidential corporate developments; friends, business associates, family members and other "tippees" of such officers, directors and employees, who traded the securities after receiving such information; employees of law, banking, brokerage and printing firms who were given such information in order to provide services to the corporation whose securities they traded; government employees who learned of such information because of their employment by the government; and other persons who misappropriated, and took advantage of, confidential information from their employers.*
>
> *Because insider trading undermines investor confidence in the fairness and integrity of the securities markets, the Commission has treated the detection and prosecution of insider trading violations as one of its enforcement priorities.[2]*

The main argument against insider trading is that it is unfair to those who do not have the privileged information. So if some executive gets rid of a stock he knows is going to be greatly decreased in worth because of bad news that no one except a few insiders knows, he takes advantage of those who bought the stock from him without full disclosure. It is the elementary ethics of honest marketing.

There is also the argument that it is the unethical misappropriation of proprietary knowledge (i.e., knowledge that only those in the firm should have, knowledge owned by the firm and not to be used by abusing one's fiduciary responsibilities to the firm). Such behavior also undermines the trust necessary to the proper functioning of a firm. But it is an unfairness to others who buy the stock. Some economists would insist that in the long run,

---

[2]http://www.sec.gov/divisions/enforce/insider.htm.

insider trading is not so bad, since the inside information would be discovered shortly, and the market would correct itself. This is true, but does not take account of the hurt to those who did the original transactions in a state of ignorance.

However, the most intriguing argument against insider trading is that it leads to inefficiency in the markets. If it were practiced as a general rule, it would drive out of the market speculators who take risks on short-term trades, which make the market more pliable. It is unfair to them, since it creates for them an uneven playing field. That concept is articulated in the last reading of the section, an excerpt from Peter Koslowski's essay on the ethics of banking: "Speculation and Insider Trading as a Problem of Business Ethics."

ETHICS IN FINANCIAL SERVICES

—RONALD DUSKA

Ronald Duska lays out the basic ethical problems facing financial markets. The article begins by defending the role of financial markets in spite of centuries of suspicion against them. Financial markets create capital and investment as well as help people to manage risk to ensure enough income so that they can live well. Thus financial markets contribute to the well-being of society. The essay explains how the markets work and examines the type of ethical problems found in the operation of those markets.

Some turn every quality or art into a means of getting wealth; this they conceive to be the end, and to the promotion of the end they think all things must contribute.

—ARISTOTLE, *POLITICS,*
BK. 1, CH. 9, 1258a13–14

"The unfettered love of money is the root of all evil." Such a claim, exaggerated as it is, reflects an ethical bias against money and money markets, and, by extension, finance and financial services that permeates many, if not most, cultures' thinking. Western philosophical culture, particularly as exemplified in Aristotle, defines the very notion of liberal as being free from concerns about money. Aristotle claims that "to be engaged in (acquiring wealth) practically is illiberal and irksome." Further, he maintains that it is " . . . justly censured; for it is unnatural, and a mode by which men gain from one another . . . For money was intended to be used in exchange, but not to increase at interest." (Aristotle, *Politics,* Bk. 1, Ch. 11, 1258b10–11, and *Politics,* Bk. 1, Ch. 10, 1258b 1.)

Major religions, such as Judaism, Christianity and Islam, at one or another point in their histories, followed this lead of Aristotle and maintained prohibitions against usury, i.e., the loaning of money at interest. Consequently from the perspective of Western culture, the notion that there could be ethics in financial services where people make money selling money is at least problematic if not downright oxymoronic.

This ethical indictment of the financial services industry even carries over in some views of contemporary popular culture. It is not helped by the egregious behavior of CEOs and financial officers of companies such as Enron, Andersen, WorldCom, ImClone, Tyco, Adelphia, Rite Aid and so forth. The early years of the 21st century have been full of behavior that erodes the trust of the public, and that turns the ordinary bias against business into an even stronger torrent of suspicion and condemnation.

However, even in spite of the Enrons and WorldComs and the behavior of the major accounting firms, we would argue that such a bias against financial markets is seriously distorted. Ethics in the financial services industry is not only present, but also necessary. A critique depending on Aristotle's view of money would be seriously flawed because, while it correctly identifies the corrupting influence of greed and a lust for the accumulation of wealth, it fails to take into account the extent to which money itself and money markets are of significant instrumental worth to society by aiding the production and distribution of goods.

Aristotle correctly noted that if a person or culture turns the pursuit of money, an instrumental good, into the ultimate goal of human beings, such a culture would be ethically corrupt. That is the moral of the story of King Midas. Nevertheless, the invention of money and the conversion of it into a commodity itself, to be used for the purchase of a multitude of other goods, was a boon to the human race, and properly utilized and constrained, financial markets, which facilitate the exchange of money, have an abidingly important and positive impact on society.

Ethics is a normative enterprise that has as its subject matter individual actions, practices, institutions and systems. Its normative nature requires it to analyze those actions, practices and systems as well as to evaluate them. Accordingly, in this section we will analyze and evaluate not only specific actions of people involved in financial services, but also the financial system itself. Any complete ethical analysis requires the analysis and evaluation of the institutions and systems of a society to see if they contribute to or frustrate individuals' fulfillment.

Consequently it is necessary to analyze and evaluate not only the actions and practices of individuals in the financial services industry, such as churning or stock manipulation, but also the ethical desirability of the entire financial system, including financial markets, financial institutions and financial instruments. From a macro point of view, a system that benefits people is ethically preferable to systems that do not provide as many benefits for people. From a micro point of view, within the financial system itself, ethical issues such as conflicts of interest, insider trading, churning, abuse of tax shelters and other issues surface frequently and their resolution depends on understanding these practices in the context of the highly complex nature of the financial environment. To help us evaluate both the system (the macro view) and the practices within the system (the micro view) it is important to begin with basic definitions, and develop a conceptual vision of how the system interconnects.

If a system is large, of course, individuals get reduced to ciphers, and their individual wants and desires play little or no role in assuring the development of equilibrium and efficiency. Given the ends of efficiency and equilibrium, individual propensities are necessarily sacrificed. Is such sacrifice justified? Yes, but solely for the sake of efficiency, an efficiency which is itself justified by something like an invisible hand argument, which assures that such efficiency will provide benefits for society in general, the greatest good for the greatest number. For the system to be justified it must provide a rising tide which lifts all boats, and do it with some semblance of fairness.

THE FINANCIAL SYSTEM

Financial systems mirror the complexities of a nation's economic system and its level of economic development, development being a normative term that implies a desirable end point. We will focus on the ethics of and in the financial system of the United States where economic development is advanced, and the financial markets, instruments and institutions set the benchmark for the rest of the world.

FINANCIAL MARKETS

Financial markets are the bedrock of the financial system. Their purpose is to allocate savings efficiently to parties who use funds for investment in real assets or financial assets. An optimal allocation function will channel savings to the most productive use of those savings. In the U.S. system the mediator in the allocation process is price, and price in a financial system is usually described in terms of an interest rate.

Efficiency of allocation is critical to assure adequate capital formation and economic growth in a modern economy. System efficiency is achieved when the price reflected in the market is an equilibrium price; that is, a market clearing price. If disequilibrium exists, rapid adjustment to a new equilibrium is guaranteed. Efficiency will occur more readily if the number of buyers and sellers is large; both parties to a transaction easily obtain information; and transaction costs are kept to a minimum.

TYPES OF MARKETS

Financial markets can be categorized according to purpose. They can be divided into money markets and capital markets. Money markets trade in securities with original maturity of one year or less; whereas capital markets trade in securities with maturity greater than one year. Money market transactions involve the buying and selling of: (1) U.S. Treasury Bills, the largest and most important money market; (2) Federal Funds, which involve inter-bank borrowing and lending, and are a critical channel for monetary policy; (3) commercial paper, short-term debt issued by financial and nonfinancial corporations; and (4) eurodollars, the market for short-term dollar deposits outside the U.S. These markets are primarily institutional, since individual investors are less likely to deal directly in the money market. Individuals' cash management transactions are facilitated through a bank or a mutual fund.

Capital markets, whose securities have maturity greater than a year, include three broad market areas—the bond, the mortgage and the stock market. The bond market includes the sale of government, corporate, municipal and international bonds. The mortgage market involves the financing of residential and commercial real estate, while equity markets involve trading in common and preferred stock.

But to understand the ethics of financial markets it is critical to understand the purposes of those markets, be that the raising of new capital or the exchange of existing instruments. Transactions to raise new capital for a corporation or government occur in what is called a

primary market or new issue market. Transactions that exchange existing investments occur in what is called a secondary market.

CAPITAL GENERATION

Obviously for the economy to prosper and grow it is important to generate capital, which
may be accomplished in a number of ways. Securities may be: (1) issued through an auction process, as with Treasury securities; (2) privately placed to a small group of sophisticated investors, as with many corporate bond issues; (3) issued through a rights offering to
existing stockholders; or (4) facilitated by an underwriter or investment banker. The most
efficient capital generation is that which costs least. The best test of efficiency in primary
markets is the net cost of the capital the market generates. The lower the cost of the capital,
the more efficient the allocation of financial resources.[1]

SECURITY EXCHANGE

Most people are probably more familiar with secondary markets than with primary markets. Secondary markets are constantly referenced in the daily media. They are either exchanges, like the New York Stock Exchange (NYSE), or over-the-counter markets.
Exchanges use the auction process for price determination through the interaction of buyers and sellers. Any exchange, be it the NYSE or the Chicago Mercantile Exchange (CME),
involves (1) a physical location; (2) a set of rules governing trading, operations and behavior; and (3) members who have purchased the right to conduct transactions.

The over-the-counter (OTC) market deals with a greater volume of trading investments
than the exchanges do with their auction process. Foreign exchange, which is the largest financial market, trades OTC. U.S. Treasury notes, bonds and bills are traded OTC. The majority of corporate and municipal bond transactions occur OTC, as do the trading in
mortgage and asset backed securities. The common stock of many prominent and recognizable companies is traded on the NYSE, but the majority of equities are traded on The
National Association of Security Dealers (NASD) systems. For example, prominent companies such as Microsoft and Cisco Systems are traded over the counter.

The OTC systems are made up of dealers, who stand ready to make a market in a particular financial asset, and brokers, who assist customers in trading. A dealer, as opposed to
a broker, carries inventory. A dealer, usually through an electronic network, posts bid and
ask prices. The dealer purchases securities at the bid price and sells them at the ask price.
The difference is referred to as the spread and it is how a dealer is compensated for the trade.

Because any exchange is susceptible to the temptation of one of the parties to profit at
the expense of the other, there are rules in place governing what constitutes fair trading.
These rules constitute one level of the ethics governing those who engage in market exchanges. For example, the U.S. over-the-counter market is regulated by a code of ethics established by the National Association of Security Dealers. (NASD is a private organization,
one of whose functions is to encourage ethical practices by its members.) The rules specified in the codes reinforce what are usually commonsense intuitions about what is ethically
acceptable behavior and what is not. If one promises to sell a customer a security at a certain

price, it is unethical to renege on that promise because a later customer offers to pay a higher price. Perhaps the most important ethical principle among brokers and dealers is "Your word is your bond." Absent adherence to that rule, it is likely the system would break down.

Besides keeping one's word, the ethics of the marketplace also demands one disclose information as fully and truthfully as possible. If people cannot be trusted to disclose the truth about a product, the market mechanism will break down, as we saw in the breakdown of trust after the Enron/WorldCom scandals. Further as we saw in the conflict of the investment companies who had advisory arms, it is unethical for a broker to give out information about a company, whose stock he is selling, which is colored to make the stock look more attractive.

FINANCIAL INSTRUMENTS AND INSTITUTIONS

Besides financial markets, there are two other critical components in the system, financial instruments and financial institutions.

1. Financial instruments are the securities that are traded. Classified according to time, money market securities are those having original maturity of one year or less while capital market instruments are those with a maturity of more than a year. Classified according to contractual reference, financial instruments are either debt or equity claims.

   Debt claims usually provide the owner with a periodic return, called a coupon interest payment, and the return of principal at the end of the contract. Examples of debt claims include the fixed income securities such as bonds and mortgages, along with money market securities and life and long term care insurance policies and annuities. The chief ethical issue in this domain will involve the responsibility to honor contracts.

   Equity claims are exemplified by common and preferred stock. Equity claims imply ownership, whereas debt claims holders have no claim to ownership. If a company is dissolved, debt holders have first legal claim on the assets. Whereas debt claims mature, most equity claims are perpetuities, and whereas debt claims come with fixed obligations as to periodic or coupon return and the return of principal, most equity claims make no fixed promise as to future cash flows. Common stock, the most familiar equity claim, may pay the owner or investor a periodic return in the form of dividends, but there is no fixed or legal obligation to make the payment.

2. Besides financial instruments, there are the financial institutions like banks, securities dealers and brokers, pension funds, accounting firms, mutual fund companies and insurance companies. These institutions are the portal for the average person to participate in the financial system because they help those people exchange financial instruments. These institutions facilitate the activity of exchange.

   From the 1930s to the 1990s U.S. financial institutions were neatly compartmentalized, with each type of institution having a specific function in the overall workings of the financial system. The landmark law that created the compartmentalization was the Glass-Steagall Act (or Banking Act) of 1933, passed by Congress as a reaction to bank failures and the perceived responsibility of banks for the Great Depression and the general market failures of the time. The Glass-Steagall Act confined banking services to making loans and taking deposits, relegated insurance services to insurance companies and home lending to savings and loan institutions. Banks were prohibited from assisting their large corporate customers in purchasing corporate stock and reselling it in the open market. In the 90s the clear demarcation of financial institutions began to get muddied. Passage of the Financial Services Modernization Act (The Gramm-Leach-Bliley Act) in 1999 has ushered in a new chapter in U.S. financial history, breaking down the barriers between financial institutions, some of the implications of which are still not clear.

FUNCTIONS OF FINANCIAL INSTITUTIONS

Financial institutions and their agents act as financial intermediaries. In a world of direct finance, where borrowers and lenders interact using primary securities, there is no need for financial institutions, but direct finance creates problems that intermediaries can help resolve. There are three types of intermediation—of denomination, maturity and risk.

Intermediation of denomination and maturity occurs where borrowers and lenders often have different desires with respect to the dollar amount of a transaction and the maturity of the loan or the investment. A financial institution, such as a bank can easily allow depositors to save in any convenient amount and then package that saving with others' savings in order to accommodate a lender's desires. With respect to maturity the intermediator can guarantee a saver one time frame, say six months, and simultaneously make a loan for a different length of time, say two years.

Financial institutions also engage in risk intermediation. The typical household saver is risk adverse and would have difficulty dealing directly with a borrower. In such a situation a bank provides a secure and risk free way for money to be transferred from the saver to the borrower, while simultaneously controlling the risk of the transaction. Insurance companies are risk intermediaries in a different way. They create pools of risk adverse people so that they can insure themselves against catastrophic events that would ruin them financially.

Besides functioning as intermediaries, financial institutions facilitate exchange by acting as depository, contractual or investment institutions. Commercial banks and thrifts, including credit unions, are the chief depository institutions, where the major source of funds is deposits sold to savers, and the major use of funds is loans to borrowers. Contractual institutions include insurance companies and pension funds where the source of funding is premiums paid to obtain various types of insurance policies or pension contributions which create annuities guaranteed by a structured contract. Investment institutions is comprised of investment companies, primarily mutual funds and broker dealers.

To sum up: the financial system is the complex array of financial markets, securities and institutions that interact in facilitating the movement of capital among savers and borrowers. The financial system is also used for mediation of risk among parties. In the best possible model, this is all accomplished in a very efficient and hopefully ethical manner.

But beyond the intermediaries such as banks, dealers, brokers and insurance professionals, there are others involved in the markets such as assessors, valuations experts, advisors, planners, arbitragers and a host of other types of practitioners. Perhaps, most important are those who keep track of the exchanges—the accountants. It has often been said that modern capitalist economics would be impossible without the extensive roles in the financial markets played by the accountants.

For a market to exist we need someone to give a picture of the product. In the case of stocks and equities it is the role of the accountant to fulfill one of the numerous functions that go along with that task.

THE ETHICS OF THE MARKET SYSTEM

Financial markets are a critical component of a modern developed economy, that is, they are the cornerstone of the free market or capitalist system, a system that historically has led to the highest overall standard of living in history. Hence the financial markets system is instrumentally beneficial in helping bring about material conditions for the good life of society. It seems clear that the free market economy and the financial system that facilitates it have become almost universally recognized as instrumentally beneficial for society.

ETHICAL PRACTICES WITHIN THE SYSTEM

But even if the macro system is ethically acceptable, there are various types of behavior on the micro level within the market system that need to be examined. Generally there is agreement that a number of practices such as fraud, stock manipulation and churning are unethical. However, there are also practices in financial dealings where it is unclear whether and how those practices are unethical. Questions can be raised about the following sorts of practices such as insider trading, tax shelters, income smoothing, conflicts of interest, independence, de-mutualization, confidentiality and privacy, conflicting loyalties between clients and companies, the responsibilities of professionalism among others.

These practices give rise to the following types of questions. Is insider trading really wrong? If so, what exactly is wrong with it? How much disclosure is necessary in sales of financial instruments? How much disclosure is necessary in financial statements that show the financial strengths and weaknesses of a company? Should mutual fund managers put themselves in unwarranted conflict of interest situations by engaging in private purchases of stocks their company trades in? Should banks be able to sell insurance and investment products, and does such a capability create unnecessary conflicts of interest for them? Should accountants do consulting for firms they audit? Is day trading merely legalized gambling? Should law firms and accounting firms join together into multi-disciplinary estate planning teams? Is it fair for mutual insurance companies to demutualize? What should the limits of privacy be in the credit industry? What climate should be created so that those interests of the broker do not conflict with those of his client? Do we need fee based advising only, or is commissioned based selling with an agent's responsibility to give a client the best possible advice? Are financial service personnel professionals or simply salespeople, and what are their responsibilities as such?

A LITANY OF UNETHICAL PRACTICES

The ethical rules in the marketplace, even the marketplace of money, are fairly straightforward. Market transactions between individuals ought to be carried on according to what was agreed upon without using others and without engaging in deception or fraud in accordance with one's role. However, human beings, being what they are, they will, for a variety of reasons fall short of fulfilling their responsibilities or what is worse greedily and selfishly use others for their own gain. What follows is a list of ethically problematic ways of behaving in the financial services industry.

Ways of being deceitful or dishonest in the financial services industry include misrepresenting the financial product, including deceptive illustrations of possible returns, concealing risk factors, withholding full disclosure, misrepresenting one's ability and other activities. Fraud is a legal concept and has specific meanings in specific instances, but generally involves "intentional misrepresentation, concealment, or omission of the truth for the purpose of deception or manipulation to the detriment of a person or organization." (Downes and Goodman, p. 148) Beyond deception and fraud, there are other ways of using a client, particularly in exchange situations, which involve coercing or manipulating the client, by fear mongering or other means.

A central concern in financial services arises from conflicts of interest. There is conflicting interest when either the broker or agent's interest is served by selling a product the client does not need or is inferior to another product, typically a product that provides less remuneration to the salesperson. There is also conflict when an agent has two clients, and service to one will be detrimental to the other. If the interests in conflict are the interests of the agent against those of the client, professionalism demands that the agent subordinate his or her interests to those of the client. When the interests in conflict are those of two parties, both of whom the agent serves, solutions are more complex.

There are particularly difficult conflict of interest situations for accounting firms arising from providing external audit function for a publicly held firm while simultaneously selling consulting services to the same firm. Also the audit function has inherent conflicts balancing confidentiality to the client and the duty to inform the public of possible illegal practices. The SEC has historically been concerned about the latter problem, but it is the mixing of auditing and consulting that concerns the SEC at the present time, particularly after the Enron debacle.

Financial planners routinely run into conflicts between the interests of their clients and the structure of fees for their services. There is an interesting juxtaposition in the field between fee-only planners and planners that sell product. A fee-only planner charges for advice, but receives no commission from the client's implementation of that advice. Most planners are not fee only, but rather do not overtly charge for their advice, but are remunerated through a commission on the implementation of that advice. This creates an interesting dilemma—does my advice purely service the needs of the client or do I shade my advice depending on the structure of a fee schedule?

In money management and investment banking, there are numerous examples of potential unethical practices. For example, money managers who trade personally in the securities their firms hold in portfolio. A manager with large holdings in a security can easily influence the price of that security as they buy and sell; therefore why not enter the market for a personal transaction before placing the firm's transaction. Investment bankers have ample opportunities to engage in practices that are either clearly a conflict of interest, and often illegal, or border on a conflict of interest. Free riding and withholding securities from the public in an initial public offering are illegal, but the temptation to compromise this rule is powerful when the issue is "hot"; that is everyone knows the price will increase once the security begins to trade in the secondary market. In December 2000 the SEC commenced an investigation against three prominent investment banking firms for selectively providing shares of "hot" IPOs to certain clients. The investigation centers on a "quid pro quo" arrangement where the client is charged higher fees for other services in exchange for IPO shares that will surely rise in value.

Another unethical practice which occurs in the financial services industry would be scalping securities: for example an investment advisor who buys a security before recommending it, then selling out after the price has risen based on the recommendation. The most prominent case occurred in the 1980s involving *The Wall Street Journal*'s "Heard on the Street" column. This column is widely read and carefully followed by investors. The articles are very specific and often list companies and recommendations. The author was accused of tipping off certain individuals about the contents of the article before it was published.

Cornering the market is obviously unethical and often illegal, especially when it is in direct violation of government regulations, as was the well-publicized case against Salomon Brothers in 1991. Salomon was one of the major primary dealers in U.S. government securities. These dealers bid in the auctions for Treasury bills, notes and bonds. The government has regulations concerning the percentage of successful bids that may go to individual firms, but firms may also bid for their customers. In one auction in early 1991 Salomon received over 80 percent of the offering under the pretense that a sizable amount of the bids were for customers. In the subsequent investigation there was evidence to suggest that Salomon had used agreements with customers that technically may not have been illegal, but surely bordered on the unethical given the intent of the government rules.

Companies can get involved in activities such as: illegal dividend payments, where "dividend payments come out of capital surplus or that make the company insolvent;" (Downes, p. 174) incestuous share dealing, buying and selling of shares in each other's companies to create a tax or other financial advantage (Downes, p. 175); compensation design, where alternative forms of payment are set up to allow agents to avoid rebating violations; discrimination in hiring and promoting; misrepresentation to new hires; invasion of privacy; and dubious claim settlement policies.

In insurance sales, there is needless replacement and defective illustrations which have been the basis of billion dollar lawsuits against Prudential, New York Life and Metropolitan Life among others. Brokers and agents get involved in churning accounts that benefit the agents at the expense of the clients. For broker/dealers there is insistence on suitability rules, which demands you know and act in behalf of the best interests of the client you are selling to. There is the prohibition for financial planners and for those with control over clients' monies, either as trustees or brokers or advisers against commingling those funds with the financial service agent's.

For those on the exchanges there is insider trading, which as the name implies, involves trading on the basis of inside information, which is viewed as unfair to other traders who do not have the information. It makes for an unequal playing field. There is free riding, in the form of withholding a new securities issue to resell later at a higher price, or in the form of buying and selling in rapid order without putting up money for the sale.

In arbitrage there is greenmail, which is "payment by a takeover target to a potential acquirer, usually to buy back acquired shares at a premium. In exchange, the acquirer agrees not to pursue the takeover bid further." (Downes, p. 164) Gun jumping involves trading securities based on information before it becomes public, or soliciting buy orders in an underwriting before the SEC registration is complete. (Downes, p. 165)

Finally, there are prohibitions against schemes such as pyramiding that build on non-existing values, such as a Ponzi Scheme, rigging the market, manipulation or running ahead, i.e., an analyst buying a stock before making the recommendation to buy to his or her client. (Downes, p. 352)

Most of these unethical practices have in common, if not downright deception, the use of one's customers or clients for the benefit of the firm, the officers of the firm or the financial services professional. There is neither time nor room to deal with all of these issues, but this litany should help us begin to understand the tremendous range of possible conflicts of interest and outright possibilities of fraud in financial interaction. What can be done to avoid such problems?

BASIC ETHICAL PRINCIPLES

Given the huge diversity of issues what is the practical way to approach them? Our experience shows there are two valuable and overarching ethical principles that can be applied to the majority of issues in financial services: (1) avoid deception and fraud, and (2) honor your commitments. What follows will be a brief discussion of how these two principles can be used to resolve a number of the ethical issues financial service professionals face.

THE AVOIDANCE OF DECEPTION AND FRAUD

Economists have developed the notion of an ideal market exchange as a transaction in which two autonomous individuals, with full information, agree to transfer goods. Ideally there is perfect information about the worth of what is being given and received in return. Such an exchange, freely entered into with full information, should maximize satisfaction on both sides. Not only is there satisfaction on both sides, the expansion of such market behavior to all agreements of exchange made freely and honored leads to the overall improvement of each trader's lot and benefits the entire society.

When the conditions of an ideal trade, which includes the freedom of the participants, and full knowledge of the pertinent details of the product, are met we have what is often called informed consent. Consent cannot be presumed if one is either forced into an exchange or lacks adequate knowledge of the product one is bargaining for.

However, real financial markets are not ideal. In real financial markets consumers are often closer to ignorance than perfect knowledge. That makes them vulnerable to the unethical machinations, which if they were to become widespread, would lead to the general demise of the health of the financial market itself.

Clearly deception undermines the "ideal exchange model." Deception leads to the deceived party getting something different and usually less valuable than they expected. The mutual satisfaction disappears. A financial system fraught with deception and fraud where one could not rely on others to honor their commitments would be an inherently unstable as well as an economically inefficient society. Hence, the acceptance of practices that utilize deception and fraud along with not honoring one's word would lead to undermining the market. This has been amply demonstrated in the host of cases that have arisen since the demise of Enron, WorldCom, Rite Aide, etc.

Empirical observations provide us with multiple examples of such failures. The reason for such failure is clear. Any rational person would be foolish to deal with a country, company or person who is deceptive and unreliable. Rational and ethical financial dealing requires people be able to trust those with whom they are dealing to be honest and abide by their commitments—even if abiding by those commitments is disadvantageous to them.

Still, because of the temptation to pursue one's interest at the expense of another, financial markets are permeated with examples of dishonest dealings. An agent tells a client that an insurance policy is a savings plan in order to make the sale and obtain the commission. A broker tells the client for whom a low risk investment is suitable that a high-risk investment will meet the client's needs in order to make the sale. A financial planner sells his client an annuity rather than a mutual fund that will bring him a better return. A financial officer gives the credit manager at a bank an inaccurate picture of the receivables of the company to secure a loan he assumes the bank would not approve if it had the true picture. All of these misrepresentations at the expense of the client (or at least without the informed consent of the client) in order to benefit the agent are essentially situations where one person gets used for the benefit of another, by being led to believe something other than the truth. That is the essence of lying, using another to benefit oneself.

But some of the most interesting cases of unethical behavior in the world of finance are not those of outright misrepresentation. A more subtle way of circumventing ideal exchange is through failure to disclose pertinent information. Often agents defend failure to disclose by saying "Not disclosing isn't lying, it's just not telling." But such a rationalization misses the point. Any action of deliberately withholding information to get another person to act contrary to the way she would if she had that information has the same deceptive structure and consequence as the overt lie. Such action doesn't allow for informed choice.

However, deciding how much to disclose is not easy. Effective salespersons are always reluctant to put negative thoughts in a buyer's mind. Pointing out the possible unsuitable features of a stock, its risk, or a variable annuity, its lower return on investment when tied to a life insurance policy, jeopardizes the sale. Aggressive intermediaries are reluctant to disclose downsides of their products. Should one disclose the downside of a product and if so how much?

The characterization of lying given above shows an approach that is helpful in determining how much to disclose. "Whenever a person is tempted not to disclose some information, that person should ask why he is not disclosing." If an agent is withholding information because of fear of losing the sale if the client knows the whole story, the agent is manipulating that client. When stock brokers, financial planners or insurance agents claim that their customers don't need all the information that is given to them, they are often rationalizing and some care needs to be taken to determine if that is really the case.

Of course, the factor that makes the issue of disclosure critical is the asymmetry of knowledge. As we have seen, in financial markets clients are often closer to ignorance than perfect knowledge and hence are entitled to enough disclosure to give informed consent. Given the complexity of financial products the seller or financial advisor usually has far greater understanding of the financial instrument than the buyer, especially when the buyer is an individual rather than an institution. Where there is asymmetry of knowledge there is a dependency relationship where the person with less knowledge is vulnerable to the person with more knowledge. In an ethical world such a vulnerable person is entitled to disclosure that will allow informed consent.

The most widely publicized issues recently involve lack of disclosure in the accounting and auditing professions. The buyer of stock in a company has the right to know the true economic picture of the company, or at least, if a true picture is impossible, a transparent picture where that person can ascertain the real value of the security. Finally, a large part of the financial market is driven by the tax codes. In a voluntary tax system we are dependent upon people acting in good faith to pay their fair share as laid out in the tax laws and tax codes. To manipulate figures so that the IRS cannot ascertain the proper tax burden, to abuse tax shelters fractures the fabric of the relationship between government and business that keeps the system running successfully.

Such dependency relationships reflect a need for a special ethical approach that permeates the world of financial markets, the world of fiduciary relationships and/or agent/principle relationships, where the client depends on the expertise, honesty and good will of the agent, broker or adviser. Such a dependency relationship puts an added responsibility on the fiduciary or agent. Fiduciaries and agents have by virtue of their relationship with their clients an ethical responsibility to look out for the best interest of their client. Technically, a fiduciary is "a person, company, or association holding assets in trust for a beneficiary. The fiduciary is charged with the responsibility of investing the money wisely for the beneficiary's benefit." An agent is "an individual authorized by another person, called the principal, to act in the latter's behalf in transactions involving a third party." (Downes, p. 12) Thus, beyond being honest, the agent or trustee has an ethical obligation to look out for the client's best interest.

Any lying or failure to disclose that harms the principal, obviously does not look out for the client's best interest, and consequently violates the agent's ethical responsibilities. But there is the responsibility to look out for the client's best interests.

Still, the responsibility to look out for a client's interests comes because the agent or fiduciary has taken it upon herself to play a certain role in the financial services industry. Hence the responsibility arises because one has made a commitment as an agent, a broker, an accountant, a banker or a planner.

The financial intermediary is more than a mere salesperson. Intermediaries make it possible to expand markets and generate growth by making financial products readily available. This means there are specific roles that need to be played in the financial markets and those roles carry specific responsibilities. In committing to those roles the financial service professional commits to those consequent responsibilities. A banker has different responsibilities from an accountant, who has different responsibilities from a broker or a mutual fund manager. But to the extent they took on those jobs, they committed to the responsibilities of those jobs.

TYPES OF ROLES IN FINANCIAL MARKETS

A number of roles have evolved to make markets more efficient. We need the creators of products and marketers of the products as well as the intermediaries. We have brokers, agents and dealers whose role is to sell. We need accountants to keep track of the exchanges and their worth. We also need accountants to give a true picture of the financial status of companies. We need auditors to attest to the accuracy or the truth of the financial statements of the companies being audited. While a broker's and agent's primary role is to make financial instruments or products available to consumers, given the complexity of the financial products available today, they often need to take on the role of an advisor. Bankers play multiple roles in the financial system. They give advice to savers, make decisions on loans and act as fiduciaries in the trust function. An emergent role in the financial services system is that of a mutual fund manager. Finally, CEOs of financial institutions have a role to maximize profit for their shareholders, and some would argue, balance that over against the interests of all the other stakeholders.

WAYS OF REGULATING BEHAVIOR

Given such a diversity of roles, it is clear that a device is necessary to spell out the obligations that arise from the assumption of such roles. There are two means of regulating, either self-policing or through state or federal laws. People in groups that regulate themselves view themselves as professionals, and develop codes of ethics that spell out the responsibilities those professionals have to their clients.

PROFESSIONALISM

Recognizing the importance of being a person of one's word, numerous people in the financial services industry have encouraged the development of a professional attitude among participants in the industry. If we look at the older paradigms of professions such as the medical, legal and teaching professions, we see that what is characteristic of those professions is the reliance of the patient, client or student on the expertise of the doctor, lawyer or teacher as well as the respective professional's concern for the well-being of the patient, client or student. In the financial market, where profit seeking is so prominent, and where the principle of enlightened self-interest is such a motivating factor, and products and instruments are so complicated, it becomes necessary to insist in some circumstances that people put their lives and or fortunes in other people's hands. Having client's welfare in their hands makes it imperative that professionals look out for the best interest of those clients, even at the expense of the professional who has the expertise.

Insurance agents, financial planners, estate planners, brokers, dealers, accountants, mutual fund managers, valuation specialists, bankers and all other financial services personnel, are experts who have others dependent upon them for their well-being. They need to look upon themselves as professionals, and upon the requirement to look out for the best interest of their clients (or of the public, as in the case of the accountant/auditor) as an ethical requirement. In short, while salespeople sell, financial service professionals, even in selling, provide a service for their clients and it is incumbent upon them that that service is in the client's best interests.

Thus, most professional codes of ethics require that transactions be carried out with integrity, fairness, competence, objectivity, professionalism, diligence and respect for clients' confidences. Those are characteristics usually demanded of professionals by the financial services industry's many codes of ethics, which govern the behavior of financial planners, accountants, tax attorneys, bankers, valuation specialists and others. In short, the codes of the professional organizations provide an excellent example of sets of ethical rules governing individual behavior.

THE LEGAL ENVIRONMENT

We could argue that self-regulation required by professional codes will lead to ethical business, and indeed it will have some effect. But the call for professionalism in the financial services marketplace with its shift of attitude toward an insistence on ethics has not taken place by itself. Human nature being what it is there will always be the necessity of government regulation, in short laws. Laws tend to codify common morality or popular custom and add the extra incentive of stipulated punishment for misbehavior. When a law based on an ethical rule is stipulated and enforced, a penalty is imposed on the violator. In this way society can legislate the most important aspects of morality.

There is a framework for indicating acceptable behavior within the financial system. Unfortunately it is fragmented, consisting of legal statutes, voluntary compliance standards, self-regulated associations, regulatory standards and codes of ethics. Financial markets and institutions went through difficult times in the late 1920s and early 1930s. Markets collapsed, fortunes were lost and public confidence was eroded. Much of the blame was placed on internal abuses, including rampant speculation, unfounded optimism supported by brokers and dealers and a general disregard for common sense and prudence. The 1933 and 1934 Securities Acts were the first serious attempt at bringing order to the financial markets. The 1933 Act applied to the primary market; that is, the markets responsible for raising capital; the 1934 Act attempted to regulate the secondary market; that is, the trading of existing securities. Legislation has evolved since the 1930s in an attempt to strengthen the integrity of market transactions and to force full disclosure in all transactions. The initial responsibility for enforcement falls on the Securities and Exchange Commission, and the regulators of the banking and insurance industries.

But by the late 1930s the intent of the 1933 and 1934 legislation was being channeled into self-regulation by the various players in the market. The New York Stock Exchange took a lead in this area, lobbying Congress to allow internal standards and enforcement to meet the goals of the 1933 and 1934 Securities Acts. The New York Stock Exchange is member owned and managed, including what is referred to as "Member Firm Regulation."

The Exchange believes that self-regulation is good business and that effective supervision is essential to the successful operation of every broker/dealer. This system of self-regulation, which Congress endorsed, begins with broker/dealer firms and places heavy reliance of their adherence to rules of conduct and the exercise of effective supervision and control over all operations and personnel. The Exchange plays a role in the process as the SEC appointed Designated Examining Authority for most of its member firms. The Exchange maintains an extensive system for monitoring and regulating the activities of members. Finally, it has the responsibility to investigate and prosecute violators of Exchange rules and the Securities Exchange Act of 1934 and the rules thereunder.

All other exchanges have the same member firm system of self-regulation. In 1937, Congress passed the Maloney Act, providing for the establishment of national securities associations to supervise the over-the-counter securities market. The OTC or dealer markets are primarily regulated by the NASD Regulation, Inc. (NASDR), which was established in 1996 as a separate, independent subsidiary of the NASD. NASDR was created as a part of an unprecedented restructuring of NASD, a major feature of which was to separate the regulation of the broker/dealer professional from the operation of the NASDAQ Stock Market. Up until 1996 the regulatory arm of the OTC markets was within the general organizational structure of the NASD and the NASDAQ market. The new structure is a positive step in self-regulation. A board composed of a 50/50 mix of public representation and industry professionals provides the governance of NASDR. This is another interesting innovation on the part of NASD.

During the last decade banks have become prominent in the sale and marketing of securities. This has created new challenges for regulators and new ethical issues. The prime investment or savings products banks have traditionally sold are deposit instruments, the majority of which are insured by the Federal Deposit Insurance Corporation (FDIC). As banks sell non-deposit products the challenge is to make certain that customers understand to which products FDIC insurance applies. Bank regulators have been promulgating additional rules and regulations to augment current broker/dealer rules when the transaction occurs through a bank.

There is plenty of evidence of regulator and internal control over the behavior of individuals responsible for the marketing and sales of securities and insurance. Most organizations within their self-regulatory structures have attempted to focus on "codes of conduct." The American Institute of Certified Public Accountants, The Institute of Management Accountants, The American Bankers Association, The Association for Investment Management and Research, The Certified Financial Planner Board of Standards, the International Association for Financial Planning, The American Institute for Chartered Property Casualty Underwriters, The Society of Financial Service Professionals, formerly the American Society of Chartered Life Underwriters, and many other professional groups in the financial service industry have codes of ethics, which lay out principles and rules of proper behavior.

What is interesting is the attempt to blend codes and regulations together. There are numerous examples. Arthur Levitt of the SEC recently encouraged the AICPA to strengthen its code governing conflicts of interest. One of the industry groups that is especially interesting is the mutual fund managers group—The Investment Company Institute—which is the national association of the U.S. investment company industry, and has published "An Investment Company Director's Guide to Oversight of Codes of Ethics and Personal Investing." The 1940 Investment Company Act reflects congressional recognition of the delicate fiduciary nature of an investment advisory relationship as well as intent to address any potential conflicts of interest that might inhibit an investment advisor's ability to render disinterested advice to its clients.

Congress, the SEC and the mutual fund industry recognized the need to reconcile these fiduciary obligations with personal investing practices. The SEC's Rule 17j-1 requires that all investment companies and their advisors adopt codes of ethics and procedures designed to detect and prevent inappropriate personal investing. This is a very positive sign in the area of money management since the mutual fund industry has become prominent and highly visible in the financial system landscape, and for them to address these complex issues through a formalized code of ethics is encouraging.

Finally, the passage of the Sarbanes-Oxley Act mandates a number of rules for corporate governance while separating auditing and other functions that might cause a conflict of interest if carried out by the same firm. The implications of that act will be huge for the financial services industry, but that is a matter for another essay.

WAYS TO ENCOURAGE ETHICAL BEHAVIOR IN THE FINANCIAL SERVICES

We have seen that there are unethical practices and that the self-regulating of the various professions as well as the laws have been utilized to improve ethical behavior in the financial services industry. But is there anything else that can be done?

First, there must be recognition of the unethical activities taking place. Then it is imperative that financial services professionals commit to, as most of their codes insist they do, putting the best interests of their clients first, and develop a strong enough character to withstand temptation. But beyond that there are other practical ways to encourage or enable ethical behavior.

One of the most common procedures being developed is the separation of the sales function from the advisor function. Fee-only planners are an example of this model. A wall between the activity of selling and advising would go a long way in cleaning up powerful temptations facing brokers and agents, but the resistance from the agents and brokers is strong, both because of the tradition of commission for sales and the high remuneration tied to those sales.

What is also critical for encouraging ethical behavior is to reduce, as much as possible, the pressures created by the corporate culture of the marketplace. A marketplace that measures success almost exclusively by profit creates pressure on companies and their managers to succeed whatever it takes. Their companies, who are in turn forced by the demands of profitability, often force financial service professionals to act in ways they see as unethical. For example, captive agents in insurance are asked to sell variable annuities they think are unsuitable. The companies produce the annuities to stay competitive. The competitive forces pressure managers, and agents are pressured to go along with their managers. Basic ethical attitudes must be compromised in order to do one's job.

What underlies this is the fact that the view that business should be concerned with profits no matter what the cost filters through the organization to the financial service professionals. Such a view needs to be replaced by a view that business should be compatible with the other values of society. The financial market system needs to concur that the business environment should not be an environment where there is a split between the personal ethical attitudes and the attitudes governing one's business life. Rather, the corporate culture, the business milieu should be one that supports personal "integrity" along with profitability.

Most of the professional codes in financial services require integrity. Usually we think of the person of "integrity" as one who is truthful, and that is certainly one meaning. But there is a fuller meaning of "integrity" where integrity means a quality whereby one's life is unified, where there is a sort of "wholeness." Such wholeness requires a culture where people can work in an environment that doesn't cause them to violate their "conscience," and which promotes their flourishing. A milieu such as Salomon Brothers pictured in *Liar's Poker* must give way to a view of enlightened self-interest concerned with the best interest of those the corporation serves.

In short a new perspective is needed. Business culture needs to be seen as a place where there is a sense of responsibility for the creation of goods and services. Financial service agents need to view themselves as agents who bring value to their clients' lives. An agent who is told to forget about the good of the client, either straight-out or subtly, cannot justify his behavior by telling himself he is helping the client. He knows he is simply lining his and the manager's pockets at the expense of the client. A professional will find such a manager's sales pushes morally repugnant and a threat to his own integrity.

For early ethicists, such as Plato and Aristotle, individual human flourishing was the main concern of ethics and setting up of a culture or environment where such flourishing was possible was the main task of societal regulation. From their perspective human beings are part of nature like everything else, and just as plants cannot flourish unless they have an environment of rich soil, so human beings cannot flourish unless their environment is rich soil. Honesty and trust and cooperation and caring are part of a rich robust human life. To live among people who lie, are untrustworthy and who do not care for one another is to live in a sort of human hell. To enter such an environment daily has a debilitating effect, and if one capitulates to that environment, one necessarily diminishes oneself.

Managers in the financial services industry and elsewhere, whose *sole* driving force is maximizing profits, are creating a business climate, in the name of "profit maximization" that will force employees to sacrifice some of their integrity. The growing pressure for businesses to be ethical in the sense of creating value is just the opposite. It is a pressure to create a business climate or culture where the honest, caring, right thing is the thing expected. And, there are those who argue, such an environment will coincidentally lead to more profit.

Ethics has become important in the culture of the financial services market. A strong view that the purpose of business activities in general and financial services in particular is the creation of value for the consumer will make it possible that ethics in the financial services industry will not only exist, but flourish.

REFERENCE

John Downes and Jordan Goodman, *Money's Complete Guide to Personal Finance and Investment Terms,* Barron's Educational Series, Woodbury, New York, 1985.

NOTE

1. Each method of capital generation is susceptible to a variety of ethically questionable activities, on numerous levels, ranging from manipulation, misuse of inside information, fraud, misrepresentation, to bribery, over or under-evaluation of assets, high pressure sales, etc.

THE RISE AND FALL OF ENRON

—C. WILLIAM THOMAS

C. William Thomas details what caused the events that gave rise to the demise of Enron and Arthur Andersen. He sees the main cause as "individual and collective greed born in an atmosphere of market euphoria and corporate arrogance." Bright people gamed the market utilizing mark-to-market accounting and complex special purpose entities. Companies' codes of ethics governing conflicts of interest were set aside; and accountants and auditors let obscure financing slide by. In the early months of 2001, the house of financial cards that Enron had constructed began to tumble, bringing its auditing firm, Arthur Andersen, along with it. As Thomas states, "The Enron implosion has wreaked more havoc on the accounting profession than any other case in U.S. history."

If you're like most, you've been astonished, disillusioned and angered as you learned of the meteoric rise and fall of Enron Corp. Remember the company's television commercial of not so long ago, ending with the reverberating phrase, "Ask why, why, why?" That question is now on everyone's lips. The Enron case is a dream for academics who conduct research and teach. For those currently or formerly involved with the company, such as creditors, auditors, the SEC and accounting regulators, it's a nightmare that will continue for a long time.

Formal investigations of Enron are now under way, headed by the company's board, the SEC, the Justice Department and Congress. The exact causes and details of the disaster may not be known for months. The purpose of this article is to summarize preliminary observations about the collapse, as well as changes in financial reporting, auditing and corporate governance that are being proposed in response by Big Five accounting firms, the AICPA and the SEC.

IN A WAY IT'S SIMPLE, IN A WAY IT'S NOT

On the surface, the motives and attitudes behind decisions and events leading to Enron's eventual downfall appear simple enough: individual and collective greed born in an atmosphere of market euphoria and corporate arrogance. Hardly anyone—the company, its employees, analysts or individual investors—wanted to believe the company was too good to be true. So, for a while, hardly anyone did. Many kept on buying the stock, the corporate mantra and the dream. In the meantime, the company made many high-risk deals, some of which were outside the company's typical asset risk control process. Many went sour in the early months of 2001 as Enron's stock price and debt rating imploded because of loss of investor and creditor trust. Methods the company used to disclose (or creatively obscure) its complicated financial dealings were erroneous and, in the view of some, downright deceptive. The company's lack of transparency in reporting its financial affairs, followed by financial restatements disclosing billions of dollars of omitted liabilities and losses, contributed to its demise. The whole affair happened under the watchful eye of Arthur Andersen LLP, which kept a whole floor of auditors assigned at Enron year-round.

THE BEGINNING PRESAGES THE END

In 1985, after federal deregulation of natural gas pipelines, Enron was born from the merger of Houston Natural Gas and InterNorth, a Nebraska pipeline company. In the process of the merger, Enron incurred massive debt and, as the result of deregulation, no longer had exclusive rights to its pipelines. In order to survive, the company had to come up with a new and innovative business strategy to generate profits and cash flow. Kenneth Lay, CEO, hired McKinsey & Co. to assist in developing Enron's business strategy. It assigned a young consultant named Jeffrey Skilling to the engagement. Skilling, who had a background in banking and asset and liability management, proposed a revolutionary solution to Enron's credit, cash and profit woes in the gas pipeline business: create a "gas bank" in which Enron would buy gas from a network of suppliers and sell it to a network of consumers, contractually guaranteeing both the supply and the price, charging fees for the transactions and assuming the associated risks. Thanks to the young consultant, the company created both a new product and a new paradigm for the industry—the energy derivative.

Lay was so impressed with Skilling's genius that he created a new division in 1990 called Enron Finance Corp. and hired Skilling to run it. Under Skilling's leadership, Enron Finance Corp. soon dominated the market for natural gas contracts, with more contacts, more access to supplies and more customers than any of its competitors. With its market power, Enron could predict future prices with great accuracy, thereby guaranteeing superior profits.

THE BEST, THE BRIGHTEST AND THE DREADED PRC

Skilling began to change the corporate culture of Enron to match the company's transformed image as a trading business. He set out on a quest to hire the best and brightest traders, recruiting associates from the top MBA schools in the country and competing with the largest and most prestigious investment banks for talent. In exchange for grueling schedules, Enron pampered its associates with a long list of corporate perks, including concierge services and a company gym. Skilling rewarded production with merit-based bonuses that had no cap, permitting traders to "eat what they killed."

One of Skilling's earliest hires in 1990 was Andrew Fastow, a 29-year-old Kellogg MBA who had been working on leveraged buyouts and other complicated deals at Continental Illinois Bank in Chicago. Fastow became Skilling's protégé in the same way Skilling had become Lay's. Fastow moved swiftly through the ranks and was promoted to chief financial officer in 1998. As Skilling oversaw the building of the company's vast trading operation, Fastow oversaw its financing by ever more complicated means.

As Enron's reputation with the outside world grew, the internal culture apparently began to take a darker tone. Skilling instituted the performance review committee (PRC), which became known as the harshest employee-ranking system in the country. It was known as the "360-degree review" based on the values of Enron—respect, integrity, communication and excellence (RICE). However, associates came to feel that the only real performance measure was the amount of profits they could produce. In order to achieve top ratings, everyone in the organization became instantly motivated to "do deals" and post earnings. Employees were regularly rated on a scale of 1 to 5, with 5s usually being fired within six months. The lower an employee's PRC score, the closer he or she got to Skilling, and the higher the score, the closer he or she got to being shown the door. Skilling's division was known for replacing up to 15% of its workforce every year. Fierce internal competition prevailed and immediate gratification was prized above long-term potential. Paranoia flourished and trading contracts began to contain highly restrictive confidentiality clauses. Secrecy became the order of the day for many of the company's trading contracts, as well as its disclosures.

HOW HIGH THEY FLY

Coincidentally, but not inconsequentially, the U.S. economy during the 1990s was experiencing the longest bull market in its history. Enron's corporate leadership, Lay excluded, comprised mostly young people who had never experienced an extended bear market. New investment opportunities were opening up everywhere, including markets in energy futures. Wall Street demanded double-digit growth from practically every venture, and Enron was determined to deliver.

In 1996 Skilling became Enron's chief operating officer. He convinced Lay the gas bank model could be applied to the market for electric energy as well. Skilling and Lay traveled widely across the country, selling the concept to the heads of power companies and to energy regulators. The company became a major political player in the United States, lobbying for deregulation of electric utilities. In 1997 Enron acquired electric utility company Portland General Electric Corp. for about $2 billion. By the end of that year, Skilling had developed the division by then known as Enron Capital and Trade Resources into the nation's largest wholesale buyer and seller of natural gas and electricity. Revenue grew to $7 billion from $2 billion, and the number of employees in the division skyrocketed to more than 2,000 from 200. Using the same concept that had been so successful with the gas bank, they were ready to create a market for anything that anyone was willing to trade: futures contracts in coal, paper, steel, water and even weather.

Perhaps Enron's most exciting development in the eyes of the financial world was the creation of Enron Online (EOL) in October 1999. EOL, an electronic commodities trading Web site, was significant for at least two reasons. First, Enron was a counterparty to every transaction conducted on the platform. Traders received extremely valuable information regarding the "long" and "short" parties to each trade as well as the products' prices in real-time. Second, given that Enron was either a buyer or a seller in every transaction, credit risk management was crucial and Enron's credit was the cornerstone that gave the energy community the confidence that EOL provided a safe transaction environment. EOL became an overnight success, handling $335 billion in online commodity trades in 2000.

The world of technology opened up the Internet, and the IPO market for technology and broadband communications companies started to take off. In January 2000 Enron announced an ambitious plan to build a high-speed broadband telecommunications network and to trade network capacity, or bandwidth, in the same way it traded electricity or natural gas. In July of that year Enron and Blockbuster announced a deal to provide video on demand to customers throughout the world via high-speed Internet lines. As Enron poured hundreds of millions into broadband with very little return, Wall Street rewarded the strategy with as much as $40 on the stock price—a factor that would have to be discounted later when the broadband bubble burst. In August 2000 Enron's stock hit an all-time high of $90.56, and the company was being touted by *Fortune* and other business publications as one of the most admired and innovative companies in the world.

THE ROLE OF MARK-TO-MARKET ACCOUNTING

Enron incorporated "mark-to-market accounting" for the energy trading business in the mid-1990s and used it on an unprecedented scale for its trading transactions. Under mark-to-market rules, whenever companies have outstanding energy-related or other derivative contracts (either assets or liabilities) on their balance sheets at the end of a particular quarter, they must adjust them to fair market value, booking unrealized gains or losses to the income statement of the period. A difficulty with application of these rules in accounting for long-term futures contracts in commodities such as gas is that there are often no quoted prices upon which to base valuations. Companies having these types of derivative instruments are free to develop and use discretionary valuation models based on their own assumptions and methods.

The Financial Accounting Standards Board's (FASB) emerging issues task force has debated the subject of how to value and disclose energy-related contracts for several years. It has been able to conclude only that a one-size-fits-all approach will not work and that to require companies to disclose all of the assumptions and estimates underlying earnings would produce disclosures that were so voluminous they would be of little value. For a company such as Enron, under continuous pressure to beat earnings estimates, it is possible that valuation estimates might have considerably overstated earnings. Furthermore, unrealized trading gains accounted for slightly more than half of the company's $1.41 billion reported pretax profit for 2000 and about one-third of its reported pretax profit for 1999.

CAPITALISM AT WORK

In the latter part of the 1990s, companies such as Dynegy, Duke Energy, El Paso and Williams began following Enron's lead. Enron's competitive advantage, as well as its huge profit margins, had begun to erode by the end of 2000. Each new market entrant's successes squeezed Enron's profit margins further. It ran with increasing leverage, thus becoming more like a hedge fund than a trading company. Meanwhile, energy prices began to fall in the first quarter of 2001 and the world economy headed into a recession, thus dampening energy market volatility and reducing the opportunity for the large, rapid trading gains that had formerly made Enron so profitable. Deals, especially in the finance division, were done at a rapid pace without much regard to whether they aligned with the strategic goals of the company or whether they complied with the company's risk management policies. As one knowledgeable Enron employee put it: "Good deal vs. bad deal? Didn't matter. If it had a positive net present value (NPV) it could get done. Sometimes positive NPV didn't even matter in the name of strategic significance." Enron's foundations were developing cracks and Skilling's house of paper built on the stilts of trust had begun to crumble.

RELATED PARTIES AND COMPLEX SPECIAL PURPOSE ENTITIES

In order to satisfy Moody's and Standard & Poor's credit rating agencies, Enron had to make sure the company's leverage ratios were within acceptable ranges. Fastow continually lobbied the ratings agencies to raise Enron's credit rating, apparently to no avail. That notwithstanding, there were other ways to lower the company's debt ratio. Reducing hard assets while earning increasing paper profits served to increase Enron's return on assets (ROA) and reduce its debt-to-total-assets ratio, making the company more attractive to credit rating agencies and investors.

Enron, like many other companies, used "special purpose entities" (SPEs) to access capital or hedge risk. By using SPEs such as limited partnerships with outside parties, a company is permitted to increase leverage and ROA without having to report debt on its balance sheet. The company contributes hard assets and related debt to an SPE in exchange for an interest. The SPE then borrows large sums of money from a financial institution to purchase assets or conduct other business without the debt or assets showing up on the company's financial statements. The company can also sell leveraged assets to the SPE and book a profit. To avoid classification of the SPE as a subsidiary (thereby forcing the entity to include the SPE's financial position and results of operations in its financial statements), FASB guidelines require that only 3% of the SPE be owned by an outside investor.

Under Fastow's leadership, Enron took the use of SPEs to new heights of complexity and sophistication, capitalizing them with not only a variety of hard assets and liabilities, but also extremely complex derivative financial instruments, its own restricted stock, rights to acquire its stock and related liabilities. As its financial dealings became more complicated, the company apparently also used SPEs to "park" troubled assets that were falling in value, such as certain overseas energy facilities, the broadband operation or stock in companies that had been spun off to the public. Transferring these assets to SPEs meant their losses would be kept off Enron's books. To compensate partnership investors for downside risk, Enron promised issuance of additional shares of its stock. As the value of the assets in these partnerships fell, Enron began to incur larger and larger obligations to issue its own stock later down the road. Compounding the problem toward the end was the precipitous fall in the value of Enron stock. Enron conducted business through thousands of SPEs. The most controversial of them were LJM Cayman LP and LJM2 Co-Investment LP, run by Fastow himself. From 1999 through July 2001, these entities paid Fastow more than $30 million in management fees, far more than his Enron salary, supposedly with the approval of top management and Enron's board of directors. In turn, the LJM partnerships invested in another group of SPEs, known as the Raptor vehicles, which were designed in part to hedge an Enron investment in a bankrupt broadband company, Rhythm NetConnections. As part of the capitalization of the Raptor entities, Enron issued common stock in exchange for a note receivable of $1.2 billion. Enron increased notes receivable and shareholders' equity to reflect this transaction, which appears to violate generally accepted accounting principles. Additionally, Enron failed to consolidate the LJM and Raptor SPEs into financial statements when subsequent information revealed they should have been consolidated.

OBSCURE DISCLOSURES REVEALED

A very confusing footnote in Enron's 2000 financial statements described the above transactions. Douglas Carmichael, the Wollman Distinguished Professor of Accounting at Baruch College in New York City, told *The Wall Street Journal* in November of 2001 that most people would be hard pressed to understand the effects of these disclosures on the financial statements, casting doubt on both the quality of the company's earnings as well as the business purpose of the transaction. By April 2001 other skeptics arrived on the scene. A number of analysts questioned the lack of transparency of Enron's disclosures. One analyst was quoted as saying, "The notes just don't make sense, and we read notes for a living." Skilling was very quick to reply with arrogant comments and, in one case, even called an analyst a derogatory name. What Skilling and Fastow apparently underestimated was that, because of such actions, the market was beginning to perceive the company with greater and greater skepticism, thus eroding its trust and the company's reputation.

IT ALL COMES TUMBLING DOWN

In February 2001 Lay announced his retirement and named Skilling president and CEO of Enron. In February Skilling held the company's annual conference with analysts, bragging that the stock (then valued around $80) should be trading at around $126 per share.

In March Enron and Blockbuster announced the cancellation of their video-on-demand deal. By that time the stock had fallen to the mid-$60s. Throughout the spring and summer, risky deals Enron had made in underperforming investments of various kinds began to unravel, causing it to suffer a huge cash shortfall. Senior management, which had been voting with its feet since August 2000, selling Enron stock in the bull market, continued to exit, collectively hundreds of millions of dollars richer for the experience. On August 14, just six months after being named CEO, Skilling himself resigned, citing "personal reasons." The stock price slipped below $40 that week and, except for a brief recovery in early October after the sale of Portland General, continued its slide to below $30 a share.

Also in August, in an internal memorandum to Lay, a company vice-president, Sherron Watkins, described her reservations about the lack of disclosure of the substance of the related party transactions with the SPEs run by Fastow. She concluded the memo by stating her fear that the company might "implode under a series of accounting scandals." Lay notified the company's attorneys, Vinson & Elkins, as well as the audit partner at Enron's auditing firm, Arthur Andersen LLP, so the matter could be investigated further. The proverbial "ship" of Enron had struck the iceberg that would eventually sink it.

On October 16 Enron announced its first quarterly loss in more than four years after taking charges of $1 billion on poorly performing businesses. The company terminated the

Raptor hedging arrangements which, if they had continued, would have resulted in it issuing 58 million Enron shares to offset the company's private equity losses, severely diluting earnings. It also disclosed the reversal of the $1.2 billion entry to assets and equities it had made as a result of dealings with these arrangements. It was this disclosure that got the SEC's attention.

On October 17 the company announced it had changed plan administrators for its employees' 401(k) pension plan, thus by law locking their investments for a period of 30 days and preventing workers from selling their Enron stock. The company contends this decision had in fact been made months earlier. However true that might be, the timing of the decision certainly has raised suspicions.

On October 22 Enron announced the SEC was looking into the related party transactions between Enron and the partnerships owned by Fastow, who was fired two days later. On November 8 Enron announced a restatement of its financial statements back to 1997 to reflect consolidation of the SPEs it had omitted, as well as to book Andersen's recommended adjustments from those years, which the company had previously "deemed immaterial." This restatement resulted in another $591 million in losses over the four years as well as an additional $628 million in liabilities as of the end of 2000. The equity markets immediately reacted to the restatement, driving the stock price to less than $10 a share. One analyst's report stated the company had burned through $5 billion in cash in 50 days.

A merger agreement with smaller cross-town competitor Dynegy was announced on November 9, but rescinded by Dynegy on November 28 on the basis of Enron's lack of full disclosure of its off-balance-sheet debt, downgrading Enron's rating to junk status. On November 30 the stock closed at an astonishing 26 cents a share. The company filed for bankruptcy protection on December 2.

THE AFTERMATH

Unquestionably, the Enron implosion has wreaked more havoc on the accounting profession than any other case in U.S. history. Critics in the media, Congress and elsewhere are calling into question not only the adequacy of U.S. disclosure practices but also the integrity of the independent audit process. The general public still questions how CPA firms can maintain audit independence while at the same time engaging in consulting work, often for fees that dwarf those of the audit. Companies that deal in special purpose entities and complex financial instruments similar to Enron's have suffered significant declines in their stock prices. The scandal threatens to undermine confidence in financial markets in the United States and abroad.

In a characteristic move, the SEC and the public accounting profession have been among the first to respond to the Enron crisis. Unfortunately, and sadly reminiscent of financial disasters in the 1970s and 1980s, this response will likely be viewed by investors, creditors, lawmakers and employees of Enron as "too little, too late."

In an "op-ed" piece for *The Wall Street Journal* on December 11, SEC Chairman Harvey Pitt called the current outdated reporting and financial disclosure system the financial "perfect storm." He stated that under the current quarterly and annual reporting system, information is often stale on arrival and mandated financial disclosures are often "arcane and impenetrable." To reassure investors and restore confidence in financial reporting, Pitt called for a joint response from the public and private sectors that included, among other things,

- A system of "current" disclosures, supplementing and updating quarterly and annual information with disclosure of material information on a real-time basis.

- Public company disclosure of significant current "trend" and "evaluative" data in addition to historical information.

- Identification of "most critical accounting principles" by all public companies in their annual reports.

- More timely and responsive accounting standard setting on the part of the private sector.

- An environment of cooperation between the SEC and registrants that encourages public companies and their auditors to seek advice on disclosure issues in advance.

- An effective and transparent system of self-regulation for the accounting profession, subject to SEC's rigorous, but nonduplicative, oversight.

- More proactive oversight by audit committees who understand financial accounting principles as well as how they are applied.

The CEOs of the Big Five accounting firms made a joint statement on December 4 committing to develop improved guidance on disclosure of related party transactions, SPEs and market risks for derivatives including energy contracts for the 2001 reporting period. In addition, the Big Five called for modernization of the financial reporting system in the United States to make it more timely and relevant, including more nonfinancial information on entity performance. They also vowed to streamline the accounting standard-setting process to make it more responsive to the rapid changes that occur in a technology-driven economy.

Since the Enron debacle, the AICPA has been engaged in significant damage control measures to restore confidence in the profession, displaying the banner "Enron: The AICPA, the Profession, and the Public Interest" on its Web site. It has announced the imminent issuance of an exposure draft on a new audit standard on fraud (the third in five years), providing more specific guidance than currently found in SAS no. 82, *Consideration of Fraud in a Financial Statement Audit.* The Institute has also promised a revised standard on reviews of quarterly financial statements, as well as the issuance, in the second quarter of 2002, of an exposure draft of a standard to improve the audit process. These standards had already been on the drawing board as part of the AICPA's response to the report of the Blue Ribbon Panel on Audit Effectiveness, issued in 2000.

In late December the AICPA issued a tool kit for auditors to use in identifying and auditing related party transactions. While it breaks no new ground, the tool kit provides, in one place, an overview of the accounting and auditing literature, SEC requirements and best practice guidance concerning related party transactions. It also includes checklists and other tools for auditors to use in gathering evidence and disclosing related party transactions.

In January the AICPA board of directors announced that it would cooperate fully with the SEC's proposal for new rules for the peer review and disciplinary process for CPA firms of SEC registrants. The new system would be managed by a board, a majority of which would be public members, enhancing the peer review process for the largest firms and requiring more rigorous and continuous monitoring. The staff of the new board would administer the reviews. In protest, the Public Oversight Board informed Pitt that it would terminate its existence in March 2002, leaving the future peer review process in a state of uncertainty. The SEC and the AICPA are now engaged in talks with the POB to reassure the board it will continue to be a vital part of the peer review process in the future.

The AICPA has also approved a resolution to support prohibitions that would prevent audit firms from performing systems design and implementation as well as internal audit outsourcing for public audit clients. While asserting that it does not believe prohibition of these services will make audits more effective or prevent financial failures, the board has stated it feels the move is necessary to restore public confidence in the profession. These prohibitions were at the center of the controversy last year between the profession and the SEC under the direction of former Chairman Arthur Levitt. Big Five CPA firms and the AICPA lobbied heavily and prevailed in that controversy, winning the right to retain these services and being required only to disclose their fees.

The impact of Enron is now being felt at the highest levels of government as legislators engage in endless debate and accusation, quarreling over the influence of money in politics. The GAO has requested that the White House disclose documents concerning appointments to President George W. Bush's Task Force on Energy, chaired by Vice-President Dick Cheney, former CEO of Halliburton. The White House has refused, and the GAO has filed suit, the first of its kind in history. Congressional investigations are expected to continue well into 2002 and beyond. Lawmakers are expected to investigate not only disclosure practices at Enron, but for all public companies, concerning SPEs, related party transactions and use of "mark-to-market" accounting.

Kenneth Lay resigned as Enron's CEO, under pressure from creditor groups. Lay, Skilling and Fastow still have much to explain. In addition, Enron's board of directors, and especially the audit committee, will be in the "hot seat" and rightfully so.

The Justice Department opened a criminal investigation and formed a national task force made up of federal prosecutors in Houston, San Francisco, New York and several other cities to investigate the possibility of fraud in the company's dealings. Interestingly, to illustrate how far-reaching Enron's ties are to government and political sources at all levels, U.S. Attorney General John Ashcroft, as well as his entire Houston office, disqualified themselves from the investigation because of either political, economic or family ties.

It appears that 2002 is shaping up to be a year of unprecedented changes for a profession that is already coping with an identity crisis.

WHERE WERE THE AUDITORS?

Arthur Andersen LLP, after settling two other massive lawsuits earlier in 2001, is preparing for a storm of litigation as well as a possible criminal investigation in the wake of the Enron collapse. Enron was the firm's second-largest client. Andersen, who had the job not only of Enron's external but also its internal audits for the years in question, kept a staff on permanent assignment at Enron's offices. Many of Enron's internal accountants, CFOs and controllers were former Andersen executives. Because of these relationships, as well as Andersen's extensive concurrent consulting practice, members of Congress, the press and others are calling Andersen's audit independence into question. Indeed, they are using the case to raise doubts about the credibility of the audit process for all Big Five firms who do such work.

So far, Andersen has acknowledged its role in the fiasco, while defending its accounting and auditing practices. In a *Wall Street Journal* editorial on December 4, as well as in testimony before Congress the following week, Joseph Berardino, CEO, was forthright in his views. He committed the firm to full cooperation in the investigations as well as to a leadership role in potential solutions.

Enron dismissed Andersen as its auditor on January 17, 2002, citing document destruction and lack of guidance on accounting policy issues as the reasons. Andersen countered with the contention that in its mind the relationship had terminated on December 2, 2001, the day the firm filed for Chapter 11 bankruptcy protection.

The fact that Andersen is no longer officially associated with Enron will, unfortunately, have little impact on forces now in place that may, in the eyes of some, determine the firm's very future. Andersen is now under formal investigation by the SEC as well as various committees of both the U.S. Senate and House of Representatives of the U.S. Congress. To make matters worse for it, and to the astonishment of many, Andersen admitted it destroyed perhaps thousands of documents and electronic files related to the engagement, in accordance with "firm policy," supposedly before the SEC issued a subpoena for them. The firm's lawyers issued an internal memorandum on October 12 reminding employees of the firm's document retention and destruction policies. The firm fired David B. Duncan, partner in charge of the Enron engagement, placed four other partners on leave and replaced the entire management team of the Houston office. Duncan invoked his Fifth Amendment rights against self-incrimination at a congressional hearing in January. Several other Andersen partners testified that Duncan and his staff acted in violation of firm policy. However, in view of the timing of the October 12 memorandum, Congress and the press are questioning whether the decision to shred documents extended farther up the chain of command. Andersen has suspended its firm policy for retention of records and asked former U.S. Senator John Danforth to conduct a comprehensive review of the firm's records management policy and to recommend improvements.

In a move to bolster its image, Andersen also has retained former Federal Reserve Chairman Paul Volcker to lead an outside board that will advise it in making "fundamental change" in its audit process. Other members of the board include P. Roy Vagelos, former chairman and CEO of Merck & Co., and Charles A. Bowsher, current chairman of the Public Oversight Board, which disbanded in March. Volcker also named a seven-member advisory panel made up of prominent corporate and accounting executives that will review proposed reforms to the firm's audit process.

Hindsight is so clear that it sometimes belies the complexity of the problem. Although fraud has not yet been proven to be a factor in Enron's misstatements, some of the classic risk factors associated with management fraud outlined in SAS no. 82 are evident in the Enron case. Those include management characteristics, industry conditions and operating characteristics of the company. Although written five years ago, the list almost looks as if it was excerpted from Enron's case:

• Unduly aggressive earnings targets and management bonus compensation based on those targets.

- Excessive interest by management in maintaining stock price or earnings trend through the use of unusually aggressive accounting practices.

- Management setting unduly aggressive financial targets and expectations for operating personnel.

- Inability to generate sufficient cash flow from operations while reporting earnings and earnings growth.

- Assets, liabilities, revenues or expenses based on significant estimates that involve unusually subjective judgments such as . . . reliability of financial instruments.

- Significant related party transactions.

These factors are common threads in the tapestry that is described of the environment leading to fraud. They were incorporated into SAS no. 82 on the basis of research into fraud cases of the 1970s and 1980s in the hope that auditors would learn from the past. Andersen will have to explain when and how it identified these factors, as well as how it responded and how it communicated with Enron's board about them.

More important, Andersen will have to explain why it delayed notifying the SEC after learning of the internal Enron memo warning of problems. In addition, it will have to explain why the Houston office destroyed the thousands of documents related to the Enron audits for 1997 through 2000. Only time will tell, but it appears the firm is in serious trouble. In the end, and also characteristic of cases like this, the chief parties likely to benefit from this process are the attorneys.

THE HUMAN FACTOR

The Enron story has produced many victims, the most tragic of which is a former vice-chairman of the company who committed suicide, apparently in connection with his role in the scandal. Another 4,500 individuals have seen their careers ended abruptly by the reckless acts of a few. Enron's core values of respect, integrity, communication and excellence stand in satirical contrast to allegations now being made public. Personally, I had referred several of our best and brightest accounting, finance and MBA graduates to Enron, hoping they could gain valuable experience from seeing things done right. These included a very bright training consultant who had lost her job in 2000 with a Houston consulting firm as a result of a reduction in force. She has lost her second job in 18 months through no fault of her own. Other former students still hanging on at Enron face an uncertain future as the company fights for survival.

The old saying goes, "Lessons learned hard are learned best." Some former Enron employees are embittered by the way they have been treated by the company that was once "the best in the business." Others disagree. In the words of one of my former students who is still hanging on: "Just for the record, my time and experience at Enron have been nothing short of fantastic. I could not have asked for a better place to be or better people to work with. Please, though, remember this: Never take customer and employee confidence for granted. That confidence is easy to lose and tough—to impossible—to regain."

RESOURCES

"A Chronology of Enron's Recent Woes." *Wall Street Journal*. December 20, 2001.

"Accounting and Auditing for Related Parties and Related Party Transactions: A Toolkit for Accountants and Auditors." www.aicpa.org.

"AICPA Statement of James G. Castellano, AICPA Chair, Barry Melancon, AICPA President and CEO." American Institute of CPAs press release. December 4, 2001.

The Associated Press. "Business: Enron Fires Arthur Andersen Accounting Firm." *Nando Times*. January 17, 2002.

Beckett, Paul, et al. "PNC Shakes Up Banking Sector; Investors Exit." *Wall Street Journal* (Heard on the Street). January 30, 2002.

Berger, Eric. "The Fall of Enron/Like Enron Employees, Lay Could Lose Nearly All/Vast Fortune from Stocks, Bonuses Susceptible to Lawsuits." *Houston Chronicle*. January 25, 2002: A19.

Brown, Ken, et al. "Andersen Fires Partner It Says Led Shredding of Documents." *Wall Street Journal*. January 16, 2002.

Browning, E. S. and Jonathan Weil. "Stocks Take a Beating as Accounting Worries Spread Beyond Enron." *Wall Street Journal*. January 30, 2002.

Clow, Robert. "Enron in Crisis." *Financial Times*. November 9, 2001: 27.

"Certified Public Scapegoat." Editorial, *New York Times*. January 25, 2002.

Eichwald, Kurt (New York Times). "Exec Abuses Criticized in Enron Report." *Waco Tribune-Herald*. February 3, 2002.

Emshwiller, John R. and Rebecca Smith. "Corporate Veil—Behind Enron's Fall, A Culture of Operating Outside Public's View." *Wall Street Journal*. December 5, 2001: A1.

Emshwiller, John R. and Rebecca Smith. "Murky Waters: A Primer on Enron Partnerships." *Wall Street Journal*. January 21, 2002: C1, C14.

Enron 401K plan lawsuit. www.enronsuit.com/defendants.html.

"The Enron Crisis: the AICPA, the Profession and the Public Interest." www.aicpa.org.

"Enron Provides Additional Information About Related Party and Off-Balance Sheet Transactions; Company to Restate Earnings for 1997–2001." Enron press release. November 8, 2001.

Flood, Mary. "Bankruptcy Tip of Iceberg in Broadening Legal Mess." *Houston Chronicle*. December 11, 2001: Business 1.

Goldberg, Laura and L. M. Sixel. "Enron on Edge of Collapse/Stock Value Plunges as Dynegy Bails Out; Bankruptcy Expected." *Houston Chronicle*. November 29, 2001: A1.

Grunder, Eric. "Market's Bullish—Or Is It?" *The Record*. December 9, 2001.

Ivanovich, David. "New Twists in Enron Fall: Local Feds, Ashcroft Recused from Inquiry." *Houston Chronicle*. January 11, 2002: A1.

Lee, Susan. "The Dismal Science: Enron's Success Story." *Wall Street Journal*. December 26, 2001: A11.

Oppel, Richard A. Jr. and Stephen Labaton. "Enron Hearings Open, Focusing on Destroyed Papers." *New York Times*. January 25, 2002.

Pitt, Harvey L. "How to Prevent Future Enrons." *Wall Street Journal*. December 11, 2001: A18.

"Power Play/Enron Timeline." *Houston Chronicle*. November 10, 2001: Business 4.

Samuelson, Robert J. "A Complicated Collapse." MSNBC. December 19, 2001.

Smith, Rebecca and John R. Emshwiller. "Fancy Finances Were Key to Enron's Success, and Now to Its Distress." *Wall Street Journal*. November 2, 2001:A1.

Statement from Big Five CEOs on Enron, PR newswire.

Swartz, Mimi. "How Enron Blew It." *Texas Monthly*. November 2001: 136–139, 171–178.

Taub, Stephen. "Angry Employees Sue Enron." www.CFO.com. November 26, 2001.

Weil, Jonathan. "After Enron, 'Mark to Market' Accounting Gets Scrutiny." *Wall Street Journal*. December 4, 2001: C1.

Weil, Jonathan. "What Enron's Financial Reports Did—and Didn't—Reveal." *Wall Street Journal*. November 5, 2001: C1.

PUBLIC ACCOUNTING: PROFESSION OR BUSINESS?

—John C. Bogle

John Bogle is the founder of the Vanguard Group. In a prescient speech evaluating the performance of the accounting industry, years before the Enron-Andersen debacle became public, Bogle speaks of the necessity of integrity in the financial markets for the sake of efficient functioning of the capitalist system. In support of a contention that now might seem more commonplace, Bogle suggests that the accountants who are asked to give us transparent and accurate information should be independent of those whom they audit so they can be objective in their assessments. Bogle sees accounting turning from a profession into a business, which means concentrating on making money more than doing one's job. He looks at the five problem areas that he sees as challenging the independence of the accounting profession: (1) the inadequacy of the Generally Accepted Accounting Principles (GAAP); (2) earnings management; (3) stock options; (4) abusive tax shelters; (5) novel forms of firm structure.

OCTOBER 16, 2000

Debates are the order of the day in the United States this month, and we've already witnessed two debates between our presidential candidates and one between our vice-presidential candidates. After what I've observed, I want to assure you that in my remarks today, I'll stay "on message," as the not-entirely-felicitous saying goes, that I will answer directly and forthrightly all questions that may be asked, that I have been given no clever one-liners by my staff, and that I will neither smirk nor sigh when my worthy opponent, if an opponent he be, has the floor. I hope this sounds like progress!

In this debate on the future of the accounting profession, I'm going to focus largely on the issue of auditor independence. While I have no business degree nor attest certificate, I've pored over more than my share of corporate and mutual fund financial statements. And while I have never worked in a controllership or treasury function nor have I been trained

"Public Accounting: Profession or Business," by John C. Bogle. Reprinted from the Seymour Jones Distinguished Lecture at the Vincent C. Ross Institute of Accounting Research, Stern School of Business, New York University (10/16/00). Reprinted with permission of the author.

as a security analyst, I have been both an eye-witness to, and active participant in, the sweep of financial history over the past 50 years and have accordingly garnered a considerable amount of study and experience in virtually all phases of American finance. Through this experience, I have developed a passionate concern about the well-being of our financial markets, and this evening I'd like to discuss my views with you. (I am, of course, speaking for myself and not for any of the organizations with which I am associated.)

The integrity of financial markets—markets that are active, liquid and honest, with participants who are fully and fairly informed—is *absolutely central* to the sound functioning of any system of democratic capitalism worth its salt. It is only through such markets that literally trillions upon trillions of dollars—the well-spring of today's powerful American economy—could have been raised in the past decade that became capital for the plant and equipment of our Old Economy and the capital for the technology and innovation of our New Economy. Only the complete confidence of investors in the integrity of the financial information they received allowed these investment needs to be met at the lowest possible cost of capital.

Sound securities markets require sound financial information. It is as simple as that. Investors require—and have a right to require—complete information about each and every security, information that fairly and honestly represents every significant fact and figure that might be needed to evaluate the worth of a corporation. Not only is accuracy required but, more than that, a broad sweep of information that provides every appropriate figure that a prudent, probing, sophisticated professional investor might require in the effort to decide whether a security should be purchased, held, or sold. *Full disclosure. Fair disclosure. Complete disclosure.* Those are the watchwords of the financial system that has contributed so much to our nation's growth, progress and prosperity.

INDEPENDENCE

It is unarguable, I think, that the independent oversight of financial figures is central to that disclosure system. Indeed independence is at integrity's very core. And, for more than a century, the responsibility for the independent oversight of corporate financial statements has fallen to America's public accounting profession. It is the auditor's stamp on a financial statement that gives it its validity, its respect, and its acceptability by investors. And only if the auditor's work is comprehensive, skeptical, inquisitive, and rigorous, can we have confidence that financial statements speak the truth.

Our government, our regulators, our corporations, and our accountants have, over this long span, properly placed the auditor's independence from his client at the keystone of our financial reporting system. And auditor independence has come to mean an absence of any and all relationships that could seriously jeopardize—either in fact or in appearance—the validity of the audit, and, therefore, of the client's financial statements. The auditor, in short, is the guardian of financial integrity. On the need to maintain, above all, this principle of independence, I hear not a single voice of dissent—not from the corporations, not from the profession, not from the regulators, not from the bar, not from the brokers and bankers—the financial market intermediaries—and not from the institutional investors who, as trustees, hold and manage the securities portfolios of their clients. So far, so good.

But being for independence is a bit like being for God, for motherhood and for the American way. For the relationship between auditor and client is complex—beginning with the fact that it is the client who *pays* the auditor for its services, creating an interdependency that is anything *but* independence. Long ago, we made a societal decision to accept that conflict because, simply put, we couldn't figure out any arrangement that was better. A system of mandatory audits by a Federal agency, for example, would probably have been intolerable even to those most disposed toward using government as the first line of attack in dealing with any other national issue.

So over the years we've developed a whole series of structures and safeguards to minimize the susceptibility of the audit firm to the dominion of the client, and put in place requirements designed to assure that the auditor remains free of entanglements that threaten his objectivity and independence. But as times have changed, these issues have become increasingly complex, and the entanglements have become more numerous. In 1997, in part as a response to these developments, Securities and Exchange Commission Chairman Arthur Levitt, in concert with the American Institute of Certified Public Accountants, established the Independence Standards Board (ISB), giving it the responsibility of establishing independence standards applicable to the audits of public entities, in order to serve the public interest and to protect and promote investors' confidence in the securities markets.

THE INDEPENDENCE STANDARDS BOARD

By agreement, the initial membership of the ISB consisted of four members from the accounting profession and four public members, one of whom would serve as chairman. The same eight individuals who joined the Board in 1997 continue to serve today, and I have been privileged to serve as one of the public members. After nearly three years of meetings with my public colleagues, let me assure you that there can be no question of their staunch and complete independence, to say nothing of their integrity, their intelligence and the dedication that they have brought to their task. *Business Week* recently stated that most of the Board members were "tied to" the profession, implying that one or more of the public members was less than independent. When I challenged its editors to specify the party or parties involved and describe any inappropriate bias, the inane allegation was promptly withdrawn. The independent members *are* independent.

While the four non-public members are of course members of the profession, I can tell you that in three years of working with them I have developed a high respect for the integrity, intelligence and dedication they too have demonstrated. Of course their point of view is hardly independent of their professional interests, but it is a serious, respectable, thoughtful, informed viewpoint, one that has helped the public members better understand, not, I think, the principles involved, but the complex issues involved in implementation—in taking sound and fair actions that give force to the principles.

I came to the Board with but a single preconception: A growing concern that many of the great professions that have served our society so well are moving rapidly toward becoming businesses, a trend that, if taken to the extreme, would undermine the sound and durable principles on which they were founded. In the dog-eat-dog, money-driven, competitive world in which we live today, I suppose it would be surprising were it not so. And surely many benefits have resulted: A greater appetite for enterprise growth, likely greater efficiency and organizational certainty, perhaps even greater creativity and innovation. Such benefits are not to be disdained. But those benefits can carry a societal cost—a diminution of traditional standards, a reduction in focus on clients and, at least in some fields, an increase in costs. But the heart of the matter is that there is a difference, however difficult to measure, between a business and a profession. When that line is crossed, we as a society are the losers.

BUSINESS VS. PROFESSION

My concerns, as you might imagine, are not mere abstractions. As I observe the mutual fund industry, in which I've spent 50 years, I see it moving from a profession—investment management—to a business—product marketing. I see fewer mutual funds that focus on sound investment principles, and more funds—often higher-risk, aggressive funds—created to meet the demands of the marketplace for the transitory fads and fashions of the day—"hot new products," if you will. I see portfolio strategies based on short-term speculation rather than long-term investment, with an attendant quantum leap in portfolio turnover. And I see costs of management soaring primarily to fund massive advertising campaigns and only partly to enhance investment research and analysis. Fund expenses have risen almost in lock-step with assets, meaning that the lion's share of the truly staggering economies of scale inherent in managing money are being arrogated by the managers rather than flowed through to the shareholders. This diversion of investment returns means that the financial interests of the clients are being subordinated to the financial interests of their trustees, whose primary concern was once acting as good stewards for those who have entrusted them with their assets. It is not a big stretch to recognize a similar pattern—albeit in a very different way—in the medical profession, where the interests of the patient seem clearly to have been superseded by the interests of the care-givers—the insurance-industry/drug-producer/private-HMO complex.

   I note the pervasiveness of the societal trend of professions to become businesses because it may help explain the similar trend in public accounting, though I would argue that the high standards of the attestation profession may, fortunately, have mitigated its full fruition. Nonetheless, over the years, attestation has come to account for only about one-third of the $26 billion of revenues of today's "Big Five" accounting firms, with tax services accounting for one-quarter. The remainder, not far from one-half of revenues, is derived from consulting, management and advisory services. The potential problem that arises from this trend, obviously, is that the desire to garner or retain a highly lucrative consulting contract from an audit client could jeopardize the auditor's independence. Admittedly, I have seen no independent studies which have directly associated audit failures with related consulting contracts. On the other hand, those relationships, if they exist, would be difficult to discover, and in any event causality would be impossible to establish. But as I testified at the SEC's hearings on Auditor Independence Requirements in July: "Studies cannot always confirm what common sense makes clear."

THE SEC'S INDEPENDENCE PROPOSAL

The SEC's proposed independence rule would, among other things, provide new—and often more appropriate—principles for determining whether an auditor is independent, largely tracking earlier standards established or being established by the ISB relating to investments in audit clients, family and employment relationships and appraisal and valuation services. These enhanced and modernized standards seem to have generated little controversy, and I hold the view that the establishment and maintenance of such independence standards should remain the province of the ISB, and that the proposed rule-making in these areas is unnecessary.

The other principal rule amendment, however, has generated a firestorm of controversy. It identifies certain management and consulting services that, if provided to an audit client, would impair the auditor's independence. The services that the public accountant would be effectively barred from providing include those which involve either a mutual or conflicting interest with the client; the auditing of one's own work; functioning as management or an employee of the client; or acting as the client's advocate. Expressed as general principles, honestly, it is unimaginable to me that any reasonable person could disagree *in the abstract* that such roles would threaten—or, at the very least, be perceived to threaten—the auditor's independence.

It must also be clear that, whether or not the auditor has the backbone to maintain its independence under these circumstances, many management and consulting arrangements could easily be perceived as representing a new element in the relationship between auditor and corporation—a *business* relationship with a *customer* rather than a *professional* relationship with a *client*. Surely this issue goes to the very core of the central issue of philosophy that I expressed earlier: The movement of auditing from profession to business, with all the potential conflicts of interest that entails. So I come down with a firm endorsement of the *substance* of the proposed SEC rule, which would in effect bar such relationships.

Of course, I have read extensive material from the opponents of that rule making the opposite case. Some arguments seem entirely worthy of consideration, especially those relating to technical—but nonetheless real—issues that engender unnecessary constraints on an auditor's entering into *any* strategic alliances or joint ventures, or that relate to the complexity in clearly defining "material direct investment" or "affiliate of the audit client" and so on. Personally, I would hope and expect that this bevy of issues will be resolved by the profession and the Commission meeting and reasoning together.

But other opposition seemed to me to be rather knee-jerk and strident (rather like those debates I mentioned at the outset). No, I for one don't believe the SEC proposals represent "an unwarranted and intrusive regulation" of the accounting profession. And, no, I for one do *not* believe that the new rules "strait-jacket" the profession. And, yes, I do believe that the growing multiplicity of inter-relationships between auditor and client is a serious threat to the concept of independence, the rock foundation of sound financial statements and fair financial markets alike. In this context, I was stunned to see this recent statement from one of the senior officers of the investment company industry group for one of the Big Five firms. "Fund companies have increasingly looked to . . . big accounting firms to help them with operational, regulatory, strategic and international decisions." If that isn't functioning as management, I'm not sure what would be.

THE FUTURE OF THE PROFESSION

While I am but a layman, I'd now like to comment on some issues that relate to the future of the profession. I begin by expressing not only my *hope,* but my expectation that public accounting will continue to operate successfully and in the public interest under the proposed SEC rules that prohibit the provision of most management and consulting services to clients. Doubtless, there are problems—serious problems—in determining the precise language and interpretation of the rules, but I'm enough of an optimist to believe that, in the environment of openness and good will on both sides, changes can be made without undermining the bedrock principle of the independence.

But there are other disturbing issues that affect the profession today, and I'd like to close by presenting just five of them. First is the question of basic accounting principles. Can the accounting principles that have served the Old Economy so well over so many years properly be applied to the New Economy? Is what is seen as a narrow accounting model applying to businesses with tangible capital equipment, hard assets and even so-called "good will" applicable to businesses in which human capital is the principal asset, information is the stock in trade and "first mover" status is the driving force in valuation? Clearly, many, indeed most, New Economy companies are valued at staggering—even infinite—multiples of any earnings that GAAP could possibly uncover. Interestingly, however, during the past seven months, at least the Internet business-to-consumer companies have reconciled that gap, as it were, in favor of GAAP.

So while that seemingly omnipotent master, "the stock market" may be telling the profession that the 1930s-based model of reporting doesn't work any more, please don't write off too hastily the possibility that the *model* may be right and the *market* wrong. And don't forget that no matter what "the market" may say today, its level on future tomorrows well down the road *will*—not *may*—be determined by earnings and dividends. Nonetheless, a re-examination of today's basic accounting principles should be a high priority. And let the chips fall where they may.

Second is the question of earnings management. I noted in a speech a year ago, we live in a world of managed earnings. While it is corporate executives who do the managing, they do so with at least the tacit approval of corporate directors and auditors, and with the enthusiastic endorsement of institutional investors with short-term time horizons, even speculators and arbitrageurs—a "happy conspiracy" as I called it then. Like it or not, corporate strategy and financial accounting alike focus on meeting the earnings expectations of "the Street" quarter after quarter. The desideratum is steady earnings growth—manage it to at least the 12% level if you can—and at all costs avoid falling short of the earnings expectations at which the corporation has hinted, or whispered, or "ballparked" before the year began. If all else fails, obscure the real results by merging, taking a big one-time write-off and relying on pooling-of-interest accounting (although that procedure will soon become unavailable). All of this creative financial engineering apparently serves to inflate stock prices, enrich corporate managers, and to deliver to institutional investors what they want.

But if the stock market is to be the arbiter of value, it will do its job best, in my judgment, if it sets its valuations based on accurate corporate financial reporting and a focus on the long-term prospects of the corporations it values. The market today seems to be focusing at least a bit more on those verities, but there is still much room for improvement. For while the accounting practices of America's corporations may well be the envy of the world, our nation's financial environment has become permeated with the concept of managed earnings. There is a "numbers game" going on, and *pro forma* operating profits permeate financial statements. *Pro forma* seems to mean, in an Alice-in-Wonderland-world, whatever the Corporation chooses it to mean, excluding such charges as amortization of good will, taxes on option exercises, equity losses in investees, in-process R&D, for example, as these costs vanish in the struggle to meet earnings expectations. Since this game is played in press releases, it is not clear where the solution lies. But I hope that the accounting profession will get involved before the coin of the realm—earnings statements with integrity—is further debased. That corporate clients may not be enamored of having the issue of managed earnings raised is—or ought to be—irrelevant.

Third is the stock option issue. Financial statements place options in a sort-of "no man's land" in which options are not treated as compensation. But, as Warren Buffett has long argued, if options *are* compensation, why aren't they charged to earnings? And if options *aren't* compensation, what are they? Surely the profession ought to play a more aggressive role in answering that question and taking a stand on proper stock option accounting. A recent study by a Wall Street firm listed four industry groups in which accounting for stock options would have reduced earnings by an average of 28% in 1997, 23% in 1998, and another 25% in 1999; 21 companies in which 1999 earnings would have been reduced from 50% to 700%(!); and 13 companies with 1999 *pro forma* (there's that word again) pre-tax stock option compensation ranging from $500 million to $1.1 billion. Quite important enough as an issue now, the question of accounting for stock options will rise to even greater importance as corporations whose stocks have faltered—even plummeted—in the recent market decline reprice their options. I hope that FASB interpretation 44 on repricing underwater options will help to deal with this issue.

ABUSIVE TAX SHELTERS

The case of overly aggressive and potentially illegal tax shelters constitutes a fourth issue. Earlier this year, Treasury Secretary Lawrence Summers excoriated the proliferation of "engineered transactions that are devoid of economic substance . . . with no goal other than to reduce a corporation's tax liabilities." The Secretary is right: Such transactions strike a blow at the integrity—here, an especially well-chosen word—of the tax system. And when companies demand—and receive—"black box" features in such transactions designed to make them impenetrable to all but those who designed them, something perilously close to fraud is going on. He challenges, I assume accurately, the professional conduct of the firms involved in the creation of abusive tax shelters and suggests sanctions on firms—here, the treasury secretary pointedly included public accountants—that issue opinions, limits on contingent fees, and excise taxes on such fee income.

It is not my place to evaluate the role of the accounting profession in these tax abuses. But it must be clear that any firm that helps develop such schemes or opines on their purported validity wins favor with the client involved, and runs a heavy risk of compromising its independence. Faustian bargains of that nature, to the extent they may exist, could even require the addition of tax services to the list of services that public accounting firms would be barred from offering to their clients. Surely, that's a high price for public accounting firms to pay.

The fifth and final issue I raise regarding independence of the future of the profession relates to the novel forms of firm structure and organizations that are now evolving. (The ISB published a Discussion Memorandum on this subject a year ago, and has received numerous comments, but has tabled the issue at the request of the SEC staff.) The traditional simple partnership model is being supplanted by alternative business structures. In one model, a group of smaller attest firms are consolidated through the sale of their non-audit practice to a third party (in a private or public offering) with the audit practice retained by the partners. An operational link remains between the two parties. In another—the "roll up" model—firms are united under a single umbrella through combination and then sale of their non-audit businesses to a third party or the public. *Byzantine* is the word that comes to mind as one looks at the organizational charts portraying these relationships. While "Byzantine" isn't necessarily bad, such dual employment surely raises important independence issues. And when CPA firms—whose integrity and independence are their stock in trade—are in fact principally investment advisory firms offering financial products sponsored by their parents, a whole other set of questions about the meaning of *professional responsibility* come to the fore.

How attest firms respond to these independence issues—and indeed whether they do— will shape the future of the profession. Most of them are clearly framed by the over-arching issue of the proper place to draw the line between business and profession. But perhaps my comments are just the ramblings of an aging Luddite who wants to bring back a proud age of tradition that will never return. In my own mutual fund industry, I *know* that the age of professional stewardship will return. While I do not understand the field of accounting nearly as well, I am confident that if financial market participants come to understand that the independent oversight of financial figures plays a critical role in our system of disclosure, that independence is at the core of integrity and that the integrity of our financial markets is essential to their well-being, the age of professional accounting too will shake off today's challenges and return to its roots.

ACCOUNTING IN CRISIS

Reform Is Urgent. Here's What Needs to Be Done

—NANETTE BYRNES, MIKE MCNAMEE, DIANE BRADY,
LOUIS LAVELLE AND CHRISTOPHER PALMERI

BusinessWeek *in January 2002 devoted an entire issue to the Enron-Andersen debacle. It proposed seven steps that must be taken to restore confidence in the accounting profession: (1) enact self-regulation with teeth; (2) bar consulting to audit clients; (3) mandate rotation of auditors; (4) impose more forensic accounting; (5) limit auditors' moves to companies; (6) reform the audit committees; (7) clean up the accounting rules. As you'll see later in this chapter, most of these recommendations actually found their way into the later Sarbanes-Oxley Act.*

A few years ago, it would hardly have seemed possible: The nation's attention, from the halls of Congress to main street, has been riveted on an accounting scandal, a subject so abstruse it rarely makes the front page. But as the tawdry chapters in the Enron fiasco unfold like some penny dreadful, with explosive revelations of hidden partnerships, shredded documents and shocking conflicts of interest, it's clear that the fall of Houston-based Enron is in a class by itself.

Everything about this debacle is huge: a $50 billion bankruptcy, $32 billion lost in market cap and employee retirement accounts drained of more than $1 billion. The lapses and conflicts on the part of Enron's auditor Arthur Andersen are equally glaring. Andersen had been Enron's outside auditor since the 1980s, but in the mid-1990s, the firm was given another assignment: to conduct Enron's internal audits as well. In effect, the firm was working on the accounting systems and controls with one hand and attesting to the numbers they produced with the other. And the ties went even deeper. Enron's own in-house financial team was dominated by former Andersen partners. Then, as the firm began its last, rapid plunge toward bankruptcy, the Andersen auditors began frantically tossing records of their work into the shredder.

For working both sides of the street, Andersen was rewarded richly. In 2000, the firm earned $25 million in audit fees from Enron, and another $27 million in consulting fees and other work. Sure, it's possible that Andersen's auditors blocked all of those connections from their minds and managed still to render an objective opinion, but even former insiders wonder how. "There were so many people in the Houston office who had their finger in the Enron pie," a former Andersen staffer says. "If they had somebody who said we can't sign this audit, that person would get fired."

As shocking as Enron is, it's only the latest in a dizzying succession of accounting meltdowns, from Waste Management to Cendant. Lynn E. Turner, former chief accountant for the SEC and now a professor at Colorado State University, calculates that in the past half-dozen years investors have lost close to $200 billion in earnings restatements and lost market capitalization following audit failures. And the pace seems to be accelerating. Between 1997 and 2000, the number of restatements doubled, from 116 to 233.

That sorry record has cast doubt on a once honored profession. Auditors have always been in the uncomfortable position of having to judge the financial integrity of the companies that pay them. But in the fast-moving 1990s, with intensifying pressure to produce ever rising earnings and stock prices, Corporate America began to push the accounting boundaries like never before. And auditors were thrust into a new role of enabler. "They began to emphasize too much, being a business partner" to the company, laments Phil Livingston, president of the Financial Executives Institute.

The accounting industry, which largely regulates itself, has steadfastly resisted change, even in the face of repeated audit failures and scandals. That's about to change. The size and scope of the Enron disaster is simply too huge to ignore. Eight congressional committees are investigating or planning hearings on the matter, and legislation is already in the works to force firms to abandon consulting to audit clients or face much stiffer legal liability. Securities & Exchange Commissioner Harvey L. Pitt, who himself has worked for the Big Five, is shaping a proposal for a new body that would remove discipline and investigation of audit failures from the current system of professional peer review. Says Representative John D. Dingell (D-Mich.), the ranking Democrat on the House Energy & Commerce Committee whose hearings begin in early February: "How to make accountants do their jobs will be one of our big interests."

Even after the flameout of Enron, the Big Five accounting firms have yet to acknowledge the need for fundamental change to their independence rules. Instead, in a joint statement issued on Dec. 4, the CEOs of the Big Five focused largely on improving the rules of accountancy. Industry leader James S. Turley, chairman of Ernst & Young, says that rather than an audit failure, Enron "at its core was a business failure." The American Institute of Certified Public Accountants (AICPA) as well as the other big firms declined to comment for this story.

Yet it's hard not to assign blame to the industry's decades-old system of peer review that again showed its ineffectiveness on Jan. 3. That's when Andersen announced that the firm and its Houston office had successfully passed the review conducted by fellow Big Five firm Deloitte & Touche. Amazingly, two weeks later on Jan. 15, Andersen fired its lead Enron auditor and put more Houston partners on leave. "What worries me," says University of Illinois accounting professor Andrew D. Bailey Jr., "is that there's another Enron coming around the bend."

To critics, there is a basic disconnect between the Big Five and the broader public outrage. "The whole culture of auditing is based on disclosure, yet the practices of the industry have defied this in recent years by embracing a fortress mentality," says former SEC commissioner Arthur Levitt Jr. who battled in 2000 very publicly with the industry over his proposal to limit consulting.

Whatever shape the final reforms take, they must reach to the heart of the conflicts that have damaged the auditing profession. As the debate begins, here are seven proposals that could go a long way to re-establishing the public trust:

1. ENACT SELF-REGULATION WITH TEETH

The Enron disaster has awakened investors to the accounting crisis. Roger C. Hamilton, a portfolio manager at John Hancock Value Funds, managed to unload his 600,000 Enron shares at $14 to $15 last fall before the stock totally collapsed, but he still suffered a substantial loss. Now Hamilton's joining the call for government oversight of the profession: "Then, I think, they would have to play by the rules of the game."

Under the current system of self-policing, it's difficult to figure out who's even in charge. Administered by the AICPA, an industry trade group, is a series of groups that are supposed to monitor auditor independence and audit quality. The Public Oversight Board (POB) is charged with ensuring that the public interest is considered in the oversight of auditors. But the POB relies entirely on the CPA firms for its funding and has no authority to investigate, no subpoena power and no power to punish infractions. An offshoot, the Quality Control Inquiry Committee (QCIC), investigates the roughly 50 cases of suspected audit failure raised in lawsuits each year. It too has no subpoena power and works entirely from public documents and anything the firms may volunteer. Separately, the AICPA runs a system of peer review. Although smaller firms have occasionally been censured by their peers, no Big Five firm has ever failed a review.

Today, even the industry has conceded that this system needs work. According to Ernst & Young chief Turley, the Big Five are working with the SEC to find a way to modify the peer-review process as well as ways to improve the quality of disciplinary proceedings. "The idea that the whole system is broken is wrong," says Charles A. Bowsher, chairman of the POB. "But with the series of alleged failures in the past two or three years, it needs to be looked at and strengthened."

That won't be enough. In light of the questions being raised about the profession's integrity, there is a rising call that oversight be taken out of the hands of the CPAs. The SEC's Pitt is contemplating transferring both auditor regulation and discipline to a new self-regulatory organization (SRO) staffed and overseen largely by outsiders who would take over the review process. The group's board would be dominated by public members. But this too may fall short if it leaves the setting of audit standards in the hands of the AICPA.

Former SEC chief accountant Lynn Turner wants any SRO to also make its findings public. Turner says a properly functioning auditor SRO would work almost like the respected National Transportation Safety Board. "When an airplane crashes in the morning, that night the NTSB is out investigating, and the airline is right there with them. Within a year they come out with a report on what went wrong and mandate certain things get fixed so it doesn't happen again," says Turner. "That's what our SRO needs to do."

But while it sounds good, creating such a body will be far from easy. First of all, to have real power it requires action by Congress, which in a shortened election year already has plenty of other things to do. How it will be funded is sure to be a topic of long and hot debate. Also, the history of SROs has been far from pristine. While the NTSB is highly effective, an auditor SRO is apt to be more like the National Association of Securities Dealers, which has had a spotty record of regulation, critics say. And any SRO must be set up in such a way, says a former senior official at the SEC, "that the whole system isn't hijacked by the firms. The accounting profession is very creative at taking over every group that's ever tried to rein it in."

2. BAR CONSULTING TO AUDIT CLIENTS

What Arthur Levitt couldn't achieve in a year of public hearings, speeches and backroom bargaining, the Enron scandal may now accomplish. "Ten years from now the auditing profession will look back at that debate on independence and consulting as a missed opportunity," says Jack T. Ciesielski, a CPA and editor of *The Analyst's Accounting Observer*. "Had they willingly gone along with some changes then, maybe they wouldn't look so bad now."

That accountants have become increasingly dependent on consulting is clear. In 1993, 31% of the industry's fees came from consulting. By 1999, that had jumped to 51%. In 2001, for example, PricewaterhouseCoopers earned only 40% of its worldwide fees from auditing, 29% coming from management consulting and most of the rest from tax and corporate finance work, reports the *International Accounting Bulletin*. More telling, in a study of the first 563 companies to file financials after Feb. 5, 2001, the University of Illinois' Bailey found that on average, for every dollar of audit fees, clients paid their independent accountants $2.69 for nonaudit consulting. Puget Energy, based in Bellevue, Wash., had the greatest imbalance, paying PricewaterhouseCoopers only $534,000 for its audit, but over $17 million in consulting fees. "That's 30 years of audit fees in one year for nonaudit," points out Bailey. Marriott International Inc. had a similar imbalance. It paid Andersen just over $1 million for its audit, but more than $30 million for information technology and other services.

The industry and others argue that conflict of interest is rarely the subject of litigation and that consulting work can provide a better understanding of the company and improve the audit. Still, in many people's minds the rising importance of consulting has contributed to a decline in auditor skepticism. It simply looks bad to have Andersen earning more on consulting to Enron than on auditing.

ACCOUNTING FAILURES AREN'T NEW—
JUST MORE FREQUENT

Investors have lost close to $200 billion in the past half-dozen years in earnings restatements and stock meltdowns following audit failures. And the pace seems to be accelerating. Between 1997 and 2000, the number of restatements jumped 100% from 116 instances to 233.

Bausch and Lomb (OCT. 23, 1995). A *BusinessWeek* investigation uncovers multiple accounting abuses by Bausch & Lomb, sparking a Securities & Exchange Commission investigation. The company later admitted that it had overstated income by $17.6 million and settled a shareholder lawsuit for $42 million.

Rite Aid (NOV. 11, 1999). KPMG resigns as auditor for Rite Aid, saying it cannot rely on the drug chain's numbers. Almost a year later, Rite Aid announced that it had overstated revenues for fiscal 1998 and 1999 by over $1 billion. In August, the company settled a suit with shareholders, but the SEC is still investigating.

Cendant (DEC. 7, 1999). Cendant agrees to pay $2.83 billion to shareholders after internal audits revealed CUC International—which merged with HFS to form Cendant in 1997—inflated income by $500 million through fraud and accounting errors. Cendant later accepts a $335 million settlement from CUC auditor Ernst & Young.

Sunbeam (MAY 15, 2001). The SEC files suit against Albert J. Dunlap and four other former Sunbeam executives, alleging accounting fraud. Earlier, auditor Arthur Andersen settled a shareholder suit for $110 million, while Dunlap settles for $15 million in January, 2002.

Waste Management (JUNE 19, 2001). Arthur Andersen agrees to pay a $7 million fine after the SEC charges it with issuing false and misleading reports on behalf of Waste Management. The reports overstated income from 1992 to 1996 by more than $1 billion. Andersen also paid part of a $229 million settlement with shareholders.

Enron (DEC. 2, 2001). Enron files the largest bankruptcy petition in U.S. history amid revelations of off-balance-sheet partnerships headed by company execs and other accounting irregularities. Six weeks earlier, Enron had restated earnings back to 1997, lopping off almost $600 million in profits.

Superior Bank (DEC. 10, 2001). The Pritzker family agrees to pay the FDIC $460 million without admitting liability after the failure of Superior Bank. The prominent Chicago family had been part-owners of Superior. Meanwhile, regulators begin investigating possible miscalculations of the bank's assets.

Dollar General (JAN. 15, 2002). Shares of Dollar General drop 13% after the company reduced earnings for the past three years by almost $200 million. The retailer took a fourth-quarter, 2000, charge of $162 million to settle shareholder suits over its accounting missteps.

3. MANDATE ROTATION OF AUDITORS

On September 11, 2001, while the world was glued to the television, Ellen Seidman, director of the Office of Thrift Supervision, testified before the Senate banking committee. Seidman was there to tell the story of the failure of Superior Bank, an Oakbrook Terrace (Ill.)-based savings and loan partly controlled by Chicago's Pritzker family, which had collapsed in spectacular fashion last July. As part of her presentation, Seidman outlined the role of auditor Ernst & Young in the failure of the bank and its write-off of $270 million and argued vigorously for auditor rotation. That would "result in a periodic 'fresh look' at the institution from an audit perspective to the benefit of investors and regulators," she said. Ernst & Young blames a large subprime loan portfolio, declining interest rates and a deteriorating economy for the bank's failure.

Fans of mandatory rotation of auditors argue that scandals like Waste Management, where income was overstated by $1.4 billion, would never occur if the auditor knew that within a few years it would be out and a competitor would be reviewing its work. Opponents say that rotation could create more problems, since new auditors need time to learn about a company. They prefer the current system of changing audit partners periodically but keeping the same firm in place.

Rotation has the advantage of being relatively inexpensive to implement. "It's a wonderful thing," says John H. Biggs, who as chief of pension giant TIAA-CREF selects a new auditor every seven years. "If you want a really good peer review, that's the way to do it. You would break through all of these independence issues very clearly and neatly with rotation."

4. IMPOSE MORE FORENSIC AUDITING

When the POB began its 2000 review of auditing effectiveness, it brought in a sleuth, Central Michigan University professor Thomas R. Weirich, to do a study of audit failures. In his review of 40 failures that led to government enforcement actions, he found in a number of cases that the Big Five auditors "did not take that extra step, do that extra work" that would have uncovered the problem. In several cases, for example, at companies that generated their bookkeeping journal entries on computer, unusual manual entries would suddenly appear at yearend, massaging the numbers. The auditors, Weirich says, "didn't ask why."

Some say that any auditor should ask that question, but one way to spur their skepticism might be to introduce some forensic auditing techniques into the average audit. Since revenue-recognition issues and the establishment of reserves are two of the most common reasons for earnings restatements, zeroing in on those hot spots could be the subject of such forensic review. The downside? Some fear that "forensic" audits might end up little more than an excuse for auditors to raise their prices.

5. LIMIT AUDITORS' MOVES TO COMPANIES

The June 19, 2001, SEC enforcement action against Arthur Andersen as auditor of Waste Management from 1993 through 1996 paints a damning picture of cronyism at the waste hauler. Besides the fact that Andersen had audited the firm since before its 1971 initial public offering, from 1971 until 1997 every chief financial officer and chief accounting officer at Waste Management had previously been an auditor at Andersen, according to the SEC.

The SEC charges that Andersen audits had begun to pick up irregularities as early as the late 1980s and that in "its original audits for 1993 through 1996, the engagement team had identified and documented numerous accounting issues underlying misstatements that the restatement ultimately addressed." But those discoveries did not prevent Andersen from giving Waste Management's inaccurate financials their blessing. When Waste Management finally came clean in February, 1998, it wiped out $1.4 billion in previous earnings.

Of course, many companies have similar rotation between their accounting staff and audit firms and never run into problems. And there are legal obstacles to limiting people's freedom to work where they like. But there is still the concern that the numbers might not be scrutinized with the necessary vigor when your old partners are adding them up. Henry R. Silverman, CEO of Cendant Corp., a franchising company based in New York, was embroiled in the 1998 accounting scandal at CUC International, a direct marketer Silverman's company had merged with that was later found to have inflated pretax income by $500 million. Silverman has a policy of not hiring people from his auditor, Deloitte & Touche. "It goes to the perception of independence," says Silverman. "It might not have anything to do with reality, but perception becomes reality."

6. REFORM THE AUDIT COMMITTEES

In 1999, an SEC blue-ribbon commission recommended that audit committees be made up solely of independent directors, each of whom should be financially literate, with at least one having accounting or financial management expertise. But when the U.S. stock exchanges moved on the recommendations and adopted new rules for listed companies, they were something else entirely.

Under the New York Stock Exchange rules, directors on the company payroll are permitted, former employees and their families can be allowed after three years and audit committee members with a "significant business relationship" with the company are also acceptable if the board determines the ties won't interfere with their judgment.

Had the SEC recommendations been adopted verbatim, half of Enron's six-member audit committee likely would have been barred from service. One member has a $72,000-a-year consulting contract with the company, and two others are employed by universities that have received significant charitable contributions from Enron, its Chairman Kenneth L. Lay, and their foundations. "The problem for corporate directors is that a lot of companies are doing what Enron did," says Russell S. Reynolds Jr., chairman and CEO of the Directorship Search Group Inc. "Nobody but maybe the CFO has the slightest idea what the magnitude of the dealings are, and the audit committees certainly don't. It's a hell of a mess." Chairman Dick Grasso says the NYSE will look to the SEC for guidance on any further changes.

7. CLEAN UP THE ACCOUNTING RULES

Accounting has become increasingly complex just as business has. "Accounting standards have become so complicated that the challenge is understanding the complicated accounting principles rather than understanding the basic aspects of a company," complains a comptroller of a major industrial conglomerate.

To many, the industry standard setter, the Financial Accounting Standards Board, is too slow to respond to change with new rules. It has been considering rules on special-purpose entities—the partnerships that were at the heart of Enron's troubles—for more than 20 years. As the debate on international accounting standards heats up over the next few years, front-and-center should be a drive toward making them clear, pertinent and timely. In need of urgent attention are clear-cut rules on materiality and how pro forma numbers are tallied and how that relates back to net income. Pitt of the SEC is one who plans to push for an overhaul of FASB. His goal: to get standards made in "months, not decades."

Would all of this have prevented the implosion at Enron? Perhaps not. For all the rules and overseers that may be created in its wake, there is, of course, no substitute for personal integrity. "You're trying to regulate human behavior, and that's going to be difficult at best and often-times impossible," says Cendant's Henry Silverman. While it may be impossible to legislate good behavior, a better monitor, the right rules and some punishment for un-ethical acts would help. Certainly they would go a long way toward restoring the public's confidence in the bruised auditing profession.

RESTORING INVESTOR CONFIDENCE
An Agenda for Change

—Henry M. Paulson Jr.

Henry Paulson was chairman and CEO of the Goldman Sachs Group. His following comments to the National Press Club on June 5, 2002, moved beyond the accounting profession specifically and addressed in addition investor confidence in the entire financial market. He suggests that changes first be made in accounting, which was beset by "pressure to produce predictable earnings and an overly complex rule set." A second area he addresses is corporate governance—Paulson gives 10 suggestions to improve corporate governance. He then turns to conflicts of interest, a sensitive area that tends to create challenges across disciplines from accountants to financial advisors, investment analysts to research firms. Ironically, it is worth noting that Goldman Sachs subsequently paid a hefty fine to the SEC for its own conflicts of interest. See the materials accompanying SEC Chairman Donaldson's speech later in this chapter.

INTRODUCTION

Good afternoon.

I come here today as the CEO of Goldman Sachs. But, perhaps even more importantly, I come here as an individual who believes passionately in the strength of our free-market system—a system that generates growth, creates jobs and wealth, rewards initiative and fosters innovation like no other in the history of the world.

Ours is an economy that has proved its resilience again and again, most recently and most dramatically as it recovered from the terrible attacks of September 11th.

Today we face another challenge—what some have called a crisis of confidence in the way in which companies do business. This, coupled with the lingering sense of vulnerability and uncertainty resulting from September 11th as well as international tensions and conflict, has seriously impaired the confidence of investors, CEOs and boards of directors alike. It has been a drag on the economy, the performance of our capital markets and corporate activity, including mergers and acquisitions and new investment.

Henry M. Paulson Jr., "Restoring Investor Confidence: An Agenda for Change." Speech to the National Press Club, Washington, DC, June 5, 2002. Reprinted with permission of the author.

This began last fall, with the collapse of Enron, at the time one of the most admired corporations in the country. That collapse rapidly became a scandal, with mounting evidence of gross mismanagement and malfeasance. One of the nation's most respected accounting firms—Arthur Andersen—was swept up in the Enron debacle, its survival still very much in the balance. In Congress and elsewhere, new and unflattering light has been shed on the practices of other companies. My own industry has come in for criticism for, among other things, the way it conducts investment research. Just six months after Enron's bankruptcy, its collapse has led to a general and often harsh examination of how we do business in America.

In my lifetime, American business has never been under such scrutiny. To be blunt, much of it is deserved.

Don't get me wrong. Our economy is not full of Enrons, ready to collapse when someone takes a close look at their books. The overwhelming majority of American corporate executives are men and women of integrity who are competent and highly committed to the long-term success of the companies that they lead. But the Enron debacle and subsequent revelations have revealed major shortcomings in the way some U.S. companies and those charged with their oversight have gone about their business. And it has, without doubt, eroded public trust.

Self-correction has already begun. And, despite the difficulties of the moment, I see the post-Enron environment as one of opportunity—a chance for all interested parties to reassess our current practices and renew our basic principles.

But we need to do so in ways that maintain the vitality of our market-driven economic system. Regulation is, of course, crucial to the proper functioning of our markets. But finding the right balance between regulation and market forces is critical. We've done it before. And I am confident that we will be able to strike such a balance yet again.

The stakes, after all, are enormous. And they transcend those of individual firms or investors. The U.S. economy and its financial markets are, rightly, the envy of the world. Since June 1981, the economy has almost doubled, productivity is up 50%, and about 40 million jobs have been created. During this same period, the stock market has appreciated by more than 2½ times. But our markets are not just beneficiaries of our remarkable economic performance. They also drive it by mobilizing capital, unlocking value, encouraging entrepreneurship, and rewarding good management. Our financial markets are the deepest, most efficient, and fairest to be found anywhere; they are models that others, in developed and developing economies alike, strive to emulate.

But they are not perfect. And it's time that we fix them.

As part of that discussion today I would like to provide some perspective on three areas: accounting policies and practices, corporate governance and conflicts of interest.

ACCOUNTING

I will begin with accounting, where we have seen by far the biggest fallout from the Enron collapse. The response is simple: the Arthur-Andersen-certified financial statements of Enron bore little or no relationship to economic reality. Moreover, a distressing—although relatively small—number of similar instances involving other firms have also come to light, as have a larger number of company-specific accounting problems.

How did all this happen?

Long bull markets always seem to result in laxity and complacency. Moreover, investors don't like surprises, and they have expressed a clear preference for companies that generate predictable earnings streams. Most businesses go through cycles or have business models that make this impossible.

Nonetheless, some CEOs feel obliged to defy gravity in an attempt to produce earnings increases quarter after quarter after quarter. This can create pressure on in-house financial staff and outside auditors. This problem is compounded by the fact that the overly complex rules-based approach underpinning U.S. GAAP is ripe for manipulation.

The combination of these two factors—pressure to produce predictable earnings and an overly complex rule set—has resulted in a few companies trying to bend the rules or circumvent them altogether. The more complex things become, the greater this temptation, and the easier it is to succeed.

So how can we strengthen our system and enhance investor confidence? First and foremost, accounting is the responsibility of corporate management . . . plain and simple.

While the exact form needs to be crafted carefully so as not to create a tidal wave of frivolous litigation, at a minimum the CEO should be required to certify that his or her company has established reasonable procedures for assessing the accuracy and completeness of its financial results and disclosures.

Next comes the question of auditor independence. Basic, simple questions must be asked. Whom does the auditing firm really believe they work for? Who hires them? Who pays them? Who gives them their directions?

Of course, existing good corporate governance standards and listing rules require that the board of directors, acting upon the recommendation of the audit committee, select auditors each year. But in practice, many boards have tended to rubber-stamp management's decision. Auditors understand that it is really management that selects them and determines their fees—a clear conflict of interest. In the post-Enron environment, the system is already beginning to self-correct to the extent that audit committees and boards feel compelled to do their job with much more zeal. But in my judgment, they must do even more.

Audit committees must develop policies and processes that ensure there is no doubt that the company's auditors report to them and work for them. A major step in that direction would be for audit committees to perform a rigorous annual review that, at a minimum, would include negotiation of audit fees and a real consideration of the factors that might cause a decision to replace the auditor. This would require an audit committee to evaluate an auditor's performance against clear criteria set in advance and it would require a practical plan to be in place if the need for replacement is determined.

On the issue of consulting services, I have a simple statement: I do not believe that auditors should provide consulting services to their audit clients because, at least in appearance, this compromises auditor independence and erodes trust.

But we must be careful in setting this rule. Some activities are so closely related to auditing that they should be permissible for audit clients because they allow the auditor to do a better job. Nothing, however, must compromise the audit firm's ability to conduct pressure-free audits.

Changes are also in order for oversight.

In recent months, we have seen the results of SEC action with several high-profile restatements of earnings. Such actions are powerful, positive steps.

But we need to go further. The SEC must be responsible for setting and enforcing auditing standards, either by establishing an independent public regulatory organization, as the Commission has already suggested, or by taking more direct responsibility itself. In any event, the current "peer review" process, which today allows audit firms to police themselves, should be replaced with an effective "audit of the auditors." This should include comprehensive reviews of specific audit work at randomly selected public companies.

Again, let's not lose sight of the fact that the SEC is the government entity charged with overall responsibility for ensuring the integrity of our financial markets. Whether it does this directly or, in the case of auditor oversight, through a public oversight body is a matter for fair debate, but it is also a matter for the SEC to determine in the first instance. However, it is imperative that any such oversight body be independent of the accounting industry, led by experienced and knowledgeable business people. The SEC must be prepared to step in directly whenever and wherever it believes the oversight body is not fulfilling its role.

Chairman Oxley of the House Financial Services Committee, among others, has proposed greater auditor oversight responsibilities for the SEC. He has also proposed strengthening the SEC with a budget increase; this is essential if it is to fulfill its mission. The SEC must have increased resources, and that means the ability to pay market-based compensation to attract and retain talented professionals.

Now I come to the most critical area—one that I believe must be addressed urgently—the U.S. rules-based accounting system.

This is where the most change is needed.

We must not lose sight of the fact that U.S. GAAP accounts for the vast majority of global economic activity, has been held up as the model for the whole world, has served us well for many years and is generally viewed as the best accounting system in the world. There is now talk of the superiority of the "European system," a less rules-based and more judgment-based approach. It is clearly different and successful in its own right. We must be willing to learn from it and to adapt our own system. The goal should be international convergence of accounting systems. To do this, we need a new approach to standard setting.

I referenced earlier the phenomenal growth in the U.S. economy over the last two decades. Indeed, the speed of innovation in the financial markets over this period has been nothing short of astonishing. This pace of change demands a nimble and practical method of ensuring that information at the core of the U.S. economy is fairly presented. We need standard-setters well versed in business complexity who understand the import of their actions and the need to address critical issues quickly. And we need a standard-setting process that is practical and efficient.

I am not an expert in the area of accounting standard-setting, but it seems to me that if the outcome of all we have been through in the past six months, all the soul searching and debate, is business as usual at the FASB, then we will have missed an enormous opportunity for improvement. I strongly encourage the SEC to take a long hard look at the way we set accounting standards in the United States, including the governance of the FASB, the selection of FASB members, the FASB standard-setting process with all of its delays, and the overall resources at the FASB's disposal, and to ask, "Are we satisfied with the results or do we need change?"

As you might expect, a number of accounting changes are being contemplated today by the FASB, some of them specifically in reaction to the Enron situation. For example, after a near 20-year debate, rules governing consolidation of special purpose entities are finally promised, and they are long overdue. But the initial proposals are complex, rules-based and lacking in underlying principle. In fact, they may make financial statements even less transparent and even more divorced from economic reality. This is not the way to move U.S. accounting standards forward.

As I said earlier, I believe that we need to focus on fundamental principles . . . principles, not details . . . to ensure that all the risks and rewards of an entity are properly recorded and disclosed to shareholders. The FASB should take a big step back and refocus its efforts on what is needed to achieve financial statement transparency. In this case, simply put, less may be more.

The FASB should begin by looking at the prevailing "historical cost" accounting model, which is hopelessly antiquated for companies principally engaged in the business of financial services or for companies that have become as heavily involved in financial instruments as Enron was.

Instead of requiring such companies to record the current, fair market value of all financial assets and liabilities in their financial statements, historical cost accounting allows them to record certain financial assets and liabilities at their historic cost. Of course, the value of financial instruments varies greatly with the fluctuations of the market. Unless companies account for those fluctuations, their financial statements can conceal tremendous losses.

In today's world, a corporation's creditworthiness can deteriorate rapidly—witness Enron, where some of the nation's largest banks were forced to fulfill billion-dollar commitments just weeks before it collapsed. Yet banks are not required to recognize the fair market value of loan commitments or outstanding loans in their financial statements, even when there has been a major erosion of economic value. Consequently, the economic cost of these outstanding liabilities is unknown to investors, regulators or the media.

I say this with the recognition that a transition to a system of fair value accounting is not without its difficulties. I also recognize that such a transition will take time. These considerations should not, however, paralyze efforts to move toward accounting practices that will best approximate economic reality.

The discipline associated with the use of fair value accounting—or, for that matter, any accounting system—includes the following:

First, we should require that any change in the methodology used to determine fair value be immediately disclosed. Secondly, and most importantly, we should require management to establish, and then to disclose, the systems and procedures necessary to ensure that fair value is properly applied. These should include the segregation and independence of financial control staff from those charged with generating revenue and the separation of professionals responsible for determining valuations from those responsible for verifying the valuations.

CORPORATE GOVERNANCE

As someone who runs a global investment bank and spends a lot of time with clients inside and outside this country, I believe that the U.S. system of corporate governance, though not perfect, is the best in the world.

Now, before I recommend some changes, let me clearly state that no form of corporate governance—no matter how well-designed—will guarantee that there won't be future failures. In a market-based economy, companies with bad business models will fail. The freedom to succeed must be accompanied by the corresponding freedom to fail. That we cannot change, nor should we. In the final analysis, the most important thing is the quality of the people involved—their competence, their experience and their integrity.

But for optimal results, competent, experienced people with integrity should be working in a corporate governance system that provides them the proper checks and balances and sufficient information to do their jobs. The three basic principles of such a system are: (1) transparency, with an emphasis on financial disclosure which reflects economic reality; (2) competence and integrity; and (3) proper alignment of interests and allocation of responsibilities among management, the board of directors and shareholders, recognizing potential conflicts and clearly disclosing their nature.

Working from these principles, it makes good sense that CEOs receive the largest portion of their compensation in equity.

But it is equally vital that they hold it for the long term. This will create the proper incentives and inspire investor and employee confidence. Share sales by top management, particularly if they represent a significant portion of the individual's ownership, fly directly in the face of the intent of an equity-based compensation program. Moreover, no matter how carefully the windows governing share sales by top management are constructed, and no matter how fulsome and transparent disclosures are, top management would have to be woefully inept not to know more about the condition of—and the prospects for—his or her company than the average shareholder.

In this regard, the business community has been given a black eye by the activities and behavior of some CEOs and other notable insiders who sold large numbers of shares just before dramatic declines in their companies' share prices. In some instances these sales preceded bankruptcy by a matter of months. Existing legal mechanisms may serve to sort out inappropriate insider selling, but given difficulties of proof, more is needed.

Executive compensation has clearly caught the public attention. There have been a few well-publicized examples of CEO overcompensation. Even when measured against a U.S. system, which pays generously relative to any other place in the world, when compensation is out of line with performance it really stands out! There have also been a few extraordinary loans to CEOs. Most shareholders don't view their company as a bank (unless it really is one!), and such a loan to a CEO does not inspire public confidence or properly align interests.

Given the public interest surrounding CEO pay, board compensation committees also face increased scrutiny, as well they should. In this regard, we should focus on the compensation of independent directors from company sources other than their directors' fees. One notorious example is Enron, which compensated at least some of its so-called independent directors through consulting fees and other arrangements that in some cases greatly exceeded their directors' fees. Even if these consulting arrangements don't actually taint directors' independence, they undermine confidence in the system.

Of course, the compensation abuses I've cited are not the norm. They are the exception. The vast majority of executive and independent director compensation stands up to scrutiny and is part of a system which has benefited this country greatly—a system that holds the board of directors accountable for hiring, firing and compensating CEOs—and puts the power to elect the board of directors in the hands of the shareholders. When CEOs are formally evaluated by competent, independent compensation committees, and their compensation is matched with the results, the system works.

Much good work has been and is being done in the area of corporate governance, including the May 2002 report by the Business Roundtable and an upcoming report by a NYSE committee on corporate governance. The key is to move quickly to implementation and, of course, for public companies to take governance very seriously, devoting more time and effort to ensure that these checks and balances are rigorous and function as intended. I would recommend the following 10-point plan, much of which already represents best practice.

First, each public company should clearly describe to its shareholders, either in its annual report or proxy statement, how its corporate governance system, with all of its checks and balances, works.

Second, all listed companies should have a majority of independent directors, both in substance and appearance.

Third, the board of directors should be required affirmatively to determine that no "independent" director has any relationship that the board believes may impair, or appear to impair, the exercise of that director's independent judgment. Additionally, the nature of that director's relationships should be fully disclosed to shareholders.

Fourth, non-management directors should be required to meet periodically without the "insiders"—including the CEO—present.

Fifth, both audit committees and compensation committees should consist entirely of independent directors.

Sixth, executive officer compensation should be aligned closely with shareholder interests by making equity a very material portion of such compensation. And compensation committees should be encouraged to develop guidelines requiring that a substantial portion of that equity be held for significant periods of time.

Seventh, all compensation plans granting stock, options or other company securities to directors or executive officers should be approved both by the compensation committee and by shareholders.

Eighth, all "compensation" or other financial relationships with the company and its executive officers or directors should be fully, fairly and promptly disclosed.

Ninth, all transactions in company securities by executive officers or directors should be disclosed within 48 hours.

Tenth, while "insiders" selling in advance of public disclosure of "bad news" is already illegal, in the case of CEOs, we should raise the bar and mandate a one-year "claw back" in the case of bankruptcy, regardless of the reason.

CONFLICTS OF INTEREST / INVESTMENT RESEARCH

Let me now turn to a third area of concern: managing conflicts of interest. I have already discussed conflicts of interest involving executives, boards, auditors, companies and shareholders, which are largely addressed by clarifying roles.

Closer to home, let me say a few words about conflicts between a company and its clients, which ultimately can lead to loss of franchise and, hence, shareholder value. An example of this is the potential conflict between the investment banking and investment research functions in an integrated investment bank. The controversy surrounding research conflicts in the investment banking industry has been widely reported in the media and has eroded investor confidence.

Conflicts are a fact of life for many, if not most, institutions throughout society, from the political arena and government to media and businesses of all types. The key is how we manage them, the disclosures we make, the systems or "firewalls" we put in place and the judgments that are made in balancing competing interests.

For an integrated investment bank such as Goldman Sachs, conflict management has always been a core competency, because it is critical to our reputation and a key to our success. Day in and day out, our business requires a proper and fair balancing of investing and issuing interests. Generally we meet these challenges. But unfortunately, particularly in the context of the technology and the telecom bubble of the late 1990s, we have not done as good a job as we might have in preserving and protecting the perception of the independence of our research analysts who play a vital role in the investing and capital allocation process.

To address this challenge, two weeks ago we at Goldman Sachs announced a number of important steps, beginning with a positive reaffirmation of the principles of integrity, independent thought, analytic rigor and transparency that underpin our research. We have codified these in a statement of Investment Research Principles. We have also appointed an Ombudsman, who is available to promptly address any conflicts which may arise, and instituted new oversight responsibilities for the audit and compensation committees of our board of directors.

Most importantly, the major part of our effort will be to continue to focus on doing better fundamental analysis. The next time something looks too good to be true, we hope to have the wisdom to see it and the courage of our conviction to act accordingly.

Integrity is the cornerstone, if not the bedrock, upon which all financial markets are based. It is also the foundation of the reputation of Goldman Sachs. In that regard, I note that recently the U.S. Securities and Exchange Commission unanimously approved sweeping changes to the rules of the NASD and NYSE designed to address investment research analyst conflicts of interest. The Commission also emphasized that additional changes may prove appropriate; the Merrill Lynch settlement is a further step in the right direction and should work to bolster investor confidence and reinforce the integrity of our markets.

CONCLUSION

My remarks here today represent my best thoughts on how to fix some of the problems facing our financial markets. They do not pretend to be comprehensive or original. In fact, many, if not most of them, have been suggested by others, including the Business Roundtable chaired by Franklin Raines, the NYSE under Dick Grasso's leadership, and the Financial Services Forum chaired by Phil Purcell.

All my suggestions have one aim: restoring trust in our system—trust in the accuracy of financial statements, trust in the integrity of corporate management, trust in the honesty of investment analysis. Without such confidence, we all lose. Investors will forgo gains, entrepreneurs will have less access to capital, there will be fewer and less attractive jobs, less business to be done and fewer tax dollars to support government programs. And the impact would fall most heavily on the less privileged. It is our job to see that our capital markets continue to be models of fairness and efficiency.

Self-correction, I'm pleased to say, is already underway. But, without overreacting, we need to move quickly to implementation to reduce uncertainty.

In retrospect, it is perhaps not surprising that the 18-year bull market we have enjoyed was also accompanied by certain excesses. Hindsight is 20/20, and it is only natural for society to look for someone to blame whenever there is a setback.

I am confident we can move beyond second-guessing and finger-pointing to attain real progress on meaningful reform. Having seen how we, as an industry and a nation, responded to the terrible attacks of September 11th, how could I not be an optimist? Working together, I am certain that we can achieve our common goal of restoring investor trust and ensuring that our financial system and economy emerge even stronger than before.

Thank you.

CONFLICTS OF INTEREST: THEY'RE NOT AS DIFFICULT AS THEY SEEM

—MARIANNE M. JENNINGS

The following reading defines succinctly what exactly a conflict of interest is, what is wrong with it and four steps to deal with a conflict: (1) admit where there is a conflict; (2) determine the type of conflict; (3) take action; and (4) develop policies to avoid or to mitigate these conflicts in the future.

Barbara Walters presented a flattering portrayal of Sir Andrew Lloyd Webber on the *20/20* news program she anchors. In addition to the positive profile, Ms. Walters' piece made note of the upcoming Broadway opening of Webber's latest musical, *Sunset Boulevard*. The following Monday those testy New York papers reported that Ms. Walters had a $100,000 investment in *Sunset Boulevard*. Upon being confronted with this information, Ms. Walters assured the public that her investment in Webber's play in no way influenced the content of the Webber piece.

Even if Ms. Walters were the very paragon of journalistic ethics, she had a conflict of interest. Her personal investment and natural desire for return on it was in conflict with her role as a journalist, which mandates a cold, hard look at the subject, a task someone with a pending investment may not be detached enough to do. When the cold, hard facts can't be looked at too closely because your personal gain might suffer, those in the business of cold, hard facts have a conflict. Ms. Walters and investment managers are alike in this regard—sometimes the cold, hard facts put a dent in compensation.

Ms. Walters' response is very typical of those who are confronted with conflicts of interest: There is always the assurance that they would never do anything to harm either of those conflicting interests. They miss the issue in conflicts. Whether you would or would not be influenced by a benefit or personal financial interest you have or are given is not the issue in conflicts of interest. The very fact that you must assure others that you are indeed to be trusted is indicative that certainly there is such a conflict. Pointing out a conflict of interest is not a comment on integrity. It is rather a commentary on the limits of human resistance to temptation.

The strange irony about conflicts of interests is that there is so much hand wringing over them when they can be handled so easily. Getting past the pervasive approach of denying the conflicts with the personal character defense is perhaps the most difficult part of resolving conflicts of interest issues. The following steps should provide some assistance in handling and resolving conflicts issues.

STEP ONE: ADMIT WHEN THERE IS A CONFLICT

React with the logic of human nature and your own long-term reputation and success, instead of reacting to a conflict of interest with the usual affront of, "How could you think that I could ever be influenced by that?" Whether you would or would not be influenced by the conflicting demand is not the issue. The issue is, why risk such an accusation?

Examples of conflicts in the investment management field include varying forms of remuneration. From churning to soft dollars, there are compensation issues in which the brokers' financial interests are torn between personal returns and client returns. Even performance-based compensation for brokers produces conflict for the broker may assume greater risk for the higher returns, and that high risk may be greater than the client's boundaries for such risk. Late last year, the SEC announced a study on brokers and their decisions to put clients in so-called B shares—those hot-selling mutual funds that have no front charge or load, but charge annual fees, versus A shares that carry a load, but that offer discounts for large purchases. With B shares brokers get a flat, fixed rate. But B shares have a redemption charge when they are sold in the six-to-eight-year time frame and higher annual fees for investors, which ultimately affects their rate of return.

In all of these scenarios, one side makes more money while the other makes less. There is a conflict of interest. The investment advisory and brokerage professions are not corrupt, but there are conflicts.

STEP TWO: DETERMINE WHAT TYPE OF CONFLICT YOU HAVE

There are two types of conflicts: those that are irreconcilable and those that can be fixed with disclosure and consent. Conflicts that are irreconcilable are those that cannot be remedied because the interests of the parties are so adverse and the issues so sensitive. For example, a law or investment firm cannot represent both sides in an acquisition or merger. The interests of the shareholders of each of the firms are too much at variance for one party to remain detached in negotiating the best arrangement for both sides. Irreconcilable conflicts exist in those circumstances where both sides need an advocate/advisor for their interests.

Many conflicts can be remedied with disclosure and consent. For example, the issue of the B shares need not be a conflict issue. But, rather, it could be a disclosure and consent issue with the disclosure involving, as it does in any area of law where full disclosure is mandated, informing the client about the returns, the advantages and the disadvantages. And the issue of soft dollars cannot be tossed lightly into the irreconcilable conflict category for there are times when the brokerage would not be able to fulfill its best execution duty without soft dollar arrangements. In this last example, and in many other conflict arrangements, the resolution comes with a discussion of the conflicting constraints with the client. Whether the client is calling the investment shots or the manager is, the disclosure discussion is necessary.

STEP THREE: TAKE ACTION

If withdrawal from handling a particular client is necessary because the differences are irreconcilable, then take the steps to withdraw. If disclosure is necessary, meet with the client and then develop a plan for ongoing disclosures, because in some situations, the disclosure cannot be made just once and it will require ongoing discussions and disclosure. Some sound advice: when in doubt, disclose and discuss. Just the fact that the issue was on the table is part of the resolution of the conflict. At a minimum, Ms. Walters should have disclosed that she had the investment interest in Mr. Webber's play before the piece ran; then the viewers could decide for themselves whether there was bias.

STEP FOUR: DEVELOP POLICIES

A firm or broker need not reinvent the wheel on every conflict. Based on the experience and type of conflict, there are some generic policies or procedures you can develop for guidance in the future. For example, a firm could develop a policy on B shares investments and how these are handled with clients.

APPLICATION OF THE MODEL

A simple example illustrates one firm's level of concern about conflicts and appearances and its long-term reputation in the community. One of the firm's large clients was redoing the landscaping in his backyard. He had received an estimate for the work, which he felt was high. Like many wealthy retirees, he was prone to complaining to anyone who would listen, including his investment managers. Upon hearing of the client's plight, one of the investment firm's principals who is married to a contractor specializing in landscaping and landscape design, offered his wife's professional opinion to the client. The landscaper wife, not thrilled with a non-profit job, went to the client's home and offered her thoughts on the client's proposed project as well as the appropriate price ranges just as a favor for her husband. The client was so impressed that he hired the wife of the principal on the spot.

From the outset, everyone involved knew the interrelationships. The principal and his spouse were just trying to help ease a client's frustrations. But, the end result is a business relationship between the spouse of an investment advisor and a client. The interest of the spouse in getting paid, and the corresponding interest of her principal husband, may be at odds with the investment goals and strategies best suited for the client. Further, the client may feel that if he does not use the spouse for his landscaping, his portfolio may not enjoy the attention he wants it to have. As is generally the case at the outset, everyone was happy, from the client who was getting better landscaping at a cheaper price to the investment firm that had a less grumpy client. Should either the landscaping or the portfolio turn sour, the interrelationships could be made to look oppressive.

The firm in this case did the right thing in steps: they acknowledged there was a conflict; they determined that the conflict was fixable by disclosure and consent; and all the principals sat down with the client and discussed the fact that they did not want him to feel pressure to use the spouse for his work. The client assured them that he was capable of saying no to anyone and firing even more people. A memo was made to the file. Finally, the firm developed some policies on business relationships for spouses and families of principals.

One of the magnificent aspects about ethics, whether we address conflicts of interest or portfolio performance representations, is that the more they are discussed and considered, the better they get and the fewer breaches we find. So it is with conflicts: talk about them, determine what type they are and then do something about them. Reliance on integrity as a defense is indefensible when resolution of the conflict itself often comes so easily.

SPEECH BY SEC CHAIRMAN: PREPARED FOR DELIVERY AT SEC PRESS CONFERENCE REGARDING GLOBAL SETTLEMENT

—WILLIAM H. DONALDSON

William Donaldson, the Chairman of the U.S. Securities and Exchange Commission, expresses "sadness and anger" about the behavior spelled out in SEC complaints about investment banking firms who pressured their research analysts to provide favorable ratings on issues the bankers were selling. The speech notes the settlement of $1.4 billion and delineates the requirements that must be met by the firms to avoid conflicts of interest. Donaldson also summarizes the requirements that, if met, will lead to better disclosure for consumers concerning the limitations of research. A chart of the payments made is included.

I am pleased to be here with some of the many people—from the SEC, the New York Attorney General's Office, the NASD, the New York Stock Exchange, and the North American Securities Administrators Association and its member states—who have worked so hard to bring to fruition the enforcement actions and settlements we announce today. These cases are an important milestone in our ongoing effort both to address serious abuses that have taken place in our markets and to restore investor confidence and public trust by making sure these abuses don't happen again in the future.

As you know, this settlement has been in the works for many months; indeed, much of the investigation and negotiation process that has resulted in today's announcement predates my arrival at the Commission. But, I believe that what we present today is a good outcome for investors and the markets.

Our unified action brings to a close a period during which the once-respected research profession became nearly unrecognizable to earlier generations of investors and analysts. As many of you know, I helped found an investment firm that bore my name and which was originally dedicated to research.

For that reason, I speak very personally, when I say that I am profoundly saddened—and angry—about the conduct that's alleged in our complaints. There is absolutely no place

This speech by U.S. SEC Chairman William H. Donaldson was delivered at SEC Press Conference regarding global settlement on April 28, 2003, in Washington, D.C.

for it in our markets and it cannot be tolerated. When an analyst signs his or her name, and places the *firm's* name, on a research report expressing strong support for an issuer, while admitting privately to doubts about the company's viability, the only appropriate reaction is outrage.

When a firm publishes favorable research about a company without revealing to its customers that that research—far from being independent—was essentially bought and paid for by the issuer, we had no choice but to conclude that the research system was broken.

To impress upon the firms the seriousness with which we regard their misconduct and to help restore investor's faith in the objectivity of research, the settlement employs a multi-pronged approach, including both monetary and non-monetary forms of relief.

The monetary relief is substantial—totaling just short of $1.4 billion. Collectively, the ten firms will disgorge illegal proceeds of nearly $400 million, and pay well in excess of $400 million in civil penalties. I am pleased to note that the penalties alone—that is, not including the disgorgement, independent research and investor education payments—are among the largest ever obtained in civil enforcement actions under the securities laws. The $150 million penalty imposed against one firm is the largest ever imposed against a broker-dealer firm in a civil action.

The $75 million penalty to be paid by another firm is the third highest paid by a brokerage firm. And the $25 million penalties to be paid by the other settling firms are easily within the top ten largest obtained by the SEC against broker-dealers. I'm confident this enforcement action has delivered a message the firms won't soon forget.

The federal regulators—the Commission, the NASD and the New York Stock Exchange—will place their share of the penalties and disgorgement—approximately $400 million—into a distribution fund for payment to harmed investors.

While there are challenges and difficulties in establishing such a fund, the Commission feels strongly that those challenges and difficulties are worth taking on and that any funds paid by the settling firms should be used to compensate the investors harmed most directly by the misconduct uncovered in our investigations. We believe this is the right thing to do, and is consistent with the message sent by Congress when it recently authorized us to use penalties to repay investors.

In accordance with the settlement agreements, a Fund Administrator will be appointed to allocate funds to individual customers of each firm based primarily on whether each customer purchased any of the limited universe of securities identified in the Commission's complaint. The Fund Administrator's plan of distribution will be subject to approval by the court.

Although the monetary relief secured in the settlement is substantial, unfortunately the losses that investors suffered in the aftermath of the market bubble that burst far exceeds the ability to compensate them fully.

They can never fully be repaid. Their loss was more than monetary. It was a loss of confidence and a loss of the hopes and dreams they had built over a lifetime. And although the monetary relief obtained in the settlement is record-breaking, the structural reforms required by the settlement are, in my view more significant and far-reaching.

The numerous obligations we impose on the defendants, taken together, will fundamentally change the role and perception of research at Wall Street firms. Indeed, I believe these reforms will go a long way towards restoring the honorable legacy of the research profession. Let me take a moment to highlight a few of the most meaningful among them.

In order to eliminate the conflicts that arise when the banking function has the opportunity or means to influence the objectivity of research analysts, the settlement:

- Requires firms to have separate reporting and supervisory structures for their research and banking operations.

- Requires that research analysts' compensation be *unrelated* to investment banking business, and instead be tied to the quality and accuracy of their research.

- Prohibits investment banking personnel from evaluating the performance of research analysts, and requires decisions concerning compensation of analysts to be documented and reviewed by an independent committee within the firm.

- Prohibits research analysts from soliciting investment banking business or participating in so called "road shows."

- Prohibits communications between firms' research and banking operations except as necessary for an analyst to advise the firm concerning the viability of a transaction. Thus, the analyst will resume the role of "gatekeeper" and shed the recently acquired identity of cheerleader or marketer.

The settlement also imposes a series of requirements that will benefit investors by providing them better information concerning the limitations of research. For instance:

- Firms must include on the first page of research reports a "warning notice" making clear that the reports are produced by firms that do investment banking business with the companies they cover, and that this may affect the objectivity of the firms' research reports; the disclosure must further state that "investors should consider the report as only a single factor in making their investment decision."

- To provide the public with the tools necessary to assess the usefulness of an analyst's research, each firm must disclose quarterly the price targets, ratings and earnings per share forecasted in its research reports. I expect that these disclosures will fuel development of private services to transform such raw data into investor-friendly report cards on the accuracy of the firms' research.

- And finally, firms must adopt policies and procedures reasonably designed to ensure that its personnel cannot and do not seek to influence the contents of research reports in order to promote investment banking business.

Another innovative and forward-looking aspect of this agreement is the commitment by the firms to purchase independent, third-party research for their customers over the next five years. Each firm will retain an independent research monitor, in consultation with the regulators, who will oversee this process to insure the research is independent, of high quality and useful to the firms' various customer bases. Each independent research monitor also will report periodically to the regulators on his or her firm's compliance with this requirement.

To better arm investors to cope with the risks inevitably associated with participating in the capital markets, the settlement also provides for the establishment of an Investor Education Fund of $80 million. This initiative is particularly important because it has meaning beyond the context of this investigation; the federal portion of this fund will support educational efforts addressing not only the possible hazards of analyst conflicts, but also a broad range of other issues associated with informed investing. The fund will make grants to organizations to develop wide-ranging, neutral and unbiased investor education programs nationwide.

In connection with the "spinning" of IPO shares—that is, the allocation of sought after, "hot" IPOs to executives of potential investment banking clients—the firms have agreed voluntarily to ban such allocations to executive officers and directors of public companies. I view this voluntary initiative as a temporary solution to the problem of spinning. In the months ahead we will explore addressing these issues with revised or new rule making.

The hallmark of our business and financial system is that the rule of law must prevail and when wrongdoing occurs, it must be confronted and punished. Today we do just that. These cases reflect a sad chapter in the history of American business—a chapter in which those who reaped enormous benefits based on the trust of investors—profoundly betrayed that trust.

The cases also represent an important new chapter in our ongoing efforts to restore investors' faith and confidence in the fairness and integrity of our markets.

To implement this global settlement, the SEC today filed separate actions against each of the firms in Federal District Court in New York City and, concurrently, the NYSE and NASD completed disciplinary proceedings pursuant to the disciplinary procedures of their respective organizations. At the state level, model settlement agreements have been finalized and the NASAA Board of Directors has recommended that all states accept the terms of the agreements. The proposed Final Judgments in the SEC actions are subject to Court approval.

Payments in Global Settlement Relating to Firm Research and Investment Banking Conflicts of Interest

Firm	Penalty ($ Millions)	Disgorgement ($ Millions)	Independent Research ($ Millions)	Investors Education ($ Millions)	Total ($ Millions)
Bear Stearns	25	25	25	5	**80**
CSFB	75	75	50	0	**200**
Goldman	25	25	50	10	**110**
J. P. Morgan	25	25	25	5	**80**
Lehman	25	25	25	5	**80**
Merrill Lynch	100*	0	75	25	**200**
Morgan Stanley	25	25	75	0	**125**
Piper Jaffray	12.5	12.5	7.5	0	**32.5**
SSB	150	150	75	25	**400**
UBS	25	25	25	5	**80**
Total ($ millions)	**487.5**	**387.5**	**432.5**	**80**	**$1,387.5**

* Payment made in prior settlement of research analyst conflicts of interest with the states securities regulators.

SUMMARY OF THE SARBANES-OXLEY ACT OF 2002

—PricewaterhouseCoopers

As you will see in a later reading in this chapter, some believe that the Sarbanes-Oxley Act of 2002 is one of the most important pieces of legislation governing the behavior of accountants, firms and financial markets since legislation in the 1930s governing markets. What follows is a summary of the main provisions of this Act.

The Sarbanes-Oxley Act of 2002 establishes new standards for corporate accountability as well as penalties for corporate wrongdoing. The legislation contains 11 titles, ranging from additional responsibilities for audit committees to tougher criminal penalties for white-collar crimes such as securities fraud. The SEC is required to issue rules implementing several of these provisions. The rules eventually issued by the SEC may go beyond the statutory requirements.

Here is a summary of each of the 11 titles:

TITLE I—PUBLIC COMPANY ACCOUNTING OVERSIGHT BOARD

- Establishes an independent, non-governmental board to oversee the audits of public companies to protect the interests of investors and further public confidence in independent audit reports.

- Defines the major responsibilities of this board.

- Requires public accounting firms to register with the board and take certain other actions in order to perform audits of public companies.

TITLE II—AUDITOR INDEPENDENCE

- Sets forth required actions by registered public accounting firms ("external auditors"), audit committees and companies that are intended to strengthen auditor independence.

- Legislates certain services, generally consistent with current independence rules, as unlawful if performed by the external auditor.

TITLE III—CORPORATE RESPONSIBILITY

- Requires audit committees to be independent and undertake specified oversight responsibilities.

- Requires CEOs and CFOs to certify quarterly and annual reports to the SEC, including making representations about the effectiveness of specified controls.

- Provides rules of conduct for companies and their officers regarding pension blackout periods and certain other matters.

- Requires the SEC to issue rules requiring attorneys in certain roles to report violations of securities laws to a company's CEO or chief legal counsel and, if no action is taken, to the audit committee.

TITLE IV—ENHANCED FINANCIAL DISCLOSURES

- Requires companies to provide enhanced disclosures, including a report on the effectiveness of internal controls and procedures for financial reporting (along with external auditor attestation of that report) and disclosures covering off-balance sheet transactions and pro forma financial information.

- Requires disclosures regarding code of ethics for senior financial officers and reporting of certain waivers.

- Requires accelerated disclosures by management, directors and principal stockholders concerning certain transactions involving company securities.

TITLE V—ANALYST CONFLICTS OF INTEREST

- Requires the SEC to adopt rules to address conflicts of interest that can arise when securities analysts recommend equity securities in research reports and public appearances.

TITLE VI—COMMISSION RESOURCES AND AUTHORITY

- Provides additional funding to the SEC.

- Gives the SEC and federal courts more authority to censure and impose certain prohibitions on persons and entities.

TITLE VII—STUDIES AND REPORTS

- Directs federal regulatory bodies to conduct studies regarding consolidation of accounting firms; credit rating agencies; violators, violations and enforcement actions involving securities laws; certain roles of investment banks and financial advisors; and certain other matters.

TITLE VIII—CORPORATE AND CRIMINAL FRAUD ACCOUNTABILITY

- Provides tougher criminal penalties for altering documents, defrauding shareholders and certain other forms of obstruction of justice and securities fraud.

- Makes debts non-dischargeable if incurred in violation of securities fraud laws.

- Protects employees of companies who provide evidence of fraud.

TITLE IX—WHITE-COLLAR CRIME PENALTY ENHANCEMENTS

- Provides that any person who attempts to commit white-collar crimes shall be treated under the law as if the person had committed the crime.

- Enhances penalties and sentencing guidelines for certain white-collar crimes such as mail and wire fraud and ERISA violations.

- Requires CEOs and CFOs to certify in their periodic reports to the SEC that their financial statements fully comply with the requirements of the Securities Exchange Act of 1934, and imposes penalties for certifying a misleading or fraudulent report.

TITLE X—CORPORATE TAX RETURNS

- Conveys the sense of the Senate that the CEO should sign a company's federal income tax return.

TITLE XI—CORPORATE FRAUD AND ACCOUNTABILITY

- Provides additional authority to regulatory bodies and courts to take various actions, including fines or imprisonment, with regard to tampering with records, impeding official proceedings, taking extraordinary payments, retaliating against corporate whistleblowers and certain other matters involving corporate fraud.

WEIGHING SARBANES-OXLEY: CHANGES APPEAR TO BE PROFOUND

—Rebecca Walker

Rebecca Walker looks at the Sarbanes-Oxley Act of 2002 and, contrary to the previous reading, contends that it will be as important as any piece of legislation since the promulgation of the U.S. Sentencing Guidelines of 1991. The reading looks at "the ways in which compliance programs are already changing," and anticipates what this will mean into the future. She predicts, for instance, that these rules will require the adoption of codes of conduct, particularly those that apply to directors and audit committees.

The effect of recent legislation and rule-making on corporate compliance will perhaps be as important as anything that has happened in this field since the promulgation of the U.S. Sentencing Guidelines for Organizations in 1991. It will undoubtedly take years to ascertain the full impact of recent legislation and rule-making that has resulted from the many corporate scandals and corporate failures of the past months.

This article attempts to take an early look at the ways in which compliance programs are already changing in the wake of recent events, and to anticipate some future implications. Because the focus of the legislation and rule-making is on codes of conduct, and because that is where the changes are currently most evident, this article will concentrate on codes. It is, however, important to note that these changes in codes of conduct seem to be indicative of more profound changes in both the way compliance programs work and how we view them.

NEW RULES AND PROPOSED RULES

The new rules and proposed rules include (i) the Sarbanes-Oxley Act of 2002 (Sarbanes-Oxley), which became law on July 30, and the Securities and Exchange Commission's (SEC) proposed regulations to implement certain provisions of that legislation, which were released on October 22, 2002 (SEC Proposed Regulations), (ii) the New York Stock Exchange's (NYSE) Corporate Governance Rule Proposals (NYSE Rule Proposals), which were submitted to the SEC on August 16, 2002, and (iii) the Nasdaq's Corporate Governance Rule Proposals (Nasdaq Rule Proposals), submitted to the SEC on October 9, 2002.[1]

Each of these undertakings, while directed at a host of corporate governance and other issues, also includes new rules for corporate compliance, generally embodied in the form of rules requiring (or requiring disclosure regarding) codes of conduct. Each approaches the issue of codes somewhat differently, but each approach has important implications for codes of conduct and compliance generally.

APPLICABILITY TO DIRECTORS

Both the NYSE Rule Proposals and the Nasdaq Rule Proposals will require listed companies to adopt codes of conduct applicable to all employees, officers and directors. Prior to these rule proposals, boards of directors often approved codes of conduct and put their official imprimatur on the establishment of the compliance program—but most codes did not apply to directors. This rule change will require many listed companies to modify the applicability of their codes to encompass directors.

Many companies are now doing this, and are also grappling with the concept of how in practice a company's code should and will apply to directors. Some employment and workplace policies have little, if any, applicability to directors. For example, a company's policies pertaining to use of the company's computer resources (which directors may never use), protecting the environment and workplace health and safety may have no applicability to directors. And, given that most directors have other full-time jobs, the code's applicability may be different in some ways for directors than for employees. To deal with this problem, some companies have included language in their codes providing that the code will be applicable to directors insofar as the directors are carrying out their duties on behalf of the company, while other companies have merely considered this implicit in the code (as, indeed, applicability to employees is also limited in many ways to their function as employees, which most companies have generally considered implicit in their codes).

Much more profound, however, than the mere reworking of a company's code, is the concept of making a code of conduct and a company's compliance program applicable to its directors. Compliance has traditionally been defined as a system of internal policies and procedures designed, implemented and enforced so as to prevent and detect violations of law, regulations and company policies by employees and other agents. Interestingly, directors have rarely been included in the "other agents" category. Indeed, very little has been said or written about the applicability of a compliance program to boards of directors, as distinguished from the role of boards in the oversight of compliance programs, a topic that has received substantial attention. The movement from viewing boards as the mere overseers of compliance to the subject of compliance programs is a fairly monumental shift in the way compliance programs are designed and perceived. It creates a new dimension in the workings of compliance programs, the full effects of which will only be known with the passage of time.

OVERSIGHT BY DIRECTORS

Since the Delaware Chancery Court's 1996 decision in *In re Caremark International Inc. Derivative Litigation,* 698 A.2d 959, there has been much discussion about the scope of a director's duty of care with respect to the oversight of a company's compliance program. The role of the board in overseeing a company's compliance program will undoubtedly be increased and formalized with the impact of recent legislation and rule-making.

Section 7(b)(i)(A) of the NYSE Rule Proposals provides that an audit committee's purpose is to assist board oversight of a company's compliance with legal and regulatory requirements. While board oversight of compliance is far from a novel concept, the NYSE Rule Proposals have already had the effect of making many boards more cognizant of their role as overseers of compliance, and of increasing boards' attentiveness to compliance programs.[2]

ROLE OF DIRECTORS IN THE FUNCTION OF THE PROGRAM

Section 301 of Sarbanes-Oxley requires the SEC to adopt a rule by April 26, 2003, directing the national securities exchanges and associations to prohibit the listing of securities of any company where the audit committee of the company has not established procedures for the receipt, retention and treatment of complaints regarding accounting, internal accounting controls or auditing matters and the confidential, anonymous submission by employees of concerns regarding questionable accounting or auditing matters.

The legislation, which makes audit committees responsible for establishing procedures to receive reports of accounting and auditing misconduct, represents a significant change with respect to the role of the audit committee in the implementation of a compliance program. In this area of compliance, the audit committee now has more than mere oversight responsibility; it must actively engage in establishing compliance procedures for reporting certain types of misconduct.

FOCUS ON UPPER MANAGEMENT

While most codes of conduct have always been applicable to all employees—from the chief executive officer down—there is, with recent corporate scandals and failures (and reflected in the recent legislation and rule-making), a new focus on the applicability of compliance programs to upper-level management. Compliance has typically been considered, in part, an educational and information tool emanating from the upper levels of management (as most agree that it must in order to be effective), informing and providing guidance to those below. Given the high level at which much of the recently reported wrongdoing has taken place, however, current legislation and rule-making are understandably focused on the applicability of the rules to those at the very top of companies.

For example, section 406 of Sarbanes-Oxley requires the SEC to adopt rules requiring issuers to disclose whether they have a code of ethics for the CFO and the controller or persons performing similar functions. The SEC's Proposed Regulations implementing this provision of Sarbanes-Oxley have expanded the applicability to include the CEO, and have asked for comments on whether the required code should also apply to the General Counsel and to others in a company. The code of ethics contemplated by Sarbanes-Oxley is a fairly generic code, including policies relating to honest and ethical conduct, conflicts of interest and compliance with rules and regulations, as well as full, fair and accurate disclosures in periodic reports. To limit the applicability to senior financial officers is thus somewhat surprising, as much of what the code of ethics concerns is presumably applicable to everyone in an organization. The NYSE Rule Proposals and Nasdaq Rule Proposals have a similar focus on upper-level management in their requirement that those waivers of a company's code of conduct made for executive officers and directors be publicly disclosed.

This focus on the highest levels of management—and on the rules applicable to them—is causing companies to rethink their codes' applicability to senior management, with a greater focus on those issues (like conflicts of interest, discussed below) where upper-level management can create the most harm. It also has important implications for the reporting procedures that are laid out in a code and that are implemented in a company's compliance program, as discussed more fully below.

Perhaps most important, this focus on potential harm caused by the most senior executives has caused corporate compliance practitioners to rethink how compliance programs protect against high-level risk. The harms that can be caused by the highest levels of management are great, and the controls oftentimes are much more difficult to implement—both from a practical perspective and from a political perspective. (The outside lawyer, the in-house lawyer and the compliance officer all report to the CEO in some manner, and so making suggestions for policing that individual is a much more difficult proposition than making suggestions for policing the sales force or the human resources department, for example.) These concerns highlight the importance of both having the audit committee involved in the oversight of the compliance program, as discussed above, and of creating appropriate reporting procedures.

REPORTING PROCEDURES

We are already seeing changes in the way companies structure reporting procedures and avenues for employees and directors to seek guidance and make disclosures regarding potentially problematic conduct. Whereas, in the past, most companies have been content to set forth avenues of reporting misconduct and disclosing conflicts that included, for example, the compliance officer, the human resources department and the legal department, many companies' recently revised codes provide additional methods for the CEO and directors to report misconduct, seek guidance or make disclosures regarding potentially problematic conduct. After all, it is likely not appropriate to have the CEO seek approval to engage in a transaction that may constitute a conflict of interest from the compliance officer, who likely reports to the CEO.

Indeed, the commentary to the SEC's Proposed Regulations implementing section 406 of Sarbanes-Oxley (the code of ethics section) notes that the persons to whom disclosures regarding conflicts of interest and reports of misconduct should be made "should have sufficient status within the company to engender respect for the code and the authority to adequately deal with the persons subject to the code, regardless of their status in the company."

(SEC Proposed Regulations n. 67 and 69.) Many companies have thus added language to their codes providing that the CEO, CFO and other high-level officers must disclose their own potential conflicts of interest directly to the audit committee or some other committee of the board and may report suspected misconduct directly to the audit committee or some other committee of the board. (There may be instances where it would not be appropriate for executive officers and directors to report suspected misconduct to the board, such as, for example, when the purported misconduct is perpetrated by lower-level employees, and the legal or compliance department is fully equipped to respond.)

As discussed above, Sarbanes-Oxley requires the SEC to prohibit the listing of any issuer whose audit committee has not established procedures for the receipt of complaints regarding accounting, internal accounting controls or auditing matters and for the confidential, anonymous submission by employees of concerns regarding questionable accounting or auditing matters. Sarbanes-Oxley also provides criminal penalties for retaliation against persons who provide law enforcement officers with information relating to the possible commission of a federal offense (with penalties of fines and up to ten years imprisonment) and for civil causes of action for persons who are discriminated against in the terms of their employment for reporting information about fraudulent activities or violations of SEC rules and regulations.

Given the additional obligations that have been placed on companies regarding reports of misconduct, some companies are for the first time developing policies to be separately disseminated to employees regarding reporting procedures and whistleblower protections. Other companies are expanding the discussion of reporting in their codes of conduct and other compliance policies. And, pursuant to the new obligations created by section 301 of Sarbanes-Oxley, the internal reporting of suspected accounting and auditing misconduct is receiving special attention.

As with other areas of recent change, the big news here may be much greater than a simple change in the language of codes of conduct or the development of separate policies regarding reporting procedures. This may instead evidence a change in how companies manage the way employees report suspected misconduct or make disclosures. There seems to be a much greater focus on ensuring that reports of suspected misconduct will reach appropriate levels within the organization and on adopting suitable safeguards to make employees feel comfortable making such reports and expressing concerns. Reporting procedures, nonretaliation provisions and promises of confidentiality are much more than buzz words these days; they are important components of effective compliance programs.

ENHANCED PUBLIC SCRUTINY

The SEC's Proposed Regulations to implement section 406 of Sarbanes-Oxley require companies to file their codes of ethics as an exhibit to their annual reports. The NYSE Rule Proposals require public companies to adopt and "disclose" codes of business conduct and ethics. Under the SEC's Proposed Regulations, the NYSE Rule Proposals and the Nasdaq Rule Proposals, waivers of codes for certain persons must be publicly disclosed. The new requirements to make codes publicly available combined with the requirements to disclose waivers for certain employees and for directors, could lead to the "watering down" of codes as companies attempt to draft codes so that waivers will rarely—if ever—be required.

Codes may also suffer from greater uniformity as companies seek to implement codes that place them firmly in step with every other company in their industry or at their level of market capitalization. Indeed, while the SEC's Proposed Regulations to implement section 406 of Sarbanes-Oxley expressly recognize that codes "do, and should, vary from company to company" and that "decisions as to the specific provisions of the code, compliance procedures and disciplinary measures for ethical breaches are best left to the company," one of the consequences of the legislation and rule-making could well be greater uniformity in all types of codes. As codes are disseminated and become publicly available, even more uniformity may result. The outcome may unfortunately be greater focus on the contents of a company's code relative to the codes of other companies and less focus on the suitability of a code to a particular company's culture history, and compliance program.

CONTENTS OF CODES

Another effect of recent rule-making may be a recasting of the contents of codes. Many companies are focusing their codes on those topics that the legislators and regulators deemed worthy of inclusion in their definitions of what constitutes a code, and some recently adopted codes address those topics either entirely or in large measure, leaving out other topics that have traditionally been included and that may be both informative to employees and helpful to companies, but were not mentioned in the legislation or rule-making. Examples include policies addressing equal employment opportunity, harassment, workplace health and safety, environmental policies, use of computer and communication resources and privacy. Because these topics were not the subject of recent rule-making, they are, in many instances, getting less attention than topics like conflicts of interest and maintaining accurate books and records.

Companies developing codes for the first time or revising their codes in light of recent rule-making should remember that codes can serve a far greater purpose than simply satisfying regulatory requirements. Codes can and should be at the heart of a company's compliance program, serving to educate employees and directors about legal obligations and company standards and about their obligations to report suspected misconduct, and setting forth the structure and parameters of a company's program to prevent and detect violations of the law. As the NYSE Rule Proposals point out, while "[n]o code of business conduct and ethics can replace the thoughtful behavior of an ethical director, officer or employee," codes "can focus the board and management on areas of ethical risk, provide guidance to personnel to help them recognize and deal with ethical issues, provide mechanisms to report unethical conduct and help to foster a culture of honesty and accountability." Codes should be drafted and revised with all of these goals in mind.

CONCLUSION

The full impact of the recent spate of rule-making and legislation on corporate compliance programs remains to be seen, and it may not be known for many years to come. What is already clear, however, is that compliance programs are in for some rather significant changes, and things are certain to look different when it is all over.

FOOTNOTES

1. With the exception of Sarbanes-Oxley, which became law on July 30, 2002, the regulations and rules discussed herein are not yet final, and are thus subject to modification.

2. In addition, section 301 of Sarbanes-Oxley requires that audit committees must have the authority to engage independent counsel and other advisors, as the audit committee deems necessary to carry out its duties. Among other things, this provision may translate into audit committees' hiring outside counsel to review a company's compliance program and report the results of that review directly to the audit committee. It is certainly not without precedent that an audit committee would ask outside counsel to review a company's compliance program, but it is somewhat unusual. This provision could make that circumstance much more commonplace.

SARBANES-OXLEY: PARDON ME IF I'M UNDERWHELMED

—DAWN-MARIE DRISCOLL

Dawn-Marie Driscoll argues that the Sarbanes-Oxley Act of 2002 will not "end up 'setting the standard' in corporate governance, financial disclosure and auditing . . . because the scandals . . . were caused by inattention to ethics and values . . . (and) you can't legislate an ethical corporate culture, a diligent board of directors or senior executives with integrity." What is needed instead is learning "how to develop corporate cultures based on values."

SEC Chairman Harvey Pitt resigned after a tenure marked by historic business ethics scandals and a flurry of attempts to do something to restore investor confidence. By all accounts, Pitt was a smart man with a deaf ear for political niceties, and at least he was smart enough not to say that the business reform legislation that Congress hurriedly passed was a case of The Emperor's New Clothes.

While I'll follow Pitt's lead and also not characterize these new initiatives quite that badly, I am underwhelmed by what they purport to do. Taken together, the Sarbanes-Oxley law and the New York Stock Exchange and Nasdaq listing requirements will not, in my opinion, end up "setting the global standard" in corporate governance, financial disclosure and auditing, as one accountancy publication predicted last September. The reason is simple: The business scandals of the past year were caused by inattention to ethics and values. You can't legislate an ethical corporate culture, a diligent board of directors or senior executives with integrity.

Let's look at what some of these new proposals contain. With a dozen sections and nearly seventy subsections, the Sarbanes-Oxley bill increases CEO accountability for financial statements, increases penalty for fraud, makes CEOs and CFOs sign off on financials and strengthens the role of the audit committee. While this all sounds admirable, we can already see what is happening in practice. CEOs and CFOs are asking those who report to them to certify their financial contributions, all the way down the line. After a while, such sign-offs will resemble the old questions at airport check-in counters: Did you pack your bag yourself and has it been with you at all times? All along, those in corporations who had a part in preparing financials—even if all they did was submit their expense reports—should have been honest about what they handed in and should have raised questions about anything they weren't sure about. Asking someone to sign a piece of paper

"Sarbanes-Oxley: Pardon Me If I'm Underwhelmed," by Dawn-Marie Driscoll. Reprinted from *Ethics Matters,* February 10, 2003, with permission of the Center for Business Ethics, Bentley College, and the author.

won't make any difference. It will create an additional workload that will add expense and perhaps little or no increased value to shareholders.

The new law also bans nine types of non-audit consulting services by outside auditors—prohibitions that audit committees could have established years ago. It requires that auditors give reports to audit committees on critical accounting policies and practices, information on alternative treatments of financial information, including the auditors' preferred treatment. The auditors must also bring to the audit committee's attention any material written communications with management, which could include disagreements as to the presentation of the company's accounts. This is surely information that auditors should have been sharing, and audit committees demanding, years ago.

Some of the stock exchanges' listing requirements purport to strengthen board independence by requiring a majority of independent directors, requiring executive sessions and tightening the definition of independence. So how is this new? Those best practice recommendations have been around for years, if boards wanted to follow them. The National Association of Corporate Directors, General Motors, the American Bar Association, TIAA-CREF and others have published corporate governance recommendations that are well-known. The 1999 Best Practices for Mutual Fund Directors report recommended that two-thirds of the board be independent, that directors have their own outside counsel and other advisers, that they meet in executive session, that former company executives *never* be board members, that boards have a lead director and set their own agenda and many other recommendations. Diligent corporate boards didn't have to wait for new legislation to benchmark themselves against the best boards—and if they had been following these recommendations, Enron, Tyco, WorldCom, Adelphia and other scandals might not have happened.

Furthermore, let's look at the behavior of some directors implicated in these scandals. To pick one example, the famous LJM off-balance sheet Enron partnerships, the Enron board:

- Approved LJM1 partnership at a *one-hour* conference call on June 28, 1999. Also on the agenda was a major stock split, an increase in shares in the company's stock compensation plan, purchase of a company jet, investment in a Middle Eastern power plant and a major corporate reorganization. The code of conduct waiver and the complicated stock hedge were approved with little study or debate and were never reviewed first by the finance committee.

- Never reviewed the second LJM partnership materials. Had the Board done so, the Directors would have learned that it named not only Andrew Fastow (CFO and LJM mastermind), but also two other senior Enron financial officers as LJM2 principals, both of whom worked for Fastow and neither of whom had obtained a code of conduct waiver to participate in LJM2.

- Relied on the company to develop and implement controls to monitor LJM.

- Did not read LJM's annual report.

Finally, the board's compensation committee asked for but never received information on senior officers' outside compensation and never followed up.

No legislation can make a board put in the time, ask hard questions, consult outside advisers or challenge management if the directors think their role is to meet periodically, have a collegial dinner and make the next plane home. Furthermore, as anyone who has participated in a telephone meeting well knows, inattention is rampant. Such meetings are fine for information updates but rarely for the conduct of serious business.

Finally, some of these "reforms" call for company codes of ethics and public disclosure of any waivers to the code. No investor should be excited about this; a study of the Fortune 1000 found that 98% already address ethics in formal documents, with 78% having a separate code of ethics. Enron, WorldCom and others all had codes of ethics and company values— but these proved to be "paper programs." These compliance mechanisms don't help employees who are faced with situations that aren't found in the rulebook. For instance, an employee might ask what do I do when my boss submits an expense voucher for prostitutes? Should I help construct a false trading room to fool visiting analysts? If the culture is not inherently ethical and is motivated by values such as greed and ego, a code of ethics, published or not, won't help. Nor will provisions requiring that waivers of the code be disclosed. There should not be any waivers to the code of ethics and to allow them indicates the reform-drafters don't understand the best practices of contemporary business ethics.

When Enron, Tyco, WorldCom and others came to light, Congressmen acted like Captain Renault in the movie *Casablanca*: "shocked, shocked" that financial scandals may have resulted from legislative loopholes passed a few years earlier, from accounting reforms buried in legislative limbo and from an underfunded SEC. Unwilling to go home to the voters and say, "Capitalism is not risk-free," they needed to pass some laws that would make everyone feel better. It won't work.

Capitalism is not risk-free, but it must not be ethics-free. Our capital market structure is built on trust. Regulators can't examine every company's books. Investors, lenders and donors have to rely on the integrity of directors and senior managers. Directors and executives have to rely on the expertise and candor of their auditors and lawyers. Auditors have to rely on what they are told by management. Employees, customers, shareholders and communities have to rely on all of the above.

There is no law or requirement that can be passed that will mandate, "Do a good job." But economic and political leaders of integrity could have stood up and, like the little child who exposed the Emperor, said, "The folks who were responsible for those business scandals were not business leaders of integrity. There is no shortcut or quick fix to that." And then those of us in the world of business ethics could have begun to educate those who want to learn how to develop corporate cultures based on values.

BOARD GOVERNANCE
POST-ENRON

—JIM CLARKE

Jim Clarke lays out the responsibilities of board members post-Enron. The specific targets of his comments are boards of community banks; but his principles apply across the board. He insists on two characteristics that every board member should have: (1) care about the institution and (2) loyalty to the institution.

Over the last two years numerous corporate failures have shaken the faith in American capitalism, many fostering an embarrassment to the free market system. In this environment corporate governance has come to be the focus of attention, and rightly it should be, but one also should keep the situation in perspective: Enron, Tyco, Adelphia and other corporate failures, that have eroded hundreds of billions of dollars of stockholder equity, may be cases of malfeasance, fraud and outright embezzlement; that is, alien to the culture in the typical community bank boardroom.

Post-Enron has already created the Sarbanes-Oxley Act and renewed scrutiny by regulators. This attention will affect board governance and place renewed pressure on boards to re-evaluate their roles. But in the end we will probably reconfirm the basic roles of the board. A board member needs to care about the business he or she oversees, and be loyal to the business—these are the roles of a board pre-Enron, and I would suspect post-Enron. I am sure the SEC, NASD, NYSE, along with the Sarbanes-Oxley legislation will again attempt to codify the role of board members, but in the end we are likely to see a reaffirmation of care and loyalty.

The role of a community bank board member is to care about the institution and ensure that they are loyal to the bank. Note that this was also the role of the Enron board. What does care mean? I would define care as the willingness and ability to conduct serious due diligence. In order to conduct serious due diligence one needs to understand the business. This was one of the failures of the Enron board—they had no idea of the complexity of the business; therefore how could they conduct due diligence. Community bank directors need to understand the basic financial concepts of the business. Audit committee members needs to have a better understanding of the financial picture. There are two solutions to this issue; stack your board with CPAs or preferably select competent individuals and provide education and training to ensure that they understand the basic balance sheet and income statement relationships.

Care relates to due diligence and this is not possible if a board member does not have the ability to understand the critical relationships in the bank. There is another issue that

---

needs to be addressed and that is the commitment to due diligence. Allow me to offer a simple example: If a board member spends five months a year in Florida and meets board obligations through a phone conference each month, that person probably does not meet the test of care and should be removed from the board.

The Sarbanes-Oxley Act and the regulatory initiatives are also concerned with the second important role of a board member which is loyalty. This is often couched in the terms of independence or conflict of interest. Loyalty is not a new concern, but rather the essence of board responsibility. Loyalty is not complicated—my first concern is the company. The more important question is: Why would I not be loyal to the company? The most obvious answer is lack of independence very often associated with a conflict of interest. Conflict of interest is a major theme in many of the solutions offered by both Congress and the regulators. In community banking conflicts often exist, and need to be addressed. Some issues are easy to address; for example, if board members or their employer are receiving revenue from the bank this could be a red flag that needs to be addressed. At a less obvious level, but equally important, are board members who depend on the board fees as an important supplement to their income—can they be independent?

Conflicts of interest and independence need to be addressed by all community banks, especially as it relates to the audit committee. In fact the initial fallout from Sarbanes-Oxley is likely to have its greatest impact on the audit committee. The touchy issue for most CEOs is eventually going to be the definition of "independence" and the ultimate interpretation of independence, because in its extreme it could be interpreted as a continual adversarial position between the CEO and the board, and this would be counterproductive in my opinion. In my experience, success in community banking depends on a partnership between the CEO and the board, especially the chairman of the board. When the CEO and the chairman of the board are on the same page success and profitability are more likely to be the result. Of all the consequences arising from Enron, it is legislation and regulation that destroy a cooperative relationship between management and the board that could be the most harmful.

ACCOUNTING FIRMS FACE BACKLASH OVER THE TAX SHELTERS THEY SOLD

—Cassell Bryan-Low

Cassell Bryan-Low describes the increasing problem of the abuse of tax shelters—a problem costing the United States government billions of dollars each year in revenue. Wherever there is legislative regulation, there will be those who invent ways to skirt the regulation by following only the letter of the law and violating the spirit of the law.

A number of things struck Henry Camferdam as unusual when he sat down in late 1999 with tax experts from Ernst & Young LLP. He and three colleagues had just sold their computer business. The meeting, at the accounting firm's downtown office here, was called to show them how they could legally shield their $70 million in profit from federal income taxes.

But first they had to sign papers agreeing not to tell anyone how the strategy worked. Only then, Mr. Camferdam says in an interview, did two Ernst & Young tax partners give a 40-minute presentation outlining the complex deal. The tax partners said the deal would be hidden from the Internal Revenue Service, according to Mr. Camferdam.

He says he didn't quite understand the plan—and wasn't allowed to take the marketing materials with him to study later. But he says he signed on, relying on the firm's reputation and the advice of his auditor and accountant who also worked for Ernst. Mr. Camferdam and his associates paid about $7 million in fees for a strategy that put their taxes at close to zero.

Now the move is beginning to look costly, both for them and for Ernst. The IRS is auditing the Ernst tax strategy, meaning that the four clients potentially face back taxes, penalties and interest of more than $20 million. They have sued Ernst in federal court in New York, alleging that the firm exploited its position as a trusted adviser, fraudulently luring them into "an illegitimate tax sham." Ernst has declined to discuss specifics of the suit, which it is fighting in court, but terms it "frivolous" and "without merit."

The dispute is just one part of a new wave of scandal hitting the accounting business. Ernst, along with nearly every other major accounting firm, is under attack for tax advice given to individuals, many of them highfliers now being pressed by the IRS to pay significant sums to cover taxes they avoided at the firms' advice. Clients are suing accountants in a sour aftermath to the profession's push in the 1990s for new markets that paid better than auditing work.

Simmering in boardrooms and courthouses for months, the issue broke into prominence this week as Sprint Corp. asked its chief executive, William Esrey, and its president, Ronald LeMay, to step down over tax-shelter deals they had gotten into. They have said they did nothing wrong and blame Ernst for providing bad advice. The accounting firm has issued a statement standing by its advice.

The IRS also is cracking down. It has pledged to close the tax loophole used by the Sprint executives and others. Last year the agency sued to force Arthur Andersen, KPMG LLP and BDO Seidman LLP to turn over shelter-related documents. The government accused the firms of flouting tax laws to help hundreds of companies and individuals avoid billions of dollars of taxes through improper shelters. The IRS has identified dozens of clients it says KPMG sold questionable tax shelters to, including former chairman of Global Crossing Ltd. Chairman Gary Winnick, Guess? Inc. Chief Executive Maurice Marciano, and New Line Cinema Chairman Robert K. Shaye. All declined to comment.

'TIDAL WAVE'

Accounting firms "are now facing a tidal wave of lawsuits over tax shelters that could do tremendous damage," says Lynn Turner, a former chief accountant at the Securities and Exchange Commission. He says this seriously threatens their credibility with clients, including wealthy executives, who may decide the advice they're getting is misleading.

The scope of the tax-avoidance problem has reached huge proportions. During 2002, the IRS got information suggesting that a million taxpayers could have been using one scheme alone—anonymous offshore bank accounts that allow them to hide money away yet gain access to it through credit or debit cards. The IRS confronts 82,100 cases of abusive devices a year, though it doesn't have the staff to pursue all of them, former IRS Commissioner Charles Rossotti wrote in a report late last year.

A federal clampdown in the 1980s on tax shelters marketed by accountants and others prompted some investors to sue their advisers. What distinguishes the recent wave of activity is the energy that large accounting firms have devoted to devising strategies themselves, as well as the scale of their marketing efforts and the size of fees earned.

The 1990s boom produced a large pool of rich potential clients, most unfamiliar with tax-law complexities. At the same time, accounting firms were looking for new revenue as that from audits flagged. A 1991 change in the profession's rules provided a helping hand: Accountants could now charge performance-based fees just like investment bankers, as opposed to the traditional hourly rate.

So big accounting firms formed teams dedicated to promoting high-margin tax strategies. Fees to the accounting firm ranged from 10% to 40% of taxes saved. The individual tax salesmen who snagged deals could get up to 10% of this. At Deloitte & Touche LLP, a large group of salesmen informally known among some members as the "Predator" group hunted clients armed with a long list of creative tax ideas. Deloitte says it does have dedicated a sales team but says it has no knowledge of that name.

"The pressure became to sell things that would be in your best interest rather than the clients'," says Robert Verzi, a former Deloitte tax partner in Atlanta who left in 2000 to join a regional firm. A Deloitte spokesman said he didn't "want to dignify such an incorrect assertion with a response."

BDO Seidman had a tax-sales team known in-house as the "wolf pack." It generated shelter sales of more than $100 million in 2000—more than half of the firm's tax revenue—according to documents filed in Chicago federal court as part of a July enforcement action.

Audit firms offered big pay packages to compete with law firms for top talent. Some tax experts moved between government posts and the accounting firms' Washington tax offices. There they ruled on tricky tax issues, interacted with regulators and often devised the strategies. Training for tax partners began to include a heavy dose of salesmanship—with coaching in voice-projection and how to make presentations.

"The pressure on the partner group to sell became severe, it became a monster that needed to be fed," says Donald M. Griswold, a former KPMG tax partner who left in 2001 and now works at a Washington law firm.

Mr. Camferdam says he saw a taste of this in his dealings with Ernst. The strategy it sold him created paper losses to offset capital gains through a complex series of transactions. They included the purchase and sale of long and short currency options, transferring them and other assets to a newly created partnership, and other steps that inflated the value of the assets before they were sold.

All of which seemed fine until one day in December, when the IRS sent him a large white hand-addressed envelope informing him he was under audit. Mr. Camferdam contends Ernst abused its position of trust. "It's like having a policeman there with you, you don't think you're committing a crime," he says in an interview.

The case shows how well these deals paid, not only for accountants but also for the lawyers and bankers brought in for their help. For accountants and lawyers, Mr. Camferdam and his three colleagues paid a fee of 4.5% of capital losses that the shelter created to shield capital gains from taxes. About one-third of that, or $1.06 million, went to Ernst.

About two-thirds of the fee, or $2.04 million, went to the law firm of Jenkens & Gilchrist, which the suit says helped develop the deal and provided a legal blessing. So-called opinion letters from law firms are vital to tax-shelter sales. The four entrepreneurs also paid lawyers Brown & Wood, now part of Sidley Austin Brown & Wood LLP, $75,000 for a second legal opinion. The opinion letters may help taxpayers who are challenged by the IRS to avoid penalties, although they're no guarantee.

Jenkens & Gilchrist declined to comment on the fees or the Camferdam suit, in which the law firm is a defendant. Sidley Austin, also a defendant, has called the lawsuit without merit.

Beyond those fees, the clients paid Deutsche Bank $3.52 million for conducting the transactions involved in the shelter. Officials of the bank, which isn't a defendant, couldn't be reached for comment.

One reason the tax maneuvers are lucrative for accounting firms is that once devised, they can be marketed to potentially thousands of clients, both corporate and individual. In the case of the Ernst shelter sold to Mr. Camferdam, at least 47 other individuals used the same transaction, generating $50 million in fees, according to his and his colleagues' suit.

Their lawyer, Blair Fensterstock, of Fensterstock & Partners LLP, says he has been contacted by a dozen other Ernst clients who say they received similar pitches.

BLIPS

KPMG partners sold a tax strategy, dubbed BLIPS, to at least 186 clients during 1999 and 2000, according to documents the IRS filed in a federal court as part of its enforcement action against the firm in July. The documents claim the strategy deprived the Treasury of about $1.28 billion in taxes. The suit says KPMG sold another strategy, known by the acronyms FLIP and OPIS, to at least 160 clients. The IRS has identified both as potentially "abusive" shelters. KPMG has maintained that the tax advice it marketed was appropriate.

Among those who bought the FLIP/OPIS strategy was Joseph J. Jacoboni, a software entrepreneur from Lake Mary, Fla. Now under IRS audit, he has accused KPMG of fraudulently misrepresenting the risks associated with the deal. In a suit in federal court in Orlando, Fla., Mr. Jacoboni contends KPMG officials assured him the strategy was bullet-proof and strictly complied with IRS rules, but told him that for reasons of confidentiality he couldn't get an independent legal review.

Mr. Jacoboni had generated $28 million in capital gains in 1997 by selling a stake in his technology company. His suit says KPMG told him it could save him millions of dollars in taxes. Mr. Jacoboni claims in the suit that he didn't understand the complex deal but went along, somewhat reluctantly, relying on the accounting firm's "blue chip" reputation.

Four years later, he learned that the IRS was auditing his 1997 tax return. In a phone call in the summer of 2001, he says in his suit, a KPMG partner told him that the firm had known for at least two years prior to the call that the IRS was challenging investments similar to the one conducted for him. His suit says this partner suggested he settle with the IRS, which he says he has since agreed to do.

The suit also alleges a "pattern of racketeering" by KPMG, naming more than 20 others that it contends were defrauded in a similar manner in 1997 and 1998. KPMG "aggressively marketed its tax strategies" through such techniques as a "Wealth Management" seminar it sponsored in Phoenix, says the suit.

KPMG say it doesn't comment on the work it performs for clients. The accounting firm has been fighting the Jacoboni lawsuit, contesting its specific allegations in court.

Tax experts at PricewaterhouseCoopers were busy designing their own deals, but in 1999, a big marketing push blew up in their face. The Treasury forced the firm to back away from a strategy known by the acronym BOSS that could have produced tens of millions of dollars in deductions.

Pricewaterhouse has scaled back its tax-shelter operations, partners say, and last summer paid about $1 million to the IRS to settle matters relating to tax-shelter registration. IRS rules require promoters to register shelters that the agency has identified as potentially abusive and to keep lists of investors; those can face stiff penalties of up to 1% of all sheltered funds. PwC says it doesn't currently sell any transactions the IRS lists as potentially abusive.

The IRS, knowing it can be years before audits identify a new type of abusive shelter, has focused increasingly on the promoters of the strategies. In a flurry of activity last year, the IRS sought tax-shelter-related information from 20 auditors and other promoters, issuing roughly

200 summonses. It has filed enforcement action against several accounting firms, including KPMG, BDO Seidman and Andersen, to force them to hand over documents—which the firms consider privileged—relating to transactions dating back to as early as 1995.

At Andersen, the agency identified at least 48 clients that invested in "potentially abusive tax-shelter transactions" with claimed deductions ranging from $10 million to $1.6 billion, according to the agency's September enforcement action against that firm in federal court in Chicago. A federal district judge in November ordered Andersen to give the IRS the documents, a potential boon to its efforts to obtain similar documents from KPMG and BDO. Both those cases are awaiting final rulings.

DECLARATION OF
MICHAEL A. HALPERT

In the following affidavit filed in the case of the United States v. KPMG, LLP, *Michael Halpert summarizes the laws governing tax shelters. The statement defines a tax shelter, and that which constitutes an abuse of those shelters. Generally they are defined as those transactions that have no discernible business use except the avoidance of a tax.*

*   *   *

II. THE LAWS GOVERNING TAX SHELTERS

4. For decades individuals and businesses have sought to arrange their financial affairs in ways to minimize their federal taxes. Some of these arrangements take "abusive" forms, in that they are not motivated by any significant business purpose, but are driven almost exclusively by the desire to achieve tax savings, without regard to the economic viability of the underlying transactions.

5. With one stated goal being to establish "transparency" for potentially abusive tax shelters, in 1984 Congress enacted the first comprehensive system to regulate the development, promotion and marketing of tax shelters. The aim of "transparency" has aspects that encompass both the organizers and the investors. The aspects that impact organizers and promoters are discussed below.

6. Beginning on September 1, 1984, 26 U.S.C. § 6111 generally requires organizers of tax shelters to register each tax shelter with the IRS, before offering to the public the opportunity to participate in the shelter. In addition, § 6112 requires organizers and sellers of potentially abusive tax shelters to maintain a list of all investors in each shelter, and make that list available to the IRS on 10 days' notice. Organizers and sellers that do not register the tax shelter under § 6111 before offering it for sale may be liable for penalties imposed by § 6707. Organizers who do not maintain or produce to the IRS upon request the list of investors required by § 6112 may be liable for penalties imposed by § 6708. The Internal Revenue Code also imposes penalties for filing incomplete or inaccurate information, for promoting abusive tax shelters (§ 6700), and for aiding or abetting others to materially understate their tax liabilities (§ 6701). United States District Courts have jurisdiction to enjoin promoters of abusive tax shelters, and the IRS has sought and obtained such injunctions against tax shelter promoters.

"Declaration of Michael A. Halpert," affidavit of Michael A. Halpert, Internal Revenue Service agent.

7. In § 6111(c), the 1984 law defined "tax shelter" generally to encompass investments in which the investor expected to achieve at least two dollars in tax savings from the arrangement for every dollar invested in the shelter.

8. In 1997 Congress amended § 6111 by adding a new subsection, § 6111(d), to cover the newly emerging forms of corporate tax shelters. That statute defines "tax shelter" to include transactions where a "significant purpose" of the structure is the avoidance or evasion of tax, where the arrangement is offered to potential participants under conditions of confidentiality, and where the aggregate promoter fees exceed $100,000.

9. In 2000, the Secretary of the Treasury promulgated temporary regulations under § 6111. Among other things, those regulations authorized the IRS to publish a list of arrangements which it considers to be tax shelters subject to the registration, disclosure and recordkeeping requirements of §§ 6111 and 6112. When the IRS publishes a notice listing such transactions as tax shelters, they are referred to as "listed transactions." Once the IRS publishes the notice, the listed transactions (and all other substantially similar arrangements) are subject to the requirements of §§ 6111 and 6112. Temp. Treas. Reg. § 301.6111-2T(b)(2), Since 2000, the IRS has from time to time published notices of such "listed transactions." . . .

10. One purpose of listing transactions is to notify promoters of the need to register the transaction under § 6111. Another purpose is to preclude investors in such transactions from attempting to use the "substantial authority" defense to the substantial understatement penalty imposed by 26 U.S.C. § 6662.

11. The temporary regulations also provide a way for an organizer or promoter to obtain an advance ruling from the IRS as to whether a particular arrangement will be considered a tax shelter under § 6111. Temp. Treas. Reg. § 301.6111-2T(b)(4)(ii).

12. The registration, reporting and recordkeeping requirements apply to "tax shelter organizers," as defined in § 6111(d). Where the shelter was registered under § 6111, that term means the person "principally responsible" for organizing the shelter. Where the shelter was not registered, that terms [sic] includes any person who participated in organizing the shelter. Under temporary Treasury Regulations, that includes anyone who performed any act, directly or through an agent, related to the establishment of the shelter, including the preparation of a tax opinion (Temp. Treas. Reg. § 301.6111-1T Q&A 28), the management of the shelter (Q&A 29), or the sale of the shelter (Q&A 31). On this last point, § 6111(d)(4) provides that an offer to participate in a shelter shall be treated as an offer for sale.

SPECULATION AND INSIDER TRADING AS A PROBLEM OF BUSINESS ETHICS

—PETER KOSLOWSKI

The stock exchange is the central institution of mediation between the supply of and demand for capital. Its function as capital market leads to a large trading of shares and obligations that causes and requires stock market speculation. The paper analyzes stock market speculation and investigates the ethical-economic evaluation of speculation and insider trading from the approach of an ethical economy.

The professional speculation at the stock exchange fulfills the economic function of carrying the burden of uncertainty about the future marketability and tradability of shares and obligations. Insider trading after tips from managers or professionals working at the stock exchange is not speculation but pseudo-speculation that does not serve the absorption of uncertainty in the economy since the insider information is already available for the public and the insider acts under knowledge about future developments. Insider trading must therefore be judged as ethically inadmissible. Although legislation prohibits insider trading in the European Union, there is no agreement on the question of whether insider trading is detrimental or not in the debate on economics and law.

What is proper conduct in the capital market, and what does justice in exchange and in pricing mean in the stock exchange?

I. INSIDER TRADING AS A FOCUS OF THE ETHICAL QUESTIONS OF THE STOCK EXCHANGE

Insider trading is not the only ethically relevant problem of the capital market. There are other aspects of proper conduct in the capital market like the ethics of the selection of stocks for investment, i.e., the economic ethics of the investor, and the ethics of the corporations listed in the stock exchange concerning their behavior toward their shareholders and the stock market. There are also questions of an ethics of the intermediaries in the stock markets like brokers and bankers transcending the insider trading problem.

The ethics of all these three groups of participants in the stock exchange, investors as suppliers of capital, corporate finance as demand for capital and the financial intermediaries as brokers between supply and demand, is touched upon in the problem of insider trading, so that the pros and cons for insider trading go to the core of an ethical economy of the capital market. The German discussion on insider trading is controversial among economists and legal scholars. The fronts in this discussion follow mostly the line separating economists and legal scholars. Whereas economists usually favor insider trading with the argument that insider trading increases the allocative efficiency of the stock market,[1] legal scholars argue in favor of its prohibition with arguments of justice, of equal justice towards all shareholders and of legal safety and stability in the stock exchange.[2]

This opposition between the points of view of economists and legal scholars in the assessment of insider trading indicates the underlying difference of normative criteria between the two disciplines. Whereas economists tend to concentrate on the aspect of the allocative function of the stock market, legal scholars favor a perspective that takes several normative criteria into account. In its attempt to synthesize the criteria of efficiency and justice, the theory of ethical economy finds itself here closer to the legal than to the purely economic approach, since the former is more open to the integration of numerous criteria.

The judgment from the perspective of ethical economy is of a higher order than the economic one, since it aims at integrating the two aspects of the good, the efficient and the just, into its reasoning. Applied to the capital market and the question of insider trading, the question of ethical economy is whether insider trading is efficient *and* just or fair, not whether it is efficient only. When the legal point of view is added to the one of ethical economy, the criteria of the legal safety and calculability of the rules and of the justiciability in cases of offenses against the rules of the stock exchange enter the picture. The law is defined by its ability to foster certainty of expectations and legal safety as well as to render conflicts justiciable.

The question of the ethical economy of the capital market and of the admissibility of insider trading is threefold. It is first the question of the institutional ethics and economics of the institution "capital market," which is part of the ethics and economics of the larger cultural sphere and the societal subsystem or concrete order of life "market economy." It is, thereby, a question of economic law, too. The ethical economy of insider trading is secondly a question of organizational ethics regarding the organizations' policies, culture and conduct, and thirdly a question of personal ethics, the organizations and individuals working within the rules of the game "stock exchange."

The system of obligations arises from the nature of the matter in three respects. The obligation is derived from the purpose or teleology of the institution, from the idea of justice and from the prerequisites of legal safety. The purpose of the sphere of culture and law in question, the idea of justice, especially of formal justice in the sense of the principle of equality and the demands of certainty in the definition of law and in jurisdiction define the obligation of ethics and of law. According to Radbruch, the idea of law arises from the purpose or teleology of the sphere to be ruled, from the principle of formal justice and from the principle of safe legal procedure.[3]

---

[1]Cf. Engel (1991) and Schneider (1993).
[2]Cf. Grunewald (1990) and Hopt (1991).
[3]Radbruch (1973), p. 114.

II. THE NATURE AND FUNCTION OF STOCK MARKET SPECULATION: BEARING UNCERTAINTY

Applied to the question of the ethics and legislation of the capital market, one must judge the problem of insider trading from the criterion of the purpose or teleology of the institution "capital market," from the criterion of formal justice or equal right of all participants in the capital market, and from the criterion of legal safety and stability.

The teleology or function of the institution of the capital market within the order of the economy is the following. The capital market fulfills two tasks in which it resembles the credit market. Like the latter, the capital market functions as the transfer process, in which savings are transferred into investment, and as the transformation process, in which investment of different terms of time periods are transformed into investments of long term ownership titles or securities. The transfer of savings and the transformation of time periods are accomplished in the capital market for shares not by the financial intermediaries of banks but by the securitization of the loans, by their marketability in the stock exchange and by the existence of speculative trading of securities. The function banks fulfill in the credit market is exercised in the stock exchange by other institutions, namely by the control of the issuing of new shares effected by the stock exchange administration or by government,[4] by the marketability of shares and securitized loans and by professional and amateur speculation about future prices of stock.

Investing in shares in the capital market is—compared to deposits in banks—an investment of higher risk. The stock market serves as the means to allocate investible funds to companies according to price differentials reflecting the expected risk and profit of the companies taking part in the stock exchange as they are seen by the market participants. The prices of shares reflect the assessment of return and risk.

Shareholders are investors bearing as owners the full risk for their invested capital. Given full publicity about the past and present record and the future strategy of the corporation, the price of its shares is formed in the market according to the assessment of the past and present performance and of the future expected return and risk.

In an ideal market, each share would have a fixed market price. Hardly any trading would take place, since the price would be the same for everyone at every period of time. In reality, however, there are huge trading volumes in the existing modern capital markets. According to Friedman, the annual trading volume on the New York Stock Exchange, for example, is normally nearly one half of the total value of listed existing shares.[5] Friedman explains this huge trading of shares by the different risk assessments of investors but does not mention the differentials in the intended duration of investment and the contingently changing decisions to divest shares. Shares are permanent or at least long-run investment. The ownership title they define remains constant, but their actual owners change in time. The periods of holding shares can be transformed at low transaction costs compared to other ownership patterns. The transformation is made possible by the marketability of shares in the stock exchange. That shares be marketable requires in turn that the supply of a given

---

[4]In Germany, the so called "anchoring principle" (*Verankerungsprinzip*) is effective. The law states that issuing bonds or shares in German Marks (DM) can only be effected by an issuing bank whose headquarters is in Germany. For the effect of this principle on decreasing international competition in the German capital market cf. Breuer (1990), p. 101.
[5]Friedman (1987), p. 323.

share find a demand for that same share at any given moment in time, even if the originally intended time periods of investment in this share do not coincide between the buyer and seller. The transformation of different periods of investment is done by trading. The supply and demand for shares, their marketability, are enormously increased by a group that, in the division of labor, professionally trades stock, the group of professional speculators.

Professional speculation creates trading volume by adding supply and demand of shares in the stock exchange that exceed the volume that would exist in the absence of speculation, when investment in shares is effected for returns from permanent investment only. Speculation is that sort of economic activity that tries to gain profit from differentials between present and future prices of stock. The speculator speculating *à la hausse* ("bull") assumes that the future price of a share will be higher than its present. Speculation *à la baisse* ("bear") speculates that the price will be lower. The bullish speculator tries to make profit by buying shares today and selling them in the future. His investment decision does not concentrate on the expected return from dividends but on the differential between future and present stock value of the share. The division of labor in the stock market between those concentrating on the returns and capital value of the stock, the investors in the proper sense, and those concentrating on the differentials of fluctuations of stock value in time, the speculators, makes sure that the investment in shares can be liquidated at any given moment of time.[6] The speculation in shares increases the marketability of shares and, thereby, the transformability of time periods of capital investment in the stock market. Professional stock market speculation decreases the risk not to be able to transform the periods of investment and divestment in shares and thereby renders an important service to the economy.

Speculation bears part of the uncertainty about future random changes of investment periods and increases the investor's independence on the time horizon of the other investors, of their time schedule for their investment or divestment in stocks. The profits from speculation are the price that the non-speculative investors must pay to the speculators for their provision of the additional trading of stocks. Professional speculation—besides having other more problematic aspects—is the intelligent gambling for profit that produces the side effect that the trading of stock is increased and the transformation of investment periods facilitated. Speculation on the spot market for stocks resembles the speculation in futures in its effect on the increase in the trading of stock.

The speculation in the forward market for commodities, currency or stock enables the hedging of prices for those commodities and stocks whose producers or investors do not want to speculate but to calculate with predictable prices for future goods. Speculation in futures serves as an insurance on future prices for the non-speculators. In the same manner, the increase in trading by speculation in stocks in the spot market is an insurance for those who want to be free in their decisions about the time period of their investment in shares. The spot market speculation in stock assures the non-speculative investors that they will be able to find demand for their shares whenever they want to divest them. In the forward market, the division of labor between the speculating and the hedging market participants stems

---

[6]Cf. Röpke (1926), p. 708.

from the fact that some people must speculate so that others can calculate with ascertained or certain future prices.[7] In the spot market for stocks, the effect of speculation is not the complete insurance of future prices but the assurance that the time periods of investment in stocks will be transformable in the future by selling or buying in the stock market.

The assurance of time transformability of shares through speculation in the stock market is economically advantageous only if speculation is not interested in price fluctuations of stock and, therefore, does not increase in the fluctuations of stock prices over time. In case professional speculation increases the price fluctuations because it makes profit out of them, the negative effect of increased price fluctuations through speculation can outweigh the welfare gains from increased marketability of shares. Economic theory distinguishes between speculation in stocks with a negative and a positive elasticity of demand for shares on expectations of stock prices. Speculation with negative elasticity of expectations describes the speculative investment in stocks that acts contrarily to the expectations of the market and, therefore, sells shares when the market expects higher future prices and buys when the market expects lower future prices. This sort of speculation decreases the fluctuations of prices of stock by contracyclical investment behavior. Speculation with a positive elasticity of demand for stock, in turn, buys and sells stock in accord with the prevalent expectations of the market, acting cyclically with the majority of the participants in the market. It thus increases the fluctuations of prices and results in negative welfare effects.

Speculation is, however, most profitable when its price anticipations are correct and when it acts contracyclically under negative elasticity of demand for stock on market expectations. It is not very profitable when it follows the market expectations with positive elasticity, and it is not profitable at all when it is wrong in its prediction about future prices. There is, therefore, a built-in tendency in speculation, brought in by the profit motive, to anticipate future price-changes of stock correctly, and there is a motive to speculate in such a way that stock market fluctuations are suppressed by the higher profitability of contracyclical speculation.

The thesis that speculation in the spot market for stocks absorbs uncertainty about future transformability of periods of investment contends that it is the function of speculation in the stock market to reduce an uncertainty of the market participants that cannot be made up for by other means. The risk of return and bankruptcy can be calculated approximately by the market, the uncertainty about future periods for which investors want to hold their investment cannot be calculated by means of the calculus of probability.[8] It can only be speculated about it.

The part of pure speculation about the uncertain and random path of stock prices being independent of returns and the part of genuine long run investment in shares as the risk bearing of owning partners should, therefore, be analytically distinguished. In actual stock market behavior, however, the speculators can only speculate by being investors in stock also. Stock market speculation is ethically admissible since it fulfills an objective function

---

[7]Cf. Nell-Breuning (1928), p. 129: Professional speculation fulfills "das Entlastungsbedürfnis derjenigen Wirtschaftskreise, 'die nicht spekulieren wollen, sondern nur kalkulieren möchten' (Terhalle)" (the favor demand of those participants in the market who do not want to speculate but would like to calculate only).

[8]See for the distinction between risk and uncertainty Knight (1921).

in the economy: the reduction of uncertainty about marketability of shares in the stock exchange. Profits from speculation are payments for this service rendered to the public in the stock exchange and are justified by the economic surplus created by speculation.

That the contribution to the common good by reducing uncertainty justifies professional speculation means in turn that speculation which does not reduce an otherwise, i.e., by other means than speculation, irreducible uncertainty is not economically and ethically justifiable. Speculation is justified as the absorption of uncertainty where there is no other way to handle it. Where uncertainty can be reduced by less costly means than speculation, this means should be used. Where speculation does not really reduce uncertainty, it is not justified.

III. INSIDER TRADING AS PSEUDO-SPECULATION AND AGIOTAGE

In the case of insider trading in the stock exchange there is no real uncertainty, since the facts of the insider information are already known uncertainty can be reduced by less costly means, i.e., by the publication of the insider information to the public. The insider produces no real good and renders no service to the stock market participants that could not be produced by the simple publication of the insider fact by the corporation affected. The insiders' speculation is a sort of pseudo-speculation, since the speculating insider does not bear uncertainty but a pseudo-uncertainty about the facts of his insider information. The insider still bears some risk—the takeover could fail to take place in the end although the insider was told so, the effects of the journalist's recommendation for a share could be less strong than he or she anticipated, etc. The insider's risk is, however, much lower than that of the other speculators acting in the same market.

Profits from professional speculation are the remuneration for the productive effect of absorbing uncertainty. Where the speculator's effort is not productive, since he or she bears only pseudo-uncertainty, it does not carry the legitimization to earn profit. The insider speculator absorbing only pseudo-uncertainty is not entitled to the profit arising from his or her insider trading. Analogous to gambling, the inside speculator plays with marked cards by reducing the element of chance and uncertainty inherent in speculation only for himself and not for all players. The inside speculator is playing the game with less uncertainty than his or her co-speculators, and the profit he or she derives from playing the game with marked cards does not correspond to his or her economic performance and productive contribution.

1. Arbitrage, Speculation, Agiotage

The productive result of insider trading speculation is neither arbitrage nor true speculation but agiotage. Arbitrage is the productive effort to earn profit from equilibrating price differences in space. The arbitrageur makes profit by lowering the price differential between different places at the same time. When the level of the interest rates for credits is low in Tokyo and high in Rome at the same date, it is profitable arbitrage to borrow money at low interest in Tokyo and to lend it at high interest rate in Rome. The arbitrageur reduces the differential between the prices at different places and equilibrates price levels between two places by removing an oversupply in one trading place and reducing a shortage—in our case a shortage of credit—in the other. Arbitrage creates welfare effects by equilibrating prices between different markets at one moment of time, speculation is the equilibration of prices at the same marketplace between different moments of time. Speculation is, so to say, arbitrage between points of time, not between points of space. Both, arbitrage and speculation, render the service of equilibrating prices to the economy.

From arbitrage and speculation, agiotage must be distinguished. Agiotage designates the activity of making profit by raising a mere surcharge (*agio*) on a given good or service without adding value to it. The price difference between the shares bought and the shares sold is just the surcharge or agio levered by the agiotageur. The insider is an agiotageur who, although he or she buys at time t and sells at time t + 1, adds no value to the goods traded, i.e., shares, since the information on which he or she bases the profit was already there at time t. The distinction between arbitrage in space and arbitrage in time or speculation as value adding economic activities on the one hand, and agiotage as surcharging without value creation on the other, permits us to classify insider trading as mere agiotage and to distinguish it from the other value adding activities in the stock exchange, i.e., as arbitrage and speculation over time.

The scholastic theorists of business ethics or scholars of the theology of business morals like Duns Scotus and particularly the Spanish natural right thinkers of early modern times already knew this distinction. Duns Scotus decided that profit is only ethically admissible if the trader or speculator has rendered some productive service to the community: "Whoever provides neither the bringing nor the storage nor the amelioration of the trading goods, nor supplies the inexperienced buyer with a guarantee of quality (through his knowledge of the merchandise), but only buys now in order to resell without fulfilling even one single of these preconditions should be exterminated from the community and exiled from it."[9] Lugo[10] and Molina[11] explained that profits from arbitrage and speculation are ethically legitimate if they add real value to the economy, but that agiotage as mere surcharging overcharges others and therefore violates the principle of justice of giving to each his or her own.[12]

2. Insider Trading and the Fiduciary Relationship

Insider speculation as mere agiotage, like reselling the same good without ameliorating it and without rendering a productive contribution to the community by the reselling, violates the nature of the matter of speculative trading. This holds true even in circumstances in which the insider trading is useful to a third party. Take the case of a firm that plans a takeover. The management or one of the shareholders can tip an insider trader to buy stock of the company to be taken over in the near future. The insider will earn an extra profit from this tip, the tipping company can stretch the buying out of the stock over a longer time period and probably acquire the stock at a lower price. Thus, the tippee or insider trader is informed by the tipper, the firm, in the firm's own interest and is induced to buy stock at the insider's profit.

---

[9]Johannes Duns Scotus: *Quaestiones in Lib. IV. Sententiarum,* vol. 9, Lyon (Laurentius Durand) 1639, reprint Hildesheim (Olms) 1968, dist. 15, q. 2, n. 23. Johannes Duns Scotus was born at Maxton (Scotland) in about 1265/66 and died at Cologne in 1308.

[10]Juan de Lugo: *De iustitia et iure,* Lyon 1670, Disp. 28, sect. 10, n. 132. J. de Lugo was born at Madrid in 1583 and died at Rome in 1660.

[11]Luis de Molina: *De iustitia et iure,* Madrid 1602, Tr. 2, disp. 410, n. 11.

[12]Cf. Nell-Breuning (1928), p. 107f.

The insider trader renders some service to the economy, namely to the firm that plans the takeover. This service, however, could also be achieved when the acquiring firm buys the stock itself or an agent buys it on its behalf under a contract of acting on behalf of the firm. The firm planning a takeover need not use the means of tipping an insider trader and, thereby, using an ethically questionable means for an end that can be reached by ethically and legally admissible means. The existence of cases where insider trading is in the interest of a third party, the tipping manager or shareholder, does not refute the thesis that insider trading is mere agiotage and not productive speculation. The tipping company has the knowledge on which the insider trading is effected and could spread it or, if this damaged its business, can withhold it[13] and act for itself by buying out the stock over time itself.

The example of insider trading by an insider buying stock for his private account in the interest of a third party demonstrates that insider trading cannot be judged unethical on the grounds only that it breaks a fiduciary duty.[14] In many cases, it does so and is then unethical on the grounds that it is an offense against the fiduciary duties. In quite a few cases, it is, however, the very person that constituted the fiduciary relationship who proliferates the insider information to another who trades in his private interest. The arguments in favor of insider trading claiming that insider trading improves the allocative function of the market by distributing information about stock are based on the fact that insider trading is not only in the interest of the insider trader or agent but can be in the interest of the principal, too.[15]

Again, neither the advantage of the inside trader nor the advantage of the principal nor some small allocative effect of the insider trading on the price formation in the stock market can be a justification for insider trading when its unethical character is due to the violation of the nature of the matter of speculation in the stock market, when it does not serve to reduce uncertainty. Since the insider information is already there, insider trading does not reduce uncertainty. Since all shareholders have the equal right to information about their company, the management may not pass information about takeovers to selected third parties for their enrichment.[16] Even the single shareholder may not pass insider knowledge to selected persons, since by doing so he or she violates the right of the other shareholders to this knowledge. The principle of equal right of the shareholder requires that either all shareholders know about the insider information and can pass it on or that none of them passes it on. When all shareholders pass it on, it will cease to be insider information.

The German and American legislation on insider trading, therefore, prohibits the shareholders to pass on their insider information, just as it prohibits the management of the firm to do so.[17] It does not take the fiduciary relationship but the principle of equal right, i.e., the

---

[13]The *Zweites Finanzmarktförderungsgesetz* (Second Law on the Improvement of the Financial Market) of August 1st, 1994, § 21, obliges all companies that are traded at that stock exchange to publish acquisitions or sales of stock of other companies exceeding or falling short of 5%, 10%, 25%, 50% or 75% of the other company's stock. The Federal Supervisory Board (*Bundesaufsichtsamt*) may, however, exempt the company from this duty if its fulfillment can cause considerable damage to it (§ 25, n° 4).

[14]Moore (1990) argues that insider trading is unethical because it breaks a fiduciary relationship. This is certainly very often the case but does not cover all cases of insider trading.

[15]The main proponent of this thesis is Manne (1966).

[16]The aspect of equal justice to all shareholders is emphasized in Hopt (1991).

[17]The German law prohibits *all* shareholders, not only the shareholders of great holdings, to proliferate insider information, cf. *Finanzmarktförderungsgesetz* § 13 no. 1,2. For the American legislation cf. Wojtek (1978), pp. 56ff.

shareholders' equal right to information, and the conditions of productive speculation in the stock market to be the reason for the legal prohibition of insider trading.

3. Insider Trading as Perverse Incentive

The conditions under which speculation in the stock market is productive and conducive to the common good by bearing uncertainty are not only violated by the detrimental effects of insider trading when it occurs; rather, the detrimental effects are intensified through perverse incentives that are furthered by legally allowing insider trading. The intermediaries in the financial markets have strong incentives to invest in the search for insider trading opportunities, if insider trading is allowed. Instead of searching for the correct anticipation of the future in speculation, they will look for insider information about a future that is not really future but already present. They will be negligent in doing proper speculation and distract their attention to insider investment opportunities.

Since the insider investment opportunities are augmented by random price fluctuations and high amplitudes of these fluctuations, the incentives of insider trading further induce the financial intermediaries to support price fluctuations instead of suppressing them. Additional "perverse" incentives to increase, instead of decrease, uncertainty for the other market participants are thus created by the legal admittance of insider trading.[18] Allowing insider trading will cause the deviation of the efforts of the financial intermediaries and speculators from investing in the reduction of uncertainty to investing in the search for insider information, i.e., for knowledge that is already there, and in strategies of increasing outside uncertainty by increasing the price fluctuations in the stock market. The "perverse incentives" of insider trading direct resources to the search for unproductive instead of productive knowledge. Knowledge that is already there but is held back from the market for the private exploitation in agiotage is unproductive knowledge.[19]

4. Insider Trading and Short-Termism

The insider knowledge in the stock market is unproductive since it is neither used for arbitrage, equilibrating price differences between different places, nor for speculation, equilibrating price differences between different time periods. Insider trading is effected in the same marketplace, and it aims at short run capital gains without bridging longer time periods. Already the short-termism of insider trading hints at the fact that it is neither the bearing of uncertainty nor real capital investment. Both, the bearing of uncertainty and capital investment, require longer time periods of investment.

Insider trading cannot, however, be banned by law because of its short-termism only. When a speculator has come to the conclusion by correct and responsible reasoning that it is economically right to end an investment after a very short term of investment due to changes of the economic conditions, this can be and is very often the efficient solution. Short terms of investment are, therefore, not per se an indicator of insider trading and no sufficient reason for an exclusion of it.[20] Here the intention, i.e.,

---

[18]Thus also Moore (1990), p. 179, Hopt (1991).

[19]For the distinction between productive and unproductive knowledge see Schäfer/Ott (1986), pp. 300ff.

[20]De George (1990) bases his critique of insider trading on its short-termism and argues for a taxation of short run capital gains with a rate of 100%.

whether the investor intends from the beginning either insider trading or serious long run investment or useful speculation in bearing uncertainty, is decisive.

5. Insider Trading and the Duty to Ad hoc Publicity

Insider information is unproductive information since its general availability is hindered only by intentionally holding it back from the market. The use of the insider information does not have an advantageous effect on the economy since it is not arbitraging between places or speculating between time periods. McGee bases his argument for the legalization of insider trading on the fact that in arbitrage business transactions the arbitrageur is not obliged to inform the potential buyer that the price of the good the arbitrageur is trying to sell is higher in another place or, in the case of speculative trade, that the price is likely to change in the future. McGee quotes Thomas Aquinas[21] who denied the duty of the seller to inform the buyer about such price differences between places or periods. McGee overlooks the underlying premise in Aquinas' argument, namely that arbitrage is economically and socially useful since it equilibrates price differences between different markets. Arbitrage will only happen if there are incentives for it in the possibility of making profit by bridging the price differences between markets. Where these incentives do not exist, no arbitrage takes place. Where the buyer would have the duty to inform the seller of grain in place A that there is a higher price for grain in place B, the seller would likely not sell him the merchandise but sell it himself in market B. The seller would, thereby, appropriate to himself the benefit of the arbitrageur's investive efforts without compensating him. For the encouragement of useful trade it is necessary to admit arbitrage in trade. That is the reason why Thomas Aquinas and the natural right theory allow it.

Where trading is only agiotage or making surplus but not arbitrage or speculation, the buyer or seller is not entitled to hold back his information and to derive profit from his knowledge about future price changes. Since the insider has not invested in productive but in unproductive knowledge, he or she is not entitled to a profit derived from the lead in knowledge that has been unjustly acquired over the competitor or is of unproductive character.

6. Detrimental Effects of Insider Trading on Allocation, Distribution and Stability

Insider trading reallocates resources from speculation to pseudo-speculation, from spreading knowledge to withholding it. There might be a minor effect of spreading knowledge to the stock exchange by the stock purchases of insider traders and some beneficial effect in the temporal extension of stock purchases in case of takeovers supported by insider traders. These beneficial allocative effects are, however, far outweighed by the misallocation of resources in the search for unproductive insider information, by the perverse incentives of insider trading to increase price fluctuations and to destabilize the stock market and by the problematic distribution pattern resulting from insider trading gains.

The perverse incentives of insider trading lead to questionable insider investments and profits. The problematic insider capital gains, their short-termism and so on, result in a so-

---

[21]McGee (1988), p. 37, about Aquinas, *Summa theologiae* II–II, q. 77, art. 3 (4).

cially destabilizing and economically and ethically questionable distribution of income. The concern of the public about the income distribution derived from insider gains[22] cannot be simply dismissed as envy.[23] Not so much the resulting distribution as the repercussions of it on the incentive structure and the allocation of productive effort in the financial markets should be the concern. Since allocation and distribution cannot be separated, huge profits from insider trading direct resources to their use in insider trading. All three economic criteria, allocation, distribution and stability, require the suppression of insider trading. The arguments from allocative efficiency, from distributional justice and from economic stability of the capital market coincide in the judgment derived from the nature of the matter, from the nature of the capital market, that the participants in the capital market have the duty to engage in productive investment and uncertainty bearing and not in the pseudo-speculation of insider trading.[24]

The effect that the prohibition of insider trading favors professional speculation at the expense of amateur speculation should not, therefore, be criticized, as by Schneider,[25] but heralded. If the prohibition of insider trading reduces the gambling element present in stock market speculation in favor of professional speculation, it decreases that part of the capital market that deals with uncertainty and reduces it to its unavoidable size. The prohibition of insider trading eliminates those factors in the stock exchange that create unnecessary and avoidable uncertainty. The stock exchange should not be a place of gambling speculation but an institution of service to the community, of serving as the mediator for capital and as bearer of uncertainty.[26]

More than 70 years ago, Nell-Breuning asked the question of whether the stock exchange needs speculation in shares or whether it could work without it.[27] The analysis of insider trading demonstrates that the stock market can work without pseudo-speculation but that speculation plays an indispensable role in bearing irreducible uncertainty. In summarizing the problem of insider trading, one can conclude that the nature and function of speculation in the stock exchange requires the strict suppression of the pseudo-speculation of insider trading, of bearing bogus uncertainty. The principle of equal justice in the legitimization of norms demands the equal right of access to information for all shareholders and speculators and therefore rules out that management or single shareholders give insider tips to third parties. Finally, the principles of economic and legal safety and stability require that insider trading be prohibited because of its perverse incentives effects. The price fluctuations in the stock market must not be augmented by forms of speculation that are not justified by the function of the capital market to bear and transform risk and uncertainty.

---

[22]The concern with the effects of financial speculation on the income distribution and distributive justice is a topic since Aristotle. Cf. Sen (1993), p. 211.

[23]Thus McGee (1988), p. 42.

[24]Grunewald (1990), p. 133, comes to the similar conclusion that insider trading must be prohibited in the interest of the proper working (*Funktionsfähigkeit*) of the capital market.

[25]Schneider (1993).

[26]Cf. Nell-Breuning's emphasis (1928), p. 23, on the "Dienstauffassung der Börse," on the awareness that the stock exchange renders a service to the economy.

[27]Nell-Breuning (1928a), p. 54.

REFERENCES

Altendorfer, Ch.: *Insidergeschäfte. Rechtsgrundlagen und Sanktionen* (Insider Trading. Legal Foundations and Sanctions), Wien (Bank-Verlag/Orac) 1992.

Andreas, K.: "Denkansätze für eine Ethik im Bankwesen" (Starting Points for an Ethics in the Banking System), in: P. Koslowski (Ed.): *Neuere Entwicklungen in der Wirtschaftsethik und Wirtschaftsphilosophie* (Recent Developments in Economic Ethics and Economic Philosophy), Berlin, Heidelberg, New York, Tokyo (Springer) 1992 (= Studies in Economic Ethics and Philosophy vol. 2), pp. 177–193.

Anger, D.: *Insiderregeln im Wertpapiergeschäft ausgewählter Länder* (Insider Laws in the Stock Exchange of Selected Countries), Diss. Erlangen-Nürnberg 1981.

Brady, F. N.: "Impartiality and Particularity in Business Ethics," in: P. Koslowski, Y. Shio-noya (Eds.): *The Good and the Economical. Ethical Choices in Economics and Management,* Berlin, Heidelberg, New York, Tokyo (Springer) 1993 (= Studies in Economic Ethics and Philosophy vol. 4), pp. 175–194.

Breuer, R.-E.: "Die Deutsche Terminbörse als Vorreiter einer Börsenlandschaft der 90er Jahre?" (The German Futures Exchange as Avantgarde for a Forward Market of the Future?), *Zeitschrift für Bankrecht und Bankwirtschaft,* 2 (1990), Nr. 3, pp. 101ff.

DeGeorge, Richard T.: "Ethics and the Financial Community: An Overview," in: O. F. Williams, F. K. Reilly, J. W. Houck (Eds.): *Ethics and the Investment Industry,* Savage (Rowman & Littlefield) 1989, pp. 197–216.

DeGeorge, Richard T.: *Business Ethics,* New York (Macmillan Publishing Company) 1990.

Dennert, J. "Insider Trading," *Kyklos,* 44 (1991), Nr. 2, pp. 181–202.

Diez-Alegría, J.: "El problema del fundamento ontológico de la obligación en la obra De iustitia de Luis de Molina" (The Problem of the Ontological Fundament of Obligation in the Work "On Justice" of Luis de Molina), *Pensamiento,* 7 (1951), pp. 147–167.

Dingeldey, Th.: *Insider-Handel und Strafrecht* (Insider Trading and Criminal Law), Köln u.a. (Heymanns) 1983.

Economic Advisory Board: *The British and German Banking System: A Comparative Study,* London 1981, pp. 388ff.

Engel, G.: "Zur Problematik eines gesetzlichen Verbots von Insider-Geschäften" (The Problem of a Legal Prohibition of Insider Trading), *Jahrbuch für Sozialwissenschaft,* 42 (1991), pp. 388–407.

Franke, G.: "Inside Information in Bank Lending and the European Insider Directive," *mimeo,* University of Konstanz 1989.

Friedman, B. M.: Article "Capital, Credit and Money Markets," in: *The New Palgrave. A Dictionary of Economics,* London (Macmillan), New York (Stockton), Tokyo (Maruzen) 1987, Vol. 1, pp. 320–327.

Gaillard, E. (Ed.): *Insider Trading. The Laws of Europe, the United States and Japan,* Deventer, Boston (Kluwer Law and Taxation) 1992.

Gay, David E. R.: Article "Dividend Policy," in: *The New Palgrave. A Dictionary of Economics,* London (Macmillan), New York (Stockton), Tokyo (Maruzen) 1987, Vol. 1, pp. 896–899.

Gesetz über den Wertpapierhandel und zur Änderung börsenrechtlicher und wertpapierrechtlicher Vorschriften (Zweites Finanzmarktförderungsgesetz) (Law on the Trading of Securities and on the Alterations of Existing Stock Exchange and Securities Regulations [Second Law on the Improvement of the Financial Market]) of July 26, 1994, German Federal Law.

Grunewald, B.: "Neue Regeln zum Insiderhandel" (New Rules Concerning Insider Trading), *Zeitschrift für Bankrecht und Bankwirtschaft,* 2 (1990), Nr. 3, pp. 128–133.

Hopt, K. J., Will, M R.: *Europäisches Insiderrecht. Einführende Untersuchung—Ausgewählte Materialien* (European Insider Law. Introduction—Selected Materials), Stuttgart (Enke) 1973.

Hopt, K. J.: "Europäisches und deutsches Insiderrecht" (European and German Insider Law), *Zeitschrift für Unternehmens- und Gesellschaftsrecht,* 20 (1991), pp. 17–73.

Jacob, A.-F. (Ed.): *Bankenmacht und Ethik* (Power of Banks and Ethics), Stuttgart (Poeschel) 1990.

Jacob, A.-F. (Ed.): *Eine Standesethik für den internationalen Finanzmanager?* (An Ethics of the Professions for the International Finance Manager?), Stuttgart (Poeschel) 1992.

Johannes Duns Scotus: *Quaestiones in Lib. IV. Sententiarum,* vol. 9, Lyon (Laurentius Durand) 1639, reprint Hildesheim (Olms) 1968.

Juan de Lugo: *De iustitia et iure,* Lyon 1670.

Kantorowicz, H.: *Der Begriff des Rechts,* Göttingen (Vandenhoeck & Ruprecht) 1963. Original: *The Definition of Law,* Cambridge (Cambridge University Press) 1958.

King, M., Roell, A.: "Insider trading," *Economic Policy. A European Forum* (1988), Nr. 6, pp. 165–193.

Knight, F.: *Risk, Uncertainty, and Profit,* New York (Houghton Mifflin) 1921.

Koslowski, P. (1982a): *Ethik des Kapitalismus.* With a comment by James M. Buchanan, Tübingen (J.C.B. Mohr [Paul Siebeck]) 1982, 6th ed. 1998. Various English translations, like: *Ethics of Capitalism,* in: P. Koslowski: *Ethics of Capitalism and Critique of Sociobiology. Two Essays with a Comment by James M. Buchanan,* Berlin, Heidelberg, New York, Tokyo (Springer) 1996, 142 pages (= Studies in Economic Ethics and Philosophy, Vol. 10). First English publication in: S. Pejovich (Ed.): *Philosophical and Economic Foundations of Capitalism,* Lexington (Lexington Books) 1983, pp. 33–64.

Koslowski, P.: *Prinzipien der Ethischen Ökonomie* (Principles of Ethical Economy), Tübingen (J.C.B. Mohr [P. Siebeck]) 1988, Reprint 1994. English translation: *Principles of Ethical Economy,* translated by David W. Lutz, Dordrecht, Boston, London (Kluwer Academic Publishers) 2000, Reihe "Issues in Business Ethics" Vol. 17, paperback edition 2001.

Koslowski, P.: *Wirtschaft als Kultur. Wirtschaftskultur und Wirtschaftsethik in der Postmoderne* (The Economy as Culture. Economic Culture and Economic Ethics in Postmodern Times), Vienna (Edition Passagen) 1989.

Koslowski, P.: *Gesellschaftliche Koordination. Eine ontologische und kulturwissenschaftliche Theorie der Marktwirtschaft* (Social Coordination. An Ontological and Cultural Theory of the Market), Tübingen (J.C.B. Mohr [Paul Siebeck]) 1991.

Koslowski, P.: *Ethik der Banken und der Börse* (The Ethics of Banking and of the Stock Exchange), Tübingen (Mohr Siebeck) 1997.

Luhmann, N.: "Kapitalismus und Utopie" (Capitalism and Utopia), *Merkur,* 48 (1994), H. 3, p. 191.

Manne, H. G.: *Insider Trading and the Stock Market,* New York (The Free Press) 1966.

Martin, D. W., Peterson, J. H.: "Insider Trading Revisited," *Journal of Business Ethics,* 10 (1991), pp. 57–61.

McGee, R. W.: "Insider Trading: An Economic and Philosophical Analysis," *Mid-Atlantic Journal of Business,* 25 (1988), pp. 35–48.

Meier, Ch.: *Wirtschaftsdelikte im Bankengewerbe* (Economic Crimes in the Banking Industry). *Eine empirische Untersuchung über Entwicklung, Erscheinungsformen, Schadensfolgen und Risikoursachen bankbezogener Wirtschaftsstraftaten,* Bern, Stuttgart (Haupt) 1986.

Molina, Luis De: *De justitia et jure* (On Justice and Natural Right and Law), Moguntiae (Madrid) 1602.

Moore, J.: "What Is Really Unethical About Insider Trading," *Journal of Business Ethics,* 9 (1990), pp. 171–182.

Neidlinger, K.: *Studien zur Geschichte der deutschen Effektenspekulation von ihren Anfängen bis zum Beginn der Eisenbahnaktenspekulation. Ein Beitrag zur Börsengeschichte* (Studies in the History of the German Speculation in Stocks and Shares from the Beginnings to the Start of the Speculation in Railway Shares. A Contribution to the History of the Stock Exchange), Jena (G. Fischer) 1930.

Nell-Breuning, O. von (1928): *Grundzüge der Börsenmoral* (Principles of the Ethics of the Stock Exchange), Freiburg i. Br. (Herder) 1928.

Nell-Breuning, O. v. (1928a): "Volkswirtschaftlicher Wert und Unwert der Börsenspekulation" (Economic Value and Nonvalue of Stock Exchange Speculation), *Stimmen der Zeit,* 114 (1928), pp. 46–56.

Pesch, H.: "Zinsgrund und Zinsgrenze" (The Reason for Interest and the Limit of the Interest Rate), *Zeitschrift für katholische Theologie,* 12 (1888), pp. 393–418.

Radbruch, G.: *Rechtsphilosophie* (Philosophy of Law), Stuttgart (Koehler) 8th ed. 1973.

Röller, W.: "Zum Selbstverständnis der Banken in einer offenen Gesellschaft" (On the Way Banks See Themselves in an Open Society), in: A.-F. Jacob: *Bankenmacht und Ethik* (Power of Banks and Ethics) (1990), pp. 1–14.

Röpke, W.: Article "Spekulation," in: *Handwörterbuch der Staatswissenschaften,* 4th ed., Jena (Gustav Fischer) 1926, Vol. 7, pp. 706–710.

Roth, W.: "Macht der Banken" (Power of Banks), in: *Tutzinger Materialen* Nr. 35, Tutzing 1986.

Schäfer, H.-B., Ott, C.: *Lehrbuch der ökonomischen Analyse des Zivilrechts* (Handbook of the Economic Analysis of Civil Law), Berlin, New York, Tokyo (Springer) 1986, pp. 300ff.

Schimmler, J.: *Spekulation, spekulative Gewinne und Preisstabilität* (Speculation, Speculative Profits, and Price Stability). *Eine Theorie der Spekulation unter besonderer Berücksichtigung der Auswirkungen spekulativer Transaktionen auf die Preisstabilität,* Meisenheim a. G. (Hain) 1974.

Schneider, Dieter: "Wider Insiderhandelsverbot und die Informationseffizienz des Kapitalmarkts" (Against the Prohibition of Insider Trading and the Informational Efficiency of the Capital Market), *Der Betrieb,* 46 (1993), H. 29, pp. 1429–1435.

Schörner, P.: *Gesetzliches Insiderhandelsverbot. Eine ordnungspolitische Analyse* (The Legal Prohibition of Insider Trading. A Political Analysis), Wiesbaden (Gabler) 1991.

Sen, A.: "Money and Value. On The Ethics and Economics of Finance," *Economics and Philosophy,* 9 (1993), pp. 203–227.

Steinmann, G.: *Theorie der Spekulation* (The Theory of Speculation), Tübingen (J.C.B. Mohr [P. Siebeck]) 1970.

Strieder, J.: *Studien zur Geschichte kapitalistischer Organisationsformen. Monopole, Kartelle und Aktiengesellschaften im Mittelalter und zu Beginn der Neuzeit* (Studies in the History of Organization in Capitalism. Monopolies, Trusts and Corporations in the Middle Ages and in the Beginning of Modern Times), München, Leipzig (Duncker & Humblot) 1925.

Thomas Aquinas, *Summa theologiae* (1267–73), Madrid (Biblioteca de Autores Cristianos) 1951.

Tuchtfeldt, E.: Article "Kapitalmarkt," in: *Handwörterbuch der Wirtschaftswissenschaft* (The Capital Market, in: Handbook of Economics), vol. 4, pp. 432–439.

Weber, Max: *Die Börse, I. Zweck und äußere Organisation* (The Stock Exchange, I. Purpose and Organisation), Göttingen (Vandenhoeck & Ruprecht) 1894 (= Göttinger Arbeiterbibliothek vol. 1, Nr. 2/3, pp. 17–48).

Weber, Max: *Die Börse, II. Der Börsenverkehr* (The Stock Exchange, II. Trading at the Stock Exchange), Göttingen (Vandenhoeck & Ruprecht) 1896 (= Göttinger Arbeiterbibliothek vol. 2, Nr. 2/3, pp. 49–80).

Weber, Wilhelm: *Wirtschaftsethik am Vorabend des Liberalismus. Höhepunkt und Abschluß der scholastischen Wirtschaftsbetrachtung durch Luis de Molina* (Business Ethics on the Eve of Liberalism. Climax and Completion of the Scholastic Examination of the Economy by Luis de Molina), Münster (Aschendorff) 1959.

Wojtek, R. J.: *Insider Trading im deutschen und amerikanischen Recht* (Insider Trading in the German and American Law), Berlin (Duncker & Humblot) 1978.

Chapter 8

ETHICAL IMPLICATIONS OF TECHNOLOGY

We must adjust to changing times and still hold to unchanging principles.

—PRESIDENT JIMMY CARTER

You say you want a revolution? Well, you know, we all want to change the world.

—JOHN LENNON AND
PAUL MCCARTNEY

Things do not change; we change.

—HENRY DAVID THOREAU

With the advent of new technology, new ethical issues emerge. That is because we consider the advances of the technology before we consider the implications. Notwithstanding issues in connection with production, marketing, finance and other areas of a firm's operations, we now have countless issues relating to ethics with which we were never before confronted. For instance, consider the implications of new technology on the following areas:

- Monitoring usage.

- Managing employee and employer expectations.

- Distinguishing between work use and personal use of technology.

- Managing flextime.

- Maintaining a virtual workplace.

- Protecting against medical concerns for telecommuters.

- Managing/balancing privacy interests.

- Monitoring the use of the Web to spread information and misinformation.

- Managing fair use/disclosure.

- Responding to accessibility issues related to the digital divide.

- Managing temporary workforces.

- Adapting to stress and changing systems.

- Managing liability issues.

- Maintaining proprietary information.

- Measuring performance.

Technology, however, does not present us with new value judgments but instead simply new ways to gather the information on which to base them. Sorting through these issues is challenging nevertheless. Consider the impact of September 11, 2001, on an employer's decision to share personal employee information with law enforcement. Private firms may be more willing today to share private information than they would have been previously. Consider more particularly the issues raised above and the implications of technology on some of these traditional workplace challenges:

- Technology allows for in-home offices, raising issues of safety, as well as privacy concerns (now there are more than 15.7 million U.S. telecommuters). (Recent efforts by OSHA to impose workplace safety standards to home offices received huge flack!)

- Technology allows for greater invasions by the employer, but also allows for additional misdeeds by employees.

- Technology blurs the lines between personal and professional lives.

- Technology allows employers to ask more of each employee—each is capable of much greater production.

- What constitutes a "workday"? When is enough enough?

- Should the ability to find something out make it relevant? (off-work activities)

- Much of the new technologies (email, voice mail) allow for faceless communication.

- Research has shown that excessive exertion of power and authority over employees may actually lead to insecurity, feelings of being overwhelmed and powerless and doubts about worthiness.[1]

Consider the following overview of the implications of the technology economy as reported in the *2001 World Employment Report,* issued by the International Labour Office:

> *More and more, boundaries are dissolving between leisure and working time, the place of work and place of residence, learning and working . . . Wherever categories such as working time, working location, performance at work and jobs become blurred, the result is the deterioration of the foundations of our edifice of agreements, norms, rules, laws, organizational forms, structures and institutions, all of which have a stronger influence on our behavioral patterns and systems of values than we are aware.[2]*

The American Management Association has conducted surveys over the past few years that evidence that roughly three-fourths of mid- to large-sized U.S. firms engage in some form of employee monitoring. Its most recent survey was conducted in 2001 and reports that the number is 77.7%, up from 30% in 1993. However, much of this monitoring is on an occasional basis rather than by regular routine. The most prevalent subject of monitoring is internet connections (62.8%) followed closely by email. Of those firms that monitor, 84% notify their workers that they do so. More interesting is the fact that 16% do not notify their workers of the monitoring. In actual numbers, estimates regarding the number of workers subject to surveillance are difficult to measure. One estimate contends that the email and/or internet use of 14 million U.S. workers are under constant surveillance each day, increasing to 27 million around the globe.[3]

Do you think about everyone who might see the emails you send? How do you know that your boss will not forward your disparaging remarks about a colleague directly to that colleague? It can be done with the touch of a key. Are there different issues that are raised by that concern as opposed to those that arose with a traditional written letter? When we

---

[1] Ashley Benigno, "Total Surveillance Is Threatening Your Health," *Asian Labour Update* (Hong Kong: Asia Monitor Resource Center, http://www.amrc.org.hk/Arch/3405.htm, accessed February 5, 2002).

[2] U. Klotz, "The Challenges of the New Economy" (October 1999), cited in *World Employment Report 2001: Life at Work in the Information Economy* (Geneva: International Labour Office, 2001), p. 145.

[3] Andrew Schulman, "One-third of U.S. Online Workforce under Internet/Email Surveillance," *Workforce Surveillance Project* (Privacy Foundation) (July 9, 2001), http://www.privacyfoundation.org/workplace/business/biz_show.asp?id=70&ac. Schulman reports that, of the 140 million workers in the United States, 40 million are online. Of that 40 million, 14 million are subject to monitoring (35%). Worldwide, 100 million of 3 billion workers are online and 27 million (27%) are subject to monitoring. (*Ibid.,* p. 2). *See also* Linda Rosencrance, "Study: Monitoring of Employee Email, Web Use Escalates," *Computerworld,* July 9, 2001.

mistakenly believe that no one is watching, we may engage in activities that we would otherwise refrain from doing. For instance, you may believe that hitting the "delete" key does actually delete an email message. However, it does not always delete that message from the server so it might have a negative impact in a lawsuit or be retrieved by your supervisor.

More than 80% of mid- to large-sized firms in the United States have internet access policies, but there remains a problem. More than 60% of these companies have disciplined employees for violations of these policies, with the leading violations being access to pornography, online chat forums, gaming, investing or shopping at work.[4]

The above concern raises but one potential dilemma in connection with new technology. In order to address some of the issues that are presented by computers specifically, the Computer Ethics Institute has created "The Ten Commandments of Computer Ethics." The Commandments include the following:

3. Thou shalt not snoop around in other people's computer files.
9. Thou shalt think about the social consequences of the program you are writing or the system you are designing.
10. Thou shalt always use a computer in ways that insure consideration and respect for your fellow humans.

Unfortunately, many of the ethical issues that arise in the area of managing information are not readily visible. When we don't completely understand the technology, we might not understand the ethical implications of our decisions. Can your employer read your email? Your first response might be "no, it doesn't have my secret password." However, experts tell us that any system is penetrable. Employers have been known to randomly read emails in order to ensure that the system is being used for business purposes. Is this ethical? Does it matter if there is a company policy that systems must be used only for business purposes, or that the employees are given notice that their email will be read? These ethical issues may be compounded by the fact that there exists a knowledge gap between people who *do* understand the technology, and others who are unable to protect themselves precisely because they do *not* understand. You might not expect to be fired for sending out an email, but if you thought about it a bit, you might have known what to expect.

Technology allows for access that was never before possible. Under previous circumstances, one could usually tell if someone had steamed open a letter over a teapot. However, today, you usually cannot discover if someone reads the email you sent yesterday to your best friend. Access can take place unintentionally, as well. In doing a routine background check, a supervisor may unintentionally uncover information of an extremely personal nature that may bear absolutely no relevance to one's work performance. This occurs because the information, though previously unavailable or too burdensome to uncover, is now freely available from a variety of sources.

Moreover, because technology allows us to work from almost anywhere on this planet, we are seldom out of the boundaries of our workplace. For instance, just because you're going to your sister's wedding, this doesn't mean that your supervisor can't reach you. Here is the tough question: Should your supervisor try to reach you just because she has the ability?

---

[4]Vasant Raval, "Ethical Behavior in the Knowledge Economy," *Information Strategy* 16, no. 3 (Spring 2000), p. 45.

Our total accessibility creates expectations, and therefore conflicts, with which we never before had to wrestle. How long is reasonable to wait before responding to an email? If someone does not hear from you within 24 hours of sending an email, is it unreasonable to resend it? Continuous accessibility blurs the lines between our personal and professional lives.

Another challenge posed by the new technology accessible in the workplace is the facelessness that results from its use. If we have to face someone as we make our decisions, we are more likely to care about the impact of that decision on that person. Conversely, when we don't get to know someone because we don't have to see that person in order to do our business, we often don't take into account the impact of our decisions on that person. They become merely a name at the other end of an email correspondence, rather than another human being. Given the ease and informality of electronic communications, we often "say" (write, email, etc.) things to each other that we would never say to someone's face, precisely because we don't have to consider the impact of what we're saying. We are more careless with our communications because they are easier to conduct—just hit a button and it's sent.

HOW DOES MONITORING WORK?

Advances in information gathering technology have allowed monitoring that perhaps was never before possible. Worldwide sales of monitoring technology are estimated at $140 million annually.[5] One example of new technology is Raytheon's Silentrunner, which allows firms to track everything that occurs on a network, including not only emails but also instant messaging (one of the new ways employees thought they had foiled email monitoring).[6] Other products allow trucking firms to track their vehicles across the nation using global positioning[7] or allow managers to test a worker's honesty by using a truth-telling monitor during telephone calls.[8]

The most prevalent internet-monitoring product in the United States is Websense, with 8.25 million users worldwide. While Websense merely *blocks* certain websites, Websense Reporter, an add-on, records all web accesses (not only attempted accesses blocked by Websense, but also all nonprohibited web surfing); 70% of Websense's customers install Reporter. MIMEsweeper is the most used email monitoring system in the United States with 6,000 corporate customers and over 6 million ultimate users worldwide. In a less publicized form of monitoring, SWS Security offers a product that allows managers to track the messages a worker receives on a portable paging device so that one could track whether the employee is being distracted by outside messages. Another provider, www.tracingamerica.com, offers the following information at the listed prices:

*   Social security numbers, $25.

*   General all around background search, $39.

---

[5]Andrew Schulman, "One-third of U.S. Online Workforce under Internet/Email Surveillance," *Workforce Surveillance Project* (Privacy Foundation) (July 9, 2001), http://www.privacyfoundation.org/workplace/business/biz_show.asp?id=70&ac.

[6]Jeffrey Brenner, "Privacy at Work? Be Serious," *Wired Magazine,* http://www.wired.com/news/business/0,1367,42029,00.html (accessed February 26, 2002).

[7]www.omnitracs.com.

[8]www.spyzone.com.

- Countywide search for misdemeanors and felonies, $35.

- Whether subject has ever spent time in prison, $25.

- Whether subject has ever served time in a federal prison, $50.

- National search for outstanding warrants for subject, $50.

- Countywide search for any civil filings filed by or against subject, $50.

- Subject's driving record at least three years back, $30.

WHY DO FIRMS MONITOR TECHNOLOGY USAGE?

There are numerous bases that support the choice of a firm to monitor. Recent research has found that monitoring serves a number of purposes for a firm:

- Managing the workplace:

  - Ensuring compliance with affirmative action.

  - Administering workplace benefits.

  - Placing workers in appropriate positions.

- Ensuring effective, productive performance:

  - Preventing loss of productivity to inappropriate technology use.

  - Recent reports evidence a rise in personal use of technology, with 85.6% of employees admitting sending or receiving personal emails at work, with 55.1% admitting to having received politically incorrect or offensive emails at work, and 62% of firms finding employees accessing sex sites during the workday.[9]

  - 13% of employees spend over two hours a day surfing nonbusiness sites.[10]

  - A recent survey in the U.K. reports that, of the workers surveyed:

    —53% behave "immorally" in email.
    —38% have used email in the pursuit of political gain within their company, at the expense of others.
    —30% admit to having sent racist, pornographic, sexist or otherwise discriminatory emails while at work.[11]

- Protecting information & guarding against theft.

- Protecting investment in equipment and bandwidth.

- Protecting against legal liability, including possible:

  - Perceptions of hostile environments.

---

[9]Elron Software, "Guide to Internet Usage and Policy" (2001), pp. 7, 17.
[10]Alan Cohen, "Worker Watchers," *Fortune/CNET Technology Review,* Summer 2001, pp. 70, 76.
[11]Institute for Global Ethics, "U.K. Survey Finds Many Workers Are Misusing Email," *Newsline* 5, no. 10 (March 11, 2002).

- Violations of software licensing laws.

- Violations regarding proprietary information or trade secrets.

- Inappropriate gathering of competitive intelligence.

- Financial fraud.

- Theft.

- Defamation/libel.

- Discrimination.

- Maintaining corporate records (including email, voice mail and so on).

- Investigating *some* personal areas (consider Infoseek executive Patrick Naughton's pursuit of a tryst with an FBI agent posing as a 13-year-old girl in a chat room).

Notwithstanding these persuasive justifications for monitoring in the workplace, there also remain several reasons to limit monitoring.

- Monitoring may create a suspicious and hostile workplace.

- Monitoring constrains effective performance (employees claim that lack of privacy may prevent "flow").

- It may be important to conduct *some* personal business at office, when necessary.

- Monitoring causes increased workplace stress and pressure, negatively impacting performance.

- Employees claim that monitoring is an inherent invasion of privacy.

- Monitoring does not always allow for workers to review and correct misinformation in data collected.

- Monitoring constrains the right to autonomy and freedom of expression.

- Monitoring intrudes upon one's right to privacy of thought ("I use a company pen; does that mean the firm has a right to read my letter to my spouse?").

In the American Management Association's 2001 survey, more than two-thirds reported that they engaged in monitoring as a result of their concerns for legal liability. Given the courts' focus in many cases on employer response to claims of sexual harassment or unethical behavior, among other complaints, firms believe that they need a way to uncover these inappropriate activities. More than 10% of firms have reported receiving a subpoena for employee email and one-third of the largest firms report firing employees for inappropriate email.[12] Without monitoring, how would they know what occurs? Moreover, as courts maintain the standard in many cases of whether the employer "knew or should have

---

[12]Dana Hawkins, "Lawsuits Spur Rise in Employee Monitoring," *U.S. News & World Reports,* August 13, 2001.

known" of wrongdoing, the state-of-the-art definition of "should have known" becomes all the more vital. If most firms use monitoring technology to uncover this wrongdoing, the definition of *should have* known will begin to include an expectation of monitoring.

Perhaps the most effective means to achieve monitoring objectives while remaining sensitive to the concerns of employees is to strive toward a balance that respects individual dignity while also holding individuals accountable for their particular roles in the organization. Ann Svendsen, director of the Center for Innovation in Management, recently published the results of her study examining the link between high trust stakeholder relationships and business value creation. Svendsen concludes that "trust, a cooperative spirit and shared understanding between a company and its stakeholders creates greater coherence of action, better knowledge sharing, lower transaction costs, lower turnover rates and organizational stability. In the bigger picture, social capital appears to minimize shareholder risk, promote innovation, enhance reputation and deepen brand loyalty."

A monitoring program developed according to the mission of the organization (i.e., with integrity), then implemented in a manner that remains accountable to the impacted employees, approaches that balance. Consider the following possible parameters for a monitoring policy that endeavors to accomplish the goals described above:

- No monitoring in private areas (i.e., restrooms).

- Limited to within the workplace.

- Employees should have access to information gathered through monitoring.

- No secret monitoring—advance notice required.

- Should only result in attainment of some business interest.

- May collect only job-related information.

- Agreement regarding disclosure of information gained through monitoring.

- Prohibition of discrimination by employers based on off-work activities.

The above parameters allow the employer to effectively and ethically supervise the work done by her or his employees, to protect against misuse of resources and to have an appropriate mechanism by which to evaluate each worker's performance, thus respecting the legitimate business interest of the employer. These guidelines may also respect the personal autonomy of the individual worker by providing for personal space within the working environment, by providing notice of where that "personal" space ends and by allowing access to the information gathered, all designed toward achievement of a personal and professional development objective.

HOW ARE FIRMS LEGALLY CONSTRAINED?

As with other areas of lightning quick advances, the law has not yet caught up with the technology involved in employee monitoring. While the law might be clear with regard to tapping a worker's telephone, it is not so clear in connection with monitoring a worker's email or text pages on a handheld device. Employee monitoring in the private-sector workplace is generally governed by state legislation and case law precedent. (The Fourth Amendment protection against an unreasonable search and seizure governs only the public-sector workplace through the Constitution's application only to state action.) From a legislative perspective, there is little, if any, protection. The Electronic Communications Privacy Act of 1986 (ECPA) prohibits the "interception" or unauthorized access of stored communications. However, its impact is to punish electronic monitoring by third parties, rather than employers, since courts have ruled that "interception" applies only to messages in transit and not to messages that have actually reached company computers. Moreover, the ECPA allows interception where consent has been granted. Therefore, a firm that secures employee consent to monitoring at the time of hire is immune from ECPA liability.

Case law recognizes the tort of intrusion into seclusion, which finds liability when one intentionally intrudes on the private affairs of another if the intrusion would be highly offensive to a reasonable person. As we begin to live more closely with technology, and the intrusions it allows, the concept of reasonableness under this formulation becomes tenuous. Additional state-by-state protection through regulation often focuses on online privacy to the exclusion of workplace privacy, though related legislation has been proposed in Washington, Maryland, Minnesota, Utah and New York.

Most recent court decisions seem to depend on whether the worker had notice that the monitoring might occur. Since the basis for finding an invasion of privacy is often the employee's legitimate and reasonable expectation of privacy, notice of monitoring would remove that expectation. This conclusion was supported in *K-Mart v. Trotti,* where the court held that search of an employee's company-owned locker was unlawful invasion since the employee used his own lock. However, in a later oft-cited case, *Smyth v. Pillsbury,* Smyth sued after a manager read his email, when Pillsbury had a policy saying that emails would *not* be read. The court concluded, "We do not find a reasonable expectation of privacy in the contents of email communications voluntarily made by an employee to his supervisor over the company email system, *notwithstanding any assurances that such communications would not be intercepted by management*" (emphasis added). The end result of *Smyth* then is to allow for monitoring even when a firm promises not to monitor. Evidence of the impact of this decision is the fact that only one state, Connecticut, requires employers to notify workers when they are being monitored.

This patchwork regime of privacy protection becomes all the more critical to maintain when one considers the implications of the European Union's personal data protection directive.[13] In addition to striving to harmonize the various means of protecting data throughout the EU, the directive also prohibits firms in the EU from transferring personal information to a non-EU country unless that country maintains adequate protections of its own.[14] In fact, the United States would not qualify as having adequate protection so the Department of Commerce negotiated a safe harbor exception for firms who maintain certain

---

[13]Council Directive 95/46, 1995 O.J. (L281).

[14]*Ibid.* at arts. 25–26.

protections of information within their possession.[15] If a firm satisfies these requirements, the directive allows the information transfer. If not, both firms can be held liable. The safe harbor requires that the receiving firm provide:

- Clear and conspicuous notice.

- Choice to opt out.

- Onward transfer only to firms with adequate protections.

- Reasonable measures to ensure reliability and protect from disclosure or loss.

- Assurance that it only process information relevant to purpose for which it was gathered.

- Access by data subject and the ability to correct misinformation.

- Mechanisms for ensuring compliance and consequences for noncompliance.

Of course, these issues are not limited to the United States. The Global Business Privacy Project has identified seven major developments of importance to businesses in connection with cyberethics:

- The European Union Privacy Directive.

- The commencement of an international privacy standards process.

- New national and global information flows.

- Information superhighway initiatives.

- Model business principles for global businesses.

- New information technology applications.

- New global interest in fashioning consumer data protection laws.[16]

In particular, the EU Privacy Directive might present challenging issues for American businesses. The Directive states that personal data may not be transferred to a non-EU state or organization unless that entity can guarantee protection of the data equivalent to the protections guaranteed by the EU Directive in EU countries. The United States does not currently protect personal information to the same extent as the European Union and therefore firms who do business in the United States might be in violation of the Directive if they transmit personal information from an EU country to their counterparts in the United States.

The Department of Commerce spent much of 2000 in the midst of high-level negotiations with the EU in order to define a "safe harbor" for American businesses who engage in data transfer. However, at press time of this text, the EU had not yet accepted the proposals by the Department of Commerce, claiming that the protections remained too vague.

---

[15]Pamela Samuelson, "Data Privacy Law: A Study of United States Data Protection," *California Law Review* 87, no. 3 (May 1999), p. 751.

[16]Global Business Privacy Project, http://www.pandab.org/global.html.

For the most up-to-date information on this topic, visit the Department of Commerce E-Commerce website.[17]

Given the nature of the legal uncertainty or instability with regard to these challenging areas of information gathering, one finds that perhaps the only source to which one should look for an answer is ethics. Yet, "the development of our moral systems has not been able to keep pace with technological and medical developments, leaving us prey individually and societally to a host of dangers."[18] As a court put it in regard to the legitimacy of police use of infrared thermal detection devices aimed at an individual's home without a warrant nor notification,

> *As technology races with ever increasing speed, our subjective expectations of privacy may be unconsciously altered . . . our legal rights to privacy should reflect thoughtful and purposeful choices rather than simply mirror the current state of the commercial technology industry.*[19]

ELECTRONIC PERFORMANCE MONITORING

As introduced above, technology invades and affects the employment relationship through employee electronic performance monitoring. Considerable controversy surrounds the issue of whether it is ethical for an employer to monitor the actions of employees through electronic surveillance. This type of monitoring may take the form of recording telephone calls of customer service representatives, electronically counting the number of keystrokes a word processor makes during the day, installing video cameras in the workplace and so on. While the employer may argue that it has the right to monitor in order to adequately and accurately appraise its employees and maintain quality levels, employees argue that the monitoring causes undue stress and pressure, and is too invasive.

Where should the line be drawn? Most of us would agree that installing video cameras in the washrooms of the workplace may be going a bit too far in order to prevent theft, knowing where to draw the line before that might be more difficult. As long as technology exists to allow for privacy invasions, should the employer have the right to use it? What constitutes humane or inhumane use of this technology?

Consider whether invasive monitoring could be made ethical or humane. It has been suggested that due notice given to employees that they will be monitored, plus the opportunity to avoid monitoring in certain situations would solve the ethical problems. For instance, if an employer chooses to monitor random phone calls made by its customer service representatives, it could notify the workers that certain calls may be monitored and these calls would be signified by a "beep" on the line during the monitoring. In addition, if a worker is making a personal call, he or she may use a "nonmonitored" phone in order to avoid a wrongful invasion of her or his privacy.

However, this may not solve all of the concerns about monitoring. Suppose you are the employer and you want to make sure that your service representatives handle calls in

---

[17]http://www.ita.doc.gov/td/ecom/menu.html.
[18]John Haas, "Thinking Ethically About Technology," http://www.nd.edu/~rbarger/haas.ethic.
[19]*State of Washington v. Young,* 123 Wash.2d 173 (1994).

a patient, tolerant and affable manner. By telling the worker which calls you are monitoring, your employees may be sure to be on their "best behavior" during those calls. Random, anonymous monitoring may better resolve your concerns (but not those of the worker). A recent study found that electronic performance monitoring has undesirable impacts on monitored workers, such as a lower perception of the fairness of the evaluation, health problems and increased stress.[20]

> *From mainframe through personal computer to internet, the electronic computer has transformed information and human communication in unanticipated ways that are giving birth to what has been variously termed cyberspace, virtual reality or hyperreality. To live in this new milieu, however, requires not virtual but real ethics, grounded in practical and public reflection on the new technolife world.*[21]

---

[20]Stephen Hawk, "The Effects of Computerized Performance Monitoring: An Ethical Perspective," *Journal of Business Ethics* 13 (1994), pp. 949–57.
[21]Carl Mitcham, "Current Issues in Modern Thought," *World & I* 11, no. 3 (March 1996), p. 314.

TECHNOLOGY AND ETHICS
Privacy in the Workplace

—Laura P. Hartman

Privacy in the workplace is one of the more troubling personal and professional issues of our time. This excerpt outlines the status of privacy in the workplace from a technological as well as a legal perspective. What was once considered as an inalienable right has now been reassessed as our society and the business world have grown ever more complex. Traditional ethical analysis offers some guidance on how to evaluate the balance between a worker's right to privacy and an employer's need for information with which to manage the workplace. But guidance is not the same as resolution: as concerns workplace privacy rights, there are many more questions than answers.

A. ETHICAL ISSUES UNIQUE TO INFORMATION TECHNOLOGY

It appears to me that in ethics the difficulties are mainly due to the attempt to answer questions without first discovering precisely what question it is which you desire to answer.

—George Edward Moore

Information technology provides us with a host of ethical challenges. New technology poses new implications for the balance of power in the workplace. We now have in-home offices, allowing for greater invasions. Moreover, the line between personal and professional lives has become blurred, as workers conduct personal business in the office and professional business at home. The office usually provides faster, cheaper and easier access to the internet, while some work must be done at home in order to be completed according to our modern, technologically enhanced pace.

Faculty members, for instance, do not go home and become people other than faculty members. We often conduct work at home such as grading, class preparation and so on. Similarly, our profession affords us a great deal of autonomy in terms of how we spend our days. We do not punch a clock or hand in a time sheet. All of my students have my home

"Technology and Ethics: Privacy in the Workplace," by Laura P. Hartman, presentation at Bentley College (February 2000). Reprinted by permission of the author.

number. My professional and personal lives are awfully blurred. (Sometimes, I wish they were not so blurred!)

Technology allows employers to ask more of each employee because now we are capable of greater production; we have greater abilities due to technology. We don't seem to know when our workday is over. I used to be a lawyer, and the understanding in that profession was, if you can work more hours, you do. This is because you will then be viewed as the preferred colleague. You will be the one who is going to get the plum assignments because you work so darn hard.

Other issues are raised by enhanced technology. For instance, should the technological ability to find something out make it relevant? With new employment-testing technology, you can find out all sorts of personal information. Through genetic testing, hair follicle testing, drug testing, your employer can find out anything it wants to know about you. Similarly, here, should the employer find out the information simply because it can?

In addition, new technology allows for a more faceless communication. If you have to fire someone, it is significantly easier to fire that person by email than to walk into her or his office. In the latter case, you see the individual—desperate, perhaps disappointed, frustrated with the fact that you've worked them so hard and now you're terminating them. It's a lot easier to be nasty when you don't have to look your stakeholders in the face.

Finally, there is research showing that the excessive exertion of power and authority may lead to what they call a "semi-schizoid response," including insecurity, "disruption of biographical continuity," feelings of being overwhelmed and powerless and doubts about worthiness. The implication is that, if someone questions you too much or takes away too much of your power, the ultimate cost may be your emotional security. Somewhat prophetically, Lawrence Lessig writes in his new bestseller, *Code,* "We have been as welcoming and joyous about the Net (and other technologies) as the earthlings were of the aliens in *Independence Day.* But at some point, we too will come to see a potential threat . . . and its extraordinary power for control."

B. Ethical Issues in the Privacy Arena

Specifically in connection with privacy, ethical issues arise with gathering information, assessing its accuracy, correcting it and disclosing it, as well as issues related to the substance of the information itself. Simply knowing that someone has personal information about you can feel invasive or violating. For that amorphous reason, privacy is a slightly difficult concept to define. Ethan Catch says it is "the ability to control what others can come to know about you." Why do we care that someone knows our personal information? We can imagine items of personal data that we simply do not want others knowing, whether or not they would actually do something with that information. We do not like people knowing things about us. It comes down to one's ability to be autonomous in controlling one's personal information.

Do you, personally, care about the information others know about you? Would you care if your boss knew of all your off-work activities? Consider Milton Hershey. Milton Hershey would tour Hershey, Pennsylvania, making note of workers' lawns that were not kept up, or homes that were not maintained. He would even hire private detectives to find out who was throwing trash in Hershey Park. Another business owner, Henry Ford, used to condition wages on workers' good behavior outside the factory. He had 150 inspectors in his "socio-logical department" to keep tabs on workers' hygiene habits and housekeeping.

Only recently did OSHA retract a statement that the occupational safety and health standards apply equally to workplaces and personal homes, when you work as a telecom-muter. Can you imagine if you had to maintain the same standards of safety in your home that your employer must maintain at the traditional workplace?

C. Status of New Technology with Regard to Workplace Privacy

A multitude of basic and inexpensive computer monitoring products allows managers to track Web use, to observe downloaded files, to filter sites, to restrict your access to certain sites and to know how much time you have spent on various sites. These include products such as WebSense, Net Access Manager, WebTrack and Internet Watchdog.

One particular firm, SpyShop.com, claims to service one-third of the Fortune 500 firms. This firm sells items such as a truth-telling device that links to a telephone. You are told that you can interview a job candidate on the phone and the device identifies those who lie. Another firm, Omnitracks, sells a satellite that fastens to the top or inside of a truck. The product allows trucking firms to locate trucks at all times. If a driver veers off the highway to get flowers for her or his partner on Valentine's Day, the firm will know what happened.

SpyZone.com sells an executive investigator kit that includes the truth phone I men-tioned earlier, as well as a pocket recording pen. Other outlets sell pinhole lens camera pens, microphones that fit in your pocket. The motto of one firm is "In God we trust. All others we monitor." That firm offers a beeper buster: a computer program that monitors calls placed to beepers within a certain vicinity. A screen on your computer will show you all the numbers so that you can determine whether the individual is being distracted during work-ing hours.

D. Competing Interests

The predominant question that I have sought to answer by my recent research is whether a balance is possible between the employer's interest in managing the workplace and the em-ployees' interest in privacy. Do employees even have a right to privacy? If one believes the answer is "no," then the entire issue becomes moot. If the employee does have some, even limited, right to privacy, one must seek to find a balance of interest. While we will return to the consideration of "rights" as we apply ethical theories, below, it is helpful to identify the proposed rights in dispute.

The employer has a right to manage the workplace. More specifically, employers want to manage the workplace so that they can place workers in the appropriate positions. They want to ensure compliance with affirmative action and administer workplace benefits. They want to ensure effective or productive performance. They need to know what their workers are doing in their workplace. The employer's perspective is as follows: "I am paying them to be there working. If they are not working, I should know that and either pay them less, or hire different workers." It seems like a relatively understandable concern.

Employees, on the other hand, want to be treated as free, equal, capable and rational individuals who have the ability to make their own decisions about the way their lives will unfold. They are interested in aiding their own personal development and valued performance (the lack of privacy may prevent "flow"); in conducting *some* personal business at the office; in being free from monitoring for performance reasons (wary of increased stress/pressure from monitoring); in being free from monitoring for privacy reasons; and in being able to review and to correct misinformation in data collected.

Consider the issue of personal work conducted at the office. I get to work some days at 7:00 A.M. and don't leave until 7:00 P.M. Last I heard, many doctors' offices are not open before or after 7:00 in the morning or night. So when is one supposed to call and make an appointment, much less ever go to an appointment, if one is punching the clock with those hours? The employer has to understand that workers must be able to call the doctor and make an appointment. Workers need to be able to conduct *involuntary* personal matters at the office. Now, one might not need to email their mother or chat on the phone with friends. Should workers still have the right to conduct that *voluntary* personal business? Perhaps the resolution lies in the precise definition of voluntary or involuntary business.

III. THE LAW, NEW TECHNOLOGY AND WORKPLACE PRIVACY

As dictated by the ethical decision-making process, one must obtain all the unbiased facts before responding to an ethical dilemma. Where new technology impacts the dilemma, the "facts" may be all the more difficult to ascertain, since we are not yet completely equipped to obtain the necessary information. For example, some scholars contend that nearly everyone who has a computer (estimated to be about 80% of the U.S. workforce) is subject to some form of information collection, no matter how much we protect ourselves. Another source reports that more than 30 million workers were subject to workplace monitoring last year, up from only 8 million in 1991. We are not yet at a point where we can even determine whether this information is realistic.

We are relatively certain about the ways in which information is collected. As of 1999, two-thirds of mid- to large-size firms conduct some form of monitoring, whether it is computer-based monitoring, video monitoring, monitoring of personal investments, or maybe simply monitoring key card access to the building or parking garage (up from 30% in 1993). Our style of working, even of communicating, has created greater possibilities for monitoring. In connection with email, for instance, more than 90 million American workers now send more than 2.8 billion email messages per day, an average of 190 emails per day, per worker. We might not be too concerned about some forms of monitoring, while other forms might feel particularly invasive.

A. Federal Legislation

More than 100 bills on privacy protection have been introduced in Congress, but only one has been approved, on the collection of personal information from kids over the internet. Also, the White House right now is only supporting privacy protections related to medical information privacy because they believe that this type of uncertainty will dissolve as firms and employees become more comfortable with the medium.

B. Constitutional Protections

The Fourth Amendment to the U.S. Constitution protects the "right of the people to be secure in their persons, houses, papers and effects, against unreasonable searches and seizures." This protection implies a reasonable expectation of privacy against intrusions *by the State, only*. As this provision of the Constitution does not apply to actions by private-sector employers, their employees must rely instead on state-by-state laws and the common law made and accepted in the courts. Similar limitation exists in connection with the First Amendment's protection of personal autonomy and the Fifth Amendment's protection against self-incrimination—each of these only protects the individual from invasions by the State. Currently, there is proposed employment-related privacy legislation in several states that would apply to private-sector employers, but those states fall in the distinct minority.

What the courts will generally consider in cases involving both the Fourth Amendment and common law privacy protections is (1) whether the employer has a legitimate business interest in obtaining the information, and (2) whether the employee has a reasonable expectation of privacy. Several examples of common law actions by the courts are illustrative of the courts' attempts at creating this balance. Perhaps more significant are the settlements reached by firms concerned about the *prospect* of a judge's decision.

C. Case Law

In one recent case, two McDonald's restaurant employees used voice-mail to transmit love messages during an affair. They believed that these messages were private since the firm told them that only they had the access codes. The franchise owner monitored the voice-mail messages and later played messages for the wife of one of the workers. The lovers sued for invasion of privacy. They settled for several million dollars, so we do not yet have any judge's decision in a situation like this.

In another case that never made it to the courts, the Minnesota Attorney General sued several banks for revealing personal information about clients to marketers in exchange for more than $4 million in fees. One bank eventually agreed to pay attorney fees plus $2.5 million to Habitat for Humanity.

While the law has not yet settled in connection with monitoring or the privacy of obtained information—hence the settlements—monitoring does seem justified by several cases where email was later used as evidence to encourage a settlement. Within the past several years, several large firms, including R. R. Donnelly, Morgan Stanley and Citicorp, have found that cases often hinged on email transmissions that people originally thought were deleted. In one case, this included an email containing 165 racial, ethnic and sexual jokes sent to the entire firm. In another, the email included sexual jokes about why beer is better than women. Had the firms enforced stringent policies about the use of email and monitored to enforce these policies, perhaps these emails would never have been sent.

A few short months ago, the *New York Times* also found itself facing some problems. They fired 24 employees at a Virginia payroll processing center for sending "inappropriate and offensive email in violation of corporate policy." The public sector is not immune from similar challenges: The U.S. Navy reported that it had disciplined more than 500 employees at a supply depot for sending sexually explicit email. It happens all the time, and it's continuing to happen. You would think that people would actually learn.

In cases where the courts have been able to address the issue, it seemed at first that *notice* of monitoring might emerge as the critical factor. Perhaps persuaded by early case law, of the 67% of mid- to large-size firms that monitor, 84% notify their employees of this activity. Notice might range from a one-line comment in the middle of an employee manual that someone receives on the first day of work, to a dialogue box reminding you that email may be monitored that pops up each time you hit the "send" button to transmit an email.

In an early case addressing this topic, the court in *K-mart v. Trotti* held that the search of an employee's company-owned locker was not appropriate because the workers were told to use their own personal lock. The basis for the decision was that the employees were left with the legitimate, reasonable expectation of privacy because it was their own lock. On the other hand, an employer's search of employee lunch buckets was held reasonable by another court only two years earlier.

In a later 1990 case, *Shoars v. Epson,* Epson won a suit filed by an employee who complained about email monitoring. In that case, the court distinguished the practice of intercepting an email transmission from storing and reading email transmissions once they had been sent, holding that the latter was acceptable. In a 1992 action, Northern Telecom settled a claim brought by employees who were allegedly secretly monitored for more than 13 years. In this case, Telecom agreed to pay $50,000 to individual plaintiffs and $125,000 for attorneys' fees.

Similarly, an employee-plaintiff in a 1995 federal action won a case against his employer, where the employer had monitored the worker's telephone for a period of 24 hours to determine whether the worker was planning a robbery. The court held that the company had gone too far and had insufficient evidence to support its claims.

One might therefore conclude that, if an employer adequately notifies workers that it will conduct monitoring, it has effectively destroyed any reasonable expectation of privacy on the part of the workers. It would now be unreasonable to expect privacy since one is told not to expect it. However, in a case where the alternative extreme was true, where a firm notified workers that it would not monitor, the court did not follow congruent logic. It did not find a reasonable expectation of privacy based on a firm's pledge not to read email.

In that case, *Smyth v. Pillsbury,* Smyth sued the firm after a manager read his email. At the time, Pillsbury had a policy saying that it would not read email. One might presume that this policy should have created this reasonable expectation of privacy. But instead, this was the first federal decision to hold that a private-sector, at-will employee has no right of privacy in the content of one's email when one sends it over the employer's computer system. The court held, "We do not find a reasonable expectation of privacy in the contents of email communications voluntarily made by an employee to his supervisor over the company email system, notwithstanding any assurances that such communications would not be intercepted by management."

IV. THE LIMITATIONS OF THE LEGAL SYSTEM: A CALL FOR ETHICS

The law offers little, if any, guidance in this area in connection with workplace monitoring, and technology as a whole. In fact, the development of our moral systems has not been able to keep pace with technological and medical developments, leaving us prey individually and societally to a host of dangers. And does this not represent our current situation in terms of technological advances?

It never occurred to most workers that some of this information was available or that they could be monitored in various ways. When employers' access to personal information is not apparent, employees do not adequately protect themselves against it. Failure to completely understand the new technology may prevent people from completely understanding their exposure or potential vulnerability.

In his State of the Union address, former President Clinton said, "Technology has to be carefully directed to assure that its reach does not compromise societal values. We have to safeguard our citizens' privacy." The primary ethical issue for analysis is whether the employee's fundamental right to privacy outweighs the employer's right to administer the workplace according to its desires. If not, is there a way to satisfy both parties? As law does not yet provide the answers, we turn to ethics for guidance.

The strongest, most persuasive and most consistent guidance in this area is based on a theory called Integrative Social Contracts Theory (ISCT), promulgated by Tom Donaldson and Tom Dunfee, both faculty in Wharton's ethics program. ISCT seeks to differentiate between those values that are fundamental across culture and theory ("hypernorms") and those values that are culturally specific, determined within moral "free space," and which are not hypernorms. In identifying values as hypernorms, Donaldson and Dunfee propose that one look to the convergence of religious, cultural and philosophical beliefs around certain core principles. Included as examples of hypernorms are freedom of speech, the right to personal freedom, the right to physical movement, and informed consent. In fact, individual privacy is at the core of many of these basic, minimal rights and is, arguably, a necessary prerequisite to many of them.

Specifically, ISCT seeks evidence of the widespread recognition of ethical principles that support a hypernorm conclusion, such as:

1. Widespread consensus that the principle is universal;
2. Component of well-known industry standards;
3. Supported by prominent nongovernmental organizations such as the International Labor Organization or Transparency International;
4. Supported by regional government organizations such as the European Union, the Organization for Economic Cooperation and Development, or the Organization of American States;
5. Consistently referred to as a global ethical standard by international media;
6. Known to be consistent with precepts of major religions;
7. Supported by global business organizations such as the International Chamber of Commerce or the Caux Roundtable;

8. Known to be consistent with precepts of major philosophies;
9. Generally supported by a relevant international community of professionals, e.g., accountants or environmental engineers;
10. Known to be consistent with findings concerning universal human values;
11. Supported by the laws of many different countries.

With regard to privacy, a key finding of a recent survey of the status of privacy in 50 countries around the world included the following conclusion:

> *Privacy is a fundamental human right recognized in all major international treaties and agreements on human rights. Nearly every country in the world recognizes privacy as a fundamental human right in their constitution, either explicitly or implicitly. Most recently drafted constitutions include specific rights to access and control one's personal information.*

Accordingly, it would appear that the value of privacy to civilized society is as great as the value of the various hypernorms to civilized existence. Ultimately, the failure to protect privacy may lead to an inability to protect personal freedom and autonomy.

The application of ISCT, however, has limitations. ISCT does not quantify critical *boundaries* for rights. If employees have a right to privacy based on a hypernorm, how far does it extend and what should happen in a conflict? Doesn't the employer have certain hypernorm-based rights that might be infringed by the protection of the employees' privacy right? To quantify the boundaries of the universal rights, one must therefore look beyond ISCT to a more fairness-based methodology.

Ethicist John Rawls's theory of distributive economic justice provides fairness-based guidance for quantifying the boundary levels of fundamental rights. Distributive justice is a teleological approach to ethical decision-making that defines ethical acts as those that lead to an equitable distribution of goods and services. To determine a fair method for distributing goods and services, Rawls suggests that one consider how we would distribute goods and services if we were under a "veil of ignorance" that prevented us from knowing our status in society (i.e., our intelligence, wealth, appearance). He asks that we consider what rules we would impose on this society if we had no idea whether we would be princes or paupers. Without knowing what role we might play in our society, would we devise a system of constant employee monitoring or complete privacy in all professional and personal endeavors? Rawls contends that those engaged in the exercise would build a cooperative system that was sensitive to the interests of all stakeholders. The reason Rawls believes that such a standard would emerge is that the members of the exercise do not know whether they would be among the employer population or employee population. Actions consistent with a system devised under a veil of ignorance are deemed ethical because of the inherent fairness of the system.

Rawls's theory of distributive justice does not provide guidance for identifying the categories of fundamental rights. What Rawls does provide is a method for establishing distribution rules that avoid market transgressions of the boundaries of ethical actions.

Conjoining ISCT and Rawlsian methods enables the identification of basic human rights and boundaries, and provides for a reasonable balance between economic and ethical consequences of privacy protection for both employees and employers. ISCT establishes the underlying or foundational hypernorms within a society, while distributive justice offers guidance on the extent of those hypernorms and the means by which to implement them.

Scholars are not in complete agreement as to whether a right to privacy is a hypernorm, though most would agree that some form of personal autonomy must be protected. As mentioned above, evidence of a hypernorm such as freedom from slavery unequivocally supports this conclusion—personal autonomy serves as a cornerstone of this protection. On the other hand, the quantification of one's right to privacy, in particular workplace privacy, is better identified using a Rawlsian analysis. A proposal for such a fairness-based balance follows.

The Implementation of an Ethical Resolution   Assuming for the purposes of this argument that privacy is a hypernorm, but one that may be limited by the employer's congruent right to managerial autonomy, how should the matter be resolved? I suggest a fairness-based decision based on two values: integrity and accountability.

Integrity, meaning consistency in values, would require that the decision-maker define her or his values, as well as create a prioritization of those values. This effort is often accomplished by a firm's mission statement or statement of values. Then, when faced with a dilemma or conflict between two or more of these values, the decision-maker will have internal as well as external guidance regarding the direction her or his decision should take. Second, no matter which direction is taken, the decision-maker must be accountable to anyone who is impacted by this decision. That would require a consideration of the impact of alternatives on each stakeholder; a balancing of that impact with the personal values addressed in the first step; and actions that represent the accountability to the stakeholders impacted by the decision.

Applying this process to a firm's response to monitoring and its impact on employee privacy, the firm may obtain guidance from its mission statement or alternative statement of values. Does monitoring satisfy or further the mission or values of the firm? Assuming that monitoring satisfies or furthers the values of the firm (since a negative relationship here would end the discussion and resolve the dilemma), the employer must impose monitoring in a manner that is accountable to those affected by the decision to monitor.

To be accountable to the impacted employees, the employer must respect their privacy rights and their right to make informed decisions about their actions. Accordingly, this model would require that the employer should give adequate notice of the intent to monitor, including the form of monitoring, its frequency and the purpose of the monitoring. In addition, to balance the employer's interests with those of the workforce, the employer should offer a means by which the employee can control the monitoring in order to create personal boundaries. In other words, if the employer is randomly monitoring telephone calls, there should be a notification device such as a beep whenever monitoring is taking place, or the employee should have the ability to block any monitoring during personal calls. This latter option would address an oft-cited challenge to notification: If employees have notice of monitoring, there is no possibility of random performance checks. However, if employees can merely block personal calls, they remain unaware of which business-related calls are being monitored.

If It Feels Wrong, It Probably Is   Ethicist Gary Marks suggests that we look to a number of questions about monitoring, and he proposes that if you answer "yes" to these questions, your monitoring is more likely to be unethical.

- Does the collection of the data involve physical or psychological harm?

- Does the technique cross a personal boundary without permission?

- Could the collection produce invalid results?

- Are you being more intrusive than necessary?

- Is the data subject prohibited from appealing or changing the information recorded?

- Are there negative effects on those beyond the data subject?

- Is the link between the information collected and the goal sought unclear?

- Is the data being used in such a way as to cause a disadvantage to the subject?

As a manager, you are not without guidance on these issues. Kevin Conlon, district counsel for the Communication Workers of America, suggests additional guidelines that may be considered in formulating an accountable process for employee monitoring:

- There should be no monitoring in highly private areas, such as restrooms;

- Monitoring should be limited to the workplace;

- Employees should have full access to any information gathered through monitoring;

- Continuous monitoring should be banned;

- All forms of secret monitoring should be banned;

- Advance notice should be given;

- Only information relevant to the job should be collected;

- Monitoring should result in the attainment of some business interest.

Moreover, in its bargaining demands for last year, the Union of the United Auto Workers demanded concessions with regard to monitoring, including:

- Monitoring only under mutual prior agreement;

- No secret monitoring: advance notice required of how, when and for what purpose employees will be monitored;

- Employees should have access to information gathered through monitoring;

- Strict limitations regarding disclosure of information gained through monitoring;

- Prohibition of discrimination by employers based on off-work activities.

* * *

From the employees' perspective, this type of resolution would respect their personal autonomy by providing for personal space, by giving notice of where that space ends, by giving them access to and the right to change or correct the information gathered and by providing for monitoring that is directed toward the personal development of the employee and not merely toward catching wrongdoers.

From the employer's perspective, this balance offers a way to effectively but ethically supervise the work done by their employees. It protects the misuse of resources, while also allowing employers to better evaluate their workers and to encourage their workers to be more effective. I contend that any program that fails to satisfy these basic elements has the potential not only for ethical lapses, but also for serious economic problems.

Vice President and current presidential candidate Al Gore, who of course is an appropriate person to quote since he "invented" the internet, claims that "new technology must not reopen the oldest threats to our basic rights: liberty and privacy. But government should not simply block or regulate all that electronic progress. If we are to move at a full speed ahead into the information age, government must do more to protect your rights—in a way that empowers you more, not less. We need an electronic bill of rights for this electronic age."

VI. CONCLUDING THOUGHTS

Before I conclude my remarks, I ask that you consider the following questions not only with regard to information technology and the impact that that technology has on your particular workplace, but also with regard to the ethical issues that arise in other areas of your work. Consider what you might be willing to quit over. What would be so damaging, so intrusive, so much of a violation of your personal space that you would simply quit right then and there? What could be so bad?

Second—and perhaps it seems extreme in this particular circumstance—what would you be willing to give your life for? You may not believe right now that information technology is going to present life-and-death ethical dilemmas. And yet when we consider the ultimate usage of some of that technology, it really does have a life-and-death impact. If you knew that it would have a fatal, negative impact, would you quit if your firm or client failed to ameliorate it? Monitoring probably does not fall within this range, but you can imagine situations where technology does allow such an extreme unethical and certainly illegal act.

The reason I want to conclude with this query is because this is really the purpose of the lecture. The world is a better place because you have thought about these questions now, rather than when you are first faced with these challenges in the workplace.

EMPLOYEE MONITORING AND COMPUTER TECHNOLOGY: EVALUATIVE SURVEILLANCE v. PRIVACY

—ADAM MOORE

In the following article, Adam Moore addresses the tension between evaluative surveillance and privacy against the backdrop of the current explosion of information technology. More specifically, and after a brief analysis of privacy rights, he argues that knowledge of the different kinds of surveillance used at any given company should be made explicit to the employees. Moreover, there will be certain kinds of evaluative monitoring that violate privacy rights and should not be used in most cases.

Too many employers practice a credo of "In God we trust, others we monitor."

—MARLENE PITURRO,
"Electronic
Monitoring"[1]

INTRODUCTION

Few would deny the profound impact, both positive and negative, that computers and digital technology are having in the modern workplace. Some of the benefits include safer working conditions, increased productivity and better communication between employees, clients and companies. The downside of this revolution can be tedious working conditions and the loss of privacy and autonomy. In the workplace there is a basic tension between surveillance technology and privacy. Companies want to monitor employees and reward effort, intelligence, productivity and success while eliminating laziness, stupidity, theft and failure. The market demands no less of most businesses. But against this pressure stands the individual within the walls of privacy—walls that protect against invasions into private domains.

Jeremy Bentham once envisioned a prison workhouse that placed overseers in a central tower with glass-walled cells and mirrors placed so that inmates could never know if they were being watched.[2] The idea was that "universal transparency" would keep the prisoners on their best behavior. Recent developments in surveillance technology are promising to turn the workplace into the modern equivalent of Bentham's workhouse. There are now computer programs that allow employers to monitor and record the number of keystrokes per minute an employee completes. Employee badges may allow the recording of movements and time spent at different locations while working. There is now the possibility of monitoring voice mail, email, and phone logs—all without the knowledge or consent of those being watched. There are even global positioning systems that allow companies to track employee movements cross-country. While employers have always sought to monitor employees it is arguably the case that digital technology has changed the game, so to speak. We may wonder, in a networked world, when this kind of surveillance technology will be used to monitor all of us? And not by just governments, although this Orwellian nightmare will be possible, but by our employers. . . .

PRIVACY

Privacy may be understood as that state where others do not have access to you or to information about you.[3] I hasten to note that there are degrees of privacy. There are our own private thoughts that are never disclosed to anyone, as well as information we share with loved ones. Furthermore, there is information that we share with mere acquaintances and the general public. These privacy relations with others can be pictured "in terms of a series of 'zones' or 'regions' . . . leading to a 'core self.' "[4] Thus, secrets shared with a loved one can still be considered private, even though they have been disclosed.

In an important article dealing with privacy, morality and the law, William Parent offers the following definition of privacy.

> *Privacy is the condition of not having undocumented personal knowledge about one possessed by others. A person's privacy is diminished exactly to the degree that others possess this kind of knowledge about him. Documented information is information that is found in the public record or is publicly available (e.g., information found in newspapers, court proceedings, and other official documents open to public inspection).*[5]

The problem with this definition is that it leaves the notion of privacy dependent upon what a society or culture takes as documentation and what information is available via the public record. Parent acts as if undocumented information is private while documented information is not, and this is the end of the matter. But surely the secret shared between lovers is private in one sense and not in another. To take another case, consider someone walking in a public park. There is almost no limit to the kinds of information that can be acquired from this public display. One's image, height, weight, eye color, approximate age and general physical abilities are all readily available. Moreover, biological matter will also be left in the public domain—strands of hair and the like may be left behind. Since this matter, and the information contained within, is publicly available it would seem that all of one's genetic profile is not private information.

Furthermore, what is publicly available information is dependent upon technology. Telescopes, listening devices, heat imaging sensors and the like open up what most would consider private domains for public consumption. What we are worried about is what should be considered a "private affair"—something that is no one else's business. Parent's conception of privacy is not sensitive to these concerns.

A right to privacy can be understood as a right to control access to oneself. It is a right to limit public access to the "core self"—and this includes personal information that one never discloses—and to information that one discloses only to family and friends. For example, suppose that I wear a glove because I am ashamed of a scar on my hand. If you were to snatch the glove away you would not only be violating my right to property—alas, the glove is mine to control—you would also violate my right to privacy; a right to restrict access to information about the scar on my hand. Similarly, if you were to focus your x-ray camera on my hand, take a picture of the scar through the glove, and then publish the photograph widely, you would violate a right to privacy.[6]

Having said something about what a right to privacy is we may ask how such rights are justified. A promising line of argument combines notions of autonomy and respect for persons. A central and guiding principle of Western liberal democracies is that individuals, within certain limits, may set and pursue their own life goals and projects. Rights to privacy erect a moral boundary that allows individuals the moral space to order their lives as they see fit.[7] Privacy protects us from the prying eyes and ears of governments, corporations and neighbors. Within the walls of privacy we may experiment with new ways of living that may not be accepted by the majority. Privacy, autonomy and sovereignty, it would seem, come bundled together.

A second but related line of argument rests on the claim that privacy rights stand as a bulwark against governmental oppression and totalitarian regimes. If individuals have rights to control personal information and to limit access to themselves, within certain constraints, then the kinds of oppression that we have witnessed in the 20th century would be near impossible. Put another way, if oppressive regimes are to consolidate and maintain power, then privacy rights (broadly defined) must be eliminated or severely restricted. If correct, privacy rights would be a core value that limits the forces of oppression.[8]

Arguably any plausible account of human well-being or flourishing will have as a component a strong right to privacy. Controlling who has access to ourselves is an essential part of being a happy and free person. This may be why "peeping Toms" and rapists are held up as moral monsters—they cross a boundary that should never be crossed without consent.

Surely each of us has the right to control our own thoughts, hopes, feelings and plans, as well as a right to restrict access to information about our lives, family and friends. I would argue that what grounds these sentiments is a right to privacy. While complete control of all our personal information is a pipe dream for many of us, simply because the information is already out there and most likely cannot or will not be destroyed, this does not detract from the view of personal information ownership. Through our daily activities we each create and leave digital footprints that others may follow and exploit—and that we do these things does not obviously sanction the gathering and subsequent disclosure of such information by others.

Whatever kind of information we are considering there is a gathering point that individuals have control over. For example, in purchasing a new car and filling out the car loan application, no one would deny we each have the right to demand that such information not be sold to other companies. I would argue that this is true for any disclosed personal information whether it be patient questionnaire information, video rental records, voting information or employment applications. In agreeing with this view, one first has to agree that individuals have the right to control their own personal information—i.e., binding agreements about controlling information presuppose that one of the parties has the right to control this information.

If I am correct about all of this, then there is a fairly strong presumption in favor of individual privacy rights—even in the workplace. What justifies a photographer taking pictures of me about the house is my consent. Most would agree that absent such consent a serious violation of privacy would have occurred. Consent is also necessary, I will argue, for employee monitoring. But therein lies the problem. Under what conditions does consent or agreement yield the appropriate sort of permission? Alas, the initial bargaining situation must be fair if we are to be morally bound by the outcome.

PRIVACY IN THE WORKPLACE

We are now in a position to consider an individual's right to privacy in the context of a working environment where evaluative surveillance is both necessary and desirable. If pay increases, promotion, profit-sharing awards and incentive pay are to be based on effort, desert and success, there must be acceptable methods of monitoring employees.

Consider the following case. In January 1990, Alana Shoars, an administrator for the electronic mail system at Epson America Inc., discovered that the company was monitoring the email messages of its employees. She was shown a batch of printouts of employee email messages—messages that she thought were protected through the use of passwords. "I glanced over at some of the printouts, and a lot of warning bells went off in my head. As far as I'd known, as email coordinator, it wasn't possible to do such a thing."[9] Upon criticizing this breach of employee privacy, Ms. Shoars was dismissed from the company for insubordination.[10]

This case represents only the tip of the iceberg with respect to employee monitoring. A survey of companies in *Macworld* concerning electronic monitoring "reported that 21.6% of the 301 participating companies admitted searching employee files, including electronic work files (73.8%), email (41.5%), network messages (27.7%) and voice mail (15.4%)."[11] And even more alarming, only 30.8% of the companies surveyed gave advance warning of the monitoring activities.[12]

In the most general terms, the case of Alana Shoars and email monitoring highlights the tension between rights to control information and individual privacy in the workplace. What was objectionable with Epson America's monitoring was not their wish to control the information that was found on the company's computer network. The objection is that their employees were not notified of the monitoring or the strict company policy forbidding personal use of the network.

Epson argued that the system was company-owned and therefore any information found in email accounts, private or otherwise, was justifiably available for inspection. Moreover, it could be argued that notification of surveillance was both unnecessary and unwise from a corporate perspective. If each instance of monitoring was known to an employee, then the data collected would be almost worthless. It would be like telling the fakes to start faking.

THIN CONSENT

Justifying employee monitoring in light of privacy rights begins with what I call thin consent. A first step in justifying a kind of monitoring is employee notification. The consent takes the following form: If your employment is to continue then you must agree to such-and-so kinds of surveillance. This is appropriately called "thin consent" because it is assumed that jobs are hard to find, the employee in question needs the job, etc. Nevertheless, quitting is a viable option. The force of such agreements or contracts is echoed by Ronald Dworkin.

> If a group contracted in advance that disputes amongst them would be settled in a particular way, the fact of that contract would be a powerful argument that such disputes should be settled in that way when they do arise. The contract would be an argument in itself, independent of the force of the reasons that might have led different people to enter the contract. Ordinarily, for example, each of the parties supposes that a contract he signs is in his own interest; but if someone has made a mistake in calculating his self-interest, the fact that he did contract is a strong reason for the fairness of holding him nevertheless to the bargain.[13]

An employee cannot consent, even thinly, to a type of monitoring if it is unknown to her. Given a fairly strong presumption in favor of privacy, thin consent would seem obligatory. Here the employee would be notified of each different type of monitoring. Individual acts of surveillance, however, would not require notification—thus slackers would not be notified to stop slacking.

Moreover, a thin consent policy for each different type of surveillance allows companies and businesses to seize the moral high ground in one important respect. There is no sneaking around riffling through office files, midnight program installations or hidden backdoor keys into email accounts. All of this is up front and in the open. Part of what makes this kind of employee monitoring distasteful is the deceit involved. Locked voice-mail accounts, email files, and desk drawers present the air of privacy when these domains are anything but private.

In any case it should be clear that thin consent is not enough to justify the array of monitoring systems that are now possible or will soon be possible—not in every case. When jobs are scarce, unemployment high and government assistance programs swamped, thin consent becomes thin indeed. In these conditions employees will be virtually forced to relinquish privacy because of the severe consequences if they don't. But notice what happens when we slide to the other extreme. Assume a condition of negative unemployment where there are many more jobs than employees and where changing jobs is relatively easy. In circumstances such as these, thin consent has become quite thick. And if employees were to agree to a certain type of monitoring in these favorable conditions most would think it justified.

As we slide from one extreme to the other—from a pro-business environment (lots of workers and few jobs yields low wage overhead) to a pro-employee environment (lots of jobs and few workers yields high employee compensation)—this method of justification becomes more plausible. What begins looking like a necessary condition ends up looking like a sufficient condition. To determine the exact point where thin consent becomes thick enough to bear the justificatory burden required is a difficult matter. The promise of actual consent depends on the circumstances. Minimally, if the conditions favor the employee then it is plausible to maintain that actual consent would be enough to override a presumption in favor of privacy.

HYPOTHETICAL THICK CONSENT

As noted above, thick consent is possible when employment conditions minimize the costs of finding a comparable job for an employee. Put another way, an employee who doesn't have to work, but agrees to anyway, has given the right kind of consent—assuming of course they have been notified of the different types of monitoring that will occur. What justifies a certain type of surveillance is that it would be agreeable to a worker in a pro-employee environment. If thin consent is obtained and the test of hypothetical thick consent is met, then we have reason to think that a strong presumption in favor of privacy has been justifiably surpassed.

We will also have to assume that the hypothetical worker making the choice is modestly interested in maintaining control over private information. If this constructed individual has nothing to hide and a general attitude of openness, then any type of surveillance will pass the test. And if I am correct about the importance of privacy with respect to sovereignty and autonomy, anyone would be interested in retaining such control. Rawls's notion of placing individuals behind a veil of ignorance may be of some service here.[14] If the individual agreeing did not know whether she was a worker, manager or owner and if we assume that anyone would be interested in retaining control over private domains, then the correct vantage point for determining binding agreements will have been attained.

The force of hypothetical contracts has been called into question by Dworkin and others— "A hypothetical contract is not simply a pale form of an actual contract; it is no contract at all."[15] Here I agree with Dworkin. The moral bindingness of hypothetical contracts has to do with the reasons for why we would choose to do this or that. Viewing it this way, hypothetical contracts are simply devices that enable us to more clearly understand the reasons, moral or otherwise, for adopting a particular institution or process. Dworkin notes,

> *There must be reasons, of course, why I would have agreed if asked in advance, and these may also be reasons why it is fair to enforce these rules against me even if I have not agreed. But my hypothetical consent does not count as a reason, independent of these other reasons, for enforcing the rules against me, as my actual agreement would have.*[16]

Thus the test of hypothetical thick consent can be understood as a way of clarifying, and allowing us to arrive at, a position that is fair and sensible. Hereafter, when I talk of hypothetical consent and the moral force of such agreements, be aware that this is simply a tool or device that is notifying us when privacy rights may be justifiably relaxed.

Taking up the Epson case again, we may ask if a policy of email monitoring would satisfy the test of hypothetical thick consent. Here we are to imagine a world where there were numerous jobs like the ones found at Epson and that moving to these other jobs would be relatively easy. Moreover, given that there is no industry-wide interest in monitoring email activity many of these other positions would not include email monitoring. If an employee would not agree under these conditions, then this type of surveillance would fail the test. Had Epson notified its employees of a company email monitoring policy, then those employees who stayed on at Epson would have given thin consent. But we should not rush to judge that such a policy would be automatically justified unless the test of hypothetical thick consent is also met. Meeting this latter test in the Epson case seems unlikely.

I take a virtue of hypothetical thick consent to be that satisfaction is determined by imagining a pro-employee situation and then asking what an employee would do in the face of some kind of surveillance. Some may charge that I am stacking the deck, however. Why not imagine a pro-business situation and then ask what an employee would do. We wouldn't have to do much imagining though, and employee consent in such conditions wouldn't justify anything. Moreover, if I am correct in positing privacy rights for each of us, then the deck is already stacked. There is a presumption in favor of individuals having control over personal information—we have privacy rights. Since employee surveillance may cross into private domains, we must consider under what conditions a privacy right may be given up or relaxed. In relatively few cases is thin consent thick enough to handle the justificatory burden. Hence, the use of hypothetical thick consent. We are imagining a case where the bargaining situation favors the employee—and if agreement is offered in these conditions, then we have reason to think that the type of surveillance in question is warranted.

I hasten to note that even in a pro-employee environment there would be certain kinds of employee monitoring that would be necessary for any business. Punching a time clock or measuring time spent working, for example, would occur in almost any business or company. Even in a pro-employee market theft would have to be minimized. It is not as if McDonald's would become so desperate for workers that they would leave the register drawers open, allow employees to come and go as they please and continue to pay wages. The market demands that businesses make a profit or at least break even. Given this, there will be certain kinds of employee monitoring that every business will use.

Moreover, there will be employment-specific monitoring as well. For example, trucking companies will have to monitor driving records and ensure that drivers maintain the appropriate skills needed to operate the big rigs. This kind of surveillance may be required by the market or by legislation of one kind or another. There may be laws that require certain licenses that make businesses liable for noncompliance. Absent laws or other government regulation, market efficiency may require certain kinds of monitoring. An example of the latter may be employee time monitoring. The hypothetical or constructed truck driver, no matter where he goes, will be subject to certain kinds of monitoring. So, even in a pro-employee environment certain kinds of surveillance will be justified—those kinds that are necessary for doing business.

So far I have been pursuing a kind of top-down strategy in presenting certain principles and considering arguments that may be marshaled to support these principles. If I am correct, thin consent will justify certain kinds of monitoring when employment conditions favor the employee. Absent such conditions actually occurring, we can imagine what an employee would choose if she were in a pro-employee environment. If she would agree to a type of monitoring from this vantage point—either because every business in her field will monitor in the way she is considering or she agrees for some other reason (maybe because the new monitoring policy will benefit her in some way)—then the monitoring is permitted. In the next section I will pursue a bottom-up strategy by presenting certain cases and then examining how the proposed model fits with these cases and our intuitions about them.

TEST CASES AND ILLUSTRATIONS

Let us begin with an easy one first. Suppose that one day an employee is approached by his boss and is informed that the company will be moving to a new building. Excited about the new digs, the employee tours the recently constructed office and is quite dismayed. It seems that management has been reading Bentham's *Panopticon* and the site has been built so that employee cubicles can be monitored by an overseer who can't himself be seen. The video cameras found in the new office have been placed so that computer screens can be watched as well as facial expressions, body motions and the like. The employee complains and asks what conceivable purpose such a system could have at an insurance company. Management replies that only someone with something to hide would object and this system of monitoring will allow hard workers to be recognized and fairly compensated.

We may now ask if such a monitoring system is justified in relation to hypothetical thick consent. I think it is clear that an individual who is modestly interested in protecting privacy and in a pro-employee environment would leave, other things being equal, and find similar employment elsewhere. The "other things being equal" exception is important because if management were to double employee salaries then maybe a deal could be made— no privacy at work for lots of cash.[17] Outside of such offers the presumption in favor of privacy rights would not have been surpassed for this type of surveillance.

Before moving on, I would like to briefly address the kinds of replies that were offered for why employees shouldn't oppose this kind of monitoring. First, that an employee should have nothing to hide is irrelevant. It is her private life that is being monitored and so it is up to her to deny access. Whether or not she has something to hide is nobody's business. We all may have perfectly normal bedroom lives and have nothing to hide in this area. Nevertheless, mounting a company video camera and wake-up siren on the bedroom wall cannot in the least bit be supported by such reasons. Employee benefit is equally, and for the same reasons, dubious.

Consider a different case. Suppose in an effort to eliminate "time theft" a company begins using "active badges" that monitor employee movements while at work. These badges are sophisticated enough to monitor time spent in a specific area. So, employees who linger in the break room, arrive late, leave early and stroll the halls, will be discovered and treated accordingly.

Few would deny that time monitoring is a necessary part of any business. Nevertheless, there will be more and less invasive ways to monitor time. Bentham's *Panopticon* with a time overseer is one of the more invasive methods. Given that there are various less invasive ways to obtain this information about employees, it would seem that a constructed individual interested in maintaining private domains would not agree to this type of surveillance. Thus for most companies such a policy would be unjustified. There may be exceptions, however. For example, the U.S. Pentagon, Arms R&D departments and the like may have to maintain this level of monitoring to ensure secrecy.[18] Monitoring college professors in this way is clearly unjustifiable.

A final case that I would like to discuss deals with remote computer monitoring. The case is provided by John Whalen.

> *A recent ad for Norton-Lambert's Close-Up/LAN software package tempted managers to "look in on Sue's computer screen. . . . Sue doesn't even know you're there!" . . . these "remote monitoring" capabilities . . . allow network administrators to peek at an employee's screen in real time, scan data files and email at will, tabulate keystroke speed and accuracy, overwrite passwords, and even seize control of a remote workstation. Products like Dynamics Corp.'s Peak and Spy; Microcom Inc.'s LANlord; Novell Inc.'s Net Ware; and Neon Software's NetMinder not only improve communications and productivity, they turn employees' cubicles into covert listening stations.*[19]

While this kind of employee monitoring may yield some benefits, the preponderance of the evidence would suggest otherwise. Some studies have shown that these monitoring systems produce fear, resentment and elevate stress levels.[20] Another study concluded that "the introduction of computerized performance monitoring may result in a workplace that is less satisfying to many employees . . . and creates a more competitive environment which may decrease the quality of social relationships."[21]

Putting aside the unsavory consequences we may ask if such monitoring passes either test under consideration. First the test of thin consent would not be passed if the employees being monitored were not notified of such practices. Given the absence of a clear pro-employee environment in most industries that would use such surveillance, even if employees were notified the consent would seem too thin. Moreover, remote computer monitoring would fail the test of hypothetical thick consent for most companies. Individuals who did not know if they were the owner, manager or employee would not agree to such privacy invasions. The presumption in favor of privacy would thus remain intact.

CONCLUSION

As noted in the opening, high-tech surveillance is promising to turn the modern workplace into an Orwellian nightmare achieving Bentham's ideal workhouse for prisoners—"universal transparency." And even if such monitoring somehow produced an overall net increase in utility, it would still be unjustifiable. Sometimes the consequences be damned. Not that I think generally good consequences could be had from such surveillance. Arguably, human beings are the most productive and creative in conditions completely opposite from those found in Bentham's *Panopticon*.

In this article I have argued that individuals have rights to privacy that shield us from the prying eyes and ears of neighbors, governments and corporations—electronic eyes and ears are no more welcome. If we begin with a fairly strong presumption in favor of privacy and test different types of employee monitoring with thin and hypothetical thick consent, many currently used kinds of surveillance will be unjustified. Arguably this consent is necessary and sufficient for overriding or relaxing privacy rights with respect to employee monitoring.[22] We will each spend at least a quarter of our lives and a large part of our most productive years at work. This environment should be constructed to promote creative and productive activity while maintaining the zones of privacy that we all cherish. Although privacy rights are not absolute, it would seem that in a networked world filled with devices that may be used to capture information about each of us, we should take privacy invasions—whether at home, on a public street or in the workplace—much more seriously.

FOOTNOTES

1. Marlene Piturro, "Electronic Monitoring," Information Center, July 1990, p. 31; quoted in Richard Spinello's *Ethical Aspects of Information Technology* (Englewood Cliffs, N.J.: Prentice Hall, 1995), p. 141.
2. J. Bentham, *Panopticon* (The Inspection House), originally published in 1791.
3. A longer version of this section appears in my article "Intangible Property: Privacy, Power, and Information Control," *American Philosophical Quarterly* 35 (1998): 365–378. I would thank the editors of *APQ* for allowing me to present this material here.
4. Alan Westin, "Privacy in the Modern Democratic State," in *Ethical Issues in the Use of Computers,* ed. D. Johnson and J. Snapper (Belmont, Calif.: Wadsworth, 1985), p. 187.
5. W. A. Parent, "Privacy, Morality, and the Law," *Philosophy and Public Affairs,* Fall 1983, pp. 269–288; reprinted in *Ethical Issues in the Use of Computers,* ed. D. Johnson and J. Snapper (Belmont, Calif.: Wadsworth, 1985), p. 203 (all page citations refer to the reprint).
6. Legal scholar William Prosser separated privacy cases into four distinct but related torts.
    Intrusion: Intruding (physically or otherwise) upon the solitude of another in a highly offensive manner. For example, a woman sick in the hospital with a rare disease refuses a reporter's request for a photograph and interview. The reporter photographs her anyway, over her objection.
    Private facts: Publicizing highly offensive private information about someone that is not of legitimate concern to the public. For example, photographs of an undistinguished and wholly private hardware merchant carrying on an adulterous affair in a hotel room are published in a magazine.
    False light: Publicizing a highly offensive and false impression of another. For example, a taxi driver's photograph is used to illustrate a newspaper article on cabdrivers who cheat the public when the driver in the photo is not, in fact, a cheat.
    Appropriation: Using another's name or likeness for some advantage without the other's consent. For example, a photograph of a famous actress is used without her consent to advertise a product.
    Dean William Prosser, "Privacy," *California Law Review* 48 (1960): 383, 389, quoted in E. Alderman and C. Kennedy, *The Right to Privacy* (New York: Alfred A. Knopf, 1995), pp. 155–56. What binds these seemingly disparate cases under the heading "privacy invasions" is that they each concern personal information control. And while there may be other morally objectionable facets to these cases—for example the taxi driver case may also be objectionable on grounds of defamation—there are arguably privacy interests at stake as well.
7. Clinton Rossiter puts the point succinctly: "Privacy is a special kind of independence, which can be understood as an attempt to secure autonomy in at least a few personal and spiritual concerns, if necessary in defiance of all the pressures of the modern society. . . . It seeks to erect an unbreachable wall of dignity and reserve against the entire world. The free man is the private man, the man who still keeps some of his thoughts and judgments entirely to himself, who feels no over-riding compulsion to share everything of value

with others, not even those he loves and trusts." C. Rossiter, *Aspects of Liberty* (Ithaca, N.Y.: Cornell University Press, 1958), quoted in Westin, "Privacy in the Modern Democratic State," p. 188.

8. For more about privacy rights see E. Hendricks, T. Hayden and J. Novik, *Your Right to Privacy* (Carbondale: Southern Illinois University Press, 1990); F. Cate, *Privacy in the Information Age* (New York: The Brookings Institution, 1997); B. Givens, *The Privacy Rights Handbook* (New York: Avon Books, 1997); Charles Fried, "Privacy," *Yale Law Journal* 77 (1968): 477; A. Westin and M. Baker, *Databanks in a Free Society* (New York: Quadrangle Press, 1972); J. Rachels, "Why Privacy Is Important," *Philosophy and Public Affairs* 4 (Summer 1975): 323–33; and Paul Weiss, *Privacy* (Carbondale: Southern Illinois University Press, 1983).

9. IDG Communications, Inc., *Infoworld,* October 22, 1990; quoted by Anne Wells Branscomb in *Who Owns Information?* (New York: Basic Books, 1994), p. 92.

10. Alana Shoars filed a wrongful termination suit. "The lower court agreed with Epson's lawyer that neither state privacy statutes nor federal statutes address confidentiality of Email in the workplace and dismissed the case." Branscomb, *Who Owns Information?* p. 93. See *Alana Shoars v. Epson America, Inc.,* No. SWC112749 (L.A. Super. Ct. 1990).

11. Branscomb, *Who Owns Information?* p. 93.

12. While the courts have ruled that employers cannot monitor their workers' personal calls, the Electronic Communications Privacy Act of 1986 grants bosses a "business-use exception," which allows supervisory and quality-control monitoring. J. Whalen, "You're Not Paranoid: They Really Are Watching You," *Wired Magazine,* March 1995. See also *Briggs v. American Filter Co.,* 704 F.2d 577 (11th Cir. 1983), *Watkins v. L. M. Berry,* 704 F.2d 579 (11th Cir. 1983), and Hendricks et al., *Your Right to Privacy,* Part 2.

13. Ronald Dworkin, *Taking Rights Seriously* (Cambridge: Harvard University Press, 1977); reprinted in *Justice: Alternative Political Perspectives,* 3rd ed., ed. James Sterba (Belmont, Calif.: Wadsworth, 1999), p. 126 (all page references refer to the reprint).

14. J. Rawls, *A Theory of Justice* (Cambridge: Harvard University Press, 1971), pp. 136–142. The hope is that Rawls's veil of ignorance will serve as a device that ensures impartiality.

15. Dworkin, *Taking Rights Seriously,* pp. 126–27.

16. *Ibid.,* p. 127.

17. Employment agreements grant rights, powers, liberties and duties to both parties. Thus an employee may trade privacy for some kind of compensation like time off or the opportunity to learn. When trade-offs such as these have occurred we may take the obligations, generated by the agreement, as prima facie—alas, the agreement may have been brokered in unfair conditions. If I am correct, fairness of conditions and binding agreements that justifiably relax rights are guaranteed when the tests of thin and hypothetical thick consent are passed.

18. Even in these cases the different types of surveillance used should be made explicit to every employee.

19. J. Whalen, "You're Not Paranoid: They Really Are Watching You," *Wired Magazine,* March 1995.

20. Richard Spinello, *Ethical Aspects of Information Technology* (Englewood Cliffs, N.J.: Prentice Hall, 1995), p. 128.

21. R. H. Irving, C. A. Higgins and F. R. Safayeni, "Computerized Performance Monitoring Systems: Use and Abuse," *Communications of the ACM,* August 1986, p. 800.

22. I take consequentialist concerns to be factored into laws or market demands. That is, hypothetical thick consent includes utility maximization arguments for requiring licenses, safety regulations and the like.

ETHICS@EMAIL: DO NEW MEDIA REQUIRE NEW MORALITY?

—Paul Soukup, S.J.

As more and more day-to-day interaction in business and academia has begun to take place through electronic mail, probably every one of its users has experienced some breakdown. By now, we have come to expect occasional hardware failures, but the human ones still catch us by surprise. That message we dashed off with no ill intent is received with hard feelings. Or it is forwarded to someone we never meant should see it. Or, unbeknown to us, it is read by our boss. Email has raised a host of ethical questions about how we treat one another and how we work, but its very newness as a medium can make the answers more obscure. Paul Soukup addresses these questions in the following article.

EMAIL vs. P-MAIL

Though it resembles its paper-based cousin, electronic mail has its own characteristics. First, it combines a conversational style with a written form. As a consequence, it suffers from problems of misinterpretation. Because it is conversational, it is seldom thought out; because it depends on text, recipients presume that it is.

Also unlike paper mail, email offers speed of delivery, permanent storage and easy replication. These characteristics can blur a number of boundaries most of us take for granted. Supposedly private comments get passed on to unintended recipients. Quickly scribbled notes find a place in permanent archives. And personal life (notes to friends, forwarded jokes, chatty comments) spills over into work time.

The intermingling of professional and personal life recalls another significant characteristic of this new medium: Someone else, often an employer, owns part or all of the structure that makes email work. Writing on the ethics and etiquette of email, Norman Shapiro and Robert Anderson note the competing interests of "an organization's desire and ability to filter, channel, record, and control messages" and the writer's desire to own the message. The question becomes, Who owns electronic mail? The sender? The receiver? The organization that provides the equipment?

OLD PRINCIPLES FOR A NEW ETHICS

Although these new questions seem to demand new laws or new ethics, the recent history of communication technology in the United States shows legal and ethical thinking lagging behind innovations. Typically, for lack of other options, we borrow guidelines from what we know. For example, when Congress needed to regulate radio and television, it required broadcasters—like railroads, in the Interstate Commerce Act—to serve the "public interest, convenience and necessity."

The discussion of email and electronic ethics is just beginning. However, several people have suggested some venerable principles to bear in mind. Dutch communication scholar and past president of the International Association for Mass Communication Research, Cees Hamelink, offers three guiding perspectives from human rights theory:

- Equality, or nondiscrimination in access and use.

- Inviolability, or the inadmissibility of intentional harm against humans.

- Liberty, or the absence of external coercion or constraints that obstruct self-determination.

To Hamelink's concerns, the Bill of Electronic Rights and Ethics adds rights to communicate, to privacy and to jurisdiction—that is, to be subject to the laws of one's own state. This document also offers the guiding principles of toleration, trust and consideration.

General principles should translate into specific actions. For example, Hamelink's principle of equality should lead to a serious consideration of universal email, a position also claimed in the right to communicate. Human beings, the argument goes, should have the means and the access to send and to receive communications. Why? The answer lies in rights principles. Rights theorists hold that the fundamental moral right is to be treated as a free and equal person capable of making decisions to advance as a human being. If today that right cannot be exercised (i.e., one can't get a job or health care or something else fundamental) without electronic communications, then one has a moral right to have email access.

Hamelink's principle of liberty lays a foundation for considerations of email censorship: Should a government or an organization limit an individual's self-expression? That same issue appears in the Bill of Electronic Rights in terms of jurisdiction. Should individuals be liable for email materials banned in one location but permitted at their point of origin?

The Telecommunications Reform Act of 1996 attempted to resolve some of these issues, particularly those dealing with obscenity; that question is currently before the courts. Lower courts have found the bill's wording too vague.

PRIVACY

Other ethical questions also remain unresolved, among them privacy. Who owns electronic mail? This issue is difficult since conflicting legal guidelines exist. On the one hand, the 1986 Electronic Communication Privacy Act prohibits access to mail transmitted over public telephone lines, just as post office correspondence is protected.

On the other hand, courts have held that private organizations may look at email within their own networks. Many companies argue they do this for the same reasons they might monitor phone calls—to improve customer service, to investigate crime or to prevent security breaches.

People have argued the merits of both sides of this issue. In the meantime, employees and system users should ask to see the privacy policy of their company. Even if privacy is company policy, users should never assume it exists. Unauthorized access can and does take place. When something calls for absolute privacy, use another medium.

ATTRIBUTION

The issue of email ownership has other ethical ramifications that might go under the heading of attribution. Who is the true author of a message and how should he or she be acknowledged?

Electronically, a letter can pass through multiple public or private machines before it arrives at its destination—and there's no evidence if it has been opened by someone else. Some email systems allow editing of the "from" line, so the author of a letter can be changed or obscured. The issues raised by these email characteristics range from forgery to anonymity to simply giving proper credit.

While the wrongness of forgery is evident, what of the use of pseudonyms? Can unsigned mail serve a purpose? Or, if the mail is signed, how should people cite it, particularly where no paper copies exist?

Perhaps the best solution in questions of attribution lies in merely considering them. Each organization should develop a policy of attribution, discussing how to give credit to work that comes through email.

Such a policy should also include guidelines for the use of anonymity appropriate to the organization. For example, in a university setting, departments may want to solicit unsigned input from students to promote risk-free brainstorming or to protect them from any real or imagined retribution for unpopular ideas.

MISINTERPRETATION

Whether it results from the medium, from the way we write electronic messages or from the way we scan them, misunderstandings occur and sometimes lead to angry responses, hurt feelings and damaged working relationships. Although this may not seem as important an ethical issue as privacy or attribution, it relates directly to the principles of trust and toleration in the Bill of Electronic Rights and Ethics.

Both senders and recipients can address this issue by writing clearly and rereading before sending. It never hurts to add interpretive cues or to separate and label opinions and emotions.

Mail recipients should presume the goodwill of their correspondents. If a message triggers an angry response, ask why and look for a possible misunderstanding. Above all, calm down before hitting the reply button.

ETIQUETTE

Politeness goes a long way toward creating a more considerate—and, therefore, more ethical—environment. Shapiro and Anderson offer a number of guidelines that make good sense.

They suggest that people sending email create single-subject messages, have in mind a model of the intended audience, keep the list of recipients to a minimum, use content labels, consciously choose a level of formality for the message, identify themselves and their affiliations and avoid criticism of third parties unless they have a chance to respond.

In receiving email, they suggest that people acknowledge messages, assume the honesty and competence of the sender, try to separate opinion from nonopinion, avoid irrelevancies and consider responding in another medium—for example, make a telephone call to clarify an email exchange that may have been confusing.

Mail recipients should not forward personal email without checking with the sender—who may or may not wish to share the correspondence. Similarly, recipients should not forward public or business email without the addition of some explanatory context.

Clearly, these proposals are only the beginning. Conversations continue almost daily on the internet, which seems the appropriate place to debate an ethics of email.

FURTHER READING

Electronic Rights and Ethics. Available online at http://www.zip.com.au/~pete/ere.html.

Hamelink, Cees. "Globalization and Human Dignity: The Case of the Information Superhighway." *Media Development* 43.1 (1996).

Shapiro, Norman Z. and Anderson, Robert H. *Towards an Ethics and Etiquette for Electronic Mail* (1985). Available online at http://www.rand.org/publications/MR/R3283.

THE ETHICAL AND LEGAL QUANDARY OF EMAIL PRIVACY

—Janice C. Sipior and Burke T. Ward

Most of us have never considered some of these issues, much less decided how we feel about them or know how our employer might feel about them. Janice Sipior and Burke Ward address some of these ethical issues and discuss how they might be resolved.

How private are employees' email messages? The answer is unclear. This lack of clarity means that protection of employee email will be at the forefront of legal controversy for at least the rest of the decade.

Privacy protection is not a new issue, and employee privacy encompasses a spectrum of issues, including:

- Drug testing.

- Searches of employees and their work areas.

- Psychological testing.

- Telephone, computer and electronic monitoring.

- Other types of employee surveillance.

The controversial nature of these areas demands that employers and employees, as well as those with whom they interact—consultants, information service support personnel, suppliers and customers—be aware of, and responsive to, expectations of and concerns about privacy. Users and organizations naive about ethical conduct and the legal parameters concerning email privacy are vulnerable to harm caused by intrusions. This article examines the potentially conflicting expectations of employers and employees regarding the ethical and legal aspects of privacy invasions in email communications. It also examines the U.S. legal system to determine the applicability of federal and state constitutional law, state common law and federal and state statutory sources in protecting email privacy.

EMAIL AND ETHICS

Organizations have an obligation to their employees, business partners, customers and society, as well as to themselves, to act ethically. However, ethical behavior is often difficult to achieve. A primary concern is actual or potential harm to individuals and groups. What is ethical and what is unethical? Answers are not straightforward. Societal standards of "good," "right" and "moral" help guide our behavior, but do not provide definitive answers for all situations. The political debate on individual and workplace privacy highlights the lack of consensus of opinion with respect to ethics and privacy. Legislatures and courts are being asked to resolve the ethical and legal questions raised by drug testing, physical searches of persons and places, electronic surveillance and other privacy issues. This article seeks to raise awareness of the ethical issues of email privacy by identifying the vulnerabilities plaguing email and the privacy expectations of employers and employees regarding their use of email.

The increasing number of computer users, applications and system interconnections, along with the increasing complexity of overall technological capabilities, means a greater chance for email privacy to be compromised. Email privacy invasions are characterized along two dimensions: sources of invasion and types of invasion. Email communications are at risk for interception from sources both internal and external to the organization. Internal sources are people employed by the organization, including executives, managers and co-workers. External sources are people with whom the organization interacts, through formal and informal relationships. Formal relationships can link service providers, consultants, suppliers and customers. Interaction may also occur in the absence of formal relationships—with competitors, corporate spies and hackers.

An invasion may be authorized or unauthorized—that is, it may be condoned by an internal authority, such as a manager, an external authority, such as a law-enforcement agency or may be a totally unauthorized privacy violation. These combinations are organized into four cells. This article focuses on internally authorized interception of email messages.

EMPLOYERS' VIEW OF EMAIL PRIVACY

Email monitoring in organizations may be viewed by employers as a necessity, as well as a right. As owners of the resources, employers may assume the right to monitor email. Such monitoring may or may not be ethically acceptable or legally permissible. But the reasons offered by employers for doing so may appear ethical and legal, including prevention of personal use or abuse of company resources, the prevention or investigation of corporate espionage or theft, cooperation with law-enforcement officials in investigations, the resolution of technical problems or other special circumstances.

A grayer area is when internal email monitoring is used to track worker performance. In this case, it is not just suspected individuals whose email is read. Hardworking employees might use email to help make a sale or to meet work deadlines; if not for their record of correspondence, their productivity and accomplishments may otherwise go unnoticed.

For publicly traded companies, an employer must ensure that employees abide by Securities and Exchange Commission rules. A company that fails to monitor performance by examining email messages sent to external destinations might be failing to protect trade secrets and proprietary information.

To achieve the positive results in these examples, all messages sent and received by employees would be subject to scrutiny. Some may regard this as an unethical disregard of employee privacy. Information an employee intends to keep private and confidential may be examined. However, an employer could argue that since the email system is owned by the employer and is to be used for the employer's purposes, the employee should not expect communications to be private. The employer would conclude that email monitoring is not unethical because employees have no reasonable expectation of privacy with respect to the employer's email system. Conversely, some may argue that monitoring is indeed an unethical invasion of an individual's privacy in light of the potential for negative consequences.

Monitoring can be a double-edged sword for those being monitored. Productive and exceptional employees, as well as employees who are unproductive, could be readily identified throughout the organization.

EMPLOYEES' VIEW OF EMAIL PRIVACY

From the employees' perspective, the content—even the existence—of email messages may be regarded as confidential, private correspondence between sender and receiver(s). This perception seems reasonable, given that email is accessed as a facility in users' computer accounts, to which access is password-controlled, providing a sense of confidentiality. Further, most people are familiar with the privacy protection of the U.S. mail and may assume it applies to email as well. Thus, users can mistakenly and reasonably assume that email messages are free from interception.

Electronic surveillance for the purpose of improving job performance, product quality and productivity takes many forms. For example, email messages are usually sent and received in directly readable, unencrypted alphanumeric form, intended for immediate reading. Employee computer screens may be viewed or messages may be intercepted without employee knowledge or consent. Email messages are thus exposed to employer scrutiny. At Epson America, Inc., an email system administrator, Alana Shoars, claimed to have been terminated in 1991 for protesting the routine practice of intercepting and printing employees' MCI email. In her case, *Shoars v. Epson America, Inc.,* she claimed Epson's invasion of privacy and her termination violated California law [16]. In another 1991 case, *Bourke v. Nissan Motor Corp.,* two software specialists contended they were forced to quit after a supervisor read their personal email correspondence, which included sexual statements [3]. They also claimed invasion of privacy and wrongful termination in violation of California law.

In both cases, the companies' right to manage their email systems was legally recognized. But because both were tried in lower-level California state courts and have not yet worked their way through the appellate process, they are of minimal value as precedents. The question remains: Were the companies' actions ethical?

Many users expect that when they press the delete key on their computers, an email message is actually deleted. However, user deletions are often archived on tape and stored for years. For example, a former employee of Borland International Inc. found, to his dismay, that deleted messages can be retrieved from the archives [14]. The employee was suspected of using a Borland-supplied MCI email account to divulge trade secrets to his future employer—and Borland rival—Symantec Corp. Borland asked MCI Communications Corp. to retrieve the former employee's deleted messages. This alleged intrusion was viewed as a property right by Borland. Since Borland paid for the email service, the employee's account became Borland's property upon his departure.

The result: pending criminal investigations of both the sender and recipient, as well as a civil suit, *Borland v. Symantec*.

Perhaps the most infamous example of retrieval of deleted messages occurred in 1987–89 during Congress's Iran-Contra investigations. Deleted IBM PROFS email correspondences between Oliver North and John Poindexter were retrieved from White House backup tapes. In testimony before the Senate, North said, "We all sincerely believed that when we sent a PROFS message to another party and punched the button 'delete' that it was gone forever. Wow, were we wrong." [9].

Regardless of the type or characteristics of email system used, the question remains: what privacy protection, if any, does an employee have in email communications? Such communications are usually made on the employer's premises, with the employer's equipment, on the employer's time and at the employer's cost—to further the employer's objectives. With such a substantial employer investment, do employees have a legitimate expectation of email privacy?

Despite employers' significant proprietary interests, employees do have expectations of privacy [10]. Given the potentially differing perceptions of employers and employees regarding email privacy and the potential problems that can result from privacy intrusions, employees and employers both need to understand the privacy protection provided by the U.S. legal system. Although ethics and law are not identical, they do come in close contact. Law is often the vehicle for formally implementing ethics into social guidelines and procedures. . . .

ELECTRONIC COMMUNICATIONS PRIVACY ACT

In an influential 1985 study, the Congressional Office of Technological Assessment (OTA) found approximately 50% of the U.S. population believed computers threaten privacy rights and supported further action to protect these rights [10]. This study inspired Congress to enact the Electronic Communications Privacy Act (ECPA) of 1986 [19]. As a society, Americans generally value privacy. However, if a societal value, such as personal privacy, is not legally protected, is it a right? By implication, the American people seem to assume they are already endowed with this right. With respect to email, the OTA stated "the existing protections are weak, ambiguous or nonexistent" [10]. This lack of protection is significant because email is vulnerable to interception, as identified by the OTA, at five specific stages:

- At the sender's terminal or electronic file.

- While being transmitted.

- When accessing the recipient's mailbox.

- When the communication is printed in hard copy.

- When retained in the files of the email service.

Relying on the 1985 study, the OTA concluded internal company email systems were not covered by federal statute [10]. Congress used the ECPA to amend existing federal wiretap protection law to include most electronic communications. Its purpose was to extend privacy protections against wiretapping to new forms of electronic communications, including email, cellular telephones and data transmission, from improper interception.

Broadly, the ECPA prohibits interception of wire, oral and electronic communications, as well as disclosure or use of such intercepted communications. The statute's broad definition of electronic communication includes email. Further, in Title II, the Equal Protection Act, subject to significant exceptions, prohibits access to and disclosure of stored electronic communications.

Two Exceptions

Whether coverage extends to monitoring the email of private-sector employers is unclear because of two exceptions in the ECPA that were part of earlier federal wiretap protection law:

Business Use or Business Extension   This exception is the basis for most of the cases brought under the ECPA [5]. To be an effective defense against employee claims of email privacy invasion, employers must demonstrate that a business use was the reason for the interception and that monitoring was conducted within the ordinary course of business [22]. In a 1983 case [22], brought under the prior federal wiretap protection law, an employer notified an employee that telephone sales calls were being monitored. This notification was interpreted to mean that the specific interception was in the ordinary course of business. The business purpose ended when it became apparent the telephone communication was personal. This exception, which can be applied to telephone communications, would seem to apply to email. If an employer wants to ensure its email system is used solely for work-related purposes, routine monitoring of the content of email messages might be included under this exception.

Prior Consent   This exception may permit telephone and email monitoring. Under it, employers may be able to protect themselves against the risk of liability by notifying employees their email may be examined. Such consent may be expressed or implied but is limited to the scope of the consent. In the aforementioned 1983 case, the consent was only to the monitoring of business calls. The court refused to extend this consent to all telephone calls.

The issue of whether the ECPA protects the privacy of email is unclear and is currently under debate in the courts. A review of relevant legal research seems to conclude that the ECPA does not afford significant privacy protection to employee email communications [5, 6]. . . .

CONCLUSIONS

Various courts and legislative bodies have sought to balance employees' expectations of personal privacy with employers' proprietary and access interests. From a managerial perspective, email—an increasingly important organizational resource touted as contributing to worker productivity—must be used in an ethical and legal manner. Since clear guidance is not provided by our legal system, organizations must formulate their own internal email privacy policies. Lacking a formal policy, employee expectations of privacy may differ from their employers' perspectives. Even with a formal policy, this balance is not easily achieved because of the dynamic nature of information technology capabilities. The rapid pace of technological advances forces the legal system to resolve conflicts for which there is no precedent.

REFERENCES

1. Baumhart, J. T. The employer's right to read employee email: Protecting property or personal prying? *The Labor Lawyer 8,* 4 (Fall 1992), 923–948.
2. Bloustein, E. J. Privacy as an aspect of human dignity: An Answer to Dean Prosser. *39 NYU Law Review, 962* 1001 (1964).
3. *Bourke v. Nissan Motor Corp.,* No. YC 003979 (Super. Ct. Cal. filed Jan. 4, 1991).
4. *Ettore v. Philco Television Broadcasting Co.,* 229 F. 2d 481 (3d Cir. 1956).
5. Griffin, J. J. The monitoring of electronic mail in the private sector workplace: An electronic assault on employee privacy rights. *Software Law Journal IV* (1991), 493–527.
6. Addressing the new hazards of the high technology workplace. *Harvard Law Review,* 104, 8 (June 1991), 1898–1916.
7. Heredia, H. F. Is there privacy in the workplace?: Guaranteeing a broader privacy right for workers under California law. *Southwestern University Law Review, 22* 1 (1992), 307–335.
8. *Luck v. Southern Pacific Transportation Co.,* 267 Cal. Rptr. 618 (Ct. App. 1990), cert. denied, 111 S. Ct. 344 (1990).
9. National Public Radio news broadcasts (1992).
10. Office of Technology Assessment (OTA), Federal Government Information Technology: Electronic Surveillance and Civil Liberties (1985).
11. *O'Connor v. Ortega,* 480 U.S. 709 (1987).
12. Privacy for Consumers and Workers Act, S. 984, H.R. 1900, (1993).
13. Restatement (Second) of Torts 652B (1977).
14. Shieh, J. and Ballard, R. Email privacy. *Educom Review* (March/April 1994), 59–62.
15. *Shoars v. Epson America, Inc.,* No. SWC 112749 (Cal. Sup. Ct. filed July 30, 1990).
16. *Shoars v. Epson America, Inc.,* No. BC 007036 (Cal. Sup. Ct. filed March 12, 1991).
17. *Skinner v. Railway Labor Executives Association,* 489 U.S. 602 (1989).
18. *Soroka v. Dayton Hudson Corp.,* 7 Cal. App. 4th 203, review granted, 4 Cal. Rptr. 2d 180 (1992).
19. 18 USC 2510–2521, 2701–1711 (1988).
20. *Vernars v. Young,* 539 F. 2d 966 (3d Cir. 1976).
21. Warren, S. D. and Brandeis, L. D. The right of privacy. *Harvard Law Review* (December 1890), 193–220.
22. *Watkins v. L. M. Berry & Co.,* 704 F. 2d 577 (11th Cir. 1983).
23. *Wilkinson v. Times Mirror Corp.,* 215 Cal. App. 3rd 1034 (Cal. App. 1 Dist. 1989).

ELEMENTS OF A SUCCESSFUL EMAIL POLICY

—GERARD PANARO

In an effort to avoid both ethical challenges and legal liability, more than two-thirds of medium- to large-sized firms in the United States have designed and implemented policies that address email and other computer resource usage. Often the policy includes no more than notice to the workforce that email or other use might be monitored. Gerard Panaro suggests additional elements that comprise a legally sufficient, defensible workplace email policy.

1. **Written policy.** First, of course, any policy should be in writing. It should make clear to employees that the security of their email is not guaranteed and that email may not be protected by privacy law. The policy should state that employees should have no expectation of privacy in the workplace. Office equipment is the property of the company and for office use; employees' use of equipment is subject to monitoring, may be accessed with or without notice, disclosed to others and used to evaluate, reward and/or discipline employees. The policy should state that messages on the system are considered to be company records.

It may be a good idea to explain to employees how email works, so they understand better why it may not be as private or confidential as they assume. Any explanations should be accurate, however. Suppose, for example, that the IT department tells employees if they delete a message on the same day it is sent or received, before it is backed up overnight, it is gone forever and irretrievable; or suppose, in response to an employee's query, who wants to recover a message s/he has inadvertently deleted, IT says it cannot be recovered. Such statements could be evidence of an expectation of privacy: an employee says s/he thought it was OK to send and receive pornographic, racial or sexual jokes so long as they were immediately deleted.

It is also recommended that if the employer uses software that enables managers to know which employees may be using the internet, and which sites they may be visiting, that this information be disclosed up front to affected employees, and they be warned to make sure their internet use is for legitimate business only.

2. **Passwords don't guarantee privacy.** Second, a written email policy will also warn that giving employees passwords, varying levels of message protection and other security measures does not necessarily create any right to privacy or guarantee no access.

Make sure employees aren't misled. In fact, consideration should be given to insisting that employees give all codes, passwords and other security information to someone in the company, in case of emergency.

3. **Reasons justifying access.** Third, it is important that the policy set forth the legitimate business reasons why email may be monitored and accessed. Every possible justification listed below may not apply to every employer, but legitimate business reasons typically include the following:

- Assess performance

- Reduce personal communications

- Improve the work product

- Protect against theft, fraud, computer crime

- Remain competitive

- Search for violations in disclosing trade secrets

- Obtain information in a business emergency or the absence of the employee

- Retrieve lost messages

- Help employees effectively use the email system

- Determine whether employee gossip hurts workplace morale

- Promote efficiency

- Provide a workplace that is free of unlawful discrimination (e.g., sexual, racial, other forms of illegal harassment)

- Insure that system is being used properly (e.g., no illegal gambling, no receipt, transmission or trafficking in obscenity, pornography, pedophilia)

- Investigate complaints of improper use (customers, other employees)

4. **Employee usage guidelines.** Fourth, the policy should establish employee usage guidelines, such as whether or not the system may be used for nonbusiness (personal) exchanges, and if so, when and to what extent. For example, the company may be willing to allow its employees to use email for personal reasons outside of normal working hours, or if the employee is willing to pay for his or her usage. It is recommended that at least some personal use of email almost has to be allowed, for at least three very practical reasons: employees can't completely control email sent to them from other sources; employees are going to make personal use of the system anyway; policing and disciplining employees for personal use will be almost impossible, will divert the company from its primary business and could backfire in the sense that it becomes so intrusive it triggers legal challenge.

5. **Violators subject to discipline.** Fifth, state in the policy that employees who violate it will be subject to discipline. There are a couple of guidelines to keep in mind here: if the company has an employment at will policy, then make sure this component of the

email policy is consistent with that policy; if the company follows a progressive discipline policy or dismisses only for cause, then the email discipline policy should likewise be consistent. The level of discipline will obviously be proportionate to the circumstances, such as nature of the violation, frequency, prior violations, etc.

6. **Dispute resolution procedure.** Sixth, consider providing in the policy a mechanism for addressing complaints. The company has to be careful here, however, to strike the right balance: on the one hand, it will want to afford employees "basic due process"; but on the other, it does not want such an elaborate system of complaints, hearings, appeals, reviews, etc., as to make the process interminable.

7. **Managerial discretion.** Seventh, spell out when managers can search for or interfere with email. This will be a crucial element of the policy, because if the company limits the circumstances under which it can access employees' email, then it risks liability if it should ever exceed its own self-imposed limits. A long list of such occasions has already been given. Certainly, the company will want to reserve the right to go into email in case of emergency, and emergency does not only refer to physical threats, such as fire or bomb scares. An emergency can be a customer or client screaming for something right away, and the person who would normally deal with the situation is out.

The company will also want the right to access employees' email when it is investigating unlawful discrimination or harassment, based on sex, race, disability or any other protected category. In fact, in view of the recent Supreme Court decisions heightening employers' liability for harassment in the workplace, and cases that have been decided in light of the Court's opinions, this business justification becomes all the more compelling.[1]

A third obvious time when the employer may want the right to monitor is when the employee's performance, evaluation and/or appraisal are in issue. Whatever the criteria decided upon, the important point is to spell them out and be sure the company adheres to them.

---

[1]In 1998, the U.S. Supreme Court decided two cases that significantly raised the stakes for employers in sexual harassment suits (and, indeed, for claims of harassment under any other protected category, such as race, age, disability, religion, etc.), *Burlington Industries, Inc. v. Ellerth,* 118 S.Ct. 2257, and *Faragher v. City of Boca Raton,* 118 S.Ct. 2275. These are the major holdings of the two decisions on when an employer is liable for sexual harassment:

- As a threshold matter, to state a claim for unlawful sexual harassment under Title VII, the federal anti-discrimination statute, a victim must be able to show that the conduct complained of was sufficiently severe and pervasive (this will be discussed further below).
- Title VII is not a "general civility code." Discourtesy, rudeness, insensitivity, simple teasing, offhand comments, isolated incidents (unless extremely serious) will not amount to unlawful sexual harassment.
- In the case of sexual harassment by a co-employee, the employer is going to be liable only if it was negligent: that is, it knew or should have known the sexual harassment was going on, and did nothing to stop it.
- In the case of sexual harassment by a supervisor that results in an actual adverse job action against the victim, the employer will always be liable, regardless of how careful it was. An employer has no defense to such "quid pro quo" harassment by a supervisor.
- In the case of sexual harassment by a supervisor that does not result in an adverse job action against the victim ("hostile environment" sexual harassment), the employer will still be subject to suit. However, it may have a defense to the claim.
- The defense consists of two elements:
  - The employer acted promptly to prevent and correct sexual harassment and
  - The employee failed to take advantage of any preventive or corrective opportunities provided by the employer (e.g., failed to complain or use the sexual harassment policy).

8. **Access by third parties.** Eighth, the policy should address the issue of third-party access. For example, a company may want to have a policy of being able to regulate the sources of email and to delete or block transmissions to employees from sources not approved. It may also wish to forbid employees from accessing or subscribing to certain sites, even if the employee is willing to pay the cost.

9. **Signed acknowledgement of having received policy.** Ninth, it is probably a good idea to have employees sign an acknowledgement or receipt form for the email policy. If the policy is incorporated in an employee handbook, a receipt for the handbook is enough; if the policy is free-standing, it may have its own receipt form.

PRACTICAL ADVICE FOR IMPLEMENTING THE POLICY

Writing a policy on email in the workplace is only the beginning. An indispensable element to its success will be how the policy is implemented. In this respect, the following steps are recommended.

Perhaps the single most practical advice to give on implementing an email policy is this: when monitoring does become necessary, *use the least intrusive means possible.* The simplest rule to follow may be that ordinarily, the company will not monitor employees' email traffic unless and until a complaint is received or there is a rational basis or articulable suspicion that the system is being misused. An employee, for example, may complain that s/he is receiving annoying or harassing email from another; an employee may complain that s/he is receiving objectionable email from an anonymous source; an enforcement agency (whether the EEOC investigating a charge, a litigant or law enforcement) may request the company's cooperation in accessing employees' email. A manager may notice that one of his or her subordinates seems to be spending an inordinate amount of time on email, a customer may call to complain that its emails have not been answered, or a manager may notice a fall-off in productivity. But whatever the source or reason, the basic rule will be: We will not monitor any employee's email unless a complaint has arisen or we have a reasonable suspicion that something is amiss.

A second way to make monitoring as unintrusive as possible, of course, is to limit those who have authority to monitor (to order monitoring), those to whom information is disseminated and/or the nature, quantity and detail of information that is monitored or disclosed. For example, the company may give the right to monitor only to the IT department, only to HR, to security or to corporate counsel. The company might even contract out the job to an independent security or investigative firm.

A third technique is to avoid any intrusion into, or dissemination of, the actual contents of email, but to monitor simply "transactional" or frequency information. To determine that an employee is abusing email, as an illustration, it may only be necessary to document that whereas the average employee sends or receives only a dozen emails a day, this employee is sending or receiving more than a hundred. It would not even be necessary to go into contents; the numbers alone would raise suspicions or prove the point.

In implementing a policy on email, especially if the policy is new, take multiple steps to make sure employees are aware of the policy and have received a copy. Some suggestions are to make the policy a part of the application process, include it with a letter offering a job, print free-standing copies of the policy and hand these out separately, even if the policy is already contained in the employee handbook; make employees sign a paper acknowledging receipt. Periodically review the policy, in light of experience, new developments, new cases, changes in technology or the business.

SUMMARY AND CONCLUSION

The law clearly recognizes and protects an employer's right to monitor employees' email (and other office communications). Indeed, the authors of law review articles and op-ed pieces in newspapers and magazines decry the lack of protection for employees' privacy interests in the workplace. Employees have no automatic privacy rights in the workplace. The key to protecting itself is for the company to have a written policy on electronic communications in the workplace, make sure employees are aware of it and to be judicious in its implementation of the policy in terms of making monitoring as little intrusive as possible.

COMPLIANCE PROGRAMS, EMAIL AND THE INTERNET

—Jeffrey M. Kaplan

Many ethics officers, in-house counsel, human resource staff and others are now being asked to assemble email/internet policies and procedures. However, because of the sudden way in which these issues have emerged, there are few published sources on establishing standards and systems to prevent and detect wrongful workplace use of these new technologies. Consider the following guidance from attorney Jeffrey Kaplan.

DEVELOPING STANDARDS

The first step in creating or enhancing a policy is determining whether to allow any personal use of email or internet in the workplace. Given the impracticality of a total ban (as well as the resentment that such an effort might engender) the trend here—exemplified by Bell South Corporation, which moved away from a "zero tolerance" policy—seems to be to allow a reasonable amount of such use.

The second step is to develop a catalog of prohibited or restricted conduct. Among the areas a company may wish to include in such a list are:

- Circulation of material with derogatory racial, religious or gender comments, or with sexual content or offensive language.

- Transmission of threatening, reckless or maliciously false communications.

- Any activity constituting or promoting a criminal offense, potentially giving rise to civil liability, or otherwise violating any laws, regulations, applicable rules or company policy.

- Transmission of copyrighted documents that are not authorized for reproduction, or, without permission, of trade secrets or any other confidential information belonging to the company.

- Use in furtherance of the business activity of any other entity or to conduct a job search.

- Use that results in additional billing or direct cost to the company.

- Use without approval to solicit funds; distribute chain letters, literature or gifts; sell merchandise or services; collect signatures, conduct membership drives, etc.

- Sending external broadcast messages.

- Use of other individuals' account names or passwords, or accessing resources to which employees have not been given access.

- Transmission of political statements not sanctioned by the company.

INTERNET CHATROOMS

Another area to consider—but which is in few, if any, policies at present—concerns participation in internet chatroom discussions relating to one's employer. Employees should be warned of the possibility of insider trading, stock manipulation and other securities law issues arising from inappropriate chatroom activities.

Finally, a policy should speak to the unique nature of email. For example, one might note, as does Boeing Co., that because the source of an email is clearly identifiable, care "must be taken to ensure such communications must not adversely affect the company or its public image or that of its customers, partners, associates, or suppliers." Similarly, one might remind employees that email messages remain part of company records long after they have been supposedly deleted, a lesson which was learned most famously in the *Microsoft* antitrust case.

COMMUNICATING COMPANY STANDARDS

As important as developing or enhancing email and internet use standards is effectively *communicating* those standards to the workforce. Among the possibilities here (in addition to including the policy in one's code of conduct) are:

- Issuing an email from top management to announce or reinforce the policy.

- Having the policy appear periodically on employees' computer screens when they log on.

- Continuously posting the policy on a company's intranet site.

- Requiring employees to acknowledge on the computer that they have read and agree to abide by the policy. (Any employee who failed to so acknowledge would presumably lose access to email and the internet.)

A company should also include discussion of these issues in its in-person training. Face-to-face communications may offer the best opportunity to make certain employees understand the dangers of misuse in this area and exactly what the company expects of them.

In addition, offensive or obscene emails are often received from outside a company rather than generated within it. Thus, an email/internet compliance program should provide means for "returning" inappropriate emails received from third parties (similar to policies requiring employees to return large gifts from vendors). For example, the policy could include sample language which, in a polite but firm manner, could be used by employees to respond to the receipt of any inappropriate email from a third party by stating that company policy prohibits the receipt of such.

ENFORCEMENT

The final element of an email/internet ethics compliance program is enforcement. There are several steps a company can take to effectively enforce its policies in this area.

First, it is important to inform employees that they should have no expectation of privacy in workplace computer communications and that the company reserves the right to monitor such communications. (According to a study by the American Management Association, 27% of large U.S. firms checked employee email in 1999—up from 15% in 1997.)

The fact that a company reserves the *right* to do this, however, does not mean that it should exercise its power in an unfettered way. That is, while many companies do conduct random checks of employees' computers, others are beginning to require some appropriate basis before taking such measures. The components of this type of procedure might include:

- An objective—but not overly legalistic—standard for authorizing such checks;

- A procedure for assuring that such a basis exists in individual cases—e.g., review by designated personnel in the Law and/or HR and/or Security departments.

Beyond monitoring through manual checking, some companies now use technologies that *automatically* monitor email and internet uses. For example, Mail Sweeper—a product of Content Technologies, Inc.—permits companies to examine outgoing messages for prohibited content.

COMPLIANCE AS A DEFENSE

The principle purpose of an email/internet use policy is, of course, to prevent and detect inappropriate behavior. However, as with other compliance fields, a good policy here can also serve as the basis—at least in some instances—of a defense to a lawsuit.

In this regard, a policy should underscore the need to report any violations by other employees. Doing so should help to minimize the likelihood of offensive email and internet usage contributing to the development of a "hostile workplace environment," and thus minimize harassment-related liability. Indeed, earlier this year, MCI Worldcom Inc. successfully defended itself against a lawsuit (*Daniels v. Worldcom*) charging racial harassment over its email system, in part, due to its having an effective email use policy. (The court's dismissal was also based upon the company's proactive and swift response to the plaintiffs' complaints.)

CONCLUSION

While companies need to have and enforce email and internet policies, there is also a real danger in instituting onerous standards, intrusive monitoring and unfair, policelike investigations. A heavy-handed approach in this area—which, regardless of what a policy says, seems to implicate *some* legitimate privacy interests—may well demoralize and alienate employees. As with all fields of compliance and ethics, care must be taken that the cure not be worse than the disease.

REASONABLE EXPECTATIONS OF PRIVACY

—Robert L. McArthur

Use of the concept of "a reasonable person and his or her expectations" is widely found in legal reasoning and in privacy cases, specifically. This legal constraint is employed in the following article to examine privacy questions associated with contemporary information technology, especially the internet. In particular, reasonable expectations of privacy while browsing the web and while sending and receiving email are analyzed.

As technology races ahead with ever increasing speed, our subjective expectations of privacy may be unconsciously altered . . . our legal rights to privacy should reflect thoughtful and purposeful choices rather than simply mirror the current state of the commercial technology industry.[1]

You already have zero privacy—get over it.[2]

In an early case before the US Supreme Court that involved electronic surveillance of a conversation from public telephones, Justice Harlan, concurring with the majority, wrote: "an enclosed telephone booth is an area where, like a home, a person has a constitutionally protected reasonable expectation of privacy."[3] As ubiquitous assaults against privacy from various kinds of information technology proliferate, Harlan's standard "the reasonable expectation of privacy" has become strained. Yet, by understanding what reasonable expectations of privacy might be, we can gain a clearer sense of where our concerns that privacy is slipping away are justified and where they are mere expressions of nostalgia for a time of heightened respect for privacy that has long ago passed from any reality.

"Reasonable Expectations of Privacy" by Robert McArthur. Copyright 2001 Kluwer Academic Publishers. Reprinted with permission from *Ethics and Information Technology*, 3: 123–128 (2001).

[1]*The State of Washington, Respondent* v. *Robert Alan Young, Appellant* 123 Wn.2d 173. Supreme Court of Washington, 1994. This case concerns the legitimacy of police use of infrared thermal detection devices aimed at a person's home without a search warrant and without notification to the home owner. The Court ruled against the police, finding that the use of such technology constitutes an invasion of the home and contravenes the Washington State Constitution and Fourth Amendment protections of privacy unless accompanied by a duly authorized search warrant. The Court affirmed the reasonable expectation of privacy in one's own home and held that this reasonable expectation is violated by warrantless infrared surveillance.

[2]Scott McNealy, CEO and founder of Sun Microsystems, quoted in Robert Scheer. Nowhere to Hide, *Yahoo Internet Life* (Special Report on Privacy) 6(10): 101, October 2000.

[3]*Katz* v. *U.S.*, 389 U.S. 347 (1967).

In general, the use of the "reasonable person" and his or her expectations is a widely used structure in legal reasoning. It is obviously normative in that it does not simply hew to socially accepted practice or to some sense of what the majority of people might have at any given moment as their subjective expectations. I will use "reasonable expectation" to mean "what a reasonable person *should* expect" in what follows.

Let me begin with a few general comments about privacy expectations. It is important to note that some expectations that people may have are quite unreasonable on their face. Suppose, for example, I am having a conversation in a public place, say, a ticket line of a movie theater. If I am talking in a normal voice, I am certain to be overheard by those around me. Any expectation, therefore, that what I am saying is "private" is entirely unreasonable. My fellow line-standers, out of politeness, might well pretend not to hear, but that does not make what I am saying private in any sense, no matter what I hope. Since I have been overheard, any other person could hear a version of my side of the conversation if it is considered interesting enough to disseminate (a matter now entirely out of my control). Or, to take another example, suppose I tell various people some intimate personal fact about my life; and, as these things go, perhaps they tell others, so that this fact becomes fairly well known. If I find that a subsequent newspaper story includes this information, I cannot reasonably claim that an invasion of privacy has occurred, since I was the original cause of the information's becoming known.[4] Two helpful principles emerge from such considerations. The first is:

> The Mischance Principle—*we cannot reasonably expect to maintain privacy over that which another person could discover, overhear, or come to know without concerted effort on his/her part to obtain this information.*[5]

Here are some further examples: undressing before a window without shades; dropping a personal letter on the sidewalk; engaging in conversation at a public gathering; displaying images or text on a computer screen that others may see (e.g., using a public-cluster terminal in a university library); reading a magazine at a bookstore in view of security cameras; carrying objects in luggage on an airplane; introducing personal information into the public record (e.g., in a trial transcript); placing my bank statement into a trash bag that has been put at roadside for pick up; having objects on one's property that can be viewed from the air.

In all of these cases, a police investigator or nosey neighbor could go looking for information, but still would not be transgressing the mischance principle since a person could come to this information entirely fortuitously. Since a passerby can easily see me if I undress by an uncurtained window, my unclothed person, at that moment, is no longer private. The case would be similar if someone in the apartment building across the street could focus on my window with his binoculars and see me undressed in sharp detail. If, on the other

---

[4]Oliver Sipple (who intervened in an attempted assassination of President Gerald Ford) brought such an action against the *San Francisco Chronicle* for including in a story that he was gay. He lost the action on the grounds that his sexual orientation was fairly widely known in the Bay Area. *Sipple* v. *Chronicle Publishing Co.* 154 Cal App. 3rd 1040 (1984). For a discussion, see Rodney A. Smolla. *Free Speech in an Open Society.* Vintage/Random House, New York, pp. 130–132, 1992.

[5]See Mark Tunik. *Practices and Principles.* Princeton University Press, Princeton, NJ, pp. 161–190, 1998. As far as I know, Tunik is the author of the mischance principle.

hand, a hidden camera were monitoring the dressing room at the health club that I frequent, the very same image of my undressed person would be considered private. The difference is explained by the mischance principle.

Next, take the trash case.[6] Searching through another's trash fits the mischance principle because a bag of trash at the curb could be torn open by a dog thus scattering the contents; and a gust of wind might blow your bank statement to my feet. So by looking at this piece of paper and learning your bank balance I am expending no effort to find the information. Consequently, you cannot claim some violation of privacy were this to happen. For that reason, if I spirit away your trash and take it to a warehouse where I go through it piece by piece (thus finding your bank statement), I am not looking at any information that is protected by some reasonable concept of privacy. I could have come to see it by mischance.

Peering in your unshaded window from across the street (but not standing on your property) is quite different from scanning your house using an infrared detector to determine whether illegal plants are being cultivated in your basement. In the first instance, the information gleaned through the window is available by mischance to anyone. In the second, one has to take actions using advanced technology devices to come to the information about heat patterns in your house (which can disclose locations and movements of persons in various rooms). The mischance principle works in a range of possible instances because it is relatively easy to figure out what precautions to take to maintain privacy against casual observation. Speaking in a barely audible whisper to a friend, for example, so as not to be overheard is exercising due caution. If I am overheard through the use of a long-range parabolic microphone, I could reasonably complain that my privacy has been transgressed. Technology has foiled my best efforts to maintain privacy, contrary to reasonable expectations.

But the context alters the case. For example, walking down the street I have a quite reasonable expectation of the privacy of my briefcase. I do not anticipate that it will be opened by strangers or even by police without proper warrants. Therefore, a document in the briefcase can properly be considered as private and should not be seen by prying eyes (unlike the situation where that same document is in a trash bag by the road). Walking through an airport is another matter. I and my briefcase are subject to search and it would be very unreasonable to suppose otherwise. The document in the briefcase can easily be seen by a passerby as the case is opened for inspection, just as a file on my laptop computer might pop up on the screen when the laptop is turned on for the gate security check. These considerations will apply in all security zones: museums, schools, courthouses, government buildings, for example. The essential difference between, say, the airport and the street is that I have chosen to take my briefcase (or laptop) and its contents into an area that I know is subject to search. In so doing, it is as though I am carrying the objects in my hand, in full view, and therefore, I cannot reasonably expect them not to be seen. I am, in effect, inviting their inspection. This, then, brings us to the second principle:

> The Voluntary Principle—*If I choose to decrease the relative amount of privacy for myself and information under my control by exposing it to view, I thereby decrease the reasonableness of any expectation that this privacy will be observed.*

---

[6]See, for example, *California v. Greenwood*, 486 U.S. 35 (1988); the case is cited and discussed by Tunik, pp. 171–172.

Decreasing the relative amount of privacy is accomplished by increasing the likelihood under the circumstances that the information will come to another's attention through mischance. Tattooing my social security number on my forehead would certainly fall into this category.

An important qualification is needed here. Winston Smith begins a journal in Orwell's *1984*.[7] Given the nature of his society, he could not realistically expect that no one would ever find his journal. Although he might hope to evade discovery, he certainly realizes that the probabilities are high that whatever he writes will be read by the authorities and that he will be duly punished for this breach. Such is the nature of any police state: privacy is either non-existent or is nearly so. In such cases we should *not* say that there is nothing reasonable about Winston's desire to be able freely to write his most personal thoughts in a private fashion; a reasonable person *should* be able to expect privacy for his journal. The mere likelihood of discovery (or certainty in Winston's case) does not eliminate a fundamental right of privacy. And it seems otiose to claim that Winston was choosing to disclose his personal views to the authorities just by writing them down, given his awareness of the prospect of their finding his journal. The authorities will find out Winston's personal views one way or the other. He clearly has no choice about that. So, I would argue, the voluntary principle is not operative in his case.

We quickly come to the point that privacy is not merely a matter of this or that person, object or bit of information, but really applies in *systemic* ways throughout a society in accord with the norms of that society and, probably, its laws. It is reasonable to expect privacy for actions inside one's home (subject to certain qualifications) because we live in a society where domestic privacy is valued and the laws that protect it are reasonably drawn. It is unreasonable to expect to maintain the privacy of the contents of one's pockets in an airport, again because our society considers strict airport security as reasonable in this age of easily disguised explosives and weapons. This reasonability, of course, stems from the social costs of airplane sabotage and highjackings and the concomitant social benefits of tight security. There is almost a paradox about our feelings in this instance. For the sake of my safety, I would like all of my fellow passengers to be completely searched to eliminate any possibility that they will be able to damage the plane that I will be on or divert it to some odd destination. At the same time, I would prefer that I not be searched. My wish to maintain privacy for my personal possessions in an airport, however, is unreasonable against the generalization of everyone's wish for their safety. In isolation my desire for privacy is reasonable, it only becomes unreasonable in the contemporary social context.

New technology begins to change the context of what we may consider private. An example is the radio station monitoring device known as Mobiltrak.[8] If I drive around in my car with the windows open and the radio blaring, I voluntarily make available to casual passersby the particular radio station to which I am tuned. They may easily hear the call numbers between musical selections or recognize the voice of an announcer. In accord with the mischance principle, a monitoring device such as Mobiltrak that picks up signals from

---

[7]George Orwell. *1984*. New American Library, New York, p. 79, 1990.
[8]See Catherine Greenan, They know what you listened to last summer on your car radio, *New York Times,* January 20, 2000. Also, www.mobiltrak.com.

my radio is recording information that would be available to a nonsnoop and so does not transgress privacy expectations. These devices are usually placed in parking lots to try to determine whether radio ads for certain stores bring customers. At the moment, all they record is the identification of the radio station to which passing cars are tuned. But it would be a fairly simple matter to combine some further identification technology so that one could match the car identity (and thus the probable driver) with the radio station. As I described the case, the information could have been gleaned without snooping with the volume turned up and the car windows open. But what if I do not open my windows and never play the radio loudly so that, in fact, it is extremely unlikely that anyone who has not been invited into my car could know my listening habits? Does Mobiltrak then transgress reasonable privacy expectations when I am cautious? I would say that it doesn't, since almost no one takes any pains to conceal their radio habits.

Another case: supermarkets now make available so-called discount cards to their patrons, who fill out applications requiring significant amounts of personal information. These cards are scanned prior to ringing up the grocery purchases (and, indeed, a few discounts are credited against the total). But the real purpose of such cards is not to save customers money but to provide information on purchases that can be aggregated into a profile. This information provides a potentially useful marketing tool once the individual's shopping predilections are known. The application of the mischance principle to this case uncovers a problem about privacy in data aggregation and storage. Imagine a supermarket that decided to compile shopper profiles by hand. Observers are posted at each cash register; as the groceries are rung up, the observer checks off each item. Prior to the end of the transaction, the observer asks for the customer's name and address. Then this information is stored in that customer's file so that clerks can look over his or her purchase history and draw conclusions about what items should be placed on sale or otherwise promoted to draw the customer back to the store. Since check-out lines are quite public, there is no problem of observation here; anyone walking by could see that I buy store-brand frozen peas, for example. My identity may be another matter, but not if I pay by credit card or with a check. If I am one of the increasingly rare cash customers, I can either volunteer my name (on the theory that all of this record keeping may offer some advantage to me), or I can refuse. If stores operated their systems by means of observers there would be no privacy concerns. The mischance and voluntary principles are satisfied; I can choose not to give my name (by paying with cash) and in any case the content of my shopping cart is already open to view. The hand-tally version of the supermarket information gathering system in all likelihood will stay small because it would be so laborious to compile the information on each customer and put it into a manageable form. By means of the scan card and the data file software now in use, however, the information is easily merged with other data files similarly gathered into a large profile on the customer.[9] So while I might be said to be voluntarily participating in the information collection by shopping at this store knowing that observers

---

[9]On the broad problems posed by data gathering, storage and sale, see, for example, Judith Wagner Decew. *In Pursuit of Privacy.* Cornell University Press, Ithaca, NY, pp. 145–153, 1997 and Helen Nissenbaum. Protecting Privacy in an Information Age. *Law and Philosophy,* 17(5–6): 559–596, 1998.

will be present, and while the information collected in each instance meets the mischance principle test, the aggregation of the information does not seem to satisfy either principle. I may not know that data gathering technology exists or that it is in wide use. And certainly no casual observer could come to know a frequency analysis of my buying habits over the past 12 months simply by looking at my shopping cart from time to time. This raises a conundrum about privacy just because it is the possibility of personal data aggregation (and possible sales to third parties) that makes the whole discount scan-card program so attractive to retailers in the first place.

One of the ways in which the voluntary principle is sometimes interpreted is that the *failure* to attempt to maintain privacy constitutes willingness for that information to become public. To return to my earlier example, by tattooing my social security number on my forehead I am *positively* increasing the likelihood of that information becoming known. If I leave my social security card around my apartment while the electrician is working, or put it on the resume that I send to 100 universities and colleges that might have job openings, I *negatively* (by my lack of due care) increase the likelihood that the number will become known.[10] This negative version of the voluntary principle seems particularly promising in sorting out what would constitute reasonable expectations of privacy in many applications of information technology.

Let us consider two examples. Is it reasonable to expect one's internet browsing to be private? Is it reasonable to expect one's email to be private? I will argue, using the negative voluntary principle as well as the mischance principle, that the answer to both questions is "no."

First, consider the internet. It is now well-known that through the use of cookies and other software, the progression of websites that one visits in any internet session can easily be tracked. A record is left in the cache history file of the computer itself in most internet browsers, even if one does not accept cookies. And since most people do accept cookies[11] companies like DoubleClick can easily keep a record of internet wanderings.[12] It therefore seems to me that logging onto the internet is analogous to browsing magazines at bookstores with security cameras in full view. In the absence of any attempts to conceal one's identity on the internet, or to block the various tracking technologies from being used, by the negative version of the voluntary principle, one is essentially exposing this information to view. I would argue that from the start, the World Wide Web was a transparent rather than a sheltered environment, more like going from shop to shop in a large mall than, say, writing in one's diary in the privacy of one's home. Given the lack of any clear social norms or

---

[10]This point is noted in Justice Harlan's opinion in *Katz* v. *U.S.* The *Katz* case is significant for the developing constitutional protection of privacy against technological intrusion because of Harlan's two-prong test: "first that a person have exhibited an actual (subjective) expectation of privacy and, second, that the expectation be one that society is prepared to recognize as 'reasonable'." An analysis of the importance of Harlan's test is developed in Richard G. Wilkins. Defining the "reasonable expectation of privacy." *Vanderbilt Law Review,* 40: 1077–1129, October 1987.

[11]"Set your web browser to accept all cookies" is standard advice from the privacy section of internet sites, e.g., *The New York Times on the Web* at www.nytimes.com. This is also the default setting of most browsers and it is reasonable to suppose that most internet users do not change the setting or even know that there is a setting to change.

[12]For an account of their activities, see www.doubleclick.com. See also, Bob Tedeschi. E-Commerce Report, *New York Times,* March 6, 2000.

laws that control access to my internet wanderings, it is therefore unreasonable to expect privacy in this domain.[13]

Finally, consider email privacy. It has become a commonplace that what one sends in an ordinary email message is far from secure. Former President Clinton, for example, told a meeting of Silicon Valley executives that he would not use email to communicate with his daughter away at college because of the transparency of this medium.[14] Standard advice in newspaper stories about email exposure is to think of an email message as a postcard, where there are numerous opportunities for the message to be read by others on its way to its intended recipient.[15] A recent survey found that 27% of all major corporations have email monitoring programs in place for employees, double the number from three years before.[16] Recently published details of the FBI "Carnivore" system suggest that this technology picks many other emails as it attempts to intercept the email of suspected criminals.[17] For many years, daily back-up tapes of computer servers all over the world captured whatever email messages happened to be there waiting to be read. Some of these tapes have a long life and are far from secure. All of these well-documented exposures of email messages suggest that there is little dependable privacy in this realm. Therefore, once again by the negative voluntary principle, using email in the face of this legendary insecurity exposes whatever one may write to the eyes of others—perhaps many others. It is not reasonable to expect privacy in email, given all of this permeability.

The extent to which expectations of privacy are reasonable takes into account the social norms governing the particular form the information may have as well as the context (like browsing a magazine in full view of an open security camera). Incursions of technology and heightened cynicism do not necessarily negate the reasonableness of privacy expectations or desires. A case in point is the privacy of medical records. After many complaints that medical records were being transferred from legitimate users—such as insurance companies—to secondary users—like credit bureaus—the Health Insurance Portability and Accountability Act of 1996 was passed by Congress.[18] The norm that one's medical history is private was well enough developed so that few people were willing to simply concede privacy here, despite the fact that security for medical information had become quite porous. In addition to raising the issue politically, many people have begun to take steps to make such records even more secure. Picking up files when one leaves a medical practice, asking for records when one changes medical insurance carriers and not providing medical information on line are all prudent steps in this direction. Although still far from the privacy of a sealed envelope moving through the U.S. Postal System or a conver-

---

[13]A useful overview of the ways in which one can control access to one's internet use is found in Anonymous. The Invisible Man. *Yahoo Internet Life,* 6(10): 108–110, October 2000.

[14]See Mark Lacey. Clinton Calls for Stronger Measures to Protect Privacy of Computer Users. *New York Times,* March 4, 2000.

[15]E.g., J. D. Biersdorpher. Q&A: Privacy Can Be Elusive in World of Email. *New York Times,* April 5, 2000.

[16]The American Manufacturing Association report is available at www.amanet.org/press/research/check email.

[17]See, e.g., *Electronic Privacy Information Center Alert* 7.15, August 3, 2000 (www.epic.org/alert/EPIC_Alert_7.15.html).

[18]The Department of Health and Human Services finally issued administrative provisions for this bill in late December 2000. See http://aspe.hhs.gov/admnsimp/index.htm or *Federal Register,* December 28, 2000, for the implementation details (which go into full effect in 2003).

sation on a landline telephone, medical information is increasingly protected and expectations of its privacy are therefore increasingly reasonable.

As a general matter, how much privacy we have and can reasonably expect to have is a function of the practices and laws of our society and underlying normative principles. The rapid advance of information technology has mounted serious challenges to our intuitive sense of privacy. Steps to protect privacy must take notice of the technological developments and the various social costs of providing such protection. Where the social costs are relatively low and the technical means are at hand, it is reasonable to expect enhanced privacy, as in the example of medical records. Where the costs are high or the technology required is unduly complex, such as in the case of email privacy, one should have lower expectations. Sorting through all of this is, obviously, a complicated matter. The mischance and voluntary principles are a useful guide to reasonableness as we all struggle to ascertain how much privacy to expect.

REFERENCES

Anonymous. The Invisible Man. *Yahoo Internet life,* 6(10): 108–110, October 2000.

J. D. Biersdorpher. Q&A: Privacy Can be Elusive in World of Email. *New York Times,* April 5, 2000.

California v. Greenwood, 486 U.S. 35 (1988).

Judith Wagner Decew. *In Pursuit of Privacy.* Cornell University Press, Ithaca, NY, 1997.

Electronic Privacy Information Center Alert 7.15, August 3, 2000 (www.epic.org/alert/EPIC_Alert_7.15.html).

Catherine Greenan. They Know What You Listened to Last Summer on Your Car Radio, *New York Times,* January 20, 2000.

Katz v. *U.S.,* 389 U.S. 347 (1967).

Mark Lacey. Clinton Calls for Stronger Measures to Protect Privacy of Computer Users. *New York Times,* March 4, 2000.

James H. Moor. Towards a Theory of Privacy in the Information Age. *Computers and Society,* 27(3): 27–32, 1997.

Helen Nissenbaum. Protecting Privacy in an Information Age. *Law and Philosophy,* 17(5–6): 559–596, 1998.

George Orwell. *1984.* New American Library, New York, 1990.

Robert Scheer. Nowhere to Hide. *Yahoo Internet Life* (Special Report on Privacy) 6(10): 101, October 2000.

Sipple v. *Chronicle Publishing Co.* 154 Cal App. 3rd 1040 (1984).

Rodney A. Smolla. *Free Speech in an Open Society.* Vintage/Random House, New York, 1992.

Bob Tedeschi. E-Commerce Report. *New York Times,* March 6, 2000.

Mark Tunik, *Practices and Principles.* Princeton University Press, Princeton, NJ, pp. 161–190, 1998.

Richard G. Wilkins. Defining the "Reasonable Expectation of Privacy". *Vanderbilt Law Review,* 40: 1077–1129, October 1987.

AS OFFICE SNOOPING GROWS, WHO WATCHES THE WATCHERS?

—Jeffrey L. Seglin

Seglin examines the nature of employee monitoring with particular attention paid to the people who will actually do the monitoring, itself. Who oversees these people, sets the standards and principles and manages the situation if something goes wrong?

Except for the shouting, it is becoming clear that the debate over employee privacy is over.

The American Management Association conducts an annual survey on electronic monitoring and surveillance in the workplace, and the latest results, released a few weeks ago, show that widespread, routine snooping on employees is no longer a threat *but a fact.* Nearly three-quarters of the large American companies that responded to the survey said they actively record and review at least one of the following: employees' phone calls, email, internet connections and computer files. That is twice the rate of snooping as in 1997. And one company in four has fired an employee over what the surveillance turned up.

So the ethical quandary over whether to monitor will soon be moot. Factors like fear of sexual harassment litigation, lost employee productivity and theft of proprietary data and software have swamped any hesitations about privacy. It is almost a cinch that your employer will be having a peek at what you're up to—if not today, then tomorrow.

If monitoring is a given, a new challenge for employers takes center stage: setting up a monitoring system that is ethical and fair to all employees, and not merely defensible in court.

A key issue, of course, is: Who will do the monitoring? And that is where things get sticky.

Two approaches are possible. Monitoring could become a full-time job for a person or department, or could be made a sidelight among other responsibilities. Each presents problems.

When policing co-workers is someone's main job, human nature creates a real danger. The designated monitor will have every incentive to find problems to justify his or her job, said N. Ben Fairweather, a research fellow at the Center for Computing and Social Responsibility in Leicester, England. Once the egregious offenders are weeded out, an effective monitoring program can easily devolve into a wild, self-perpetuating array of witch hunts and speed traps—an ethically unjustifiable state of affairs, however one may feel about monitoring in the abstract.

More often, monitoring is assigned to people or departments that mainly do something else. Typically, the job goes to information-technology people, for no better reason than that they are usually the only ones who have the necessary access to hardware and software and know how it all works, on the snoop's side as well as the user's.

But think again of human nature. Making snooping a sideline is likely to lead to wild inconsistency, occasional incompetence or outright capriciousness in the way monitoring is applied and policies are enforced.

I don't mean to suggest that technical people are reckless or capricious. Only a fool would make such an observation and expect his office internet connection to ever work smoothly again.

It's just that the do-it-in-your-spare-time approach is doomed from the outset. People will naturally devote most of their time and attention to their principal responsibilities—the ones that figure in whether they get promotions and raises—and turn to monitoring only when they have the time and inclination. Inevitably, that means inconsistent enforcement, which can be worse than none at all.

"Generally, in all areas of corporate management, the idea of having a policy is a good one, but it's not enough," said Jeffrey D. Neuburger, a lawyer specializing in technology-related issues at Brown Raysman Millstein Felder & Steiner, a Manhattan firm. "If you don't enforce it, you're almost better off not having a policy, because you get charged with this standard that you're telling the world that you're going to live under."

Mr. Neuburger's point is one both of fairness and of vulnerability in court. A company sued by an employee over a claim of sexual harassment can find itself in trouble, for example, if it can be demonstrated that the company adopted a policy against viewing internet pornography on office computers but did not consistently enforce the policy. It won't do much for the company's defense to have some harried systems analyst testify that checking the logs for naughty downloads was item No. 137 on her weekly to-do list.

A survey earlier this year by Elron Software, a publisher of monitoring software, shows that internet policy enforcement is far from airtight. One-tenth of workers responding to the survey said they had seen co-workers viewing adult Web sites on the job; more than half of that 10% said their companies had explicit policies forbidding it.

If full-time snoops are prone to overzealousness and part-timers to inconsistency, what is the right way to manage routine monitoring? There isn't one.

The ethical approach is to use snooping the way the police are supposed to use searches and telephone taps: only when warranted. "There might be a need for monitoring, but only *after* the organization has good grounds for suspecting that there is abuse," Dr. Fairweather said.

In other words, he snoops fairest who snoops least, and then only with cause.

CYBERLIABILITY: AN ENTERPRISE WHITE PAPER

—Elron Software

This cyberliability overview explores the risks to employers from internet connections and delineates the various types of risks posed. In addition, though the balance of rights and responsibilities between employees and employers remains somewhat vague (see chapter introduction), the following discussion outlines the parameters of that relationship in regard to cyber issues.

THE PROBLEM: RISKS FROM INTERNET CONNECTIVITY SKYROCKET

As with all technological advances, the benefits of internet connectivity are coupled with associated risks. These hazards take a variety of forms, from non-business Web surfing to confidential data leaks from emails. The range of connectivity risks and costs is summarized on the following page.

CYBERLIABILITY

Of all the internet risks, cyberliability exposes organizations to the highest level of danger. The most common scenario involves employees who use the internet to find/share information they find interesting with co-workers/outside parties. These users believe that their electronic communications are casual, but may soon discover that these e-documents are as binding as those written on company letterhead.

To make matters worse, once an email is sent, it can be discovered in at least six different places (sender desktop, sender mail server, sender ISP, recipient ISP, recipient mail server and recipient desktop). The situation is similar for the "cookie trail" left by Web surfers. In the end, emails or Web surfing that contain offensive or company confidential information can quickly result in:

- Legal fees *(including costs to prepare, litigate and settle cases).*

- Depressed stock price.

- Negative effect on brand, reputation and corporate confidence.

Risks and Resulting Costs of Connecting to the internet

Resulting Costs	Risks					
	Offensive Material or Spam	Libelous or Defamatory Material	Confidential Data Leaks	Excessive Personal Email	Excessive Personal Web Surfing	Excessive Personal Newsgroups, FTP, Chat
Cyberliability						
Legal liability: case preparation fees	√	√	√			
Legal liability: settlement or damages	√	√	√			
Damaged company image	√	√	√	√	√	√
Lower shareholder value	√	√	√	√	√	√
Other risks						
Decreased employee productivity	√		√	√	√	√
Lost sales due to network slowdowns				√	√	√

CYBERLIABILITY:

Legal proceedings and related costs due to unmanaged internet use, including email, Web surfing, ftp, newsgroups and spam.

Combine the casual atmosphere of internet communications with this substantial electronic paper trail, and it's easy to see why the use of "e-evidence" has skyrocketed within the following categories of litigation:

- Discrimination
- Harassment
- Obscenity and pornography
- Defamation and libel
- Information leaks
- Spam

A complete listing of cyberliability cases and press coverage could fill several volumes. Below, please find a handful of recent examples:

1. Discrimination

- A Federal court in New York has allowed a class action discrimination suit based on racist emails. The defendant is a large Wall Street brokerage firm and the plaintiffs are seeking $60 million in damages. *(Owens and Hutton v. Morgan Stanley & Co., Inc.,* Case No 96 Civ 9747)

- Female warehouse employees alleged that a hostile work environment was created in part by inappropriate email. Plaintiffs ask for $60 million in damages; case settles out of court. *(Harley v. McCoach,* 928 F. Supp. 533, E.D. Pa. 1996)

2. Harassment

- International Microcomputer Software pays a former employee $105,000 after she received sexually harassing messages on the firm's electronic bulletin board, even though the company reported the incident to authorities and launched an internal investigation. (Staff Writer, CNET News.com, April 14, 1999)

- Chevron settles sexual harassment lawsuit for $2.2 million over email postings such as: "25 reasons why beer is better than women." (Jerry Adler, *Newsweek,* "When Email Bites Back," November 23, 1998)

3. Information Leaks

- The Justice Department's anti-trust lawsuit against Microsoft Inc. is based in large part on internal email messages about efforts to insert a bug into Microsoft products to disable competitor's products. (*Wall Street Journal,* John R. Wilke, August 27, 1998)

- The defense contractor Raytheon sued 21 "John Doe" employees for posting company confidential information on the internet. Two workers have since been identified and have elected to resign. (Staff Writer, CNET News.com, April 6, 1999, 1:30 P.M. PT)

- The restaurant chain Shoney's is demanding that Yahoo reveal the identity of 100 people who posted confidential information concerning restaurant closings and an alleged pending bankruptcy filing on message boards. (Staff Writer, CNET News.com, April 12, 1999, 5:00 A.M. PT)

4. Offensive Content

- The New York Times dismissed 23 employees at an administrative center for violating the company's email policy regarding "offensive or disruptive messages, including photographs, graphics and audio materials." (Staff writer, *NYTimes,* December 1, 1999)

- The Xerox Corp. fired approximately 40 people for viewing pornographic sites at work. (Richard Mullins, *Rochester Democrat and Chronicle,* October 7, 1999)

- At least six employees of the U.S. Navy Naval Supply Systems Command (NAVSUP) have been, or are expected to be, suspended for circulating "inappropriate, adult humor material" in emails. Another 500 were reported disciplined. (Staff writer, *The Sentinel,* December 4, 1999)

5. Defamation and Libel

- Wade Cook Financial sues members of a bulletin board for libelous statements about the company. (Liz Enbysk, *ZDNET Anchordesk,* March 10, 1999)

- An insurance company is sued for circulating an email that accused an employee of using her corporate credit card to defraud the company. (*Meloff v. New York Life Insurance Co.,* 51 F.3d 372, 2nd Cir. 1992)

6. Spam

- GTE blamed spam for the shutdown of one of its mail servers. Several individuals also complained over the year that they were personally shut down after spammers used the individual's email addresses as forged return addresses. (John C. Dvorak, *PC Magazine,* March 24, 1998)

MONITORING INTERNET USAGE: EMPLOYER RIGHTS AND RESPONSIBILITIES

Employer's Right to Monitor

Most experts agree that an employer has both the right and the responsibility to manage employee internet use. Ed Cavazos, senior vice president and general counsel of Interliant, a data network/internet service provider in Houston says:

> *In most cases companies are well within their rights when they monitor or block their employees' Net activity. There are no laws on the books that can be interpreted as prohibiting an employer from watching what its employees do on the internet. The Electronic Communications Privacy Act (ECPA) generally prevents employers from monitoring personal communications, such as private phone calls, unless there is reason to believe that a crime has occurred or certain other exceptions.* However, the ECPA does support an employer's right to monitor stored electronic communications, such as voicemail and email messages in order to protect its business, rights or property. (PC World, *November 1997*)

The Written Policy

There is no legislation that requires employers to require a written policy before monitoring email and web usage. However, having each employee read and sign your Internet Usage Policy is an extra step that the courts have found to reinforce the employer's rights:

- After being terminated for inappropriate emails, two employees later filed a lawsuit for violation of privacy which was then dismissed by the California Court of Appeals. The court concluded that the employees have no reasonable expectation of privacy in their email messages. The employees had acknowledged and agreed to the employer's policies that stated that the use of company computers was for business purposes only. *(Bourke v. Nissan Motor Corp.,* No YC-003979, Cal. Ct. App., June 1993)

- A company president allegedly spent eight hours reviewing employee emails. The plaintiffs used disparaging nicknames for the president and alleged he was having an affair with another co-worker. Although the company did not have a published policy that prohibited personal email messages, the court held that an employer's storing and reviewing of email messages on a company server did not violate the wiretapping statute. *(Restuccia v. Burk Technology,* Civil Action No 95-2125, 1996, LEXIS 367, Mass. Super. Ct., Middlesex County, December 13, 1996)

INTERNET USAGE POLICY QUIZ

Experts agree that the best way to minimize the risks of cyberliability is to create and enforce an Internet Usage Policy that supports your unique corporate culture. As stated earlier, few employees purposely try to damage an organization with their internet usage—most intend only to share humor or promote positive company information.

Internet Usage Policy Quiz

1. Does your Internet Usage Policy give specific guidelines for the following corporate communications:
   - ❑ Web surfing   ❑ Email   ❑ FTP
   - ❑ Newsgroups   ❑ Chat rooms   ❑ Spam
2. Do you periodically generate usage reports to get feedback on compliance?
   - ❑ Weekly   ❑ Monthly   ❑ Bimonthly   ❑ Not at all
3. Have you posted your policy and given each employee a copy?   ❑ Yes ❑ No
4. Have you vigorously enforced and promoted your policy?   ❑ Yes ❑ No
5. Have you been consistent in your treatment of policy offenders?   ❑ Yes ❑ No
6. Have you periodically updated your policy to reflect current technology and business trends?
   - ❑ Annually   ❑ Semi-annually   ❑ Not at all

If you answered "no" to any of the questions above, your policy is in need of an update.

Index